NEW!

for Psychology

Engaging Every Student. | **Supporting Every Instructor.** | **Setting the New Standard for Teaching and Learning.**

Achieve for Psychology sets a whole new standard for integrating **assessments**, **activities**, and **analytics** into your teaching. It brings together all of the features that instructors and students loved about our previous platform, LaunchPad—interactive e-book, LearningCurve adaptive quizzing and other assessments, interactive learning activities, extensive instructor resources—in a powerful new platform that offers:

- A cleaner, more intuitive, **mobile-friendly** interface.
- Powerful analytics.
- Self-regulated learning and goal-setting surveys.
- A fully integrated iClicker classroom response system, with questions available for each unit or the option to integrate your own.
- A **NEW Video Collection for Introductory Psychology!**

Our resources were **co-designed with instructors and students**, on a foundation of *years* of **learning research**, and rigorous testing over multiple semesters. The result is superior content, organization, and functionality. Achieve's pre-built assignments engage students both *inside and outside of class*. And Achieve is effective for students of *all levels* of motivation and preparedness, whether they are high achievers or need extra support.

Macmillan Learning offers **deep platform integration** of Achieve with all learning management systems (LMS) providers, including Blackboard, Brightspace, Canvas, and Moodle. With integration, students can access course content and their grades through one sign-in. And you can pair Achieve with course tools from your LMS, such as discussion boards and chat and Gradebook functionality. LMS integration is also available with Inclusive Access. For more information, visit MacmillanLearning .com/College/US/Solutions/LMS-Integration or talk to your local sales representative.

Achieve was built with accessibility in mind. Macmillan Learning strives to create products that are usable by all learners and meet universally applied accessibility standards. In addition to addressing product compatibility with assistive technologies such as screen reader software, alternative keyboard devices, and voice recognition products, we are working to ensure that the content and platforms we provide are fully accessible. For more information visit Macmillanlearning.com/college/us/our-story /accessibility

Mobile: Based on user data, we know that lots of students use parts of Achieve on a mobile device. As such, activities such as e-book readings, videos, and LearningCurve adaptive quizzes are easily used across devices with different screen sizes.

Achieve for Psychology: Assessments

LearningCurve Adaptive Quizzing

Based on extensive learning and memory research, and proven effective for hundreds of thousands of students, LearningCurve focuses on the core concepts in every chapter, providing individualized question sets and feedback for correct and incorrect responses. The system adapts to each student's level of understanding, with follow-up quizzes targeting areas where the student needs improvement. Each question is tied to a learning objective and linked to the appropriate section of the e-book to encourage students to discover the right answer for themselves. LearningCurve has consistently been rated the #1 resource by instructors and students alike.

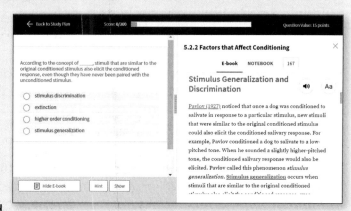

- LearningCurve's game-like quizzing promotes retrieval practice through its unique delivery of questions and its point system.

- Students with a firm grasp on the material get plenty of practice but proceed through the activity relatively quickly.

- Unprepared students are given more questions, therefore requiring that they do what they should be doing anyway if they're unprepared — practice some more.

- Instructors can monitor results for each student and the class as a whole, to identify areas that may need more coverage in lectures and assignments.

E-book

Macmillan Learning's e-book is an interactive version of the textbook that offers highlighting, bookmarking, and note-taking. Built-in, low-stakes self-assessments allow students to test their level of understanding along the way, and learn even more in the process thanks to the *testing effect*. Students can download the e-book to read offline, or to have it read aloud to them. Achieve allows instructors to assign chapter sections as homework.

Test Bank

Test banks for Macmillan Learning's psychology textbooks offer thousands of questions, all meticulously reviewed. Instructors can assign out-of-the-box exams or create their own by:

- Choosing from thousands of questions in our database.
- Filtering questions by type, topic, difficulty, and Bloom's level.
- Customizing multiple-choice questions.
- Integrating their own questions into the exam.

Exam/Quiz results report to a Gradebook that lets instructors monitor student progress individually and classwide.

Practice Quizzes

Practice Quizzes mirror the experience of a quiz or test, with questions that are similar but distinct from those in the test bank. Instructors can use the quizzes as is or create their own, selecting questions by type, topic, difficulty, and Bloom's level.

Achieve for Psychology: Activities

Achieve is designed to support and encourage active learning by connecting familiar activities and practices out of class with some of the most effective and approachable in-class activities, curated from a variety of active learning sources.

New! Video Collection for Introductory Psychology

This collection offers classic as well as current, in-demand clips from high-quality sources, with original content to support *Discovering Psychology,* Ninth Edition. In addition to the new video collection, this edition includes a brand new **Tell Me More** video feature in which master teacher Susan Nolan breaks out a compelling topic from each chapter of the text.

PBS Newshour/boclips

Accompanying assessment makes these videos assignable, with results reporting to the Achieve Gradebook. Our faculty and student consultants were instrumental in helping us create this diverse and engaging set of clips. All videos are closed-captioned and found only in Achieve.

Immersive Learning Activities

Focusing on student engagement, these immersive learning activities invite students to apply what they are learning to their own lives, or to play the role of researcher — exploring experimental methods, analyzing data, and developing scientific literacy and critical thinking skills.

Think Like a Scientist A renewed emphasis on scientific literacy can be seen in the updated "Think Like a Scientist" feature in Achieve. Students are placed in real-life scenarios that walk through the steps of scientific thinking — combining video, text, and assessment to develop and hone critical thinking skills.

Studying Implicit Biases

Can implicit and explicit biases be changed by diversity training? In one study, researchers examined implicit beliefs among faculty members in the sciences by giving male and female participants an IAT before and after a half-hour diversity training session (Jackson & others, 2014). Participants were also asked about their explicit attitudes, their conscious beliefs about women in the sciences.

So, researchers examined the effects of two variables—gender (female and male) and diversity training (pre-training and post-training)—on two other variables—implicit attitudes about women in science using an IAT and explicit attitudes about women in science.

Klaus Tiedge/age fotostock

Slide 10 / 22   Previous   Next

Concept Practice Tutorials

Achieve includes dozens of these dynamic, interactive mini-tutorials that teach and reinforce the course's foundational ideas. Each of these brief activities (only 5 minutes to complete) addresses one or two key concepts, in a consistent format—review, practice, quiz, and conclusion.

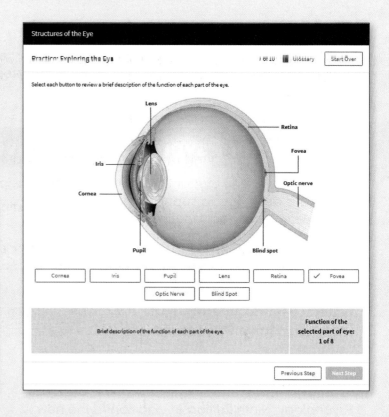

Instructor Activity Guides

Instructor Activity Guides provide instructors with a structured plan for using Achieve's active learning opportunities in both face-to-face and remote learning courses. Each guide offers step-by-step instructions—from pre-class reflection to in-class engagement to post-class followup. The guides include suggestions for discussion questions, group work, presentations, and simulations, with estimated class time, implementation effort, and Bloom's taxonomy level for each activity.

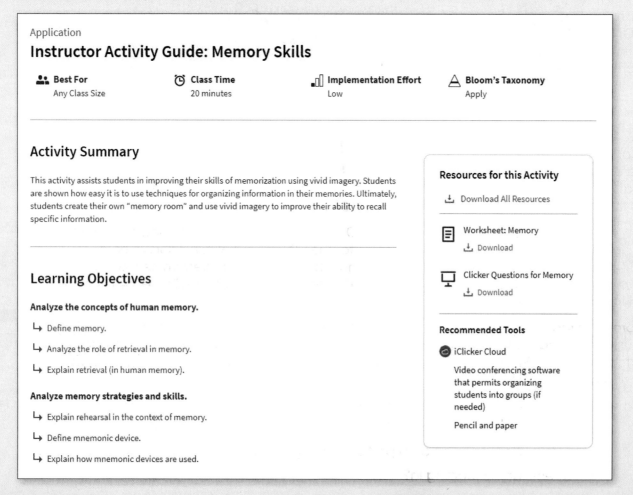

Application

Instructor Activity Guide: Memory Skills

Best For	Class Time	Implementation Effort	Bloom's Taxonomy
Any Class Size	20 minutes	Low	Apply

Activity Summary

This activity assists students in improving their skills of memorization using vivid imagery. Students are shown how easy it is to use techniques for organizing information in their memories. Ultimately, students create their own "memory room" and use vivid imagery to improve their ability to recall specific information.

Learning Objectives

Analyze the concepts of human memory.

↳ Define memory.

↳ Analyze the role of retrieval in memory.

↳ Explain retrieval (in human memory).

Analyze memory strategies and skills.

↳ Explain rehearsal in the context of memory.

↳ Define mnemonic device.

↳ Explain how mnemonic devices are used.

Resources for this Activity

⤓ Download All Resources

Worksheet: Memory
⤓ Download

Clicker Questions for Memory
⤓ Download

Recommended Tools

◉ iClicker Cloud

Video conferencing software that permits organizing students into groups (if needed)

Pencil and paper

iClicker Classroom Response System

Achieve seamlessly integrates iClicker, Macmillan Learning's highly acclaimed classroom response system. iClicker can help make any classroom—in person or virtual—more lively, engaging, and productive:

- iClicker's attendance feature helps you make sure students are actually attending in-person classes.
- Instructors can choose from flexible polling and quizzing options to engage students, check their understanding, and get their feedback in real time.
- iClicker allows students to participate using laptops, mobile devices, or in-class remotes.
- iClicker easily integrates your instructors' existing slides and polling questions—there is no need to re-enter them.
- Instructors can take advantage of the questions in our In-Class Activity Guides, and our book-specific questions within Achieve to improve the opportunities for all students to be active in class.

Achieve for Psychology: Analytics

Learning Objectives, Reports, and Insights

Content in Achieve is tagged to specific Learning Objectives, aligning the coursework with the textbook and with the APA Learning Goals and Outcomes. Reporting within Achieve helps students see how they are performing against objectives, and it helps instructors determine if any student, group of students, or the class as a whole needs extra help in specific areas. This enables more efficient and effective instructor interventions.

Achieve provides reports on student activities, assignments, and assessments at the course level, unit level, subunit level, and individual student level, so instructors can identify trouble spots and adjust their efforts accordingly. Within Reports, the Insights section offers snapshots with high-level data on student performance and behavior, to answer such question as:

- What are the top Learning Objectives to review in this unit?
- What are the top assignments to review?
- What's the range of performance on a particular assignment?
- How many students aren't logging in?

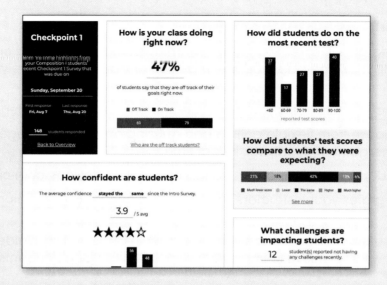

Achieve's **Innovation Lab** offers surveys that help students self-direct, and develop confidence in, their own learning:

- The **Intro Survey** asks students to consider their goals for the class and how they plan to manage their time and learning strategies.

- **Checkpoint surveys** ask students to reflect on what's been working and where they need to make changes.

- **Each completed survey generates a report** that reveals how each student is doing, beyond the course grade.

These tools help instructors engage their students in a discussion on soft skills, such as metacognition, effective learning and time management strategies, and other non-cognitive skills that impact student success.

Additional Instructor Resources in Achieve: All Within One Place

Image Slides and Tables

Presentation slides feature chapter photos, illustrations, and tables and can be used as is or customized to fit an instructor's needs. Alt text for images is available upon request via WebAccessibility@Macmillan.com

Instructor's Resource Manual

Downloadable Word manuals include a range of resources, such as chapter outlines or summaries, teaching tips, discussion starters, sample syllabi, assignment suggestions, and classroom activities.

Lecture Slides

Accessible, downloadable presentation slides provide support for key concepts and themes from the text and can be used as is or customized to fit an instructor's needs.

Customer Support

Our Achieve Client Success Team—dedicated platform experts—provides collaboration, software expertise, and consulting to tailor each course to fit your instructional goals and student needs. Start with a demo at a time that works for you to learn more about how to set up your customized course. Talk to your sales representative or visit www.macmillanlearning.com/college/us/contact-us/training-and-demos for more information.

Pricing and bundling options are available at the Macmillan student store: store.macmillanlearning.com/

NINTH EDITION

DISCOVERING PSYCHOLOGY

SUSAN A. NOLAN
Seton Hall University

SANDRA E. HOCKENBURY

worth publishers
Macmillan Learning

New York

Senior Vice President, Content Strategy: Charles Linsmeier
Program Director, Social Sciences: Shani Fisher
Senior Executive Program Manager: Carolyn Merrill
Development Editor: Michael Kimball
Associate Development Editor: Nick Rizzuti
Editorial Assistant: Allison Curley
Executive Marketing Manager: Kate Nurre
Marketing Assistant: Steven Huang
Director of Media Editorial and Assessment: Noel Hohnstine
Media Editor: Stefani Wallace
Senior Director, Content Management Enhancement: Tracey Kuehn
Senior Managing Editor: Lisa Kinne
Senior Content Project Manager: Edward Dionne
Senior Workflow Project Manager: Paul Rohloff
Production Supervisor: Robert Cherry
Director of Design, Content Management: Diana Blume
Design Services Manager: Natasha Wolfe
Cover Design Manager: John Callahan
Interior Design: Lumina Datamatics, Inc.
Art Manager: Matthew McAdams
Illustrations: Eli Ensor
Senior Media Permissions Manager: Christine Buese
Photo Researcher: Richard Fox, Lumina Datamatics, Inc.
Permissions Editor: Michael McCarty
Director of Digital Production: Keri deManigold
Lead Media Project Manager: Joseph Tomasso
Composition: Lumina Datamatics, Inc.
Printing and Binding: LSC Communications

Library of Congress Control Number: 2021940749

ISBN-13: 978-1-319-24722-5
ISBN-10: 1-319-24722-9

International Edition:
ISBN-13: 978-1-319-46676-3
ISBN-10: 1-319-46676-1

Printed in the United States of America

1 2 3 4 5 6   26 25 24 23 22 21

Worth Publishers
120 Broadway
New York, NY 10271
www.macmillanlearning.com

To Sandy Hockenbury, for your
friendship and mentorship
—S. A. N.

To Laura, for the love and laughter
along the way
—S. E. H.

ABOUT THE AUTHORS

Susan A. Nolan is Professor of Psychology at Seton Hall University in New Jersey, where she was a 2020 College of Arts and Sciences Teacher of the Year. Susan researches the interpersonal consequences of mental illness and the role of gender in science careers. Her research has been funded by the National Science Foundation. Susan was the 2021 president of the Society for the Teaching of Psychology. She also is a past president of the Eastern Psychological Association (EPA) and a Fellow of the EPA, the American Psychological Association (APA), and the Association for Psychological Science. She holds an A.B. from the College of the Holy Cross and a Ph.D. from Northwestern University.

Susan is fascinated by the applications of psychology to the "real world," both locally and globally. She served as a representative from the APA to the United Nations for five years, and was the 2020 recipient of the Fukuhara Award for Advanced International Research and Service from the International Council of Psychologists. She was a 2015–2016 U.S. Fulbright Scholar in Bosnia and Herzegovina, where she and her husband have a home. She is an avid traveler. Susan uses the examples she encounters through these experiences in the classroom, in this textbook, and in the statistics textbooks that she co-authors.

Sandra E. Hockenbury is a science writer who specializes in psychology. Sandy received her B.A. from Shimer College and her M.A. from the University of Chicago, where she was also a research associate at the Institute of Social and Behavioral Pathology. Prior to co-authoring *Psychology* and *Discovering Psychology*, Sandy worked for several years as a psychology editor in both academic and college textbook publishing. Sandy has also taught as an adjunct faculty member at Tulsa Community College.

Sandy's areas of interest include positive psychology, cross-cultural psychology, and the intersection of Buddhist philosophy, neuroscience, and psychology. She is a member of the American Psychological Association, the Association for Psychological Science, and the American Association for the Advancement of Science. An avid hiker, Sandy has twice served as a volunteer with Nomads Clinic, a nonprofit organization that brings medical care to remote areas in the Himalayan regions of Nepal and the Tibetan Plateau.

Brief Contents

Contents

Klaus Vedfelt/Getty Images

CULTURE AND HUMAN BEHAVIOR 14
What Is Cross-Cultural Psychology?

CRITICAL THINKING 30
How to Think Like a Scientist

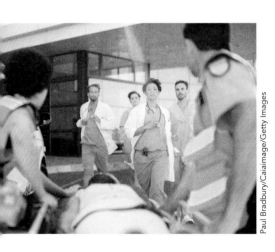

Paul Bradbury/Caiaimage/Getty Images

Erik Isakson/Tetra images/Getty images

3   Sensation and Perception

Ugurhan Betin/Exactostock-1672/Superstock

4 Consciousness and Its Variations

Sergey Sikharulidze/Alamy Stock Photo

5 Learning

Amril Izan Imran/Alamy Stock Photo

6 Memory

red_bred_Creatas Video+/Getty Images Plus

7 Thinking, Language, and Intelligence

John Warburton Lee/SuperStock

FOCUS ON NEUROSCIENCE 276
Dopamine Receptors and Obesity: Eating to Stimulate Brain Reward?

CRITICAL THINKING 281
Emotion in Nonhuman Animals: Laughing Rats, Affectionate Elephants, and Smiling Dolphins?

IN FOCUS 284
Detecting Lies

IN FOCUS 287
Focus on Emotion Regulation

ddea/Getty Images

Emma McIntyre/Getty Images

10 Gender and Sexuality

Design Pics Inc/Alamy Stock Photo

11 Personality

Jen Lombardo/Alamy Stock Photo

12 Social Psychology

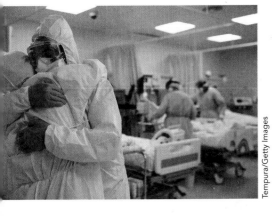

Tempura/Getty Images

13 Stress, Health, and Coping

aetb/Creatas Video+/Getty Images

14 Psychological Disorders

Adam Weiss/Gallery Stock

15 Therapies

APPENDIX A Statistics: Understanding Data

APPENDIX B Industrial/Organizational Psychology

To the Instructor

The future is disco. That might sound counterintuitive, that a dance style from the past is the future, but "disco" was our working nickname for *Discovering Psychology*, Ninth Edition. And we've made some important, accessible, and compelling updates to this new edition text that are all about the future of psychology—online learning; diversity, equity, and inclusion; neuroscience; and scientific literacy.

The Future Is Disco! "Disco" was our working nickname for the ninth edition of *Discovering Psychology*. We've made important, accessible, and compelling updates throughout the text that are all about the future of psychology—online learning; diversity, equity, and inclusion; neuroscience; and scientific literacy.

What's New in the Ninth Edition

We began the revision process with the thoughtful recommendations and feedback we received from hundreds of faculty using the text, from reviewers, from colleagues, and from students. We also had face-to-face dialogues with our own students. As you'll quickly see, the ninth edition marks a major step in the evolution of *Discovering Psychology*. We'll begin by summarizing the biggest changes to this edition.

The Highlights

Online Learning First, we introduce Achieve for Psychology, Macmillan Learning's new online platform that will engage every student with assessment, activities, and analytics. For more information, go to achieve.macmillanlearning.com.

As the pandemic taught us, the future is learning with technology. The new Achieve platform, with its standard-setting LearningCurve adaptive quizzing, is the future of online learning, asynchronous learning, and homework. This new platform is user-friendly and houses new features to help with remote teaching and learning—including the new introductory psychology video collection with lots of contemporary options and a brand new **Tell Me More** video feature in which master teacher Susan Nolan breaks out a compelling topic from each chapter of the text.

Diversity, Equity, and Inclusion We have always been concerned with diversity, equity, and inclusion, but never more so than in this new edition of *Discovering Psychology*. We appreciate the good social change happening in the world today and support that with a new chapter, Gender and Sexuality (Chapter 10). The chapter contains updated language throughout based on extensive feedback from GLAAD, and covers everything from updated research on changes in gender stereotypes and cognitive gender differences to new research on intersex people, gender identity, and sexual orientation. There is also new and updated diversity, equity, and inclusion coverage throughout the text, including updated diversity research, increased inclusion of the contributions of pioneering psychologists from underrepresented groups, and increased coverage of research by psychologists from a diverse range of backgrounds, including BIPOC people, LGBTQ+ people, and people from countries around the world. (Please see the list of chapter-by-chapter changes, below, for more details on these updates and additions.)

Tell Me More Videos The new Tell Me More videos show master teacher Susan Nolan breaking down compelling topics for each chapter. Highlights include Susan discussing teenage risk taking for the chapter on lifespan development, the gender mosaic for the chapter on gender and sexuality, cognitive dissonance and COVID for the chapter on social psychology, and discrimination and mental health for the chapter on psychological disorders.

Neuroscience The new understanding that neuroscience research provides is an obvious part of the future of psychology. To help explain that, this edition welcomed the expertise of neuroscientist Abigail A. Baird, Professor of Psychological Science at Vassar College. Professor Baird is also the Principal Investigator of the Laboratory for Adolescent Science, where she conducts award-winning neuroscience research on real-world questions. The result of her work on *Discovering Psychology* is a thoroughly revised Chapter 2 (Neuroscience and Behavior)—including beautifully revised art throughout. There are also dozens of new references—including expanded coverage of glial cells and new coverage of the microbiome. In addition, Focus on Neuroscience boxes in each chapter reflect exciting advances in the discipline.

Scientific Literacy A hallmark of *Discovering Psychology* since the first edition, we've built on the scientific literacy feature through every edition since. The Myth or Science feature, Critical Thinking boxes, and Think Like a Scientist digital activities have all been updated for the ninth edition and continue to support this emphasis on psychology as a science. This edition also adds new coverage of scientific literacy—including the topics of preregistration, effect size, open science, the replication crisis, and the problem of WEIRD samples.

COVID Coverage Besides all of these updates, we cover psychological aspects of COVID in targeted places throughout the text. This coverage includes mentions of the loss of the sense of smell for some who contracted COVID (in the chapter on sensation and perception), a new In Focus box called Contact Tracing and the Shortcomings of Memory, and new research on personality change and "growth," including that due to COVID. The Stress, Health, and Coping chapter begins with a new prologue called Stress and Health in the Time of COVID and includes new research on stress and coping during a pandemic. The chapter on psychological disorders has a new In Focus box called Mental Health During the Pandemic and the chapter on therapies includes new research on the increased demand for mental health care during the pandemic, including unequal access for people from marginalized groups, and the use of mobile phone apps and other online sources for eHealth during the pandemic. Finally, the appendix about industrial/organizational psychology contains new research on workplace challenges in the pandemic, including policies related to diversity, updated coverage concerning the popularity of remote work, and a discussion of Zoom fatigue.

Achieve for Psychology

Achieve for Psychology was built to engage students with active learning experiences that increase success. Use Achieve for Psychology to engage every student in an immersive online learning experience. Faculty can use Achieve to:

- Build each student's background knowledge with LearningCurve, an adaptive game-like quiz that motivates students and adapts to their needs based on their performance.

- Assign reading in our interactive e-book, which is accessible and downloadable.

- Access the **new** Introductory Psychology Video Collection, which provides updated clips rich with activities and assessment.

- Engage students during class with iClicker's flexible polling and quizzing options to check understanding and get feedback from students in real time.

- Help students apply knowledge and extend their understanding of psychology with immersive learning and assess this learning with practice quizzes.

Macmillan offers Faculty Support every step of the way:

- Pre-built assignments help you get started by creating a course with a variety of activities to engage students both inside and outside of class. Many of these pre-built assignments were created to help current Launch Pad users transition to Achieve.

- In-Class Instructor Activity Guides help engage students through active learning

- Insights and Reporting provide powerful analytics, viewable in an elegant dashboard, that offer you a window into student progress and facilitate lessons that are specifically tailored to students' needs.

Upgrade to Achieve and you will find all of the things you love about Launch-Pad: Learning Curve, the Integrated e-book, and Immersive Learning Activities. The upgrade includes the new Introductory Psychology Video Collection, more powerful instructor analytics, iClicker classroom response system, and LMS integration.

NEW! Achieve: Read & Practice

Achieve: Read & Practice is the marriage of Worth's LearningCurve adaptive quizzing and our mobile, accessible e-book in one easy-to-use and affordable product.

With Achieve: Read & Practice, instructors can arrange and assign chapters and sections from the e-book in any sequence they prefer, assign the readings to their class, and track student performance.

Assignments come with LearningCurve quizzes offering individualized and adaptive question sets, immediate feedback, and e-book references for correct and incorrect answers. If students struggle with a particular topic, they are encouraged to reread the material and check their understanding by answering a few short additional questions before being given the option to quiz themselves again.

The Read & Practice Gradebook provides analytics for student performance individually and for the whole class, by chapter, section, and topic, helping instructors prepare for class and one-on-one discussions.

Pricing and bundling options are available at the Macmillan student store: store.macmillanlearning.com/.

Major Chapter Revisions

As you page through our new edition, you will encounter new examples, boxes, photos, and illustrations in every chapter. In fact, there are hundreds of new references, the vast majority of which are from the last few years. Below are highlights of the most significant changes:

Chapter 1: Introduction and Research Methods

- New coverage of Mamie Phipps Clark, including more information about the work Clark did with her husband, Kenneth Clark, and the fact that Kenneth Clark received acclaim for the work that Mamie Phipps Clark had spearheaded (also with a new photo of Mamie Phipps Clark and Kenneth Clark).
- Inclusion of community psychology as a major specialty area
- New or updated coverage of terms concerning scientific literacy: preregistration, effect size, open science, the replication crisis, and the problem of WEIRD samples
- Think Like a Scientist box updated with new example related to the debunked practice of "energy healing," which was featured as "science" on the Netflix show *Goop Lab*

Chapter 2: Neuroscience and Behavior

- New Prologue about Gabby Giffords and her recovery from a gunshot wound to the left side of her brain
- New biological and neurological art throughout the chapter—including new figures for the overview of the nervous system, glial cells, the parts of the neuron, action potential, spinal reflexes, the endocrine system, and the cerebral hemispheres
- New Critical Thinking box about the gut–brain connection (i.e., the microbiome)
- Updated and reorganized Focus on Neuroscience: Imaging the Brain
- New Psych for Your Life box on Concussions: Assessment, Treatment, and Cumulative Impact

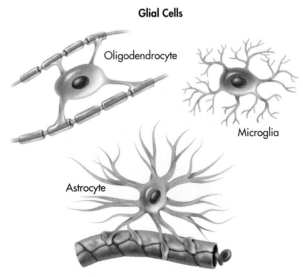

Glial Cells

Oligodendrocyte

Microglia

Astrocyte

Chapter 3: Sensation and Perception

- New Focus on Neuroscience box concerning synesthesia
- Updated biological art throughout the chapter

Chapter 4: Consciousness and Its Variations

- Updated data on drivers distracted by the use of cell phones or who are impaired while tired, and new example of pedestrians distracted while using cell phones
- New information about the dangers of vaping (including lung injuries), particularly from the use of unregulated e-cigarettes
- New information about the rising trend of microdosing, as well as research on its (lack of) effectiveness

Chapter 5: Learning

Design Pics Inc/Alamy Stock Photo

- New section, Beyond Pavlov, discusses Charles Henry Turner, often referred to as the first African American psychologist
- Expanded information on Rosalie Raynor, the research partner and wife of John Watson, whose contributions have long been overlooked; clarification about myths related to the conditioning of Little Albert
- New Focus on Neuroscience: Fear Conditioning
- New section, Mirror Neurons and Observational Learning, with new key term for mirror neurons

Chapter 6: Memory

- New photo example for recency effect involving Mariah Carey not remembering the words to "Auld Lang Syne"
- New In Focus box related to the pandemic, Contact Tracing and the Shortcomings of Memory
- Updated Alzheimer's disease research for the Focus on Neuroscience box Mapping Brain Changes

Chapter 7: Thinking, Language, and Intelligence

Jalil Ahmad/Reuters/Newscom

- New functional fixedness photo example of teenage Afghani girls making inexpensive ventilators during the pandemic
- New section, A Compromise: General and Multiple Intelligences, which introduces the Carroll three-stratum module and Cattel–Horn–Carroll theory of intelligence
- New section, Changing Ideas of Intelligence, on the future of intelligence research
- New information in the text and photo example of Leta Hollingworth, who first used "gifted" as a descriptor for intelligence
- New coverage of Robert Williams, who created the Black Intelligence Test of Cultural Homogeneity

Chapter 8: Motivation and Emotion

- New In Focus box, Focus on Emotion Regulation
- New organization for theories of motivation, now separate sections for Classic Theories of Motivation and Contemporary Theories of Motivation
- New coverage of Dweck's research concerning achievement goal theory

Chapter 9: Lifespan Development

- New Prologue about the unique lifespan perspective of an obituary writer for *The New York Times*, along with an example of the story arc of a life, that of lawyer, ordained minister, and civil rights activist Dovey Johnson Roundtree
- Updated Focus on Neuroscience box: The Adolescent Brain: A Work in Progress

Chapter 10: Gender and Sexuality

- Language updated throughout the chapter based on extensive feedback from GLAAD
- New section on toxic masculinity with new photo related to the gender difference in mask-wearing during the pandemic
- New information about Leta Hollingworth's 100-year-old research questioning a gender difference in cognition
- Updated research in the Critical Thinking box Gender Differences: Women in Science, Technology, Engineering, and Mathematics Fields
- Updated research on intersex people
- New research and historical information on transgender people
- Updated research on sexual orientation, including asexuality and the rising rates of people who identify as bisexual
- New Psych for Your Life, Strengthening Intimate Relationships

RoBeDeRo/Getty Images

Chapter 11: Personality

- New coverage on Karen Horney and her groundbreaking work
- Added information about Melanie Klein's important contributions to psychoanalysis, as well as her debates with Anna Freud
- Discussion of the fact that the Big Five theory of personality may not apply in many non-WEIRD cultures
- New information and research about the HEXACO model of personality, and the benefits of this model across cultures and languages
- Addition of the dark triad (and tetrad) and the light triad of personality
- Addition of research on personality change and "growth," including that due to COVID

Chapter 12: Social Psychology

- New prologue on the Sirens, an all-women motorcycle club that breaks stereotypes, including by volunteering their time to deliver breast milk to babies in need
- New emphasis on the importance of culture to social psychology research, including mention of important articles by Hector Betancourt and Steven Regeser Lopez and by Stanley Sue
- Inclusion of James Jackson and his groundbreaking work on the psychology of Black Americans
- New Focus on Neuroscience box about how ingroup bias helps us ignore our friends' bad behavior, but not strangers' bad behavior
- New research on cognitive dissonance during the pandemic, microaggressions, and overcoming prejudice at both individual and institutional levels
- Inclusion of "intersectionality" as a new key term
- New examples and research related to the pandemic in the Psych for Your Life box on persuasion

GoodLifeStudio/Getty Images

Chapter 13: Stress, Health, and Coping

- New Prologue, Stress and Health in the Time of COVID
- New research on stress and coping during a pandemic
- New research on social and cultural sources of stress
- New research on stress and chromosomes concerning Black women and institutional racism

Chapter 14: Psychological Disorders

- New research on the stigma associated with psychological disorders among different cultural groups
- New research on predicting future episodes of depression
- New coverage of Indian-born psychiatrist Shekhar Saxena, an advocate for increasing access to treatment and reducing stigma globally
- New In Focus box, Mental Health During the Pandemic
- New Focus on Neuroscience box, Hearing and Seeing Within Your Own Mind, about internal speech

Chapter 15: Therapies

- New photo of Tiffany Haddish with a caption concerning the Black community and treatment for mental illness
- New research on the increased demand for mental health care during the pandemic, including unequal access for different groups, and the use of mobile phone apps, and other online sources for eHealth during the pandemic
- New coverage of Carolyn Attneave, "the most well-known psychologist of American Indian background" (LaFromboise & Trimble, 1996)
- New coverage of Martha Bernal, the first U.S. Latina psychologist and a vocal proponent of *multicultural training* for psychologists
- New Table 15.7, Psychological First Aid, about tools that can help others in emergency situations

Appendix A: Statistics

- New Prologue about a failed replication: The (supposed) power of a hot coffee (with updated tables and figures throughout the appendix)
- Expanded information on open science
- New Psych for Your Life about questions to ask when reading about a study in the news

Appendix B: Industrial/Organizational Psychology

- New Prologue on Brittany Graziosi, whose career trajectory captures many of the changes in today's workplace
- Discussion of social movements that affect the workplace, including #MeToo and global antiracism movements
- New research and coverage of workplace challenges in the pandemic, including policies for women
- Updated and new coverage concerning remote work and its popularity, especially during the pandemic, as well as Zoom fatigue

Brittany Graziosi

Features of *Discovering Psychology*

For all that is new in the ninth edition, we were careful to maintain the unique elements that have been so well received in the previous editions. Every feature and element in our text was carefully developed and serves a specific purpose. Described below are the main features of *Discovering Psychology* and a discussion of how these features enhance the learning process.

The **In Focus** boxes explore interesting topics in more depth than the chapter's organization would allow. These boxes highlight interesting research, answer questions that students commonly ask, or show students how psychological research can be applied in their own lives. A few of our favorite In Focus boxes include the following:

- Evolution, Biological Preparedness, and Conditioned Fears: What Gives You the Creeps?, p. 160
- Changing the Behavior of Others: Alternatives to Punishment, p. 167
- Contact Tracing and the Shortcomings of Memory, p. 209
- Detecting Lies, p. 284
- Interpersonal Attraction and Liking, p. 407
- Mental Health During the Pandemic, p. 478
- Increasing Access During the Pandemic: Meeting the Need for Mental Health Care, p. 532

Emphasis on Scientific Literacy

Students come to psychology with many preconceived ideas, some absorbed from popular culture, about the human mind and behavior. These notions are often inaccurate. Our **Myth or Science?** feature helps dispel some of these popular but erroneous beliefs.

Each chapter begins with a list of "Is It True?" questions that reflect popular beliefs about human behavior. Each question is answered in the body of the chapter. A margin note signals the student to find the explanation and indicates whether the statement is "myth" or "science."

One important goal for introductory psychology is to teach students how to distinguish fact from opinion, and research-based, empirical findings from something heard from friends or encountered on the Internet.

Is it true that striking a "power pose" for just a few minutes can affect your hormones and profoundly change your life?

Think Like a Scientist Model and Digital Feature

To help students learn to develop their scientific thinking skills and become critical consumers of information, a unique feature of *Discovering Psychology* is a set of **Think Like a Scientist** digital activities and also available with Achieve. We developed each digital activity specifically for *Discovering Psychology*, providing students with the opportunity to apply their critical thinking and scientific thinking skills. These immersive learning activities combine video, audio, text, and assessment to help students hone and master scientific literacy skills they will use well beyond the introductory course. In these activities, one for each chapter, students will be invited to critically explore questions they encounter in everyday life, such as "Can you learn to tell when someone is lying?" and "Are some people 'left-brained' and some people 'right-brained'?" For the ninth edition, *Think Like a Scientist* activities have been updated to improve accessibility and to reflect recent research.

If you saw a crime take place, would you be a good witness? Go to Achieve to **Think Like a Scientist** about **Eyewitness Testimony.**

These activities employ a simple four-step model introduced in the Critical Thinking box "How to Think Like a Scientist" in Chapter 1. These four steps include:

1. Identify the Claim

2. Evaluate the Evidence

3. Consider Alternative Explanations

4. Consider the Source of the Research or Claim

The *Think Like a Scientist* digital activities are designed to teach and develop a skill set that will persist long after the final exam grades are recorded. We hope to develop a set of transferable skills that can be applied to analyzing dubious claims in any subject area—from advertisements to politics. We think students will enjoy completing these activities—and instructors will value them. Each chapter of *Discovering Psychology* includes a *Think Like a Scientist* digital activity. Some of our favorites include Eyewitness Testimony (Chapter 6), Lie Detection (Chapter 8), Employment-Related Personality Tests (Chapter 11), Coping with Stress (Chapter 13), and Tracking Mental Illness Online (Chapter 14).

This objective is reinforced by the latest revision of the APA Guidelines for the Undergraduate Psychology Major, which identifies Scientific Literacy and Critical Thinking as one of its five key goals. *Discovering Psychology* supports optimal expectations for student performance with clear connections to the American Psychological Association's Guidelines for the Undergraduate Major. (Please ask your sales rep for a full list of these connections.) Scientific literacy and critical thinking skills can help students in a variety of careers and in a variety of majors, and they can help ensure that students become critical consumers of scientific information in the world around them.

Because we carefully guide students through the details of specific experiments and studies, they develop a solid understanding of how scientific evidence is gathered and the interplay between theory and research. And because we rely on original rather than secondary sources, students get an accurate presentation of both classic and contemporary psychological studies.

Emphasis on Critical Thinking

Another important goal of *Discovering Psychology* is to encourage the development of critical thinking skills. To that end, we give students an understanding of how particular topics evolve. In doing so, we also demonstrate the process of challenging preconceptions, evaluating evidence, and revising theories based on new evidence. In short, every chapter shows the process of psychological research—and the important role played by critical thinking in that enterprise.

Beyond discussions in the text proper, every chapter includes one or more **Critical Thinking** boxes. These boxes are carefully designed to encourage students to think

CRITICAL THINKING

about the broader implications of psychological research—to strengthen and refine their critical thinking skills by developing their own positions on questions and issues that don't always have simple answers. Each Critical Thinking box ends with two or three questions that you can use as a written assignment or for classroom discussion. These are some of our favorite Critical Thinking boxes:

• How to Think Like a Scientist, p. 30

• Does Exposure to Media Violence *Cause* Aggressive Behavior?, p. 180

• The Persistence of Unwarranted Beliefs, p. 240

• Emotion in Nonhuman Animals: Laughing Rats, Affectionate Elephants, and Smiling Dolphins?, p. 281

• The Effects of Child Care on Attachment and Development, p. 328

• Do Personality Factors Cause Disease?, p. 455

• Should Social Media Help to Diagnose Disorders?, p. 472

Cultural Coverage

As you can see in Table 1, we weave cultural coverage throughout discussions in the text. We also highlight specific topics in **Culture and Human Behavior** boxes. These boxes increase student awareness of the importance of culture in many areas of human experience, showing students how cultural influences shape behavior and attitudes. Here are some highlights from the Culture and Human Behavior boxes:

CULTURE AND HUMAN BEHAVIOR

- What Is Cross-Cultural Psychology?, p. 14
- Culture's Effects on Early Memories, p. 196
- Where Does the Baby Sleep?, p. 307
- Explaining Failure and Murder: Culture and Attributional Biases, p. 405
- The Stress of Adapting to a New Culture, p. 445

TABLE 1

Integrated Cultural Coverage

In addition to the topics covered in the Cultural and Human Behavior boxes, this table highlights some of the other cultural influences addressed throughout the text.

Page(s)	Topic	Page(s)	Topic
23	The problem of WEIRD samples in psychology research	352–353	Discussion of variations in gender identity and gender expression globally
7–9	The groundbreaking work of Mamie Phipps Clark and Kenneth Clark that showed the harmful effects of segregation on children	354	Discussion of the Yogyakarta Principles, global human rights guidelines related to the LGBTQ community
11–13	Culture, social loafing, and social striving	382	Lexical approach to understanding personality traits globally
96	Cross-cultural research on the language of smell in non-Western groups	405–406	Cross-cultural research on the universality of the five-factor model of personality
101	Cross-cultural research on effects of ethnicity and culture on pain perception	400, 405, 416–417, 428, 429	Discussion of the importance of culture to social psychology
147	Research collaboration between Tibetan Buddhist monks and Western neuroscientists	400	James Jackson's groundbreaking work on the psychology of Black Americans
265	Spontaneous development of sign languages in a Nicaraguan school and a Bedouin village as cross-cultural evidence of innate human predisposition to develop language	430	Attributional biases in individualistic versus collectivistic cultures
267	Native language and infant language development	432	Cultural differences in interpersonal attraction
267	Cross-cultural research on infant-directed speech	412	Expanded research on microaggressions
272–273	Historical misuse of IQ tests to evaluate immigrants	409	Discussion of intersectionality
273	Wechsler's recognition of the importance of culture and ethnicity in developing the WAIS intelligence test	449	Stress and institutional racism
		503	Description of the World Health Organization's *International Classification of Diseases*
257–258	Robert Williams as a pioneer in understanding race and intelligence	568–569	Mechanisms for increasing access to mental health care worldwide
281–282	Rapid gains in IQ scores in different nations		
298	Role of globalization in the increase of obesity in developing countries worldwide	B-10, B-12	Discussion of global antiracist movements and their impact on the workplace
380	Cultural differences in the effectiveness of different parenting styles		

Gender Coverage

Besides the new chapter to this edition, Gender and Sexuality, we cover gender influences and gender differences in many chapters. Table 2 highlights some of the integrated coverage of gender-related issues and topics in *Discovering Psychology.* To help identify the contributions made by female researchers, the full names of researchers are provided in the References section at the end of the text. When researchers are identified using initials instead of first names (as APA style recommends), many students automatically assume that the researchers are male.

Neuroscience Coverage

Psychology and neuroscience have become intricately intertwined. Especially in the past decade, the scientific understanding of the brain and its relation to human behavior has grown dramatically. The imaging techniques of brain science — PET scans, MRIs, functional MRIs, and diffusion MRIs — have become familiar terminology to many students, even if they don't completely understand the differences among them. To reflect that growing trend, we have increased our neuroscience coverage to show students how an understanding of the brain can help explain the complete range of human behavior, from the ordinary to the

 FOCUS ON NEUROSCIENCE

TABLE 2

Integrated Gender Coverage

Page(s)	Topic
4	Titchener's inclusion of female graduate students in his psychology program in the late 1800s
6	Contributions of Mary Whiton Calkins to psychology
6	Contributions of Margaret Floy Washburn to psychology
6	Christine Ladd Franklin's activism against Titchener's exclusion of women from professional organizations
8–9	Contributions of Mamie Phipps Clark related to the harm segregation caused children
67	Sex differences and the brain
91	Gender differences in incidence of color blindness
101	Gender differences in the perception of pain
136	Gender differences in dream content
153–154	Expanded discussion of Rosalie Raynor's role in her research with John Watson
166	Women as research assistants in Pavlov's laboratories
253, 344	Contributions of Leta Hollingworth, including related to gender and intelligence
284	Test performance and the influence of gender stereotypes
298	Gender differences in sedentary lifestyles
300–301	Sex differences in the pattern of human sexual response
343	Definitions of gender, gender role, and gender identity

Page(s)	Topic
343	Discussion of toxic masculinity
343–345	Gender differences in childhood behavior
343–350	Development of gender identity and gender roles
345–348	Theories of gender-role development
349–350	Variations in gender identity
360–362	Gender and accelerated puberty in father-absent homes
371–373	Expanded and new coverage of Karen Horney, Melanie Klein, and Anna Freud related to psychoanalysis and gender
432	Gender similarities and differences in interpersonal attraction
435–436	Misleading effect of gender stereotypes
486–488	Gender differences in providing social support and effects of social support
487–488	Gender differences in responding to stress — the "tend-and-befriend" response
531	Contributions of Carolyn Attneave, groundbreaking American Indian psychologist
538	Contributions of Martha Bernal, groundbreaking Latina psychologist and a proponent of multicultural training for psychologists
B-10	Discussion of the #MeToo movement and its impact on the workplace

unusual. Each chapter contains one or more **Focus on Neuroscience** discussions that are designed to complement the broader chapter discussion. Here are some highlights from the ninth edition:

- Imaging the Brain, p. 56
- Synesthesia, p. 84
- The Sleep-Deprived Emotional Brain, p. 121
- Assembling Memories: Echoes and Reflections of Perception, p. 215
- Seeing Faces and Places in the Mind's Eye, p. 231
- The Adolescent Brain: A Work in Progress, p. 318
- The Mysterious Placebo Effect, p. 450
- The Hallucinating Brain, p. 501

Psych for Your Life

 PSYCH FOR YOUR LIFE

Among all the sciences, psychology is unique in the degree to which it speaks to our daily lives and applies to everyday problems and concerns. The **Psych for Your Life** feature at the end of each chapter presents the findings from psychological research that address a wide variety of problems and concerns. In each of these features, we present research-based information in a form that students can use to enhance everyday functioning. As you can see in the following list, topics range from strengthening close relationships to coping with stress:

- Successful Study Techniques, p. 33
- Ten Steps to Boost Your Memory, p. 223
- Strengthening Intimate Relationships, p. 359
- Raising Psychologically Healthy Children, p. 333
- Minimizing the Effects of Stress, p. 463
- Five Questions to Ask When You Read a Study in the News, p. A-12

The Pedagogical System

The pedagogical system in *Discovering Psychology* was carefully designed to help students identify important information, test for retention, and learn how to learn.

A special student preface titled **To the Student** describes the complete pedagogical system and demonstrates how students can make the most of it.

The pedagogical system has four main components: (1) Advance Organizers, (2) Chapter Reviews, (3) Concept Maps, and (4) Achieve *and* Achieve: Read & Practice for *Discovering Psychology*, Ninth Edition. Major sections are introduced by an **Advance Organizer** that identifies the section's *Key Theme* followed by a bulleted list of *Key Questions*.

Several other in-chapter pedagogical aids support the Advance Organizers and Concept Reviews. A clearly identified **Chapter Outline** provides an overview of topics and organization. Each chapter begins with a carefully chosen **Prologue**, and the stories we tell reflect one of the most effective teaching methods: the narrative approach. In addition to engaging the reader, each story serves as a pedagogical springboard to illustrating important concepts and ideas. Every story is used to connect new ideas, terms, and ways of looking at behavior to information with which the student is already familiar. Within the chapter, **key terms** are set in boldface type and defined in the margin. *Pronunciation guides* are included for difficult or unfamiliar words. Because students often have trouble identifying the most important theorists and researchers, names of **key people** are set in boldface type within the chapter. The **Chapter Review** provides a page-referenced list of key people and key terms.

Concept Maps are visual reviews that encourage students to review and check their learning at the end of the chapter. The hierarchical layout shows how themes, concepts, and facts are related to one another. Chapter photos are included as visual cues to important chapter information.

Updated connections to the American Psychological Association Guidelines, with references to the APA/IPI recommendations can be found in with the online Instructor Resources. We believe the ninth edition beautifully reflects the *American Psychological Association (APA) Introductory Psychology Initiative (APA/IPI)*. The APA released the results of the initiative in August 2020 and encourages instructors to adopt seven integrative themes. The APA also approved seven learning outcomes. *Discovering Psychology,* Ninth Edition, and the Achieve course will help faculty incorporate these seven themes into the classroom; Macmillan offers a downloadable instructor's resource with tagging suggestions.

Instructor's Resources

- The **Instructor's Resource Manual** contains a wealth of helpful materials that instructors can use to plan their courses, including lecture guides, suggestions for engaging activities for both in-person and asynchronous learning, advice for teaching students with a range of backgrounds and experience levels, and suggestions for additional videos and current events to help demonstrate the connections between psychology and students' everyday lives. The Instructor's Resource Manual is available in Achieve or for download from macmillanlearning.com.

- Macmillan also provides a downloadable guide to the Connections to the APA Guidelines for the Undergraduate Psychology Major and Connections to the APA Guidelines for the APA/IPI Initiatives.

- **Test Bank**, revised by Samantha Spitler, includes over 5,000 multiple-choice and essay questions. Each question is linked to specific textbook content, learning objectives, APA outcomes, and Bloom's taxonomy levels. The test bank is integrated into Achieve, making it easy to track students' progress with Achieve's analytics. It is also available at macmillanlearning.com

- There are fully updated **Lecture Slides** available for each chapter, which include figures, art, and tables from the book. These can be used as is or easily modified to suit each instructor's course needs. The lecture slides are available for download at macmillanlearning.com

- **iClicker questions** are available for every chapter to promote active learning in class, offering a range of different question types and polls that students can interact with using iClicker remotes or their smartphones, laptops, and tablets using the Reef mobile app.

Acknowledgments

Many talented people contributed to this project. First, we would like to acknowledge the efforts of our supplements team, who created materials specifically devoted to our book. Our thanks to:

- **Abigail A. Baird,** Vassar College, for bringing her neuroscience expertise to the ninth edition—especially her revisions to the chapters concerning Neuroscience and Behavior, Sensation and Perception, and Lifespan Development, as well as the new and beautiful neurological art found in those chapters.

- **Alex Schmider,** the Associate Director for Transgender Representation at GLAAD, for his thoughtful and careful suggestions for revising the language in the Gender and Sexuality chapter, making it more accurate and more inclusive.

- **Graphic World** for carefully updating the Test Bank and Practice Quizzes for this edition.
- **Claudia Cochran-Miller** at El Paso Community College and **Marie Waung** at the University of Michigan at Dearborn for their contributions to the appendix on industrial/organizational psychology.
- **Marie D. Thomas** at California State University, San Marcos, for her contributions to the student-friendly statistics appendix.

As colleagues who care as much as we do about teaching, they have our gratitude for their hard work and commitment to excellence.

We are indebted to our colleagues who acted as reviewers throughout the development of the ninth edition of *Discovering Psychology*. Their thoughtful suggestions and advice helped us refine and strengthen this edition. To the reviewers, thank you for your feedback, reviews, and ideas. Your contributions have influenced the new edition greatly:

- **Allison Allen,** Indiana University Southeast
- **Adolfo Alvarez,** The University of Texas at El Paso
- **Jamie Arnold,** Temple College
- **Kathleen Bartolini,** Middlesex Community College—Lowell
- **Kathleen Cain,** Gettysburg College
- **Netali Chopra,** College of Dupage
- **Diana Ciesko,** Valencia College
- **Madison Clement,** University of New Hampshire—Main Campus
- **Mary Ann Constantini,** Eastern Gateway Community College
- **Barry Davis,** South Florida Bible College and Theological Seminary
- **Eugene DeRobertis,** Brookdale Community College
- **Julia Dickinson,** Chabot College
- **Lisa Fozio-Thielk,** Waubonsee Community College
- **Marc Gentzler,** Valencia College
- **Brett Heintz,** Delgado Community College
- **Brooke Hindman,** Greenville Technical College
- **Monique Johnson Dixon,** St. Philip's College
- **Dylan Kreischer,** Indiana State University
- **Shannon Lance,** Front Range Community College
- **Margaret Jelinek Lewis,** Lone Star College—Tomball
- **Jessica Mahoney,** Front Range Community College
- **Cade Mansfield,** Weber State University
- **Richard Marmer,** American River College
- **Rene Meyers,** North Central Kansas Technical College
- **Ry Mittlestadt,** Front Range Community College
- **Cynthia Nicodemus,** Howard Community College
- **Natasha Otto,** Morgan State University
- **Timothy B. Patrick,** Indiana University Bloomington
- **Laura Sherrick,** Front Range Community College
- **Maria Shpurik,** Florida International University

- **Jeannine Stamatakis,** Lincoln University
- **Elayne Thompson,** Harper College
- **Jill Urban-Bollis,** Illinois Valley Community College
- **Christine Weinkauff-Duranso,** Univ North Georgia — Oconee

The remarkable people who make up Worth Publishers have a well-earned reputation for producing college textbooks and supplements of the highest quality. Special thanks to executive vice president Charles Linsmeier for his enthusiasm, humor, and unfailing support of our project. We greatly benefited from the strong guidance, good judgment, and clarifying insights of our senior executive program manager, Carolyn Merrill. Our talented development editor, Michael Kimball, has a rare ability to both zero in on details and see the big picture. His input consistently made the narrative clearer and more compelling. Thanks also go to editorial assistant Allison Curley, who expertly and cheerfully kept track of countless details and managed the enormous image program with great ease. Next up is associate development editor Nick Rizzuti, whose help with reviews for content and diversity was indispensable. And his thoughtful development work made the new **Tell Me More** videos possible. The beautiful design for the ninth edition reflects the creative talents of designers at Lumina Datamatics, Inc. We never cease to be impressed by their ability to create the seamless interaction of text, graphics, boxes, and features that you see on every page of *Discovering Psychology*. The stunning graphics of this edition represent the combined talents of illustrator Eli Ensor, art manager Matthew McAdams, senior media permissions manager and photo editor Christine Buese, and photo researcher Richard Fox, whose creative efforts to find just the right image are greatly appreciated.

By any standard, senior director of content management enhancement Tracey Kuehn is an unbelievably talented and dedicated person. Senior managing editor Lisa Kinne effectively tackled and resolved the inevitable problems that accompany a project of this complexity. One of the heroes in this project was senior content project manager Edward Dionne. Without Ed's enormous patience, insightful decision making, and unflappable attention to the workflow during a pandemic, we would still be working on this text! Kate Daly was masterful, as always, in her excellent copyedits throughout the text.

Perhaps the greatest unsung heroes in college textbook publishing are the media editors. At Worth Publishers, those editors work tirelessly to set the standard by which all other publishers are judged. With conscientious attention to a multitude of details, director of media editorial and assessment Noel Hohnstine and media editor Stefani Wallace expertly assembled the integrated program of print, video, and digital supplements that accompanies our text. Psychology marketing manager Kate Nurre helped launch the ninth edition with her expertly coordinated advertising, marketing, and sales support efforts.

A few personal acknowledgments are in order. Susan is immensely grateful to her husband, Ivan Bojanic, for his love and support, and for patiently enduring endless tales of fascinating psychology research. She also thanks Kaylise Algrim, Tahra Anglade, and Prachi Pathak for their invaluable research assistance and insightful feedback. In particular, Susan is immensely grateful to MaryClare Colombo, whose extraordinary research assistance went well beyond typical expectations for the job. Her thoughtful input and creative ideas made this a better book. Susan thanks, too, her colleagues and friends at Seton Hall University and in the psychology teaching community more broadly, as well as the many students whose reactions to the material covered in the Introduction to Psychology course have shaped her teaching and writing. Finally, Susan is indebted to Seton Hall University Department of Psychology secretary Willie Yaylaci for her ongoing friendship and support.

Sandy would like to thank the friends and family members who kindly allowed us to share their stories with you. Sadly, Fern and Erv are no longer with us, but they live on in our memories, as well as in the personal stories we continue to tell about them. Last but surely not least, Sandy's daughter Laura has lived with this project since birth and is now in grad school working her way to becoming a psychologist in her own right. Laura, thank you for your idealism, your generous heart, and for being true to yourself.

We hope that your class is an enjoyable and successful one as you introduce your students to the most fascinating and personally relevant science that exists.

To the Student

Learning from *Discovering Psychology*

Welcome to psychology! Our names are **Susan Nolan** and **Sandy Hockenbury**. We're the authors of your textbook. Our favorite course to teach is introductory psychology. Every aspect of this book has been carefully designed to help you get the most out of your introductory psychology course. Before you begin reading, take a few minutes to familiarize yourself with the special features and learning aids in this book.

Learning Aids in the Text

■ **KEY THEME**

You can enhance your chances for success in psychology by using the learning aids that have been built into this textbook.

= **KEY QUESTIONS**

* What are the functions of the Prologue, "Myth or Science?" questions, Advance Organizers, Key Terms, Key People, and Concept Maps?
* What are the functions of the different types of boxes in this text, and why should you read them?
* Where can you go to access a virtual study guide at any time of the day or night, and what study aids are provided?

First, read and think about the **Myth or Science?** questions at the beginning of each chapter. In the course of reading the chapter, you'll find out which statements are popular myths—and which are actually true and based on scientific evidence.

Next, take a look at the **Chapter Outline** at the beginning of each chapter, which overviews the main topics in the chapter.

Then, read the chapter **Prologue**. The Prologues are true stories about real people. In each chapter, we return to the people and stories introduced in the Prologue to illustrate important themes and concepts.

You will notice several special elements. The beginning of each major section includes an **Advance Organizer**—a short section preview that looks like the one above.

The **Key Theme** provides you with a preview of the material in the section to come. The **Key Questions** will help you focus on some of the most important material in the section. Keep the questions in mind as you read the section.

The visual **Concept Maps** at the end of each chapter give you a hierarchical layout showing how themes, concepts, and facts are related to one another. Use the visual Concept Maps to review the information in each section.

Special Features in the Text

Each chapter in *Discovering Psychology* has several boxes that focus on different kinds of topics. They present important information that you may be expected to know for class discussion or tests. There are four types of boxes:

* **Critical Thinking** boxes ask you to stretch your mind a bit by presenting issues that are provocative or controversial. They will help you actively question the implications of the material that you are learning.

* **Culture and Human Behavior** boxes highlight cultural differences in thinking and behavior. They will help to make you aware of the ways in which people's behavior, including your own, has been influenced by cultural factors.

 Achieve

Can you identify the emotions represented by different facial expressions? Go to **Achieve** and try **Concept Practice: Facial Expressions of Emotion.**

(l) Ekman & Matsumoto, Japanese and Caucasian Facial Expressions of Emotions
(r) Ana Blazic Pavlovic/Shutterstock

 CRITICAL THINKING

 CULTURE AND HUMAN BEHAVIOR

- **In Focus** boxes present interesting information or research. Think of them as sidebar discussions. They deal with topics as diverse as human pheromones, whether animals dream, and why snakes and spiders give so many people the creeps.

- **Focus on Neuroscience** sections provide clear explanations of intriguing studies that use brain imaging techniques to study psychological processes. Among the topics that are highlighted: schizophrenic hallucinations, mental images, drug addiction, and romantic love.

The **Psych for Your Life** sections at the end of each chapter provide specific suggestions to help apply chapter information to real-life concerns. These suggestions are based on psychological research, rather than opinions, anecdotes, or pop psych self-help philosophies.

Especially important is the Psych for Your Life section at the end of Chapter 1, which provides a list of research-based study techniques that you can use to help you succeed in psychology and other courses. In addition, the Psych for Your Life sections for Chapters 5, 6, and 8 deal with setting and achieving goals and enhancing motivation and memory, so you may want to skip ahead and read them after you finish this To the Student section. We hope that all of the Psych for Your Life sections make a difference in your life.

Also at the back of this text is a **Glossary** containing the definitions for all **key terms** in the book and the pages on which they are discussed in more detail.

That's it! We hope you enjoy reading and learning from the ninth edition of *Discovering Psychology*. Have a great semester!

DISCOVERING PSYCHOLOGY

Is it true . . .

▶ That the field of psychology focuses primarily on treating people with psychological problems and disorders?

▶ That Sigmund Freud was the first psychologist?

▶ That striking a "power pose" for just a few minutes can affect your hormones?

▶ That reading something over and over is the most effective way to prepare for a test?

▶ That when two behaviors are "linked," "related," or tend to occur together, it's safe to assume that one behavior caused the other?

▶ That psychologists are not allowed to trick you into taking part in a study?

Introduction and Research Methods

PROLOGUE

~

The First Exam

"So let's talk about the upcoming exam," your author Sandy began. "What are you planning to do to prepare?"

Janelle started, "I like to study by testing myself. Will we have the chance to take practice tests?"

Sandy responded, "Thanks, Janelle. That's a great technique, and one backed by research. And yes, we'll definitely have practice tests. Anyone else?"

"I'm going to work on my test anxiety in addition to studying," Derek piped up. "I actually started doing energy healing to reduce my stress levels. My girlfriend swears by it."

"How does energy healing work, and what's it supposed to do?" Sandy asked.

"An energy healer moves their hands around your body, mostly without touching you," Derek said. "It was on a Netflix show called *The Goop Lab* if you want to see it. The healer tries to release energy from a part of your body where your energy might be stuck. In my case, they're trying to release it to reduce stress and anxiety. I figured it couldn't hurt, so why not try it?"

"I'm not aware of any research on energy healing for test anxiety," Sandy said carefully. "But let's look it up and see what we find out."

Later in the chapter, we'll share what we found out about energy healing. More

Klaus Vedfelt/Getty Images

CHAPTER 1

important, we'll discuss what psychologists have discovered about the most effective ways to study. You'll also see how psychological research can help you critically evaluate new ideas and claims that you encounter outside the classroom.

As you'll discover, psychology has a lot to say about many of the questions that are of interest to college students. In this introductory chapter, we'll explore the scope of contemporary psychology as well as psychology's historical origins. The common theme connecting psychology's varied topics is its reliance on a solid foundation of scientific evidence. By the end of the chapter, you'll have a better appreciation of the scientific methods that psychologists use to answer questions, big and small, about behavior and mental processes.

Welcome to psychology!

psychology The scientific study of behavior and mental processes.

Introduction: What Is Psychology?

■ KEY THEME

Psychology's origins and history helped to shape its current status as the science of behavior and mental processes.

⹀ KEY QUESTIONS

- What are the goals and scope of contemporary psychology?
- What roles did Wundt, Titchener, and James play in establishing psychology?
- What were the early schools of thought and approaches in psychology, and how did their views differ?

Psychology is formally defined as *the scientific study of behavior and mental processes.* But this definition is deceptively simple. As you'll see in this chapter, the scope of contemporary psychology is broad—ranging from the behavior of a single brain cell to the behavior of a crowd of people or even entire cultures.

Many people think that psychologists are primarily—or even exclusively—interested in studying and treating psychological disorders and problems, but that's a myth. Psychologists are just as interested in "normal," everyday behaviors and mental processes—topics like learning and memory, emotions and motivation, relationships and loneliness. And, psychologists seek ways to use the knowledge that they discover through scientific research to optimize human performance and potential in many different fields, from classrooms to workplaces to the military.

The four basic goals of psychology are to *describe, predict, explain,* and *control* or *influence* behavior and mental processes. To illustrate how these goals guide psychological research, think about our chapter opening Prologue. Most people, like Derek, have an intuitive understanding of what the word *stress* refers to. Psychologists, however, seek to go beyond intuitive or "common sense" understandings of human experience.

Here's how psychology's goals might help guide research on stress:

1. *Describe:* Trying to objectively *describe* the experience of stress, a psychologist studies the sequence of emotional responses that occur during stressful experiences.

2. *Predict:* A psychologist investigates responses to different kinds of challenging events, hoping to be able to *predict* the kinds of events that are most likely to evoke a stress response.

3. *Explain:* Seeking to *explain* why some people are more vulnerable to the effects of stress than others, a psychologist studies the different ways in which people respond to natural disasters.

4. *Control, change, or influence:* After studying the effectiveness of different coping strategies, a psychologist helps people use those coping strategies to better *control* their reactions to stressful events.

How did psychology evolve into today's diverse and rich science? We begin this introductory chapter by stepping backward in time to describe the origins of psychology and its historical development. Indeed, the early history of psychology is the history of a field struggling to define itself as a separate and unique scientific discipline. The early psychologists debated such fundamental issues as:

- What is the proper subject matter of psychology?
- What methods should be used to investigate psychological issues?
- Should psychological findings be used to change or enhance human behavior?

These debates helped set the tone of the new science, define its scope, and set its limits. Over the past century, the shifting focus of these debates has influenced the topics studied and the research methods used.

MYTH ◀ SCIENCE

Is it true that the field of psychology focuses primarily on treating people with psychological problems and disorders?

Carmine Marinelli/Newscom

⌃ **What Do Psychologists Study?** It's International Pillow Fight Day, and these young members of a flash mob join the fun in Vancouver, British Columbia. What motivated them to show up? What kind of emotions might they be feeling? How does the presence of like-minded others affect their behavior? Whether studying the behavior of a crowd of people or a single brain cell, psychologists rely on the scientific method to guide their investigations.

Psychology's Origins: The Influence of Philosophy and Physiology

The earliest origins of psychology can be traced back several centuries to the writings of the great philosophers. More than 2,000 years ago, the Greek philosopher Aristotle wrote about topics such as sleep, dreams, the senses, and memory. Many of Aristotle's ideas remained influential until the beginnings of modern science in the seventeenth century (Kheriaty, 2007).

At that time, the French philosopher René Descartes (1596–1650) proposed the idea that mind and body were separate entities that interact to produce sensations, emotions, and other conscious experiences. Today, psychologists continue to explore the relationship between mental activity and the brain.

Philosophers also laid the groundwork for another issue that would become central to psychology, the *nature–nurture issue.* For centuries, philosophers debated which was more important: the inborn *nature* of the individual or the environmental influences that *nurture* the individual. This debate was sometimes framed as nature *versus* nurture. Today, however, psychologists understand that "nature" and "nurture" are impossible to unravel (Sameroff, 2010). So, while some psychologists do investigate the relative influences of *heredity versus environmental factors* on behavior, today's researchers also focus on the dynamic *interaction* between environmental factors and genetic heritage (Dick et al., 2015; Norouzitallab et al., 2019; Szyf, 2013).

The early philosophers could advance the understanding of human behavior only to a certain point. Their methods were limited to intuition, observation, and logic.

The eventual emergence of psychology as a science hinged on advances in other sciences, particularly physiology. *Physiology* is a branch of biology that studies the functions and parts of living organisms, including humans. In the 1600s, physiologists were becoming interested in the human brain and its relation to behavior. By the early 1700s, it was discovered that damage to one side of the brain produced a loss of function in the opposite side of the body. By the early 1800s, the idea that different brain areas were related to different behavioral functions was being vigorously debated. Collectively, the early scientific discoveries made by physiologists helped to establish the foundation for an idea that was to prove critical to the emergence of psychology—namely, that scientific methods could be applied to answering questions about behavior and mental processes.

For an overview of psychology today, go to **Achieve** and watch **Video: What Is Psychology?**

⌃ **Nature and Nurture?** Both father and daughter are clearly enjoying the experience of making music together. The child's interest in music is likely an expression of her natural tendencies, as well as the result of her father's encouragement and teaching.

Wilhelm Wundt: The Founder of Psychology

By the second half of the 1800s, the stage had been set for the emergence of psychology as a distinct scientific discipline. The leading proponent of this idea was a German physiologist named **Wilhelm Wundt** (Gentile & Miller, 2009). Wundt used scientific methods to study fundamental psychological processes, such as mental reaction times in response to visual or auditory stimuli. For example, Wundt tried to measure precisely how long it took a person to consciously detect the sight and sound of a bell being struck.

A major turning point in psychology occurred in 1874, when Wundt outlined the connections between physiology and psychology in his landmark text, *Principles of Physiological Psychology* (Diamond, 2001). He argued that psychology should be established as a separate scientific discipline that would use experimental methods to study mental processes.

Wundt achieved that goal in 1879, when he established the first psychology research laboratory at the University of Leipzig. Wundt's experiments were simple by today's standards but groundbreaking for the time. For example, participants might be asked to press a key when they saw a white circle but not a black circle, and trained students would measure the participants' reaction times. The experiment would be repeated with more complex stimuli and the reaction times compared (Robinson, 2001). Many mark the opening of Wundt's psychology lab as the formal beginning of psychology as an experimental science (Kohls & Benedikter, 2010).

⌃ **Wilhelm Wundt (1832–1920)** German physiologist Wilhelm Wundt is generally credited as being the founder of psychology as an experimental science.

Wundt defined psychology as the study of consciousness and emphasized the use of experimental methods to study and measure it. Until he died in 1920, Wundt exerted a strong influence on the development of psychology as a science (Wong, 2009).

Edward B. Titchener: Structuralism

One of Wundt's most devoted students was a young Englishman named **Edward B. Titchener**. After earning his doctorate in Wundt's laboratory, Titchener began teaching at Cornell University in New York. There he established a psychology laboratory that ultimately spanned 26 rooms.

Titchener shared many of Wundt's ideas about the nature of psychology. Eventually, however, Titchener developed his own approach, which he called *structuralism*, and it became the first major school of thought in psychology. **Structuralism** *held that even our most complex conscious experiences could be broken down into elemental "structures," or component parts, of sensations and feelings.* To identify these structures of conscious thought, Titchener trained research participants in a procedure called *introspection.* The participants viewed a simple stimulus, such as a book, and then tried to reconstruct their sensations and feelings immediately after viewing it. (In psychology, a *stimulus* is anything perceptible to the senses, such as a sight, sound, smell, touch, or taste.) They might first report on the colors they saw, then the smells, and so on, in the attempt to create a total description of their conscious experience (Titchener, 1896).

In addition to being distinguished as the first school of thought in early psychology, Titchener's structuralism holds the dubious distinction of being the first school to disappear. Titchener's death in 1927 essentially marked the end of structuralism as an influential school of thought in psychology. But even before Titchener's death, structuralism was often criticized for relying too heavily on introspection as a method.

As noted by Wundt and other scientists, introspection had significant limitations. First, introspection was an unreliable method of investigation. Different participants often provided very different introspective reports about the same stimulus. Even participants well trained in introspection varied in their responses to the same stimulus from trial to trial.

Second, introspection could not be used to study children or animals. Third, complex topics, such as learning, development, mental disorders, and personality, could not be investigated using introspection. Ultimately, the methods and goals of structuralism were too limited to accommodate the rapidly expanding interests of the field of psychology.

William James: Functionalism

By the time Titchener arrived at Cornell University, psychology was already well established in the United States. The main proponent of psychology in the United States was one of Harvard's most outstanding teachers — **William James**. James had become intrigued by the emerging science of psychology after reading one of Wundt's articles. But there were other influences on the development of James's thinking.

Like many other scientists and philosophers of his generation, James was fascinated by the idea that different species had evolved over time (Menand, 2001). Many nineteenth-century scientists in England, France, and the United States were *evolutionists* — that is, they believed that species had not been created all at once but rather had changed over time (Caton, 2007).

Published in 1859, **Charles Darwin's** groundbreaking work, *On the Origin of Species,* gathered evidence from different scientific fields to provide a compelling account of evolution through natural selection. James and his fellow thinkers actively debated the notion of evolution, which came to have a profound influence on James's ideas (Richardson, 2006). Like Darwin, James stressed the importance of adaptation to environmental challenges.

▲ **Edward B. Titchener (1867–1927)**
In contrast to faculty at other psychology programs, Edward Titchener welcomed women into his graduate program at Cornell. In fact, more women completed their psychology doctorates under Titchener's direction than under any other male psychologist of his generation (Evans, 1991). Despite this, Christine Ladd-Franklin, a prominent researcher of color vision, pushed back against psychology organizations that excluded women. She fought Titchener with a letter-writing campaign to accept women to the all-male Society of Experimentalists (Vaughn, 2010). Unfortunately, Titchener never gave in, and the first women were only admitted after his death. Ladd-Franklin did, however, crash one meeting, having warned Titchener in advance of her intentions.

structuralism Early school of psychology holding that even our most complex conscious experiences could be broken down into elemental "*structures,*" or component parts, of sensations and feelings.

By the late 1870s, James was teaching psychology classes and writing a comprehensive textbook of psychology, a task that would take him more than a decade. James's *Principles of Psychology* was finally published in 1890. Despite its length of more than 1,400 pages, *Principles of Psychology* quickly became the leading psychology textbook. In it, James discussed such diverse topics as brain function, habit, memory, sensation, perception, and emotion.

James's ideas became the basis for a new school of psychology called functionalism. **Functionalism** *emphasized studying the purpose, or function, of behavior and mental experiences*. It stressed the importance of how behavior *functions* to allow people and animals to adapt to their environments. Unlike structuralists, functionalists did not limit their methods to introspection. They expanded the scope of psychological research to include direct observation of living creatures in natural settings. They also examined how psychology could be applied to areas like education, child rearing, and the work environment.

Both the structuralists and the functionalists thought that psychology should focus on the study of conscious experiences. But the functionalists had very different ideas about the nature of consciousness and how it should be studied. Rather than trying to identify the essential structures of consciousness at a given moment, James saw consciousness as an ongoing stream of mental activity that shifts and changes.

Like structuralism, functionalism no longer exists as a distinct school of thought in contemporary psychology. Nevertheless, functionalism's twin themes of the importance of the adaptive role of behavior and the application of psychology to enhance human behavior are still important in modern psychology.

William James (1842–1910)
Harvard professor William James was instrumental in establishing psychology in the United States. James's ideas became the basis of another early school of psychology, called *functionalism*, which stressed studying the adaptive and practical functions of human behavior.

After James: Prominent Early Psychologists Historically, any list of prominent early psychologists consisted of primarily White men, with a few exceptions. But many other people made important contributions that were buried by history (Cramblet Alvarez et al., 2019). Among the overlooked are two people who tried valiantly, through their work, to call attention to important omissions — Robert V. Guthrie and Pauline Elizabeth Scarborough. In 1976, **Robert V. Guthrie** (1932–2005), a Black American psychologist, wrote a book for which part of the title was *Even the Rat Was White*. Guthrie highlighted important contributions by early Black American psychologists and described the significant obstacles they faced.

Pauline Elizabeth Scarborough (1935–2015), a Russian-born American psychologist, championed the inclusion of women in the story of U.S. psychology. She and psychologist Laurel Furumoto documented the lives of the first 25 female psychologists in the United States. She also explored the way that women's changing social status affected the field of psychology (Scarborough, 2005).

Throughout the book, we'll do our best to highlight overlooked psychologists from underrepresented groups — those who are women, members of racial and ethnic minorities, or part of the LGBTQ community. In this section, you'll learn about Kenneth and Mamie Clark. Mamie Clark's story, in particular, has been hidden for far too long (Aldridge & Christensen, 2013; Cramblet Alvarez et al., 2019). For now, back to James.

Like Wundt, James profoundly influenced psychology through his many students. Two of James's most notable students were G. Stanley Hall and Mary Whiton Calkins.

In 1878, **G. Stanley Hall** received the first Ph.D. in psychology awarded in the United States. Hall founded the first psychology research laboratory in the United States at Johns Hopkins University in 1883. Most important, in 1892, Hall founded the American Psychological Association and was elected its first president (Anderson, 2012). Today, the American Psychological Association (APA) is the world's largest professional organization of psychologists, with more than 120,000 members. (The Association for Psychological Science, founded in 1988, has more than 35,000 members.)

functionalism Early school of psychology that emphasized studying the purpose, or function, of behavior and mental experiences.

Mary Whiton Calkins (1863–1930)
Mary Whiton Calkins had a distinguished professional career. She established a psychology laboratory at Wellesley College and became the first woman president of the American Psychological Association.

In 1890, **Mary Whiton Calkins** was assigned the task of teaching experimental psychology at a new women's college in the United States—Wellesley College. Calkins studied with James at nearby Harvard University. She completed all the requirements for a Ph.D. in psychology. However, Harvard refused to grant her the Ph.D. degree because she was a woman, and at the time Harvard was not a coeducational institution (Pickren & Rutherford, 2010).

Although never awarded the degree she had earned, Calkins made several notable contributions to psychology. She conducted research in dreams, memory, and personality. In 1891, she established a psychology laboratory at Wellesley College. At the turn of the twentieth century, she wrote a well-received textbook titled *Introduction to Psychology*. In 1905, Calkins was elected president of the American Psychological Association—the first woman, but far from the last, to hold that position.

For the record, the first U.S. woman to earn an official Ph.D. in psychology was **Margaret Floy Washburn**, Edward Titchener's first doctoral student at Cornell University. Washburn strongly advocated the scientific study of the mental processes of different animal species. In 1908, she published an influential text titled *The Animal Mind.* Her book summarized research on sensation, perception, learning, and other "inner experiences" of different animal species. Like Mary Whiton Calkins, Washburn taught at a women's college, Vassar College, which she also had attended as a student.

One of G. Stanley Hall's notable students was **Francis C. Sumner**. Sumner was the first Black American psychologist to receive a Ph.D. in psychology, awarded by Clark University in 1920. Later, at Howard University in Washington, D.C., Sumner chaired a psychology department that produced more Black American psychologists than all other U.S. colleges and universities combined (Guthrie, 2000, 2004). One of Sumner's most famous students was **Kenneth Bancroft Clark**. Kenneth Clark, together with his wife, psychologist **Mamie Phipps Clark**, conducted research on the negative effects of racial discrimination. Their work was instrumental in the U.S. Supreme Court's 1954 decision to end segregation in schools (Jackson, 2006). Mamie Clark's contributions were long overlooked, including the fact that the segregation research was initially her project, rather than

Margaret Floy Washburn (1871–1939) After becoming the first woman in the United States to earn an official Ph.D. in psychology, Washburn went on to a distinguished career in psychology, publishing more than 100 papers and an influential textbook on animal behavior. She was the second woman to be elected president of the American Psychological Association.

Francis C. Sumner (1895–1954) In 1920, Sumner became the first Black American psychologist to earn a Ph.D. in psychology. Sumner later joined Howard University and helped create a strong psychology program that led the country in training Black American psychologists (Belgrave & Allison, 2010).

Mamie Phipps Clark (1917–1983) and Kenneth Clark (1914–2005) Mamie Phipps Clark and Kenneth Clark met as students at Howard University. They were partners in marriage and in research. They also applied their research to the broader community. Together, the Clarks founded the Northside Center for Childhood Development in the Harlem neighborhood of New York City, which Mamie Clark directed for more than 30 years. Mamie Clark also contributed to the start of the Head Start program, part of the U.S. Department of Health and Human Services, which focuses on early childhood education and health in lower-income communities (Karera & Rutherford, 2017).

Kenneth's (Aldridge & Christensen, 2013; Cramblet Alvarez et al., 2019). In fact, Kenneth Clark spoke out about Mamie Clark's contributions to the research that the Supreme Court cited, noting: "The record should show that was Mamie's primary project that I crashed. I sort of piggybacked on it" (Nyman, 2010, p. 76). In 1970, Kenneth became the first Black American president of the American Psychological Association (Belgrave & Allison, 2010).

Sigmund Freud: Psychoanalysis

Wundt, James, and other early psychologists emphasized the study of conscious experiences. But at the turn of the twentieth century, new approaches challenged the principles of both structuralism and functionalism.

In Vienna, Austria, a physician named **Sigmund Freud** was developing an intriguing theory of personality based on uncovering causes of behavior that were *unconscious,* or hidden from the person's conscious awareness. Freud's school of thought, called **psychoanalysis**, is *a personality theory and form of psychotherapy that emphasizes the role of unconscious factors in determining behavior and personality.* Freud himself was a neurologist, *not* a psychologist. Nevertheless, psychoanalysis had a strong influence on psychological thinking in the early part of the century.

Freud's psychoanalytic theory of personality and behavior was based largely on his work with his patients and on insights derived from self-analysis. Freud believed that human behavior was motivated by unconscious conflicts that were almost always sexual or aggressive in nature. Past experiences, especially childhood experiences, were thought to be critical in the formation of adult personality and behavior. According to Freud (1904), glimpses of these unconscious impulses are revealed in everyday life in dreams, memory blocks, slips of the tongue, and spontaneous humor. Freud believed that when unconscious conflicts became extreme, psychological disorders could result.

Freud's psychoanalytic theory of personality also provided the basis for a distinct form of psychotherapy. Many of the fundamental ideas of psychoanalysis, such as the importance of unconscious influences and early childhood experiences, continue to influence psychologists and other professionals in the mental health field. We'll explore Freud's theory in more depth in the chapters on personality and therapies.

Ivan Pavlov, John B. Watson, and B.F. Skinner: Behaviorism

The course of psychology changed dramatically in the early 1900s, when another approach emerged as a dominating force. **Behaviorism** *emphasized the study of observable behaviors, especially as they pertain to the process of learning.* It rejected the emphasis on consciousness promoted by structuralism and functionalism. It also flatly rejected Freudian notions about unconscious influences, claiming that such ideas were unscientific and impossible to test. Instead, behaviorism contended that psychology should focus its scientific investigations strictly on *overt behavior* — observable behaviors that could be objectively measured and verified.

Behaviorism is another example of the influence of physiology on psychology. Behaviorism grew out of the pioneering work of a Russian physiologist named **Ivan Pavlov**. Pavlov demonstrated that dogs could learn to associate a neutral stimulus, such as the sound of a ticking metronome, with an automatic behavior, such as reflexively salivating to food. Once an association between the sound of the metronome and the food was formed, the sound of the metronome alone would trigger the salivation reflex in the dog. Pavlov enthusiastically believed he had discovered the mechanism by which all behaviors were learned.

In the United States, a young, dynamic psychologist named **John B. Watson** shared Pavlov's enthusiasm. Watson (1913) championed behaviorism as a new school of psychology. Structuralism was still an influential perspective, but Watson

psychoanalysis Personality theory and form of psychotherapy that emphasizes the role of unconscious factors in determining personality and behavior.

behaviorism School of psychology that emphasizes the study of observable behaviors, especially as they pertain to the process of learning.

Is it true that Sigmund Freud was the first psychologist?

Clark University Archives

⌃ **Sigmund Freud (1856–1939) and G. Stanley Hall (1844–1924)** In 1909, Freud *(front left)* and several other psychoanalysts were invited by G. Stanley Hall *(front center)* to participate in Clark University's twentieth-anniversary celebration (Hogan, 2003). Hall helped organize psychology in the United States. He established the first psychology research laboratory in the United States and also founded the American Psychological Association. Listening in the audience was William James, who later wrote to a friend that Freud struck him as "a man obsessed with fixed ideas" (Rosenzweig, 1997). Carl Jung *(front right),* who later developed his own theory of personality, also attended this historic conference.

Ivan Pavlov (1849–1936)

John B. Watson (1878–1958)

B.F. Skinner (1904–1990)

△ **Three Key Scientists in the Development of Behaviorism** Building on the pioneering research of Russian physiologist Ivan Pavlov, U.S. psychologist John B. Watson founded the school of behaviorism. Behaviorism advocated that psychology should study observable behaviors, not mental processes. Following Watson, B.F. Skinner continued to champion the ideas of behaviorism. Skinner became one of the most influential psychologists of the twentieth century.

Carl Rogers (1902–1987)

Abraham Maslow (1908–1970)

△ **Two Leaders in the Development of Humanistic Psychology** Carl Rogers and Abraham Maslow were key figures in establishing humanistic psychology. Humanistic psychology emphasized the importance of self-determination, creativity, and human potential (Serlin, 2012). The ideas of Carl Rogers have been particularly influential in modern psychotherapy. Abraham Maslow's theory of motivation emphasized the importance of psychological growth.

strongly objected to both its method of introspection and its focus on conscious mental processes. As Watson (1924) wrote in his classic book, *Behaviorism:*

> Behaviorism, on the contrary, holds that the subject matter of human psychology *is the behavior of the human being.* Behaviorism claims that consciousness is neither a definite nor a usable concept. The behaviorist, who has been trained always as an experimentalist, holds, further, that belief in the existence of consciousness goes back to the ancient days of superstition and magic.

Behaviorism's influence on U.S. psychology was enormous. The goal of the behaviorists was to discover the fundamental principles of *learning* — how behavior is acquired and modified in response to environmental influences. For the most part, the behaviorists studied animal behavior under carefully controlled laboratory conditions.

Although Watson left academic psychology in the early 1920s, behaviorism was later championed by an equally forceful proponent — the famous U.S. psychologist **B.F. Skinner**. Like Watson, Skinner believed that psychology should restrict itself to studying outwardly observable behaviors that could be measured and verified. In compelling experimental demonstrations, Skinner systematically used reinforcement or punishment to shape the behavior of rats and pigeons.

Between Watson and Skinner, behaviorism dominated psychology in the United States for almost half a century. During that time, the study of conscious experiences was largely ignored as a topic in psychology (Baars, 2005). In the chapter on learning, we'll look at the lives and contributions of Pavlov, Watson, and Skinner in greater detail.

Carl Rogers and Abraham Maslow: Humanistic Psychology

For several decades, behaviorism and psychoanalysis were the perspectives that most influenced the thinking of U.S. psychologists. In the 1950s, a new school of thought emerged, called **humanistic psychology**, *that emphasized each person's unique potential for psychological growth and self-direction.* Because humanistic psychology was distinctly different from both psychoanalysis and behaviorism, it was sometimes referred to as the "third force" in U.S. psychology (Waterman, 2013; Watson et al., 2011).

Humanistic psychology was largely founded by U.S. psychologist **Carl Rogers** (Elliott & Farber, 2010). Like Freud, Rogers was influenced by his experiences with his psychotherapy clients. However, rather than emphasizing unconscious conflicts, Rogers emphasized the *conscious* experiences of his clients, including each person's unique potential for psychological growth and self-direction. In contrast to the behaviorists, who saw human behavior as being shaped and maintained by external causes, Rogers emphasized self-determination, free will, and the importance of choice in human behavior (Elliott & Farber, 2010; Kirschenbaum & Jourdan, 2005).

Abraham Maslow was another advocate of humanistic psychology. Maslow developed a theory of motivation that emphasized psychological growth, which we'll discuss in the motivation and emotion chapter. Like psychoanalysis, humanistic psychology included not only influential theories of personality but also a form of psychotherapy.

The debates among the key thinkers in psychology's history shaped the development of psychology as a whole. Each of the schools had an impact on the topics and methods of psychological research. That impact has been a lasting one. In the next sections, we'll touch on some of the more recent developments in psychology's evolution. We'll also explore the diversity that characterizes contemporary psychology.

humanistic psychology School of psychology that emphasizes each person's unique potential for psychological growth and self-direction.

neuroscience The study of the nervous system, especially the brain.

Contemporary Psychology

■ KEY THEME
As psychology has developed as a scientific discipline, the topics it investigates have become progressively more diverse.

≡ KEY QUESTIONS
- How do the perspectives in contemporary psychology differ in emphasis and approach?
- How do psychiatry and psychology differ, and what are psychology's major specialty areas?

Over the past decades, the range of topics in psychology has become progressively more diverse. And, as psychology's knowledge base has increased, psychology itself has become more specialized. Rather than being dominated by a particular approach or school of thought, today's psychologists tend to identify themselves according to: (1) the *perspective* they emphasize in investigating psychological topics and (2) the *specialty area* in which they have been trained and practice.

Major Perspectives in Psychology

Any given topic in contemporary psychology can be approached from a variety of perspectives (see photo on next page). Each perspective discussed here represents a different emphasis or point of view that can be taken in studying a particular behavior, topic, or issue. As you'll see in this section, the influence of the early schools of psychology is apparent in the first four perspectives that characterize contemporary psychology.

The Biological Perspective As we've already noted, physiology has played an important role in psychology since it was founded. Today, that influence continues, as is shown by the many psychologists who take the biological perspective. The *biological perspective* emphasizes studying the physical bases of human and animal behavior, including the nervous system, endocrine system, immune system, and genetics. More specifically, **neuroscience** refers to *the study of the nervous system, especially the brain.* Sophisticated brain-scanning techniques allow neuroscientists to study the structure and activity of the intact, living brain in increasing detail. In the next chapter, we'll describe these techniques and explain how psychologists use them as research tools.

BSIP SA/Alamy Stock Photo

▲ The Biological Perspective The physiological aspects of behavior and mental processes are studied by biological psychologists. Psychologists and other scientists who specialize in the study of the brain and the rest of the nervous system are called neuroscientists. Here, Swiss neuroscientist Juliane Britz uses a device called an *electro-encephalogram* to monitor brain wave activity in a research participant (Britz et al., 2014).

The Psychodynamic Perspective The key ideas of Freud's theory of psychoanalysis continue to be influential among some psychologists, especially in the mental health field. Today, psychologists who take the *psychodynamic perspective* may or may not follow Freud or take a psychoanalytic approach. However, they do tend to emphasize the importance of unconscious influences, early life experiences, and interpersonal relationships in explaining the underlying dynamics of behavior or in treating people with psychological problems.

The Behavioral Perspective Watson and Skinner's contention that psychology should focus on observable behaviors and the fundamental laws of learning is evident today in the *behavioral perspective*. Contemporary psychologists who take the behavioral perspective continue to study how behavior is acquired or modified by environmental causes. Many psychologists who work in the area of mental health also emphasize the behavioral perspective in explaining and treating psychological disorders.

The Humanistic Perspective The influence of the work of Carl Rogers and Abraham Maslow continues to be seen among contemporary psychologists who take the humanistic perspective (Serlin, 2012; Waterman, 2013). The *humanistic perspective* focuses on the motivation of people to grow psychologically, the influence of interpersonal relationships on a person's self-concept, and the importance of choice and self-direction in striving to reach one's potential. Like the psychodynamic perspective, the humanistic perspective is most often emphasized among psychologists working in the mental health field.

The Positive Psychology Perspective The humanistic perspective's emphasis on psychological growth and human potential contributed to the recent emergence of a new perspective. *Positive psychology* is a field of psychological research and theory focusing on the study of positive emotions and psychological states, positive individual traits, and the social institutions that foster those qualities in individuals and communities (Csikszentmihalyi & Nakamura, 2011; Peterson, 2006; Seligman et al., 2005). By studying the conditions and processes that contribute to the optimal functioning of people, groups, and institutions, positive psychology seeks to counterbalance psychology's traditional emphasis on psychological problems and disorders (McNulty & Fincham, 2012).

Topics that fall under the umbrella of positive psychology include personal happiness, optimism, creativity, resilience, character strengths, and wisdom. Positive psychology is also focused on developing therapeutic techniques, with varying levels of success, that increase personal well-being rather than just alleviating the troubling symptoms of psychological disorders (Snyder et al., 2011; White et al., 2019).

Studying Behavior from Different Psychological Perspectives Psychologists can study a particular behavior, topic, or issue from different perspectives. For example, taking the biological perspective, a psychologist might study whether there are biological differences between parkour athletes and other people, such as the ability to stay focused in the face of dangerous situations. A psychologist taking the behavioral perspective might look at the types of rewards that reinforce their parkour behavior. And, a psychologist who took the positive psychology perspective might investigate how meeting the challenge of making a difficult jump contributed to self-confidence and personal growth.

The Cognitive Perspective During the 1960s, psychology experienced a return to the study of how mental processes influence behavior. Often referred to as "the cognitive revolution" in psychology, this movement represented a break from traditional behaviorism. Cognitive psychology focused once again on the important role of mental processes in how people process and remember information, develop language, solve problems, and think.

The development of the first computers in the 1950s contributed to the cognitive revolution. Computers gave psychologists a new model for conceptualizing human mental processes — human thinking, memory, and perception could be understood in terms of an information-processing model.

The Cross-Cultural Perspective More recently, psychologists have taken a closer look at how cultural factors influence patterns of behavior — the essence of the *cross-cultural perspective*. By the late 1980s, *cross-cultural psychology* had emerged in full force as large numbers of psychologists began studying the diversity of human behavior in different cultural settings and countries (Kitayama & Uskul, 2011; P. Smith, 2010). In the process, psychologists discovered that some well-established psychological findings were not as universal as they had thought.

For example, one well-established psychological finding was that people exert more effort on a task when working alone than when working as part of a group, a phenomenon called *social loafing*. First demonstrated in the 1970s, social loafing was a consistent finding in several psychological studies conducted with participants in the United States and Europe. But when similar studies were conducted with Chinese participants, the opposite was found to be true (Hong et al., 2008). Chinese participants worked harder on a task when they were part of a group than when they were working alone, a phenomenon called *social striving*.

Today, psychologists are keenly attuned to the influence of cultural factors on behavior (Hall et al., 2016). Although many psychological processes *are* shared by all humans, it's important to keep in mind that there are cultural variations in behavior. Thus, we have included Culture and Human Behavior boxes throughout this textbook to help sensitize you to the influence of culture on behavior—including your own. We describe cross-cultural psychology in more detail in the Culture and Human Behavior box, "What Is Cross-Cultural Psychology?"

The Evolutionary Perspective *Evolutionary psychology* refers to the application of the principles of evolution to explain psychological processes and phenomena (Al-Shawaf et al., 2019; D. M. Buss, 2009, 2011). The *evolutionary perspective* reflects a renewed interest in the work of English naturalist Charles Darwin. As noted previously, Darwin's (1859) first book on evolution, *On the Origin of Species*, played an influential role in the thinking of many early psychologists.

The theory of evolution proposes that the individual members of a species compete for survival. Because of inherited differences, some members of a species are better adapted to their environment than are others. Organisms that inherit characteristics that increase their chances of survival in their particular habitat are more likely to survive, reproduce, and pass on their characteristics to their offspring. But individuals that inherit less useful characteristics are less likely to survive, reproduce, and pass on their characteristics. This process reflects the principle of *natural selection:* The most adaptive characteristics are "selected" and perpetuated in the next generation.

Psychologists who take the evolutionary perspective assume that psychological processes are also subject to the principle of natural selection. That is, psychological processes that helped individuals adapt to their environments also helped them survive, reproduce, and pass those abilities on to their offspring (Confer et al., 2010). However, as you'll see in later chapters, some of those processes may not necessarily be adaptive in our modern world (Loewenstein, 2010; Tooby & Cosmides, 2008).

∧ **The Evolutionary Perspective** The evolutionary perspective analyzes behavior in terms of how it increases a species' chances to survive and reproduce. Comparing behaviors across species can often lead to new insights about the adaptive function of a particular behavior. For example, close bonds with caregivers are essential to the primate infant's survival—whether that infant is a Barbary macaque at a wildlife preserve or a human infant at a family picnic.

CULTURE AND HUMAN BEHAVIOR

What Is Cross-Cultural Psychology?

People around the globe share many attributes: We all eat, sleep, form families, seek happiness, and mourn losses. Yet the *way* in which we express our human qualities can vary considerably among cultures (Triandis, 2005). *What* we eat, *where* we sleep, and *how* we form families, define happiness, and express sadness can differ greatly in different cultures.

Culture refers to *the attitudes, values, beliefs, and behaviors shared by a group of people and communicated from one generation to another* (Cohen, 2009, 2010). Studying the differences among cultures and the influences of culture on behavior are the fundamental goals of *cross-cultural psychology.*

Cultural identity is influenced by many factors, including ethnicity, nationality, race, religion, and language. As we grow up within a given culture, we learn our culture's *norms,* or unwritten rules of behavior. And, we tend to act in accordance with those internalized norms without thinking. For example, according to the dominant cultural norms in the United States, babies usually sleep separately from their parents. But in many cultures around the world, it's taken for granted that babies will sleep in the same bed as their parents (Barry, 2019; Mindell et al., 2010a, 2010b). Members of these other cultures are often surprised and even shocked at the U.S. practice of separating babies from their parents at night. (In the chapter on lifespan development, we discuss this topic at greater length.)

Ethnocentrism is *the belief that one's own culture or ethnic group is superior to all others and the related tendency to use one's own culture as a standard by which to judge other cultures.* Ethnocentrism may be a natural tendency, but it can prevent us from understanding the behaviors of others (Bizumic et al., 2009). Ethnocentrism may also prevent us from being aware of how our behavior has been shaped by our own culture.

Extreme ethnocentrism can lead to intolerance toward other cultures. If we believe that our way of seeing things or behaving is the only proper one, other ways of behaving and thinking may seem laughable, inferior, wrong, or even immoral.

In addition to influencing how we behave, culture affects how we define our sense of self (Markus & Kitayama, 1991, 1998, 2010). For the most part, the dominant cultures of the United States, Canada, Australia, New Zealand, and Europe can be described as individualistic cultures. **Individualistic cultures** *emphasize the needs and goals of the individual over the needs and goals of the group* (Henrich, 2014; Markus & Kitayama, 2010). In individualistic societies, the self is seen as *independent,* autonomous, and distinctive. Personal identity is defined by individual achievements, abilities, and accomplishments.

In contrast, **collectivistic cultures** *emphasize the needs and goals of the group over those of the individual.*

Social behavior is more heavily influenced by cultural norms and social context than by individual preferences and attitudes (Liu et al., 2019; Owe et al., 2013; Talhelm et al., 2014). In a collectivistic culture, the self is seen as being much more *interdependent* with others. Relationships with others and identification with a larger group, such as the family or tribe, are key components of personal identity. The cultures of Asia, Africa, Mexico, and Central and South America tend to be collectivistic. About two-thirds of the world's population live in collectivistic cultures (Triandis, 2005).

The distinction between individualistic and collectivistic societies is useful in cross-cultural psychology. However, most cultures are neither completely individualistic nor completely collectivistic but fall somewhere between the two extremes. And, psychologists are careful not to assume that these generalizations are true of every member or every aspect of a given culture (Kitayama & Uskul, 2011). Psychologists also recognize that there is a great deal of individual variation among the members of every culture (Heine & Norenzayan, 2006). It's important to keep that qualification in mind when cross-cultural findings are discussed.

The Culture and Human Behavior boxes that we have included in this book will help you learn about human behavior in other cultures. They will also help you understand how culture affects *your* behavior, beliefs, attitudes, and values.

Dave Stamboulis/AGE Fotostock

∧ **The Roots of Collectivistic Culture?** Even within a given society, people's cultural values may vary. Thomas Talhelm and his colleagues (2014) found that Chinese people from northern China, where wheat is traditionally grown, are more individualistic than Chinese people from southern China, where rice is grown, despite sharing the same ethnic, educational, and socioeconomic background. The explanation? As this photo of villagers in southwest China harvesting rice shows, rice farming requires an extraordinary level of cooperation and coordination among villagers, characteristics that are highly valued in collectivistic cultures. In contrast, wheat farmers can succeed without help from their neighbors.

Specialty Areas in Psychology

Many people think that psychologists primarily diagnose and treat people with psychological problems or disorders. In fact, psychologists who specialize in *clinical psychology,* or *counseling psychology,* are trained in the diagnosis, treatment, causes, and prevention of psychological disorders, leading to a doctorate in clinical psychology or counseling psychology, respectively. Although the doctorate is the typical degree for a psychologist in the United States, Canada, and many other countries, in most of the world, clinical or counseling psychologists have a master's degree.

In contrast, a *psychiatrist* has earned a medical degree, either an M.D. or D.O., followed by several years of specialized training in the treatment of mental disorders. **Psychiatry** is *a medical specialty focused on the diagnosis, treatment, causes, and prevention of mental and behavioral disorders.* As physicians, psychiatrists can hospitalize people, order biomedical therapies, and prescribe medications. Clinical psychologists are not medical doctors and cannot order medical treatments. However, in the United States, a few states have passed legislation allowing clinical psychologists to prescribe medications after specialized training (Riding-Malon & Werth, 2014).

As you'll learn, contemporary psychology is a diverse discipline that ranges far beyond the treatment of psychological problems. This diversity is reflected in **Table 1.1**, which shows the range of psychology's different specialties.

culture The attitudes, values, beliefs, and behaviors shared by a group of people and communicated from one generation to another.

ethnocentrism The belief that one's own culture or ethnic group is superior to all others and the related tendency to use one's own culture as a standard by which to judge other cultures.

individualistic cultures Cultures that emphasize the needs and goals of the individual over the needs and goals of the group.

collectivistic cultures Cultures that emphasize the needs and goals of the group over the needs and goals of the individual.

psychiatry Medical specialty focused on the diagnosis, treatment, causes, and prevention of mental and behavioral disorders.

TABLE 1.1

Major Specialties in Psychology

Specialty	Major Focus
Applied psychology	Applying the findings of basic psychology to diverse areas; examples include sports psychology, media psychology, forensic psychology, rehabilitation psychology, and military psychology.
Biological psychology	Exploring relationships between psychological processes and the body's physical systems; *neuroscience* refers specifically to the study of the brain and the rest of the nervous system.
Clinical psychology	Focusing on the causes, diagnosis, treatment, and prevention of psychological disorders.
Cognitive psychology	Researching mental processes, including reasoning and thinking, problem solving, memory, perception, mental imagery, and language.
Community psychology	Promoting research-based social justice, as well as positive cultural, political, and economic change at community, national, and international levels (Jason et al., 2019).
Counseling psychology	Helping people adjust, adapt, and cope with personal and interpersonal challenges; improving well-being, alleviating distress and maladjustment, and resolving crises.
Developmental psychology	Studying physical, social, and psychological changes that occur at different ages and stages of the lifespan.
Educational psychology	Applying psychological principles and theories to methods of learning.
Experimental psychology	Studying basic psychological processes, including sensation and perception, and principles of learning, emotion, and motivation.
Health psychology	Researching psychological factors in the development, prevention, and treatment of illness; stress and coping; promoting health-enhancing behaviors.
Industrial/organizational psychology	Understanding the relationship between people and work.
Personality psychology	Explaining the nature of human personality, including the uniqueness of each person, traits, and individual differences.
School psychology	Applying psychological principles and findings in primary and secondary schools.
Social psychology	Understanding how an individual's thoughts, feelings, and behavior are affected by social environments and the presence of other people.

Nearly 7,000 doctorates were awarded in psychology in the United States in 2017, an increase of 25% over the previous decade. Women earned about three-quarters of these doctorates, and people of color earned about one-third of them. Of the approximately 7,000 doctorates about 37% were earned in clinical psychology and another 8% in counseling psychology (Christidis et al., 2019).

The Scientific Method

■ **KEY THEME**
The scientific method is a set of assumptions, attitudes, and procedures that guides all scientists, including psychologists, in conducting research.

≡ KEY QUESTIONS
- What assumptions and attitudes are held by psychologists?
- What characterizes each step of the scientific method?
- How does a hypothesis differ from a theory?

Whatever their approach or specialty, psychologists are trained as scientists. And, like other scientists, they rely on the scientific method to guide their research. The **scientific method** refers to *a set of assumptions, attitudes, and procedures that guide researchers in creating questions to investigate, in generating evidence, and in drawing conclusions.*

Like all scientists, psychologists are guided by the basic scientific assumption that *events are lawful.* When this scientific assumption is applied to psychology, it means that psychologists assume that behavior and mental processes follow consistent patterns. Psychologists are also guided by the assumption that *events are explainable.* Thus, psychologists assume that behavior and mental processes have a cause or causes that can be understood through careful, systematic study.

Psychologists are also *open-minded.* They are willing to consider new or alternative explanations of behavior and mental processes. However, their open-minded attitude is tempered by a *healthy sense of scientific skepticism.* That is, psychologists critically evaluate the evidence for new findings, especially those that seem contrary to established knowledge.

The Steps in the Scientific Method: Systematically Seeking Answers

Like any science, psychology is based on **empirical evidence**—*verifiable evidence that is the result of objective observation, measurement, and experimentation.* As part of the overall process of producing empirical evidence, psychologists follow the four basic steps of the scientific method. In a nutshell, these steps are:

- Formulate a specific question that can be tested.
- Design a study to collect relevant data.
- Analyze the data to arrive at conclusions.
- Report the results.

Following the basic guidelines of the scientific method does not guarantee that valid conclusions will always be reached. However, these steps help guard against bias and minimize the chances for error and faulty conclusions. Let's look at some of the key concepts associated with each step of the scientific method.

Step 1. Formulate a Testable Hypothesis   Once a researcher has identified a question or an issue to investigate, they must formulate a hypothesis that can be tested empirically. Formally, a **hypothesis** is *a tentative statement that describes the relationship between two or more variables.* A hypothesis is often stated as a specific prediction that can be empirically tested, such as "the use of electronic media like smartphones or video games is associated with lower psychological well-being in adolescents."

A **variable** is simply *a factor that can vary, or change, in ways that can be observed, measured, and verified.* The psychologist must provide an operational definition of each variable to be investigated. An **operational definition** is *a precise description of how the variable in a study will be measured, manipulated, or changed.* Operational definitions

scientific method   A set of assumptions, attitudes, and procedures that guides researchers in creating questions to investigate, in generating evidence, and in drawing conclusions.

empirical evidence   Verifiable evidence that is based upon objective observation, measurement, and/or experimentation.

hypothesis (high-POTH-uh-sis) A tentative statement that describes the relationship between two or more variables.

variable   A factor that can vary, or change, in ways that can be observed, measured, and verified.

operational definition   A precise description of how the variables in a study will be measured, manipulated, or changed.

are important because many of the concepts that psychologists investigate—such as memory, happiness, or stress—can be defined and measured in more than one way.

For example, how would you test the hypothesis that "the use of electronic media like smartphones or video games is associated with lower psychological well-being in adolescents"? To test that specific prediction, you would need to formulate an operational definition of each variable. How could you operationally define *use of electronic media*? *Well-being*? What could you objectively observe and measure?

To investigate the impact of social networks on college students, Jean Twenge and Keith Campbell (2019) analyzed data from online surveys of more than 200,000 adolescents in the United States and the United Kingdom. They operationally defined *use of electronic media* as the *participant's number of hours spent on various types of electronic media*.

How was *well-being* operationally defined? Twenge and Campbell used data from several samples. They found that adolescents with higher use of electronic media tended to be less confident, optimistic, cheerful, and energetic (Tennant et al., 2007). **Figure 1.1** shows part of their results. For one sample in the United Kingdom, psychological well-being decreased as hours spent on a smartphone increased.

Step 2. Design the Study and Collect the Data

This step involves deciding which research method to use for collecting data. There are two basic types of designs used in research—*descriptive* and *experimental*. Each research approach answers different kinds of questions and provides different kinds of evidence. Ideally, researchers say in advance exactly how they plan to collect and analyze their data, a process called *preregistration*. Researchers preregister the details of their study on a time-stamped Web site so that they cannot tweak their process later to achieve their desired results.

Descriptive research includes research strategies for observing and describing behavior, including identifying the factors that seem to be associated with a particular phenomenon. For example, Laura Stockdale and Sarah Coyne (2020) documented the reasons that young people used social media, such as Twitter and Instagram. They found the three main reasons to be a search for connections with other people, a search for

Are Hands-Free Mobile Phones Safer? Hypotheses are often generated from everyday observations. For example, many people assume that hands-free devices are safe to use while driving, since they don't require the driver to actually look at the phone or take their hands off the wheel to operate them. In fact, a number of U.S. states and other countries, including the United Kingdom, have banned the use of mobile phones while driving, unless they're hands-free. You could test that assumption by turning it into a formal hypothesis—that hands-free devices are safe to use when driving. However, studies have found that talking on a hands-free phone while driving was just as distracting as talking on a handheld phone (Stavrinos et al., 2018; Strayer et al., 2006). Hands-free or not, using a mobile phone while driving was much more distracting than conversing with a passenger or listening to music or the radio (Strayer et al., 2013). You'll learn why in the discussion of multitasking in the chapter on variations in consciousness.

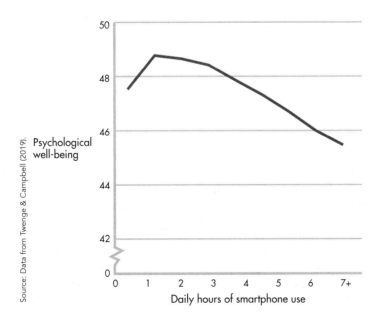

FIGURE 1.1 Electronic Media Use and Psychological Well-Being This graph illustrates the association between smartphone use and psychological well-being among adolescents in the United Kingdom (Twenge & Campbell, 2019). Overall, the more adolescents used their smartphones, the less optimistic, confident, cheerful, and energetic they tended to be. There were similar associations for the use of video games and computers.

information, and boredom. Descriptive research answers the *who, what, where,* and *when* kinds of questions about behavior. Who engages in a particular behavior? What factors or events seem to be associated with the behavior? Where does the behavior occur? When does the behavior occur? How often does the behavior occur? In the next section, we'll discuss commonly used descriptive methods, including *naturalistic observation, surveys, case studies,* and *correlational studies.*

In contrast, *experimental research* is used to show that one variable causes change in a second variable. In an experiment, the researcher deliberately varies one factor and then measures the changes produced in a second factor. Ideally, all experimental conditions are kept as constant as possible except for the factor that the researcher systematically varies. Then, if changes occur in the second factor, those changes can be attributed to the variations in the first factor.

Step 3. Analyze the Data and Draw Conclusions Once observations have been made and measurements have been collected, the raw data need to be analyzed and summarized. Researchers use **statistics,** *a branch of mathematics, to analyze, summarize, and interpret the data they have collected.*

Researchers rely on statistics to determine whether their results support their hypotheses. They also use statistics to determine whether their findings are **statistically significant,** *a mathematical indication that the research results are not very likely to have occurred by chance if there truly isn't anything to be found.* As a rule, statistically significant results provide evidence for a hypothesis. Appendix A provides a more detailed discussion of the use of statistics in psychology research.

Keep in mind that even though a finding is statistically significant, it may not be practically significant. If a study involves a large number of participants, even small differences among groups of participants may result in a statistically significant finding. But the actual average differences may be so small as to have little practical significance or importance.

For example, Reynol Junco (2012) surveyed nearly 2,000 college students and found a statistically significant relationship between amount of time spent on social media and grade point average (GPA): Students who spent a lot of time on social media tended to have lower grades than students who spent less time. However, the practical, *real-world* significance of this relationship was low: It turned out that a student had to spend 93 minutes per day more than the average of 106 minutes for the increased time to have even a small (0.12 percentage point) impact on GPA. So remember that a statistically significant result is simply one that is not very likely to have occurred by chance if there's no actual finding. In this example, the data would be unlikely to result in a statistically significant finding if there's not actually a relationship between time spent on social media and GPA. But whether the finding is significant in the everyday sense of being important is another matter altogether.

How do we know if a finding is important in the everyday sense? Researchers can calculate another statistic, called effect size. **Effect size** is *a statistic that tells us, in general terms, whether a particular finding is small, medium, or large.* It gives us a sense of how meaningful a finding is in practical terms. The social media study we just described is an example of a finding that is statistically significant, but has a very small effect size. From a practical standpoint, the finding is not that meaningful.

A statistical technique called *meta-analysis* is sometimes used in psychology to analyze the results of many research studies on a specific topic. **Meta-analysis** *involves pooling the effect sizes of several studies into a single analysis.* By creating one large pool of data to be analyzed, meta-analysis can help reveal overall trends that may not be evident in individual studies.

Meta-analysis is especially useful when a particular issue has generated a large number of studies with inconsistent results. For example, many studies have looked at the factors that predict success in college. British psychologist Michelle Richardson and her colleagues (2012) pooled the results of over 200 research studies investigating personal characteristics that were associated with success in college. "Success in college" was operationally defined as cumulative GPA. They found that *motivational factors* were

statistics A branch of mathematics used by researchers to analyze, summarize, and interpret the data they have collected.

statistically significant A mathematical indication that research results are not very likely to have occurred by chance if there truly isn't anything to be found.

effect size A statistic that tells us, in general terms, whether a particular finding is small, medium, or large.

meta-analysis A statistical technique that involves pooling the effect sizes of several research studies into a single analysis.

the strongest predictor of college success, outweighing test scores, high school grades, and socioeconomic status. Especially important was a trait they called *performance self-efficacy,* the belief that you have the skills and abilities to succeed at academic tasks. We'll talk more about self-efficacy in the chapter on motivation and emotion.

Step 4. Report the Findings For advances to be made in any scientific discipline, researchers must share their findings with other scientists. In addition to reporting their results, psychologists provide a detailed description of the study itself, including who participated in the study, how variables were operationally defined, how data were analyzed, and so forth. In recent years, there's been a movement toward what is called open science (Christensen et al., 2020). **Open science** refers to *the use of transparent research practices, including sharing the procedures of a study, the specifics of how the statistics were calculated, and the research data.* It's a way of crowdsourcing research (Baranski, 2015).

Describing the precise details of the study makes it possible for other investigators to **replicate**, *or repeat, the study in order to increase confidence in the validity of the original findings.* Replication is an important part of the scientific process generally and the open science movement more specifically. Replication works best when researchers are open about their process, allowing for others to repeat their study. When a study is replicated and the same basic results are obtained again, scientific confidence that the results are accurate is increased. Conversely, if the replication of a study fails to produce the same basic findings, confidence in the original findings is reduced.

Replication guards against the possibility that a particular finding was a fluke, an isolated finding, or valid for only a select group of participants. And many studies in psychological science, as well as in other fields like medical science, have failed to replicate, a situation often called the *replication crisis.* Consider this example: A team of researchers found that holding a "power pose" (see photo) for two minutes significantly increased feelings of power and willingness to take risks and even affected hormones related to dominance and stress (Carney et al., 2010). The findings were widely publicized and were the subject of a TED Talk by Amy Cuddy (2012) with over 40 million views. Subsequent researchers were unable to replicate the original findings (Ranehill et al., 2015; Smith & Apicella, 2017). One study even found that power poses were associated with *lower* feelings of power (Garrison et al., 2016). But Cuddy pushed back. Although the effects on hormones appear not to have replicated, she and her colleagues reported solid evidence for the impact of power posing on attitudes and emotions (Cuddy et al., 2018). This situation isn't unique. In one giant crowdsourced study, 270 researchers from all over the world attempted to replicate 100 well-known psychology studies (Open Science Collaboration, 2015). Only 36 percent of these studies replicated.

Future research may call Cuddy's more recent power posing findings into question or produce new evidence to support the idea that "power posing" does have an impact on hormones. The same may be true for the studies in the giant replication initiative. However, the lack of replication in these cases casts doubt on the strength of these findings. Does a failed replication invalidate the original study? Not necessarily. There may be a subtle difference between the two studies that led to the difference in findings, further fine-tuning our understanding of a psychological concept. Exploring why a study did not replicate may lead psychologists to better understand the phenomenon that they are studying. As psychologist Lisa Feldman Barrett (2015) observed, "Failure to replicate is not a bug; it is a feature. It is what leads us along the path—the wonderfully twisty path—of scientific discovery." Others applaud the collaboration and creativity that the open science movement has brought to the field (Vazire, 2018; Wagenmakers et al., 2018). It's an exciting time to be a psychological scientist!

Like all scientists, psychologists present their research at academic conferences and/or write a paper summarizing the study and submit

open science The use of transparent research practices, including sharing the procedures of a study, the specifics of how the statistics were calculated, and the research data.

replicate To repeat a study in order to increase confidence in the validity of the original findings.

Is it true that striking a "power pose" for just a few minutes can affect your hormones?

⌃ **The Importance of Replication: How Powerful Is the Power Pose Effect?** In her popular TED Talk on "power posing," Amy Cuddy (2012), pictured here, described research showing that holding a power pose like the one in the photo above for two minutes could significantly impact attitudes, hormones, and behavior (Carney et al., 2010). Later researchers were unable to replicate the original study, casting doubt on the strength of the original finding (Simmons & Simonsohn, 2017). But Cuddy and her colleagues (2018) have responded, noting that the biological findings haven't held up, but the finding that power posing affects attitudes and emotions appears to be solid.

ELIZABETH D. HERMAN/The New York Times/Redux Pictures

theory A tentative explanation that tries to integrate and account for the relationship of diverse findings on the same topic.

it to one of the many psychology journals for publication. Before accepting papers for publication, most psychology journals send the paper to other knowledgeable psychologists to review and evaluate in a process called *peer review*. If the study conforms to the principles of sound scientific research and contributes to the existing knowledge base, the paper is accepted for publication.

Throughout this text, you'll see citations that look like this: (Cushen et al., 2019). These citations identify the sources of the research and ideas that are being discussed. The citation tells you the author or authors of the study—for "Cushen et al.," Cushen is the first author and "et al." means "other colleagues"—and the year (2019) in which the study was published. You can find the complete reference in the alphabetized References section at the back of this text. The complete reference lists the authors' full names, the article title, the journal or book in which the article was published, and the DOI, or digital object identifier. The DOI is a permanent Internet address for journal articles and other digital works posted on the Internet. If you want to read any of the original sources that we cite, find it in the References section, then search for the DOI or for the title of the article or book in your university library's online databases or on Google Scholar, the free search engine for scholarly works. Where can you find Google Scholar? Just google it!

Figure 1.2 shows you how to decipher the different parts of a typical journal reference.

Building Theories: Integrating the Findings from Many Studies

As research findings accumulate from individual studies, eventually theories develop. A **theory**, or *model,* is *a tentative explanation that tries to account for diverse findings on the same topic*. Note that theories are *not* the same as hypotheses when applied to research, although they're often used interchangeably in everyday language. A hypothesis is a specific question or prediction to be tested. In contrast, a theory integrates and summarizes numerous research findings and observations on a particular topic. Along with explaining existing results, a good theory often generates new predictions and hypotheses that can be tested by further research (Higgins, 2004).

As you encounter different theories, try to remember that theories are *tools* for explaining behavior and mental processes, not statements of absolute fact. As with any tool, the value of a theory is determined by its usefulness. A useful theory is one that furthers the understanding of behavior, allows testable predictions to be made, and

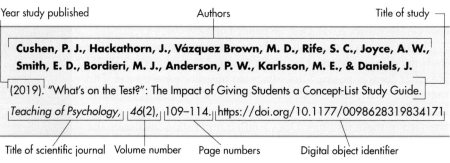

Year study published   Authors   Title of study

Cushen, P. J., Hackathorn, J., Vázquez Brown, M. D., Rife, S. C., Joyce, A. W., Smith, E. D., Bordieri, M. J., Anderson, P. W., Karlsson, M. E., & Daniels, J.

(2019). "What's on the Test?": The Impact of Giving Students a Concept-List Study Guide.

Teaching of Psychology, 46(2), 109–114. https://doi.org/10.1177/0098628319834171

Title of scientific journal   Volume number   Page numbers   Digital object identifier

FIGURE 1.2 How to Read a Journal Reference You can find the complete source for each citation that appears in a chapter in the References section at the end of this text. The reference above is in the usual format you'll see if you look for an article through your university library database or through Google Scholar. In the back of this text, we included first names as well, to highlight that many women, as well as men, conduct research in psychological science. This figure shows the different components of a typical journal reference. In the chapter itself, the citation for this particular reference reads (Cushen et al., 2019). In this study, students either received a study guide for their exams or were encouraged to create their own. Students did worse on their exams, on average, when they received a study guide than when they did not. Our advice? Create your own study guide!

stimulates new research. Often, more than one theory proves to be useful in explaining a particular area of behavior or mental processes, such as the development of personality or the experience of emotion.

It's also important to remember that theories often reflect the *self-correcting nature of the scientific enterprise.* In other words, when new research findings challenge established ways of thinking about a phenomenon, theories are expanded, modified, and even replaced. Thus, as the knowledge base of psychology evolves and changes, theories evolve and change to produce more accurate and useful explanations of behavior and mental processes. The open science movement can help these changes occur more quickly and efficiently.

Descriptive Research

■ KEY THEME
Descriptive research is used to systematically observe and describe behavior.

≡ KEY QUESTIONS
- What are naturalistic observation and case study research, and why and how are they conducted?
- What is a survey, and why is random selection important in survey research?
- What are the advantages and disadvantages of each descriptive method?

Descriptive research *uses scientific procedures for systematically observing and describing behavior.* Using descriptive research designs, researchers can answer important questions, such as when certain behaviors take place, how often they occur, and whether they are related to other factors, such as a person's age, ethnic group, or educational level. Descriptive research can provide a wealth of information about behavior, especially behaviors that would be difficult or impossible to study experimentally.

There are many different research designs, but two basic strategies deserve special mention. **Longitudinal design** is *a research strategy that tracks a particular variable or set of variables in the same group of participants over time, sometimes for years.* For example, a longitudinal study of the effect of college-readiness programs on academic achievement might compare the academic records of participants who enrolled in college-readiness programs versus participants who did not, following all the participants from high school through college graduation.

In contrast, **cross-sectional design** is *a research strategy for studying a variable or set of variables among a group of participants at a single point in time.* Often, the participants are of different ages or developmental stages. For example, to study the effect of aging on memory, developmental psychologists might compare memory abilities in participants aged 25, 45, and 55, looking for age-related differences.

Naturalistic Observation: The Science of People- and Animal-Watching

The systematic observation and recording of behaviors as they occur in their natural settings is the descriptive method called **naturalistic observation**. Usually, researchers engaged in naturalistic observation try to avoid being detected by their subjects, whether people or nonhuman animals. The basic goal of naturalistic observation is to detect the behavior patterns that exist naturally—patterns that might not be apparent in a laboratory or if the subjects knew they were being watched.

As you might expect, psychologists very carefully define the behaviors that they will observe and measure before they begin their research. Often, to increase the accuracy of the observations, two or more observers are used. In some studies, observations are recorded so that the researchers can carefully analyze the details of the behaviors being studied.

descriptive research Research that uses scientific procedures for systematically observing and describing behavior.

longitudinal design Research strategy that tracks a particular variable or set of variables in the same group of participants over time, sometimes for years.

cross-sectional design Research strategy for studying a variable or set of variables among a group of participants at a single point in time.

naturalistic observation The systematic observation and recording of behaviors as they occur in their natural setting.

Noelia Ramon-TellingLife/Getty Images

⋏ **Naturalistic Observation: Studying the Effects of Drones on Kangaroo Behavior**
Drones are increasingly used to monitor wildlife, including kangaroos. But what are the effects of these looming devices on the animals' behavior? Australian researcher Elizabeth Brunton and her colleagues (2019) observed wild kangaroos without a drone present and then while a drone flew overhead. They found that kangaroos appeared to be more vigilant when drones were present, but only ran away when drones flew as low as 30 meters (about 98 feet). The researchers recommend that drones monitoring kangaroos be kept at high altitudes—and more research.

Abby Solomon: More Than a Case Study Abby Solomon, a young woman who lives in Austin, Texas, and is passionate about her hometown's world-class music scene, has a rare genetic disorder that leads her to be extremely thin (Rascoe, 2018). Her condition has led to chronic pain and a series of surgeries. It also led to the discovery of a hormone that might one day help to treat obesity.

One advantage of naturalistic observation is that it allows researchers to study human behaviors that cannot ethically be manipulated in an experiment. For example, suppose that a psychologist wants to study bullying behavior in children. It would not be ethical to deliberately create a situation in which one child is aggressively bullied by another child. However, it *would* be ethical to study bullying by observing aggressive behavior in children in their classrooms, as Carlos Santoyo and Brenda Mendoza (2018) did in a study in Mexico.

As a research tool, naturalistic observation can be used wherever patterns of behavior can be openly observed—from the rain forests of the Amazon to restaurants, city streets, and classrooms. Because the observations occur in the natural setting, the results of naturalistic observation studies can be generalized to real-life situations with more confidence than can the results of studies using artificially manipulated or staged situations.

Case Studies: Details, Details, Details

A **case study** is *an intensive, in-depth investigation of an individual, a family, or some other social unit.* Case studies involve compiling a great deal of information from numerous sources to construct a detailed picture of the person. The individual may be extensively interviewed, and their friends, family, and co-workers may be interviewed as well. Psychological and biographical records, neurological and medical records, and even school or work records may be examined. Other sources of information can include psychological testing and observations of the person's behavior. Clinical psychologists and other mental health specialists routinely use case studies to develop a complete profile of a psychotherapy client.

Case studies are also used in psychological research investigating rare, unusual, or extreme conditions. These kinds of case studies often provide psychologists with information that can be used to help understand normal behavior or develop treatments for more common conditions. For example, Abby Solomon suffers from a rare, painful genetic disorder that results from "the thin gene" (Kennedy, 2016; Rascoe, 2018). She weighs about 100 pounds (45 kilograms), and feels hungry almost all the time, but feels full after just a few bites. Abby willingly collaborates with researchers who want to understand more about her condition, and this research has led to remarkable results (though not for Abby directly). Research into her condition led to the discovery of a hormone that might one day help treat obesity.

While case studies can provide invaluable information, they also have limitations. The most important limitation is that the findings on people with rare or unusual conditions might not apply to people in the broader population.

Surveys: (A) Always (B) Sometimes (C) Never (D) Huh?

How much time do you spend studying and preparing for class? Is it more, less, or about the same amount of time as other students at your college? Do you think other students are managing their time better than you are?

How could you find out the answers to such questions? A direct way to find out about the behavior, attitudes, and opinions of people is simply to ask them, and one way to do that is with a survey. A **survey** is *a structured set of questions designed to investigate the opinions, behaviors, or characteristics of a particular group.* One key advantage offered by survey research is that information can be gathered from a much larger group of people than is possible with other research methods.

Typically, surveys involve carefully constructed questionnaires. Questionnaires may be paper, Internet-based, computer-based, or administered in person or over the telephone by a trained interviewer.

Surveys are seldom administered to everyone within the particular group or population under investigation. Instead, researchers usually select a **sample**—a *segment of the population used to represent the group that is being studied.* Selecting a sample that is representative of the larger group is the key to getting accurate survey results. A **representative sample** is *a selected segment that very closely parallels the larger population being studied on relevant characteristics.* Relevant characteristics are factors such as age, gender, race, marital status, and educational level.

case study An intensive, in-depth investigation of an individual, a family, or some other social unit.

survey A structured set of questions designed to investigate the opinions, behaviors, or characteristics of a particular group.

sample A selected segment of the population used to represent the group that is being studied.

representative sample A selected segment that very closely parallels the larger population being studied on relevant characteristics.

How do researchers select participants so that their sample is representative of the larger group? Well, to tell the truth, they usually don't. In fact, psychology research relies too much on what are often called WEIRD samples (Henrich et al., 2010). WEIRD stands for Western, Educated, Industrialized, Rich, and Democratic (WEIRD) societies. If you live in a WEIRD society, as most reading this book do, it might seem pretty normal. It's not. People from WEIRD countries make up only 12 percent of the world's population. Yet an analysis of a major psychology journal found that 95 percent of participants were from WEIRD countries (Rad et al., 2018). When drawing conclusions from a study, remember they only apply to people like those in the study, not to everyone in the world.

Do researchers ever use representative samples? Sometimes, in the rare cases in which they can draw from the entire population. In such cases, the goal is to *randomly select* the sample participants. **Random selection** is *a process by which every member of the larger group has an equal chance of being selected for inclusion in the sample*. Such a situation is unusual, but sometimes occurs. To illustrate, let's look at the National Survey of Student Engagement (NSSE, 2016), a survey of almost 300,000 U.S. college students and 22,000 Canadian college students. The NSSE surveys students in their first and last years of college about the nature and quality of their educational experience. **Table 1.2** shows how the randomly selected sample surveyed in the NSSE compares to the broader population of U.S. undergraduates enrolled in four-year institutions.

What did the NSSE find? Among other findings, the survey showed that many first-year students struggled with managing their time and mastering challenging course material. About one in five (20 percent) of first-year college students had difficulty learning course material *and* had difficulty getting help. The survey also found that students who spent the most time preparing for class were the most likely to stay in college and graduate.

One potential problem with surveys and questionnaires is that people do not always answer honestly, especially when they are asked questions about sexual activity, drug or alcohol use, or illegal activities. The tendency to respond in socially desirable ways can be addressed in a carefully designed survey. One strategy is to rephrase the question and ask for the same information in a different way at different points during the survey. Researchers can then compare the responses to make sure that the participant is responding honestly and consistently. There is some evidence that participants are more likely to respond honestly to Internet or computer-administered surveys than to surveys that are administered in person (Dennis & Li, 2007).

TABLE 1.2

Comparing a Sample to the Larger Population

	U.S. 4-Year-College Population	NSSE Sample
Enrollment Status		
Full-time	83%	89%
Part-time	17%	11%
Gender		
Female	55%	65%
Male	45%	35%
Race/Ethnicity		
African American/Black	12%	10%
American Indian/Alaska native	1%	1%
Asian/Asian American/Pacific Islander	6%	5%
Caucasian/White	58%	65%
Hispanic	14%	12%
Multiracial/Multiethnic	3%	4%
International	4%	4%

Source: Data from NSSE, 2016.

How closely did the NSSE sample match important characteristics of U.S. undergraduates enrolled at four-year institutions as a whole? You can see for yourself by comparing the two columns in this table. Clearly, the random selection process used in the NSSE resulted in a sample that very closely approximated the characteristics of the larger population.

Correlational Studies: Looking at Relationships and Making Predictions

■ KEY THEME
Correlational studies show how strongly two factors are related.

⊐ KEY QUESTIONS
- What is a correlation coefficient?
- What is the difference between a positive correlation and a negative correlation?
- Why can't correlational studies be used to demonstrate cause-and-effect relationships?

Along with answering the *who, what, where,* and *when* questions, the data gathered by descriptive research techniques can be analyzed to show how various factors are related. A **correlational study** *examines how strongly two variables are related to, or associated with, each other*. Correlations can be used to analyze the data gathered by any type of descriptive method, and are also used to analyze the results of experiments.

random selection Process by which every member of the larger group has an equal chance of being selected for inclusion in the sample.

correlational study A study that examines how strongly two variables are related to, or associated with, each other.

FIGURE 1.3 Study Strategies and Grade-Point Average The graph shows the percentages of students reporting regular use of self-testing, according to grade-point average (GPA). The most common reason for self-testing was to determine how well information had been learned.

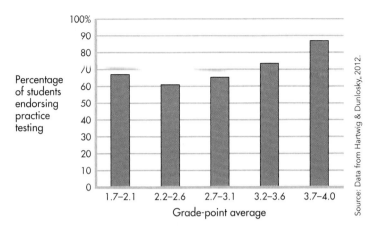

Source: Data from Hartwig & Dunlosky, 2012.

To illustrate, let's look at a correlational study conducted by psychologists Marissa K. Hartwig and John Dunlosky (2012). Hartwig and Dunlosky were interested in identifying the study habits most strongly linked to academic success. They surveyed 324 college students at a large state university. They used self-reported GPA as the operational definition of *academic achievement.* **Figure 1.3** shows some of the survey results. Once the data were collected, Hartwig and Dunlosky used a statistical procedure to calculate a figure called a *correlation coefficient.*

A **correlation coefficient** is *a numerical indicator of the strength of the relationship between two variables.* A correlation coefficient always falls in the range from −1.00 to +1.00. The correlation coefficient has two parts—the number and the sign. The number indicates the *strength* of the relationship, and the sign indicates the *direction* of the relationship between the two variables.

More specifically, the closer a correlation coefficient is to 1.00, whether it is positive or negative, the stronger the correlation or association is between the two factors. Hence, a correlation coefficient of +.90 or −.90 represents a very strong association, meaning that the two factors almost always occur together. A correlation coefficient of +.10 or −.10 represents a very weak correlation, meaning that the two factors seldom occur together. (Correlation coefficients are discussed in greater detail in Appendix A on statistics, at the back of this book.)

Notice that correlation coefficients do not function like the algebraic number line. A correlation of −.80 represents a stronger relationship than does a correlation of +.10. The plus or minus sign in a correlation coefficient simply tells you the direction of the relationship between the two variables.

> **Will Using More Emojis Get You More Dates?** Psychologist Amanda Gesselman and her colleagues (2019) analyzed survey data from over 5,000 adults who participated in the "Singles in America" study. The researchers found a positive correlation between how often participants reported using emojis in text messages to potential dates and the number of first dates they went on in the past year. Can you conclude that using emojis when texting potential dates causes more people to go out with you? No. A positive correlation exists, but you cannot conclude that one causes the other. It could be the reverse. Maybe going on more first dates causes you to use more emojis because you're happier. :) Or maybe a third variable is causing both increases. Maybe people who are more fun both use more emojis and go on more first dates.

A **positive correlation** is *a finding that two factors vary in the same direction, that is, increasing or decreasing together.* That is, the two factors increase or decrease together. For example, Hartwig and Dunlosky (2012) found that there was a strong positive correlation between GPA and use of self-testing as a study strategy. That is, as the use of self-testing *increased,* so did GPA. Other study strategies, such as using flashcards, rereading, or highlighting, were *not* associated with an increase in GPA. Wondering why not? Stay tuned—we'll discuss that very question in the Psych for Your Life section at the end of the chapter.

In contrast, a **negative correlation** is *a finding in which the two variables move in opposite directions, one increasing as the other decreases.* In a study investigating the relationship between multitasking and GPA, Reynol Junco and Shelia Cotten (2012) found that there was a *negative correlation* between time spent sending text messages while studying and GPA: As time spent texting while studying *increased,* GPA *decreased.*

What can we conclude about the relationship between academic achievement and sending texts while studying? Or GPA and self-testing? Does the evidence allow us to conclude that texting while studying *causes* a decrease in grade-point average? Or that using self-testing as a study strategy *causes* people to achieve higher GPAs?

Not necessarily. Consider the negative correlation between GPA and time spent texting while studying. It could be that a third variable was responsible for the associations between texting and GPA. Perhaps students who send texts while studying do so because they lack academic motivation or are uninterested in the subject matter. In other words, it might be that a lack of academic motivation or interest, rather than sending texts, was actually responsible for the lower grades.

Similarly, consider the positive correlation between self-testing and GPA. We cannot conclude that using self-tests in itself *causes* an increase in GPA. It's entirely possible that people who are more academically motivated are also more likely to actively test their mastery of class material, which after all, takes more effort than simply rereading or high-lighting material in a textbook. Thus, it could be that highly motivated students are more likely to use self-testing as a study strategy than students who are less motivated.

Here is the critical point: Even if two factors are very strongly correlated, *correlation does not necessarily indicate causality.* A correlation tells you only that two factors seem to be related or that they co-vary in a systematic way. Although two factors may be very strongly correlated, correlational studies cannot be used to demonstrate a true cause-and-effect relationship. As you'll see in the next section, the experimental method is the only scientific strategy that can provide compelling evidence of a cause-and-effect relationship between two variables.

Experimental Research

■ KEY THEME

The experimental method is used to demonstrate a cause-and-effect relationship between two variables.

⹀ KEY QUESTIONS

- What roles do the independent variable and dependent variable play in an experiment?
- What is the testing effect?
- How can experimental controls help minimize the effects of confounding variables?

So far, we've noted a number of factors that are associated with higher or lower college grades. But all of these factors—such as time spent sending texts and on Facebook—are *correlational,* meaning that while they are linked, they do not necessarily indicate that the two factors are causally related.

In contrast to descriptive research and correlational studies, **experimental research** is *a method of investigation used to demonstrate cause-and-effect relationships by purposely manipulating one factor thought to produce change in another factor.* In an experiment, an **independent variable**, or predictor variable, is *a factor that is purposely manipulated to produce change.* The researcher then measures the changes, if any, that are produced in the **dependent variable**, *a second factor, also called the* outcome variable, *that is observed and measured for change in an experiment.* The dependent variable is so named because changes in it "depend on" variations in the independent variable.

To the greatest degree possible, all other conditions in the experiment are kept exactly the same for all participants. Thus, when the data are analyzed, any changes that are measured in the dependent variable can be attributed to the deliberate manipulation of the independent variable. In this way, an experiment can provide evidence of a cause-and-effect relationship between the independent and dependent variables.

In designing experiments, psychologists try to anticipate and control for **confounding variables**, *which are extraneous variables that are not the focus of the experiment but could affect the outcome of an experiment.* Confounding variables might produce inaccurate

correlation coefficient A numerical indicator of the strength of the relationship (the *correlation*) between two variables.

positive correlation A finding that two factors vary systematically in the same direction, that is, increasing or decreasing together.

negative correlation A finding in which the two variables move in opposite directions, one increasing as the other decreases.

experimental research A method of investigation used to demonstrate cause-and-effect relationships by purposely manipulating one factor thought to produce change in another factor.

independent variable A factor that is purposely manipulated to produce change in an experiment; also called a *predictor variable.*

dependent variable The factor that is observed and measured for change in an experiment; also called the *outcome variable.*

confounding variable Extraneous variables that are not the focus of the experiment but could affect the outcome of an experiment.

experimental results by influencing changes in the dependent variable. Confounding variables in a psychology experiment could include unwanted variability in such factors as age, gender, ethnic background, race, health, occupation, personal habits, education, and so on. We've already talked about confounding variables, just in a different context. The third variables we referred to in our discussion of correlation are actually confounding variables. Third variables are not the focus of a correlational study, but can explain a relation between two other variables. For example, it's possible that an engaging personality explained the correlation between emoji use and first dates. Fun people may both use more emojis and have more first dates.

To illustrate how experimental research works, let's look at a topic of interest to most university students: What types of study strategies are most effective?

In most educational settings, learning is thought to take place during study, instruction, and practice. Tests, in contrast, are neutral experiences and simply assess what has been learned. But some studies seemed to suggest that being tested on new information helped students learn and remember it better than simply studying it (see Bae et al., 2019; Roediger & Butler, 2011). Psychologists Henry Roediger and Jeffrey Karpicke (2006) set out to investigate the effects of testing on learning and memory.

Experimental Design: Studying The Effects of Testing

How could you experimentally study the difference between learning due to studying and learning due to testing? In a classic study, Roediger and Karpicke (2006) designed an experiment that compared the effects of repeated testing with the effects of repeated study periods. They predicted that students who repeatedly took tests after studying would have better long-term memory of the new information than students who repeatedly studied, but were not tested on, the same material. The hypothesis, then, was that "repeated testing improves learning more than repeated studying."

The participants were 60 college undergraduates aged 18 to 24. The researchers used *random assignment* to assign participants to one of two groups: either the *experimental group* or the *control group*. **Random assignment** is *a process of assigning participants to experimental conditions so that all the participants have an equal chance of being assigned to any of the conditions or groups in the study.* Random assignment is often confused with random selection, which we discussed previously. Random selection is one way to choose a sample of participants, but it's rarely used. Random assignment is common, and what researchers do once they have their participants. Random assignment helps ensure that any potential differences among the participants are spread out evenly across all experimental conditions.

In every experiment, there are at least two conditions of the independent variable, a *control condition* and a *treatment condition*. The treatment condition is the particular condition, substance, or situation that the researchers wish to test to see whether it will affect the dependent variable. The **experimental group** is *the group of participants exposed to the treatment condition*. It's important that experiments also include a **control group**, *the group exposed to the control condition of the independent variable*. The control group serves as a baseline against which changes in the experimental group can be compared. In a typical experiment, the participants in the control group go through all the experimental phases but are not exposed to the specific treatment that the experimental group experiences.

In this study, the independent variable was "learning technique." And, the independent variable had two conditions: The treatment condition was "repeated testing," and was experienced by the participants in the experimental group. The control condition was "repeated study," and was experienced by participants in the control group. The *dependent variable* was the score earned on a final test.

Here's how the experiment was conducted. All of the participants were given a short prose passage to study. Participants in the *control group* read the passage for five minutes, and took a two-minute break. They then studied the passage again for five minutes before taking another two-minute break. They repeated this process for a total of four consecutive study periods. Note that this is the standard test-preparation method: to repeatedly study the same material until you feel certain that you have mastered it.

≈ Achie√e

To better understand how the experimental method is used to answer questions about human behavior and mental processes, go to **Achieve** and watch **Video: Experimental Design.**

random assignment The process of assigning participants to experimental conditions so that all participants have an equal chance of being assigned to any of the conditions or groups in the study.

experimental group Group of participants who are exposed to all experimental conditions, including the treatment condition of the independent variable; also called *experimental condition*.

control group Group of participants exposed to the control condition of the independent variable; also called *control condition*.

testing effect The finding that practicing retrieval of information from memory produces better retention than restudying the same information for an equivalent amount of time.

Participants in the *experimental group* were given the same prose passage to learn. They were also allotted five minutes to study the passage, and then took a two-minute break. But rather than restudying the passage, they took a test on the material: They were given a blank sheet of paper and were allowed 10 minutes to write down as much information from the prose passage as they could remember. After another two-minute break, without studying the material again, they were given the same test, followed by a two-minute break. This procedure was followed for a total of one study period and three test periods. **Figure 1.4** shows the setup of the experiment.

At the end of the session, all of the participants filled out a short questionnaire asking them to predict how well they would remember the material in a week. A week later, all participants were tested on the material.

How do you think the two groups would compare on a test of their retention of the material a week later? Conventional wisdom would suggest that the control group members, who studied the material in four periods for a total of 20 minutes, would have learned the material much better than the participants in the experimental group, who, after all, had only studied the material for a total of five minutes.

What were the results on the test one week later? Despite having studied the material only one-fourth as long as the control group, the experimental group trounced the control group: They remembered 61 percent of the material in the passage, while the control group remembered only 40 percent. Results are shown in **Figure 1.5**. Interestingly, the control group participants were much more confident of their ability to remember the information than the experimental group.

Were you surprised by the results? In fact, the basic results have been replicated by many different researchers (see Bjork et al., 2013; Rowland, 2014). Multiple studies have supported what has been dubbed the **testing effect**: *the finding that practicing retrieval of information from memory produces better retention than restudying the same information for an equivalent amount of time.* In other words, testing—rather than simply being a neutral assessment of what has been learned—is a powerful learning tool in its own right (Batsell et al., 2017; Roediger & Karpicke, 2018; Roediger & Nestojiko, 2015). More recent research has expanded our knowledge of the testing effect. For example, research showed that being tested on previously learned information actually boosts our ability to learn similar, new information (Yang et al., 2018).

We'll discuss some of the reasons for the testing effect in the chapter on memory. In Psych for Your Life at the end of this chapter, we'll describe some of the other ways in which the testing effect has been explored. And, we'll discuss additional ways in which you can use psychological research to improve your own memory for new information.

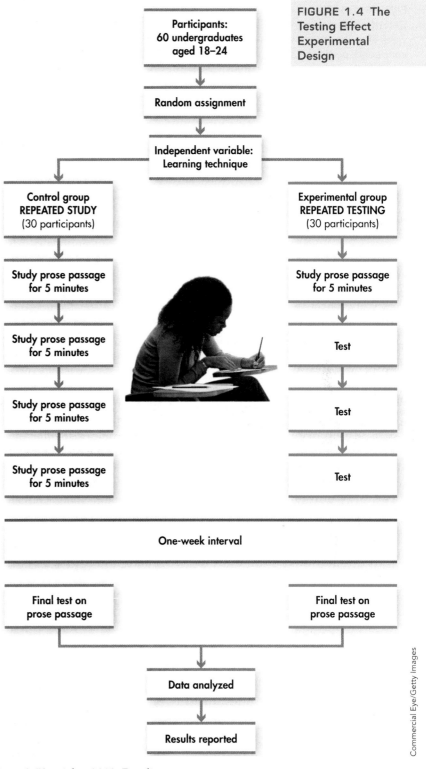

FIGURE 1.4 The Testing Effect Experimental Design

Participants: 60 undergraduates aged 18–24

Random assignment

Independent variable: Learning technique

Control group REPEATED STUDY (30 participants)

Experimental group REPEATED TESTING (30 participants)

Study prose passage for 5 minutes | Study prose passage for 5 minutes

Study prose passage for 5 minutes | Test

Study prose passage for 5 minutes | Test

Study prose passage for 5 minutes | Test

One-week interval

Final test on prose passage | Final test on prose passage

Data analyzed

Results reported

Commercial Eye/Getty Images

MYTH ◀ SCIENCE

Is it true that reading something over and over is the most effective way to prepare for a test?

FIGURE 1.5 Effects of Testing on Retention: Experimental Results One week after the experimental sessions concluded, participants were tested to see how much they retained from material they had studied. As you can see, the participants who were repeatedly tested remembered much more of the information than the students who had repeatedly studied the same material.

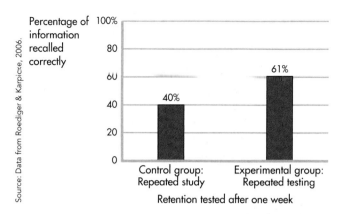

Source: Data from Roediger & Karpicke, 2006.

Percentage of information recalled correctly

40% Control group: Repeated study
61% Experimental group: Repeated testing

Retention tested after one week

double-blind technique An experimental control in which both the participants and the researchers are "blind," or unaware of the treatment or condition to which the participants have been assigned.

demand characteristics In a research study, subtle cues or signals expressed by the researcher that communicate the kind of response or behavior that is expected from the participant.

placebo A fake substance, treatment, or procedure that has no known direct effects.

placebo effect Any change attributed to a person's beliefs and expectations rather than to an actual drug, treatment, or procedure.

Experimental Controls

Some experiments involve extra controls to increase the reliability of their findings. One important safeguard is the **double-blind technique**, *an experimental control in which both the participants and the researchers are "blind," or unaware of the treatment or condition to which the participants have been assigned.* It is often used when researchers are testing the effectiveness of a procedure or drug treatment.

Using a double-blind technique helps guard against the possibility that the researcher inadvertently becomes an extraneous or confounding variable in the study. This can happen when a researcher, without realizing it, displays **demand characteristics**, *subtle cues or signals expressed by the researcher that communicate the kind of response or behavior that is expected from the participant.* A behavior as subtle as the researcher slightly smiling or frowning when dealing with some participants, but not others, could bias the outcome of a study.

Such studies also often involve the use of a **placebo**, *a fake substance, treatment, or procedure that has no known direct effects.* Although it is inactive, a placebo can produce real effects (see Wager & Atlas, 2015). A **placebo effect** is *any change that can be attributed to beliefs and expectations rather than to an actual drug, treatment, or procedure.* We'll talk more about a possible placebo effect with respect to antidepressant medications in the chapter on therapies.

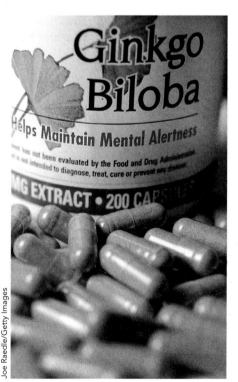

Joe Raedle/Getty Images

› Can Ginkgo Biloba Enhance Your Mental Abilities? The herbal supplement *ginkgo biloba* is marketed as a "cognitive enhancer" that supposedly improves memory, alertness, and concentration, especially in older adults. However, studies of ginkgo don't support those claims (see Birks & Evans, 2009; Daffner, 2010; Snitz et al., 2009).

For example, one student in our class asked us whether we believed that the herb ginkgo biloba could improve memory. To test that notion, psychologist Paul Solomon and his colleagues (2002) used a placebo in a double-blind study to test whether ginkgo biloba improved memory and concentration in older adults. Participants in the experimental group took the manufacturer's recommended daily dose of ginkgo biloba for six weeks, while those in the control group took an identical dose of placebo capsules.

The researchers who interacted with the participants did not know which participants received the real and which received the fake ginkgo biloba. The researchers who did know the group assignments did *not* interact with or evaluate the participants. Memory and other cognitive abilities were assessed at the beginning and end of the six-week study.

Can you predict the results of the ginkgo biloba experiment? At the end of the six-week study, the test scores of *both* groups rose. However, there were no significant differences between the improvement in the ginkgo biloba and placebo groups. So why did both groups improve? The researchers concluded that it was probably due to the *practice effect*. The participants' experience with the tests—the practice they got by simply taking the mental ability tests twice—was the most likely reason that test scores improved in both groups. This experiment illustrates the importance of the control group: Without a control group for comparison, the improvement in the experimental group might have been attributed to the drug. But since the control group participants *also* improved, there must have been another explanation.

Limitations of Experiments and Variations in Experimental Design

A well-designed and carefully executed experiment can provide convincing evidence of a cause-and-effect relationship between the independent and dependent variables. But experiments do have limitations. Because experiments are often conducted in highly controlled laboratory situations, they are sometimes criticized for having little to do with actual behavior. That is, the results may not *generalize* well, meaning that the results cannot be applied to real-world situations or to more general populations beyond the participants in the study. To minimize this, experiments are sometimes carried out in natural settings, rather than in a laboratory. A second potential limitation is that the phenomena the researchers want to study may be impossible or unethical to control experimentally.

A study investigating the effects of a naturally occurring event on the research participants is a **natural experiment**. Researchers carefully observe and measure the impact of a naturally occurring event or condition on their study participants (Leatherdale, 2019; Rutter, 2008). Although these are not true experiments, psychologists can use natural experiments to study people in everyday settings such as students in classrooms, diners in restaurants, or drivers in traffic. But they also can study the effects of disasters, epidemics, or other events.

Psychology graduate student Mengtian Zhao and her colleagues (2019) conducted a study in which participants role-played being in the path of a tornado. Participants indicated the level of risk they perceived from the tornado and how likely they were to seek shelter. The study was a natural experiment. The researchers collected data before, and then again after, a major tornado hit Oklahoma City (so major that 24 people died in the tragedy). The researchers found that participants who responded just after the devastating tornado rated the risk as higher and their likelihood of seeking shelter as higher, on average, than those who responded before the tragedy. The research was correlational, though, so the researchers couldn't conclude that the tornado *caused* changes in participant reports. It could be that something else changed during the time before the tornado hit. Maybe other world events led people to become more risk averse.

Of course, researchers can't randomly assign large numbers of participants to particular periods of time—some before a destructive tornado and some just after. Instead, the researchers took advantage of a naturally occurring disaster in which people are essentially randomly assigned to that point in time—before and after the tornado struck. Zhao and her colleagues took advantage of the naturally occurring weather disaster to assess perceptions of risk and behavioral intentions before and after it occurred.

Before leaving the topic of research methods, one contemporary trend deserves special mention: the increasing use of brain-imaging techniques in virtually every area of psychology. To help highlight the importance of neuroscience, chapters include special Focus on Neuroscience features.

This brief introduction to research methods will give you some idea of how psychologists conduct research. But we hope it also illustrates some of the ways in which scientists—and others—evaluate claims and evidence. In the Critical Thinking box "How to Think Like a Scientist," we offer several suggestions to help you evaluate claims that you encounter both inside and outside the classroom.

natural experiment A study investigating the effects of a naturally occurring event on the research participants.

THINK LIKE A **SCIENTIST**
Could you have been part of an experiment without realizing it? Go to Achieve: Resources to **Think Like a Scientist** about **Contagious Online Emotions.**

Achieve

David Mabe/Alamy Stock Photo

⌃ **Using a Natural Experiment to Study How People Perceive Risk from a Tornado** We can't always randomly assign people to conditions—such as before or after a tornado strikes. But we can collect data just before and just after a naturally occurring event. Mengtian Zhao and her colleagues (2019) did just that. They collected data just before and after a major tornado hit Oklahoma City. Study participants engaged in a role-playing exercise in which they rated the risk of a hypothetical approaching tornado and rated how likely it was that they would seek shelter. Those who participated before the Oklahoma tornado hit gave higher ratings to both variables, on average, than those who participated after it hit.

🗨 CRITICAL THINKING

How to Think Like a Scientist

Do you remember Derek from the Prologue? He wanted to know whether energy healing could reduce his test anxiety. Energy healing involves using light touch or moving hands just above the body to treat various conditions and ailments (supposedly)—yes, including anxiety.

How can you evaluate the claims you encounter, like this one about energy healing? Both in class and out, it's important to engage in **critical thinking**, *actively questioning statements rather than blindly accepting them.*

Critical thinkers are open to new information, ideas, and claims. However, this open-mindedness is tempered by a healthy sense of skepticism (J. C. Smith, 2010). The critical thinker might ask "What evidence supports this claim?"

In this chapter, we've detailed the ways that psychologists conduct research, including the different ways they test hypotheses. You can think of the claims you encounter in the news, on social media, on shows (like the Netflix series *The Goop Lab,* where Derek heard the claim about energy healing), or in conversation as hypotheses, too. When you encounter an idea or statement that is presented as factual, try to *think like a scientist.*

Like a scientist, you can follow these four steps to determine the validity of a particular claim. Research demonstrates that those who use reasoning to evaluate facts are less likely to fall for misinformation (Pennycook & Rand, 2019):

1. Identify the Claim
Some claims are so vague that they are impossible to test scientifically. During an episode of *The Goop Lab,* an energy healer explained to *Goop* founder Gwyneth Paltrow and her team how it works: "You have energy that's bound up in the muscles and ligaments and spine and fascia and organs when you're under stress. So I show up and actually influence how energy's moving so that your body can heal faster in your physical being, your emotional being, your mind, your soul." Superficially, it *sounds* convincing, but can you imagine an experiment that would actually test the claim that a healer's hands can influence your body's "energy" to heal you? Try to restate the claim in terms of a hypothesis that could be supported or disproved by empirical evidence. How would you define the variables that could be objectively measured?

2. Evaluate the Evidence
If you're getting information from a non-scientific source, like *The Goop Lab,* check whether it cites or links to a scientific source, such as an academic journal article. (We'll talk more about sources in section 4 of this box.) As you have learned, the scientific method includes key safeguards in experimental design, such as random assignment, the presence of a control group, and researchers who are "blind" to participants' conditions. So when evidence is offered in support of a particular position, scrutinize it and look for those basic safeguards.

Consider also the nature of the evidence that may be offered. When words like "link," "tie," or "association" are used, the evidence is probably correlational, rather than experimental. But as you learned in the section on Correlational Studies, just because two events are correlated does not mean that they are causally linked.

MYTH ◀ SCIENCE

Is it true that when two behaviors are "linked," "related," or tend to occur together, it's safe to assume that one behavior caused the other?

Ethics in Psychological Research

■ KEY THEME
Psychological research conducted in the United States is subject to ethical guidelines developed by the American Psychological Association (APA).

⹀ KEY QUESTIONS
• What are five key provisions of the APA ethics code for research involving human participants?
• Why do psychologists sometimes conduct research with nonhuman animal subjects?

You might wonder what would happen if you were to volunteer to participate in a psychology experiment or study. Are psychologists allowed to manipulate or control you without your knowledge or consent? Could a psychologist force you to reveal your innermost secrets? Could they administer electric shocks?

The answer to all of these questions is "no." The American Psychological Association (APA) has developed a strict code of ethics for conducting research with both human participants and animal subjects. This code is contained in a document called *Ethical Principles of Psychologists and Code of Conduct* (APA, 2002, 2010, 2017a). You can go to the Web site apa.org/ethics to download a copy of the document.

critical thinking Actively questioning statements rather than blindly accepting them.

People may report that they feel better after an energy healing session. But is such a conclusion justified? *No.* You cannot conclude that any correlation between energy healing and self-reports of improvement occurred because of the energy healing. In addition, any self-reports of improvement may be a placebo effect.

We can't measure the impact of a healer's hands on "energy" within the body. But we can conduct an experiment comparing energy healing to a control group to see if they lead to different outcomes. Researchers conducted a scientific review of the research on Reiki, perhaps the best known type of energy healing, on anxiety and depression (Joyce & Herbison, 2015). The researchers found just three experiments, the only kind of research that can determine cause and effect, on this topic. The data from these experiments did not provide evidence for the effectiveness of energy healing.

It also is important to remember that *testimonials are not evidence* (Coltheart & McArthur, 2012). Distinguish between empirical evidence that can be objectively observed, measured, and shared, like the review we just described, and private opinions, based on feelings or personal experience. For example, *The Goop Lab* presents John, who credits energy healing for ridding him of numbness below his chest that he experienced after his recovery from cancer (Paltrow et al., 2020). "But," one reporter wrote, "this kind of nerve damage often fades with time, and the show doesn't say how many people try it without success" (Wilson, 2020).

3. Consider Alternative Explanations

Especially if a claim is highly unusual, seems to contradict accepted scientific theories, or has no plausible explanation, *consider alternative explanations.* A claim demonstrating improvement in a condition or skill could, in fact, have many different explanations. Maybe Derek felt less anxious after energy healing. The improvement *could* be due to the treatment. But it could also be due to the placebo effect (see page 28).

4. Consider the Source of the Research or Claim

Typically, scientific research is reported in a peer-reviewed scientific journal or at an academic conference *before* the results are released to the media. So, when research is reported in the popular media or on the Internet, consider the source of the research. Although publication in a scientific journal, like the review we described above, is no guarantee that the results will hold up over time, you can at least be certain that the research has been carefully evaluated by other scientists in the field. When a claim has no apparent ties to legitimate educational or scientific enterprises, you should be especially cautious. In general, it's worth considering the researchers' motives. If the people or company making the claim have the potential to profit from its use, the source may not be objective.

Whether the claims you encounter come from friends, instructors, or celebrities on a Netflix series, remember these four steps — and think like a scientist before blindly accepting them.

CRITICAL THINKING QUESTIONS

- Why might other people want to discourage you from thinking critically?
- In what situations is it probably most difficult or challenging for you to exercise critical thinking skills? Why?
- What can you do or say to encourage others to use critical thinking in evaluating questionable claims or assertions?

In general, psychologists must respect the dignity and welfare of participants. Psychologists cannot deceptively expose research participants to conditions that might cause either physical or emotional harm. At most institutions, any psychological research using human participants or animal subjects is scrutinized by an institutional review board before approval is granted (Fisher & Vacanti-Shova, 2012).

Here are highlights of five key provisions in the most recent APA ethical principles regulating research with human participants:

- **Informed consent and voluntary participation.** The psychologist must inform the participants of the purpose of the research, including any important factor that might influence a person's willingness to participate in the study, such as potential risks, discomfort, or unpleasant emotional experiences. The psychologist must also explain that participants are free to decline to participate or to withdraw from the research at any time.

- **Students as research participants.** When research participation is a course requirement or an opportunity for extra credit, the student must be given the choice of an alternative activity to fulfill the course requirement or earn extra credit.

- **The use of deception.** Psychologists can use deceptive techniques as part of the study only when two conditions have been met: (1) when it is not feasible

MYTH ◀ SCIENCE

Is it true that psychologists are not allowed to trick you into taking part in a study?

comparative psychology The branch of psychology that studies the behavior of nonhuman animals.

to use alternatives that do not involve deception and (2) when the potential findings justify the use of deception because of their scientific, educational, or applied value.

- **Confidentiality of information.** In their writing, lectures, or other public forums, psychologists may not disclose personally identifiable information about research participants.

- **Information about the study and debriefing.** All participants must be provided with the opportunity to obtain information about the nature, results, and conclusions of the research. Psychologists are also obligated to *debrief* the participants and to correct any misconceptions that participants may have had about the research.

What about research involving nonhuman animal subjects? Only a fraction of psychological research studies conducted in a given year involve animal subjects—typically about 7 to 8 percent. About 90 percent of those studies involve rodents or birds, typically rats, mice, and pigeons. Why are animals used in psychological research? Two of the main reasons are listed below.

1. **Many psychologists are interested in the study of animal behavior for its own sake.**

   The branch of psychology that focuses on the study of the behavior of nonhuman animals is called **comparative psychology**. Some psychologists also do research in *animal cognition,* which is the study of animal learning, memory, thinking, and language (Zentall & Wasserman, 2012). And research is also pursued for its potential benefit to the animals themselves. For example, psychological research on animal behavior has been used to improve the quality of life of animals in zoos and to increase the likelihood of survival of endangered species in the wild (Blumstein & Fernandez-Juricic, 2010; Frank et al., 2019; Goulart et al., 2009).

2. **Animal subjects are sometimes used for research that could not feasibly be conducted on human participants.**

   There are many similarities between human and animal behavior, but animal behavior tends to be less complex. Thus, it is sometimes easier to identify basic principles of behavior by studying animals. Psychologists can also observe some animals throughout their entire lifespan. To track such changes in humans would take decades of research. Finally, psychologists can exercise greater control over animal subjects than over human participants. If necessary, researchers can control every aspect of the animals' environment and even their genetic background (Ator, 2005).

   The use of nonhuman animal subjects in psychological research is also governed by specific ethical guidelines (APA, 2012; Perry & Dess, 2012). The American Psychological Association publishes the *Guidelines for Ethical Conduct in the Care and Use of Nonhuman Animals in Research,* which you can read at apa.org/science /leadership/care/guidelines.aspx. The APA guidelines for animal care have been praised as being the most comprehensive set of guidelines of their kind. In addition, psychologists must adhere to federal and state laws governing the use and care of research animals.

> **Psychological Research Helping Animals** Comparative psychologist Rebecca Snyder is the curator of giant panda research and management at Zoo Atlanta. Collaborating with scientists at Chengdu Zoo in Sichuan province in China, Snyder and her colleagues have studied topics as diverse as spatial memory in adult giant pandas, play behavior in cubs, and reproductive behavior (Perdue et al., 2009; M. Wilson et al., 2009; Snyder et al., 2016). Knowledge gained from such research not only improves the quality of life of pandas in zoos, but also can be applied to conservation efforts in the wild (Perdue et al., 2013). Many zoos consult comparative psychologists to help design appropriate housing and enrichment activities for all sorts of animals. For more on the psychological and behavioral research at Zoo Atlanta, visit zooatlanta.org/research/

Zhang Jun/Xinhua News Agency/Newscom

Closing Thoughts

Remember the students in the chapter Prologue who wanted help with studying for tests? Many students come to psychology courses with questions about personal experiences, seeking help for common problems or explanations for common and uncommon behaviors. As you'll see throughout this book, psychological research has produced many useful insights into behavior and mental processes. At the end of each chapter, we present research-based strategies that *you* can implement to improve your everyday life.

At several points in this chapter, we've described research on factors affecting academic success in college. Fortunately, psychologists have identified several techniques that anyone can use to improve their mastery of new information. We discuss these techniques in the next section, Psych for Your Life.

 **PSYCH FOR YOUR LIFE**

Successful Study Techniques

Psychologists have conducted thousands of research studies investigating learning and memory. In the chapter on memory, we'll provide strategies to improve your ability to memorize lists of items and other types of content. For now, here are five research-based suggestions that you can use to help you study more effectively—and succeed in this course and others.

1. Focus your attention

Many students think they are good multitaskers. But do you remember the correlational research on multitasking during studying? The psychological research is clear: Attention is a limited resource (Chun et al., 2011; Wammes et al., 2019). So, when you sit down to study, put your phone and other devices on "silent" and try to avoid going online except for topic-related material. If you find it hard to stay on task, set a timer and challenge yourself to read for 30 minutes without interruption. You'll be amazed at how much more efficient your studying is.

2. Engage your mind: Be an active reader

One of the most common study techniques used by students is to highlight or underline text in handouts and textbooks. Highlighting and underlining can be helpful, but *only* if done properly (Dunlosky et al., 2013; Miyatsu et al., 2018).

Research has found that you're more likely to remember text marked by highlighting or underlining. The problem is that you are *less* likely to remember material that you don't mark. Thus, if you highlight the wrong material, highlighting may be more harmful than helpful. It's also a problem if you highlight *too much* material. One early study found a negative correlation between the amount of text highlighted and test scores: The more material students highlighted, the lower their test scores (Fowler & Barker, 1974).

So, be an active reader—and a selective highlighter, highlighting only the most important information. In this textbook, the Key Questions at the beginning of each section will help you identify the most important points.

3. In the classroom, take notes by hand, not on your laptop

Many students take notes on a laptop or tablet, but research suggests that taking notes by hand increases conceptual understanding and factual retention of the material (Mitchell & Zheng, 2019; Mueller & Oppenheimer, 2014). Students also had higher test scores when they studied from their handwritten notes versus studying from typed notes, even though their typed notes included more information. The explanation?

▲ **Using a Laptop in Class?** It may *seem* more efficient to use your laptop or tablet to take notes in class, but you'll actually remember the material better if you pay close attention and take notes by hand (Glass & Kang, 2019; Mueller & Oppenheimer, 2014). You'll also be less likely to be distracted by online temptations like social media or shopping sites.

Students who typed on a laptop tended to simply transcribe verbatim what they heard. In contrast, note-takers using longhand had to listen, digest, and summarize the information in their own words. Doing so required them to deeply engage with the material, which led to better memory for the information.

Here's another problem with using your laptop to take notes in class: You may be tempted to go online. In one study, students were randomly assigned to use their electronic devices in some lectures but not in others (Glass & Kang, 2019). The researchers found that students did worse on exams when they could use their devices in the lectures than when it was forbidden. Even more important, this was true among the students who chose not to use their laptops. They were likely distracted by their classmates' use of social media devices. The moral of the story: Unless your laptop is required for the class, best to leave it at home or in your backpack, and try not to sit where you can see others' screens.

4. Practice retrieval: Use the testing effect to your advantage

Earlier in the chapter, we described an experiment that demonstrated the power of the *testing effect* — the finding that retrieving information from memory produces better retention than restudying the same information (Roediger & Karpicke, 2006, 2018; Roediger & Butler, 2011). Hundreds of experiments have shown that tests do more than simply assess learning; they are powerful tools in their own right (Batsell et al., 2017; Bjork et al., 2013). In fact, practice tests enhance memory for all types of information, including learning new skills (Dunlosky et al., 2013).

Yet another benefit of practice tests has been found: They can help you overcome the test anxiety that leads you to choke during an exam. Psychologists have long known that stress impairs memory retrieval (Wolf, 2017; Wolf & Kluge, 2017). But Amy Smith and her colleagues (2016) found that preparing for an exam with practice tests can actually "stress-proof" your exam performance. Participants in the study took an exam after being subjected to a stressful experience. The participants who studied by using practice tests outperformed participants who simply reviewed the material. In fact, stress actually *improved* exam performance in those who used practice testing.

Why is practice testing such a powerful study technique? Practice testing allows you to identify the gaps that exist in your knowledge so that you can better allocate your study time (Roediger et al., 2011). Practice tests also allow you to practice the very skills that you will need to succeed — retrieving information you've learned from memory (Roediger et al., 2012; Yang et al., 2018).

Take advantage of any practice quizzes that may be offered by your professor or in study guides. Challenge yourself to write out the definitions for each of the boldfaced key terms in your text, and then to come up with new examples if you can. Or read a section of material, close your book, and write down ten key points from that section. Go back and check your work against the material.

5. Space out your study time: The benefits of distributed vs. massed practice

Psychologists call it "massed practice." Students call it "cramming." A common strategy for time-challenged students, massed practice involves trying to study as much as possible in a short period of time, typically right before an exam. Interestingly, massed practice *is* effective — but *only* in the short term (Bjork et al., 2013). Typically, information learned through cramming is forgotten very quickly.

A much more effective study strategy is what psychologists call *distributed practice,* which means that you learn the information over several sessions, separated in time. Countless studies have shown that information learned over distributed sessions is much better retained than information learned in a single session (see Soderstrom et al., 2016; Soderstrom & Bjork, 2015). One reason may be that the time between sessions gives you a chance to organize and incorporate new information into your memory (Carpenter et al., 2012).

We hope you find these suggestions helpful, both in psychology and in your other courses. Welcome to psychology!

⬑ CHAPTER REVIEW

Introduction and Research Methods

 **Achieve,** Macmillan Learning's online study platform, features the full e-book of *Discovering Psychology,* the **LearningCurve** adaptive quizzing system, videos, and a variety of activities to boost your learning. Visit **Achieve** at macmillanlearning.com.

KEY PEOPLE

Mary Whiton Calkins, p. 8
Kenneth Bancroft Clark, p. 8
Mamie Phipps Clark, p. 8
Charles Darwin, p. 6
Sigmund Freud, p. 9

Robert V. Guthrie, p. 7
G. Stanley Hall, p. 7
William James, p. 6
Abraham Maslow, p. 10
Ivan Pavlov, p. 9

Carl Rogers, p. 10
Pauline Elizabeth Scarborough, p. 7
B.F. Skinner, p. 10
Francis C. Sumner, p. 8

Edward B. Titchener, p. 6
Margaret Floy Washburn, p. 8
John B. Watson, p. 9
Wilhelm Wundt, p. 5

KEY TERMS

psychology, p. 4
structuralism, p. 6
functionalism, p. 7
psychoanalysis, p. 9
behaviorism, p. 9
humanistic psychology, p. 10
neuroscience, p. 11
culture, p. 14
ethnocentrism, p. 14
individualistic cultures, p. 14
collectivistic cultures, p. 14
psychiatry, p. 15
scientific method, p. 16

empirical evidence, p. 16
hypothesis, p. 16
variable, p. 16
operational definition, p. 16
statistics, p. 18
statistically significant, p. 18
effect size, p. 18
meta-analysis, p. 18
open science, p. 19
replicate, p. 19
theory, p. 20
descriptive research, p. 21
longitudinal design, p. 21

cross-sectional design, p. 21
naturalistic observation, p. 21
case study, p. 22
survey, p. 22
sample, p. 22
representative sample, p. 22
random selection, p. 23
correlational study, p. 23
correlation coefficient, p. 24
positive correlation, p. 24
negative correlation, p. 24
experimental research, p. 25
independent variable, p. 25

dependent variable, p. 25
confounding variable, p. 25
random assignment, p. 26
experimental group, p. 26
control group, p. 26
testing effect, p. 27
double-blind technique, p. 28
demand characteristics, p. 28
placebo, p. 28
placebo effect, p. 28
natural experiment, p. 29
critical thinking, p. 30
comparative psychology, p. 32

Origins of Psychology

Psychology: The scientific study of behavior and mental processes
Psychology's goals: To describe, explain, predict, and influence behavior and mental processes

The work of early philosophers and psychologists provided a foundation for the birth of psychology as an experimental science.

Wilhelm Wundt (1832–1920)
Founded psychology as experimental science

Edward B. Titchener (1867–1927)
Structuralism: Structures of thought; introspection

William James (1842–1910)
Functionalism: Adaptive role of behavior

Robert V. Guthrie (1932–2005) and **Pauline Elizabeth Scarborough** (1935–2015)

Highlighted members of marginalized groups who were overlooked in psychology.
Mary Whiton Calkins (1863–1930)
Margaret Floy Washburn (1871–1939)
Francis C. Sumner (1895–1954)
Kenneth Bancroft Clark (1914–2005)
Mamie Phipps Clark (1917–1983)

Sigmund Freud (1856–1939)
Psychoanalysis: Unconscious influences on behavior

Ivan Pavlov (1849–1936)
John B. Watson (1878–1958)
B.F. Skinner (1904–1990)
Behaviorism: Observable behaviors that can be objectively measured and verified

Carl Rogers (1902–1987)
Abraham Maslow (1908–1970)
Humanistic psychology: Psychological growth, human potential, self-direction

Contemporary Psychology

Perspectives:
• Biological
• Psychodynamic
• Behavioral
• Humanistic
• Positive psychology
• Cognitive
• Cross-cultural
• Evolutionary psychology

Specialty areas:
• Applied
• Biological
• Clinical
• Cognitive
• Community
• Counseling
• Developmental
• Educational
• Experimental
• Health
• Industrial/organizational
• Personality
• School
• Social

The Scientific Method

Systematic procedure to collect **empirical evidence**

1. Generate an empirically testable **hypothesis; operationally define** all **variables**
2. Design study and collect data
3. Analyze data and draw conclusions
4. Report the findings

Use **statistics** to analyze findings and determine whether they are **statistically significant;** use **meta-analysis** to combine and analyze data from effect sizes.

Open science promotes transparency in research. For example, publishing details of study design so that study can be **replicated.**

Develop **theories** to integrate and explain various findings and observations.

ELIZABETH D. HERMAN/The New York Times/Redux Pictures

Research Methods

Must conform to American Psychological Association codes of ethics

Requirements for research with human participants:
- Informed consent
- Voluntary participation
- Deception allowable only when no other alternatives and if justified by study's potential merit
- Confidentiality of personal information
- Debriefed at conclusion of study

Requirements for research with nonhuman subjects:
- Acceptable scientific purpose
- Must increase knowledge about species, behavior, or benefit the health or welfare of humans or nonhuman animals
- Must meet local, state, and federal guidelines regulating care of research animals

Zhang Jun/Xinhua News Agency/Newscom

Descriptive research methods: Systematically observe and describe behavior.

Naturalistic observation

Case studies

Surveys, questionnaires

Correlational studies:
- Determine strength of relationship between two factors; cannot provide evidence of causality
- The relationship is expressed as a numerical **correlation coefficient.**
- A **positive correlation** indicates that two factors vary in the same direction.
- A **negative correlation** indicates that two factors vary in opposite directions.

Experimental method: Manipulates **independent variable** and measures the effects on **dependent variable;** used to demonstrate a cause-and-effect relationship

Natural experiments: Investigate effects of naturally occurring events

Experimental controls:
- **Random assignment** of research participants to experimental or control group
- **Double-blind** experimental design to guard against experimenter bias and **demand characteristics**
- Anticipate potential influence of **extraneous variables**

Experimental group: Exposed to treatment condition of the independent variable

Control group: Not exposed to treatment condition of the independent variable

Placebo control group: (in some experiments): Exposed to fake version of the experimental condition

Measure effects, if any, on **dependent variable**

Commercial Eye/Getty Images

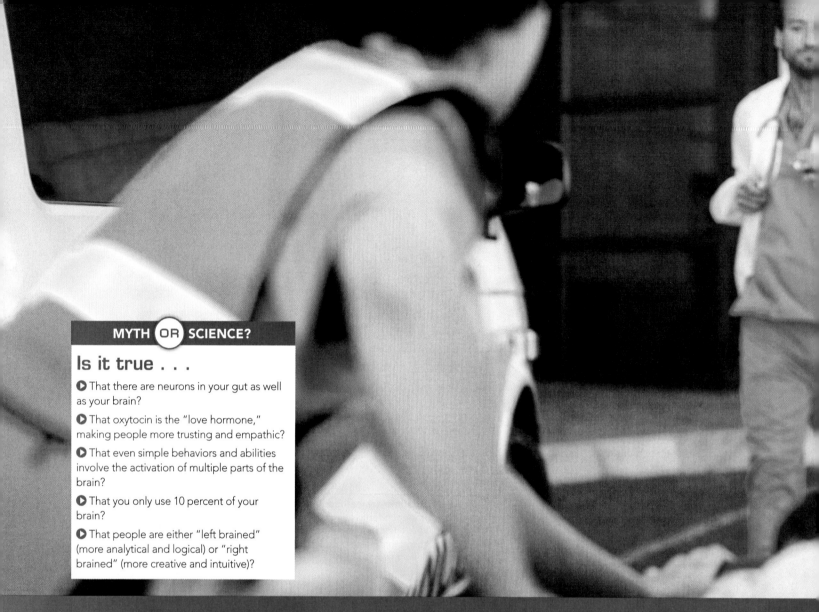

MYTH OR SCIENCE?

Is it true . . .

▶ That there are neurons in your gut as well as your brain?

▶ That oxytocin is the "love hormone," making people more trusting and empathic?

▶ That even simple behaviors and abilities involve the activation of multiple parts of the brain?

▶ That you only use 10 percent of your brain?

▶ That people are either "left brained" (more analytical and logical) or "right brained" (more creative and intuitive)?

Neuroscience and Behavior

PROLOGUE

Gabby's Story

It's Saturday, January 8, just before 10:00 A.M., and Congresswoman Gabrielle Giffords is planning a casual gathering to talk with residents in her home district. Congresswoman Giffords — called Gabby by friends, colleagues, and constituents — is known for her upbeat and approachable personality. She prides herself on connecting with the people who elected her and has hosted more than 20 gatherings like the one planned for today. Close to 10 A.M., Gabby arrives at a parking lot outside a Safeway supermarket in Tucson, Arizona, where her staff set up

a table underneath flags of Arizona and the United States. She sends out a Tweet: "My 1st Congress on Your Corner starts now. Please stop by to let me know what is on your mind or tweet me later." As always, Gabby is excited to speak with her constituents.

There are already about 20 people waiting to meet Gabby, among them a local doctor, a homemaker, a Vietnam veteran, a retired construction worker, and his wife. A man wearing sneakers and a dark sweatshirt approaches the table, telling a staff member that he is eager to speak with the congresswoman, and takes a place in line. Gabby speaks animatedly with the first person in line, adjusting her red blazer when he asks for

a photo together. Next, an older couple ask questions about Medicare. Suddenly, the man in the dark sweatshirt steps out of the line. He approaches the congresswoman with a semiautomatic handgun and shoots her in the head at point-blank range. Congresswoman Giffords drops to the ground, motionless. The man then fires 30 shots into the crowd, killing 6 and injuring 13 before running out of bullets. While attempting to reload, the gunman is overpowered by people in the crowd.

Bystanders rush to help the wounded. A doctor and nurse who had been shopping in the Safeway triage a nine-year-old girl and begin giving CPR. Twenty-year-old Daniel Hernandez, one of Gabby's newest interns and a trained nursing

CHAPTER **2**

assistant, runs to Gabby's side and applies pressure to her wounds. Congresswoman Giffords is hurried to the University Medical Center along with others who are critically wounded. Within minutes of her arrival, trauma surgeons begin working to save her life.

Initial reports are dire. National Public Radio announces, "Congresswoman Gabrielle Giffords of Arizona has been shot and killed during a public event in Tucson, Arizona." This news is then "confirmed" by CNN and several other reputable news outlets. Everyone fears the worst. Giffords's husband, astronaut Mark Kelly, boards a plane for home while praying for the best. A bullet has entered the back of Gabby's head and exited above her

left eye, a fatal type of gunshot wound in 95 percent of cases.

Hours of complex surgery is needed to reduce the swelling and bleeding within Gabby's brain. Surgeons also remove bone fragments and portions of her brain that are beyond repair. Gabby's husband arrives at the hospital just as she is being moved out of surgery and into the intensive care unit. She will survive, but she will be in a coma for four to six months. Doctors explain that the bullet destroyed most of Gabby's brain on the left side. While Gabby's life has been saved, the quality of that life hangs in the balance. It is impossible to know if she will ever speak, move, or even act like the person she was before the shooting. 〜

biological psychology The scientific study of the biological bases of behavior and mental processes.

neuroscience The study of the nervous system, especially the brain.

Introduction: Neuroscience and Behavior

Biological psychology is *the scientific study of the biological bases of behavior and mental processes*. At the heart of biological psychology is **neuroscience**, defined in Chapter 1 as *the study of the nervous system, especially the brain*. Neuroscience has become an essential part of the field of psychology, impacting virtually every area of research (Schwartz et al., 2016). You will see references to important neuroscience findings throughout this text that will help you understand some of the "mechanics" that support the most interesting aspects of human behavior.

This chapter will lay an important foundation for the rest of the book by helping you develop an understanding of the nervous system and its relationship to behavior. Look at **Figure 2.1** to get a sense of the overall nervous system. Learning more about the brain helps us to understand the inner workings of what makes us "human." For example, what happens within the brain when you sleep, dream, or meditate (Chapter 4)? How does the brain contribute to the ways in which emotions and personality affect your vulnerability to infection (Chapter 13)? How do medications work in the brain to alleviate many symptoms associated with these disorders (Chapter 14)?

We'll start by looking at *neurons*, the basic cells of the nervous system. We'll consider the organization of the nervous system and a closely linked communication network, the *endocrine system*. We'll then move on to a guided tour of the brain and explore how certain brain areas are specialized to handle different functions. In Psych for Your Life, at the end of the chapter, we'll help you better understand what a concussion is, how it is assessed, and importantly, what is most relevant for recovery.

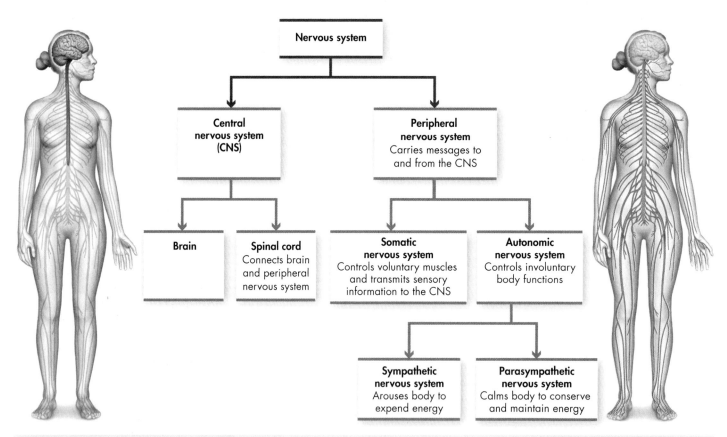

FIGURE 2.1 The Organization of the Nervous System We will spend a lot of time learning about the human nervous system in this chapter, so it is important to know how it is organized. The human nervous system is divided into several important subsystems. There are two major subdivisions, the central nervous system and the peripheral nervous system, both of which include additional components or subsystems. The central nervous system includes the brain and the spinal cord. The peripheral nervous system is home to the somatic nervous system and the autonomic nervous system. The autonomic nervous system is further divided into the sympathetic nervous system and parasympathetic nervous system.

The Neuron: The Basic Unit of Communication

■ KEY THEME
Information in the nervous system is transmitted by specialized cells called neurons.

≡ KEY QUESTIONS
• What are the basic components of the neuron, and what are their functions?
• What are glial cells, and what is their role in the nervous system?
• What is an action potential, and how is it produced?

Communication throughout the nervous system takes place via **neurons** — *cells that are highly specialized to receive and transmit information from one part of the body to another.* Most neurons, especially those in your brain, are extremely small. A bit of brain tissue no larger than a grain of rice contains about 10,000 neurons! Your entire brain contains an estimated 90 *billion* neurons (Azevedo et al., 2009; Herculano-Houzel, 2009).

Neurons vary greatly in size and shape, reflecting their specialized functions. There are three basic types of neurons, each of which is responsible for relaying a different kind of information. A **sensory neuron** *conveys information about the environment, such as light or sound, from specialized receptor cells in the sense organs to the brain.* Sensory neurons also carry information from the skin and internal organs to the brain. A **motor neuron** *communicates information to the muscles and glands of the body.* Simply blinking your eyes activates thousands of motor neurons. Finally, an **interneuron** *communicates information between neurons.* Of note, most of the neurons in the human nervous system are interneurons, and many of them connect to other interneurons. This relatively large number of interneurons is part of what makes the human brain so sophisticated: such dense connections allow for lots of information from different sources to be integrated very quickly.

Characteristics of the Neuron

Most neurons have three basic components: a *cell body, dendrites,* and an *axon* (see **Figure 2.2**). The **cell body** is *the part of the neuron containing structures that process nutrients, providing the energy the neuron needs to function;* also called the *soma.* The cell body also contains the *nucleus,* which in turn contains the cell's genetic material — twisted strands of DNA called *chromosomes.*

Short branching fibers called *dendrites* extend from the cell bodies of most neurons. **Dendrites** are *the part of the neuron that receives messages from other neurons.* The term

neurons Cells that are highly specialized to receive and transmit information from one part of the body to another.

sensory neuron A type of neuron that conveys information about the environment, such as light or sound, from specialized receptor cells in the sense organs to the brain.

motor neuron A type of neuron that communicates information to the muscles and glands of the body.

interneuron A type of neuron that communicates information between neurons.

cell body The part of a neuron that contains structures that process nutrients, providing the energy the neuron needs to function; also called the *soma*.

dendrites The part of the neuron that *receives* messages from other neurons.

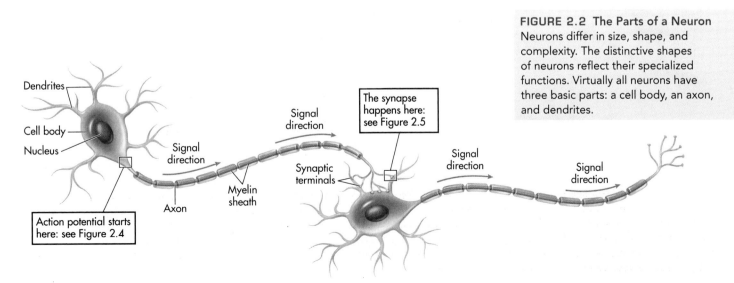

FIGURE 2.2 The Parts of a Neuron
Neurons differ in size, shape, and complexity. The distinctive shapes of neurons reflect their specialized functions. Virtually all neurons have three basic parts: a cell body, an axon, and dendrites.

axon The part of the neuron that carries information *from* the neuron *to* other cells in the body, including other neurons, glands, and muscles.

glial cells (glia) (GLEE-ull) Cells that provide the structural and functional support for neurons throughout the nervous system.

myelin sheath (MY-eh-lin) A white, fatty covering wrapped around the axons of some, but not all, neurons in the brain.

dendrite comes from a Greek word meaning "tree." And, the intricate branching of the dendrites does often resemble the branches of a tree. Dendrites with many branches have a greater surface area, which increases the amount of information the neuron can receive. Some neurons have thousands of dendrites.

An **axon** is *the part of the neuron that carries information from the neuron to other cells in the body, including other neurons, glands, and muscles.* The axon is a single elongated tube that extends from the cell body in most neurons. (Some neurons do not have axons.) In contrast to the potentially large number of dendrites, a neuron has only one axon. However, many axons have branches near their tips that allow the neuron to communicate information to more than one target.

Axons can vary enormously in length. Most axons are very small, some just a few thousandths of an inch long. Other axons are quite long. For example, the longest axon in your body is that of the motor neuron that controls your big toe. This axon extends from the base of your spine to your foot. If you happen to be a seven-foot-tall basketball player, this axon could be four feet long! For most of us, though, this axon is closer to three feet long.

Glial Cells

Along with neurons, the human nervous system is made up of other specialized cells. *Glia* is Greek for "glue," and **glial cells** are *cells that provide the structural and functional support for neurons throughout the nervous system.* Glial cells are abundant in the human brain, making up about 50 percent of the brain's total volume (von Bartheld et al., 2016; see **Figure 2.3**).

There are several different kinds of glial cells, each with its own specialized function (see Critical Thinking box) (Jäkel & Dimou, 2017). For example, *oligodendrocytes, microglia,* and *astrocytes* are different types of glial cells.

- Oligodendrocytes form the **myelin sheath**, *a white fatty covering that is wrapped around the axons of some, but not all, neurons in the brain.* In much the same way that insulating plastic on electrical wires prevents interference when wires contact each other, myelin helps insulate one axon from the axons of other neurons. Rather than forming a continuous coating of the axon, however, the myelin sheath occurs in segments that are separated by small gaps. The small gaps are called the *nodes of Ranvier,* or simply *nodes.* Neurons with myelinated axons communicate their messages up to 50 times faster than do unmyelinated neurons (Fields, 2013).

- Microglia are specialized cells that do a lot of the brain's "clean-up" work. They break down and remove dead or damaged cells as part of the brain's immune response. When there is an increased presence of microglia, it is often a sign of infection, trauma, or stroke (Davies & Miron, 2018).

- Astrocytes are the most common glial cells, and they have many functions (Ben Haim & Rowitch, 2017). They provide critical structural support for neurons, provide neurons with nutrients, and help to keep the neurons healthy. Astrocytes also supply nutrients to the cells that keep toxic substances (like infections and viruses) from entering the brain's bloodstream. Finally, unlike other cells in the brain, glial cells are capable of dividing throughout life.

The importance of myelin becomes readily apparent when it is damaged. For example, *multiple sclerosis* is an autoimmune disease in which the immune system mistakenly eats away at patches of the myelin sheath. This degeneration causes the transmission of neural messages to be slowed or interrupted, resulting in disturbances in sensation and movement. Muscle weakness, loss of coordination, and blurred vision are among the more common symptoms of multiple sclerosis.

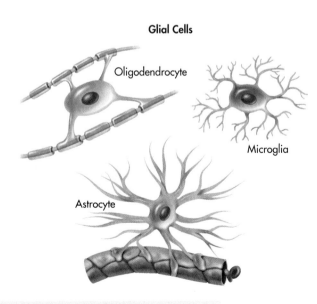

Glial Cells

Oligodendrocyte

Microglia

Astrocyte

FIGURE 2.3 Glial Cells There are many kinds of glial cells, or *glia.* They play an active role in brain functioning.

CRITICAL THINKING

The Gut–Brain Connection?

Science continues to show us that the different systems of the body are interconnected and cannot be completely understood without keeping this in mind. The gut–brain connection is one very important example of this phenomenon. The expression "a gut decision" refers to a cognitive process that occurs without a lot of conscious thought. If you've ever made a gut decision, you likely have used both of your brains. Huh, you might think, I have two brains? You have spent a lot of this chapter learning about the brain, but it is worth taking a moment to appreciate that after the brain, the second-largest number of neurons in the human body can be found in the gut. The enteric nervous system (ENS) earned its nickname as "the second brain" because there are hundreds of millions of neurons in your digestive system that communicate with your brain, more neurons than any other part of the peripheral nervous system (Schemann et al., 2020).

Is it true that there are neurons in your gut as well as your brain?

It's important to remember that our gut is also responsible for digesting our food, something critical for survival. Many researchers have suggested that the high number of neurons in the gut probably evolved to make sure that digestion ran smoothly without us having to consciously attend to that process. It is also the case that during a fight-or-flight response, the big brain can tell the gut brain to slow or stop digestion. Fight or flight requires that all of the body's energy be dedicated to survival at that moment. If you are about to be killed by a bear, you probably don't need to finish digesting your breakfast, and that energy might be better used to survive. (This is also an important reminder about the dangers of chronic intense stress.)

Communication between your brain and gut is a two-way street. Your emotional state is highly influenced by the neurons in your gut. But the neurons in your gut can't help you read the words in this book or compose your next text message; however, the ENS acts like emotional radar, helping to determine your general state of mind. Further, the neurons in the gut are critical for giving you emotional input that helps you understand what feels "right" or "wrong." UCLA researcher Michael Gershon, at New York-Presbyterian Hospital/Columbia University Medical Center, has said, "Everyday emotional well-being may rely on messages from the brain above and the brain below" (Hadhazy, 2010; Rao & Gershon, 2016).

Lots of different types of microorganisms (bacteria, viruses, protozoa, and fungi) live inside both your small and large intestines; this makes up something called the microbiome. The microbiome of the gut also produces many neurotransmitters, including norepinephrine and dopamine, that are used by the brain for cognitive and emotional processes (Strandwitz, 2018).

Because the gut is directly linked to the brain in multiple ways, "It's almost unthinkable that the gut is not playing a critical role in mind states," says gastroenterologist Emeran Mayer, M.D., director of the Center for Neurobiology of Stress at the University of California, Los Angeles (Carpenter, 2012). Many scientists have suggested that the gut influences the brain through changes in the immune system (Carpenter, 2012). Irritation in the gut is thought to cause changes to the chemistry in the brain, and at the same time, there is evidence that certain brain states can disrupt the gut's microbiome (Mayer et al., 2015). The idea that the immune system might be one of the primary ways in which the gut and brain communicate makes sense, because the immune system is based primarily in the gut (Verheijden & Boeckxstaens, 2018).

Regardless of the ways in which the gut and brain communicate, understanding the microbiome might lead to new treatments for many psychological disorders. For example, research has documented gut–brain connections that may influence major depressive disorder (Bastiaanssen et al., 2020). First, there is evidence that factors that alter the microbiome—stress, certain medications, an unhealthy diet—might contribute to the development of depression. Second, depressed people tend to have lower levels of certain beneficial bacteria in their microbiome than do nondepressed people. Third, in some cases, it seems that the microbiome limits the effectiveness of or contributes to side effects from certain antidepressant medications. New treatments, such as probiotics that increase healthy bacteria, might alleviate depression by altering the microbiome. These researchers conclude: "Although research is in its very early days, with much yet to be understood, the microbiome is offering new avenues for developing potentially novel strategies for managing [major depressive disorder]" (Bastiaanssen et al., 2020). The same may be true for a range of psychological disorders.

CRITICAL THINKING QUESTIONS

- Is it possible that what you eat may impact your mood or ability to concentrate?
- Could the immune system play a role in psychiatric illnesses?
- Why do so many people have a hard time trusting their "gut instinct"?

Communication Within the Neuron: The Action Potential

As humans, the complex ways in which we communicate, reason, and remember make us a unique species. The massive amount of communication within the human brain makes these abilities possible. It is not simply the large number of neurons in the brain, it is also the fact that each neuron "talks to" about 1,000 other neurons (Hyman, 2005). When you take this all into consideration, there are typically 100 trillion connections within the human brain (Pakkenberg & Gundersen, 1997; Pakkenberg et al., 2003; Eroglu & Barres, 2010). That's the number 10 followed by 13 zeros!

stimulus threshold The minimum level of stimulation required to activate a particular neuron.

action potential A brief electrical impulse that transmits information along the axon of a neuron.

resting potential The state in which a neuron is prepared to activate and communicate its message if it receives sufficient stimulation.

The *flexibility* of these connections between neurons is as remarkable as the large number of connections. This communication between networks of neurons resembles the communication between people within larger social groups. In these cases, people often change whom they talk to and/or the groups with which they spend time. The human brain uses a similar strategy, responding to a person's needs by changing which individual cells and groups of cells "talk" to each other.

But exactly *how* do neurons transmit information? Neurons only "speak" when spoken to, meaning that a neuron will only become active if it is stimulated by another source. Each neuron requires a minimum level of stimulation from other neurons or sensory receptors to activate it. *The minimum level of stimulation required to activate a particular neuron* is called the neuron's **stimulus threshold**. When the stimulus threshold is reached, the dendrites relay this signal to the cell body (soma). The neuron's soma then generates *a brief electrical impulse that transmits information along the axon of a neuron,* called an **action potential**.

Once an action potential is initiated, it is like rolling a ball down a hill; it is *self-sustaining* and continues to the end of the axon. There is no "maybe" when it comes to neurons being stimulated. Either the neuron is sufficiently stimulated and an action potential occurs, or the neuron is not sufficiently stimulated and an action potential does not occur. This principle is referred to as the *all-or-none law.* It's a bit like a hot-tempered person: if they are pushed (stimulated) enough, they "blow their top," but can be perfectly calm if not bothered.

The specific electrochemical mechanisms responsible for the action potential are nothing short of miraculous. Simply, the action potential is produced by the movement of electrically charged chemicals, called *ions,* across the membrane of the axon. Some ions are negatively charged, while others are positively charged. Let's look at the sequence for this to happen.

The state in which a neuron is prepared to activate and communicate its message if it receives sufficient stimulation is called its **resting potential** (see **Figure 2.4**). While waiting to be activated, the neuron is said to be *polarized.* This means that there is a difference in the electrical charge between the inside and the outside of the axon. More specifically, there is a greater concentration of negative ions inside the neuron. Thus, the axon's interior is more negatively charged than the exterior fluid surrounding the axon. At resting potential, the negative electrical charge is about −70 millivolts (thousandths of a volt). You can think of the axon's membrane as a gatekeeper that controls the balance of positive and negative ions on the interior and exterior of the axon. As the gatekeeper, the axon membrane opens and closes *ion channels* that allow ions to flow into and out of the axon.

In this polarized condition (negative inside–positive outside condition) are different concentrations of two particular ions: sodium and potassium. While the neuron is in resting potential, the fluid surrounding the axon contains a larger concentration of *sodium* ions than does the fluid within the axon. The fluid within the axon contains a larger concentration of *potassium* ions than is found in the fluid outside the axon.

An *action potential* first causes the neuron to *depolarize:* At each successive axon segment, sodium ion channels open for a mere thousandth of a second. The sodium ions rush to the axon's interior from the surrounding fluid, and then the sodium ion channels close. Less than a thousandth of a second later, the potassium ion channels open, allowing potassium to flow out of the axon and into the fluid surrounding it. Then the potassium ion channels close. This sequence of depolarization and ion movement continues down the entire length of the axon.

As this ion exchange occurs, the relative balance of positive and negative ions separated by the axon membrane changes. The electrical charge on the inside of the axon momentarily changes from the −70 millivolts of the *resting potential* to a positive charge of about +30 millivolts. The result is a brief positive electrical impulse that progressively occurs at each segment down the axon—the electrochemical wave known as the *action potential.*

(a)

1. Resting Potential

- Inside the cell is negatively charged
- Outside the cell is positively charged
- A –70 millivolts charge inside the cell
- Sodium and potassium channels are closed

2. Stimulus Threshold

- The cell body receives a critical amount of stimulation from other cells
- The action potential is initiated
- Neuron is considered polarized

3. Depolarization

- Sodium channels open
- Positively charged sodium ions flow into the neuron
- Inside the cell becomes positively charged
- Outside the cell becomes negatively charged
- Sodium channels close

4. Repolarization

- Potassium channels open
- Positive potassium ions flow out of the cell
- Inside the cell becomes negatively charged
- Outside the cell becomes positively charged

5. Refractory Period

- Positive potassium ions continue to leave the neuron
- Outside the cell becomes more positively charged
- Inside the cell becomes more negatively charged
- Neuron returns to resting potential

1. Resting Potential

- Neuron is ready to fire again

(b)

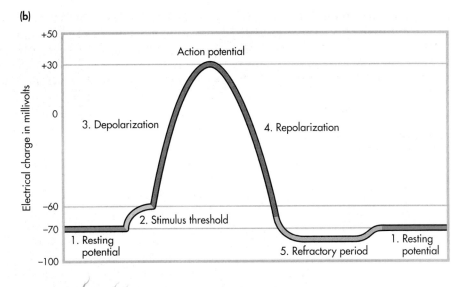

(c)

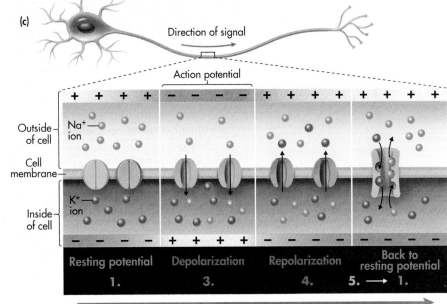

Direction of signal

FIGURE 2.4 Communication Within the Neuron: The Action Potential The action potential is a series of events that take place both inside and outside the neuron. The series of steps involved in the action potential are described by number in Part A. Those same steps, displayed in the same colors, are visually represented in Part B. The chemical exchanges that take place inside and outside the cell membrane in Part A are also visually displayed in the breakout of Part C—with matching by colors and numbers.

After the action potential, the neuron enters a *refractory period,* lasting a thousandth of a second or less, during which the neuron cannot "fire," or generate another action potential. Instead, the neuron *repolarizes* and reestablishes the negative inside–positive outside condition (potassium reenters the neuron and sodium leaves it). Like depolarization, repolarization occurs progressively at each segment down the axon. This process reestablishes the *resting potential* (–70 millivolts inside the neuron) conditions so that the neuron is capable of firing again.

Because action potentials are generated in mere thousandths of a second, a single neuron can potentially generate hundreds of neural impulses per second. Just how fast do neural impulses zip around your body? The fastest nerve impulses are known to travel at upward of 270 miles per hour. Myelin formation increases with frequently used connections between different brain regions, as well as when we learn new motor behaviors (Long & Corfas, 2014; McKenzie et al., 2014). In the slowest neurons, messages creep along at about 2 miles per hour. This variation in communication speed is due to at least three factors: the axon diameter, the myelin

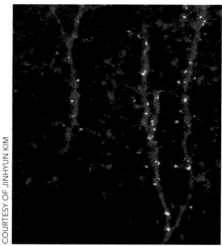

COURTESY OF JINHYUN KIM

▲ **The Brain Capturing a Thought** In the brain, as in the rest of the nervous system, information is transmitted by electrical impulses that speed from one neuron to the next (Kim et al., 2012). In this striking image, you can clearly see the synaptic connections (bright yellow dots) between the axons of the presynaptic or "sending" neurons (blue) and the dendrites of the postsynaptic or "receiving" neurons (red).

synapse (SIN-aps) The point of communication between two neurons.

synaptic gap (sin-AP-tick) A tiny fluid-filled space between the presynaptic and postsynaptic neurons.

axon terminals Small branches at the end of the axon.

synaptic vesicles (sin-AP-tick VESS-ick-ullz) Tiny sacs in the axon terminal.

neurotransmitters Chemical messengers manufactured by a neuron.

synaptic transmission (sin-AP-tick) The entire process of transmitting information at the synapse.

reuptake The process by which neurotransmitter molecules detach from the receptor and are reabsorbed by the presynaptic neuron so they can be recycled and used again.

sheath, and the distance the signal needs to travel. The larger the axon's diameter, the faster it conducts action potentials. Of note, myelinated neurons communicate much faster than unmyelinated neurons because the action potential "jumps" from node to node rather than progressing down the entire length of the axon. It should not surprise you that the neural signal for a simple reflexive behavior like pulling your hand away from a hot stove travels much faster than the complex group of signals involved in reading these words and understanding their meaning (Frijns et al., 1997; Haggard et al., 2002).

Communication Between Neurons: Bridging the Gap

■ KEY THEME
Communication between neurons takes place at the synapse, the junction between two adjoining neurons.

═ KEY QUESTIONS
- How is information communicated at the synapse?
- What is a neurotransmitter, and what is its role in synaptic transmission?
- What are seven important neurotransmitters, and how do psychoactive drugs affect synaptic transmission?

The primary function of a neuron is to communicate information to other cells, most notably other neurons. *The point of communication between two neurons* is called the **synapse**. At this communication junction, the message-*sending* neuron is referred to as the *presynaptic neuron*. The message-*receiving* neuron is called the *postsynaptic neuron*. For cells that are specialized to communicate information, neurons have a surprising characteristic: They don't touch each other. *A tiny fluid-filled space between the presynaptic and postsynaptic neurons,* called the **synaptic gap**, is only 20 to 40 nanometers wide. How small is that? For comparison, the thickness of a single sheet of paper is about 100,000 nanometers.

How do neurons communicate? In most cases, when the presynaptic neuron is activated, it generates an action potential that travels to the end of the axon. **Axon terminals** are *small branches at the end of the axon. Tiny sacs in the axon terminal,* called **synaptic vesicles**, hold special *chemical messengers manufactured by the neuron,* called **neurotransmitters**.

When the action potential reaches the axon terminals, some of the synaptic vesicles "dock" on the axon terminal membrane and then release their neurotransmitters into the synaptic gap. These chemical messengers cross the synaptic gap and attach to *receptor sites* on the dendrites of the receiving or postsynaptic neuron. This journey across the synaptic gap takes just a few millionths of a second. *The entire process of transmitting information at the synapse* is called **synaptic transmission** (**Figure 2.5**).

What happens to the neurotransmitter molecules after they've attached to the receptor sites of the postsynaptic neuron? Like many of us, neurons are very "green" and prefer to recycle, repurpose, and reuse whenever possible. **Reuptake** is *the process by which neurotransmitter molecules detach from the receptor and are reabsorbed by the presynaptic neuron so they can be recycled and used again.* Reuptake also occurs with many of the neurotransmitters that failed to attach to a receptor and were left floating in the synaptic gap. Neurotransmitter molecules that are not reabsorbed or that remain attached to the receptor site are broken down or destroyed by enzymes.

Some neurons produce only one type of neurotransmitter, but others manufacture three or more. Each neurotransmitter has a chemically distinct shape. Like a key in a lock, a neurotransmitter's shape must precisely match that of a receptor site on the postsynaptic neuron for the neurotransmitter to affect that neuron. And, the postsynaptic neuron can have many differently shaped receptor sites on its dendrites and other surfaces. Thus, a given neuron may receive several different neurotransmitters.

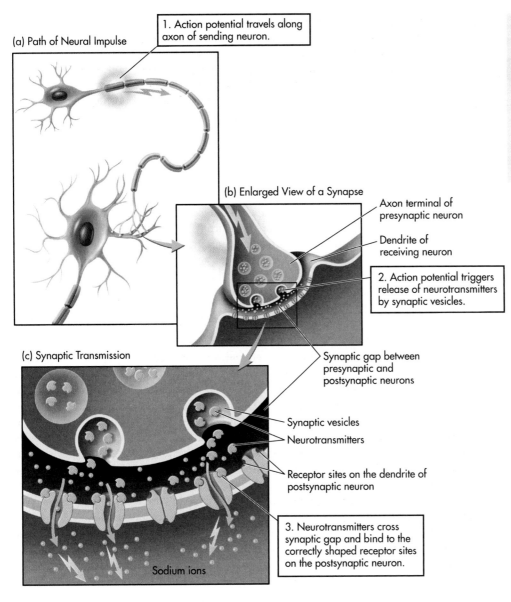

(a) Path of Neural Impulse

1. Action potential travels along axon of sending neuron.

(b) Enlarged View of a Synapse

Axon terminal of presynaptic neuron

Dendrite of receiving neuron

2. Action potential triggers release of neurotransmitters by synaptic vesicles.

(c) Synaptic Transmission

Synaptic gap between presynaptic and postsynaptic neurons

Synaptic vesicles

Neurotransmitters

Receptor sites on the dendrite of postsynaptic neuron

3. Neurotransmitters cross synaptic gap and bind to the correctly shaped receptor sites on the postsynaptic neuron.

Sodium ions

FIGURE 2.5 Communication Between Neurons: The Process of Synaptic Transmission Follow the steps in this progressive graphic to trace the sequence of synaptic transmission. Neurotransmitters are released by the sending, or presynaptic, neuron; cross the tiny fluid-filled space called the synaptic gap; and attach to receptor sites on the receiving, or postsynaptic, neuron.

Depending upon the receptor to which it binds, a neurotransmitter communicates either an excitatory or an inhibitory message to a postsynaptic neuron. An *excitatory message* increases the likelihood that the postsynaptic neuron will activate and generate an action potential. An *inhibitory message* decreases the likelihood that the postsynaptic neuron will fire.

Neurotransmitters and Their Effects

Your ability to perceive, feel, think, move, act, and react depends on the delicate balance of neurotransmitters in your nervous system. Yet neurotransmitters are present in only infinitesimal amounts in brain tissue — roughly equivalent to a pinch of salt dissolved in an Olympic-sized swimming pool.

Specific neurotransmitters are associated with particular psychological processes and problems (see **Table 2.1**). However, the connection between a particular neurotransmitter and a particular effect is *not* a simple one-to-one relationship. Most behaviors are the result of the complex interaction of different neurotransmitters. Further, neurotransmitters sometimes have different effects in different areas of the brain.

TABLE 2.1

Summary of Important Neurotransmitters

Neurotransmitter	Primary Roles
Acetylcholine	Learning, memory Muscle contractions
Dopamine	Movement Thought processes Rewarding sensations
Serotonin	Emotional states Sleep Sensory perception
Norepinephrine	Physical arousal Learning, memory Regulation of sleep
Glutamate	Excitatory messages
GABA	Inhibitory messages
Endorphins	Pain perception Positive emotions

REUTERS/Alamy Stock Photo

Acetylcholine and Simone Biles
Acetylcholine is the neurotransmitter used during any physical activity. This means that all movements rely on acetylcholine, from walking down the street to doing a double back flip with three twists, known as "The Biles II." In fact, it is so critical for functional movement that a drug can cause paralysis if it interferes with acetylcholine. For example, the drug Botox causes a mild paralysis of very specific muscles for a relatively short time. More seriously, a drug like curare causes severe paralysis by stopping all movements, including those needed for breathing.

Important Neurotransmitters The first neurotransmitter discovered was *acetylcholine,* the most abundant neurotransmitter and one that is found in all motor neurons. **Acetylcholine** is *a neurotransmitter that is the chemical means by which neurons communicate with muscles.* This type of communication is critical to nervous system regulation of muscular function. For example, acetylcholine stimulates muscles in the heart and stomach to contract, keeping you alive and nourished. All movement involves acetylcholine, from a simple eye blink to a complex back flip.

Acetylcholine is also found in many neurons in the brain, where it serves an important role in memory, learning, and general intellectual functioning. People with *Alzheimer's disease,* which is characterized by progressive loss of memory and deterioration of intellectual functioning, have a severe depletion of several neurotransmitters in the brain, most notably acetylcholine.

Dopamine is *a neurotransmitter involved in movement, attention, learning, and pleasurable or rewarding sensations.* More specifically, dopamine has been linked to the *anticipation* of reward, the feeling that something good is about to happen (Dubol et al., 2018). For example, if you like rollercoasters, try to think of when your excitement is sincerely highest. Many think it is during the ride, but most people are just holding on for dear life. The most intense excitement actually takes place during that slow, ticking ride up to the top—just before the first big drop. This anticipation of excitement and/or reward is a powerful motivational force in people that will be discussed in greater depth in Chapter 8. Recognizing how truly dazzling this feeling can be to the human brain helps us better understand why drugs such as cocaine and nicotine are so psychologically addictive (Linnet, 2020). Because of their ability to increase the brain's dopamine activity, these drugs tap into one of the most intense motivational circuits in the human brain (Kawa et al., 2019).

In addition to learning and motivation, dopamine plays a critical role in movement. The degeneration of the neurons that produce dopamine in one brain area causes *Parkinson's disease,* which is characterized by rigidity, muscle tremors, poor balance, and difficulty in initiating movements. Symptoms of Parkinson's can be alleviated by a drug called *L-dopa,* which converts to dopamine in the brain. This is a highly effective treatment, but use of drugs that affect the dopamine system can also contribute to symptoms of psychosis, which will be addressed in greater detail in the chapter on psychological disorders.

Serotonin and *norepinephrine* are found in many brain areas. **Serotonin** is *a neurotransmitter involved in sleep, sensory perceptions, moods, and emotional states*—particularly those associated with feeling "calm" and physically and emotionally "satisfied" (Deneris & Wyler, 2012). Low levels of serotonin are often seen in people with depression (Cowen & Browning, 2015). It is not surprising, then, that some antidepressant drugs, like *Prozac,* increase the availability of serotonin in certain brain regions. **Norepinephrine** is *a neurotransmitter implicated in the activation of neurons throughout the brain and helps the body gear up in the face of danger or threat.*

The most abundant neurotransmitters in the brain are two closely related neurotransmitters, *glutamate* and *gamma-aminobutyric acid,* abbreviated GABA. In a delicate balancing act, **glutamate** is *a neurotransmitter that conveys excitatory messages.* **GABA** is *a neurotransmitter that communicates inhibitory messages.* Glutamate is involved in learning, memory, and sensory processes (Morris, 2013). Too much glutamate can overstimulate the brain, causing seizures and cell death. Glutamate is also implicated in Alzheimer's disease, neurological diseases, and schizophrenia.

Like a dimmer switch, GABA regulates the level of neural activity in the brain. Too much GABA impairs learning, motivation, and movement, but too little GABA can lead to seizures (McCarthy, 2007). Alcohol makes people feel relaxed and less inhibited partly by increasing GABA activity and decreasing glutamate, reducing overall brain activity.

Endorphins are *a class of neurotransmitter that is produced by the brain and released in response to pain and stress.* They are chemically similar to synthetic drugs like morphine, heroin, and other opioid drugs. The endorphins produced by your brain are thought to be more potent than their synthetic counterparts, but you cannot release endorphins at will, which is why synthetic opioids exist and are highly addictive. Endorphins are implicated in the pain-reducing effects of *acupuncture,* an ancient Chinese medical technique that involves inserting needles at various locations in the body (Kemmer, 2007;

Zhao, 2008). Also associated with positive mood, endorphins are thought to give some people a "runner's high" from intense and prolonged physical exertion.

How Drugs Affect Synaptic Transmission

Much of what is known about different neurotransmitters has been learned from observing the effects of drugs and other substances. Many drugs, especially those that affect moods or behavior, work by affecting the normal functioning of neurotransmitters in the synapses (Volkow et al., 2011a, 2011b).

Some drugs increase or decrease the amounts of neurotransmitters released by neurons. For example, the venom of a black widow spider bite causes acetylcholine to be released continuously by motor neurons, causing severe muscle spasms. Drugs may also affect the length of time the neurotransmitters remain in the synaptic gap, either increasing or decreasing the amount available to the postsynaptic receptor.

One way in which drugs can prolong the effects of the neurotransmitters is by blocking the reuptake of the neurotransmitters by the sending neuron. For example, the antidepressants Prozac, Zoloft, and Paxil are *selective serotonin reuptake inhibitors,* also called *SSRIs.* These medications selectively target and inhibit the reuptake of serotonin, increasing the availability of serotonin in the brain. Similarly, the illegal drug cocaine produces its exhilarating rush by interfering with the reuptake of dopamine (Volkow et al., 2011a, 2011b).

Drugs can also *mimic* specific neurotransmitters. An *agonist* is a drug or other chemical that binds to a receptor and facilitates synaptic transmission. Often, agonist drugs are chemically similar to a specific neurotransmitter and produce the same effect. For example, nicotine is chemically similar to acetylcholine. It occupies acetylcholine receptor sites, stimulating skeletal muscles and causing the heart to beat more rapidly.

Alternatively, an *antagonist* is a drug that binds to a receptor and blocks synaptic transmission. For example, the drug *naloxone* is an opioid antagonist. It blocks endorphin receptors, and it can quickly reverse the effects of heroin, oxycodone, or other opioid drugs (Rich et al., 2011). Naloxone is so effective at reversing the effects of opioid drugs that most first responders carry it in a nasal spray called Narcan. It is easy enough to use that the surgeon general suggests that anyone who spends time near opioids should keep Narcan on hand (Ryan & Dunne, 2018). **Figure 2.6** summarizes the effects of drugs on synaptic transmission.

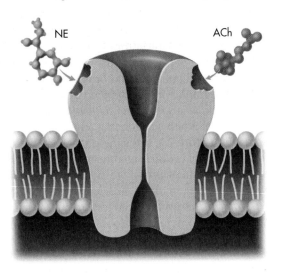

acetylcholine (uh-seet-ull-KO-leen) A neurotransmitter that is the chemical means by which neurons communicate with muscles.

dopamine (DOPE-uh-meen) A neurotransmitter involved in movement, attention, learning, and pleasurable or rewarding sensations.

serotonin (ser-uh-TONE-in) A neurotransmitter involved in sleep, sensory perceptions, moods, and emotional states.

norepinephrine (nor-ep-in-EF-rin) A neurotransmitter implicated in the activation of neurons throughout the brain and helps the body gear up in the face of danger or threat.

glutamate A neurotransmitter that conveys excitatory messages.

GABA (gamma-aminobutyric acid) A neurotransmitter that communicates *inhibitory* messages.

endorphins (en-DORF-inz) A class of neurotransmitter that is produced by the brain and released in response to pain and stress.

FIGURE 2.6 How Drugs Affect Synaptic Transmission Drugs affect brain activity by interfering with neurotransmitter function in the synapse. Drugs may also affect synaptic transmission by increasing or decreasing the amount of a particular neurotransmitter that is produced.

The Nervous System and the Endocrine System: Communication Throughout the Body

■ KEY THEME
Two major communication systems in the body are the nervous system and the endocrine system.

⚎ KEY QUESTIONS
- What are the divisions of the nervous system, and what are their functions?
- How is information transmitted in the endocrine system, and what are its major structures?
- How do the nervous and endocrine systems interact to produce essential human behaviors, including the fight-or-flight response?

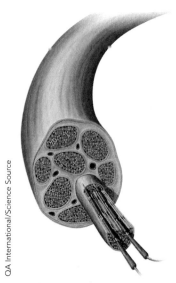

QA International/Science Source

▲ **Nerves and Neurons Are Not the Same** Pictured above is a cross section of a peripheral nerve. Unlike neurons, nerves are composed of bundles of different types of axons. Within these bundles are individual myelinated axons. In the peripheral nervous system, the myelin is formed by glial cells. Blood vessels may even be seen within this peripheral nerve (highlighted by the dark red and dark blue colors).

nervous system A system of up to 1 *trillion linked* neurons throughout your body in a complex, organized communication network.

nerves Large bundles of neuron axons that carry information in the peripheral nervous system.

central nervous system (CNS) The division of the nervous system that consists of the brain and spinal cord.

spinal reflexes Simple, automatic behaviors that occur without any brain involvement.

peripheral nervous system (per-IF-er-ull) The division of the nervous system that includes all the nerves lying outside the central nervous system.

somatic nervous system The subdivision of the peripheral nervous system that communicates sensory information received by sensory receptors along sensory nerves *to* the central nervous system.

The **nervous system** is *a system of up to 1 trillion linked neurons throughout your body in a complex, organized communication network.* The human nervous system is divided into two main divisions. the *central nervous system* and the *peripheral nervous system.* For even simple behaviors to occur, such as curling your toes or scratching your nose, these two divisions must function as a single integrated unit. Yet each of these divisions is highly specialized and performs different tasks.

The neuron is the most important transmitter of messages in the central nervous system. **Nerves** are *large bundles of neuron axons that carry information in the peripheral nervous system.* Unlike neurons, many nerves are large enough to be seen easily with the unaided eye.

The Central Nervous System

The **central nervous system (CNS)** is *the division of the nervous system that consists of the brain and the spinal cord.* The central nervous system is so critical to your ability to function that it is entirely protected by bone—the brain by your skull and the spinal cord by your spinal column. Surrounding and protecting the brain and the spinal cord are three layers of membranous tissues, called the *meninges.* As an added measure of protection, the brain and spinal cord are suspended in *cerebrospinal fluid* to protect them from being jarred. Cerebrospinal fluid also fills four hollow cavities in the brain, called *ventricles.* The inner surfaces of the ventricles are lined with *neural stem cells,* specialized cells that generate neurons in the developing brain (see Chapter 9).

The central nervous system is the central processing center. Every action, thought, feeling, and sensation you experience is processed through the central nervous system. The most important element of the central nervous system is, of course, the brain, which acts as the command center (see later in this chapter).

Also important to the CNS, the spinal cord handles both incoming and outgoing messages. Sensory receptors send messages along sensory nerves to the spinal cord, then up to the brain. To activate muscles, the brain sends signals down the spinal cord that are relayed out along motor nerves to the muscles.

Although most behaviors are controlled by your brain, **spinal reflexes** are *simple automatic behaviors that occur without any brain involvement.* For example, the *withdrawal reflex* occurs when you touch a painful stimulus, such as something hot or sharp. As shown in **Figure 2.7**, this simple reflex involves a loop of rapid communication among *sensory neurons,* which communicate sensation to neighboring neurons within the spinal cord; *interneurons,* which relay information within the spinal cord; and *motor neurons,* which signal the muscles to react.

Spinal reflexes are crucial to your survival. The additional few seconds that it would take you to consciously process sensations and decide how to react could result in serious injury. Spinal reflexes are also important as indicators that the neural pathways in your spinal cord are working correctly. That's why physicians test spinal reflexes during neurological examinations by tapping just below your kneecap for the knee-jerk spinal reflex.

The Peripheral Nervous System

The *peripheral nervous system* is the other major division of your nervous system. The **peripheral nervous system** is *the division of the nervous system that includes all the nerves lying outside the central nervous system* (i.e., the brain and the spinal cord). Those nerves extend to the outermost borders of your body, including your skin. The communication functions of the peripheral nervous system are handled by its two subdivisions: the *somatic nervous system* and the *autonomic nervous system.*

The **somatic nervous system** is *the subdivision of the peripheral nervous system that receives information from sensory receptors along sensory nerves and communicates it to the central nervous system.* And, it carries messages *from* the central nervous system along motor nerves to perform voluntary muscle movements. When you send a quick text message to friends letting them know that you will be late for dinner because you

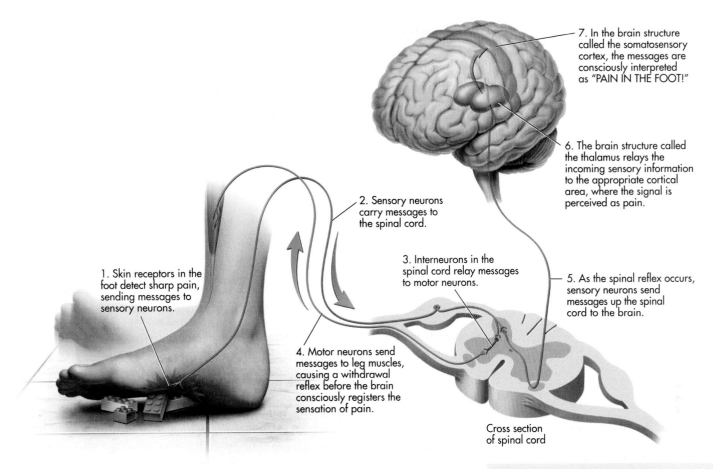

7. In the brain structure called the somatosensory cortex, the messages are consciously interpreted as "PAIN IN THE FOOT!"

6. The brain structure called the thalamus relays the incoming sensory information to the appropriate cortical area, where the signal is perceived as pain.

2. Sensory neurons carry messages to the spinal cord.

3. Interneurons in the spinal cord relay messages to motor neurons.

5. As the spinal reflex occurs, sensory neurons send messages up the spinal cord to the brain.

1. Skin receptors in the foot detect sharp pain, sending messages to sensory neurons.

4. Motor neurons send messages to leg muscles, causing a withdrawal reflex before the brain consciously registers the sensation of pain.

Cross section of spinal cord

are reading an amazing psychology textbook, for example, messages from the brain are communicated down the spinal cord and then out to the muscles via the somatic nervous system.

The **autonomic nervous system** is *the subdivision of the peripheral nervous system that regulates involuntary functions, such as heartbeat, blood pressure, breathing, and digestion.* These processes occur with little or no conscious involvement. This is an efficient way to manage these functions, because if you had to mentally command your heart to beat or your stomach to digest the food you had for lunch, it would be difficult to focus your attention on anything else.

However, the autonomic nervous system is not completely self-regulating. By engaging in physical activity or purposely tensing or relaxing your muscles, you can increase or decrease autonomic activity. Emotions and mental imagery also influence your autonomic nervous system. Given this, it should not surprise you that many autonomic functions can be harmed by chronic stress, which you will learn more about in the chapter on stress, health, and coping.

The involuntary functions regulated by the autonomic nervous system are controlled by two different branches: the *sympathetic* and *parasympathetic nervous systems.* These two systems control many of the same organs in your body but cause them to respond in opposite ways (see **Table 2.2**).

The **sympathetic nervous system** is *the branch of the autonomic nervous that is the body's emergency system, rapidly activating bodily systems to meet threats or emergencies.* When you are frightened, your breathing accelerates, your heart beats faster, digestion stops, and the bronchial tubes in your lungs expand. All these physiological responses increase the amount of oxygen available to your brain and muscles. Your pupils dilate to increase your field of vision, and your mouth becomes dry because salivation stops. These and other bodily changes collectively represent the *fight-or-flight response*—they physically prepare you to fight or to flee from a perceived danger. We'll discuss the fight-or-flight response in greater detail in the chapters on emotion and stress.

FIGURE 2.7 A Spinal Reflex A *spinal reflex* is a simple, involuntary behavior that is processed in the spinal cord without brain involvement. If you accidentally step on some loose Legos, you'll instantly lift your foot away from the painful stimulus—an example of the withdrawal reflex. The sequence shown here illustrates how the withdrawal reflex can occur before the brain processes the conscious perception of pain.

autonomic nervous system (aw-toe-NAHM-ick) The subdivision of the peripheral nervous system that regulates *involuntary* functions, such as heartbeat, blood pressure, breathing, and digestion.

sympathetic nervous system The branch of the autonomic nervous system that is the body's emergency system, rapidly activating bodily systems to meet threats or emergencies.

TABLE 2.2

The Sympathetic and Parasympathetic Branches of the Autonomic Nervous System

Sympathetic Nervous System	Body Part	Parasympathetic Nervous System
Body's Response: Fight or Flight		Body's Response: Rest and Digest
Dilates pupils	Eyes	Contracts pupils
Inhibits salivation	Mouth	Stimulates salivation
Rapid/shallow breathing	Lungs	Slower/deeper breathing
Increases heart rate	Heart	Decreases heart rate
Increases sweat	Palms	Decreases sweat
Inhibits digestion	Stomach/intestines	Stimulates digestion

The two subdivisions of the autonomic nervous system operate at the unconscious level. Arousal of the sympathetic nervous system prepares the body for fight or flight from dangerous or frightening situations. The parasympathetic nervous system calms the body and is responsible for stimulating many of the processes that keep the body alive, such as resting and digesting.

While the sympathetic nervous system mobilizes your body's physical resources, the **parasympathetic nervous system** is *the branch of the autonomic nervous system that conserves and maintains your physical resources.* It calms you down after an emergency. Acting much more slowly than the sympathetic nervous system, the parasympathetic nervous system gradually returns your body's systems to normal.

Although the sympathetic and parasympathetic nervous systems produce opposite effects, they act together, keeping the nervous system in balance (see **Figure 2.8**). Each division handles different functions, yet the whole nervous system works in unison so that both automatic and voluntary behaviors are carried out smoothly.

The Endocrine System

The **endocrine system** is *the system of glands, located throughout the body, that secrete hormones into the bloodstream* (see **Figure 2.9**). Like the nervous system, the endocrine system uses chemical messengers to transmit information from one part of the body to another. The endocrine system is not part of the nervous system, but interacts with it in important ways.

Endocrine glands communicate information from one part of the body to another via **hormones**, *chemical messengers secreted into the bloodstream.* The hormones circulate throughout the bloodstream until they reach specific hormone receptors on target organs or tissue. Hormones regulate physical processes and influence behavior. For example, metabolism, growth rate, digestion, blood pressure, and sexual development and reproduction are all regulated by the endocrine hormones. Hormones also have effects on the brain, where they act as neurotransmitters and are involved in emotional responses and stress.

The signals that trigger the secretion of hormones are regulated by the brain, primarily by a brain structure called the **hypothalamus**, *a complex structure that is found just beneath the thalamus (where its name comes from); it is the direct link between the endocrine system and the nervous system via the pituitary gland.* The hypothalamus is often called "the master switchboard" and directly regulates the release of hormones by the pituitary gland, which is often called "the master gland." The **pituitary gland** is *a pea-sized gland just under the brain that regulates the production of other hormones by many of the glands in the endocrine system.*

parasympathetic nervous system The branch of the autonomic nervous system that conserves and maintains your physical resources.

endocrine system (EN-doe-krin) The system of glands, located throughout the body, that secrete hormones into the bloodstream.

hormones Chemical messengers secreted into the bloodstream primarily.

hypothalamus (hi-poe-THAL-uh-muss) A complex structure that is found just beneath the thalamus (where its name comes from); it is the direct link between the endocrine system and the nervous system via the pituitary gland.

pituitary gland (pih-TOO-ih-tare-ee) A pea-sized gland just under the brain that regulates the production of other hormones by many of the glands in the endocrine system.

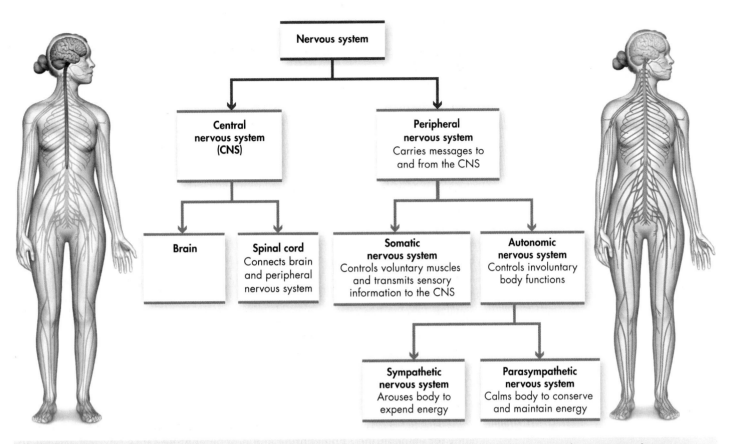

FIGURE 2.8 The Organization of the Nervous System The human nervous system is divided into several important subsystems. There are two major subdivisions, the central nervous system and the peripheral nervous system, both of which include additional components or subsystems. The central nervous system includes the brain and the spinal cord. The peripheral nervous system is home to the somatic nervous system and the autonomic nervous system. The autonomic nervous system is further divided into the sympathetic nervous system and parasympathetic nervous system.

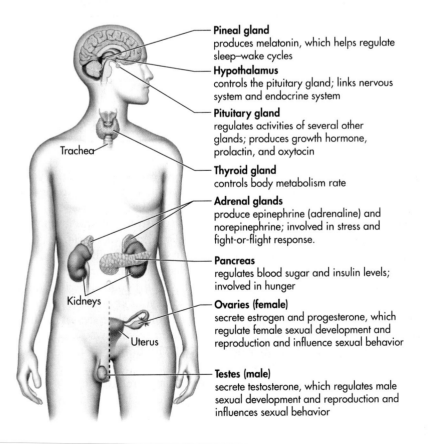

FIGURE 2.9 The Endocrine System The endocrine system and the nervous system are directly linked by the hypothalamus, which controls the pituitary gland. In turn, the pituitary gland releases hormones that affect the hormone production of several other endocrine glands. Shown here are the location and main functions of several important endocrine glands.

oxytocin A hormone involved in reproduction, social motivation, and social behavior that is produced by the hypothalamus and released into the bloodstream by the pituitary gland.

adrenal glands A pair of endocrine glands that produce hormones involved in the human stress response and play a key role in the fight-or-flight response.

MYTH ◄ SCIENCE

Is it true that oxytocin is the "love hormone," making people more trusting and empathic?

The pituitary gland also produces some hormones that act directly. For example, the pituitary produces *growth hormone,* which stimulates normal skeletal growth during childhood. The pituitary gland can also secrete endorphins to reduce the perception of pain. In nursing mothers, the pituitary produces *prolactin,* the hormone that stimulates milk production.

Another important hormone is **oxytocin**, *a hormone involved in reproduction, social motivation, and social behavior, produced by the hypothalamus and released into the bloodstream by the pituitary gland.* Breastfeeding is an example of the complex interaction among behavior, the nervous system, and the endocrine system. In nursing mothers, nerve impulses from sensory receptors in the skin are sent to the hypothalamus, which signals the release of oxytocin. Oxytocin produces the let-down reflex, causing stored milk to begin flowing. During childbirth, oxytocin signals the uterus to contract.

Oxytocin also has brain-based effects on behavior (Carter, 2014). It promotes bonding between reproductive partners, between parent and infant, and even between dogs and owners (Nagasawa et al., 2015). Early research found that it also promotes empathy, trust among group members, and sensitivity to social cues (see Miller, 2013). These findings gave oxytocin its reputation as "the love hormone," but that is a myth. Oxytocin is actually involved in *many* aspects of social motivation and behavior. In some circumstances, oxytocin can promote aggression or other antisocial behavior (de Dreu et al., 2011; Olff et al., 2013). And, other researchers have found that some people respond to oxytocin with increased social anxiety rather than increased feelings of trust (Bartz et al., 2011; Olff et al., 2013).

The **adrenal glands** are *a pair of endocrine glands that are involved in the stress response and play a key role in the fight-or-flight response.* When activated, the sympathetic nervous system stimulates the adrenal glands, which produce *epinephrine* and *norepinephrine.* (You may be more familiar with the word *adrenaline,* which is another name for epinephrine.) Epinephrine and norepinephrine cause physical arousal and also act as neurotransmitters, stimulating activity at the synapses in the sympathetic nervous system.

A Guided Tour of the Brain

■ KEY THEME
The brain is a highly complex, integrated, and dynamic system of interconnected neurons.

≡ KEY QUESTIONS
- What are neural pathways, and why are they important?
- What is functional and structural plasticity?
- How is the human brain organized?

The most complex mass of matter in the universe sits right behind your eyes and between your two ears—your brain. Not even the Internet can match the human brain for speed and sophistication of information transmission.

Our knowledge of the brain benefits immensely from the development of sophisticated scanning techniques, described in the Focus on Neuroscience, "Imaging the Brain," later in the chapter. In this part of the chapter, we'll take you on a guided tour of the human brain. As such, our first goal is to familiarize you with the basic organization and structures of the brain. Our second goal is to give you a sense of how the brain works. In later chapters, we'll add to your knowledge of the brain as we discuss the brain's involvement in specific psychological processes. Learning about the human brain is not that different from learning your way around a university campus. At first, it can seem overwhelming, but with time and practice you realize it's not that hard to remember the campus layout.

In terms of learning about the human brain, it makes some sense that simple human behaviors require the interaction of fewer brain regions, while complex

Geoff Tompkinson/Science Source

▲ The Human Brain Weighing roughly three pounds, the human brain is about the size of a small cauliflower and has the consistency of tofu. Although your brain makes up only about 2 percent of your total body weight, it uses some 20 percent of the oxygen your body needs while at rest (Raichle, 2015). The oxygen is used in breaking down glucose to supply the brain with energy.

human behaviors require the interaction of more brain regions (Breakspear, 2017). It is true that even simple behaviors involve activation of multiple parts of the brain. For example, perceiving the color blue requires the interaction of fewer brain regions than understanding the fact that blue whales communicate with each other. Keep in mind that while certain functions are associated with particular brain regions, specific functions seldom correspond neatly to a single specific brain site. Most psychological processes, especially complex ones, involve *multiple* brain structures and regions. Even seemingly simple tasks—such as listening to music, catching a ball, or watching a movie—involve the smoothly coordinated synthesis of information among many different areas of your brain (Turk-Browne, 2013). Thus, contrary to what some people claim, it's *not* true that you "use only 10 percent of your brain." Hopefully, you would not be willing to turn over 90 percent of your brain to anyone who asks! As neuroscientist Barry Gordon (2008) observes, "We use virtually every part of the brain, and the brain is active almost all the time."

Brain activity among the estimated 90 billion neurons of the human brain is linked by millions of miles of neural connections. Many brain functions involve the activation of *neural pathways* that link different brain structures (Jbabdi & Behrens, 2012; Park & Friston, 2013). Neural pathways are formed by groups of neuron cell bodies in one area of the brain that project their axons to other brain areas (Seung, 2012). These neural pathways form communication networks and circuits that link different brain areas.

The Dynamic Brain: Plasticity and Neurogenesis

Before embarking on our tour, we need to describe one last important characteristic of the brain: its remarkable capacity to change in response to experience. Until the mid-1960s, neuroscientists believed—and taught—that by early adulthood the brain's physical structure was *hardwired,* or fixed for life. But today it's known that the brain's physical structure is literally sculpted by experience (Wenger et al., 2017). The brain's ability to change function and structure is referred to as *neuroplasticity,* or simply *plasticity.* (The word *plastic* originally comes from a Greek word, *plastikos,* which means the quality of being easily shaped or molded.)

One form of plasticity is **functional plasticity**, which refers to *the brain's ability to shift functions from damaged to undamaged brain areas.* When talking about functional plasticity, neuroscientists are usually referring to changes in the axons that allow brain regions to communicate. Depending on the location and degree of brain damage, stroke or accident victims often need to relearn once-routine tasks such as speaking, walking, and reading. If the rehabilitation is successful, undamaged brain areas gradually assume the ability to process and execute the tasks (Pascual-Leone et al., 2005). Functional plasticity allowed Gabby Giffords, whom you met in the chapter's Prologue, to regain the ability to speak. With extensive therapy, uninjured portions of her brain took over the task of providing speech.

In addition to shifting functions from one area to another, the human brain is capable of *structural plasticity.* **Structural plasticity** refers to *the brain's ability to change its physical structure in response to learning, active practice, or environmental influences.*

Even subtle changes in your environment or behavior can lead to structural changes in the brain. For example, just seven days after learning how to juggle, young adults showed measurable changes in brain regions involved in perceiving, remembering, and anticipating complex visual motions (Driemeyer et al., 2008). So did senior citizens (Boyke et al., 2008). If you spent (or are spending) your first year at college, that experience has also been shown to produce changes in the brain regions involved with emotion and empathy (Bennett & Baird, 2006). Even mental activity changes the brain: 10 weeks of foreign-language training resulted in measurable changes in the amount of gray matter in the hippocampus, a brain structure associated with memory formation (Bellander et al., 2016). In another study, tiny structural changes in one brain region were detected after study participants spent just *two hours* playing a new video game that involved spatial learning and memory (Sagi et al., 2012).

MYTH ▶ SCIENCE

Is it true that even simple behaviors and abilities involve the activation of multiple parts of the brain?

MYTH ◀ SCIENCE

Is it true that you only use 10 percent of your brain?

functional plasticity The brain's ability to shift functions from damaged to undamaged brain areas.

structural plasticity The brain's ability to change its physical structure in response to learning, active practice, or environmental influences.

magnetic resonance imaging (MRI) An imaging technique that produces highly detailed images of the body's structures and tissues, using electromagnetic signals generated by the body in response to magnetic fields.

diffusion MRI (dMRI) An imaging technique that maps neural connections in the brain by tracking the movement of water molecules along myelinated axons.

positron-emission tomography (PET) An imaging technique that provides color-coded images of brain activity by tracking the brain's use of a radioactively tagged compound, such as glucose, oxygen, or a drug.

functional magnetic resonance imaging (fMRI) An imaging technique that uses magnetic fields to map brain activity by measuring changes in the brain's blood flow and oxygen levels.

Imaging the Brain

Brain-scan images have become so commonplace in popular media that it's easy to forget just how revolutionary brain imaging technology has been in the field of neuroscience (Mather et al., 2013a, 2013b; Nowogrodzki, 2018). Here, we'll look at six commonly used brain imaging techniques and examine how they're used in psychological research. In terms of how the brain is studied, techniques tend to focus on either brain structure or brain function (hardware vs. software, if you will).

Structural Imaging Techniques

Computed tomography (CT), formerly known as computerized axial tomography (CAT), has been around since the 1970s, making it among the first technologies to visualize the human brain in a living person. CT scans use repetitive X-ray images taken from different directions to create two-dimensional images, or slices, that computer algorithms convert to a three-dimensional image of the region being scanned. Although CT scans are not rich with detail, they have been used to assess or rule out stroke, traumatic brain injury, and tumors (Devulapalli et al., 2018).

Magnetic resonance imaging (MRI) is *an imaging technique that produces highly detailed images of the body's structures and tissues, using electromagnetic signals generated by the body in response to magnetic fields.* MRI uses a technique that does not expose people to radiation and as such is virtually harmless. While a person lies in a magnetic tube, their brain is bombarded with powerful but harmless magnetic fields. A computer analyzes the electromagnetic signals generated by brain-tissue molecules in response to the magnetic fields. The result is a series of digital images, detailed slices of the brain's structure. The incredibly detailed images produced by this technique revolutionized the way scientists visualized and investigated the structure of the human brain (Wintermark et al., 2015).

Diffusion MRI (dMRI) is *an imaging technique that maps neural connections in the brain by tracking the movement of water molecules along myelinated axons.* It is a relatively new way of using magnetic resonance and allows neuroscientists to produce detailed three-dimensional

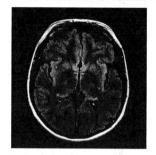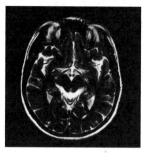

⌃ Magnetic Resonance Imaging MRI scans produce digital images showing detailed "slices" of the brain's structures. The detailed images produced by MRIs revolutionized the way scientists visualized and investigated the structure of the human brain (Wintermark et al., 2015).

George Mdivanian / Alamy Stock Photo

images of the brain's neural pathways (Chi, 2014; Glasser et al., 2016; Van Essen & Glasser, 2016). Using dMRI, it is possible to visualize both the size and direction of these neural pathways in the brain (Asken et al., 2018).

Functional Imaging Techniques

Electroencephalography (EEG) is the oldest of any brain imaging technique, dating to 1924. With this technique, scientists and clinicians place small electrodes on the scalp that detect electrical charges caused by brain activity. An EEG measures brain activity and can notice any abnormalities in the electrical charges in your brain. EEG is the only imaging technique that measures brain activity in real time (Hordacre et al., 2016). This technique is most often used to diagnose epilepsy or sleep disorders. Because electrical changes are collected from the scalp, it is not always possible to know the exact location of the observed brain activity. But recent advances have made it possible to better localize signals from the surface of the brain and even measure activity in subcortical areas like the amygdala and hippocampus (Michel & Brunet, 2019).

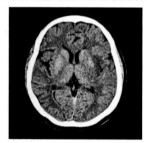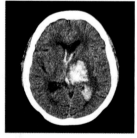

⌃ Computed Tomography CT scanning is often used as a quick, relatively safe, and inexpensive way to determine if there has been a significant brain injury. Despite the relatively low resolution of CT scans, it is easy to see that the brain on the left does not show any significant abnormalities, while the scan on the right shows clear evidence of a significant brain event. In this case, further evaluation revealed that the patient had suffered a stroke (bleeding) deep in the brain.

Puwadol Jaturawutthichai/Shutterstock

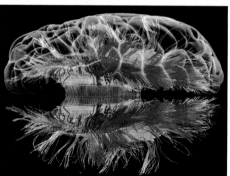

Pasieka/Science Source

⌃ Diffusion MRI dMRI tracks the movement of water through brain tissue to provide detailed three-dimensional images of the brain's neural pathways (Chi, 2014; Van Essen & Glasser, 2016). Overlaid on a model of the human brain, this dMRI scan clearly shows the intricate neural connections in the left and right cerebral hemispheres. The neural fibers of the *corpus callosum*, which connects the two hemispheres of the brain, are shown in red.

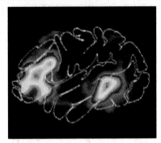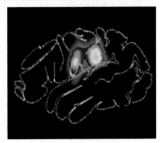

Unpracticed   Practiced

▲ **Positron-Emission Tomography** PET scans provide color-coded images of the brain's activity. Red and yellow colors highlight areas with the highest level of activity, while green and blue colors indicate lower levels of brain activity. These scans show the brain regions active while participants learned a new language task (left) and performing the language task after it had been well learned (right).

Dr. Marcus E. Raichle, Professor of Radiology & Neurology/Washington University School of Medicine

Positron-emission tomography (PET) is *an imaging technique that provides color-coded images of brain activity by tracking the brain's use of a radioactively tagged compound, such as glucose, oxygen, or a drug.* PET is based on the fact that increased activity in a particular brain region is associated with increased blood flow and energy consumption in that region. This change in energy consumption draws more of the radioactively tagged compound to the area, allowing the brain's activity to be visualized (Pagani et al., 2019).

Functional Magnetic Resonance Imaging (fMRI) is *an imaging technique that uses magnetic fields to map brain activity by measuring changes in the brain's blood flow and oxygen levels.* fMRI

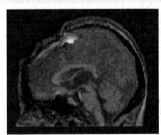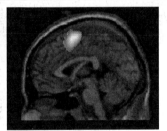

Patient   Controls

▲ **Functional MRI** fMRI combines the ability to produce a detailed image of the brain's structures with the capacity to track the brain's functioning. Here, fMRI was used to record the brain activity of a patient in a vegetative state (Owen et al., 2006). Researchers asked them to imagine playing tennis and other tasks. The scans compare their brain activity to that of normal volunteers (controls) performing the same tasks. In both, regions known to be involved in movement and spatial navigation were active. The fMRI scans confirmed that the patient was conscious of their surroundings and able to respond to spoken commands.

Reprinted by permission from American Association for the Advancement of Science: Figure 1 from Owen, Adrian M.; Coleman, Martin R.; Boly, Melanie; Davis, Matthew H.; Laureys, Steven; Pickard, John D. (2006). Detecting awareness in the vegetative state. *Science, 313*(5792), 1402. https://doi.org/10.1126/science.1130197. Permission conveyed through Copyright Clearance Center, Inc.

combines the ability to produce the most detailed images of the brain's structures with the capacity to track very specific brain activity (van der Zwaaga et al., 2016; Eickenberg et al., 2017). Scientists often compare what brain activity looks like during a specific task stimulus to either a very different stimulus or to a period of relative rest. Alternating between different types of stimuli over time lets scientists isolate which part of the brain is responding to which type of stimulus.

Limitations of Brain Imaging Studies

Neuroscientists and psychologists use brain imaging technology in many kinds of research, and we'll highlight its use throughout this text. It's not unusual to see fMRI scans in the media, sometimes used to illustrate claims that the brain is the source for particular characteristics or behaviors (Poldrack & Farah, 2015). Brain imaging has revolutionized psychology and neuroscience, but it is essential to understand that brain imaging also has limitations (Poldrack et al., 2017; Satel & Lilienfeld, 2013). When you consider the results of brain imaging studies, including those presented in this textbook, maintain a healthy level of skepticism (an important part of scientific literacy). It is important to keep in mind that functional brain imaging may not increase our understanding of a real-time human behavior. For example, although brain imaging might point to a particular brain structure as being crucially involved in, say, fear or romantic love, knowing this may not advance our understanding of the psychological experience of fear or romantic love (Decety & Cacioppo, 2010). This is particularly true because there is not always one particular brain area that responds the same way in everyone. Our experiences play a role in our brain activity. In a discussion of interpretations of fMRI output, researchers explained that, "[f]or example, the meaning of concepts like patriotism, memory or beauty will vary considerably between individuals, with different histories, so that the brain activity induced by the same word will depend upon its context" (Shulman & Rothman, 2019).

To be truly useful, brain imaging of a particular behavior must also be interpreted within the context of existing psychological knowledge about the behavior (Beck, 2010; Kihlstrom, 2010). The colorful images that often accompany fMRI studies can be given too much importance. These visual depictions of brain imaging results are not evidence of the brain "lighting up." Instead, these images show how likely the change in brain activity tracks (in a particular brain region) with changes during a specific behavior task (and is not just random activity).

Looking at Brain-Scan Images

What should you notice when you look at the brain-scan images in this text? First, read the text description so you understand the task or condition being measured. Second, read the brain-scan caption for specific details or areas of the brain to notice. Third, carefully compare the treatment scan with the control scan if both are shown. Fourth, keep the limitations of brain-scan technology in mind. Finally, remember that human experience is much too complex to be captured by a single snapshot of brain activity (Miller, 2010).

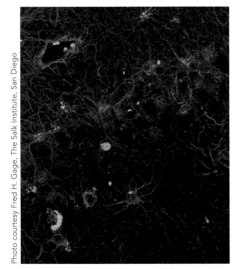

▲ Neurogenesis in the Adult Human Brain New neurons, shown in green, can be seen amid already established neurons, shown in red. In one area of the adult hippocampus, researchers found that each cubic centimeter of brain tissue contained 100 to 300 new neurons (Eriksson et al., 1998). A later study by Kristy Spalding and her colleagues (2013) confirmed that more than 1,000 new neurons are generated each day, even in older adults.

An even more dramatic example of the brain's capacity to change is **neurogenesis**—*the development of new neurons.* For many years, scientists believed that humans did not experience neurogenesis after birth (Kempermann, 2012a).

It's now believed that in humans, neurogenesis is limited to two brain regions: the hippocampus and the *olfactory bulb,* which is responsible for odor perception. These newly generated neurons are incorporated into existing neural networks, possibly playing a key role in learning and memory (Kempermann, 2012b; Marín-Burgin et al., 2012), although their function in the human brain is still being investigated (Duque & Spector, 2019; Gage, 2019).

In the next section, we'll begin our guided tour of the brain. Following the general sequence of the brain's development, we'll start with the structures at the base of the brain that are the oldest in terms of evolution and the most critical for survival. Then we'll work our way up to more recently evolved and increasingly complex brain regions, which are responsible for nuanced social and emotional behavior.

The Brainstem: Hindbrain and Midbrain Structures

■ KEY THEME
The brainstem includes the hindbrain and midbrain, located at the base of the brain.

≡ KEY QUESTIONS
- What are the key structures of the hindbrain and midbrain, and what are their functions?
- Why might damage to the brainstem likely be lethal?

The major regions of the brain are illustrated in **Figure 2.10,** which can serve as a map to keep you oriented during our tour. At the base of the brain lie the hindbrain and, directly above it, the midbrain. The **brainstem** is *a region of the brain made up of the hindbrain and the midbrain.*

FIGURE 2.10 Major Regions of the Brain Situated at the base of the brain, the hindbrain has functions that include coordinating movement and posture, regulating alertness, and maintaining vital life functions. The midbrain helps process sensory information. In combination, the hindbrain and the midbrain comprise the brainstem. The forebrain is the largest brain region and is involved in more sophisticated behaviors and mental processes.

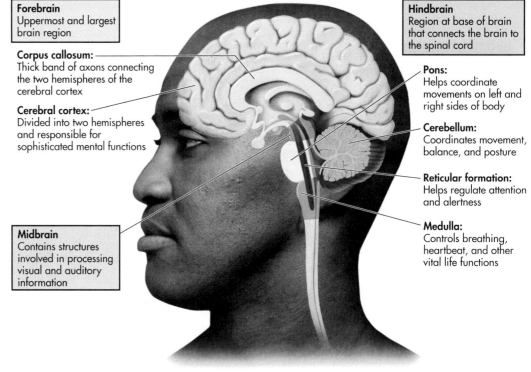

Forebrain
Uppermost and largest brain region

Corpus callosum:
Thick band of axons connecting the two hemispheres of the cerebral cortex

Cerebral cortex:
Divided into two hemispheres and responsible for sophisticated mental functions

Midbrain
Contains structures involved in processing visual and auditory information

Hindbrain
Region at base of brain that connects the brain to the spinal cord

Pons:
Helps coordinate movements on left and right sides of body

Cerebellum:
Coordinates movement, balance, and posture

Reticular formation:
Helps regulate attention and alertness

Medulla:
Controls breathing, heartbeat, and other vital life functions

The Hindbrain The **hindbrain** is *a region at the base of the brain containing several structures that regulate basic life functions.* It connects the spinal cord with the rest of the brain. Sensory and motor pathways pass through the hindbrain to and from regions that are situated higher up in the brain.

Three structures make up the hindbrain—the medulla, the pons, and the cerebellum. The **medulla** is *a hindbrain structure that controls vital life functions.* It is situated at the base of the brain directly above the spinal cord and contains centers controlling vital functions that you don't have to think about, like breathing, heart rate, and blood pressure. The medulla also controls a number of vital reflexes, including swallowing, coughing, vomiting, and sneezing. Because the medulla is involved in such critical life functions, damage to this brain region can rapidly prove fatal. When any portion of the brain swells, it puts pressure on the brainstem and potentially damages it. This should help you understand why a blow to any part of the head can be lethal. This is also why a portion of Gabby Giffords's skull had to be removed in order to keep her alive after her injury. The initial injury to her brain, as well as the surgeries meant to improve her condition, all created swelling that would have been lethal otherwise.

Above the medulla is a mound of tissue called the *pons* that represents the uppermost level of the hindbrain. The **pons** is *a hindbrain structure that connects the medulla to the two sides of the cerebellum and helps coordinate and integrate movements on each side of the body.* Located just behind the pons is the **cerebellum**, *a large, two-sided hindbrain structure at the back of the brain that is responsible for muscle coordination and equilibrium.* On each side of the pons, a large bundle of axons connects it to the cerebellum. The word *pons* means "bridge," and the pons is a bridge of sorts: Information from various other brain regions located higher up in the brain is relayed to the cerebellum via the pons. The pons also contains centers that play an important role in regulating breathing.

The cerebellum functions in the control of balance, muscle tone, and coordinated muscle movements. It is also involved in the learning of habitual or automatic movements and motor skills, such as typing, writing, or backhanding a tennis ball. Jerky, uncoordinated movements can result from damage to the cerebellum. Simple movements, such as walking or standing upright, may become difficult or impossible. The cerebellum is also one of the brain areas affected by alcohol consumption, which is why a person who is intoxicated may stagger and have difficulty walking a straight line or standing on one foot.

At the core of the medulla and the pons is the **reticular formation**, *a network of nerve fibers located in the center of the medulla that helps regulate attention, arousal, and sleep; also called the* reticular activating system. It is composed of many groups of specialized neurons that project up to higher brain regions and down to the spinal cord.

The Midbrain The **midbrain** is *an important relay station that contains centers involved in the processing of auditory and visual sensory information.* The primary function of the midbrain is to help you automatically adjust to sights and sounds around you. Think of how fast your head whips around when a noise startles you. That's your midbrain trying to keep you alive. After passing through the midbrain level, auditory information and visual information are relayed to sensory processing centers farther up in the forebrain region, which will be discussed next.

The Forebrain

■ KEY THEME
The forebrain includes the limbic system and cerebral cortex.

⹅ KEY QUESTIONS
- What are the four lobes of the cerebral cortex, and what are their functions?
- What is the limbic system?
- What functions are associated with the thalamus and amygdala?

neurogenesis The development of new neurons.

brainstem A region of the brain made up of the hindbrain and the midbrain.

hindbrain A region at the base of the brain containing several structures that regulate basic life functions.

medulla (muh-DOOL-uh) A hindbrain structure that controls vital life functions.

pons A hindbrain structure that connects the medulla to the two sides of the cerebellum and helps coordinate and integrate movements on each side of the body.

cerebellum (sair-uh-BELL-um) A large, two-sided hindbrain structure at the back of the brain that is responsible for muscle coordination and equilibrium.

reticular formation (reh-TICK-you-ler) A network of nerve fibers located in the center of the medulla that helps regulate attention, arousal, and sleep; also called the *reticular activating system*.

midbrain An important relay station that contains centers involved in the processing of auditory and visual sensory information.

forebrain The largest and most complex brain region, which contains centers for complex behaviors and mental processes; also called the *cerebrum*.

limbic system A group of forebrain structures that form a border around the brainstem and are involved in emotion, motivation, learning, and memory.

hippocampus A large forebrain structure that is part of the limbic system and embedded in the temporal lobe in each cerebral hemisphere.

thalamus (THAL-uh-muss) A rounded forebrain structure located within each cerebral hemisphere that processes sensory information (except smell).

Situated above the midbrain is the **forebrain**, *the largest and most complex brain region, which contains centers for complex behaviors and mental processes; also called the* cerebrum. In humans, the forebrain represents about 90 percent of the brain. The human forebrain is known to be larger in humans (proportionally) than in most species. (It is also possible that the opposite is true and that the larger forebrain contributed to the development of those complex societies.). This larger forebrain may be a result of the complex societies in which humans live. Regardless, many contemporary human neuroscientists have described the human brain as an essentially "social organ" (Adolphs, 2010).

The Limbic System Above the hindbrain is the **limbic system**, *a group of forebrain structures that form a border around the brainstem and are involved in emotion, motivation, learning, and memory.* The word *limbic* means "border," and as you can see in **Figure 2.11**, the structures that make up the limbic system form a border of sorts between the survival-related functions of the brainstem and the more complex functions of the forebrain. Next, we'll briefly consider some key limbic system structures and the roles they play in behavior.

The Hippocampus The **hippocampus** is *a large forebrain structure that is part of the limbic system and embedded in the temporal lobe in each cerebral hemisphere* (see Figure 2.11). The word *hippocampus* comes from a Latin word meaning "sea horse." If you have a vivid imagination, the hippocampus does look a bit like the curved tail of a sea horse. The hippocampus plays an important role in your ability to form new memories of events and information (Moscovitch et al., 2016). In Chapter 6, we'll take a closer look at the role of the hippocampus and other brain structures in memory.

The Thalamus The word *thalamus* comes from a Greek word meaning "inner chamber." And indeed, the **thalamus** is *a rounded forebrain structure located within each cerebral hemisphere that processes sensory information (except smell).* The thalamus processes and distributes motor information and sensory information going to and from the cerebral cortex. **Figure 2.12** depicts some of the neural pathways going from the thalamus to the different lobes of the cerebral cortex. You will learn a lot more about the role of the thalamus in the chapter on sensation and perception.

The Hypothalamus *Hypo* means "beneath" or "below." As its name implies, the hypothalamus is located below the thalamus. Although it is only about the size of a peanut, the hypothalamus contains more than 40 neural pathways. Along with helping regulate

FIGURE 2.11 Key Structures of the Forebrain and Limbic System In the cross-sectional view shown here, you can see the locations and functions of four important subcortical brain structures. In combination, these structures make up the *limbic system,* which regulates emotional control, learning, and memory.

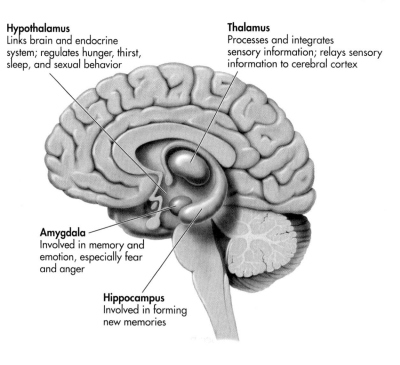

Hypothalamus
Links brain and endocrine system; regulates hunger, thirst, sleep, and sexual behavior

Thalamus
Processes and integrates sensory information; relays sensory information to cerebral cortex

Amygdala
Involved in memory and emotion, especially fear and anger

Hippocampus
Involved in forming new memories

the *pituitary gland* (discussed earlier in this chapter), the hypothalamus regulates both divisions of the autonomic nervous system, increasing and decreasing such functions as heart rate and blood pressure. It also helps regulate a variety of behaviors related to survival, such as eating, drinking, frequency of sexual activity, fear, and aggression.

The Amygdala The **amygdala** is *an almond-shaped cluster of neurons at the base of the temporal lobe.* The amygdala is involved in a variety of emotional responses, including fear, anger, and disgust. In animal studies, electrical stimulation of the amygdala produces behaviors associated with fear or rage, while destruction of the amygdala reduces or disrupts such behaviors (Haller, 2018). The best way to understand what the amygdala does is to think about it as the brain's "lookout," constantly screening the world around you for anything relevant to your survival (Phelps, 2006).

It's long been known that the amygdala is involved in the detection of threatening stimuli, but neuroscientists have discovered that the amygdala has a broader role. Brain imaging studies have shown that the amygdala responds to many different types of emotional stimuli, appealing as well as upsetting (Cunningham & Brosch, 2012). For example, studies of humans looking at facial expressions consistently show significantly increased amygdala activity in response to facial expressions, especially ones expressing fear (Diano et al., 2017). Since the amygdala plays a role in our survival, it is not surprising that it is highly sensitive to fearful faces that could signal danger.

The amygdala is also involved in learning and forming memories, especially those with a strong emotional component (Tambini et al., 2017). In future chapters, we'll take a closer look at the amygdala's role in memory and emotion.

The Cerebral Cortex The **cerebral cortex** is *the wrinkled outer portion of the forebrain, which contains the most sophisticated brain centers.* The word *cortex* means "bark," and the cerebral cortex is only about a quarter of an inch thick, much like the bark of a tree. It is composed mainly of neuron cell bodies, unmyelinated axons and capillaries, giving it a light grayish appearance—which is why the cerebral cortex is sometimes described as being composed of *gray matter.* Extending inward from the cerebral cortex are myelinated axons that are often referred to as *white matter.* These axons have a whitish appearance because the myelin insulating these axons is made of a fatty substance (not unlike what you see when looking at an uncooked steak). These myelinated axons connect the regions of the cerebral cortex to each other as well as other brain regions (like the limbic system).

Numerous folds and grooves characterize the human cerebral cortex. The purpose of these ridges and valleys is nothing short of genius. Imagine a flat three-foot by three-foot piece of paper. You can compact the surface area of this piece of paper by scrunching it up into a wad. In much the same way, the grooves and bulges of the cerebral cortex allow about three square feet of surface area to be packed into the small space of the human skull.

The nearly symmetrical left and right halves of the cerebral cortex are the **cerebral hemispheres**. *The thick band of axons that connects the two cerebral hemispheres and acts as a communication link between them* is the **corpus callosum** (see **Figure 2.13**). The corpus callosum serves as the primary communication link between the left and right cerebral hemispheres. Its enormous size reflects just how much information passes between the hemispheres on a regular basis. We will return to how functions differ between the two hemispheres, but first let's take a look at what you will find in them. Each cerebral hemisphere can be roughly divided into four regions, or *lobes: the occipital, parietal, temporal,* and *frontal lobes* (see **Figure 2.14**).

The **occipital lobe** is *an area at the back of each cerebral hemisphere that is the primary receiving area for visual information.* The occipital lobe includes the *primary visual cortex,*

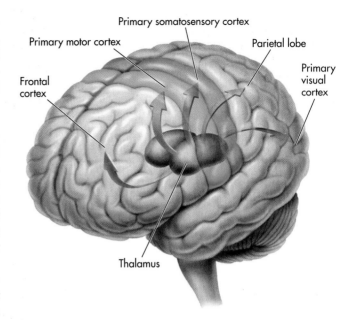

FIGURE 2.12 The Thalamus Almost all sensory and motor information going to and from the cerebral cortex is processed through the thalamus. This figure depicts some of the neural pathways from different regions of the thalamus to specific lobes of the cerebral cortex.

amygdala (uh-MIG-dull-uh) An almond-shaped cluster of neurons at the base of the temporal lobe.

cerebral cortex (suh-REE-brull or SAIR-uh-brull) The wrinkled outer portion of the forebrain, which contains the most sophisticated brain centers.

cerebral hemispheres The nearly symmetrical left and right halves of the cerebral cortex.

corpus callosum A thick band of axons that connects the two cerebral hemispheres and acts as a communication link between them.

occipital lobe (ock-SIP-it-ull) An area at the back of each cerebral hemisphere that is the primary receiving area for visual information.

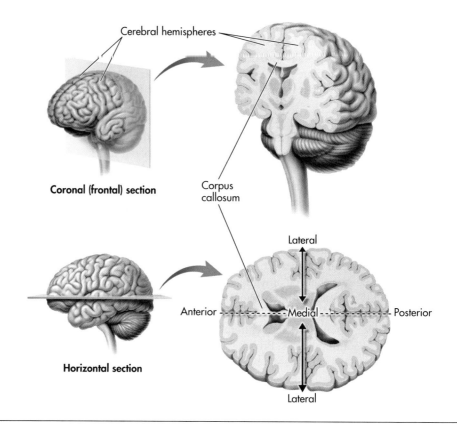

FIGURE 2.13 The Cerebral Hemispheres and the Corpus Callosum The two hemispheres of the cerebral cortex can be clearly seen in this side-to-side cross-sectional view of the brain. The main communications link connecting the two cerebral hemispheres is the *corpus callosum,* a thick, broad bundle of some 300 million myelinated neuron axons.

Cerebral hemispheres

Corpus callosum

Coronal (frontal) section

Lateral

Anterior -------- Medial -------- Posterior

Lateral

Horizontal section

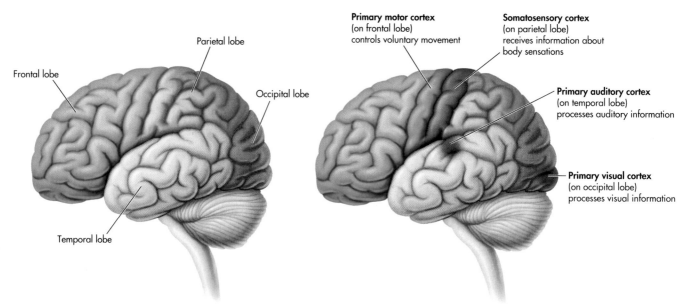

Parietal lobe

Frontal lobe

Occipital lobe

Temporal lobe

Primary motor cortex (on frontal lobe) controls voluntary movement

Somatosensory cortex (on parietal lobe) receives information about body sensations

Primary auditory cortex (on temporal lobe) processes auditory information

Primary visual cortex (on occipital lobe) processes visual information

FIGURE 2.14 Lobes of the Cerebral Cortex Each hemisphere of the cerebral cortex can be divided into four regions, or *lobes.* Each lobe is associated with distinct functions. The association areas, also called the *association cortex,* make up most of the rest of the cerebral cortex.

where visual information received from the eyes is processed. The occipital lobe also contains the *visual association cortex,* which enables us to make sense of visual stimuli received in the primary visual cortex. For example, consider this visual stimulus: + (a plus sign). Your primary visual cortex detects two lines that intersect, whereas your visual association cortex may tell you that it is a symbol frequently used in math.

These association areas exist in all of the brain's lobes and are critically important for making sense of the world we live in. In just one example of this, the occipital lobe of humans contains an association area that is specifically tuned to detecting faces because faces are essential in human communication. If this area is damaged, people may not recognize faces of people they have known for years *using their vision,* but they often recognize them by relying on another sense, such as the sound of their voice (Maguinness & von Kriegstein, 2017).

The **parietal lobe** is *an area on each hemisphere of the cerebral cortex above the temporal lobe that processes the body's sensations.* This *somatosensory* information includes touch, temperature, pressure, and information from receptors in the muscles and joints. A band of tissue on the parietal lobe, called the *primary somatosensory cortex,* receives information from touch receptors in different parts of the body (Orban, 2016).

Each part of the body is represented on the somatosensory cortex, but this representation is not equally distributed (see **Figure 2.15**). Instead, body parts are represented in

parietal lobe (puh-RYE-ut-ull) An area on each hemisphere of the cerebral cortex, located above the temporal lobe, that processes the body's sensations.

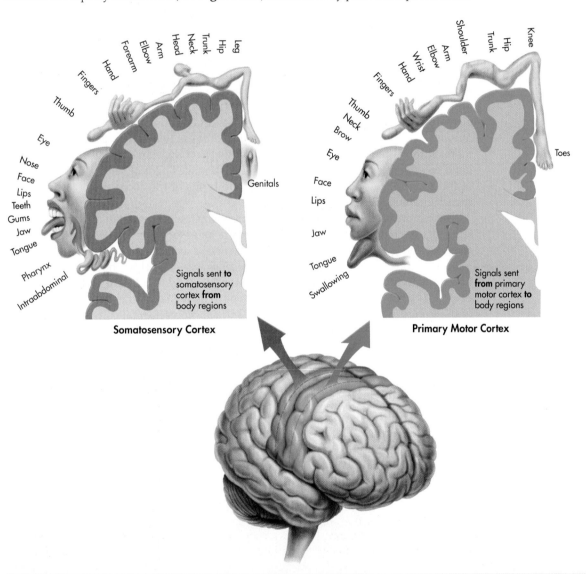

FIGURE 2.15 The Body's Representation on the Somatosensory Cortex and the Primary Motor Cortex This illustration depicts the right cerebral hemisphere. Because of the brain's *contralateral organization,* the right side of the brain processes functions for the left side of the body and vice versa. Touch, temperature, pressure, and pain sensations for different areas of the body occur at distinct locations on the parietal lobe's *somatosensory cortex.* Similarly, the initiation of movement for different parts of the body occurs at distinct locations on the frontal lobe's *primary motor cortex.* If body parts were proportional to their representation on the somatosensory cortex and primary motor cortex, they would look like the misshapen human figures on the outer edges of the drawings.

temporal lobe An area on each hemisphere of the cerebral cortex, near the temples, that is the primary receiving area for auditory information.

frontal lobe The largest lobe of each cerebral hemisphere; it processes voluntary muscle movements and is involved in thinking, planning, and emotional control.

cortical localization The idea that particular brain areas are associated with specific functions.

aphasia (uh-FAYZH-yuh) The partial or complete inability to articulate ideas or understand spoken or written language because of brain injury or damage.

Broca's area A brain region in the frontal lobe of the dominant hemisphere, usually the left, that is critical for speech production.

Wernicke's area A brain region in the left temporal lobe of the dominant hemisphere, usually the left, that is crucial for the comprehension of language.

proportion to their sensitivity to somatic sensations. For example, on the left side of Figure 2.15, you can see that your hands and face, which are very responsive to touch, have much greater representation on the somatosensory cortex than do the backs of your legs, which are far less sensitive to touch. The association areas in the parietal lobe also help you process information about how you are positioned relative to the environment around you as well as things like the amount of pressure or quality of touch sensations (Kaas et al., 2018).

The **temporal lobe** is *an area on each hemisphere of the cerebral cortex, near the temples, that is the primary receiving area for auditory information.* It contains the *primary auditory cortex,* which receives basic auditory information from the ears. As with the other lobes, the association cortex in the temporal lobes helps your brain recognize and give meaning to the difference between a musical note and baby's cry. As we will read shortly, there is an association area in the left temporal lobe that is the central location for understanding spoken language (Notter et al., 2019).

The **frontal lobe** is *the largest lobe of each cerebral hemisphere; it processes voluntary muscle movements and is involved in thinking, planning, and emotional control.* Damage to this area of the brain can affect many functions. The muscle movements of different body parts are represented in a band of tissue on the frontal lobe called the primary motor cortex. The degree of representation on the *primary motor cortex* for a particular body part reflects the diversity and precision of its potential movements, as shown on the right side of Figure 2.15. Thus, it's not surprising that almost one-third of the primary motor cortex is devoted to the hands and another third is devoted to facial muscles. The disproportionate representation of these two body areas on the primary motor cortex is reflected in the human capacity to produce an extremely wide range of hand movements and facial expressions. It also makes a lot of sense when you think of the importance of communication, both in terms of the coordination required for speech and for kissing!

There is an additional portion of the frontal lobe that is located in front of the motor strip, just behind your forehead. This region is an association area called the *prefrontal cortex* and it is often thought of as the "central executive" of the human brain. The prefrontal cortex received this nickname because it coordinates a number of cognitive functions in humans such as thinking, attention, and regulating emotion (Hacker et al., 2019). The prefrontal cortex also helps us to understand other people's minds, one of the things that makes humans unique. In fact, the prefrontal cortex is so essential to your personality—what makes you "you"—that serious injury to this region often produces massive changes in personality and behavior (see photo).

> **Focus on the Frontal Lobes: Phineas Gage** Early interest in the frontal lobes was sparked by the case of Phineas Gage, a railroad foreman. In 1848, a freak explosion shot a 13-pound, three-and-a-half-foot-long iron bar through his skull, piercing his brain. After the accident, the formerly conscientious, soft-spoken foreman was said to have become bad-tempered and irresponsible. After Gage's death in 1861, his physician proposed that Gage's personality changes were caused by damage to his frontal lobes (Harlow, 1869). More than a century later, neuroscientists studying Gage's skull confirmed that his left frontal lobe had been severely damaged (Damasio et al., 1994; Ratiu & Talos, 2004). A more recent model points to probable damage to white matter connections between Gage's frontal lobe and other brain regions associated with emotion and memory (van Horn et al., 2012). This disconnection may have contributed to Gage's personality changes after the accident. Interestingly, new research suggests that Gage went on to make a full recovery in the years after his accident (Kean, 2014; Macmillan, 2000; Macmillan & Lena, 2010).

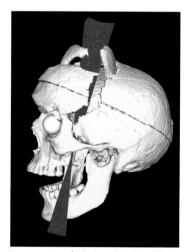

Image courtesy of John Darrell Van Horn, Ph.D., Institute of Neuroimaging and Informatics, University of Southern California. Figure 1B from Van Horn, John Darrell; Irimia, Andrei; Torgerson, Carinna M.; Chambers, Micah C.; Kikinis, Ron; & Toga, Arthur W. (2012). Mapping connectivity damage in the case of Phineas Gage. *PLOS ONE, 7(5):* e37454. https://doi.org/10.1371/journal.pone.0037454

Specialization in the Cerebral Hemispheres

■ **KEY THEME**
Although they have many functions in common, the two hemispheres of the cerebral cortex are specialized for different tasks.

═ **KEY QUESTIONS**
- How did Broca, Wernicke, and Sperry contribute to our knowledge of the brain?
- Why would the corpus callosum be surgically severed, and what effects would that produce?
- How are the functions of the right and left cerebral hemispheres unique?

If you held a human brain in your hand, the two cerebral hemispheres would appear to be symmetrical. Although the left and right hemispheres are very similar in appearance, they are not identical. Anatomically, one hemisphere may be slightly larger than the other. There are also subtle differences in the sizes of particular structures, in the distribution of gray matter and white matter, and in the patterns of folds and grooves that make up the surface of the cerebral cortex (Ocklenburg & Güntürkün, 2012).

In some instances, the functioning of the left and right hemispheres is symmetrical, meaning that the same functions are located in roughly the same places on each hemisphere. Examples of such functional symmetry include the primary motor cortex and the somatosensory cortex, discussed in the previous section. With regard to other important processes, however, the left and right cerebral hemispheres do differ—with each cerebral hemisphere specialized for particular abilities.

As you'll see in this section, the first discoveries about the differing abilities of the two brain hemispheres were made more than 100 years ago by two important pioneers in brain research, Pierre Paul Broca and Karl Wernicke.

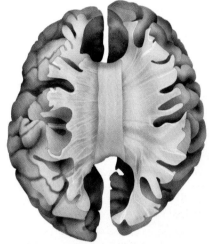

▲ **The Corpus Callosum** In the drawing, the top of the brain has been cut away, exposing the thick fibers of the corpus callosum, which connect the left and right hemispheres.

Language and the Left Hemisphere: The Early Work of Broca and Wernicke

Phrenology was a popular pseudoscience in the 1800s and early 1900s that "read" bumps on the skull to map character traits onto the brain. Although phrenology was wrong about the significance of bumps on the skull, its popularity did help inspire scientific speculation about *cortical localization* (Finger, 2010). **Cortical localization** refers to *the idea that particular brain areas are associated with specific functions.* During the late 1800s physicians were also becoming increasingly aware of a condition called **aphasia**, *the partial or complete inability to articulate ideas or understand spoken or written language because of brain injury or damage.*

In the 1860s, speculation that some language functions were localized to the left frontal lobe was confirmed by French surgeon and neuroanatomist **Pierre Paul Broca**. Broca treated several patients who had difficulty speaking but who could comprehend written or spoken language—a condition later called *Broca's aphasia.* Autopsies of these patients revealed a consistent finding—damage to what is today referred to as **Broca's area**, *a brain region in the frontal lobe of the dominant hemisphere, usually the left, that is critical for speech production* (see **Figure 2.16**).

About a decade after Broca's discovery, a young German neurologist named **Karl Wernicke** discovered another area in the left hemisphere that, when damaged, produced a different type of language disturbance. Unlike Broca's patients, Wernicke's patients had great difficulty understanding spoken or written communications, a condition now called *Wernicke's aphasia.* They could speak quickly and easily, but their speech made no sense. Autopsies of these patients' brains revealed consistent damage to a part of the brain called **Wernicke's area**, *a brain region in the temporal lobe of the dominant hemisphere, usually the left, that is crucial for the comprehension of language* (see Figure 2.16).

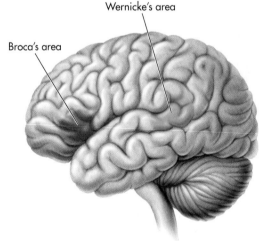

Wernicke's area

Broca's area

FIGURE 2.16 Broca's and Wernicke's Areas of the Cerebral Cortex Broca's area, located on the lower frontal lobe, is involved in the production of speech. Wernicke's area, found in the temporal lobe, is important in the comprehension of written or spoken language. Damage to either of these areas will produce different types of speech disturbances, or *aphasia*. In most people, both areas are found in the left hemisphere.

lateralization of function The notion that specific psychological or cognitive functions are processed primarily on one side of the brain

Courtesy of Dr. William D. Hopkins/Georgia State University

▲ **Left-Handed Orangutans** Like humans, many animals display a preference for one hand or paw (Ocklenburg & Güntürkün, 2012). Unlike humans, who are predominantly right-handed, animals tend to vary by species, population, and task (Hopkins & Cantalupo, 2005; Grant, 2014). For example, orangutans, like the one shown here, tend to be left-handed, but gorillas, chimpanzees, and bonobos tend to be right-handed (Hopkins et al., 2011; Prieur et al., 2016a, 2016b). Handedness is discussed in more detail in the In Focus box "Brain Myths."

THINK LIKE A **SCIENTIST**

Can you be classified as right-brained or left-brained? Go to Achieve: Resources to **Think Like a Scientist** about **The Right Brain Versus the Left Brain.**

Achieve

The discoveries of Broca and Wernicke provided the first compelling clinical evidence that language and speech functions are performed primarily by the left cerebral hemisphere. If similar brain damage occurs in the same locations on the *right* hemisphere of most people, these severe disruptions in language and speech are usually *not* seen.

The notion that specific psychological or cognitive functions are processed primarily on one side of the brain is termed **lateralization of function**. Speech and language functions are *lateralized* on the left hemisphere. The left hemisphere exerts greater control over speech and language abilities in virtually all right-handed and the majority of left-handed people (Häberling et al., 2016). However, although damage to either Broca's area or Wernicke's area often produces aphasia, it's now known that speech and language functions are *not* localized to just these two areas. Rather, they are widely distributed throughout the brain (Tremblay & Dick, 2016). It's also worth remembering that both Broca's area and Wernicke's area are association cortex, because their specialized functions are the result of the synthesis of information from multiple brain regions.

At the beginning of this chapter, we described the symptoms experienced by Gabby Giffords in the weeks and months following her traumatic brain injury. Gabby, who is right-handed, lost most of the tissue in her left hemisphere, including both Broca's area and Wernicke's area. These are the most critical regions for creating and understanding language. Of course, as we know from Gabby's story, the brain's plasticity means that people sometimes recover some degree of language usage. For example, Gabby struggles with finding the words she wants to use, as well as performing the motor functions needed to speak clearly. As her recovery has progressed, these errors have become less frequent.

For Gabby, music therapy has been critical to her recovery. Compelling video footage from her early recovery shows a speech therapist working with her to say the word "light." The only word she can say, though, is "chicken," which Gabby finds frustrating to the point of tears. Next, the therapist begins to sing "This Little Light of Mine," and Gabby sings the word "light" through her tears (along with the song's other lyrics). Gabby can sing "light" because music (including its lyrics) is represented in both hemispheres of the brain (unlike language, which is almost entirely represented in the left hemisphere).

Most neuroscientists agree that few things activate the brain as extensively as music does (Whitehead & Armony, 2018). In studies of brain function, the right hemisphere shows a higher degree of specialization for musical appreciation or responsiveness—but not necessarily for musical ability, which involves the use of the left hemisphere as well (Oechslin et al., 2018). It is important to keep in mind that things as fundamental (and yet complex) as music require a lot of coordination—both between brain regions in each hemisphere and between the two hemispheres (Koelsch, 2018).

Cutting the Corpus Callosum: The Split Brain

In the 1960s, psychologist and neuroscientist **Roger Sperry** (1982) and his colleagues recruited patients who each had their corpus callosum cut to reduce the spread of epilepsy seizures. While this procedure is no longer used, it provided Sperry and his colleagues with information to begin to unravel the puzzle of the left and right hemispheres.

Because the two hemispheres were no longer connected by the corpus callosum, information projected to the *right* hemisphere was not perceived by the *left* hemisphere, and vice versa. If a split-brain participant was asked to verbally identify an image, they could do so only if the information was sent to their left—verbal—hemisphere. If the information was sent to their right—nonverbal—hemisphere, they would deny having seen anything.

Over the past decades, researchers have gained numerous insights about the brain's lateralization of functions by studying split-brain patients, using both brain imaging techniques with typical participants and behavioral techniques (Gazzaniga, 2005; Hugdahl & Westerhausen, 2010). These different specialized abilities of the two hemispheres are highlighted in **Table 2.3**.

As you look at Table 2.3, it's important to keep two points in mind. First, the differences between the left and right hemispheres are almost always relative differences, *not*

TABLE 2.3

Specialized Abilities of the Two Hemispheres

General Function	Left-Hemisphere Dominance	Right-Hemisphere Dominance
Vision	Words Letters	Geometric patterns Faces Emotional expression
Hearing	Language sounds	Nonlanguage sounds, music
Memory	Verbal memory	Nonverbal memory
Language	Speech Grammar rules Reading Writing Arithmetic	Emotional tone of speech
Spatial ability and perception		Geometry Sense of direction Distance Mental rotation of shapes

Most people are left-hemisphere dominant for speech and language tasks and right-hemisphere dominant for visual and spatial tasks. Although the hemispheres display some specialized abilities, many functions are symmetrical and performed the same way on both hemispheres (Häberling et al., 2016).

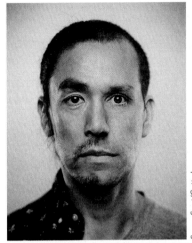

What a Split-Brain Person Sees When a person with a split brain looks quickly at a photo-combination of two different faces (called a chimeric face), the information from each side of the photo only goes to one brain hemisphere. This means the split-brain person's left hemisphere is only aware of an Asian man, while the right hemisphere only sees a White man. If the split-brain patient is asked to describe who they are looking at, their likely answer is "an Asian man."

absolute differences. In other words, *both* hemispheres of your brain are activated to some extent as you perform virtually any task (Toga & Thompson, 2003; Behrmann & Plaut, 2015). In a typical brain, the left and right hemispheres function in an integrated fashion, constantly exchanging information (Allen et al., 2007). Thus, Table 2.3 indicates the hemisphere that typically displays greater activation or exerts greater control over a particular function. Misconceptions about the roles played by the left and right hemispheres are common in the popular media and even in education (Howard-Jones, 2014). The In Focus box "Brain Myths" explores some of the most common misperceptions about the brain. Second, many functions of the cerebral hemispheres, such as those involving the primary sensory and motor areas, *are* symmetrical. They are located in virtually the same place and function very similarly in both the left and the right hemispheres.

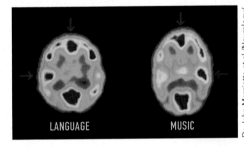

Specialization in the Left and Right Hemispheres The red arrow at the top of each PET scan points to the front of the brain. The red and yellow colors indicate the areas of greatest brain activity. Listening to speech involves a greater degree of activation of the language areas of the left hemisphere. Listening to music involves more activation in right-hemisphere areas. Notice, however, that there is some degree of activity in both hemispheres during these tasks.

Closing Thoughts

In our exploration of neuroscience and behavior, we've traveled from the activities of individual neurons to the complex interaction of the billions of neurons that make up the human nervous system, most notably the brain. We've also explored the ways in which the endocrine system works closely with the brain and the body to help out with just about every aspect of human behavior.

Although the nervous system is highly specialized, even simple behaviors involve the highly integrated interaction of trillions of synapses. Your ability to process new information and experiences, your memories of previous experiences, your sense of who you are and what you know, your actions and reactions—all depend upon the harmony of

● IN FOCUS

Brain Myths

Is It True That Some People Are "Right-Brained" and Other People "Left-Brained"?

To investigate this question, researchers compared more than a thousand fMRI scans taken while participants rested. There was *no* evidence that participants relied more on the left or right hemisphere, as you would expect if some people were "left-brained" and others "right-brained" (Nielsen et al., 2013).

It certainly seems as if some people are more logical and analytical, while others are more creative, especially in the way that they make decisions or tackle problems. Remember, though, that the two hemispheres are highly interconnected in the normal intact human brain. Unless the corpus callosum has been surgically sliced, virtually all humans rely on the smooth, integrated functioning of *both* left and right hemispheres to speak, learn, and generally navigate everyday life. In fact, the more complex the task, the greater the likelihood that both hemispheres will be involved in performing it (Allen et al., 2007; S. H. Lee et al., 2019).

What About Left-Handed People? Is It True That They Are Right-Hemisphere-Dominant?

Only about 10 to 13 percent of the population identify themselves as left-handed (Basso, 2007). Unlike right-handed people, who tend to use their right hand for virtually all tasks requiring dexterity, most left-handers actually show a pattern of *mixed* handedness. Strong left-handedness is extremely rare (Wolman, 2005).

It's a myth that left-handers have a fundamentally different brain organization from right-handers (Häberling et al., 2016). About 75 percent of left-handers are *left-hemisphere dominant* for language, just like right-handers. The remaining 25 percent are either right-hemisphere dominant for language or bilateral, using *both* hemispheres for speech and language functions. Just for the record, about 5 percent of right-handed people are also either right-hemisphere or bilaterally specialized for language (Knecht et al., 2000; Ocklenburg & Güntürkün, 2012).

Is the Right Brain Responsible for Creativity and Intuition? Can You Train Your Right Brain?

The right hemisphere is specialized for holistic processing, but it is a myth that the right hemisphere is any more "intuitive" or "creative" than the left hemisphere (Gazzaniga, 2005). In fact, a recent study found that a task requiring a *creative* solution involved greater left hemisphere activation than a task that required a *noncreative* solution (Aziz-Zadeh et al., 2013). There is also no evidence that any teacher, however skilled, could somehow selectively "educate" one side of your brain in isolation from the other (Goswami, 2006). While it is true that each hemisphere is specialized for different abilities, you rely on the integrated functioning of *both* hemispheres to accomplish most tasks. This is true especially for such cognitively demanding tasks as artistic creativity, musical performance, or finding innovative solutions to complex problems.

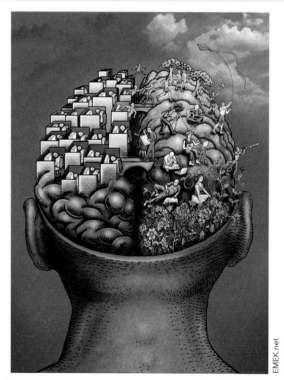

▲ **Left Brain, Right Brain?** As this image rather playfully suggests, many people see the two hemispheres as representing diametrically opposed ways of thinking and behaving: The left brain is cold, rational, and analytical; the right brain is emotional, artistic, and free-spirited. But how much truth is there to this myth?

EMEK.net

- Why were many cultures historically fearful of left-handed people?

- Is there any benefit to learning to write with both hands?

- Why do you think left-handed children who were forced to write with their right hand very often developed problems with their speech?

> **MYTH ◀ SCIENCE**
>
> Is it true that people are either "left brained" (more analytical and logical) or "right brained" (more creative and intuitive)?

the nervous system. We also explored the geography of the brain itself, starting at the most survival-related portions (hindbrain) and working up to the regions involved with more complex cognitive functions (the prefrontal cortex). Finally, we learned that while many regions of cerebral cortex have specific functions, it also takes the coordination of many cortical regions (across both hemispheres) to produce human behavior.

The story of Gabby's injury illustrated what can happen when that harmony is disrupted. Gabby survived her injury, but many people who experience traumatic brain injuries die or are left with even more severe impairments in their ability to function.

What happened to Gabby? Fortunately, her story has a relatively happy ending. Gabby was luckier than many people who survive severe traumatic brain injuries—she was young, strong, and otherwise healthy. Gabby's recovery was also aided by her high level of motivation, her willingness to work hard, excellent medical care, and an incredibly supportive social network. In fact, Gabby's husband Mark (and his NASA mantra, "The sky is not always the limit") was a critical part of her recovery. After being discharged from the hospital, Gabby began months of intensive speech and physical therapy. She has also participated in music therapy as she relearned how to play the French horn, an instrument she played in high school.

Today, more than nine years after her injury, Gabby has come a very long way. She still has limits on the use of her right arm and leg, but she has made remarkable progress with regard to her speech. She continues to serve the country and has begun to make regular public speeches on the issues that matter to her. Thus, Gabby's story illustrates a final theme—the brain's remarkable *plasticity*.

JIM WATSON/Getty Images

Gabby's Recovery Gabby Giffords resigned from Congress in 2012 to focus on her recovery, which continues to this day. She has, however, maintained an active role in U.S. politics. At the 2020 Democratic convention, she addressed viewers, saying, "I put one foot in front of the other. I found one word and then I found another. My recovery is a daily fight but fighting makes me stronger. Words once came easily. Today I struggle to speak. But I have not lost my voice." In keeping with her remarkable spirit, Gabby marked the three-year anniversary of her survival by going skydiving.

PSYCH FOR YOUR LIFE

Concussions, Assessment, Treatment, and Cumulative Impact

If you're playing football or hockey, you probably wear a helmet. If you're walking to class or rehearsing a play, you probably don't wear a helmet. You might be surprised to know that, according to a comprehensive study of college undergraduates, 64 percent of concussions happen *outside* of athletics, with the majority being the result of falls (Breck et al., 2019). In terms of athletics, it is not surprising to know that the sport with the highest incidence of concussion is boys' football, but it might surprise you to know that the sport with the second highest concussion count is actually girls' soccer (boys' soccer comes in third). If that did not surprise you, then how about this: the *only* sport with more concussions in practice than in competition is cheerleading!

Given these findings, all of us would benefit from understanding how concussions happen, how they are diagnosed, and how they are treated. The brain is actually highly susceptible to injury—even though it's encased in bone and cushioned by cerebrospinal fluid. Just a quarter-inch of bone and membranes protect the brain from harm. A sharp blow to the head or the rapid acceleration and sudden deceleration of the head (e.g., whiplash) can cause the brain to shake, twist, or literally crash into the skull. Helmets may help protect the brain from a direct impact to the skull, but they are not as helpful with something like whiplash. Just think of how different it is to bang on a can of soda relative to shaking it and you'll get a sense of what happens to the brain with a concussion.

When an injury disrupts normal brain functioning, a *traumatic brain injury* (or *TBI*) may be diagnosed. A *concussion* is the most common, and mildest, type of TBI—more than 1 million cases every year in the United States alone (Rabinowitz et al., 2014). Auto accidents, falls, and sports injuries are the most common causes of concussion when all age groups (not only university students) are considered.

After a concussion, the brain damage may not be readily evident on a CT or MRI scan. The brain may have twisted, bounced and/or collided with the skull, damaging axons and disrupting brain chemistry, any of which can significantly impair brain function. Even without brain imaging evidence, there are obvious changes in behavior of people with a concussion that are described in **Table 2.4** (Guay et al., 2016). According to the U.S. Centers for Disease Control and Prevention (2019a), diagnosing a concussion relies on signs that are both observed and reported (by the person who was injured). Keep in mind: Symptoms of a concussion may be evident immediately, but it is also possible for symptoms to show up hours or days later.

TABLE 2.4

Changes in Behavior After a Concussion

Observed Signs of Concussion	Self-Reported Concussion Symptoms
Can't recall events prior to or after a hit or fall	Headache or "pressure" in head
Appears dazed or stunned	Nausea or vomiting
Forgets an instruction; is confused about an assignment or position; or is unsure of the game, score, or opponent	Balance or dizziness, or double or blurry vision
Moves clumsily	Bothered by light or noise
Answers questions slowly	Feeling sluggish, hazy, foggy, or groggy
Loses consciousness (even briefly)	Confusion, difficulty concentrating on memory problems
Shows mood, behavior, or personality changes	Just not "feeling right" or "feeling down"

Source: Information from Centers for Disease Control and Prevention (2019a).

Most people recover from concussions within a few weeks, but if symptoms do not improve (or if they get worse) within a few weeks or months after the initial injury, *post-concussion syndrome* may be an issue. Post-concussion syndrome is thought to be more common in people who have a history of multiple concussions, but the Centers for Disease Control and Prevention (2019b) offer recommendations that may help people avoid it. The most important thing to do after a concussion is rest. The brain needs time to heal, and the body provides resources to reduce inflammation that may be causing TBI symptoms. To be clear, rest includes reducing overall activity and getting plenty of sleep at night. Activities can be added back to a young person's schedule, but only if they do not induce or exacerbate concussion symptoms.

Health care professionals who treat high school and college athletes now use scores on the Acute Concussion Evaluation (ACE) to determine readiness to return to play, with hopes of ensuring that athletes are fully healed and not suffering from post-concussion syndrome (Gioia et al., 2008). The ACE quantifies symptoms using a checklist that covers four areas (physical, cognitive, emotional, and sleep) and results in a numeric score. This assessment can be used repeatedly to see how people with concussions improve over time.

Repeated concussions can lead to a serious brain disease called *chronic traumatic encephalopathy,* or *CTE*. CTE is a progressive degenerative brain disease that can be diagnosed only after death (Hay et al., 2016). As of now, it has been reported almost exclusively among retired professional athletes. Health professionals and researchers are still working to improve our understanding of CTE, but we know its symptoms consistently include depression and anxiety, poor judgment, lack of impulse control, and problems with memory, concentration, and attention—all of which worsen over time.

Researchers hope that future work will help identify ways to protect people, especially young people, against the worst effects of head impacts. As CTE researcher and neurologist Robert Stern (2016) observed, "We need to take very seriously the notion that hitting your head over and over again may have long-term consequences."

▼ CHAPTER REVIEW

Neuroscience and Behavior

 Achieve, Macmillan Learning's online study platform, features the full e-book of *Discovering Psychology*, the **LearningCurve** adaptive quizzing system, videos, and a variety of activities to boost your learning. Visit **Achieve** at macmillanlearning.com.

KEY PEOPLE

Pierre Paul Broca, p. 65   Roger Sperry, p. 66   Karl Wernicke, p. 65

KEY TERMS

biological psychology, p. 40

neuroscience, p. 40

neurons, p. 41

sensory neuron, p. 41

motor neuron, p. 41

interneuron, p. 41

cell body, p. 41

dendrites, p. 41

axon, p. 42

glial cells (glia), p. 42

myelin sheath, p. 42

stimulus threshold, p. 44

action potential, p. 44

resting potential, p. 44

synapse, p. 46

synaptic gap, p. 46

axon terminals, p. 46

synaptic vesicles, p. 46

neurotransmitters, p. 46

synaptic transmission, p. 46

reuptake, p. 46

acetylcholine, p. 48

dopamine, p. 48

serotonin, p. 48

norepinephrine, p. 48

glutamate, p. 48

GABA (gamma-aminobutyric acid), p. 48

endorphins, p. 48

nervous system, p. 50

nerves, p. 50

central nervous system (CNS), p. 50

spinal reflexes, p. 50

peripheral nervous system, p. 50

somatic nervous system, p. 50

autonomic nervous system, p. 51

sympathetic nervous system, p. 51

parasympathetic nervous system, p. 52

endocrine system, p. 52

hormones, p. 52

hypothalamus, p. 52

pituitary gland, p. 52

oxytocin, p. 54

adrenal glands, p. 54

functional plasticity, p. 55

structural plasticity, p. 55

magnetic resonance imaging (MRI), p. 56

diffusion MRI (dMRI), p. 56

positron emission tomography (PET), p. 57

functional magnetic resonance imaging (fMRI), p. 57

neurogenesis, p. 58

brainstem, p. 58

hindbrain, p. 59

medulla, p. 59

pons, p. 59

cerebellum, p. 59

reticular formation, p. 59

midbrain, p. 59

forebrain, p. 60

limbic system, p. 60

hippocampus, p. 60

thalamus, p. 60

amygdala, p. 61

cerebral cortex, p. 61

cerebral hemispheres, p. 61

corpus callosum, p. 61

occipital lobe, p. 61

parietal lobe, p. 63

temporal lobe, p. 64

frontal lobe, p. 64

cortical localization, p. 65

aphasia, p. 65

Broca's area, p. 65

Wernicke's area, p. 65

lateralization of function, p. 66

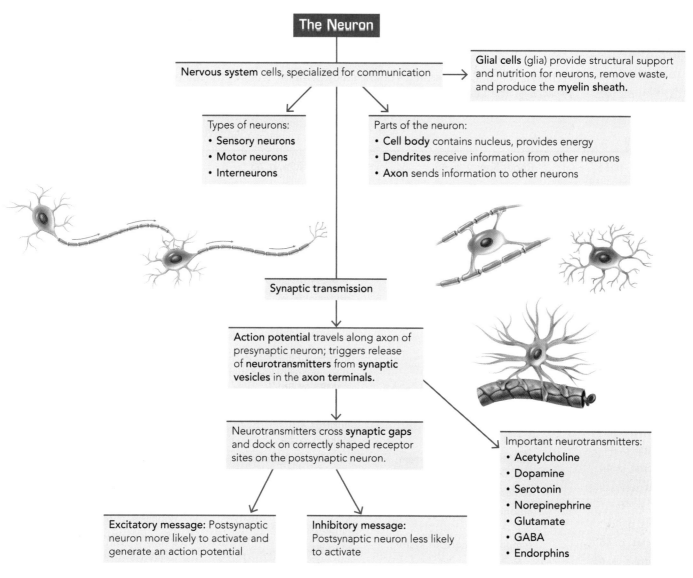

The Neuron

Nervous system cells, specialized for communication →

Glial cells (glia) provide structural support and nutrition for neurons, remove waste, and produce the myelin sheath.

Types of neurons:
• Sensory neurons
• Motor neurons
• Interneurons

Parts of the neuron:
• Cell body contains nucleus, provides energy
• Dendrites receive information from other neurons
• Axon sends information to other neurons

Synaptic transmission

Action potential travels along axon of presynaptic neuron; triggers release of neurotransmitters from synaptic vesicles in the axon terminals.

Neurotransmitters cross synaptic gaps and dock on correctly shaped receptor sites on the postsynaptic neuron.

Important neurotransmitters:
• Acetylcholine
• Dopamine
• Serotonin
• Norepinephrine
• Glutamate
• GABA
• Endorphins

Excitatory message: Postsynaptic neuron more likely to activate and generate an action potential

Inhibitory message: Postsynaptic neuron less likely to activate

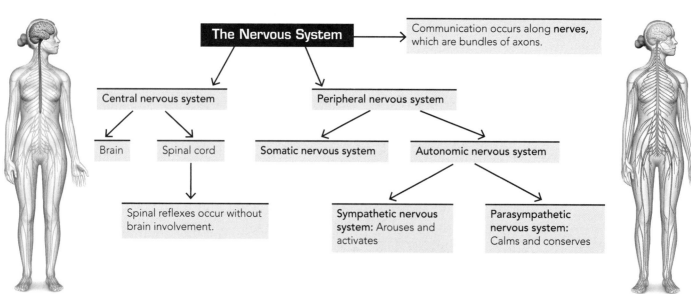

The Nervous System

Communication occurs along nerves, which are bundles of axons.

Central nervous system

Peripheral nervous system

Brain

Spinal cord

Somatic nervous system

Autonomic nervous system

Spinal reflexes occur without brain involvement.

Sympathetic nervous system: Arouses and activates

Parasympathetic nervous system: Calms and conserves

The Endocrine System → Communication through hormones released into the bloodstream → **Hypothalamus:** Links brain and endocrine system; hunger, thirst, sleep, sexual behavior →

Important glands
• Pineal gland
• Pancreas
• Thyroid
• **Adrenal glands**
• **Pituitary gland**

The Brain

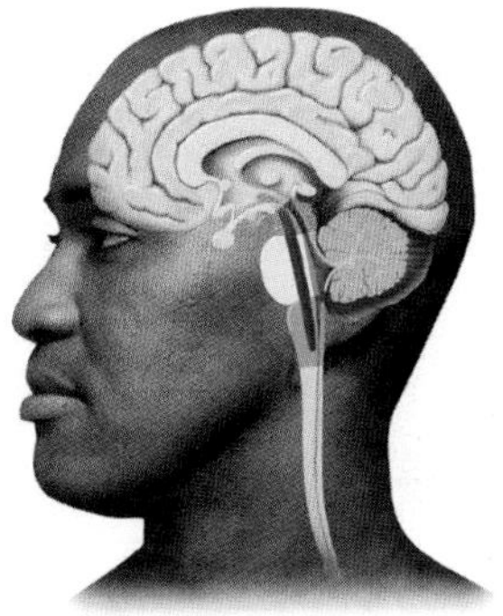

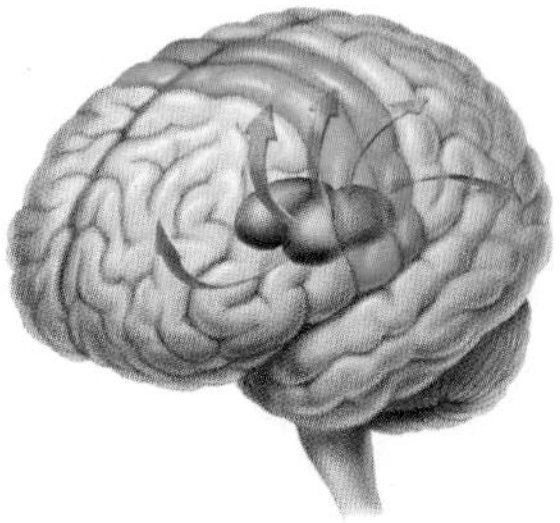

A complex, integrated, and dynamic system of interconnected neurons

Capable of changing in response to environmental stimulation; characterized by:
Functional plasticity: Capacity to shift functions from damaged to undamaged brain areas
Structural plasticity: Capacity to change physical structure
Neurogenesis: Capacity to develop new neurons through the lifespan

Jupiter Images/Photos.com/Alamy

Brainstem

Hindbrain: Connects spinal cord and brain

Midbrain: Preliminary processing of auditory and visual information

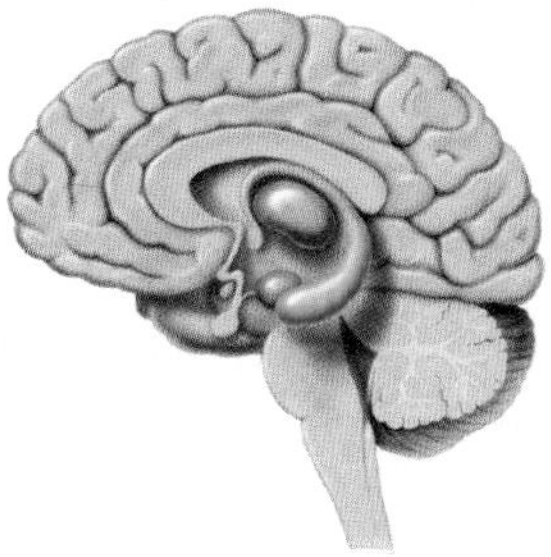

Medulla: Controls vital life functions
Pons: Coordinates movement on left and right side of body
Cerebellum: Coordinates movements, balance, and posture
Reticular formation: Regulates attention, alertness, and sleep

Forebrain

Limbic system: Structures beneath the cerebral cortex

Hippocampus: Memory
Thalamus: Relays sensory information; awareness and attention
Hypothalamus: Links brain and endocrine system; hunger, thirst, sleep, sexual behavior
Amygdala: Emotional responses and memory

Cerebral cortex: Wrinkled outer portion of forebrain Divided into two **cerebral hemispheres,** connected by **corpus callosum**

Occipital lobe: Primary visual cortex; processes visual information
Parietal lobe: Somatosensory cortex; processes touch and other body information
Temporal lobe: Primary auditory cortex; processes auditory information
Frontal lobe: Primary motor cortex; controls voluntary movement

Specialization in the Cerebral Hemispheres → Pierre Paul Broca (1824–1880)
Karl Wernicke (1848–1905)
Provided evidence for **cortical localization:** functions localized in the brain; and **lateralization of function:** some functions processed by one side of brain

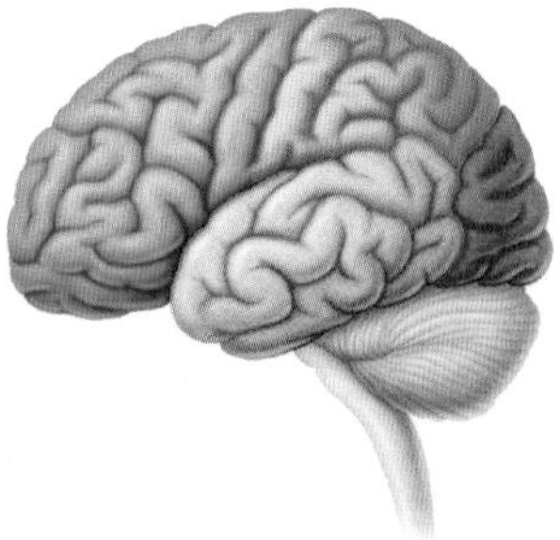

Roger Sperry (1913–1994)
Split-brain research

Left cerebral hemisphere: language, especially grammar, writing, reading; arithmetic; verbal memory

Right cerebral hemisphere: visual-spatial tasks, patterns, faces, emotional expression, music

MYTH OR SCIENCE?

Is it true . . .

▶ That an object's color is not a fundamental property of the object?

▶ That pheromones can make some people irresistible to possible romantic partners?

▶ That different tastes are detected on different parts of your tongue?

▶ That some people continue to feel sensations from a body part after it has been amputated?

▶ That there is a scientific basis for ESP?

▶ That magnets can relieve pain?

Sensation and Perception

PROLOGUE

Learning to See

Mike was just three years old when a jar of chemicals, left in an old storage shed, exploded in his face. The blast destroyed his left eye and severely damaged his right eye. For more than four decades, Mike May was completely blind (Kurson, 2007). Despite his blindness, Mike accomplished much more than most people ever dream of achieving. Always athletic, Mike wrestled and played soccer in high school and college. As an adult, he earned a master's degree in international affairs from Johns Hopkins University, went to work

for the CIA, and then became a successful businessperson.

He also learned to skydive, windsurf, water ski, and snow ski. How does a blind person ski down mountains? With a guide skiing in front of him shouting "left" or "right" to identify obstacles, Mike hurtled down the most difficult black diamond slopes at speeds up to 65 miles per hour. In fact, Mike won several medals in national and international championships for blind downhill speed skiing. It was through skiing that Mike met his wife, Jennifer. An accomplished skier herself, she volunteered to be his guide at a ski slope.

In his forties, Mike started a successful company that develops global positioning

devices — along with other mobility devices — for the blind. The portable navigation system gives visually impaired people information about their location, landmarks, and streets whenever they travel (Kurson, 2007). Beyond this, Mike's keen sensory world of touch, sounds, and aroma was on the verge of expanding: A new surgical technique offered the chance to restore the vision in Mike's right eye. As the bandages were removed, Mike described "a whoosh! Of light blasting into my eye" (May, 2002). For the first time since he was 3 years old, Mike May could see.

The first time Mike could see Jennifer, he explained, "It was incredible, but the

Erik Isakson/Tetra images/Getty Images

truth is, I knew exactly what she looked like . . . [t]he same with my kids. Now, seeing other people that I can't touch, well, that's interesting because I couldn't see them before."What exactly could Mike see? Anatomically, his right eye was now normal, but his vision was closer to 20/1,000 than 20/20. He could see colors, shapes, lines, shadows, and light and dark patches, but his view of the world was quite blurry.

The structures of his eye were working, but his brain did not know how to interpret the signals it was receiving. As neuropsychologist Ione Fine (2002) explained, "Most people learn the language of vision between the age of birth and two years old. Mike has had to learn it as an adult."

What was it like the first time he went skiing after his surgery? Mike was dazzled by the sight of the dark green trees, the snow, and the distant peaks against the blue sky (May, 2004).

Surprisingly, Mike found it easier to ski with his eyes closed, with Jennifer skiing ahead and shouting out directions. With his eyes open, he was overwhelmed by all the visual stimuli and the frightening sense that objects were rushing toward him. This chapter discusses the ways in which our brains interpret the information our senses detect and make it possible for us to navigate our daily lives. At the end of this chapter, we will come back to Mike's story. ∿

⊙ IN THIS CHAPTER:

Sensation and Perception When listening to music, sensation involves the detection and experience of the sounds coming through the earbuds. Perception involves how the children interpret the sensory information as a song.

Introduction: What Are Sensation and Perception?

Glance around you. Notice the incredible variety of colors, shades, shadows, and images. Listen carefully to the diversity of sounds, loud and soft, near and far. Focus on everything that's touching you—your clothes, your shoes, the chair you're sitting on. Now, inhale deeply through your nose and identify the aromas in the air.

With these simple observations, you gathered information from four of your senses: vision, hearing, touch, and smell. Where does that information come from? Put simply, your senses are the gateways through which your brain receives all its information about the environment. It's a process that is so natural and automatic that we typically take it for granted until it is disrupted by illness or injury. Nevertheless, as Mike's story demonstrates, people with a limited or nonfunctional sense are amazingly adaptive. Often, they learn to compensate for the missing environmental information by relying on their other senses.

In this chapter, we will explore the overlapping processes of *sensation* and *perception*. **Sensation** refers to *the process of detecting a physical stimulus, such as light, sound, heat, or pressure.* **Perception** refers to *the process of integrating, organizing, and interpreting sensations.* Here's a simple example to contrast the two terms. Your eyes' physical response to light, colors, and shapes exemplifies *sensation*. Integrating and organizing those sensations so that you interpret the light, colors, and shapes as a painting, a flag, or some other object represents *perception*. Mike's visual world reflects this distinction. His eye was accurately transmitting visual information from his environment (*sensation*), but his brain was unable to make sense out of the information (*perception*).

Where does the process of sensation leave off and the process of perception begin? There is no clear boundary line between the two processes as we experience them.

Basic Principles of Sensation

■ KEY THEME
Sensation is the result of neural impulses transmitted to the brain from sensory receptors that have been stimulated by physical energy from the external environment.

⹂ KEY QUESTIONS
- What is a sensory threshold, and what are two main types of sensory thresholds?
- What is the process of transduction?
- How do sensory adaptation and Weber's law demonstrate that sensation is relative rather than absolute?

We're accustomed to thinking of the senses as being quite different from one another. However, all our senses involve some common processes. All sensation is a result of **sensory receptors**, *specialized cells unique to each sense organ that respond to a particular form of sensory stimulation.*

Imagine listening to music with a close friend. Your experience of hearing the music is a response to the physical energy of vibrations in the air, or sound waves. The feeling of sipping your milkshake comes from the pressure of the straw against your lips. The sweet taste of the milkshake is a response to the physical energy of dissolvable chemicals in your mouth, just as the distinctive aroma of burgers and fries is a response to airborne chemical molecules that you inhale through your nose. And the red color of the ketchup is a response to the physical energy of light waves reflecting from the sauce on your fries.

Sensory Thresholds We do not have an infinite capacity to detect all levels of energy. To be sensed, a stimulus must first be strong enough to be detected—loud enough to be heard, concentrated enough to be smelled, bright enough to be seen.

sensation The process of detecting a physical stimulus, such as light, sound, heat, or pressure.

perception The process of integrating, organizing, and interpreting sensations.

sensory receptors Specialized cells unique to each sense organ that respond to a particular form of sensory stimulation.

absolute threshold The smallest possible strength of a stimulus that can be detected half the time.

difference threshold The smallest possible difference between two stimuli that can be detected half the time; also called *just noticeable difference*.

transduction The process by which physical energy is converted into a coded neural signal that can be processed by the nervous system.

The point at which a stimulus is strong enough to activate a sensory receptor cell is called a *threshold.* There are two general kinds of sensory thresholds for each sense — the absolute threshold and the difference threshold.

The **absolute threshold** refers to *the smallest possible strength of a stimulus that can be detected half the time.* Why just half the time? The level for detection varies from person to person and from trial to trial. Because of this variability, researchers have arbitrarily set the limit as the minimum level of stimulation that can be detected half the time. Under ideal conditions (which rarely occur in normal daily life), our sensory abilities are far more sensitive than you might think (see **Table 3.1**).

The other important threshold involves detecting the *difference* between two stimuli. The **difference threshold** is *the smallest possible difference between two stimuli that can be detected half the time.* Another term for the difference threshold is *just noticeable difference,* which is abbreviated *jnd.*

The just noticeable difference will *vary* depending on its relation to the original stimulus. Imagine holding a small rock (the original stimulus). If a second small rock is placed in your hand, you will notice an increase in weight. But if you start off holding a heavy rock (the original stimulus), you might not detect an increase in weight when the same small rock is balanced on it. Weber's law is a principle of sensation holding that the size of a just noticeable difference is a constant proportion of the size of the initial stimulus. So, whether we can detect a change in the strength of a stimulus depends on the intensity of the *original* stimulus. This idea underscores that our psychological experience of sensation is *relative.*

Sensory receptors convert these different forms of physical energy into electrical impulses that are transmitted via neurons to the brain. *The process by which physical energy is converted into a coded neural signal that can be processed by the nervous system* is called **transduction**. These neural signals are sent from the sensory organs (like your eyes) to the brain, where perceptual processes organize and interpret the coded messages. **Figure 3.1** illustrates the steps involved in sensation and perception.

We are constantly being bombarded by many different forms of energy. For instance, at this very moment radio and television waves are bouncing around the atmosphere

TABLE 3.1

Absolute Thresholds

Sense	Absolute Threshold
Vision	A candle flame seen from 30 miles away on a clear, dark night
Hearing	The tick of a watch at 20 feet
Taste	One teaspoon of sugar in two gallons of water
Smell	One drop of perfume throughout a three-room apartment
Touch	A bee's wing falling on your cheek from a height of about half an inch

These classic examples of the absolute threshold for each sense were provided by psychologist Eugene Galanter (1962). In each case, people are able to sense these faint stimuli at least half the time.

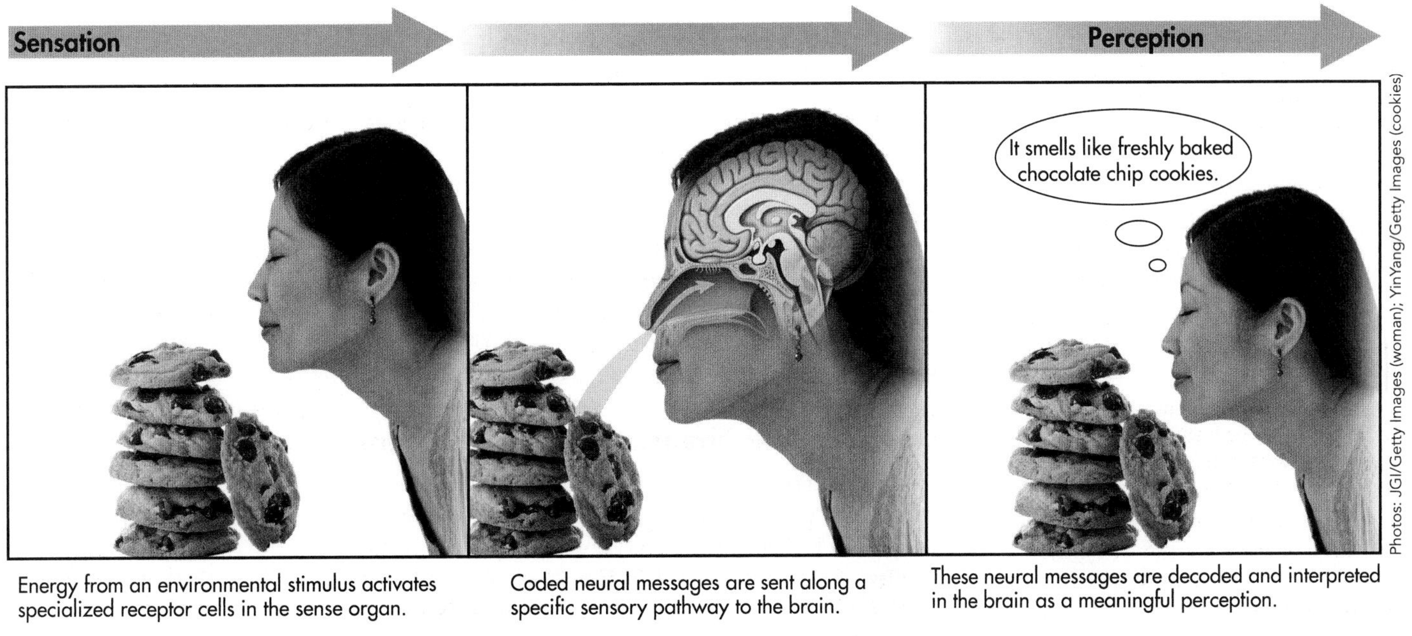

FIGURE 3.1 The Basic Steps of Sensation and Perception The first thing that happens is a stimulus activates receptor cells in the sense organ. Those neurons send a message along a sensory pathway to the brain, which is then decoded by the brain as a perception.

Sensation → Perception

It smells like freshly baked chocolate chip cookies.

Energy from an environmental stimulus activates specialized receptor cells in the sense organ.

Coded neural messages are sent along a specific sensory pathway to the brain.

These neural messages are decoded and interpreted in the brain as a meaningful perception.

Photos: JGI/Getty Images (woman); YinYang/Getty Images (cookies)

sensory adaptation The gradual decline in sensitivity to a constant stimulus.

wavelength The distance from one wave peak to another.

and passing through your body. However, human sensory receptors are so highly specialized that they are sensitive only to very specific types of energy (which is good, or you might be seeing *SpongeBob SquarePants* reruns in your brain when you least expect it). So, for any type of stimulation to be sensed, the stimulus energy must first be in a form that can be detected by our sensory receptor cells. Otherwise, transduction cannot occur.

Sensory Adaptation   Suppose your best friend has invited you over for tacos. As you walk in the front door, you're almost overwhelmed by the odor of onions, chilies, and garlic cooking on the stove. However, after just a few moments, you no longer notice the smell. Why? Because your sensory receptor cells become less responsive to a constant stimulus. *The gradual decline in sensitivity to a constant stimulus* is called **sensory adaptation**. Once again, we see that our experience of sensation is relative—in this case, relative to the *duration of exposure.*

Because of sensory adaptation, we become accustomed to constant stimuli, which allows us to quickly notice new or changing stimuli. This makes sense. If we were continually aware of all incoming stimuli, we'd be so overwhelmed with sensory information that we couldn't focus our attention. For example, once you manage to plant your tush on the sofa, you don't need to be constantly reminded that the sofa is beneath you.

Vision: From Light to Sight

How a Pit Viper Sees a Bird at Night   Does the world look different to other species? In many cases, yes. Each species has evolved a unique set of sensory capabilities. Pit vipers see infrared light, which we sense only as warmth. The bird here has been photographed through an infrared viewer. The image shows how a pit viper uses its infrared vision to detect warm-blooded prey at night (Van Dyke & Grace, 2010). Similarly, many insect and bird species can detect ultraviolet light, which is invisible to humans.

■ **KEY THEME**
Vision is the most-used human sense, so it is important to understand how it works.

▪ **KEY QUESTIONS**
- What is the visible spectrum?
- What are the key structures of the eye and their functions?
- What are rods and cones, and how do their functions differ?

A lone caterpillar on the screen door, the pile of dirty laundry in the corner, the intricate play of color and texture in a painting by Monet. The sense organ for vision is the eye, which contains receptor cells that are sensitive to the physical energy of *light.* But before we can talk about how the eye functions, we need to briefly discuss some characteristics of light as the visual stimulus.

What We See: The Nature of Light

Light is just one of many different kinds of electromagnetic energy that travel in the form of waves. Other forms of electromagnetic energy include X-rays, microwaves, and the infrared signals or radio waves transmitted by your TV's remote control. The various types of electromagnetic energy differ in **wavelength**, *the distance from one wave peak to another.*

Humans are capable of seeing only a minuscule portion of the electromagnetic energy range. In **Figure 3.2**, notice that the visible portion of the electromagnetic energy spectrum can be further divided into different wavelengths. As we'll discuss in more detail later, the different wavelengths of visible light correspond to our psychological perception of different colors.

How We See: The Human Visual System

Imagine you're watching your author Susan's cat Milla, shown in **Figure 3.3**, sun herself in a nearby window. How do light waves bouncing off Milla's fur culminate in the visual image of a brown cat with green eyes?

First, light waves reflected from the cat enter your eye, passing through the *cornea, pupil,* and *lens.* The *cornea,* a clear membrane that covers the front of the eye, helps

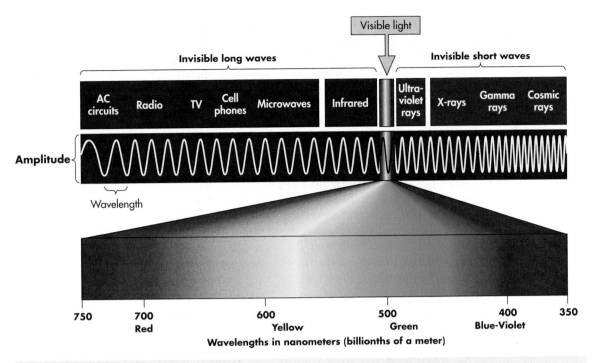

FIGURE 3.2 The Electromagnetic Spectrum We are surrounded by different kinds of electromagnetic energy waves, yet we see only a tiny portion—less than 1 percent—of the entire spectrum of electromagnetic energy. Some electronic instruments, like radio and television, are specialized receivers that detect a specific wavelength range. Similarly, the human eye is sensitive to a specific and very narrow range of wavelengths.

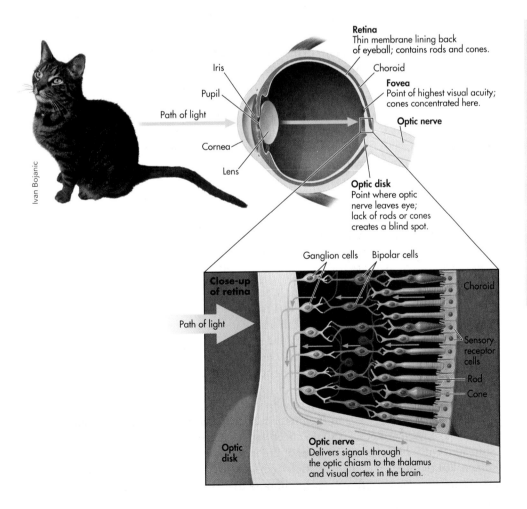

FIGURE 3.3 Path of Light in a Human Eye Reflected light waves pass through your cornea, pupil, and lens. The iris controls the amount of light entering the eye by controlling the size of the pupil. The lens changes shape to focus the incoming light onto the retina. As the light strikes the retina, the light energy activates the rods and cones. Signals from the rods and cones are collected by the bipolar cells, which transmit the information to the ganglion cells. The ganglion cell axons are bundled together to form the optic nerve, which transmits the information to the brain. The optic nerve leaves the eye at one point, creating a blind spot in our visual field. (For a demonstration of the blind spot, see Figure 3.4.)

pupil The opening in the middle of the iris that changes size to let in different amounts of light.

lens A transparent structure, located behind the pupil, that actively focuses, or bends, light as it enters the eye.

accommodation The process by which the lens changes shape to focus incoming light so that it falls on the retina.

retina (RET-in-uh) A thin, light-sensitive membrane located at the back of the eye, which contains the sensory receptors for vision.

rods The long, thin, blunt sensory receptors of the eye that are highly sensitive to light, but not to color.

cones The short, thick, pointed sensory receptors of the eye that detect color.

fovea (FOE-vee-uh) A small area in the center of the retina, composed entirely of cones, where visual information is most sharply focused.

blind spot The point at which the optic nerve leaves the eye, producing a small gap in the field of vision.

⌃ Ultraviolet Rays and Cataracts
People who live at high altitudes, as this blind woman in Nepal does, are more susceptible to developing cataracts. The long-term exposure to ultraviolet rays while living in the mountains can accelerate the degeneration and cause damage to the cornea, lens, and retina.

gather and direct incoming light. The **pupil** is *the opening in the middle of the iris that changes size to let in different amounts of light.* The pupil is surrounded by the *iris,* the colored structure that we refer to when we describe a person's eye color. The iris is actually a ring of muscular tissue that contracts or expands to precisely control the size of the pupil. In dim light, the iris widens the pupil to let light in; in bright light, the iris narrows the pupil.

The **lens** is *a transparent structure, located behind the pupil, that actively focuses, or bends, light as it enters the eye.* **Accommodation** is *the process by which the lens changes shape to focus the incoming light so that the light falls on the retina.* If the eyeball is abnormally shaped, the lens may not properly focus the incoming light on the retina, resulting in a visual disorder. In nearsightedness, or *myopia,* distant objects appear blurry because the light reflected off the objects focuses in front of the retina. In farsightedness, or *hyperopia,* objects near the eyes appear blurry because light reflected off the objects is focused behind the retina. During middle age, another form of farsightedness often occurs, called *presbyopia.* Presbyopia is caused when the lens becomes brittle and inflexible. In *astigmatism,* an abnormally curved eyeball results in blurry vision for lines in a particular direction. Corrective glasses remedy these conditions by intercepting and bending the light so that the image falls properly on the retina. Surgical techniques like LASIK correct visual disorders by reshaping the cornea so that light rays focus more directly on the retina.

The Retina: Rods and Cones

The **retina** is *a thin, light-sensitive membrane located at the back of the eye which contains the sensory receptors for vision* (see Figure 3.3). Contained in the retina are the *rods* and *cones.* **Rods** are *the long, thin, blunt sensory receptors of the eye that are highly sensitive to light, but not to color.* They are primarily responsible for peripheral vision and night vision. **Cones** are *the short, thick, pointed sensory receptors of the eye that detect color.* They are responsible for color vision and visual acuity. Each eye contains about 7 million cones, but 125 million rods. Because these sensory receptor cells respond to light, they are often called *photoreceptors.* When exposed to light, the rods and cones undergo a chemical reaction that results in electrical signals being generated by the bipolar and ganglion neurons.

Rods and cones react differently to *changes* in the amount of light. Rods adapt relatively slowly, reaching maximum sensitivity to light in about 30 minutes. In contrast, cones adapt quickly to bright light, reaching maximum sensitivity in about 5 minutes. That's why it takes several minutes for your eyes to adapt to the dim light of a darkened room but only a few moments to adapt to the brightness when you switch on the lights.

You may have noticed that it is difficult or impossible to distinguish colors in very dim light. This difficulty occurs because only the cones are sensitive to the different wavelengths that produce the sensation of color, and cones require much more light than rods do to function effectively. Cones are also specialized for seeing fine details and for vision in bright light.

The **fovea** is *a small area in the center of the retina, composed entirely of cones, where visual information is most sharply focused.* Cones are scattered throughout the rest of the retina, but they become progressively less common toward the periphery. There are no rods in the fovea. Images that do not fall on the fovea tend to be perceived as blurry or indistinct. One part of the retina, the *blind spot,* lacks rods and cones altogether. That is why we have a **blind spot,** *the point at which the optic nerve leaves the eye, producing a small gap in the field of vision.* To experience the blind spot, try the demonstration in **Figure 3.4**.

Why don't we notice this hole in our visual field? The most compelling explanation is that the brain actually fills in the missing background information (Ramachandran, 1992a, 1992b; Weil & Rees, 2010). In effect, signals from neighboring neurons fill in the blind spot with the color and texture of the surrounding visual information (Supèr & Romeo, 2011).

Design Pics Inc/Alamy Stock Photo

FIGURE 3.4 Demonstration of the Blind Spot Hold this book a few feet in front of you. Close your right eye and stare at the spider with your left eye. Slowly bring the book toward your face. At some point the moth will disappear because you have focused it onto the part of your retina where the blind spot is located. Notice, however, that you still perceive the spider web. That's because your brain has filled in information from the surrounding area (Komatsu, 2006).

Processing Visual Information

■ KEY THEME
Signals from the rods and cones undergo preliminary processing in the retina before they are transmitted to the brain.

≡ KEY QUESTIONS
- What are the bipolar and ganglion cells, and how do their functions differ?
- How is visual information transmitted from the retina to the brain?
- What properties of light correspond to color perceptions, and how is color vision explained?

Visual information is processed primarily in the brain. However, before visual information is sent to the brain, it undergoes some preliminary processing in the retina by specialized neurons called *ganglion cells*. This preliminary processing of visual data in the cells of the retina is possible because the retina develops from a bit of brain tissue that migrates to the eye during fetal development (Hubel, 1995).

When the numbers of rods and cones are combined, there are over 130 million receptor cells in each retina. However, there are only about 1 million ganglion cells. How do just 1 million ganglion cells transmit messages from 130 million visual receptor cells?

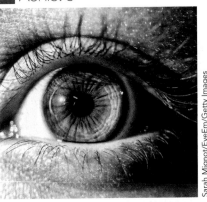

🅜 Achie√e

Can you identify the major structures and basic functions of the eye? Go to **Achieve** and try **Concept Practice: Structures of the Eye**.

Visual Processing in the Retina Information from the sensory receptors, the rods and cones, is first collected by specialized neurons, called *bipolar cells.* Look back at the lower portion of Figure 3.3. The bipolar cells then funnel the collection of raw data to the ganglion cells. Each ganglion cell receives information from the photoreceptors that are located in its *receptive field* in a particular area of the retina. In this early stage of visual processing, each ganglion cell combines, analyzes, and encodes the information from the photoreceptors in its receptive field before transmitting the information to the brain (Ringach, 2009).

Signals from rods and signals from cones are processed differently in the retina. For the most part, a single ganglion cell receives information from only one or two cones but might well receive information from a hundred or more rods. The messages from

optic nerve The thick nerve that exits from the back of the eye and carries visual information to the visual cortex in the brain.

optic chiasm (KY az-ulim) The point in the brain where the optic nerve fibers from each eye meet and partly cross over to the opposite side of the brain.

these many different rods are combined in the retina before they are sent to the brain. Thus, the brain receives less specific visual information from the rods and messages of much greater visual detail from the cones.

As an analogy to how rod information is processed, imagine listening to a hundred people trying to talk at once over the same telephone line. You would hear the sound of many people talking, but individual voices would be blurred. Now imagine listening to the voice of a single individual being transmitted across the same telephone line. Every syllable and sound would be clear and distinct. In much the same way, cones use the ganglion cells to provide the brain with more specific visual information than is received from rods.

Because of this difference in how information is processed, cones are especially important in *visual acuity*—the ability to see fine details. Visual acuity is strongest when images are focused on the fovea because of the high concentration of cones there.

From Eye to Brain How is information transmitted from the ganglion cells of the retina to the brain? The 1 million axons of the ganglion cells are bundled together to form the **optic nerve,** *the thick nerve that exits from the back of the eye and carries visual information to the visual cortex in to the brain.* The optic nerve has about the same diameter as a pencil. The **optic chiasm** is *the point in the brain where the optic nerve fibers from each eye meet and partly cross over to the opposite side of the brain.* For each eye, the axons from the right visual field cross over and project to the left side of the brain, and the axons from the left visual field cross over and project to the right side of the brain (see **Figure 3.5**).

From the optic chiasm, most of the optic nerve axons project to the brain structure called the thalamus. (For more on the brain structures involved in vision, see the chapter on neuroscience.) This primary pathway seems to be responsible for processing information about form, color, brightness, and depth. A smaller number of axons follow a detour to areas in the midbrain before they make their way to the thalamus. This secondary pathway seems to be involved in processing information about the location of an object.

From the thalamus, the signals are sent to the visual cortex, where they are decoded and interpreted. When those additional levels of processing fail, usually due to damage to the occipital cortex, a rare phenomenon called *blindsight* can emerge. Blindsight describes a condition where an individual believes that they cannot see. This phenomenon is particularly interesting because it highlights the distinction between sensation and perception. The sensory input from the eyes and thalamus are intact, so individuals sense visual stimuli. However, perception is not possible because

FIGURE 3.5 Neural Pathways from Eye to Brain The bundled axons of the ganglion cells form the optic nerve, which exits the retina at the optic disk. The optic nerves from the left and right eyes meet at the optic chiasm, then split apart. For each eye, the nerve fibers from the right visual field cross over and project to the left side of the brain, and the nerve fibers from the left visual field cross over and project to the right side of the brain. Most of the nerve fibers travel to the thalamus and then on to the visual cortex of the occipital lobe.

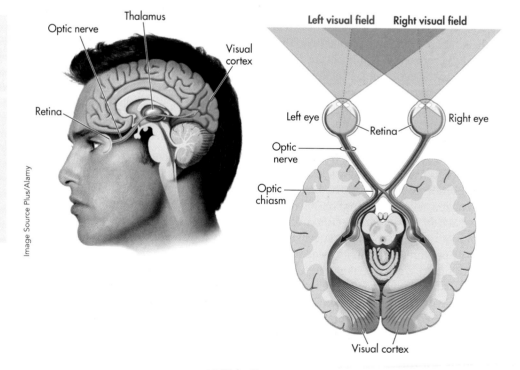

Image Source Plus/Alamy

the occipital cortex is damaged. For example, if you hold up a ball and ask some-one with blindsight what they "see," they will say, "nothing." However, if you gently tossed the ball toward the person with blindsight, they would either catch it or bat it away—even though they cannot "see" it. This is because their eyes and thalamus are intact and can produce simple reflexes without perceptual awareness in the cortex (Ajina & Bridge, 2017).

Most of the receiving neurons in the visual cortex of the brain are highly specialized. Each responds to a particular type of visual stimulation—such as angles, edges, lines, and other forms—and even to the movement and distance of objects (Hubel & Wiesel, 2005; Livingstone & Hubel, 1988). These neurons are sometimes called *feature detectors* because they detect, or respond to, particular features or aspects of more complex visual stimuli. Reassembling the features into a recognizable image involves additional levels of processing that rely on the visual cortex communicating fluently with other parts of the brain.

Understanding exactly how neural responses of individual feature detection cells become integrated into the visual perceptions of faces and objects is a major goal of contemporary neuroscience (Celesia, 2010; Mahon & Caramazza, 2011). Experience also plays an important role in the development of perception, especially visual percep-tion (Huber et al., 2015). In the Focus on Neuroscience box, we explore another percep-tual phenomenon, the fascinating experience of synesthesia.

Color Vision

We see images of an apple, a banana, and an orange because these objects reflect light waves. But why do we perceive that the apple is red and the banana yellow? What makes an orange orange?

The Experience of Color: What Makes an Orange Orange? Color is *the perceptual experience of different wavelengths of light, involving hue, saturation (purity), and brightness (intensity).* To explain how we perceive color, we must discuss the three properties of the light wave—hue, saturation, and brightness. *Hue* varies with the wavelength of light; different wavelengths are perceived as different colors. *Saturation* corresponds to the purity of the wavelength; a color produced by a single wavelength will appear vivid, while a color produced by a mix of wavelengths will appear faded. *Brightness* corresponds to the amplitude of the wavelength; the higher the amplitude, the brighter the color appears to be. Some of you might be familiar with these terms from software filters that adjust these aspects of photos to improve their appearance.

So what makes an orange orange? Intuitively, it seems obvious that the color of any object is a property that can't be separated from the object—unless we spill paint or spaghetti sauce on it. In reality, *color is a learned perception in the brain* (Werner et al., 2007). Color is not a fundamental property of any object.

Our perception of color is primarily determined by the wavelength of light that an object reflects. If your T-shirt is red, it's red because the cloth is *reflecting* only the wavelength of light that corresponds to the red portion of the spectrum. The T-shirt is *absorbing* the wavelengths that correspond to all other colors. An object appears white because it *reflects* all the wavelengths of visible light and absorbs none. An object appears black when it *absorbs* all the wavelengths of visible light and reflects none. Of course, in everyday life, our perceptions of color are also strongly affected by the amount or type of light falling on an object or the textures and colors that surround it (Purves, 2009; Shevell & Kingdom, 2008).

How We See Color Color vision has interested scientists for hundreds of years. The first scientific theory of color vision, proposed by Hermann von Helmholtz (1821–1894) in the mid-1800s, was called the *trichromatic theory.* A rival theory, the *opponent-process theory,* was proposed in the late 1800s. Each theory was capable of explaining some aspects of color vision, but neither could explain all aspects of color vision. Technological

▲ **When Red + Blue + Green = White** When light waves of different wavelengths are combined, the wavelengths are added together, producing the perception of a different color. When green light is combined with red light, yellow light is produced. When the wavelengths of red, green, and blue light are added together, we perceive the blended light as white. If you're wondering why mixing paints together produces a muddy mess rather than pure white, it's because the wavelengths are *subtracted* rather than added. Each color of pigment absorbs a different part of the color spectrum, and each time a color is added, less light is reflected. Thus, the mixed color appears darker. If you mix all three primary colors together, they absorb the entire spectrum—so we perceive the splotch as black.

MYTH ▶ SCIENCE

Is it true that an object's color is not a fundamental property of the object?

color The perceptual experience of different wavelengths of light, involving hue, saturation (purity), and brightness (intensity).

FOCUS ON NEUROSCIENCE

Synesthesla

The word *synethesia* is a combination of the Greek words for together *(syn)* and perception *(aesthesis)*, alluding to the meaning of the word as perceiving multiple senses together. Specifically, synesthesia is a condition in which one sense is perceived simultaneously alongside another sense or senses. Any combination of senses can be involved in synesthesia, but the most common type of synesthesia is when words or numbers are also perceived as colors. It is important to keep in mind that these perceptions are unique for each person with synesthesia. For example, they might see the word *bicycle* as lavender or the letter *A* as dark green. Neuropsychologists call this particular blending of senses word–color synesthesia.

The condition of synesthesia was reported as early as the nineteenth century. Even early researchers noticed that synesthesia seemed to run in families, which would suggest a genetic basis for the condition. But it was only early in this century that research confirmed synesthesia as an actual biological condition (Ramachandran & Hubbard, 2001). The neurologist Richard Cytowic is among a group of researchers who have suggested universal standards for understanding the condition of synesthesia (Cytowic, 1995; Cytowic & Eagleman, 2009):

1. Synesthesia is outside of a person's control. The perceptions occur involuntarily.

2. Synesthesia results in actual sensory experiences. It does not just occur in the mind. For example, a person does not imagine the color green but actually "sees" the color green.

3. Synesthesia is consistent. This means that if you see the color blue when you hear the name Grace, this will always be the case.

4. People who experience synesthesia are more likely to remember the second perception than the first. If someone sees the color blue when they hear the name Grace, they're more likely to remember the color blue than the name Grace when they see her.

5. Synesthesia is often accompanied by intense emotional experiences.

Today neuroscientists agree that there is a neural basis for synesthesia, which results from atypical connections in the brain that allow multiple sensory inputs to be perceived simultaneously (Rothen & Terhune, 2012). However, there is no consensus on the precise brain circuitry or neural mechanisms involved in the experience of synesthesia. Synesthesia experts Cytowic and Eagleman (2009) favor the explanation that synesthesia results from additional neural activity among existing connections rather than the idea that people with synesthesia have *more* connectivity in their brains than others.

Other researchers disagree with Cytowic and Eagleman. For example, Ramachandran and Hubbard have proposed that synesthesia does in fact result from increased connectivity (or hyperconnectivity) between the brain regions that supply the perceptual experiences involved in synesthesia (Weiss et al., 2001; Ramachandran & Hubbard, 2001). A number of brain imaging studies seem to support this idea. Dovern and colleagues (2012) have published a compelling series of brain studies, using fMRI images supporting the idea that the brains of people with synesthesia do in fact show hyperconnectivity. For example, brain images have shown that people who experience the word–color form of synesthesia, have an increased number of connections between the brain regions that process color information (in the occipital lobe) and the brain regions that process language comprehension (in the temporal lobe). These connections are not seen in control participants who do not experience synesthesia. Neuroscientists may need more time to reach a consensus on the precise brain basis of synesthesia. However, they would all agree that it is one of the most fascinating (and thankfully harmless) irregularities in human perception.

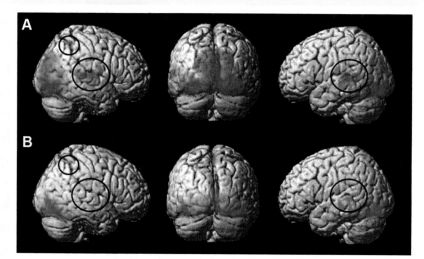

❮ Synesthesia and Hyperconnectivity A person with synesthesia perceives one sense simultaneously with another sense or senses. Researchers have suggested that synesthesia results from hyperconnectivity between brain regions that process perceptions (Weiss et al., 2001; Ramachandran & Hubbard, 2001). These brain images show this increased activity in the occipital lobe and the temporal lobe in part A compared with part B. Reprinted by permission of the *Journal of Neuroscience*, Figure 3 from Dovern, Anna; Fink, Gereon R.; Fromme, A. Christina B.; Wohlschläger, Afra M.; Weiss, Peter H.; & Riedl, Valentin. (2012). Intrinsic network connectivity reflects consistency of synesthetic experiences. Journal of Neuroscience, 32, 7614–7621. https://doi.org/10.1523/JNEUROSCI.5401-11.2012. Permission conveyed through Copyright Clearance Center, Inc.

advances in the past few decades have allowed researchers to gather direct physiological evidence to test both theories. The resulting evidence indicates that *both* theories of color vision are accurate. Each theory describes color vision at a different stage of visual processing (Hubel, 1995).

The Trichromatic Theory As you'll recall, only the cones are involved in color vision. The **trichromatic theory of color vision** is the *theory that sensation of color results because cones are especially sensitive to red light (long wavelengths), green light (medium wavelengths), or blue light (short wavelengths)*. For the sake of simplicity, we will refer to the three varieties of cones as red-sensitive, green-sensitive, and blue-sensitive cones, but keep in mind that there is some overlap in the wavelengths to which a cone is sensitive (Purves, 2009). A given cone will be very sensitive to one of the three colors and only slightly responsive to the other two.

When a color other than red, green, or blue strikes the retina, it stimulates a *combination* of cones. For example, if yellow light strikes the retina, both the red-sensitive and green-sensitive cones are stimulated; purple light evokes strong reactions from red-sensitive and blue-sensitive cones. The trichromatic theory of color vision received compelling research support in 1964, when George Wald showed that different cones were indeed activated by red, blue, and green light.

The trichromatic theory provides a good explanation for the most common form of color blindness: red–green color blindness. People with red–green color blindness cannot discriminate between red and green. That's because they have normal blue-sensitive cones, but their other cones are *either* red-sensitive or green-sensitive (Carroll et al., 2009). Thus, red and green look the same to them. Because red–green color blindness is so common, stoplights are designed so that the location of the light as well as its color provides information to drivers. In vertical stoplights the red light is always on top, and in horizontal stoplights the red light is always on the far left.

The Opponent-Process Theory The trichromatic theory cannot account for all aspects of color vision. One important phenomenon that the theory does not explain is the afterimage. An afterimage is a visual experience that occurs after the original source of stimulation is no longer present.

Afterimages can be explained by the opponent-process theory of color vision, which proposes a different mechanism of color detection from the one set forth in the trichromatic theory. The **opponent-process theory of color vision** is the *theory that color vision is the product of opposing pairs of color receptors: red–green, blue–yellow, and black–white; when one member of a pair is stimulated, the other is inhibited*. The members of each color pair *oppose* each other. If red is stimulated, green is inhibited; if green is stimulated, red is inhibited. Green and red cannot be stimulated simultaneously. The same is true for the blue–yellow pair. In addition, black and white act as an opposing pair. Color, then, is sensed and encoded in terms of its proportion of red *or* green and blue *or* yellow.

trichromatic theory of color vision
Theory that the sensation of color results because cones are especially sensitive to red light (long wavelengths), green light (medium wavelengths), or blue light (short wavelengths).

opponent-process theory of color vision
Theory that color vision is the product of opposing pairs of color receptors: red–green, blue–yellow, and black–white; when one member of a pair is stimulated, the other is inhibited.

PicturesWild/Shutterstock

❮ **The Most Common Form of Color Blindness** To someone with the most common form of red–green color blindness, these two photographs look almost exactly the same. People with this type of color blindness have normal blue-sensitive cones, but their other cones are sensitive to either red *or* green. Because of the way red–green color blindness is genetically transmitted, it is much more common in men than in women. About 8 percent of the male population is born with red–green color deficiency, and about a quarter of these males experience only the colors coded by the blue–yellow cones. People who are completely color blind and see the world only in shades of black, white, and gray are extremely rare (Shevell & Kingdom, 2008).

For example, red light evokes a response of RED-YES–GREEN-NO in the red–green opponent pair. Yellow light evokes a response of BLUE-NO–YELLOW-YES. Colors other than red, green, blue, and yellow activate one member of each of these pairs to differing degrees. Purple stimulates the *red* of the red–green pair plus the *blue* of the blue–yellow pair. Orange activates *red* in the red–green pair and *yellow* in the blue–yellow pair.

Afterimages can be explained when the opponent-process theory is combined with the general principle of sensory adaptation (Jameson & Hurvich, 1989). If you stare continuously at one color, sensory adaptation eventually occurs and your visual receptors become less sensitive to that color. What happens when you subsequently stare at a white surface?

If you remember that white light is made up of the wavelengths for *all* colors, you may be able to predict the result. The receptors for the original color have adapted to the constant stimulation, and, temporarily, they do not respond to that color. Instead, only the receptors for the opposing color will be activated, and you perceive the wavelength of only the *opposing* color. For example, if you stare at a patch of green, your green receptors eventually become "tired." The wavelengths for both green and red light are reflected by the white surface, but since the green receptors are "off," only the red receptors are activated.

An Integrated Explanation of Color Vision At the beginning of this section, we said that current research has shown that *both* the trichromatic theory and the opponent-process theory of color vision are accurate. How can both theories be right? It turns out that each theory correctly describes color vision at a *different level* of visual processing.

As described by the *trichromatic theory,* the cones of the retina do indeed respond to and encode color in terms of red, green, and blue. But recall that signals from the cones and rods are partially processed in the ganglion cells before being transmitted along the optic nerve to the brain. Researchers now believe that an additional level of color processing takes place in the ganglion cells (Demb & Brainard, 2010).

As described by the *opponent-process theory,* the ganglion cells respond to and encode color in terms of opposing pairs (DeValois & DeValois, 1975; Solomon & Lennie, 2007). In the brain, the thalamus and visual cortex also encode color in terms of opposing pairs. Consequently, both theories contribute to our understanding of the process of color vision. Each theory simply describes color vision at a different stage of visual processing (Hubel, 1995; Werner et al., 2007).

Hearing: From Vibration to Sound

■ KEY THEME
Auditory sensation, or hearing, results when sound waves are collected in the outer ear, amplified in the middle ear, and converted to neural messages in the inner ear.

≡ KEY QUESTIONS
• How do sound waves produce different auditory sensations?
• What are the key structures of the ear and their functions?
• How do place theory and frequency theory explain pitch perception?

The scientific term for the sense of hearing is **audition**. Hearing is the first sense that humans develop. Fascinating research has shown that infants' hearing develops while they are still in utero (Mehler et al., 1978). Hearing their mother's voice while still in the womb helps the brain become organized for learning language (Uchida-Ota et al., 2019). The ability to sense and perceive very subtle differences in sound is important to physical survival, social interactions, and language development. Most of the time, all of us are bathed in sound—so much so that moments of near-silence can seem almost eerie.

Achieve

Go to **Achieve** and watch **Video: Vision: How We See** to review visual processing and how we perceive color.

audition The scientific term for the sense of hearing.

What We Hear: The Nature of Sound

Whether it's the ear-splitting screech of metal on metal or the subtle whir of a grasshopper's wings, *sound waves* are the physical stimuli that produce our sensory experience of sound. Usually, sound waves are produced by the rhythmic vibration of air molecules, but sound waves can be transmitted through other media, such as water, too. Our perception of sound is directly related to the physical properties of sound waves (see **Figure 3.6**).

One of the first things that we notice about a sound is how loud it is. *Loudness* is determined by the intensity, or *amplitude,* meaning the height, of a sound wave and is measured in units called *decibels.* Zero decibels represents the loudness of the softest sound that humans can hear, or the absolute threshold for hearing. As decibels increase, perceived loudness increases.

Pitch refers to *the relative highness or lowness of a sound, determined by the frequency of a sound wave.* **Frequency** refers to *the rate of vibration, or number of waves per second,* and is measured in units called *hertz.* Hertz simply refers to the number of wave peaks per second. The faster the vibration, the higher the frequency. A higher-frequency wave produces a tone that is higher in pitch. If you pluck the high E and the low E strings on a guitar, you'll notice that the low E vibrates far fewer times per second than does the high E.

Most of the sounds we experience do not consist of a single frequency but are *complex,* consisting of several sound-wave frequencies. The *complexity* of a sound wave, or its unique combination of frequencies, produces the distinctive quality, or *timbre,* of a sound, which enables us to distinguish easily between the same note played on a saxophone and on a piano. Every human voice has its own distinctive timbre, which is why you can immediately identify a friend's voice on the telephone from just a few words.

How We Hear: The Path of Sound

The ear is made up of the outer ear, the middle ear, and the inner ear. Sound waves are *collected* in the outer ear, *amplified* in the middle ear, and *transduced,* or *transformed into neural messages,* in the inner ear (see **Figure 3.7**).

The **outer ear** is *the part of the ear that collects sound waves; it includes the pinna, the ear canal, and the eardrum.* The pinna is that oddly shaped flap of skin and cartilage that's attached to each side of your head. The pinna helps us pinpoint the location of a sound. But the pinna's primary role is to catch sound waves and funnel them into the ear canal. Animals who have relatively large, and often rotating, pinnas—such as deer and rabbits—tend to be prey and have to be able to pick up the sounds of stealthy predators looking for them as their next meal. The sound wave travels down the ear canal and then bounces into the **eardrum,** *a tightly stretched membrane that vibrates when hit by sound waves.*

The eardrum separates the outer ear from the **middle ear,** *the part of the ear that amplifies sound waves; it consists of three small bones: the hammer, the anvil, and the stirrup.* Each bone sets the next bone in motion. The joint action of these three bones almost doubles the amplification of the sound. The innermost bone, the stirrup, transmits the amplified vibration to the *oval window.* If the tiny bones of the middle ear are damaged or become brittle, as they sometimes do in old age, *conduction deafness* may result. Conduction deafness can be helped by a hearing aid, which amplifies sounds.

Like the eardrum, the oval window is a membrane, but it is many times smaller than the eardrum. The oval window separates the middle ear from the **inner ear,** *the part of the ear where sound is transduced into neural impulses; it consists of the cochlea and semicircular canals.* As the oval window vibrates, the vibration is next relayed to an inner structure called the **cochlea,** *the coiled, fluid-filled inner-ear structure that contains the basilar membrane and hair cells.* The word *cochlea* comes from the Greek word for "snail," and the spiral shape of the cochlea does resemble a snail's shell.

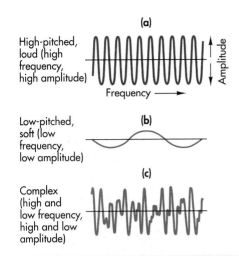

FIGURE 3.6 Characteristics of Sound Waves The length of a wave, its height, and its complexity determine the loudness, pitch, and timbre that we hear. The sound produced by **(a)** would be high-pitched and loud. The sound produced by **(b)** would be soft and low. The sound in **(c)** is complex, like the sounds we usually experience in the natural world.

pitch The relative highness or lowness of a sound, determined by the frequency of a sound wave.

frequency The rate of vibration, or the number of sound waves per second.

outer ear The part of the ear that collects sound waves; includes the pinna, the ear canal, and the eardrum.

eardrum A tightly stretched membrane that vibrates when hit by sound waves.

middle ear The part of the ear that amplifies sound wave; it consists of three small bones: the hammer, the anvil, and the stirrup.

inner ear The part of the ear where sound is transduced into neural impulses; it consists of the cochlea and semicircular canals.

cochlea (COKE-lee-uh or COCK-lee-uh) The coiled, fluid-filled inner-ear structure that contains the basilar membrane and hair cells.

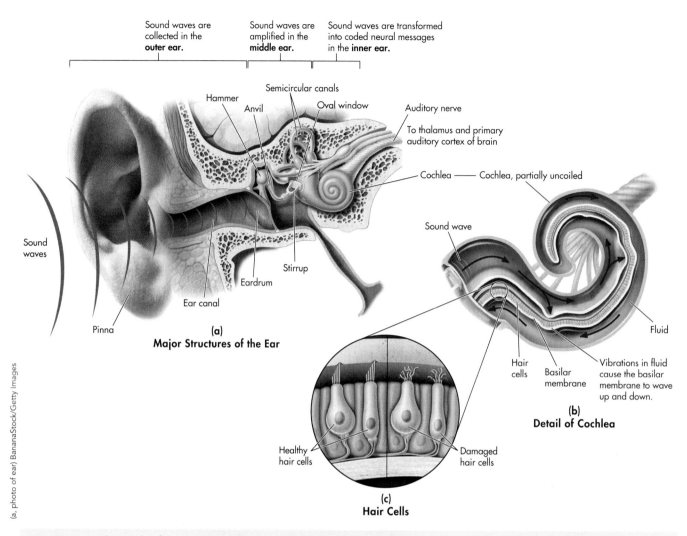

FIGURE 3.7 **The Path of Sound Through the Human Ear** The path that sound waves take through the major structures of the human ear is shown in **(a)**. After being caught by the outer ear, sound waves are funneled down the ear canal to the eardrum, which transfers the vibrations to the structures of the middle ear. In the middle ear, the vibrations are amplified and transferred in turn to the oval window and on to the fluid-filled cochlea in the inner ear **(b)**. As the fluid in the cochlea vibrates, the basilar membrane ripples, bending the hair cells, which appear as rows of yellow tips in the top right section of the color-enhanced scanning electron micrograph **(c)**. The bending of the hair cells stimulates the auditory nerve, which ultimately transmits the neural messages to the auditory cortex in the brain.

basilar membrane (BAZ-uh-ler or BAYZ-uh-ler) The membrane within the cochlea of the ear that contains the hair cells.

hair cells The hair-like sensory receptors for sound, which are embedded in the basilar membrane.

frequency theory The view that the basilar membrane vibrates at the same frequency as the sound wave.

place theory The view that different frequencies cause larger vibrations at different locations along the basilar membrane.

Although the cochlea is a very complex structure, it is quite tiny — no larger than a pea.

As the fluid in the cochlea ripples, the vibration in turn is transmitted to the **basilar membrane**, *the membrane within the cochlea of the ear that contains the hair cells. The hair-like sensory receptors for sound, which are embedded in the basilar membrane* are called **hair cells**.

The hair cells bend as the basilar membrane ripples. It is here that transduction finally takes place: The physical vibration of the sound waves is converted into neural impulses. As the hair cells bend, they stimulate the cells of the auditory nerve, which carries the neural information to the thalamus and the auditory cortex in the brain (Hackett & Kaas, 2009; Recanzone & Sutter, 2008).

You may have experienced temporary damage to your hair cells after attending a loud and prolonged event, such as a music concert, and your ears ring for hours (sometimes days). Your ears are ringing because the hair cells have been bent for so long that they are having a hard time "getting up." Their bent position continues to stimulate

TABLE 3.2

Decibel Levels of Some Common Sounds

Decibels	Examples	Exposure Danger
140	Shotgun blast, jet plane	Any exposure is dangerous
120	Speakers at rock concert, sandblasting, thunderclap	Immediate danger
100	Chain saw, pneumatic drill	2 hours
90	Truck traffic, noisy home appliances, lawn mower	Less than 8 hours
80	Subway, heavy city traffic, alarm clock at 2 feet	More than 8 hours
70	Busy traffic, noisy restaurant	Critical level begins with constant exposure
50	Light traffic at a distance, refrigerator	
30	Quiet library, soft whisper	
0	Lowest sound audible to human ear	

⌄ Damage to the hair cells is cumulative, and noise exposure, not age, is the leading cause of hearing loss. One survey found that 12–15 percent of school-age children have some hearing deficits due to noise exposure (Harrison, 2012). Along with exposure to environmental noise, phones and other personal music players can also expose the listener to dangerously high levels of noise (Breinbauer et al., 2012). As a general rule, if others can hear what you are listening to with your earbuds or headphones, the volume is too high.

JGI/Jamie Grill/Blend Images/Getty Images

the auditory nerve even in the absence of actual sound, which most people experience as ringing or buzzing (Strimbu et al., 2019). Over time or with prolonged exposure to loud noise, the hair cells may lose their flexibility altogether, and in doing so significantly reduce a person's hearing (Wu et al., 2020).

Damage to the hair cells or auditory nerve can result in *nerve deafness*. Exposure to loud noise can cause nerve deafness (see **Table 3.2**). Hearing aids are of no use in this form of deafness because the neural messages cannot reach the brain. However, nerve deafness *can*, in some cases, be treated with a *cochlear implant*, which is an electronic device surgically implanted behind the ear (see photo).

Kathy deWitt/Alamy

Distinguishing Pitch How do we distinguish between the low-pitched throb of a bass guitar and the high-pitched tones of a piccolo? Remember, pitch is determined by the *frequency* of a sound wave. The basilar membrane is a key structure involved in our discrimination of pitch. Two complementary theories describe the role of the basilar membrane in the transmission of differently pitched sounds.

Frequency theory is *the view that the basilar membrane vibrates at the same frequency as the sound wave.* Thus, a sound wave of about 100 hertz would excite each hair cell along the basilar membrane to vibrate 100 times per second, and neural impulses would be sent to the brain at the same rate. However, there's a limit to how fast neurons can fire. Individual neurons cannot fire faster than about 1,000 times per second. But we can sense sounds with frequencies that are many times higher than 1,000 hertz. A child, for example, can typically hear pitches ranging from about 20 to 20,000 hertz.

So how do we hear higher-pitched sounds above 3,000 hertz? **Place theory** is *the view that different frequencies cause larger vibrations at different locations along the basilar membrane.* High-frequency sounds, for example, cause maximum vibration near the stirrup end of the basilar membrane. Lower-frequency sounds cause maximum

‹ Restoring Hearing Cochlear implants convert sound into electrical impulses that directly stimulate the auditory nerve via electrodes implanted in the cochlea. Cochlear implants do *not* restore normal hearing (Farris-Trimble et al., 2014). However, their use can allow hearing-impaired individuals to perceive speech and other everyday sounds (Clark et al., 2013; O'Donoghue, 2013).

⌄ Can Snakes Hear? Snakes have functional inner ears, but they don't have outer ears. So how do snakes hear? With their jaws. When a desert viper rests its head on the ground, a bone in its jaw picks up minute vibrations in the sand. From the jaw, these vibrations are transmitted along a chain of tiny bones to the cochlea in the inner ear, allowing the snake to hear the faint footsteps of a mouse or other prey (Freidel et al., 2008).

Andy Hunger/AGE Fotostock

olfaction Scientific name for the sense of smell.

gustation Scientific name for the sense of taste.

vibration at the opposite end. Thus, different pitches excite different hair cells along the basilar membrane. Higher-pitched sounds are interpreted according to the place where the hair cells are most active.

Both frequency theory and place theory are involved in explaining pitch (Kaas et al., 2013). Frequency theory helps explain low frequencies. Place theory helps explain high-pitched sounds. For midrange pitches, both place and frequency are involved.

The Chemical and Body Senses: Smell, Taste, Touch, and Position

■ KEY THEME
Chemical stimuli produce the sensations of smell and taste, while pressure and other stimuli are involved in touch, pain, position, and balance sensations.

≡ KEY QUESTIONS
- How do airborne molecules result in the sensation of an odor?
- What are the primary tastes, and how does the sensation of taste arise?
- How do fast and slow pain systems differ, and what is the gate-control theory of pain?
- How are body sensations of movement, position, and balance produced?

Olfaction is *the scientific name for the sense of smell.* **Gustation** is *the scientific name for the sense of taste.* The senses of smell and taste are closely linked. If you've ever temporarily lost your sense of smell because of a bad cold, you've probably noticed that your sense of taste was also disrupted. Even a hot fudge sundae tastes bland.

Smell and taste are linked in other ways, too. Unlike vision and hearing, which involve sensitivity to different forms of energy, the sensory receptors for taste and smell are specialized to respond to different types of *chemical* substances. That's why smell and taste are sometimes called the "chemical senses" (Travers & Travers, 2009).

People can get along quite well without a sense of smell. A surprisingly large number of people are unable to smell specific odors or lack a sense of smell completely, a condition called *anosmia.* In fact, a common symptom of COVID-19 is the loss of the sense of smell, typically for several weeks but much longer in some cases. Fortunately, humans gather most of their information about the world through vision and hearing. However, many animal species depend on chemical signals as their primary source of information.

Even for humans, smell and taste can provide important information about the environment. Tastes help us determine whether a particular substance is to be savored or spat out. Smells, such as the odor of a smoldering fire, leaking gas, or spoiled food, alert us to potential dangers.

▼ **What Does Popcorn Smell Like?**
English and other European languages have many abstract words that can be used to describe sights, tastes, and textures, but very few words for odors. Typically, odors are described as "smelling like" other objects, such as "smells moldy" or "smells lemony."

The same is not true of all languages, however. Two hunter-gatherer groups in the tropical rain forest of Malaysia and Thailand have rich odor vocabularies, and easily outscore English-speakers in identifying odors (Majid & Burenhult, 2014; Wnuk & Majid, 2014). For example, the Jahai people of Malaysia use the word *p?us* (pronounced pa-OOS) to describe the smell of old huts, day-old food, and cabbage (Majid, 2014). In a new study, members of another hunter-gatherer group in the Malaysia rain forest were better able to name odors than a neighboring group that cultivated rice (Majid & Kruspe, 2018). Thus, the olfactory expertise of hunter-gatherers may reflect the importance of smells in their culture.

How We Smell (Don't Answer That!)

The sensory stimuli that produce our sensation of an odor are *molecules in the air.* These airborne molecules are emitted by the substance we are smelling. We inhale them through the nose and through the opening in the palate at the back of the throat. In the nose, the molecules encounter millions of *olfactory receptor cells* located high in the nasal cavity. Many species use airborne chemical signals, called *pheromones,* to communicate information about territory, mating strategies, and so forth. What about humans? The In Focus box "Do Pheromones Influence Human Behavior?" explores this question.

Unlike the sensory receptors for hearing and vision, the olfactory receptors are constantly being replaced. Each cell lasts for only about 30 to 60 days. Like synaptic receptors, each odor receptor seems to be specialized to respond to molecules of a different chemical structure. When these olfactory receptor cells

Nutnarin Khetwong/Shutterstock

Do Pheromones Influence Human Behavior?

Many animals, including primates, communicate by releasing **pheromones,** *chemical signals that have evolved for communication with other members of the same species* (Drea, 2015; Wyatt, 2015). Pheromones may mark territories, advertise sexual status, or serve as warning signals. From insects to mammals, pheromones are used to communicate aggression, alarm, and fearful states (Radulescu & Mujica-Parodi, 2013). Pheromones are also extremely important in regulating sexual attraction, mating, and reproductive behavior in many animals (Wyatt, 2009). A lusty male cabbage moth, for example, can detect pheromones released from a sexually receptive female cabbage moth that is several miles away.

Do humans produce pheromones as other animals do? Early evidence for the existence of human pheromones comes from studies of the female menstrual cycle by University of Chicago biopsychologist Martha McClintock (1992). While still a college student, McClintock (1971) set out to scientifically investigate the folk notion that women who live in the same dorm eventually develop synchronized menstrual periods. McClintock found that the more time women spent together, the more likely their cycles were to be in sync. Later research showed that smelling an unknown chemical substance in underarm sweat from female donors synchronized the recipients' menstrual cycles with the donors' cycles (Preti et al., 1986; Stern & McClintock, 1998). But other studies find no evidence for menstrual synchrony among women (see Doty, 2014; Ziomkiewicz, 2006).

Since these findings, McClintock and other researchers have made a number of discoveries in their quest to identify human pheromones, which they prefer to call *human chemosignals.* The most likely candidates are chemicals found in steroid compounds that are naturally produced by the human body and found in sweat, armpit hair, blood, and semen. One study in McClintock's lab showed that exposure to a chemical compound in the perspiration of breast-feeding mothers significantly increased sexual motivation in other non–breast-feeding women (Spencer et al., 2004). The study's authors speculate that the presence of breast-feeding women acts as a social signal—an indicator that the social and physical environment is one in which pregnancy and breast-feeding will be supported.

Later studies found that the same chemical affected women's, but not men's, mood and attitudes. For example, it was shown

❮ **The Scent of Attraction** Some perfume manufacturers claim that their products contain human pheromones that will make you "irresistible" to members of the opposite sex. But is there any evidence that pheromones affect human sexual attraction?

Mario Castello/AGE Fotostock

to increase women's attraction to men at a speed-dating event (Saxton et al., 2008), improve positive mood (Bensafi et al., 2004), and increase generosity and positive mood in women playing an economic game (Perrotta et al., 2016). There is also evidence that human chemosignals are involved in communicating emotional states, including stress, anxiety, and fear (see Radulescu & Mujica-Parodi, 2013). For example, women watched either a frightening video or a neutral video while being exposed to either "neutral sweat" or "fear sweat." Regardless of which video the women watched, women who were exposed to the "fear sweat" were more likely to react with fearful expressions than the women who were exposed to the neutral sweat (de Groot et al., 2014).

It is a myth that pheromones make people irresistible to potential romantic partners. But, it

MYTH ◄ SCIENCE

Is it true that pheromones can make some people irresistible to possible romantic partners?

may be that these consciously undetectable chemosignals play an important role in communicating and synchronizing emotional states among people in groups (de Groot et al., 2014).

are stimulated by the airborne molecules, the stimulation is converted into neural messages that pass along their axons, bundles of which make up the *olfactory nerve.*

So far, hundreds of different odor receptors have been identified (Gottfried, 2010). Humans have about 350 different olfactory receptors, far fewer than the 1,000 different receptors in mice and rats. And scientists have identified only about 10 to 20 percent of the odor molecules that activate these receptors (Ravindran, 2016). We don't have a separate receptor for each of the estimated 10,000 different odors that we can detect, however. Rather, each receptor is like a letter in an olfactory alphabet. Just as different combinations of letters in the alphabet are used to produce recognizable words,

pheromones Chemical signals that have evolved for communication with other members of the same species; also called *chemosignals.*

Courtesy of Noam Sobel

▲ **Can Humans Track a Scent?** Dogs are famous for their ability to track a scent. Humans? Not so much. However, it turns out that people are better trackers than you might think. Scientists embedded a long line of chocolate-scented twine into the ground and then tested whether college students could track the scent using olfaction alone (Porter et al., 2007). To block all other sensory cues, participants wore eye masks, earmuffs, thick pads, and work gloves. Although the human trackers were able to locate and follow the trail, their average speed was only about one inch per second. However, after only a few days of practice, the trackers' speed doubled.

different combinations of olfactory receptors produce the sensation of distinct odors. Thus, the airborne molecules activate specific combinations of receptors. In turn, the brain identifies an odor by interpreting the *pattern* of olfactory receptors that are stimulated (Shepherd, 2006).

As shown in **Figure 3.8**, the olfactory nerves directly connect to the **olfactory bulb**, *the enlarged ending of the olfactory cortex at the front of the brain where the sensation of smell is registered.* Axons from the olfactory bulb form the *olfactory tract.* These neural pathways project to different brain areas, including the temporal lobe and structures in the limbic system (Gottfried, 2010; Shepherd, 2006). The projections to the *temporal lobe* are thought to be part of the neural pathway involved in our conscious recognition of smells. The projections to the *limbic system* are thought to regulate our emotional response to odors.

The direct connection of olfactory receptor cells to areas of the cortex and limbic system is unique to our sense of smell. Olfaction is unique among the senses in that the receptor cells for smells are actually neurons and have a direct connection to the brain—specifically, to the parts of the brain responsible for emotions and memory. This direct connection may be part of why certain smells can bring up very deep and specific memories for people without conscious effort.

Olfactory function tends to decline with age. About half of those aged 65 to 80 have a significant loss of olfactory function, a number that increases to two-thirds of people aged 80 and older (Lafreniere & Mann, 2009; Rawson, 2006). At any age, air pollution, smoking, and exposure to some industrial chemicals can decrease the ability to smell.

Although humans are highly sensitive to odors, many animals display even greater sensitivity. Dogs, for example, have about 200 million olfactory receptor cells, compared with the approximately 12 million receptors that humans have (Sela & Sobel, 2010). A dog's incredible sense of smell has been used to detect different types of cancer in humans (Edwards et al., 2017). More recently, dogs have detected olfactory changes

FIGURE 3.8 The Olfactory System Inhaled through the nose or the mouth, airborne molecules travel to the top of the nasal cavity and stimulate the olfactory receptors. When stimulated, these receptor cells communicate neural messages to the olfactory bulb, which is part of the olfactory cortex of the brain where the sense of smell is registered.

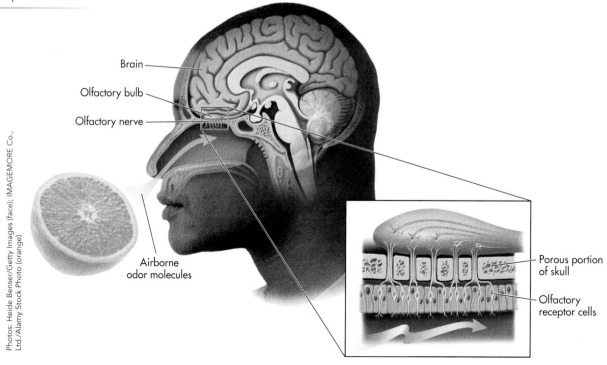

Photos: Heide Benser/Getty Images (face); IMAGEMORE Co., Ltd./Alamy Stock Photo (orange)

Brain

Olfactory bulb

Olfactory nerve

Airborne odor molecules

Porous portion of skull

Olfactory receptor cells

that precede seizures and alert a person to a seizure onset (Catala et al., 2019). All this said, humans are more sensitive to smell than most people realize (McGann, 2017; Shepherd, 2004).

Taste

Our sense of taste, or *gustation*, results from the stimulation of special taste receptors by chemical substances in food and drink. When dissolved by saliva, these chemicals activate the **taste buds**, *the specialized sensory receptors for taste that are located on the tongue and inside the mouth and throat.*

The surface of the tongue is covered with thousands of little bumps with grooves in between (see **Figure 3.9**). These grooves are lined with the taste buds. Contrary to popular belief, there is no "tongue map" in which different regions of the tongue are specialized to respond to sweet, sour, salty, and bitter tastes. Instead, responsiveness to the five basic tastes is present in all tongue areas. Each taste bud shows maximum sensitivity to one particular taste and lesser sensitivity to other tastes (Chandrashekar et al., 2006). When activated, special receptor cells in the taste buds send neural messages along pathways to the thalamus in the brain. In turn, the thalamus directs the information to several regions in the cortex (Shepherd, 2006).

There were long thought to be four basic taste categories: sweet, salty, sour, and bitter. However, scientists identified the receptor cells for a fifth basic taste, *umami* (Chaudhari et al., 2000). Loosely translated, *umami* means "yummy" or "delicious" in Japanese. *Umami* is the distinctive taste of monosodium glutamate and is associated with meat and other protein-rich foods. It's also responsible for the savory flavor of Parmesan and other aged cheeses, mushrooms, and seaweed.

From an evolutionary view, these five basic tastes supply the information we need to seek out nutrient-rich foods and avoid potentially hazardous substances (Chandrashekar et al., 2006; Eisenstein, 2010). Sweet tastes attract us to energy-rich foods, *umami* to protein-rich nutrients. Bitter or sour tastes warn us to avoid many toxic

olfactory bulb (ole-FACK-tuh-ree) The enlarged ending of the olfactory cortex at the front of the brain where the sensation of smell is registered.

taste buds The specialized sensory receptors for taste that are located on the tongue and inside the mouth and throat.

Is it true that different tastes are detected on different parts of your tongue?

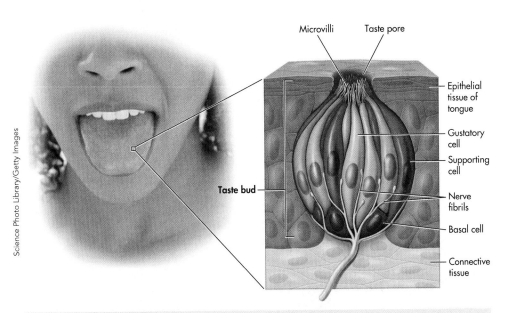

FIGURE 3.9 Taste Buds Embedded in the surface of the tongue are thousands of taste buds, the sensory receptor organs for taste. Taste buds are located in the grooves of the bumps on the surface of the tongue. Each taste bud contains an average of 50 taste receptor cells. When activated, the taste receptor cells send messages to adjoining sensory neurons, which relay the information to the brain. Taste buds, like the olfactory neurons, are constantly being replaced. The life expectancy of a particular taste bud is only about 10 days.

Maren Caruso/Getty Images

Expensive Taste Although wine experts may be able to discern subtle differences among wines, amateurs may not be as objective. To determine the effect of *price* on perceived quality, researchers asked participants to decide which tasted better: a $90 bottle of wine or one that cost $10 (Plassmann et al., 2008). Although the wine in the two bottles was identical, participants overwhelmingly thought the $90 bottle tasted better. Their subjective, verbal rating was confirmed by brain scans: Activity in a brain region associated with pleasant sensations was much higher when they sipped the wine that they thought was more expensive. Thus, many different factors affect taste, not the least of which is your expectation of just how good something is likely to taste.

pain The unpleasant sensory and emotional experience associated with actual or potential bodily damage.

gate-control theory of pain Theory that physiological and psychological factors cause spinal gates to open and relay to the brain patterns of stimulation that are perceived as pain.

or poisonous substances (Peyrot des Gachons et al., 2011). Sensitivity to salty-tasting substances helps us regulate the balance of electrolytes in our diets.

Evolutionary influences are also apparent in the taste receptors of different animal species (Breslin, 2013). Animals vary in their ability to sense different tastes. For example, cats, who almost exclusively eat meat, do not have functioning sweet receptors. But dogs, rats, and raccoons, who eat a variety of different foods, are attracted to sweet-tasting foods (Jiang et al., 2012). Young human children have also shown a consistent preference for sweet-tasting liquids and foods. It is thought that this evolved to attract younger people to higher-calorie sources of nutrition during the most important phases of their physical growth (Petty et al., 2020). It's also hard to mention children and taste and not think of the "picky eater." There are a number of behavioral reasons children choose to avoid particular foods—such as the texture and/or appearance of the food, as well as parental attention. There may also be sensory issues related to taste that make it hard for children to enjoy brussels sprouts. Given that younger people have an average of 10,000 taste buds relative to the 5,000 seen in most older adults, foods may simply stimulate a more intense sensory response in children (Segovia et al., 2002).

Most tastes are complex and result from the activation of different combinations of basic taste receptors. Taste is just one aspect of *flavor,* which involves several sensations, including the aroma, temperature, texture, and appearance of food (Shepherd, 2006).

The Skin and Body Senses

While vision, hearing, smell, and taste provide you with important information about your environment, another group of senses provides you with information that comes from a source much closer to home: your own body. In this section, we'll first consider the *skin senses,* which provide essential information about your physical status and your physical interaction with objects in your environment. We'll next consider the *body senses,* which keep you informed as to your position and orientation in space.

Touch   We usually don't think of our skin as a sense organ. But the skin is in fact the largest and heaviest sense organ; it is also the largest organ in the human body overall. The skin of an average adult covers about 20 square feet of surface area and weighs about six pounds.

There are many different kinds of sensory receptors in the skin. Some of these sensory receptors are specialized to respond to just one kind of stimulus, such as pressure, warmth, or cold (McGlone & Reilly, 2010). Other skin receptors respond to more than one type of stimulus (Delmas & Rodat-Despoix, 2011).

Sensory receptors are distributed unevenly among different areas of the body, which is why sensitivity to touch and temperature varies from one area of the body to another. Your hands, face, and lips, for example, are much more sensitive to touch than are your back, arms, and legs. That's because your hands, face, and lips are much more densely packed with sensory receptors. The reason there are more sensory receptors in these areas has a lot to do with their various functions. Think of all the complex things we do with our hands, faces, and lips. If you recall the drawing of the homunculus in Chapter 2 (see Figure 2.15), the figure shows you how much of the brain is devoted not only to the sensory aspects of these regions, but also to the perceptual experiences they evoke. Given all the different ways that actions with our hands or faces can be interpreted, it's a good thing there is such a density of sensory receptors in these areas.

Pain   From the sharp sting of a paper cut to the dull ache of a badly sprained ankle, a wide variety of stimuli can trigger pain. Traditionally, **pain** is defined as *the unpleasant sensory and emotional experience associated with actual or potential bodily damage* (Peirs & Seal, 2016).

Although unpleasant, pain is important to our survival, reminding us to avoid a hot stove or nurse an injured wrist.

Your body's specialized sensory receptors for pain are found in the skin, muscles, and internal organs are called nociceptors. *Nociceptors* are actually small sensory fibers, called *free nerve endings.* You have millions of nociceptors throughout your body, mostly in your skin (see **Table 3.3**). Your fingertips may have as many as 1,200 nociceptors per square inch. Your muscles and joints have fewer nociceptors, and your internal organs have the smallest number of nociceptors.

Fast and Slow Pain Systems Have you ever stubbed your toe on a piece of furniture? If so, your injury triggered two types of nociceptors. One type activates the myelinated fibers of the *fast pain system,* which transmits the sharp, intense, but short-lived pain of the immediate injury. These pain signals travel up the spinal cord to the brain, first to the thalamus, then to the somatosensory cortex, where the sensory aspects of the pain message are interpreted, such as the location and intensity of the pain.

In most cases, acute pain gradually diminishes to a burning, dull throbbing sensation, caused by the activation of the unmyelinated fibers of the *slow pain system* (Guindon & Hohmann, 2009). While less intense than the pain signals carried by the fast pain system, the slow pain system is longer lasting. In contrast to the fast pain system, slow pain messages travel first to the hypothalamus and thalamus and then to limbic system structures, such as the amygdala. Its connections to the limbic system suggest that the slow pain system is more involved in the emotional aspects of pain.

Factors That Influence the Experience of Pain There is considerable individual variation in the experience of pain (Denk et al., 2014; Jensen & Turk, 2014). Pain signals are integrated in the brain with psychological and cognitive factors that determine how the information is interpreted and the pain ultimately perceived (Wiech, 2016). The classic **gate-control theory of pain**, is the *theory that physiological and psychological factors cause spinal gates to open and relay to the brain patterns of stimulation that are perceived as pain* (Melzack & Wall, 1965, 1996; Katz & Rosenblum, 2015). If, because of psychological, social, or situational factors, the brain signals the gates to open, pain is experienced or intensified. If the brain signals the gates to close, pain is reduced.

Psychological factors that can intensify the experience of pain include anxiety, fear, and a sense of helplessness (Edwards et al., 2009). Feelings of depression and sadness can also intensify the experience of pain (Berna et al., 2010).

On the other hand, positive mood and a sense of control can reduce the perception of pain (Ong et al., 2015). As one example, consider the athlete who has trained to minimize the experience of pain during competition. The experience of pain is also influenced by social and situational factors, along with cultural beliefs about the meaning of pain and the appropriate response to pain (Bosch & Cano, 2013; Gatchel et al., 2011).

Today, some pain researchers conceptualize the perception of pain as one that is *actively constructed,* determined by expectations and personal experience (Wiech, 2016). We discuss some helpful strategies that you can use to minimize pain in the Psych for Your Life section at the end of the chapter.

Sensitization: Unwarranted Pain One of the most frustrating aspects of pain management is that it can continue even after an injury has healed, such as after recovering from a spinal cord injury or severe burns. An extreme example of this phenomenon is *phantom limb pain,* in which a person continues to experience intense painful sensations in a limb that has been amputated (Wolff et al., 2011).

How can phantom limb pain be explained? Basically, the neurons involved in processing the pain signals undergo *sensitization.* Earlier in the chapter, we discussed *sensory adaptation,* in which sensory receptors become gradually less responsive to steady stimulation over time. Sensitization is the opposite of adaptation. In sensitization, pain pathways in the brain become increasingly *more* responsive over time. It's like a broken volume-control knob on your stereo that you can turn up but not down or off.

TABLE 3.3

Sensitivity of Different Body Areas to Pain

Most Sensitive	Least Sensitive
Back of the knee	Tip of the nose
Neck region	Sole of the foot
Bend of the elbow	Ball of the thumb

Source: Information from Geldard (1972).

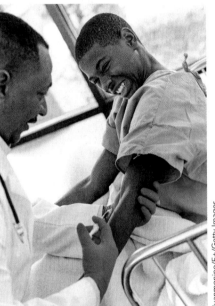

Juanmonino/E+/Getty Images

⌃ Individual Differences in Pain Perception and Tolerance People respond to pain very differently (Denk et al., 2014). Women tend to have a lower pain threshold than men, rating pain as more unpleasant and displaying more intense physiological responses to painful stimuli (Jarrett, 2011). Ethnicity, race, and culture also influence the response to pain (see Jarrett, 2011; Palit et al., 2013). Such differences may reflect cultural beliefs, social expectations, and actual physiological differences among ethnic groups (Rahim-Williams et al., 2012). Moreover, research has documented stereotype-driven differences in treatment of pain with many doctors showing higher empathy and a higher likelihood of treatment for White people than Black people, despite the fact that Black people often report higher levels of pain than White people (Tait & Chibnall, 2014).

MYTH ▶ SCIENCE

Is it true that some people continue to feel sensations from a body part after it has been amputated?

proprioception The sense of body movement and position.

ESP (extrasensory perception) Perception of information by some means other than through the normal processes of sensation.

parapsychology The scientific investigation of claims of paranormal phenomena and abilities.

As the pain circuits undergo sensitization, pain begins to occur in the absence of any sensory input. The result can be the development of persistent, *chronic pain* that continues even after the injury has healed (Denk et al., 2014; Wolff et al., 2011). In the case of phantom limb pain, sensitization has occurred in the pain transmission pathways from the site of the amputation. The sensitized pathways produce painful sensations that feel as though they are coming from a limb that is no longer there.

Proprioception: Movement, Position, and Balance Stand in a dark room and touch your right ear. If you could do that, you have just demonstrated **proprioception**—*the sense of body movement and position*. Specialized neurons in the muscles and joints, called *proprioceptors,* continuously communicate changes in body position and muscle tension to the brain (Proske & Gandevia, 2016). Your *vestibular system* maintains your sense of balance, posture, and position in space (Eatock & Songer, 2011). How? Changes in gravity, motion, and body position are detected by hair-like receptor cells embedded in fluid in the *semicircular canals* and *vestibular sacs* in the inner ear (see Figure 3.7 on page 87).

Maintaining your equilibrium requires the integration of knowledge from the proprioceptors, the vestibular system, and other senses, especially vision. When visual information conflicts with vestibular information, dizziness and disorientation may result. Thus, one strategy to combat motion sickness is to minimize sensory conflicts by focusing on a fixed point in the distance.

In the first part of this chapter, we described how the body's senses respond to stimuli in the environment. **Table 3.4** summarizes these different sensory systems. Next, we'll look at the process of perception—how we make sense of the information that we receive from our environment. One long-standing question in psychology is whether information can be perceived *without* the involvement of normal sensory systems, a process called *extrasensory perception,* or *ESP.* We take a close look at this issue in the Critical Thinking box, "ESP: Can Perception Occur Without Sensation?"

TABLE 3.4

Summary Table of the Senses

Sense	Stimulus	Sense Organ	Sensory Receptor Cells
Hearing (audition)	Sound waves	Ear	Hair cells in cochlea
Vision	Light waves	Eye	Rods (light/dark) and cones (color) in retina
Smell (olfaction)	Airborne odor molecules	Nose	Hair-like receptor cells at top of nasal cavity
Taste (gustation)	Chemicals dissolved in saliva	Mouth, tongue	Taste buds
Touch	Pressure	Skin	Pacinian corpuscle
Pain	Tissue injury or damage; varied	Skin, muscles, and organs	Nociceptors
Body position and movement (proprioception)	Movement of the body	None; muscle and joint tissue	Proprioceptors in muscle and joint tissue
Balance and spatial orientation (vestibular sense)	Changes in position, gravity	Semicircular canals and vestibular sacs	Hair-like receptor cells in semicircular canals and vestibular sacs

CRITICAL THINKING

ESP: Can Perception Occur Without Sensation?

ESP, or **extrasensory perception**, means the *perception of information by some means other than through the normal processes of sensation.*

Do you believe in ESP? If you do, you're not alone (Ridolfo et al., 2010). Surveys conducted by the Associated Press and the Gallup Poll have found that close to 50 percent of American adults "believe in ESP" (Fram, 2007; D. Moore, 2005).

Forms of ESP include *telepathy*, which is the *direct communication between the minds of two individuals; clairvoyance,* the perception of a remote object or event, such as "sensing" that a friend has been injured in a car accident; *psychokinesis*, the ability to influence a physical object without touching it; and *precognition,* the ability to predict future events (Bem, 2016; Cardeña, 2018).

The general term for such unusual abilities is *paranormal phenomena. Paranormal* means "outside the range of normal experience."

Is it true that there is a scientific basis for ESP?

Thus, **parapsychology** refers to *the scientific investigation of claims of paranormal phenomena and abilities* (Cardeña et al., 2015; Zingrone et al., 2015). It is a myth that there is a scientific basis for ESP, and very few psychologists conduct any kind of parapsychological research.

Have you ever felt as if you had just experienced ESP? Many people have had the experience of dreaming something only to realize that something very similar to their dream actually happens in the days following the dream. Are people who experience this capable of precognitive dreaming?

Do such experiences "prove" that ESP exists? Two less extraordinary concepts can explain such occurrences: coincidence and the fallacy of positive instances. *Coincidence* describes an event that occurs simply by chance. For example, you have over a thousand dreams per year, most of which are about familiar people and situations. By mere chance, *some* aspect of *some* dream will occasionally correspond with waking life.

The *fallacy of positive instances* is the tendency to remember coincidental events that seem to confirm our belief about unusual phenomena and to forget all the instances that do not. For example, think of the number of times you've had a dream that did *not* come true. Such situations are far more common than their opposites, but we quickly forget about the hunches that are not confirmed.

Why do people attribute chance events to ESP? Research has shown that believers in ESP are less likely to accurately estimate the probability of an event occurring by chance alone. Nonbelievers tend to be more realistic about the probability of events being the result of simple coincidence or chance (Dagnall et al., 2007; Rogers et al., 2009).

Parapsychologists attempt to study ESP in the laboratory under controlled conditions. Many initially convincing demonstrations of ESP are later shown to be the result of research design problems or of the researcher's unintentional cuing of the participant. Another problem involves *replication*. To be considered valid, experimental results must be able to be replicated, or repeated, by other scientists under identical laboratory conditions. Replication is especially problematic in parapsychology research (Hyman, 2010).

The Ganzfeld Technique Clairvoyance and telepathy experiments often involve use of the *ganzfeld* technique (Baptista et al., 2015). The research subject lies in a quiet room, with their eyes and ears covered to block external sensory stimuli, while a "sender" in another room attempts to communicate information.

Jeremy Walker/Science Source

Research in parapsychology continues, however (Cardeña, 2018; Mossbridge & Radin, 2018). Psychologist Daryl Bem (2011) tested precognition in a series of nine experiments involving more than 1,000 participants. Bem's strategy was to "time-reverse" standard psychological tasks, changing the normal order of cause and effect.

For example, participants taking a memory test better remembered words that they practiced *after* taking the test. In another experiment, participants predicted the location of a target image on a computer screen *before* they saw it.

In all, eight of Bem's nine experiments showed small but statistically significant effects in favor of precognition. These, and similar findings from Bem's series of experiments, could not be easily explained (Judd & Gawronski, 2011).

Bem's research sparked a flurry of media attention, including an appearance on *The Colbert Report*. It also triggered a firestorm of reaction from psychologists and other scientists. Much of the criticism focused on the statistical methods used to analyze the data (see Palmer, 2015). So far, replication attempts have been mostly unsuccessful (Baruš & Rabier, 2014; Galak et al., 2012; Howard, 2018). Undaunted, Bem and his colleagues (2015) published their own meta-analysis of 90 replication attempts, concluding that the results showed solid support for the existence of precognition.

Of course, the history of science is filled with examples of phenomena that were initially scoffed at and later found to be real, such as the notion that moods affect health and immune system functioning. So keep an open mind about ESP, but also maintain a healthy sense of scientific skepticism (Schooler et al., 2018). In the final analysis, all psychologists, including those who accept the possibility of ESP, recognize the need for evidence that meets the requirements of the scientific method.

CRITICAL THINKING QUESTIONS

- Why do you think that people who believe in ESP are less likely to attribute events to chance than people who don't think ESP is a real phenomenon?
- Can you think of any reasons why replication might be particularly elusive in research on extrasensory perception?
- Why is replication important in all psychological research, but particularly so in studies attempting to prove extraordinary claims, like the existence of ESP?

Do you have psychic powers? Go to LaunchPad: Resources to **Think Like a Scientist** about **ESP.**

bottom-up processing Emphasizes sensory receptors in detecting the basic features of a stimulus; attention focuses on the parts of the pattern before moving to the whole.

top-down processing Emphasizes the observer's experience in arriving at meaningful perceptions; attention moves from the whole to part of the pattern.

Gestalt psychology (geh-SHTALT) School of psychology that maintained sensations are actively processed according to consistent perceptual rules, producing meaningful whole perceptions, or *gestalts*.

figure–ground relationship Gestalt principle stating that a perception is automatically separated into the *figure*, which is the main element of the scene, and the *ground*, which is its background.

Perception

■ KEY THEME

Perception refers to the process of integrating, organizing, and interpreting sensory information into meaningful representations.

≡ KEY QUESTIONS

- What are bottom-up and top-down processing, and how do they differ?
- What is Gestalt psychology?
- What Gestalt principles explain how we perceive objects and their relationship to their surroundings?

As we've learned, our senses are constantly registering a diverse range of stimuli from the environment and transmitting that information to the brain. Perception is the means by which we make use of the raw sensory information the brain receives. In order to make meaning of the world around us, we must organize, interpret, and relate the information acquired by our senses to existing knowledge. It is important to understand that while sensation is quite similar across individuals, perception is far more individualized. For example, two people may have the same sensory experience while looking at a two intersecting lines but they undoubtedly perceive it differently. Because of perception, one person may think the lines look like a mathematical symbol for multiplication, while the other person may perceive the letter *X*. Music is another example where this happens. One person's favorite music might be thrash metal while that might sound like "noise" to another person. To make use of this raw sensory data, we must organize, interpret, and relate the data to existing knowledge.

Psychologists sometimes refer to this flow of sensory data from the sensory receptors to the brain as *bottom-up processing*. **Bottom-up processing** *emphasizes sensory receptors in detecting the basic features of a stimulus; attention focuses on the parts of the pattern before moving to the whole.* Bottom-up processing is often at work when we're confronted with an ambiguous stimulus. We aren't immediately sure what it is as a whole, so we assemble individual features. For example, if you saw two lines that started out far apart and converged at the bottom "v" you might think it is the letter *v* (and this would be confirmed in a top-down way if it was part of a word "verb"). However, based on top-down processing, the "v" could also be an indication of direction in a video game—especially if it is surrounded by other directional cues.

But as we interact with our environment, many of our perceptions are shaped by *top-down processing*. **Top-down processing** *emphasizes the observer's experience in arriving at meaningful perceptions; attention moves from the whole to part of the pattern.* Cultural experiences also affect perceptual processes, as discussed in the Culture and Human Behavior box, "Ways of Seeing: Culture and Top-Down Processes."

One useful way to think about visual perception is to consider the basic perceptual questions we must answer in order to survive in an ever-changing environment. Whether it's a bulldozer or a bowling ball, we need to identify objects, locate objects in space, and, if they are moving, track their motion. Thus, our perceptual processes must help us organize our sensations to answer three basic, important questions: (1) What is it? (2) How far away is it? (3) Where is it going?

In the next few sections, we will look at what psychologists have learned about the principles we use to answer these perceptual questions. Much of our discussion concerns **Gestalt psychology**, a *school of psychology that maintained sensations are actively processed according to consistent perceptual rules, producing meaningful whole perceptions, or gestalts.* Founded by German psychologist **Max Wertheimer** in the early 1900s, the Gestalt psychologists emphasized that we perceive whole objects or figures (*gestalts*) rather than isolated bits and pieces of sensory information (Wertheimer, 1923). Roughly translated, the German word *Gestalt* means a unified whole, form, or shape. Although the Gestalt school of psychology no longer formally exists, the pioneering work of the Gestalt psychologists established many basic perceptual principles (S. Palmer, 2002).

CULTURE AND HUMAN BEHAVIOR

Ways of Seeing: Culture and Top-Down Processes

Do people in different cultures perceive the world differently? In Chapter 1, we described two types of cultures. People in *individualistic* cultures tend to emphasize independence, whereas people in *collectivistic* cultures tend to see humans as being enmeshed in complex relationships. This social perspective is especially pronounced in the East Asian cultures of Korea, Japan, and China, where a person's sense of self is highly dependent upon their social context (Beins, 2011). Consequently, East Asians pay much closer attention to the social context in which their own actions, and the actions of others, occur (Nisbett, 2007; Varnum et al., 2010).

James Warwick/Getty Images

The Cultural Eye of the Beholders

Do these cultural differences in social perspective influence visual perception and memory? Take a few seconds to look at the photo on the right. Was your attention drawn by the tiger or its surroundings?

In one study, Hannah Faye Chua and her colleagues (2005) used sophisticated eye-tracking equipment to monitor the eye movements of U.S. and Chinese students while they looked at similar photographs that showed a single focal object against a realistic, complex background. The results showed that their eye movements differed: The U.S. students looked sooner and longer at the focal object in the foreground than the Chinese students did. In contrast, the Chinese students spent more time looking at the background than the U.S. students did. And, the Chinese students were also less likely to recognize the foreground objects when they were placed in front of a new background.

Rather than separating the object from its background, the Chinese students tended to see—and remember—object and background as a single perceptual image. Many psychologists believe that this pattern of results reflects the more "holistic" perceptual style that characterizes collectivistic cultures (Boduroglu et al., 2009; Boland et al., 2008).

In another, similar experiment, researchers found that U.S. participants tended to focus their attention on the object alone, whereas the East Asian participants alternated looking at the object and the background, paying more attention to the *relationship* between the object and background (Goh et al., 2009). "Culture," the researchers observed, "may operate as a top-down mechanism that guides and interacts with basic neuro-perceptual processes."

The Perception of Shape: What Is It?

When you look around your world, you don't see random edges, curves, colors, or splotches of light and dark. Rather, you see countless distinct objects against a variety of backgrounds. Although to some degree we rely on size, color, and texture to determine what an object might be, we rely primarily on an object's *shape* to identify it.

Figure–Ground Relationship How do we organize our perceptions so that we see an object as separate from other objects? The **figure–ground relationship** is a *Gestalt principle stating that a perception is automatically separated into the figure, which is the main element of the scene, and the ground, which is its background.*

You can experience the figure–ground relationship by looking at a coffee cup on a table. The coffee cup is the figure, and the table is the ground. Notice that usually the figure has a definite shape, tends to stand out clearly, and is perceptually meaningful in some way. In contrast, the ground tends to be less clearly defined, even fuzzy, and usually appears to be behind and farther away from the figure.

The separation of a scene into figure and ground is not a property of the actual elements of the scene at which you're looking. Rather, your ability to separate a scene into figure and ground is a psychological accomplishment. To illustrate, look at the classic example shown in **Figure 3.10**. This perception of a single image in two different ways is called a *figure–ground reversal.*

FIGURE 3.10 A Classic Example of Figure–Ground Reversal Figure–ground reversals illustrate the psychological nature of our ability to perceptually sort a scene into the main element and the background. If you perceive the white area as the figure and the dark area as the ground, you'll perceive a vase. If you perceive the dark area as the figure, you'll perceive two faces.

FIGURE 3.11 The Gestalt Principles of Organization (a) *The law of similarity* is the tendency to perceive objects of a similar size, shape, or color as a unit or figure. A mixed array of fruits and vegetables. (b) The *law of proximity* is the tendency to perceive objects that are close to one another as a single unit. (c) The *law of continuity* is the tendency to group elements as a single unit or figure when appear to flow in the same direction. (d) The *law of closure* is the tendency to fill in the gaps in an incomplete image. (e) The *law of symmetry* is the tendency to perceive symmetrical objects as part of the same group.

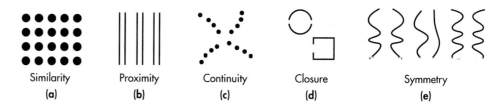

Similarity (a)   Proximity (b)   Continuity (c)   Closure (d)   Symmetry (e)

Perceptual Grouping Many of the forms we perceive are composed of a number of different elements that seem to go together (Glicksohn & Cohen, 2011). It would be more accurate to say that we actively organize the elements to try to produce the stable perception of well-defined whole objects. This is what perceptual psychologists refer to as "the urge to organize." What principles do we follow when we attempt to organize visual elements?

The Gestalt psychologists studied how the perception of visual elements becomes organized into patterns, shapes, and forms. They identified several laws, or principles, that we tend to follow in grouping elements together to arrive at the perception of forms, shapes, and figures (see **Figure 3.11**). The Gestalt principles, which include *similarity, closure, good continuation,* and *proximity,* help us more efficiently remember groups of objects and perceive the relationships among them (Corbett, 2017).

The ability to efficiently organize elements into stable objects helps us perceive the world accurately. In effect, we actively and automatically construct a perception that reveals "the essence of something."

Depth Perception: How Far Away Is It?

■ KEY THEME
Perception of distance and motion helps us gauge the position of stationary objects and predict the path of moving objects.

≡ KEY QUESTIONS
- What are the monocular and binocular cues for distance or depth perception, and how does binocular disparity explain our ability to see three-dimensional forms in two-dimensional images?
- What visual cues help us perceive distance and motion?
- Why do we perceive the size and shape of objects as unchanging despite changes in sensory input?

Being able to perceive the distance of an object has obvious survival value, especially regarding potential threats, such as snarling dogs or oncoming trains. But simply walking through your house or apartment also requires that you accurately judge the distance of furniture, walls, other people, and so forth. Otherwise, you'd be constantly bumping into doors, walls, and tables. *The use of visual cues to perceive the distance or the three-dimensional characteristics of an object* is called **depth perception**.

Monocular Cues We use a variety of cues to judge the distance of objects. Requiring the use of only one eye (*mono* means "one"), **monocular cues** are *distance or depth cues that can be processed by either eye alone.* Artists use monocular cues, sometimes called *pictorial cues,* to create the perception of distance or depth in paintings. These cues include:

1. *Relative size.* If two or more objects are assumed to be similar in size, the object that appears larger is perceived as being closer.
2. *Overlap.* When one object partially blocks or obscures the view of another object, the partially blocked object is perceived as being farther away.
3. *Aerial perspective.* Faraway objects appear hazy or blurred by the atmosphere.
4. *Texture gradient.* As a surface with a distinct texture extends into the distance, the details of the surface texture gradually become less clearly defined.

depth perception The use of visual cues to perceive the distance or the three-dimensional characteristics of an object.

monocular cues (mah-NOCK-you-ler) Distance or depth cues that can be processed by either eye alone.

Texture Gradient, Overlap, and Aerial Perspective Monocular cues are used to judge the distance of objects. Crisp orange-red poppies appear against a background of lavender flowers that become increasingly fuzzy, an example of texture gradient. Similarly, the hills at the top of the image are just blurs of color, creating an impression of even greater distance through aerial perspective. And, the poppies are perceived as being closer than the lavender flowers that they overlap.

Relative Size and Linear Perspective Monocular cues provide depth cues that create the illusion of a palm tree-lined road receding into the distance. Linear perspective is evident in the near-convergence of the palm trees as the road narrows. And, the palm trees appear to decrease in size, an example of relative size contributing to the perception of distance.

Motion Parallax This photograph of waiters in India passing a tray from one train car to the next captures the visual flavor of motion parallax. Objects that whiz by faster are perceptually judged as being closer, as in the case here of the blurred ground and grass. Objects that pass by more slowly are judged as being farther away, as conveyed by the clearer details of the distant buildings and trees.

5. *Linear perspective.* Parallel lines seem to meet in the distance. The closer together the lines appear to be, the greater the perception of distance.

6. *Motion parallax.* When you are moving, you use the speed of passing objects to estimate the distance of the objects. Nearby objects seem to zip by faster than do distant objects. When you are riding on a commuter train, for example, houses and parked cars along the tracks seem to whiz by, while the distant downtown skyline seems to move slowly.

Binocular Cues Binocular cues are *distance or depth cues that require the use of both eyes.* One binocular cue is *convergence*—the degree to which muscles rotate your eyes to focus on an object. The more the eyes converge, or rotate inward, to focus on an object, the greater the strength of the muscle signals and the closer the object is perceived to be. For example, if you hold a coin about six inches in front of your nose, you'll notice the slight strain on your eye muscles as your eyes converge to focus on the coin. If you hold the coin at arm's length, less convergence is needed. Perceptually, the information provided by these signals from your eye muscles is used to judge the distance of an object.

Another binocular distance cue is *binocular disparity.* Because our eyes are set a couple of inches apart, a slightly different image of an object is cast on the retina of each eye. When the two retinal images are very different, we interpret the object as being close by. When the two retinal images are more nearly identical, the object is perceived as being farther away (Parker, 2007).

binocular cues (by-NOCK-you-ler) Distance or depth cues that require the use of both eyes.

perceptual constancy The tendency to perceive objects, especially familiar objects, as constant and unchanging despite changes in sensory input.

size constancy The perception that a familiar object remains the same shape regardless of the image produced on our retinas.

shape constancy The perception that a familiar object remains the same shape regardless of the image produced on the retina.

▲ **A Photo Finish and the Perception of Motion** When we perceive movement, the image of the horses moves across the retina. Our eye muscles make very small movements to keep the galloping horses in focus.

FIGURE 3.12 How Many Right Angles Do You See? Most people find 12 right angles in this drawing of a slightly tilted cube. But look again. There are no right angles in the drawing. Shape constancy leads you to perceive an image of a cube with right angles, despite the lack of sensory data to support that perception.

To experience how binocular disparity affects distance perception, hold a pen just in front of your nose. Close your left eye, then your right. Because the images from the two eyes are very different, the binocular disparity leads you to perceive the pen as being very close. Now focus on an object across the room and close each eye again. Because the images are much more similar, you perceive the object as farther away. With both eyes open, the two images are fused.

The Perception of Motion: Where Is It Going?

In addition to the ability to perceive the distance of stationary objects, we need the ability to gauge the path of moving objects, whether it's a baseball whizzing through the air, an approaching car, or an egg about to roll off the counter. How do we perceive movement?

As we follow a moving object with our gaze, the image of the object moves across the retina. Our eye muscles make microfine movements to keep the object in focus. We also compare the moving object to the background, which is usually stationary. When the retinal image of an object enlarges, we perceive the object as moving toward us. Our perception of the speed of the object's approach is based on our estimate of the object's rate of enlargement (Harris et al., 2008). Neural pathways in the brain combine information about eye-muscle activity, the changing retinal image, and the contrast of the moving object with its stationary background. The end result? We perceive the object as moving.

Psychologically, we tend to make certain assumptions when we perceive movement. For example, we typically assume that the *object*, or figure, moves while the background, or frame, remains stationary (Rock, 1995). Thus, as you visually follow a car as it drives down a road you are about to cross, you perceive the car as moving and not the buildings around it, which serve as the background.

Perceptual Constancies

Consider this scenario. As you're driving on a flat stretch of highway, a red SUV zips past you and speeds far ahead. As the distance between you and the SUV grows, its image becomes progressively smaller until it is no more than a dot on the horizon. Yet, even though the image of the SUV on your retinas has become progressively smaller, you don't perceive the vehicle as shrinking. Instead, you perceive its shape, size, and brightness as unchanged.

The tendency to perceive objects, especially familiar objects, as constant and unchanging despite changes in sensory input is called **perceptual constancy**. Without this perceptual ability, our perception of reality would be in a continual state of flux. If we simply responded to retinal images, our perceptions of objects would change as lighting, viewing angle, and distance from the object changed from one moment to the next. Instead, color, size, and shape constancy promote a stable view of the world.

Size and Shape Constancy **Size constancy** is *the perception that an object remains the same size despite its changing image on the retina*. When our distance from an object changes, the image of the object that is cast on the retinas of our eyes also changes, yet we still perceive it to be the same size. The example of the red SUV illustrates the perception of size constancy. As the distance between you and the red SUV increased, you could eventually block out the retinal image of the vehicle with your hand, but you don't believe that your hand has suddenly become larger than the SUV. Instead, your brain automatically adjusts your perception of the vehicle's size by combining information about retinal image size and distance.

Shape constancy is *the perception that a familiar object remains the same shape regardless of the image produced on our retinas*. Try looking at a familiar object, such as a door, from different angles. Your perception of the door's rectangular shape remains constant despite changes in its retinal image. Shape constancy has a greater influence on your perceptions than you probably realize (see **Figure 3.12**).

Perceptual Illusions

■ KEY THEME
Perceptual illusions underscore the idea that we actively construct our perceptual representations of the world according to psychological principles.

☰ KEY QUESTIONS
- How can the Müller-Lyer and moon illusions be explained?
- What do perceptual illusions reveal about perceptual processes?
- What roles do perceptual sets, learning experiences, and culture play in perception?

Our perceptual processes are largely automatic and unconscious. On the one hand, this arrangement is mentally efficient. With a minimum of cognitive effort, we decipher our surroundings, answering important perceptual questions and making sense of the environment. On the other hand, because perceptual processing is largely automatic, we can inadvertently arrive at the wrong perceptual conclusion. *The misperception of the true characteristics of an object or an image* is called a **perceptual illusion**.

The perceptual contradictions of illusions are not only fascinating but can also shed light on how the normal processes of perception guide us to perceptual conclusions. Given the basics of perception that we've covered thus far, you're in a good position to understand how and why some famous illusions seem to occur.

The Müller-Lyer Illusion

Look at the center line made by the corners of the walls in (a) and (c) in **Figure 3.13**. Which line is longer? If you said (c), then you've just experienced the **Müller-Lyer illusion**, *a famous visual illusion involving the misperception of the identical length of two lines, one with arrows pointed inward, one with arrows pointed outward*. In fact, the two center lines are the same length, even though they *appear* to have different lengths. You can confirm that they are the same length by measuring them. The same illusion occurs when you look at a simple line drawing of the Müller-Lyer illusion, shown in parts (b) and (d) of Figure 3.13.

The Müller-Lyer illusion is caused in part by visual depth cues that promote the perception that the center line in (c) is *farther* from you (Gregory, 1968; Rock, 1995). When you look at (c), the center line is that of a wall jutting away from you. When you look at drawing (d), the outward-pointing arrows create much the same visual effect—a corner jutting away from you. In Figure 3.13 (a) and (b), visual depth cues promote the perception of *lesser* distance—a corner that is jutting toward you.

Size constancy also seems to play an important role in the Müller-Lyer illusion. Because they are the same length, the two center lines in the photographs and the line drawings produce retinal images that are the same size. However, as we noted in our earlier discussion of size constancy, if the retinal size of an object stays the same but the perception of its distance increases, we will perceive the object as being larger.

The same basic principle seems to apply to the Müller-Lyer illusion. Although all four center lines produce retinal images that are the same size, the center lines in images (c) and (d) are embedded in visual depth cues that make you perceive them as farther away.

Keep in mind that the arrows pointing inward or outward are responsible for creating the illusion in the Müller-Lyer illusion. Take away those potent depth cues and the Müller-Lyer illusion evaporates. You perceive the two lines just as they are—the same length. For more on the Müller-Lyer illusion, see the Culture and Human Behavior box on the next page.

The Moon Illusion

The **moon illusion** is *a visual illusion involving the misperception that the moon is larger when it is on the horizon than when it is directly overhead*. A full moon appears much larger when viewed on the horizon against buildings and trees than it does when viewed in the clear sky overhead. But the moon, of course, doesn't shrink as it rises. In fact, *the retinal size of the full moon is the same in all positions*. What causes this illusion?

perceptual illusion The misperception of the true characteristics of an object or an image.

Müller-Lyer illusion A famous visual illusion involving the misperception of the identical length of two lines, one with arrows pointed inward, one with arrows pointed outward.

moon illusion A visual illusion involving the misperception that the moon is larger when it is on the horizon than when it is directly overhead.

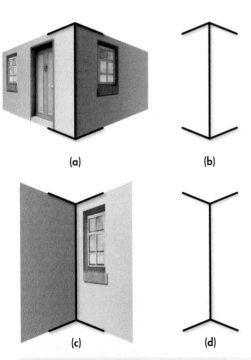

(a)   (b)

(c)   (d)

FIGURE 3.13 The Müller-Lyer Illusion Compare the two drawings of buildings. Which *corner* line is longer? Now compare the two line drawings. Which *center* line is longer? In reality, the center lines in the buildings and the line drawings are all exactly the same length, which you can prove to yourself with a ruler.

CULTURE AND HUMAN BEHAVIOR

Culture and the Müller-Lyer Illusion: The Carpentered-World Hypothesis

Since the early 1900s, it has been known that people in industrialized societies are far more susceptible to the Müller-Lyer illusion than are people in some nonindustrialized societies (Matsumoto & Juang, 2008; Phillips, 2011). How can this difference be explained?

Cross-cultural psychologist Marshall Segall and his colleagues (1963, 1966) proposed the *carpentered-world hypothesis*. They suggested that people living in urban, industrialized environments have a great deal of perceptual experience in judging lines, corners, edges, and other rectangular, manufactured objects. Thus, people in carpentered cultures would be more susceptible to the Müller-Lyer illusion, which involves arrows mimicking a corner that is jutting toward or away from the perceiver.

In contrast, people who live in noncarpentered cultures more frequently encounter natural objects. In these cultures, perceptual experiences with straight lines and right angles are relatively rare. Segall predicted that people from these cultures would be less susceptible to the Müller-Lyer illusion.

To test this idea, Segall and his colleagues (1963, 1966) compared the responses of people living in carpentered societies, such as Evanston, Illinois, with those of people living in noncarpentered societies, such as remote areas of Africa. The results confirmed their hypothesis. The Müller-Lyer illusion was stronger for those living in carpentered societies. Could the difference in illusion susceptibility be due to some sort of biological difference rather than a cultural difference? To address this issue, psychologist V. Mary Stewart (1973) compared groups of White and Black American schoolchildren living in Evanston, Illinois. Regardless of race, all of the children living in the city were equally susceptible to the Müller-Lyer illusion. Stewart also compared groups of Black African children in five different areas of Zambia—ranging from the very carpentered capital city of Lusaka to rural, noncarpentered areas of the country. Once again, the African children living in the

▲ **A Noncarpentered Environment** People who live in urban, industrialized environments have a great deal of perceptual experience with straight lines, edges, and right angles. In contrast, people who live in a noncarpentered environment, like the village shown here, have little experience with right angles and perfectly straight lines (Phillips, 2011). Are people who grow up in a noncarpentered environment equally susceptible to the Müller-Lyer illusion?

robertharding/Alamy Stock Photo

carpentered society of Lusaka were just as susceptible to the illusion as the Evanston children, but the African children living in the noncarpentered countryside were not.

These findings provided some of the first evidence for the idea that culture could shape perception. As Segall (1994) later concluded, "Every perception is the result of an interaction between a stimulus and a perceiver shaped by prior experience." Thus, people who grow up in very different cultures might well perceive aspects of their physical environment differently.

REUTERS/Darryl Webb

▲ **The Moon Illusion** Why does the moon appear to be much larger when it's viewed on the horizon than when it's viewed higher in the sky? Part of the explanation has to do with our perception of the distance of objects at different locations on the horizon—here the runner, the trees, and the moon itself.

Part of the explanation has to do with our perception of the distance of objects at different locations in the sky (Ozkan & Braunstein, 2010). Researchers have found that people perceive objects on the horizon as farther away than objects that are directly overhead in the sky. The horizon contains many familiar distance cues, such as buildings, trees, and the smoothing of the texture of the landscape as it fades into the distance. The moon on the horizon is perceived as being *behind* these depth cues, so the depth perception cue of overlap adds to the perception that the moon on the horizon is farther away.

The moon illusion also involves the misapplication of the principle of size constancy. The moon looks larger when the perception of its distance increases. Remember, the retinal image of the moon is the *same* in all locations. Thus, even though the retinal image of the moon remains constant, we perceive the moon as being larger because it seems farther away on the horizon (Kaufman et al., 2007).

If you look at a full moon on the horizon through a cardboard tube, you'll remove the distance cues provided by the horizon. The moon on the horizon shrinks immediately—and looks the same size as it does when directly overhead.

The Effects of Experience on Perceptual Interpretations

Our educational, cultural, and life experiences shape what we perceive. As a simple example, consider a climbing wall in a gym. If your knowledge of climbing is limited, the posts, ropes, arrows, and lines look like a meaningless jumble of equipment. But if you are an expert climber, you see handgrips and footgrips, belays, overhangs, and routes of varying difficulty. Our different perceptions of a climbing wall are shaped by our prior learning experiences. Learning experiences can vary from person to person and from culture to culture.

Perception can also be influenced by an individual's expectations, motives, and interests. The term **perceptual set** refers to *the tendency to perceive objects or situations from a particular frame of reference.* Perceptual sets usually lead us to reasonably accurate conclusions. If they didn't, we would develop new perceptual sets that were more accurate. But sometimes a perceptual set can lead us astray. For example, someone with an avid interest in UFOs might readily interpret unusual cloud formations as a fleet of alien spacecraft.

People are especially prone to seeing *faces* in ambiguous stimuli, as in the photo here. Why? One reason is that the brain is wired to be uniquely responsive to faces or face-like stimuli (Leopold & Rhodes, 2010; Pascalis & Kelly, 2009). The primate brain has been found to contain individual neurons that respond exclusively to faces or face-like images (Tsao, 2006; Tsao et al., 2006). This specialized face-recognition system allows us to identify an individual face out of the thousands that we can recognize (Kanwisher & Yovel, 2009).

But this extraordinary neural sensitivity also makes us more liable to false positives, seeing faces that aren't there. Vague or ambiguous images with face-like blotches and shadows can also trigger the brain's face-recognition system. Thus, we see faces where they don't exist at all — except in our own minds.

Closing Thoughts

From reflections of light waves to perceptual illusions, the world you perceive is the result of complex interactions among distinctly dissimilar elements — environmental stimuli, sensory receptor cells, neural pathways, and brain mechanisms. Equally important are the psychological and cultural factors that help shape your perception of the world. The world we experience relies not only on the functioning of our different sensory systems but also on neural pathways sculpted by years of learning experiences from infancy onward (Huber et al., 2015).

Mike May spent more than four decades totally blind, but never seemed to lack vision. He sought out a life of change and adventure — and he found it. Rather than expecting his surgery to fundamentally change his life, he simply welcomed the opportunity for new experiences. Throughout his life, Mike wrote, "I have sought change and thrive on it. I expected new and interesting experiences from getting vision as an adult but not that it would change my life" (May, 2004). As Mike points out, "My life was incredibly good before I had my operation. I've been very fortunate and had incredible opportunities, and so I can say that life was incredible. It was fantastic as a non-seeing person, and life is still amazing now that I have vision. That's been consistent between not seeing and seeing. Experiencing life to its fullest doesn't depend on having sight" (May, 2002).

In the next section, we'll provide you with some tips that we think you'll find useful in influencing your perceptions of painful stimuli.

⌄ Now I Can See After regaining some sight, Mike May said, "I gained some new elements of my personality and lifestyle without rejecting the blindness. I am not even simply a visually impaired person. I am Mike with his quirky sense of humor, graying hair, passion for life, and rather unusual combination of sensory skills."

Alyson Aliano

PSYCH FOR YOUR LIFE

Strategies to Control Pain

Pain specialists use a variety of techniques to control pain, including *hypnosis* and *pain-killing drugs* (Flor, 2014). We'll discuss both of these topics in the next chapter. Another pain-relieving strategy is *acupuncture*.

Acupuncture is a pain-relieving technique that has been used in traditional Chinese medicine for thousands of years. Acupuncture involves inserting tiny, sterile needles at specific points in the body. The needles are then twirled, heated, or stimulated with a mild electrical current. Exactly how this stimulation diminishes pain signals or the perception of pain has yet to be completely explained (Moffet, 2008, 2009). Some research has shown that acupuncture stimulates the release of endorphins in the brain (Field, 2009). Evidence suggests that psychological factors also play a significant role in the pain-relieving effects of acupuncture. A meta-analysis of dozens of studies found that acupuncture was significantly more effective than sham acupuncture or usual-care treatment in relieving pain associated with chronic headaches, arthritis, and chronic back, neck, and shoulder pain (Avins, 2012; Vickers et al., 2012). Similar results were found in a meta-analysis of postoperative pain (Wu et al., 2016).

But what about everyday pain, such as the pain that accompanies a sprained ankle or a trip to the dentist? There are several simple techniques that you can use to help cope with minor pain.

Acupuncture for Pain Relief Acupuncture is a pain-relieving technique that involves inserting tiny needles at specific points in the body. The needles are then twirled, heated, or stimulated with a mild electrical current. In fact, a meta-analysis showed that acupuncture was more effective than the usual treatments for chronic headaches, arthritis, and chronic back pain (Avins, 2012; Vickers et al., 2012).

Self-Administered Strategies

1. Distraction

By actively focusing your attention on some nonpainful task, you can often reduce pain (Edwards et al., 2009). For example, you can mentally count backward by sevens from 901, draw different geometric figures in your mind, or focus on the details of a picture or other object. Intently listening to an interesting podcast or calming music can also reduce discomfort (Loewy & Spintge, 2011; North & Hargreaves, 2009).

2. Imagery

Creating a vivid mental image can help control pain (Pincus & Sheikh, 2009). Usually people create a pleasant and progressive scenario, such as walking along the beach or hiking in the mountains. Try to imagine all the different sensations involved, including the sights, sounds, aromas, touches, and tastes. The goal is to become so absorbed in your fantasy that you distract yourself from sensations of pain.

3. Relaxation

Deep relaxation can be a very effective strategy for deterring pain sensations (Edwards et al., 2009; Turk & Winter, 2006). One simple relaxation strategy is deep breathing: Inhale deeply, then exhale very slowly and completely, releasing tension throughout your body. As you exhale, consciously note the feelings of relaxation and warmth you've produced in your body.

4. Meditation

Several studies have shown that practicing meditation is an effective way to minimize pain (see Flor, 2014; Grant et al., 2010, 2011). Meditation may reduce the subjective experience of pain through multiple pathways, including relaxation, distraction, and inducing a sense of detachment from the painful experience (Jacob, 2016; Zeidan & Vago, 2016). Apparently, you do not need to be an expert to benefit from meditation's pain-relieving effects. Fadel Zeidan and his colleagues (2011) found that after just four 20-minute training sessions in a simple meditation technique, participants' ratings of the unpleasantness of a painful stimulus dropped by 57 percent. (We'll discuss meditation in more detail in the next chapter.)

5. Positive self-talk and reappraisal

This strategy involves making positive coping statements, either silently or out loud, during a painful episode or procedure. Examples of positive self-talk include statements such as, "It hurts, but I'm in control" and "I'm uncomfortable, but I can handle it."

Self-talk can also include reappraising or redefining the pain (Edwards et al., 2009). Substituting realistic and constructive thoughts about the pain experience for threatening or helpless thoughts can significantly reduce pain. For example, an athlete in training might say, "The pain means my muscles are getting stronger."

Can Magnets Relieve Pain?

Our students frequently ask us about different *complementary and alternative medicines (CAMs)*. Complementary and alternative medicines are a diverse group of health care systems, practices, or products that are *not* currently considered to be part of conventional medicine. Scientific evidence exists for some CAM therapies, such as massage (Moyer et al., 2004). Therapies that are scientifically proven to be safe and effective usually become adopted by the mainstream health care system. However, the effectiveness and safety of many CAMs have not been proven by well-designed scientific studies.

Magnets are one popular CAM that have been used for many centuries to treat pain. But can magnets relieve pain? To date, there is *no* evidence supporting the idea that magnets relieve pain (Natural Standard Monographs, 2009). The pain relief that some people experience could be due to a placebo effect, or expectations that pain will decrease. Or the relief could come from whatever holds the magnet in place, such as a warm bandage or the cushioned insole (Weintraub et al., 2003).

One final note: The techniques described here are not a substitute for seeking appropriate medical attention, especially when pain is severe, recurring, or of unknown origin. If pain persists, seek medical attention.

Is it true that magnets can relieve pain?

CHAPTER REVIEW

Sensation and Perception

 **Achieve,** Macmillan Learning's online study platform, features the full e-book of *Discovering Psychology*, the **LearningCurve** adaptive quizzing system, videos, and a variety of activities to boost your learning. Visit **Achieve** at macmillanlearning.com.

KEY PEOPLE

Max Wertheimer, p. 98

KEY TERMS

sensation, p. 76
perception, p. 76
sensory receptors, p. 76
absolute threshold, p. 77
difference threshold, p. 77
transduction, p. 77
sensory adaptation, p. 78
wavelength, p. 78
pupil, p. 80
lens, p. 80
accommodation, p. 80
retina, p. 80
rods, p. 80
cones, p. 80
fovea, p. 80
blind spot, p. 80

optic nerve, p. 82
optic chiasm, p. 82
color, p. 83
trichromatic theory of color vision, p. 85
opponent-process theory of color vision, p. 85
audition, p. 86
pitch, p. 87
frequency, p. 87
outer ear, p. 87
eardrum, p. 87
middle ear, p. 87
inner ear, p. 87
cochlea, p. 87
basilar membrane, p. 88

hair cells, p. 88
frequency theory, p. 89
place theory, p. 89
olfaction, p. 90
gustation, p. 90
pheromones, p. 91
olfactory bulb, p. 92
taste buds, p. 93
pain, p. 94
gate-control theory of pain, p. 95
proprioception, p. 96
ESP (extrasensory perception), p. 97
parapsychology, p. 97
bottom-up processing, p. 98

top-down processing, p. 98
Gestalt psychology, p. 98
figure–ground relationship, p. 99
depth perception, p. 100
monocular cues, p. 100
binocular cues, p. 101
perceptual constancy, p. 102
size constancy, p. 102
shape constancy, p. 102
perceptual illusion, p. 103
Müller-Lyer illusion, p. 103
moon illusion, p. 103
perceptual set, p. 105

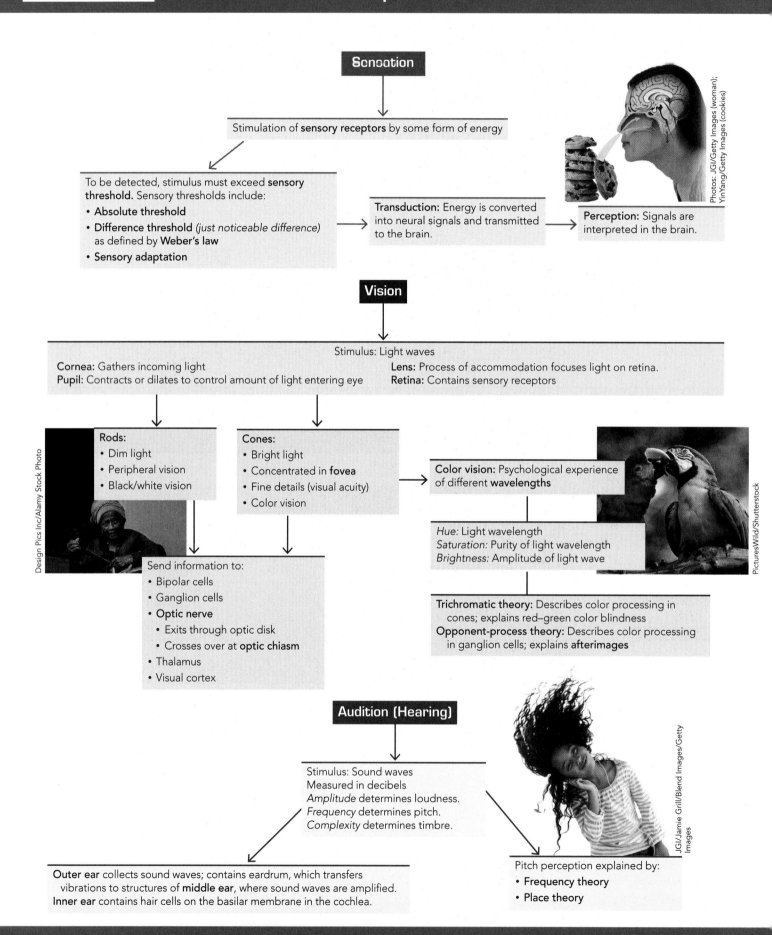

Sensation

Stimulation of **sensory receptors** by some form of energy

To be detected, stimulus must exceed **sensory threshold.** Sensory thresholds include:
- **Absolute threshold**
- **Difference threshold** (*just noticeable difference*) as defined by **Weber's law**
- **Sensory adaptation**

Transduction: Energy is converted into neural signals and transmitted to the brain.

Perception: Signals are interpreted in the brain.

Photos: JGI/Getty Images (woman); YinYang/Getty Images (cookies)

Vision

Stimulus: Light waves

Cornea: Gathers incoming light
Pupil: Contracts or dilates to control amount of light entering eye

Lens: Process of accommodation focuses light on retina.
Retina: Contains sensory receptors

Design Pics Inc/Alamy Stock Photo

Rods:
- Dim light
- Peripheral vision
- Black/white vision

Cones:
- Bright light
- Concentrated in **fovea**
- Fine details (visual acuity)
- Color vision

Color vision: Psychological experience of different **wavelengths**

Hue: Light wavelength
Saturation: Purity of light wavelength
Brightness: Amplitude of light wave

PicturesWild/Shutterstock

Send information to:
- Bipolar cells
- Ganglion cells
- **Optic nerve**
  - Exits through optic disk
  - Crosses over at **optic chiasm**
- Thalamus
- Visual cortex

Trichromatic theory: Describes color processing in cones; explains red–green color blindness
Opponent-process theory: Describes color processing in ganglion cells; explains **afterimages**

Audition (Hearing)

Stimulus: Sound waves
Measured in decibels
Amplitude determines loudness.
Frequency determines pitch.
Complexity determines timbre.

JGI/Jamie Grill/Blend Images/Getty Images

Outer ear collects sound waves; contains eardrum, which transfers vibrations to structures of **middle ear**, where sound waves are amplified.
Inner ear contains hair cells on the basilar membrane in the cochlea.

Pitch perception explained by:
- Frequency theory
- Place theory

Chemical and Body Senses

Smell (olfaction): When stimulated by airborne chemicals, receptor cells transmit signals along axons to **olfactory bulb** and on to other brain regions.

Proprioception: Sensory neurons called *proprioceptors* detect changes in body position and movement.

Taste (gustation): When stimulated by chemicals in saliva, **taste buds** send neural messages to the thalamus and on to other brain regions.

Vestibular system: Receptor cells in semicircular canals and vestibular sacs detect changes in body position and help maintain balance and equilibrium.

Courtesy of Noam Sobel

Pain: Stimulation of free nerve endings, called **nociceptors,** trigger:
- Fast pain system—sharp, intense pain
- Slow pain system—dull, chronic pain

Gate-control theory of pain describes how psychological and other factors affect the experience of pain.

Perception

The process of integrating, organizing, and interpreting sensory information

Top-down processing, Bottom-up processing

Gestalt psychology emphasized perception of whole forms, or gestalts.

Gestalt principles of perception and organization:
- **Figure–ground relationship**
- Law of similarity
- Law of closure
- Law of good continuation
- Law of proximity

Depth perception

Monocular cues:
- Relative size
- Overlap
- Aerial perspective
- Texture gradient
- Linear perspective
- Motion parallax

Binocular cues:
- Convergence
- Binocular disparity

Perceptual principles

Perceptual constancy: Objects are perceived as stable despite changes in sensory input.
- **Size constancy**
- **Shape constancy**
- **Color constancy**

Perceptual illusions:
- **Müller-Lyer illusion**
- **Moon illusion**

Motion perception:
- Induced motion
- Stroboscopic motion

Perception is influenced by experience.
Perceptual set is the tendency to perceive objects from a particular frame of reference.

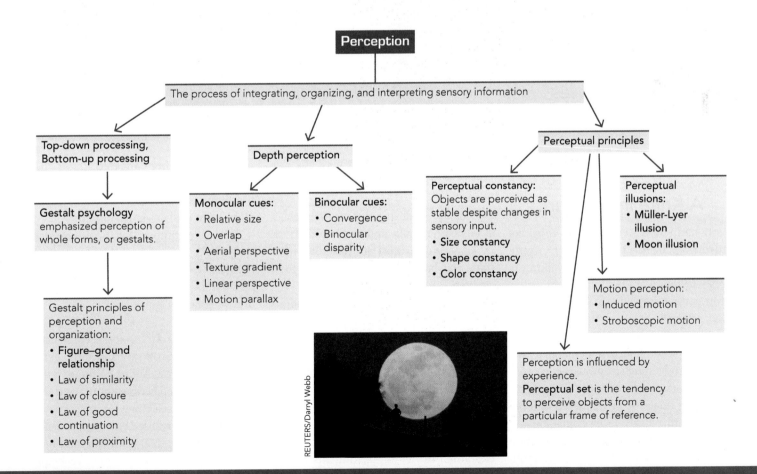

REUTERS/Darryl Webb

MYTH OR SCIENCE?

Is it true . . .

▶ That multitasking is an efficient way to get things done?

▶ That you can have coherent conversations with people who are talking in their sleep?

▶ That sleeping pills are an effective way to treat chronic insomnia?

▶ That it can be dangerous to wake a sleepwalker?

▶ That you can be hypnotized against your will?

▶ That meditation is a drowsy, trancelike state that is no different from simple relaxation?

▶ That e-cigarettes are *not* addictive?

Consciousness and Its Variations

PROLOGUE
~

A Knife in the Dark

Scott had some sleepwalking episodes growing up, but his parents weren't overly concerned about them. Sleepwalking is pretty common among kids. "I remember Scott getting dressed at midnight, glassy-eyed, saying he had to go to school," Scott's mother recalled.

Scott's sister, Laura, remembers a particularly frightening sleepwalking incident when Scott was in college "and stressing" about finals. Scott wandered into the kitchen with a glazed facial expression and reached for the doorknob. Laura quickly leaned around him to lock the deadbolt.

That's when Scott grabbed her. "His face looked almost demonic when he reacted to me."

Scott eventually married his high school sweetheart, Yarmila, and had two children. By all accounts, Scott and Yarmila's marriage was happy, revolving around their children.

However, Scott was under tremendous pressure at his job. He often worked night after night with three hours of sleep or less. To stay alert and focused at work, he resorted to taking caffeine tablets. After several nights in a row with very little sleep, Scott would "crash" early to catch up on his sleep.

Finally, at dinner one night, Scott explained to his family that his team's

project was being canceled. Later that night, Yarmila fell asleep on the couch in the family room. Scott kissed her good night, went upstairs, and "crashed."

Less than an hour later, Scott was startled awake by the sound of their dogs barking wildly. Disoriented, he rushed downstairs. Two police officers, guns drawn, yelled at him to get facedown on the floor.

"What's going on?" Scott asked, confused.

For an hour, Scott sat handcuffed in the back of a police car. At first he thought that Yarmila had been seriously hurt and that the police were searching for the perpetrator. But then he realized Yarmila was dead.

It was almost 2:00 A.M. when a Phoenix Police Department detective began

CHAPTER 4

Ugurhan Betin/Exactostock-1672/Superstock

interrogating Scott. "What set you off?" the detective asked.

Scott replied, "Obviously, you think I killed her. I don't know what makes you think that."

"Because a neighbor saw you do it."

"I'm sorry. I don't remember doing it," Scott answered, then paused. "How did she die?"

"Well, the neighbor says you stabbed her and dragged her over to the pool and held her under the water. What did she do to set you off like that?"

"Nothing."

"Nothing went wrong?"

"I love my wife. I love my kids."

Scott had stabbed Yarmila 44 times, then left her floating facedown in the pool. But he had no memory of his actions.

Could Scott have unknowingly committed such violent acts while he was sleepwalking? Is it possible for someone to carry out complex actions, like driving, while asleep?

In this chapter, we'll tackle those questions and others as we explore variations in our experience of consciousness. As you'll see, psychologists have learned a great deal about our daily fluctuations of consciousness. Psychologists have also gained insight into the different ways that alterations in consciousness can be induced, such as through the use of hypnosis, meditation, or psychoactive drugs. We'll return to Scott's story to help illustrate some of these concepts. ∿

consciousness Personal awareness of mental activities, internal sensations, and the external environment.

attention The capacity to selectively focus awareness on particular stimuli in your external environment or on your internal thoughts or sensations.

Phoenix Police Department, Public Records

▲ **Murder while sleepwalking?** Scott Falater had a history of sleepwalking. After a neighbor witnessed Scott killing his wife, Yarmila, late one night, Scott claimed to have no memory of his actions. Could Scott really have murdered Yarmila without awareness? Could he have unknowingly committed this horrific crime while sleepwalking? This tragic murder led to questions about the nature of consciousness.

▲ **William James and the Stream of Consciousness** We now often use the phrase "stream of consciousness," first used by prominent early psychologist William James. James explained that consciousness "does not appear to itself chopped up in bits. . . . It is nothing jointed; it flows. A "river" or a "stream" are the metaphors by which it is most naturally described. In talking of it hereafter, let us call it the stream of thought, or consciousness, of subjective life."
—*William James (1892)*

Introduction: Consciousness: Experiencing the "Private I"

■ KEY THEME
The topic of consciousness includes understanding waking awareness, where you focus your attention, and the dangers when attention is split.

⹀ KEY QUESTIONS
- What did William James mean by the phrase "stream of consciousness"?
- What are the functions of consciousness?
- How is attention defined, and how do the limitations of attention affect human thought and behavior?

The nature of consciousness is difficult to define precisely. For our purposes, we'll use a simple definition: **Consciousness** is your *personal awareness of mental activities, internal sensations, and the external environment.*

Take a few moments to pay attention to your own experience of consciousness. You'll notice that the contents of your awareness shift from one moment to the next. Among other activities, your mental experience might include *focused attention* on this textbook; *awareness of internal sensations,* such as hunger or a throbbing headache; or *planning* and *active problem-solving,* such as mentally rehearsing an upcoming meeting with your adviser.

Even though your conscious experience is constantly changing, you don't experience your personal consciousness as disjointed. Rather, your experience of consciousness has a sense of continuity. This characteristic of consciousness led the influential psychologist **William James** (1892) to describe consciousness as a "stream" or "river." Despite the changing focus of our awareness, our experience of consciousness as an unbroken "stream" helps provide us with a sense of personal identity that has continuity from one day to the next.

Our definition of consciousness refers to waking awareness. However, psychologists also study other types of conscious experience, which we'll consider later in the chapter. But first, we'll take a closer look at the nature of awareness.

Attention: The Mind's Spotlight

Lost in your thoughts, you don't notice when your friend asks you a question. "Are you listening?" your friend asks impatiently.

But what *is* attention? In reality, you are always "paying attention" to *something*—just not always the stimuli that you're *supposed* to be paying attention to. For example, when your mind "wanders," you are focusing on your internal environment—your daydreams or thoughts—rather than your external environment (Smilek et al., 2010).

Like consciousness, *attention* is one of the oldest topics in psychology (Raz, 2009). And, like consciousness, attention is difficult to define precisely.

For our purposes, we'll define **attention** as *the capacity to selectively focus awareness on particular stimuli in your external environment or on your internal thoughts or sensations* (Chun et al., 2011; Posner & Rothbart, 2007). Most of the time, we deliberately control our attentional processes, which helps us regulate our thoughts and feelings. For example, we may deliberately turn our attention to a pleasant thought or memory when troubled by a painful memory (Baumeister & Masicampo, 2010; Baumeister et al., 2011).

Psychologists have identified a number of characteristics of attention, some of which have important implications for our daily life. These are:

1. *Attention has a limited capacity.*

We cannot pay attention to *all* of the sights, sounds, and other sensations in our external environments. Similarly, the range of potential thoughts, memories, or fantasies available to us at any given time is overwhelming. Thus, we focus our attention on the information that is most relevant to our goals (Ristic & Enns, 2015).

2. *Attention is selective.*

Attention is often compared to a spotlight that we shine on particular stimuli while ignoring others (Dijksterhuis & Aarts, 2010). A classic example of the selective nature of attention is the *cocktail party effect* (Hill & Miller, 2010; Pashler, 1998). At a noisy party, you monitor multiple streams of auditory information, but focus your attention on your own conversation. But should someone nearby mention your name, you'll shift your attention and miss what is next said in your own conversation.

3. *Attention can be "blind."*

Given the limited, selective nature of attention, it's not surprising that we sometimes completely miss what seem to be obvious stimuli in our field of vision or hearing. For example, magicians use a strategy called *misdirection* to deliberately draw the audience's attention away from the "method," or secret action, and toward the "effect," which refers to what the magician wants the audience to perceive (Macknik et al., 2008). To experience a bit of magic firsthand, direct your attention to **Figure 4.1**, and try the demonstration before you read on.

Magicians also exploit a phenomenon called *inattentional blindness*, which occurs when we simply don't notice some significant object or event that is in our clear field of vision (Mack & Rock, 2000). Because we have a limited capacity for attention, the more attention we devote to one task, the less attention we have for another. That is why we may fail to notice an event or object, especially if it is unexpected or unusual, when we are engaged in one task that demands a great deal of our attention.

For example, if a clown on a unicycle crossed your path while you were walking across campus, do you think you would notice? Psychologist Ira Hyman enlisted a student to dress up as a clown and slowly unicycle across a busy campus square (Hyman et al., 2010). Researchers later stopped people whose paths had crossed with the unicycling clown and asked them whether they had seen him. Most of the people who were walking alone, in pairs, or who were listening to music *did* remember seeing the clown. However, fully three-fourths of those talking on their phones failed to notice the clown.

Finally, *change blindness* is also relatively common. Change blindness refers to not noticing when something changes, such as when a friend gets a haircut or shaves his beard (Rosielle & Scaggs, 2008). Were you fooled by the magic trick in Figure 4.1? If so, you can blame change blindness.

Think you're good at paying attention? Go to **Achieve** and try **Video Activity: Attention.**

FIGURE 4.1[A] Can We Read Your Mind? We'd like you to participate in a mind-reading experiment. Please follow all directions as carefully as you can. First, pick one of the six cards below and remember it.

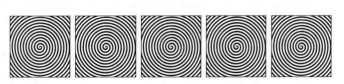

Say its name aloud several times so you won't forget it. Once you're sure you'll remember it, cross out one of the spirals in the row to the right. Then turn to page 115.

The Perils of Multitasking

Multitasking refers to paying attention to two or more sources of stimuli at once—such as doing homework while watching television, or talking on the phone while cooking dinner. In essence, multitasking involves the *division of attention.* So, it is a myth that multitasking is an efficient way to get things done. When attention is divided among different tasks, each task receives less attention than it would normally (Borst et al., 2010; Lavie, 2010; Poljac et al., 2018). Some people *are* better at handling multiple tasks than others (Goel & Schnusenberg, 2019; Seegmiller et al., 2011). However, people generally underestimate the costs of multitasking. When you attempt to do two things at once—such as talk on the phone while studying—your performance on *both* tasks is impaired (Finley et al., 2014).

In general, tasks that are very different are least likely to interfere with each other. There is evidence that visual and auditory tasks draw on independent, different attention resources—at least for simple, well-rehearsed tasks. For example, listening to the radio (an auditory task) interferes less with driving (a visual task) than would a second visual task (Borst et al., 2010). However, this is *not* the case when one of the tasks requires a great deal of concentration. Absorption in a visual task can produce inattentional deafness, and absorption in an auditory task can produce inattentional blindness (Macdonald & Lavie, 2011).

The perils of divided attention are especially obvious when people use cell phones. As demonstrated by the unicycling clown study, using a cell phone seems to absorb a great deal of attentional resources. Because cell phone conversations are so engrossing, they are especially likely to produce inattentional blindness (Chabris & Simons, 2010). One study found that driving was more impaired when drivers were talking on a cell phone than when the same drivers were legally drunk (Strayer et al., 2006). Unsurprisingly, texting and browsing social media while driving are also quite dangerous (Hashash et al., 2019). And, it turns out, using a hands-free device while driving does not improve safety. It's the *attention* devoted to the conversation that is dangerously distracting to drivers (see Baumeister et al., 2011; Drews et al., 2008). In fact, in the United States, 9 percent of deaths in traffic accidents were caused by driver distraction, often because of cell phone use (National Highway Traffic Safety Administration, 2017). And globally, the World Health Organization (2020b) reports that drivers using cell phones are four times as likely to be involved in a traffic accident as drivers not using cell phones.

Inattention among pedestrians using cell phones is just as dangerous (Simmons et al., 2020). In one study, researchers set up video cameras to record pedestrians and cars at several intersections that had crosswalks, but no traffic lights (Zhang et al., 2019).

MYTH ◀ **SCIENCE**

Is it true that multitasking is an efficient way to get things done?

THINK LIKE A SCIENTIST

Are you good at working on several tasks at once? Go to Achieve: Resources to **Think Like a Scientist** about **Multitasking.**

🏔 Achieve

❯ **Inattention Blindness.** Surprisingly, sometimes we don't notice obvious stimuli in our environment, which is called inattentional blindness. Here, the boy walking next to this body of water is so absorbed in his smartphone that he doesn't notice the two ducks hanging out sunning themselves.

Mona Cauley/Shutterstock

Pedestrians using cell phones while crossing were slower to leave the curb when it was safe to cross, less likely to look around at traffic, and more likely to have close calls than pedestrians not using cell phones.

Cycles of Consciousness: Circadian Rhythms and Sleep

■ KEY THEME
Consciousness, like many other body functions, varies in a systematic way over the course of every 24-hour period.

≡ KEY QUESTIONS
- What are circadian rhythms, and how do they regulate body functions?
- What are the different stages of sleep, and how do they progress through the night?
- What evidence suggests that we have a biological need for sleep?

Throughout the course of each day, consciousness ebbs and flows in a natural rhythm. The most dramatic of these variations, of course, is our daily cycle of sleep and wakefulness. But sleep and wakefulness are only the most obvious of the cyclic changes that mark our days—and our nights.

Biological and Environmental "Clocks" That Regulate Consciousness

What time do you usually wake up? When do you naturally feel most alert? Sleepiest? From body temperature to mental alertness, more than 100 body processes rhythmically peak and dip at consistent times each day. This variation is called a **circadian rhythm**, *a roughly 24-hour long cycle of fluctuations in biological and psychological processes.*

Your many circadian rhythms are controlled by a master biological clock—a tiny cluster of neurons in the *hypothalamus* in the brain (see **Figure 4.2**). In humans, light detected by special photoreceptors in the eye sends signals via the optic nerve to this cluster of neurons in the hypothalamus (Drouyer et al., 2007).

Environmental cues help keep circadian rhythms synchronized. The most important environmental cue is sunlight. As the sun sets, the decrease in available light is detected by the hypothalamus, which then triggers an increase in the production of a hormone called *melatonin.* Melatonin is manufactured by the *pineal gland,* an endocrine gland located in the brain. Increased blood levels of melatonin cause sleepiness, so you feel sleepy in the evening. Bright light *suppresses* the production of melatonin. Shortly before sunrise, when available light is increased, the pineal gland all but stops producing melatonin, and you soon wake up. In this way, sunlight regulates the hypothalamus so it keeps your circadian rhythms synchronized. Exposure to artificial light, including that generated by computer or tablet screens, also influences circadian rhythms (Dijk et al., 2012; Tähkämö et al., 2019).

Exposure to environmental time signals is necessary for us to stay synchronized to a 24-hour day. In the absence of external time cues, our internal body clock drifts to its

Want to Sleep Better? Turn Off That Screen! Smartphone, tablet, and laptop screens all emit blue light, which mimics daylight, increasing alertness and suppressing melatonin, leading to problems sleeping (Twenge et al., 2019). When researchers compared the effects of reading a print book with reading a light-emitting e-book 2 hours before bedtime, they found that the e-book readers took longer to fall asleep, had disrupted sleep patterns, and were less alert the next day than the print book readers (Chang et al., 2015).

circadian rhythm (ser-KADE-ee-en) A roughly 24-hour-long cycle of fluctuations in biological and psychological processes.

FIGURE 4.2 The Biological Clock
Special photoreceptors in the retina regulate the effects of light on the body's circadian rhythms (Menaker, 2003). In response to morning light, signals from these special photoreceptors are relayed via the optic nerve to neurons in the hypothalamus. In turn, these neurons reduce the pineal gland's production of melatonin, a hormone that causes sleepiness. As blood levels of melatonin decrease, mental alertness increases. Daily exposure to bright light, especially sunlight, helps keep the body's circadian rhythms synchronized and operating on a 24-hour schedule.

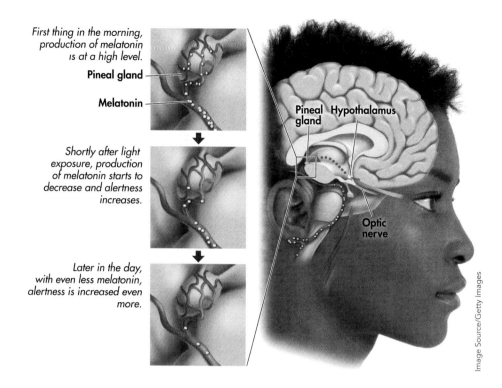

First thing in the morning, production of melatonin is at a high level.

Pineal gland

Melatonin

Shortly after light exposure, production of melatonin starts to decrease and alertness increases.

Later in the day, with even less melatonin, alertness is increased even more.

Pineal gland   Hypothalamus

Optic nerve

Image Source/Getty Images

> **Circadian Rhythms and People Who Are Blind** This woman, who has been blind since birth, confidently navigates her environment with the help of her guide dog. Many people with total blindness have desynchronized circadian rhythms because they're unable to detect the sunlight that normally sets the body's internal biological clock. Like sighted people deprived of all environmental time cues, blind people can experience desynchronized melatonin, body temperature, and sleep–wake circadian cycles. Consequently, about 60 percent of blind people suffer from recurring bouts of insomnia and other sleep problems (Arendt et al., 2005; Mistlberger & Skene, 2005).

Africa Studio/Shutterstock

natural—or *intrinsic*—rhythm. Interestingly, our intrinsic circadian rhythm is about 24.2 hours, or slightly *longer* than a day (Czeisler & Gooley, 2007). When there are no external time cues, our normally coordinated circadian rhythms become desynchronized.

When environmental signals are out of sync with your internal body clock, such as when you travel and cross multiple time zones, you may experience symptoms of *jet lag.* You experience physical and mental fatigue, confusion or problems concentrating, depression or irritability, and disrupted sleep. Jet lag tends to be more severe in an eastward direction (moving your clock forward and shortening your day) than travel in a westward direction (moving your clock back and lengthening your day), probably because of our natural tendency toward days that are slightly longer than 24 hours (Roach & Sargent, 2019). Professional athletes are not immune to this phenomenon: eastward travel impaired performance of Major League Baseball teams in the United States more than westward travel (Song et al., 2017).

The Dawn of Modern Sleep Research

The invention of the electroencephalograph by German psychiatrist Hans Berger in the 1920s gave sleep researchers an important tool (Stern, 2001). The **electroencephalograph**, or EEG, is *an instrument that uses electrodes placed on the scalp to measure and record the brain's rhythmic electrical activity.* These rhythmic patterns of electrical activity are referred to as *brain waves.* Sleep researchers firmly established that brain-wave activity systematically changes throughout sleep by studying the graphic record of EEGs.

electroencephalograph (e-lec-tro-en-SEFF-uh-low-graph) An instrument that uses electrodes placed on the scalp to measure and record the brain's rhythmic electrical activity.

Most people tend to think of sleep as an "either/or" condition—the brain is *either* awake and active *or* asleep and idle. In fact, sleep researchers know that the sleeping brain doesn't just shut down during sleep. The sleeping brain remains active, although its patterns of activity are distinctly different from the patterns displayed by the waking brain (Colwell, 2011; Nir et al., 2011; Vyazovskiy et al., 2011).

Sleep researchers distinguish between two basic types of sleep. **REM sleep**, or *rapid-eye-movement sleep*, is a *type of sleep during which rapid eye movements (REM) and dreaming usually occur and voluntary muscle activity is suppressed*. In contrast, during **NREM sleep**, or *non-rapid-eye-movement sleep*, is *quiet, typically dreamless sleep in which rapid eye movements are absent*. Usually pronounced as "non-REM sleep," it is further divided into three stages, as we'll describe shortly (Stevner et al., 2019).

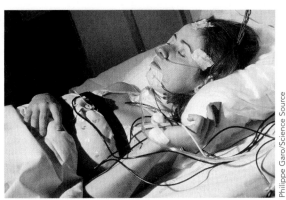

Wired for Sleep Using electrodes pasted to the scalp, the *electroencephalogram* (EEG) detects changes in the brain's electrical activity. Other instruments record eye and muscle movements, respirations, heart rate, and body temperature. Although it may look uncomfortable, most people involved in sleep studies become oblivious to the electrodes and wires as they drift into sleep (Carskadon & Rechtschaffen, 2005).

The Onset of Sleep

Awake and reasonably alert as you prepare for bed, your brain generates **beta brain waves**, a *brain-wave pattern associated with alert wakefulness*. After your head hits the pillow and you close your eyes, your muscles relax. Your brain's electrical activity gradually gears down, generating slightly larger and slower **alpha brain waves**, a *brain-wave pattern associated with relaxed wakefulness and drowsiness*.

During this drowsy, presleep phase, you may experience odd but vividly realistic sensations called *hypnagogic hallucinations,* like hearing a loud crash or feeling as if you are flying. Perhaps the most common hypnagogic hallucination is the vivid sensation of falling. This is often accompanied by a *myoclonic jerk,* an involuntary but harmless full-body spasm that jolts the person awake. But sometimes, hypnagogic imagery reflects everyday experience or preoccupations. For example, about a third of participants who learned a new video game, *Alpine Racer II,* reported hypnagogic images related to the skiing game (Schwartz, 2010; Wamsley et al., 2010). Psychologist Melissa Burkley (2019) described the "magic" of a hypnogogic state, during which "you get the best of both worlds. You experience the creatively rich visions and ideas normally found in deep sleep, but you are still aware enough to consciously process and remember the experiences" (p. 26).

The First 90 Minutes of Sleep and Beyond

The course of a normal night's sleep follows a relatively consistent cyclical pattern. As you drift off to sleep, you enter NREM sleep and begin a progression through the three NREM sleep stages (see **Figure 4.3**). Each progressive NREM sleep stage is characterized by corresponding decreases in brain and body activity (Stevner et al., 2019).

NREM Sleep   As the alpha brain waves of drowsiness are replaced by even slower *theta brain waves,* you enter the first stage of sleep. Lasting only a few minutes, stage 1 is a transitional stage during which you gradually disengage from the sensations of the surrounding world. During stage 1 NREM, you can quickly regain conscious alertness if needed.

Stage 2 represents the onset of true sleep. Stage 2 sleep is defined by the appearance of *sleep spindles,* brief bursts of brain activity that last a second or two, and *K complexes,* single high-voltage spikes of brain activity (see Figure 4.3). Other than these occasional sleep spindles and K complexes, brain activity continues to slow down. Theta waves are predominant in stage 2, but larger, slower brain waves, called *delta brain waves,* also begin to emerge, and their activity gradually increases.

You now enter the deepest stage of sleep—stage 3, or *slow-wave sleep,* so called because this stage of sleep is dominated by "slow" delta brain waves. During the night's first episode of stage 3 NREM, delta waves eventually come to represent 100 percent of brain activity. At that point, heart rate, blood pressure, and breathing rate drop to their lowest levels. Not surprisingly, the sleeper is almost completely oblivious to the world.

REM sleep Type of sleep during which rapid eye movements (REM) and dreaming usually occur and voluntary muscle activity is suppressed.

NREM sleep Quiet, typically dreamless sleep in which rapid eye movements are absent.

beta brain waves Brain-wave pattern associated with alert wakefulness.

alpha brain waves Brain-wave pattern associated with relaxed wakefulness and drowsiness.

◉ IN FOCUS

What You Really Want to Know About Sleep

Why do I yawn?

The notion that too little oxygen or too much carbon dioxide causes yawning is not supported by research. However, yawning is typically followed by an *increase* in activity level and some evidence suggests that yawning regulates and increases your level of arousal. Hence, you frequently yawn after waking up in the morning, while attempting to stay awake in the late evening, or when you're bored.

Is yawning contagious?

Seeing, hearing, or thinking about yawning can trigger a yawn. More than half of adults will yawn when they're shown videos of other people yawning. Blind people will yawn more frequently in response to audio recordings of yawning. Some psychologists believe that contagious yawning is related to our ability to feel empathy for others. (Have you yawned yet?) Interestingly, chimpanzees and macaques, both highly social animals, display contagious yawning. So do domestic dogs, which in a recent study were shown to "catch" yawns from human strangers. From an evolutionary perspective, such observations lend support to the idea that contagious yawning may have evolved as an adaptive social cue, allowing groups to signal and coordinate times of activity and rest. In support of that view, a study found that chimpanzees yawn more after viewing videos of other chimpanzees yawning—but *only* if the chimps were members of their own social group.

Why do I get sleepy?

A naturally occurring compound in the body called *adenosine* may be the culprit. In studies with cats, prolonged wakefulness sharply

increases adenosine levels, which reflect energy used for brain and body activity. As adenosine levels shoot up, so does the need for sleep. Slow-wave NREM sleep reduces adenosine levels. In humans, the common stimulant drug caffeine blocks adenosine receptors, promoting wakefulness.

Sometimes in the morning when I first wake up, I can't move. I'm literally paralyzed! Is this normal?

REM sleep is characterized by paralysis of the voluntary muscles, which keeps you from acting out your dreams. **Sleep paralysis** is *a temporary condition in which a person is unable to move upon awakening in the morning or during the night.* A relatively common phenomenon, the paralysis of REM sleep carries over to the waking state for up to 10 minutes. If preceded by an unpleasant dream or hypnagogic experience, this sensation can be frightening. Sleep paralysis can also occur as you're falling asleep. In either case, the sleep paralysis lasts for only a few minutes. So, if this happens to you, relax—voluntary muscle control will soon return.

Do people who are deaf and use sign language sometimes "sleep-sign" during sleep?

Yes.

Do the things people say when they talk in their sleep make any sense?

MYTH ◀ SCIENCE

Is it true that you can have coherent conversations with people who are talking in their sleep?

Sleeptalking typically occurs during NREM stage 3. There are many anecdotes of partners who have supposedly engaged their sleeptalking mates in extended conversations, but it is a myth that coherent conversations with sleeptalkers are possible. Sleep researchers have been unsuccessful in having extended dialogues with people who chronically talk in their sleep. As for the truthfulness of the sleeptalker's utterances, they're reasonably accurate insofar as they reflect whatever the person is responding to while asleep. By the way, not only do people talk in their sleep, but they can also sing or laugh in their sleep. In one case we know of, a little boy sleep-sang "Frosty the Snowman."

Sources: Campbell & de Waal (2011); Campbell et al. (2009); Cartwright (2004); Empson (2002); Joly-Mascheroni et al. (2008); Landolt (2008); Platek et al. (2005); Pressman (2007); Rétey et al. (2005); Romero et al. (2013); Takeuchi et al. (2002).

Claudio Peri/EPA/Shutterstock

Noises as loud as 90 decibels may fail to wake them. However, their muscles are still capable of movement.

It can easily take 15 minutes or longer to regain full waking consciousness from stage 3. When people are briefly awakened by sleep researchers during stage 3 NREM and asked to perform some simple task, they often don't remember it the next morning.

Thus far, the sleeper is immersed in deeply relaxed stage 3 NREM sleep. Now, the sequence reverses. In a matter of minutes, the sleeper cycles back from stage 3 to stage 2 and enters a dramatic new phase: the night's first episode of REM sleep.

sleep paralysis A temporary condition in which a person is unable to move upon awakening in the morning or during the night.

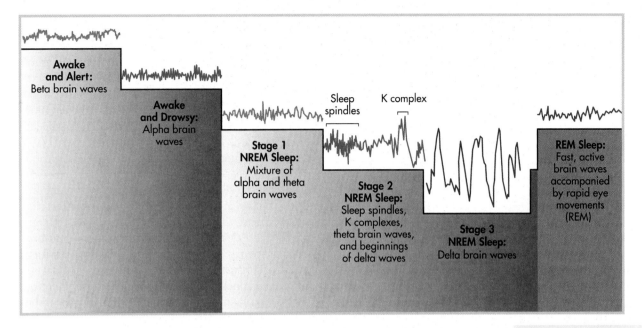

REM Sleep

During REM sleep, the brain becomes more active, generating smaller and faster brain waves. Visual and motor neurons in the brain activate repeatedly, just as they do during wakefulness. Dreams usually occur during REM sleep. Although the brain is very active, voluntary muscle activity is suppressed, which prevents the dreaming sleeper from acting out their dreams.

REM sleep is accompanied by considerable physiological arousal. The sleeper's eyes dart back and forth behind closed eyelids—the rapid eye movements. Heart rate, blood pressure, and respirations can fluctuate up and down, sometimes extremely. Muscle twitches occur. In both sexes, sexual arousal may occur, which is not necessarily related to dream content. From the beginning of stage 1 NREM sleep through the completion of the first episode of REM sleep, about 90 minutes have elapsed.

FIGURE 4.3 The First 90 Minutes of Sleep From wakefulness to the deepest sleep of stage 3 NREM, the brain's activity, measured by EEG recordings, progressively diminishes, as demonstrated by larger and slower brain waves. Over the course of the night, the sleeper continually experiences 90-minute cycles of alternating NREM and REM sleep.

Source: Data from Carskadon & Dement (2005).

Beyond the First 90 Minutes of Sleep

Throughout the rest of the night, the sleeper cycles between NREM and REM sleep. Each sleep cycle lasts about 90 minutes on average, with about five cycles of NREM and REM sleep occurring during a typical night. Just before and after REM periods, the sleeper typically shifts position.

Stage 3 NREM, slow-wave sleep, usually occurs only during the first few 90-minute cycles. As the night progresses, REM sleep episodes become increasingly longer, and less time is spent in NREM sleep. In a later section, we'll look at dreaming and REM sleep in more detail.

Changing Sleep Patterns over the Lifespan

Circadian rhythms seem to develop before birth. During the third trimester of prenatal development, active (REM) and quiet (NREM) sleep cycles emerge. The typical 90-minute sleep cycles gradually emerge over the first few years of life, and the typical 90-minute sleep cycles of alternating REM and NREM sleep are established by age 5 (Grigg-Damberger et al., 2007).

As any parent knows, sleep patterns change throughout childhood and adolescence. Over the lifespan, total sleep time decreases, as does the percentage of a night's sleep spent in deeper slow-wave sleep. The percentage of REM sleep increases during childhood and adolescence, remains stable throughout adulthood, and then decreases during late adulthood (Ohayon et al., 2004).

▲ Sleep-Deprived Adolescents Circadian rhythms shift in adolescence. Adolescents tend to fall asleep later and wake up later. The majority of teenagers worldwide do not get the 8.5 to 9 hours of sleep that they need to feel fully rested. In the United States, more than two-thirds of teenagers report that they get less than 7 hours of sleep on school nights, which is probably why they tend to sleep about 2 hours longer on weekends. Consequences of regular sleep loss include poor school performance, increased risk of accidents and injuries, and depressed mood (Colrain & Baker, 2011; Galván, 2020).

Don Johnston_MA/Alamy Stock Photo

Question: When Does an 800-Pound Predator Sleep? Answer: Any time it wants to! Sleep patterns vary widely across species. For example, sleep duration in mammals varies from a low of 3 hours a day in grazing animals like horses to up to 20 hours a day in bats (Siegel, 2005, 2009). One explanation is that sleep patterns result from evolutionary adaptation to a particular ecological niche. Thus, animals with few predators, like polar bears, have the luxury of sleeping long hours out in the open and even taking daytime naps after a meal. In contrast, giraffes take short naps throughout the day, often keeping one eye open to stay alert for predators.

Why Do We Sleep?

It may seem obvious: We sleep because we're tired and need rest. Thus, it may surprise you to learn that sleep researchers aren't really sure *why* we sleep. Sleep initiates a process that clears metabolic waste products from the brain (Xie et al., 2013). Sleep is also thought to maintain immune system function, improve brain function, enhance learning and consolidate memory, and help regulate moods and emotion (Frank & Heller, 2019; Krueger et al., 2017).

However, these explanations don't account for the enormous variability in sleep patterns across different species. Some researchers take the view that the sleep patterns exhibited by different animals, including humans, are the result of *evolutionary adaptation* (Roth et al., 2010; Siegel, 2009). According to this view, different sleep patterns evolved as a way of conserving energy and preventing a particular species from interacting with the environment when doing so is most hazardous.

Another important function of sleep deserves special mention. Sleep plays a critical role in strengthening new memories and in integrating new memories with existing memories (Frank & Heller, 2019; Walker, 2010). Sleep seems to be especially important in preserving emotional memories and memories of details that are relevant to personal goals and preoccupations (Pace-Schott et al., 2015; Stickgold & Walker, 2013).

Sleep researchers are finding that the strengthening and enhancement of new memories during sleep is a very active process. That process seems to work like this: New memories formed during the day are *reactivated* during the 90-minute cycles of sleep that occur throughout the night. This process of repeatedly reactivating these newly encoded memories during sleep strengthens the neuronal connections that contribute to forming long-term memories (Wamsley et al., 2010; Yang et al., 2014). Along with helping solidify new memories, sleep is also critical to integrating the new memories into existing networks of memories (Stickgold & Walker, 2013; Walker & Robertson, 2016).

Rather than an all-encompassing theory explaining why we sleep, today's sleep researchers recognize that sleep serves a host of vital functions. Studying sleep from multiple perspectives—psychological, physiological, and neurological—yields a dynamic understanding of how sleep occurs, how it is regulated, and how it contributes to optimal functioning (Krueger et al., 2017).

The Effects of Sleep Deprivation The importance of sleep is demonstrated by *sleep deprivation studies.* After being deprived of sleep for just one night, research participants develop *microsleeps,* which are episodes of sleep lasting only a few seconds that occur during wakefulness. People who go without sleep for a day or more also experience disruptions in mood, mental abilities, reaction time, perceptual skills, and complex motor skills (Bonnet, 2005).

David R. Frazier Photolibrary, Inc./Alamy Stock Photo

The Perils of Driving While Drowsy According to studies reported by the National Highway Traffic Safety Administration (2017), drowsiness is officially blamed for tens of thousands of traffic accidents in the United States each year—and more than 800 deaths. But researchers think that this official figure underestimates the true number of deaths that involve a drowsy driver, which may be in the range of 6,000 to 8,000 deaths in the United States alone (National Highway Traffic Safety Administration, 2017). And one survey found that about 20 percent of U.S. drivers reported having fallen asleep behind the wheel at least once (Covington, 2020). The best way to avoid an accident if you're sleepy? Get off the road and rest. Opening windows and turning up the radio and air conditioning are not effective ways to maintain alertness.

🧠 FOCUS ON NEUROSCIENCE

The Sleep-Deprived Emotional Brain

Whether they are children or adults, people often react with more emotional when they're not getting adequate sleep (Cote et al., 2019; Ma et al., 2015). Is this because they're simply tired, or do the brain's emotional centers become more reactive in response to sleep deprivation?

To study this question, researcher Seung-Schik Yoo and his colleagues (2007) deprived some participants of sleep for 35 hours while other participants slept normally. Then, all of the participants observed a series of images ranging from emotionally neutral to very unpleasant and disturbing while undergoing an fMRI brain scan.

Compare the two fMRI scans shown here. The orange and yellow areas indicate the degree of activation in the *amygdala*, a key component of the brain's emotional centers. Compared to the adequately rested participants, the amygdala activated 60 percent more strongly when the sleep-deprived participants looked at the aversive images.

Yoo's research clearly shows that the sleep-deprived brain is much more prone to strong emotional reactions to negative stimuli. Later research has shown that sleep deprivation also affects how we respond to *positive* stimuli. The same team of researchers found that sleep-deprived participants responded with heightened activity in the brain's reward circuits to images of *pleasant* scenes, such as cute bunnies or ice cream sundaes (Gujar et al., 2011). The implication?

Unrealistically positive responses may lead sleep-deprived people to engage in risky or addictive behavior.

As sleep scientist Matthew Walker (2011) observes, "When functioning correctly, the brain finds the sweet spot on the mood spectrum. But the sleep-deprived brain will swing to both extremes, neither of which is optimal for making wise decisions."

So, when you're consistently operating on too little sleep, monitor your emotional reactions so that you don't overreact and say or do something that you will regret later—such as after you've caught up on your sleep.

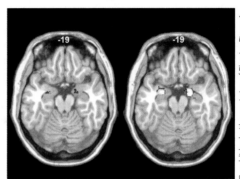

Republished with permission of Elsevier, Figure 1, Part A, from Yoo, Seung-Schik; Gujar, Ninad; Hu, Peter; Jolesz, Ferenc A.; & Walker, Matthew P. (2007). The human emotional brain without sleep: A prefrontal-amygdala disconnect. *Current Biology, 17,* 877–878. Copyright 2007, Permission conveyed through Copyright Clearance Center, Inc.

Sleep Control   Sleep Deprivation

Getting less than an optimal amount of sleep also has a wide range of effects (Walker, 2017). When sleep is restricted to 4 hours or less in laboratory studies, concentration, reaction time, and memory are impaired (Ma et al., 2015). Motor skills—including driving skills—decrease, producing a greater risk of accidents. As discussed in the Focus on Neuroscience box "The Sleep-Deprived Emotional Brain," moods, especially negative moods, become much more volatile (Harvey, 2011). Harmful changes occur in hormone levels, including stress hormone levels (Balbo et al., 2010). The immune system's effectiveness is diminished, increasing susceptibility to colds and infections (Irwin, 2015). Finally, metabolic changes occur, including changes linked to obesity and diabetes (Van Cauter et al., 2008).

When sleep-deprived, people tend to consume more calories and gain weight (Markwald et al., 2013; Zhu et al., 2019). One explanation is that sleep deprivation tends to increase the appeal of high-calorie foods. As compared to food choices made when they were well rested, people who were sleep-deprived tended to prefer high-calorie treats like potato chips and desserts over nourishing but low-calorie foods like apple slices (Greer et al., 2013).

Sleep researchers have also selectively deprived people of different components of normal sleep. To study the effects of *REM deprivation,* researchers wake sleepers whenever the monitoring instruments indicate they are entering REM sleep. After several nights of being selectively deprived of REM sleep, the participants are allowed to sleep uninterrupted. What happens? They experience *REM rebound*—the amount of time spent in REM sleep increases by as much as 50 percent. Similarly, when people are selectively deprived of NREM stage 3, they experience *NREM rebound,* spending more time in NREM sleep (Borbély & Achermann, 2005; Tobler, 2005). Thus, it seems that the brain needs to experience the full range of sleep states, making up for missing sleep components when given the chance.

Dreams and Mental Activity During Sleep

■ KEY THEME

A dream is an unfolding sequence of perceptions, thoughts, and emotions that is experienced as a series of actual events during sleep.

⁼ KEY QUESTIONS

- How does brain activity change during dreaming sleep, and how are those changes related to dream content?
- What do people dream about, and why don't we remember most dreams?
- How do the psychoanalytic, activation–synthesis, and neurocognitive models explain the nature and function of dreams?

Dreams have fascinated people since the beginning of time. By adulthood, about 2 hours of a good night's sleep is spent dreaming. Assuming you live to a ripe old age, you'll devote about six years of your life to dreaming.

Although dreams may be the most interesting brain productions during sleep, they are not the most common. More prevalent is *sleep thinking*—vague, thoughtlike ruminations about real events that usually occurs during NREM slow-wave sleep (McCarley, 2007). Sometimes, sleep thinking interferes with sleep, such as when anxious students toss and turn during the night before an important exam.

In contrast to sleep thinking, a **dream** is *an unfolding sequence of thoughts, perceptions, and emotions that typically occurs during REM sleep and is experienced as a series of real-life events* (Domhoff, 2005a, 2005b). However bizarre the details or illogical the events, the dreamer accepts them as reality. In a recurring segment on *The Late Late Show,* celebrities read fans' tweets describing their dreams about them, and they are often quite bizarre. In one episode, the Jonas Brothers read a fan's description of her dream in which the Jonas Brothers were her cousins, and Nick Jonas asked to borrow money from her to buy tacos (Martin, 2020). To the fan, this dreamed event probably felt quite real.

It was once thought that dreams occurred exclusively during REM sleep, but new research reveals that dreams also occur during NREM sleep (Foulkes & Domhoff, 2014; Siclari et al., 2017). When awakened during active REM sleep, people report a dream about 90 percent of the time, even people who claim that they never dream. The dreamer is usually the main participant in these events, and at least one other person is involved in the dream story. But sometimes the dreamer is simply the observer of the unfolding dream story.

People usually have four or five dreaming episodes each night. The first REM episode of the night is the shortest, lasting only about 10 minutes. Subsequent REM episodes average around 30 minutes and tend to get longer as the night continues. Early morning dreams, which can last 40 minutes or longer, are the dreams most likely to be recalled.

PET and fMRI scans reveal that the brain's activity during REM sleep is distinctly different from its activity during either wakefulness or NREM slow-wave sleep (Fuller et al., 2006; Nofzinger, 2006).

Dream Themes and Imagery

Although almost everyone can remember having had a bizarre dream, research on dream content shows that bizarre dream stories tend to be the exception, not the rule. *Most* dreams are about everyday settings, people, activities, and events.

In reviewing studies of dream content, researcher William Domhoff (2005b, 2010) has concluded that so-called common dream themes, like being naked in a public place, flying, or failing an exam, are actually quite rare in dream reports. Analyzing thousands of dream reports, Domhoff (2007, 2011) found that negative feelings were more common than positive feelings. Apprehension and fear were the most frequently reported emotions, followed by happiness and confusion. Instances of aggression were more common than instances of friendliness, and the dreamer was more likely to be the victim of aggression than the aggressor. Women were more likely to experience emotions in their dreams, and men more likely to experience physical aggression.

dream An unfolding sequence of thoughts, perceptions, and emotions that typically occurs during REM sleep and is experienced as a series of real-life events.

The emotional tone of the average dream pales in comparison with the intensity of a **nightmare**, *a vivid and frightening or unpleasant anxiety dream that occurs during REM sleep.* Nightmares often awaken the sleeper. Typically, the dreamer feels helpless or powerless in the face of being aggressively attacked or pursued. Although fear, anxiety, and even terror are the most commonly experienced emotions, some nightmares involve intense feelings of sadness, anger, disgust, or embarrassment (Nielsen & Zadra, 2005). As a general rule, nightmares are *not* indicative of a psychological or sleep disorder unless they occur frequently, cause difficulties returning to sleep, or cause daytime distress (Levin & Nielsen, 2007; Nielsen et al., 2006).

nightmare A vivid and frightening or unpleasant anxiety dream that occurs during REM sleep.

activation–synthesis model of dreaming The theory that brain activity during sleep produces dream images (*activation*), which are combined by the brain into a dream story (*synthesis*).

The Significance of Dreams

Why do we dream? Do dreams contain symbolic or hidden messages? Three models of the nature and function of dreaming offer insights.

Sigmund Freud: Dreams as Fulfilled Wishes

Sigmund Freud believed that sexual and aggressive instincts are the motivating forces that dictate human behavior (see Chapter 1). Because these instinctual urges are so consciously unacceptable, sexual and aggressive thoughts, feelings, and wishes are pushed into the unconscious, or *repressed.* Freud believed that these repressed urges and wishes could surface in dream imagery.

Freud (1904) believed that dreams have two components: the *manifest content,* or the dream images themselves, and the *latent content,* the disguised psychological meaning of the dream. For example, Freud (1911) believed that dream images of swords and other elongated objects were *phallic symbols,* representing the penis, while cupboards and ovens symbolized the vagina.

In some types of psychotherapy today, especially those that follow Freud's ideas, dreams are still seen as an important source of information about psychological conflicts (Meltzer, 2018; Pesant & Zadra, 2004). However, Freud's belief that dreams represent the fulfillment of repressed wishes has not been substantiated by psychological research. Furthermore, research does not support Freud's belief that the dream images themselves—the manifest content of dreams—are symbols that disguise the dream's true psychological meaning (Domhoff, 2003, 2011).

The Activation–Synthesis Model of Dreaming

Researchers J. Allan Hobson and Robert W. McCarley first proposed a new model of dreaming in 1977. Called the **activation–synthesis model of dreaming**, *this theory maintains that brain activity during sleep produces dream images (activation), which are combined by the brain into a dream story (synthesis)* (see **Figure 4.4**). Since it was first proposed, the model has evolved as new findings have been reported (see Hobson, 2017; McCarley, 2007).

According to the activation–synthesis model, dreams occur when brainstem circuits at the base of the brain activate and trigger higher brain regions, including visual, motor, and auditory pathways. Limbic system structures involved in emotion, such as the amygdala and hippocampus, are also activated during REM sleep. When we're awake, these brain structures and pathways process stimuli from the external world. But rather than responding to the external environment, the dreaming brain is responding to its own internally generated signals (Hobson, 2005).

In the absence of external sensory input, the activated brain combines, or *synthesizes*, these internally generated sensory signals and imposes meaning on them. According to this model, then, dreaming is essentially the brain synthesizing and integrating memory fragments, emotions, and sensations that are internally triggered (Hobson et al., 1998, 2011).

According to the activation–synthesis model, dream images are not symbols to be decoded. Rather, the meaning of dreams can be uncovered by understanding the deeply personal way the dreamer, once awake, makes sense of the chaotic progression of dream images.

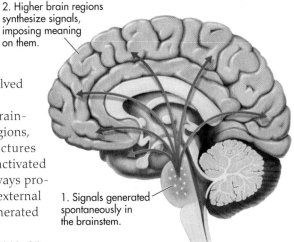

Activation–Synthesis Model of Dreaming

2. Higher brain regions synthesize signals, imposing meaning on them.

1. Signals generated spontaneously in the brainstem.

FIGURE 4.4 The Activation–Synthesis Model of Dreaming In the activation–synthesis model of dreaming, the brainstem produces signals for dream images (activation). The higher regions of the brain then impose some meaning on these dream images (synthesis), often in the form of a dream story.

neurocognitive model of dreaming
Model that emphasizes the continuity between waking and dreaming cognition.

sleep disorder A serious and consistent sleep disturbance that interferes with daytime functioning and causes subjective distress.

insomnia A condition in which a person regularly experiences an inability to fall asleep, to stay asleep, or to feel adequately rested by sleep.

The Neurocognitive Theory of Dreaming In contrast to the activation–synthesis model, the **neurocognitive model of dreaming** *emphasizes the continuity between waking and dreaming cognition.* According to William Domhoff (2005a, 2010, 2011), dreams are not a "cognitive mishmash" of random fragments of memories, images, and emotions generated by lower brainstem circuits, as the activation–synthesis model holds. Rather, dreams reflect our interests, personality, and individual worries (Nir & Tononi, 2010).

Further, the activation–synthesis model rests on the assumption that dreams result from brain activation during REM sleep. However, as Domhoff and other dream researchers point out, people also dream during NREM sleep, at sleep onset, and even experience dreamlike episodes while awake but drowsy (Foulkes & Domhoff, 2014; Siclari et al., 2017).

Like dreams, Domhoff (2011) notes, waking thought can also be marked by spontaneous mental images, rapid shifts of scene or topic, and unrealistic or fanciful thoughts. Thus, dreams are not as foreign to our waking experience as the activation–synthesis model claims. Instead, dreams mirror our waking concerns, and do so in a way that is remarkably similar to normal thought processes (Foulkes & Domhoff, 2014).

Sleep Disorders

■ KEY THEME
Sleep disorders are surprisingly common, take many different forms, and interfere with a person's daytime functioning.

⹀ KEY QUESTIONS
- What is a sleep disorder?
- What are insomnia, sleep apnea, and narcolepsy?
- What kinds of behavior are displayed in the different parasomnias?

Almost everyone *occasionally* experiences disrupted sleep. In contrast, a **sleep disorder** is *a serious and consistent sleep disturbance that interferes with daytime functioning and causes subjective distress* (Kryger et al., 2020; Thorpy, 2012; Thorpy & Plazzi, 2010).

Insomnia

Insomnia, the most common sleep disorder, is not defined solely based on how long a person sleeps. Why? Put simply, because people vary in how much sleep they need to feel refreshed. Rather, **insomnia** is *a condition in which a person regularly experiences an inability to fall asleep, to stay asleep, or to feel adequately rested by sleep.* Regularly taking 30 minutes or longer to fall asleep is considered to be a symptom of insomnia. These disruptions must also produce daytime sleepiness, fatigue, impaired social or occupational performance, or mood disturbances (Bootzin & Epstein, 2011).

One common cause of some kinds of insomnia is hyperarousal (Vargas et al., 2020; Wassing et al., 2016). Excitement about an upcoming event or the use of stimulants, like nicotine and caffeine, can make it hard to fall asleep. Often, insomnia can be traced to anxiety over stressful life events, such as job, school, or relationship difficulties. Sometimes, worry about inadequate sleep can itself cause insomnia. In fact, sometimes cues associated with sleep, such as getting into bed, become automatically associated with a fear of not sleeping (Perogamvros et al., 2020). This fear then fuels insomnia. We'll learn more about these kinds of automatic associations in the chapter on learning.

Although the *occasional* use of prescription "sleeping pills" can be helpful to treat isolated episodes of insomnia, it is a myth that the frequent use, or use for chronic insomnia, is helpful. Along with having harmful side effects, they do not offer a long-term solution to the problem, because the insomnia returns if the pills are not used. In *Psych for Your Life*, we'll describe one effective behavioral treatment for insomnia and give you several suggestions to improve the quality of your sleep.

Roz Chast/The New Yorker Collection/www.cartoonbank.com

MYTH ◄ SCIENCE

Is it true that sleeping pills are an effective way to treat chronic insomnia?

Obstructive Sleep Apnea: Blocked Breathing During Sleep

Excessive daytime sleepiness is a key symptom of the second most common sleep disorder. **Obstructive sleep apnea (OSA)** is *a sleep disorder in which the person repeatedly stops breathing during sleep*. In OSA, the sleeper's airway becomes narrowed or blocked, causing very shallow breathing or repeated pauses in breathing. Each time breathing stops, oxygen blood levels decrease and carbon dioxide blood levels increase, triggering a momentary awakening. Over the course of a night, 300 or more sleep apnea episodes can occur (Schwab et al., 2005).

Obstructive sleep apnea disrupts the quality and quantity of a person's sleep, causing daytime grogginess, poor concentration, memory and learning problems, and irritability (Weaver & George, 2005). Sleep apnea can also cause physical health problems, including weight gain, high blood pressure, and diabetes.

Sleep apnea can often be treated with lifestyle changes, such as avoiding alcohol or losing weight (Hoffstein, 2005; Powell et al., 2005). Moderate to severe cases of sleep apnea are usually treated with *continuous positive airway pressure* (CPAP), using a device that increases air pressure in the throat so that the airway remains open (Grunstein, 2005).

Narcolepsy: Blurring the Boundaries Between Sleep and Wakefulness

Narcolepsy is *a sleep disorder characterized by excessive daytime sleepiness and brief lapses into episodes of sleep throughout the day*. Narcolepsy can occur even among those with adequate nighttime sleep. These involuntary sleep episodes, called *sleep attacks* or *microsleeps,* typically last from a few seconds to several minutes, and can send the person with narcolepsy directly into REM sleep (Mahoney et al., 2019). About 70 percent of people with narcolepsy experience episodes during which they suddenly lose voluntary muscle control. These episodes are often triggered by laughter or strong emotion, and can last from several seconds to several minutes.

The Parasomnias: Undesired Arousal or Actions During Sleep

We tend to think of sleep as an "either/or" phenomenon—we are either asleep or we are awake. But as the *parasomnias* show, sometimes sleep and waking states overlap or "bleed" into one another (Colwell, 2011; Mahowald & Schenk, 2005). In the parasomnias, some parts of the brain—like those involved in judging, thinking, or forming new memories—are asleep, but other, more primitive parts of the brain become activated. The brain is *partially* awake—awake enough to carry out the actions, but not awake enough to be consciously aware of performing the actions (Cartwright, 2010).

The **parasomnias** are a *category of sleep disorders characterized by undesirable physical arousal, behaviors, or events during sleep or sleep transitions* (Pavlova & Latreille, 2019; Schenck, 2007). All of the parasomnias are characterized by a lack of conscious awareness during the behaviors and total amnesia for behaviors or events upon awakening.

Unlike nightmares, which typically occur during REM sleep, parasomnias occur during NREM stage 3 slow-wave sleep during the first half of a night's sleep. They can be triggered by a wide range of stimuli, including sleep deprivation, stress, erratic sleep schedules, sleeping medications, stimulants, pregnancy, and tranquilizers.

Sleep Terrors   Also called *night terrors,* **sleep terrors** are *a sleep disturbance involving an episode of increased physiological arousal, panic, frightening hallucinations, and no recall of the episode*. Sleep terrors begin with a sharp increase in physiological arousal—restlessness, sweating, and a racing heart. The person abruptly sits up in bed and may let out a panic-stricken scream. Sleep terrors usually involve the terrifying sensation that one is being choked or crushed or is falling. Although sufferers may appear to be awake, they are terrified and disoriented and are usually impossible to calm (Mahowald & Schenck, 2005). Sleep terrors are most common in children, but a small percentage of adults also experience them.

obstructive sleep apnea (OSA) (APP-nee-uh) A sleep disorder in which the person repeatedly stops breathing during sleep.

narcolepsy (NAR-ko-lep-see) A sleep disorder characterized by excessive daytime sleepiness and brief lapses into episodes of sleep throughout the day.

parasomnias (pare-uh-SOM-nee-uz) Category of sleep disorders characterized by undesirable physical arousal, behaviors, or events during sleep or sleep transitions; includes *sleepwalking, sleep terrors, sleepsex,* and *sleep-related eating disorder.*

sleep terrors Sleep disturbance involving an episode of increased physiological arousal, panic, frightening hallucinations, and no recall of the episode; also called *night terrors.*

David Walter Banks for The New York Times/Redux

⌃ **Life with Narcolepsy** College student Kailey Profeta was diagnosed with narcolepsy when she was 9 years old (Barrow, 2018). She was homeschooled for years until doctors developed a combination of medications that would keep her awake during the day and let her sleep at night. She graduated from high school at the top of her class, but life with narcolepsy is not easy. "What I feel like on a regular day is what a normal person would feel after not sleeping for 7 days—that's how tired narcoleptics feel. Narcolepsy affects my life a lot, but I'm still me," Kailey says. To listen to Kailey's story and to hear more first-person accounts of life with narcolepsy, go to http://www.nytimes.com/interactive/2018/well/patient-voices-narcolepsy.html

Is it true that it can be dangerous to wake a sleepwalker?

Eros Hoagland/Redux

▲ **Warning: May Cause Sleep-Driving and Sleep-Eating** *Ambien®*, a widely prescribed sleeping pill, was originally marketed as being less addictive and having fewer side effects than older medications. But Ambien users have reported waking up to find the oven turned on and food strewn around the kitchen and in their bed. Other Ambien users have reported driving while asleep, waking up only after being arrested on the side of the road (Saul, 2007a, 2007b). In general, Ambien appears to increase the odds of experiencing parasomnias (Ben-Hamou et al., 2011). The U.S. Food and Drug Administration now requires that Ambien and other sleeping medications warn of sleep-driving, sleep-eating, and sleep-walking as potential side effects. For more information about sleep disorders, visit the American Academy of Sleep Medicine's Web site, www.SleepEducation.org, or the National Sleep Foundation's Web site, www.SleepFoundation.org.

Sleepwalking and Other Complex Behaviors During Sleep The Prologue story about Scott described several key features of another parasomnia— *sleepwalking*. **Sleepwalking** *is a sleep disturbance characterized by an episode of walking or performing other actions during stage 3 NREM sleep.* Fairly common in childhood, sleepwalking can occur in adulthood, too. About 4 percent of adults regularly sleepwalk (Hughes, 2007). Surprisingly, a sleepwalker can engage in elaborate and complicated behaviors, such as unlocking locks, opening windows, dismantling equipment, using tools, and even driving. Recall that Scott's attack occurred early in the night, shortly after he had "crashed," or fallen asleep, as is most commonly the case with sleepwalking. The attack had no apparent motive, and he had no memory of it when he was awakened, which is a characteristic of parasomnias (Cartwright, 2004).

It's difficult to rouse sleepwalkers from deep sleep. In most cases, sleepwalkers respond to verbal suggestions and can be gently led back to bed without incident. But it is true that sleepwalkers sometimes respond aggressively if touched or interrupted (Pressman, 2007). Scott reacted violently to being interrupted while sleepwalking at least once while he was growing up, and his attack on his wife may have been caused by her trying to wake him up and guide him back to the house (Cartwright, 2004, 2007).

Sleepwalking is also involved in *sleep-related eating disorder*, which involves sleepwalking to the kitchen, eating compulsively, and then awakening the next morning with no memory of having done so. Although sugary foods are most commonly consumed, the sleepwalker can also voraciously eat bizarre items, like raw bacon, dry pancake mix, coffee grounds, or cat food sandwiches.

Also called *sexsomnia, sleepsex* involves abnormal sexual behaviors and experiences during sleep. Without realizing what they are doing, sleepers initiate sexual behavior, such as masturbation, groping or fondling their bed partner, or even sexual intercourse (Trajanovic & Shapiro, 2010). Such behavior is usually described as "robotic," aggressive, impersonal, and as being out of character with the individual's waking behavior (Schenck et al., 2007). As is the case in other parasomnias, the person typically has no memory of his actions the next day (Schenck, 2007).

Finally, no discussion of the parasomnias would be complete without at least a mention of the colorfully titled *exploding head syndrome*. As its name implies, the unfortunate sufferer reports the sensation of loud noises that sound like gunshots or a bomb exploding inside their head while falling asleep or waking up (Sharpless, 2015a). Although painless, episodes are usually accompanied by extreme arousal and fear. Exploding head syndrome was once thought to be extremely rare, but a recent survey found that about one in five university students had experienced one or more episodes, and it seems to be even more common among the middle-aged and elderly (Davidson & Davenport, 2016). The cause is unknown, although some researchers believe that stress is a risk factor. Psychologist and exploding head syndrome researcher Brian Sharpless (2015b) likens it to a "brain hiccup." He speculates that the sensation occurs when auditory neurons fire rather than shut down as the brain transitions between sleep and wakefulness.

Hypnosis

■ **KEY THEME**

During hypnosis, people respond to suggestions with changes in perception, memory, and behavior.

▬ **KEY QUESTIONS**

- What characteristics are associated with responsiveness to hypnotic suggestions?
- What are some important effects of hypnosis?
- How has hypnosis been explained?

sleepwalking A sleep disturbance characterized by an episode of walking or performing other actions during stage 3 NREM sleep.

What is hypnosis? **Hypnosis** is formally defined as *a cooperative social interaction in which the hypnotized person responds to the hypnotist's suggestions with changes in perception, memory, thoughts, and behavior* (American Psychological Association, 2005).

The word *hypnosis* is derived from the Greek *hypnos,* meaning "sleep." However, rather than being a sleeplike trance, hypnosis produces a highly focused, absorbed state of attention that minimizes competing thoughts and attention (Oakley & Halligan, 2013). It is also characterized by increased responsiveness to suggestions, vivid images and fantasies, and a willingness to accept distortions of logic or reality. During hypnosis, people temporarily suspend their sense of initiative and voluntarily accept and follow the hypnotist's instructions (Hilgard, 1986a). However, they typically remain aware of who they are, where they are, and the events that are transpiring.

People vary in their responsiveness to hypnotic suggestions (see Nash, 2008). The best candidates are individuals who approach the experience with positive, receptive attitudes. About 15 percent of adults are highly susceptible to hypnosis, and 10 percent are difficult or impossible to hypnotize.

Effects of Hypnosis

Deeply hypnotized people sometimes experience profound changes in their subjective experience of consciousness. They may report feelings of detachment from their bodies, profound relaxation, or sensations of timelessness.

Sensory changes that can be induced through hypnosis include hallucinations, temporary blindness, deafness, or a complete loss of sensation in some part of the body (Kihlstrom, 2007). For example, when the suggestion is made to a highly responsive person that their arm is numb and cannot feel pain, they will not consciously experience the pain of a pinprick or of having their arm immersed in ice water. This property of hypnosis has led to its use as a technique in pain control (Adachi et al., 2014; Jensen & Patterson, 2014). Painful dental and medical procedures, including surgery, have been successfully performed with hypnosis as the only anesthesia (Hilgard et al., 1994; Salazar et al., 2010).

Hypnosis can also influence behavior outside the hypnotic state. A **posthynpotic suggestion** is *an instruction given during hypnosis asking a person to carry out a specific behavior following the hypnotic session.* For example, under hypnosis, a student was given the posthypnotic suggestion that the number 5 no longer existed. He was brought out of hypnosis and then asked to count his fingers. He counted 11 fingers! Counting again, the baffled young man was at a loss to explain his results. We discuss the three main explanations for hypnosis in the Critical Thinking box, "Is Hypnosis a Special State of Consciousness?"

Limits and Applications of Hypnosis

Although the effects of hypnosis can be dramatic, there are limits to the behaviors that can be influenced by hypnosis. First, contrary to popular belief, you cannot be hypnotized against your will. Second, hypnosis cannot make you perform behaviors that are contrary to your morals and values. Thus, you're very unlikely to commit criminal or immoral acts under the influence of hypnosis—unless, of course, you find such actions acceptable (Hilgard, 1986b).

Can hypnosis be used to help you lose weight, stop smoking, or stop biting your nails? Hypnosis is not a magic bullet. However, research *has* shown that hypnosis can be helpful in modifying problematic behaviors, especially when used as part of a structured treatment program (Lynn et al., 2010). For example, when combined with cognitive-behavioral therapy or other supportive treatments, hypnosis has been shown to help motivated people quit smoking (Elkins et al., 2006; Green et al., 2006; Lynn & Kirsch, 2006). There is not strong evidence, however, for hypnotherapy as a treatment on its own for people who want to quit smoking (Barnes et al., 2010). In children and adolescents, hypnosis can be an effective treatment for such habits as thumb-sucking, nail-biting, and compulsive hair-pulling (Rhue, 2010).

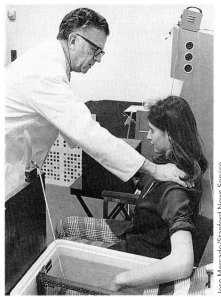

Jose Mercado/Stanford News Service

⌃ **Hypnotic Suppression of Pain** In this classic photo taken at the Stanford Laboratory of Hypnosis Research, psychologist Ernest Hilgard (1904–2001) instructs this hypnotized young woman that she will feel no pain in her arm. Her arm is then immersed in circulating ice water for several minutes, and she reports that she does not experience any pain. In contrast, a nonhypnotized participant perceives the same experience as extremely painful and can keep their arm in the ice water for no more than a few seconds.

MYTH ◄ SCIENCE

Is it true that you can be hypnotized against your will?

hypnosis (hip-NO-sis) A cooperative social interaction in which the hypnotized person responds to the hypnotist's suggestions with changes in perception, memory, thoughts, and behavior.

posthypnotic suggestion An instruction given during hypnosis asking a person to carry out a specific behavior following the hypnotic session.

CRITICAL THINKING

Is Hypnosis a Special State of Consciousness?

Are the changes in perception, thinking, and behaviors that occur during hypnosis the result of a "special" or "altered" state of consciousness? Psychologist **Ernest R. Hilgard** (1986a, 1991, 1992) believed that the hypnotized person experiences **dissociation**—*the splitting of consciousness into two or more simultaneous streams of mental activity.* According to Hilgard, a hypnotized person consciously experiences one stream of mental activity that complies with the hypnotist's suggestions. But a second, dissociated stream of mental activity is also operating, processing information that is unavailable to the consciousness of the hypnotized person (Sadler & Woody, 2010). Hilgard (1986a, 1992) referred to this second, dissociated stream of mental activity as the hidden observer. (The phrase hidden observer does not mean that the hypnotized person has multiple personalities.) Let's consider the evidence for three competing points of view on this issue.

The State View: Hypnosis Involves a Special State

The "state" explanation contends that hypnosis is a unique state of consciousness, distinctly different from normal waking consciousness (Wagstaff, 2014). The state view is perhaps best represented by Hilgard's theory described above. So according to this theory, the hypnotized young woman shown on the previous page reported no pain because the painful sensations were dissociated from awareness.

The Non-State View: Ordinary Psychological Processes

Some psychologists reject the notion that hypnotically induced changes involve a "special" state of consciousness. According to the *social cognitive view of hypnosis*, people are responding to the *social demands* of the hypnosis situation. They act the way they think good hypnotic participants are supposed to act, conforming to the expectations of the hypnotist, their own expectations, and situational cues (Lynn & Green, 2011). In this view, the "hypnotized" young woman in the photo reported no pain because that's what she expected to happen during the hypnosis session.

To back up the social cognitive theory of hypnosis, Nicholas Spanos and his colleagues (1991, 1994, 2005) amassed an impressive array of evidence showing that highly motivated people often perform just as well as hypnotized people in demonstrating pain reduction, amnesia, age regression, and hallucinations.

The Imaginative Suggestibility View

Challenging the social cognitive view, however, are the results of numerous brain imaging studies showing that hypnosis can produce alterations in brain function (see Oakley & Halligan, 2013). For example, in one study, hypnotized participants were given instructions to

Meditation

■ **KEY THEME**

Meditation involves using a mental or physical technique to induce a state of focused attention and heightened awareness.

≡ **KEY QUESTIONS**
- What are two general types of meditation?
- What are some effects of meditation?

Meditation refers to *a group of techniques that induce an altered state of focused attention and heightened awareness.* Taking many forms, meditation has been an important part of religious practices throughout the world for thousands of years (Nelson, 2001; Wallace, 2009). However, meditation can also be practiced as a secular technique, independent of any religious tradition or spiritual context (Carmody, 2015).

Common to all forms of meditation is the goal of *controlling or training attention* (Davis & Thompson, 2015; Tang & Posner, 2015). There are literally hundreds of different meditation techniques, but they can be divided into two general categories (Slagter et al., 2011). *Focused attention techniques* involve focusing awareness on a visual image or an object, the sensation of breathing, or a sound, word, or phrase. Sometimes a short word or religious phrase, called a *mantra,* is repeated mentally.

Focused attention techniques involve monitoring and regulating the quality of attention. It may sound simple, but try it: Sit quietly and try to focus your attention on a simple stimulus in your own environment—perhaps a pebble or even a blank Post-it Note. You'll quickly realize how hard it is to maintain focus on the object, to notice when your attention is distracted by thoughts or other environmental stimuli, and to return your focus to the chosen object.

dissociation The splitting of consciousness into two or more simultaneous streams of mental activity.

meditation A group of techniques that induce an altered state of focused attention and heightened awareness.

"drain" color from a visual image made up of colored rectangles or, conversely, to "add" color to a visual image made up of gray rectangles, like those shown to the right. The brain function of hypnotized participants reflected the hypnosis-induced visual hallucination—*not* the actual images that participants viewed (Kosslyn et al., 2000).

Psychologists Irving Kirsch and Wayne Braffman (2001) dismiss the social cognitive view that hypnotized people are merely acting. But they also contend that brain imaging studies don't necessarily prove that hypnosis is a unique state. Rather, Kirsch and Braffman maintain that such studies emphasize individual differences in *imaginative suggestibility*—the degree to which a person is able to experience an imaginary state of affairs as if it were real (Kirsch, 2014b; Kirsch et al., 2011).

Braffman and Kirsch (1999) have shown that many highly suggestible participants were just as responsive to suggestions when they had *not* been hypnotized as when they had been hypnotized. "Hypnotic responses reveal an astounding capacity that some people have to alter their experience in profound ways," Kirsch and Braffman (2001) write. "Hypnosis is only one of the ways in which this capacity is revealed. It can also be evoked—and almost to the same extent—without inducing hypnosis."

Despite the controversy over how best to explain hypnotic effects, psychologists do agree that hypnosis can be an effective therapeutic technique (Lynn et al., 2010). And, increasingly, cognitive neuroscientists are using hypnosis as a tool to manipulate subjective awareness (Oakley & Halligan, 2013).

Colored rectangles   **Gray rectangles**

CRITICAL THINKING QUESTIONS

- Does the fact that highly motivated people can "fake" hypnotic effects invalidate the notion of hypnosis as a unique state of consciousness? Why or why not?

- What kinds of evidence could provide support for the notion that hypnosis is a unique state of consciousness?

In contrast, *open monitoring techniques* involve monitoring the content of experience from moment to moment (Slagter et al., 2011). Rather than concentrating on an object, sound, or activity, the meditator engages in present-centered awareness of the "here and now." When distracting thoughts arise—as they surely will—the practitioner notes the thought and returns to a state of open, nonreflective awareness. *Mindfulness,*

David Sutherland/Alamy Stock Photo

Aleksandr Davydov/Alamy Stock Photo

▲ **Meditation in Different Cultures** (Left) Like this group in Hanoi, Vietnam, many people throughout Asia begin their day with *tai chi*, often meeting in parks and other public places. Tai chi is a form of meditation that involves a structured series of slow, smooth movements. Sometimes described as "meditation in motion," tai chi has been practiced for over 2,000 years.

(Right) These young Americans are practicing zazen, or "just sitting," a form of open monitoring meditation (Austin, 2009). Originating in China, Zen is found in many Asian countries, especially Japan, Korea, and Vietnam. Over the past few decades, Zen Buddhism has become increasingly popular in the United States and other Western countries.

a meditation technique that has become increasingly popular in psychological research and clinical practice, is a form of open monitoring meditation. Definitions vary, but in simple terms, mindfulness meditation involves focusing attention on the present experience with nonjudgmental acceptance (Kabat-Zinn, 2013; Quaglia et al., 2015).

In practice, focused attention and open monitoring techniques often overlap, especially when people are just learning to meditate. For example, beginning mindfulness meditation often starts with focused attention on your breath to calm or "settle" the mind and reduce distractions (Shapiro & Carlson, 2009). Only gradually do practitioners transition to a more open attentiveness to whatever occurs in awareness, whether it be a sensation, thought, or feeling.

Many people falsely believe that meditation involves entering a sort of trancelike state that resembles drowsiness or hypnosis. In fact, mindfulness meditators report the *opposite* effect—a state of heightened awareness and sensitivity to thoughts, internal sensations, and external stimuli such as sounds and smells (Davis & Thompson, 2015; Ricard, 2010).

Scientific Studies of the Effects of Meditation

Much of the early research on meditation investigated its use as a relaxation technique that relieved stress and improved cardiovascular health. The meditation technique that was most widely used in this early research was *transcendental meditation,* or *TM,* a focused attention technique that involved mentally repeating a mantra given to the practitioner by a teacher. Many studies showed that even beginning meditators practicing TM experienced a state of lowered physical arousal, including a decrease in heart rate, lower blood pressure, and changes in brain waves associated with relaxation (Alexander et al., 1994; Benson, 2010).

Contemporary research on meditation is more wide-ranging and has increased dramatically in recent years (Creswell, 2017). Today, researchers hope to learn more about the nature of conscious experience as well as meditation's effects on attention, emotional control, health, and the brain (Tang et al., 2015; van Vugt, 2015). Some psychologists are using meditation to study how intensive mental training affects basic psychological processes, such as attention and memory (Ricard et al., 2014; Slagter et al., 2011). And, brain imaging technology has allowed neuroscientists to document brain changes *during* meditation and brain changes that seem to result as an *effect* of meditation (Tang et al., 2015; Zeidan, 2015).

One difficulty in studying meditation is that there are literally hundreds of different meditation techniques (Sedlmeier et al., 2012). Many of today's research studies involve mindfulness techniques, partly because they can be easily taught in a secular context (Davidson, 2010). But even mindfulness-based practices can vary a great deal (Chiesa & Malinowski, 2011). And, study participants may range from novice meditators to people who have practiced meditation for decades. These qualifications need to be kept in mind. However, carefully controlled studies have found that meditation can:

- improve concentration, perceptual discrimination, and attention (Baird et al., 2014; Lutz et al., 2009; MacLean et al., 2010).

- increase working memory and attention in U.S. military personnel before deployment (Jha et al., 2010, 2015).

- improve emotional control and well-being (Arch & Landy, 2015; Farb et al., 2010; Sahdra et al., 2011).

- reduce the symptoms of stress, anxiety, and depression (Hoge et al., 2018; Irving et al., 2015; Saeed et al., 2019).

Are years of disciplined practice needed to experience the benefits of meditation practice? *No.* In one study, university students with no prior meditation experience learned mindfulness meditation and practiced it for just 20 minutes a day for four days (Zeidan et al., 2010). As compared to a matched control group, the meditation group significantly improved on several cognitive tasks and sharply improved their ability to focus and sustain attention.

MYTH ◀ SCIENCE

Is it true that meditation is a drowsy, trancelike state that is no different than simple relaxation?

Jeff Miller/University of Wisconsin-Madison

⌃ Studying the Well-Trained Mind
Neuroscientist and psychologist Richard Davidson confers with Buddhist monk Matthieu Ricard during an EEG study that monitored brain waves during different meditative practices (Lutz et al., 2004). Ricard, a former molecular biologist, helped design the studies, held under the auspices of the Mind and Life Institute (mindandlife.org). Davidson and other psychologists have brought the methods of contemporary psychology, including brain imaging, to study the effects of meditative practice on mind and behavior (Creswell, 2017; Davidson & Kazniak, 2015). If you would like to try a simple meditation technique, turn to page 464 in Chapter 13.

Increasingly, meditative practice is also incorporated into psychotherapy (Kuykens et al., 2016). Today, many psychologists are studying the use of meditation techniques to help tackle psychological problems ranging from eating disorders and substance abuse to major depressive disorder, anxiety, and even more serious disorders (see Bowen et al., 2015; Creswell, 2017; Jaconsen et al., 2019). However, meditation researchers caution that mindfulness practice is not a cure-all, and may even have negative effects (Van Dam et al., 2018a, 2018b). More research is needed to better understand ways in which meditation can improve health and well-being (Baer et al., 2019; Davidson & Dahl, 2018). We return to the topic of meditation in the chapter on stress and health, and discuss mindfulness-based therapies in the chapter on therapies.

Psychoactive Drugs

▪ KEY THEME
Psychoactive drugs alter consciousness by changing arousal, mood, thinking, sensations, and perceptions.

⹀ KEY QUESTIONS
- What are four broad categories of psychoactive drugs?
- What are some common properties of psychoactive drugs?
- What factors influence the effects, use, and abuse of drugs?

A **psychoactive drug** is *a chemical substance that affects brain function and alters consciousness, perception, mood, or behavior*. In this section, we will look at the characteristics of four broad categories of psychoactive drugs:

1. *Depressants*—drugs that depress, or inhibit, brain activity.

2. *Opioids*—drugs that are chemically similar to morphine and that relieve pain and produce euphoria.

3. *Stimulants*—drugs that stimulate, or excite, brain activity.

4. *Psychedelic drugs*—drugs that distort sensory perceptions.

Common Effects of Psychoactive Drugs

Addiction is a broad term that refers to a condition in which a person feels psychologically and physically compelled to take a specific drug. People experience **physical dependence**, *a condition in which a person has physically adapted to a drug so that they must take it regularly in order to avoid withdrawal symptoms*. Many physically addictive drugs gradually produce **drug tolerance**, *a condition in which increasing amounts of a physically addictive drug are needed to produce the original, desired effect.*

When a person becomes physically dependent on a drug, abstaining from the drug produces *withdrawal symptoms*—unpleasant physical reactions to the lack of the drug, plus an intense craving for it. Withdrawal symptoms are alleviated by taking the drug again. Often, the withdrawal symptoms are opposite to the drug's action, a phenomenon called the drug rebound effect. For example, withdrawing from stimulating drugs, like the caffeine in coffee, may produce depression and fatigue. Withdrawal from opioid painkillers may produce pain and discomfort.

Each psychoactive drug has a distinct biological effect. Psychoactive drugs may influence many different bodily systems, but their consciousness-altering effects are primarily due to their effect on the brain. Typically, these drugs influence brain activity by altering synaptic transmission among neurons. As we discussed in Chapter 2, drugs affect synaptic transmission by increasing or decreasing neurotransmitter amounts or by blocking, mimicking, or influencing a particular neurotransmitter's effects (see Figure 2.6). Chronic drug use can also produce long-term changes in brain structures and functions, as discussed in the Focus on Neuroscience box, "The Addicted Brain: Diminishing Rewards."

psychoactive drug A chemical substance that affects brain function and alters consciousness, perception, mood, or behavior.

physical dependence A condition in which a person has physically adapted to a drug so that they must take it regularly in order to avoid withdrawal symptoms.

drug tolerance A condition in which increasing amounts of a physically addictive drug are needed to produce the original, desired effect.

Timothy Hiatt/Getty Images

∧ Juice Wrld and the Danger of Mixing Drugs Rapper Juice Wrld died of an accidental overdose due, in part, to a dangerous mix of oxycodone and codeine. The combination produced a lethal additive drug effect, depressing his brain's vital life functions to the point that his heart stopped.

FOCUS ON NEUROSCIENCE

The Addicted Brain: Diminishing Rewards

Addictive drugs include alcohol, cocaine, heroin, nicotine, and the amphetamines. Although their effects are diverse, these addictive drugs share one thing in common: They all activate dopamine-producing neurons in the brain's reward system (Volkow et al., 2016). The initial dopamine surge in response to an addictive drug is a powerful brain reward, one that prompts the person to repeat the drug-taking behavior.

The brain's reward system evolved to reinforce behaviors that promote survival, such as eating and sex. Many pleasurable activities, including exercising, listening to music, and even looking at an attractive person, can cause a temporary increase in dopamine.

But in contrast to naturally rewarding activities and substances, addictive drugs hijack the brain's reward system. Initially, the drug produces the intense dopamine-induced feelings of euphoria. But with repeated drug use, the brain's reward pathways *adapt* to the high dopamine levels. One result is that the availability of dopamine receptors is down-regulated, or greatly reduced (Volkow et al., 2016). Along with decreased dopamine activity, other biochemical changes dampen or inhibit the brain's reward circuits, reducing the pleasurable effects of the abused substance. These adaptations create the conditions for *drug tolerance*—more of the substance is now needed to produce a response that is similar to the drug's original effect (Nestler & Malenka, 2004).

As the brain's reward circuits down-regulate to counter the dopamine surge, another change occurs. The normally reinforcing experiences of everyday life are no longer satisfying or pleasurable. Emotionally, the addict experiences depression, boredom, and apathy—along with intense cravings. The addicted person needs the substance not to get high but just to feel "normal."

Because the neurons in the brain's reward system have physically changed, they can remain hypersensitive to such cues associated with

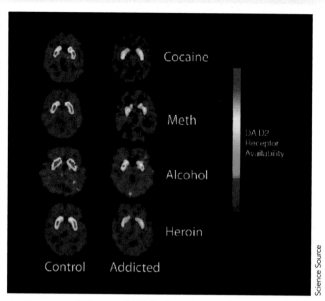

Common Effects of Addictive Drugs The intoxicating effects of all addictive drugs are produced by rapidly increasing dopamine levels in the brain's reward system (Volkow et al., 2016). As the brain adjusts to the effects of repeated drug use, long-term changes occur in the brain's reward circuitry. The number of dopamine receptors is indicated by orange and yellow in the scans above. Substance abuse sharply reduces the number of dopamine receptors in the brain's reward system, as you can see by comparing the control scans of non-users on the left to the scans on the right of people who are addicted to various substances.

the abused substance for months and even years after drug use has ended. Simply being exposed to drug-related stimuli or stressful life events can trigger craving—and relapse (Volkow et al., 2006, 2011b).

The biological effects of a drug can vary considerably from person to person. An individual's race, gender, age, and weight may influence the intensity of a particular drug's effects. For example, many East Asians and Asian Americans have a specific genetic variation that makes them much more responsive to alcohol's effects. In turn, this heightened sensitivity to alcohol is associated with significantly lower rates of alcohol dependence seen among people of Asian heritage as compared to other ethnic groups (Cook et al., 2005; Kufahl et al., 2008).

Psychological and environmental factors can also influence a drug's effects. An individual's response to a drug can be greatly affected by their personality characteristics, mood, expectations, and experience with the drug, as well as the setting in which the drug is taken (Kufahl et al., 2008). And, the effects of psychoactive drugs are especially unpredictable when combined.

Drug abuse, more formally termed *substance use disorder*, refers to *recurrent substance use that involves impaired control, disruption of social, occupational, and interpersonal functioning, and the development of craving, tolerance, and withdrawal symptoms* (American Psychiatric Association, 2013). In the United States, alcohol is, by far, the most widely abused substance (Substance Abuse and Mental Health Services Administration, 2019).

drug abuse (formally called *substance use disorder*) Recurrent substance use that involves impaired control, disruption of social, occupational, and interpersonal functioning, and the development of craving, tolerance, and withdrawal symptoms.

Drug overdoses are now the leading cause of accidental death in the United States. In 2015, the number of deaths due to overdoses from all classes of drugs topped 50,000, exceeding deaths due to guns or automobile accidents (Olaisen et al., 2019). About 70 percent of those overdose deaths were due to *opioids*—prescription painkillers and heroin (Wilson et al., 2020). We'll look at these drugs after we introduce the depressants.

The Depressants: Alcohol, Barbiturates, and Tranquilizers

■ KEY THEME
Depressants inhibit central nervous system activity, while opioids are addictive drugs that relieve pain and produce euphoria.

⁼ KEY QUESTIONS
- What are the physical and psychological effects of alcohol?
- How do barbiturates and tranquilizers affect the body?
- What are the effects of opioids and how do they affect the brain?

The **depressants** are *a category of psychoactive drugs that depress or inhibit brain activity*. In general, depressants produce drowsiness, sedation, or sleep. Depressants also relieve anxiety and lower inhibitions. All depressant drugs are potentially physically addictive. Further, the effects of depressant drugs are *additive,* meaning that the sedative effects are increased when depressants are combined.

Alcohol Weddings, parties, and other social gatherings often include alcohol, a tribute to its relaxing and social lubricating properties. Alcohol has widespread effects on the brain, and abuse is associated with changes in brain circuits involved in cognition, motivation, and self-control (Volkow et al., 2017). Used in small amounts, alcohol reduces tension and anxiety. But even though it is legal for adults and readily available in most countries alcohol also has a high potential for abuse—and high social cost. Consider these statistics:

- Excessive alcohol consumption accounts for an estimated 90,000 deaths annually in the United States. And, it is a factor in the deaths of over 1,800 U.S. university students each year (National Institute on Alcohol Abuse and Alcoholism, 2017, 2020). And globally, alcohol is a factor in about 3 million deaths a year, about 5 percent of all deaths (World Health Organization, 2018).

- Alcohol is involved in more than half of all assaults, homicides, and motor vehicle accidents in the United States (Advokat et al., 2014). Intoxicated drivers are the cause of more than 10,000 traffic deaths each year in the United States and 370,000 worldwide (National Center for Statistics and Analysis, 2019a; World Health Organization, 2018).

- Alcohol intoxication is often a factor in domestic and partner violence, child abuse, sexual assault, and public violent behavior (Easton et al., 2007; Shepherd, 2007; World Health Organization, 2018).

- Drinking during pregnancy is a leading cause of birth defects. It is the most common cause of intellectual disability worldwide (Niccols, 2007; World Health Organization, 2018).

An estimated 15 million Americans, including 3 million between the ages of 18 and 25, are either dependent upon alcohol or have serious alcohol problems (Substance Abuse and Mental Health Services Administration, 2019). Worldwide, almost 240 million men and 50 million women have alcohol use disorders, with the highest rates in Europe, North America, and South America (World Health Organization, 2018). They drink heavily on a regular basis and suffer social, occupational, and health problems as a result.

However, the numerous adverse health and social consequences associated with excessive drinking—health problems, injuries, accidents, violence—are not limited to those who are alcohol-dependent. In fact, most of those who periodically drink heavily or drive while intoxicated do *not* meet the formal criteria for alcohol dependence (Woerle et al., 2007; World Health Organization, 2018).

depressants A category of psychoactive drugs that depress or inhibit brain activity.

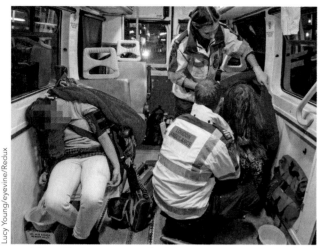

⌃ A Deadly Drug Binge-drinking can lead to tragedy: Acute alcohol poisoning kills six people in the United States every day. Only a third of those who die from overdosing on alcohol were dependent on alcohol. Although the alcohol-related deaths of binge-drinking university students tend to receive the most notice, most alcohol overdoses occur among middle-aged, non-Hispanic white men (Centers for Disease Control and Prevention, 2015a).

What Are Alcohol's Psychological Effects? People are often surprised that alcohol is classified as a depressant. Initially, alcohol produces a mild euphoria, talkativeness, and feelings of good humor and friendliness, leading many people to think of alcohol as a stimulant. But these subjective experiences occur because alcohol *lessens inhibitions* by depressing the brain centers responsible for judgment and self-control. Reduced inhibitions and self-control contribute to the aggressive and violent behavior sometimes associated with alcohol abuse. And, impaired judgment and poor impulse control create deadly results when an intoxicated person gets behind the wheel of a car. However, the loss of inhibitions affects individuals differently, depending on their environment and expectations regarding alcohol's effects.

How Does Alcohol Affect the Body? As a general rule, it takes about one hour to metabolize the alcohol in one drink, which is defined as 1 ounce of 80-proof whiskey, 4 ounces of wine, or 12 ounces of beer. All three drinks contain the same amount of alcohol; the alcohol is simply more diluted in beer than in hard liquor.

Factors such as body weight, gender, food consumption, and the rate of alcohol consumption affect blood alcohol levels. A slender person who quickly consumes three drinks on an empty stomach will become more than twice as intoxicated as a heavier person who consumes three drinks with food. Women typically metabolize alcohol more slowly than do men. If a man and a woman of equal weight consume the same number of drinks, the woman will become more intoxicated. **Table 4.1** shows the behavioral effects and impairments associated with different blood alcohol levels.

Binge drinking is a particularly risky practice. *Binge drinking* is defined as five or more drinks in a row for men, or four or more drinks in a row for women (Cooke et al., 2010). Every year, several university students die of alcohol poisoning after ingesting large amounts of liquor in a short amount of time. Less well publicized are the other negative effects associated with binge drinking, including aggression, sexual assaults, accidents, and property damage (Mitka, 2009; Wechsler & Nelson, 2008; World Health Organization, 2018).

TABLE 4.1

Behavioral Effects of Blood Alcohol Levels

Blood Alcohol Level	Behavioral Effects
0.05%	Lowered alertness; release of inhibitions; impaired judgment
0.10%	Slowed reaction times; impaired motor function; less caution
0.15%	Large, consistent increases in reaction time
0.20%	Marked depression in sensory and motor capability; obvious intoxication
0.25%	Severe motor disturbance; staggering; sensory perceptions greatly impaired
0.30%	Stuporous but conscious; no comprehension of the world around them
0.35%	Surgical anesthesia; minimal level causing death
0.40%	About half of people at this level die

❮ This Is Fun? According to a national survey of U.S. university students, about one-third engaged in binge drinking in the previous month (National Institute on Alcohol Abuse and Alcoholism, 2020). Binge drinking involves rapid consumption of alcohol leading to intoxication—usually four drinks for women and five for men over the course of about two hours. Despite the deaths from alcohol poisoning of several university students each year, binge drinking and public drunkenness remain common at spring break celebrations. One survey found that university students in the United States spent $5.5 billion a year on alcohol, more than they spend on textbooks, soft drinks, tea, milk, juice, and coffee combined (Nelson et al., 2005).

In a person who is physically dependent on alcohol, withdrawal causes a rebound effect in the brain. The severity of the withdrawal symptoms depends on the level of physical dependence. With a low level of dependence, withdrawal may involve disrupted sleep, anxiety, and mild tremors ("the shakes"). At higher levels of physical dependence on alcohol, withdrawal may involve confusion, hallucinations, and severe tremors or seizures. Collectively, these severe symptoms are called *delirium tremens,* or the *DTs.* In cases of extreme physical dependence, alcohol withdrawal, in the absence of medical supervision, can cause seizures, convulsions, and even death.

Barbiturates and Tranquilizers **Barbiturates** and tranquilizers are *a category of depressant drugs that reduce anxiety and produce sleepiness.* Barbiturates depress activity in the brain centers that control arousal, wakefulness, and alertness. They also depress the brain's respiratory centers. *Tranquilizers* have similar effects, but are less potent and are typically used to treat anxiety.

Like alcohol, barbiturates at low doses cause relaxation, mild euphoria, and reduced inhibitions. Larger doses produce a loss of coordination, impaired mental functioning, and depression. High doses can produce unconsciousness, coma, and death. Because of the additive effect of depressants, barbiturates combined with alcohol are particularly dangerous.

Barbiturates produce both physical and psychological dependence. Withdrawal from low doses of barbiturates produces irritability and REM rebound nightmares. Withdrawal from high doses of barbiturates can produce hallucinations, disorientation, restlessness, and life-threatening convulsions.

The Opioids: From Poppies to Demerol

Also called *narcotics* or *opiates,* the **opioids** are *a category of psychoactive drugs that are chemically similar to morphine and have strong pain-relieving properties.* Natural opioids include *opium,* which is derived from the opium poppy, a flowering plant; *morphine,* the active ingredient in opium; and *codeine,* which can be derived from either opium or morphine. Synthetic and semisynthetic opioids include *heroin, methadone, oxycodone,* and the prescription painkillers *OxyContin®, Vicodin®, Percodan®, Demerol®,* and *fentanyl.*

Opioids produce their powerful effects by mimicking the brain's own natural painkillers, called *endorphins.* Opioids occupy endorphin receptor sites in the brain. When used medically, opioids alter an individual's reaction to pain by reducing the brain's perception of pain. It was once believed that people who took medically prescribed opioids rarely developed drug tolerance or addiction. In the short term, opioids can be helpful for pain relief. But the repeated use of any opioid leads to the development of tolerance and some degree of physical dependence (Volkow et al., 2018). *Most* patients who take opioid painkillers for a short period of time do not become addicted. Nevertheless, it is true that physicians and researchers today are more aware of the addictive potential of these drugs.

Among the most dangerous opioids is *heroin.* When injected into a vein, heroin reaches the brain in seconds, creating an intense rush of euphoria that is followed by feelings of contentment, peacefulness, and warmth. Withdrawal is not life-threatening, but it does produce unpleasant rebound effects. Withdrawal symptoms include an intense craving for heroin, fever, chills, muscle cramps, and gastrointestinal problems.

Heroin is not the most commonly abused opioid. That distinction belongs to the prescription pain pills, especially *OxyContin,* which combines the synthetic opioid *oxycodone* with a time-release mechanism. Street users discovered that crushing the OxyContin tablets easily destroyed the time-release mechanism. The resulting powder can be snorted, smoked, or diluted in water and injected—resulting in a rapid, intense high.

The synthetic opioids are now the most commonly prescribed class of medications in the United States (Volkow et al., 2018). Abuse of OxyContin and similar prescription pain pills such as Vicodin, hydrocodone, and oxycodone has skyrocketed in recent years,

barbiturates (barb-ITCH-yer-its) A category of depressant drugs that reduce anxiety and produce sleepiness.

opioids (OH-pee-oidz) A category of psychoactive drugs that are chemically similar to morphine and have strong pain-relieving properties; also called *opiates* or *narcotics.*

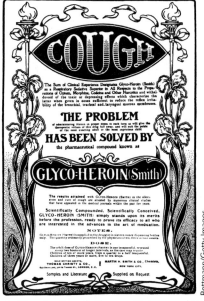

▲ **Heroin Cough Syrup** Opium and its derivatives, including heroin, morphine, and codeine, were legal in the United States until 1914. In the late nineteenth and early twentieth centuries, opioids were commonly used in over-the-counter medications for a variety of ailments from sleeplessness to "female problems" (Musto, 1991). This ad for "Glyco-Heroin" cough syrup appeared in 1904. Codeine is still used in some prescription cough syrups, and like other opioids, can be dangerous when abused.

∧ **Mac Miller and the Danger of Synthetic Drugs** Rapper Mac Miller died of an accidental drug overdose due, in part, to a dangerous mix of cocaine, fentanyl, and alcohol. Fentanyl is a synthetic opioid that is up to 100 times more potent than morphine.

becoming a national health crisis. Prescription pain pills are especially dangerous when mixed with other drugs, such as alcohol or barbiturates. Deaths from accidental overdose of opioids quadrupled between 1999 and 2010, with the number of deaths staying at that high rate since then (National Institute on Drug Abuse, 2020). Prescription opioids accounted for most of this increase (Volkow et al., 2014).

As access to prescription opioids has become more strictly controlled, heroin use and overdose deaths have skyrocketed (Kolodny et al., 2015; Wilson et al., 2020). Much of the increase is due to people turning to heroin—a cheaper and more potent high—after first becoming addicted to prescription painkillers (Martins et al., 2017). In some cases, people have died from unknowingly ingesting heroin that had been combined with *fentanyl,* a synthetic painkiller that is up to a hundred times more potent than morphine. The medical use of fentanyl is typically restricted to short-term use post-surgery or for people suffering severe pain. Many people are not intending to take fentanyl. Often, people who think they're buying OxyContin, oxycodone, heroin, cocaine, or other drugs are unknowingly buying a product that has been replaced with or laced with fentanyl (Centers for Disease Control and Prevention, 2020; National Institute on Drug Abuse, 2016). Why? Greed. Fentanyl is cheaper than most other drugs. Perhaps due in part to unintentional ingestion of fentanyl, overdose from opioids alone is now the second leading cause of accidental death in the United States, second only to motor vehicle accidents (Centers for Disease Control and Prevention, 2015b; Volkow & McLellan, 2011).

The Stimulants: Caffeine, Nicotine, Amphetamines, and Cocaine

■ KEY THEME
Stimulant drugs increase brain activity, while the psychedelic drugs create perceptual distortions, alter mood, and affect thinking.

= KEY QUESTIONS
- What are the general effects of stimulants and the specific effects of caffeine, nicotine, amphetamines, and cocaine?
- What are the effects of mescaline, LSD, and marijuana?
- What are the "club drugs," and what are their effects?

Stimulants are *a category of psychoactive drugs that increase brain activity, arouse behavior, and increase mental alertness.* Stimulants vary in legal status, the strength of their effects, and the manner in which they are taken. All stimulant drugs, however, are at least mildly addicting.

Caffeine and Nicotine **Caffeine** is *a stimulant drug found in coffee, tea, cola drinks, chocolate, and many over-the-counter medications.* Caffeine is the most widely used psychoactive drug in the world and is found in such common sources as coffee, tea, cola drinks, chocolate, and certain over-the-counter medications. Caffeine promotes wakefulness, mental alertness, vigilance, and faster thought processes by stimulating the release of dopamine in the brain's prefrontal cortex.

Caffeine also produces its mentally stimulating effects by blocking *adenosine* receptors in the brain. As noted earlier, adenosine levels gradually increase the longer a person is awake. When adenosine levels reach a certain level in your body, the urge to sleep greatly intensifies. Caffeine staves off the urge and promotes alertness by blocking adenosine's sleep-inducing effects (Roehrs & Roth, 2008).

Yes, coffee drinkers, there is ample scientific evidence that caffeine is physically addictive. However, because the brain-reward effects of caffeine are mild, coffee lovers are not likely to ransack the nearest Starbucks or take hostages if deprived of their favorite espresso. However, they will experience withdrawal symptoms if they abruptly stop their caffeine intake. Headaches, irritability, drowsiness, and fatigue can last a week or longer (Juliano & Griffiths, 2004; Reissig et al., 2009).

stimulants A category of psychoactive drugs that increase brain activity, arouse behavior, and increase mental alertness.

caffeine (kaff-EEN) A stimulant drug found in coffee, tea, cola drinks, chocolate, and many over-the-counter medications.

Chelsea Lauren/Getty Images

Taken to excess, caffeine can produce anxiety, restlessness, and increased heart rate, and can disrupt normal sleep patterns. Excessive caffeine use can also contribute to the incidence of sleep disorders, including the NREM parasomnias, like sleepwalking (Cartwright, 2004). Recall that Scott, whose story we told in the Prologue, had been taking caffeine pills for several weeks before his sleepwalking episode. Because Scott never drank coffee or other caffeinated beverages, his caffeine tolerance would have been low. Especially when combined with sleep deprivation, irregular sleep schedules, and high levels of stress—all of which Scott experienced—excessive caffeine intake can trigger sleepwalking and other NREM parasomnias. At least one sleep expert believes that Scott's high caffeine use may have contributed to his outburst of sleep violence (Cartwright, 2007).

For some people, a cup of coffee and a cigarette go hand in hand. Cigarettes contain **nicotine**, *a potent and addictive stimulant drug found in all tobacco products, including smokeless tobacco.* Like caffeine, nicotine increases mental alertness and reduces fatigue or drowsiness. Brain imaging studies show that nicotine increases neural activity in many brain areas, including the frontal lobes, thalamus, hippocampus, and amygdala (Rose et al., 2003). Thus, it's not surprising that smokers report that tobacco enhances mood, attention, and arousal.

When cigarette smoke is inhaled, nicotine reaches the brain in seconds. But over the next hour or two, nicotine's desired effects diminish. For the addicted person, smoking becomes a finely tuned and regulated behavior that maintains steady brain levels of nicotine. At regular intervals ranging from about 30 to 90 minutes, the smoker lights up, avoiding the withdrawal effects that are starting to occur. For the pack-a-day smoker, that averages out to some 70,000 "hits" of nicotine every year.

A new development in nicotine delivery is "vaping," or the use of electronic or "e-cigarettes" (Dawkins & Corcoran, 2014). E-cigarettes are battery-powered devices that heat liquid nicotine and mimic the look and feel of smoking, from a glowing tip to the hazy, smokelike vapor that is inhaled. E-cigarettes also are used to deliver tetrahydrocannabinol (THC) or cannabidiol (CBD), both ingredients in marijuana. (We'll discuss marijuana in the section on psychedelic drugs.)

The use of e-cigarettes is controversial. Some public health researchers support their use because they believe that e-cigarettes are less harmful than regular cigarettes, especially if people use e-cigarettes to help them quit smoking (King et al., 2020). But it's a myth that e-cigarettes are not addictive. Researchers point out that nicotine in any form is highly addictive, that dangerous chemicals may be present in the vapor, and that the long-term effects are unknown (Fairchild & Bayer, 2015). Moreover, there have been recent, alarming reports of lung injuries among even young, healthy people who vape, some of which have been deadly (King et al., 2020). These illnesses are particularly prevalent among those who buy their vaping products on the streets as opposed to from legitimate sources. In the United States, the Centers for Disease Control issued a warning against using such bootleg vaping products (Kaplan, 2019).

People who start smoking or vaping for nicotine's stimulating properties often continue in order to avoid the withdrawal symptoms. Along with an intense craving for nicotine, withdrawal symptoms include jumpiness, irritability, tremors, headaches, drowsiness, "brain fog," and light-headedness.

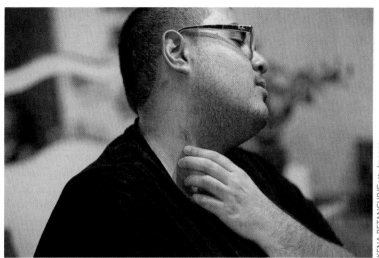

The Dangers of Vaping 22-year-old Gregory Rodriguez became dangerously ill as a result of vaping THC. The New York City resident spent almost two weeks in the hospital and suffered serious damage to his lungs. Here he shows the scars from where tubes were inserted in his neck to help keep his blood oxygenated. As tobacco use has fallen, "vaping" of tobacco products as well as ingredients from marijuana has increased, particularly among young people. In 2018, just 3.2 percent of adults in the United States used e-cigarettes, far fewer than used regular cigarettes (Creamer et al., 2019). In 2019, by contrast, 10.5 percent of middle schoolers and 27.5 percent of high school students did so, more than used regular cigarettes (Cullen et al., 2020). In recent years, numerous cases of lung injuries related to vaping, such as that experienced by Rodriguez, were reported, often using bootleg—or unregulated—vaping products (Christiani, 2019). Many of those affected by these lung injuries died.

MYTH ◀ SCIENCE

It is a myth that e-cigarettes are *not* addictive.

nicotine A potent and addictive stimulant drug found in all tobacco products, including smokeless tobacco.

amphetamines (am-FET-uh-meenz) A class of stimulant drugs that arouse the central nervous system and suppress appetite.

cocaine An illegal stimulant derived from the leaves of the coca plant, which is found in South America.

Amphetamines and Cocaine Like caffeine and nicotine, amphetamines and cocaine are addictive substances that affect brain dopamine and stimulate brain activity, increasing mental alertness and reducing fatigue (Wang et al., 2015). However, amphetamines and cocaine also elevate mood and produce a sense of euphoria. When abused, both drugs can produce severe psychological and physical problems.

Sometimes called "speed" or "uppers," **amphetamines** are *a class of stimulant drugs that arouse the central nervous system and suppress appetite.* They were once widely prescribed as diet pills. *Benzedrine* and *Dexedrine* are prescription amphetamines. Tolerance to the appetite-suppressant effects occurs quickly, so progressive increases in amphetamine dosage are required to maintain the effect. Consequently, amphetamines are no longer prescribed for weight control.

Using any type of amphetamines for an extended period of time is followed by "crashing"—withdrawal symptoms of fatigue, deep sleep, intense mental depression, and increased appetite. This is another example of a drug rebound effect. Users also become psychologically dependent on the drug for the euphoric state, or "rush," that it produces, especially when injected.

Cocaine is *an illegal stimulant derived from the leaves of the coca plant, which is found in South America.* (The coca plant is not the source of cocoa or chocolate, which is made from the beans of the *cacao* tree.) Psychologically, cocaine produces intense euphoria, mental alertness, and self-confidence. These psychological responses occur because cocaine blocks the reuptake of three different neurotransmitters—dopamine, serotonin, and norepinephrine. Blocking reuptake *potentiates,* or increases the effects of, these neurotransmitters.

The effects of cocaine depend partly on the form in which it is taken. A concentrated form of cocaine, called "crack," is smoked. When smoked or injected, cocaine reaches the brain in seconds, and effects peak in about five minutes. If inhaled, or "snorted," cocaine takes several minutes to be absorbed through the nasal membranes, and peak blood levels are reached in 30 to 60 minutes. Chronic cocaine use produces a wide range of psychological disorders.

Methamphetamine, also known as *meth,* is an illegal drug that can be easily manufactured in home or street laboratories. Providing an intense high that is longer lasting and less expensive than that of cocaine, methamphetamine is highly addictive. It can also cause extensive brain damage.

Extensive neurological damage, especially to the frontal lobes, adds to the cognitive and social skill deficits that are evident in heavy methamphetamine users (Homer et al., 2008). Depression, emotional instability, and impulsive and violent behavior are also common. Finally, some research suggests that it may take years for the brain to recover from damage caused by methamphetamine abuse (Bamford et al., 2008). Even after months of abstinence, PET scans of former meth users show significant reductions in the number of dopamine receptors (Volkow et al., 2001).

> **Cocaine Toothache Drops?** Cocaine was legal in the United States until 1914. Like the opioids, it was widely used as an ingredient in over-the-counter medicines (Jonnes, 1999). Cocaine derivatives, such as novocaine and lidocaine, are used medically as anesthetics. Cocaine was also part of Coca-Cola's original formula in 1888. It was replaced in 1903 with another stimulant, caffeine.

Psychedelic Drugs: Mescaline, LSD, and Marijuana

The term *psychedelic drug* was coined in the 1950s. **Psychedelic drugs** are *a category of psychoactive drugs that create sensory and perceptual distortions, alter mood, and affect thinking.* Psychedelic literally means "mind manifesting."

Mescaline and LSD Naturally occurring psychedelic drugs have been used in religious rituals for thousands of years. **Mescaline** is *a psychedelic drug derived from the peyote cactus.* Another psychedelic drug, called *psilocybin,* is derived from *Psilocybe* mushrooms, which are sometimes referred to as "magic mushrooms" or "shrooms."

In contrast to these naturally occurring psychedelics, **LSD** *(lysergic acid diethylamide)* is *a powerful synthetic psychedelic drug.* First synthesized in the late 1930s, LSD is far more potent than mescaline or psilocybin. Just 25 micrograms, or one-millionth of an ounce, of LSD can produce profound psychological effects with relatively few physiological changes.

LSD and psilocybin are very similar chemically to the neurotransmitter *serotonin,* which is involved in regulating moods and sensations (see Chapter 2). LSD binds to serotonin receptors in the brain (Wacker et al., 2017). Similarly, psilocybin stimulates serotonin receptor sites in the somatosensory cortex and other brain regions (Carhart-Harris et al., 2014; Kupferschmidt, 2014a).

The effects of a psychedelic experience vary greatly, depending on an individual's personality, current emotional state, surroundings, and the other people present. A "bad trip" can produce extreme anxiety, panic, and even psychotic episodes. Tolerance to psychedelic drugs may occur after heavy use. However, even heavy users of LSD do not develop physical dependence, nor do they experience withdrawal symptoms if the drug is not taken.

One large-scale mental health survey of nearly 20,000 participants who had used psychedelic drugs found no increased risk of developing psychological problems (Johansen & Krebs, 2015). However, adverse reactions to LSD can include flashbacks (recurrences of the drug's effects), depression, long-term psychological instability, and prolonged psychotic reactions (Advokat et al., 2014). In a psychologically unstable or susceptible person, even a single dose of LSD can precipitate a psychotic reaction.

On the other hand, some clinical trials have shown that LSD, psilocybin, or other psychedelic drugs, given under carefully controlled conditions, may be helpful in the treatment of psychological disorders, including anxiety, substance abuse, and depression (Aday et al., 2020; Chi & Gold, 2020). For example, two carefully controlled, rigorous studies found that a single dose of psilocybin, taken in a therapeutic context, rapidly relieved anxiety and depression in cancer patients (Griffiths et al., 2016; Ross et al., 2016). The improvements in mood, mental health, and quality of life persisted for months after the experience. Although promising, such treatments are still experimental (Reiff et al., 2020).

Another growing area of research surrounds the practice of microdosing, taking tiny amounts of a psychedelic such as LSD or psilocybin to treat psychological disorders, increase creativity, or enhance cognitive functioning. The boom in microdosing followed media reports, including a widely read 2015 article in *Rolling Stone* and popular online communities on sites like Reddit (Jarrett, 2019). Despite the hype, the effects of a microdose are so small that most people are unable to tell whether they have been given a microdose or a placebo (Turk, 2019). Although some researchers are currently conducting carefully controlled studies of microdosing, there is not strong evidence yet of its effectiveness. Moreover, there also is some evidence that it can increase negative emotions (Polito & Stevenson, 2019).

John Mitchell/Alamy Stock Photo

Peyote-Inspired Visions The Huichol Indians of Mexico have used peyote in religious ceremonies for hundreds of years. Huichol yarn paintings, like the one shown here, often depict imagery and scenes inspired by traditional peyote visions. These visions resemble the geometric shapes and radiating patterns of hallucinations induced by psychedelic drugs. Today, peyote is used as a sacrament in the religious ceremonies of the Native American Church, a religion with more than 300,000 members (Swan & Big Bow, 1995). Such ritual use of peyote is not generally associated with psychological or cognitive problems (see Halpern et al., 2005).

psychedelic drugs (sy-kuh-DEL-ick) A category of psychoactive drugs that create sensory and perceptual distortions, alter mood, and affect thinking.

mescaline (MESS-kuh-lin) A psychedelic drug derived from the peyote cactus.

LSD (lysergic acid diethyl-amide) A powerful synthetic psychedelic drug.

Medical Marijuana Marijuana has been used as a medicine for thousands of years in China, Egypt, and other countries. Marijuana is illegal at the federal level in the United States. But by 2020, 47 states, the District of Columbia, and Puerto Rico had legalized marijuana use in some form. One unexpected finding: the average death rate for opioid overdose was 25 percent lower in states with legalized medical marijuana than in states without legal access to marijuana (Bachhuber et al., 2014). Another study found that hospitalizations for opioid abuse and dependence dropped by an average of 23 percent in states that approved medical marijuana (Shi, 2017). Although correlational, such studies suggest that the availability of medical marijuana for chronic pain may be associated with less use—and abuse—of narcotic painkillers.

Marijuana The common hemp plant, *Cannabis sativa,* is used to make rope and cloth. But when its leaves, stems, flowers, and seeds are dried and crushed, the mixture is called marijuana, one of the most widely used (mostly) illegal drugs. Formally, **marijuana** is *a psychoactive drug derived from the hemp plant.* Marijuana's active ingredient is the chemical *tetrahydrocannabinol,* abbreviated *THC.* When marijuana is smoked, THC reaches the brain in less than 30 seconds. One potent form of marijuana, *hashish,* is made from the resin of the hemp plant.

To lump marijuana with the highly psychedelic drugs mescaline and LSD is somewhat misleading. At high doses, marijuana can sometimes produce sensory distortions that resemble a mild psychedelic experience. Low to moderate doses of THC typically produce a sense of well-being, mild euphoria, and a dreamy state of relaxation. Taste, touch, and smell may be enhanced; time perception may be altered.

The brain has receptor sites that are specific for THC. A naturally occurring brain chemical, called *anandamide,* is structurally similar to THC and binds to the THC receptors (Mechoulam et al., 2014). Anandamide appears to be involved in regulating the transmission of pain signals and may reduce painful sensations. Active ingredients in marijuana have been shown to be involved in several psychological processes, including mood, memory, cognition, appetite, and neurogenesis (see Mechoulam & Parker, 2013).

Marijuana and its active ingredient, THC, have been shown to be helpful in the treatment of pain, epilepsy, hypertension, nausea, glaucoma, arthritis, and asthma (National Academies of Science, Engineering, and Medicine, 2017; Rabgay et al., 2020). In cancer patients, THC can prevent the nausea and vomiting caused by chemotherapy (Vale, 2019). One compound in marijuana is *cannabidiol,* or *CBD,* which appears to have no psychoactive effects but has shown promise in treating seizure disorders and other conditions.

In recent years, however, CBD has surged in popularity for a range of uses beyond those supported by the evidence. As of 2019, more than 1,000 products were being sold in stores, in restaurants and bars, and on the Internet (Hurd, 2020). Researchers have raised concerns about mislabeled or tainted CBD products and the lack of evidence for many of the health claims for these products (White, 2019). And CBD can have side effects, including gastrointestinal problems and sleepiness. One researcher calls the unregulated CBD market "a significant threat to public health" and calls for rules and regulations to enhance its safety.

Also on the negative side, marijuana interferes with muscle coordination and perception and may impair driving ability. Marijuana has also been shown to interfere with learning, memory, and cognitive functioning (Cohen et al., 2019; Harvey et al., 2007). In addition, although some people use marijuana to help them fall asleep, research has uncovered a backlash—increased fatigue the next day (Goodhines et al., 2019).

Most marijuana users do not develop physical dependence. Chronic users of high doses can develop some tolerance to THC and may experience withdrawal symptoms when its use is discontinued (Volkow et al., 2017). Such symptoms include irritability, restlessness, insomnia, tremors, and decreased appetite.

Designer "Club" Drugs: Ecstasy and the Dissociative Anesthetic Drugs

Some drugs don't fit into neat categories. The "club drugs" are a loose collection of psychoactive drugs that are popular at dance clubs, parties, and the all-night dance parties called "raves." Many of these drugs are *designer drugs,* meaning that they were synthesized in a laboratory rather than derived from naturally occurring compounds.

marijuana A psychoactive drug derived from the hemp plant.

In this section, we'll take a look at three of the most popular club drugs—*ecstasy, ketamine,* and *PCP.*

The initials *MDMA* stand for the long chemical name of the drug better known as *ecstasy.* **Ecstasy** (or **MDMA**) is a *synthetic club drug that combines stimulant and mild psychedelic effects.* Its popularity, however, results from its emotional effects: Feelings of euphoria, friendliness, and increased well-being are common (Bedi et al., 2010). Ecstasy's side effects hint at the problems that can be associated with its use: dehydration, rapid heartbeat, tremors, muscle tension and involuntary teeth-clenching, and hyperthermia (abnormally high body temperature). Rave partygoers who take MDMA in crowded, hot surroundings are particularly at risk for collapse or death from dehydration and hyperthermia.

The "love drug" effects of ecstasy may result from its unique effect on serotonin in the brain. Along with causing neurons to release serotonin, MDMA also blocks serotonin reuptake, amplifying and prolonging serotonin effects (Braun, 2001). Although flooding the brain with serotonin may temporarily enhance feelings of emotional well-being, some research has suggested that long-term use of ecstasy may damage the brain's serotonin system and cause depression, anxiety, and mood disturbances (Benningfield & Cowan, 2013). However, MDMA is also being studied as a potential treatment for posttraumatic stress disorder when used as part of psychotherapy (see Vermetten & Yehuda, 2020).

Another class of drugs found at dance clubs and raves is the *dissociative anesthetics,* including phencyclidine, better known as *PCP* or *angel dust,* and *ketamine* (street name *Special K*). **Dissociative anesthetics** are a *class of drugs that reduce sensitivity to pain and produce feelings of detachment and dissociation rather than actual hallucinations.* Feelings of detachment from reality—including distortions of space, time, and body image— are common. Generally, PCP has more intense and longer effects than ketamine does. Ketamine has also shown promise in the treatment of depression (Duman 2018; McGirr et al., 2015). We discuss the experimental use of ketamine for treatment-resistant depression in the chapter on therapies.

Closing Thoughts

Internal biological rhythms and external environmental factors influence the natural ebb and flow of your consciousness over the course of any given day. Beyond those natural oscillations, hypnosis and meditation are techniques that can profoundly alter your experience of consciousness. Meditation, in particular, produces numerous benefits that can help you cope more effectively with life's demands. Some psychoactive drugs, including widely available substances like caffeine, can also influence your experience of consciousness in beneficial ways. But other psychoactive substances, although producing dramatic alterations in consciousness, do so with the potential risk of damaging the finely tuned balance of the brain's neurotransmitters and reward system.

Both natural and deliberate factors seem to have played a role in the extreme breach of consciousness that Scott Falater claimed to experience. Severe disruptions in his normal sleep patterns, his out-of-character use of caffeine, and intense work-related stresses combined to trigger sleepwalking, a parasomnia that Scott had demonstrated when he was younger. And that Scott reacted violently when his wife tried to guide him back to bed also had precedent: Scott had reacted aggressively earlier in his life when his sister tried to intervene during one of his sleepwalking episodes.

Scott Falater's trial for murdering his wife drew international attention. In the end, the Arizona jury convicted Falater of first-degree, premeditated murder. Falater was sentenced to life in prison with no possibility of parole. Today, Scott Falater is incarcerated in the Arizona State Prison Complex at Yuma, where he works as an educational aide and library clerk.

MDMA or **ecstasy** Synthetic club drug that combines stimulant and mild psychedelic effects.

dissociative anesthetics Class of drugs that reduce sensitivity to pain and produce feelings of detachment and dissociation, rather than actual hallucinations; includes the club drugs phencyclidine (PCP) and ketamine.

 **PSYCH FOR YOUR LIFE**

Overcoming Insomnia

In this section, we'll provide some simple tips to help you minimize sleep problems. If you frequently suffer from insomnia, we'll also describe an effective treatment that you can implement on your own—*stimulus control therapy.*

Preventing Sleep Problems

You may not realize the degree to which your daily habits can contribute to or even create sleeping difficulties. The following four strategies can help you consistently get a good night's sleep.

1. Monitor your intake of stimulants.

Many people aren't aware of how much caffeine they're ingesting. Coffee, tea, soft drinks, chocolate, and many over-the-counter medications contain significant amounts of caffeine. Monitor your caffeine intake, and avoid caffeine products for at least 4 hours before going to bed. Some people are very sensitive to caffeine's stimulating effects and may need to avoid caffeine for up to 10 hours before bedtime. Beyond caffeine, some herbal teas and supplements contain ginseng, ephedrine, or other stimulants that can keep you awake.

2. Establish a quiet bedtime routine.

Avoid stimulating mental or physical activity for at least an hour before your bedtime. That means no suspenseful television shows, violent videos, exciting video games, or loud arguments right before bedtime. Ditto for strenuous exercise. Although regular exercise is an excellent way to improve your sleep, exercising within 3 hours of bedtime may keep you awake. Finally, soaking in a very warm bath shortly before bed promotes deep sleep by raising your core body temperature.

3. Create the conditions for restful sleep.

Your bedroom should be quiet, cool, and dark. If you live in a noisy environment, invest in a pair of earplugs or some sort of "white noise" source, such as a fan or a white-noise smartphone app, for your bedroom. Turn off or mute all devices that can potentially disrupt your sleep, including phones and computers. And, limit your exposure to all types of electronic screens before bedtime. Remember, the blue light emitted by tablets, laptops, and smartphones can trick your brain into thinking it's morning, triggering alertness rather than sleepiness (Chang et al., 2015).

4. Establish a consistent sleep–wake schedule.

Although this is probably the single most effective strategy to achieve high-quality sleep, it's also the most challenging for a lot of university students. Try to go to bed at about the same time each night and get up at approximately the same time every morning so that your circadian rhythms stay in sync. Exposure to bright lights or sunlight shortly after awakening in the morning helps keep your internal clock set.

Many students try to "catch up" on their sleep by sleeping in on the weekends. Unfortunately, this strategy can work against you by producing a case of the "Monday morning blues," which is a self-induced case of jet lag caused by resetting your circadian rhythms to the later weekend schedule.

If you've tried all these suggestions and are still troubled by frequent insomnia, you may need to take a more systematic approach, as outlined in the next section.

Stimulus Control Therapy

Without realizing it, you can sabotage your ability to sleep by associating mentally arousing activities and stimuli with your bedroom, such as watching TV or videos, text messaging, reading, surfing the Internet, doing homework or paperwork, and so on. Over time, your bed and bedroom become stimuli that trigger arousal rather than drowsiness and the rapid onset of sleep. In turn, this increases the amount of time that you're lying in bed awake, thrashing around, and trying to force yourself to sleep.

Stimulus control therapy is an *insomnia treatment involving specific guidelines to create a strict association between the bedroom and rapid sleep onset*. It is designed to help you (1) establish a consistent sleep–wake schedule and (2) associate your bedroom and bedtime with falling asleep rather than other activities (Morin et al., 2006). To achieve improved sleep, you must commit to the following rules with *no* exceptions for at least two weeks:

- Only sleep and sex are allowed in your bedroom. None of the sleep-incompatible activities mentioned above are allowed in your bed or bedroom.
- Only go to bed when you are sleepy, not tired or wiped out, but *sleepy*.
- Once in bed, if you're still awake after 15 minutes, don't try to force yourself to go to sleep. Instead, get out of bed and go sit in another room. Only go back to bed when you get sleepy.
- Get up at the *same* time *every* morning, including weekends, regardless of how much sleep you got the night before.
- No daytime napping.

Strictly adhering to these rules can be challenging given the realities of work, family, school, and other personal commitments. However, those situations are much easier to manage when you are adequately rested.

Keeping a *sleep diary* can help you track your sleep and sleep-related behaviors. It will also increase your awareness of your sleep habits and the factors that interfere with restorative sleep. You can go to sleepfoundation.org/articles/nsf-official-sleep-diary to download a sleep diary from the National Sleep Foundation. Other sleep diaries can easily be found with an Internet search. Sleep well!

stimulus control therapy Insomnia treatment involving specific guidelines to create a strict association between the bedroom and rapid sleep onset.

◤ CHAPTER REVIEW

Consciousness and Its Variations

 **Achieve,** Macmillan Learning's online study platform, features the full e-book of *Discovering Psychology*, the **LearningCurve** adaptive quizzing system, videos, and a variety of activities to boost your learning. Visit **Achieve** at macmillanlearning.com.

KEY PEOPLE

Sigmund Freud, p. 123   Ernest R. Hilgard, p. 128   William James, p. 112

KEY TERMS

consciousness, p. 112
attention, p. 112
circadian rhythm, p. 115
electroencephalograph, p. 116
REM sleep, p. 117
NREM sleep, p. 117
beta brain waves, p. 117
alpha brain waves, p. 117
sleep paralysis, p. 118
dream, p. 122
nightmare, p. 123
activation–synthesis model of
    dreaming, p. 123

neurocognitive model of
    dreaming, p. 124
sleep disorder, p. 124
insomnia, p. 124
obstructive sleep apnea (OSA),
    p. 125
narcolepsy, p. 125
parasomnias, p. 125
sleep terrors, p. 125
sleepwalking, p. 126
hypnosis, p. 127
posthypnotic suggestion,
    p. 127

dissociation, p. 128
meditation, p. 128
psychoactive drug, p. 131
physical dependence, p. 131
drug tolerance, p. 131
drug abuse, p. 132
depressants, p. 133
barbiturates, p. 135
opioids, p. 135
stimulants, p. 136
caffeine, p. 136
nicotine, p. 137

amphetamines, p. 138
cocaine, p. 138
psychedelic drugs,
    p. 139
mescaline, p. 139
LSD, p. 139
marijuana, p. 140
MDMA (ecstasy), p. 141
dissociative anesthetics,
    p. 141
stimulus control therapy,
    p. 143

CONCEPT MAP › Consciousness and Its Variations

Consciousness

The immediate awareness of internal and external stimuli

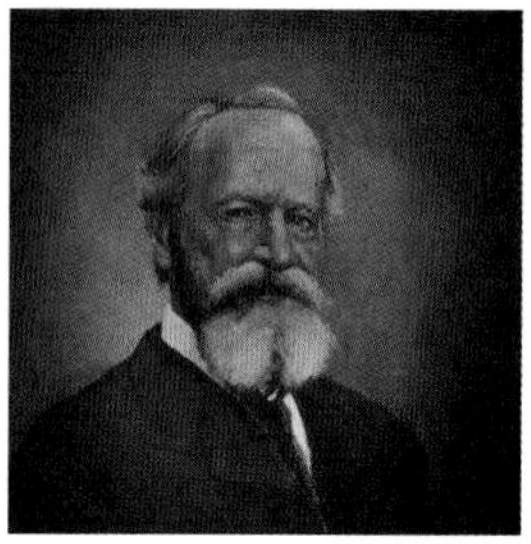

William James (1842–1910)
Described subjective experience of consciousness as ongoing stream of mental activity

Attention is the capacity to selectively focus awareness on particular stimuli.
- Has limited capacity
- Disrupted by inattentional blindness, change blindness, multitasking

Cycles of Consciousness

Circadian rhythms:
- Daily fluctuations in biological and psychological processes
- A cluster of neurons in the hypothalamus responds to light and triggers pineal gland to release melatonin

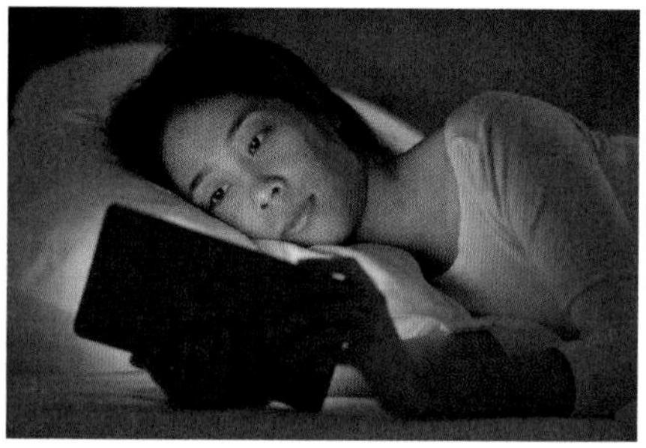

TORWAISTUDIO/Shutterstock

Sleep

Sleep onset:
- Alert wakefulness (**beta brain waves**)
- Drowsiness (**alpha brain waves**)

NREM sleep:
- Stage 1: transition from drowsiness to light sleep
- Stage 2: sleep spindles; K complexes
- Stage 3 (slow-wave sleep): delta brain waves; deep sleep

REM sleep:
- Rapid eye movement
- Dreaming
- Heightened brain and body activity

Functions of Sleep:
- Evolutionary adaptation
- Memory formation
- Mood regulation, immune system functioning, and metabolism

Don Johnston_MA/Alamy Stock Photo

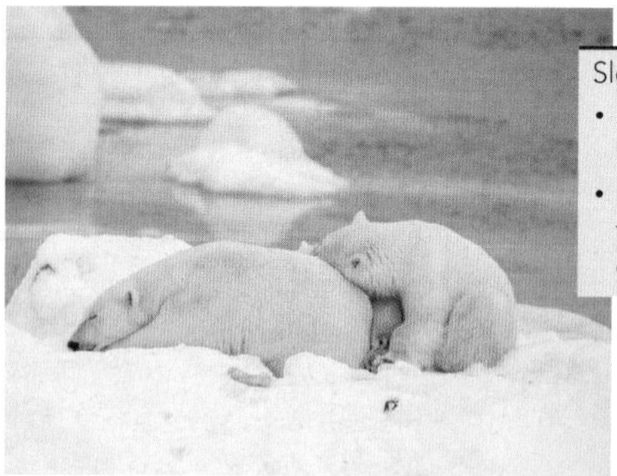

Sleep patterns:
- Nightly: five 90-minute NREM/REM cycles with longer REM episodes as sleep progresses
- Lifespan: typical cycles emerge by age 5; total sleep time, slow-wave sleep, and REM decrease through late adulthood

Dreams and Mental Activity During Sleep

Sleep thinking
Dreams
Nightmares

Significance of dreams:
Sigmund Freud (1856–1939)
Psychoanalytic theory of dreams
- Dream images symbolize repressed wishes and urges.

Activation–synthesis model of dreaming
- Dreams are subjective awareness of internally generated signals during sleep.

Neurocognitive model of dreaming
- Emphasizes continuity of waking and dreaming cognition.

Sleep Disorders

Disruptions in amount, quality, or timing of sleep
- Insomnia
- Obstructive sleep apnea
- Narcolepsy

Parasomnias: Undesirable physical arousal, behaviors, or events during sleep
- Sleep terrors
- Sleepwalking
- Sleep-related eating disorder
- Sleepsex
- Exploding head syndrome

Eros Hoagland/Redux

Hypnosis

A cooperative social interaction in which the participant responds to suggestions made by the hypnotist

Effects of hypnosis:
- Sensory, perceptual changes
- **Posthypnotic suggestions**
- Memory changes
- **Dissociation**

Explaining hypnosis:
- Hypnosis as a special state of consciousness: **Ernest Hilgard** (1904–2001) proposed that hypnosis involves a dissociation of consciousness into two streams of mental activity. He calls one of these streams the *hidden observer*
- The *social cognitive view:* Hypnosis is due to ordinary psychological processes
- The *imaginative suggestibility view:* Hypnosis is due to capacity to imagine and heightened suggestibility

Limitations of hypnosis:
- Not all people are capable of being hypnotized.
- Cannot hypnotize a person against their will
- Cannot hypnotically induce immoral or criminal acts

Meditation

Mental or physical techniques used to induce a state of focused attention and heightened awareness

Forms of meditation:
- Focused awareness
- Open monitoring, including mindfulness

Aleksandr Davydov/Alamy Stock Photo

Effects of meditation:
- Improves attention, concentration, memory, and emotional control
- Reduces physiological arousal and stress

Psychoactive Drugs

Alter synaptic transmission in the brain and induce changes in arousal, mood, thinking, sensation, and perception

Drug abuse involves:
- **Physical dependence**
- **Drug tolerance**
- Withdrawal symptoms
- Rebound effect

Depressants: Addictive drugs that inhibit central nervous system activity
- Alcohol
- **Barbiturates**

"Club" drugs: Synthetic drugs used at dance clubs, parties, and "raves"
- **MDMA (ecstasy)**
- **Dissociative anesthetics** include PCP and ketamine

Psychedelic drugs: Create perceptual distortions, alter mood and thinking
- **Mescaline**
- **LSD**
- **Marijuana**

Opioids: Addictive drugs that relieve pain and produce feelings of euphoria
- Opium
- Morphine
- Codeine
- Heroin
- Methadone
- Prescription painkillers

Stimulants: Addictive drugs that increase brain activity
- **Caffeine**
- **Nicotine**
- **Amphetamines**
- **Cocaine**
- **Methamphetamines**

RJ Sangosti/Getty Images

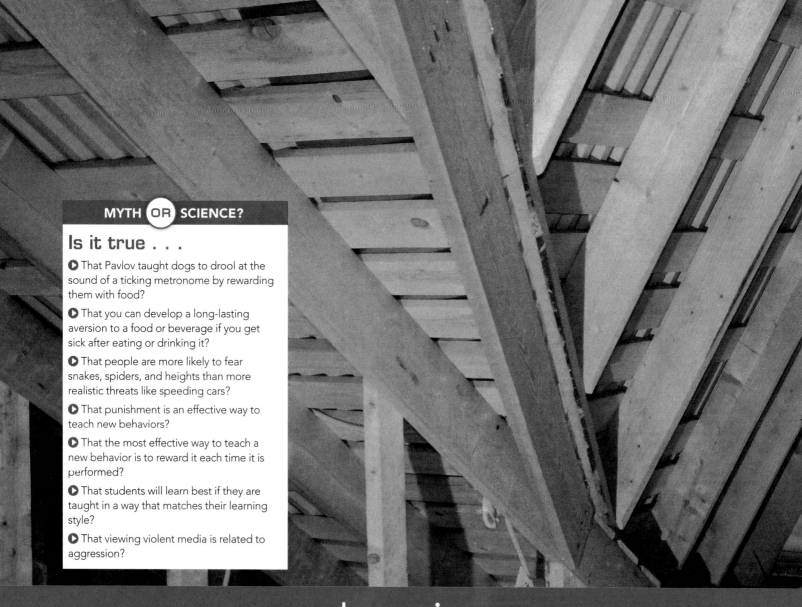

Learning

PROLOGUE

The Killer Attic

Your author Sandy's parents, Erv and Fern, were married for more than 50 years. Sometimes it seems truly amazing that they managed to stay together for so long, as you'll see from this true story.

On a warm summer morning in Chicago, Erv and Fern made plans for the day. The lawn needed mowing and someone had to go to the post office. Fern, who didn't like driving, said that she would mow the lawn if Erv would go to the post office. Erv, who didn't like yard work, agreed to the deal.

When Erv returned, he parked the car around the corner under some large shade trees so that it would stay cool. Walking through the front door, he noticed that the attic fan was squeaking loudly. Erv retrieved the stepladder and oil from the basement, propped the ladder under the attic's trapdoor, and gingerly crawled up into the attic to oil the fan, leaving the trapdoor open.

Meanwhile, Fern walked past the garage on the way into the house and noticed the car was still gone. "Why isn't Erv back yet?" She then noticed the stepladder and the open attic door. Muttering that Erv never put anything

away, Fern latched the trapdoor shut and dragged the ladder back down to the basement.

Erv, who had crawled to the other side of the attic to oil the fan, never heard the attic trapdoor shut. It was very hot in the well-insulated, airless attic, so he tried to work fast. After oiling the fan, he crawled back to the trapdoor—only to discover that it was latched shut from the outside! "Fern," he hollered, "open the door!"

Outside, Fern couldn't hear Erv over the noise of the lawn mower. She stopped to talk to a neighbor, leaving the lawn mower idling. He offered Fern a cold beer, and the two of them leaned over

Sergey Sikharulidze/Alamy Stock Photo

the fence, laughing and talking. From a small, sealed attic window, Erv jealously watched the whole scene. He could already see the tabloid headlines: LAUGHING WIFE DRINKS BEER WHILE HUSBAND COOKS IN ATTIC!

Finally, Fern finished the lawn and walked back to the house. Hearing the back door open, Erv began to yell.

"Fern, let me out! I'm going to suffocate up here!"

"Erv! Is that you? Where are you?" she called, looking around.

"I'm in the attic! Let me out!"

Once Fern was reassured that Erv had suffered no ill effects, she burst out laughing. Ever since, whenever Erv went up into the attic, he posted a sign on the ladder that read MAN IN THE ATTIC! In fact, for years afterward, Erv got nervous whenever he had to go up into the attic.

For her part, Fern began carefully checking on Erv's whereabouts before closing the attic door. But she still laughs when she tells the story of the "killer attic."

Erv and Fern both learned from their experience, as is reflected in the changes in their behavior. Learning new behaviors can occur in many ways, but it almost always helps us adapt to changing circumstances, as you'll see in this chapter. ∿

Conditioning, Learning, and Behavior Psychologists have identified general principles of learning that explain how people and animals acquire new behaviors. These principles apply to simple responses, but they can also help explain how we learn complex skills, such as the proper way to shoot a bow and arrow, as these girls are learning in Java, Indonesia.

Introduction: What Is Learning?

■ KEY THEME

Learning refers to a relatively enduring change in behavior or knowledge as a result of experience.

☰ KEY QUESTIONS
- What is conditioning?
- What are three basic types of learning?

What do we mean when we say that Fern and Erv have "learned" from their experience with the killer attic? In the everyday sense, *learning* often refers to formal methods of acquiring new knowledge or skills, such as learning in the classroom or learning to play the flute.

In psychology, however, the topic of learning is much broader. In general, psychologists formally define **learning** as *a process that produces a relatively enduring change in behavior or knowledge as a result of an individual's experience*. For example, Erv has learned to feel anxious and uncomfortable whenever he needs to enter the attic. He's also learned to take simple precautions, such as posting his MAN IN THE ATTIC! sign, to avoid getting locked in the attic again. As Erv's behavior demonstrates, the learning of new behaviors often reflects adapting to your environment. As the result of experience, you acquire new behaviors or modify old behaviors so as to better cope with your surroundings.

In this broad sense of the word, learning occurs in every setting, not just in classrooms. And learning takes place at every age. For example, during the global pandemic, we all finally learned the proper way to wash our hands, no matter how old we were. Further, the psychological study of learning is not limited to humans. From arachnids to zebras, learning is an important aspect of the behavior of virtually all animals.

Psychologists have often studied learning by observing and recording the experiences of animals in carefully controlled laboratory situations. Using animal subjects, researchers can precisely control the conditions under which a particular behavior is learned. The goal of much of this research has been to identify the general principles of learning that apply across a wide range of species, including humans.

Much of this chapter will focus on a very basic form of learning, called *conditioning*. **Conditioning** is *the process of learning associations between environmental events and behavioral responses*. This description may make you think conditioning has only a limited application to your life. In fact, however, conditioning is reflected in most of your everyday behavior, from simple habits like washing your hands regularly to emotional reactions and complex skills like merging your car onto a busy highway.

In this chapter, we'll look at three basic types of learning—classical conditioning, operant conditioning, and observational learning. As you'll see in the next section, *classical conditioning* explains how certain stimuli can trigger a reflexive, automatic response, as the attic now triggers mild anxiety in Erv. And, as you'll see in a later section, *operant conditioning* is useful in understanding how we acquire new, voluntary actions, such as Erv's posting his sign whenever he climbs into the attic. Finally, we'll consider the process of *observational learning*, or how we acquire new behaviors by observing the actions of others.

Classical Conditioning: Associating Stimuli

■ KEY THEME
Classical conditioning is a process of learning associations between stimuli.

☰ KEY QUESTIONS
- How did Pavlov discover and investigate classical conditioning?
- How does classical conditioning occur?
- What factors can affect classical conditioning?

learning A process that produces a relatively enduring change in behavior or knowledge as a result of an individual's experience.

conditioning The process of learning associations between environmental events and behavioral responses.

One of the major contributors to the study of learning was not a psychologist but a Russian physiologist who was awarded a Nobel Prize for his work on digestion (Miyata, 2009).

Ivan Pavlov's (1849–1936) involvement with psychology began as a result of an observation he made while investigating the role of saliva in digestion, using dogs as his experimental subjects.

In order to get a dog to produce saliva, Pavlov (1904) put food on the dog's tongue. After he had worked with the same dog for several days in a row, Pavlov noticed something curious. The dog began salivating *before* Pavlov put the food on its tongue. In fact, the dog began salivating when Pavlov entered the room or even at the sound of his approaching footsteps. But salivating is a *reflexive response*—a largely involuntary, automatic response to an external stimulus. (A *stimulus* is anything perceptible to the senses, such as a sight, sound, smell, touch, or taste.) The dog should salivate only *after* the food is presented, not before. Why would the response occur before the stimulus was presented? What was causing this unexpected behavior?

If you own a dog, you've probably observed the same basic phenomenon. Your dog gets excited and begins to slobber when you shake a box of dog biscuits, even before you've given them a doggie treat. In everyday language, your pet has learned to anticipate food in association with some signal—namely, the sound of dog biscuits rattling in a box.

Pavlov's extraordinary gifts as a researcher enabled him to recognize the important implications of what had at first seemed a problem—a reflexive response (salivation) that occurred *before* the appropriate stimulus (food) was presented. He also had the discipline to systematically study how such associations are formed. Pavlov abandoned his research on digestion and devoted the remaining 30 years of his life to investigating different aspects of this phenomenon. Let's look at what he discovered in more detail.

Principles of Classical Conditioning

The process of conditioning that Pavlov discovered was the first to be extensively studied in psychology. Thus, it's called *classical conditioning* (Hilgard & Marquis, 1940). It's also known as *Pavlovian conditioning*. **Classical conditioning** is formally defined as *the basic learning process that involves repeatedly pairing a neutral stimulus with a response-producing stimulus until the neutral stimulus elicits the same response.* Classical conditioning deals with behaviors that are elicited automatically by some stimulus. *Elicit* means "draw out" or "bring forth." That is, the stimulus doesn't produce a new behavior but rather *causes an existing behavior to occur*.

Classical conditioning almost always involves some kind of reflexive behavior. Remember, a reflexive response is a relatively simple, unlearned behavior, governed by the nervous system, that occurs *automatically* when the appropriate stimulus is presented. Examples of reflexes include sneezing, yawning, shivering when you're cold, or salivating when you smell a tasty treat. In Pavlov's (1904) original studies of digestion, the dogs salivated reflexively when food was placed on their tongues. But when the dogs began salivating in response to the sight of Pavlov or to the sound of his footsteps, a new, *learned* stimulus elicited the salivary response. Thus, in classical conditioning, a *new* stimulus–response sequence is learned.

How does this kind of learning take place? Essentially, classical conditioning is a process of learning an *association between two stimuli*. Classical conditioning involves pairing a *neutral* stimulus (e.g., the sight of Pavlov) with an *unlearned, natural* stimulus (food in the mouth) that automatically elicits a reflexive response (the dog salivates). If the two stimuli (Pavlov + food) are repeatedly paired, eventually the neutral stimulus (Pavlov) elicits the same basic reflexive response as the natural stimulus (food)—even in the absence of the natural stimulus. So, when the dog in the laboratory started salivating at the sight of Pavlov *before* the food was placed on its tongue, it was because the dog had formed a new, *learned association* between the sight of Pavlov and the food.

Pavlov used special terms to describe each element of the classical conditioning process. *The natural stimulus that reflexively elicits a response without the need for prior learning* is called the **unconditioned stimulus** (or **UCS**). In this example, the unconditioned stimulus is the food in the dog's mouth. *The unlearned, reflexive response that is elicited by an unconditioned stimulus* is called the **unconditioned response** (or **UCR**). The unconditioned response is the dog's salivation.

To learn more about his discovery, Pavlov (1927) controlled the stimuli that preceded the presentation of food. For example, in one set of experiments, he used a ticking metronome as a neutral stimulus. Pavlov also used other stimuli such as a

classical conditioning The basic learning process that involves repeatedly pairing a neutral stimulus with a response-producing stimulus until the neutral stimulus elicits the same response.

unconditioned stimulus (UCS) The natural stimulus that reflexively elicits a response without the need for prior learning.

unconditioned response (UCR) The unlearned, reflexive response that is elicited by an unconditioned stimulus.

Sovfoto/Getty Images

⌃ **Ivan Pavlov** During Pavlov's four decades of research, more than 140 scientists and students worked in his laboratories under his direction. Twenty of his co-researchers were women, and included his daughter, V. I. Pavlova.

conditioned stimulus (CS) A formerly neutral stimulus that acquires the capacity to elicit a reflexive response.

conditioned response (CR) The learned, reflexive response to a previously neutral stimulus.

MYTH ◀ SCIENCE

Is it true that Pavlov taught dogs to drool at the sound of a ticking metronome by rewarding them with food?

buzzer and a light, but contrary to popular belief, he never actually used a bell (Todes, 2014). The metronome functioned as a neutral stimulus because dogs don't normally salivate to the sound of a metronome. Pavlov first started the metronome and then gave the dog food. After this procedure was repeated several times, the dog began to salivate when the metronome started ticking, before the food was put in its mouth. At that point, the dog was *classically conditioned* to salivate to the sound of a metronome alone. That is, the dog had *learned a new association* between the sound of the metronome and the presentation of food. So, the idea that Pavlov was rewarding the dogs with food is a myth.

Pavlov called the metronome's sound the *conditioned stimulus*. The **conditioned stimulus** (or **CS**) is *a formerly neutral stimulus that acquires the capacity to elicit a reflexive response.* He called the dog's salivation to the metronome's sound the **conditioned response** (or **CR**), which is *the learned, reflexive response to a previously neutral stimulus.* The steps of Pavlov's conditioning process are outlined in **Figure 5.1**.

Classical conditioning terminology can be confusing. You may find it helpful to think of the word *conditioned* as having the same meaning as "learned." Thus, the "conditioned stimulus" refers to the "learned stimulus," the "unconditioned response" refers to the "unlearned response," and so forth.

FIGURE 5.1 The Process of Classical Conditioning The diagram shows Pavlov's classical conditioning procedure. As you can see, classical conditioning involves the learning of an association between a neutral stimulus (the ticking metronome) and a natural stimulus (food).

Before Conditioning:

Prior to conditioning, the dog notices the ticking of the metronome but does not salivate. Here, the metronome is a neutral stimulus. Food placed in the dog's mouth (the **UCS**) naturally produces the salivation response (the **UCR**).

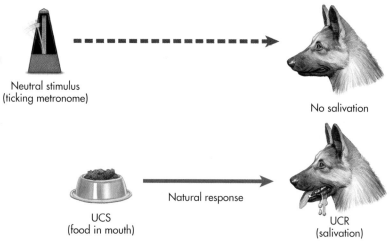

Neutral stimulus (ticking metronome)

No salivation

Natural response

UCS (food in mouth)

UCR (salivation)

During Conditioning:

In the conditioning phase, the neutral stimulus (the ticking metronome) is repeatedly sounded immediately before food is placed in the dog's mouth (the **UCS**), which produces the natural response of salivation (the **UCR**).

Neutral stimulus (ticking metronome)   +   UCS (food in mouth)

Natural response

UCR (salivation)

After Conditioning:

The ticking metronome is no longer neutral. It is now called a conditioned stimulus or **CS** because, when the metronome ticks, the dog reacts with a conditioned response or **CR**: The dog salivates even though no food is present. The salivation response is the **CR**.

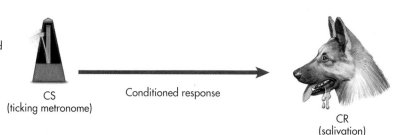

CS (ticking metronome)

Conditioned response

CR (salivation)

It's also important to note that, in this case, the unconditioned response and the conditioned response describe essentially the same behavior—the dog's salivating. The label that is applied depends on which stimulus elicits the response. If the dog is salivating in response to a *natural* stimulus that was not acquired through learning, the salivation is an *unconditioned* response. If, however, the dog has learned to salivate to a *neutral* stimulus that doesn't normally produce the automatic response, the salivation is a *conditioned* response.

Beyond Pavlov

Pavlov's revolutionary work on classical conditioning was soon taken up by other researchers. Among them was **Charles Henry Turner** (1867–1923), an African American zoologist and a leader in the civil rights movement. Like Pavlov, Turner was not a psychologist, but he conducted research that used classical conditioning and he published his work in psychology journals (Abramson, 2003a, 2003b). In fact, based on the publication of an 1892 paper, "Psychological Notes Upon the Gallery Spider," he has been referred to as the first African American psychologist. Despite his accomplishments, Turner has long been underrecognized. He spent much of his career teaching high school, having been thwarted in his attempts to find a position at a university. Yet, he published more than most university professors at the time—without a laboratory or research assistants.

In one groundbreaking study, Turner (1914) wanted to determine whether moths of a certain species could hear. He first found that only 3 of 78 moths responded to sound, leading him to wonder whether they were deaf or simply had a "sluggish temperament" (p. 331). He used Pavlovian techniques to find out. Initially, the moths did not respond when Turner played a sound on an organ pipe. Then, he played the sound and immediately spent several minutes handling each moth (UCS). (We can assume that Turner would not have wanted to harm the moths, given that he wanted to monitor their future behavior, and he also uses the word *gently* in his description of his intervention.) The moths, understandably, were agitated by being handled (UCR). This pairing of the sound and the handling was repeated multiple times over a couple of days. After conditioning, each time the sound was played (CS), most of the moths would respond by furiously flapping their wings (CR). Turner now had evidence that the moths could indeed hear.

Factors That Affect Conditioning

Pavlov (1928) discovered many factors that could affect the strength of the conditioned response (Bitterman, 2006). For example, he discovered that the more frequently the conditioned stimulus and the unconditioned stimulus were paired, the stronger the association between the two.

Pavlov also discovered that the *timing* of stimulus presentations affected the strength of the conditioned response. He found that conditioning was most effective when the conditioned stimulus was presented immediately *before* the unconditioned stimulus. Pavlov and other researchers found that the optimal time interval could vary in different conditioning situations but was rarely more than a few seconds.

Stimulus Generalization and Discrimination Pavlov (1927) noticed that once a dog was conditioned to salivate in response to a particular stimulus, new stimuli that were similar to the original conditioned stimulus could also elicit the conditioned salivary response. For example, Pavlov conditioned a dog to salivate to a low-pitched tone. When he sounded a slightly higher-pitched tone, the conditioned salivary response would also be elicited. Pavlov called this phenomenon *stimulus generalization*. **Stimulus generalization** is *the occurrence of a learned response not only to the original stimulus but to other, similar stimuli as well*. If you own a dog that tends to salivate and get excited when you shake a box of dog biscuits, you may have noticed that your dog also drools when you shake a bag of cat food. If so, that would be an example of stimulus generalization.

Just as a dog can learn to respond to similar stimuli, so too can it learn the opposite— to *distinguish* between similar stimuli. For example, Pavlov repeatedly gave a dog some

⌃ **Charles Henry Turner (1867–1923)** Although trained as a zoologist, Charles Henry Turner conducted most of his research on topics related to psychology and learning, working with a number of species. His work was referred to by famed behaviorist John Watson as "ingenious." In addition to demonstrating that moths could hear, he used learning techniques to demonstrate that bees could see color, training bees to fly into different colored boxes. (He even used his bees to teach behavioral principles to high school students!) Turner invented and published his method for teaching bees to fly to targets 10 years before used by another researcher, the German-Austrian Karl von Frisch. Today, the technique is still called the "von Frisch technique," another instance of Turner's groundbreaking work not receiving the credit it is due.

stimulus generalization The occurrence of a learned response not only to the original stimulus but to other, similar stimuli as well.

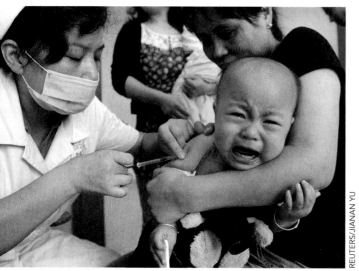

REUTERS/JIANAN YU

▲ **Classical Conditioning in Early Life: White Coats and Doctor Visits** Most infants receive several vaccinations in their first few years of life. The painful injection (a UCS) elicits fear and distress (a UCR). After a few office visits, the clinic, nurse, or even the medical staff's white lab coats can become a conditioned stimulus (CS) that elicits fear and distress—even in the absence of a painful injection.

FIGURE 5.2 Extinction and Spontaneous Recovery in Pavlov's Laboratory This demonstration involved a dog that had already been conditioned to salivate (the CR) to just the sight of meat powder (the CS). During the extinction phase, meat powder (the CS) was repeatedly presented at three-minute intervals and held just out of the dog's reach. As you can see in the graph, over the course of six trials, the amount of saliva secreted by the dog quickly decreased to zero. This indicates that *extinction* had occurred. After a two-hour rest period, meat powder (the CS) was presented again and, the dog secreted saliva once more, evidence for the *spontaneous recovery* of the conditioned response.

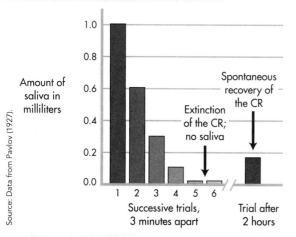

Source: Data from Pavlov (1927).

food following a high-pitched tone but did not give the dog any food following a low-pitched tone. The dog learned to distinguish between the two tones, salivating to the high pitched tone but not to the low-pitched tone. This phenomenon, **stimulus discrimination**, is *the occurrence of a learned response to a specific stimulus but not to other, similar stimuli.* So, if your dog eventually stops drooling when you shake a bag of cat food, stimulus discrimination has taken place.

Higher Order Conditioning   Pavlov (1927) also found that a conditioned stimulus could itself function as an unconditioned stimulus. **Higher order conditioning**, or *second order conditioning,* is a *procedure in which a conditioned stimulus from one learning trial functions as the unconditioned stimulus in a new conditioning trial.* Pavlov repeatedly paired a new neutral stimulus (a black square) with an existing conditioned stimulus (a ticking metronome). Eventually, the black square *alone* began producing the conditioned response (salivation), even though it had never been paired with food. It acquired its ability to produce the conditioned response only by being paired with the original conditioned stimulus.

Consider this example: Like most babies, your author Sandy's daughter Laura hated shots. Each painful injection (UCS) made her cry (UCR). Soon Laura developed a conditioned response—just the sight of a doctor's white jacket (CS) triggered crying (CR). To illustrate higher order conditioning, imagine if Laura reacted with fear when she saw a white-jacketed restaurant server bringing coffee. If Laura responded with fear the next time she smelled coffee, higher order conditioning would have taken place. The coffee aroma had never been paired with the original UCS, the painful injection, but it became a CS by being paired with the first CS, the white jacket, and produced the CR.

Extinction and Spontaneous Recovery   Once learned, can conditioned responses be eliminated? Pavlov (1927) found that conditioned responses could be gradually weakened. If the conditioned stimulus (the ticking metronome) was repeatedly presented *without* being paired with the unconditioned stimulus (the food), the conditioned response seemed to gradually disappear. Pavlov called this process **extinction**, which is formally defined as *the gradual weakening and apparent disappearance of conditioned behavior.*

Pavlov also found that the dog did not simply return to its unconditioned state following extinction (see **Figure 5.2**). If the animal was allowed a period of rest (such as a few hours) after the response was extinguished, the conditioned response would reappear when the conditioned stimulus was again presented. This process, called **spontaneous recovery**, is *the reappearance of a previously extinguished conditioned response after a period of time without exposure to the conditioned stimulus.* The phenomenon of spontaneous recovery demonstrates that extinction is not unlearning. That is, the learned response may seem to disappear, but it is *not* eliminated or erased (Archbold et al. 2010; Rescorla, 2001).

From Pavlov to Watson: The Founding of Behaviorism

■ KEY THEME
Behaviorism was founded by John Watson, who redefined psychology as the scientific study of behavior.

≡ KEY QUESTIONS
- What were the fundamental assumptions of behaviorism?
- How did Watson use classical conditioning to explain and produce conditioned emotional responses?
- How did Watson apply classical conditioning techniques to advertising?

Over the course of three decades, Pavlov systematically investigated different aspects of classical conditioning. Pavlov believed he had discovered the mechanism by which all learning occurs, but he did not apply his findings to human behavior. That task was to be taken up by psychologist **John Watson**.

Watson believed that the early psychologists were following the wrong path by focusing on the study of subjective mental processes, which could not be objectively observed (Berman & Lyons, 2007). Instead, Watson (1913) strongly advocated that psychology should be redefined as *the scientific study of behavior,* which, unlike mental processes, *could* be objectively observed. As described in Chapter 1, Watson founded a new school, or approach, in psychology, called *behaviorism.* Specifically, **behaviorism** is *the school of psychology and theoretical viewpoint that emphasizes the study of observable behaviors, especially as they pertain to the process of learning.* Pavlov's discovery of the conditioned response provided the model Watson had been seeking to investigate and explain human behavior (Evans & Rilling, 2000; Watson, 1916).

Watson believed that virtually *all* human behavior is a result of conditioning and learning. Boldly, Watson (1924) proclaimed:

> I should like to go one step further now and say, "Give me a dozen healthy infants, well-formed, and my own specified world to bring them up in and I'll guarantee to take any one at random and train him to become any type of specialist I might select—doctor, lawyer, artist, merchant-chief and yes, even beggar-man and thief, regardless of his talents, penchants, tendencies, abilities, vocations, and race of his ancestors."

Needless to say, Watson never actually carried out such an experiment, and his boast clearly exaggerated the role of the environment to make his point. Yet, Watson, along with his second wife, **Rosalie Rayner**, tried to raise his own children according to these principles. Rayner was a rising psychologist in her own right, but a scandalous affair with Watson led to the end of his career as a professor and the end of her graduate career before she received her degree (Smirle, 2013). Watson and Rayner married and continued conducting research, much of it as collaborators. They raised their two sons according to strict behaviorist principles. Rayner sometimes questioned their child-rearing protocol, explaining that "[i]n some respects I bow to the great wisdom in the science of behaviorism, and in others I am rebellious . . . I cannot restrain my affection for the children completely." Sadly, both sons eventually attempted suicide, one of them dying that way. Rayner herself never received the attention she deserved, likely because most of her published articles were coauthored with Watson.

Nevertheless, Watson's influence on psychology cannot be overemphasized. Behaviorism was to dominate psychology in the United States for more than 50 years. And, as you'll see in the next section, Watson did carry out a famous and controversial experiment to demonstrate how human behavior could be classically conditioned.

Conditioned Emotional Reactions

Watson believed that, much as Pavlov's dogs reflexively salivated to food, human emotions could be thought of as reflexive responses involving the muscles and glands. In studies with infants, Watson (1919) identified three emotions that he believed represented inborn and natural unconditioned reflexive responses—fear, rage, and love. According to Watson, each of these innate emotions could be reflexively triggered by a small number of specific stimuli. For example, he found two stimuli that could trigger the reflexive fear response in infants: a sudden loud noise and a sudden dropping motion.

The Famous Case of Little Albert Watson's interest in the role of classical conditioning in emotions set the stage for one of the most famous and controversial experiments in the history of psychology. In 1920, Watson and Rayner set out to demonstrate that classical conditioning could be used to deliberately establish a conditioned emotional response in a human subject. Their subject was a baby known as "Little Albert."

Watson and Rayner (1920) first assessed Little Albert when he was only nine months old. Little Albert was a healthy, unusually calm baby who showed no fear when presented with a tame white rat, a monkey, masks, and even burning newspapers! But, as with other infants whom Watson had studied, fear could be triggered in Little Albert by a sudden loud sound—clanging a steel bar behind his head (see **Figure 5.3**). In this case, the sudden clanging noise is the unconditioned stimulus, and the unconditioned response is fear.

stimulus discrimination The occurrence of a learned response to a specific stimulus but not to other, similar stimuli.

higher order conditioning Procedure in which a conditioned stimulus from one learning trial functions as the unconditioned stimulus in a new conditioning trial; also called *second order conditioning.*

extinction (in classical conditioning) The gradual weakening and apparent disappearance of conditioned behavior.

spontaneous recovery The reappearance of a previously extinguished conditioned response after a period of time without exposure to the conditioned stimulus.

behaviorism School of psychology and theoretical viewpoint that emphasizes the study of observable behaviors, especially as they pertain to the process of learning.

Before Conditioning:

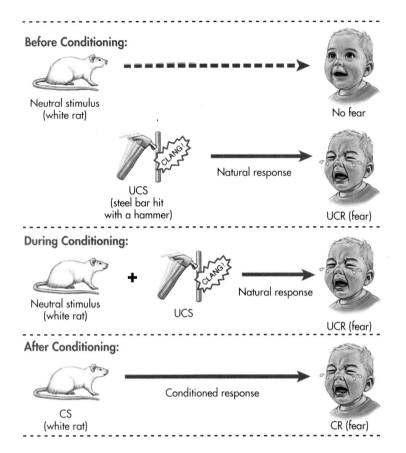

Neutral stimulus
(white rat)

No fear

UCS
(steel bar hit
with a hammer)

Natural response

UCR (fear)

During Conditioning:

Neutral stimulus
(white rat)

+

UCS

Natural response

UCR (fear)

After Conditioning:

CS
(white rat)

Conditioned response

CR (fear)

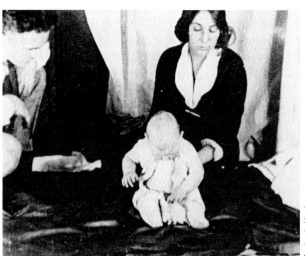

FIGURE 5.3 A Classically Conditioned Fear Response In the photograph below, Rosalie Rayner (1898–1935) holds Little Albert as John Watson (1878–1958) looks on. Little Albert is petting the tame white rat, clearly not afraid of it. But, after being repeatedly paired with the UCS (a sudden, loud noise), the white rat becomes a CS. After conditioning, Little Albert is terrified of the tame rat.

Benjmain Harris

Two months after their initial assessment, Watson and Rayner attempted to condition Little Albert to fear the tame white rat (the conditioned stimulus). Watson stood behind Little Albert and clanged the steel bar with a hammer whenever Little Albert reached toward the rat. Just as before, of course, the unexpected loud CLANG! (the unconditioned stimulus) startled and terrified Little Albert (the unconditioned response). After only seven pairings of the loud noise and the white rat, the white rat alone triggered the conditioned response—extreme fear—in Little Albert. Figure 5.3 shows the conditioning process.

Watson and Rayner also found that stimulus generalization had taken place. Along with fearing the rat, Little Albert was now afraid of other furry animals, including a dog and a rabbit. He had even developed a classically conditioned fear response to a variety of fuzzy objects, both white in color and nonwhite—a sealskin coat, cotton, Watson's hair, and a white-bearded Santa Claus mask!

Although the Little Albert study has attained legendary status in psychology, it had several problems (Griggs, 2014; Harris 1979, 2011; Paul & Blumenthal, 1989). One criticism is that the experiment was not carefully designed or conducted. For example, Albert's fear and distress were not objectively measured by an outside observer or a carefully defined behavioral measure. Instead, they were subjectively evaluated by Watson and Rayner, whose judgments may have been influenced by their own expectations.

Moreover, those telling the story of Little Albert over the years have left out details that make his story less straightforward. For example, Watson himself wore the Santa Claus mask and crawled toward Little Albert, a behavior that may have been scarier than the white beard (Harris, 2011). And Albert continued to enjoy touching the hair of the women working in the lab, inconsistent with a clear narrative of generalization.

The experiment is also open to criticism on ethical grounds. Watson and Rayner (1920) did not extinguish Little Albert's fear of furry animals and objects, even though they believed that such conditioned emotional responses would "persist and modify personality throughout life." Such an experiment could not ethically be conducted today.

Whether Watson and Rayner had originally intended to extinguish the fear is not completely clear (see Paul & Blumenthal, 1989). Watson (1930) later wrote that he and Rayner could not try to eliminate Albert's fear response because the infant had been adopted by a family in another city shortly after the experiment had concluded. As you'll see in the chapter on therapies, a psychologist named **Mary Cover Jones** (1924a, 1924b) *did* use classical conditioning to extinguish the fears of a very young child.

Generations of psychologists have wondered what happened to Little Albert. After years of detective work, two candidates have been suggested: Douglas Merritt, who died at age 6 of a neurological disease (Beck et al., 2009, 2010), and Albert Barger, who lived to the ripe old age of 86 (Powell et al., 2014). Both were the sons of women working at the hospital where the experiment was conducted.

You can probably think of situations, objects, or people that evoke a strong classically conditioned emotional reaction in you, such as fear, anger, happiness, or sadness. In this chapter's Prologue, we saw that Erv became classically conditioned to feel anxious whenever he entered the attic. The attic (the original neutral stimulus) was coupled with being trapped in extreme heat (the UCS), which produced fear (the UCR). Following the episode, Erv found that going into the attic (now a CS) triggered mild fear and anxiety (the CR). Like Erv, many people experience a conditioned fear response to objects, situations, or locations that are associated with some kind of traumatic experience or event.

▲ **Classically Conditioned Emotional Reactions** After being involved in a serious auto accident, many people develop a conditioned emotional response to the scene of the accident. Just driving past the intersection where the accident occurred can make them feel fearful or anxious. In this example, can you identify the UCS, UCR, CS, and CR?

Other Classically Conditioned Responses

Under the right conditions, virtually any automatic response can become classically conditioned. For example, some aspects of sexual responses can become classically

---

IN FOCUS

Watson, Classical Conditioning, and Advertising

From shampoos to soft drinks, advertising campaigns often use sexy models to promote their products. Today, we take this advertising tactic for granted. But it's actually yet another example of Watson's influence. After being banned from academia, Watson married Rayner and joined an advertising agency (Buckley, 1989; Carpintero, 2004).

Watson was a pioneer in the application of classical conditioning principles to advertising. "To make your consumer react," Watson told his colleagues at the ad agency, "tell him something that will tie him up with fear, something that will stir up a mild rage, that will call out an affectionate or love response, or strike at a deep psychological or habit need" (quoted in Buckley, 1982).

For example, a Pebeco toothpaste campaign targeted the newly independent young woman who smoked. The ad raised the fear that attractiveness might be diminished by the effects of smoking—and Pebeco toothpaste was promoted as a way of increasing sexual attractiveness. One ad read, "Girls! Don't worry any more about smoke-stained teeth or tobacco-tainted breath. You can smoke and still be lovely if you'll just use Pebeco twice a day." And in an ad for Johnson & Johnson Baby Powder, Watson tried to stimulate an anxiety response in mothers by creating doubts about their ability to care for their infants.

Following in Watson's footsteps, ad campaigns today pair products with images of adorable babies, cuddly kittens, happy families, or other "natural" stimuli that elicit warm, emotional responses. If classical conditioning occurs, the product by itself will also elicit a warm, emotional response.

Are such procedures effective? In a word, yes. Attitudes toward a product or a particular brand can be influenced by advertising and marketing campaigns that use classical conditioning methods (Hofmann et al., 2010).

▲ **Classical Conditioning in Contemporary Advertising** Taking a cue from John Watson, classical conditioning is widely used in today's commercials and print ads, pairing emotion-evoking images with otherwise neutral stimuli, like soft drinks or new cars. See if you can identify the UCS, UCR, CS, and CR in this striking billboard.

placebo response An individual's psychological and physiological response to what is actually a fake treatment or drug; also called *placebo effect.*

conditioned, sometimes inadvertently. To illustrate, suppose that a neutral stimulus, such as the scent of a particular cologne, is regularly paired with the person with whom you are romantically involved. You, of course, are most aware of the scent when you are physically close to your partner in sexually arousing situations. After repeated pairings, the initially neutral stimulus—the particular cologne scent—can become a conditioned stimulus. Now, the scent of the cologne evokes feelings of romantic excitement or mild sexual arousal even in the absence of your lover or, in some cases, long after the relationship has ended. And, in fact, a wide variety of stimuli can become "sexual turn-ons" through classical conditioning.

Classical conditioning also seems to be involved in some instances of placebo response (Babel, 2019; Benedetti et al., 2010, 2016). Also called *placebo effect,* a **placebo response** is *an individual's psychological and physiological response to what is actually a fake treatment or drug.* We'll discuss this phenomenon in more detail in the chapter on stress, health, and coping.

Contemporary Views of Classical Conditioning

■ KEY THEME
Contemporary learning researchers acknowledge the importance of both cognitive factors and evolutionary influences in classical conditioning.

⹀ KEY QUESTIONS
- How has the involvement of cognitive processes in classical conditioning been demonstrated experimentally?
- What is meant by the phrase "the animal behaves like a scientist" in classical conditioning?
- How do taste aversions challenge the basic conditioning principles, and what is biological preparedness?

The traditional behavioral perspective holds that classical conditioning results from a simple association of the conditioned stimulus and the unconditioned stimulus. Mental or cognitive processes such as thinking, anticipating, or deciding were not needed to explain the conditioning process. However, according to the *cognitive perspective* (see Chapter 1), mental processes as well as external events are important components in the learning of new behaviors. In the next section, we'll look at research on cognitive processes in classical conditioning.

Cognitive Aspects of Classical Conditioning: Reliable Signals

Learning theorist **Robert A. Rescorla** demonstrated that classical conditioning involves more than learning the simple association of two stimuli. In one classic study, one group of rats heard a tone (the conditioned stimulus) that was paired 20 times with a brief electric shock (the unconditioned stimulus). A second group of rats not only experienced 20 tone–shock pairings but also experienced an *additional* 20 shocks with *no* tone that were randomly interspersed with the tone–shock pairings (Rescorla, 1968). Then Rescorla tested for the conditioned fear response by presenting the tone alone to each group of rats. Because each group had received 20 tone–shock pairings, both groups should have displayed the same levels of conditioned fear. However, the rats in the first group displayed a much stronger fear response to the tone than did the rats in the second group. Why?

According to Rescorla (1988), classical conditioning depends on the *information* the conditioned stimulus provides about the unconditioned stimulus. For learning to occur, the conditioned stimulus must be a *reliable signal* that predicts the presentations of the unconditioned stimulus—as it was for the first group of rats. But for the second group, the tone was an unreliable signal. Sometimes the tone preceded the shock, and sometimes the shock occurred without warning.

Rescorla concluded that the rats in both groups were *actively processing information* about the reliability of the signals they encountered. Rather than merely associating two closely paired stimuli, as Pavlov suggested, the animals assess the *predictive value* of stimuli.

Applying this interpretation to classical conditioning, we can conclude that Pavlov's dogs learned that the metronome was a signal that *reliably predicted* that food would follow.

According to this view, animals use cognitive processes to draw inferences about the signals they encounter in their environments. Rescorla's research suggests that "the animal behaves like a scientist, detecting causal relations among events and using a range of information about those events to make the relevant inferences" (Rescorla, 1980). Put simply, classical conditioning seems to involve *learning the relationships between events* (Rescorla, 1988, 2003). We now know that verbal information can lead to the same type of learning about relationships between events as classical conditioning (see the Focus on Neuroscience box on the next page, "Fear Conditioning").

Evolutionary Aspects of Classical Conditioning: Biological Predispositions to Learn

According to Darwin's *theory of evolution by natural selection,* both the physical characteristics and the natural behavior patterns of any species have been shaped by evolution to maximize adaptation to the environment. Thus, just as physical characteristics vary from one species to another, so do natural behavior patterns.

The presence of natural behavior patterns creates an important "exception" to the well-established principles of classical conditioning, which traditional behaviorists believed applied to virtually all learning situations (Lockard, 1971; Seligman, 1970). As you'll see in this section about a phenomenon known as a *taste aversion,* these natural behavior patterns can affect how an animal learns new behaviors.

Taste Aversions and Classical Conditioning: Spaghetti? No, Thank You!

A few years ago, our friend Tom ate a large plateful of spaghetti at a highly rated restaurant. But in the middle of the night, Tom came down with a nasty stomach virus. As a result, Tom developed a *taste aversion*—he avoided eating spaghetti and felt queasy whenever he smelled tomato sauce. **Taste aversion** is formally defined as *a classically conditioned dislike for and avoidance of a particular food that develops when an organism becomes ill after eating the food.*

Such learned taste aversions are relatively common. Our students have told us about episodes of motion sickness, morning sickness, or illness that resulted in taste aversions to foods as varied as cotton candy, strawberries, and tacos. In some cases, a taste aversion can persist for years.

At first glance, it seems as if taste aversions can be explained by classical conditioning. In Tom's case, a neutral stimulus (spaghetti) was paired with an unconditioned stimulus (a stomach virus), which produced an unconditioned response (nausea). Now a conditioned stimulus, the spaghetti sauce alone elicits the conditioned response of nausea.

But notice that this explanation seems to violate two basic principles of classical conditioning. First, the conditioning did not require repeated pairings. Conditioning occurred in a *single pairing* of the conditioned stimulus and the unconditioned stimulus. Second, the time span between these two stimuli was *several hours,* not a matter of seconds. Is this possible? The anecdotal reports of people who develop specific taste aversions seem to suggest it is. But such reports lack the objectivity and systematic control that a scientific explanation of behavior requires.

Enter psychologist **John Garcia**, who demonstrated that taste aversions could be produced in laboratory rats under controlled conditions (Garcia et al., 1966). Garcia's procedure was straightforward. Rats first drank saccharin-flavored water (the neutral stimulus). Hours later, the rats were injected with a drug (the unconditioned stimulus) that produced gastrointestinal distress (the unconditioned response). After the rats recovered from their illness, they refused to drink the flavored water again. The rats had developed a taste aversion to the saccharin-flavored water, which had become a conditioned stimulus.

At first, many psychologists were skeptical of Garcia's findings because they seemed to violate the basic principles of classical conditioning (Davis & Riley, 2010). Several leading psychological journals refused to publish Garcia's research, saying the results were unconvincing or downright impossible (Garcia, 1981, 2003). But Garcia's results have been replicated many times. In fact, based on later research, we now know that it is true that taste

Tony Camacho/Science Source

⌃ **Classical Conditioning and Survival** Animals quickly learn the signals that predict the approach of a predator. In classical conditioning terms, they learn to associate the approach of a predator (the unconditioned stimulus) with particular sounds, smells, or sights (the originally neutral stimuli that become conditioned stimuli). To survive, animals that are vulnerable to predators, such as this alert meerkat, use environmental signals to predict events in their environment. A rustle in the underbrush, the shadow of an eagle's wings, or a glimpse of a hyena tells the animal that it's time to flee.

taste aversion A classically conditioned dislike for and avoidance of a particular food that develops when an organism becomes ill after eating the food.

⚒ FOCUS ON NEUROSCIENCE

Fear Conditioning

If you could ask your amygdala about its one true purpose, it might answer that it was committed to keeping you alive. The amygdala does this by helping you learn instant conditioned responses to potentially dangerous stimuli (LeDoux, 2014; Fullana, et al., 2015). Many of you have had a *single* experience with something that was painful enough to create an enduring conditioned response. For example, a bite from a dog would make many people cautious around dogs in the future, if not outright afraid. Basically, the amygdala reminds you that you got lucky surviving that previous unpleasant experience (a dog bite), so don't try it again. This fear conditioning is a type of classical conditioning, and your amygdala makes it nearly impossible to forget any truly negative experiences (Fullana et al., 2015).

One important aspect of human life, however, is that we rarely gain direct experience with things that are potentially dangerous. Still, an emotionally intense movie can often leave us with an unpleasant feeling about something we have never directly encountered—for example, ghost stories or that creepy house down the street. As you have read about, there are cognitive aspects of classical condition; so, it should not surprise you that, given the great ability humans have for communication, we can form close associations between stimuli with which we do not have direct experience. Let's consider what this looks like in the brain.

Neuroscientist Elizabeth Phelps has demonstrated that, in the absence of actual experience, humans use verbal information to create a conditioned response for things with which they have no prior association. In her now classic study, participants attached an electrode to their wrist that they were told could deliver an unpleasant (but not painful) shock while they underwent fMRI scans (Phelps et al., 2001). (In actuality, participants never received a shock.) Participants were told they would view a series of blue squares, yellow squares, and the word *rest*. They were then told that one color (which varied as part of the study design) would serve as a threatening stimulus and signal an unpleasant event (a potential mild shock to their hand), while the other color would serve as a safe stimulus and signal no potential threat.

In the study, no participant had a preexisting negative association between the blue or yellow squares and negative outcomes. Further, the colored shapes didn't possess any symbolic qualities normally associated with threat (no crosses or red octagons). Most importantly, as we explained previously, despite the threat of a shock, no one was actually shocked, even when the "threat" color was presented. The research results showed that participants who viewed the threat color tended to have increased activity in the amygdala as compared with those who viewed the safe color. This increased brain activity was correlated with increases in how much participants sweat, a physiological reaction associated with the human experience of fear (LeDoux, 2014). The study demonstrated that verbal information can reliably produce activity in the amygdala that is nearly indistinguishable from that produced by classical fear conditioning.

MYTH ▶ SCIENCE

Is it true that you can develop a long-lasting aversion to a food or beverage if you get sick after eating or drinking it?

> **John Garcia (1917–2012)** John Garcia, the son of immigrants from Spain, grew up working on farms in northern California. In his late 20s, Garcia enrolled at a community college. At the age of 48, Garcia earned his Ph.D. in psychology from the University of California, Berkeley (Garcia, 1997). Garcia was one of the first researchers to experimentally demonstrate the existence of taste aversions and other "exceptions" to the general laws of classical conditioning. His research emphasized the importance of the evolutionary forces that shape the learning process.

aversions could develop even when a full 24 hours separated the presentation of the flavored water and the drug that produced illness (Davis & Riley, 2010).

Conditioned taste aversions also challenged the notion that any stimulus can become a conditioned stimulus. As Pavlov (1928) wrote, "Any natural phenomenon chosen at will may be converted into a conditioned stimulus . . . any visual stimulus, any desired sound, any odor, and the stimulation of any part of the skin." But if this were the case, why was it that only the spaghetti sauce became a conditioned stimulus that triggered Tom's nausea, not the restaurant, the tablecloth, or his dining companions?

Contrary to what Pavlov suggested, Garcia and his colleagues demonstrated that the particular conditioned stimulus that is used *does* make a difference in classical conditioning (Garcia & Koelling, 1966). In another series of experiments, Garcia found that rats did *not* learn to associate a taste with a painful event, such as a shock. Nor did they learn to associate a flashing light and noise with illness. Instead, rats were much more likely to associate a *painful stimulus,* such as a shock, with *external stimuli,* such as flashing lights and noise. And rats were much more likely to associate a *taste stimulus* with *internal stimuli* — the physical discomfort of illness. Garcia and Koelling (1966) humorously suggested that a sick rat, like a sick person, speculates, "It must have been something I ate."

Why is it that certain stimuli are more easy to associate than others? One factor that helps explain Garcia's results is **biological preparedness**—*the idea that an organism is innately predisposed to form associations between certain stimuli and responses* (Freeman & Riley, 2009). Apparently, both humans and rats are biologically prepared to learn taste aversions relatively easily. But if the particular stimulus and response combination is *not* one that an animal is biologically prepared to associate, then the association may not occur or may occur only with great difficulty (see the In Focus box on the next page, "Evolution, Biological Preparedness, and Conditioned Fears: What Gives You the Creeps?").

Associations that are easily learned may reflect the evolutionary history and survival mechanisms of the particular animal species (Freeman & Riley, 2009). For example, rats in the wild eat a wide variety of foods. If a rat eats a new food and gets sick several hours later, it's likely to survive longer if it learns from this experience to avoid that food in the future (Kalat, 1985; Seligman, 1970).

That different species form some associations more easily than others also probably reflects the unique sensory capabilities and feeding habits that have evolved as a matter of environmental adaptation. Bobwhite quail, for instance, rely primarily on vision for identifying potential meals. In contrast, rats have relatively poor eyesight and rely primarily on taste and odor cues to identify food. Given these species differences, it shouldn't surprise you that quail, but not rats, can easily be conditioned to develop an aversion to blue-colored water—a *visual* stimulus. On the other hand, rats learn more readily than quail to associate illness with sour water—a *taste* stimulus (Wilcoxon et al., 1971). In effect, quail are biologically prepared to associate visual cues with illness, while rats are biologically prepared to associate taste cues with illness.

Taste aversion research emphasizes that the study of learning must consider the unique behavior patterns and capabilities of different species. As the result of evolution, animals have developed unique forms of behavior to adapt to their natural environments (Bolles, 1985). These natural behavior patterns and unique characteristics ultimately influence what an animal is capable of learning—and how easily it can be conditioned to learn a new behavior.

Operant Conditioning: Associating Behaviors and Consequences

■ KEY THEME
Operant conditioning deals with the learning of active, voluntary behaviors that are shaped and maintained by their consequences.

⚌ KEY QUESTIONS
- How did Edward Thorndike study the acquisition of new behaviors, and what conclusions did he reach?
- What were B. F. Skinner's key assumptions?
- How are positive reinforcement and negative reinforcement similar, and how are they different?

Classical conditioning can help explain the acquisition of many learned behaviors, including emotional and physiological responses. However, recall that classical conditioning involves reflexive behaviors that are automatically elicited by a specific stimulus. Most everyday behaviors don't fall into this category. Instead, they involve nonreflexive, or *voluntary,* actions that can't be explained with classical conditioning.

In the next section, we'll track the investigation of how voluntary behaviors are acquired. Building on Edward L. Thorndike's pioneering work with animals, B. F. Skinner identified and developed the model of *operant conditioning,* another form of conditioning that explains how we acquire and maintain voluntary behaviors.

biological preparedness The idea that an organism is innately predisposed to form associations between certain stimuli and responses.

⌃ Saving a Species by Creating a Taste Aversion The endangered northern quoll is an Australian marsupial that seems to have a particular fondness for cane toads, a highly invasive, nonnative species. Quolls have been decimated by their habit of eating cane toads, whose skin, glands, and internal organs contain a deadly poison.

University of Sydney ecologist Stephanie O'Donnell and her colleagues (2010) successfully created a conditioned taste aversion to teach quolls to avoid eating cane toads. They fed young quolls tiny, dead cane toads that were laced with a nausea-inducing drug. The juvenile cane toads, weighing less than a tenth of an ounce, did not contain enough poison to kill the quolls, but the drug made the quolls extremely nauseated. Did a taste aversion develop? Yes, and the quolls with taste aversions survived up to five times longer in the wild than control group quolls who were not exposed to the sickness-inducing toads.

IN FOCUS

Evolution, Biological Preparedness, and Conditioned Fears: What Gives You the Creeps?

Does this photo make you uncomfortable?

A *phobia* is an extreme, irrational fear of a specific object, animal, or situation. It was once believed that all phobias were acquired through classical conditioning, as was Little Albert's fear of the rat. But many people develop phobias without experiencing a traumatic event in association with the object of their fear. Obviously, other forms of learning, such as observational learning, are involved in the development of some fears (Bruchey et al., 2010).

Psychologist Martin Seligman (1971) noticed that phobias are selective. Extreme, irrational fears of snakes, spiders, heights, and small enclosed places (like Erv and Fern's attic) are relatively common. But very few people have phobias of stairs, ladders, electrical outlets, or sharp objects, though these things are more likely to be associated with traumatic experiences.

Seligman proposed that humans are biologically prepared to develop fears of objects or situations—such as snakes, spiders, and heights—that may once have posed a threat to humans' evolutionary ancestors. As Seligman (1971) put it, "The great majority of phobias are about objects of natural importance to the survival of the species." According to this view, people don't commonly develop phobias of knives, stoves, or cars because they're not biologically prepared to do so.

Experimental evidence supports an evolutionary explanation for the most common phobias (Coelho & Purkis, 2009; Öhman, 2009).

Nicolas Reusens/Getty Images

Both humans and monkeys acquire conditioned fear responses pictures of snakes and spiders more rapidly than they do to pictures of neutral objects, like mushrooms and flowers (Öhman & Mineka, 2001, 2003).

Are such findings the result of frightening experiences with snakes or spiders? Apparently not. It turns out that we are more likely to develop certain types of fears. Research has shown that preschoolers and even infants are faster at spotting images of snakes and spiders among photos of flowers, frogs, or caterpillars (LoBue, 2010; LoBue & DeLoache, 2008, 2010). They are also more likely to associate snakes and spiders with fearful stimuli, like angry faces or voices (DeLoache & LoBue, 2009).

MYTH ▶ SCIENCE

Is it true that people are more likely to fear snakes, spiders, and heights than more realistic threats like speeding cars?

Öhman and Mineka (2003) suggest that because poisonous snakes, reptiles, and insects have been associated with danger throughout the evolution of mammals, there is an evolved "fear module" in the brain that is highly sensitized to such evolutionarily relevant stimuli. According to this explanation, individuals who more rapidly detected such dangerous animals would have been more likely to learn to avoid them and survive to reproduce and pass on their genes to future generations (Coelho & Purkis, 2009; Öhman et al., 2007).

▲ **Thorndike's Puzzle Box** Thorndike constructed a total of 15 different puzzle boxes, which varied in how difficult they were for a cat to escape from. In a simple box like this one, a cat merely had to step on a treadle at the front of the cage to escape. More complex boxes required the cat to perform a chain of three responses—step on a treadle, pull on a string, and push a bar up or down (Chance, 1999).

Thorndike and the Law of Effect

Edward L. Thorndike (1874–1949) was the first psychologist to systematically investigate animal learning and how voluntary behaviors are influenced by their consequences. In an important series of experiments, Thorndike (1898) put hungry cats in cages that he called "puzzle boxes," with a dish of food placed outside. A cat could escape the cage by a simple act, such as pulling a loop or pressing a lever that would unlatch the cage door.

Thorndike found that when the cat was first put into the puzzle box, it would engage in random behaviors to escape. Eventually, the cat would accidentally pull on the loop or step on the lever, opening the door latch. After several trials in the same puzzle box, a cat could escape very quickly. The cats gradually learned to associate certain responses with successfully gaining the food reward.

Thorndike's observations led him to formulate the **law of effect**, a *learning principle in which responses followed by satisfying effects are strengthened (more likely to occur again), but responses followed by dissatisfying effects are weakened (less likely to occur again).*

Thorndike's description of the law of effect was an important first step in understanding how active, voluntary behaviors can be modified by their consequences. Thorndike, however, never developed his ideas on learning into a formal model or system (Hearst, 1999). That task would be taken up by another American psychologist, B. F. Skinner (Rutherford, 2012).

B. F. Skinner and the Search for "Order in Behavior"

From the time he was a graduate student in psychology until his death, the famous American psychologist **B. F. Skinner** searched for the "lawful processes" that would explain "order in behavior" (Skinner, 1956, 1967). Like John Watson, Skinner was a staunch behaviorist. Skinner strongly believed that psychology should restrict itself to studying only phenomena that could be objectively measured and verified—outwardly observable behavior and environmental events.

Skinner acknowledged that Pavlov's classical conditioning could explain the learned association of stimuli in certain reflexive responses (Iversen, 1992). But classical conditioning was limited to existing behavioral responses that were reflexively elicited. To Skinner, the most important form of learning was demonstrated by *new* behaviors that were actively *emitted* by the organism, such as the active behaviors produced by Thorndike's cats in trying to escape the puzzle boxes.

Skinner (1953) coined the term **operant** to describe any *"active behavior that operates upon the environment to generate consequences."* In everyday language, our actions often have consequences that can lead to us performing an action more or less. Indeed, Skinner's principles of operant conditioning explain how we acquire the wide range of *voluntary* behaviors that we perform in daily life. But as a behaviorist who rejected mentalistic explanations, Skinner avoided the term *voluntary* because it would imply that behavior was due to a conscious choice or intention (Moore, 2005b).

Reinforcement: Increasing Future Behavior

In a nutshell, Skinner's **operant conditioning** is *the basic learning process that involves changing the probability that a response will be repeated by manipulating the consequences of that response.* One possible consequence of a behavior is reinforcement. **Reinforcement** is *the occurrence of a stimulus or an event following a response that increases the likelihood* of that response being repeated. Notice that reinforcement is defined by the effect it produces—increasing or strengthening the occurrence of a behavior in the future.

Let's look at reinforcement in action. Suppose you put your money into a soft-drink vending machine and push the button. Nothing happens. You push the button again. Nothing. You try the coin-return lever. A shower of coins is released. In the future, if another vending machine swallows your money without giving you what you want, what are you likely to do? Hit the coin-return lever, right?

In this example, pushing the coin return lever is the *operant*—the active response you emitted. The shower of coins is the *reinforcing stimulus,* or *reinforcer*—the stimulus or event that is sought in a particular situation. In everyday language, a reinforcing stimulus is typically something desirable, satisfying, or pleasant. Skinner, of course, avoided such terms because they reflected subjective emotional states.

One last component of the operant conditioning model remains to be described. The **discriminative stimulus** is *a specific stimulus that increases the likelihood of a particular response because it indicates that reinforcement is likely to occur.* For example, when you hear the "ding" of a text message on your phone, you're likely to swipe the screen. You've learned from experience that doing so is likely to be reinforced with a message from a friend. In this case, the "ding" is a discriminative stimulus.

As this example illustrates, we learn from experience to associate certain environmental stimuli with reinforcement—or its absence. That is, discriminative

▲ **Burrhus Frederic Skinner (1904–1990)** After spending a year trying to be a writer, Skinner decided psychological research was a better way to learn about human nature (Moore, 2005a). As Skinner (1967) later wrote, "A writer might portray human behavior accurately, but he did not understand it. . . . The relevant science appeared to be psychology, though I had only the vaguest idea of what that meant."

law of effect Learning principle in which responses followed by satisfying effects are strengthened (more likely to occur again), but responses followed by dissatisfying effects are weakened (less likely to occur again).

operant Any "active behavior that operates upon the environment to generate consequences" (Skinner, 1953).

operant conditioning The basic learning process that involves changing the probability that a response will be repeated by manipulating the consequences of that response.

reinforcement The occurrence of a stimulus or event following a response that increases the likelihood of that response being repeated.

discriminative stimulus A specific stimulus that increases the likelihood of a particular response because it indicates that reinforcement is likely to occur.

TABLE 5.1

Comparing Positive and Negative Reinforcement

Process	Operant Behavior	Consequence	Effect on Behavior
Positive reinforcement	Studying to *win* an academic award	*Win* academic award	Increase studying in the future
Negative reinforcement	Studying to *avoid* losing academic scholarship	*Avoid* loss of academic scholarship	Increase studying in the future

Both positive and negative reinforcement increase the likelihood of a behavior being repeated. Positive reinforcement involves a behavior that leads to a reinforcing or rewarding event. In contrast, negative reinforcement involves a behavior that leads to the avoidance of or escape from an aversive or undesired event.

∨ **Negative Reinforcement** Negative reinforcement occurs when a behavior leads to the avoidance of an aversive, or undesired stimulus. Avoiding the unwanted stimulus reinforces the behavior, which will then typically be repeated. For example, the people in this photo are using insect repellant to avoid bug bites. If it works, it will reinforce this behavior, the use of the insect repellant, which will increase the likelihood that they will use the spray in future situations where there may be bugs.

RealPeopleGroup/Getty Images

stimuli can also signal that certain operant behaviors are *unlikely* to be reinforced. Thus, you've learned that you're more likely to be reinforced for screaming at the top of your lungs at a football game (one discriminative stimulus) than in the middle of class (a different discriminative stimulus).

Positive and Negative Reinforcement There are two forms of reinforcement: *positive reinforcement* and *negative reinforcement*. Both affect future behavior, but they do so in different ways (see **Table 5.1**). It's easier to understand these differences if you note at the outset that Skinner did not use the terms *positive* and *negative* in their everyday sense of meaning "good" and "bad" or "desirable" and "undesirable." Instead, think of the words *positive* and *negative* in terms of their mathematical meanings. *Positive* is the equivalent of a plus sign (+), meaning that something is added. *Negative* is the equivalent of a minus sign (−), meaning that something is subtracted or removed.

Positive reinforcement is *a situation in which a response is followed by the addition of a reinforcing stimulus, increasing the likelihood that the response will be repeated in similar situations.* Everyday examples of positive reinforcement in action are easy to identify. Here are some examples:

- Your backhand return of the tennis ball (the operant) is low and fast, and your tennis coach yells, "Excellent!" (the reinforcing stimulus).

- You watch a film version of *Hamilton* and write a short paper about it (the operant) for 10 bonus points (the reinforcing stimulus) for your history class.

- You post a cat photo on social media (the operant), and you get many "likes" from your friends (the reinforcing stimulus).

In each example, if the addition of the reinforcing stimulus has the effect of making you more likely to repeat the operant in similar situations in the future, then positive reinforcement has occurred.

It's important to point out that what constitutes a *reinforcing stimulus* can vary from person to person, species to species, and situation to situation. Although gold stars and stickers may be reinforcing to a third-grader, they would probably have little reinforcing value to the average adult in the workplace.

It's also important to note that the reinforcing stimulus is not necessarily something we usually consider positive or desirable. For example, most teachers would not think of a scolding as being a reinforcing stimulus to children. But to children, adult attention can be a powerful reinforcing stimulus. If a child receives attention from the teacher only when they misbehave, then the teacher may unwittingly be reinforcing misbehavior. The child may actually increase disruptive behavior in order to get the sought-after reinforcing stimulus—adult attention—even if it's in the form of being scolded. To reduce the child's disruptive behavior, the teacher would do better to reinforce the child's appropriate behavior by paying attention to them when they're *not* being disruptive, such as when they are working quietly.

Negative reinforcement is *a situation in which a response results in the removal of, avoidance of, or escape from an aversive, or undesired, stimulus, increasing the likelihood that the response will be repeated in similar situations.* Remember that the word *negative* in the phrase *negative reinforcement* is used like a mathematical minus sign (−).

For example, you take two aspirin (the operant) to remove a headache (the aversive stimulus). Thirty minutes later, the headache is gone. Are you now more likely to take aspirin to deal with bodily aches and pain in the future? If you are, then negative reinforcement has occurred.

Aversive stimuli typically involve physical or psychological discomfort that an organism seeks to escape or avoid. Consequently, behaviors are said to be negatively reinforced when they let you either (1) *escape* aversive stimuli that are already present or (2) *avoid* aversive stimuli before they occur. That is, we're more likely to repeat the same escape or avoidance behaviors in similar situations in the future. The headache example illustrates the negative reinforcement of *escape behavior*. By taking two aspirin, you "escaped" the headache. Locking up your bicycle so it won't get stolen illustrates the negative reinforcement of *avoidance behavior*. Here are some more examples of negative reinforcement involving escape or avoidance behavior:

- You make digital backups of important files (the operant) to avoid losing the data if your computer's hard drive should fail (the aversive stimulus).

- You dab some hydrocortisone cream on an insect bite (the operant) to escape the itching (the aversive stimulus).

- You install a new battery (the operant) in the smoke detector to escape the annoying beep (the aversive stimulus).

In each example, if escaping or avoiding the aversive event has the effect of making you more likely to repeat the operant in similar situations in the future, then negative reinforcement has taken place.

Positive reinforcement and negative reinforcement increase the likelihood of a behavior being repeated, but through different means.

Primary and Conditioned Reinforcers

Skinner also distinguished two kinds of reinforcing stimuli: primary and conditioned. A **primary reinforcer** is *a stimulus or event that is naturally or inherently reinforcing for a given species*. That is, even if an individual has not had prior experience with the particular stimulus, the stimulus or event still has reinforcing properties. For example, food, water, adequate warmth, and sexual contact are primary reinforcers for most animals, including humans.

A **conditioned reinforcer**, also called a *secondary reinforcer,* is *a stimulus or event that has acquired reinforcing value by being associated with a primary reinforcer.* The classic example of a conditioned reinforcer is money. Money is reinforcing not because those flimsy bits of paper have value in and of themselves, but because we've learned that we can use them to acquire primary reinforcers and other conditioned reinforcers. Awards, frequent-flyer points, and university degrees are just a few other examples of conditioned reinforcers. Technology can be a reinforcer. One study even found that smartphones were a better reinforcer than food (O'Donnell & Epstein, 2019). University students deprived of both food and their smartphones worked more diligently on a computer task to earn up to two minutes of smartphone use than to earn a snack such as a Kit Kat bar or Doritos. Although smartphone use might be seen in this particular situation as positive reinforcement, other researchers have viewed it as negative reinforcement. People increase a behavior, smartphone use, to reduce an unpleasant sensation, such as anxiety or fear of missing out (FOMO, for short) (Elhai et al., 2019).

Conditioned reinforcers need not be as tangible as money or university degrees. Conditioned reinforcers can be as subtle as a smile, a touch, or a nod of recognition. Looking back at the Prologue, for example, Fern was reinforced by the laughter of her friends and relatives each time she told "the killer attic" tale — so she kept telling the story!

THINK LIKE A SCIENTIST

Can wearable technology help you break a bad habit or form a good one? Go to Achieve: Resources to **Think Like a Scientist** about **Positive and Negative Reinforcement.**

 Achieᴠe

▲ **Types of Reinforcers** Primary reinforcers, like food when you're hungry, are naturally reinforcing—you don't have to learn their value. In contrast, the value of conditioned reinforcers, like grades and awards, has to be learned through their association with primary reinforcers. But conditioned reinforcers can be just as reinforcing as primary reinforcers. As proof, U.S. soccer player Megan Rapinoe shows off the gold medal that she won, along with her team, at the 2012 Olympic Games in London.

positive reinforcement A situation in which a response is followed by the addition of a reinforcing stimulus, increasing the likelihood that the response will be repeated in similar situations.

negative reinforcement A situation in which a response results in the removal of, avoidance of, or escape from an aversive, or undesired, stimulus, increasing the likelihood that the response will be repeated in similar situations.

primary reinforcer A stimulus or event that is naturally or inherently reinforcing for a given species.

conditioned reinforcer A stimulus or event that has acquired reinforcing value by being associated with a primary reinforcer; also called a secondary reinforcer.

punishment The presentation of a stimulus or event following a behavior that acts to decrease the likelihood of the behavior being repeated.

positive punishment A situation in which an operant is followed by the presentation or addition of an aversive stimulus; also called *punishment by application*.

negative punishment A situation in which an operant is followed by the removal or subtraction of a reinforcing stimulus; also called *punishment by removal*.

 Achieve

Is Maria's preference for this blue blouse based on classical or operant conditioning? Go to **Achieve** and try **Concept Practice: Conditioning in Daily Life**.

Punishment and negative reinforcement are two different processes that produce *opposite* effects on a given behavior. Punishment decreases the future performance of the behavior, while negative reinforcement *increases* it.

Punishment: Using Aversive Consequences to Decrease Behavior

■ KEY THEME
Punishment is a process that decreases the future occurrence of a behavior.

≡ KEY QUESTIONS
- How does punishment differ from negative reinforcement?
- What factors influence the effectiveness of punishment?
- What effects are associated with the use of punishment to control behavior, and what are some alternative ways to change behavior?

Positive and negative reinforcement are processes that *increase* the frequency of a particular behavior. The opposite effect is produced by punishment. **Punishment** is *the presentation of a stimulus or event following a behavior that acts to decrease the likelihood of the behavior's being repeated*. Many people tend to confuse punishment and negative reinforcement, but these two processes produce entirely different effects on behavior (see **Table 5.2**). Negative reinforcement *always increases* the likelihood that an operant will be repeated in the future. Punishment *always decreases* the future performance of an operant.

Skinner (1953) identified two types of aversive events that can act as punishment. **Positive punishment**, also called *punishment by application*, is *a situation in which an operant is followed by the presentation of an aversive stimulus*. The word *positive* in the phrase *positive punishment* signifies that something is added or presented in the situation. In this case, it's an aversive stimulus. Here are some everyday examples of punishment by application:

- An employee wears shorts to work (the operant) and is reprimanded by his supervisor for dressing inappropriately (the punishing stimulus).
- Your cat jumps up on the kitchen counter (the operant), and you loudly shake a metal can filled with coins (the punishing stimulus).
- You are late to class (the operant), and your instructor responds with a sarcastic remark (the punishing stimulus).

Here's an example of positive punishment applied more broadly. Concerned about teenagers loitering on busy train platforms, Japanese rail stations installed devices that emit a high-frequency tone that only young people can typically hear (Richarz, 2018). If a young person lingers too long in a station, they are punished by the annoying sound, and their behavior—lingering in the train station—is reduced.

In each of these examples, if the presentation of the punishing stimulus has the effect of decreasing the behavior it follows, then punishment has occurred. Although the punishing stimuli in these examples were administered by other people, punishing stimuli also occur as natural consequences for some behaviors. Inadvertently touching a hot stove or a sharp object (the operant) can result in a painful injury (the punishing stimulus).

The second type of punishment is **negative punishment**, also called *punishment by removal, a situation in which an operant is followed by the removal or subtraction of a reinforcing stimulus* (see **Table 5.3**). In this case, it is the loss or withdrawal of a reinforcing stimulus following a behavior. That is, the behavior's consequence is the loss of some privilege,

TABLE 5.2

Comparing Punishment and Negative Reinforcement

Process	Operant	Consequence	Effect on Behavior
Punishment	Wear a warm but unstylish flannel shirt	A friend makes the hurtful comment, "Nice shirt. Whose couch did you steal to get the fabric?"	Decrease wearing the shirt in the future
Negative reinforcement	Wear a warm but unstylish flannel shirt	Avoid feeling cold and uncomfortable all day	Increase wearing the shirt in the future

possession, or other desirable object or activity. Here are some everyday examples of punishment by removal:

- After they speed through a red light (the operant), their driver's license is suspended (loss of reinforcing stimulus).

- Because they were flirting with another person (the operant), they get dumped by their partner (loss of reinforcing stimulus).

In each example, if the behavior decreases in response to the removal of the reinforcing stimulus, then punishment has occurred. It's important to stress that, like reinforcement, punishment is defined by the effect it produces. In everyday usage, people often refer to a particular consequence as a punishment when, strictly speaking, it's not. Why? Because the consequence has *not* reduced future occurrences of the behavior.

Skinner (1953) as well as other researchers have noted that several factors influence the effectiveness of punishment (Horner, 2002). For example, punishment is more effective if it immediately follows a response than if it is delayed. Punishment is also more effective if it consistently, rather than occasionally, follows a response (Lerman & Vorndran, 2002; Spradlin, 2002). Though speeding tickets and prison sentences are commonly referred to as punishments, these aversive consequences are inconsistently applied and often administered only after a long delay. Thus, they don't always effectively decrease specific behaviors.

It's a myth that punishment is an effective way to teach new behaviors. Even when punishment works, its use has several drawbacks (see B. Smith, 2012). First, punishment may decrease a specific response, but it doesn't necessarily teach or promote a more appropriate response to take its place. Second, punishment that is intense may produce undesirable results, such as complete passivity, fear, anxiety, or hostility (Lerman & Vorndran, 2002). For example, spanking, defined as hitting a child on the buttocks, arms, or legs with an open hand without causing a bruise or physical harm, is a common form of discipline in many cultures (UNICEF, 2014). Some researchers believe that mild and occasional spanking is not necessarily harmful, especially when used as a backup for other forms of discipline (Oas, 2010). However, many studies have demonstrated that spanking is associated with negative outcomes. In a wide-ranging meta-analysis of studies involving more than 100,000 children, Elizabeth Gershoff and Andrew Gorgan-Kaylor (2016) found that spanking was associated with aggressive

TABLE 5.3

Types of Reinforcement and Punishment

	Reinforcing stimulus	Aversive stimulus
Stimulus presented	Positive reinforcement	Positive punishment
Stimulus removed	Negative punishment	Negative reinforcement

To identify the type of reinforcement or punishment that has occurred, determine whether the stimulus is *reinforcing* or *aversive* and whether it was *presented* or *removed* following the operant.

MYTH ◀ SCIENCE

Is it true that punishment is an effective way to teach new behaviors?

⌃ Honk More, Wait More Enormous traffic jams in Mumbai, India, have led to a serious honking problem (Pallavi, 2020). Motorists honk even when the light is red, leading to a serious noise pollution problem. But the Mumbai police have come up with a solution based on negative punishment. They installed noise meters near major intersections. When the decibel level of the honking reaches a certain level, the red-light timer resets to 90 seconds and a sign proclaims "Honk More, Wait More." The punishment was the loss of the reinforcing stimulus of a green light. When drivers ceased honking, they avoided losing time. (Like many situations in which punishment and reinforcement are used, we could reframe this situation as positive punishment, which also leads to the reduction of a behavior—honking. With this reframe, the punishment is the addition of the longer red light as an aversive stimulus.) A viral video demonstrated the immediate decrease in honking and spawned the hashtag #HonkResponsibly (https://twitter.com/MumbaiPolice/status/1223090017397960705).

TABLE 5.4

Components of Operant Conditioning

	Discriminative Stimulus	Operant Response	Consequence	Effect on Future Behavior
Definition	The environmental stimulus that precedes an operant response	The actively emitted or voluntary behavior	The environmental stimulus or event that follows the operant response	Reinforcement increases the likelihood of operant being repeated; punishment or lack of reinforcement decreases the likelihood of operant being repeated.
Examples	Wallet on college sidewalk	Give wallet to security	Receive $50 reward from wallet's owner	Positive reinforcement: *More likely* to turn in lost items to authorities
	Gas gauge almost on "empty"	Fill car with gas	Avoid running out of gas	Negative reinforcement: *More likely* to fill car when gas gauge shows empty
	Informal social situation at work	Tell an off-color, sexist joke	Receive reprimand for sexism and inappropriate workplace behavior	Positive punishment: *Less likely* to tell off-color, sexist jokes in workplace
	ATM/banking machine	Insert bank card	Bank card taken away by broken machine that eats your bank card and doesn't dispense cash	Negative punishment: *Less likely* to use that machine in the future

The examples given here illustrate the three key components involved in operant conditioning. The basic operant conditioning process works like this: In the presence of a specific discriminative stimulus, an operant response is emitted, which is followed by a consequence. Depending on the consequence, we are either more or less likely to repeat the operant when we encounter the same or a similar discriminative stimulus in the future.

and antisocial behavior, mental health problems, low self-esteem, and poor relationships with parents. Finally, the effects of punishment are likely to be temporary (Estes & Skinner, 1941, Skinner, 1938). A child who is sent to their room for teasing their younger sibling may well repeat the behavior when their parent's back is turned. As Skinner (1971) noted, "Punished behavior is likely to reappear after the punitive consequences are withdrawn." For some suggestions on how to change behavior without using a punishing stimulus, see the In Focus box on the next page, "Changing the Behavior of Others: Alternatives to Punishment."

We have now discussed all three fundamental components of operant conditioning (see **Table 5.4**). In the presence of a specific environmental stimulus (the *discriminative stimulus*), we emit a particular behavior (the *operant*), which is followed by a consequence (*reinforcement* or *punishment*). If the consequence is either positive or negative reinforcement, we are *more* likely to repeat the operant when we encounter the same or similar discriminative stimuli in the future. If the consequence is some form of punishment, we are *less* likely to repeat the operant when we encounter the same or similar discriminative stimuli in the future.

Next, we'll build on the basics of operant conditioning by considering how Skinner explained the acquisition of complex behaviors.

Shaping and Maintaining Behavior

■ KEY THEME
New behaviors are acquired through shaping and can be maintained through different patterns of reinforcement.

⁼ KEY QUESTIONS
• How does shaping work?
• What is the partial reinforcement effect, and how do the four schedules of reinforcement differ in their effects?
• What is behavior modification?

operant chamber or **Skinner box**
B. F. Skinner invented this experimental apparatus to scientifically study the relationship between environmental events and active behaviors.

B. F. Skinner invented the **operant chamber**, more popularly known as the **Skinner box**, *to scientifically study the relationship between environmental events and active behaviors.* An operant chamber is *a small cage with a food dispenser.* Attached

● IN FOCUS

Changing the Behavior of Others: Alternatives to Punishment

Although punishment may temporarily decrease the occurrence of a problem behavior, it doesn't promote more desirable or appropriate behaviors in its place. Throughout his life, Skinner remained strongly opposed to the use of punishment. Instead, he advocated the greater use of positive reinforcement to strengthen desirable behaviors (Dinsmoor, 1992; Skinner, 1971). Here are four strategies that can be used to reduce undesirable behaviors without resorting to punishment.

Strategy 1: Reinforce an Incompatible Behavior

The best method to reduce a problem behavior is to reinforce an *alternative* behavior that is both constructive and incompatible with the problem behavior. For example, if you're trying to decrease a child's whining, respond to their requests (the reinforcer) only when they talk in a normal tone of voice.

Strategy 2: Stop Reinforcing the Problem Behavior

Technically, this strategy is called *extinction*. The first step in effectively applying extinction is to observe the behavior carefully and identify the reinforcer that is maintaining the problem behavior. Then eliminate the reinforcer.

Suppose a friend keeps interrupting you while you are trying to study, asking you if you want to play a video game or just hang out. You want to extinguish his behavior of interrupting your studying. In the past, trying to be polite, you've responded to their behavior by acting interested (a reinforcer). You could eliminate the reinforcer by acting uninterested and continuing to study while they talk.

It's important to note that when the extinction process is initiated, the problem behavior often *temporarily* increases. This situation is more likely to occur if the problem behavior has only occasionally been reinforced in the past. Thus, once you begin, be consistent in nonreinforcement of the problem behavior.

Strategy 3: Reinforce the Nonoccurence of the Problem Behavior

This strategy involves setting a specific time period after which the individual is reinforced if the unwanted behavior has *not* occurred. For example, if you're trying to reduce bickering between children, set an appropriate time limit, and then provide positive reinforcement if they have *not* squabbled during that interval.

Strategy 4: Remove the Opportunity to Obtain Positive Reinforcement

It's not always possible to identify and eliminate all the reinforcers that maintain a behavior. For example, a child's obnoxious behavior might be reinforced by the social attention of siblings or classmates.

In a procedure called *time-out from positive reinforcement*, the child is removed from the reinforcing situation for a short time, so that the access to reinforcers is eliminated. When the undesirable behavior occurs, the child is immediately sent to a time-out area that is free of distractions and social contact. The time-out period begins as soon as the child's behavior is under control. For children, a good rule of thumb is one minute of time-out per year of age.

Enhancing the Effectiveness of Positive Reinforcement

Often, these four strategies are used in combination. However, remember the most important behavioral principle: *Positively reinforce the behaviors that you want to increase.* There are several ways in which you can enhance the effectiveness of positive reinforcement:

- Make sure that the reinforcer is *strongly* reinforcing to the individual whose behavior you're trying to modify.
- The positive reinforcer should be delivered *immediately* after the preferred behavior occurs.
- The positive reinforcer should initially be given *every* time the preferred behavior occurs. When the desired behavior is well established, *gradually reduce the frequency of reinforcement.*
- Use a *variety* of positive reinforcers, such as tangible items, praise, special privileges, recognition, and so on. Minimize the use of food as a positive reinforcer.
- Capitalize on what is known as the *Premack principle*—a more preferred activity (e.g., painting) can be used to reinforce a less preferred activity (e.g., picking up toys).
- Encourage the person to engage in *self-reinforcement* in the form of pride, a sense of accomplishment, and feelings of self-control.

Stretch Photography/Blend Images/Corbis

▲ **Using Reinforcement in the Classroom** Teachers at all levels use positive reinforcement to increase desired behaviors. Often, conditioned reinforcers, like stickers or gold stars, can be exchanged for other, more tangible rewards, like a new pencil or classroom privileges.

shaping The operant conditioning procedure of selectively reinforcing successively closer approximations of a goal behavior until the goal behavior is displayed.

continuous reinforcement A schedule of reinforcement in which every occurrence of a particular response is followed by a reinforcer.

partial reinforcement A situation in which the occurrence of a particular response is only sometimes followed by a reinforcer.

▲ **The Skinner Box** Popularly called a Skinner box after its inventor, an operant chamber is used to experimentally study operant conditioning in laboratory animals.

to the cage is a device that automatically records the number of operants made by an experimental animal, usually a rat or pigeon. For a rat, the typical operant is pressing a bar, for a pigeon, it is pecking at a small disk. Food pellets are usually used for positive reinforcement. Often, a light in the cage functions as a discriminative stimulus. When the light is on, pressing the bar or pecking the disk is reinforced with a food pellet. When the light is off, these responses do not result in reinforcement.

When a rat is first placed in a Skinner box, it typically explores its new environment, occasionally nudging or pressing the bar in the process. The researcher can accelerate the rat's bar-pressing behavior through a process called shaping. **Shaping** is *the operant conditioning procedure of selectively reinforcing successively closer approximations of a goal or behavior until the goal behavior is displayed.* For example, the researcher might first reinforce the rat with a food pellet whenever it moves to the half of the Skinner box in which the bar is located. Other responses would be ignored. Once that response has been learned, reinforcement is withheld until the rat moves even closer to the bar. Then the rat might be reinforced only when it touches the bar. Step by step, the rat is reinforced for behaviors that correspond ever more closely to the final goal behavior—pressing the bar.

Skinner believed that shaping could explain how people acquire a wide variety of abilities and skills—everything from tying shoelaces to operating sophisticated computer programs.

The Partial Reinforcement Effect: Building Resistance to Extinction

Once a rat had acquired a bar-pressing behavior, Skinner found that the fastest way to strengthen the response was to immediately reinforce *every* occurrence of bar pressing. This pattern of reinforcement, called **continuous reinforcement**, is *a schedule of reinforcement in which every occurrence of a particular response is followed by a reinforcer.* In everyday life, of course, it's common for responses to be reinforced only sometimes—a pattern called **partial reinforcement**, *a situation in which the occurrence of a particular response is only sometimes followed by a reinforcer.* For example, practicing your basketball skills isn't followed by putting the ball through the hoop on every shot. Sometimes you're reinforced by making a basket, and sometimes you're not.

❯ **Training Service Dogs with Operant Conditioning** This photo shows a service dog opening a door for a person using a wheelchair. The dog was trained using operant conditioning principles. A trainer shaped the dog's behavior using positive reinforcement. For example, if the dog approached the door, they received a treat. Next, they only received the treat for touching the rope, then pulling the rope, then pulling it enough to open the door. Each time they came closer to the desired behavior, they received a treat.

Now suppose that despite all your hard work, your basketball skills are dismal. If practicing free throws was *never* reinforced by making a basket, what would you do? You'd probably eventually quit playing basketball. This is an example of **extinction**, *a phenomenon that occurs when a learned response no longer results in reinforcement, and the likelihood of the behavior's being repeated gradually declines.*

Skinner (1956) first noticed the effects of partial reinforcement when he began running low on food pellets one day. Rather than reinforcing every bar press, Skinner tried to stretch out his supply of pellets by rewarding responses only periodically. He found that the rats not only continued to respond but actually increased their rate of bar pressing.

One important consequence of partially reinforcing behavior is that partially reinforced behaviors tend to be more resistant to extinction than are behaviors conditioned using continuous reinforcement. So, it's a myth that the most effective way to teach a new behavior is to reinforce it every time. This phenomenon is called the **partial reinforcement effect**, *the phenomenon in which behaviors that are conditioned using partial reinforcement are more resistant to extinction than behaviors that are conditioned using continuous reinforcement.* For example, when Skinner shut off the food-dispensing mechanism, a pigeon conditioned using continuous reinforcement would continue pecking at the disk 100 times or so before the behavior decreased significantly, indicating extinction. In contrast, a pigeon conditioned with partial reinforcement continued to peck at the disk thousands of times! If you think about it, this is not surprising. When pigeons, rats, or humans have experienced partial reinforcement, they've learned that reinforcement may yet occur, despite delays and nonreinforced responses, if persistent responses are made.

In everyday life, the partial reinforcement effect is reflected in behaviors that persist despite the lack of reinforcement. Gamblers may persist despite a string of losses, writers will persevere in the face of repeated rejection slips, and the family dog will continue begging for the scraps of food that it has only occasionally received at the dinner table in the past.

The Schedules of Reinforcement Skinner (1956) found that specific preset arrangements of partial reinforcement produced different patterns of responses. Collectively, these different reinforcement arrangements are called **schedules of reinforcement**, *the delivery of a reinforcer according to a preset pattern based on the number of responses or the time interval between responses* (see **Figure 5.4**).

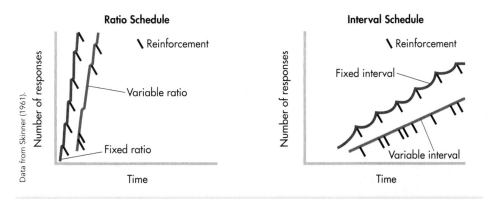

FIGURE 5.4 Schedules of Reinforcement and Response Patterns Different patterns of responding are produced by the four basic schedules of reinforcement. In the left graph, The predictable nature of a *fixed-ratio schedule* (the red line) produces a high rate of responding, with a pause after the reinforcer is delivered. The unpredictable nature of *variable-ratio schedules* (purple) also produces high, steady rates of responding, but with hardly any pause between reinforcers. In the right graph, *Fixed-interval schedules* (red) produce a scallop-shaped pattern of responding. The unpredictable nature of *variable-interval schedules* (purple) produces a moderate but steady rate of responding.

extinction (in operant conditioning) A phenomenon that occurs when a learned response no longer results in reinforcement, and the likelihood of the behavior's being repeated gradually declines.

partial reinforcement effect The phenomenon in which behaviors that are conditioned using partial reinforcement are more resistant to extinction than behaviors that are conditioned using continuous reinforcement.

schedule of reinforcement The delivery of a reinforcer according to a preset pattern based on the number of responses or the time interval between responses.

MYTH ◀ SCIENCE

Is it true that the most effective way to teach a new behavior is to reward it each time it is performed?

▲ **Superstitious Rituals: Behaviors Shaped by Accidental Reinforcement** Like many athletes, LeBron James has developed a superstitious pregame routine. His ritual is a complex sequence that includes carefully choreographed handshakes with teammates and culminates with James tossing chalk high into the air.

Skinner (1948) pointed out that superstitions may result when a behavior is accidentally reinforced—that is, when reinforcement is just a coincidence. So although it was really just a fluke that wearing your "lucky" shirt was followed by a win, the illusion of reinforcement can shape and strengthen behavior. One study found that engaging in superstitious behaviors improved performance, probably because doing so enhanced self-confidence (Damisch et al., 2010).

behavior modification The application of learning principles to help people develop more effective or adaptive behaviors.

There are two basic types of schedules, ratio schedules and interval schedules. In *ratio* schedules, reinforcement is delivered after a certain number of responses, such as a peck on a light or a press of a bar. If you are paid a commission for making a certain number of sales, regardless of how long it takes you, you are being reinforced on a ratio schedule.

In *interval* schedules, reinforcement is delivered after a certain interval, or amount of time, has elapsed. If you are paid on an hourly basis, regardless of how many sales you close, you are being reinforced on an interval schedule.

In the preceding examples, reinforcement schedules are fixed, meaning predictable and consistent. But schedules can also be variable. In variable schedules, reinforcement occurs after an average number of responses or average time interval, which varies from trial to trial. So although reinforcement will eventually be delivered, any individual response may or may not be reinforced. Therefore, there is hardly any pause after reinforcement.

Variable-ratio schedules of reinforcement produce high, steady rates of responding that are very resistant to extinction. Posting on social media hoping to receive a "like" or retweet is one example, but the classic example of variable-ratio schedules in real life is gambling (Schüll, 2012). Each response—a spin of the roulette wheel, a toss of the dice, or a pull of the slot machine handle—could be the big one, and the more often you respond, the more opportunities you have to win.

Variable-interval schedules tend to produce moderate but steady rates of responding. In daily life, we experience variable-interval schedules when we have to wait for events that follow an approximate, rather than a precise, schedule. For example, parents often unwittingly reinforce a whining child on a variable-interval schedule. From the child's perspective, the whining usually results in the desired request, but how long the child has to whine before getting reinforced can vary. Thus, the child learns that persistent whining will eventually pay off.

Schedules of reinforcement are powerful influences on behavior. According to Skinner (1974), behavior is determined and controlled by environmental stimuli and your history of reinforcement—*not* by conscious choices.

Applications of Operant Conditioning

The In Focus box on alternatives to punishment earlier in the chapter described how operant conditioning principles can be applied to reduce and eliminate problem behaviors. These examples illustrate **behavior modification**, *the application of learning principles to help people develop more effective or adaptive behaviors.*

Behavior modification techniques have been successfully applied in many different settings (see Kazdin, 2008). Coaches, parents, therapists, and teachers all routinely use operant conditioning. For example, behavior modification has been used to reduce public smoking by teenagers (Jason et al., 2009), decrease problem behaviors in schoolchildren (Dunlap et al., 2010; Schanding & Sterling-Turner, 2010), and improve social skills and reduce self-destructive behaviors in people with autism spectrum disorders (Makrygianni & Reed, 2010).

Employers also use behavior modification. For example, one large retailer increased productivity by allowing employees to choose their own reinforcers. A casual dress code and flexible work hours proved to be more effective reinforcers than money (Raj et al., 2006). The principles of operant conditioning have also been used in the specialized training of animals, such as Seeing Eye dogs and capuchin monkeys who assist people who are disabled.

A movement called gamification advocates turning daily life into a kind of virtual reality game, in which "points" or other conditioned reinforcers are awarded to reward healthy or productive behaviors

Using Operant Conditioning to Train "HeroRATs" African giant pouched rats are well equipped to sniff out unexploded land mines. They are too light to set the mines off and they have a powerful sense of smell, able to detect TNT from two feet away. They are also relatively easy to train using operant conditioning (Poling et al., 2010). Reinforced with bits of banana, rats learn to scratch the dirt when they smell TNT. A Belgian nonprofit agency has trained dozens of rats to sweep minefields in Cambodia, Mozambique, and Angola. You can watch video of the "HeroRATs" in action at www.apopo.org

Taylor Weidman/Getty Images

(Campbell, 2011). Gamification has become increasingly common in business, education, medicine, and even government. For example, some businesses give reductions on health insurance premiums to employees who rack up enough points on specially equipped pedometers that monitor their daily activity level. Activity trackers that award points or certificates for meeting fitness or dietary goals are another example. The danger? Marketing professionals are already studying ways to use gamification to influence consumer preferences and buying decisions (Schell, 2010). In each of these examples, the systematic use of reinforcement, shaping, and extinction increased the occurrence of desirable behaviors and decreased the incidence of undesirable behaviors. In the chapter on therapies, we'll look at behavior modification techniques in more detail.

Contemporary Views of Operant Conditioning

■ KEY THEME
In contrast to Skinner, today's psychologists acknowledge the importance of both cognitive and evolutionary factors in operant conditioning.

≡ KEY QUESTIONS
- How did Tolman's research demonstrate the involvement of cognitive processes in learning?
- What are cognitive maps, latent learning, and learned helplessness?
- How do an animal's natural behavior patterns affect the conditioning of operant behaviors?

In our discussion of classical conditioning, we noted that contemporary psychologists acknowledge the important roles played by cognitive factors and biological predispositions in classical conditioning. The situation is much the same with operant conditioning. The basic principles of operant conditioning have been confirmed in thousands of studies. However, our understanding of operant conditioning has been broadened by the consideration of cognitive factors and the recognition of the importance of natural behavior patterns.

Cognitive Aspects of Operant Conditioning

In Skinner's view, operant conditioning did not need to invoke cognitive factors to explain the acquisition of operant behaviors. Words such as *expect, prefer, choose,* and *decide* could not be used to explain how behaviors were acquired, maintained, or extinguished. Similarly, Thorndike and other early behaviorists believed that complex, active behaviors were no more than a chain of stimulus–response connections.

However, not all learning researchers agreed with Skinner and Thorndike. **Edward C. Tolman** (1898–1956) firmly believed that cognitive processes played an important role in the learning of complex behaviors — even in the lowly laboratory rat. According to Tolman, although such cognitive processes could not be observed directly, they could still be experimentally verified and inferred by careful observation of outward behavior (Tolman, 1932).

Much of Tolman's research involved rats in mazes. When Tolman began his research in the 1920s, many studies of rats in mazes had been done. In a typical experiment, a rat would be placed in the "start" box. A food reward would be put in the "goal" box at the end of the maze. The rat would initially make many mistakes in running the maze. After several trials, it would eventually learn to run the maze quickly and with very few errors.

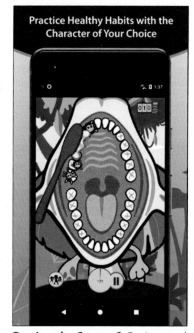

^ Gaming the System? Business, education, medicine, and government organizations use *gamification* to engage and motivate people to perform certain behaviors. Chomper-Chums, a dental-hygiene app for smartphones, was developed by a U.S. dental insurance company. Different cartoon animals, including a lion and an alligator, teach children how to floss and brush their teeth. Children earn coins they can use to buy food to feed the animals. Users may choose healthy foods like an apple or a carrot or less-healthy foods like ice cream or a hot dog to feed the animals (though the animals become less healthy if they are fed unhealthy snacks). Children who regularly use the app are awarded the "Super Smile Award," which they can use to choose new adventures for the animals. The insurance company clearly wants to save money paying for dental treatments, so they have turned good oral hygiene into a fun game, which benefits the children, too.

"Well, you don't look like an experimental psychologist to me."

Sam Gross/www.CartoonStock.com

cognitive map Tolman's term for the mental representation of the layout of a familiar environment.

latent learning Tolman's term for learning that occurs in the absence of reinforcement but is not behaviorally demonstrated until a reinforcer becomes available.

But what had the rats learned? According to traditional behaviorists, the rats had learned a *sequence of responses,* such as "first corner—turn left; second corner—turn left; third corner turn right," and so on. Each response was associated with the "stimulus" of the rat's position in the maze. And the entire sequence of responses was "stamped in" by the food reward at the end of the maze.

Tolman (1948) disagreed with that view. He noted that several investigators had reported as incidental findings that their maze-running rats had occasionally taken their own shortcuts to the food box. In one case, an enterprising rat had knocked the cover off the maze, climbed over the maze wall and out of the maze, and scampered directly to the food box (Lashley, 1929; Tolman et al., 1946). To Tolman, such reports indicated that the rats had learned more than simply the sequence of responses required to get to the food. Tolman believed instead that the rats eventually built up, through experience, a *cognitive map* of the maze. **Cognitive map** is *Tolman's term* for *the mental representation of the layout of a familiar environment.*

As an analogy, think of the route you typically take to get to your psychology classroom. If a hallway along the way were blocked off for repairs, you would use your cognitive map of the building to come up with an alternative route to class. Tolman showed experimentally that rats, like people, seem to form cognitive maps (Tolman, 1948). And, like us, rats can use their cognitive maps to come up with an alternative route to a goal when the customary route is blocked (Tolman & Honzik, 1930a).

Tolman challenged the prevailing behaviorist model on another important point. According to Thorndike, for example, learning would not occur unless the behavior was "strengthened," or "stamped in," by a rewarding consequence. But Tolman showed that this was not necessarily the case. In a classic experiment, three groups of rats were put in the same maze once a day for several days (Tolman & Honzik, 1930b). For group 1, a food reward awaited the rats at the end of the maze. Their performance in the maze steadily improved; the number of errors and the time it took the rats to reach the goal box showed a steady decline with each trial. The rats in group 2 were placed in the maze each day with *no* food reward. They consistently made many errors, and their performance showed only slight improvement. The performance of the rats in groups 1 and 2 was exactly what the traditional behaviorist model would have predicted.

Now consider the behavior of the rats in group 3. These rats were placed in the maze with no food reward for the first 10 days of the experiment. Like the rats in group 2, they made many errors as they wandered about the maze. But, beginning on day 11, they received a food reward at the end of the maze. As you can see in **Figure 5.5**, there was a dramatic improvement in group 3's performance from day 11 to day 12. Once the rats had discovered that food awaited them at the end of the maze, they made a beeline for the goal. On day 12, the rats in group 3 ran the maze with very few errors, improving their performance to the level of the rats in group 1 that had been rewarded on every trial!

Tolman concluded that *reward*—or reinforcement—is *not necessary* for learning to take place (Tolman & Honzik, 1930b). The rats in group 3 had learned the layout of the maze and formed a cognitive map of it simply by exploring it for 10 days. However, they had not been motivated to *demonstrate* that learning until a reward was introduced. Rewards, then, seem to affect the *performance* of what has been learned rather than learning itself. **Latent learning** is *Tolman's term for learning that occurs in the absence of reinforcement but is not behaviorally demonstrated until a reinforcer becomes available* (Soderstrom & Bjork, 2015).

From these and other experiments, Tolman concluded that learning involves the acquisition of knowledge rather than simply changes in outward behavior. According to Tolman (1932), an organism essentially learns "what leads to what." It learns to "expect" that a certain behavior will lead to a particular outcome in a specific situation.

Tolman is now recognized as an important forerunner of modern cognitive learning theorists (Gleitman, 1991; Olton, 1992). Many contemporary cognitive learning theorists follow Tolman in their belief that operant conditioning involves the *cognitive representation* of the relationship between a behavior and its consequence. Today, operant conditioning is seen as involving the cognitive *expectancy* that a given consequence will follow a given behavior (Bouton, 2007; Dickinson & Balleine, 2000).

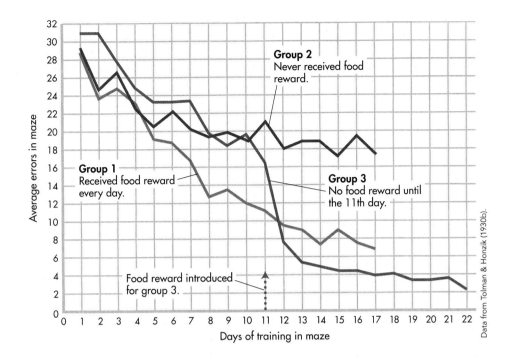

FIGURE 5.5 Latent Learning Beginning on day 1, the rats in group 1 received a food reward at the end of the maze, and the number of errors they made steadily decreased each day. The rats in group 2 never received a food reward; they made many errors as they wandered about in the maze. The rats in group 3 did not receive a food reward on days 1 through 10. Beginning on day 11, they received a food reward at the end of the maze. Notice the sharp decrease in errors on day 12 and thereafter. According to Tolman, the rats in group 3 had formed a cognitive map of the maze during the first 11 days of the experiment. Learning had taken place, but this learning was not demonstrated until reinforcement was present—a phenomenon that Tolman called *latent learning*.

Learned Helplessness: Expectations of Failure and Learning to Quit

Cognitive factors, particularly the role of expectation, are involved in another learning phenomenon, called *learned helplessness.* Learned helplessness was discovered by accident. Psychologists were trying to find out if classically conditioned responses would affect the process of operant conditioning in dogs. The dogs were strapped into harnesses and then exposed to a tone (the neutral stimulus) paired with an unpleasant but harmless electric shock (the UCS), which elicited fear (the UCR). After conditioning, the tone alone—now a CS—elicited the conditioned response of fear.

In the classical conditioning setup, the dogs were unable to escape or avoid the shock. But the next part of the experiment involved an operant conditioning procedure in which the dogs *could* escape the shock. The dogs were transferred to a special kind of operant chamber called a *shuttlebox,* which has a low barrier in the middle that divides the chamber in half. In the operant conditioning setup, the floor on one side of the cage became electrified. To escape the shock, all the dogs had to do was learn a simple escape behavior: Jump over the barrier when the floor was electrified. Normally, dogs learn this simple operant very quickly.

However, when the classically conditioned dogs were placed in the shuttlebox and one side became electrified, the dogs did *not* try to jump over the barrier. Rather than perform the operant to escape the shock, they just lay down and whined. Why?

To Steven F. Maier and **Martin Seligman** (b. 1942), two young psychology graduate students at the time, the explanation of the dogs' passive behavior seemed obvious. During the tone–shock pairings in the classical conditioning setup, the dogs *had learned that shocks were inescapable.* No active behavior that they engaged in—whether whining, barking, or struggling in the harness—would allow them to avoid or escape the shock. In other words, the dogs had "learned" to be helpless: They had developed the *cognitive expectation* that their behavior would have no effect on the environment.

To test this idea, Seligman and Maier (1967) used dogs in sets of three. The first dog could escape shocks by pushing a panel. The second dog was "yoked" to the first and could only escape the shocks if the first dog pushed the panel. The third dog was the control, receiving no shocks. After training, the dogs were transferred to the shuttlebox.

▲ Learned Helplessness on the Field In humans, learned helplessness can be produced when negative events are perceived as uncontrollable. Even highly trained athletes who believe that they have no control over the factors that led to their loss or poor performance are less likely to believe that they can succeed in the future (Coffee et al., 2009). They're also less likely to persist in the face of failure (Le Foll et al., 2008).

As predicted, the first and third dogs quickly learned to escape the shock delivered by the electrified floor by jumping over the barrier. But the second dog did not try to escape the shock, having learned that its efforts were futile. The name of this phenomenon is **learned helplessness**—*a phenomenon in which exposure to inescapable and uncontrollable aversive events produces passive behavior* (Maier et al., 1969).

Learned helplessness has been demonstrated in many different species, including primates, cats, rats, and fish (LoLordo, 2001). In humans, numerous studies found that exposure to uncontrollable, aversive events can produce passivity and learned helplessness. For example, researchers found that high school students who perceived their teachers to be controlling in the classroom tended to have higher levels of learned helplessness, which in turn predicted lower levels of academic achievement (Filippello et al., 2020). Similarly, university students who have experienced failure in previous academic settings may feel that academic tasks are beyond their control. Thus, when faced with the demands of exams, papers, and studying, rather than rising to the challenge, they may experience feelings of learned helplessness (Au et al., 2010). Such students may be prone to engage in self-defeating responses, such as procrastinating or giving up prematurely.

How can learned helplessness be overcome? In their early experiments, Seligman and Maier discovered that if they forcibly dragged the dogs over the shuttlebox barrier when the floor on one side became electrified, the dogs would eventually overcome their passivity and begin to jump over the barrier on their own (LoLordo, 2001; Seligman, 1992). For students who experience academic learned helplessness, establishing a sense of control over their schoolwork is the first step. Seeking knowledge about course requirements and assignments and setting goals, however modest, that can be successfully met can help students begin to acquire a sense of mastery over environmental challenges (Glynn et al., 2005).

Learned helplessness has been shown to play a role in psychological disorders, particularly depression, and in the ways that people respond to stressful events. For example, across a range of populations, including lower-caste women in India and Black people in the United States, discrimination has been shown to lead to learned helplessness, which in turn can lead to depression (Khubchandani et al., 2018; Madubata et al., 2018).

In the chapter on stress, health, and coping, we will take up the topic of learned helplessness again.

Operant Conditioning and Biological Predispositions: Misbehaving Chickens

Skinner and other behaviorists firmly believed that the general laws of operant conditioning applied to all animal species—whether they were pecking pigeons or bar-pressing rats. As Skinner (1956) wrote:

> Pigeon, rat, monkey, which is which? It doesn't matter. Of course, these species have behavioral repertoires which are as different as their anatomies. But once you have allowed for differences in the ways in which they make contact with the environment, and in the ways in which they act upon the environment, what remains of their behavior shows astonishingly similar properties.

However, psychologists studying operant conditioning, like those studying classical conditioning, found that an animal's natural behavior patterns *could* influence the learning of new behaviors. Consider the experiences of Keller and Marian Breland, two of Skinner's students at the University of Minnesota. Using operant conditioning, the Brelands trained thousands of animals of many different species to perform all sorts of complex tricks for shows and commercials (Bihm et al., 2010a, 2010b).

learned helplessness A phenomenon in which exposure to inescapable and uncontrollable aversive events produces passive behavior.

instinctive drift The tendency of an animal to revert to instinctive behaviors that can interfere with the performance of an operantly conditioned response.

But the Brelands weren't always successful in training the animals. For example, they tried to train a raccoon to pick up two coins and deposit them into a metal box. The raccoon easily learned to pick up the coins but seemed to resist putting them into the box. Rather than dropping the coins in the box, it would dip the coins in the box and take them out again. As time went on, this behavior became more persistent, even though the raccoon was not being reinforced for it. In fact, the raccoon's "misbehavior" was actually *preventing* it from getting reinforced for correct behavior (Bailey & Bailey, 1993).

The Brelands noted that such nonreinforced behaviors seemed to reflect innate, instinctive responses. Raccoons in the wild instinctively clean and moisten their food by dipping it in streams or rubbing it between their forepaws. These natural behaviors interfered with the operant behaviors the Brelands were attempting to condition. This phenomenon is called **instinctive drift**, *the tendency of an animal to revert to its instinctive behaviors that can interfere with the performance of an operantly conditioned response* (Bailey & Bailey, 1993).

The biological predisposition to perform such natural behaviors was strong enough to overcome the lack of reinforcement. These instinctual behaviors also *prevented the animals from engaging in the learned behaviors that would result in reinforcement.* Clearly, reinforcement is not the sole determinant of behavior. And, inborn or instinctive behavior patterns can interfere with the operant conditioning of arbitrary responses.

Before you go on to the next section, take a few minutes to review **Table 5.5** and make sure you understand the differences between classical and operant conditioning. Beyond conditioning, what about more complex types of learning, such as learning new concepts in school or skills in a workplace? Some educators believe that students differ with regard to the mode of instruction or study that is most effective for them, differences that are sometimes called *learning styles* (Pashler et al., 2008). We take a look at the claims of learning styles theories in the Critical Thinking box, "Do 'Learning Styles' Affect Learning?"

Joseph Scherschel/Getty Images

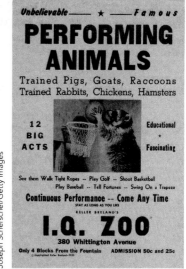

Robert E. Bailey

▲ **The IQ Zoo** Keller and Marian Breland's "IQ Zoo" was one of the most popular roadside attractions in the United States. Among its stars were basketball-playing raccoons, reindeer who operated a printing press, and chickens who played tic-tac-toe. Beyond entertainment, the Brelands were pioneers in the development of animal training and behavior modification techniques. Marian Breland was one of the first psychologists to use positive reinforcement to teach basic self-help skills to people with developmental disabilities and also helped train marine mammals for the U.S. Navy (Bihm et al., 2010a, 2010b).

TABLE 5.5

Comparing Classical and Operant Conditioning

	Classical Conditioning	Operant Conditioning
Type of behavior	Reflexive, involuntary behaviors	Nonreflexive, voluntary behaviors
Source of behavior	Elicited by stimulus	Emitted by organism
Basis of learning	Associating two stimuli: CS + UCS	Associating a response and the consequence that follows it
Responses conditioned	Physiological and emotional responses	Active behaviors that operate on the environment
Extinction process	Conditioned response decreases when the CS is repeatedly presented without the UCS	Responding decreases with elimination of reinforcing consequences
Cognitive aspects	Expectation that CS reliably predicts the UCS	Performance of behavior influenced by the expectation of reinforcement or punishment
Evolutionary influences	Innate predispositions influence how easily an association is formed between a particular stimulus and response	Behaviors similar to natural or instinctive behaviors are more readily conditioned

CRITICAL THINKING

Do "Learning Styles" Affect Learning?

When you want to learn something new, do you ask the teacher to show you, tell you, or let you try it? Do you best remember new information by writing it down, saying it out loud, or physically acting it out?

These types of questions are used to assess individual learning styles in classrooms in many countries. Although definitions vary, in general **learning styles** have been defined as *the idea, not supported by research, that people differ with regard to what mode of instruction is most effective for them* (Pashler et al., 2008; Willingham et al., 2015).

Research on learning styles theories is complicated because there are so many different theories, each with its own classification system. One review identified more than 84 different learning styles theories (Evans & Waring, 2012)! Despite this variety, all of the learning styles theories assert (1) that people learn in different ways, and (2) that learning is optimized when learners are instructed in their preferred learning style (Pashler et al., 2008; Rogowsky et al., 2015). Surveys have found widespread acceptance of learning styles theories among educators (Dekker et al., 2012; Howard-Jones, 2014).

Students obviously differ in their abilities and in the ways they approach new information. So it seems like common sense that matching an individual learner's preferences would help them learn new information (Knoll et al., 2017; Newton, 2015). Many people do believe that teaching to "learning styles" helps people learn better (Nancekivell et al., 2020). But does it? Let's look at two studies that directly tested this hypothesis.

First, Laura Massa and Richard Mayer (2006) assessed college students and non–college-educated participants and classified

Helping Students Learn According to learning style theorists, students learn more if the instructional style matches their individual learning style. But research suggests that all students benefit when teachers use a variety of sensory modalities—like this high school teacher who is using a physical model to teach students about the brain (Lethaby & Harris, 2016). The belief in learning styles can also have unexpected negative consequences. As Kris Vasquez (2009) points out, "Students may come to believe that their label defines what is possible for them, and in an ironic self-fulfilling prophecy, become limited by a tool that is meant to offer opportunity."

them into two groups: *verbalizers*, who preferred to receive instruction with words, and *visualizers*, who preferred to receive information with pictures. Participants worked on a computer-based lesson that provided help screens with pictures or help screens with text.

Learning styles theories would predict that the visualizers would perform better when supported with visual help options

Observational Learning: Imitating the Actions of Others

■ KEY THEME
In observational learning, we learn through watching and imitating the behaviors of others.

⩵ KEY QUESTIONS
- How did Albert Bandura demonstrate the principles of observational learning?
- What four mental processes are involved in observational learning?
- How has observational learning been shown in nonhuman animals?

Classical conditioning and operant conditioning emphasize the role of direct experiences in learning, such as directly experiencing a reinforcing or punishing stimulus following a particular behavior. But much human learning occurs *indirectly,* by watching what others do and then imitating it. **Observational learning** is *learning that occurs through observing the actions of others.*

Humans develop the capacity to learn through observation at a very early age. Studies of infants, some as young as two to three days, have shown that they will imitate a variety of actions, including opening their mouths, sticking out their tongues, and making other facial expressions (Leighton & Heyes, 2010).

learning styles The idea, not supported by research, that people differ with regard to what mode of instruction is most effective for them.

observational learning Learning that occurs through observing the actions of others.

and more poorly when given verbal, text-based support. Conversely, the verbalizers would be predicted to perform better when supported with text-based support and more poorly with visual support.

But in three different experiments, and using multiple measures, Massa and Mayer found no support for that hypothesis. Instead, they found that adding diagrams and illustrations to a written lesson helped *both* visualizers and verbalizers. These results are consistent with what Mayer (2001) has called the *multimedia effect:* Whatever their learning preference, people tend to learn better from words combined with pictures than from just words or just pictures.

Let's look at another study, by Beth Rogowsky and her colleagues (2015). Participants completed a popular learning style inventory that asked questions like, "Do you better remember new information by reading about it or listening to a discussion about it?" Based on their answers, participants were divided into two groups, *auditory learning style* and *visual learning style.* Participants were randomly assigned to either listen to a nonfiction audiobook or read an e-book version of the same book. They were later tested on their comprehension.

Learning styles theories would predict that the students would learn best when their preference matched the way information was delivered—that is, that the visual learners would learn more from the e-book and less from the audiobook and that the auditory learners would learn more from the audiobook and less from the e-book. But the results failed to support this hypothesis: There was no statistically significant relationship between learning style preference and instructional method. That is, this study did not provide evidence that auditory learners learn more from listening to an audiobook than from reading an e-book or that visual learners learn more from reading an e-book than from listening to an audiobook.

The bottom line? Students do differ in terms of their learning preferences and cognitive abilities. But the idea that there are individual learning styles is a myth. To date there is no good evidence supporting the hypothesis that students will learn more, or learn more effectively, if they are taught only in a way that matches their preferences or abilities (Clark, 2020; Lethaby & Harries, 2016; Willingham et al., 2015).

MYTH ◀ SCIENCE

Is it true that students will learn best if they are taught in a way that matches their learning style?

Without question, though, students tend to learn more when lessons have variety and involve many different sense modalities (Lethaby & Harries, 2016). So, rather than tailoring instruction to the requirements of individual learning styles, educators should present material in the way that best suits the content they are trying to convey (Riener & Willingham, 2010).

CRITICAL THINKING QUESTIONS

- What are some reasons that learning styles became so popular, despite the lack of evidence?
- How might learning style labels be self-limiting—that is, how might the label affect students' educational choices?
- How might learning style labels negatively affect teachers' instructional efforts in the classroom?

Psychologist **Albert Bandura** (1974) showed that observational learning involves active cognitive processes, not mere "mechanical copying," in a famous experiment involving the imitation of aggressive behavior. Four-year-old children separately watched a short film showing an adult playing aggressively with a Bobo doll—a large, inflated balloon doll that stands upright because the bottom is weighted with sand (Bandura, 1965). All the children saw the adult hit, kick, and punch the Bobo doll in the film.

However, there were three different versions of the film, each with a different ending. Some children saw the adult *reinforced* with soft drinks, candy, and snacks after performing the aggressive actions. Other children saw a version in which the aggressive adult was *punished* for the actions with a scolding and a spanking by another adult. Finally, some children watched a version of the film in which the aggressive adult experienced *no consequences.*

After seeing the film, each child was allowed to play alone in a room with several toys, including a Bobo doll. The playroom was equipped with a one-way window so that the child's behavior could be observed. Bandura found that the consequences the children observed in the film made a difference. Children who watched the film in which the adult was punished were much less likely to imitate the aggressive behaviors than were children who watched either of the other two film endings.

Bandura (1965) explained these results much as Tolman explained latent learning. Reinforcement is *not* essential for learning to occur. Rather, the *expectation of reinforcement* affects the *performance* of what has been learned.

▲ **Albert Bandura (1925–2021)**
Bandura contends that most human behavior is acquired through observational learning rather than through trial and error or direct experience of the consequences of our actions. Watching and processing information about the actions of others, including the consequences that occur, influence the likelihood that the behavior will be imitated.

Courtesy of Albert Bandura

⌃ The Classic Bobo Doll Experiment
In Bandura's classic study of observational learning, children watched a film showing an adult playing aggressively with an inflated Bobo doll. If they saw the adult rewarded with candy for the aggressive behavior or experience no consequences, the children were much more likely to imitate the behavior than if they saw the adult punished for the aggressive behavior (Bandura, 1965; Bandura et al., 1963).

✿ Achie/e

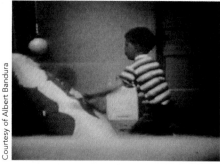

Courtesy of Albert Bandura

To view video clips of Bandura's classic study, go to **Achieve** and try **Concept Practice: Bandura's Bobo Doll Experiment.**

Bandura (1986) suggests that four cognitive processes interact to determine whether imitation will occur. First, you must pay *attention* to the other person's behavior. Second, you must *remember* the other person's behavior so that you can perform it at a later time. That is, you must form and store a mental representation of the behavior to be imitated. Third, you must transform this mental representation into *actions that you are capable of reproducing.* These three factors—attention, memory, and motor skills—are necessary for learning to take place through observation.

Fourth, there must be some *motivation* for you to imitate the behavior. This factor is crucial to the actual performance of the learned behavior. You are more likely to imitate a behavior if there is some expectation that doing so will produce reinforcement or reward. Thus, all the children were capable of imitating the adult's aggressive behavior. But the children who saw the aggressive adult being rewarded were much more likely to imitate the aggressive behavior than were the children who saw the adult punished. **Table 5.6** summarizes other factors that increase the likelihood of imitation.

From hamsters to great apes, many animal species have been found to learn novel behaviors through observation (Kendal et al., 2010; Reader & Biro, 2010). Even guppies can learn foraging behavior and escape routes from other guppies (Reader et al., 2003). And, just as with humans, motivational factors can influence observational learning. In one study, orangutans imitated the behavior of both humans and other orangutans, but they were more likely to imitate high-status or dominant models than low-status models (Russon & Galdikas, 1995).

TABLE 5.6

Factors That Increase Imitation

You're more likely to imitate:
- People who are rewarded for their behavior
- Warm, nurturing people
- People who have control over you or have the power to influence your life
- People who are similar to you in terms of age, sex, and interests
- People you perceive as having higher social status
- When the task to be imitated is not extremely easy or difficult
- If you lack confidence in your own abilities in a particular situation
- If the situation is unfamiliar or ambiguous
- If you've been rewarded for imitating the same behavior in the past

Source: Research from Bandura (1977, 1986, 1997).

Mirror Neurons and Observational Learning

Italian neuroscientist Giacomo Rizzolatti accidentally discovered *mirror neurons* (Winerman, 2005). He was studying which part of the brain fired when macaque monkeys performed certain actions, such as reaching for food like a peanut. But Rizzolatti and his team noticed something surprising: The same neurons that were activated when the monkeys held the peanut were *also* activated when the researcher held the peanut (even if it was before the monkey held the peanut). The same was true for the monkeys' brains when the researcher put the peanut in their own mouth and when the monkey put the peanut in their own mouth. The researchers were witnessing observational learning, but also something more. What was going on?

Rizzolatti and his colleagues had discovered **mirror neurons**, *brain cells that become activated both when individuals perform a motor act and when they observe the same motor act done by another individual* (Rizzolatti et al., 1996; Rizzolatti & Sinigaglia, 2016). The discovery of mirror neurons suggests that our brains have a hardwired (or built-in) capacity for imitation, a capacity that is the foundation for many critically important social behaviors, possibly even empathy. When we imitate someone doing something or even just observe them, we share their experience to some degree. As reporter Lea Winerman (2005) observes, "You're walking through a park when out of nowhere, the man in front of you gets smacked by an errant Frisbee. Automatically, you recoil in sympathy."

So far, we know more about mirror neurons in monkeys than in humans (Campbell & Cunnington, 2017). But mirror neurons might be the key to understanding why observational learning is so effective. In fact, researchers believe that we acquired this ability for empathy through the mirror neuron system as a result of evolution (de Waal & Preston, 2017). Moreover, understanding what happens when our mirror neuron system doesn't work might be a key to understanding some types of psychological disorders, such as autism spectrum disorder (Jeon & Lee, 2018).

Applications of Observational Learning

Bandura's finding that children will imitate film footage of aggressive behavior has more than just theoretical importance. One obvious implication has to do with the effects of negative behaviors that are depicted in films, social media, and television shows. Is there any evidence that television and other media can increase negative or destructive behaviors in viewers?

An important implication of Bandura's research is the relationship between media images of violence and behavior. We examine that relationship in the Critical Thinking box, "Does Exposure to Media Violence *Cause* Aggressive Behavior?" Given the potential impact of negative media images, let's look at the flip side. Is there any evidence that television and other media can encourage socially desirable behavior?

Consider the MTV reality series, *16 and Pregnant,* which featured the struggles of pregnant teens and young mothers. Some feared that the show was glamorizing teenage pregnancy. However, researchers Melissa Kearney and Phillip Levine (2014) found that teen birth rates in areas where the show was aired dropped 5.7 percent in the 18 months after its introduction. They also registered thousands of tweets and large spikes in Google searches for information about birth control shortly after each episode aired. It's important to note that the study is *correlational,* so it's impossible to say that viewing the TV show directly caused a drop in teen pregnancy. However, the findings highlight ways in which media can influence social outcomes in positive ways.

An effective application of observational learning has been using television and radio dramas to promote social change and healthy behaviors in Asia, Latin America, Africa, and the United States (Media for Health, 2011; Population Communications International, 2004). Pioneered by Mexican television executive Miguel Sabido, the first such attempt was a long-running serial drama that used observational learning principles to promote literacy among adults. The main storyline centered on a group of people in a literacy self-instruction group. In the year before the televised series, about 90,000 people were enrolled in such literacy groups. In the year during the series, enrollment jumped to 840,000 (Bandura, 1997). Since the success of this program, the nonprofit group PCI Media Impact (2018) has

Mirror neurons Brain cells that become activated both when individuals perform a motor act and when they observe the same motor act done by another individual.

^ **Animal Culture and Observational Learning** Like humans, nonhuman animal species, acquire and transmit distinct "cultures" or behavior patterns through observational learning (Allen et al., 2013; van de Waal et al., 2013). For example, wild adult vervet monkeys developed a preference for pink corn over blue corn after researchers treated the blue corn with a bitter-tasting substance (van de Waal et al., 2013). The colors were switched for nearby vervet monkey groups, who quickly became partial to the blue corn. After several months, the researchers stopped treating the corn, but the monkeys still ate only the preferred color of corn. And, so did infant monkeys who had never been exposed to bitter-tasting corn of either color. Imitating their mothers, they ate the same color corn that she did, and ignored the other corn.

CRITICAL THINKING

Does Exposure to Media Violence *Cause* Aggressive Behavior?

Bandura's early observational learning studies showed preschoolers enthusiastically mimicking the movie actions of an adult pummeling a Bobo doll. His research provided a powerful paradigm to study the effects of "entertainment" violence. Bandura found that observed actions were most likely to be imitated when:

- They were performed by a high-status, attractive model.
- The model is rewarded for his or her behavior.
- The model is not punished for his or her actions.

Over the past five decades, more than 1,000 studies have investigated the relationship between media depictions of violence and increases in aggressive behavior in the real world (see Bushman & Anderson, 2007; Bushman et al., 2014). We'll highlight some key findings here.

How Prevalent Is Violence in the Media?

An alarming amount of violence is depicted on American television and in movies. On average, American youth witness 1,000 rapes, murders, and assaults on television annually (Parents Television Council, 2007). More troubling, much of the violent behavior is depicted in ways that are known to *increase* the likelihood of imitation. For example, violent behavior is not punished and is often perpetrated by the "good guys." The long-term consequences of violence are rarely shown.

Is Exposure to Media Violence Linked to Aggressive Behavior?

Numerous research studies show that exposure to media violence produces short-term increases in laboratory measures of aggressive thoughts and behavior. And, hundreds of correlational studies demonstrate a link between exposure to violent media and aggressive behavior (see Anderson et al., 2010; Bushman et al., 2014; Murray, 2008).

Reviewing the accumulation of decades of research evidence, the American Psychological Association Task Force Assessment of Violent Video Games concluded that playing violent video games is related to increased aggressive behavior as well as reduced empathy toward others, although they did not find evidence for a link with criminal behavior (Calvert et al., 2017).

 MYTH ▶ SCIENCE

Is it true that viewing violent media is related to aggression?

What About Violent Video Games?

Many people wonder about the effects of violent digital games, especially "first-person shooter" games. Several comprehensive meta-analyses concluded that violent digital games increased aggressive thoughts, feelings, and behavior, although the increase was likely a small effect (see Anderson et al., 2010; Mathur & Vander-Weele, 2019; Prescott et al., 2018).

But other researchers strongly disagree with these conclusions (Ferguson, 2018; Ivory et al., 2015). For example, some researchers have *not* found an increase in aggression, including when violent and nonviolent games are carefully matched in terms of competitiveness and other factors (see Hilgard et al., 2019; Przbylski et al., 2014). Researchers also have not found long-term increases in violence; in one study of more than 3,000 children in Singapore, playing aggressive video games was not statistically related to measures of aggression two years later (Ferguson

Swen Pförtner/AP Images

& Wang, 2019). And, during the era in which video games increased in popularity and graphic violence, violent crime steadily *declined*, rather than increased, as you would expect if digital games were as dangerous as some claim (Ferguson, 2014), Some have even observed positive effects on social behavior of violent video games in which players must cooperate with each other (Halbrook et al., 2019).

So Does Violent Media *Cause* Violent Behavior?

Based on their review of the evidence, some psychologists, like Brad Bushman and his colleagues (2009), flatly concluded that "exposure to violent media increases aggression and violence." But many other psychologists are more cautious in their conclusions (Elson & Ferguson, 2014a, 2014b; Ivory et al., 2015).

It's important to note that the vast majority of studies on media violence and aggressive behavior are *correlational* (Ferguson & Kilbourn, 2009; Savage & Yancey, 2008). As you learned in Chapter 1, correlation does not necessarily imply causation. Even if two factors are strongly correlated, some other variable could be responsible for the association between the two factors. Experimental studies, on the other hand, *are* designed to demonstrate causality. However, most experimental studies involve artificial measures of aggressive behavior, which may *not* accurately measure the likelihood that a participant will act aggressively in real life.

Psychologists on both sides of the debate agree on one important point: Violent behavior is a complex phenomenon that is unlikely to have a single cause. They also generally agree that some viewers *are* highly susceptible to the negative effects of media violence (see Huesmann et al., 2013). Some researchers think that the time has come to go beyond the question of *whether* media violence causes aggressive behavior and focus instead on investigating the factors that are most likely to be associated with its harmful effects (Feshbach & Tangney, 2008; Ferguson & Konijn, 2015).

CRITICAL THINKING QUESTIONS

- Given the evidence, what conclusions can you draw about the effect of violent media and digital games on aggressive behavior?
- Why is it so difficult to design an experimental study that would demonstrate that violent media causes aggressive behavior?
- Given the general conclusion that some, but not all, viewers are likely to become more aggressive after viewing violent media, what should be done about media violence?

developed over 100 productions in 50 countries around the world. For a look at some of these programs, check out pcimedia.org/our-programs.

Education-entertainment programs are designed to fulfill the optimal conditions for observational learning to occur (Bandura, 2002). The programs are engaging, so viewers become involved in the dramas and pay *attention.* To ensure that the modeled messages are *remembered,* each episode concludes with a summary of the key points and issues. To enhance the viewers' *ability* to carry out the modeled behaviors, a variety of support programs and groups are put in place when the series airs. And *motivating* people to change their behaviors in line with the modeled behaviors is accomplished by depicting the benefits of doing so. Research studies have confirmed the positive impact of these popular shows (see Banerjee et al., 2019; Gessen-Edelsburg et al., 2010; Singhal et al., 2004). Beyond the effects of media depictions on behavior, observational learning has been applied in a wide variety of fields—such as education, job training, psychotherapy, counseling, and medicine use observational learning to help teach appropriate behaviors.

Closing Thoughts

One theme throughout this chapter has been the quest to discover general laws of learning that would apply across virtually all species and situations. John Watson was convinced that these laws were contained in the principles of classical conditioning. B. F. Skinner contended that they were to be found in the principles of operant conditioning. In a sense, they were both right. Thousands of experiments have shown that behavior can be influenced by classical and operant conditioning procedures. By and large, the general principles of classical and operant conditioning hold up quite well across a wide range of species and situations.

But you've also seen that the general principles of classical and operant conditioning are just that—general, not absolute. Such researchers as John Garcia and Marian and Keller Breland recognized the importance of a species' evolutionary and biological heritage in acquiring new behaviors. Other researchers, such as Edward Tolman and Robert Rescorla, drew attention to the important role played by cognitive processes in learning. And Albert Bandura's investigations of observational learning underscored that classical and operant conditioning principles could not account for all learning.

Another prominent theme has been the adaptive nature of learning. Faced with an ever-changing environment, an organism's capacity to learn is critical to adaptation and survival. Clearly, there are survival advantages in learning that a neutral stimulus can signal an important upcoming event, as in classical conditioning. An organism also enhances its odds of survival by being responsive to the consequences of its actions, as in operant conditioning. And, by observing the actions and consequences experienced by others, behaviors can be acquired through imitation. These basic learning principles are demonstrated with such consistency across so many species. In the final analysis, it's probably safe to say that the most important consequence of learning is that it promotes the adaptation of many species, including humans, to their unique environments.

 PSYCH FOR YOUR LIFE

Using Learning Principles to Improve Your Self-Control

Self-control often involves choosing between two reinforcers: (1) a long-term reinforcer that will provide gratification at some point in the future or (2) a short-term reinforcer that provides immediate gratification but gets in the way of obtaining a long-term reinforcer. Objectively, the benefits of the long-term reinforcer typically far outweigh the benefits associated with the short-term, immediate reinforcer. Yet despite our commitment to the long-term goal, sometimes we choose a short-term reinforcer that conflicts with it (Galla & Duckworth, 2015). Why?

Mediae Company Ltd.

⌃ **Makutano Junction** Regularly watched by over 7 million viewers in Kenya alone, *Makutano Junction* is an award-winning soap opera that teaches as it entertains. Set in a small Kenyan town, it uses dramatic stories, humor, and appealing characters to educate viewers about such serious topics as mental and physical health, family life and relationships, government corruption, and even modern farming practices. Viewers can send text messages to request additional information about topics covered on the show, such as how to prevent malaria or how to live with HIV or AIDS (P. Smith, 2010). Some 30,000 messages are received every year. You can watch episodes on YouTube or at the Makutano Junction Web site: http://www.makutanojunction.org/en/thesoap.html

The Shifting Value of Reinforcers

The key is that *the relative value of reinforcers can shift over time* (Ainslie, 1975, 1992; Rachlin, 1974, 2000). Suppose you sign up for an 8:00 A.M. class that meets every Tuesday morning. Every Monday night as you set your alarm, you weigh the value of two different reinforcers. You'd like to get a good grade in the class (long-term reinforcer). But you'd also like to sleep in (short-term reinforcer). Neither reinforcer is immediately available, and it's obvious that earning a good grade outweighs the value of one hour of extra sleep. But when your alarm rings on Tuesday morning, the reinforcer of extra sleep is immediately available, increasing its value. Meanwhile, the value of a good grade has not changed. At the moment you make your decision, you choose whichever reinforcer has the greater apparent value to you. In other words, you'll probably stay in your bed.

When you understand how the values of reinforcers shift over time, the tendency to cave in to available short-term reinforcers starts to make more sense. The availability of an immediate, short-term reinforcer can temporarily outweigh the value of a long-term reinforcer in the distant future (Steel, 2007). How can you counteract these momentary surges in the value of short-term reinforcers? Fortunately, there are several strategies that can help you overcome the temptation of short-term reinforcers and improve your self-control (Fishbach & Converse, 2010; Kruglanski et al., 2010).

Strategy 1: Precommitment

Precommitment involves making an advance commitment to your long-term goal, one that will be difficult to change when a conflicting reinforcer becomes available (Fujita & Roberts, 2010). In the case of getting to class on time, a precommitment could involve setting multiple alarms and putting them far enough away that you will be forced to get out of bed to shut each of them off.

Strategy 2: Self-Reinforcement

Sometimes long-term goals seem so far away that your sense of potential future reinforcement seems weak compared with immediate reinforcers. One strategy to increase the value of the long-term reinforcer is to use self-reinforcement for current behaviors related to your long-term goal (Fishbach & Converse, 2010). For example, promise yourself that if you spend two hours studying in the library, you'll reward yourself by watching a movie.

It's important, however, to reward yourself only *after* you perform the desired behavior. If you say to yourself, "Rather than study tonight, I'll go to this party and make up for it by studying tomorrow," you've blown it. You've just reinforced yourself for *not* studying! This would be akin to trying to increase bar-pressing behavior in a rat by giving the rat a pellet of food *before* it pressed the bar. Obviously, this contradicts the basic principle of positive reinforcement in which behavior is *followed* by the reinforcing stimulus.

Strategy 3: Stimulus Control

Remember, environmental stimuli can act as discriminative stimuli that "set the occasion" for a particular response (Duckworth et al., 2016; Kruglanski et al., 2010). In effect, the environmental cues that precede a behavior can acquire some control over future occurrences of that behavior. So be aware of the environmental cues that are likely to trigger unwanted behaviors, such as studying in the kitchen (a cue for eating) or in an easy chair in the living room (a cue for watching television). Then replace those cues with others that will help you achieve your long-term goals.

For example, always study in a specific location, whether it's in the library, in an empty classroom, or at a table or desk in a certain corner of your apartment. Over time, these environmental cues will become associated with the behavior of studying.

Strategy 4: Focus on the Delayed Reinforcer

The cognitive aspects of learning also play a role in choosing behaviors associated with long-term reinforcers (Mischel, 1996; Mischel et al., 2004). When faced with a choice between an immediate and a delayed reinforcer, focus your attention on the delayed reinforcer. You'll be less likely to impulsively choose the short-term reinforcer (Kruglanski et al., 2010).

Practically speaking, this means that if your goal is to save money for school, don't fantasize about a new car or expensive shoes. Focus instead on the delayed reinforcement of achieving your long-term goal (Kross & Mischel, 2010). Imagine yourself proudly walking across the stage and receiving your college degree. Visualize yourself fulfilling your long-term career goals. Practicing mindfulness, a focus on an acceptance of your present circumstances, can help provide the self-control necessary to resist the short-term reinforcer (Smith et al., 2019).

Strategy 5: Observe Good Role Models

Observational learning is another strategy you can use to improve self-control (Maddux et al., 2010). In a series of classic studies, psychologist Walter Mischel found that children who observed others choose a delayed reinforcer over an immediate reinforcer were more likely to choose the delayed reinforcer themselves (Kross & Mischel, 2010; Mischel, 1996). So look for good role models. Observing others who are currently behaving in ways that will ultimately help them realize their long-term goals can make it easier for you to do the same.

⬈ CHAPTER REVIEW

Learning

 **Achieve,** Macmlllan Learning's online study platform, features the full e-book of *Discovering Psychology,* the **LearningCurve** adaptive quizzing system, videos, and a variety of activities to boost your learning. Visit **Achieve** at macmillanlearning.com.

KEY PEOPLE

Albert Bandura, p. 177

John Garcia, p. 157

Mary Cover Jones, p. 155

Ivan Pavlov, p. 149

Rosalie Rayner, p. 153

Robert A. Rescorla, p. 156

Martin Seligman, p. 173

B. F. Skinner, p. 161

Edward L. Thorndike, p. 160

Edward C. Tolman, p. 171

Charles Henry Turner, p. 151

John Watson, p. 153

KEY TERMS

learning, p. 148

conditioning, p. 148

classical conditioning, p. 149

unconditioned stimulus (UCS), p. 149

unconditioned response (UCR), p. 149

conditioned stimulus (CS), p. 150

conditioned response (CR), p. 150

stimulus generalization, p. 151

stimulus discrimination, p. 152

higher order conditioning (second-order conditioning), p. 152

extinction (in classical conditioning), p. 152

spontaneous recovery, p. 152

behaviorism, p. 153

placebo response, p. 156

taste aversion, p. 157

biological preparedness, p. 159

law of effect, p. 160

operant, p. 161

operant conditioning, p. 161

reinforcement, p. 161

discriminative stimulus, p. 161

positive reinforcement, p. 162

negative reinforcement, p. 162

primary reinforcer, p. 163

conditioned reinforcer, p. 163

punishment, p. 164

positive punishment, p. 164

negative punishment, p. 164

operant chamber (Skinner box), p. 166

shaping, p. 168

continuous reinforcement, p. 168

partial reinforcement, p. 168

extinction (in operant conditioning), p. 169

partial reinforcement effect, p. 169

schedules of reinforcement, p. 169

behavior modification, p. 170

cognitive map, p. 172

latent learning, p. 172

learned helplessness, p. 174

instinctive drift, p. 175

learning styles, p. 176

observational learning, p. 176

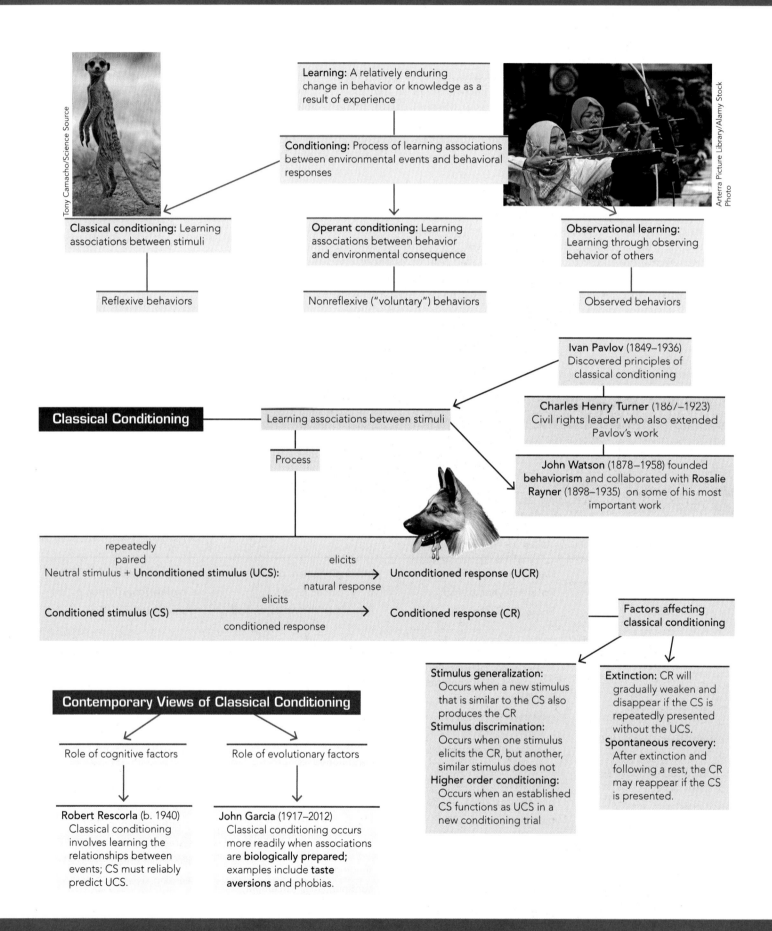

Learning: A relatively enduring change in behavior or knowledge as a result of experience

Conditioning: Process of learning associations between environmental events and behavioral responses

Classical conditioning: Learning associations between stimuli

Operant conditioning: Learning associations between behavior and environmental consequence

Observational learning: Learning through observing behavior of others

Reflexive behaviors

Nonreflexive ("voluntary") behaviors

Observed behaviors

Tony Camacho/Science Source

Arterra Picture Library/Alamy Stock Photo

Classical Conditioning

Learning associations between stimuli

Ivan Pavlov (1849–1936) Discovered principles of classical conditioning

Charles Henry Turner (186/–1923) Civil rights leader who also extended Pavlov's work

John Watson (1878–1958) founded **behaviorism** and collaborated with **Rosalie Rayner** (1898–1935) on some of his most important work

Process

repeatedly paired
Neutral stimulus + Unconditioned stimulus (UCS): →(elicits / natural response)→ Unconditioned response (UCR)

Conditioned stimulus (CS) →(elicits / conditioned response)→ Conditioned response (CR)

Factors affecting classical conditioning

Stimulus generalization: Occurs when a new stimulus that is similar to the CS also produces the CR
Stimulus discrimination: Occurs when one stimulus elicits the CR, but another, similar stimulus does not
Higher order conditioning: Occurs when an established CS functions as UCS in a new conditioning trial

Extinction: CR will gradually weaken and disappear if the CS is repeatedly presented without the UCS.
Spontaneous recovery: After extinction and following a rest, the CR may reappear if the CS is presented.

Contemporary Views of Classical Conditioning

Role of cognitive factors

Role of evolutionary factors

Robert Rescorla (b. 1940) Classical conditioning involves learning the relationships between events; CS must reliably predict UCS.

John Garcia (1917–2012) Classical conditioning occurs more readily when associations are **biologically prepared;** examples include **taste aversions** and phobias.

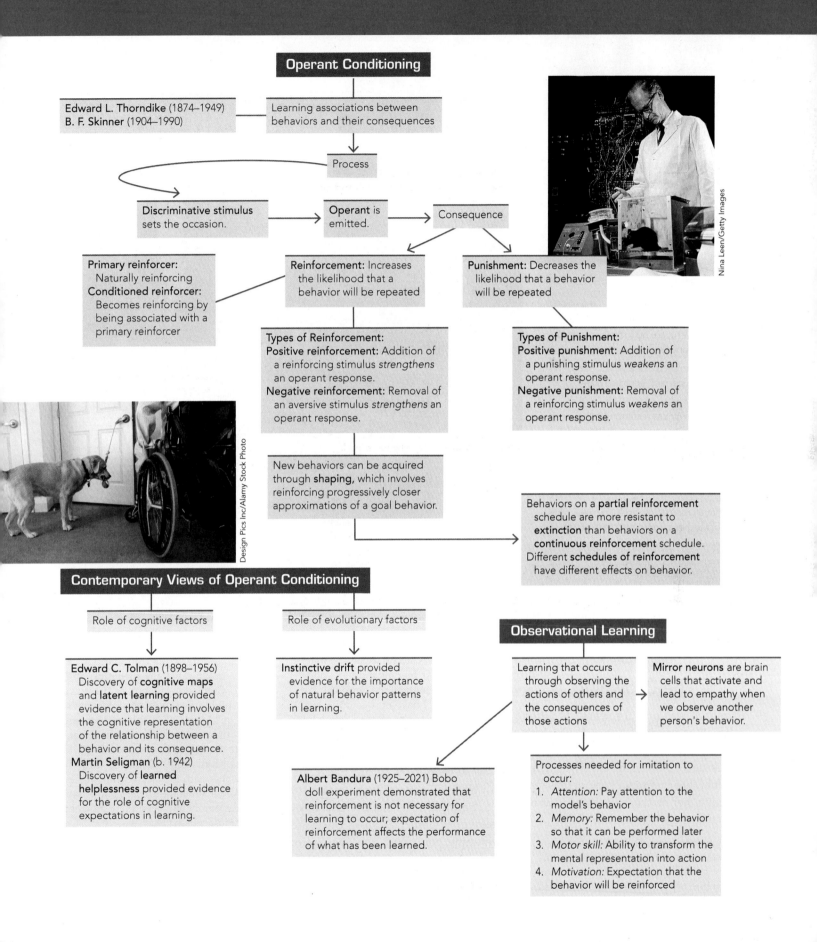

Operant Conditioning

Edward L. Thorndike (1874–1949)
B. F. Skinner (1904–1990)

Learning associations between behaviors and their consequences

Process

Discriminative stimulus sets the occasion.

Operant is emitted.

Consequence

Primary reinforcer:
  Naturally reinforcing
Conditioned reinforcer:
  Becomes reinforcing by being associated with a primary reinforcer

Reinforcement: Increases the likelihood that a behavior will be repeated

Punishment: Decreases the likelihood that a behavior will be repeated

Types of Reinforcement:
Positive reinforcement: Addition of a reinforcing stimulus *strengthens* an operant response.
Negative reinforcement: Removal of an aversive stimulus *strengthens* an operant response.

Types of Punishment:
Positive punishment: Addition of a punishing stimulus *weakens* an operant response.
Negative punishment: Removal of a reinforcing stimulus *weakens* an operant response.

New behaviors can be acquired through **shaping,** which involves reinforcing progressively closer approximations of a goal behavior.

Behaviors on a **partial reinforcement** schedule are more resistant to **extinction** than behaviors on a **continuous reinforcement** schedule. Different **schedules of reinforcement** have different effects on behavior.

Nina Leen/Getty Images

Design Pics Inc/Alamy Stock Photo

Contemporary Views of Operant Conditioning

Role of cognitive factors

Role of evolutionary factors

Edward C. Tolman (1898–1956)
Discovery of **cognitive maps** and **latent learning** provided evidence that learning involves the cognitive representation of the relationship between a behavior and its consequence.
Martin Seligman (b. 1942)
Discovery of **learned helplessness** provided evidence for the role of cognitive expectations in learning.

Instinctive drift provided evidence for the importance of natural behavior patterns in learning.

Albert Bandura (1925–2021) Bobo doll experiment demonstrated that reinforcement is not necessary for learning to occur; expectation of reinforcement affects the performance of what has been learned.

Observational Learning

Learning that occurs through observing the actions of others and the consequences of those actions

Mirror neurons are brain cells that activate and lead to empathy when we observe another person's behavior.

Processes needed for imitation to occur:
1. *Attention:* Pay attention to the model's behavior
2. *Memory:* Remember the behavior so that it can be performed later
3. *Motor skill:* Ability to transform the mental representation into action
4. *Motivation:* Expectation that the behavior will be reinforced

Is it true . . .

► That "flashbulb memories," the vivid memories you form after an important, dramatic event, are no more accurate than other memories?

► That memory is like a video recorder—it preserves a perfect record of your experience?

► That eyewitness testimony is the most reliable form of courtroom evidence?

► That it's common to completely repress memories of traumatic events but that such events can be accurately remembered under hypnosis?

► That all memories, even complex ones, are located in a single part of the brain?

Memory

PROLOGUE

The Drowning

Elizabeth was only 14 years old when her mother drowned. Although Elizabeth remembered many things about visiting her Uncle Joe's home in Pennsylvania that summer, her memory of the details surrounding her mother's death had always been hazy. As she explained:

> In my mind I've returned to that scene many times, and each time the memory gains weight and substance. I can see the cool pine trees, smell their fresh tarry breath, feel the lake's algae-green water on my skin, taste Uncle Joe's iced tea with fresh-squeezed lemon. But the death itself was always vague and unfocused. I never saw my mother's body, and I could not imagine her dead. The last memory I have of my mother was her tiptoed visit the evening before her death, the quick hug, the whispered, "I love you."

Some 30 years later, at her Uncle Joe's 90th birthday party, Elizabeth was told by a relative that she had been the one to discover her mother's body in Uncle Joe's swimming pool. With this realization, memories that had eluded Elizabeth for decades began to come back:

> The memories began to drift back, slow and unpredictable, like the crisp piney smoke from the evening campfires. I could see myself, a thin, dark-haired girl, looking into the flickering blue-and-white pool. My mother, dressed in her nightgown, is floating facedown. "Mom? Mom?" I ask the question several times, my voice rising in terror. I start screaming. I remember the police cars, their lights flashing, and the stretcher with the clean, white blanket tucked in around the edges of the body. The memory had been there all along, but I just couldn't reach it.

As the memory crystallized, it suddenly made sense to Elizabeth why she had always felt haunted by her vague memories of the circumstances surrounding her mother's death. And it also seemed to

CHAPTER 6

explain, in part, why she had always been so fascinated by the topic of memory.

However, several days later, Elizabeth learned that the relative had been wrong—it was *not* Elizabeth who discovered her mother's body, but her aunt Pearl. Other relatives confirmed that Aunt Pearl had been the one who found Elizabeth's mother in the swimming pool. Yet Elizabeth's memory had seemed so real! How could she remember something that never happened?

The Elizabeth in this story is none other than psychologist Elizabeth Loftus, an internationally recognized expert on memory distortions, including those that occur in everyday life and those experienced by eyewitnesses to crimes and accidents.

In this chapter, we'll consider the psychological and biological processes that underlie how memories are formed and forgotten. As you'll see, memory distortions such as the one Elizabeth Loftus experienced are relatively common. By the end of this chapter, you'll have a much better understanding of the memory process, including the reason that Elizabeth's "memory" of finding her mother's body seemed so real. ❀

memory The mental processes that enable you to encode, retain, and retrieve information over time.

encoding The process of transforming information into a form that can be entered into and retained by the memory system.

storage The process of retaining information in memory so that it can be used at a later time.

retrieval The process of recovering information stored in memory so that we are consciously aware of it.

stage model of memory A model describing memory as consisting of three distinct stages: sensory memory, short-term memory, and long-term memory.

sensory memory The stage of memory that registers information from the environment and holds it for a very brief period of time.

▲ **Memories Can Involve All Your Senses** Think back to a particularly memorable experience from your high school years. Can you conjure up vivid memories of smells, sights, sounds, or emotions associated with that experience? In the years to come, these friends may remember many sensory details associated with their senior prom.

FIGURE 6.1 Overview of the Stage Model of Memory The stage model of memory describes three distinct stages—sensory memory, short-term memory, and long-term memory. The idea behind the stage model is that information is transferred from one memory stage to another (see arrows).

Introduction: What Is Memory?

■ KEY THEME
Memory is a group of related mental processes that are involved in acquiring, storing, and retrieving information.

⹀ KEY QUESTIONS
* What are encoding, storage, and retrieval?
* What is the stage model of memory?
* What are the nature and function of sensory memory?

Like Elizabeth's memories of her uncle's home, memories can be vivid and evoke intense emotions. We can conjure up distinct memories that involve all our senses, including smells, sounds, and even tactile sensations. For example, close your eyes and try to recall the feeling of rain-soaked clothes against your skin, the smell of popcorn, and the sound of the half-time buzzer during a high school basketball game.

Memory refers to *the mental processes that enable you to encode, retain, and retrieve information over time*. Rather than being a single process, memory involves three fundamental processes: *encoding, storage,* and *retrieval.*

Encoding refers to *the process of transforming information into a form that can be entered into and retained by the memory system.* For example, to memorize the definition of a key term that appears in this textbook, you would visually *encode* the patterns of lines and dots on the page as meaningful words that could be retained by your memory. **Storage** is *the process of retaining information in memory so that it can be used at a later time.* **Retrieval** is *the process of recovering information stored in memory so that we are consciously aware of it.*

The Stage Model of Memory

No single model has been shown to capture all aspects of human memory (Baddeley et al., 2009; Tulving, 2007). However, the basic workings of memory are explained by the **stage model of memory**. In this model, shown in **Figure 6.1**, memory involves three distinct stages: *sensory memory, short-term memory,* and *long-term memory* (Atkinson & Shiffrin, 1968; Shiffrin & Atkinson, 1969). The stage model is based on the idea that information is *transferred* from one memory stage to another.

The first stage of memory is **sensory memory**, *the stage of memory that registers information from the environment and holds it for a very brief period of time* (Treisman & Lages, 2013). After three seconds or less, the information fades. Think of your sensory memory as an internal camera that continuously takes "snapshots" of your surroundings. With each snapshot, you momentarily focus your attention on specific details. Almost instantly, the snapshot fades, only to be replaced by another.

Sensory Memory		Short-Term Memory		Long-Term Memory
• Environmental information is registered		• New information is transferred from sensory memory	**Encoding and Storage** →	• Information that has been encoded in short-term memory is stored
• Large capacity for information	**Attention** →	• Old information is retrieved from long-term memory		• Unlimited capacity for information
• Duration: 1/4 second to 3 seconds		• Limited capacity for information	← **Retrieval**	• Duration: potentially permanent
		• Duration: approx. 20 seconds		

During the very brief time the information is held in sensory memory, you "select," or pay *attention* to, just a few aspects of all the environmental information being registered. While studying, for example, you focus your attention on one page of your textbook, ignoring other environmental stimuli. The information you select from sensory memory is important because this information is transferred to the second stage of memory, *short-term memory.*

Short-term memory refers to *the active stage of memory in which information is stored for up to about 20 seconds* (Peterson & Peterson, 1959). This working memory system temporarily holds all the information you are currently thinking about or consciously aware of. Over the course of any given day, vast amounts of information flow through your short-term memory. Most of this information quickly fades and is forgotten in a matter of seconds. However, some of the information that is actively processed in short-term memory may be encoded for storage in long-term memory.

Long-term memory is *the stage of memory that represents the long-term storage of information.* This third memory stage represents what most people typically think of as memory—the long-term storage of information, potentially for a lifetime. It's important to note that the transfer of information between short-term and long-term memory goes two ways. Not only does information flow from short-term memory to long-term memory, but much information also flows in the other direction, from long-term memory to short-term memory.

Consider a routine cognitive task, such as carrying on a conversation. Such tasks involve processing current sensory data and retrieving relevant stored information, such as the meaning of individual words. In the next few sections, we'll describe each of the stages of memory in more detail.

▲ The Interaction of Memory Stages in Everyday Life Imagine cooking a favorite dish from memory. How might each of your memory stages be involved in the food preparation? What kinds of information would be transferred from sensory memory and retrieved from long-term memory?

Sensory Memory: Fleeting Impressions of the World

You're engrossed in watching a suspenseful movie. From another room, your roommate calls out, "Where'd you put my car keys?" You respond with, "What?" A split second later, the question registers in your mind. Before the other person can repeat the question, you reply, "Oh. They're on your desk."

You could answer the question because your *sensory memory* registered and preserved the other person's words for a few fleeting seconds—just long enough for you to recall what had been said to you while your attention was focused on the movie. Sensory memory stores a detailed record of a sensory experience, but only for a few seconds at the most.

The Duration of Sensory Memory: It Was There Just a Split Second Ago! The characteristics of visual sensory memory were first identified largely through the research of psychologist **George Sperling** in 1960. In his experiment, Sperling flashed the images of 12 letters on a screen for one-twentieth of a second. The letters were arranged in four rows of three letters each. Participants focused their attention on the screen and, immediately after the screen went blank, reported as many letters as they could remember.

On average, participants could report only four or five of the 12 letters. However, several participants claimed that they had actually seen *all* the letters but that the complete image had faded from their memory as they spoke, disappearing before they could verbally report more than four or five letters. Sperling's classic experiment demonstrated that our visual sensory memory holds a great deal of information very briefly, for about half a second. This information is available just long enough for us

short-term memory The active stage of memory in which information is stored for up to about 20 seconds.

long-term memory The stage of memory that represents the long-term storage of information.

to pay attention to specific elements that are significant to us at that moment. This meaningful information is then transferred from the very brief storage of sensory memory to the somewhat longer storage of short-term memory.

Types of Sensory Memory: Pick a Sense, Any Sense! Memory researchers believe there is a separate sensory memory for each sense — vision, hearing, touch, smell, taste, and so on (Werkhoven & van Erp, 2013). Of the different senses, however, visual and auditory sensory memories have been the most thoroughly studied. *Visual sensory memory* is sometimes referred to as *iconic memory* because it is the brief memory of an image, or *icon*. *Auditory sensory memory* is sometimes referred to as *echoic memory*, meaning a brief memory that is like an *echo*.

Researchers have found slight differences in the duration of sensory memory for visual and auditory information. Your visual sensory memory typically holds an image of your environment for about one-quarter to one-half second before it is replaced by yet another overlapping "snapshot." This is easy to demonstrate. Quickly wave a pencil back and forth in front of your face. Do you see the fading image of the pencil trailing behind it? That's your visual sensory memory at work. It momentarily holds the snapshot of the environmental image you see before it is almost instantly replaced by another overlapping image.

Your auditory sensory memory holds sound information a little longer, up to three or four seconds. This brief auditory sensory trace for sound allows you to hear speech as continuous words, or a series of musical notes as a melody, rather than as disjointed sounds. It also explains why you can "remember" something that you momentarily don't "hear," as in the example of your roommate asking you where the car keys were.

An important function of sensory memory is to very briefly store sensory impressions so that they overlap slightly with one another. This is why we perceive the world around us as continuous rather than as a series of disconnected visual images or disjointed sounds.

▲ **Perception and Sensory Memory Traces** Because your visual sensory memory holds information for a fraction of a second before it fades, rapidly presented stimuli overlap and appear continuous. Thus, you perceive the separate blades of a rapidly spinning windmill as a smooth blur of motion. Similarly, you perceive a lightning bolt streaking across the sky as continuous even though it is actually three or more separate bolts of electricity.

Short-Term Memory and Working Memory: The Workshop of Consciousness

■ KEY THEME
Short-term memory provides temporary storage for information transferred from sensory and long-term memory.

▭ KEY QUESTIONS
• What are the duration and capacity of short-term memory?
• How can you overcome the limitations of short-term memory?
• What are the main components of Baddeley's model of working memory?

You can think of *short-term memory* as the "workshop" of consciousness. It is the stage of memory in which information transferred from sensory memory *and* information retrieved from long-term memory become conscious. When you recall a past event or mentally add two numbers, the information is temporarily held and processed in your short-term memory. Your short-term memory also allows you to make sense out of this sentence by holding the beginning of the sentence in active memory while you read the rest of the sentence. Thus, short-term memory provides temporary storage for information that is currently being used in some conscious cognitive activity.

The Duration of Short-Term Memory: Going, Going, Gone! Information in short-term memory lasts longer than information in sensory memory, but its duration is still very short. Estimates vary, but generally you can hold most types of information in short-term memory up to about 20 seconds before it's forgotten (Peterson & Peterson, 1959). However, information can be maintained in short-term memory if it is *rehearsed*, or repeated, over and over. Consciously rehearsing information will maintain it in short-term memory. This process is called **maintenance rehearsal**, *the mental or verbal repetition of information in order to maintain it beyond the usual 20-second duration of short-term memory.* For example, suppose that you decide to order a pizza for yourself and some friends. You look up the number and mentally rehearse it until you can dial the phone.

Information that is *not* actively rehearsed is rapidly lost. Why? One possible explanation is that information that is not maintained by rehearsal simply fades away, or *decays*, with the passage of time. Another potential cause of forgetting in short-term memory is *interference* from new or competing information (Baddeley, 2002; Nairne, 2002). For example, if you are distracted by one of your friends asking you a question before you dial the pizza place, your memory of the phone number will quickly evaporate. Interference may also explain the irritating experience of forgetting someone's name just moments after you're introduced to them. If you engage the new acquaintance in conversation without rehearsing their name, the conversation may "bump" the person's name out of your short-term memory.

The Capacity of Short-Term Memory: So That's Why There Were Seven Dwarfs!

Along with the relatively short duration, short-term memory also has a relatively limited capacity. This is easy to demonstrate. Take a look at the nearby rows of numbers. If you've got a friend handy who's willing to serve as your research participant, simply read the numbers out loud, one row at a time, and ask your friend to repeat them back to you in the same order. Try to read the numbers at a steady rate, about one per second. Note each row that they correctly remember.

How many numbers could your friend repeat accurately? Most likely, they could correctly repeat between five and nine numbers. That's what psychologist George Miller (1956) described as the limits of short-term memory in a classic paper titled "The Magical Number Seven, Plus or Minus Two." Miller believed that the capacity of short-term memory is limited to about seven items, or bits of information, at one time (Cowan, 2015). It's no accident that local telephone numbers are seven digits long (Cowan et al., 2004).

So what happens when your short-term memory storage is full? New information *displaces*, or bumps out, currently held information. One way to avoid the loss of information from short-term memory is by consciously repeating the information you want to remember. This repetition keeps the current information active in short-term memory and prevents it from being displaced by new information.

Although the capacity of your short-term memory is limited, there are ways to increase the amount of information you can hold in short-term memory at any given moment. To illustrate this point, let's try another short-term memory demonstration. Read this sequence of letters: U A V F C I D B D S A I. Now close your eyes and try to repeat the letters out loud in the same order.

How many letters could you remember? Unless you have an exceptional short-term memory, you probably could not repeat the whole sequence correctly. Now try this sequence of letters: D V D F B I U S A C I A.

You probably managed the second sequence with no trouble at all, even though it is made up of exactly the same letters as the first sequence. The ease with which you handled the second sequence demonstrates **chunking**—*increasing the amount of information that can be held in short-term memory by grouping related items together into a single unit, or chunk.* The first letter sequence was perceived as 12 separate items and probably exceeded your short-term memory's capacity. But the second letter sequence was perceived as only four "chunks" of information, which you easily remembered: DVD, FBI, USA, and CIA. Thus, chunking can increase the amount of information held in short-term memory. But to do so, chunking also often involves the retrieval of meaningful information from *long-term memory*, such as the meaning of the initials FBI (Baddeley et al., 2010).

Row 1 — 8 7 4 6
Row 2 — 3 4 9 6 2
Row 3 — 4 2 7 7 1 6
Row 4 — 5 1 4 0 8 1 3
Row 5 — 1 8 3 9 5 5 2 1
Row 6 — 2 1 4 9 7 5 2 4 8
Row 7 — 9 3 7 1 0 4 2 8 9 7
Row 8 — 7 1 9 0 4 2 6 0 4 1 8

▲ **Demonstration of Short-Term Memory Capacity**

maintenance rehearsal The mental or verbal repetition of information in order to maintain it beyond the usual 20-second duration of short-term memory.

chunking Increasing the amount of information that can be held in short-term memory by grouping related items together into a single unit, or *chunk*.

The basic principle of chunking is incorporated into many numbers that we need to remember. Long strings of identification numbers, such as Social Security numbers or credit card numbers, are usually broken up by hyphens or spaces so that you can chunk them easily.

Not every memory researcher accepts that short-term memory is limited to exactly seven items, plus or minus two. Over the half-century since the publication of Miller's classic article, researchers have challenged the seven-item limit (Cowan et al., 2007; Jonides et al., 2008). Current research suggests that the true "magical number" is more likely to be *four plus or minus one* rather than *seven plus or minus two* (Cowan, 2010, 2015).

Cognitive psychologist Nelson Cowan (2001, 2005, 2010) believes that the type of stimuli used in many short-term memory tests has led researchers to overestimate its capacity. Typically, such memory tests use lists of letters, numbers, or words. According to Cowan, many people *automatically* chunk such stimuli to help remember them. For example, even seemingly random numbers may be easily associated with a date, an address, or another familiar number sequence.

To overcome this tendency, Jeffrey Rouder and his colleagues (2008) used a simple visual stimulus instead of a sequence of numbers, letters, or words. The memory task? Remembering the position of colored squares on a computer screen. In this and similar studies, participants could hold only three or four items in their short-term memory at a time. Thus, most researchers today believe that the capacity of short-term memory is no more than about three to four items at a time when chunking is not an option (Cowan, 2010, 2015; Mandler, 2013).

Whether the "magic number" is four or seven, the point remains: Short-term memory has a limited number of mental "slots" for information. Chunking can increase the amount of information held in each slot, but the number of slots is still limited.

From Short-Term Memory to Working Memory

Our discussion of short-term memory has so far focused on just one type of information—verbal or acoustic codes, that is, speech-like stimuli that we can mentally recite. Lists of numbers, letters, words, or other items fall into this category.

But suppose you're shopping with a friend who asks whether you think a particular chair will fit in their dorm room. To answer, you need to call up a mental image of their room from your long-term memory and mentally manipulate it as you imagine placing the chair in different locations. Thus, along with holding information in our short-term memory, we also use short-term memory to temporarily store and manipulate information, whether it be mental images or mental arithmetic.

Many memory researchers differentiate between *short-term memory*, which refers to the simple temporary storage of information, and *working memory*, which refers to actively processing and manipulating the information that you are holding in awareness, as in this example (Hardman & Cowan, 2016). The terms *working memory* and *short-term memory* are often used interchangeably. But **working memory** specifically refers to *the temporary storage and active, conscious manipulation of information needed for complex cognitive tasks, such as reasoning, learning, and problem solving*. In contrast, short-term memory is more likely to be used when the focus is on simpler memory processes, such as rehearsing lists of syllables, words, or numbers (Baddeley, 2010). And, working memory is also more likely to involve the recall and manipulation of information held in long-term memory (Corkin, 2013).

The best-known model of working memory was developed by British psychologist Alan Baddeley. In Baddeley's (1992, 2007) model of working memory, there are three main components (see **Figure 6.2**). One component, called the *phonological loop,* is specialized for auditory material, such as lists of numbers or words. This is the aspect of working memory that is often tested by standard memory tasks (Mueller et al., 2003). The second component, called the *visuospatial sketchpad,* is specialized for spatial or visual material, such as remembering the layout of a room or city. Each component functions independently (Fougnie et al., 2015).

The third component is what Baddeley calls the *central executive,* which controls attention, integrates information, and manages the activities of the phonological loop

For an overview of memory processes and an explanation of working memory, go to **Achieve** and watch **Video: Models of Memory.**

working memory The temporary storage and active, conscious manipulation of information needed for complex cognitive tasks, such as reasoning, learning, and problem solving.

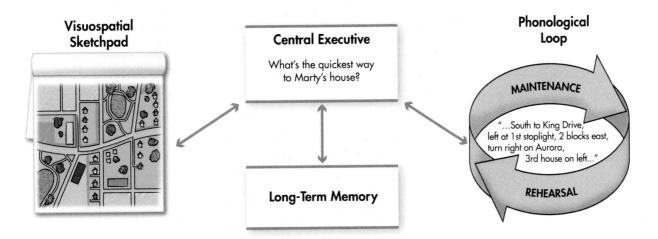

Visuospatial Sketchpad

Central Executive

What's the quickest way to Marty's house?

Long-Term Memory

Phonological Loop

MAINTENANCE

"...South to King Drive, left at 1st stoplight, 2 blocks east, turn right on Aurora, 3rd house on left..."

REHEARSAL

FIGURE 6.2 Baddeley's Model of Working Memory: How Do I Get to Marty's House? Suppose you are trying to figure out the fastest way to get to a friend's house. In Baddeley's model of working memory, you would use the phonological loop to verbally recite the directions. Maintenance rehearsal helps keep the information active in the phonological loop. You would use the visuospatial sketchpad to imagine your route and any landmarks along the way. The central executive actively processes and integrates information from the phonological loop, the visuospatial sketchpad, and long-term memory.

and the visuospatial sketchpad. The central executive also initiates retrieval and decision processes as necessary and integrates information coming into the system. There are many ways in which this system helps us in everyday life. For example, imagine you have a class in a building on campus to which you have never been. Using a handy map, you will make use of both your visuospatial sketchpad and your phonological loop to get to class. You use your phonological loop to hold onto the name of the building you are looking for, as well as the names of nearby buildings to use as points of reference (or landmarks). Noticing the buildings and streets you pass in relation to your destination relies on your visuospatial sketchpad. The central executive works to integrate and briefly retain the information from your phonological loop and your visuospatial sketchpad. While individuals vary on which system they rely on more, there is no doubt that both play an important role in working memory.

Long-Term Memory

■ KEY THEME
Once encoded, an unlimited amount of information can be stored in long-term memory, which has different memory systems.

⩵ KEY QUESTIONS
* What methods can be used to improve the effectiveness of encoding?
* How do procedural, episodic, and semantic memories differ, and what are implicit and explicit memory?
* How does the semantic network model explain the organization of long-term memory?

Long-term memory refers to the storage of information over extended periods of time. Technically, any information stored longer than the roughly 20-second duration of short-term memory is considered to be stored in long-term memory. In terms of maximum duration, some long-term memories last a lifetime.

In contrast to the limited capacities of sensory memory and short-term memory, the amount of information that can be held in long-term memory is limitless. Granted, it doesn't always feel limitless, but consider this: Every day, you remember the directions to your school; the names of hundreds of friends, relatives, and acquaintances; and how to make breakfast. Retrieving information from long-term memory happens quickly and with little effort — most of the time.

Encoding Long-Term Memories How does information get "into" long-term memory? One important function that takes place in short-term memory is *encoding,* or transforming the new information into a form that can be retrieved later (see **Figure 6.3**). As a student, you may have tried to memorize dates, facts, or definitions by simply

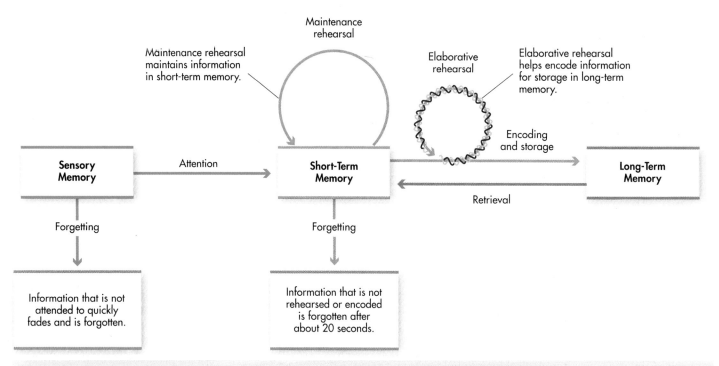

FIGURE 6.3 The Role of Sensory and Short-Term Memory in the Stage Model of Memory In the stage model of memory, information that is not attended to in sensory memory quickly fades and is forgotten. Information that does receive attention moves on to short-term memory. In short-term memory, information that is not rehearsed or encoded is forgotten after about 20 seconds. Information that receives elaborative rehearsal is encoded and stored in long-term memory (and can later be retrieved for short-term memory). This is how we encode long-term memories.

repeating them to yourself over and over. This strategy reflects an attempt to use maintenance rehearsal to encode material into long-term memory. However, maintenance rehearsal is *not* an effective strategy for encoding information into long-term memory.

A much more effective encoding strategy is **elaborative rehearsal**, *rehearsal that involves focusing on the* meaning *of information to help encode and transfer it to long-term memory.* With elaborative rehearsal, you relate the information to other information you already know. That is, rather than simply repeating the information, you *elaborate* on the new information in some meaningful way.

Elaborative rehearsal significantly improves memory for new material. This point is especially important for students, because elaborative rehearsal is a helpful study strategy. Here's an example of how you might use elaborative rehearsal to improve your memory for new information. In the chapter on neuroscience, we discussed three brain structures that are part of the limbic system: the *hypothalamus,* the *hippocampus,* and the *amygdala.* If you tried to memorize the definitions of these structures by reciting them over and over to yourself, you engaged in the not-so-effective memory strategy of maintenance rehearsal.

But if you elaborated on the information in some meaningful way, you would be more likely to recall it. For example, you could think about the limbic system's involvement in emotions, memory, and motivation by constructing a simple story. "I knew it was lunchtime because my hypothalamus told me I was *h*ungry, *t*hirsty, and cold. My hippocampus helped me remember a new restaurant that opened on *campus,* but when I got there I had to wait in line and my *a*mygdala reacted with *a*nger." The story may be a bit silly, but many studies have shown that elaborative rehearsal leads to better retention (Lockhart & Craik, 1990).

Creating this simple story to help you remember the limbic system illustrates two additional factors that enhance encoding. First, applying information to yourself, called the *self-reference effect,* improves your memory for information. Second, the use of *visual imagery,* especially vivid images, also enhances encoding (Kesebir & Oishi, 2010; Paivio, 2007).

elaborative rehearsal Rehearsal that involves focusing on the meaning of information to help encode and transfer it to long-term memory.

The fact that elaborative rehearsal results in more effective encoding and better memory of new information has many practical applications for students. As you study:

- Make sure you understand the new information by restating it in your own words.

- Actively question new information.

- Think about the potential applications and implications of the material.

- Relate the new material to information you already know, searching for connections that make the new information more meaningful.

- Generate your own examples of the concept, especially examples from your own experiences.

At the end of the chapter, in the Psych for Your Life section, we'll give you more suggestions for strategies you can use to improve your memory.

Types of Information in Long-Term Memory

There are three major categories of information stored in long-term memory—*procedural memory, episodic memory,* and *semantic memory* (Tulving, 1985, 2002). **Procedural memory** is a *category of long-term memory that includes memories of different skills, operations, and actions.* Texting, riding a bike, and making scrambled eggs are all examples of procedural information stored in long-term memory. We begin forming procedural memories early in life when we learn to walk, talk, feed ourselves, and so on.

Often, we can't recall exactly when or how we learned procedural information. And usually it's difficult to describe procedural memories in words. For example, try to describe *precisely* and *exactly* what you do when you comb your hair, play the guitar, or ride a bicycle. A particular skill may be easy to demonstrate but very difficult to describe.

In contrast to procedural memory, **episodic memory** is a *category of long-term memory that includes memories of particular events, including the time and place that they occurred* (Gallo & Wheeler, 2013; Tulving, 2002). Your memory of attending a friend's wedding or your first day at university would both be examples of episodic memories.

The third category is **semantic memory**, a *category of long-term memory that includes memories of general knowledge, concepts, facts, and names.* Semantic memory represents your personal encyclopedia of accumulated data and trivia stored in your long-term memory. Typically, you store semantic memories in long-term memory *without* remembering when or where you originally acquired the information. For example, can you remember when or where you learned that there are different time zones across the United States? Or when you learned that there are nine innings in a baseball game?

Closely related to episodic memory is *autobiographical memory,* which refers to the events of your life—your personal life history (Fivush, 2011). Your autobiographical memory includes your episodic memories about your life. But it also includes the semantic memories that relate to your life story, such as knowing when and where your parents met or when and where you were born (Tulving & Szpunar, 2009).

In many ways, your sense of self is shaped by your autobiographical memory (Ross & Wang, 2010). Some people have an extraordinary ability to remember the events of their lives. For example, Jill Price can tell you exactly what she was doing on any particular date since 1980 (McRobbie, 2017). Price is one of a handful of people who have hyperthymesia, better known as Highly Superior Autobiographical Memory, or HSAM (Parker et al., 2006). People with HSAM have memory and cognitive abilities that are, in general, no better than average (LePort et al., 2016, 2017). But they have an extraordinary ability to retrieve memories from their own past. One study found that people with HSAM tend to become deeply absorbed in imaginative fantasies, suggesting that they might be more likely than others to obsessively replay memories of past experiences (Patihis, 2016).

Julio Aguilar/Getty Images Sport/Getty Images

⌃ Types of Information Stored in Long-Term Memory A memorable basketball game involves all three types of long-term memory. Remembering how to dribble and shoot a basketball are examples of *procedural memory.* Knowing the rules of the game would be an example of *semantic memory.* And, the vivid memory of an intense play during a basketball game, such as these players trying to get a rebound, would be an example of an *episodic memory.*

procedural memory Category of long-term memory that includes memories of different skills, operations, and actions.

episodic memory Category of long-term memory that includes memories of particular events, including the time and place that they occurred.

semantic memory Category of long-term memory that includes memories of general knowledge, concepts, facts, and names.

explicit memory Information or knowledge that can be consciously recollected; also called *declarative memory*

The majority of middle-aged and older people are most likely to remember events and experiences that occurred in adolescence and early adulthood—a phenomenon called the *reminiscence bump* (Koppel & Berntsen, 2015; Koppel & Rubin, 2016). One explanation is that this developmental period includes memories of events that are crucially important in the formation of an adult identity, such as high school and university experiences, early professional choices, and relationships (Conway & Holmes, 2004).

As you'll see in the Culture and Human Behavior box on earliest memories, autobiographical memory is also shaped by cultural experience.

Implicit and Explicit Memory: Two Dimensions of Long-Term Memory

Studies with patients who have suffered different types of amnesia as a result of damage to particular brain areas have led memory researchers to recognize that long-term memory is *not* a simple, unitary system. Instead, long-term memory appears to be composed of separate but interacting subsystems and abilities (Slotnick & Schacter, 2007).

What are these subsystems? One basic distinction that has been made is between *explicit memory* and *implicit memory.* Memory *with* awareness is **explicit memory**, *information or knowledge that can be consciously recollected; also called* declarative memory. Thus, remembering what you did last New Year's Day or the

---

CULTURE AND HUMAN BEHAVIOR

Culture's Effects on Early Memories

For most adults, earliest memories are for events that occurred between the ages of 2 and 4 (Bauer et al., 2014). These early memories mark the beginning of autobiographical memory, which provides the basis for the development of an enduring sense of self (Fivush, 2011; Markowitsch & Staniloiu, 2011). Do cultural differences in the sense of self influence the content of our earliest memories?

Comparing the earliest memories of European American university students and Taiwanese and Chinese university students, developmental psychologist Qi (pronounced "chee") Wang (2001, 2006) found a number of significant differences. First, the average age for earliest memory was much earlier for the U.S.-born students than for the Taiwanese and Chinese students.

Wang also found that the Americans' memories were more likely to be discrete, one-point-in-time events reflecting individual experiences or feelings, such as "I remember getting stung by a bee when I was 3 years old. I was scared and started crying." In contrast, the earliest memories of both the Chinese and Taiwanese students were of general, routine activities with family, schoolmates, or community members, such as playing in the park or eating with family members.

For Americans, Wang notes, the past is like a drama in which the self plays the lead role. Themes of self-awareness and individual autonomy were more common in the American students' memories, which tended to focus on their own experiences, emotions, and thoughts.

In contrast, Chinese and Taiwanese students were more likely to include other people in their memories. Rather than focusing exclusively on their own behavior and thoughts, their earliest memories were typically brief accounts that centered on collective activities. For the Chinese and Taiwanese students, the self is not easily separated from its social context.

> **Culture and Earliest Memories** Psychologist Qi Wang (2013) found that the earliest memories of Chinese and Taiwanese adults tended to focus on routine activities that they shared with other members of their family or social group rather than individual events. Perhaps years from now, these children will remember learning to dance with their preschool friends.

Philipp Engelhorn/laif/Redux

Wang (2013, 2014) believes that cultural differences in autobiographical memory are formed in very early childhood, through interaction with family members. For example, *shared reminiscing*—the way that mothers talk to their children about their past experiences—differs in Eastern and Western cultures (Fivush, 2011). When Asian mothers reminisce with their children, they tend to talk about group settings or situations, and to de-emphasize emotions, such as anger, that might separate the child from the group. In comparison, Western mothers tend to focus more on the child's individual activities, accomplishments, and emotional reactions (Ross & Wang, 2010). As Katherine Nelson and Robyn Fivush (2004) observe, such conversations about the personal past "provide children with information about how to be a 'self' in their culture."

topics discussed in your last psychology class are both examples of explicit memory. Explicit memories are also called *declarative memories* because, if asked, you can "declare" the information.

In contrast, memory *without* awareness is **implicit memory**, *information or knowledge that affects behavior or task performance but cannot be consciously recollected; also called nondeclarative memory*. Implicit memories cannot be consciously recollected, but they still affect your behavior, knowledge, or performance of some task. For example, imagine that we asked you to type the following phrase with your eyes closed: "most zebras cannot be extravagant." Easy, right? Now, without looking at a keyboard, try reciting, from left to right, the seven letters of the alphabet that appear on the bottom row of a keyboard. Can you do it? Your authors are both expert typists, and neither one of us could do this. Chances are, you can't either. (In case you're wondering, the letters are ZXCVBNM.)

Here's the point: Your ability to type the phrase "most zebras cannot be extravagant" without looking demonstrates that you *do* know the location of the letters *Z, X, C, V, B, N*, and *M*. But your inability to recite that knowledge demonstrates that your memory of each key's location cannot be consciously recollected. Even though you're not consciously aware of implicit memories, they can still affect your behavior and attitudes. For example, a teenager might have forgotten being frightened by an angry Chihuahua as a young toddler. Yet even in the absence of an explicit memory of the incident, the implicit memory might lead them to feel nervous around small dogs years later (Squire & Dede, 2015). Procedural memories, including skills and habits, typically reflect implicit memory processes. **Figure 6.4** summarizes the different types of long-term memory.

implicit memory Information or knowledge that affects behavior or task performance but cannot be consciously recollected; also called *nondeclarative memory*.

clustering Organizing items into related groups, or clusters, during recall from long-term memory.

semantic network model A model that describes units of information in long-term memory as being organized in a complex network of associations.

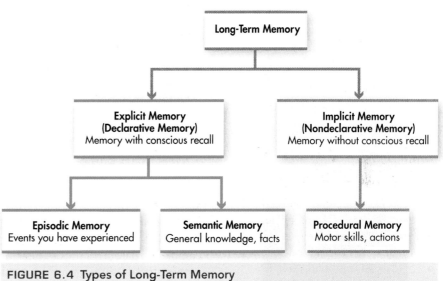

FIGURE 6.4 Types of Long-Term Memory

Although much of the memory research covered in this chapter centers on explicit memory, psychologists and neuroscientists have become increasingly interested in implicit memory. As we'll see in a later section, there is growing evidence that implicit memory and explicit memory involve different brain regions (Squire & Dede, 2015). Some memory theorists believe that implicit memory and explicit memory are two distinct memory systems (Kihlstrom et al., 2007; Tulving, 2002).

The Organization of Information in Long-Term Memory Exactly how information is organized in long-term memory is not completely understood by memory researchers. Nonetheless, memory researchers know that information in long-term memory is *clustered* and *associated*.

Clustering means *organizing items into related groups, or* clusters, *during recall from long-term memory*. Before reading further, try the demonstration in **Figure 6.5**. Even though the words are presented in random order, but you probably recalled groups of vehicles, fruits, and furniture when you wrote them down. In other words, you organized the bits of information by clustering them into related categories.

Different bits and pieces of information in long-term memory are also logically linked, or associated. For example, what's the first word that comes to your mind in response to the word *red*? When we asked our students that same question, their top five responses were "blue," "apple," "color," "green," and "rose." Even if you didn't answer with one of the same associations, your response was based on some kind of logical association that you could explain if asked.

Memory researchers have developed several models to show how information is organized in long-term memory. One of the best-known is the **semantic network model**, *a*

chair	apple
boat	car
footstool	airplane
orange	lamp
pear	banana
peach	dresser
bed	sofa
bus	bookcase
train	truck
plum	table
grapes	strawberry
motorcycle	bicycle

FIGURE 6.5 Clustering Demonstration Study the words on this list for one minute. Then count backward by threes from 108 to 0. When you've completed that task, write down as many of the words from the list as you can remember.

retrieval The process of recovering information stored in memory so that we are consciously aware of it.

retrieval cue A clue, prompt, or hint that helps trigger recall of a given piece of information stored in long-term memory.

model that describes units of information in long-term memory as being organized in a complex network of associations (Collins & Loftus, 1975). When one concept is activated in the semantic network, it can *spread* in any number of directions, *activating* other associations in the semantic network. For example, the word *red* might activate "blue" (another color), "apple," "fire truck" (objects that are red), or "alert" (as in the phrase, "red alert"). In turn, these associations can activate other concepts in the network.

The semantic network model is a useful way of conceptualizing how information is organized in long-term memory. However, keep in mind that it is just a metaphor, not a physical structure in the brain. Nevertheless, the fact that information *is* organized in long-term memory has important implications for the retrieval process, as you'll see in the next section.

Retrieval: Getting Information from Long-Term Memory

■ KEY THEME
Retrieval refers to the process of accessing and retrieving stored information in long-term memory.

≡ KEY QUESTIONS
- What are retrieval cues, and how do they work?
- What do tip-of-the-tongue experiences tell us about the nature of memory?
- How is retrieval tested, and what is the serial position effect?

So far, we've discussed some of the important factors that affect encoding and storing information in memory. In this section, we will consider factors that influence the retrieval process. Before you read any further, try the demonstration in **Figure 6.6**. After completing part (a) of the demonstration, try part (b) on the next page. We'll refer to this demonstration throughout this section, so please take a shot at it. After you've completed both parts of the demonstration, continue reading.

The Importance of Retrieval Cues

Retrieval refers to *the process of recovering information stored in memory so that we are consciously aware of it.* There's a vast difference between what is stored in our long-term memory and what we can actually access. In many instances, our ability to retrieve stored memory hinges on having an appropriate **retrieval cue**, *a clue, prompt, or hint that helps trigger recall of a given piece of information stored in long-term memory.*

⌃ Reminders and Retrieval Cues
Smartphone reminders can be potent retrieval cues, triggering recall of a bit of information held in long-term memory, like a pending appointment or the deadline for an assignment.

FIGURE 6.6(a) Demonstration of Retrieval Cues

Instructions: Spend 3 to 5 seconds reading each of the following sentences, and read through the list only once. As soon as you are finished, cover the list and write down as many of the sentences as you can remember (you need not write "can be used" each time). Please begin now.

A brick can be used as a doorstop.
A ladder can be used as a bookshelf.
A wine bottle can be used as a candleholder.
A pan can be used as a drum.
A fork can be used to comb hair.
A guitar can be used as a canoe paddle.
A leaf can be used as a bookmark.
An orange can be used to play catch.
A newspaper can be used to swat flies.
A T-shirt can be used as a coffee filter.
A sheet can be used as a sail.
A boat can be used as a shelter.
A bathtub can be used as a punch bowl.

A flashlight can be used to hold water.
A rock can be used as a paperweight.
A knife can be used to stir paint.
A pen can be used as an arrow.
A barrel can be used as a chair.
A rug can be used as a bedspread.
A CD can be used as a mirror.
A scissors can be used to cut grass.
A board can be used as a ruler.
A balloon can be used as a pillow.
A shoe can be used to pound nails.
A dime can be used as a screwdriver.
A lampshade can be used as a hat.

Now that you've recalled as many sentences as you can, go to Figure 6.6(b) on the next page.

Source: Research from Bransford & Stein (1993).

How did you do on the first part of the demonstration, in Figure 6.6(a)? If your performance on the demonstration was typical, the importance of retrieval cues should have been vividly illustrated. After generating a number of answers, you probably reached a point at which you couldn't remember any more pairs. At that point, you experienced **retrieval cue failure**, which refers to *the inability to recall long-term memories because of inadequate or missing retrieval cues.*

You should have done much better on the demonstration in Figure 6.6(b) than the demonstration in Figure 6.6(a). Why the improvement? In part (b) you were presented with retrieval cues that helped you access your stored memories.

This exercise demonstrates the difference between information that is *stored* in long-term memory versus the information that you can *access.* Many of the items on the list that you could not recall in part (a) were not forgotten. They were simply inaccessible — until you had a retrieval cue to help jog your memory. This exercise illustrates that many memories only *appear* to be forgotten. With the right retrieval cue, you can often access stored information that seemed to be completely unavailable.

Common Retrieval Glitches: The Tip-Of-The-Tongue Experience

Quick — what is the name of the actor who plays Wonder Woman in the recent *Wonder Woman* films? Who won the most recent season of NBC's popular show *The Voice*? If popular culture isn't your thing, how about this question: Who wrote the book *I Know Why the Caged Bird Sings*?

Did any of these questions leave you feeling as if you knew the answer but just couldn't quite recall it? If so, you experienced the common, and frustrating, **tip-of-the-tongue (TOT) experience** *a memory phenomenon that involves the sensation of knowing that specific information is stored in long-term memory, but being temporarily unable to retrieve it.* Subjectively, it feels as if the information is very close, but just out of reach — or on the tip of your tongue (Schwartz, 2002, 2011).

TOT experiences appear to be universal, and the "tongue" metaphor is used to describe the experience in many cultures (Brennen et al., 2007; Schwartz, 2002). On average, people have about one TOT experience per week, and TOT experiences with particular words tend to recur (D'Angelo & Humphreys, 2015). Although people of all ages experience such word-finding memory glitches, TOT experiences tend to be more common among older adults than younger adults (Farrell & Abrams, 2011).

When experiencing this sort of retrieval failure, people can almost always dredge up partial responses or related bits of information from their memory. About half

retrieval cue failure The inability to recall long-term memories because of inadequate or missing retrieval cues.

tip-of-the-tongue (TOT) experience A memory phenomenon that involves the sensation of knowing that specific information is stored in long-term memory, but being temporarily unable to retrieve it.

Lokibaho/Getty Images

❮ A "Tip-of-the-Fingers" Experience
American Sign Language (ASL) users sometimes have a "tip-of-the-fingers" experience when they are sure they know a sign but can't retrieve it. During a TOT experience, people are often able to remember the first letter or sound of the word they're struggling to remember. Similarly, ASL users tend to remember the hand shape, which appears as the signer begins to make the sign, rather than later parts of the sign, like the hand movement. For words that are finger-spelled, ASL users were more likely to recall the first letters than later letters (Thompson et al., 2005).

recall A test of long-term memory that involves retrieving information without the aid of retrieval cues; also called *free recall.*

cued recall A test of long-term memory that involves remembering an item of information in response to a retrieval cue.

recognition A test of long-term memory that involves identifying correct information out of several possible choices.

serial position effect The tendency to retrieve information more easily from the beginning and the end of a list rather than from the middle.

Instructions: *Do not* look back at the list of sentences in Figure 6.6(a). Use the following list as retrieval cues, and now write as many sentences as you can. Be sure to keep track of how many you can write down.

flashlight	lampshade
sheet	shoe
rock	guitar
CD	scissors
boat	leaf
dime	brick
wine bottle	knife
board	newspaper
pen	pan
balloon	barrel
ladder	rug
T-shirt	orange
fork	bathtub

FIGURE 6.6(b) Demonstration of Retrieval Cues

> **A Demonstration of the Primacy Effect** On New Year's Eve in 2009, Mariah Carey infamously couldn't remember most of the words to "Auld Lang Syne," She remembered the opening easily enough, but was soon just singing the first line over and over again. Most people correctly remember the words at the beginning of "Auld Lang Syne" but—like Mariah—have difficulty recalling the words and phrases in the middle.

the time, people can accurately identify the first letter of the target word and the number of syllables in it. They can also often produce words with similar meanings or sounds. While momentarily frustrating, about 90 percent of TOT experiences are eventually resolved, often within a few minutes.

Tip-of-the-tongue experiences illustrate that retrieving information is not an all-or-nothing process. Often, we remember bits and pieces of what we want to remember. In many instances, information is stored in memory but is not accessible without the right retrieval cues. TOT experiences also emphasize that information stored in memory is *organized* and connected in relatively logical ways. As you mentally struggle to retrieve the blocked information, logically connected bits of information are frequently triggered. In many instances, these related tidbits of information act as additional retrieval cues, helping you access the desired memory.

Testing Retrieval: Recall, Cued Recall, and Recognition The demonstration in Figure 6.6(a) illustrated the use of recall as a strategy to measure memory. **Recall** is *a test of long-term memory that involves retrieving information without the aid of retrieval cues; also called* free recall. This is the memory measure that's used on essay tests. Other than the essay questions themselves, an essay test provides no additional retrieval cues to help jog your memory.

The demonstration in Figure 6.6(b) used a different memory measurement, **cued recall**, *a test of long-term memory that involves remembering an item of information in response to a retrieval cue.* Fill-in-the-blank and matching questions are examples of cued-recall tests.

A third memory measurement is **recognition**, *a test of long-term memory that involves identifying correct information out of several possible choices.* Multiple-choice tests involve recognition as a measure of long-term memory. The multiple-choice question provides you with one correct answer and several wrong answers. If you have stored the information in your long-term memory, you should recognize the correct answer.

Cued-recall and recognition tests are clearly to the student's advantage. Because these kinds of tests provide retrieval cues, the likelihood that you can access stored information is increased.

The Serial Position Effect
Notice that the demonstration in Figure 6.6(a) did not ask you to recall the sentences in any particular order. Instead, you could recall the items in any order. Take another look at your answers to Figure 6.6(a). Do you notice any sort of pattern to the items that you did recall?

Most people are least likely to recall items from the middle of the list. This pattern of responses is called the **serial position effect**, which refers to the *tendency to retrieve information more easily from the beginning and the end of a list rather than from the middle.* There are two parts to the serial position effect. The tendency to recall the first items in a list is called the *primacy effect,* and the tendency to recall the final items in a list is called the *recency effect.*

The primacy effect is especially prominent when you have to engage in *serial recall,* that is, when you need to remember a list of items in their original order. Remembering speeches, telephone numbers, and directions are a few examples of serial recall.

The Encoding Specificity Principle

■ KEY THEME
According to the encoding specificity principle, re-creating the original learning conditions makes retrieval easier.

⹀ KEY QUESTIONS
• How can context and mood affect retrieval?
• What role does distinctiveness play in retrieval, and how accurate are flashbulb memories?

One of the best ways to increase access to information in memory is to re-create the original learning conditions. This simple idea is formally called the **encoding specificity principle**, *the principle that retrieval is more likely to be successful when the conditions of information retrieval are similar to the conditions of information encoding* (Tulving, 1983).

For example, have you ever had trouble remembering some bit of information during a test but immediately recalled it as you entered the library where you normally study? When you intentionally try to remember some bit of information, such as the definition of a term, you often encode much more into memory than just that isolated bit of information. As you study in the library, at some level you're aware of all kinds of environmental cues including the sights, sounds, and aromas within that particular situation. *The environmental cues in a particular context can become encoded as part of the unique memories you form while in that context.* These same environmental cues can act as retrieval cues to help you access the memories formed in that context.

This particular form of encoding specificity is called the **context effect**, *the tendency to recover information more easily when the retrieval occurs in the same setting as the original learning of the information.* Thus, the environmental cues in the library where you normally study act as additional retrieval cues that help jog your memory. Of course, it's too late to help your test score, but the memory was there.

Encoding takes a different form with **mood congruence**, *an encoding specificity phenomenon in which a given mood tends to evoke memories that are consistent with that mood.* In other words, a specific emotional state can act as a retrieval cue that evokes memories of events involving the same emotion. So, when you're in a positive mood, you're more likely to recall positive memories. When you're feeling blue, you're more likely to recall negative or unpleasant memories.

Flashbulb Memories: Vivid Events, Accurate Memories?

If you rummage around your own memories, you'll quickly discover that highly unusual, surprising, or even bizarre experiences are easier to retrieve from memory than are routine events (Geraci & Manzano, 2010). Such memories are said to be characterized by a high degree of *distinctiveness.* That is, the encoded information represents a unique, different, or unusual memory.

Various events can create vivid, distinctive, and long-lasting memories that are sometimes referred to as *flashbulb memories* (Brown & Kulik, 1982; Hirst & Phelps, 2016). Just as a camera flash captures the specific details of a scene, a **flashbulb memory** is thought to involve the *recall of very specific images or details surrounding a vivid, rare, or significant event; details may or may not be accurate.*

Do flashbulb memories actually capture specific details, like the details of a photograph, that are unaffected by the passage of time? Emotionally charged national or

encoding specificity principle The principle that retrieval is more likely to be successful when the conditions of information retrieval are similar to the conditions of information encoding.

context effect The tendency to recover information more easily when the retrieval occurs in the same setting as the original learning of the information.

mood congruence An encoding specificity phenomenon in which a given mood tends to evoke memories that are consistent with that mood.

flashbulb memory The recall of very specific images or details surrounding a vivid, rare, or significant personal event; details may or may not be accurate.

⌃ **Flashbulb Memories** Can you remember where you were when you learned of the death of Ruth Bader Ginsburg? Of the outcome of the 2020 U.S. presidential election? Supposedly, shocking national or international events can trigger distinctive, long-term flashbulb memories. Meaningful personal events, such as your high school graduation or wedding day, are also said to produce vivid flashbulb memories. Even though they are distinctive, we don't remember flashbulb memories any more accurately than other memories.

Hill Street Studios/Sarah Golonka/Blend Images/Alamy Stock Photo

international events have provided a unique opportunity to study flashbulb memories. On September 12, 2001, a day after the World Trade Center attacks, psychologists Jennifer Talarico and David Rubin (2003, 2007) asked university students to complete questionnaires about how they learned about the terrorist attacks. For comparison, students also described an ordinary, everyday event that had recently occurred.

Over the next year, students were periodically asked to again describe their memories of the 9/11 attacks and of the ordinary event. When the researchers compared these accounts to the original, September 12 reports, they discovered that both the flashbulb and everyday memories had decayed over time, with an increasing number of inconsistent details. But when asked to rate the vividness and accuracy of both memories, only the ratings for the ordinary memory declined. Despite being just as inconsistent as the ordinary memories, the students perceived their flashbulb memories of 9/11 as being more accurate.

A similar pattern was observed in a 10-year, longitudinal study involving 3,000 participants in seven different U.S. cities who described how they learned of the 9/11 attacks (Hirst et al., 2015). Within the first year after the attack, participants rapidly forgot details. Despite inconsistencies between original reports and memories of the event, participants' confidence in the accuracy of their memories remained high. Interestingly, proximity to the attacks was not associated with more accurate memories, but *was* associated with confidence levels. People who lived in New York at the time of the attacks had much higher levels of confidence in their memories, but their memories were no more accurate than those of non–New Yorkers.

Although flashbulb memories can seem incredibly vivid, they appear to function just as normal, everyday memories do (Hirst & Phelps, 2016). We remember flashbulb memories no more accurately than other memories. We remember some details, forget some details, and think we remember some details. What does seem to distinguish flashbulb memories from ordinary memories is the high degree of confidence the person has in the accuracy of these memories. But clearly, confidence in a memory is *no* guarantee of accuracy. We'll come back to that important point shortly.

Forgetting: When Retrieval Fails

■ KEY THEME
Forgetting is the inability to retrieve information that was once available.

⹂ KEY QUESTIONS
- What discoveries were made by Hermann Ebbinghaus?
- How do encoding failure, interference, and decay contribute to forgetting, and how can prospective memory be improved?
- What is repression and why is the topic controversial?

Forgetting is so common that life is filled with reminders to safeguard against forgetting important information. Cars are equipped with beeping tones so you don't forget to fasten your seatbelt. Dentists call or text you the day before your appointment so that it doesn't slip your mind.

Although forgetting can be annoying, it does serve several adaptive functions (Nørby, 2015). Forgetting irrelevant information improves the efficiency of cognitive processes. Our minds would be cluttered if we remembered every conversation and meal we'd ever had, and every bus we'd missed. And, because people tend to forget negative experiences, forgetting helps us maintain our emotional equilibrium (Walker et al., 2003).

Psychologists define **forgetting** as *the inability to remember information that was previously available*. Note that this definition does not refer to the "loss" or "absence" of once-remembered information. While it's tempting to think of forgetting as the gradual loss of information from long-term memory over time, this compelling explanation of forgetting is too simplistic. Psychologists have identified several factors that are

MYTH ▶ SCIENCE

Is it true that "flashbulb memories," the vivid memories you form after an important, dramatic event, are no more accurate than other memories?

forgetting The inability to recall information that was previously available.

involved in forgetting, but exactly how—and why—forgetting occurs is still not completely understood.

Hermann Ebbinghaus: The Forgetting Curve

German psychologist **Hermann Ebbinghaus** began the scientific study of forgetting in the 1870s. Because there was a seven-year gap between obtaining his doctorate and his first university teaching position, Ebbinghaus couldn't use university students for experimental subjects (Erdelyi, 2010; Fancher, 1996). So to study forgetting, Ebbinghaus had to rely on the only available research subject: himself.

Ebbinghaus's goal was to determine how much information was forgotten after different lengths of time. But he wanted to make sure that he was studying the memory and forgetting of completely new material rather than information that had preexisting associations in his memory. So Ebbinghaus (1885) created new material to memorize: thousands of nonsense syllables. A *nonsense syllable* is a three-letter combination, made up of two consonants and a vowel, such as WIB or MEP. Ebbinghaus carefully noted how many times he had to repeat a list of 13 nonsense syllables before he could recall the list perfectly.

Once he had learned the nonsense syllables, Ebbinghaus tested his recall of them after varying amounts of time, ranging from 20 minutes to 31 days. He plotted his results in the now-famous *forgetting curve,* shown in **Figure 6.7**.

The Ebbinghaus forgetting curve reveals two distinct patterns in the relationship between forgetting and the passage of time. First, much of what we forget is lost relatively soon after we originally learned it. How quickly we forget material depends on several factors, such as how well the material was encoded in the first place, how meaningful the material was, and how often it was rehearsed.

In general, if you learn something in a matter of minutes, most forgetting will occur very soon after the original learning—also in minutes. However, if you spend many sessions over days or weeks encoding new information into memory, the period of most rapid forgetting will be the first several weeks or months after such learning.

Second, the Ebbinghaus forgetting curve shows that the amount of forgetting eventually levels with very little difference between how much Ebbinghaus forgot eight hours later and a month later. The information that is *not* quickly forgotten seems to be remarkably stable in memory over long periods of time.

The forgetting curve was nicely illustrated in a study comparing the memories of people who binge-watched episodes of a TV series with people who watched episodes weekly (Horvath et al., 2017). The binge-watchers had a better memory for program

Hermann Ebbinghaus (1850–1909) After earning his Ph.D. in philosophy in 1873, Ebbinghaus worked as a private tutor for several years. It was during this time that he conducted his famous research on the memory of nonsense syllables. In 1885, he published his results in *Memory: A Contribution to Experimental Psychology*. Ebbinghaus observed, "Left to itself, every mental content gradually loses its capacity for being revived. Facts crammed at examination time soon vanish, if they were not sufficiently grounded by other study and later subjected to a sufficient review."

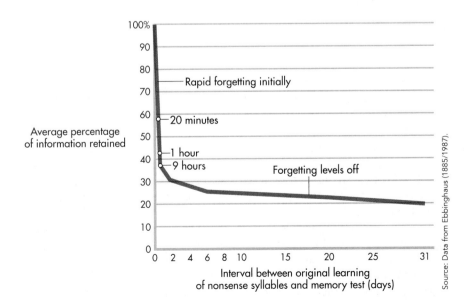

FIGURE 6.7 The Ebbinghaus Forgetting Curve Ebbinghaus's research demonstrated the basic pattern of forgetting: relatively rapid loss of some information, followed by stable memories of the remaining information.

Dan Reynolds/www.CartoonStock.com

details 24 hours after watching the episodes, but their memory performance declined sharply over the following 140 days. The weekly viewers had a poorer memory for program details 24 hours after viewing the last episode, but their performance did not decline as much over the long-term.

Although common, the pattern of forgetting that Ebbinghaus identified is *not* universal. Under some conditions, memory for new information actually *improves* over time (Erdelyi, 2010; Roediger, 2008). One well-documented way to increase memory for new information over time is to frequently practice retrieving the information. More specifically, as explained in the chapter on introduction and research methods, repeatedly *testing* yourself for the new information is a reliable way to improve your memory for that information (Karpicke & Roediger, 2008). One explanation is that retrieving the information on a test reactivates and strengthens the original memory (Hardt et al., 2010; Smolen et al., 2016). Another possibility is that you learn more effective retrieval cues as you repeatedly test yourself over the same material (Pyc & Rawson, 2010).

Why Do We Forget?

Ebbinghaus was a pioneer in the study of memory. His major contribution was to identify a basic pattern of forgetting: rapid forgetting of some information relatively soon after the original learning, followed by stability of the memories that remain. But what causes forgetting? Psychologists have identified several factors that contribute to forgetting, including encoding failure, decay, interference, and motivated forgetting.

Encoding Failure: It Never Got to Long-Term Memory
Without rummaging through your loose change, take a look at **Figure 6.8**. Which drawing accurately depicts the face of a U.S. penny?

When this task was presented to participants in one study, fewer than half of them picked the correct drawing (Nickerson & Adams, 1982). The explanation? Even though you may have handled thousands of pennies, you've probably never looked carefully at one. Chances are that you've encoded only the most superficial characteristics of a penny—its size, color, and texture—into your long-term memory.

In a follow-up study, William Marmie and Alice Healy (2004) allowed participants to study an unfamiliar coin for short periods of time, ranging from 15 seconds to 60 seconds. Even with only 15 seconds devoted to focusing on the coin's appearance, participants were better able to remember the details of the *unfamiliar* coin than the all-too-familiar penny. In effect, Marmie and Healy (2004) confirmed that lack of attention at the time of encoding was responsible for the failure to accurately remember the appearance of a penny.

As these simple demonstrations illustrate, one of the most common reasons for forgetting is called **encoding failure**, *the inability to recall specific information because*

FIGURE 6.8 Test for Memory of Details of a Common Object Which of these drawings is an accurate picture of a real penny? Even though most people in the United States may have handled thousands of pennies, you've probably never looked carefully at one. Chances are that you've encoded only the most superficial characteristics of a penny—its size, color, and texture—into your long-term memory. The real penny is the first one here, A.

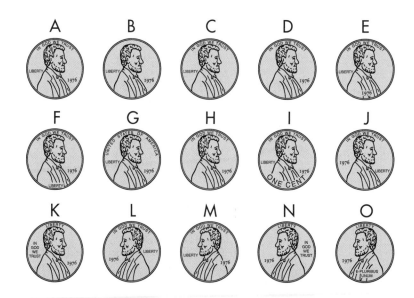

of insufficient encoding of the information for storage in long-term memory. Encoding failure explains why you forget a person's name two minutes after being introduced to them: The information was momentarily present in your short-term memory, but was never encoded into long-term memory.

Encoding failure can also help explain everyday memory failures due to *absentmindedness.* Absentmindedness occurs because you don't pay enough attention to a bit of information at the time when you should be encoding it, such as in which aisle you parked your car at the mall. Absentminded memory failures often occur because your attention is *divided.* Rather than focusing your full attention on what you're doing, you're also thinking about other matters (McVay & Kane, 2010).

Research has shown that divided attention at the time of encoding tends to result in poor memory for the information (Craik et al., 1996; Riby et al., 2008; Smallwood et al., 2007). Such absentminded memory lapses are especially common when you're performing habitual actions that don't require much thought, such as parking your car in a familiar parking lot or setting down your cell phone or keys when you come home.

Absentmindedness is also implicated in another annoying memory problem—forgetting to do something in the future, such as returning a library book or taking a medication on schedule. *Remembering to do something in the future* is called **prospective memory**. In contrast to other types of memories, the crucial component of a prospective memory is *when* something needs to be remembered, rather than *what.*

Rather than encoding failure, prospective memory failures are due to *retrieval cue failure*—the inability to recall a memory because of missing or inadequate retrieval cues. For example, you forget to submit your credit card payment on time and incur a late fee. The problem with this sort of scenario is that there is no strong, distinctive retrieval cue embedded in the situation. This is why ovens are equipped with timers that buzz and why reminder programs are popular smartphone apps. Such strategies provide distinctive retrieval cues that will hopefully trigger those prospective memories at the appropriate moment. **Table 6.1** lists additional suggestions to help minimize prospective memory failures.

Decay Theory: Fading with the Passage of Time   **Decay theory**, is *the view that forgetting is due to normal brain processes that occur over time.* The idea is that when a new memory is formed, it creates a *memory trace*—a distinct structural or chemical change in the brain. Over time, the normal metabolic processes of the brain are thought to erode the memory trace, especially if it is not "refreshed" by frequent rehearsal. The gradual fading of memories, then, would be similar to the fading of letters on billboards or newsprint exposed to environmental elements, such as sunlight.

Although decay theory makes sense intuitively, too much evidence contradicts it (Jonides et al., 2008). Look again at the Ebbinghaus forgetting curve in Figure 6.8. If memories simply faded over time, you would expect to see a steady decline in the amount of information remembered with the passage of time. Instead, once the information held in memory stabilizes, it changes very little over time. In other words, the *rate* of forgetting actually *decreases* over time (Wixted, 2004).

Beyond that point, many studies have shown that information can be remembered decades after it was originally learned, even though it has not been rehearsed or recalled since the original memory was formed (Custers & Ten Cate, 2011). As we discussed earlier, the ability to access memories is strongly influenced by the kinds of retrieval cues provided when memory is tested. If the memory trace simply decayed over time, the presentation of potent retrieval cues should have no effect on the retrieval of information or events experienced long ago—but it does!

So have contemporary memory researchers abandoned decay theory as an explanation of forgetting? Not completely. Although decay is not regarded as the primary cause of forgetting, many of today's memory researchers believe that it contributes to forgetting (Altmann, 2009; Portrat et al., 2008).

TABLE 6.1

Eight Suggestions for Avoiding Prospective Memory Failure

1	Be proactive! Create a reminder the instant you realize that you need to do something in the future.
2	Make reminder cues and make sure that they tell you *what* you are supposed to remember to do.
3	Make reminder cues OBVIOUS by posting them where you will definitely see them, such as on your mirror, refrigerator or coffeepot, front or back door, computer monitor, and so on.
4	Put a notepad or Post-it Notes and a pencil in lots of convenient places (your dresser, your car, the kitchen counter, etc.).
5	For tasks you need to remember to do in the next few hours, buy small battery-operated kitchen timers.
6	Leave yourself a voice mail message.
7	Use the calendar reminder and follow-up features on your computer or use a free Internet reminder service (e.g., www.memotome.com).
8	Smartphone users, check out the many reminder apps that are available for iPhone, Android, or other models.

encoding failure The inability to recall specific information because of insufficient encoding of the information for storage in long-term memory.

prospective memory Remembering to do something in the future.

decay theory The view that forgetting is due to normal brain processes that occur over time.

interference theory The theory that forgetting is caused by one memory competing with or replacing another memory.

retroactive interference Backward-acting memory interference in which a new memory interferes with remembering an old memory.

proactive interference Forward-acting memory interference in which an old memory interferes with remembering a new memory.

suppression Motivated forgetting that occurs consciously, a deliberate attempt to not think about and remember specific information.

repression Motivated forgetting that occurs unconsciously, a memory that is blocked and unavailable to consciousness.

⌄ **Motivated Forgetting** Car accidents, serious illnesses, surgeries, and other traumatic events are painful to relive in memory. Some researchers believe that by voluntarily directing our attention away from memories of such traumatic events, we can eventually *suppress* our memory of the experiences, making them difficult or impossible to consciously retrieve (Anderson et al., 2011; Hulbert et al., 2016).

Getty Images

Interference Theory: Memories Interfering with Memories

Interference theory, *the theory that forgetting is caused by one memory competing with or replacing another memory* (Nørby, 2015). The most critical factor is the similarity of the information. The more similar the information is in two memories, the more likely it is that interference take place.

There are two basic types of interference, *retroactive interference* and *proactive interference*. **Retroactive interference** is *backward-acting memory interference in which a new memory interferes with remembering an old memory.* It occurs when a *new* memory (the combination for the new lock you just bought for your bicycle) interferes with remembering an *old* memory (the combination for the lock you've been using at the gym).

Proactive interference is *forward-acting memory interference, in which an old memory interferes with remembering a new memory.* It occurs when an old memory (your previous zip code) interferes with remembering a new memory (your new zip code). Name mix-ups are a common and often embarrassing example of proactive interference, such as when parents call children by their sibling's name or when you address a new partner with the name of an ex. One survey found that people were most likely to confuse the names of those who fell into the same relationship category, such as mixing up the names of family members or mixing up the names of friends (Deffler et al., 2016). Name mix-ups were also more likely when names sounded similar, such as "Dawn" and "Donna." One incidental finding was that people also frequently called family members by the dog's name.

Motivated Forgetting: Forgetting Unpleasant Memories

Motivated forgetting refers to the idea that we forget because we are motivated to forget, usually because a memory is unpleasant or disturbing. **Suppression** *is motivated forgetting that occurs consciously, a deliberate attempt to not think about and remember specific information.* For example, after seeing a disturbing report of a horrendous crime or massacre on the evening news, you consciously avoid thinking about it, turning your attention to other matters. According to some researchers, over time and with repeated effort, pushing an unwanted memory out of awareness may make the memory less accessible (Hulbert et al., 2016; Nørby, 2015).

Another form of motivated forgetting is fundamentally different and much more controversial. **Repression** can be defined as *motivated forgetting that occurs unconsciously, a memory that is blocked and unavailable to consciousness* (Langnickel & Markowitsch, 2006). One obvious problem is determining whether a memory has been "repressed" or simply forgotten. For example, several studies have found that people better remember positive life experiences than negative life experiences (Lambert et al., 2010). Is that because unhappy experiences have been "repressed"? Or is it simply that people are less likely to think about, talk about, dwell on, or rehearse unhappy memories?

Among psychologists, repression is an extremely controversial topic (see Erdelyi, 2006a, 2006b). At one extreme are those who believe that true repression *never* occurs (Hayne et al., 2006). At the other extreme are those who are convinced that repressed memories are at the root of many psychological problems, particularly repressed memories of childhood sexual abuse (Gleaves et al., 2004). This latter contention gave rise to a form of psychotherapy involving the recovery of repressed memories. Later in the chapter, we'll explore this controversy in the Critical Thinking box "The Memory Wars: Recovered or False Memories?"

Imperfect Memories: Errors, Distortions, and False Memories

■ KEY THEME
Memories can be easily distorted so that they contain inaccuracies. Confidence in a memory is no guarantee that the memory is accurate.

⹂ KEY QUESTIONS
- What is the misinformation effect?
- What are schemas, and how can they contribute to memory distortions?
- What is source confusion, and how can it distort memories?

People usually remember the essence of their experience, but the failings of human memory can be disturbing. It is a myth that human memory functions like a video recorder that captures a perfect copy of visual and auditory information (Schacter & Loftus, 2013). Instead, memory details can change over time. You can vividly remember the details of an event—and yet be completely *wrong*. Confidence in a memory is no guarantee that the memory is accurate.

How do errors and distortions creep into memories? A new memory is not simply recorded, but *actively constructed*. Forming a new memory involves organizing and encoding different types of information, such as sensory details and the time and place of the event. When you later attempt to retrieve those details, you *reconstruct*, or rebuild, the details of the memory (Bartlett, 1932; Stark et al., 2010). Several factors can contribute to errors or distortions during the process of constructing or reconstructing a memory.

At the forefront of research on memory distortions is **Elizabeth Loftus**, whose story we told in the Prologue. Loftus is one of the most widely recognized authorities on eyewitness memory and the different ways it can go awry (see Loftus, 2007, 2011).

> **misinformation effect** A memory-distortion phenomenon in which your existing memories can be altered if you are exposed to misleading information.

MYTH ◄ SCIENCE

Is it true that memory is like a video recorder—it preserves a perfect record of your experience?

Courtesy Elizabeth Loftus

❮ Elizabeth Loftus (b. 1944) Renowned memory researcher Elizabeth Loftus was a pioneer in research about the flaws in our memories. Loftus (2002) wrote that "Psychological studies have shown that it is virtually impossible to tell the difference between a real memory and one that is a product of imagination or some other process. Our job as researchers in this area is to understand how it is that pieces of experience are combined to produce what we experience as 'memory.'"

The Misinformation Effect: The Influence of Post-Event Information on Misremembering
Let's start by considering a classic Loftus study (Loftus & Palmer, 1974). Participants watched a film of an automobile accident and then answered a series of questions. The critical question in the series was: "About how fast were the cars going when they *contacted* each other?" For some participants, the word *contacted* was replaced with *hit*. Other participants were given the words *bumped*, *collided*, or *smashed*.

Depending on the specific word used in the question, participants gave very different speed estimates. As shown in **Table 6.2**, the participants who were given the word *smashed* estimated speeds averaging 9 m.p.h. faster than participants who were given the word *contacted*. A week later, participants who were given the word *smashed* were also more likely to report seeing broken glass, although no broken glass was shown in the film. Notice what happened: After the initial memory was formed, new information (the word *smashed*) distorted the reconstruction of the memory.

The use of suggestive questions is just one example of how the information a person gets *after* an event can change what the person later remembers about the event. The **misinformation effect** is *a memory-distortion phenomenon in which your existing memories can be altered if you are exposed to misleading information*. Literally hundreds of studies have demonstrated the different ways that the *misinformation effect* can be produced

TABLE 6.2

Estimated Speeds

Word Used in Question	Average Speed Estimate
smashed	41 m.p.h.
collided	39 m.p.h.
bumped	38 m.p.h.
hit	34 m.p.h.
contacted	32 m.p.h.

Source: Research from Loftus & Palmer (1974).

AP Photo/Chuck Burton

◂ **Eyewitness Misidentification: Convicting the Innocent**
Ronald Cotton spent more than 10 years serving a life-plus-54-years sentence for raping a university student, Jennifer Thompson-Cannino, in her North Carolina apartment. When she first saw Cotton in a police lineup, Thompson-Cannino was not certain that he was the rapist. But by the time of the trial, after repeated questioning by the police, Thompson-Cannino was "absolutely sure" that Cotton was the rapist (Garrett, 2011). So certain was she, that when shown the actual perpetrator, who had confessed the crime to another inmate, she said she had never seen him before in her life. Ten years after Cotton's conviction, he was freed when DNA evidence conclusively proved that he had not committed the crime and identified the other prisoner as the rapist. Today, Cotton and Thompson-Cannino are close friends and fellow activists, writing a memoir together and speaking widely to educate law enforcement personnel and others about eyewitness testimony and wrongful convictions (Thompson-Cannino & Cotton, 2009). Scores of studies have shown that eyewitness misidentification is the leading cause of wrongful conviction (see Loftus, 2013; Smalarz & Wells, 2015; The Innocence Project, 2015).

(Loftus, 1996, 2005). Basically, the research procedure involves three steps. First, participants are exposed to a simulated event, such as an automobile accident or a crime. Next, after a delay, half of the participants receive misinformation, while the other half receive no misinformation. In the final step, all of the participants try to remember the details of the original event.

In study after study, Loftus and other researchers have confirmed that post-event exposure to misinformation can distort the recollection of the original event by eyewitnesses (see Davis & Loftus, 2007; Frenda et al., 2011). It is a myth that eyewitness testimony is the most reliable form of courtroom evidence. People have recalled stop signs as yield signs, normal headlights as broken, barns along empty roads, a blue vehicle as being white, and Minnie Mouse when they really saw Mickey Mouse! Whether it is in the form of suggestive questions, misinformation, or other exposure to conflicting details, such post-event experiences can distort eyewitness memories (Brewer & Wells, 2011). For more on eyewitnesses and misremembering, see the In Focus box, "Contract Tracing and the Shortcomings of Memory."

Schemas and Memory Distortions: The Influence of Existing Knowledge on What Is Remembered

Now that we know that information presented after a memory is formed can change the contents of that memory, let's consider the opposite effect: Can the knowledge you had *before* an event occurred influence your later memory of the event? If so, how?

Since you were a child, you have been actively forming mental representations called **schemas**—*organized clusters of information about particular topics.* The topic can be almost anything—an object (a phone), a setting (a movie theater), or a concept (freedom). Schemas are useful in organizing and forming new memories, helping you to quickly integrate new experiences into your knowledge base. But schemas can also contribute to memory distortions by prompting us to fill in missing details with schema-consistent information.

Apparently, preexisting schemas can distort memories for events within *seconds* (Strickland & Keil, 2011). In one study, participants watched videos showing athletes kicking, throwing, or hitting a ball. In some videos, the actual point of contact was *not* shown, just the ball flying into the distance. Nevertheless, within seconds of viewing the video, participants believed that they had seen the causal action that had only been implied by the film. Essentially, they "filled in" the missing moment of contact because, based on prior experience, that interpretation simply made sense.

MYTH ◂ SCIENCE

Is it true that eyewitness testimony is the most reliable form of courtroom evidence?

 Achieve

wake	
Presented	**New**
This word was presented in the original list.	This word is new (not presented in the original list).

Go to **Achieve** and test the effects of schemas on your memory with **Concept Practice: How Reliable Is Your Memory?**

schemas (SKEE-muh) Organized clusters of information about particular topics.

IN FOCUS

Contact Tracing and the Shortcomings of Memory

Recent history has reintroduced us to the fraught nature of information obtained from eyewitness and first-person accounts of events. Following the massive spread of the COVID-19 virus, the phrase "contact tracing" became a part of our daily world. Simply, contact tracing means determining the people with whom an infected person has had contact. Once identified, these people can then be tested (and treated and/or isolated to prevent further spread). Contact tracing has been a pillar of public health for decades and is particularly essential for new infections when there is either no vaccine or not enough vaccines for everyone (Müller and Kretzschmar, 2021).

The COVID-19 virus is particularly contagious because of the ease with which it can be passed between people, making contact tracing even more essential. Maryanne Garry and colleagues (2021) remind us how important it is to recognize the challenges of human memory with regard to contact tracing. Fortunately, there is a model for contact tracers to follow — that of criminal investigators as they try to elicit accurate memories from eyewitnesses. For example, contact tracers should avoid leading questions that might result in a particular response and use instructions that can enhance memory. So, a contact tracer might say "Try to place yourself back at the church, in your mind — think about what you could see, what you could hear, how you were feeling, and so on" (Garry et al., 2021).

Beyond applying research on memory to interview protocols, contact tracers can make better use of technology to improve the accuracy of memory related to contact tracing (Garry et al., 2021). For example, contact tracers can encourage people to use apps on their smartphones, such as the calendar, reminders, or even running-map apps, to jog their memory of where they had been. There are also smartphone apps designed for contact tracing that record each person who passes within two meters, as long as they also have the app on a device they are carrying when contact happens. The contacts, however, are known only to the app maker, which can make it difficult to get accurate and specific information to public health workers in a time frame that prevents contagion. These apps have other serious limitations, including the imperfect accuracy of GPS and the difficulties in recruiting enough people to participate.

Contact-tracing apps may eventually improve, allowing the field to follow the lead of law enforcement agencies, which have moved away from eyewitness accounts and now lean more heavily on forensic and photographic evidence. Following the 2021 siege on the United States Capitol, the Federal Bureau of Investigation relied on more than 140,000 images and videos posted on the Internet to pursue individuals who were involved in the insurrection (Bennett et al., 2021; Spocchia, 2021). The need for unbiased information is particularly notable in this example because of the politically charged nature of the incident. As a result, it would be hard to find truly objective witnesses to the events that took place at the Capitol on January 6, 2021. Therefore, law enforcement is relying on objective technology, including analyses of photos and videos posted to social media, in their investigation (Johnson, 2021). The use of objective information in law enforcement is critically important to keeping people safe without the wrongful convictions that have been all too common when eyewitness testimony is the sole source of information.

Source Confusion: Misremembering the Source of a Memory Have you ever confidently remembered hearing something on television only to discover that it was really a friend who told you the information? Or felt sure that an event happened at one time and place only to learn later that it really happened at a *different* time and place? If so, you can blame your faulty memories on a phenomenon called **source confusion**, *a memory distortion that occurs when the true source of the memory is forgotten* (M. Johnson et al., 2012; Lindsay, 2008).

Source confusion can help explain the misinformation effect: False details that were provided *after* the event become confused with authentic details of the original memory. In one study, participants were shown digitally doctored photos of famous news events, such as the violent 1989 Tiananmen Square protests in Beijing, China. Details from the *fake* photos were incorporated into participants' original memories of the actual news event (Sacchi et al., 2007). Importantly, the participants were just as confident of their *false* memories as they were when recalling their *accurate* memories of other details of the news event.

Elizabeth's story in the Prologue also demonstrated how confusion about the source of a memory can give rise to an extremely vivid, but inaccurate, recollection. Accurate memories of her uncle's home, such as the smell of the pines and the feel of the lake water, became blended with Elizabeth's fantasy of finding her mother's body. The result was a **false memory,** which is *a distorted or fabricated recollection of something that did not*

In essence, all memory is false to some degree. Memory is inherently a reconstructive process, whereby we piece together the past to form a coherent narrative that becomes our autobiography. In the process of reconstructing the past, we color and shape our life's experiences based on what we know about the world.

—*Daniel M. Bernstein &
Elizabeth F. Loftus, 2009*

source confusion A memory distortion that occurs when the true source of the memory is forgotten.

false memory A distorted or fabricated recollection of something that did not actually occur.

Stuart Franklin/Magnum Photos

Stuart Franklin/Magnum Photos and courtesy of Elizabeth Loftus and Dario Sacchi

⋀ Which Is the Real Photo? The photograph of an unknown young man bravely defying oncoming tanks in an antigovernment protest in China's Tiananmen Square (left) has become an iconic image of individual courage and the global struggle for human rights. But after people who remembered the original image correctly were shown the doctored image on the right, their memories changed to incorporate the crowds of onlookers in the fake photo (Sacchi et al., 2007).

actually occur. Importantly, a false memory feels "real" and is often accompanied by all the emotional impact of a real memory.

Forming False Memories: From the Plausible to the Impossible

■ KEY THEME
A variety of techniques can create false memories for events that never happened.

≡ KEY QUESTIONS
• What is the *lost-in-the-mall* technique, and how does it produce false memories?
• What is imagination inflation, and how has it been demonstrated?
• What factors contribute to the formation of false memories?

Up to this point, we've talked about how misinformation, source confusion, and the mental schemas we've developed can change or add details to a memory that already exists. However, memory researchers have gone beyond changing a few details here and there. Since the mid-1990s, an impressive body of research has accumulated showing how false memories can be created for events that *never* happened (Frenda et al., 2011; Loftus & Cahill, 2007). We'll begin with another Loftus study that has become famous—the *lost-in-the-mall* study.

Imagination Inflation: Remembering Being Lost in the Mall   In a classic experiment, Loftus and Jacqueline Pickrell (1995) gave each of 24 participants written descriptions of four childhood events that had been provided by a parent or other older relative. Three of the events had really happened, but the fourth did not. The false story went like this: At the age of 5 or 6, the person got lost for an extended period of time in a shopping mall, became very upset and cried, was rescued by an elderly person, and ultimately was reunited with the family. (Family members verified that the participant had never actually been lost in a shopping mall as a child.)

After reading the four event descriptions, the participants wrote down as many details as they could remember about each event. About two weeks later, participants were interviewed and asked to recall as many details as they could about each of the four events. Approximately one to two weeks after that, participants were interviewed a second time and asked once again what they could remember about the four events.

By the final interview, 6 of the 24 participants had created either full or partial memories of being lost in the shopping mall. How entrenched were the false memories for those who experienced them? Even after being debriefed at the end of the study, some of the participants continued to struggle with the vividness of the false memory.

"I totally remember walking around in those dressing rooms and my mom not being in the section she said she'd be in," one participant said (Loftus & Pickrell, 1995).

The research strategy of using information from family members to help create or induce false memories of childhood experiences has been dubbed the *lost-in-the-mall technique* (Loftus, 2003). By having participants remember real events along with imagining false events, researchers have created a wide variety of false memories. For example, participants have been led to believe that as a child they had been saved by a lifeguard from nearly drowning (Heaps & Nash, 2001). Or that they had knocked over a punch bowl at a wedding reception (Hyman & Pentland, 1996).

One key factor in the creation of false memories is the power of imagination. Put simply, imagining the past as different from what it was can change the way you remember it. Several studies have shown an effect called **imagination inflation**, *a memory phenomenon in which vividly imagining an event markedly increases confidence that the event actually occurred* (Garry & Polaschek, 2000; Thomas et al., 2003).

How does imagining an event—even one that never took place—help create a memory that is so compelling? Several factors seem to be involved. First, repeatedly imagining an event makes the event seem increasingly familiar. People then misinterpret the sense of familiarity as an indication that the event really happened (Sharman et al., 2004). Second, people experience source confusion—that is, subtle confusion as to whether a retrieved "memory" has a real or an imagined event as its source. Over time, people may misattribute their memory of imagining the false event as being a memory of the actual event. Third, vivid sensory and perceptual details can make the imagined events feel more like real events (Thomas et al., 2003).

Beyond personal history, could the same techniques be used to manipulate people's memories of actual political events? Yes. In an ingenious study, the online magazine *Slate* invited thousands of readers to participate in a survey about political events (Frenda et al., 2013; Saletan, 2010). As part of the survey, five photographs were shown. In each set of five photos, one had been doctored so that it showed an event that had never actually occurred. For example, one phony photo depicted Barack Obama shaking hands with Iranian president Mahmoud Ahmadinejad. (In reality, Obama has never been in the same room with Ahmadinejad.)

Over 5,000 *Slate* readers participated in the study. When asked how they felt about each of the five political events depicted, fully 50 percent reported that they remembered the false event happening—and more than half of this group said that they remembered seeing it on the news! As Steven Frenda and his colleagues (2013) wrote, "*Slate* readers became participants in the largest false memory experiment ever conducted."

All of the examples described so far involve creating false memories of relatively innocuous events, like getting lost as a child or seeing two politicians together. But what about more memorable, consequential events? Could false memories of more serious events, such as committing a crime and being arrested for it, also be created? Psychologists Julia Shaw and Stephen Porter (2015) showed that they could be created—and relatively easily. Just three 40-minute sessions of suggestive questioning were sufficient to convince fully 70 percent of participants that they had committed a serious crime—assault, assault with a weapon, or theft—during adolescence. The memories themselves were vivid and rich in complex detail.

Such findings have an important, real-world application (Howe & Knott, 2015). The Innocence Project (2015), a nonprofit group that investigates false convictions, found that false confessions are a common problem. More than 25 percent of the times when DNA evidence showed someone had been wrongly convicted, false confessions were involved.

imagination inflation A memory phenomenon in which vividly imagining an event markedly increases confidence that the event actually occurred.

Can Real Photos Create False Memories? Psychologist D. Stephen Lindsay and his colleagues (2004a, 2004b) had participants look at their first-grade class photo and read a description of a prank that they were led to believe had occurred in the first grade—putting "Slime" in their teacher's desk. After a week of trying to remember the prank, 65 percent of the participants reported vivid, detailed memories of the prank. In contrast, only about a quarter (23 percent) of participants who tried to remember the prank but did not view a school photo developed false memories of the pseudo-event. Viewing an actual school photo like the one shown here, Lindsay believes, added to the legitimacy of the pseudo-event, making it seem more probable. It also provided vivid sensory details that blended with the imagined details to create elaborate and subjectively compelling false memories. Real photos can lend credibility to imaginary events (Strange et al., 2011).

False Memories of Political Events That Never Happened

For an experiment on false memory, researchers doctored an actual photo of Barack Obama shaking hands with a man in a suit (left) to make it appear that he was shaking hands with Iranian president Mahmoud Ahmadinejad (right). When shown the doctored photo on the right, half of those participating in an online survey at *Slate* magazine said that they remembered Obama meeting Ahmadinejad—and some even remembered seeing a story about it on the news (Frenda et al., 2013). In reality, Obama and Ahmadinejad have never met.

Many of these confessions had been obtained through interrogations that incorporated strategies that are now known to produce false memories (Shaw & Porter, 2015).

Table 6.3 summarizes factors known to contribute to the formation of false memories. Research demonstrating the ease with which memories can be created and manipulated has raised questions in another important area—that of psychotherapy for serious psychological problems. We explore this controversy in the Critical Thinking box, "The Memory Wars: Recovered or False Memories?"

Distorted memories can ring true and feel just as real as accurate memories (Bernstein & Loftus, 2009; Clifasefi et al., 2007). In the chapter Prologue, you saw how easily Elizabeth Loftus created a false memory. You also saw how quickly she became convinced of the false memory's authenticity and the strong emotional impact it had

CRITICAL THINKING

The Memory Wars: Recovered or False Memories?

Repressed memory therapy, recovery therapy, recovered memory therapy, trauma therapy—these are some of the names of a therapy introduced in the 1990s and embraced by many psychotherapists, counselors, social workers, and other mental health workers. Proponents of the therapy claimed they had identified the root cause of a wide assortment of psychological problems: repressed memories of sexual abuse that had occurred during childhood.

This therapeutic approach assumed that incidents of sexual and physical abuse experienced in childhood, especially when perpetrated by a trusted caregiver, were so psychologically threatening that the victims repressed all memories of the experience (Gleaves et al., 2004; McNally & Geraerts, 2009). Despite being repressed, these unconscious memories of unspeakable traumas were thought to continue to cause psychological and physical problems, ranging from low self-esteem to eating disorders, substance abuse, and major depressive disorder.

The goal of repressed memory therapy was to help adult incest survivors "recover" their repressed memories of childhood sexual abuse. Reliving these painful experiences would help them begin "the healing process" of working through their anger and other intense emotions (Bass & Davis, 1994). Survivors were encouraged to confront their abusers and, if necessary, break all ties with their abusive families.

The Controversy: The "Recovery" Methods

The validity of the memories recovered in therapy became the center of a highly charged public controversy that has been dubbed "the memory wars" (Loftus, 2004; Patihis et al., 2014). A key issue was the methods used to help people unblock, or recover, repressed memories. Some recovered memory therapists used hypnosis, dream analysis, guided imagery, intensive group therapy, and other highly suggestive techniques to recover the long-repressed memories (Lynn et al., 2015; Thayer & Lynn, 2006).

Many patients supposedly recovered memories of repeated incidents of physical and sexual abuse, sometimes beginning in early infancy, ongoing for years, and involving multiple victimizers. Even more disturbing, some patients recovered vivid memories of years of alleged ritual satanic abuse involving secret cults practicing cannibalism, torture, and ritual murder (Loftus & Davis, 2006; Sakheim & Devine, 1992).

In more than twenty-five years of doing several hundred studies involving perhaps 20,000 people, we had distorted a significant portion of the subjects' memories. And the mechanism by which we can convince people they were lost, frightened, and crying in a mall is not so different than the mechanism by which therapists might unwittingly encourage memories of sexual abuse.

—*Elizabeth Loftus (2003)*

The Critical Issue: Recovered or False Memories?

Are traumatic memories likely to be repressed? It is well established that in documented cases of trauma, most survivors are troubled by the *opposite* problem—they cannot forget their traumatic memories (Iyadurai et al., 2019). Rather than being unable to remember the experience, trauma survivors suffer from recurring flashbacks, intrusive thoughts and memories of the trauma, and nightmares. This pattern is a key symptom of posttraumatic stress disorder (PTSD), which we'll discuss in the chapter on disorders.

While it is relatively common for a person to be unable to remember *some* of the specific details of a traumatic event or to be troubled by memory problems after the traumatic event, such

TABLE 6.3

Factors Contributing to False Memories

Factor	Description
Misinformation effect	Erroneous information received after an event leading to distorted or false memories of the event
Schema distortion	The tendency to fill in missing memory details with information that is consistent with preexisting knowledge
Source confusion	Forgetting or misremembering the true source of a memory
Imagination inflation	Unfounded confidence in a false or distorted memory caused by vividly imagining the false event
False familiarity	Increased feelings of familiarity due to repeatedly imagining an event
Blending fact and fiction	Using vivid, authentic details to add to the legitimacy and believability of a false event
Suggestion	Hypnosis, guided imagery, or other highly suggestive techniques

THINK LIKE A SCIENTIST

If you saw a crime take place, would you be a good witness? Go to Achieve: Resources to **Think Like a Scientist** about **Eyewitness Testimony.**

 Achie√e

on her. However, we don't want to leave you with the impression that all memories are highly unreliable. In reality, most memories tend to be quite accurate about the main things that happened. When memory distortions occur spontaneously in everyday life, they usually involve limited bits of information.

memory problems do *not* typically include difficulty in remembering the trauma itself (McNally, 2007). Memory researchers agree that a person might experience amnesia for a single traumatic incident but are skeptical that anyone could repress *all* memories of *repeated* incidents of abuse, especially when those incidents occurred over a period of several years (McNally & Geraerts, 2009).

Critics of repressed memory therapy contend that many of the supposedly "recovered" memories are actually *false memories* that were produced by the well-intentioned but misguided use of suggestive therapeutic techniques (Davis & Loftus, 2009). It is a myth that it's common to completely repress memories of traumatic events, but that such events can be accurately remembered under hypnosis. In fact, memory experts object to the use of hypnosis and other highly suggestive techniques to recover repressed memories (Gerrie et al., 2004; McNally & Geraerts, 2009). Understandably so. As you've seen in this chapter, compelling research shows the ease with which misinformation, suggestion, and imagination can create vivid—but completely *false*—memories.

MYTH ◀ SCIENCE

Is it true that it's common to completely repress memories of traumatic events, but that such events can be accurately remembered under hypnosis?

What Conclusions Can Be Drawn?

After years of debate, some areas of consensus have emerged (Allen, 2005; Colangelo, 2007). First, there is no question that physical and sexual abuse in childhood is a serious social problem that also contributes to psychological problems in adulthood (Hillberg et al., 2011).

Second, some psychologists contend it is *possible* for memories of childhood abuse to be completely forgotten, only to surface many years later in adulthood (Colangelo, 2007). Nevertheless, it's clear that repressed memories that have been recovered in psychotherapy need to be regarded with caution (Piper et al., 2008).

Third, the details of memories can be distorted with disturbing ease (Herndon et al., 2014). Consequently, the use of highly suggestive techniques to recover memories of abuse raises serious concerns about the accuracy of such memories. As we have noted repeatedly in this chapter, a person's confidence in a memory is no guarantee that the memory is indeed accurate. False or fabricated memories can seem just as detailed, vivid, and real as accurate ones (Gerrie et al., 2004; Lampinen et al., 2005).

Fourth, keep in mind that every act of remembering involves reconstructing a memory. Remembering an experience is not like replaying a movie captured with your cell phone. Memories can change over time. Without our awareness, memories can grow and evolve, sometimes in unexpected ways.

Finally, psychologists and other therapists have become more aware of the possibility of inadvertently creating false memories in therapy (Davis & Loftus, 2009). Guidelines have been developed to help mental health professionals avoid unintentionally creating false memories in clients (American Psychological Association Working Group, 1998; Colangelo, 2007).

CRITICAL THINKING QUESTIONS

- Why is it difficult to determine the accuracy of a "memory" that is recovered in therapy?
- How could the phenomenon of source confusion be used to explain the production of false memories?

memory trace or **engram** The hypothetical brain changes associated with a particular stored memory.

The Search for the Biological Basis of Memory

■ KEY THEME
Early researchers believed that memory was associated with physical changes in the brain, but these changes were discovered only in the past few decades.

▪ KEY QUESTIONS
- How are memories both localized and distributed in the brain?
- How do neurons change when a memory is formed?

Do you remember the name *Ivan Pavlov*? We hope so. As you should recall from the chapter on learning, Pavlov was the Russian physiologist who classically conditioned dogs to salivate to the sound of a metronome and other neutral stimuli. Without question, learning and memory are intimately connected. Learning an adaptive response depends on our ability to form new memories in which we associate environmental stimuli, behaviors, and consequences.

Pavlov (1927) believed that the memory involved in learning a classically conditioned response would ultimately be explained as a matter of changes in the brain. However, Pavlov only speculated about the kinds of brain changes that would produce the memories needed for classical conditioning to occur. Other researchers would take up the search for the physical changes associated with learning and memory. In this section, we look at some of the key discoveries that have been made in trying to understand the biological basis of memory.

The Search for the Elusive Memory Trace

American physiological psychologist **Karl Lashley** (1890–1958) set out to investigate Pavlov's speculations in the 1920s. Lashley began the search for the **memory trace**, or **engram**—*the hypothetical brain changes associated with a particular stored memory*. Guiding Lashley's research was his belief that memory was *localized*, meaning that a particular memory was stored in a specific brain area (Lashley, 1929; Josselyn et al., 2015).

Lashley first looked for the specific location of the memory trace that a rat forms for running a maze. Once a rat had learned to run the maze, Lashley surgically removed tiny portions of the rat's cerebral cortex. After the rat recovered, Lashley tested the rat in the maze again. Obviously, if the rat could still run the maze, then the portion of the brain removed did not contain the memory.

Over the course of 30 years, no matter which part of the cortex Lashley removed, the rats were still able to run the maze (Lashley, 1929, 1950). At the end of his professional career, Karl Lashley concluded that memories are not localized in specific locations but instead are *distributed,* or stored, throughout the brain.

Lashley was wrong, but not completely wrong. Some memories *do* seem to be localized at specific spots in the brain. Some 20 years after Lashley's death, psychologist **Richard F. Thompson** (1930–2014) and his colleagues resumed the search for the location of the memory trace that would confirm Pavlov's speculations.

Thompson classically conditioned rabbits to perform a very simple behavior—an eyeblink. By repeatedly pairing a tone with a puff of air administered to the rabbit's eye, he classically conditioned rabbits to blink reflexively in response to the tone alone (Thompson, 1994, 2005).

Thompson discovered that after a rabbit had learned this simple behavior, there was a change in the brain activity in a small area of the rabbit's *cerebellum,* a lower brain structure involved in physical movements. When this tiny area of the cerebellum was removed, the rabbit's memory of the learned response disappeared. It no longer blinked at the sound of the tone. However, the puff of air still caused the rabbit to blink reflexively, so the reflex itself had not been destroyed.

Thompson and his colleagues had confirmed Pavlov's speculations. The long-term memory trace of the classically conditioned eyeblink was formed and stored in a very localized region of the cerebellum.

Combined, the findings of Lashley and Thompson indicate that memories have the potential to be *both localized* and *distributed*. Very simple memories (Thompson's research) may be localized in a specific area, whereas more complex memories (Lashley's research) are distributed throughout the brain. A complex memory involves clusters of information, and each part of the memory may be stored in the brain area that originally processed the information (Greenberg & Rubin, 2003; Josselyn et al., 2015).

Adding support to Lashley's and Thompson's findings, brain imaging technology has confirmed that many kinds of memories are distributed in the human brain. When we are performing a relatively complex memory task, multiple brain regions are activated—evidence of the distribution of memories involved in complex tasks (Khan & Muly, 2011).

The Focus on Neuroscience box describes a clever study that explored how memories involving different sensory experiences are assembled when they are retrieved.

Is it true that all memories, even complex ones, are located in a single part of the brain?

FOCUS ON NEUROSCIENCE

Assembling Memories: Echoes and Reflections of Perception

If we asked you to remember the theme from *Star Wars*, you would "hear" the song in your head. Conjure up a memory of your high school cafeteria, and you "see" it in your mind. Memories can include a great deal of sensory information—sounds, sights, and even odors, textures, and tastes. How are such rich sensory aspects of an experience incorporated into a memory that is retrieved?

Researchers set out to investigate this question using a simple memory task and fMRI (Wheeler et al., 2000; Herholz et al., 2012). Participants studied names for common objects that were paired with either a picture or a sound associated with the word. For example, the word *dog* was either paired with a picture of a dog or the sound of a dog barking. The researchers then used fMRI to measure brain activity when the volunteers were instructed to recall the words they'd memorized.

The results? Retrieving the memory activated a subset of the same brain areas that were involved in perceiving the sensory stimulus. Participants who had memorized the word *dog* with a *picture* of a dog showed a high level of activation in the *visual cortex* when they retrieved the memory. And participants who had memorized the word *dog* with the *sound* of a barking dog showed a high level of activation in the *auditory cortex* when they retrieved the memory.

Of course, many of our memories are highly complex, involving not just sensations but also thoughts and emotions. Neuroscientists assume that such complex memories involve networks of neurons that are widely distributed throughout the brain. However, they still don't completely understand how all these neural records are bound together and interrelated to form a single, highly elaborate memory (Josselyn et al., 2015).

Perception   Recall

Picture

(a)   (b)

Sound

(c)   (d)

Courtesy of Mark E. Wheeler, Randy L. Buckner, and Steven E. Petersen

‹ Retrieving the Memory of a Sensory Experience Top row: (a) Perceiving a picture activates areas of the visual cortex. (b) When the memory of the picture is recalled, it reactivates some of the same areas of the visual cortex *(arrow)* that were involved in the initial perception of the picture. Bottom row: (c) Perceiving a sound activates areas of the auditory cortex. (d) When the memory of the sound is recalled, it reactivates some of the same areas of the auditory cortex *(arrow)* that were involved in the initial perception of the sound.

long-term potentiation A long-lasting increase in synaptic strength between two neurons.

amnesia (am-NEE-zha) Severe memory loss.

retrograde amnesia Loss of memory, especially for episodic information of recent events.

memory consolidation The gradual, physical process of converting new long-term memories to stable, enduring memory codes.

The Role of Neurons in Long-Term Memory

What exactly is localized or distributed? The notion of a memory trace suggests that some change must occur in the workings of the brain when a new long-term memory is stored. Logically, two possible changes could occur. First, the *functioning* of the brain's neurons could change. Second, the *structure* of the neurons could change. Given those two possibilities, the challenge for memory researchers has been to identify the specific neurons involved in a given memory, a task that is virtually impossible with the human brain because of its enormous complexity. What this task required was a creature with a limited number of neurons that is also capable of learning new memories.

Enter *Aplysia*, a gentle, seaweed-munching sea snail that resides off the California coast. The study of *Aplysia* over the past 30 years has given memory researchers important insights into the brain changes involved in memory. Why *Aplysia*? Because *Aplysia* has only about 20,000 good-sized neurons. That was a key reason why memory researcher **Eric Kandel** (b. 1929; 2006, 2009) chose this unassuming creature to study the neuronal changes that occur when a new memory is formed for a simple classically conditioned response.

If you give *Aplysia* a gentle squirt with a Waterpik, followed by a mild electric shock to its tail, the snail reflexively withdraws its gill flap. When the process is repeated several times, *Aplysia* wises up and acquires a new memory of a classically conditioned response—it withdraws its gill when squirted with the WaterPik alone. This learned gill-withdrawal reflex seems to involve a circuit of just three neurons: one that detects the water squirt, one that detects the tail shock, and one that signals the gill-withdrawal reflex (see **Figure 6.9**).

When *Aplysia* acquires this new memory through repeated training trials, significant changes occur in the three-neuron circuit (Kandel, 2001). First, the *function* of the neurons is altered: There is an increase in the amount of the neurotransmitters produced by the neurons. Second, the *structure* of the snail's neurons changes: The number of interconnecting branches between the neurons increases, as does the number of synapses, or communication points, on each branch. These changes allow the neurons involved in the particular memory circuit to communicate more easily. Collectively, these changes are called **long-term potentiation**, which refers to *a long-lasting increase in synaptic strength between two neurons* (Baudry et al., 2011; Smolen et al., 2016).

The same kinds of brain changes have been observed in more sophisticated species. Chicks, rats, and rabbits also show structural and functional neuron changes associated with new learning experiences and memories. And, as you may recall from the Psych for Your Life section in the chapter on neuroscience, there is ample evidence that the same kinds of changes occur in the human brain.

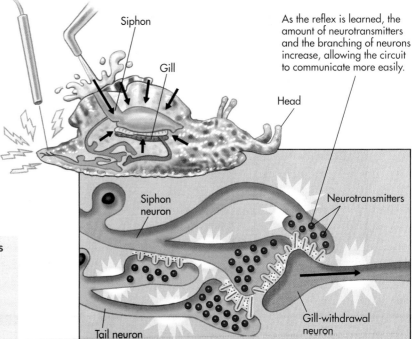

As the reflex is learned, the amount of neurotransmitters and the branching of neurons increase, allowing the circuit to communicate more easily.

FIGURE 6.9 How Neurons Change as *Aplysia* Forms a New Memory When *Aplysia* is repeatedly squirted with water, and each squirt is followed by a mild shock to its tail, the snail learns to withdraw its gill flap if just squirted with the water. Conditioning leads to structural and functional changes in the three neurons involved in the memory circuit.

In terms of our understanding of the memory trace, what do these findings suggest? Although there are vast differences between the nervous system of a simple creature such as *Aplysia* and the enormously complex human brain, some tentative generalizations are possible. Forming a memory seems to produce distinct functional changes and structural changes in specific neurons. These changes create a memory circuit. Each time the memory is recalled, the neurons in this circuit are activated. As the structural and functional changes in the neurons strengthen the communication links in this circuit, the memory becomes established as a long-term memory (Kandel, 2006, 2009).

Processing Memories in the Brain: Clues from Amnesia

■ KEY THEME
Important insights into the brain structures involved in normal memory have been provided by case studies of people with amnesia caused by damaged brain tissue.

≡ KEY QUESTIONS
• Who was H. M., and what did his case reveal about normal memory processes?
• What brain structures are involved in normal memory?
• What are dementia and Alzheimer's disease?

Before today's sophisticated brain imaging technology, researchers studied individuals who had sustained a brain injury or had part of their brain surgically removed for medical reasons. Often, such individuals experienced **amnesia**, or *severe memory loss*. By relating the type and extent of amnesia to the specific damaged brain areas, researchers uncovered clues as to how the human brain processes memories.

Retrograde Amnesia: Disrupting Memory Consolidation One type of amnesia is retrograde amnesia. *Retrograde* means "backward moving." People with **retrograde amnesia** experience a *loss of memory, especially for episodic information of recent events*. Retrograde amnesia often results from a blow to the head. Boxers sometimes suffer such memory losses after years of fighting. Head injuries from automobile and motorcycle accidents are another common cause of retrograde amnesia. Typically, memories of the events that immediately preceded the injury are completely lost, as in the case of accident victims who cannot remember details about what led up to the accident. It is important to remember, however, that it is not really possible to erase a person's entire memory. Memories are thought to be stored throughout the entire brain. Damage to the brain undoubtedly disrupts a person's access to some memories, but it does not erase their entire memory. The only brain process capable of this full erasure is the type of pervasive atrophy you see in many types of dementia, a topic we will address shortly.

Apparently, establishing a long-term memory is like creating a Jell-O mold—it needs time to "set" before it becomes solid. This process of "setting" a new memory permanently in the brain is called memory consolidation (Dudai et al., 2011). More specifically, **memory consolidation** is *the gradual, physical process of converting new long-term memories to stable, enduring memory codes* (Medina et al., 2008). If memory consolidation is disrupted before the process is complete, the vulnerable memory may be lost (Dudai, 2004).

In humans, memory consolidation can be disrupted by brain trauma, such as a sudden blow, concussion, electric shock, or encephalitis (Riccio et al., 2003). Similarly, many drugs, such as alcohol and the benzodiazepines, interfere with memory consolidation. In contrast, stimulants and the

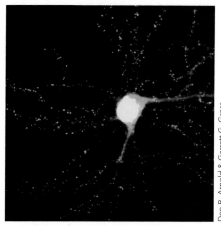

▲ **Making Memories in the Brain: Changing Synaptic Connections**
Forming a new memory involves physical changes in the brain. New synaptic connections are created, and old synaptic connections are weakened or eliminated. This photo shows a single rat neuron (Gross et al., 2013). The bright green and red spots dotting the dendrites extending from the cell body are synapses. As the brain processes information, synapses change. Ultimately, new memories are reflected in the evolving patterns of synaptic structure.

Don B. Arnold & Garrett G. Gross

Tony Ding/AP Images

❮ **Disrupting the Consolidation of Memories** Head injuries are common in football and many other sports. University of Michigan running back Chris Evans, shown here, was diagnosed with a concussion after being hit from both sides in a game against the University of Illinois. In one study, football players who were questioned immediately after a concussion or other head injury could remember how they were injured and the name of the play just performed. But if questioned 30 minutes later for the same information, they could not. Because the head injury had disrupted the memory consolidation process, the memories were permanently lost (Yarnell & Lynch, 1970). Refer back to Figure 6.3 on page 194 about encoding long-term memories and you will be reminded that information (like the name of a play just run) has to be rehearsed or it is forgotten in about 20 seconds. It is hard for the brain to rehearse anything while it is attending to a potentially lethal injury.

anterograde amnesia Loss of memory caused by the inability to store new memories.

stress hormones that are released during emotional arousal tend to *enhance* memory consolidation (Nielson & Lorber, 2009).

Anterograde Amnesia: Disrupting the Formation of Explicit Memories

Another form of amnesia is **anterograde amnesia**—the *loss of memory caused by the inability to store new memories. Anterograde* means "forward moving." The most famous case study of anterograde amnesia lasted over 50 years. It was of a man who for years was known only by his initials—H. M. But the need to protect H. M.'s privacy ended when Henry Molaison died at the age of 82 on December 2, 2008.

In 1953, Molaison was 27 years old and had a history of severe, untreatable epileptic seizures. Molaison's doctors located the brain area where the seizures seemed to originate. With no other options available at the time, the decision was made to surgically remove portions of the *medial* (inner) *temporal lobe* on each side of Molaison's brain, including the brain structure called the *hippocampus* (Scoville & Milner, 1957). Portions of the left and right *amygdala* were also removed (Annese et al., 2014).

After the experimental surgery, the frequency and severity of Molaison's seizures were greatly reduced. However, it was quickly discovered that Molaison's ability to form new memories of events and information had been destroyed. Although the experimental surgery had treated Molaison's seizures, it also dramatically revealed the role of the hippocampus in forming new explicit memories for episodic and semantic information.

Psychologists **Brenda Milner** (1970) and **Suzanne Corkin** (2013) studied Molaison extensively over the past 50 years. He was well aware of his memory problem. When Suzanne Corkin (2002) once asked him, "What do you do to try to remember?" Molaison quipped, "Well, that I don't know because I don't remember [chuckle] what I tried."

"Henry Molaison, aged 60, at MIT in 1986. Photograph by Jenni Ogden, first published in her book "Trouble in Mind: Stories from a Neuropsychologist's Casebook."

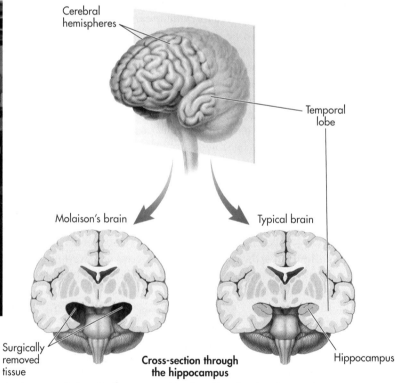

Cerebral hemispheres

Temporal lobe

Molaison's brain

Typical brain

Surgically removed tissue

Cross-section through the hippocampus

Hippocampus

⌃ **Henry Gustav Molaison: The Real H. M. (1926–2008)** At the age of nine, Molaison jarred his head badly when he was hit by a bicyclist. Not long after, he began experiencing seizures. By early adulthood, Molaison's seizures had increased in both severity and frequency. In an effort to control the seizures, an experimental surgery was performed, removing the hippocampus, the surrounding cortical tissue, and the amygdala on each side of Molaison's brain. Because of the profound anterograde amnesia caused by the surgery, Molaison became one of the most intensive case studies in psychology and neuroscience. Over the next half century, Molaison participated in hundreds of studies that fundamentally altered the scientific understanding of memory. Molaison died on December 2, 2008, but his contributions to science continue. Neuroscientist Jacopo Annese and his team (2014) dissected Molaison's brain, slicing it into 2,400 micro-thin slices in a marathon, three-day session that was streamed online. Photographs of each slice were taken to create a virtual 3-D digital model of Molaison's brain.

Despite having a delightful sense of humor and appearing normal, Molaison lived in the eternal present. Corkin could talk with Molaison for 15 minutes, then leave the room for two or three minutes before coming back, and he wouldn't remember having even met Corkin before. Some psychologists and doctors treated Molaison for years, even decades, and Molaison always acted as if he were meeting them for the first time (Corkin, 2013; MacKay, 2014).

For the most part, Molaison's short-term memory worked just fine. In fact, he could fool you. If Molaison actively repeated or rehearsed information, he could hold it in short-term memory for an hour or more (Nader & Wang, 2006). Yet just moments after he switched his attention to something else and stopped rehearsing the information, it was gone forever. However, Molaison's long-term memory was partially intact. He could retrieve long-term memories from *before* the time he was 16 years old, when the severe epileptic seizures began.

In general, Molaison was unable to acquire new long-term memories of events (episodic information) or general knowledge (semantic information). Still, every now and then, Molaison surprised his doctors and visitors with some bit of knowledge that he acquired after the surgery.

Molaison's case suggests that the hippocampus is not involved in most short-term memory tasks, nor is it the storage site for already established long-term memories. Instead, the critical role played by the hippocampus seems to be the *encoding* of new memories for events and information and the *transfer* of those new memories from short-term to long-term memory.

Implicit and Explicit Memory in Anterograde Amnesia Molaison's case and those of other patients with anterograde amnesia have contributed greatly to our understanding of implicit versus explicit memories. To refresh your memory, *implicit memories* are memories without conscious awareness. In contrast, *explicit memories* are memories with conscious awareness.

Molaison could not form new episodic or semantic memories, which reflects the explicit memory system. But he *could* form new procedural memories, which reflects the implicit memory system. For example, when given the same logical puzzle to solve several days in a row, Molaison solved it more quickly each day. This improvement showed that he *implicitly* "remembered" the procedure involved in solving the puzzle. But if you asked Molaison if he had ever seen the puzzle before, he would answer "no" because he could not consciously (or *explicitly*) remember having learned how to solve the puzzle. This suggests that the hippocampus is less crucial to the formation of new implicit memories, such as procedural memories, than it is to the formation of new explicit memories.

Were Molaison's memory anomalies an exception? Not at all. Studies conducted with other people who have sustained damage to the hippocampus and related brain structures showed the same anterograde amnesia (see Bayley & Squire, 2002; Squire & Dede, 2015). Like Molaison, these patients are unable to form new explicit memories, but their performances on implicit memory tasks, which do not require conscious recollection of the new information, are much closer to normal. Such findings indicate that implicit and explicit memory processes involve different brain structures and pathways.

Brain Structures Involved in Memory Along with the hippocampus, several other brain regions involved in memory include the cerebellum, the amygdala, and the frontal cortex (see **Figure 6.10**). As you saw earlier, the *cerebellum* is involved in classically conditioning simple reflexes, such as the eyeblink reflex. The cerebellum is also involved in procedural memories and other motor skill memories.

Suzanne Corkin (1937–2016) For nearly 50 years, MIT neuropsychologist Suzanne Corkin (2013) evaluated different aspects of Molaison's memory abilities along with Brenda Milner (b., 1918). In looking back on Molaison's life, Corkin (2002) commented, "We all understand the rare opportunity we have had to work with him, and we are grateful for his dedication to research. He has taught us a great deal about the cognitive and neural organization of memory. We are in his debt."

marc marnie/AP Images

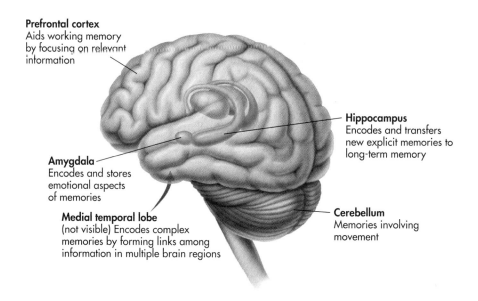

FIGURE 6.10 Brain Structures Involved in Human Memory Shown here are some of the key brain structures involved in encoding and storing memories. The labels describe the various functions of the different brain structures.

Prefrontal cortex
Aids working memory by focusing on relevant information

Amygdala
Encodes and stores emotional aspects of memories

Medial temporal lobe
(not visible) Encodes complex memories by forming links among information in multiple brain regions

Hippocampus
Encodes and transfers new explicit memories to long-term memory

Cerebellum
Memories involving movement

The *amygdala*, which is situated very close to the hippocampus, is involved in encoding and storing the emotional qualities associated with particular memories, such as fear or anger (Hamann, 2009; McGaugh, 2004). For example, normal monkeys are afraid of snakes. But if the amygdala is damaged, a monkey loses its fear of snakes and other natural predators.

The *frontal lobes* are involved in retrieving and organizing information that is associated with autobiographical and episodic memories (Greenberg & Rubin, 2003). The *prefrontal cortex* seems to play an important role in working memory by focusing on and selecting relevant information (D'Esposito & Postle, 2015; Lara & Wallis, 2015; McNab & Klingberg, 2008).

The *medial temporal lobes*, like the frontal lobes, do not actually store the information that comprises our autobiographical memories. Rather, they are involved in encoding complex memories, by forming links among the information stored in multiple brain regions (Greenberg & Rubin, 2003; Shrager & Squire, 2009). As we described in the Focus on Neuroscience, "Assembling Memories," retrieving a memory activates the same brain regions that were involved in initially encoding the memory.

Dementia: Losing Memory, Losing the Self Understanding how the brain processes and stores memories has important implications. **Dementia** is a broad term that refers to the *progressive deterioration and impairment of memory, reasoning, language, and other cognitive functions as the result of disease, injury, or substance abuse.* These cognitive disruptions occur to such an extent that they interfere with the person's ability to carry out daily activities. Dementia is not itself a disease. Rather, it describes a group of symptoms that often accompany a disease or a condition. Dementia has long been associated with aging. Repeated head injuries, strokes, and brain diseases such as Parkinson's disease can increase the risk of dementia (Alzheimer's Association, 2016; *The Lancet*, 2015).

The most common cause of dementia is **Alzheimer's disease (AD)**, *a progressive disease that destroys the brain's neurons, gradually impairing memory, thinking, language, and other cognitive functions, resulting in the complete inability to care for oneself.* It is the most common cause of dementia, and it is estimated that about 5.4 million Americans suffer from AD. That number is expected to dramatically escalate as "baby boomers" age. The disease usually doesn't begin until after age 60, but the risk goes up with age. About 15 percent of men and women in the 65–74

dementia Progressive deterioration and impairment of memory, reasoning, language, and other cognitive functions as the result of disease, injury, or substance abuse.

Alzheimer's disease (AD) A progressive disease that destroys the brain's neurons, gradually impairing memory, thinking, language, and other cognitive functions, resulting in the complete inability to care for oneself.

Steve Liss/Getty Images

∧ **The Nun Study of Aging and Alzheimer's Disease** Neurologist David Snowdon is shown here having a laugh during a card game with Sister Esther, who is 106 years old. Since 1986, Snowdon (2002, 2003) has studied 678 elderly Roman Catholic nuns, an ideal research group because their lifestyles and environment are so similar. Although the study is ongoing, several findings have already emerged (see K. Riley et al., 2005; Tyas et al., 2007a, 2007b).

For example, the outward signs of Alzheimer's disease (AD) and the degree of brain damage evident at death are not perfectly correlated. Although some nuns had clear brain evidence of AD, they did not display observable cognitive and behavior declines prior to their deaths. Other nuns had only mild brain evidence of AD but showed severe cognitive and behavioral declines.

Interestingly, the sisters who displayed better language abilities when they were young women were less likely to display AD symptoms. This held true regardless of how much brain damage was evident at the time of death (Iacono et al., 2009).

age group have AD. About a third of adults age 85 and older have AD (Alzheimer's Association, 2016).

The cause or causes of Alzheimer's disease are still unknown, but it is known that the brains of AD patients develop an abundance of two abnormal structures—*protein plaques* and *fibrous tangles* (Ballard et al., 2011). The *plaques* are dense deposits of protein and other cell materials outside and around neurons. The plaques interfere with the ability of neurons to communicate, damaging the neurons to the point that they die. The *tangles* are twisted fibers that build up inside the neuron and interrupt the flow of nourishment to the neuron, ultimately causing the neuron to die. Although most older people develop some plaques and tangles in their brains, the brains of AD patients have them to a much greater extent (Petersen, 2002).

The Focus on Neuroscience box vividly portrays the progressive loss of neurons that causes the symptoms of AD. Some people have developed systems to deal with their forgetfulness and declining cognitive abilities (Kleinfeld, 2016). For example, Geri Taylor, a former nurse, was diagnosed with Alzheimer's disease when she was just 69. Determined to maintain an active life, Taylor keeps detailed notes on her iPhone and uses it to take photos of places so she won't get lost.

In the early stages of AD, the symptoms of memory impairment are often mild, such as forgetting the names of familiar people, forgetting the location of familiar places, or forgetting to do things. But as the disease progresses, memory loss and confusion become more pervasive. The person becomes unable to remember what

🧠 FOCUS ON NEUROSCIENCE

Mapping Brain Changes in Alzheimer's Disease

The hallmark of Alzheimer's disease is its relentless, progressive destruction of neurons in the brain, turning once-healthy tissue into a tangled, atrophied mass. This progressive loss of brain tissue is dramatically revealed in the MRI images shown below. Created by neuroscientist Paul Thompson and his colleagues (2003), these high-resolution "brain maps" represent composite images of the progressive effects of Alzheimer's disease (AD) in 12 patients over the course of two years. In these color-coded images, blue corresponds to normal tissue (no loss), red indicates up to 10 percent tissue loss, and white indicates up to 20 percent tissue loss.

Thompson likens the progression of AD to that of molten lava flowing around rocks—the disease leaves islands of brain tissue

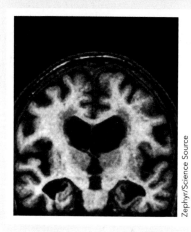

Zephyr/Science Source

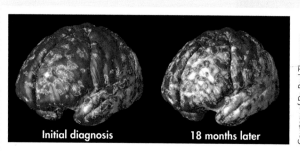

Initial diagnosis   18 months later

Courtesy of Dr. Paul Thompson, Laboratory of Neuro-Imaging and the Imaging Genetics Center at UCLA

unscathed. The disease first attacks the temporal lobes, affecting areas involved in memory, especially short-term memory. Next affected are the frontal areas, which are involved in thinking, reasoning, self-control, and planning ahead. You can also see significant internal loss in the limbic areas, which are involved in regulating emotion. The photo above shows the brain of someone with Alzheimer's disease. The ventricles, which hold the cerebral spinal fluid, are large compared with a typical brain because they have been ravaged by the disease. Recently, neuroscientists started using the pattern and amount of atrophy in different brain regions as a way to diagnose Alzheimer's disease (Frenzel et al., 2020). Previously, it could only be diagnosed following a postmortem examination of the patient's brain. There is also increasing evidence that specific patterns of brain change may be associated with the different patterns of symptoms seen among Alzheimer's disease patients.

month it is or the names of family members. Frustrated and disoriented by the inability to retrieve even simple information, the person can become agitated and moody. In the last stage of AD, internal brain damage has become widespread, and the person becomes increasingly unable to carry out the simplest tasks. The person no longer recognizes loved ones and is unable to communicate in any meaningful way. At the closing stages, the person becomes completely incapacitated. Ultimately, AD is fatal (Alzheimer's Association, 2016).

Closing Thoughts

Human memory is at once both perfectly ordinary and quite extraordinary. With next to no mental effort, you form and recall countless memories as you go through daily life. Psychologists have made enormous progress in explaining how those memories are encoded, stored, retrieved, and forgotten.

Perhaps the most fascinating aspect of human memory is its fallibility. Memory is surprisingly susceptible to errors and distortions. Under some conditions, completely false memories can be experienced, such as Elizabeth Loftus's memory of discovering her mother's body in the swimming pool. Such false memories can be so compelling that they feel like authentic memories, yet confidence in a memory is not proof of the memory's truth.

Many mysteries of human memory remain, including exactly how memories are stored in and retrieved from the brain. Nevertheless, reliable ways of improving memory in everyday life have been discovered. In the Psych for Your Life, section, we provide several suggestions to enhance your memory for new information.

PSYCH FOR YOUR LIFE

Ten Steps to Boost Your Memory

There are many simple and effective strategies that can help boost your memory for important information. Before reading further, flip back to the chapter on introduction and research methods and review the research-based study strategies described there. (You *do* remember those suggestions, don't you?) Knowing what you now know about human memory, you should have a better understanding of *why* those strategies are effective. To recap, those strategies included the following:

- Focus your attention.
- Be an active reader.
- Take notes by hand.
- Practice retrieval.
- Use flashcards and practice tests correctly.
- Space out your study time.

   Want to improve your memory? Read on for 10 simple and effective memory-boosting techniques.

1. Commit the necessary time.

The more time you spend learning material, the better you will understand it and the longer you will remember it. Budget enough time to read the assigned material carefully. If you read material faster than you can comprehend it, you not only won't understand the material, you also won't remember it.

2. Organize the information.

We have a strong natural tendency to organize information in long-term memory into categories. You can capitalize on this tendency by actively organizing information you want to remember. One way to accomplish this is by outlining chapters or your lecture notes. Use the chapter headings and subheadings as categories, or, better yet, create your own categories. Under each category, list and describe the relevant terms, concepts, and ideas. This strategy can double the amount of information you can recall.

3. Elaborate on the material.

You've probably noticed that virtually every term or concept in this text is formally defined in just a sentence or two. But we also spend a paragraph or more explaining what the concept means. To remember the information you read, you have to do the same thing — engage in *elaborative rehearsal* and actively process the information for meaning. Actively question new information and think about its implications. Form memory associations by relating the material to what you already know. Try to come up with examples that relate to your own life.

4. Explain it to a friend.

After you read a section of material, stop and summarize what you have read in your own words. When you think you understand it, try explaining the information to a friend or family member. As you'll quickly discover, it's hard to explain material that you don't really understand! Memory research has shown that explaining new material in your own words forces you to integrate the new information into your existing knowledge base — an excellent way to solidify new information in your memory (Kornell, 2008).

5. Use visual imagery.

Two memory codes are better than one (Paivio, 1986). Rather than merely encoding the information verbally, use mental imagery (Carretti et al., 2007; Sadoski, 2005).

Much of the information in this text easily lends itself to visual imagery. Use the photographs and other illustrations to help form visual memories of the information. Better yet, try drawing or sketching the information. Jeffrey Wammes and his colleagues (2016) found that drawing words resulted in better memory than forming mental images of words, writing words, seeing photos of words, or describing words. The researchers speculated that drawing created a memory trace that integrated visual imagery, motor memory, and elaboration in a seamless way, making the memory easier to retrieve later.

6. Reduce interference within a topic.

If you occasionally confuse related terms and concepts, it may be because you're experiencing *interference* in your memories for similar information. To minimize memory interference for related information, first break the chapter into manageable sections, then learn the key information one section at a time. As you encounter new concepts, compare them with previously learned concepts, looking for differences and similarities. By building distinct memories for important information as you progress through a topic, you're more likely to distinguish between concepts so they don't get confused in your memory.

7. Counteract the serial position effect.

The *serial position effect* is the tendency to have better recall of information at the beginning and end of a sequence. To counteract this effect, spend extra time learning the information that falls in the middle. Once you've mastered a sequence of material, start at a different point each time you review or practice the information.

8. Use contextual cues to jog memories.

Ideally, study in the setting in which you're going to be tested. If that's not possible, when you're taking a test and a specific memory gets blocked, imagine that your books and notes are in front of you and that you're sitting where you normally study. Simply imagining the surroundings where you learned the material can help jog those memories.

9. Use a mnemonic device for remembering lists.

A *mnemonic device* is a method or strategy to aid memory. Some of the most effective mnemonic devices use visual imagery (Foer, 2011). For example, the *method of loci* is a mnemonic device in which you remember items by visualizing them at specific locations in a familiar setting, such as the different rooms in your house or at specific locations on your way to work or school. To recall the items, mentally revisit the locations and imagine the specific item at that location.

Another mnemonic that involves creating visual associations is the *peg-word method*. First, you learn an easily remembered list containing the peg words, such as: 1 is bun, 2 is shoe, 3 is tree, 4 is door, 5 is hive, 6 is sticks, 7 is heaven, 8 is gate, 9 is vine, 10 is a hen, and you can keep going as needed. Then, you create a vivid mental image associating the first item you want to remember with the first peg word, the next item with the next peg word, and so on. To recall the list, use each successive peg word to help retrieve the mental image.

10. Finally, sleep on it to help consolidate those memories.

As we discussed in the chapter about consciousness and its variations, numerous studies have demonstrated that sleep helps you consolidate new memories. (Don't try this as an excuse in class.) A good night's sleep also helps you integrate new memories into existing networks, making it more likely that you'll recall the new information when you need to (Stickgold & Walker, 2013). In other words, all-night cram sessions just before an exam are one of the *least* effective ways to learn new material. And, speaking of sleep, not getting enough sleep also disrupts memory, interfering with the encoding of new material (Abel et al., 2013).

> **Memory Superstar Joshua Foer** Journalist Joshua Foer (2011) visited a memory competition expecting to find people with special memory abilities. Instead, he encountered a group of "mental athletes"—people with ordinary minds who had trained their memories to accomplish incredible feats, such as reciting hundreds of random digits or pages of poetry. Told that anyone could develop an expert memory with training, he set out to prove it and devoted months to training his own memory. A year later, he won the USA Memory Championship and even set a new U.S. record by memorizing the position of cards in a deck in 1 minute, 40 seconds. Foer's secret? Mnemonic techniques, like the method of loci—and lots and lots of practice. Foer explains his method in his TED Talk, available at: ted.com/talks/joshua_foer_feats_of_memory_anyone_can_do

Merlijn Doomernik/Hollandse Hoogte/Redux

CHAPTER REVIEW

Memory

Achieve, Macmillan Learning's online study platform, features the full e-book of *Discovering Psychology,* the **LearningCurve** adaptive quizzing system, videos, and a variety of activities to boost your learning. Visit **Achieve** at macmillanlearning.com.

KEY PEOPLE

Suzanne Corkin, p. 218

Hermann Ebbinghaus, p. 203

Eric Kandel, p. 216

Karl Lashley, p. 214

Elizabeth Loftus, p. 207

Brenda Milner, p. 218

George Sperling, p. 189

Richard F. Thompson, p. 214

KEY TERMS

memory, p. 188

encoding, p. 188

storage, p. 188

retrieval, p. 188

stage model of memory, p. 188

sensory memory, p. 188

short-term memory, p. 189

long-term memory, p. 189

maintenance rehearsal, p. 191

chunking, p. 191

working memory, p. 192

elaborative rehearsal, p. 194

procedural memory, p. 195

episodic memory, p. 195

semantic memory, p. 195

explicit memory, p. 196

implicit memory, p. 197

clustering, p. 197

semantic network model, p. 197

retrieval, p. 198

retrieval cue, p. 198

retrieval cue failure, p. 199

tip-of-the-tongue (TOT) experience, p. 199

recall, p. 200

cued recall, p. 200

recognition, p. 200

serial position effect, p. 200

encoding specificity principle, p. 201

context effect, p. 201

mood congruence, p. 201

flashbulb memory, p. 201

forgetting, p. 202

encoding failure, p. 204

prospective memory, p. 205

decay theory, p. 205

interference theory, p. 206

retroactive interference, p. 206

proactive interference, p. 206

suppression, p. 206

repression, p. 206

misinformation effect, p. 207

schemas, p. 208

source confusion, p. 209

false memory, p. 209

imagination inflation, p. 211

memory trace (engram), p. 214

long-term potentiation, p. 216

amnesia, p. 217

retrograde amnesia, p. 217

memory consolidation, p. 217

anterograde amnesia, p. 218

dementia, p. 220

Alzheimer's disease (AD), p. 220

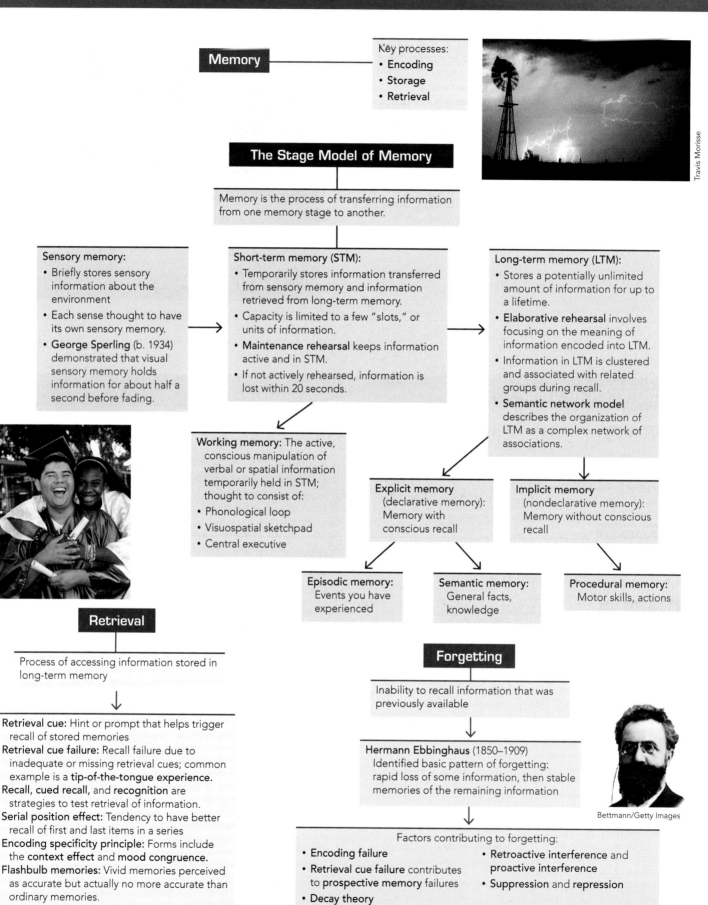

Memory

Key processes:
- Encoding
- Storage
- Retrieval

Travis Morisse

The Stage Model of Memory

Memory is the process of transferring information from one memory stage to another.

Sensory memory:
- Briefly stores sensory information about the environment
- Each sense thought to have its own sensory memory.
- **George Sperling** (b. 1934) demonstrated that visual sensory memory holds information for about half a second before fading.

Short-term memory (STM):
- Temporarily stores information transferred from sensory memory and information retrieved from long-term memory.
- Capacity is limited to a few "slots," or units of information.
- **Maintenance rehearsal** keeps information active and in STM.
- If not actively rehearsed, information is lost within 20 seconds.

Long-term memory (LTM):
- Stores a potentially unlimited amount of information for up to a lifetime.
- **Elaborative rehearsal** involves focusing on the meaning of information encoded into LTM.
- Information in LTM is clustered and associated with related groups during recall.
- **Semantic network model** describes the organization of LTM as a complex network of associations.

Working memory: The active, conscious manipulation of verbal or spatial information temporarily held in STM; thought to consist of:
- Phonological loop
- Visuospatial sketchpad
- Central executive

Hill Street Studios/Sarah Golonka/Blend Images/Alamy Stock Photo

Explicit memory (declarative memory): Memory with conscious recall

Implicit memory (nondeclarative memory): Memory without conscious recall

Episodic memory: Events you have experienced

Semantic memory: General facts, knowledge

Procedural memory: Motor skills, actions

Retrieval

Process of accessing information stored in long-term memory

Retrieval cue: Hint or prompt that helps trigger recall of stored memories

Retrieval cue failure: Recall failure due to inadequate or missing retrieval cues; common example is a **tip-of-the-tongue experience.**

Recall, cued recall, and **recognition** are strategies to test retrieval of information.

Serial position effect: Tendency to have better recall of first and last items in a series

Encoding specificity principle: Forms include the **context effect** and **mood congruence.**

Flashbulb memories: Vivid memories perceived as accurate but actually no more accurate than ordinary memories.

Forgetting

Inability to recall information that was previously available

Hermann Ebbinghaus (1850–1909) Identified basic pattern of forgetting: rapid loss of some information, then stable memories of the remaining information

Bettmann/Getty Images

Factors contributing to forgetting:
- Encoding failure
- **Retrieval cue failure** contributes to **prospective memory** failures
- Decay theory
- **Retroactive interference** and **proactive interference**
- **Suppression** and **repression**

Imperfect Memories

Elizabeth Loftus (b. 1944) and other researchers have identified several factors that can contribute to **false memories:**
- **Misinformation effect**
- Preexisting **schemas** can distort memories for new information.
- **Source confusion**
- **Imagination inflation** can produce a sense of false familiarity.
- Blending fact and fiction
- Suggestion

Stuart Franklin/Magnum Photos

The Search for the Biological Basis of Memory

Karl S. Lashley (1890–1958)
- Concluded memories are *distributed* rather than *localized* as a **memory trace** in the brain

Richard F. Thompson (1930–2014)
- Showed that memory for a simple conditioned reflex is *localized* in the brain
- Memories can be both distributed and localized.

Eric Kandel (b. 1929)
- Showed that forming a new memory produces functional and structural changes in neurons
- As memory becomes established, **long-term potentiation** occurs.

Insights about how memory is processed in the brain have come from studying people with **amnesia,** which can be caused by injury or brain surgery.

Retrograde amnesia: Backward-acting amnesia disrupts process of **memory consolidation.**

Dementia is the progressive deterioration of cognitive functions, especially memory and reasoning; occurs as a result of a disease or other physical condition.

Most common cause of dementia is **Alzheimer's disease (AD),** which is characterized by beta-amyloid plaques and neurofibrillary tangles in the brain.

Anterograde amnesia: Forward-acting amnesia disrupts ability to form new memories.

Most famous case of anterograde amnesia was that of Henry Molaison (1926–2008), known as H. M.

Brenda Milner (b. 1918) and **Suzanne Corkin** (1937–2016) Studies of H. M. showed that **explicit memory** and **implicit memory** involve different brain regions.

Blue Planet Archive/Marc Chamberlain

Brain structures involved in memory:
- Hippocampus
- Cerebellum
- Amygdala
- Frontal lobes, including the prefrontal cortex
- Medial temporal lobes

cognition The mental activities involved in acquiring, retaining, and using knowledge.

thinking The manipulation of mental representations of information in order to draw inferences and conclusions.

mental image A mental representation of objects or events that are not physically present.

▲ **Tempt's Art** A creative team, including programmers and neuroscientists, used their problem-solving abilities to help Tempt communicate. The EyeWriter allows Tempt to create art once again, including this sculpture that he designed. Tempt explained, "I can't even begin to describe how good it feels to be able to rock styles again, and through my art I've been able to raise awareness about my disease" (Barlow et al., 2012).

▲ **Thinking** What types of cognitive activities might be required to plan and implement a new furniture line? Jordanian graphic designer Abdelrahman Asfour, who turns car parts into furniture, is highly creative (Arar, 2017). But he must also be able to draw on existing knowledge, analyze new information, effectively solve problems, and make good decisions.

Introduction: Thinking, Language, and Intelligence

■ KEY THEME
Thinking is a broad term that refers to how we use knowledge to analyze situations, solve problems, and make decisions.

≡ KEY QUESTIONS
• What are some of the basic characteristics of mental images?
• How do we manipulate mental images?
• What are concepts, and how are they formed?

Cognition is a general term that refers to *the mental activities involved in acquiring, retaining, and using knowledge.* In previous chapters, we've looked at fundamental cognitive processes such as perception, learning, and memory. These processes are critical in order for us to acquire and retain new knowledge.

In this chapter, we focus on how we *use* that knowledge to analyze situations, solve problems, make decisions, and use language. As you'll see, such cognitive abilities are widely regarded as key dimensions of *intelligence*—a concept that we will also explore.

The Building Blocks of Thought: Mental Imagery and Concepts

In the most general sense, *thinking* is involved in all conscious mental activity, whether it is acquiring new knowledge, reasoning, planning ahead, or daydreaming. More narrowly, we can say that **thinking** involves *the manipulation of mental representations of information in order to draw inferences and conclusions.* Thinking, then, involves active mental processes and is often directed toward some goal, purpose, or conclusion.

What exactly is it that we think *with*? Two important forms of mental representations are *mental images* and *concepts.* We'll look first at mental images.

Mental Images Do you think Tempt, the artist described in the Prologue, creates a mental image of a drawing before sketching it out with his eyes? When we're creating something new or encountering new information, we often develop mental images. Formally, a **mental image** is *a mental representation of objects or events that are not physically present.* Does the brain process mental images in the same way that it processes physical perceptions? We discuss this question in the Focus on Neuroscience box on the next page, "Seeing Faces and Places in the Mind's Eye."

We often rely on mental images to accomplish some cognitive task. For example, try reciting the letters of the alphabet that consist of only curved lines. To accomplish this task, you have to mentally visualize and then inspect an image of each letter of the alphabet.

Typically, the term *mental images* refers to visual "pictures." However, people can also form mental representations that involve senses other than vision (Cattaneo & Vecchi, 2008; Kollndorfer et al., 2015; Palmiero et al., 2009). For example, you can probably easily create a mental representation for the taste of a chocolate milk shake, the smell of freshly popped popcorn, or the feel of cold, wet clothing sticking to your skin. Sometimes thinking involves the *manipulation* of mental images. For example, try the problem in **Figure 7.1** and then continue reading.

Just as it takes time to rotate a physical object, it takes time to mentally rotate an image. Furthermore, the greater the degree of rotation required, the longer it takes you to rotate the image mentally and the greater the brain activity that occurs (Seurinck et al., 2011; Wohlschläger & Wohlschläger, 1998).

Collectively, research seems to indicate that we manipulate mental images in much the same way we manipulate the actual objects they represent (Gardony et al., 2014;

FIGURE 7.1 Manipulating Mental Images Two of these threes are backward. Which ones? Determining which 3s were backward required you to mentally *rotate* each one to an upright position. The one in the middle had to be rotated 180 degrees, which probably took you longer than it did to mentally rotate the one on the far left which had to be rotated only 60 degrees.

Rosenbaum et al., 2001). However, mental images are not perfect duplicates of our actual sensory experience. The mental images we use in thinking have some features in common with actual visual images, but they are not like photographs. Instead, they are *memories* of visual images. And, like other memories, visual images are actively constructed and potentially subject to error (Cattaneo & Vecchi, 2008).

FOCUS ON NEUROSCIENCE

Seeing Faces and Places in the Mind's Eye

Until the advent of sophisticated brain-scanning techniques, studying mental imagery relied on cognitive tasks, such as measuring how long participants reported it took to scan a mental image (see Kosslyn et al., 2001). Today, however, psychologists use brain imaging techniques to study mental imagery. One important issue is whether mental images activate the same brain areas that are involved in perception. Remember, perception takes place when the brain registers information that is received directly from sensory organs.

Previously, researchers found that perceiving certain types of scenes or objects activates specific brain areas. For example, when we look at *faces*, specific brain areas such as the *fusiform face area (FFA)* are activated (Axelrod & Yovel, 2015; Epstein & Kanwisher, 1998). When we look at pictures of *places*, a different brain area, called the *parahippocampal place area*, or *PPA*, is activated (Cant & Goodale, 2011; Kanwisher, 2001). Given these findings, the critical question is this: If we simply *imagine* faces or places, will the same brain areas be activated?

To answer that question, psychologists Kathleen O'Craven and Nancy Kanwisher (2000) used fMRI to compare brain activity during perception and mental imagery. Study participants underwent fMRI scans while they looked at photographs of familiar faces and places (scenes from their college campus). Next, the participants were asked to close their eyes and form a vivid mental image of each of the photographs they had just viewed.

Two key findings emerged from the study. First, as you can see from the fMRI scans of two participants shown here, *imagining* a face or place activated the same brain region that is activated when *perceiving* a face or a place.

Second, compared to imagining a face or place, actually perceiving a face or place evoked a stronger brain response, as indicated by the slightly larger red and yellow areas in the perception fMRIs (upper row).

Other neuroscientists have confirmed that there is considerable overlap in the brain areas involved in visual perception and mental images (Ganis et al., 2004; Naselaris et al., 2015). Clearly, perception and imagination share common brain mechanisms. So, at least as far as the brain is concerned, "the next best thing to being there" might just be closing your eyes . . . and going there in your mind's eye.

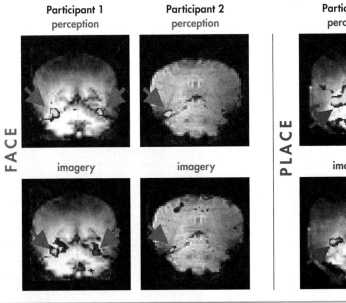

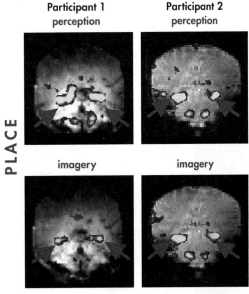

‹ **Brain Activation During Perception and Mental Imagery** Shown here are the fMRIs of two participants in O'Craven and Kanwisher's (2000) study. Notice that the same brain areas are activated while perceiving or imagining a familiar face. Likewise, the same brain areas are activated while perceiving or imagining a familiar place. Also notice that the brain activation is slightly stronger in the perception condition than in the mental imagery condition.

Courtesy of O'Craven and Kanwisher

concept A mental category of objects or ideas based on properties they share.

prototype The most typical instance of a particular concept.

Concepts Along with mental images, thinking also involves the use of concepts. A **concept** is *a mental category of objects or ideas based on properties they share.* Concepts provide a kind of mental shorthand, economizing the cognitive effort required for thinking and communicating.

Using concepts makes it easier to communicate with others, remember information, and learn new information. For example, the concept "food" might include anything from a sardine to a rutabaga. Although they are very different, we can still group rutabagas and sardines together because they share the central feature of being edible. If someone introduces us to a new delicacy and tells us it is *food,* we immediately know that it is something to eat — even if it is something we've never seen before.

Adding to the efficiency of our thinking is our tendency to organize the concepts we hold into orderly hierarchies composed of main categories and subcategories (Markman & Gentner, 2001; Voorspoels et al., 2011). A general concept, such as "furniture," can be mentally divided into a variety of subcategories: tables, chairs, lamps, and so forth. As we learn the key properties that define a general concept, we also learn how members of the concept are related to one another.

How are concepts formed? Sometimes we form a concept by learning the *rule* or *features* that define the particular concept. These rules are logical but rigid. If the defining features, or *attributes,* are present, then the object is included as a member or example of that concept. For some concepts, this rigid all-or-nothing categorization procedure works well. For example, a substance can be categorized as a solid, liquid, or gas.

However, sometimes we form a concept as a result of everyday experience rather than by logically determining whether an object or event fits a specific set of rules. The rules or attributes that define these concepts are *not* sharply defined. Therefore, it's often easier to classify some members of concepts than others. To illustrate this point, think about the defining features or rules that you usually associate with the concept "vehicle." With virtually no hesitation, you can say that a car, truck, and bus are all examples of this concept. How about a sled? A wheelbarrow? A raft? An elevator? It probably took you a few seconds to determine whether these objects were also vehicles. Why are some examples easier to classify than others?

According to psychologist Eleanor Rosch (1978), some members are better representatives of a concept than are others. *The most typical instance of a particular concept* is called a **prototype** (Mervis & Rosch, 1981; Rosch, 1978). According to prototype theories of classification, we tend to determine whether an object is an instance of a concept by comparing it to the prototype we have developed rather than by logically evaluating whether the defining features are present or absent (Minda & Smith, 2001, 2011).

The more closely an item matches the prototype, the more quickly we can identify it as being an example of that concept (Rosch & Mervis, 1975). For example, it usually takes us longer to identify an olive or a coconut as being a fruit because they are so

⌄ Are These Mammals? The more closely an item matches the prototype of a concept, the more quickly we can identify the item as being an example of that concept. Because bats, dolphins, and the rather peculiar-looking African long-tailed pangolin don't fit our prototype for a mammal, it takes us longer to decide whether they belong to the category "mammal" than it does to classify animals that are closer to the prototype.

Top-Pics TBK/Alamy Stock Photo

ArchMan/Shutterstock

Abaca Press/Sipa USA/Lahad Datu/Sabah/Malaysia/Newscom

dissimilar from our prototype of a typical fruit, like an apple or an orange. Similarly, it's easier to identify cars and trucks than wheelbarrows and elevators as vehicles.

Some researchers believe that we don't classify a new instance by comparing it to a single "best example" or prototype. Instead, they believe that we store **exemplars**, *individual instances of a concept or category, held in memory.* (Nosofsky & Zaki, 2002; Voorspoels et al., 2008). Then, when we encounter a new object, we compare it to the exemplars that we have stored in memory to determine whether it belongs to that category (Nosofsky et al., 2011). So, if you're trying to decide whether a coconut is a fruit, you compare it to your memories of other items that you know to be fruits. Is it like an apple? An orange? How about a peach? Or a cantaloupe? The more varied exemplars we have stored in our memory, the easier it is to categorize a new object (Wahlheim & DeSoto, 2016).

As the two building blocks of thinking, mental images and concepts help us impose order on the phenomena we encounter and think about. We often rely on this knowledge when we engage in complex cognitive tasks, such as solving problems and making decisions, which we'll consider next.

Solving Problems and Making Decisions

■ KEY THEME

Problem solving refers to thinking and behavior directed toward attaining a goal that is not readily available.

⁑ KEY QUESTIONS

- What are some advantages and disadvantages of each problem-solving strategy?
- What is insight, and how does it work?
- How can functional fixedness and mental set interfere with problem solving?

In the Prologue, you learned about a team of people engaged in problem solving as they tackled an incredible challenge—finding an affordable way for Tempt, a paralyzed artist, to draw using only his eyes and brain. But most of our problem solving isn't this dramatic. From fixing flat tires to figuring out how to pay for college classes, we all engage in problem solving so routinely that we often don't even notice the processes we follow. Formally, **problem solving** refers to *thinking and behavior directed toward attaining a goal that is not readily available* (Novick & Bassok, 2005; Wang & Chiew, 2010).

Before you can solve a problem, you must develop an accurate understanding of it. In the case of Tempt, the problem was clear. He needed a tool to help him draw without using his hands. Correctly identifying the problem is a key step in successful problem solving (Bransford & Stein, 1993). If your representation of the problem is flawed, your attempts to solve it will also be flawed.

Problem-Solving Strategies

As a general rule, people tend to attack a problem in an organized or systematic way. Usually, the strategy you select is influenced by the nature of the problem and your degree of experience, familiarity, and knowledge about the problem you are confronting (Chrysikou, 2006; Leighton & Sternberg, 2013). In this section, we'll look at some of the common strategies used in problem solving.

Trial and Error: A Process of Elimination
Trial and error is *a problem-solving strategy that involves attempting different solutions and eliminating those that do not work.* When there is a limited range of possible solutions, trial and error can be a useful problem-solving strategy. If you were trying to develop a new curry recipe, for example, you might use trial and error to fine-tune the seasonings.

When the range of possible answers or solutions is large, however, trial and error can be time-consuming. For example, Tempt's team used a trial-and-error process to get the

exemplars Individual instances of a concept or category, held in memory.

problem solving Thinking and behavior directed toward attaining a goal that is not readily available.

trial and error A problem-solving strategy that involves attempting different solutions and eliminating those that do not work.

⌃ Trial and Error Even an expert mixologist like LaTanya White, owner of a Florida cocktail catering company, needs to adjust a drink's ingredients—tasting a cocktail before finalizing the recipe to be sure that the flavors are just right. Drink recipes are often developed through a process of trial and error.

St Petersburg Times/ZUMA Press/Tampa/FL/USA/Newscom

algorithm A problem-solving strategy that involves following a specific rule, procedure, or method that inevitably produces the correct solution.

heuristic A problem-solving strategy that involves following a general rule of thumb to reduce the number of possible solutions.

insight The sudden realization of how a problem can be solved.

Caiaimage/Rafal Rodzoch/Getty Images

▲ **Heuristics at Work** Tackling an engine repair job requires effective problem solving. This mechanic might use heuristics to enhance her chances of success. For example, she might start by checking for the most common engine problems.

eye tracker to comfortably stay on his face. Too tight and it was uncomfortable. Too loose and it would slide down his nose. After several tries, his team realized they could have Tempt recline more, raise the computer screen, and use gravity to keep the glasses on.

Algorithms: Guaranteed to Work Unlike trial and error, an **algorithm** is *a problem-solving strategy that involves following a specific rule, procedure, or method that inevitably produces the correct solution*. Mathematical formulas are examples of algorithms. For instance, the formula used to convert temperatures from Celsius to Fahrenheit (multiply *C* by 9/5, then add 32) is an algorithm.

Even though an algorithm may be guaranteed to eventually produce a solution, using an algorithm is not always practical. For example, imagine that while rummaging in a closet you find a combination lock with no combination attached. Using an algorithm will eventually produce the correct combination. You can start with 0–0–0, then try 0–0–1, followed by 0–0–2, and so forth, and systematically work your way through combinations to 39–39–39. But this solution would take a while, because there are 64,000 potential combinations to try. So, although using an algorithm to generate the correct combination for the combination lock is guaranteed to work eventually, it's not a very practical approach to solving this particular problem.

Heuristics: Rules of Thumb In contrast to an algorithm, a **heuristic** is *a problem-solving strategy that involves following a general rule of thumb to reduce the number of possible solutions*. Although heuristic strategies are not guaranteed to solve a given problem, they tend to simplify problem solving because they reduce the number of possible solutions. With a more limited range of solutions, you can use trial and error to eventually arrive at the correct one. In this way, heuristics may serve an adaptive purpose by allowing us to use patterns of information to solve problems quickly and accurately (Gigerenzer & Gaissmeier, 2011; Gigerenzer & Goldstein, 2011). For example, Tempt's team used their scientific expertise to guide what they actually tried, applying heuristics based on their training to the problem of how to make the EyeWriter work.

Here's another example. You might choose a restaurant based on the numbers of stars in online reviews. This strategy is likely better than choosing a restaurant at random, but it does not guarantee success. Perhaps quality has declined since the restaurant earned those stars.

One common heuristic is to break a problem into a series of *subgoals*. This strategy is often used in writing a term paper. Choosing a topic, locating information about the topic, organizing the information, and so on become a series of subproblems. As you solve each subproblem, you move closer to solving the larger problem. Another useful heuristic involves *working backward* from the goal. Starting with the end point, you determine the steps necessary to reach your final goal. For example, when making a budget, people often start off with the goal of spending no more than a certain total each month, then work backward to determine how much of the target amount they will allot for each category of expenses.

Perhaps the key to successful problem solving is *flexibility*. A good problem solver recognizes that a particular strategy is unlikely to yield a solution — and knows to switch to a different approach (Bilalić et al., 2008; Ionescu, 2012). And, sometimes, the reality is that a problem may not have a single "best" solution.

Insight **Insight** is *the sudden realization of how a problem can be solved* (Ohlsson, 2010; Weisberg, 2015). Sometimes an insight will occur when you recognize how the problem is similar to a previously solved problem. Or an insight can involve the sudden realization that an object can be used in a novel way. Try your hand at the two problems in **Figure 7.2**. The solution to each of those problems is often achieved by insight.

Insights rarely occur through the conscious manipulation of concepts or information. In fact, you're usually not aware of the thought processes that lead to an insight. Increasingly, cognitive psychologists and neuroscientists are investigating nonconscious processes, including unconscious problem solving, insight, and intuition (Gilhooly, 2016; Hogarth, 2010; Horr et al., 2014).

Problem 1	Six drinking glasses are lined up in a row. The first three are full of water, the last three are empty. By handling and moving only one glass, change the arrangement so that no full glass is next to another full one, and no empty glass is next to another empty one.
Problem 2	A woman who lived in a small town married 20 different men in that same town. All of them are still living, and she never divorced any of them. Yet she broke no laws. How could she do this?

FIGURE 7.2 A Demonstration of Insightful Solutions The solutions to these problems are often characterized by sudden flashes of insight. See if you have the "That's it!" experience in solving these problems without looking at the solutions on page 236.

Source: Problem 1 information from Ashcraft (1994);
Problem 2 information from Sternberg (1986).

functional fixedness The tendency to view objects as functioning only in their usual or customary way.

mental set The tendency to persist in solving problems with solutions that have worked in the past.

Insight typically involves perceiving a pattern in the information you're considering, but not consciously. The perception of such patterns is based on your expertise in a given area and your memories of related information. Sometimes people call this a "hunch" or an educated guess. It is a new idea that integrates new information with existing knowledge stored in long-term memory. Once a hunch is formed, conscious analytical thought processes take over. For example, an experienced doctor might integrate both obvious and subtle clues to recognize a pattern in a patient's symptoms, a pattern that takes the form of a hunch. With a hunch consciously formulated, the doctor might order lab tests to confirm or disprove their tentative diagnosis. Such hunches are likely to be accurate only in contexts in which you already have a broad base of knowledge and experience (Jones, 2003; M. Lieberman, 2000).

Obstacles to Solving Problems: Thinking Outside the Box

Sometimes, past experience or expertise in a particular domain can interfere with effective problem solving. If we always do something in a particular way, we may not be open to new or better solutions. When we can't move beyond old, inappropriate heuristics, ideas, or problem-solving strategies, *fixation* can block new, more effective approaches (Moss et al., 2011; Storm & Angello, 2010).

The tendency to view objects as functioning only in their usual or customary way is called **functional fixedness**. Functional fixedness often prevents us from seeing the full range of ways in which an object can be used. To get a feel for how functional fixedness can interfere with your ability to find a solution, try the problem in **Figure 7.3**.

For example, consider the problem of single-use plastic bags, which clog landfills and waterways and take decades to degrade. Hundreds of cities have dealt with the problem by passing ordinances banning or restricting their use. Functional fixedness kept people from thinking of the bags as anything but trash. But it turns out that the indestructible nature of these single-use bags can be advantageous: The bags can be turned into "plarn," a plastic yarn that can be repurposed to create durable, waterproof sleeping mats for the homeless. A Chicago-based group, New Life for Old Bags, estimates that it takes between 600 and 700 plastic bags to create one six-foot by two-foot sleeping mat. The finished mats are distributed to homeless shelters throughout the city (Franklin, 2016; Stuart, 2013).

Another common obstacle to problem solving is **mental set**— *the tendency to persist with solutions that have worked in the past* (Öllinger et al., 2008). Obviously, if a solution has worked in the past, there's good reason to consider using it again. However, if we approach a problem with a rigid mental set, we may not see other possible solutions (Kershaw & Ohlsson, 2004).

FIGURE 7.3 Overcoming Functional Fixedness Here's a classic problem for you to solve. You have two candles, some thumbtacks, and a box of matches. Using just these objects, try to figure out how to mount the candles on a wall. (The solution is on page 237.)

Source: Research from Duncker (1945).

Jalil Ahmad/Reuters/Newscom

⌃ **Overcoming Functional Fixedness** A team of teenage girls from Afghanistan is trying to build an inexpensive ventilator for use with COVID patients (Hadid, 2020). The girls, who call their team the "Afghan Dreamers," are adapting a design from MIT to build a ventilator using materials that are easily found locally, such as car parts. For example, they use windshield wiper motors to run their ventilator. Finding new uses for familiar objects is the essence of overcoming functional fixedness.

FIGURE 7.4 Mental Set The equations on the left, expressed in Roman numerals, are obviously incorrect. Your task is to transform each incorrect equation into a correct equation by moving ONE matchstick in each equation. The matchstick can only be moved once. Only Roman numerals and the three arithmetic operators +, −, or = are allowed. Take your best shot at solving the equations before looking at the solutions on page 238. Remember, in the Roman numeral system, I = 1; II = 2; III = 3; IV = 4; V = 5. (The solution is on page 238.)

Source: Research from Duncker (1945).

| Problem 1 | Pour the water in glass number 2 into glass number 5. |
| Problem 2 | The woman is a minister. |

⌃ **Solutions to Figure 7.2**

Ironically, mental set is sometimes most likely to block insight in areas in which you are already knowledgeable or well trained. Before you read any further, try solving the simple arithmetic problems in **Figure 7.4**. If you're having trouble coming up with the answer, it's probably because your existing training in solving arithmetic problems is preventing you from seeing the equations from a different perspective than what you have been taught (Knoblich & Öllinger, 2006; Öllinger et al., 2008).

Mental sets can sometimes suggest a useful heuristic. But they can also prevent us from coming up with new, and possibly more effective, solutions. If we try to be flexible in our thinking and overcome the tendency toward mental sets, we can often identify simpler solutions to many common problems.

Decision-Making Strategies

◼ KEY THEME
Different cognitive strategies are used when making decisions, depending on the type and number of options available to us.

≡ KEY QUESTIONS
- What are the single-feature model, the additive model, and the elimination-by-aspects model of decision making?
- Under what conditions is each strategy most appropriate?
- How do we use the availability and representativeness heuristics to help us estimate the likelihood of an event?

Who hasn't felt like flipping a coin when faced with an important or complicated decision? Fortunately, most of the decisions we make in everyday life are relatively minor. But every now and then we have to make a decision where much more is at stake. When a decision is important or complex, we're more likely to invest time, effort, and other resources in considering different options.

The decision-making process becomes complicated when each option involves the consideration of several features. It's rare that one alternative is superior in every category. So, what do you do when each alternative has pros and cons? In this section, we'll describe three common decision-making strategies.

The Single-Feature Model One decision-making strategy is called the *single-feature model*. In order to simplify the choice among many alternatives, you base your decision on a single feature. When the decision is a minor one, the single-feature model can be a good decision-making strategy. For example, faced with an entire supermarket aisle of laundry detergents, you could simplify your decision by deciding to buy the cheapest brand. When a decision is important or complex, however, making decisions on the basis of a single feature can increase the riskiness of the decision.

The Additive Model A better strategy for complex decisions is to systematically evaluate the important features of each alternative. One such decision-making model is called the *additive model*.

In this model, you first generate a list of the factors that are most important to you. For example, suppose you need off-campus housing. Your list of important factors might include cost, proximity to campus, compatibility with roommates, or having a private bathroom. Then, you rate each alternative for each factor using an arbitrary scale, such as from 1 to 10. If a particular factor has strong advantages or appeal, such as compatible roommates, you give it the maximum rating (10). If a particular factor has strong disadvantages, such as distance from campus, you give it the minimum rating (1). Finally, you add up the ratings for each alternative. This strategy can often reveal the best overall choice. If the decision involves a situation in which some factors are more important than others, you can emphasize the more important factors by multiplying their ratings.

availability heuristic A strategy in which the likelihood of an event is estimated on the basis of how readily available other instances of the event are in memory.

The Elimination-by-Aspects Model Psychologist Amos Tversky (1972) proposed another decision-making model called the *elimination-by-aspects model*. Using this model, you evaluate all the alternatives one characteristic at a time, typically starting with the feature you consider most important. If a particular alternative fails to meet that criterion, you scratch it off your list of possible choices, even if it possesses other desirable attributes. As the range of possible choices is narrowed down, you continue to compare the remaining alternatives, one feature at a time, until just one alternative is left.

For example, suppose you want to buy a new laptop. You might initially eliminate all the models that aren't powerful enough to run the software you need to use, then the models outside your budget, and so forth. Continuing in this fashion, you would progressively narrow down the range of possible choices to the one choice that satisfies all your criteria.

Good decision makers adapt their strategy to the demands of the specific situation. And, when the decision is complex, people often use *more than one* strategy. Of course, it's not always as straightforward as this. Other factors, such as our emotions, play in to our decision making, too (Lerner et al., 2015).

^ **Solution to Figure 7.3**

Decisions Involving Uncertainty: Estimating the Probability of Events

Some decisions involve a high degree of uncertainty. In these cases, you need to make a decision, but you are unable to predict with certainty that a given event will occur. Instead, you have to estimate the probability of an event occurring. But how do you actually make that estimation?

For example, imagine that you're running late for an important appointment. You may be faced with this decision: "Should I risk a speeding ticket to get to the appointment on time?" In this case, you would have to estimate the probability of a particular event occurring—getting pulled over for speeding. Or, in a more extreme example, imagine that you're deciding whether to ski in the backcountry of Colorado, where the risk of avalanche is high. Almost 30 people per year die in avalanches in the United States, with more deaths occurring in Colorado than in any other state (Blevins, 2019). Behavioral scientists are trying to understand how people decide to enter dangerous territory in spite of the risks.

In such instances, we often estimate the likelihood that certain events will occur, and then gamble. In deciding what the odds are that a particular gamble will go our way, we tend to rely on two rule-of-thumb strategies to help us estimate the likelihood of events: the *availability heuristic* and the *representativeness heuristic* (Kahneman, 2003; Tversky & Kahneman, 1982).

The Availability Heuristic The **availability heuristic** is *a strategy in which the likelihood of an event is estimated on the basis of how readily available other instances of the event are in memory.* When instances of an event are easily recalled, we tend to consider the event as being more likely to occur. So, we're less likely to exceed the speed limit if we can readily recall that a friend recently got a speeding ticket. On the other hand, the

Jody Watt/Media Bakery

^ **Vivid Images and the Availability Heuristic: Sharks & Selfies!** Almost every summer, shark attacks make media headlines. But how likely are you to die in a shark attack? In 2019, there were two deaths due to shark attack (Naylor & Bowling, 2020). In contrast, in the United States alone, 857 bicyclists were killed in collisions with motor vehicles in 2018 (National Center for Statistics and Analysis, 2019b). And about 100 people a year die while taking selfies, leading to headlines like this one: "More people die taking selfies than by shark attacks" (Bansal et al., 2018; Keeley, 2019). How does the availability heuristic explain why people are afraid to go to the beach after a well-publicized shark sighting, yet they are more than willing to regularly ride bikes or take selfies?

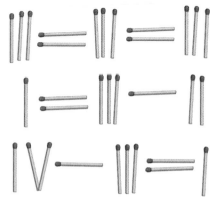

⌃ Solution to Figure 7.4 Most people try to correct the equations in Figure 7.4 by moving a matchstick that changes one of the numbers. Why? Because solving the math problems that we are assigned in school almost always involves manipulating the numbers, not the arithmetic signs. While this assumption is a useful one in solving the vast majority of math problems—especially the ones that you are assigned as homework—it is an example of a mental set that can block you from arriving at new, creative solutions to problems.

availability heuristic can lead us to more readily recall a good outcome. In the case of backcountry skiing, skiers who view other skiers' social media reports of successful exploits in avalanche-prone areas will more easily recall adventures that end safely—and be tempted to make risky decisions themselves (Blevins, 2016). With COVID-19, we may be tempted to remember the times we were in stores without getting the disease and discount a friend's experience contracting it from dinner out at a restaurant.

However, when a rare event makes a vivid impression on us, we may overestimate its likelihood (Tversky & Kahneman, 1982). State lottery commissions capitalize on this cognitive tendency by running many TV commercials showing that lucky person who won the $100 million Powerball. A vivid memory is created, which leads viewers to an inaccurate estimate of the likelihood that the event will happen to them.

The key point here is that the less accurately our memory of an event reflects the actual frequency of the event, the less accurate our estimate of the event's likelihood will be. That's why the lottery commercials don't show the other 50 million people staring dejectedly at their TV screens because they did *not* win the $100 million.

The Representativeness Heuristic The **representativeness heuristic** is *a strategy in which the likelihood of an event is estimated by comparing how similar it is to the prototype of the event* (Kahneman & Tversky, 1982; Kahneman, 2003). Remember, a *prototype* is the most typical example of an object or an event.

Like the availability heuristic, the representativeness heuristic can lead to inaccurate judgments. Consider the following description:

> Maria is a perceptive, sensitive, introspective woman. She is very articulate but measures her words carefully. Once she's certain she knows what she wants to say, she expresses herself easily and confidently. She has a strong preference for working alone.

On the basis of this description, is it more likely that Maria is a successful fiction writer or that Maria is a registered nurse? Most people guess that she is a successful fiction writer. Why? Because the description seems to mesh with what many people think of as the typical characteristics of a writer.

However, when you compare the number of registered nurses (which is very large) to the number of successful fiction writers (which is very small), it's actually much more likely that Maria is a nurse. Thus, the representativeness heuristic can produce faulty estimates if: (1) we fail to consider possible variations from the prototype or (2) we fail to consider the approximate number of prototypes that actually exist. And this happens all the time. A woman we know wrote on social media: "The bus driver I ride with every day just asked me if I am a college poetry teacher. I told him no and asked why he thought that, to which he replied, 'you look laid back and wear jeans to work.'"

What determines which heuristic is more likely to be used? Research suggests that the availability heuristic is most likely to be used when people rely on information held in their long-term memory to determine the likelihood of events occurring. On the other hand, the representativeness heuristic is more likely to be used when people compare different variables to make predictions (Harvey, 2007).

Some argue that models of decision making such as those based on heuristics are not general enough (Oppenheimer & Kelso, 2015). These models may explain individual decisions, but they don't offer a broad explanation of how we process information to make decisions. A developing area of research is generating great interest in information-processing theories, which focus on "basic cognitive building blocks" like attention, perception, and memory to help us understand decision making.

The Critical Thinking box "The Persistence of Unwarranted Beliefs" (on page 240) discusses some of the other psychological factors that can influence the way in which we evaluate evidence, make decisions, and draw conclusions.

representativeness heuristic A strategy in which the likelihood of an event is estimated by comparing how similar it is to the prototype of the event.

Language and Thought

■ KEY THEME

Language is a system for combining arbitrary symbols to produce an infinite number of meaningful statements.

≡ KEY QUESTIONS

- What are the characteristics of language?
- What are the stages of language development?
- What are the effects of bilingualism?
- What has research found about the cognitive abilities of nonhuman animals?

The human capacity for language is surely one of the most remarkable of all our cognitive abilities. With little effort, you produce hundreds of new sentences every day. And you understand the vast majority of the thousands of words contained in this chapter without consulting a dictionary. Human language has many special qualities—qualities that make it flexible, versatile, and complex. **Language** can be formally defined as *a system for combining arbitrary symbols to produce an infinite number of meaningful statements.* We'll begin our discussion of the relationship between language and thought by describing these special characteristics of language.

The Characteristics of Language

The purpose of language is to communicate—to express meaningful information in a way that can be understood by others. To do so, language requires the use of *symbols.* These symbols may be written or spoken words. But they may also be other sounds. Several countries use whistling languages as well as spoken languages (Meyer, 2015). In Turkey, for example, about 10,000 people speak kuş dili, or "bird language," in which the Turkish language is communicated through musical whistling noises (Fezehai, 2019). The language developed as a way to communicate across vast distances in rural farming villages and is dying out as mobile phones become more popular. Symbols also may be formalized gestures, as in American Sign Language and other sign languages.

A few symbols may be similar in form to the meaning they signify, such as the English words *boom* and *pop.* However, for most words, the connection between the symbol and the meaning is completely *arbitrary* (Pinker, 1995, 2007). For example, *ton* is a small word that stands for a vast quantity, whereas *nanogram* is a large word that stands for a very small quantity. Because the relationship between the symbol and its meaning is arbitrary, language is tremendously flexible (Pinker, 1994, 2007). New words can be invented, such as *selfie, podcast,* and *crowdfund.* And the meanings of words can change and evolve, such as *spam, troll,* and *catfish.*

The meaning of these symbols is *shared* by others who speak the same language. That is, speakers of the same language agree on the connection between the sound and what it symbolizes. Consequently, a foreign language sounds like a stream of meaningless sounds because we do not share the memory of the connection between the arbitrary sounds and the concrete meanings they symbolize.

Further, language is a highly structured system that follows specific rules. Every language has its own unique *syntax,* or set of rules for combining words. Although you're usually unaware of these rules as you're speaking or writing, you immediately notice when a rule has been violated.

The rules of language help determine the meaning that is being communicated. For example, word-order rules are important in determining the meaning of an English phrase. "The boy ate the giant pumpkin" has an entirely different meaning from "The giant pumpkin ate the boy." In other languages, meaning may be conveyed by different rule-based distinctions, such as specific pronouns, the class or category of words, or word endings.

▲ **Sign Language** Sign language, used by hearing-impaired people, meets all the formal requirements for language, including syntax, displacement, and generativity. The similarities between spoken language and sign language have been confirmed by brain imaging studies. The same brain regions are activated in hearing people when they speak as in deaf people when they use sign language (Hickok et al., 2001; Lubbadeh, 2005). The same is true in deaf people when they read written words and when they view signs (Moreno et al., 2018).

language A system for combining arbitrary symbols to produce an infinite number of meaningful statements.

CRITICAL THINKING

The Persistence of Unwarranted Beliefs

Is it true that people tend to cling to their beliefs even when they are presented with solid evidence that contradicts those beliefs?

Throughout this text, we show that many claims fail when subjected to scientific scrutiny (Boudry et al., 2015). However, once a belief, for example in energy healing as we discussed in Chapter 1, is established, the presentation of contradictory evidence often has little impact (Lester, 2000). Ironically, contradictory evidence can actually *strengthen* a person's established beliefs (Lord et al., 1979). For example, in one study, participants were given the accurate information that the flu vaccine does not cause the flu (Nyhan & Reifler, 2015). Those who were already worried about getting the flu from the vaccine were not reassured. In fact, they were even *less* likely to say they would get the flu vaccine after learning this information. How do psychologists account for this phenomenon?

Several psychological studies have explored how people deal with evidence, especially evidence that contradicts their beliefs (see Ross & Anderson, 1982; Zusne & Jones, 1989). The four obstacles to logical thinking described here can account for much of the persistence of unwarranted beliefs (Risen & Gilovich, 2007).

Obstacle 1: The Belief-Bias Effect

The *belief-bias effect* occurs when people accept only the evidence that conforms to their belief, rejecting or ignoring any evidence that does not. For example, in a classic study conducted by Warren Jones and Dan Russell (1980), ESP (extrasensory perception) believers and ESP disbelievers watched two attempts at telepathic communication. In each attempt, a "receiver" tried to indicate what card the "sender" was holding.

In reality, both attempts were rigged. One attempt was designed to appear to be a successful demonstration of telepathy, with a significant number of accurate responses. The other attempt was designed to convincingly demonstrate failure. In this case, the number of accurate guesses was no more than chance and could be produced by simple random guessing.

Following the demonstration, the participants were asked what they believed had taken place. Both believers and disbelievers indicated that ESP had occurred in the successful attempt. But only the believers said that ESP had also taken place in the clearly *unsuccessful* attempt. In other words, the ESP believers ignored or discounted the evidence in the failed attempt. This is the essence of the belief-bias effect.

Obstacle 2: Confirmation Bias

Confirmation bias is *the tendency to seek out evidence that confirms an existing belief while ignoring evidence that might contradict or undermine that belief* (Gilovich, 1997; Masnick & Zimmerman, 2009). For example, we tend to visit Web sites that support our own viewpoints and read blogs and editorial columns written by people who interpret events from our perspective. At the same time, we avoid the Web sites, blogs, and columns written by people who don't see things our way (Ruscio, 1998).

People also tend to believe evidence that confirms what they *want* to believe is true, a bias that is sometimes called the *wishful thinking bias* (Bastardi et al., 2011). Faced with evidence that seems to contradict a hoped-for finding, people may object to the study's methodology. And, evaluating evidence that seems to confirm a

> **Giving Birth to a New Language** In 1977, a special school for deaf children opened in Managua, Nicaragua. The children quickly developed a system of gestures for communicating with one another. Since then, the system of gestures has evolved into a unique new language with its own grammar and syntax—*Idioma de Signos Nicaragense* (Senghas et al., 2004; Siegal, 2004). Another unique sign language spontaneously developed in a remote Bedouin village where a large number of villagers share a form of hereditary deafness (Fox, 2008; Sandler et al., 2005). Like Nicaraguan Sign Language, *Al-Sayyid Bedouin Sign Language* has its own syntax and grammatical rules, which differ from other languages in the region. The spontaneous evolution of these two unique sign languages vividly demonstrates the human predisposition to develop rule-based systems of communication (Meir et al., 2010).

Another important characteristic of language is that it is creative, or *generative*. That is, you can generate an infinite number of new and different phrases and sentences.

A final important characteristic of human language is called *displacement*. You can communicate meaningfully about ideas, objects, and activities that are not physically present. You can refer to activities that will take place in the future, that took place in the past, or that will take place only if certain conditions are met. ("If I take on extra shifts at work, maybe I can go on spring break with my friends.") You can also carry on a vivid conversation about abstract ideas ("What is justice?") or strictly imaginary topics ("If you were going to spend a year in space, what would you bring along?").

wished-for finding, people may overlook flaws in the research or argument. For example, parents with children in day care may be motivated to embrace research findings that emphasize the benefits of day care for young children and discount findings that emphasize the benefits of home-based care.

Obstacle 3: The Fallacy of Positive Instances

The *fallacy of positive instances* is the tendency to remember uncommon events that seem to confirm our beliefs and to forget events that disconfirm our beliefs. Often, the occurrence is really nothing more than coincidence. For example, you find yourself thinking of an old friend. A few moments later, the phone rings and it's them. You remember this seemingly telepathic event but forget all the times that you've thought of your old friend and they did not call. In other words, you remember the positive instance but fail to notice the negative instances when the anticipated event did not occur (Gilovich, 1997).

Obstacle 4: The Overestimation Effect

The tendency to overestimate the rarity of events is referred to as the *overestimation effect*. Suppose a "psychic" comes to your class of 23 students. Using their psychic abilities, the visitor "senses" that two people in the class were born on the same day. A quick survey finds that, indeed, two people share the same month and day of birth. This is pretty impressive evidence of clairvoyance, right? After all, what are the odds that two people in a class of 23 would have the same birthday?

When we perform this "psychic" demonstration in class, our students usually estimate that it is very unlikely that 2 people in a class

of 23 will share a birthday. In reality, the odds are *1 in 2*, or 50–50 (Martin, 1998). Our students' overestimation of the rarity of this event is an example of the *overestimation effect*.

Thinking Critically About the Evidence

On the one hand, it is important to keep an open mind. Simply dismissing an idea as impossible shuts out the consideration of evidence for new and potentially promising ideas or phenomena. At one time, for example, scientists thought it impossible that rocks could fall from the sky (Hines, 2003).

On the other hand, the obstacles described here underscore the importance of choosing ways to gather and think about evidence that will help us avoid unwarranted beliefs and self-deception.

The critical thinking skills we described in the chapter Introduction and Research Methods are especially useful in this respect. The "How to Think Like a Scientist" Critical Thinking box provided guidelines that can be used to evaluate all claims, including pseudoscientific or paranormal claims. In particular, it's important to stress again that good critical thinkers strive to evaluate all the available evidence before reaching a conclusion, not just the evidence that supports what they want to believe.

CRITICAL THINKING QUESTIONS
- How can using critical thinking skills help you avoid these obstacles to logical thinking?
- Beyond the logical fallacies described here, what might motivate people to maintain beliefs in the face of contradictory evidence?

All your cognitive abilities are involved in understanding and producing language. Using learning and memory, you acquire and remember the meaning of words. You interpret the words you hear or read (or see, in the case of American Sign Language and other sign languages) through the use of perception. You use language to help you reason, represent and solve problems, and make decisions (Polk & Newell, 1995).

The Effect of Language on Perception

Language requires the use of your cognitive abilities, but what exactly is the relationship between language and thought? Benjamin Whorf (1956) believed that a person's language determines the very structure of their thoughts and perceptions. Your language, he claimed, determines how you perceive and "carve up" the phenomena of your world. He argued that people who speak very different languages have completely different worldviews. *The hypothesis that differences among languages cause differences in the thoughts of their speakers* is the **linguistic relativity hypothesis**; also called the *Whorfian hypothesis*.

To illustrate his hypothesis, Whorf contended that people native to Arctic regions had many different words for "snow"; they "would say that falling snow, slushy snow, and so on are sensuously and operationally different" (Whorf, 1956). But English, he pointed out, has only the "all-inclusive" word *snow*. But think carefully about Whorf's example. Is it really true that English-speaking people have a limited capacity to describe snow?

confirmation bias The tendency to seek out evidence that confirms an existing belief while ignoring evidence that might contradict or undermine that belief.

linguistic relativity hypothesis The hypothesis that differences among languages cause differences in the thoughts of their speakers; also called the *Whorfian hypothesis*.

Is it true that, unlike English speakers, people who are native to Arctic regions have dozens of words for snow?

© Edward Gibson, MIT Brain and Cognitive Sciences

∧ **Can You Count Without Number Words?** Cognitive neuroscientist Edward Gibson traveled to a remote Amazon village to confirm previous research by anthropologist and linguist Daniel Everett (2005, 2008) that suggested that the Pirahã people lacked the ability to count and had no comprehension of numbers. According to Gibson, the Pirahã are capable of learning to count, but did not develop a number system because numbers are simply not useful in their culture (Frank et al., 2008).

Or do not discriminate between different types of snow? The English language includes *snowflake, snowfall, slush, sleet, flurry, blizzard,* and *avalanche.* Avid skiers have many additional words to describe snow, from *powder* to *mogul* to *hardpack.* It is a myth that English speakers do not have dozens of words for snow.

More generally, people with expertise in a particular area tend to perceive and make finer distinctions than nonexperts do. Experts are also more likely to know the specialized terms that reflect those distinctions (Pinker, 1994, 2007). Despite expert/nonexpert differences in noticing and naming details, we don't claim that the expert "sees" a different reality than a nonexpert. In other words, our perceptions and thought processes influence the language we use to describe those perceptions (Rosch, 1987; Pinker, 2007). Notice that this conclusion is the exact *opposite* of the linguistic relativity hypothesis.

Whorf also pointed out that many languages have different color-naming systems. English has names for 11 basic colors: *black, white, red, green, yellow, blue, brown, purple, pink, orange,* and *gray.* However, some languages have only a few color terms. Would people who had just a few words for colors carve up and perceive the electromagnetic spectrum differently?

Eleanor Rosch set out to answer this question (Heider & Olivier, 1972). The Dani-speaking people of New Guinea have words for only two colors. *Mili* is used for the dark, cool colors of black, green, and blue. *Mola* is used for light, warm colors, such as white, red, and yellow. According to the Whorfian hypothesis, the people of New Guinea, who have names for only two classes of colors, should perceive color differently than English-speaking people, who have names for 11 basic colors.

Rosch showed Dani speakers a brightly colored chip. Thirty seconds later, she asked them to pick out the color they had seen from an array of other colors. Despite their lack of specific words for the colors they had seen, the Dani did as well as English speakers on the test. The Dani people used the same word to label red and yellow, but they still distinguished between the two. Rosch concluded that the Dani people perceived colors in much the same way as English-speaking people.

Whorf's strong contention that language *determines* perception and the structure of thought has not been supported. However, cultural and cognitive psychologists today are actively investigating the ways in which language can *influence* perception, thought, and memory (Fausey et al., 2010; Frank et al., 2008; Majid et al., 2004).

A striking demonstration of the influence of language comes from studies of remote indigenous peoples living in the Amazon region of Brazil (Everett, 2005, 2008; Gordon, 2004). The language of the Pirahã people, an isolated tribe of fewer than 200 members, has no words for specific numbers (Frank et al., 2008). Rather than identifying quantities by exact numbers, individuals used relative terms like "few," "more," and "many." Individuals were capable of learning to count, suggesting that this lack of number words did not affect their ability to perceive exact quantities. But they were unable to complete simple arithmetic tasks.

Such findings demonstrate how language categories can affect *how* individuals think about particular concepts. And most researchers today discuss thinking and language as interacting — each influencing the other and both being influenced by culture (ojalehto & Medin, 2015).

Language Development

According to linguist Noam Chomsky (1965), every child is born with a biological predisposition to learn language — *any* language. In effect, children possess a "universal grammar" — a basic understanding of the common principles of language organization. Infants are innately equipped not only to understand language but also to extract grammatical rules from what they hear. The key task in the development of language is to learn a set of grammatical rules that allows the child to produce an unlimited number of sentences from a limited number of words.

At birth, infants can distinguish among the speech sounds of all the world's languages, no matter what language is spoken in their homes (Kuhl, 2004; Werker &

Desjardins, 1995). And shortly after birth, infants prefer speech over other sounds that humans make (Shultz et al., 2014). But infants lose the ability to distinguish among all possible speech sounds by 10 to 12 months of age. Instead, they can distinguish only among the speech sounds that are present in the language to which they have been exposed (Kuhl et al., 1992; Yoshida et al., 2010). Thus, during the first year of life, infants begin to master the sound structure of their own native language.

People in every culture, especially parents, use a style of speech called *motherese, parentese,* or *infant-directed speech,* with babies (Bryant & Barrett, 2007; Kuhl, 2004). Infant-directed speech is characterized by very distinct pronunciation, a simplified vocabulary, short sentences, high pitch, and exaggerated intonation and expression. Characteristics of infant-directed speech appear to be universal. For example, researchers studied a remote culture in Kenya that had no exposure to Western languages like English (Bryant et al., 2012). The Kenyan adults reliably identified when recorded English speakers were communicating with a child versus an adult, even though they couldn't understand the words being said. Furthermore, the Kenyan adults often understood the general intent of what was being said to the child. For example, they could tell when a parent was trying to get an infant's attention.

The adult use of infant-directed speech seems to be instinctive. Deaf mothers who use sign language modify their hand gestures when they communicate with infants and toddlers in a way that is very similar to the infant-directed speech of hearing mothers (Koester & Lahti-Harper, 2010).

The Stages of Language Development

The stages of language development appear to be universal (Kuhl, 2004). In virtually every culture, infants follow the same sequence of language development and at roughly similar ages.

At about 3 months of age, infants begin to "coo," repeating vowel sounds such as *ahh-hhh* or *ooooo,* varying the pitch up or down. At about 5 months of age, infants begin to *babble.* They add consonants to the vowels and string the sounds together in sometimes long-winded productions of babbling, such as *ba-ba-ba-ba, de-de-de-de,* or *ma-ma-ma-ma.*

When infants babble, they are not simply imitating adult speech. Infants all over the world use the *same* sounds when they babble, including sounds that do not occur in the language of their parents and other caregivers. At around 9 months of age, babies begin to babble more in the sounds specific to their language. Babbling, then, seems to be a biologically programmed stage of language development (Gentilucci & Dalla Volta, 2007; Petitto et al., 2004).

Before they are a year old, most infants can understand simple commands, such as "Bring Daddy the block," even though they cannot *say* the words *bring, Daddy,* or *block.* This reflects the fact that an infant's **comprehension vocabulary** (*the words that are understood by an infant or child*) is much larger than their **production vocabulary** (*the words that an infant or child understands and can speak*). Generally, infants acquire comprehension of words more than twice as fast as they learn to speak new words.

Somewhere around their first birthday, infants produce their first real words. First words usually refer to concrete objects or people that are important to the child, such as *mama, daddy,* or *ba-ba* (bottle). First words are also often made up of the syllables that were used in babbling.

During the *one-word stage,* babies use a single word and vocal intonation to stand for an entire sentence. With the proper intonation and context, *baba* can mean "I want my bottle!" "There's my bottle!" or "Where's my bottle?"

Around their second birthday, toddlers begin putting words together. During the *two-word stage,* they combine two words to construct a simple "sentence," such as "Mama go." During this stage, the words used are primarily content words—nouns, verbs, and sometimes adjectives or adverbs. Articles (*a, an, the*) and prepositions (such as *in, under, on*) are omitted. Two-word sentences reflect the first understandings of grammar. Although these utterances include only the most essential words, they basically follow a grammatically correct sequence.

At around 2½ years of age, children move beyond the two-word stage. They rapidly increase the length and grammatical complexity of their sentences. There is a dramatic

comprehension vocabulary The words that are understood by an infant or child.

production vocabulary The words that an infant or child understands and can speak.

▲ **Deaf Babies Babble with Their Hands** Deaf babies whose parents use American Sign Language (ASL) babble with their hands, rather than their voices (Petitto et al., 2001; Petitto & Marentette, 1991). Just as hearing babies repeat the same syllables over and over, deaf babies repeat the same simple hand gestures. Hearing babies born to deaf parents who are exposed only to sign language also babble with their hands (Petitto et al., 2004). Here, a baby repeats the sign for "A."

bilingualism Fluency in two or more languages.

increase in the number of words they can comprehend and produce. By the age of 3, the typical child has a production vocabulary of more than 3,000 words. Acquiring about a dozen new words per day, a child may have a production vocabulary of more than 10,000 words by school age (Bjorklund, 1995).

The ability to learn so many new words so quickly doesn't last. There appears to be a critical period during which it's easiest to learn a new language, including learning proper pronunciation and grammar (DeKeyser, 2000). Beginning around age 6 or 7, the ability to learn a new language declines. One study, for example, found a correlation between age and success in learning English among Spanish- and Chinese-speaking immigrants to the United States (Hakuta et al., 2003). The researchers found that the older the age at arrival in the United States, the lower the eventual success in learning English.

The Bilingual Mind: Are Two Languages Better Than One?

How many languages can you speak fluently? In many countries, **bilingualism**, or *fluency in two or more languages*, is the norm. (Some researchers prefer the term *multilingual* to refer to people who speak more than two languages.) In fact, estimates are that about two-thirds of children worldwide are raised speaking two or more languages (Bialystok et al., 2009).

At one time, especially in the United States, raising children as bilingual was discouraged. Educators believed that children who simultaneously learned two languages would be confused and not learn either language properly. Such confusion, they believed, could lead to delayed language development, learning problems, and lower intelligence (see García & Náñez, 2011). Some professionals still hold these beliefs, including, in one study, nurses in Sweden (Nayeb et al., 2015). The nurses sometimes delayed referrals for real speech problems, attributing difficulties to bilingualism.

Some research has found neither benefits nor drawbacks to speaking multiple languages over speaking one language (Nichols et al., 2020). But other research has found that bilingualism has many cognitive benefits (Kroll et al., 2014). This is true particularly in the case of *balanced proficiency*, when speakers are equally proficient in two languages (García & Náñez, 2011). Several studies have found that bilingual speakers are better able to control attention and inhibit distracting information than people who are fluent in just a single language (Bialystok, 2011). Why? It turns out that *both* languages are constantly active to some degree in the brain of a bilingual speaker, even in a situation where only one language is spoken. Thus, the bilingual speaker must be a "mental juggler," and the resulting cognitive workout pays off in increased mental agility.

This cognitive flexibility may also have social benefits: Research suggests that bilingual people are better at taking the perspective of others, such as imagining how another person might view a particular situation (Liberman et al., 2016; Rubio-Fernández & Glucksberg, 2012).

Bilingualism also seems to pay off in preserving brain function in old age (Alladi et al., 2013). Like education, exercise, and mental stimulation, speaking two (or more) languages fluently seems to build up what researchers call a *cognitive reserve* that can help protect against cognitive decline in late adulthood (Bialystok et al., 2012; Costa & Sebastián-Gallés, 2014).

Animal Communication and Cognition

Chimpanzees "chutter" to warn of snakes and "chirp" to let others know that a leopard is nearby. Prairie dogs make different sounds to warn of approaching coyotes, dogs, hawks, and even humans wearing blue shirts versus humans wearing yellow shirts (Connell et al., 2019; Slobodchikoff et al., 2009). Even insects have complex communication systems. For example, honeybees perform a "dance" to report information about the distance, location, and quality of a pollen source to their hive mates (J. Riley et al., 2005).

Clearly, animals communicate with one another, but can they master language? Some psychologists think that, although animals can vocalize and communicate, language itself is "uniquely human" (Berwick et al., 2013). But others think that animal language is possible. Some of the most promising results have come from the research of psychologists Sue Savage-Rumbaugh and Duane Rumbaugh (Lyn et al., 2006).

∧ **Prairie Dogs** Prairie dogs use a sophisticated system of vocal communication to describe predators. Their high-pitched calls contain specific information about what the predator is, how big it is, and how fast it is approaching (Connell et al., 2019; Slobodchikoff et al., 2009).

Chuck Haney/DanitaDelimont.com

These researchers began working with a rare chimpanzee species called the *bonobo* in the mid-1980s (Savage-Rumbaugh & Lewin, 1994).

A bonobo named Kanzi was able to learn symbols and also to comprehend spoken English. Altogether, Kanzi understands elementary syntax and more than 500 spoken English words. And, Kanzi can respond to new, complex spoken commands, such as "Put the ball on the pine needles" (Segerdahl et al., 2006). Because these commands are spoken by an assistant out of Kanzi's view, he cannot be responding to nonverbal cues.

Research evidence suggests that nonprimates also can acquire limited aspects of language. For example, Louis Herman (2002) trained bottle-nosed dolphins to respond to sounds and gestures, each of which stands for a word. This artificial language incorporates syntax rules, such as those that govern word order. And honeyguides, a type of bird in Mozambique, respond to vocalizations made by people searching for honey (Spottiswoode et al., 2016). The birds respond to specific sounds made by people seeking beehives, which are often hidden in trees. The people foraging for honey were three times as likely to find honey if they made these sounds to request guidance from the birds. What's in it for the birds? They learned that humans have tools to open the hives, and the birds eat leftover beeswax once the people have taken the honey.

Going beyond language, psychologists today study many aspects of animal behavior. *The study of animal learning, memory, thinking, and language* is referred to as **animal cognition** or **comparative cognition** (Shettleworth, 2010; Wasserman & Zentall, 2006). It is a myth that humans are the only animals to have language, use tools, and plan ahead.

Rather than focusing on whether nonhuman animals can develop human capabilities, such as language, comparative psychologists today study a wide range of cognitive abilities in many different species. For example, Western scrub jays can remember the past and anticipate the future (Clayton et al., 2003). They survive harsh winters by remembering precisely where they stored the food they gathered months earlier (Raby et al., 2007; van der Vaart et al., 2011). Recent research on owls and pigeons might help explain why birds seem so smart. Researchers found a structure in the birds' brains that functions much like the cortex in the brains of mammals, including primates and humans (Stacho et al., 2020). And we already knew that primates are smart. For example, bonobos and chimpanzees can remember events in a movie after viewing it just once (Kano & Hirata, 2015). Their eyes focused on the location of the action they expected to see — a human in an ape suit emerging through a door.

What about the animals with which many of us share our lives? Dogs, in particular, seem to have convinced their owners that they are "smart," and their responsiveness to training makes them willing research participants. Since 2000, there has been a dramatic increase in research on dogs' cognitive abilities, and we've learned a lot (Arden et al., 2016; Miklósi & Kubinyi, 2016). For example, dogs can distinguish between people who are stingy with food rewards and people who are generous with food rewards (Bray et al., 2014). They remember this information, and later they will approach the generous person even if that person clearly has less food to offer than the stingy person. Dogs also seem to distinguish among numbers up to nine (Roberts & Macpherson, 2016). As demonstrated by fMRI, dogs can separately understand words and the tone in which they are spoken. In one study, dogs' brains didn't react to praise unless both the words and the tone in which they were spoken matched (Andics et al., 2017).

But contrary to popular belief, dogs' cognitive skills may not be especially human-like. For example, in a study on dogs' responses to human emergencies, researchers observed the behavior of dogs in a room in which the dog's owner appeared to be trapped under a bookcase. None of the dogs sought help from an experimenter

animal cognition or **comparative cognition**
The study of animal learning, memory, thinking, and language.

MYTH ◄ SCIENCE

Is it true that humans are the only animals to have language, use tools, and plan ahead?

Irene Pepperberg with Alex Over 30 years of research, Irene Pepperberg and an African gray parrot named Alex revolutionized ideas about avian intelligence and animal communication. Along with his remarkable language abilities, Alex also displayed an understanding of simple concepts, including an understanding of bigger and smaller, similarity and difference. Shown a green block and a green ball and asked "What's the same?" Alex would respond, "Color." Alex could even accurately label quantities up to the number six (Pepperberg, 2007). Alex died in 2007, but Pepperberg's research with gray parrots continues. Visit alexfoundation.org to learn more.

© Arlene Levin-Rowe

Lending a Trunk Elephants, highly social animals, seem to understand the nature of cooperation. In this experiment, Asian elephants had to pull two ends of the same rope simultaneously to drag buckets of tasty corn within reach. Researchers found that the elephants quickly learned to coordinate their efforts, and would wait at their rope end as long as 45 seconds for an elephant partner. They also appeared to understand that there was no point to pulling if the partner lacked access to the rope (Plotnik et al., 2011).

THINK LIKE A **SCIENTIST**

Can online brain games make you smarter? Go to Achieve Resources to **Think Like a Scientist** about **Brain Exercises.**

Achieve

intelligence The global capacity to think rationally, act purposefully, and deal effectively with the environment.

mental age A measurement of intelligence in which an individual's mental level is expressed in terms of the average abilities of a given age group.

intelligence quotient (IQ) A measure of general intelligence derived by comparing an individual's score with the scores of others in the same age group.

in the next room (Macpherson & Roberts, 2006). Based on the overall body of research on dog cognition, psychologist Clive Wynne (2016) concluded that dogs aren't cognitively unique as compared with other species, but they do have "exquisite sensitivity to human action," which can make it seem as though they have special cognitive skills.

Can nonhuman animals "think"? Do they consciously reason? Such questions may be unanswerable. More important, many comparative psychologists today take a different approach. Rather than trying to determine whether animals can reason, think, or communicate like humans, these researchers are interested in the specific cognitive capabilities that different species have evolved to best adapt to their ecological niche (de Waal & Ferrari, 2010; Shettleworth, 2010).

Measuring Intelligence

■ KEY THEME

Intelligence is defined as the global capacity to think rationally, act purposefully, and deal effectively with the environment.

≡ KEY QUESTIONS
- What roles did Binet, Terman, and Wechsler play in the development of intelligence tests?
- How did Binet, Terman, and Wechsler differ in their beliefs about intelligence and its measurement?
- Why are standardization, validity, and reliability important components of psychological tests?

Up to this point, we have talked about a broad range of cognitive abilities—the use of mental images and concepts, problem solving and decision making, and the use of language. All these mental abilities are aspects of what we commonly call *intelligence.*

What exactly is intelligence? We will rely on a formal definition developed by psychologist David Wechsler. Wechsler (1944, 1977) defined **intelligence** as *the global capacity to think rationally, act purposefully, and deal effectively with the environment.* Although many people commonly equate intelligence with "book smarts," notice that Wechsler's definition is much broader. To Wechsler, intelligence is reflected in effective, rational, and goal-directed behavior.

The Development of Intelligence Tests

Can intelligence be measured? Intelligence tests attempt to measure general mental abilities, rather than accumulated knowledge or aptitude for a specific subject or area. In the next several sections, we will describe the evolution of intelligence tests, including the qualities that make any psychological test scientifically acceptable.

Alfred Binet: Identifying Students Who Needed Special Help
In the early 1900s, the French government passed a law requiring all children to attend school. Faced with the need to educate children from a wide variety of backgrounds, the French government commissioned psychologist **Alfred Binet** to develop procedures to identify students who might require special help.

With the help of French psychiatrist Théodore Simon, Binet devised a series of tests to measure different mental abilities. Binet deliberately did not test abilities, such as reading or mathematics, that the students might have been taught. Instead, he focused on elementary mental abilities, such as memory, attention, and the ability to understand similarities and differences.

Binet arranged the questions on his test in order of difficulty, with the simplest tasks first. He found that brighter children performed like older children. This observation led Binet to the idea of a **mental age,** *a measurement of intelligence in which an individual's mental level is expressed in terms of the average abilities of a given age group.* Mental age is different from a child's chronological age. A bright 7-year-old might answer the same number of questions as an average 9-year-old, whereas a less capable 7-year-old might do only as well as an average 5-year-old.

It is somewhat ironic that Binet's early tests became the basis for modern intelligence tests. First, Binet did *not* believe that he was measuring an inborn or permanent level of intelligence (Foschi & Cicciola, 2006; Kamin, 1995). Rather, he believed that his tests could help identify children who could benefit from special help (Newton & McGrew, 2010).

Second, Binet believed that intelligence was too complex a quality to describe with a single number (Siegler, 1992). He steadfastly refused to rank "normal" children on the basis of their scores, believing that such rankings would be unfair. He recognized that many individual factors, such as a child's level of motivation, might affect the child's score. Finally, Binet noted that an individual's score could vary from time to time (Gould, 1993; Kaufman, 2009).

Lewis Terman and the Stanford–Binet Intelligence Test
There was enormous interest in Binet's test in the United States, which was translated and adapted by Stanford University psychologist **Lewis Terman**. Terman's revision was called the *Stanford–Binet Intelligence Scale.* First published in 1916, the Stanford–Binet was for many years the standard for intelligence tests in the United States.

Terman adopted the **intelligence quotient,** or **IQ**, *a measure of general intelligence derived by comparing an individual's score with the scores of others in the same age group.* This number was derived by dividing the individual's mental age by the chronological age and multiplying the result by 100. Thus, a child of average intelligence, whose mental age and chronological age were the same, would have an IQ score of 100. A 10-year-old child with a mental age of 13 would have an IQ of 130 (13/10 × 100). A child with a chronological age of 10 and a mental age of 7 would have an IQ of 70 (7/10 × 100). It was Terman's use of the intelligence quotient that resulted in the popularization of the phrase "IQ test."

World War I and Group Intelligence Testing
When the United States entered World War I in 1917, the U.S. military was faced with the need to rapidly screen 2 million army recruits. Using a group intelligence test designed by one of Terman's students, army psychologists developed the Army Alpha and Beta tests, which were later adapted for civilian use. The result was a tremendous surge in the intelligence-testing movement (Anastasi & Urbina, 1997; Kamin, 1995). However, the indiscriminate use of the tests also resulted in skepticism and hostility.

For example, immigrants were screened as they arrived at Ellis Island. The result was sweeping generalizations about the intelligence of different nationalities and races. Yet, few talked about the language and cultural differences that may have affected scores. For example, as part of an intelligence test, immigrants were asked to interpret pictures. One picture showed a group of children digging a hole, a dead rabbit on the ground beside them. Many immigrants, based on their experience living in countries in which people eat rabbits, "thought the children had killed the rabbit for dinner. Very few recognized immediately that the children were holding a funeral for their late, lamented pet" (Ellis Island Museum, 2018).

Despite concerns about the misuse of the so-called IQ tests, the tests quickly became popular. Contrary to Binet's contention, it soon came to be believed that the IQ score was a fixed, inborn characteristic that was resistant to change (Gould, 1993).

Terman and other American psychologists believed that a high IQ predicted more than success in school. To investigate the relationship between IQ and success in life, Terman (1926) followed the eventual careers of 1,500 California schoolchildren with "genius" IQ scores. Some of the findings of this landmark study are described in the In Focus box (on page 249), "Does a High IQ Score Predict Success in Life?"

▲ **Alfred Binet** French psychologist Alfred Binet (1857–1911) is shown here with an unidentified child and an instrument from his laboratory that was used to measure his young participants' breathing rates while they performed different tasks (Cunningham, 1997). Although Binet developed the first systematic intelligence tests, he did not believe that he was measuring innate ability. Instead, he believed that his tests could identify schoolchildren who could benefit from special help.

Binet Archives, at Henri-Poincaré Archives (Nancy, France, CNRS/University of Lorraine)

▼ **Testing Immigrants at Ellis Island** This photograph, taken in 1917, shows an examiner administering a mental test to a newly arrived immigrant at the U.S. immigration center on Ellis Island. According to one intelligence "expert" of the time, 80 percent of the Hungarians, 79 percent of the Italians, and 87 percent of the Russians were "feeble-minded" (see Kamin, 1995). The new science of "mental testing" was used to argue for restrictions on immigration.

The Drs. Nicholas and Dorothy Cummings Center for the History of Psychology, The University of Akron

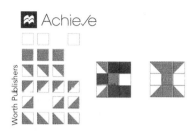

Achieve

Go to **Achieve** to try questions that are much like the Wechsler Adult Intelligence Scale (WAIS) items in **Concept Practice: Wechsler Intelligence Tasks.**

David Wechsler and the Wechsler Intelligence Scales The next major advance in intelligence testing came as a result of a young psychologist's dissatisfaction with the Stanford–Binet and other intelligence tests in widespread use. **David Wechsler** (1896–1981) was in charge of testing adults of widely varying cultural and socioeconomic backgrounds and ages at a large hospital in New York City. He designed a new intelligence test, called the *Wechsler Adult Intelligence Scale (WAIS)*, which was first published in 1955.

The WAIS had two advantages over the Stanford–Binet. First, the WAIS was specifically designed for adults, rather than for children. Second, Wechsler's test provided scores on 11 subtests measuring different abilities. The subtest scores were grouped to provide an overall verbal score and performance score. The *verbal score* represented scores on subtests of vocabulary, comprehension, knowledge of general information, and other verbal tasks. The *performance score* reflected scores on largely nonverbal subtests, such as identifying the missing part in incomplete pictures, arranging pictures to tell a story, or arranging blocks to match a given pattern.

The design of the WAIS reflected Wechsler's belief that intelligence involved a variety of mental abilities. Because the WAIS provided an individualized profile of the participants' strengths and weaknesses on specific tasks, it marked a return to the attitudes and goals of Alfred Binet (Fancher, 1996; Sternberg, 1990).

The subtest scores on the WAIS also proved to have practical and clinical value. For example, a pattern of low scores on some subtests combined with high scores on other subtests might indicate a specific learning disability (Kaufman, 1990). Researchers have observed a particular pattern in the WAIS scores of people with autism spectrum disorder (Kanai et al., 2012). And someone who did well on the performance subtests but poorly on the verbal subtests might be unfamiliar with the culture rather than deficient in these skills (Aiken, 1997). That's because many items included on the verbal subtests draw on cultural knowledge.

Wechsler's test also provided an overall, global IQ score, but he changed the way that the IQ score was calculated. On the Stanford–Binet and other early tests, the IQ represented mental age divided by chronological age. But this approach makes little sense when applied to adult participants. Although a 12-year-old typically answers more questions than an 8-year-old because of developmental differences, such year-by-year age differences lose their meaning in adulthood.

Instead, Wechsler calculated the IQ by comparing an individual's score with the scores of others in the same general age group, such as young adults. The average score for a particular age group was statistically fixed at 100. The range of scores is statistically defined so that two-thirds of all scores fall between 85 and 115—the range considered to indicate "normal" or "average" intelligence. This procedure proved so successful that it was adopted by the administrators of other tests, including the current version of the Stanford–Binet. Today, IQ scores continue to be calculated by this method.

The WAIS was revised in 1981, 1997, and, most recently, in 2008. The fourth edition of the WAIS is known as WAIS-IV. Since the 1960s, the WAIS has remained the most commonly administered intelligence test. Wechsler also developed two tests for children: the *Wechsler Intelligence Scale for Children (WISC)* and the *Wechsler Preschool and Primary Scale of Intelligence (WPPSI)*.

Principles of Test Construction: What Makes a Good Test?

Many kinds of psychological tests measure various aspects of intelligence or mental ability. An **achievement test** is *a test designed to measure a person's level of knowledge, skill, or accomplishment in a particular area*, such as mathematics or a foreign language. In contrast, an **aptitude test** is *a test designed to assess a person's capacity to benefit from education or training*. The overall goal of an aptitude test is to predict your ability to learn certain types of information or perform certain skills.

Any psychological test must fulfill certain requirements to be considered scientifically acceptable. The three basic requirements of good test design are standardization, reliability, and validity. Let's briefly look at what each of those requirements entails.

achievement test A test designed to measure a person's level of knowledge, skill, or accomplishment in a particular area.

aptitude test A test designed to assess a person's capacity to benefit from education or training.

IN FOCUS

Does a High IQ Score Predict Success in Life?

In 1921, Lewis M. Terman identified 1,500 California girls and boys between the ages of 8 and 12 who had IQs above 140, the minimum IQ score for genius-level intelligence. Terman's goal was to track these children by conducting periodic surveys and interviews to see how genius-level intelligence would affect the course of their lives.

Within a few years, Terman (1926) showed that the highly intelligent children tended to be socially well adjusted, as well as taller, stronger, and healthier than average children, with fewer illnesses and accidents. Not surprisingly, those children performed exceptionally well in school.

But how did Terman's "gifted" children fare in the real world as adults? As a group, they showed an astonishing range of accomplishments (Terman & Oden, 1947, 1959). In 1955, when average income was $5,000 a year, the average income for the group was $33,000. Two-thirds had graduated from college, and a sizable proportion had earned advanced academic or professional degrees.

However, not all of Terman's participants were so successful. To find out why, Terman's colleague Melita Oden compared the 100 most successful men (the "A" group) and the 100 least successful men (the "C" group) in Terman's sample. Despite their high IQ scores, only a handful of the C group were professionals, and, unlike the A group, the Cs were earning only slightly above the national average income. In terms of their personal lives, the Cs were less healthy, had higher rates of alcoholism, and were three times more likely to be divorced than the As (Terman & Oden, 1959).

Given that the IQ scores of the A and C groups were essentially the same, what accounted for the difference in their levels of accomplishment? Terman noted that, as children, the As were much more likely to display "prudence and forethought, will power, perseverance, and the desire to excel." As adults, the As were rated differently from the Cs on only three traits: They were more goal-oriented, had greater perseverance, and had greater self-confidence. Overall, the As seemed to have greater ambition and a greater drive to achieve. In other words, *personality factors* seemed to account for the differences in level of accomplishment between the A group and the C group (Terman & Oden, 1959).

Stanford University Archives

"With the exception of moral character, there is nothing as significant for a child's future as his grade of intelligence."

—*Lewis M. Terman (1916)*

Recent research supports the importance of personality factors. Positive life outcomes such as health and financial success were found to be better associated with grades and achievement tests than with IQ (Borghans et al., 2016). Why? Personality traits such as the capacity to plan are closely linked with grades and achievement tests, and these traits on their own have been shown to be important predictors of life outcomes.

As the general success of Terman's gifted children demonstrates, high intelligence can certainly contribute to success in life. But intelligence alone is not enough. Although IQ scores do reliably predict academic success, success in school is no guarantee of success beyond school. Many different personality factors are involved in achieving success: motivation, emotional maturity, commitment to goals, creativity, and—perhaps most important—a willingness to work hard (Furnham, 2008; Lubinski & Benbow, 2021). None of these attributes are measured by traditional IQ tests.

Standardization   If you answer 75 of 100 questions correctly, what does that score mean? Is it high, low, or average? For an individual's test score to be interpreted, it has to be compared against some sort of standard of performance.

Standardization is *the administration of a test to a large, representative sample of people under uniform conditions for the purpose of establishing norms.* The scores of this group establish the *norms,* or the standards against which an individual score is compared and interpreted.

For IQ tests, such norms closely follow a pattern called the **normal curve,** or **normal distribution,** *a bell-shaped distribution of individual differences in a normal population in which most scores cluster around the average score.* Most scores cluster around the average score. As scores become more extreme, fewer instances of the scores occur. In **Figure 7.5,** you can see the normal distribution of IQ scores on the

standardization The administration of a test to a large, representative sample of people under uniform conditions for the purpose of establishing norms.

normal curve or **normal distribution** A bell-shaped distribution of individual differences in a normal population in which most scores cluster around the average score.

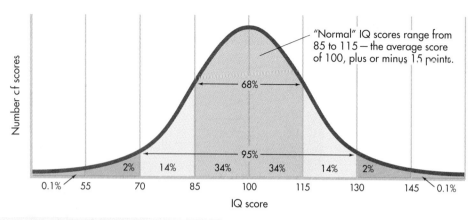

WAIS-IV. About 68 percent of participants taking the WAIS-IV will score between 85 and 115, the IQ range for "normal" intelligence. Less than 1 percent of the population have extreme scores that are above 145 or below 55.

Reliability   A good test must also have **reliability**, *the ability of a test to produce consistent results when administered on repeated occasions under similar conditions.* How do psychologists determine whether a psychological test is reliable? One method is to administer two similar, but not identical, versions of the test at different times. Another procedure is to compare the scores on one half of the test with the scores on the other half of the test. A test is considered reliable if the test and retest scores are highly similar when such strategies are used.

Validity   Finally, a good test must demonstrate **validity**, *the ability of a test to measure what it is intended to measure.* One way to establish the validity of a test is by demonstrating its predictive value. For example, if a test is designed to measure mechanical aptitude, people who received high scores should ultimately prove more successful in mechanical jobs than people who received low scores.

FIGURE 7.5 The Normal Curve of Distribution of IQ Scores The distribution of IQ scores on the WAIS-IV in the general population tends to follow a bell-shaped normal curve, with the average score defined as 100. Notice that 68 percent of the scores fall within the "normal" IQ range of 85 to 115. Ninety-five percent of the general population score between 70 and 130, while fewer than 1 percent score lower than 55 or higher than 145. (Because of rounding, percentages add up to more than 100 percent.)

The Nature of Intelligence

▪ KEY THEME
Psychologists do not agree about the basic nature of intelligence, including whether it is a single, general ability and whether it includes skills and talents as well as mental aptitude.

⹀ KEY QUESTIONS
- How do the concepts of general intelligence, multiple intelligences, and the triarchic theory of intelligence differ in their understanding of intelligence?
- How do the combined models of cognitive abilities represent a compromise among the other models of intelligence?
- What are some of the newest perspectives on intelligence?

The Wechsler Adult Intelligence Scale and the Stanford–Binet Intelligence Scale are standardized, reliable, and valid. But do they adequately measure intelligence? The question is not as simple as it sounds. Over the years, there has been considerable disagreement among psychologists about the nature of intelligence, including how intelligence should best be defined and measured (Gardner, 2011; Neisser et al., 1996). As you'll see in the next section, psychologists have struggled with the challenge of how to define intelligence for over a with some degree of agreement only occurring in recent years.

Theories of Intelligence

reliability The ability of a test to produce consistent results when administered on repeated occasions under similar conditions.

validity The ability of a test to measure what it is intended to measure.

Much of the controversy over the definition of *intelligence* has centered on two key issues. First, is intelligence a single, general ability, or is it better described as a cluster of different mental abilities? Or is it a combination of both a general ability and a cluster of different abilities? And second, should the definition of intelligence be restricted to the mental abilities measured by IQ and other intelligence tests? Or should intelligence be defined more broadly?

These issues have been debated for more than a century, and although there is increasing consensus, there are still disagreements. In this section, we'll describe three influential approaches to understanding intelligence, including a combined model that currently has the most research support. We'll also discuss some ideas about how views of intelligence might continue to change.

Intelligence as a General Ability Some psychologists have suggested that a common factor, or general mental capacity, is at the core of different mental abilities. This approach originated with British psychologist **Charles Spearman** (1863–1945). Although Spearman agreed that an individual's scores could vary on tests of different mental abilities, he found that the scores on different tests tended to be similar. That is, people who did well or poorly on a test of one mental ability, such as verbal ability, tended also to do well or poorly on the other tests.

Spearman recognized that particular individuals might excel in specific areas. However, Spearman (1904) also believed there was a factor he called the *g* **factor** or **general intelligence**, *the notion of a general intelligence factor that is responsible for a person's overall performance on tests of mental ability.* Psychologists who follow this approach think that intelligence can be described as a single measure of general cognitive ability, or *g* factor (Gottfredson, 1998). Thus, these psychologists believe that general mental ability could accurately be expressed by a single number, such as the IQ score.

Multiple Intelligences Other theorists have described intelligence as made up of different mental abilities, even though researchers have long argued that these models do not match with existing research (e.g., Lohman, 1998). Howard Gardner and Robert Sternberg have proposed the best-known of these theories. **Howard Gardner** (b. 1943) described intelligence as different mental abilities that operate independently, instead of as one general intelligence that can be measured as a single score.

Rather than one intelligence, Gardner (1993, 1998a) believes there are "multiple intelligences." To Gardner, "an intelligence" is the ability to solve problems, or to create products, that are valued within one or more cultural settings (1998b, 2011). Gardner's theory includes eight distinct, independent intelligences, which include linguistic (or language-related) intelligence, musical intelligence, and interpersonal intelligence.

Some of the abilities emphasized by Gardner, such as logical-mathematical intelligence, might be tapped by a standard intelligence test. However, other abilities, such as bodily-kinesthetic intelligence or musical intelligence, do not seem to be reflected on standard intelligence tests, although they are highly valued across many different cultures. Currently, the consensus among intelligence theorists is that Gardner's theory, despite its popularity, is not supported by research (Visser et al., 2006).

Robert Sternberg (b. 1949; 2012b, 2014) agrees with Gardner that intelligence is a much broader quality than is reflected in the narrow range of mental abilities measured by a conventional IQ test. However, Sternberg (1988, 1995) disagrees with Gardner's notion of multiple, independent intelligences. He believes that some of Gardner's intelligences are more accurately described as specialized talents, whereas intelligence is a more general quality. Sternberg (1988) points out that you would manage just fine if you were tone-deaf and lacked "musical intelligence" in most societies. However, if you didn't have the ability to reason and plan ahead, you would be unable to function in any culture.

The **triarchic theory of intelligence** is *Robert Sternberg's (1997, 2012c) theory that there are three distinct forms of intelligence: analytic, creative, and practical.* The theory emphasizes both the universal aspects of intelligent behavior and the importance of adapting to a particular social and cultural environment. Sternberg refers to the combination of the three types of abilities as *successful intelligence.*

Analytic intelligence refers to the mental processes used in learning how to solve problems, such as picking a problem-solving strategy and applying it. *Creative intelligence* is the ability to deal with novel situations by drawing on existing skills and knowledge.

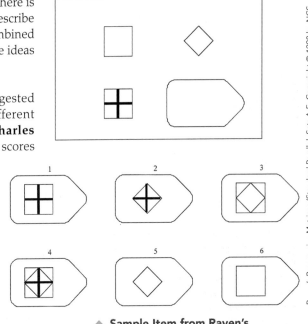

▲ **Sample Item from Raven's Progressive Matrices Test** John Raven, one of Charles Spearman's students, developed a nonverbal test of logic and higher-level abstract thinking to test general mental ability. The Raven test consists of matrix problems that become progressively more difficult. The instructions are simple: Choose the item that best completes the pattern. Because the test does not rely upon previously learned information, many cognitive psychologists regard it as an especially pure test of Spearman's *g* factor (Holyoak, 2005). (Were you able to solve this item? The correct answer is option 2.)

g **factor** or **general intelligence** The notion that a general intelligence factor is responsible for a person's overall performance on tests of mental ability.

triarchic theory of intelligence Robert Sternberg's theory that there are three distinct forms of intelligence: analytic, creative, and practical.

Bartosz Hadyniak/E+/Getty Images

Steven Kingsman/Icon Sportswire

We'll explore the topic of creativity in more detail in the Psych for Your Life section at the end of the chapter. *Practical intelligence* involves the ability to adapt to the environment and often reflects what is commonly called "street smarts." Several studies, however, have failed to find evidence that practical intelligence is a different ability and that Sternberg's model is different from a general model of intelligence (Brody, 2003; Gottfredson, 2003). Most current research supports the idea of general intelligence, though with different types of intelligence underneath the "general" umbrella. The most commonly accepted theories of intelligence at present are combined, or hierarchical, models.

A Compromise: General and Multiple Intelligences

There are several models that combine the idea of intelligence as a general trait (e.g., Spearman) with the idea of multiple intelligences (e.g., Gardner and Sternberg). And these combined models have received more support in recent years than either general intelligence or multiple intelligence theories alone. Two of the better-known combined models are the Carroll Three-Stratum model and the Cattell–Horn–Carroll (CHC) theory of intelligence, the second of which Sternberg himself (2012a) refers to as "the most widely accepted theory" of intelligence.

The Carroll Three-Stratum model and CHC theory are similar. The first was developed by John Carroll, and the second combined Carroll's theory with another theory from Raymond Cattell and John Horn (Carroll, 1997; McGrew, 2009). These combined models break intelligence into three layers (or "strata," as the theorists call the layers). The first layer is the broadest and represents general intelligence, or *g*. The second layer includes broad abilities, such as reading and writing, cognitive processing speed, and quantitative knowledge. The third layer includes narrow abilities that fall under the category of each broad ability. For example, the broad ability of cognitive processing speed breaks down into several narrower categories including skill with numbers and reading speed.

Supporters see combined theories as bridging the gap between intelligence researchers and those who work in the field, measuring intelligence for specific purposes such as in schools (McGrew, 2009). There are conflicting views on their usefulness, however (Canivez & Youngstrom, 2019; Wasserman, 2019; Zaboski et al., 2018). For now, these combined theories are the most accepted in the field, although intelligence researchers continue to call for more studies. The latest theories about intelligence are growing out of new research on cognition and neuroscience (Kaufman et al., 2013; Savi et al., 2019; van der Maas et al., 2017). As we'll see in the next section, new ideas about the nature of intelligence continue to emerge.

Changing Ideas of Intelligence

It is likely that how we think about intelligence will continue to change. Initially, intelligence was measured to predict something, such as how someone would do in school or in a particular job. Then, for a number of years, psychologists thought about intelligence scores as a direct measure of someone's innate abilities. But more and more, many researchers now see measures of intelligence as quantifying a range of specific cognitive abilities (Kovacs & Conway, 2019). In addition, some researchers see these cognitive abilities as shaped by culture and social interactions, rather than being innate (Heyes, 2020).

In line with these more recent perspectives on intelligence, psychologist Philip Ackerman (2017) points out that what a successful adult is expected to be good at has changed over the years. Ackerman asks about the challenges in creating an ideal intelligence test: "Do we give credit only to those who can retrieve correct information from long-term memory, or is the person who [achieves] skills at rapid information search and retrieval from the Internet or other sources equal in ability?" (p. 995). A successful adult might be skilled at synthesizing various online reviews before buying a product, but they might never need to interpret a printed road map. Ackerman wonders about the possible benefits of an "open-book" intelligence test, noting that such a test would not help with some abilities, like spatial skills or comprehension, but might more accurately reflect the skills that contribute to success today.

⌃ **Gardner's Theory of Multiple Intelligences** According to Howard Gardner, many mental abilities are not adequately measured by traditional intelligence tests. As Gardner (2003) explains, "Different tasks call on different intelligences or combinations of intelligence. To perform music intelligently involves a different set of intelligences than preparing a meal, planning a course, or resolving a quarrel." Examples might include the spatial intelligence reflected in the clay pots of this talented Nepalese artist and the extraordinary bodily-kinesthetic intelligence of U.S. soccer player Carli Lloyd.

The Extremes of Intelligence

There is a wide range of diversity in how high people fall on intelligence scales. At one extreme, **intellectual disability** is a *neurodevelopmental disorder in which deficits in mental abilities impair functioning such that standards of personal independence are not met.* It is a condition in which individuals generally have an IQ score of 70 or below. According to the American Association on Intellectual and Developmental Disability (2010), a person with an intellectual disability has difficulties in functioning in three areas: (a) conceptual skills such as the use of language and the ability to understand time; (b) social skills; and (c) practical skills such as the ability to take care of personal hygiene and health.

Individuals are said to be *gifted* when they possess an exceptional amount of natural ability or talent, especially when it becomes evident in childhood. More specifically, **intellectual giftedness** is *a condition in which individuals have an IQ of 130 or higher and exceptional abilities in areas related to intelligence.* As compared with the low functioning associated with intellectual disability, those who are intellectually gifted tend to be highly successful. **Leta Hollingworth**, who studied under pioneering psychologists James Cattell and Edward Thorndike, was a pioneer herself. Hollingworth studied intellectual giftedness. In fact, she came up with the term "gifted," now widely used in this context (Held, 2010). Further, many of her then-groundbreaking ideas are now mainstream. Hollingworth's work emphasized the roles of education and the environment, and not just genetics, in the development of giftedness.

Earlier in the chapter, the In Focus box "Does a High IQ Score Predict Success in Life?" explored Lewis Terman's research tracking life outcomes for gifted children. Another, more recent, study similarly tracked a large group of highly gifted young adolescents through age 40 (Makel et al., 2016). Just as Terman found, the group's accomplishments on the whole were "extraordinary." More than one-third had earned doctoral degrees and nearly 10 percent held patents. Many became leaders in business, medicine, or law. But giftedness alone was not enough to *guarantee* an extraordinary outcome. Researchers noted that most noteworthy accomplishments are achieved when high ability is coupled with commitment, motivation, and the opportunity to be challenged in their education (Lubinski & Benbow, 2021; Wai et al., 2010).

The Roles of Genetics and Environment in Determining Intelligence

■ KEY THEME

Both genes and environment contribute to intelligence, but the relationship is complex.

⚌ KEY QUESTIONS

- How are twin studies used to measure genetic and environmental influences on intelligence?
- What is a heritability estimate, and why can't it be used to explain differences between groups?
- How do social, cultural, and psychological factors affect performance on intelligence tests?

Given that psychologists do not agree on the definition or nature of intelligence, it probably won't surprise you to learn that psychologists also do not agree on the *origin of intelligence.* On the surface, the debate comes down to this: Do we essentially *inherit* our intellectual potential from our parents, grandparents, and great-grandparents? Or is our intellectual potential primarily determined by our *environment* and upbringing?

It is a myth that intelligence is primarily determined by heredity. Virtually all psychologists agree that *both* heredity and environment are important in determining intelligence level. Where psychologists disagree is in identifying how much of intelligence is determined by heredity and how much by environment. The implications of this debate have provoked some of the most heated arguments in the history of psychology.

intellectual disability Neurodevelopmental disorder in which deficits in mental abilities impair functioning such that standards of personal independence are not met (formerly called *mental retardation*).

intellectual giftedness A condition in which individuals have an IQ of 130 or higher and exceptional abilities in areas related to intelligence.

▲ **Leta Hollingworth (1886–1939)** Leta Hollingworth, the creator of the now widely used term "gifted," studied intellectual giftedness. She was the first to write a major book on giftedness. Her research upended the idea that the brightest children were self-sufficient, and led to the development of curricula geared toward gifted students. Many of her groundbreaking findings and ideas are now mainstream. (She was also renowned for her work on the psychology of women, which we discuss in the chapter on gender and sexuality.) Hollingworth's work received a great deal of recognition, including, in an indication of the sexism of the time, inclusion on the prestigious American Men in Science list.

MYTH ◀ SCIENCE

Is it true that intelligence is primarily determined by heredity?

CULTURE AND HUMAN BEHAVIOR

Performing with a Threat in the Air: How Stereotypes Undermine Performance

Your anxiety intensifies as you walk into the testing center. You know how much you've prepared for this test. You should feel confident, but you can't ignore the nagging awareness that not everyone expects you to do well. Can your performance be influenced by your awareness of those expectations?

As psychologist **Claude Steele** (b. 1946; 1997) discovered, if those expectations are negative, being aware of that fact can cause you to perform below your actual ability level. Steele coined the term **stereotype threat**, *a psychological predicament in which fear that you will be evaluated in terms of a negative stereotype about a group to which you belong creates anxiety and self-doubt, lowering performance.*

For example, one common stereotype is that women perform poorly in math, especially advanced mathematics. Multiple studies have shown that when women are reminded of their gender before taking an advanced mathematics test, their scores are lower than would be expected (see Steele et al., 2007). Even mathematically gifted women show a drop in scores when they are made aware of gender stereotypes (Good et al., 2008; Kiefer & Sekaquaptewa, 2007).

In one study (Shih et al., 1999, 2006), mathematically gifted Asian American female college students were randomly assigned to three groups. Group 1 filled out a questionnaire about their Asian background, designed to remind them of their Asian identity. Group 2 filled out a questionnaire designed to remind them of their female identity. Group 3 was the control group and filled out a neutral questionnaire.

The results? The students who were reminded of their racial identity as Asians scored significantly higher on the exam than the students who were reminded of their gender as women. The control group of female students who filled out the neutral questionnaire scored in the middle of the other two groups.

Members of virtually any group can experience a decline in performance due to stereotype threat (Schmader et al., 2008). As Steele (1997) explained, stereotype "can affect the members of any group about whom a negative stereotype exists, whether it's skateboarders, older adults, White men, or gang members. Where bad stereotypes about these groups apply, members of these groups can fear being reduced to that stereotype."

How does being reminded of a negative stereotype undermine a person's performance? First, there's the fear that you might confirm the stereotype, which creates psychological stress, self-doubt, and anxiety

Linda A. Cicero/Stanford News Service

‹ **"A Threat in the Air"** Researcher Claude Steele and his colleagues have studied stereotype threat, the idea that our performance can fall below our abilities if we are aware of the negative expectations, or stereotypes, about a group to which we belong. What Steele called "a threat in the air" can affect members of any group, such as a woman who performs more poorly on a mathematics exam when reminded of negative stereotypes about women and math.

(Schmader et al., 2009). In turn, physiological arousal and distracting thoughts interfere with concentration, memory, and problem-solving abilities (Mrazek et al., 2011; Schmader, 2010).

Some research has not found support for the existence of stereotype threat in all situations. For example, researchers did not find support for stereotype threat based on race for U.S. soldiers taking an aptitude test or based on gender for women in the United States answering quantitative reasoning questions (Cullen et al., 2004; Finnigan & Corker, 2016). Some researchers believe there is publication bias in the original research—suggesting that only studies that support stereotype threat are published (Flore & Wicherts, 2015; Flore et al., 2019). Other researchers also consider the possibility that stereotype threat is limited to certain circumstances or that it is occurring all of the time, even for those who are not reminded of the relevant stereotype (Ganley et al., 2013; Pennington et al., 2019).

In the circumstances in which stereotype threat seems to take place, how can it be counteracted? Some research has shown that simply being aware of how stereotype threat can affect your performance helps minimize its negative effects (Johns et al., 2005; Nadler & Clark, 2011). Reminding yourself of *positive* aspects of your social identity, such as your identity as a university student, can boost performance (Shih et al., 2012). Such interventions have had lasting effects in a variety of student populations (G. Cohen et al., 2012).

---

stereotype threat A psychological predicament in which fear that you will be evaluated in terms of a negative stereotype about a group to which you belong creates anxiety and self-doubt, lowering performance.

or "culture-free." However, it is now generally recognized that it is virtually impossible to design a test that is completely culture-free (Greenfield, 2003). As cross-cultural psychologist Patricia Greenfield (1997) argues, ability tests "reflect the values, knowledge, and communication strategies of their culture of origin." Within that culture, the intelligence test may be a valid measure. Thus, a test will tend to favor the people from the culture in which it was developed. For example, in a test that asks people to identify objects, no Canadian adults were able to identify the *mitre*, a headpiece worn by the Archbishop of Canterbury for public ceremonies in England (Roberts, 2003). That doesn't mean these Canadian adults are less intelligent than the 55 percent of British test-takers who did correctly identify that object.

Cultural differences may also be involved in *test-taking behavior* (Sternberg, 1995, 2012b). People from different cultural backgrounds may use strategies in solving problems or organizing information that are different from those required on standard intelligence tests (Miller-Jones, 1989). In addition, such cultural factors as motivation, attitudes toward test taking, and previous experiences with tests can affect performance and scores on tests.

Closing Thoughts

So, what conclusions can we draw about the debates surrounding intelligence, including the role of heredity in mental ability?

First, it's clear that the IQ score of any individual—regardless of their racial, social, or economic group—is the result of a complex interaction among genetic and environmental factors. Second, environmental factors are much more likely than genetic factors to account for average IQ differences among distinct groups of people. Third, within *any* given group of people, IQ differences among people are due both to environmental influences and to genetic influences. And finally, IQ scores reflect what IQ tests are designed to measure—a particular group of mental abilities.

As we've seen throughout this chapter, we draw on *many* different types of mental abilities to solve problems, adapt to our environment, and communicate with others. Cognitive flexibility and creative thinking also contribute to our ability to successfully adapt to our particular environment. Can you learn to be more creative? We invite you to attend "A Workshop on Creativity" in the Psych for Your Life section.

Testing, Testing, Testing . . . Virtually all university students will be evaluated with standardized tests at some point. Although great pains are taken to make tests as unbiased and objective as possible, many factors, both personal and situational, can affect performance on tests. Cultural factors, familiarity with the testing process, and anxiety or nervousness are just a few of the factors that can skew test results. So perhaps the best way to view standardized tests is as just one of many possible indicators of a student's level of knowledge—and of their potential to learn.

 PSYCH FOR YOUR LIFE

A Workshop on Creativity

Creativity can be defined as *a group of cognitive processes used to generate useful, original, and novel ideas or solutions to problems* (Hennessey & Amabile, 2010; Runco, 2007). Notice that usefulness, along with originality, is involved in judging creativity. An idea can be highly original, but if it lacks usefulness, it is not regarded as creative.

Although we typically think of creativity in terms of artistic expression, the act of creativity is almost always linked to the process of solving some problem. In that sense, creativity can occur in virtually any area of life. Mick Ebeling, who was named one of the Top 50 Most Creative People of 2014, sees utility as a primary catalyst for creativity (Allen, 2015). His organization, Not Impossible Labs, describes its goal as developing solutions to "real-world problems," like the inability of a person with paralysis to communicate. As you learned in the chapter Prologue, that practical goal spurred Ebeling and his team to create the highly original EyeWriter, which allows the artist Tempt to draw using only eye movement.

Can you learn to be more creative? It is a myth that there's nothing you can do to increase creativity. In general, creativity experts agree that you can. Although there is no simple formula that guarantees creative success, a few basic ingredients are central to the process of creative thinking.

1. Choose the goal of creativity.

Psychologists have found that virtually everyone possesses the intelligence and cognitive processes needed to be creative (Weisberg, 1988, 1993). But the creative individual values creativity as a personal goal. Without the personal goal of creativity, the likelihood of doing something creative is slim (Hennessey, 2010).

Is it true that you're either creative or you're not—there's nothing you can do to increase creativity?

creativity A group of cognitive processes used to generate useful, original, and novel ideas or solutions to problems.

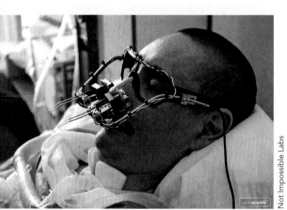

Not Impossible Labs

▲ **The EyeWriter** Tempt is once again using the EyeWriter because it is more efficient than the BrainWriter. The main drawback to the EyeWriter is that "it's tiring—incredibly tiring" to use (Rodriguez, 2017). So, the team at Not Impossible Labs continues to seek creative solutions to help Tempt and others like him to communicate and create.

2. Reinforce creative behavior.

People are most creative when motivated by their own interest, the enjoyment of a challenge, and a personal sense of satisfaction and fulfillment (Amabile, 1996, 2001; Gilson & Madjar, 2011). This is called *intrinsic motivation.* In contrast, when people are motivated by external rewards, such as money or grades, they are displaying *extrinsic motivation.*

Researchers used to believe that extrinsic rewards made creative behavior much less likely. However, rewards can increase creative behavior in a person who has some training in generating creative solutions to problems (Eisenberger et al., 1998).

3. Engage in problem finding.

In many cases, the real creative leap involves recognizing that a problem exists. This is referred to as *problem finding* (Kaufman & Sternberg, 2010). We often overlook creative opportunities by dismissing trivial annoyances rather than recognizing them as potential problems to be solved.

For example, consider the minor annoyance experienced by a man named Art Fry. Fry, a researcher for 3M Corporation, regularly sang in his church choir. To locate the hymns quickly during the Sunday service, Fry used little scraps of paper to mark their places. But the scraps of paper would sometimes fall out when Fry stood up to sing (Kaplan, 1990).

While sitting in church, Fry recognized the "problem" and came up with a relatively simple solution. If you put a substance that is sticky, but not *too* sticky, on the scraps of paper, they'll stay on the page, and you can take them off when they are not needed anymore.

If you haven't already guessed, Art Fry invented Post-it Notes. The formula for the adhesive had been discovered years earlier at 3M, but nobody could imagine a use for a glue that did not bond permanently. The mental set of the 3M researchers was to find *stronger* glues, not weaker ones. Fry's story demonstrates the creative value of recognizing problems instead of simply dismissing them.

A technique called *bug listing* is one useful strategy to identify potential problems. Bug listing involves creating a list of things that annoy or bug you. Such everyday annoyances are problems in need of creative solutions.

4. Acquire relevant knowledge.

Creativity requires a good deal of preparation (Weisberg, 1993). Acquiring a solid knowledge base increases your potential for recognizing how to creatively extend your knowledge or apply it in a new way. As the famous French chemist Louis Pasteur said, "Chance favors the prepared mind."

5. Try different approaches.

Creative people are flexible in their thinking. They step back from problems, turn them over, and mentally play with possibilities. This is called *divergent thinking* because it involves moving away (or diverging) from the problem and considering it from a variety of perspectives (Baer, 1993).

Looking for analogies is one technique to encourage divergent thinking. In problem solving, an *analogy* is the recognition of some similarity or parallel between two objects or events that are not usually compared. Similarities can be drawn in terms of the objects' operations, functions, purposes, materials, or other characteristics.

Or stop thinking about the problem for a while. Research has even shown that creative people, including writers and scientists, often come up with creative ideas when they let their minds wander (Gable et al., 2019).

6. Exert effort and expect setbacks.

Flashes of insight or inspiration can play a role in creativity, but they usually occur only after a great deal of work. Whether you're trying to write a brilliant term paper or design the next *Animal Crossing* video game, creativity requires more effort and persistence than most people think (Lucas & Nordgren, 2015). Famous inventor

Dean Kamen described his laborious creative process:"I work all day. I work all night. I work all weekend. I get obsessed with something and don't give up till I've figured out how to do it. . . . I don't think people realize there is no easy way" (George, 2018).

Finally, the creative process is typically filled with obstacles and setbacks. For example, the best-selling novelist Stephen King endured years of rejection of his manuscripts before his first book was published. And discrimination may also be an obstacle to the creative process for members of some groups. Virginia Jaramillo, an abstract painter who is Latina, got her first solo show at age 81 in 2020. During the years in which her work was ignored, she told a reporter, people would say "Oh, wow, I never knew that you did this kind of work." And she would respond, "Where have you been?" (Loos, 2020). In the face of obstacles and setbacks, the creative person perseveres.

To summarize our workshop on creativity, we'll use the letters of the word *create* as an acronym. Thus, the basic ingredients of *creativity* are:

- **C**hoose the goal of creativity.
- **R**einforce creative behavior.
- **E**ngage in problem finding.
- **A**cquire relevant knowledge.
- **T**ry different approaches.
- **E**xert effort and expect set backs.

⬛ CHAPTER REVIEW

Thinking, Language, and Intelligence

 **Achieve,** Macmillan Learning's online study platform, features the full e-book of *Discovering Psychology*, the **LearningCurve** adaptive quizzing system, videos, and a variety of activities to boost your learning. Visit **Achieve** at macmillanlearning.com.

KEY PEOPLE

Alfred Binet, p. 246	Charles Spearman, p. 251	Robert Sternberg, p. 251	David Wechsler, p. 248
Howard Gardner, p. 251	Claude Steele, p. 258	Lewis Terman, p. 247	Robert Williams, p. 257
Leta Hollingworth, p. 253			

KEY TERMS

cognition, p. 230	functional fixedness, p. 235	bilingualism, p. 244	reliability, p. 250
thinking, p. 230	mental set, p. 235	animal cognition (comparative cognition), p. 245	validity, p. 250
mental image, p. 230	availability heuristic, p. 237	intelligence, p. 246	g factor (general intelligence), p. 251
concept, p. 232	representativeness heuristic, p. 238	mental age, p. 246	triarchic theory of intelligence, p. 251
prototype, p. 232	language, p. 239	intelligence quotient (IQ), p. 247	intellectual disability, p. 253
exemplars, p. 233	confirmation bias, 240	achievement test, p. 248	intellectual giftedness, p. 253
problem solving, p. 233	linguistic relativity hypothesis, p. 241	aptitude test, p. 248	heritability, p. 254
trial and error, p. 233	comprehension vocabulary, p. 243	standardization, p. 249	stereotype threat, p. 258
algorithm, p. 234	production vocabulary, p. 243	normal curve (normal distribution), p. 249	creativity, p. 259
heuristic, p. 234			
insight, p. 234			

Cognition:
The mental activities involved in acquiring, retaining, and using knowledge

Thinking:
The manipulation of mental representations of information in order to draw inferences and conclusions

Mental images:
Manipulated in the same way as actual objects

Concepts:
Mental categories of objects or ideas based on shared properties
- Some are defined by strict rules or specific features.
- Some develop out of everyday experience.
- New instances are classified by comparing them to **prototypes** or **exemplars**.

REUTERS/Muhammad Hamed

Jody Watt/Media Bakery

Solving Problems and Making Decisions

Problem-solving strategies:
- **Trial and error:** Try different solutions, eliminate those that don't work.
- **Algorithm:** Follow a specific rule or procedure that always produces the correct solution.
- **Heuristics:** Follow a rule of thumb to reduce number of potential solutions.
- **Insight:** Reach solutions through sudden realization of correct answer.

Decision-making models:
- Single-feature model
- Additive model
- Elimination-by-aspects model

When events are uncertain, decision-making strategies that involve estimating the likelihood of an event:
- **Availability heuristic:** How easily can you remember similar instances?
- **Representativeness heuristic:** How similar is the current situation to your prototype for an event?

Obstacles to problem-solving:
- **Functional fixedness**
- **Mental set**

Language and Thought

Language characteristics:
- Meaning is conveyed by arbitrary symbols whose meaning is shared by speakers of the same language
- Rule-based system
- Generative
- Involves displacement

Language development:
- Stages include cooing, babbling, one-word stage, two-word stage.
- **Comprehension vocabulary** is larger than **production vocabulary**.

Benefits of **bilingualism** include:
- Improved ability to focus attention, ignore distractions, and take the perspective of others
- Helps preserve cognitive function in late adulthood

Linguistic relativity hypothesis: Do differences among languages cause differences in the thoughts of their speakers?

Animal cognition, or **comparative cognition**, is the study of animal learning, memory, thinking, and language.

Steven Kingsman/Icon Sportswire

Measuring Intelligence

Intelligence: The global capacity to think rationally, act purposefully, and deal effectively with the environment

```
"Normal" IQ scores range from
85 to 115 — the average score
of 100, plus or minus 15 points.
```

Number of scores

68%

95%

| 0.1% | 2% | 14% | 34% | 34% | 14% | 2% | 0.1% |
| 55 | 70 | 85 | 100 | 115 | 130 | 145 |

IQ score

History of intelligence tests

Alfred Binet (1857–1911)
- Developed the first widely accepted intelligence test
- Originated idea of **mental age** as different from chronological age

Lewis Terman (1877–1956)
- Translated and adapted Binet's test for the United States
- Defined **intelligence quotient (IQ)**, a measure of general intelligence derived by comparing an individual's score with the scores of others in the same age group

David Wechsler (1896–1981)
- Developed the **Wechsler Adult Intelligence Scale (WAIS)**

Psychological tests include **achievement tests** and **aptitude tests**. Requirements:
- **Standardization:** Norms are established by administering test to a large, representative sample of people under uniform conditions; norms usually reflect **normal curve** or **normal distribution** of scores.
- **Reliability:** Test produces consistent results when administered on repeated occasions under similar conditions.
- **Validity:** Test measures what it is purported to measure.

Hero Images/Corbis

The Nature of Intelligence

Is intelligence a single factor or a cluster of different abilities? How narrowly should intelligence be defined?

General Intelligence
- **Charles Spearman** (1863–1945)
- Intelligence as a single factor called **general intelligence**, or the *g* **factor**

Multiple Intelligences
- **Howard Gardner** (b. 1943)
- **Robert Sternberg** (b. 1949): **Triarchic theory of intelligence** which involves analytic, creative, and practical mental abilities

Combined Models
- Carroll Three-Stratum model
- Cattell–Horn–Carroll (CHC) model
- A layered model with general intelligence at the top and other intelligences under that umbrella in a second and third layer

Effects of culture on measurements of intelligence:
- Average IQ scores of the dominant social group tend to be higher than the average IQ scores of other groups.
- Intelligence tests can be culturally biased.
- **Robert Williams** (1930–2020) studied the cultural unfairness of traditional intelligence tests

Claude Steele (b. 1946)
- **Stereotype threat** can lower test scores in people who are aware that they belong to negatively viewed groups.

- Intelligence, as measured by IQ, is the result of a complex interaction between heredity and the environment.
- **Heritability:** the percentage of variation within a given population that is due to heredity.
- There is more variation within groups than between groups.
- At the extremes are **intellectual disability,** defined as an IQ of 70 or below, and **intellectual giftedness,** defined as an IQ of 130 or above.
- **Leta Hollingworth** (1886–1939) was a pioneer in giftedness research

MYTH OR SCIENCE?

Is it true . . .

▶ That people need to satisfy basic needs before they can try to achieve higher needs?

▶ That obesity is primarily due to genetics?

▶ That women are more emotional than men?

▶ That facial expressions, such as smiles, are learned and vary from one culture to another?

▶ That polygraphs, or lie detector tests, are a valid way to detect lying?

▶ That if you "put on a happy face," you will actually feel happier?

Motivation and Emotion

PROLOGUE

One Step, One Breath

A steep staircase hewn out of solid rock, the trail seemed to rise straight up the Himalayan mountainside. To the left, the canyon walls dripped with moisture. To the right, the trail dropped sharply to the roaring Budhi Gandaki River hundreds of feet below. The rocky trail was coated with mud and, in some spots, fast-running water. Dismayed, your author Sandy gazed up the trail. Her hiking boots were soaked

through. Her wet hair was matted to her forehead. And she was tired from long days of trekking through rain, mud, and sleet. But there was no way back. The only option was to go forward.

"What am I *doing* here?" Sandy thought. It was her second trip to Nepal as a non-medical volunteer with a small group of doctors and nurses holding health clinics in remote Himalayan villages in Nepal. There were no roads here. Transportation was on foot, and all supplies were carried by donkeys, by yaks, or on human backs. For several days it had rained, soaking

through "waterproof" duffels and raingear. Determined, Sandy and her group trekked on, despite their discomfort and fatigue. Guides reassured the group that the rain would dissipate once higher, drier altitudes were reached. Moods lifted with the clouds, as clear skies revealed that these deep valleys were surrounded by stunning snow-covered peaks.

The last clinic was held in Samagaon, near Nepal's border with Tibet. Villagers began lining up at dawn. Their weathered faces marked by curiosity, trepidation, or friendly grins, the older villagers waited

John Warburton Lee/SuperStock

CHAPTER 8

patiently while the children shrieked with excitement. When the clinic finally closed, nearly 350 villagers had been treated.

The next day brought more rain. Unable to go forward over a high pass as planned, the volunteers had to retrace their steps, and the trails were even more treacherous, some nearly washed out by landslides. One particular staircase was especially daunting. The trail was narrow and slippery, the river below running fast and loud. "I'll never make it," Sandy thought. From halfway up the trail, Pasang, a guide and

translator, called "Never look at the top! Just look two steps ahead, and the way will be easy. One step at a time."

Sandy topped the staircase with relief. Giving up was *not* an option. She had made it.

Why would people leave their comfortable homes to travel to a remote part of the world as volunteers? What kept them going despite fear and fatigue? These are the types of questions that we'll cover in this chapter in our exploration of the two closely linked topics, *motivation* and *emotion.*

Introduction: Motivation

■ **KEY THEME**

Motivation refers to the forces acting on or within an organism to initiate and direct behavior.

≡ **KEY QUESTIONS**

- What three characteristics are associated with motivation?
- How is emotion related to the topic of motivation?
- How do instinct, drive, incentive, arousal, and humanistic theories explain the general principles of motivation?
- What motivated you to sign up for college? Or to enroll in this class?

The topic of **motivation** includes *the biological, emotional, cognitive, or social forces that activate and direct behavior.* There are three basic characteristics commonly associated with motivation: activation, persistence, and intensity.

Activation is demonstrated by the initiation or production of behavior, such as your decision to improve your understanding of psychology by reading this chapter. *Persistence* is demonstrated by continued efforts or the determination to achieve a particular goal, often in the face of obstacles, as evidenced by the volunteers slogging their way up steep, muddy trails, despite cold rain and wet equipment. Finally, *intensity* is seen in the greater vigor of responding that usually accompanies motivated behavior.

Motivation is closely tied to emotional processes, and vice versa. Emotions can drive a behavior, such as when we lash out in anger. Most of the volunteers made the arduous trek through the Himalayas because of the joy and satisfaction they experienced when they helped heal a sick woman or an injured child. We'll take a look at emotion in the second half of the chapter. But first, we'll begin our exploration of motivation with a brief survey of the most influential theories. We'll start by revisiting some of the first "classic" theories of motivation that continue to inform psychological science, and then we will explore some of the contemporary theories that are helping us advance our understanding of what drives humans to do what they do!

"Could you give me a little push?"

Classic Theories of Motivation

■ **KEY THEME**

Classic theories of motivation highlight the essential building blocks of human motivation.

≡ **KEY QUESTIONS**

- How did William James's work lay the groundwork for understanding human motivation?
- How do drive, incentive, arousal, and humanistic theories clarify the basic principles of motivation?
- How does Maslow's hierarchy of needs explain human motivation?

Classic theories of motivation are important to consider as a group because these early theories were focused on *what* it is that motivates us. These theories have continued to be relevant because of their focus on the fundamental mechanisms of what produces and sustains motivation. In the next section, we will review contemporary theories of motivation.

Instinct Theories: Inborn Behaviors as Motivators

Inspired by Charles Darwin's landmark theory of evolution, early psychologists, like William James (1890) and William McDougall (1908), proposed that people were primarily driven by *instincts*. **Instinct theories** are *the view that certain human behaviors*

motivation The biological, emotional, cognitive, or social forces that activate and direct behavior.

instinct theories The view that certain human behaviors are innate and due to evolutionary programming.

drive theories The view that behavior is motivated by the desire to reduce internal tension caused by unmet biological needs.

homeostasis (home-ee-oh-STAY-sis) The idea that the body monitors and maintains internal states, such as energy supplies, at relatively constant levels.

drive A need or internal motivational state that activates behavior to reduce the need and restore homeostasis.

incentive theories The view that behavior is motivated by the pull of external goals, such as rewards.

are innate and due to evolutionary programming. Just as animals display automatic and innate instinctual behavior patterns called *fixed action patterns,* such as migration or mating rituals, human behavior was also thought to be motivated by inborn instinctual behavior patterns, a few of which are very common. Yawning is a great example of a fixed-action pattern in humans. Yawning is an instinctual response to needing more oxygen, and it motivates us (as well as those around us) to take in more air (Krestel et al., 2018). Once initiated, this instinctive, biologically based response must run its course from beginning to end. Think about it: Have you really ever stopped mid-yawn? And did you yawn just now reading about it? Instinctual behavior is that powerful.

Table 8.1 lists some of the human instincts that William James (1890) included in his famous text, *Principles of Psychology.* By the early 1900s, thousands of instincts had been proposed to account for just about every conceivable human behavior (Bernard, 1924). The obvious problem with the early instinct theories was that merely describing and labeling behaviors did not explain their relationship to motivation. By the 1920s, instinct theories had fallen out of favor as a singular explanation of human motivation. But the more general idea that some human behaviors are innate remained important in understanding motivation. Today, psychologists taking the *evolutionary perspective* consider how our evolution has endowed us with many instinctual biologically based behaviors that continue to contribute to our understanding of motivation (Cosmides & Tooby, 2013).

Drive Theories: Biological Needs as Motivators

Beginning in the 1920s, instinct theories were replaced by **drive theories**, *the view that behavior is motivated by the desire to reduce internal tension caused by unmet biological needs.* These unmet biological needs, such as hunger and thirst, "drive" or "push" us to behave in ways that will lead to a reduction in the drive.

Drive theorists believed that drives are triggered by the internal mechanisms of homeostasis. **Homeostasis** is *the idea that the body monitors and maintains internal states, such as energy supplies, at relatively constant levels.* If internal conditions deviate from the optimal level, the body initiates processes to bring the condition back to the normal or optimal range. Thus, the body automatically tries to maintain a "steady state," which is what *homeostasis* means. According to drive theorists, a **drive** is *a need or internal motivational state that activates behavior to reduce the need and restore homeostasis.*

Today, the drive concept remains useful in explaining motivated behaviors that clearly have biological components, such as hunger, thirst, and sexuality. However, drive theories also have limitations. For example, eating behavior can be motivated by factors other than the biological drive of hunger: People often eat when they're not hungry and don't eat when they *are* hungry. And how could drive theories account for the motivation to buy a lottery ticket, run a marathon, or study something as complicated as human behavior?

Incentive Theories: Goal Objects as Motivators

Building on the base established by drive theories, incentive theories emerged in the 1940s and 1950s. **Incentive theories** hold *the view that behavior is motivated by the pull of external goals, such as rewards.* Incentive theories drew heavily from well-established learning principles, such as *reinforcement,* and the work of influential learning theorists, such as Pavlov, Watson, Skinner, and Tolman (see the chapter on learning).

When combined, drive and incentive theories account for a broad range of the "pushes" and "pulls" motivating many of our behaviors. But even in combination, drive and incentive explanations of motivation still had limitations. In some situations, such as playing a rapid-response video game, our behavior seems to be directed toward *increasing* tension and physiological arousal. Some of you may choose to watch scary movies, knowing that they might frighten you, which is not a desirable experience for most people. If you think about it, the decision to watch a scary movie is not motivated by either an internal

TABLE 8.1

James's List of Human Instincts

Attachment	Resentment
Fear	Curiosity
Disgust	Shyness
Rivalry	Sociability
Greediness	Bashfulness
Suspicion	Secretiveness
Hunting	Cleanliness
Play	Modesty
Shame	Love
Anger	Parental love

In his famous text, *Principles of Psychology*, William James (1890) devoted a lengthy chapter to the topic of instinct. With an air of superiority, James noted that "no other mammal, not even the monkey, shows so large an array of instincts" as humans. The table shows some of the human instincts identified by James.

⌄ **Motivation and Drive Theories**
After a grueling Ultimate frisbee championship game, players, including Hannah Babcock and Sawyer Wood, both shown here, are likely motivated to rest, cool off, and hydrate. Drive theories of motivation are useful in explaining biological motives like hunger, thirst, and fatigue, but are less useful in explaining psychological motives. For example, how could we explain their motivation to play competitive frisbee?

Portland Press Herald/Getty Images

biological drive or an external incentive. In order to fully understand why some of us enjoy choosing to scare ourselves, we need to consider arousal theory.

Sensation Seeking People who enjoy high-risk activities are usually sensation seekers. For them, the rush of adrenaline they feel when they push the outer limit is an exhilarating and rewarding experience.

Arousal Theory: Optimal Stimulation as a Motivator

Racing your car along a barren stretch of highway, checking out a haunted house at Halloween, shooting down the Super Slide at a water park—none of these activities seems to involve tension reduction, the satisfaction of some biological need, or the lure of some reward. Rather, performing the activity itself seems to motivate us. Why?

Arousal theory is *the view that people are motivated to maintain a level of arousal that is optimal—neither too high nor too low* (Hebb, 1955). When arousal is too low, we experience boredom and become motivated to *increase* arousal by seeking out stimulating experiences (Berlyne, 1960, 1971). But when arousal is too high, we seek to *reduce* arousal in a less stimulating environment. The large number of theories for motivation reflect how much variation there is among individuals in terms of what increases or decreases motivation. What is universally clear, however, is that the most people function best at a middle level of arousal (rather than an extremely high or low arousal). The idea that there is an ideal level of arousal for performing a task successively is described by the Yerkes–Dodson law. Robert Yerkes and John Dodson looked at the effects of administering shocks to Japanese dancing mice while they were performing cognitive tasks. The researchers found that low levels of shock improved learning among the mice, while high levels of shock created arousal levels that decreased performance on learning tasks (Yerkes & Dodson, 1908). Although these original findings are more than a century old, they continue to inform thinking about human motivation and our understanding that there is an optimal level of arousal, as well as less-than-optimal levels (Garger et al., 2020; Rowland & van Lankveld, 2019).

For example, we have all been in a classroom where our interest in the new material we are learning increases our arousal, making it easier to remember the material. Unfortunately, we have also been in a classroom in which the complexity of the material or the demeanor of the teacher increases our arousal past the point of being helpful, making it harder to learn the material.

That the optimal level of arousal varies from person to person is especially evident in *sensation seekers*. According to psychologist Marvin Zuckerman (1979, 2007, 2009), **sensation seeking** is *the degree to which an individual is motivated to experience high levels of sensory and physical arousal associated with varied and novel activities*. Although such experiences can sometimes involve physical or social risks, sensation seekers aren't necessarily drawn to danger—but rather to the experience of novelty or excitement. For example, university students who study abroad score significantly higher on sensation seeking than university students who stay in their country of origin (Maultsby & Stutts, 2019). Like people, animals also seem to seek out novel environmental stimulation. Rats, cats, dogs, and other animals actively explore a new environment.

Humanistic Theories: Human Potential as a Motivator

In the late 1950s, humanistic theories of motivation were championed by psychologists Carl Rogers and Abraham Maslow. **Humanistic theories of motivation** are *the view that emphasizes the importance of psychological and cognitive factors in motivation, especially the notion that people are motivated to realize their personal potential* (Sheldon, 2008). Motivation was thought to be affected by how we perceive the world, how we think about ourselves and others, and our beliefs about our abilities and skills (Rogers, 1961, 1977).

Although innate and universal, the motivation to strive toward your highest potential could be jeopardized by the absence of a supportive environment—personal, social, and cultural (King, 2008). Next, we'll consider the best-known humanistic model of motivation, Maslow's *hierarchy of needs*.

arousal theory The view that people are motivated to maintain a level of arousal that is optimal—neither too high nor too low.

sensation seeking The degree to which an individual is motivated to experience high levels of sensory and physical arousal associated with varied and novel activities.

humanistic theories of motivation The view that emphasizes the importance of psychological and cognitive factors in motivation, especially the notion that people are motivated to realize their personal potential.

Maslow's Hierarchy of Needs: Psychological Needs as Motivators

What motivates you to study long hours for an important exam? To get up early to join a friend for breakfast? To push yourself to achieve a new "personal best" at a favorite sport? Rather than being motivated by a biological need or drive like hunger, such behaviors are more likely motivated by the urge to satisfy *psychological needs.*

A major turning point in the discussion of human needs occurred when humanistic psychologist **Abraham Maslow** developed his model of human motivation. Maslow acknowledged the importance of biological needs as motivators. But once basic biological needs are satisfied, he believed, "higher" psychological needs emerge.

The **hierarchy of needs** is *Maslow's levels of motivation that progress from basic physical needs to psychological needs to self-fulfillment needs* (summarized in **Figure 8.1**; Maslow, 1954, 1968). It is important to note that Maslow himself never used a pyramid to show his ideas (Bridgman et al., 2019). Later theorists framed his ideas first by using a ladder or staircase and still later the pyramid typically used today. Maslow believed that people are motivated to satisfy the needs at each level of the hierarchy before moving up to the next level. The lowest levels of Maslow's hierarchy emphasize fundamental physiological and biological needs. Once these basic needs are met, safety becomes centrally important and includes a need to feel secure.

Once an individual feels safe and secure in a physical sense, the needs for belonging and love make up the next level of the Maslow's hierarchy. Once people have fulfilled their need to belong and feel accepted by others, they feel motivated to achieve different goals. This need for esteem focuses on a sense of accomplishment and/or pride about one's achievements.

At the next level, the hierarchy changes its focus to more intangible (abstract) needs that are more related to social and psychological growth. The first of these is the need to achieve *self-actualization,* which Maslow (1970) described as "the full use and exploitation of talents, capacities, [and] potentialities." In plain language, this means that you have lived up to your potential and have become the person you truly would like to be. When you live in a way that does not feel authentic—whether that be in terms of your academic, professional, or relationship status—your self-actualization needs are not being met.

Maslow's model of motivation generated considerable research, especially during the 1970s and 1980s. Some researchers found support for Maslow's ideas (see Graham &

hierarchy of needs Maslow's levels of motivation that progress from basic physical needs to psychological needs to self-fulfillment needs.

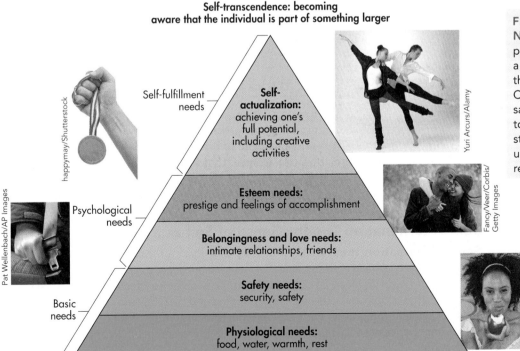

FIGURE 8.1 Maslow's Hierarchy of Needs Abraham Maslow believed that people are innately motivated to satisfy a progression of needs, beginning with the most basic physiological needs. Once the needs at a particular level are satisfied, the individual is motivated to satisfy the needs at the next level, steadily progressing upward. The ultimate goal is self-actualization, the realization of personal potential.

Balloun, 1973). But others criticized his model on several points (see Bridgman, 2019; Fox, 1982; Neher, 1991; Wahba & Bridwell, 1976).

First, Maslow's core assumption that we must satisfy needs at one level before moving to the next level has *not* been supported by empirical research (Sheldon et al., 2001). Second, Maslow's concept of self-actualization is vague and almost impossible to define in a way that would allow it to be tested scientifically. Third, self-actualization is an "elitist, indvidualistic" goal that may not be prized across cultures (Compton, 2018). Even Maslow admitted that self-actualization is rarely achieved, which calls into question its status as a universal and innate goal that motivates all people.

Perhaps Maslow's most important contribution was to encourage psychology to focus on the motivation and development of psychologically healthy people (King, 2008). In advocating that idea, he helped focus attention on psychological needs as motivators. The work he inspired helped achieve a better understanding of the human needs for belonging and for love.

The Need to Belong   According to an influential theory proposed by psychologists Roy Baumeister and Mark Leary (1995), the *need to belong* is a *fundamental* human motivation—as essential to human survival as food and shelter. They define **the need to belong** as *the drive to form and maintain lasting positive relationships that are characterized by mutual concern and caring.* To meet our belongingness needs, such relationships should include frequent, positive interactions and persistent caring.

Closely connected to the need to belong is the *need for affiliation,* or the need to associate with like-minded people in social groups (Neel et al., 2016). In combination, belongingness and affiliation are essential to both thriving in our personal lives and surviving as a species. From an evolutionary perspective, social bonds are key to the survival of humans of all ages, and this may be why social isolation is so threatening.

People differ in their need for affiliation (Dufner et al., 2015). Nevertheless, the importance of social bonds is revealed when the needs to belong and affiliate are not met. Social isolation can lead to the pain of loneliness, which has a negative effect on both psychological and physical well-being (Cacioppo et al., 2015a, 2015b; Holt-Lunstad et al., 2015).

Similarly, social rejection by other group members, sometimes called *ostracism,* can be emotionally devastating (Williams, 2007, 2009). In fact, the emotional pain of social rejection activates *physical* pain areas in the brain (MacDonald & Leary, 2005). Perhaps this is not surprising. Just as physical pain signals potential or actual damage to our physical body, social pain alerts us that the close ties that we rely on for survival are under threat (Eisenberger, 2015).

Contemporary Theories of Motivation

Contemporary theories of motivation build on our understanding of *what* motivates us by focusing on and providing important insights about *why* we are motivated. Together, these contemporary theories generally relate to this idea: People are motivated by the belief that there are rewards they can achieve. That said, there are many variations on the rewards that motivate people, so let's take a closer look at the different contemporary theories of motivation.

Self-Determination Theory: Sense of Self as a Motivator

Self-determination theory (SDT) is *Deci and Ryan's theory that optimal human functioning can occur only if the psychological needs for autonomy, competence, and relatedness are satisfied* (Ryan & Deci, 2012a, 2012b, 2017). Much like Maslow's theory, SDT's premise is that people are actively growth oriented and that they move toward a unified sense of self and integration with others. And, it incorporates other researchers' work on the importance of social relationships, belongingness, competence, and achievement motivation.

the need to belong   The drive to form and maintain lasting positive relationships that are characterized by mutual concern and caring.

self-determination theory (SDT)   Deci and Ryan's theory that optimal human functioning can occur only if the psychological needs for autonomy, competence, and relatedness are satisfied.

To realize optimal psychological functioning and growth throughout the lifespan, Ryan and Deci contend that three innate and universal psychological needs must be satisfied:

- *Autonomy*—the need to determine, control, and organize our own behavior and goals so that they are in harmony with our own interests and values

- *Competence*—the need to learn and master appropriately challenging tasks

- *Relatedness*—the need to feel attached to others and experience a sense of belongingness, security, and intimacy

An important aspect of Deci and Ryan's theory is the importance of autonomy as a basic motive. Deci and Ryan's definition of *autonomy* emphasizes the need to feel that your activities are self-chosen and self-endorsed (Niemiec et al., 2010; Ryan & Deci, 2011). This reflects the importance of self-determination in Deci and Ryan's theory.

How does a person satisfy the needs for autonomy, competence, and relatedness? In a supportive social, psychological, and physical environment, an individual will pursue interests, goals, and relationships that tend to satisfy these psychological needs. In turn, this enhances the person's psychological growth and intrinsic motivation (Sheldon & Ryan, 2011). **Intrinsic motivation** is *the desire to engage in tasks that are inherently satisfying and enjoyable, novel, or optimally challenging.* Basically, intrinsic motivation is the desire to do something for its own sake. The doctors, nurses, and other volunteers who traveled to Nepal in the Prologue story displayed intrinsic motivation, taking time away from work and family to contribute their efforts to helping others in a distant land.

In contrast, **extrinsic motivation** is *the external factors or influences on behavior, such as rewards, consequences, or social expectations.* Of course, much of our behavior in daily life is driven by extrinsic motivation (Ryan & La Guardia, 2000). According to SDT, the person who has satisfied the needs for competence, autonomy, and relatedness actively *internalizes* and *integrates* different external motivators as part of their identity and values (Ryan & Deci, 2012, 2017). In effect, the person incorporates societal expectations, rules, and regulations as values or rules that they personally endorse.

In support of self-determination theory, Deci and Ryan have compiled an impressive array of studies, including cross-cultural studies (Deci & Ryan, 2000, 2012a, 2012b, 2017). From an evolutionary perspective, they argue, the needs for autonomy, competence, and relatedness have adaptive advantages. For example, the need for relatedness promotes resource sharing, mutual protection, and the division of work, increasing the likelihood that both the individual and the group will survive.

Achievement Goal Theory: Success as a Motivator

Achievement motivation is *the desire to direct your behavior toward excelling, succeeding, or outperforming others at some task* (Conroy, 2017; Murray, 1938). Achievement goal theory has been studied in many different contexts. Hundreds of studies have shown that measures of achievement motivation generally correlate well with various areas of success, such as school grades, job performance, and worker output (Senko et al., 2008). This is understandable, since people who score high in achievement motivation expend their greatest efforts when faced with moderately challenging tasks. In striving to achieve the task, they often choose to work long hours and have the capacity to delay gratification and focus on the goal. They also tend to display original thinking, seek expert advice, and value feedback about their performance (McClelland, 1985).

Within achievement goal theory, researchers now make an important distinction between a person's motivation to master something and a person's motivation to perform something. These different motivations have very different goals and end up inspiring different outcomes (Dweck & Leggett, 1988). Mastery goals are focused on just what they sound like, learning to do something well. Performance goals, however, focus on simply showing others that you can do something. This distinction turns out to have a significant impact on long-term educational outcomes as well as self-esteem. People who pursue a goal because they are motivated by learning perform better than people who are motivated by simply demonstrating an ability to others (Dweck & Grant, 2008; Elliot & Dweck, 1988).

intrinsic motivation The desire to engage in tasks that are inherently satisfying and enjoyable, novel, or optimally challenging.

extrinsic motivation External factors or influences on behavior, such as rewards, consequences, or social expectations.

achievement motivation The desire to direct your behavior toward excelling, succeeding, or outperforming others at some task.

THE WORLD'S #1 MOTIVATIONAL SPEAKER

Make me proud before I die.

I'm begging.

Roz Chast The New Yorker Collection/The Cartoon Bank

⌃ Extraordinary Achievement Motivation Thousands of students from 120 countries compete each year in the Google Science Fair. Showing off their trophies—and their grins—are some recent winners: 14-year-old Viney Kumar, from Australia, who invented a signaling system for emergency vehicles; 15-year-old Ann Makosinski, from Canada, who designed a flashlight without batteries or moving parts; 16-year-old Elif Bilgin, from Turkey, who developed a method to create bioplastics from banana peels; and 17-year-old Eric Chen, from the United States, who discovered a new approach to finding better anti-flu medications.

The key difference between these two styles has been more recently described as representing a "fixed" mindset (performance goals) versus a "growth" mindset (mastery goals). People who are motivated by learning, or are encouraged by those around them (e.g., parents and teachers), often end up with a growth mindset. A growth mindset is based on the idea that abilities can be developed and improved with effort and experience. This mastery version of motivation, and the belief that you *can* improve an aspect of yourself, are consistently associated with higher levels of self-esteem (Dweck & Grant, 2008).

People with a fixed mindset (associated with performance goals) are more likely to perceive abilities as unchangeable. As a result, they are more likely to see effort as a waste of time (even the effort to master something). This does not encourage personal or intellectual growth and is more about "studying for the test" rather than "learning the material." It might sound like that is just about schoolwork, but the idea can be applied to many life situations.

When it is broadly defined as "the desire for excellence," achievement motivation is found in many, if not all, cultures. In early cross-cultural research, psychologist David McClelland explored how differences in achievement motivation at the national level have influenced economic development (McClelland, 1961, 1976; McClelland & Winter, 1971).

Other researchers have looked at cultural differences in achievement motivation. In individualistic cultures, like those that characterize North American and European countries, the need to achieve emphasizes personal, individual success rather than the success of the group. In these cultures, achievement motivation is also closely linked with succeeding in competitive tasks (Markus et al., 2006; Morling & Kitayama, 2008).

In collectivistic cultures, like those of many Asian countries, achievement motivation tends to have a different focus. Instead of being oriented toward the individual, achievement orientation is more *socially* oriented (Bond, 1986; Kitayama & Park, 2007). For example, the Japanese student who strives to do well academically is typically not motivated by the desire for personal recognition. Rather, the student's behavior is more likely to be motivated by the desire to enhance the social standing of his or her family by gaining admission to a top university (Kitayama & Park, 2007).

Hunger and Eating

▪ KEY THEME
Hunger is a biological motive, but eating behavior is motivated by a complex interaction of biological, social, and psychological factors.

⹃ KEY QUESTIONS
• What is energy homeostasis, and how is food converted to energy?
• What signals regulate eating behavior?
• What chemical signals are involved in the long-term regulation of a stable body weight?

It seems simple: You're hungry, so you eat. But in reality, what, how much, and how often you eat is influenced by an array of psychological, biological, social, and cultural factors.

For example, think about what you ate yesterday. Now contrast your choices with food preferences in other cultures. A typical diet for the Dusan of Borneo is anteater, snake, and rat meat that have spoiled to the point of liquefaction, consumed with rice. In Nepal, the trekkers were offered Tibetan butter tea, a thick brew of tea, salt, yak butter, and yak milk. Clearly, cultural experience shapes our food choices.

In the next several sections, we look at what researchers have learned about the factors that trigger hunger and motivate eating behavior.

Energy Homeostasis: Calories Consumed Equals Calories Expended

How is food converted to energy in the body? The food that you eat is broken down by enzymes, gradually absorbed in your intestines, and converted into amino acids, fatty acids, and simple sugars. The simple sugar glucose provides the main source of energy for all mammals, including humans. The hormone insulin, secreted by the pancreas, helps control blood levels of glucose and promotes the uptake of glucose by the muscles and other body tissues.

About one-third of your body's energy is expended for the routine physical activities of daily life. The remaining two-thirds of your body's energy is used for continuous bodily functions such as generating body heat, heartbeat, respiration, and brain activity. When you are resting, the rate at which your body uses energy for vital body functions is referred to as your basal metabolic rate (BMR). Energy that is not needed to meet your immediate bodily needs is stored in the form of body fat.

Often, there is considerable daily variation in what, when, how often, and how much we eat. Yet despite this variability in eating behavior, our body weight tends to stay relatively constant (Bessesen, 2011). Your typical or average body weight is called your *baseline body weight,* which is maintained by a process called *energy homeostasis.*

Signals That Regulate Eating

Why do we eat? About 30 minutes before you eat, you experience a *slight* increase in blood levels of insulin and a *slight* decrease in blood levels of glucose. In experimental studies with both humans and rats, these small changes reliably predict the initiation of eating (Chaput & Tremblay, 2009). Once the meal is begun, blood glucose levels return to their baseline level.

A more important internal signal is *ghrelin,* an appetite-stimulating hormone manufactured by cells lining the stomach. Blood levels of ghrelin rise sharply before and fall abruptly after meals. It also seems to be involved in the long-term regulation of energy balance and weight. When people diet and lose weight, ghrelin levels—and feelings of hunger—increase.

Eating is also triggered by psychological factors. Both *classical conditioning* and *operant conditioning,* described in the chapter on learning, affect eating behavior. For example, in much the same way as Pavlov's dogs were conditioned to salivate at the sound of a ticking metronome, your feelings of hunger have been classically conditioned by experience. Time of day or other stimuli, such as your kitchen or a campus cafeteria, can become associated with the anticipation of eating and trigger the physiological signals that increase your sense of hunger (Davidson et al., 2000). Operant conditioning is also involved in the many ways that eating behaviors are positively reinforced.

Why do we *stop* eating? *Satiation* is the feeling of fullness and diminished desire to eat that follows eating. One satiation signal involves *stretch receptors* in the stomach that communicate sensory information to the brainstem. The sensitivity of the stomach's stretch receptors is increased by a hormone called *cholecystokinin,* thankfully abbreviated as *CCK.*

Psychological factors play a role in satiation, too. As you eat a meal, food becomes less appealing, especially the specific food that you are eating. By the fourth piece of pizza, the pizza's appeal begins to diminish. This phenomenon is termed *sensory-specific satiety* (Havermans et al., 2009; Maier et al., 2007). But if a *different* appealing food becomes available, your willingness to eat returns. Restaurants are well aware of this, which is why servers will bring a tempting platter of scrumptious desserts to your table after you've finished a large and otherwise satisfying dinner.

Long-Term Signals That Regulate Body Weight

Many different chemical messengers are involved in monitoring and maintaining a steady body weight over time. One important signal is **leptin**, a *hormone produced by fat cells that signals the hypothalamus, regulating hunger and eating behavior.* Along with

JORGE UZON/AFP/Newscom

▲ **Delicious or Disgusting?** The need to eat is a universal human motive. However, culture influences *what* we eat, *when* we eat, and *how* we eat (Rozin, 1996, 2007). This upscale restaurant in Mexico City serves *chapulines* (grasshoppers, left) and *gusanos del maguey* (caterpillars). High in protein and readily available, insects are standard fare in many countries.

leptin Hormone produced by fat cells that signals the hypothalamus, regulating hunger and eating behavior.

Daniele Venturelli/Getty Images

⌃ **Health at Every Size** Here, super-model and body activist Ashley Graham walks the runway during Fashion Week in Milan, Italy. Graham is a vocal advocate for body positivity and the Health at Every Size movement.

Robert Llewellyn

⌃ **Calculating Your BMI: Where Do You Weigh In?** You can calculate your BMI (body mass index) using the handy calculator at this Web site: http://tinyurl.com/b53foz

BMI is often used as a "quick and dirty" measure of obesity because it can be easily calculated. However, many researchers prefer measures of waist circumference, because it indicates the amount of abdominal fat—which is considered to be the most damaging to physical health.

MYTH ◄ **SCIENCE**

Is it true that obesity is primarily due to genetics?

insulin, which is secreted by the pancreas, the amount of leptin in the bloodstream rises with increasing fat stores. When the level of these hormones in the brain increases, food intake is reduced and the body's fat stores shrink over time. When fat stores shrink, blood levels of leptin decrease, triggering eating behavior.

Another signal that triggers eating behavior is a neurotransmitter, *neuropeptide Y,* abbreviated NPY. If you lose weight, decreased leptin and insulin levels promote the secretion of NPY by the hypothalamus (Powley, 2009). In turn, increased brain levels of neuropeptide Y trigger eating behavior, reduce body metabolism, and promote fat storage.

In combination, these long-term and short-term eating-related signals provide a feedback loop that is monitored by the hypothalamus. Food intake and BMR are adjusted in response to these internal signals. Over time, your average weight tends to remain stable because the calories you consume closely match the calories you expend.

Set-point theory is the *theory that humans and other animals have a natural weight, called the set-point weight, that the body maintains.* Your body vigorously defends this set-point weight from becoming lower or higher by regulating feelings of hunger and body metabolism (Geary, 2020; Major et al., 2007). Interestingly, in spite of the well-documented notion of a set point for body weight, most people tend to drift to a heavier average body weight as they get older (Chooi et al., 2019).

Excess Weight and Obesity

The "thin ideal" is pervasive in many cultures, including in the United States. In fact, over the past decades, performers, models, beauty pageant winners, and even cartoon characters have become progressively thinner (Grabe et al., 2008). But there is an enormous gap between the cultural *ideal* of a slender body and the cultural *reality* of expanding waistlines in many countries.

How is healthy weight determined? For statistical purposes, **body mass index (BMI)** is *a numerical measure of body fat and weight status based on height and weight.* For adults, the body mass index provides a single numerical value that reflects your weight in relation to your height (see photo). A healthy BMI falls between 18 and 25. Generally, people with a BMI between 25 and 29.9 are considered *overweight.* However, a high BMI could be due to muscle or bone rather than fat. It is possible to have a high BMI and still be very healthy, as are many athletes and bodybuilders. Therefore, some researchers prefer waist circumference as a measure of overweight because it indicates the amount of abdominal fat tissue, which is thought to be the most unhealthy. According to this measure, healthy weight is indicated by a waist circumference of 40 inches or less in adult males and 35 inches or less in adult women. For either sex, waist circumference should be less than half your height in inches. In contrast, **obesity** is a *condition characterized by excessive body fat and a body mass index equal to or greater than 30.0* (Chooi et al., 2019).

More than one-third of the adult U.S. population is overweight. Another third of adults—over 97 million people—are considered medically obese, with a BMI of 30 or above (Ogden et al., 2015). Beyond the United States, rapidly increasing rates of obesity have become a global health problem. In developing countries, the percentage of obesity has quadrupled since 1980 (Blüher, 2019; Budnik & Henneberg, 2017).

Why Do People Become Overweight or Obese? Genetics is one important factor in excess body weight. Research suggests that multiple genes are involved in creating susceptibility to obesity (Albuquerque et al., 2016; Friedman, 2009). People with a family history of obesity are two to three times more likely to become obese than people with no such family history.

Even people who are not genetically susceptible to obesity can become overweight when they habitually take in more calories than they expend. And, in the United States, daily caloric intake has steadily increased over the past two decades for both adults and children (Lobstein et al., 2015; Piernas & Popkin, 2011). At the same time, physical activity has *decreased.* For example, in the United States, from 1994 to 2010, the number of women who reported *no* physical activity during their leisure hours jumped from about 20 percent to over 50 percent. For men, the percentage rose from about 11 percent to 43 percent (Ladabaum et al., 2014).

But why are people motivated to eat more than they need to sustain their daily activity level? Some researchers think this tendency might be a leftover from our evolutionary past. Our prehistoric human ancestors, relying upon the availability of wild game or plant foods, experienced periods of both plentiful food and food shortages. According to King (2013), prehistoric humans would have consumed as much food as possible during times of abundance as a survival mechanism. However, unlike our evolutionary ancestors, who had to hunt game or forage for seeds, nuts, and fruits, today's humans simply don't need to expend physical energy to acquire the food they need to meet their physical needs. Although this evolutionary perspective may account for some instances of overeating, it has also been shown that many people overeat simply because eating calorie-dense foods that are high in sugar, salt, and fat is inherently rewarding (Carr & Epstein, 2011; Yokum & Stice, 2019).

It is also critically important to consider relatively recent changes in U.S. society that have spurred an association between socioeconomic status (SES) and obesity. Although this might not be immediately intuitive, the relationship between SES and obesity is clear. In the United States, food that is considered "healthy," "organic," or "not genetically modified" has become increasingly expensive (Auld & Powell, 2009; Kern et al., 2017). At the same time, less expensive food that is both lower in nutritional value and higher in unhealthy fat is increasingly available from fast food restaurants (Powell et al., 2007). Increased consumption of fast food, as well as poor quality food from convenience stores, among low-SES Americans is a multifaceted issue not only because the food is less expensive, but it is also does not require preparation; something that is a significant consideration among parents who are working long hours at minimum wage jobs and/or parents who are trying to care for large, often multigenerational, families.

Even so, not everyone who overeats gains weight. Why not? For one, people vary greatly in their basal metabolic rate. Metabolism also decreases with age, so fewer calories are required to meet your basic energy needs. Thus, it's not surprising that many people begin to gain weight in early and middle adulthood.

Surprisingly, not getting enough sleep is another factor that affects metabolic rate. Multiple studies have shown that inadequate sleep disrupts metabolism, including secretion of the hunger-related hormones leptin and ghrelin (Lin et al., 2020; Taheri et al., 2004). People who sleep fewer than seven hours a night have higher BMIs than people who sleep nine hours or more, and those who sleep less are much more likely to be overweight or obese (Paunio, 2012; Watson et al., 2012). Sleep-deprived people also tend to prefer calorie-rich foods like chocolate and potato chips over healthier fare (Greer et al., 2013).

When a person is overweight, metabolic changes occur and the normal mechanisms of homeostasis are disrupted. For example, many obese people experience *leptin resistance,* in which the normal mechanisms through which leptin regulates body weight and energy balance are disrupted (Enriori et al., 2006; Lin et al., 2020; Morrison, 2008).

Although dieting can reduce weight, it also affects metabolism. Although any diet that reduces caloric intake will result in weight loss, maintaining the lower weight can be challenging. Many overweight or obese dieters experience *weight cycling,* or *yo-yo dieting*—the weight lost through dieting is regained in weeks or months and maintained until the next attempt at dieting.

One reason this occurs is because the human body is much more effective at vigorously defending against weight *loss* than it is at protecting against weight *gain* (Keel et al., 2007). As caloric intake is reduced and fat cells begin to shrink, the body actively defends against weight loss by decreasing metabolic rate. With energy expenditure reduced, far fewer calories are needed to maintain the excess weight. In effect, the body is using energy much more efficiently. If dieters continue to restrict caloric intake, weight loss will plateau in a matter of weeks. When they go off the diet, their now more energy-efficient bodies quickly utilize the additional calories, and they regain the weight they lost (Engber, 2019). The Focus on Neuroscience box, "Dopamine Receptors and Obesity," explains how the brain's reward system is implicated in eating behavior, particularly in those who are overweight.

set-point theory Theory that humans and other animals have a natural body weight, called the *set-point weight*, that the body maintains.

body mass index (BMI) A numerical measure of body fat and weight status based on height and weight.

obesity Condition characterized by excessive body fat and a body mass index equal to or greater than 30.0.

FOCUS ON NEUROSCIENCE

Dopamine Receptors and Obesity: Eating to Stimulate Brain Reward?

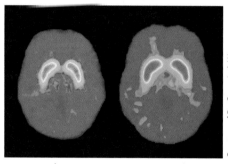

Courtesy of Dr. Gene-Jack Wang, Brookhaven National Laboratory

Obese   Normal

In the Neuroscience and Behavior chapter, we noted that dopamine brain pathways are involved in the reinforcing feelings of pleasure and satisfaction. In the chapter Consciousness and Its Variations, we also noted that many addictive drugs produce their pleasurable effects by increasing brain dopamine levels. These pleasurable effects are most reinforcing in people who have low levels of dopamine brain receptors (Volkow et al., 2007, 2011b). Given that eating can be highly reinforcing and produces pleasurable sensations, could the same mechanisms also play a role in obesity?

In a landmark study, researchers compared dopamine receptors in normal-weight and obese individuals. As shown in the scans here, obese individuals had significantly fewer dopamine receptors, colored red, than the normal-weight individuals. And, among the obese people in the study, the number of dopamine receptors *decreased* as BMI *increased* (DiFeliceantonio & Small, 2019; Wang et al., 2001, 2004). Thus, it could be that compulsive or binge eating compensates for reduced dopamine function by stimulating the brain's reward system (Volkow & Wise, 2005; Yokum & Stice, 2019).

But is the lower number of dopamine receptors a *cause* or a *consequence* of obesity? In one study, a group of rats was allowed to eat as much as they wanted of rat chow—a nutritionally complete but boring diet (Johnson & Kenny, 2010). Another group of rats, genetically identical to the first group, was offered a "cafeteria diet" of high-fat, sugary foods that are freely available in the modern U.S. diet: sausage, bacon, cheesecake, pound cake, chocolate, and frosting.

The rats on the junk-food diet rapidly became overweight, eating up to twice as many calories as the rats fed only the boring rat chow.

Refusing nutritious, low-calorie food, the rats became compulsive eaters. Like drug addicts seeking a high despite negative consequences, they would eat the junk food even when it was paired with a mild electric shock.

Even more interesting was what happened to the rats' brain chemistry. Much like the brain changes associated with drug addiction, dopamine response in the junk-food-addicted rats was significantly reduced. In humans, too, a significant reduction in dopamine response has been observed in conjunction with weight gain (Stice & Yokum, 2016).

Such results imply that obesity can be a vicious circle: People eat more to compensate for reduced brain rewards, but overeating reduces the dopamine reward system levels even further. These findings help explain why people continue to overeat despite suffering the unhealthy consequences of obesity. And the research allows us to begin to think about ways to improve the health of those suffering from obesity.

Emotion

■ KEY THEME

Emotions are complex psychological states that serve many functions in human behavior and relationships.

≡ KEY QUESTIONS

* What are the three components of emotion, and what functions do emotions serve?
* How do evolutionary psychologists view emotion?
* What are the basic emotions?

Most people would agree that laughing and crying are both expressions of emotion, but it's often hard for people to define exactly what emotion means. Given all of the words we have for our emotions, it's hard to deny that emotion is important. When we have a personal reaction to an object, event, person, or memory, we are experiencing emotion. The dread of hearing your parents say that they are "disappointed" in you, the euphoria when someone you like returns your text message, the sadness you feel when you remember the loss of a friend—these are all examples of what it means to experience emotion. Emotions impact and inform our life from the earliest days of infancy to the final days of our lives. But what, exactly, *is* emotion, and why is it so critical to human survival?

Emotion is *a complex psychological state that involves three distinct but related components: a cognitive experience, a physiological response, and a behavioral* or *expressive response.* Humans have emotion for two important reasons: (1) to help us understand the meaning of survival-related information from our experiences; and (2) to communicate with other humans and understand their experiences, most often through facial expressions. For example, fear can save your life if it makes you run away from a dangerous situation and then avoid that same situation (or ones like it) in the future. By offering a friendly facial expression, you can convey kinship with another human. Conversely, an angry facial expression could convince a potential rival to keep their distance, as you are ready to fight if need be.

It's worth knowing that emotions may be informed by moods, but moods are actually distinct from emotions. Generally, emotions are intense but rather short-lived. Emotions are also more likely to have a specific cause that is more easily identified, to be directed toward some particular object, and to motivate a person to take some sort of action. In contrast, a *mood* involves a milder emotional state that is more general and pervasive, such as gloominess or contentment. Moods may last for a few hours or even days (Gendolla, 2000). Emotions are more easily provoked and generally more difficult to regulate. There is an extent to which the expression of emotion (particularly facial expressions) is universal, whereas moods are not known to have consistent expression (Davidson et al., 1994). And while most people are not aware of what causes a mood state, people are more likely to understand what causes a specific emotion (Ekman & Davidson, 1994). This again underscores the survival function that emotion serves.

Emotional processes are closely tied to motivational processes. Like the word *motivation,* the root of the word *emotion* is the Latin word *movere,* which means "to move." Often emotions do move us to act. For example, consider the anger that motivates you to seek out a new job when you feel you've been treated unfairly. Emotions often *motivate* behavior (Damasio & Carvalho, 2013). Most of us direct our lives so as to maximize the experience of positive emotions and minimize the experience of negative emotions (Gendolla, 2017).

Psychologists have become increasingly focused on the important functions of emotion. Emotional responses inform individuals about the world around them and motivate them to act accordingly. Research has highlighted the importance of emotions in many different areas of human behavior, including rational decision making, purposeful behavior, and setting appropriate goals (Lerner et al., 2015; Mikels et al., 2011). Most of our choices are guided by emotion, sometimes without our conscious awareness (Kouider et al., 2011). In fact, the idea that emotion has a strong influence on our decision making has become so widely accepted that Daniel Kahneman was awarded the 2002 Nobel Prize in Economics for his work that has shown how essential emotion is to making decisions (Arnott & Gao, 2019; Kahneman, 2003).

Before we go further into our understanding of emotion, it is important to note that the ability to regulate emotion may be as important as the ability to experience it. The proper regulation of emotion is often thought of as *emotional intelligence.* Emotional intelligence relies on the capacity to understand and manage your own emotional experiences, as well as to perceive, understand, and respond appropriately to the emotional responses of others (by regulating your own behavior). People who are low in emotional intelligence may have superior reasoning powers, but they sometimes experience one failure in life after another (Mayer et al., 2004; Van Heck & den Oudsten, 2008). Why? People low in emotional intelligence lack the ability to manage their own emotions, understand the emotional responses of others, and respond appropriately to the emotions of other people. In contrast, people who are high in emotional intelligence are adept at understanding the emotions of other people and use their emotions to help inform and regulate their own behavior (Mayer et al., 2008; Telle et al., 2011).

emotion A complex psychological state that involves three distinct but related components: a cognitive experience, a physiological response, and a behavioral or expressive response.

The Many Functions of Emotion Two friends share news, smiles, and laughter as they patiently wait their turns at the medical clinic in an isolated village in Tsum Valley, Nepal. Emotions play an important role in relationships and social communication.

Sandy Hockenbury

basic emotions The most fundamental set of emotion categories, which are biologically innate, evolutionarily determined, and culturally universal.

Evolutionary Explanations of Emotion

One of the earliest scientists to systematically study emotions was **Charles Darwin**. Darwin published *The Expression of the Emotions in Man and Animals* in 1872, only a year after his book on the evolution of humans, *The Descent of Man* (1871). Darwin (1872) described the facial expressions, body movements, and postures used to express specific emotions in animals and humans. He argued that emotions reflect evolutionary adaptations to the problems of survival and reproduction.

Like Darwin, today's evolutionary psychologists believe that emotions are the product of evolution (Cosmides & Tooby, 2013; Damasio & Carvalho, 2013). Emotions help us solve adaptive problems posed by our environment. They "move" us *toward* potential resources, and they move us *away from* potential dangers. Fear prompts us to flee an attacker or evade a threat. Anger moves us to turn and fight a rival. Love propels us to seek out a mate and care for our offspring. Disgust prompts us to avoid a sickening stimulus. Obviously, the capacity to feel and be moved by emotion has adaptive value: An organism that quickly responds to rewards or threats is more likely to survive and successfully reproduce.

Darwin (1872) also pointed out that emotional displays serve the important function of informing other organisms about an individual's internal state. When facing an aggressive rival, the snarl of a baboon signals its readiness to fight. A wolf rolling submissively on its back telegraphs its willingness to back down and avoid a fight. A parent's facial expression of sadness or fear elicits helping behavior from young children and lays the foundation for a range of prosocial behaviors (Walle et al., 2020).

In this chapter, we'll consider each of the components of emotion in turn, and then review how theorists have proposed these different components work together to produce the rich emotional lives of humans. Let's begin with the component that is most familiar to most of you: the cognitive, or subjective, experience of emotion.

The Cognitive Experience of Emotion

Basic emotions are *the most fundamental set of emotion categories, which are biologically innate, evolutionarily determined, and culturally universal.* What are these basic emotions? As shown in **Table 8.2**, fear, disgust, surprise, happiness, anger, and sadness are most commonly cited as the basic emotions (Ekman & Cordaro, 2011; Matsumoto & Hwang, 2011a).

Each basic emotion represents a sequence of responses that is innate and hard-wired in the brain (Gu et al., 2019; Tooby & Cosmides, 2000; Vytal & Hamann, 2010). But your emotional experience is not limited to pure forms of each basic emotion. Rather, each basic emotion represents a family of related emotional states (Ekman & Cordaro, 2011). For example, consider the many types of angry feelings, which can range from mild annoyance to bitter resentment or fierce rage.

Furthermore, psychologists recognize that emotional experience can be complex and multifaceted. People often experience a *blend* of emotions. In more complex situations, people may experience *mixed emotions,* in which very different emotions are experienced simultaneously or in rapid succession (Heavey et al., 2017). One way to think about this is to make an analogy between emotional experience and the way we experience color: There are not only primary and secondary colors—as there are primary and secondary emotions—but there are also many combinations that vary in terms of color and intensity (Plutchik, 2001).

Emotion Experience, Culture, and Gender In diverse cultures, psychologists have found general agreement regarding the subjective experience and meaning of different basic emotions. Canadian psychologist James Russell (1991) compared emotion descriptions by people from several different cultures. He found that emotions were most commonly classified according to two dimensions: (1) the degree to which the emotion is *pleasant* or *unpleasant* and (2) the level of *activation,* or arousal, associated with the emotion. For example, joy and contentment are both pleasant emotions, but joy is associated with a higher degree of activation (Feldman Barrett & Russell, 1999).

TABLE 8.2

The Basic Emotions

Fear	Disgust
Surprise	Happiness
Anger	Sadness

The six emotions shown here represent the universal set of basic emotions (Ekman & Cordaro, 2011). Other possible candidates are contempt or disdain, pride, and excitement.

While these may be the most fundamental dimensions of emotion, cultural variations in classifying emotions do exist. For example, Hazel Rose Markus and Shinobu Kitayama (1991, 1994) found that Japanese participants classified emotions in terms of not two but three important dimensions. Along with the pleasantness and activation dimensions, **interpersonal engagement** is the *emotion dimension reflecting the degree to which emotions involve a relationship with another person or other people* (Kitayama et al., 2000). Japanese participants rated anger and shame as being about the same in terms of unpleasantness and activation, but they rated shame as being much higher than anger on the dimension of interpersonal engagement.

Why would the Japanese emphasize interpersonal engagement as a dimension of emotion? Japan is a collectivistic culture, so a person's identity is seen as interdependent with those of other people, rather than independent, as is characteristic of the more individualistic cultures. Thus, social context is an important part of private emotional experience (Kitayama & Park, 2007; Mesquita et al., 2016).

Many people wonder if there are sex differences when it comes to emotional experience. Historically, both men and women believed that women were "more emotional" than men (Barrett & Bliss-Moreau, 2009; Vigil, 2009). In reality, emotion is just not that simple; there is no single way to define "more emotional." Studies have looked at sex differences in responses to watching emotional videos. In one study, researchers found that men generally showed larger increases in their heart rate (physiological arousal), but women were more likely to report feeling higher levels of arousal compared to the men (Deng et al., 2016). This suggests that woman may be higher in emotional expressivity (Keltner & Horberg, 2015). Interestingly, these sex differences were only significant for specific emotions such as anger, amusement, and pleasure. Women, however, did show higher heart rates relative to men when watching videos that induced sadness (Deng et al., 2016). It is hard to know if these sex differences are the result of differences in biological makeup or social experience and expectation (Kret & de Gelder, 2012).

❮ Socially Engaged Emotions in Japan Closeness and interdependence are fostered by Japanese child-rearing practices, and some psychologists believe they also form the basis for such other-focused emotions as *amae*, an emotion central to Japanese culture (Markus & Kitayama, 1991). *Amae* can be defined as the sense of being lovingly cared for and unconditionally accepted by another person. *Amae* can be achieved only within a reciprocal, interdependent relationship with someone else. Thus, *amae* is a prototypical example of a socially engaged emotion—an other-focused emotion that creates and fosters interdependence with significant others (Rothbaum et al., 2007; Yamaguchi & Ariizumi, 2006).

amana images inc./Alamy

MYTH ◀ SCIENCE

Is it true that women are more emotional than men?

The Expression of Emotion: Making Faces

■ KEY THEME
The behavioral components of emotion include facial expressions and nonverbal behavior.

⹂ KEY QUESTIONS
• What evidence supports the idea that facial expressions for basic emotions are universal?
• How does culture affect the behavioral expression of emotion?
• How can emotional expression be explained in terms of evolutionary theory?

Every day, we witness the behavioral components of emotions in ourselves and others. We laugh with pleasure, slam a door in frustration, or frown at a clueless remark. But of all the ways that we express and communicate our emotional responses, facial expressions are the most important. In fact, recognizing faces and facial expressions is so important to humans that there is a brain region within devoted to these functions called the fusiform face area (Guyer et al., 2008; Sergent et al., 1992).

In *The Expression of the Emotions in Man and Animals,* Darwin (1872) argued that human emotional expressions are innate and culturally universal. He also noted the continuity of emotional expression between humans and many other species, citing it as evidence

interpersonal engagement Emotion dimension reflecting the degree to which emotions involve a relationship with another person or other people.

Science History Images/Alamy Stock Photo

⌃ **Which Is the "True" Smile?**
Psychologist and emotion researcher Paul Ekman demonstrates the difference between a fake smile (right) and the true smile (left). If you were able to pick out the true smile, it was because you, like most people, are able to decipher the subtle differences in the facial muscles, especially around the eyes and lips. In fact, research has found that people instinctively respond to true smiles with genuine smiles of their own. Polite smiles are more likely to elicit the same (Heerey & Crossley, 2013).

🔹 Achie√e

Can you identify the emotions represented by different facial expressions? Go to **Achieve** and try **Concept Practice: Facial Expressions of Emotion.**

(l) Ekman & Matsumoto, Japanese and Caucasian Facial Expressions of Emotions
(r) Ana Blazic Pavlovic/Shutterstock

anthropomorphism The attribution of human traits, motives, emotions, or behaviors to nonhuman animals or inanimate objects.

of the common evolutionary ancestry of humans and other animals. But do nonhuman animals actually experience emotions? We explore this question in the Critical Thinking box, "Emotion in Nonhuman Animals: Laughing Rats, Affectionate Elephants, and Smiling Dolphins?"

Of course, humans are the animals that exhibit the greatest range of facial expressions. Psychologist **Paul Ekman** has studied the facial expression of emotions for more than four decades. Ekman (1980) estimates that the human face is capable of creating more than *7,000* different expressions. This enormous flexibility allows us considerable versatility in expressing emotion in all its subtle variations.

To study facial expressions, Ekman and his colleague Wallace Friesen (1978) coded different facial expressions by painstakingly analyzing the facial muscles involved in producing each expression. In doing so, they precisely classified the facial expressions that characterize the basic emotions of happiness, sadness, surprise, fear, anger, and disgust. When shown photographs of these facial expressions, research participants correctly identified the emotion being displayed (Ekman, 1982, 1992, 1993).

Ekman concluded that facial expressions for the basic emotions are innate and probably hard-wired in the brain. Further evidence comes from children who are born blind and deaf. Despite their inability to observe or hear others, they express joy, anger, and pleasure using the same expressions as sighted and hearing children (Goodenough, 1932; Matsumoto & Hwang, 2011b). Similarly, the spontaneous facial expressions of children and young adults who were born blind do not differ from those of sighted children and adults (Galati et al., 1997, 2003).

Emotional Expression, Culture, and Gender   Facial expressions for the basic emotions seem to be universal across different cultures (Waller et al., 2008). Ekman (1982) and other researchers showed photographs of facial expressions to people in 21 different countries. Despite their different cultural experiences, all the participants identified the emotions being expressed with a high degree of accuracy (see Ekman, 1998). Even the inhabitants of remote, isolated villages in Papua New Guinea—who had never been exposed to movies or other aspects of Western culture—identified the emotions being expressed. However, more recent research has enriched our understanding of emotional expression. Many aspects of facial expressions are universal, but there are also cultural and gender-based differences that Ekman's original work reported. Specifically, research has reported reliable differences in facial expressions called "dialects" (see Elfenbein & Ambady, 2002; Frank & Stennett, 2001). In the same ways that a single spoken language can be spoken in more than one way (e.g., British English vs. Canadian English vs. Australian English); a single emotion can be expressed in slightly different ways. For example, while facial expressions of happiness look reliably similar across cultures, it is also the case that Chinese participants are more likely to rely on the eyes when it comes to facial expressions relative to Western Caucasians, who typically use their eyebrows and mouths to create the same facial expressions (Jack et al., 2012). Future research will undoubtedly continue to improve our understanding of subtle, but important, differences in cultural "dialects" when it comes to communicating emotion.

Other aspects of emotional expression, such as tone of voice and nonverbal expression, also seem to be easily understood across widely different cultures. As anyone who has ever been the target of a sarcastic remark is well aware, the human voice very effectively conveys emotional messages. Several studies have found that people from different cultures can accurately identify the emotion being expressed by tone of voice alone, even when the actual words used were unintelligible (Russell et al., 2003; Scherer et al., 2001). Similarly, people from different cultures were able to accurately evaluate the emotional content of video clips depicting an emotional conversation between two

CRITICAL THINKING

Emotion in Nonhuman Animals: Laughing Rats, Affectionate Elephants, and Smiling Dolphins?

Do animals experience emotions? If you've ever frolicked with a playful puppy or shared the contagious contentment of a cat purring in your lap, the answer seems obvious. But before you accept that answer, remember that emotion involves three components: physiological arousal, behavioral expression, and subjective experience. In many animals, fear and other "emotional" responses appear to involve physiological and brain processes that are similar to those involved in human emotional experience. In mammals, it's also easy to observe behavioral responses when an animal is menaced by a predator or by the anger in aggressive displays.

One problem in establishing whether animals experience emotion is the difficulty of determining the nature of an animal's subjective experience (Kuczaj, 2013). Even Darwin (1871) readily acknowledged this problem, writing, "Who can say what cows feel, when they surround and stare intently on a dying or dead companion?"

Anthropomorphism: Happy Dolphins?

Despite the problem of knowing just what an animal is feeling, we often *think* that we do. For example, one reason that dolphins are so appealing is the wide, happy grin they seem to wear. But the dolphin's "smile" is *not* a true facial expression—it's simply the bony curvature of its mouth. If you comment on the friendly, happy appearance of the dolphins frolicking at SeaWorld or another aquarium, you're *projecting* those human emotions onto the dolphins.

You also just committed **anthropomorphism**—*the attribution of human traits, motives, or behaviors to nonhuman animals or inanimate objects.* The tendency of people to anthropomorphize is understandable when you consider how extensively most of us were conditioned as children via books, cartoons, and Disney characters to believe that animals are just like people, only with fur or feathers.

From a scientific perspective, anthropomorphism can hinder progress in understanding animal emotions. By assuming that an animal thinks and feels as we do, we run the risk of distorting or

∧ **Laughing Rats?** Rats are sociable, playful creatures. They emit distinct, high-pitched chirps when they play, anticipate treats, and engage in positive social interactions. They also chirp when they're tickled by researchers like neuroscientist Jaak Panksepp (2000, 2007). But when infant rats are separated from their mothers, or when they're cold, they emit a distress cry that is much lower in frequency than the ultrasonic chirps that are associated with pleasant experiences.

∧ **Affectionate Elephants** Elephants form tightly knit family groups. When reunited after a long separation, elephants perform an elaborate greeting ceremony—trumpeting, flapping their ears, and exuberantly intertwining their trunks. Female elephants are intensely devoted to their offspring, and family members often touch one another with what looks like affection (Bradshaw et al., 2005).

obscuring the reality of the animal's own unique experience (de Waal, 2011; Hauser, 2000). Instead, we must acknowledge that other animals are not happy or sad in the same way that humans subjectively experience happiness or sadness.

Animals clearly demonstrate diverse emotions—fear, anger, surprise. But to understand how they subjectively *experience* such feelings—and, indeed, whether they do at all—raises questions that cannot be fully answered at this time. Nonetheless, it seems safe to assume that more primitive animals, like fish, turtles, and snakes, probably do not possess a level of self-awareness that would allow them to experience complex emotions like grief, empathy, or altruism (Hauser, 2000). For more sophisticated animals, like dolphins, primates, and elephants, the evidence is more compelling (Bekoff, 2007; Kuczaj, 2013; Lyn & Savage-Rumbaugh, 2013).

One subjective aspect of the scientific method is how to interpret evidence and data. In the case of the evidence for animal emotions, the scientific debate is far from over. Although the lack of a definitive answer can be frustrating, keep in mind that such scientific debates play an important role in avoiding erroneous conclusions and shaping future research.

CRITICAL THINKING QUESTIONS

• What evidence would lead you to conclude that primates, dolphins, or elephants experience emotions?

• Would you accept different evidence to conclude that a six-month-old human infant can experience emotions? If so, why?

• Is it possible to be completely free of anthropomorphic tendencies in studying animal emotions?

     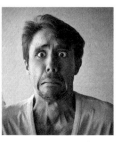

| Happiness | Surprise | Sadness | Anger | Disgust | Fear |

Photos from Left to Right: Cultura Creative RF/Alamy Stock Photo; Aaron Amat/Alamy Stock Photo; Bulat Silvia/Alamy Stock Photo; Pongtorn Hiranlikit/Alamy Stock Photo; frantic/Alamy Stock Photo; michele piacquadio/Alamy Stock Photo

⌃ Basic Emotions and Universal Facial Expressions Paul Ekman and his colleagues have precisely calibrated the muscles used in facial expressions for basic emotions. Ekman showed that people in a wide variety of cultures—even those with no experience of Western culture—were able to identify facial expressions for each of the basic emotions.

Is it true that facial expressions, such as smiles, are learned and vary from one culture to another?

display rules Social and cultural regulations governing emotional expression, especially facial expressions.

people, even though the dialogue was scrambled (Sneddon et al., 2011). Some body language seems to be universal.

However, some specific nonverbal gestures, which are termed *emblems,* vary across cultures. For example, shaking your head means "no" in the United States but "yes" in southern India and Bulgaria. Nodding your head means "yes" in the United States, but in Japan it could mean "maybe" or even "no way!"

In many situations, you adjust your emotional expressions to make them appropriate in that particular social context. For example, even if you are deeply angered by your supervisor's comments at work, you might consciously restrain yourself and maintain a neutral facial expression. **Display rules** are *social and cultural regulations governing emotional expression, especially facial expressions* (Ekman et al., 1987; Ambady et al., 2006).

Consider a classic experiment in which a hidden camera recorded the facial expressions of Japanese and American participants as they watched films that showed grisly images of surgery, amputations, and so forth (Ekman et al., 1987; Friesen, 1972). When they watched the films alone, the Japanese and American participants displayed virtually identical facial expressions, grimacing with disgust and distaste at the gruesome scenes. But when a scientist was present while the participants watched the films, the Japanese participants masked their negative facial expressions of disgust or fear with smiles. Why? In Japan an important display rule is that you should not reveal negative emotions in the presence of an authority figure so as not to offend the higher-status individual.

Display rules can also vary for different groups within a given culture. In many cultures, including the United States, women are allowed a wider range of emotional expressiveness and responsiveness than men (Fischer et al., 2004). For example, for men, it's considered "unmasculine" to be too open in expressing certain emotions, such as sadness (Johnson et al., 2011). Even as gender norms continue to move in a more fluid direction, women still tend to be more likely to display positive facial expression more frequently and for longer durations, while men are more likely to communicate negative emotions using facial expressions in day-to-day life outside the laboratory (McDuff et al., 2017).

So what overall conclusions emerge from the research findings on emotional expressions? First, Paul Ekman and other researchers have amassed considerable evidence that facial expressions for the basic emotions—happiness, sadness, anger, fear, surprise, and disgust—are hard-wired into the brain. They also contend that the basic emotions are biologically determined, the result of evolutionary processes. Second, these emotional expressions serve the adaptive function of communicating internal states to friends and enemies. Like the survival of other social animals, human survival depends on recognizing and responding quickly to the emotional states of others. Third, although facial expressions for the basic emotions may be biologically programmed, cultural influence, gender-role expectations, and other learning experiences shape how, when, and whether emotional responses are displayed.

The Neuroscience of Emotion

◼ KEY THEME
Emotions are associated with distinct patterns of responses by the sympathetic nervous system and in the brain.

⹀ KEY QUESTIONS
- How is the sympathetic nervous system involved in intense emotional responses?
- What brain structures are involved in emotional experience, and what neural pathways make up the brain's fear circuit?
- How does the evolutionary perspective explain the dual brain pathways for transmitting fear-related information?

Psychologists have long studied the physiological aspects of emotion. Early research focused on the autonomic nervous system's role in triggering physiological arousal. More recently, brain imaging techniques have identified specific brain regions involved in emotional experience. In this section, we'll look at both areas of research. We'll also explore how we regulate our emotions in the In Focus box on page 287.

Emotion and the Sympathetic Nervous System: Hot Heads and Cold

Feet The pounding heart and churning stomach that occur when you experience an intense emotion like fear reflect the activation of the sympathetic branch of the *autonomic nervous system.* When you are threatened, the *sympathetic nervous system* triggers the *fight-or-flight response,* a rapidly occurring series of automatic physical reactions that involves the hypothalamus signaling the amygdala in the brain and the adrenal glands (adrenaline) in the body. Breathing and heart rate accelerate, and blood pressure surges. You perspire, your mouth goes dry, and the hairs on your skin may stand up, giving you the familiar sensation of goose bumps. Your pupils dilate, allowing you to take in a wider visual field. Blood sugar levels increase, providing a burst of energy. Digestion stops as blood is diverted from the stomach and intestines to the brain and skeletal muscles, sometimes causing the sensations of light-headedness or "butterflies" fluttering in your stomach. The polygraph, or "lie detector," measures these physiological reactions associated with emotional arousal (see the In Focus box, "Detecting Lies").

The sympathetic nervous system is also activated by other intense emotions, such as excitement, passionate love, or extreme joy. Obviously, not all emotions involve intense physical reactions. And some emotions, such as contentment, are characterized by decreased physical arousal and the slowing of some body processes (Levenson et al., 1990, 1992, 2017).

Research has shown that there are differing patterns of physiological arousal for different emotions (Ekman, 2003). In a series of classic studies, psychologist Robert W. Levenson (1992) found that fear, anger, and sadness are all associated with accelerated heart rate. But comparing anger and fear showed differences that confirm everyday experience. Anger produces greater increases in blood pressure than fear. And although anger produces an increase in skin temperature, fear produces a *decrease* in skin temperature. Perhaps that's why when we are angry, we speak of "getting hot under the collar," and when fearful, we feel clammy and complain of having "cold feet."

Levenson believes that these differing patterns of sympathetic nervous system activation are universal, reflecting biological responses to the basic emotions that are hard-wired by evolution into all humans (Levenson, 1992, 2003; Levenson et al., 2017). Supporting this contention, Levenson found that male and female participants as well as young and elderly participants experience the *same* patterns of autonomic nervous system activity for different basic emotions. And, it seems that people in different cultures associate certain patterns of physical sensations with certain emotions. When asked to describe the way that basic emotions such as fear, anger, sadness, and happiness "felt"

THINK LIKE A **SCIENTIST**

Can you learn to tell when someone is lying? Go to Achieve: Resources to **Think Like a Scientist** about **Lie Detection.**

 Achieve

Eric Engman/ZUMA Press/Newscom

▲ **Arousal and Intense Emotion** A young woman sheds tears of joy at reuniting with her fiancé, who holds an engagement ring. Many intense emotions involve the activation of the sympathetic nervous system. Although emotions like extreme joy, fear, and grief subjectively feel very different, they all involve increases in heart rate, breathing, and blood pressure.

Detecting Lies

The *polygraph*, commonly called a *lie detector*, doesn't really detect lies or deception. Rather, a polygraph measures physiological changes associated with emotions like fear, tension, and anxiety. Heart rate, blood pressure, respiration, and other indicators are monitored during a polygraph interview. The polygraph is based on the assumption that lying is accompanied by anxiety, fear, and stress. When people show arousal patterns typically associated with anxiety or fear, lying is inferred (Grubin, 2010; Meijer & Verschuere, 2010).

There are many potential problems with using a polygraph to detect lying. First, there is no unique pattern of physiological arousal associated specifically with lying (Vrij et al., 2010). Second, some people can lie without experiencing anxiety or arousal. This produces a false negative result—the liar is judged to be telling the truth. Third, people may be innocent of any wrong-doing but still be fearful or anxious when asked incriminating questions—especially if they believe that they are suspected of a crime. Truth-tellers can be as nervous as liars, especially if they have reason to believe that negative consequences will follow if they are disbelieved (Vrij et al., 2010). This can lead to false pos-

MYTH ◄ SCIENCE

Is it true that polygraphs, or lie detector tests, are a valid way to detect lying?

itive results—innocent people are judged as being guilty. It is a myth that polygraph tests are a valid way to detect lying. In fact, they are more likely to wrongly identify innocent people as guilty than guilty people as innocent (Bashore & Rapp, 1993; National Research Council, 2003).

Finally, interpreting polygraph results can be highly subjective. In one study, polygraph results were compared to later confessions of guilt in criminal cases. Lying was accurately detected by the polygraph examiners at a rate just slightly better than flipping a coin (Phillips, 1999).

In the scientific community, it is generally agreed that polygraphs are not a valid method to detect lies and that their results should not be used as evidence (National Research Council, 2003). Because of the polygraph's high error rate, many states do not allow polygraph tests as evidence in court. However, the U.S. government uses polygraph testing in several agencies, including the CIA, FBI, and Border Patrol (Holden, 2001).

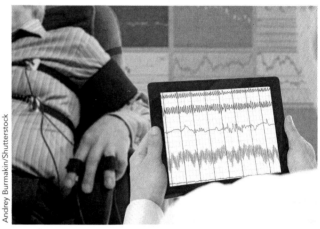

Andrey Burmakin/Shutterstock

▲ **Administering a Polygraph Exam** Although commonly called "lie detectors," polygraphs don't actually detect lies. Rather, polygraphs record changes in physiological measures of arousal, such as respiration, heart rate, and skin conductivity. Because of their high error rate, polygraph test results are not admissible in court in several states and are no longer allowed to be used in pre-employment screening by employers in the private sector. Nevertheless, polygraph tests are widely used in the United States to screen job applicants and employees in law enforcement and many government agencies, including the CIA, FBI, and Border Patrol.

Microexpressions: Fleeting Indicators of Deceit

Emotion researcher Paul Ekman (2003) has found that deception is associated with a variety of nonverbal cues, such as fleeting facial expressions, vocal cues, and nervous body movements. Especially revealing are the fleeting facial expressions, called *microexpressions*, that last about 1/25 of a second. When people lie and try to control their facial expressions, microexpressions of fear, guilt, or anxiety often "leak" through (Ekman & O'Sullivan, 2006). Even so, no single nonverbal cue indicates that someone is lying, and not all researchers have found evidence that deception is revealed in microexpressions (Vrij, 2015). However, people who are skilled at decoding nonverbal cues—like clinical psychologists—are better than other people at detecting deception (Bond, 2008; Ekman et al., 1999).

in the body, Finnish psychologist Lauri Nummenmaa and his colleagues (2014) found a high degree of agreement in participants from Finland, Sweden, and Taiwan (see **Figure 8.2**).

The Emotional Brain: Fear and the Amygdala

Sophisticated brain imaging techniques have led to an explosion of new knowledge about the brain's role in emotion (Kemp et al., 2015; Kragel & LaBar, 2016). Of all the emotions, the brain processes involved in *fear* have been most thoroughly studied. Many brain areas are implicated in emotional responses, but especially important is the brain structure called the **amygdala**, *an almond-shaped cluster of neurons at the base of the temporal lobe*.

amygdala (uh-MIG-dull-uh) An almond-shaped cluster of neurons at the base of the temporal lobe.

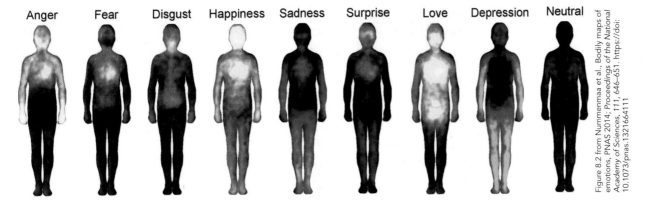

Anger Fear Disgust Happiness Sadness Surprise Love Depression Neutral

Figure 8.2 from Nummenmaa et al., Bodily maps of emotions, PNAS 2014; *Proceedings of the National Academy of Sciences*, 111, 646–651. https://doi: 10.1073/pnas.1321664111

The amygdala is part of the *limbic system,* a group of brain structures involved in emotion, memory, and basic motivational drives, such as hunger, thirst, and sex. Neural pathways connect the amygdala with many other brain structures (Cunningham & Brosch, 2012; Pessoa & Adolphs, 2010).

Several studies have shown that the amygdala is a key brain structure in the emotional response of fear in humans (LeDoux, 2007; Pedersen et al., 2019). For example, brain imaging techniques have demonstrated that the amygdala activates when you view threatening or fearful faces, or hear people make nonverbal sounds expressing fear (Morris et al., 1999; Öhman et al., 2007). Even when people simply anticipate a threatening stimulus, the amygdala activates as part of the fear circuit in the brain (Phelps et al., 2001; Pedersen et al., 2019).

In rats, amygdala damage disrupts the neural circuits involved in the fear response. For example, rats with a damaged amygdala can't be classically conditioned to acquire a fear response (LeDoux, 2007). In humans, damage to the amygdala also disrupts elements of the fear response. For example, people with amygdala damage lose the ability to distinguish between friendly and threatening faces (Adolphs et al., 1998; Bas-Hoogendam et al., 2020).

Activating the Amygdala: Direct and Indirect Neural Pathways Let's use an example to show how the amygdala participates in the brain's fear circuit. Imagine that your niece sneaks up behind you at a family picnic and pokes you in the back with a long stick. As you quickly wheel around, she shouts, "Look what I found in the woods!" Dangling from the stick is a wriggling, three-foot-long snake. You let out a yell and jump out of your seat to get away from the threat. As she bursts into hysterical laughter, you quickly realize that the real-looking snake is made of rubber, and your niece is trolling you.

Even if you don't have a prankster niece, you've probably experienced a sudden fright in which you instantly reacted to a threatening stimulus, like an oncoming car. Typically, you respond instinctively, without taking time to consciously or deliberately evaluate the situation.

So how can you respond to potentially dangerous stimuli before you've had time to think about them? Let's stay with our example. When you saw the dangling snake, the visual stimulus was first routed to the *thalamus* (see **Figure 8.3**). This sensory information about a potentially threatening stimulus is routed from the thalamus along two pathways simultaneously (LeDoux, 1996, 2000).

The first pathway bypasses the cortex, taking a shortcut from the thalamus directly to the amygdala. This is a "quick-and-dirty" route that transmits crude, almost archetypal, information about the stimulus directly to the amygdala. This rapid transmission allows the brain to start to respond to the possible danger represented by a snake *before* you have time to consciously think about the stimulus. This response is critically important because it is survival related—remember from the chapter on neuroscience that the amygdala is the brain's burglar alarm—so it needs to be activated as soon as possible in dangerous situations.

FIGURE 8.2 Mapping Emotions in the Body As expressions like "cold feet" or "butterflies in the stomach" reflect, emotions are often associated with physical sensations. Finnish psychologist Lauri Nummenmaa and his colleagues (2014) investigated this phenomenon in a clever study. Participants were shown blank silhouettes of bodies and, in response to emotion-evoking words, images, or films, they were asked to color in the areas of their body where sensations became stronger or weaker. The body maps show regions where activation increased (warm colors) and decreased (cool colors) when each emotion was felt. While the number of participants is not large enough to draw sweeping conclusions, the results do hint that there may be culturally universal associations of specific emotions with specific body areas. Try this exercise yourself the next time you feel angry, happy, or experience another strong emotion. Do the "body maps" found in this research agree with your own experience of different emotions?

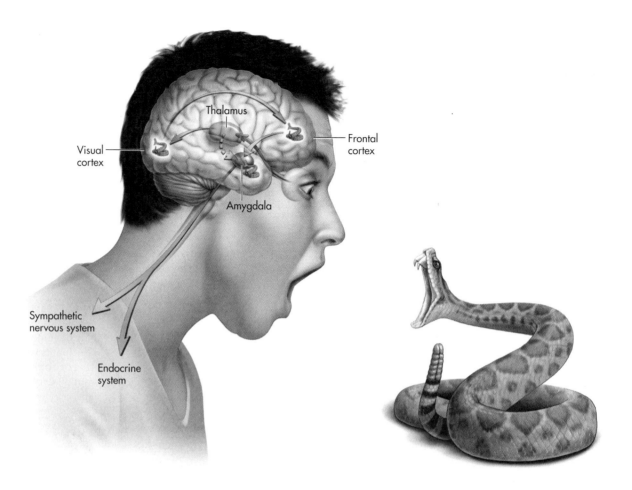

FIGURE 8.3 Fear Circuits in the Brain When you're faced with a potentially threatening stimulus—like a snake dangling from a stick—information arrives in the thalamus and is relayed simultaneously along two pathways. Crude, archetypal information rapidly travels the direct route to the amygdala, triggering an almost instantaneous fear response. More detailed information is sent along the pathway to the visual cortex, where the stimulus is interpreted. If the cortex determines that a threat exists, the information is relayed to the amygdala along the longer, slower pathway. The amygdala triggers other brain structures, such as the hypothalamus, which activate the sympathetic nervous system and the endocrine system's release of stress hormones.

What happens next? The amygdala sends information along neural pathways projecting to other brain regions that are part of the fear circuit. In turn, this triggers arousal of the sympathetic nervous system and the release of stress hormones (LeDoux, 1995, 2000).

The result? You respond instantly to the threat—"SNAKE!"—by leaping backward, heartbeat and breathing accelerating. But even as you respond physically to the threat, information is also speeding along the second neural pathway that reaches the amygdala by traveling through the cortex. The visual cortex registers a more detailed and accurate representation of the visual stimulus, then sends this information to the prefrontal cortex, where it is interpreted within the context of what is happening around you. That's when you realize that the "snake" is actually just a rubber toy. Following this cognitive judgment, the prefrontal cortex sends a "false alarm" message to the amygdala (Braunstein et al., 2017; Loos et al., 2020). But note that information traveling along the thalamus→visual cortex→frontal cortex→amygdala route takes about twice as long to reach the amygdala as the information traveling along the direct thalamus→amygdala route. Since both pathways are simultaneously activated, the alarm response is already in full swing before any brain-based efforts to regulate behavior from the cortex reach the amygdala. That said, the prefrontal cortex does have some influence on a person's complete behavioral response, meaning that the prefrontal cortex can "chime in" and help you regulate your response as it happens.

These dual alarm pathways serve several adaptive functions. The direct thalamus→amygdala pathway rapidly triggers a nearly instantaneous response to threats that, through evolution, we are biologically prepared to fear, such as snakes. The idea of an automatic evolutionarily adaptive response is also supported by the fact that people also detect and react more quickly to angry or threatening faces than they do to friendly or neutral faces (Öhman & Mineka, 2001; Ren et al., 2019; Schupp et al., 2004). From

IN FOCUS

Focus on Emotion Regulation

Emotion is powerful and important to humans, so it makes sense that harnessing the power of emotion is central to emotional health and well-being (Braunstein et al., 2017; Kobylińska & Kusev, 2019). Humans do this through emotion regulation, which is a person's ability to understand and manage emotional experience and emotional expression (McRae & Gross, 2020). As shown in the image below almost all forms of emotion regulation rely on communication and coordination among a number of regions in the prefrontal cortex, as well between the prefrontal regions and the limbic system (the amygdala most specifically). There are two areas where emotional health and well-being relies critically on emotion regulation: (1) creating and maintaining close interpersonal relationships (Lindsey, 2020), and (2) coping with aversive life events (Ochsner et al., 2002).

The importance of emotional regulation within the context of relationships begins pretty much from birth. As we will discuss in greater depth in the chapter on lifespan development, the process of initial attachment between infant and caregiver relies on both parties regulating their emotion. Obviously, given the greater life experience of the caregiver (relative to the infant), they are expected to be more skilled in emotion regulation and to help these skills emerge in the developing child (Grolnick et al., 1998). In fact, understanding the emotions of others and responding in kind requires emotion regulation and tends to be a strong predictor of friendship success during childhood and adolescence (Masten et al., 2012). It also turns out that the emotional regulation strategies that you acquire through these early relationships (together with individual life experience) significantly predict the success of romantic relationships in later life (Marroquín & Nolen-Hoeksema, 2015).

Emotion regulation is also central to coping with adverse life events. One of the most studied methods for doing this coping is called reappraisal, which involves reframing how you think about an event in order to reduce the negative emotions that follow negative life events (Ochsner et al., 2002). Reappraisal involves using areas of the prefrontal cortex to support thoughtful processes that help control the negative emotion often associated with adverse events. It is important to note that reappraisal is different from ignoring or forgetting, which both require a lot more effort and are not as effective in terms of long-term psychological health. Reappraisal works because it is deliberate, or mindful, behavior. The prefrontal cortex, which is the control center of the brain, provides a different interpretation of negative emotional signals sent from the limbic system when you are trying to cope with upsetting experiences.

If you understand the saying, "what doesn't kill you makes you stronger" in relation to negative life events, then you understand the function of reappraisal. This saying means that you can shift your focus and pay attention to positive aspects of the experience instead of simply being upset or hurt by negative life events. In doing this, you gain valuable life experience when it comes to coping with negative life events. For example, imagine you get lost on your way to dinner with your friends. Most people would feel frustrated and have negative thoughts such as this: "Why am I so bad at finding my way around?" or "My friend is going to be so irritated with me if I am late." If you used reappraisal instead, you would *deliberately* focus on equally valid thoughts such as this: "I actually learned a new way to get around town" or "My friends like me more for my personality than my punctuality, so they will cut me some slack." The ability to cope with our emotional reactions to negative life events in a healthy way underscores just how important emotion regulation is to our psychological health and well-being.

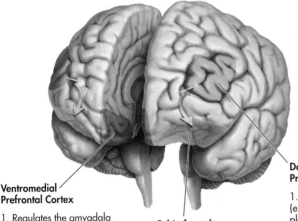

Ventromedial Prefrontal Cortex

1. Regulates the amygdala
2. Inhibits emotional response
3. Contributes to decision making and self-control

Orbitofrontal Prefrontal Cortex

1. Receives connections from the thalamus
2. Sensitive to how rewards inform decisions
3. Helps regulate social behavior

Dorsolateral Prefrontal Cortex

1. Executive function center (e.g., working memory, planning, abstract reasoning)
2. Oversees many aspects of social cognition
3. Close connections to orbitofrontal prefrontal cortex and thalamus

❮ **Prefrontal Brain Regions Support Emotional and Behavioral Regulation** Different portions of the prefrontal cortex have different jobs that all contribute to emotional and behavioral regulation. The dorsolateral prefrontal cortex coordinates and contributes thoughtful input to help understand the situation. The dorsolateral prefrontal cortex works very closely with almost all subregions of the prefrontal cortex, but has a particularly close relationship to the orbitofrontal cortex. The orbitofrontal prefrontal cortex is the portion of the brain that sits just over the eyeballs and does a great deal to help us regulate our behavior. It communicates fluently with the thalamus and is highly sensitive to rewards, both of which help us manage our behavior. The ventromedial prefrontal cortex is located on the inside surface of the brain and has strong connections to the amygdala. It is both informed by its response and helps quiet the amygdala when it is a "false alarm." This connectivity contributes a great deal of what allows us to regulate our emotional responses.

the point of view of survival, it is clearly advantageous to respond quickly in situations of potential danger. In contrast, the indirect pathway allows more complex stimuli to be evaluated in the cortex and help to moderate the amygdala's alarm system and learn from the experience.

Theories of Emotion: Explaining Emotion

■ KEY THEME

Emotion theories emphasize different aspects of emotion, but all have influenced the direction of emotion research.

≡ KEY QUESTIONS

- What are the basic principles and key criticisms of the James–Lange theory of emotion?
- How do the facial feedback hypothesis and other contemporary research support aspects of the James–Lange theory?
- What are the two-factor theory and the cognitive appraisal theory of emotion, and how do they emphasize cognitive factors in emotion?

For more than a century, American psychologists have actively debated theories to explain emotion (Manstead & Parkinson, 2015; Reisenzein, 2015). Like many controversies in psychology, the debate helped shape the direction of psychological research.

In this section, we'll look at the most influential theories of emotion. As you'll see, while most theories agree on the components that contribute to emotion, few agree on the order in which the components occur or the relative importance of each — cognitive experience, physiological arousal, or expressive behavior.

The James–Lange Theory of Emotion: Do You Run Because You're Afraid? Or Are You Afraid Because You Run?

Imagine that you're walking through a park on a nice sunny day. A large dog, off their leash, comes running toward you. The distance between you and the dog quickly disappears. The dog is rather large, and you cannot tell if it is friendly.

Your heart starts pounding and you think you should run. The dog's owner appears, though, and calls "Bunny" to come. The dog responds immediately, returning to the owner, who quickly leashes the dog and apologizes to you for what happened. As you stand there, listening to how "sweet" the dog actually is, your hands are trembling so much you hide them by folding your arms. As you continue to exchange pleasantries about "Bunny," you realize that your palms are sweating and your eyes are wide. You finally continue on your way and start to talk yourself down, realizing that you were not in actual danger.

In this example, all three emotion components are clearly present. You experienced a subjective feeling that you labeled as "fear." You experienced physical arousal — trembling, sweating, and pounding heart. And you expressed the fear by tightening your muscles, folding your arms into your body and widening your eyes. What caused this constellation of effects that you experienced as fear?

William James (1842–1910) was among the first to propose a plausible explanation of emotion (James, 1884). Danish psychologist Carl Lange proposed a very similar theory at about the same time (see James, 1894; Lange & James, 1922). Thus, the **James–Lange theory of emotion** is *the theory that emotions arise from the perception of body changes* (see **Figure 8.4**).

Consider our example again. According to the James–Lange theory, you felt afraid *because* your heart pounded and you began to sweat. James believed that emotion follows this sequence: (1) We perceive a stimulus; (2) physiological and behavioral changes occur, which (3) we experience as a particular emotion.

James–Lange theory of emotion The theory that emotions arise from the perception of body changes.

facial feedback hypothesis The view that expressing a specific emotion, especially facially, causes the subjective experience of that emotion.

"Hey, don't worry, he's friendly"

1. STIMULUS: Unkown dog is running toward you in a park

2. Physiological arousal and behavioral changes.

3. Subjective experience of emotion

FIGURE 8.4 The James–Lange Theory of Emotion According to William James, we don't tremble and run because we are afraid, we are afraid because we tremble and run. James believed that body signals trigger emotional experience. These signals include physiological arousal and feedback from the muscles involved in behavior.

In 1927, the famous physiologist **Walter Cannon** (1871–1945) challenged the James–Lange theory (Dror, 2014). First, Cannon pointed out that body reactions are similar for many emotions, yet our subjective experience of various emotions is very different. For example, both fear and rage are accompanied by increased heart rate, but we have no difficulty distinguishing between the two emotions.

Second, Cannon (1927) argued that our emotional reaction to a stimulus is often faster than our physiological reaction. It can take several seconds for the physiological changes caused by activation of the sympathetic nervous system to take effect, but the subjective experience of emotion is often virtually instantaneous.

Third, artificially inducing physiological changes does not necessarily produce a related emotional experience (Reisenzein & Stephan, 2014). In one early test of the James–Lange theory, conducted by Spanish researcher Gregorio Marañon (1924), participants were injected with the hormone *adrenaline,* (also called *epinephrine*) which activates the sympathetic nervous system. When asked how they felt, the participants simply reported the physical changes produced by the drug, saying, "My heart is beating very fast." Some reported feeling "as if" they should be feeling an emotion, but they said they did not feel the emotion itself: "I feel *as if* I were afraid."

Evidence Supporting the James–Lange Theory Research on the **facial feedback hypothesis** is *the view that expressing a specific emotion, especially facially, causes the subjective experience of that emotion* (Soussignan, 2004; Winkielman et al., 2015). Supporting this are studies showing that when people mimic the facial expressions characteristic of a given emotion, such as anger or fear, they tend to report *feeling* the emotion (Laird & Lacasse, 2014; Schnall & Laird, 2003).

The basic explanation for this phenomenon is that the facial muscles send feedback signals to the brain. In turn, the brain uses this information to activate and regulate emotional experience, intensifying or lessening emotion (Izard, 1990a, 1990b). In line with this explanation, Paul Ekman and Richard Davidson (1993) demonstrated that deliberately creating a "happy" smile produces brain-activity changes similar to those caused by spontaneously producing a happy smile in response to a real event, a finding that continues to be supported (Marsh et al., 2019).

MYTH ▶ SCIENCE

Is it true that if you "put on a happy face," you will actually feel happier?

creative ways to overcome obstacles. If you see yourself as competent and capable, you are more likely to strive for higher personal goals (Bayer & Gollwitzer, 2007; Wood & Bandura, 1991).

People tend to avoid challenging situations or tasks that they *believe* exceed their capabilities (Bandura, 2008). If self-doubts occur, motivation quickly dwindles because the task is perceived as too difficult or threatening. So how do you build your sense of self-efficacy, especially in situations in which your confidence is shaky?

According to Bandura (1991, 2006), the most effective way to strengthen your sense of self-efficacy is through *mastery experiences*—experiencing success at moderately challenging tasks in which you have to overcome obstacles and persevere. As you tackle a challenging task, you should strive for progressive improvement rather than perfection on your first attempt. Understand that setbacks serve a useful purpose in teaching that success usually requires sustained effort. If you experienced only easy successes, you'd be more likely to become disappointed and discouraged and to abandon your efforts when you did experience failure.

A second strategy is *social modeling,* or *observational learning.* In some situations, the motivation to succeed is present, but you lack the knowledge of exactly how to achieve your goals. In such circumstances, it can be helpful to observe and imitate the behavior of someone who is already competent at the task you want to master (Bandura, 1986, 1990). For example, if you're not certain how to prepare effectively for a test or a class presentation, watch fellow students who *are* successful.

Implementation Intentions: Turning Goals into Actions

Suppose your sense of self-efficacy is strong, but you still have trouble putting your intentions into action. For example, have you ever made a list of New Year's resolutions and looked back at it six months later? If you're like most people, you'll wonder what went wrong.

How can you bridge the gap between good intentions and effective, goal-directed behavior? German psychologist Peter Gollwitzer (1999, 2014) points out that many people have trouble *initiating* the actions required to fulfill their goals and then *persisting* in these behaviors until the goals are achieved. Gollwitzer and his colleagues (2008, 2010) have identified some simple yet effective techniques that help people translate their good intentions into actual behavior.

Step 1: Form a goal intention.

This step involves translating vague general intentions ("I'm going to do my best") into a specific, concrete, and binding goal. Express the specific goal in terms of "I intend to achieve_____," filling in the blank with the particular behavior or outcome that you wish to achieve. For example, suppose you resolve to exercise more regularly. Transform that general goal into a much more specific goal intention, such as "I intend to work out at the campus gym on Monday, Wednesday, and Friday." Forming the specific goal intention enhances your sense of personal commitment to the goal, and it also heightens your sense of obligation to realize the goal.

Step 2: Create implementation intentions.

This step involves *making a specific plan for turning your good intention into reality.* The trick is to specify exactly where, when, and how you will carry out your intended behavior. Mentally link the intended behaviors to specific situational cues, such as saying, "After my psychology class, I will go to the campus athletic center and work out for 45 minutes." By linking the behavior to specific situational cues, you're more likely to initiate the goal behavior when the critical situation is encountered (Webb & Sheeran, 2007). The ultimate goal of implementation intentions is to create a new automatic link between a specific situation and the desired behavior—and, ultimately, to create new habits or routines in your life (Adriaanse et al., 2011).

As simple as this seems, research has demonstrated that forming specific implementation intentions is very effective (Legrand et al., 2017; Parks-Stamm et al., 2007).

Mental Rehearsal: Visualize the Process

The mental images you create in anticipation of a situation can strongly influence your sense of self-efficacy and self-control as well as the effectiveness of your implementation intentions (Knäuper et al., 2009). For example, students sometimes undermine their own performance by vividly imagining their worst fears, such as becoming overwhelmed by anxiety during a class presentation or going completely blank during a test. However, the opposite is also possible. Mentally visualizing yourself dealing *effectively* with a situation can enhance your performance (Conway et al., 2004; Libby et al., 2007). Athletes, in particular, are aware of this and mentally rehearse their performance prior to competition.

So, strive to control your thoughts in an optimistic way by mentally focusing on your capabilities and a positive outcome, not your limitations and worst fears. The key here is not just imagining a positive outcome. Instead, imagine and mentally rehearse the *process*—the skills you will effectively use and the steps you will take—to achieve the outcome *you* want. Go for it!

CHAPTER REVIEW

Motivation and Emotion

 **Achieve,** Macmillan Learning's online study platform, features the full e-book of *Discovering Psychology,* the **LearningCurve** adaptive quizzing system, videos, and a variety of activities to boost your learning. Visit **Achieve** at macmillanlearning.com.

KEY PEOPLE

Walter Cannon, p. 289

Charles Darwin, p. 278

Paul Ekman, p. 280

William James, p. 288

Abraham Maslow, p. 269

KEY TERMS

motivation, p. 266

instinct theories, p. 266

drive theories, p. 267

homeostasis, p. 267

drive, p. 267

incentive theories, p. 267

arousal theory, p. 268

sensation seeking, p. 268

humanistic theories of motivation, p. 268

hierarchy of needs, p. 269

the need to belong, p. 270

self-determination theory (SDT), p. 270

intrinsic motivation, p. 271

extrinsic motivation, p. 271

achievement motivation, p. 271

leptin, p. 273

set-point theory, p. 274

body mass index (BMI), p. 274

obesity, p. 274

emotion, p. 277

basic emotions, p. 278

interpersonal engagement, p. 279

anthropomorphism, p. 281

display rules, p. 282

amygdala, p. 284

James–Lange theory of emotion, p. 288

facial feedback hypothesis, p. 289

two-factor theory of emotion, p. 290

cognitive appraisal theory of emotion, p. 290

self-efficacy, p. 291

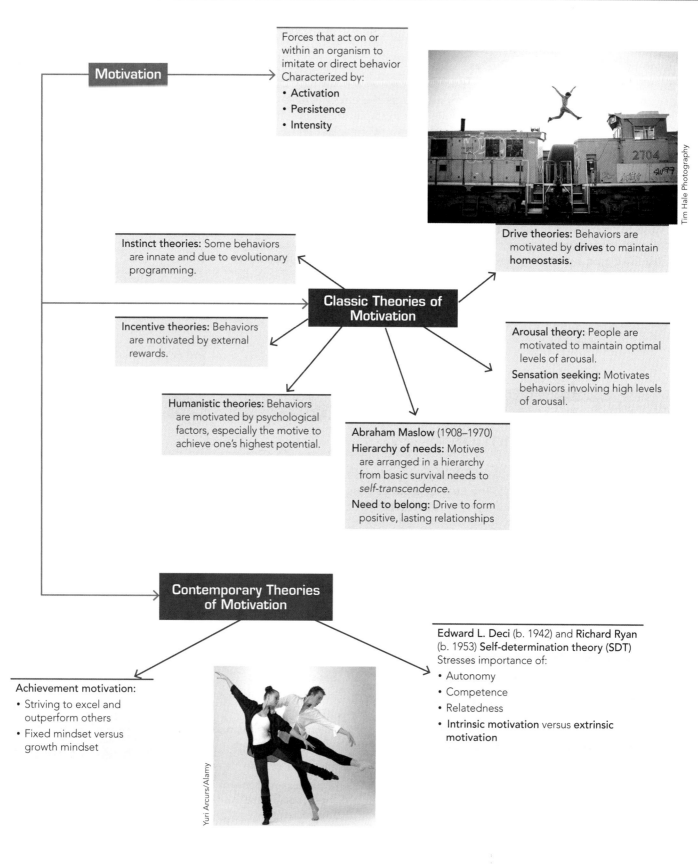

Motivation

Forces that act on or within an organism to imitate or direct behavior Characterized by:
- Activation
- Persistence
- Intensity

Tim Hale Photography

Instinct theories: Some behaviors are innate and due to evolutionary programming.

Drive theories: Behaviors are motivated by **drives** to maintain **homeostasis.**

Classic Theories of Motivation

Incentive theories: Behaviors are motivated by external rewards.

Arousal theory: People are motivated to maintain optimal levels of arousal.

Sensation seeking: Motivates behaviors involving high levels of arousal.

Humanistic theories: Behaviors are motivated by psychological factors, especially the motive to achieve one's highest potential.

Abraham Maslow (1908–1970)

Hierarchy of needs: Motives are arranged in a hierarchy from basic survival needs to *self-transcendence.*

Need to belong: Drive to form positive, lasting relationships

Contemporary Theories of Motivation

Achievement motivation:
- Striving to excel and outperform others
- Fixed mindset versus growth mindset

Edward L. Deci (b. 1942) and **Richard Ryan** (b. 1953) **Self-determination theory (SDT)** Stresses importance of:
- Autonomy
- Competence
- Relatedness
- **Intrinsic motivation** versus **extrinsic motivation**

Yuri Arcurs/Alamy

Hunger and Eating

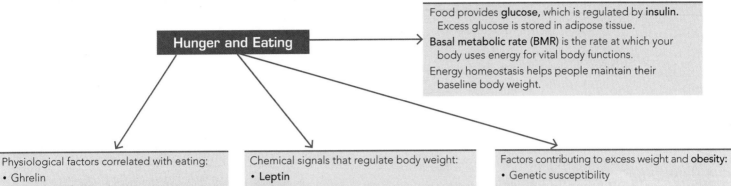

Food provides **glucose,** which is regulated by **insulin.**
Excess glucose is stored in adipose tissue.

Basal metabolic rate (BMR) is the rate at which your body uses energy for vital body functions.

Energy homeostasis helps people maintain their baseline body weight.

Physiological factors correlated with eating:
• Ghrelin

Psychological factors that trigger eating:
• Classically conditioned stimuli
• Positive reinforcement

Satiation signals:
• Cholecystokinin (CCK)
• Sensory-specific satiety

Chemical signals that regulate body weight:
• **Leptin**
• **Insulin**
• Neuropeptide Y
• Ghrelin

Explaining long-term weight regulation:
• **Set-point theory**

Factors contributing to excess weight and **obesity:**
• Genetic susceptibility
• Overeating
• Sedentary lifestyles
• Individual differences in BMR
• Inadequate sleep
• Leptin resistance
• Weight cycling due to frequent dieting
• Socio-economic status (SES)

Emotion

Theories of Emotion

The Neuroscience of Emotion

Two-factor theory: Theorists:
Stanley Schachter and Jerome Singer
• Emotion results from applying a cognitive label to feelings of arousal.

Charles Darwin
(1809–1882) emphasized that emotions reflect evolutionary adaptations to problems of survival and reproduction.
Functions of emotion include:
• Trigger-motivated behavior
• **Emotional intelligence** contributes to rational decision making and purposeful behavior.
• May involve arousal of sympathetic nervous system

Components:
• Cognitive experience
• Physiological response
• Behavioral or expressive response

Cognitive appraisal theory: Theorists:
Craig Smith and Richard Lazarus
• Emotions are triggered by cognitive evaluations of events.

James–Lange theory: Theorist: William James (1842–1910)
• Emotion results from perception of biological and behavioral responses.
• **Facial feedback hypothesis:** Facial expression of emotion creates subjective experience of the emotion.
• Challenged by **Walter Cannon** (1871–1945)

• **Sympathetic nervous system:** Emotion can be felt throughout the body.
• The **amygdala** is activated during fear.
• The **prefrontal cortex** is critical for emotion regulation.

Basic emotions:
• Biologically determined and culturally universal
• Include fear, disgust, surprise, happiness, anger, and sadness

Culture and emotion:
• Collectivistic cultures emphasize emotions involving **interpersonal engagement.**
• Emotional expression is regulated by cultural **display rules.**

Paul Ekman (b. 1934):
• Analyzed facial expressions
• Demonstrated that facial expressions for basic emotions are culturally universal

Eric Engman/ZUMA Press/Newscom

Sandy Hockenbury

MYTH OR SCIENCE?

Is it true . . .

▶ That the genes you inherit provide an unchanging "blueprint" that determines your physical characteristics, abilities, and personality traits?

▶ That just a few hours after birth, infants already prefer their mothers to strangers?

▶ That most adolescents have poor relationships with their parents?

▶ That the number of sexual partners among millennials is higher than previous generations?

▶ That many middle-aged people experience a "midlife crisis"?

▶ That dying people go through five predictable stages—denial, anger, bargaining, depression, and acceptance?

Lifespan Development

PROLOGUE

An Obituary: The Arc of a Life

Margalit Fox wrote obituaries for *The New York Times*, receiving praise for her witty, moving life stories of both the famous (Maya Angelou) and the obscure (the inventor of the plastic pink flamingo lawn ornament). The stories Fox told spanned the lives of many notable people, including the long and productive life of Dovey Johnson Roundtree, who was born in 1914 and died in 2018. Fox's obituary of Roundtree tells the 104-year story of her many life stages, highlighting her pro-social work as a minister, a lawyer, and a civil

rights activist (Fox, 2018a). As Fox explained, each person profiled in an obituary shared a trait: They had each "put a wrinkle in the social fabric and changed the world" (Cowen, 2016). In many ways, Fox and other obituary writers are channeling developmental psychologists, the psychological scientists who study the stages of human life.

Fox (2018a) began the trajectory of Roundtree's life with the detail that she was born in North Carolina to a family "of slender means." Her father died during the influenza pandemic when she was just a few years old and the family soon after moved in with her grandparents. Roundtree grew up in the segregated south, where her family's life was marked by threats and violence from the Ku Klux

Klan. Despite these challenges, Roundtree was enormously successful in her studies and it helped that education was prized in her family. Roundtree went on to attend the renowned Spelman College, a historically black college and university (HBCU), working three jobs to pay for her education.

After college, Roundtree became the important activist whom Fox described in her *Times* obit. For example, Roundtree successfully lobbied for an end to "colored tables" in the dining hall while in the Women's Army Auxiliary Corps (Fox, 2018a). She soon went to law school at Howard University, another HBCU, and overcame heated objections to become the first Black person to be admitted to Washington DC's Women's Bar Association. (Roundtree

ddea/Getty Images

CHAPTER **9**

was married around this time, but her all-consuming focus on the law led to an early end to her marriage.)

As an attorney, Roundtree litigated a groundbreaking case involving a Black woman on a bus who was arrested after ignoring an order to give her seat to a White man, several years before Rosa Parks became famous for the same action. Roundtree won the case, and segregation was banned on interstate buses—"a civil rights watershed." Soon, Roundtree added another degree, this one from Howard's divinity school, and became an ordained minister. Roundtree remained a successful lawyer into her 80s.

Fox (2018a) ends Roundtree's obituary with a story, "In her 90s, Ms. Roundtree lost her sight to diabetes, from which she had suffered for many years. That did not keep her, in November 2008, from going to the polls in Charlotte, the city where the Klan had rampaged past her home. There, with the help of a sighted friend, she cast her ballot for Barack Obama."

Fox describes her love for her own work: "Writing daily obits only reinforced what I had long suspected: It is the best beat in journalism. The reason is simple: In following their subjects from cradle to grave, obits are the most narrative genre in any daily paper" (Fox, 2018b). And the stories Fox told were stories that highlighted the arc of a life, including so many of the stages and topics we address in this chapter. ∿

⊘ **IN THIS CHAPTER:**

- INTRODUCTION: Developmental Psychology
- Genetic Contributions to Development
- Prenatal Development
- Development During Infancy and Childhood
- Adolescence
- Adult Development
- Late Adulthood and Aging
- Closing Thoughts
- PSYCH FOR YOUR LIFE: Raising Psychologically Healthy Children

297

developmental psychology The study of how people change physically, cognitively, and socially throughout the lifespan.

Introduction: Developmental Psychology

◼ KEY THEME

Developmental psychology is the study of how people change over the lifespan.

⹀ KEY QUESTIONS
- What are some of the key themes in developmental psychology?
- How do we learn about people over the course of their lifespan?

One way to look at the overall development of your life is to think of your life as a story, much like the stories told by Margalit Fox in her compelling obituaries. Like Dovey Johnson Roundtree, you are the main character. Your life story so far has a distinct plot, occasional subplots, and a cast of supporting characters, including family, friends, and lovers. Like every other person's life story, yours has been influenced by factors beyond your control. One such factor is the unique combination of genes you inherited from your biological mother and father. Another is the historical era during which you grew up. Your individual development has also been shaped by the cultural, social, and family contexts within which you were raised.

The patterns of your life story, and the life stories of countless other people, are the focus of **developmental psychology**—*the study of how people change physically, cognitively, and socially throughout the lifespan.* Developmental psychologists investigate the influence of biological, environmental, social, cultural, and behavioral factors on development at every age and stage of life.

When most of us think about developmental psychology, we most often envision children, and maybe teens, but it is important to understand that development starts before a person is born and continues until the very end of their life. "Arrested development" is a memorable phrase, but it's not really possible. Human development is a lot like a ball rolling down a hill that has many peaks and valleys that influence, but never halt, its path. Human development is a flexible process, allowing

❯ **Continuity and Change over the Lifespan** The twin themes of continuity and change throughout the lifespan are evident in the changing nature of relationships. Childhood friendships center on sharing activities, while peer relationships in adolescence emphasize sharing thoughts and feelings. Early adulthood brings the challenge of forming intimate relationships and, for some, beginning a family. Close relationships with friends and family continue to contribute to psychological well-being in middle and late adulthood.

Caiaimage/Paul Bradbury/Getty Images

Mint Images/Tim Pannell/Getty Images

Blend Images/Alamy

Erickson Stock/Blend Images

human infants to follow an infinite number of developmental paths. Ideally, the developmental path is determined by environmental demands that not only serve the individual's survival (e.g., quickly learning to communicate their needs and form attachments with caregivers) but also encourage long-term outcomes (e.g., learning the specific demands of your culture) that result in a person's eventual reproductive success.

The impact of these factors on individual development is greatly influenced by attitudes, perceptions, and personality characteristics. For example, the adjustment to middle school may be a breeze for one child but a nightmare for another. We are influenced by the events we experience, but we also shape the meaning and consequences of those events. Along with studying common patterns of growth and change, developmental psychologists look at the ways in which people differ in their development and life stories. As we'll note several times in this chapter, the typical pattern of development can also vary across cultures (Kagan, 2011; Molitor & Hsu, 2011).

Developmental psychologists often conceptualize the lifespan in terms of basic stages of development (see **Table 9.1**). Many stages of the lifespan are defined by age, and as such some of life's transitions are rather abrupt, such as entering the workforce, becoming a parent, or retiring. And some aspects of development, such as prenatal development and language development, are closely tied to critical periods, during which a child is maximally sensitive to environmental influences.

Still, most of our physical, cognitive, and social changes occur gradually. As we trace the typical course of human development in this chapter, the theme of gradually unfolding changes throughout the ages and stages of life will become more evident. Another important theme in developmental psychology is the interaction between heredity and environment. There is no aspect of human development that can be fully understood without considering the role of *both* nature and nurture. We are born with a specific genetic potential that we inherit from our biological parents, but our environment influences how, when, and whether that potential is expressed. In turn, our genetic inheritance influences the ways in which we experience and interact with the environment (Diamond, 2009; Meaney, 2010).

TABLE 9.1

Major Stages of the Lifespan

Stage	Age Range
Prenatal	Conception to birth
Infancy and toddlerhood	Birth to 2 years
Early childhood	2 to 6 years
Middle childhood	6 to 12 years
Adolescence	12 to 18 years
Emerging adulthood	18 to 25 years
Young adulthood	25 to 40 years
Middle adulthood	40 to 65 years
Late adulthood	65 years to death

The Chapters in Your Life Story If you think of your life as an unfolding story, then the major stages of the human lifespan represent the different "chapters" of your life. Each chapter is characterized by fundamentally different physical, cognitive, and social transitions, challenges and opportunities, demands and adjustments. Comparing different life stories reveals many striking similarities in the developmental themes of any given stage. Nevertheless, every life story is unique.

Genetic Contributions to Development

■ KEY THEME

Your genotype consists of the chromosomes inherited from your biological parents, but your phenotype—the actual characteristics you display—results from the interaction of genetics and environmental factors.

⹂ KEY QUESTIONS
- What are DNA, chromosomes, and genes?
- What role does the environment play in the relationship between genotype and phenotype?
- What is epigenetics?

You began your life as a **zygote**, *the single cell formed at conception from the union of the egg cell and sperm cell.* For perspective, a zygote is no larger than the period at the end of this sentence. Packed in that tiny cell was the unique set of genetic instructions that you inherited from your biological parents. Today, that same set of genetic information is found in the nucleus of nearly every cell of your body.

The genetic data you inherited from your biological parents are encoded in the chemical structure of each **chromosome**, *a long, threadlike structure composed of twisted parallel*

zygote The single cell formed at conception from the union of the egg cell and sperm cell.

chromosome A long, threadlike structure composed of twisted parallel strands of DNA.

> **The 23 Pairs of Human Chromosomes**
Each person's unique genotype is represented in the 23 pairs of chromosomes found in the nucleus of almost all human body cells. This photograph, taken through a microscope, depicts a *karyotype*, which shows one cell's complete set of chromosomes. By convention, the chromosomes are arranged in pairs from largest to smallest, numbered from 1 to 22. **Sex chromosomes** are the *chromosomes, designated as X or Y, that determine biological sex; the 23rd pair of chromosomes in humans.* The sex chromosomes in this karyotype are XX, indicating a female. A male karyotype would have an XY combination.

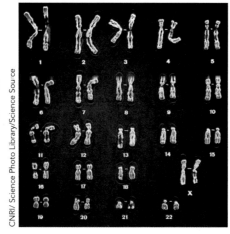

strands of DNA. Chromosomes are found in the cell nucleus. As depicted in **Figure 9.1**, **deoxyribonucleic acid**, abbreviated **DNA** is *the double-stranded molecule that encodes genetic instructions.* Put simply, DNA stores the inherited information that guides the development of all living organisms.

Each of your chromosomes contains thousands of DNA segments, each one is a **gene**, *a unit of DNA on a chromosome that encodes instructions for making a particular protein molecule.* Each gene is a unit of DNA that alone, or most often in combination with other genes, make up an individual's *genotype.*

At fertilization, your biological mother's egg cell and your biological father's sperm cell each contributed 23 chromosomes. This set of 23 chromosome pairs represents your **genotype**, *the genetic makeup of an individual organism.* With the exception of the reproductive cells (sperm or eggs), every cell in your body contains a complete, identical copy of your genotype.

From Genotype to Phenotype

While the term *genotype* refers to an organism's unique genetic makeup, the term **phenotype** refers to *the observable traits or characteristics of an organism as determined by the interaction of genetics and environmental factors.* At one time, the genotype was commonly described as a "genetic blueprint," which implied that the genotype was a fixed, master plan, like an architectural blueprint. It was thought that a person's inherited genotype directed and controlled virtually all aspects of development as it unfolded over the lifespan (Dar-Nimrod & Heine, 2011). But research has shown that the genetic blueprint analogy is *not* completely accurate.

The first problem with the genotype-as-blueprint analogy is that genes don't *directly* control development, traits, or behaviors (Zhang & Meaney, 2010). Rather, genes direct the production of the thousands of different proteins that are the building blocks of all body tissues and structures—which ultimately *do* influence your development and behavior.

Second, environmental factors influence the phenotype you display. For example, even if your genotype contains a copy of the dominant "freckles" gene, you will

MYTH ◄ **SCIENCE**

Is it true that the genes you inherit provide an unchanging "blueprint" that determines your physical characteristics, abilities, and personality traits?

deoxyribonucleic acid (DNA) The double-stranded molecule that encodes genetic instructions.

sex chromosomes Chromosomes, designated as X or Y, that determine biological sex; the 23rd pair of chromosomes in humans.

gene A unit of DNA on a chromosome that encodes instructions for making a particular protein molecule.

genotype (JEEN-oh-type) The genetic makeup of an individual organism.

phenotype (FEEN-oh-type) The observable traits or characteristics of an organism as determined by the interaction of genetics and environmental factors.

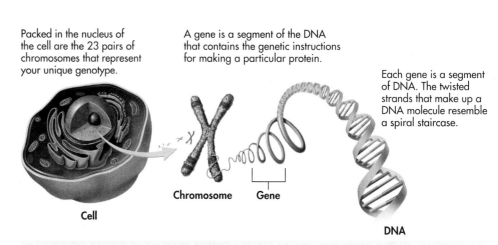

FIGURE 9.1 **Chromosomes, Genes, and DNA** Each chromosome contains thousands of genes, and each gene is a unit of DNA instructions. Incredibly fine, the strands of DNA in a single human cell would be more than three inches long if unraveled. If the DNA present in one person were unraveled, it would stretch from Earth to Pluto and back—*twice!*

not develop freckles unless the expression of that dominant gene is triggered by a specific environmental factor: sunlight. On the other hand, if you carry two recessive "no freckles" genes, you won't develop freckles no matter how much time you spend in the sunlight.

Here's the important point: *Different genotypes react differently to environmental factors* (Buil et al., 2015; Masterpasqua, 2009). Thus, psychologists and other scientists often speak of *genetic predispositions* to develop in a particular way (Champagne & Mashoodh, 2009). In other words, people with a particular genetic configuration will be more or less sensitive to particular environmental factors. For example, think of people you know who sunburn easily, such as redheads or people with very fair skin. Their genotype is especially sensitive to the effects of ultraviolet light. One person's freckle factory is another person's light tan—or searing sunburn.

The Science of Epigenetics

Each of us started life as a single-celled zygote that divided and multiplied. Each new cell contained the exact same set of genetic instructions. Yet some of those cells developed into bones, eyes, joints, or other specialized tissues. Why are cells so different? How does the zygote develop into a complex, differentiated organism?

The dramatic differences among the size, shape, and function of cells are due to *which* genes are "expressed," or activated. Put simply, cells develop differently because different genes are activated at different times. Some genes are active for just a few hours, others for a lifetime. Many genes are *never* expressed. For example, humans carry all of the genes to develop a tail, but we don't develop a tail because those genes are never activated.

What triggers a gene to activate? Gene expression can be triggered by the activity of *other* genes, internal chemical changes, or by external environmental factors, such as sunlight in our earlier freckles example. Thus, gene expression is *flexible,* responsive to both internal and external factors (Meaney, 2010; Szyf, 2013).

Scientists have only recently begun to understand the processes that regulate gene expression. This field is called **epigenetics**—*the study of the cellular mechanisms that control gene expression and of the ways that gene expression impacts health and behavior* (Meaney, 2010; Zhang & Meaney, 2010).

To help illustrate epigenetic influences, consider identical twins, who develop from a single zygote. Each twin inherits exactly the same set of genes. Yet, as twins develop, differences in physical and psychological characteristics become evident. These differences are due to epigenetic changes—differences in the expression of each twin's genes, *not* to their underlying DNA, which is still identical (Champagne & Mashoodh, 2009; Fraga et al., 2005).

Epigenetic research is providing new insights into *how* the environment affects gene expression and the phenotype (Champagne, 2010; Szyf & Bick, 2013). For example, in one series of studies, newborn rats that were genetically predisposed to be nervous and high-strung were shown to develop into calm, stress-resistant adult rats when raised by genetically unrelated, attentive mother rats (Meaney, 2001, 2010). Conversely, newborn rats that were genetically predisposed to be calm and stress resistant grew up to be nervous and high-strung when they were raised by *inattentive,* genetically unrelated mother rats.

The important point is that although the rats' DNA did *not* change, chemical "markers" that control gene expression *did* change. The rats' upbringing set in motion a cascade of epigenetic changes that changed their brain chemistry and "reprogrammed" their future behavior (see Hyman, 2009; Sapolsky, 2004). Surprisingly, the influence of their upbringing extended to the *next* generation: The calm, stress-resistant rats grew up to be attentive mothers to their own offspring.

Interactions among genes and between the genotype and environmental influences are two critical factors in the relationship between genotype and phenotype. Beyond these factors, genes can also *mutate,* or spontaneously change, from one generation to the next. Further, DNA itself can be damaged by environmental factors, such as exposure to chemical toxins. Just as a typo in a recipe can ruin a dish, errors in the genetic code can lead to birth defects or genetic disorders.

epigenetics The study of the cellular mechanisms that control gene expression and of the ways that gene expression impacts health and behavior.

prenatal stage The stage of development before birth that is divided into the germinal, embryonic, and fetal periods.

germinal period The first two weeks of prenatal development.

embryonic period The second period of prenatal development, extending from the third week through the eighth week.

Prenatal Development

■ KEY THEME
During the prenatal stage, the single-celled zygote develops into a full-term fetus.

☰ KEY QUESTIONS
- What are the three stages of prenatal development?
- How does the brain develop?
- What are teratogens?

At conception, chromosomes from the biological mother and father combine to form a single cell—the fertilized egg, or *zygote.* Over the relatively brief span of nine months, that single cell develops into the estimated trillion cells that make up a newborn baby. This **prenatal stage** *is the stage of development before birth that is divided into the germinal, embryonic, and fetal periods* (see photos).

The Germinal and Embryonic Periods

The **germinal period**, also called the *zygotic period,* represents *the first two weeks of prenatal development.* During this time, the zygote undergoes rapid cell division before becoming implanted on the wall of the mother's uterus. By the end of the two-week germinal period, the single-celled zygote has developed into a cluster of cells called the *embryo.*

The **embryonic period** is *the second period of prenatal development, extending from the third week through the eighth week.* During this time of rapid growth and intensive cell differentiation, the organs and major systems of the body form. Genes on the sex chromosomes and hormonal influences also trigger the initial development of the sex organs.

Protectively housed in the fluid-filled *amniotic sac,* the embryo's lifeline is the umbilical cord. Extending from the placenta on the mother's uterine wall to the embryo's abdominal area, the *umbilical cord* delivers nourishment, oxygen, and water and carries away carbon dioxide and other wastes. The *placenta* is actually a disk-shaped, vascular organ that acts as a filter, preventing the mother's blood from directly mingling with that of the developing embryo.

The placenta also filters out harmful agents from the mother's blood, although it is not always successful. *Agents or substances that can potentially harm the developing fetus*

(a) Dr. G. Moscoso/Science Source (b) Petit Format/Nestle/ Science Source (c) Petit Format/Nestle/Science Source

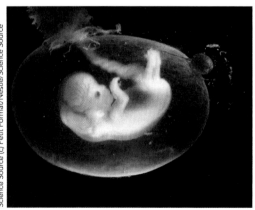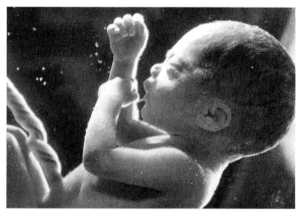

⌃ **Prenatal Development** Although it is less than an inch long, the beginnings of arms, legs, and fingers can already be distinguished in the seven-week-old embryo (*left*). The amniotic sac can be clearly seen in this photograph. The fetus at four months (*middle*) measures 6 to 10 inches long, and the mother may be able to feel the fetus's movements. Notice the well-formed umbilical cord. Near full term (*right*), the eight-month-old fetus gains body fat to help the newborn survive outside the mother's uterus.

are called **teratogens**. Generally, the greatest vulnerability to teratogens occurs during the embryonic stage, when major body systems are forming. But many substances, including cocaine, prescription and over-the-counter drugs, cigarette smoke, and alcohol, can damage the developing fetus at *any* stage before birth. Even small amounts of teratogens in drinking water, such as lead or traces of prescription drugs, can have negative impact on embryonic development (Kaushik et al., 2016; Rodrigues et al., 2016). Known teratogens include the following:

- Exposure to radiation

- Toxic chemicals and metals, such as mercury, PCBs, and lead

- Viruses and bacteria, such as German measles (rubella), genital herpes, and human immunodeficiency virus (HIV)

- Prescription painkillers and other prescription and nonprescription drugs

- Addictive drugs, including heroin, sedatives, cocaine, amphetamines, and methamphetamine

- Maternal smoking and exposure to secondhand smoke

- Alcohol

Alcohol deserves special mention. Although drinking alcohol at any point during pregnancy can harm the fetus, the greatest risk is during the first trimester of prenatal development, when the brain and major organs are developing. Excessive drinking can cause *fetal alcohol spectrum disorders,* which are characterized by physical and mental problems (Bakoyiannis et al., 2014; Sokol et al., 2003). Symptoms include abnormal facial features, poor coordination, learning disabilities, behavior problems, and intellectual disability. Binge drinking is especially harmful to the developing fetus, but most researchers believe that there is *no* safe level of alcohol use during pregnancy.

Finally, the mother's psychological state can affect the unborn child. Chronic stress, depression, and anxiety are associated with low birth weight and premature birth (see Dunkel Schetter, 2011). Poor nutrition, lack of sleep, and other unhealthy behaviors can also affect the unborn child's growth and development.

By the end of the embryonic period, the embryo has grown from a cluster of a few hundred cells no bigger than the head of a pin to over an inch in length. Now weighing about an ounce, the embryo looks distinctly human, even though its head accounts for about half its body size.

Prenatal Brain Development

By three weeks after conception, a sheet of primitive neural cells has formed. Just as you might roll a piece of paper to make a tube, this sheet of neural cells curls to form the hollow *neural tube.* The neural tube is lined with **stem cells**, which are *cells that can divide indefinitely, renew themselves, and give rise to a variety of other types of cells.* At four weeks, this structure is about the size of a grain of salt. At seven weeks it is about a quarter-inch long.

The neural stem cells divide and multiply, producing other specialized cells that eventually give rise to neurons and glial cells. Gradually, the top of the neural tube thickens into three bulges that will eventually form the three main regions of the brain: the *hindbrain, midbrain,* and *forebrain* (see **Figure 9.2**).

During peak periods of brain development, new neurons are being generated at the rate of 250,000 per minute (McDonald, 2009). The developing brain cells multiply, differentiate, and begin their migration to their final destination. Guided by the fibers of a special type of glial cell, the newly generated neurons travel to specific locations (Bystron et al., 2008). They join with other developing neurons and begin forming the structures of the developing nervous system.

teratogens Agents or substances that can potentially harm the developing fetus.

stem cells Cells that can divide indefinitely, renew themselves, and give rise to a variety of other types of cells.

Tom Williams/AP Images

▲ **Waterborne Teratogens** Residents of Flint, Michigan, started noticing problems with their water in 2014. It was discolored and smelled bad. Over the next couple of years, researchers discovered why. The water in Flint was contaminated, and contained high levels of lead, a potent teratogen that can lead to birth defects. In this photo, a volunteer loads bottled water into a truck to distribute to Flint residents whose water was unsafe to drink. As of early 2021, Flint residents continue to struggle with this issue.

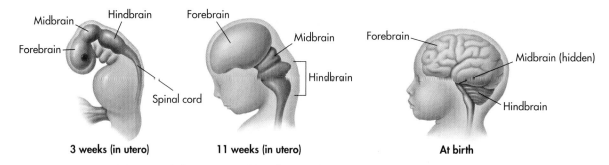

FIGURE 9.2 The Sequence of Fetal Brain Development The human brain begins as a fluid-filled neural tube at about three weeks after conception. The hindbrain structures are the first to develop, followed by midbrain structures. The forebrain structures develop last, eventually coming to surround and envelop the hindbrain and midbrain structures.

The Fetal Period

The third month heralds the beginning of the **fetal period**—*the third and longest period of prenatal development, extending from the ninth week until birth.* The main task during the next seven months is for body systems to grow and reach maturity in preparation for life outside the mother's body. By the end of the third month, the fetus can move its arms, legs, mouth, and head. The fetus becomes capable of reflexive responses, such as fanning its toes if the sole of the foot is stroked and squinting if its eyelids are touched. During the fourth month, the mother experiences *quickening*—she can feel the fetus moving.

The fetal brain is constantly changing, forming as many as 2 million synaptic connections per second. The fetus now has distinct sleep–wake cycles and periods of activity (Mirmiran et al., 2003). During the sixth month, the fetus's brain activity becomes similar to that of a newborn baby.

During the final two months of the fetal period, the fetus will double in weight, gaining an additional three to four pounds of body fat. This additional body fat will help the newborn adjust to changing temperatures outside the womb. As birth approaches, growth slows, and the fetus's body systems become more active.

At birth, the newborn's brain is only about one-fourth the size of an adult brain, weighing less than a pound. After birth, the neurons grow in size and continue to develop new dendrites and interconnections with other neurons. *Myelin* forms on axons in key areas of the brain, such as those involved in motor control (Jakovcevski et al., 2009). Axons also grow longer, and the branching at the ends of the axons becomes more dense.

Development During Infancy and Childhood

■ **KEY THEME**
Although physically helpless, newborn infants are equipped with reflexes and sensory capabilities that enhance their chances for survival.

≡ **KEY QUESTIONS**
• How do the senses and the brain develop after birth?
• What roles do temperament and attachment play in social and personality development?

The newly born infant enters the world with an impressive array of physical and sensory capabilities. Initially, their behavior is mostly limited to reflexes that enhance chances for survival. Touching the newborn's cheek triggers the *rooting reflex*—the infant turns toward the source of the touch and opens their mouth. Touching the newborn's lips evokes the *sucking reflex*. If you put a finger on each of the newborn's palms, they will respond with the *grasping reflex*—the baby will grip your fingers so tightly that they

fetal period The third and longest period of prenatal development, extending from the ninth week until birth.

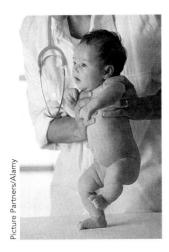
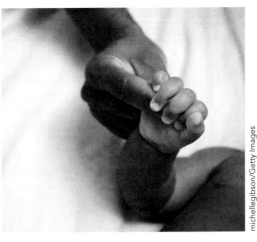

Picture Partners/Alamy

michellegibson/Getty Images

> **Newborn Reflexes** When this two-week-old baby (*left*) is held upright with their feet touching a flat surface, they display the *stepping reflex*, moving their legs as if trying to walk. Another reflex that is present at birth is the *grasping reflex* (*right*). The infant's grip is so strong that they can support their own weight. Thought to enhance the newborn's chances for survival, these reflexive responses drop out during the first few months of life as the baby develops voluntary control over movements.

can be lifted upright. As motor areas of the infant's brain develop over the first year of life, the rooting, sucking, and grasping reflexes are replaced by voluntary behaviors. It is also worth noting that many of these reflexes are simply adorable and make us want to pay attention to and take care of the babies in our social worlds. Anyone who has had a baby grasp their finger knows this to be true.

The newborn's senses—vision, hearing, smell, and touch—are keenly attuned to people. In a classic study, Robert Fantz (1961) demonstrated that the image of a human face holds the newborn's gaze longer than do other images. Other researchers have also confirmed the newborn's visual preference for the human face (Pascalis & Kelly, 2009). Newborns only 10 *minutes* old will turn their heads to continue gazing at the image of a human face as it passes in front of them, but they will not visually follow other images (Turati, 2004).

And newborns quickly learn to differentiate between their mothers and strangers. Within just hours of their birth, newborns display a preference for their mother's voice and face over that of a stranger (Bushnell, 2001). And at two days old, infants preferred the smell of their mother to that of a woman they did not know (Marin et al., 2015). For their part, mothers become keenly attuned to their infant's appearance, smell, and even skin texture. Fathers, too, are able to identify their newborn from a photograph after just minutes of exposure (Bader & Phillips, 2002).

Vision is the least developed sense at birth. A newborn infant is extremely nearsighted, meaning they can see close objects more clearly than distant objects. The optimal viewing distance for the newborn is about 6 to 12 inches, the perfect distance for a nursing baby to focus easily on their mother's breast and face, which helps them learn to make eye contact (Brazelton & Cramer, 1990). It is worth noting that the breast is a perfect bull's eye. Regardless of skin tone, the nipple is a darker color, which helps the infant find their food source quickly.

The interaction between adults and infants seems to compensate naturally for the newborn's poor vision. When adults interact with very young infants, they almost always position themselves so that their face is about 8 to 12 inches away from the baby's face. Adults also have a strong natural tendency to exaggerate head movements and facial expressions, such as smiles and frowns, again making it easier for the baby to see them.

Physical Development

By the time infants begin crawling, at about seven to eight months of age, their view of the world, including distant objects, will be as clear as that of their parents. The increasing maturation of the infant's visual system reflects the development of their brain. At birth, their brain is an impressive 25 percent of its adult weight. In contrast, their birth weight is only about 5 percent of their eventual adult weight. During infancy, their brain will grow to about 75 percent of its adult weight, while their body weight will reach only about 20 percent of their adult weight.

During the prenatal period, the top of the body develops faster than the bottom. For example, the head develops before the legs. If you've ever watched a three-month-old baby

MYTH ▶ SCIENCE

Is it true that just a few hours after birth, infants already prefer their mothers to strangers?

Matteo Omied/Alamy Stock Photo

^ The Nearsighted Newborn Classic research by psychologist Robert Fantz and his colleagues (1962) showed that the newborn comes into the world very nearsighted, having approximately 20/300 vision. The newborn's ability to detect the contrast of object edges and boundaries is also poorly developed (Stephens & Banks, 1987). As this image illustrates, even by age three months, the infant's world is still pretty fuzzy.

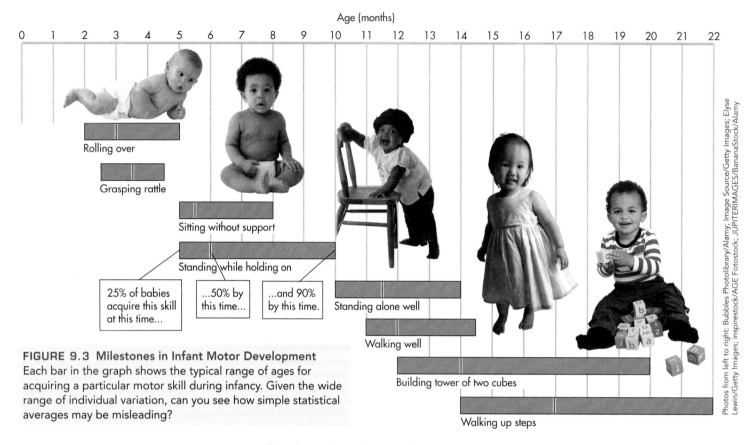

Age (months)

0 1 2 3 4 5 6 7 8 9 10 11 12 13 14 15 16 17 18 19 20 21 22

Rolling over

Grasping rattle

Sitting without support

Standing while holding on

25% of babies acquire this skill at this time...

...50% by this time...

...and 90% by this time.

Standing alone well

Walking well

Building tower of two cubes

Walking up steps

Photos from left to right: Bubbles Photolibrary/Alamy; Image Source/Getty Images; Elyse Lewin/Getty Images; inspirestock/AGE Fotostock; JUPITERIMAGES/BananaStock/Alamy

FIGURE 9.3 Milestones in Infant Motor Development
Each bar in the graph shows the typical range of ages for acquiring a particular motor skill during infancy. Given the wide range of individual variation, can you see how simple statistical averages may be misleading?

pulling themselves along the floor by their arms, you've probably noticed that an infant's motor skills also develop unevenly and follow the same general pattern. Motor skill development tends to follow a "top to bottom" sequence. The infant develops control over their head, chest, and arms before developing control over the lower part of their body (Kopp, 2011). Infants also develop motor control from the center of their bodies outward. They gain control of their abdomen before their elbows, knees, hands, or feet.

The basic *sequence* of motor skill development is universal, but the *average ages* can be a little deceptive (see **Figure 9.3**). As any parent knows, infants vary a great deal in the ages at which they master each skill. For example, virtually all infants are walking well by 15 months of age, but some infants will walk as early as 10 months. Each infant has their own timetable of physical maturation and developmental readiness to master different motor skills.

Social and Personality Development

From birth, forming close social and emotional relationships with caregivers is essential to the infant's physical and psychological well-being. Although physically helpless, the young infant does not play a passive role in forming these relationships. As you'll see in this section, the infant's individual traits play an important role in the development of the relationship between infant and caregiver.

Temperamental Qualities: Babies Are Different! Infants come into the world with very distinct and consistent behavioral styles. Some babies are consistently calm and easy to soothe. Other babies are fussy, irritable, and hard to comfort. Some babies are active and outgoing; others seem shy and wary of new experiences. Psychologists refer to these *inborn predispositions to consistently behave and react in a certain way* as an infant's **temperament**.

Interest in infant temperament was triggered by a classic longitudinal study launched in the 1950s by psychiatrists Alexander Thomas and Stella Chess. The focus of the study was on how temperamental qualities influence adjustment throughout life. Chess and Thomas rated young infants on a variety of characteristics, such as activity level, mood, regularity in sleeping and eating, and attention span. They found that about two-thirds of the babies could be classified into one of three broad temperamental patterns: *easy, difficult,* and *slow-to-warm-up.* The remaining third of the infants were characterized as *average* babies because they did not

temperament Inborn predispositions to consistently behave and react in a certain way.

fit neatly into one of these three categories (Thomas & Chess, 1977). Before we get into further description of these temperamental "types," it is important to understand that the descriptors are about behavior and not babies themselves. Babies who are described as "difficult" may need more soothing than "easy" babies, but all babies need emotional interaction with their caretakers that fits their temperament, something that even Thomas and Chess acknowledged in their later research (Thomas et al., 1982).

Easy babies readily adapt to new experiences, generally display positive moods and emotions, and have regular sleeping and eating patterns. *Difficult* babies tend to be intensely emotional, irritable and fussy, and prone to crying. They also tend to have irregular sleeping and eating patterns. *Slow-to-warm-up* babies have a low activity level, withdraw from new situations and people, and adapt to new experiences very gradually. After studying the same children from infancy through childhood, Thomas and Chess (1986) found that these broad patterns of temperamental qualities are remarkably stable.

❮ **Temperamental Patterns** Most babies can be categorized into one of three broad temperamental patterns. An "easy" baby is usually easy to soothe, calm, cheerful, and readily adaptable to new situations. "Slow-to-warm-up" babies tend to adapt to new situations and experiences very slowly, but once they adapt, they're fine. "Difficult" babies are more likely to be emotional, irritable, and fussy. It is important to understand that none of these temperament types are "bad" or "wrong." These words are descriptors that help the adults around infants understand an infant's needs, which we will discuss in greater detail in the section about attachment. Which category do you think the baby shown here might fit into? Why?

CULTURE AND HUMAN BEHAVIOR

Where Does the Baby Sleep?

In most U.S. families, infants sleep in their own beds (Mindell et al., 2010a). It may surprise you to discover that the United States is very unusual in this respect. In one survey of 100 societies, the United States was the *only one* in which babies slept in separate rooms. Another survey of 136 societies found that in two-thirds of the societies, infants slept in the same beds as their mothers. In the remainder, infants generally slept in the same room as their mothers (Huang et al., 2010; Morelli et al., 1992).

In one of the few in-depth studies of co-sleeping in different cultures, Gilda Morelli and her colleagues (1992) compared the sleeping arrangements of several middle-class U.S. families with those of Mayan families in a small town in Guatemala. They found that babies in the Mayan families slept with their mothers until they were two or three, usually until another baby was about to be born. At that point, toddlers moved to the bed of another family member, usually the father or an older sibling. Children continued to sleep with other family members throughout childhood. Co-sleeping can actually help infants learn to self-soothe, which then makes it easier for them to transition to sleeping alone (Barry, 2019).

When infants and toddlers sleep alone, bedtime marks a separation from their families. To ease the child's transition to sleeping, "putting the baby to bed" may involve bedtime rituals, including rocking, singing lullabies, or reading stories (Morrell & Steele, 2003). Small children take comforting items, such as a favorite blanket or teddy bear, to bed with them to ease the stressful transition to falling asleep alone.

In contrast, the Mayan babies did not take cuddly items to bed, and no special routines marked the transition between wakefulness and sleep. Mayan parents were puzzled by the very idea. Instead, the Mayan babies simply went to bed when their parents did or fell asleep in the middle of the family's social activities. Morelli and her colleagues (1992) found that the different sleeping customs of the U.S. and Mayan families reflect different cultural values. Some of the U.S. babies slept in the same room as their parents when they were first born, which the

⌃ **Culture and Co-Sleeping** Even in the United States, sleeping arrangements vary by racial and ethnic groups. Stephanie Milan and her colleagues (2007) found that Latino and Black preschoolers were more likely to sleep with a sibling or parent than were White preschoolers.

parents felt helped foster feelings of closeness and emotional security in the newborns (Barry, 2019). Nonetheless, most of the U.S. parents moved their babies to a separate room when they felt that the babies were ready to sleep alone, usually by the time they were three to six months of age. These parents explained their decision by saying that it was time for the baby to learn to be "independent" and "self-reliant."

In contrast, the Mayan parents felt that it was important to develop and encourage the infant's feelings of *interdependence* with other members of the family. Thus, in both Mayan and U.S. families, sleeping arrangements reflect cultural goals for child rearing and cultural values for relations among family members.

attachment The emotional bond that forms between an infant and caregiver(s), especially their parents.

More recently, researchers have examined the physiological basis of temperament. For example, after decades of research, Jerome Kagan (2010a, 2010b) classified temperament in terms of *reactivity. High-reactive* infants react intensely to new experiences, strangers, and novel objects. They tend to be tense, fearful, and inhibited. At the opposite pole are *low-reactive* infants, who tend to be calmer, uninhibited, and bolder. Sociable rather than shy, low-reactive infants are more likely to show interest than fear when exposed to new people, experiences, and objects.

Virtually all temperament researchers agree that individual differences in temperament have a genetic and biological basis (Gagne et al., 2009; Zentner & Shiner, 2012). However, researchers also agree that environmental experiences can modify a child's basic temperament (Stack et al., 2010). As Kagan (2004) points out, "Temperament is not destiny. Many experiences will affect high and low reactive infants as they grow up. Parents who encourage a more sociable, bold persona and discourage timidity will help their high reactive children develop a less-inhibited profile."

Because cultural attitudes affect child-rearing practices, infant temperament can also be affected by cultural beliefs (Kagan, 2010a, 2010b). For example, cross-cultural studies of temperament have found that infants who display temperamental characteristics related to shyness are treated with greater maternal approval and warmth in Eastern Asian and Latino cultures (Kim et al., 2008; Varela et al., 2009). That same temperamental style is seen as less desirable in Western cultures, however, and is often met with parental disappointment, rejection, and concern (Tani et al., 2014; van Zalk et al., 2011). Thus, the development of temperamental qualities is yet another example of the complex interaction among genetic and environmental factors.

Attachment: Forming Emotional Bonds Not long after World War II, Austrian psychiatrist Rene Spitz dramatically showed the detrimental effects of institutionalization on children who were deprived of a relationship with a warm, loving caregiver. Although provided with adequate nutrition, many infants failed to thrive. Psychologist **Harry Harlow** (1905–1981) showed that it wasn't just human children who suffered from the lack of care. Infant rhesus monkeys who were raised in isolation from other monkeys showed severe pathology such as repetitive and self-harming behaviors. When offered the choice between a wire figure holding bottled milk and a cloth-covered figure, the monkeys would cling to the cloth-covered figure even though it did not provide food. The conclusion: All primates, including human primates, seek out what Harlow (1958) termed *contact comfort* (see photo).

Harlow's findings helped stimulate research on the emotional bond that forms between infants and their caregivers during the first year of life. **Attachment** is *the emotional bond that forms between an infant and caregiver(s), especially their parents.* As conceptualized by attachment theorist John Bowlby (1969, 1988) and psychologist **Mary Ainsworth** (1979), attachment relationships serve important functions throughout infancy and, indeed, the lifespan. Ideally, the parent or caregiver functions as a *secure base* for the infant, providing a sense of comfort and security—a safe haven from which the infant can explore and learn about the environment. According to attachment theory, an infant's ability to thrive physically and psychologically depends in large part on the quality of attachment (Ainsworth et al., 1978).

Generally, when parents are consistently warm, responsive, and sensitive to their infant's needs, the infant develops a *secure attachment* to their parents (Belsky, 2006). The infant's expectation that their needs will be met by their caregivers is the most essential ingredient in forming a secure attachment to them. And, studies have confirmed that sensitivity to the infant's needs is associated with secure attachment across diverse cultures (van IJzendoorn & Sagi-Schwartz, 2008; Vaughn et al., 2007).

In contrast, *insecure attachment* may develop when an infant's parents are neglectful, inconsistent, or insensitive to their moods or behaviors. Insecure attachment seems to reflect an ambivalent or detached emotional relationship between an infant and their parents (Ainsworth, 1979; Isabella et al., 1989).

How do researchers measure attachment? The most commonly used procedure, called the *Strange Situation,* was devised by Ainsworth. The Strange Situation is typically used with infants who are between one and two years old (Ainsworth et al., 1978). In

Nina Leen/Getty Images

△ **The Importance of "Contact Comfort" in Infancy** Rhesus monkeys who were separated in infancy from their mothers preferred cloth mothers over wire mothers—even when the wire mothers provided nourishment through an attached feeding bottle. As U.S. psychologist Harry Harlow (1958) concluded, such findings demonstrated the importance of physical contact or "contact comfort" in infancy. (Such studies would be considered unethical and would not be allowed today.)

this technique, the baby and their mother are brought into an unfamiliar room with a variety of toys. A few minutes later, a stranger enters the room. The mother stays with the baby for a few moments and then departs, leaving the baby alone with the stranger. After a few minutes, the mother returns, spends a few minutes in the room, leaves, and returns again. Through a one-way window, observers record the infant's behavior throughout this sequence of separations and reunions.

Psychologists assess attachment by observing the child's behavior toward their mother during the Strange Situation procedure. When their mother is present, the *securely attached* baby will use her as a "secure base" from which to explore the new environment, periodically returning to her side. They will show distress when their mother leaves the room and will greet her warmly when she returns. A securely attached baby is easily soothed by their mother (Ainsworth et al., 1978; Lamb et al., 1985).

In contrast, an *insecurely attached* infant is less likely to explore the environment, even when their mother is present. In the Strange Situation, insecurely attached infants may appear either very anxious or completely indifferent. Such infants tend to ignore or avoid their mothers when they are present. Some insecurely attached infants become extremely distressed when their mothers leave the room. When insecurely attached infants are reunited with their mothers, they are hard to soothe and may resist their mothers' attempts to comfort them.

In studying attachment, psychologists have typically focused on the infant's bond with the mother, since the mother is often the infant's primary caregiver. Still, it's important to note that most fathers are also directly involved with the basic care of their infants and children. As is the case with mothers, children are more likely to be securely attached to fathers who are involved with their care and sensitive to their needs (Brown et al., 2012). In homes where both parents are present, children who are attached to one parent are usually also attached to the other (Furman & Simon, 2004). Finally, infants are capable of forming attachments to other consistent caregivers in their lives, such as relatives or workers at a day-care center. Thus, an infant can form *multiple* attachments.

The quality of attachment during infancy is associated with a variety of long-term effects (Bornstein, 2014; Groh et al., 2016). Preschoolers with a history of being securely attached tend to be more prosocial, empathic, and socially competent than are preschoolers with a history of insecure attachment (Rydell et al., 2005). Adolescents who were securely attached in infancy tend to have fewer problems, do better in school, and have more successful relationships with their peers than do adolescents who were insecurely attached in infancy (Laible, 2007; Sroufe, 2002; Sweeney, 2007). University students in Iran who reported secure attachments to their parents and friends were more likely to also report feeling empathy toward others and having an ability to understand another person's perspective (Teymoori & Shahrazad, 2012).

Because attachment in infancy seems to be so important, psychologists have extensively investigated the impact of day care on attachment. In a Critical Thinking box later in the chapter, we'll take a close look at this issue.

Mary Ainsworth (1913–1999) Best known for developing the *Strange Situation* procedure to measure attachment, Mary Ainsworth originated the concept of the *secure base*. She was also the first researcher in the United States to make extensive, systematic, naturalistic observations of mother–infant interactions in their own homes. Her findings often surprised contemporary psychologists. For example, Ainsworth provided the first evidence demonstrating the importance of the caregiver's responsiveness to the infant's needs (Bretherton & Main, 2000).

Dr. Patricia Crittenden

LWA/Dann Tardif/Getty Images

The Importance of Attachment Secure attachment in infancy forms the basis for emotional bonds in later childhood. At one time, attachment researchers focused only on the relationship between mothers and infants. Today, the importance of the attachment relationship between fathers and children is also recognized (Lucassen et al., 2011).

sensorimotor stage The first stage of cognitive development, from birth to about age 2, the period during which infants acquire knowledge through sensing and manipulating objects.

object permanence The understanding that an object continues to exist even when it can no longer be seen.

preoperational stage The second stage of cognitive development, which lasts from about age 2 to age 7, and is characterized by increasing use of symbols and prelogical thought processes.

symbolic thought The ability to use words, images, and symbols to represent the world.

Cognitive Development

■ KEY THEME

According to Piaget's theory, children progress through four distinct cognitive stages, and each stage marks a shift in how they think and understand the world.

≡ KEY QUESTIONS

- What are Piaget's four stages of cognitive development?
- What are three criticisms of Piaget's theory?
- How do Vygotsky's ideas about cognitive development differ from Piaget's theory?

Just as children advance in motor skill and language development, they also develop increasing sophistication in cognitive processes — thinking, remembering, and processing information. The most influential theory of cognitive development is that of Swiss psychologist **Jean Piaget**. Originally trained as a biologist, Piaget (1961) combined a boundless curiosity about the nature of the human mind with a gift for scientific observation (Boeree, 2006).

Piaget (1952, 1972) believed that children *actively* try to make sense of their environment rather than passively soaking up information about the world. To Piaget, many of the "cute" things children say actually reflect their sincere attempts to make sense of their world. Piaget was known to refer to children as "little scientists" who are naturally motivated to conduct experiments in order to explore and learn about their worlds. In fact, Piaget carefully observed his own three children in developing his theory and published three books about them (Boeree, 2006).

According to Piaget, children progress through four distinct cognitive stages: the *sensorimotor stage,* from birth to age 2; the *preoperational stage,* from age 2 to age 7; the *concrete operational stage,* from age 7 to age 11; and the *formal operational stage,* which begins during adolescence and continues into adulthood. As a child advances to a new stage, their thinking is *qualitatively different* from that of the previous stage. In other words, each new stage represents a fundamental shift in *how* the child thinks and understands the world.

Piaget saw cognitive development as more qualitative than quantitative. This means that as child develops and matures, they do not simply acquire more information. Rather, they develop a new understanding of the world in each progressive stage, building on the understandings acquired in the previous stage (Piaget, 1961). As the child *assimilates* new information and experiences, meaning that they add on to existing knowledge, they eventually change their way of thinking, meaning they acquire, or accommodate, new knowledge (Piaget, 1961).

Elie Bernager/Getty Images

> **This Tastes Different!** During the sensorimotor stage, infants and toddlers rely on their basic sensory and motor skills to explore and make sense of the world around them. Piaget believed that infants and toddlers acquire very practical understandings about the world as they touch, feel, taste, push, pull, twist, turn, and manipulate the objects they encounter.

Piaget (1971) believed that these stages were biologically programmed to unfold at their respective ages. He also believed that children in every culture progressed through the same sequence of stages at roughly similar ages. However, Piaget also recognized that hereditary and environmental differences could influence the rate at which a given child progressed through the stages.

The Sensorimotor Stage In Piaget's theory, the **sensorimotor stage** is *the first stage of cognitive development, from birth to about age 2, the period during which infants acquire knowledge about the world through actions that allow them to directly experience and manipulate objects.* Infants discover a wealth of very practical sensory knowledge, such as what objects look like and how they taste, feel, smell, and sound.

Infants in this stage also expand their practical knowledge about motor actions—reaching, grasping, pushing, pulling, and pouring. In the process, they gain a basic understanding of the effects their own actions can produce, such as pushing a button to turn on the television or knocking over a pile of blocks to make them crash and tumble.

At the beginning of the sensorimotor stage, the infant's motto seems to be "Out of sight, out of mind." An object exists only if they can directly sense it. For example, if a four-month-old infant knocks a ball underneath the couch and it rolls out of sight, they will not look for it. Piaget interpreted this response to mean that to the infant, the ball no longer exists.

However, by the end of the sensorimotor stage, children acquire a new cognitive understanding, called object permanence. **Object permanence** is *the understanding that an object continues to exist even if it can't be seen*. Now the infant will actively search for a ball that they have watched roll out of sight (Mash et al., 2006). Achieving object permanence reflects the ability to hold something in mind, a schema according to Piaget (Perry et al., 2008). This is a critical milestone in child development. The ability to hold schemas in mind forms the basis of working memory and the foundation of cognitive development. Research shows that recognizing object permanence is a product of frontal lobe maturation (Baird et al., 2002; Bell & Fox, 1992). This connection is not surprising, given that the frontal lobe is known for supporting and coordinating many aspects of cognition (see the neuroscience and behavior chapter for a review).

⌃ **Object Permanence** At the beginning of the sensorimotor stage, an object only "exists" for an infant if they can see it, as with this infant. If the infant's sister hides the toy, the toy will no longer exist for her younger sibling.

The Preoperational Stage In Piaget's theory, the **preoperational stage** is *the second stage of cognitive development, which lasts from about age 2 to age 7 and is characterized by increasing use of symbols and prelogical thought processes.* In Piaget's theory, the word *operations* refers to logical mental activities. Thus, the "preoperational" stage is a prelogical stage.

The hallmark of preoperational thought is the child's capacity to engage in symbolic thought. **Symbolic thought** refers to *the ability to use words, images, and symbols to represent the world*. One indication of the expanding capacity for symbolic thought is the child's impressive gains in language during this stage.

The child's increasing capacity for symbolic thought is also apparent in their use of fantasy and imagination while playing. A discarded box becomes a spaceship, a house, or a fort as children imaginatively take on the roles of different characters. Some children even create an imaginary companion (Taylor et al., 2009, 2013).

Still, the preoperational child's understanding of symbols remains immature. A two-year-old shown a picture of a flower, for example, may try to smell it. A young child may be puzzled by the notion that a map symbolizes an actual

❮ **Preoperational Thinking: Manipulating Mental Symbols** The young child's increasing capacity for symbolic thought is delightfully reflected in symbolic play and deferred imitation. In *symbolic play*, one object stands for another. A hairbrush can become a microphone. *Deferred imitation* is the capacity to repeat an action observed earlier, such as pretending to be a famous singer onstage.

egocentrism The inability to take another person's perspective or point of view.

irreversibility The inability to mentally reverse a sequence of events or logical operations.

centration The tendency to focus, or *center*, on only one aspect of a situation and ignore other important aspects of the situation.

conservation The understanding that two equal quantities remain equal even if the form or appearance is rearranged, as long as nothing is added or subtracted.

location. In short, preoperational children are still actively figuring out the relationship between symbols and the actual objects they represent.

The thinking of preoperational children often displays **egocentrism**, *the inability to take another person's perspective or point of view*. Thus, the young child genuinely thinks that Grandma would like a new Lego set or a video game for her upcoming birthday because that's what they want. Egocentric thought is also operating when the child silently nods their head in answer to Grandpa's question on the telephone.

The preoperational child's thought is also characterized by irreversibility and centration. In Piaget's theory, **irreversibility** is *the inability to take another person's perspective or point of view*. It means that the child cannot mentally reverse a sequence of events or logical operations back to the starting point. For example, if a child watches you flatten a ball of clay, they will not understand that the flattened clay could be easily rolled back into the ball seen at the beginning of the task. **Centration** refers to *the tendency to focus, or center, on only one aspect of a situation, and ignore other important aspects of the situation*.

The classic demonstration of both irreversibility and centration involves a task devised by Piaget. Ideally, you would want to find a five-year-old, two identical transparent containers, a third transparent container that is a different shape from the other two, and some colored liquid. Next, pour an equal amount of liquid into each container while your five-year-old friend watches. Now, make sure that the child agrees there is the same amount of liquid in each container. Then, while your pint-sized scientist is watching, pour the liquid from one container into a third container that is taller and thinner than the two identical containers. Now, ask the child if the two containers still have the same amount of liquid in them. Any preoperational child will insist—in spite of having watched you pour the same exact liquid from the original container—that the taller, thinner container "has more." You can try this experiment over and over with different containers. If the third container is taller or shorter than the original two containers, the preoperational child will insist that the amount of liquid has changed—even though they watched you pour it from its original container.

This classic demonstration illustrates the preoperational child's inability to understand conservation. The principle of **conservation** is *the understanding that two equal quantities remain equal even if the form or appearance is rearranged, as long as nothing is added or subtracted* (Piaget & Inhelder, 1974). Because of *centration,* the child cannot simultaneously consider the height and the width of the liquid in the container. Instead, the child focuses on only one aspect of the situation, the height of the liquid. And because of *irreversibility,* the child cannot cognitively reverse the series of events, mentally returning the poured liquid to its original container. Thus, they fail to understand that the two amounts of liquid are still the same.

▲ **Piaget's Conservation Task** A five-year-old compares the liquid in the two short glasses, then watches as liquid is poured into a tall, narrow glass. When asked which has more, the girl insists that there is more liquid in the tall glass. As Piaget's classic task demonstrates, the average five-year-old doesn't grasp this principle of conservation.

The Concrete Operational Stage In Piaget's theory, the **concrete operational stage** is *the third stage of cognitive development, which lasts from about age 7 to adolescence and characterized by the ability to think logically about concrete objects and situations.* Children are much less egocentric in their thinking, can reverse mental operations, and can focus simultaneously on two aspects of a problem. In short, they understand the principle of conservation. When presented with two rows of pennies, each row equally spaced, concrete operational children understand that the number of pennies in each row remains the same even when the spacing between the pennies in one row is increased or decreased.

As the name of this stage implies, thinking and use of logic tend to be limited to concrete reality—to tangible objects and events. Children in the concrete operational stage often have difficulty thinking logically about hypothetical situations or abstract ideas. For example, an eight-year-old will explain the concept of friendship in very tangible terms, such as "Friendship is when someone plays with me." In effect, the concrete operational child's ability to deal with abstract ideas and hypothetical situations is limited to their personal experiences and actual events.

The Formal Operational Stage In Piaget's theory, the **formal operational stage** is *the fourth stage of cognitive development, which lasts from adolescence through adulthood and is characterized by thinking logically about abstract principles and hypothetical situations.* In terms of problem solving, the formal operational adolescent is much more systematic and logical than the concrete operational child (Kuhn & Franklin, 2006). Formal operational thought reflects the ability to think logically even when dealing with abstract concepts or hypothetical situations (Kuhn, 2008; Piaget, 1972; Piaget & Inhelder, 1958). In contrast to the concrete operational child, the formal operational adolescent explains *friendship* by emphasizing more global and abstract characteristics, such as mutual trust, empathy, loyalty, consistency, and shared beliefs (Harter, 1990).

But, like the development of cognitive abilities during infancy and childhood, formal operational thought emerges as a unique stage. However, unlike other stages, formal operational thought continues to increase in sophistication throughout adolescence and adulthood. Although an adolescent may deal effectively with abstract ideas in one domain of knowledge, their thinking may not reflect the same degree of sophistication in other areas. Piaget (1973) acknowledged that even among many adults, formal operational thinking is often limited to areas in which they have developed expertise or a special interest. **Table 9.2** summarizes Piaget's stages of cognitive development.

Criticisms of Piaget's Theory Piaget's theory has inspired hundreds, if not thousands, of research studies, and he is considered one of the most important scientists of the 20th century (Perret-Clermont & Barrelet, 2008). Generally, scientific research has supported Piaget's most fundamental idea: that infants, young children, and older children use distinctly different cognitive abilities to construct their understanding of the world. However, other aspects of Piaget's theory have been challenged.

Criticism 1: Piaget underestimated the cognitive abilities of infants and young children. To test for object permanence, Piaget would show an infant an object, cover it with a cloth, and then observe whether the infant tried to reach under the cloth for the object. Using this procedure, Piaget found that it wasn't until an infant was about nine months old that they behaved as if the object continued to exist after it was hidden.

But what if the infant "knew" that the object was under the cloth but simply lacked the physical coordination to reach for it? How could you test this hypothesis? Rather than using manual tasks to assess object permanence and other cognitive abilities,

concrete operational stage The third stage of cognitive development, which lasts from about age 7 to adolescence and is characterized by the ability to think logically about concrete objects and situations.

formal operational stage The fourth stage of cognitive development, which lasts from adolescence through adulthood and is characterized by thinking logically about abstract principles and hypothetical situations.

THINK LIKE A **SCIENTIST**

Children's cognition is also affected by environmental factors. For example, what classroom decor better helps kindergarten students learn? Go to Achieve Resources to **Think Like a Scientist** about **Learning Environments.**

 Achieve

 Achieve

Worth Publishers

Do differences in reasoning mark different stages of development? Go to **Achieve** and watch **Video: Cognitive Development.**

TABLE 9.2

Piaget's Stages of Cognitive Development

Stage	Characteristics of the Stage	Major Change of the Stage
Sensorimotor (0–2 years)	Acquires understanding of object permanence. First understandings of cause-and-effect relationships.	Development proceeds from reflexes to active use of sensory and motor skills to explore the environment.
Preoperational (2–7 years)	Symbolic thought emerges. Language development occurs (2–4 years). Thought and language both tend to be egocentric. Cannot solve conservation problems.	Development proceeds from understanding simple cause-and-effect relationships to prelogical thought processes involving the use of imagination and symbols to represent objects, actions, and situations.
Concrete operations (7–11 years)	Reversibility attained. Can solve conservation problems. Logical thought develops and is applied to concrete problems. Cannot solve complex verbal problems and hypothetical problems.	Development proceeds from prelogical thought to logical solutions to concrete problems.
Formal operations (adolescence through adulthood)	Logically solves all types of problems. Thinks scientifically. Solves complex verbal and hypothetical problems. Is able to think in abstract terms.	Development proceeds from logical solving of concrete problems to logical solving of all classes of problems, including abstract problems.

Renée Baillargeon developed a method based on *visual* tasks. Baillargeon's research is based on the premise that infants, like adults, will look longer at "surprising" events that appear to contradict their understanding of the world (Baillargeon et al., 2011, 2012).

Figure 9.4 shows a classic test of object permanence (Baillargeon & DeVos, 1991). Studies like this one demonstrated that children displayed object permanence as young as two and a half months of age, more than six months earlier than the age at which Piaget believed infants first showed evidence of object permanence.

Piaget's discoveries laid the groundwork for our understanding of cognitive development. However, as developmental psychologists Jeanne Shinskey and Yuko Munakata (2005) observe, today's researchers recognize that "what infants appear to know depends heavily on how they are tested."

Criticism 2: Piaget underestimated the impact of the social and cultural environment on cognitive development. In contrast to Piaget, the Russian psychologist **Lev Vygotsky** (1896–1934) believed that cognitive development is strongly influenced by social and cultural factors. Vygotsky formulated his theory of cognitive development at about the same time Piaget formulated his. However, Vygotsky's writings did not become available in the West until many years after his untimely death at age 38 from tuberculosis in 1934 (Rowe & Wertsch, 2002; van Geert, 1998).

Vygotsky agreed with Piaget that children may be able to reach a particular cognitive level through their own efforts. However, Vygotsky (1978, 1987) argued that

FIGURE 9.4 Testing Object Permanence in Babies How can you test object permanence in infants who are too young to reach for a hidden object? Three-and-a-half-month-old infants initially watched a possible event: The short carrot passes from one side of the panel to the other without appearing in the window. In the impossible event, the tall carrot does the same. Because the infants are surprised and look longer at the impossible event, Baillargeon and DeVos (1991) concluded that the infants had formed a mental representation of the existence, height, and path of each carrot as it moved behind the panel—the essence of object permanence (Baillargeon, 2004).

Possible Event   Impossible Event

children are able to attain higher levels of cognitive development through the support and instruction that they receive from other people. Researchers have confirmed that social interactions, especially with older children and adults, play a significant role in a child's cognitive development (Psaltis et al., 2009; Wertsch, 2008). Not surprisingly, it has also been shown that the social "boost" that benefits children is maximally effective when it is culturally specific (Taber, 2020). This is emphasized in the way that Vygostky's approach describes the child as a "little apprentice."

An important idea here was the notion of the **zone of proximal development**, *Vygotsky's theory about the gap between what children can accomplish on their own and what they can accomplish with the help of others who are more competent* (Holzman, 2009). Note that the word *proximal* means "nearby," indicating that the assistance provided goes just slightly beyond the child's current abilities. Such guidance can help "stretch" the child's cognitive abilities to new levels.

Cross-cultural studies have shown that cognitive development is strongly influenced by the skills that are valued and encouraged in a particular environment, such as the ability to weave, hunt, or collaborate with others (Saxe & de Kirby, 2014; Wells, 2009). Such findings suggest that Piaget's stages are not as universal and culture-free as some researchers had once believed (Cole & Packer, 2011).

Criticism 3: Piaget overestimated the degree to which people achieve formal operational thought processes. Researchers have found that many adults display abstract-hypothetical thinking only in limited areas of knowledge and that some adults never display formal operational thought processes at all (see Kuhn, 2008; Molitor & Hsu, 2011). University students, for example, may not display formal operational thinking when given problems outside their major, as when a philosophy major is presented with a physics problem (DeLisi & Staudt, 1980). Late in his life, Piaget (1972, 1973) suggested that formal operational thinking might not be a universal phenomenon but, instead, is the product of an individual's expertise in a specific area.

Rather than distinct stages of cognitive development, some developmental psychologists emphasize the **information-processing model of cognitive development**, a *model that views cognitive development as a process that is continuous over the lifespan and that studies the development of basic mental processes such as attention, memory, and problem solving* (Courage & Howe, 2002; Craik & Bialystok, 2006; Munakata et al., 2006). Through life experiences, we continue to acquire new knowledge, including more sophisticated cognitive skills and strategies. In turn, this improves our ability to process, learn, and remember information.

With the exceptions that have been noted, Piaget's observations of the changes in children's cognitive abilities are fundamentally accurate. His description of the distinct cognitive changes that occur during infancy and childhood ranks as one of the most important contributions to developmental psychology.

Adolescence

■ KEY THEME
Adolescence is the stage that marks the transition from childhood to adulthood.

= KEY QUESTIONS
- What factors affect the timing of puberty?
- What characterizes adolescent relationships with parents and peers?
- What is Erikson's psychosocial theory of lifespan development?

Adolescence is *the transitional stage between late childhood and the beginning of adulthood, during which sexual maturity is reached*. Although it can vary by individual, culture, and gender, adolescence usually begins around age 11 or 12. It is a transition marked by sweeping physical, social, and cognitive changes as the individual moves toward independence and adult responsibilities. Outwardly, the most noticeable changes that occur during adolescence are the physical changes that accompany the development of sexual

zone of proximal development Vygotsky's theory about the gap between what children can accomplish on their own and what they can accomplish with the help of others who are more competent.

information-processing model of cognitive development Model that views cognitive development as a process that is continuous over the lifespan and that studies the development of basic mental processes such as attention, memory, and problem solving.

adolescence The transitional stage between late childhood and the beginning of adulthood, during which sexual maturity is reached.

maturity. We'll begin by considering those changes, then turn to the aspects of social development during adolescence. Following that discussion, we'll consider some of the cognitive changes of adolescence, including identity formation.

Physical and Sexual Development

Nature seems to have a warped sense of humor when it comes to **puberty**, *the stage of adolescence in which an individual reaches sexual maturity and becomes physiologically capable of sexual reproduction.* As you may well remember, physical development during adolescence sometimes proceeds unevenly. Feet and hands get bigger before legs and arms do. The torso typically develops last, so hoodies sometimes don't fit quite right. And the left and right sides of the body can grow at different rates. References to being "awkward" abound when it comes to adolescence. It is a time when different portions of the body, brain, and behavior are all changing at different rates. It is easy to think of the awkward physical changes that are part of adolescence, but it is equally important to remember that there are changes in behavior (and the underlying brain networks that support adolescent behavior) that are happening at the same time. Although this makes a lot of sense in terms of development, it can be confusing to the adolescent and those around them.

Although nature's game plan for physical change during adolescence may seem haphazard, puberty actually tends to follow a predictable sequence for each sex. These changes are summarized in **Table 9.3**.

Primary and Secondary Sex Characteristics   The physical changes of puberty fall into two categories. Internally, puberty involves the development of the **primary sex characteristics**, which are the *sex organs that are directly involved in reproduction.* For example, the female's uterus and the male's testes enlarge in puberty. Externally, adolescents also develop **secondary sex characteristics**, *sexual characteristics that develop during puberty and are not directly involved in reproduction but differentiate between the sexes.* Secondary sex characteristics include changes in height, weight, and body shape; the appearance of body hair and voice changes; and, in girls, breast development.

As you can see in Table 9.3, females are typically about two years ahead of males in terms of physical and sexual maturation. For example, *the period of accelerated growth*

▲ **Girls Get a Head Start** These two eighth-graders are the same age! In terms of the progress of sexual and physical maturation, girls are usually about two years ahead of boys.

Dennis MacDonald/PhotoEdit

puberty The stage of adolescence in which an individual reaches sexual maturity and becomes physiologically capable of sexual reproduction.

primary sex characteristics Sex organs that are directly involved in reproduction.

secondary sex characteristics Sexual characteristics that develop during puberty and are not directly involved in reproduction but differentiate between the sexes.

TABLE 9.3

The Typical Sequence of Puberty

Girls	Average Age	Boys	Average Age
Ovaries increase production of estrogen and progesterone.	9	Testes increase production of testosterone.	10
Internal sex organs begin to grow larger.	9½	External sex organs begin to grow larger.	11
Breast development begins.	10	Production of sperm and first ejaculation	13
Peak height spurt	12	Peak height spurt	14
Peak muscle and organ growth, including widening of hips	12½	Peak muscle and organ growth, including broadening of shoulders	14½
Menarche (first menstrual period)	12½	Voice lowers.	15
First ovulation (release of fertile egg)	13½	Facial hair appears.	16

Source: Data from Brooks-Gunn & Reiter (1990).

during puberty, involving rapid increases in height and weight, is called the **adolescent growth spurt**. It occurs about two years earlier in females than in males.

The statistical averages in Table 9.3 are informative, but—because they are only averages—they cannot convey the normal range of individual variation in the timing of pubertal events (see Ellis, 2004). For example, *a female's first menstrual period, which occurs during puberty*, termed **menarche**, typically occurs around age 12 or 13, but menarche may take place as early as age 9 or 10 or as late as age 16 or 17 (Biro et al., 2018). For boys, the testicles typically begin enlarging around age 11 or 12, but the process can begin before age 9 or after age 14 (Kahn, 2019).

Thus, it's entirely possible for some adolescents to have already completed physical and sexual maturation before their classmates have even begun puberty. Yet they would all be considered well within the normal age range for puberty (Sun et al., 2002).

Less obvious than the outward changes associated with puberty are the sweeping changes occurring in another realm of physical development: the adolescent's brain. We discuss these developments in the Focus on Neuroscience.

Factors Affecting the Timing of Puberty Although you might be tempted to think that the onset of puberty is strictly a matter of biological programming, researchers have found that both genetic and environmental factors play a role in the timing of puberty (Zhu et al., 2018). Genetic evidence includes the observation that girls usually experience menarche at about the same age their mothers did (Ersoy et al., 2005). And, not surprisingly, the timing of pubertal changes tends to be closer for identical twins than for nontwin siblings (Mustanski et al., 2004).

Environmental factors, such as nutrition and health, also influence the onset of puberty. Generally, well-nourished and healthy children begin puberty earlier than do children who have experienced serious health problems or inadequate nutrition. As living standards and health care have improved, the average age of puberty has steadily been decreasing in many countries over the past century. For example, 150 years ago the average age of menarche in the United States and other developed countries was about 17 years old. Today it is about 13 years old. Boys, too, are beginning the physical changes of puberty about a year earlier today than they did in the 1960s (Irwin, 2005).

Body size, nutrition, and degree of physical activity are also related to the timing of puberty (Aksglaede et al., 2009; Cheng et al., 2012). In general, heavier children and those with poorer dietary habits begin puberty earlier than do lean children and those who tend to eat healthier food. Girls who are involved in physically demanding athletic activities where their body size tends to be below average, such as gymnastics, figure skating, dancing, and competitive running, can experience delays in menarche of up to two years beyond the average age (Brooks-Gunn, 1988; Georgopoulos et al., 2004).

Interestingly, the timing of puberty is also influenced by the absence of the biological father in the home. Several studies have found that girls, and to a lesser extent boys, raised in homes in which the biological father is absent tend to experience puberty earlier than children raised in homes where the father is present (Bogaert, 2005, 2008; Gaml-Sørensen et al., 2021; Neberich et al., 2010).

Why would the absence of a father affect the timing of puberty? A stressful home environment may play a role (Gaml-Sørensen et al., 2021). In families marked by marital conflict and strife, girls enter puberty earlier, regardless of whether the father remains or leaves (Saxbe & Repetti, 2009). In general, negative and stressful family environments are associated with an earlier onset of puberty, whereas positive family environments are associated with later physical development (Ellis & Essex, 2007; James et al., 2012).

Effects of Early Versus Late Maturation Adolescents tend to be keenly aware of the physical changes they are experiencing as well as of the *timing* of those changes compared with their peer group. Most adolescents are "on time," meaning that the maturational changes are occurring at roughly the same time for them as for others in their peer group.

adolescent growth spurt The period of accelerated growth during puberty, involving rapid increases in height and weight.

menarche (meh-NAR-kee) A female's first menstrual period, which occurs during puberty.

🧠 FOCUS ON NEUROSCIENCE

The Adolescent Brain: A Work in Progress

For many adolescents, the teenage years, especially the early ones, seem to seesaw between moments of exhilaration and exasperation. Impressive instances of insightful behavior are counterbalanced by impulsive decisions made with little or no consideration of the potential risks or consequences. Much of the erratic and risky behavior that characterizes adolescence can be better understood by taking a closer look at the still developing adolescent brain (Giedd, 2008; Casey, 2015).

To track changes in the adolescent brain, neuroscientists Jay Giedd, B. J. Casey, Elizabeth Sowell, and their colleagues have used MRI to repeatedly scan the brains of typical children and teenagers. One striking insight produced by their studies is that the human brain goes through not one but two distinct spurts of brain development—one during prenatal development and one during late childhood just prior to puberty (Giedd, 2008; Gogtay et al., 2004; Lenroot & Giedd, 2006).

Earlier in the chapter, we described how new neurons are produced at an astonishing rate during the first months of prenatal development. By the sixth month of prenatal development, there is a vast overabundance of neurons in the fetal brain. During infancy and early childhood, the brain's outer gray matter continues to develop and grow. The tapestry of interconnections between neurons becomes much more intricate as dendrites and axon terminals multiply and branch to extend their reach. White matter also increases as groups of neurons develop myelin, the white, fatty covering that insulates some axons, speeding communication between neurons.

Outwardly, these brain changes are reflected in the increasing cognitive and physical capabilities of the child. The key to understanding how the brain develops after childhood comes down to two simple ideas: (1) "use it or lose it" and (2) "It gets better with practice." As the brain develops, circuits that are regularly used stay, while circuits that are not used get pruned. These regularly used circuits support progressively complicated behavior that is part of maturing, so they need to communicate with increasing numbers of brain regions. As with any new skill, these communications can be awkward at first and require a lot of energy. Over time, however, the circuits become refined and increasingly nimble. As the brain becomes more coordinated, it also becomes more structurally efficient, meaning that you require less to do more. As an analogy, when you are first learning to ride a bike, you need to focus all your energy and attention on balancing, pedaling, and steering properly. Once you become proficient at riding a bike, however, you can talk, sightsee, and (should you choose) learn to do cool tricks on your bike. This is not all that different from brain development.

By six years of age, the child's brain is about 95 percent of its adult size. The longitudinal MRI studies of typical children and adolescents have shown that a second wave of gray matter overproduction occurs just prior to puberty. This late childhood surge of cortical gray matter is not due to the production of new neurons. Rather, the size, complexity, and connections among neurons all increase. This increase in gray matter peaks at about age 11 for girls and age 12 for boys (Toga et al., 2006). And this surge is followed by a second round of pruning neurons during the teenage years (Gerber et al., 2009; Toga et al., 2006).

The color-coded series of brain images below shows the course of brain development from ages 5 to 20 (Gogtay et al., 2004). Red and yellow indicate more gray matter; blue and purple indicate less gray matter.

The MRI images reveal that as the brain matures, neuronal connections are pruned and gray matter diminishes in a back-to-front wave—

Courtesy of the authors

⌃ Effects of Early Versus Late Maturation As anyone who remembers seventh-grade gym class can attest, the timing of puberty varies widely. Early maturation can have different effects for boys and girls. Early-maturing boys tend to be successful in athletics and popular with their peers, but they are more susceptible to risky behaviors, such as drug, alcohol, or steroid use (McCabe & Ricciardelli, 2004). Early-maturing girls tend to have more negative feelings about the arrival of puberty and body changes, have higher rates of teenage pregnancy, and may be embarrassed or harassed by unwanted attention from older males (Adair & Gordon-Larsen, 2001; Ge et al., 2003; Grower et al., 2019).

However, for some adolescents, maturation may be out of sync with their peers, experiencing the visible byproducts of puberty noticeably earlier or later than the majority of their peers. Generally speaking, off-time maturation is stressful for both boys and girls, who may experience teasing, social isolation, and exclusion from social activities (Conley & Rudolph, 2009).

Being off-time has different effects for girls and boys. Girls who develop early and boys who develop late are most likely to have problems. For example, early-maturing girls tend to be more likely than late-maturing girls to have negative feelings about their body image and pubertal changes, such as menarche (Ge et al., 2003; Copeland et al., 2019). Compared to late-maturing girls, early-maturing girls are less likely to have received factual information concerning development. They may also feel embarrassed by unwanted attention from older males (Brooks-Gunn & Reiter, 1990; Grower et al., 2019). Early-maturing girls also have higher rates of sexual risk taking, drug and alcohol use, and delinquent behavior, and are at greater risk for unhealthy weight gain later in life (Adair & Gordon-Larsen, 2001; Belsky et al., 2010).

Early maturation can be advantageous for boys, but it is also associated with risks. Early-maturing boys tend to be popular with their peers. However, although they are more successful in athletics than late-maturing peers, they are also more susceptible to behaviors that put their health at risk, such as steroid use (McCabe & Ricciardelli, 2004).

with the frontal lobes maturing last. As pruning occurs, the connections that remain are strengthened and reinforced, and this is reflected by the steady increases in the amount of white matter in the brain (Giedd, 2009; Schmithorst & Yuan, 2010). The enormous growth and improved coordination of the frontal lobes is the cornerstone of the relationship between neural and behavioral maturation during adolescence. As we have talked about in previous chapters, the mature prefrontal cortex is essential for a number of critical behaviors, including impulse control, judgment, problem solving, and socialization. Importantly, this region of the brain is not fully mature until the conclusion of adolescence. The prolonged development and organization of the prefrontal cortex throughout adolescence provides the brain-based scaffolding for the changes in both thinking and feeling that make adult behavior possible. Mature behavior is both produced and regulated by the prefrontal cortex. Given the immensity of change that takes place during adolescence, it makes sense that the prefrontal cortex waits to fully mature in order to accommodate the cognitive and behavioral demands placed on adolescents.

Basically, the frontal lobe is what makes us humans as a species and individuals in our own worlds.

And when does the prefrontal cortex reach full maturity? According to the MRI studies, not until people reach their mid-twenties (Bennett & Baird, 2006; Gogtay et al., 2004). This suggests that an adolescent's occasional impulsive or immature behavior is at least partly a reflection of a brain that still has a long way to go to reach full adult maturity (Casey, 2013; Casey & Caudle, 2013). During early adolescence, hormonal changes drive increased activity in the limbic system, resulting in a significant increase in emotionality and impulsivity. These changes are functional in that they motivate adolescents to try new things, explore, and learn about their worlds. Remember, however, that the parts of the brain responsible for exercising judgment are still maturing (Luna et al., 2013). The result is a "mismatch" between behavioral drives and the ability to regulate them that is thought to produce a lot of the impulsive, unpredictable—and often risky behaviors for which adolescents are known (Steinberg, 2010).

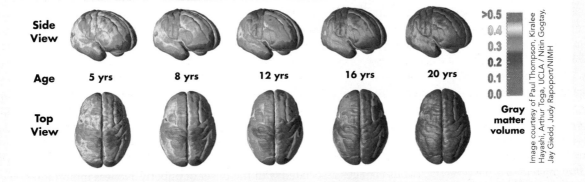

Early-maturing boys are also more prone to feelings of depression, problems at school, and drug or alcohol use (see Hayatbakhsh et al., 2009; Mendle & Ferrero, 2012).

Social Development

The changes in adolescents' bodies are accompanied by changes in their social interactions, most notably with parents and peers. Contrary to what many people think, parent–adolescent relationships are generally positive. In fact, most teenagers report that they admire their parents and turn to them for advice (Steinberg, 1990, 2001; Branje, 2018). As a general rule, when parent–child relationships have been good before adolescence, they continue to be relatively smooth during adolescence. Adolescents who perceive their relationships with their parents as being warm and supportive have higher self-esteem and are most likely to follow their parents' guidance and stay out of trouble (Branje, 2018; Fosco et al., 2012; McElhaney et al., 2008). However, some friction seems to be inevitable as children make the transition to adolescence. And, many developmental psychologists view the increased conflict in early and middle adolescence as healthy, a necessary stage in the adolescent's development of increased autonomy.

Although parents remain influential throughout adolescence, relationships with friends and peers become increasingly important (Albert et al., 2013; Somerville, 2013). Adolescents usually encounter greater diversity among their peers as they make the transitions to middle school and high school. To a much greater degree than during childhood, the adolescent's social network, social context, and community influence their values, norms, and expectations. It is also worth noting that this shift in where

MYTH ◀ SCIENCE

Is it true that most adolescents have poor relationships with their parents?

adolescents get their information is functional: Most teenagers will join the social worlds of their peers rather than their parents.

Susceptibility to peer influence peaks during early adolescence (Dishion & Tipsord, 2011). As they grow older, adolescents' maturation helps them better attend to the information that is most functional for their development. Most often, the best information comes from both peers and parents. (Cook et al., 2009; Sumter et al., 2009).

Parents often worry that peer influences will lead to undesirable behavior, but researchers have found that peer relationships tend to *reinforce* the traits and goals that parents fostered during childhood (Steinberg, 2001). Peers can also influence one another in positive ways (Allen et al., 2008). Friends often exert pressure on one another to study, earn good grades, attend university, and engage in prosocial behaviors. This positive influence is especially true for peers who are strong students (Cook et al., 2007).

Romantic and sexual relationships also become increasingly important throughout the adolescent years. One national survey showed that by the age of 12, about one-quarter of adolescents reported having had a "special romantic relationship," although not necessarily a relationship that included sexual intimacy. By age 15, that percentage increased to 50 percent, and reached 70 percent by the age of 18 (Connolly & McIsaac, 2009).

Social and cultural factors influence when, why, and how adolescents engage in romantic and sexual behaviors. The beginning of dating, for example, coincides more strongly with cultural and social expectations and norms, such as when friends begin to date, than with an adolescent's degree of physical maturation (see Collins, 2003). In fact, there are stark cultural differences in the age at which adolescents begin to date. For example, 80 percent of Israeli 14-year-olds report some type of dating, as compared to only 50 percent of North Americans of the same age (Connolly & McIsaac, 2009).

The physical and social developments we've discussed so far are the more obvious changes associated with the onset of puberty. No less important, however, are the changes related to cognition and identity formation that allow the adolescent to think and reason in new, more complex ways.

⌃ Peer Relationships in Adolescence Although parents often worry about the negative impact of peers, peers can also have a positive influence on one another. These boys from Memphis, Tennessee, volunteered to clean up their community during an annual event, the Martin Luther King Servathon.

Identity Formation: Erikson's Theory of Psychosocial Development

When psychologists talk about **identity,** they are referring to *a person's sense of self, including their memories, experiences, and the values and beliefs that guide their behavior*. Our sense of personal identity gives us an integrated and continuing sense of self over time.

Identity formation is a process that continues throughout the lifespan. As we embrace new and different roles over the course of our lives, we define ourselves in new and different ways (Erikson et al., 1986; McAdams & Olson, 2010).

For the first time in the lifespan, the adolescent possesses the cognitive skills necessary for dealing with identity issues in a meaningful way (Sebastian et al., 2008). Beginning in early adolescence, self-definition shifts. Preadolescent children tend to describe themselves in very concrete social and behavioral terms, reflecting Piaget's theory of cognitive development. An eight-year-old might describe themselves by saying, "I play with Mark, and I like to ride my bike." In contrast, adolescents use more abstract self-descriptions that reflect personal attributes, values, beliefs, and goals (Phillips, 2008). Thus, a 14-year-old might say, "I have strong religious beliefs, love animals, and hope to become a veterinarian."

Some aspects of personal identity involve characteristics over which the adolescent really has no control, such as gender, race, ethnic background, and socioeconomic level. For most people and for most of these characteristics, these identity characteristics are fixed and already internalized by the time an individual reaches the adolescent years.

identity A person's sense of self, including their memories, experiences, and the values and beliefs that guide their behavior.

Beyond such fixed characteristics, the adolescent begins to evaluate themselves on several different dimensions. Social acceptance by peers, academic and athletic abilities, work abilities, personal appearance, and romantic appeal are some important aspects of self-definition. Another challenge facing the adolescent is to develop an identity that is independent of their parents while retaining a sense of connection to their family. Thus, the adolescent has not one but several self-concepts that they must integrate into a coherent and unified whole to answer the question, "Who am I?"

The adolescent's task of achieving an integrated identity is one important aspect of psychoanalyst **Erik Erikson's** (1902–1994) influential theory of psychosocial development. Briefly, Erikson (1968) proposed that each of eight stages of life is associated with a particular psychosocial conflict that can be resolved in either a positive or a negative direction (see **Table 9.4**). Relationships with others play an important role in determining the outcome of each conflict. According to Erikson, the key psychosocial conflict facing adolescents is *identity versus role confusion.*

To successfully form an identity, adolescents must not only integrate various dimensions of their personality into a coherent whole but also define the roles that they will adopt within the larger society on becoming an adult (Bohn & Berntsen, 2008). To accomplish this, adolescents grapple with a wide variety of issues, such as selecting a potential career and formulating religious, moral, and political beliefs. They must also adopt social

∧ **Identity Formation** It is during adolescence that we develop an integrated sense of self and interest in future adult roles. For example, a love of animals might translate into a desire to one day become a veterinarian. This identity formation is a process that continues throughout the lifespan.

TABLE 9.4

Erik Erikson's Psychosocial Stages of Development

Life Stage	Psychosocial Conflict	Positive Resolution	Negative Resolution
Infancy (birth to 18 months)	Trust vs. mistrust	Reliance on consistent and warm caregivers produces a sense of predictability and trust in the environment.	Physical and psychological neglect by caregivers leads to fear, anxiety, and mistrust of the environment.
Toddlerhood (18 months to 3 years)	Autonomy vs. doubt	Caregivers encourage independence and self-sufficiency, promoting positive self-esteem.	Overly restrictive caregiving leads to self-doubt in abilities and low self-esteem.
Early childhood (3 to 6 years)	Initiative vs. guilt	The child learns to initiate activities and develops a sense of social responsibility concerning the rights of others; promotes self-confidence.	Parental overcontrol stifles the child's spontaneity, sense of purpose, and social learning; promotes guilt and fear of punishment.
Middle and late childhood (6 to 12 years)	Industry vs. inferiority	Through experiences with parents and "keeping up" with peers, the child develops a sense of pride and competence in schoolwork and home and social activities.	Negative experiences with parents or failure to "keep up" with peers leads to pervasive feelings of inferiority and inadequacy.
Adolescence	Identity vs. role confusion	Through experimentation with different roles, the adolescent develops an integrated and stable self-definition; forms commitments to future adult roles.	An apathetic adolescent or one who experiences pressures and demands from others may feel confusion about their identity and role in society.
Young adulthood	Intimacy vs. isolation	By establishing lasting and meaningful relationships, the young adult develops a sense of connectedness and intimacy with others.	Because of fear of rejection or excessive self-preoccupation, the young adult is unable to form close, meaningful relationships and becomes psychologically isolated.
Middle adulthood	Generativity vs. stagnation	Through child rearing, caring for others, productive work, and community involvement, the adult expresses unselfish concern for the welfare of the next generation.	Self-indulgence, self-absorption, and a preoccupation with one's own needs lead to a sense of stagnation, boredom, and a lack of meaningful accomplishments.
Late adulthood	Ego integrity vs. despair	In reviewing their life, the older adult experiences a strong sense of self-acceptance and meaningfulness in their accomplishments.	In looking back on their life, the older adult experiences regret, dissatisfaction, and disappointment about their life and accomplishments.

Source: Research from Erikson (1964a).

moral reasoning The aspect of cognitive development that has to do with how an individual reasons about moral decisions.

roles involving interpersonal relationships, sexuality, and long-term commitments such as marriage and parenthood (Kerpelman & Pittman, 2018).

In Erikson's (1968) theory, the adolescent's path to successful identity achievement begins with *role confusion,* which is characterized by little sense of commitment on any of these issues. This period is followed by a *moratorium period,* during which the adolescent experiments with different roles, values, and beliefs. Gradually, by choosing among the alternatives and making commitments, the adolescent arrives at an *integrated identity.*

The Development of Moral Reasoning

The aspect of cognitive development that has to do with how an individual reasons about moral decisions is **moral reasoning**. Adolescents and adults often face moral decisions on difficult interpersonal and social issues (Hart, 2005). What is the right thing to do at a given time and place? How is the best possible outcome achieved for all? The adolescent's increased capacities to think abstractly, imagine hypothetical situations, and compare ideals to the real world all affect their thinking about moral issues (Baird, 2007; Kagan & Sinnott-Armstrong, 2007; Turiel, 2010).

The most influential theory of moral development was proposed by **Lawrence Kohlberg** (1927–1987). Kohlberg's interest in moral development may have been triggered by his experiences as a young adult. Kohlberg (1976, 1984) used hypothetical moral dilemmas to investigate moral reasoning, such as whether a husband should steal a drug he could not afford to cure his dying wife. Kohlberg analyzed the responses of children, adolescents, and adults to such hypothetical moral dilemmas, focusing on the *reasoning* that they used to justify their answers rather than the answers themselves. He concluded that there are distinct *stages* of moral development. As with Piaget's stages of cognitive development, Kohlberg (1981) believed that moral development unfolded in an age-related, step-by-step fashion.

Kohlberg proposed three distinct *levels* of moral reasoning: *preconventional, conventional,* and *postconventional.* Each level is based on the degree to which a person conforms to conventional standards of society. Furthermore, each level has two *stages* that represent different degrees of sophistication in moral reasoning. **Table 9.5** describes the characteristics of the moral reasoning associated with each of Kohlberg's levels and stages.

Kohlberg's belief that the development of abstract thinking in adolescence naturally and invariably leads people to the formation of idealistic moral principles has not been supported. Only a few exceptional people display the philosophical ideals in Kohlberg's highest level of moral reasoning. In fact, because clear-cut expressions of "universal moral principles" were so rare, Kohlberg and his colleagues eventually cut stage 6 from the theory (Gibbs, 2003; Rest, 1983). The normal course of changes in moral reasoning for most people seems to be captured by Kohlberg's first four stages (Colby & Kohlberg, 1984). By adulthood, the predominant form of moral reasoning is conventional moral reasoning, reflecting the importance of social roles and rules.

Kohlberg's theory has been criticized on several grounds (see Krebs & Denton, 2005, 2006). Probably the most important criticism of Kohlberg's theory is that moral *reasoning* doesn't always predict moral *behavior* (Baird & Roellke, 2015). People don't necessarily respond to real-life dilemmas as they do to the hypothetical dilemmas that are used to test moral reasoning. Further, people can, and do, respond at different levels to different kinds of moral decisions. People are *flexible* in their real-world moral behavior: The goals that people pursue affect the types of moral judgments they make (Krebs & Denton, 2005).

Similarly, Kohlberg's theory is a theory of cognitive development, focusing on the type of conscious reasoning that people use to make moral decisions. However, moral decisions in the real world are often affected by nonrational processes, such as emotional responses, custom, or tradition (Haidt, 2007, 2010).

⌃ **Lawrence Kohlberg (1927–1987)** After graduating from high school in the United States in 1945, Kohlberg joined the Merchant Marine. In Europe, he witnessed the aftermath of World War II and met many Holocaust survivors. After finishing his service in the Merchant Marine, Kohlberg helped smuggle Jewish refugees into what was then British-controlled Palestine. He was caught and briefly imprisoned by the British but escaped and eventually made his way back to the United States (Schwartz, 2004). Years later, Kohlberg (1988) wrote, "My experience with illegal immigration into Israel raised all sorts of moral questions, issues which I saw as issues of justice. When is it permissible to be involved with violent means for supposedly just ends?" Kohlberg was to be preoccupied with themes of justice and morality for the rest of his life.

‹ **Moral Development: Developing a Sense of Right and Wrong** As adolescents develop new cognitive abilities, they become more aware of moral issues in the world. Their newly acquired ability to imagine hypothetical situations and compare abstract ideals to the reality of situations often leads teenagers to question authority or take action against perceived injustices. These young protesters marched in Philadelphia to demand action to slow climate change.

TABLE 9.5

Kohlberg's Levels and Stages of Moral Development

I. Preconventional Level

Moral reasoning is guided by external consequences. No internalization of values or rules.

Stage 1: Punishment and Obedience

"Right" is obeying the rules simply to avoid punishment because others have power over you and can punish you.

Stage 2: Mutual Benefit

"Right" is an even or fair exchange so that both parties benefit. Moral reasoning guided by a sense of "fair play."

II. Conventional Level

Moral reasoning is guided by conformity to social roles, rules, and expectations that the person has learned and internalized.

Stage 3: Interpersonal Expectations

"Right" is being a "good" person by conforming to social expectations, such as showing concern for others and following rules set by others so as to win their approval.

Stage 4: Law and Order

"Right" is helping maintain social order by doing one's duty, obeying laws simply because they are laws, and showing respect for authorities simply because they are authorities.

III. Postconventional Level

Moral reasoning is guided by internalized legal and moral principles that protect the rights of all members of society.

Stage 5: Legal Principles

"Right" is helping protect the basic rights of all members of society by upholding legalistic principles that promote the values of fairness, justice, equality, and democracy.

Stage 6: Universal Moral Principles

"Right" is determined by self-chosen ethical principles that reflect the person's respect for ideals such as nonviolence, equality, and human dignity. If these moral principles conflict with democratically determined laws, the person's self-chosen moral principles take precedence.

Sources: Research from Kohlberg (1981) and Colby et al., (1983).

Gender, Culture, and Moral Reasoning Other challenges to Kohlberg's theory questioned whether it was as universal as its proponents claimed. Psychologist Carol Gilligan (1982) pointed out that Kohlberg's early research was conducted entirely with male participants and relied on stories with main characters who are male, yet it became the basis for a theory applied to both males *and* females. Thus, Gilligan believes that Kohlberg's model reflects a male perspective that may not accurately depict the development of moral reasoning in women (Baird & Roellke, 2015).

To Gilligan, Kohlberg's model is based on an *ethic of individual rights and justice,* which is a more common perspective for men. In contrast, Gilligan (1982) developed a model of women's moral development that is based on an *ethic of care and responsibility.*

But *do* women use different criteria in making moral judgments? In a meta-analysis of studies on gender differences in moral reasoning, Sara Jaffee and Janet Shibley Hyde (2000) found only slight differences between male and female responses. Instead, evidence suggested that *both* men and women used a mix of care and justice perspectives. Thus, Kohlberg's theory did *not* adequately reflect the way that humans actually experienced moral decision making.

Despite Kohlberg's belief that the stages of moral development were universal, culture also affects moral reasoning (Graham et al., 2011; Haidt, 2007). Kohlberg's moral decisions focus on issues of harm, fairness, and justice. In many cultures, however, other domains are equally deemed to be morally important. For example, religious or spiritual

emerging adulthood In industrialized countries, the distinct stage of the lifespan from the late teens through the 20s, characterized by exploration and flexibility in social roles, vocational choices, and relationships.

purity, loyalty to one's family or social group, respect for those in authority, and respect for tradition may also be seen as issues of morality.

Some cross-cultural psychologists also argue that Kohlberg's stories and scoring system reflect a Western emphasis on *individual* rights and justice that is not shared in many cultures (Shweder et al., 1997). For example, Kohlberg's moral stages do not reflect the sense of interdependence and the concern for the overall welfare of the group that is more common in collectivistic cultures. Cultural psychologist Harry Triandis (1994) reports an example of a response that does not fit into Kohlberg's moral scheme. In response to the scenario in which the husband steals the drug to save his wife's life, a man in New Guinea said, "If nobody helped him, I would say that *we* had caused the crime." Thus, there are aspects of moral reasoning in other cultures that do not seem to be reflected in Kohlberg's theory (Haidt, 2007; Shweder & Haidt, 1993).

Adult Development

■ KEY THEME
Development throughout adulthood is marked by exploration, physical changes, and the adoption of new social roles.

▪ KEY QUESTIONS
- What is emerging adulthood?
- What physical changes take place in adulthood?
- What are some general patterns of adult social development?

You can think of the developmental changes you experienced during infancy, childhood, and adolescence as early chapters in your life story. Those early life chapters helped set the tone for the primary focus of your life story—adulthood. During the half-century or more that constitutes adulthood, self-definition evolves as people achieve independence and take on new roles and responsibilities.

Emerging Adulthood

At one time, adolescence marked the end of childhood and the beginning of adulthood. Even as recently as the mid-1970s, most young people moved into the adult roles of stable work, marriage, and parenthood shortly after high school (Arnett, 2000, 2004). In the United States and other industrialized countries today, however, most young adults do not fully transition to adult roles until their late twenties. One reason is the need for additional education or training before entering the adult workforce. According to developmental psychologist Jeffrey Jensen Arnett (2000, 2004, 2010), **emerging adulthood** is, *in industrialized countries, the distinct stage of the lifespan from the late teens through the 20s, characterized by exploration and flexibility in social roles, vocational choices, and relationships.*

According to Erikson's (1964) theory, the identity conflict should be fully resolved by the end of adolescence. However, Arnett (2010) contends that in today's industrialized cultures, identity is not fully resolved until the mid- or late twenties. Instead, Arnett writes, "It is during emerging adulthood, not adolescence, that most young people explore the options available to them in love and work and move towards making enduring choices." Indeed, research suggests that many 18-year-olds are still developing cognitive control, the ability to rein in impulsivity and risk taking, until their twenties (Cohen et al., 2016; Wood et al., 2018).

Many emerging adults feel "in between": They are no longer adolescents, but not quite adults. Although some find this instability unsettling and disorienting, several studies have found that well-being and self-esteem steadily rise over the course of emerging adulthood for most people (Galambos et al., 2006; Schulenberg & Zarrett, 2006), especially for those who report having positive peer relationships (Sanchez-Queija et al., 2017).

Although some emerging adults establish long-term, stable relationships, in general relationships during emerging adulthood are often characterized by exploration. "Hooking up" during the college and post-college years is common (see the In Focus box). Compared to their parents and grandparents, today's emerging adults are waiting much longer to get

⌄ Emerging Adulthood According to Jeffrey Jensen Arnett (2004, 2010), the years from 18 to the mid- to late 20s are a time of exploration in relationships as well as vocational choices and social roles. Marriage is often postponed until the late 20s or even the 30s, after education is complete and careers are established.

Cultura RM/Alamy

Sources: Data from U.S. Census Bureau (2016); Vespa et al., (2013)

FIGURE 9.5 The Median Age at First Marriage The average age at first marriage is about six years older for young adults today than it was in the 1970s. Part of the explanation for this trend is that more people are postponing marriage in order to complete a university education. Among young adults in the 25-to-34 age range, 26 percent of men and 33 percent of women have earned a bachelor's degree or higher.

married. As **Figure 9.5** shows, in 1970 the median age for a first marriage in the United States was 23 for men and 21 for women. By 2016 those figures had increased to about 30 for men and 27 for women. Many emerging adults postpone marriage until their late twenties or early thirties so they can finish their education and become established in a career (Bernstein, 2010). When planning their futures, emerging adults, especially young women, also consider the potential difficulties in achieving a balance between work and family (Coyle et al., 2015).

Emerging adults also actively explore different career options (Hamilton & Hamilton, 2006). On average, emerging adults hold down an average of seven different jobs during their twenties (Arnett, 2004).

Is emerging adulthood a universal period of development? The answer appears to be no. According to Arnett (2011), emerging adulthood exists only in cultures in which adult responsibilities and roles are postponed until the twenties. This pattern occurs most typically in industrialized or post-industrialized countries. Even within industrialized countries, however, emerging adulthood may not characterize the developmental trajectory of all young adults. For example, members of minoritized groups, immigrants, and young adults who enter directly into the workforce rather than seeking college or university education are all less likely to experience emerging adulthood as a distinct period of exploration and change.

Physical Changes in Adulthood

Your unique genetic heritage greatly influences the unfolding of certain physical changes during adulthood, such as when your hair begins to thin and turn gray. Such genetically influenced changes can vary quite a bit from one person to another and are often influenced by their life experiences (epigenetics).

However, genetic heritage is *not* destiny. The lifestyle choices that people make in young and middle adulthood influence the aging process through many processes including epigenetics. Staying physically and mentally active, avoiding tobacco products and other harmful substances, and eating a healthy diet can both slow and minimize the physical declines that are typically associated with aging.

Another potent environmental force is simply the passage of time. With each decade after age 20, the efficiency of various body organs declines. For example, lung capacity decreases, as does the amount of blood pumped by the heart, though these changes are usually not noticeable until late adulthood.

Physical strength typically peaks in *early adulthood,* the twenties and thirties. By *middle adulthood,* roughly from the forties to the mid-sixties, physical strength and endurance gradually decline. Physical and mental reaction times also begin to slow during middle adulthood. During *late adulthood,* from the mid-sixties on, physical stamina and reaction time tend to decline further and faster.

Significant reproductive and hormonal changes also occur during adulthood. **Menopause** is *the natural cessation of menstruation and the end of reproductive capacity in women.* It occurs anytime from the late thirties to the early fifties. For some women, menopause involves unpleasant symptoms, such as *hot flashes,* which are rapid and extreme

REUTERS/Finbarr O'Reilly

⌃ Emerging Adulthood Many emerging adults hold a range of jobs while they explore possible careers. Here, 22-year-old Ndeye Astou Fall works at a call center in Senegal speaking with clients from across the French-speaking world.

menopause The natural cessation of menstruation and the end of reproductive capacity in women.

IN FOCUS

Hooking Up on Campus

Pop culture and the news media alike have been abuzz about today's hookup culture. In the words of *New York Times* reporter Kate Taylor (2013), "It is by now pretty well understood that traditional dating in college has mostly gone the way of the landline."

"Hooking up" refers to a no-strings-attached sexual encounter that can range from kissing and cuddling to sexual intercourse, but is not accompanied by the expectation of a committed relationship or even future interactions. On many college campuses, hooking up appears to be very common. Researcher Lisa Wade (2017) studied hookup culture in about 100 students over the course of a semester. One of these students called it "an established norm," and another reported that "Hook up culture = social life." Other studies have shown that a majority of students reported hooking up at least once while they were in university, and more than half had hooked up during the previous year (Owen et al., 2011; Reiber & Garcia, 2010).

Yet, hooking up is probably not as common as many people think. A survey of more than 24,000 students found that a third of students reported no hookups. And students who did hook up did so only about twice per year (Wade, 2017).

There's nothing new about sexual activity among young adults. In fact, the number of sexual partners for members of the millennial generation is actually about the same as for baby boomers at the same age. So, contrary to the buzz about the hookup culture, millennials are not exhibiting a spike in partners (Twenge et al., 2015). But hooking up does differ in some key ways from other types of sexual activity.

THE DAY THE COMPUTER AND THE COFFEE MAKER HOOKED UP.

Liza Donnelly/The New Yorker Collection/The Cartoon Bank

MYTH ◄ SCIENCE

Is it true that the number of sexual partners among millennials is higher than previous generations?

Wade emphasizes that hooking up is deliberately "meaningless." In fact, those engaging in a hookup sometimes emphasize the lack of meaning by publicly announcing that they do not care about the other person after having sex with them and have no interest in engaging in future interactions (Vedantam et al., 2017). Indeed, one college junior said about her regular hookup that "we don't really like each other in person, sober" (Taylor, 2013).

Perhaps not surprisingly, alcohol use is strongly implicated in hooking-up behavior. Alcohol consumption precedes almost two-thirds of hookups (Fielder & Carey, 2010; Vander Ven & Beck, 2009). As Wade explains, "If the students have been drinking, that helps send the message that [the sex] is meaningless" (Vedantam et al., 2017).

Although hooking up is widely accepted on college campuses, among heterosexual people, both women and men overestimate the degree to which the other sex is comfortable with hooking up (Reiber & Garcia, 2010). Today's young adults haven't given up on the hope of creating a long-term, committed relationship. Indeed, one U.S. college senior who was interviewed about hooking up described a romantic relationship she had during a study-abroad experience and said it made her hopeful that she would one day have such a relationship back home (Taylor, 2013). However, for now, university students are immersed in what appears to be a larger cultural shift toward more flexible, less clearly defined relationships (Bisson & Levine, 2009).

---

increases in body temperature (Umland, 2008). Other symptoms may include night sweats and disturbances in sex drive, sleep, eating, weight, and motivation. Emotional symptoms may include depression, sadness, and emotional instability (Freeman, 2010).

Cultural stereotypes reinforce the notion that menopause is mostly a negative experience (APA, 2007). However, many postmenopausal women develop a new sense of identity, become more assertive, and pursue new aspirations (Fahs, 2007). In many cultures, postmenopausal women are valued for their experience and wisdom (Jeste & Lee, 2019; Robinson, 2002).

Middle-aged men do not experience an abrupt end to their reproductive capability. However, they do experience a gradual decline in testosterone levels, a condition sometimes called *andropause* (Hochreiter et al., 2005). Decreased levels of the hormone testosterone cause changes in physical and psychological health. These changes include loss of lean muscle, increased body fat, weakened bones, reduced sexual motivation and function, and cognitive declines (Harman, 2005). Emotional problems such as depression and irritability may also occur (Zitzmann, 2020).

Does the loss of reproductive capability trigger a "midlife crisis" in women, or especially, in men? No. Consistently, psychological research has shown that there is no such thing as a midlife crisis (see Clay, 2003; Sneed et al., 2012). Instead, most men and women who experienced a "crisis" of depression or despair during middle age *also* experienced depression, anxiety, and similar crises in young adulthood (Wethington, 2000).

Social Development in Adulthood

The "traditional" track of achieving intimacy in adulthood was once to find a mate, get married, and start and raise a family. Today, however, the structure of U.S. families varies widely (see **Figure 9.6**). Just over half of all adults are currently married, a decline of 5 percentage points since 1995, whereas the percentage of those cohabiting increased from 3 to 7 percent in that time period (Graf, 2019). Currently, more than 20 percent of U.S. children are being raised by a single parent, far higher than the global rate of 7 percent (Kramer, 2019).

Given that more than half of all first marriages end in divorce, the phenomenon of remarrying and starting a second family later in life is not unusual. As divorce has become more common, the number of single parents and stepfamilies has also risen. And among married couples, some opt for a child-free life together.

Such diversity in adult relationships reflects the fact that adult social development does not always follow a predictable pattern. As you travel through adulthood, your life story may include many unanticipated twists in the plot and changes in the cast of characters. Just as the "traditional" family structure has its joys and heartaches, so do other configurations of intimate and family relationships. In the final analysis, *any* relationship that promotes the overall sense of happiness and well-being of the people involved is a successful one.

The Transition to Parenthood Although it is commonly believed that children strengthen the marital bond, marital satisfaction and time together tend to decline after the birth of the first child (Doss et al., 2009; Lawrence et al., 2010).

With the birth or adoption of your first child, you take on a commitment to nurture the physical, emotional, social, and intellectual well-being of the next generation, fundamentally changing your identity. This change can be a struggle, especially if the transition to parenthood was more of a surprise than a planned event (Grussu et al., 2005).

Parenthood is further complicated by the fact that children are not born speaking fluently, so you can't immediately enlighten them about the constraints of adult life. Instead, you must continually strive to adapt lovingly and patiently to your child's needs while managing all the other priorities in your life (Nelson-Coffey, 2018).

Not all couples experience a decline in marital satisfaction after the birth of a child. The hassles and headaches of child rearing can be minimized if the marital relationship is warm and positive, and if both husband and wife share household and child-care responsibilities (Tsang et al., 2003). The transition to parenthood is also smoother if you're blessed with a child who is born with a good disposition. Parents of babies with an "easy" temperament find it less difficult to adjust to their new role and maintain a healthy marital relationship (Mehall et al., 2009). The relationship between infant temperament and an easy transition to parenthood is also predicted by individual differences in the psychosocial health and well-being of the parents themselves (Brenning et al., 2019).

That many couples are marrying at a later age and waiting until their thirties to start a family also seems to be advantageous. Becoming a parent at an older age and waiting longer after marriage to start a family may ease the adjustment to parenthood. Why? Largely because the couple is more mature, the marital relationship is typically more stable, and finances are more secure (Hatton et al., 2010; Nelson et al., 2014).

In developed societies, dual-career families have become increasingly common. However, the career tracks of men and women often differ if they have children. Although today's fathers are more actively involved in child rearing than were fathers in previous generations, women in heterosexual couples still tend to have primary responsibility for child care (Meier et al., 2006). Thus, married heterosexual women with children are much more likely than are single women or childless women to interrupt

Is it true that many middle-aged people experience a "midlife crisis"?

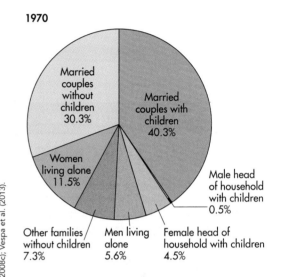

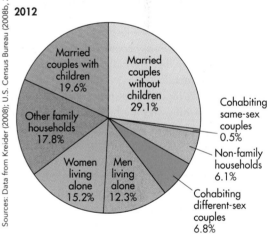

Sources: Data from Kreider (2008); U.S. Census Bureau (2008a, 2008b, 2008c); Vespa et al. (2013).

FIGURE 9.6 The Changing Structure of U.S. Families and Households In a relatively short time, U.S. households have undergone a metamorphosis. Between 1970 and 2012, the number of U.S. households increased from 63 million to 115 million, but the average household size decreased from 3.1 to 2.6 persons. As the living arrangements of U.S. families have become more diversified, the U.S. Census Bureau modified the categories it uses to classify households. Hence, the two pie charts differ slightly. Notice that single-parent family groups have doubled. Today, single mothers or fathers represent 9 percent of all households. In contrast, the number of married couples with children has sharply decreased.

their careers, leave their jobs, or switch to part-time work because of child-rearing responsibilities. As a consequence, women with children tend to earn less than women with no children (Gangl & Ziefle, 2009).

Many working parents are concerned about the effects of nonparental care on their children. Earlier in the chapter, we discussed the importance of attachment relationships between young children and their primary caregivers. In the Critical Thinking box, we take a close look at what psychologists have learned about the effects of day care on attachment and other aspects of development.

Do adults, particularly women, experience greater stress because of the conflicting demands of career, marriage, and family? Not necessarily. Generally, multiple roles seem to provide both men and women with a greater potential for increased feelings of self-esteem, happiness, and competence (Cinamon et al., 2007). The critical factor

CRITICAL THINKING

The Effects of Child Care on Attachment and Development

The majority of children under the age of 5 in the United States—more than 11 million children—are in some type of child care (Phillips & Lowenstein, 2011). Does extensive day care during the first years of life create insecurely attached infants and toddlers? Does it produce negative effects in later childhood? Let's look at the evidence.

Developmental psychologist Jay Belsky (1992, 2001, 2002) sparked considerable controversy when he first published studies showing that infants under a year old were more likely to demonstrate insecure attachment if they experienced over 30 hours of day care per week. Based on his research, Belsky contended that children who entered full-time day care before their first birthday were "at risk" to be insecurely attached to their parents.

However, the proportion of insecurely attached infants in day care is only slightly higher than the proportion typically found in the general population (Lamb et al., 1992). In other words, most of the children who had started day care in infancy were securely attached, just like most of the children who had not experienced extensive day care during infancy (Phillips & Lowenstein, 2011).

Researchers agree that the quality of child care is a key factor in facilitating secure attachment in early childhood and preventing problems in later childhood (NICHD, 2003a, 2003b; Vandell et al., 2010). Many studies have found that children who experience high-quality child care tend to be more sociable, better adjusted, and more academically competent than children who

‹ Individual Attention
Individual attention from consistent caregivers or teachers helps foster the young child's sense of predictability and security in the care setting.

Design Pics Inc/Alamy Stock Photo

experience low-quality care, even well into their teens (Belsky et al., 2007; Vandell et al., 2010).

Child care is just one aspect of a child's developmental environment. Sensitive parenting and the quality of caregiving in the child's home have been found to have an even greater influence on social, emotional, and cognitive development than the quality of child care (Belsky et al., 2007).

Clearly, then, day care in and of itself does not necessarily lead to undesirable outcomes (Belsky, 2009). The critical factor is the *quality* of care (Phillips & Lowenstein, 2011). High-quality day care can benefit children, even when it begins in early infancy. In contrast, low-quality care can contribute to social and academic problems in later childhood (Muenchow & Marsland, 2007). Unfortunately, in many areas of the United States, high-quality day care is not readily available or is prohibitively expensive (Phillips & Lowenstein, 2011).

Characteristics of High-Quality Child Care

- The setting meets state and local standards and is accredited by a professional organization.
- Warm, responsive caregivers encourage children's play and learning.
- Groups of children and adults are consistent over time.
- Groups are small enough to provide individual attention.
- A minimum of two adults care for no more than 8 infants, 12 toddlers, or 20 four- and five-year-olds.
- Caregivers are trained in principles of child development and learning.
- Developmentally appropriate learning materials and toys are available that offer interesting, safe, and achievable activities.

Sources: National Institute of Child Health and Human Development (2006); National Association for the Education of Young Children (2009); National Association of Child Care Resource & Referral Agencies (2010).

CRITICAL THINKING QUESTIONS

- Why is it difficult to definitively measure the effects of day care on children?
- Given the benefits of high-quality child care, should the availability of affordable, high-quality care be a governmental priority? How will the effects of the COVID-19 pandemic change what high-quality child care is?

seems to be not the *number* of roles that people take on but the *quality* of their experiences on the job, in marriage, and as a parent (Lee & Phillips, 2006; Plaisier et al., 2008). When experiences in different roles are positive and satisfying, psychological well-being is enhanced. However, when work is dissatisfying, finding high-quality child care is difficult, and making ends meet is a never-ending struggle, stress can escalate, and psychological well-being can plummet—regardless of sex (Bakker et al., 2008).

Although marital satisfaction declines when people first become parents, it rises again after children leave home (Gorchoff et al., 2008). Thus, most parents do *not* experience feelings of sadness, emptiness, and loss when their last child leaves home, often called the "empty nest syndrome" (Bouchard, 2014). Successfully launching your children into the adult world represents the attainment of the ultimate parental goal. There is also more time to spend in leisure activities with your spouse. Not surprisingly, then, marital satisfaction tends to increase steadily once children are out of the nest and flying on their own. Relatively recent is the new phenomenon of *boomerang kids*—adult children returning home after a brief period on their own because of economic pressures or, more recently, to escape the social isolation of the pandemic. In some cases, the return of adult children can have a negative impact on marital relationships (Bouchard, 2014; Umberson et al., 2005).

▲ **Single-Parent Families** Today, more than 20 percent of all children are being raised by a single parent (Graf, 2019). Many single parents provide their children with a warm, stable, and loving environment. In terms of school achievement and emotional stability, children in stable, single-parent households do just as well as children with two parents living in the same home.

Late Adulthood and Aging

■ KEY THEME
Late adulthood does not necessarily involve a steep decline in physical or cognitive capabilities.

≡ KEY QUESTIONS
- What cognitive changes take place in late adulthood?
- What factors influence social development in late adulthood?

The average life expectancy for men in the United States is currently about 76 years, and for women, about 81 years (Arias, 2016). Globally, average life expectancies have increased and are currently about 67 for men and 71 for women (He et al., 2016). Thus, the stage of late adulthood can easily last a decade or more. From about 15 percent of the population in 2015, the percentage of U.S. residents over the age of 65 is projected to grow to about 22 percent by 2050 (He et al., 2016). The world population is aging, too. Globally, the number of people aged 80 and older is expected to grow from 69 million in 2014 to 379 million in 2050 (Harper, 2014).

Although we experience many physical and sensory changes throughout adulthood, that's not to say that we completely fall apart when we reach our sixties, seventies, or even eighties. Contrary to many young people's misconceptions of late adulthood, *most* older adults live healthy, active, and self-sufficient lives (National Institute on Aging, 2007; Wurtele, 2009). Even adults 85 years and older report good health and functioning despite increasing prevalence of disease and impairment (Collerton et al., 2009). For many people, good health and well-being reach well into the latest stages of adulthood (Charles & Carstensen, 2010).

Cognitive Changes

During which decade of life do you think people reach their intellectual peak? If you answered the twenties or thirties, you may be surprised by the results of research. There is a lot of variability in terms of the age at which different cognitive abilities are at their peak (Hartshorne & Germine, 2015). One study of business executives found that older executives performed more poorly, on average, than younger executives on some measures of cognitive ability but performed better on others (Klein et al., 2015).

Decades of work by K. Warner Schaie (1995, 2005) and his colleagues has shown that mental abilities remain relatively stable until about the age of 60. And in terms of mental

MICHAEL FRANCIS MCELROY/Tribune News Service/Newscom

▲ **A Lifetime of Experience to Share**
Like many other senior adults, Lillian Williams derives great personal satisfaction from her work as a volunteer "Foster Grandparent," shown here reading to a student at a school in Fort Lauderdale, Florida. Contributing to their communities, taking care of others, and helping people both younger and older than themselves are important to many older adults.

abilities related to what we do—our jobs and our hobbies—we might even see improved cognitive functioning as we age (Ackerman, 2014). After age 60, slight declines begin to appear on tests of general intellectual abilities, such as logical reasoning, math skills, word recall, and the ability to mentally manipulate images (Alwin, 2009, Siegler et al., 2009).

But even after age 60, most older adults maintain their previous levels of ability. A longitudinal study of adults in their seventies, eighties, and nineties found that there were slight but significant declines in memory, perceptual speed, and fluency. However, measures of knowledge, such as vocabulary, remained stable up to age 90 (Singer et al., 2003; Zelinski & Kennison, 2007). Similarly, the ability to speak and understand language tends to remain stable as people age (Shafto & Tyler, 2014). When declines in mental abilities occur during old age, Schaie (2005) found that the explanation is often simply a lack of practice or experience with the kinds of tasks used in mental ability tests. Even just a few hours of training on mental skills can improve test scores for most older adults.

Some research suggests that physiological functioning of the brain begins to slow with age (Salthouse, 2009). Neurons appear to become less efficient at communicating with one another, and this seems to result in slowed and sometimes inhibited cognitive performance (Bucur et al., 2008). According to one hypothesis, older brains appear to *compensate* for this decline in processing speed by outsourcing some of the work to other parts of the brain (Dennis & Cabeza, 2008). However, the need to recruit more regions of the brain comes at a price—slower processing.

Is it possible to minimize declines in mental and physical abilities in old age? In a word, *yes.* Consistently, research has found that those who are better educated and engage in physical, mental, and social activities throughout older adulthood show the smallest declines in mental abilities (Anguera et al., 2013; Lindenberger, 2014; Smith et al., 2014). However, dysfunctional social relationships can have *negative* effects. In one study of more than 10,000 people living in the United Kingdom, close relationships that caused worry and stress predicted a decline in mental abilities eight years later (Liao et al., 2014). Aerobic exercise, however, has strong research support for its effectiveness in improving cognitive functioning in late adulthood (Hertzog et al., 2009). The Focus on Neuroscience "Boosting the Aging Brain" provides a look at an experiment that demonstrated the remarkable effects of a moderate exercise program on the brains of elderly adults.

In contrast, the greatest intellectual declines tend to occur in older adults with unstimulating lifestyles, such as people who live alone, are dissatisfied with their lives, and engage in few activities (see Calero-Garcia et al., 2007; Newson & Kemps, 2005; Zhou et al., 2018).

Social Development

One theory of social development in late adulthood holds that older adults gradually "disengage," or withdraw, from vocational, social, and relationship roles as they face the prospect of their lives ending (Lange & Grossman, 2010). But consider the actor Betty White, born in 1922. Closing in on a century of life, White continues to have close friendships, to engage in animal rights activism, and to act, including in Pixar's *Toy Story 4* in 2019, where she played a stuffed animal named for her—the toy tiger, Bitey White (Truitt, 2019).

What Betty White epitomizes is the **activity theory of aging**, *the psychosocial theory that life satisfaction in late adulthood is highest when people maintain the level of activity they displayed earlier in life* (Lange & Grossman, 2010).

Just like younger adults, older adults differ in the level of activity they find personally optimal. Some older adults pursue a busy lifestyle of social activities, travel, university classes, and volunteer work. Other older adults are happier with a quieter lifestyle: reading, pursuing hobbies, or simply puttering around their homes. Such individual preferences reflect lifelong temperamental and personality qualities that continue to be evident as a person ages.

For many older adults, caregiving responsibilities can persist well into late adulthood. Sandy's mother, Fern, for example, spent a great deal of time helping out with her young grandchildren and caring for some of her older relatives. She was not unusual in that respect. Many older adults who are healthy and active find themselves taking care of other older adults who are sick or have physical limitations.

Along with satisfying social relationships, the prescription for psychological well-being in old age includes achieving what Erik Erikson called *ego integrity*—the feeling that one's life has been meaningful (Erikson et al., 1986). Older adults experience ego integrity when they look back on their lives and feel satisfied with their

activity theory of aging The psychosocial theory that life satisfaction in late adulthood is highest when people maintain the level of activity they displayed earlier in life.

🧠 FOCUS ON NEUROSCIENCE

Boosting the Aging Brain

Does staying physically active improve cognitive functioning and brain health in old age? Or are people with better cognitive functioning and brain health more likely to stay physically active?

To answer this question, researchers randomly assigned sedentary but healthy participants to two groups: *an aerobic exercise group* that walked three times a week, and a *stretching and toning group* that focused on nonaerobic exercise (Erickson et al., 2011). After a year of regular exercise, *both* groups improved on measures of spatial memory, on average, which is good news for those who engage in less-active exercise programs. It's also possible that all the participants benefited from the social interaction during their respective exercise classes (Dause and Kirby, 2019).

Were there any structural effects on the elderly brains? Because of its involvement in memory (see Chapter 6), researchers looked for changes in the *hippocampus*. The stretching and toning group showed, on average, a 1.4 percent decline in hippocampal volume over the one-year study period, which is about average for this age group.

In contrast, participants in the aerobic exercise group *increased* the volume of their hippocampus by an average of 2 percent. Two percent may not sound like a large increase. However, because the hippocampus typically shrinks about 1–2 percent annually in older adults, a 2 percent gain is roughly equivalent to reversing two years of tissue loss.

This study is notable for several reasons. First, it showed that even in late adulthood, behavioral interventions can affect brain structure (Dause and Kirby, 2019). Second, it showed that aerobic exercise is *neuroprotective*—it helps keep the brain healthy and may protect brain tissue from age-related deterioration. And third, it showed that a very moderate, simple exercise program can significantly improve cognitive abilities and brain health—even in late adulthood.

The bottom line: Declines in cognitive abilities and brain functions are neither inevitable nor unalterable (Voss et al., 2010; Ballesteros et al., 2018; Horowitz et al., 2020). And, you don't have to be a highly conditioned athlete with expensive equipment to reap the benefits of aerobic exercise. All you need is a good pair of shoes and a safe place to walk, ideally with a close friend or two.

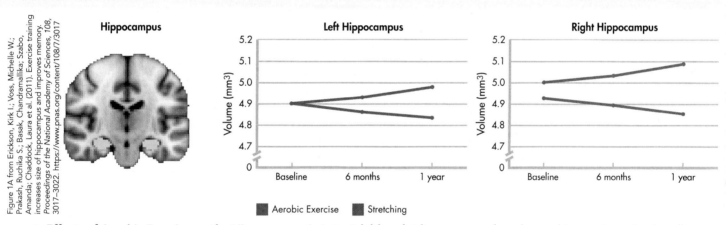

Figure 1A from Erickson, Kirk I.; Voss, Michelle W.; Prakash, Ruchika S.; Basak, Chandramallika; Szabo, Amanda; Chaddock, Laura et al. (2011). Exercise training increases size of hippocampus and improves memory. *Proceedings of the National Academy of Sciences, 108,* 3017–3022. https://www.pnas.org/content/108/7/3017

▲ **Effects of Aerobic Exercise on the Hippocampus in Late Adulthood** After one year of regular aerobic exercise—simply walking three times a week—elderly participants (purple line) increased the size of their left and right hippocampus (brain region, highlighted in yellow) by an average of 2 percent. In contrast, the stretching-and-toning group (orange line) showed about a 1.5 percent decline in the hippocampal volume, which is normal for this age group.

accomplishments, accepting whatever mistakes or missteps they may have made (Torges et al., 2008, 2009).

In contrast, those who are filled with regrets or bitterness about past mistakes, missed opportunities, or bad decisions experience *despair*—a deep sense of disappointment in life. Often the theme of ego integrity versus despair emerges as older adults engage in a *life review,* thinking about or retelling their life story to others (Bohlmeijer et al., 2007; Kunz & Soltys, 2007).

Dying and Death

It is tempting to view death as the special province of the very old. Of course, death can occur at any point during the lifespan. It's also tempting to assume that older adults have come to a special understanding about death—that they view the prospect of dying with wisdom and serenity. In reality, attitudes toward death in old age show the same diversity that is reflected in other aspects of adult development. Not all older adults are accepting of death, even when poor health has severely restricted their activities (Jun et al., 2010).

As psychologist Robert Kastenbaum (1992) wrote, "Everyone lives in relationship to death at every point in the lifespan." In other words, long before encountering old age, each individual has a personal history of thinking about death. Some people are obsessed with issues of life and death from adolescence or early adulthood onward, while others, even in advanced old age, take more of a one-day-at-a-time approach to living. And, feelings about and attitudes toward death are also influenced by cultural, philosophical, and religious beliefs (Gire, 2011; Rosenblatt, 2007).

In general, worries about death tend to peak in middle adulthood, then *decrease* in late adulthood (Neimeyer et al., 2004; Russac et al., 2007). At any age, people respond with a wide variety of emotions when faced with the prospect of imminent death, such as when they are diagnosed with a terminal illness.

The scientific study of death and dying owes much to pioneering psychiatrist **Elisabeth Kübler-Ross** (1926–2004). Based on interviews with hundreds of terminally ill patients, Kübler-Ross (1969) proposed that the dying go through five stages. First, they *deny* that death is imminent, perhaps insisting that their doctors are wrong or denying the seriousness of their illness. Second, they feel and express *anger* that they are dying. Third, they *bargain*—they try to "make a deal" with doctors, relatives, or God, promising to behave in a certain way if only they may be allowed to live. Fourth, they become *depressed.* Finally, they *accept* their fate.

Although Kübler-Ross's research did much to sensitize the public and the medical community to the emotional experience of dying, it now seems clear that dying individuals do *not* necessarily progress through the predictable sequence of stages that she described (Kastenbaum, 2000, 2005).

Rather, dying is as individual a process as living is. People cope with the prospect of dying much as they have coped with other stressors in their lives. Faced with impending death, some older adults react with passive resignation, others with bitterness and anger. Some people plunge into activity and focus their attention on external matters, such as making funeral arrangements, disposing of their property, or arranging for the care of other family members. And others turn inward, searching for the meaning of their life's story as the close of the final chapter draws near (Kastenbaum, 2000).

But even in dying, our life story doesn't just end. Each of us leaves behind a legacy of memories in the minds of those who survive us. As we live each day, we are building our legacy through our words, our actions, and the many choices we make along the way.

Each of us began life being completely dependent on others for our survival. Over the course of our lifespan, others come to depend on us. It is those people whose lives we have touched in some way, whether for good or for ill, who will remember us. In this sense, the final chapter of our lives will be written not by us, but by those whose life stories have intersected with our own.

Closing Thoughts

Traditionally, development in childhood has received the most attention from developmental psychologists. Yet, as we have emphasized throughout this chapter, development is a lifelong process. Throughout this chapter, you've seen that every life is a unique combination of universal and individualized patterns of development.

Thinking back to this chapter's Prologue, we can see how the best obituaries describe human development across the lifespan, as did Margalit Fox's story of the remarkable life of Dovey Johnson Roundtree. "Because what does an obit do?" Fox asked. "It's charged with taking subjects from the cradle—John Doe was born on January 1st, 1900—to the grave—John Doe died yesterday" (Cowan, 2016). In this chapter, we covered something Fox understands intuitively, the arc of human lives from the perspective of psychological science.

Some aspects of development unfold in a predictable fashion, but every life story (including Dovey Roundtree's, including yours) is influenced by unexpected events and plot twists. Despite predictable changes, the wonderful thing about development over the lifespan is that you never really know what the next chapter of your life story may hold.

MYTH ◀ SCIENCE

Is it true that dying people go through five predictable stages—denial, anger, bargaining, depression, and acceptance?

Margaret Thomas/The Washington Post/Getty Images

∧ **The Arc of a Life** The story of Dovey Johnson Roundtree, groundbreaking civil rights activist, lawyer, and minister, was told in her obituary (Fox, 2018a). *The New York Times* obituary editor explained that writers "try to trace the arc of a life, from birth—in part to suggest what may have driven a person to succeed, to achieve, to find fame" (Takenaga, 2018). In many ways, obituary writers are capturing a life through the lens of developmental psychology.

 **PSYCH FOR YOUR LIFE**

Raising Psychologically Healthy Children

Unfortunately, kids don't come with owners' manuals. Maybe that's why if you walk into any bookstore and head for the "parenting" section, you'll see shelves of books offering advice on topics ranging from "how to toilet-train your toddler" to "how to talk to your teenager." We're not going to attempt to cover that range here. However, we will present some basic principles of parenting that have been shown to foster the development of children who are psychologically well adjusted, competent, and in control of their own behavior.

Basic Parenting Styles and Their Effects on Children

Psychologist Diana Baumrind (1971, 1991, 2005) has described three basic parenting styles: authoritarian, permissive, and authoritative. These parenting styles differ in terms of (1) parental control and (2) parental responsiveness to the child's needs and wishes.

The **authoritarian parenting style** is a *parenting style in which parents are demanding and unresponsive toward their children's needs or wishes.* Authoritarian parents believe that they should shape and control the child's behavior so that it corresponds to an absolute set of standards. Put simply, they expect children to obey the rules, no questions asked. Rules are made without input from the child, and they are enforced by punishment, often physical.

At the opposite extreme is the **permissive parenting style,** a *parenting style in which parents are extremely tolerant and not demanding; permissive-indulgent parents are responsive to their children, while permissive-indifferent parents are unresponsive* (Maccoby & Martin, 1983). *Permissive-indulgent parents* are responsive, warm, and accepting of their children but impose few rules and rarely punish their children. *Permissive-indifferent parents* are both unresponsive and uncontrolling. Establishing firm rules and consistently enforcing them is simply too much trouble for permissive-indifferent parents. If taken to an extreme, the lack of involvement of permissive-indifferent parenting can amount to child neglect.

The **authoritative parenting style** is a *parenting style in which parents set clear standards for their children's behavior but are also responsive to their children's needs and wishes.* Authoritative parents are warm, responsive, and involved with their children. They set clear standards for mature, age-appropriate behavior and expect their children to be responsive to parental demands. However, authoritative parents also feel a *reciprocal* responsibility to consider their children's reasonable demands and points of view. Thus, there is considerable give-and-take between parent and child. Rules are firm and consistently enforced, but the parents discuss the reasons for the rules with the child.

How do these different parenting styles affect young children? Baumrind (1971) found that the children of authoritarian parents are likely to be moody, unhappy, fearful, withdrawn, unspontaneous, and irritable. The children of permissive parents tend to be more cheerful than the children of authoritarian parents, but they are more immature, impulsive, and aggressive. In contrast, the children of authoritative parents are likely to be cheerful, socially competent, energetic, and friendly. They show high levels of self-esteem, self-reliance, and self-control (Buri et al., 1988). They also tend to be happier and have better overall mental health (Raboteg-Saric & Sakic, 2014; Uji et al., 2014).

Decades of research has shown that parenting styles affect children's competence, adjustment, behavior, and self-esteem (Heaven & Ciarrochi, 2008; Simons & Conger, 2007). Consistently, research has shown that authoritative parenting is associated with higher grades, lower rates of delinquent behavior, and lower rates of substance abuse, on average, than authoritarian or permissive parenting (Grusec, 2011; Turner et al., 2009).

Why does an authoritative parenting style provide such clear advantages over other parenting styles? First, when children perceive their parents' requests as fair and reasonable, they are more likely to comply with the requests. Second, the children are more likely to *internalize* (or accept as their own) the reasons for behaving in a certain way and thus to achieve greater self-control (Martinez & Garcia, 2008).

authoritarian parenting style Parenting style in which parents are demanding and unresponsive toward their children's needs or wishes.

permissive parenting style Parenting style in which parents are extremely tolerant and not demanding; permissive-indulgent parents are responsive to their children, while permissive-indifferent parents are unresponsive.

authoritative parenting style Parenting style in which parents set clear standards for their children's behavior but are also responsive to their children's needs and wishes.

induction A discipline technique that combines parental control with explaining why a behavior is prohibited.

In contrast, authoritarian parenting tends to promote rebellion and resentment. Because compliance is based on external control and punishment, children may not learn to control their own behavior (Gershoff, 2002). In a study that included participants from China, India, Italy, Kenya, Thailand, and the Philippines, authoritarian parenting produced anxiety and aggression in children (Gershoff et al., 2010).

Finally, the child with permissive parents may never learn self-control. And because permissive parents have low expectations, the child may well live up to those expectations by failing to strive to fulfill their potential (Baumrind, 1971). However, there is some evidence that the permissive parenting style has benefits in some cultures, including countries in South America and Southern Europe (see Garcia & Gracia, 2009; Martinez & Garcia, 2008). So, it may be that the effectiveness of particular parenting styles, like many other aspects of development, is affected by culture.

How to Be an Authoritative Parent: Some Practical Suggestions

Authoritative parents are high in both responsiveness and control. How can you successfully achieve that balance? Here are several suggestions based on psychological research.

1. Let your children know that you love them.

Attention, hugs, and other demonstrations of physical affection, coupled with a positive attitude toward your child, are *some* of the most important aspects of parenting, aspects that have enduring effects (Steinberg, 2001). Children who experience warm, positive relationships with their parents are more likely to become happy adults with stable marriages and good relationships with friends (Hardy et al., 2010). So the question is simple: Have you hugged your kids today?

2. Listen to your children.

Let your children express their opinions, and respect their preferences when it's reasonable to do so. In making rules and decisions, ask for their input and give it genuine consideration. Strive to be fair and flexible, especially on issues that are less than earthshaking, such as which clothes they wear to school.

3. Use induction to teach as you discipline.

The most effective form of discipline is called **induction**, *a discipline technique that combines parental control with explaining why a behavior is prohibited* (Hoffman, 1977). It *induces* understanding in the child. Put simply, induction involves consistently explaining (a) the reason for prohibiting or performing certain behaviors, (b) the *consequences* of the action for the child, and (c) the *effect* of the child's behavior on others. When parents use induction, the child begins to learn that their parents' actions are not completely arbitrary or unfair. The child is also more likely to internalize the reasoning and apply it in new situations (Kerr et al., 2004; Sorkhabi, 2010).

4. Work with your child's temperamental qualities.

Think back to our earlier discussion of temperamental qualities. Be aware of your child's natural temperament and work with it, not against it. If your child is very active, for example, it is unrealistic to expect them to sit quietly during a four-hour plane or bus trip. Knowing that, you can increase the likelihood of positive experiences by planning ahead. Bring coloring books, picture books, or small toys to occupy the young child in a restaurant or at a family gathering. Take frequent "exercise stops" on a long car trip. If your child is unusually sensitive, shy, or "slow-to-warm-up," give them plenty of time to make the transition to new situations and provide lots of preparation so that they know what to expect.

5. Understand your child's age-related cognitive abilities and limitations.

Some parents make the mistake of assuming that children think in the same way adults do. They may see a toddler or even an infant as purposely "misbehaving," "being naughty," or "rebelling" when the little one is simply doing what one-year-olds or three-year-olds do. Your expectations for appropriate behavior should be geared to the child's age and developmental stage. Having a thorough understanding of the information in this chapter is a good start. You might also consider taking a developmental psychology or child development class. Or go to your university or local library and check out some of the developmental psychology texts. By understanding your child's cognitive abilities and limitations at each stage of development, you're less likely to misinterpret behavior or to place inappropriate demands on them.

6. Don't expect perfection, and learn to go with the flow.
Accidents happen. Mistakes occur. Children get cranky or grumpy, especially when they're tired or hungry. Don't get too bent out of shape when your child's behavior is less than perfect. Be patient. Moments of conflict with children are a natural, inevitable, and healthy part of growing up. Look at those moments as part of the process by which a child achieves autonomy and a sense of self.

Finally, effective parenting is an ongoing process in which you, as the parent, should be regularly assessing your impact on your child. It's not always easy to combine responsiveness with control, or flexibility with an appropriate level of firmness. When you make a mistake, admit it not just to yourself but also to your child. In doing so, you'll teach your child how to behave when they make a mistake. As you'll discover, children are remarkably forgiving—and resilient.

◤ CHAPTER REVIEW

Lifespan Development

 **Achieve,** Macmillan Learning's online study platform, features the full e-book of *Discovering Psychology,* the **LearningCurve** adaptive quizzing system, videos, and a variety of activities to boost your learning. Visit **Achieve** at macmillanlearning.com.

KEY PEOPLE

Mary Ainsworth, p. 308

Erik Erikson, p. 321

Harry Harlow, p. 308

Lawrence Kohlberg, p. 322

Elisabeth Kübler-Ross, p. 332

Jean Piaget, p. 310

Lev Vygotsky, p. 314

KEY TERMS

developmental psychology, p. 298

zygote, p. 299

chromosome, p. 299

deoxyribonucleic acid (DNA), p. 300

sex chromosomes, p. 300

gene, p. 300

genotype, p. 300

phenotype, p. 300

epigenetics, p. 301

prenatal stage, p. 302

germinal period, p. 302

embryonic period, p. 302

teratogens, p. 303

stem cells, p. 303

fetal period, p. 304

temperament, p. 306

attachment, p. 308

sensorimotor stage, p. 310

object permanence, p. 311

preoperational stage, p. 311

symbolic thought, p. 311

egocentrism, p. 312

irreversibility, p. 312

centration, p. 312

conservation, p. 312

concrete operational stage, p. 313

formal operational stage, p. 313

zone of proximal development, p. 315

information-processing model of cognitive development, p. 315

adolescence, p. 315

puberty, p. 316

primary sex characteristics, p. 316

secondary sex characteristics, p. 316

adolescent growth spurt, p. 317

menarche, p. 317

identity, p. 320

moral reasoning, p. 322

emerging adulthood, p. 324

menopause, p. 325

activity theory of aging, p. 330

authoritarian parenting style, p. 333

permissive parenting style, p. 333

authoritative parenting style, p. 333

induction, p. 334

Genetic Contributions to Your Life Story

The **genotype** is a person's unique set of inherited genetic information, which is found in every body cell except reproductive cells.
- Genetic information is encoded in **chromosomes,** which are made of **deoxyribonucleic acid (DNA).**
- Each chromosome includes thousands of DNA segments called **genes.**

The **phenotype** is the collection of characteristics that an organism actually displays and is the result of gene–environment interaction.
- Environmental factors trigger gene expression.
- Different genotypes react differently to environmental factors.
- **Epigenetics** is the study of the factors that control gene expression.
- Most characteristics involve the interaction of multiple genes.

Prenatal Development

Germinal period: Conception to week 2: Single-celled **zygote** divides and develops into multicellular embryo.
Embryonic period: Week 3: to week 8: Major body systems form; period of greatest vulnerability to **teratogens;** brain development begins.
Fetal period: Week 9 to birth: Body systems mature.

Picture Partners/Alamy

Development During Infancy and Childhood

Physical development:
- Many reflexes are present at birth.
- Newborn sensory abilities are not fully developed.
- Motor skills develop in a universal sequence, although ages of acquisition vary.

Personality and social development:
Temperament seems to be inborn and biologically based but can be modified by environmental influences; basic temperamental patterns include easy, difficult, slow-to-warm-up.
Attachment refers to the emotional bond between infants and caregivers.
Mary Ainsworth (1913–1999) devised the Strange Situation to measure attachment.
Harry Harlow (1905–1981) demonstrated attachment in rhesus monkeys.

Cognitive development:
Jean Piaget (1896–1980) proposed that children progress through distinct stages of cognitive development.
- **Object permanence** is acquired through the **sensorimotor stage.**
- **Symbolic** thought is acquired during the **preoperational stage.** Preoperational thought is **egocentric** and characterized by **irreversibility** and **centration.** The preoperational child cannot grasp the principles of **conservation.**
- Children become capable of logical thought during the **concrete operational stage.**
- During the **formal operational stage,** the adolescent can engage in logical mental operations involving abstract concepts.

Lev Vygotsky (1896–1934) stressed the importance of social and cultural influences in cognitive development.
- **Zone of proximal development:** Children can progress to higher cognitive levels through the assistance of others who are more competent.

The **information-processing model of cognitive development** emphasizes basic mental processes and stresses that cognitive development is a process of continuous change.

Dennis MacDonald/PhotoEdit

Physical development:
• **Puberty** involves the development of **primary** and **secondary sex character-istics**, including **menarche** in girls.
• Girls experience the **adolescent growth spurt** at a younger age than boys.

Erik Erikson (1902–1994) proposed a theory of psychosocial development stressing that every stage of life is marked by a particular psychosocial conflict. **Identity** versus role confusion is associated with adolescence.

Development of moral reasoning:
Lawrence Kohlberg (1927–1987) proposed a theory of moral development in which children progressed from preconventional to conventional and ultimately postconventional moral reasoning. Criticisms of Kohlberg's theory include:
• Moral decisions are often affected by emotional or other nonrational factors.
• Carol Gilligan theorized that males and females reason differently about moral dilemmas, but evidence shows that the **moral reasoning** of men and women does not differ.
• Kohlberg's theory emphasizes individual rights, a perspective that is not shared by cultures that emphasize interdependence.

Cultura RM/Alamy

Adult Development

Emerging adulthood and adulthood:
Key developmental tasks are forming committed, intimate relationships and *generativity*—contributing to future generations through work and family life.
• In industrialized countries, **emerging adulthood** lasts from the late teens to the mid- to late twenties and is characterized by exploration of social roles, vocational choices, and relationships.
• U.S. families are increasingly diverse.
• Marital satisfaction often declines after children are born but often rises after they leave home.

Late adulthood and aging:
• Mental abilities begin to decline slightly at around age 60.
• Cognitive decline can be minimized when older adults are better edu-cated, physically healthy, and engage in physical and mental activity.
• **Activity theory of aging:** Life satisfaction in late adulthood is highest when people maintain their previous levels of activity.
• Erikson identified ego integrity versus despair as the key psychosocial conflict of old age.

MICHAEL FRANCIS MCELROY/Tribune News Service/Newscom

Dying and death:
• **Elisabeth Kübler-Ross** (1926–2004) proposed a five-stage model of dying: denial, anger, bargaining, depression, and acceptance.
• Individuals respond in diverse ways to impending death.

MYTH **OR** SCIENCE?

Is it true . . .

▶ That most gender differences are caused by biological factors?

▶ That most women are more emotional than men?

▶ That girls score just as highly as boys on national tests of math skills?

▶ That transgender people are lesbians or gay men?

▶ That once they are in their 70s and 80s, very few adults are sexually active?

Gender and Sexuality

PROLOGUE
~

People Are People

James is the kind of guy people are drawn to — extraverted, smart, funny, caring, interesting. A talented writer and artist, James works at the local food pantry and manages the town's community garden. You know the type: He's the caretaker, the peacemaker, the organizer.

James is also a transgender man. He was assigned female at birth, but knew himself to be and identified as male very early in life. "I remember being a little kid and trying to get my friends to refer to me

as a boy," he says. His early identification as male evoked a range of reactions. His friends awkwardly attempted to ignore it. His parents insisted he call himself a "tomboy" instead of a boy, firmly correcting him again and again.

It wasn't until middle school that James first heard the term *transgender,* but at that point he didn't apply it to himself. James just wanted to live his life in accord with his sense of self — as a boy, not a girl.

A turning point came a few years ago, when James was 22 years old. Dressed in women's clothes — "a figure-fitting tank top and everything" — James was working at the community garden. A young boy,

trying to be chivalrous, offered to shovel for him. James was annoyed. "Don't treat me like a woman," he responded.

Later that day, another staff member who overheard James's reaction asked James point-blank if he had ever thought he might be transgender. Thoughtful, James went home and did some research. "Oh my god," he realized, "this explains everything!"

James was relieved to learn that there was a term for his experience — and that he shared it with many other people. Matter-of-factly, he began to live as a man, first swapping out his feminine clothes for masculine clothes, then slowly but surely

GENDER

CHAPTER 10

Emma McIntyre/Getty Images

started telling his friends and family that he is transgender.

The news elicited a range of reactions from anger and confusion to complete acceptance. His brother was among those who accepted James unconditionally. He said, "Well, I never really saw you as a sister in the first place, so I don't think anything is changing other than pronouns."

In the past several years, James has become a transgender activist. He has spoken at an LGBTQ equality and justice lobbying event in his state capital about the struggles, including homelessness, sometimes suffered by LGBTQ youth. He wants people to know that he's more than

his gender identity, saying, "It's society that really makes our lives revolve around being transgender, not us."

What James's story illustrates is that who we are in this life—our identity—is not determined by any single characteristic or quality. James is transgender, but that's not all James is, just as you are defined by more than a single characteristic. Nonetheless, James's story illustrates that sexual orientation and gender identity are potent forces that shape and direct each of our lives, including the relationships we form. In this chapter, we'll explore how gender stereotypes and gender roles affect all of our lives. We'll also explore the spectrum of human sexuality. ~

James A young man living in a rural area in upstate New York, James is an avid gardener, writer, and artist. He's a volunteer and an activist in his community. He's also transgender. James wants people to realize that there are many parts of his identity as a person. He explained that people "shouldn't really be focused on this term transgender because a lot of people seem to stick us in a category." He wants people to see beyond the label and get to know him as a person.

Photograph: Gene Fischer "James, Teen Shelter", 2013 www.genefischer.com

Gender Nonconformity Around the world, attitudes toward people with nontraditional gender identities and gender expression are changing (Fontanella et al., 2014; Rubin et al., 2020). Although people who don't conform to gender expectations still experience prejudice and discrimination, there is increasing acceptance of the many ways in which gender is experienced and expressed among both cisgender and transgender people.

RoBeDeRo/Getty Images

Introduction: Gender and Sexuality

■ KEY THEME

Although the words are sometimes used interchangeably, *sex* refers to the biological aspects of being male, female, or intersex, while *gender* refers to the psychological, social, and cultural aspects of masculinity and femininity.

≡ KEY QUESTIONS

* What are gender roles?
* How do the terms *gender identity* and *sexual orientation* differ in meaning?

As our description of James's life demonstrates, gender and sexuality are important components of everyone's personal identity. As you read this chapter, we encourage you to think about how *your* life has been shaped by your sex, gender, gender identity, and sexual orientation. Some of the information we present in this chapter may challenge your preconceptions about sexual attitudes and behavior. Certain topics related to gender and sexuality are controversial for some people. However, our primary goal in this chapter is to present research findings in an unbiased and even-handed fashion.

Before we begin, we need to clarify terminology. The English language is less than precise in the arena of gender and sexuality. For example, the word *sex* can be used to describe an activity, as in the phrase "having sex." But the word *sex* is also used to indicate whether someone is biologically male, female, or intersex. In this sense, the term **sex** refers to *biologically determined physical characteristics, such as differences in genetic composition and reproductive anatomy and function* (Pryzgoda & Chrisler, 2000).

In contrast, **gender** refers to *the cultural, social, and psychological meanings that are associated with masculinity and femininity* (Wood & Eagly, 2009). Think of "male" and "female" as designating the main biological categories of *sex*, while "masculine" and "feminine" designate the social, cultural, and psychological categories of *gender.*

Gender roles consist of *the behaviors, attitudes, and personality traits that are designated as either masculine or feminine in a given culture.* **Gender identity** refers to *a person's psychological sense of self as male or female* (Egan & Perry, 2001). Finally, **sexual orientation** refers to *the direction of a person's emotional and erotic attraction, whether toward members of the opposite sex, the same sex, both sexes, or neither sex.*

By the time most people reach adulthood, both gender identity and sexual orientation are well established. Gender identity can develop as young as two or three years old, whereas sexual orientation often develops later, with increases in attraction to the same gender or other genders. Often without our awareness, our behaviors, attitudes, and aspirations have been strongly influenced by the gender-role expectations of our particular culture. But it's important to note that biological sex, gender identity, and sexual orientation are independent of one another. For example, James's gender identity is male, despite the fact that his biological sex at birth was female. Like most transgender people, he prefers the pronouns — *he, him, his* — that match his gender identity rather than his biological sex. (Cisgender people are those whose gender identity matches their biological sex.) Further, as a transgender man who is attracted to women, James' sexual orientation is heterosexual.

In this chapter, we'll take a close look at the development and consequences of male and female gender roles. We'll also examine how sexuality develops. Later in the chapter, we'll consider some of the ways in which the expression of sexuality can become disrupted and psychologically troubling. In Psych for Your Life, at the end of the chapter, we'll look at ways to strengthen intimate relationships.

Gender Stereotypes and Gender Roles

■ **KEY THEME**
Gender-role stereotypes are the beliefs and expectations that people hold about the characteristics and behaviors of each sex.

KEY QUESTIONS
- How do men and women compare in personality characteristics and emotionality?
- How do men and women compare in terms of cognitive abilities?

The beliefs and expectations people hold about the typical characteristics, preferences, and behavior of men and women are referred to as **gender-role stereotypes**. Stereotypes, which we'll explore more in the social psychology chapter, are characteristics associated with the members of a particular group, sometimes inaccurately. In our culture, gender-role stereotypes for men and women are very different. Women are thought (and expected) to be more emotional, nurturing, and patient than are men. Men are thought (and expected) to be more aggressive, decisive, and mechanically minded than are women (Rudman & Glick, 2012). Both women and men are sometimes perceived more negatively when they do not adhere to traditional gender-role stereotypes (Brescoll & Uhlmann, 2005).

People often assume that gender stereotypes are derogatory toward women. In the United States, however, both men and women view the female gender-role stereotype more positively than the male gender-role stereotype (T. L. Lee et al., 2010). Still, psychologists Peter Glick and Susan Fiske (2001, 2003) argue that accepting positive stereotypes of women can produce a type of prejudice called *benevolent sexism.* While benevolent sexism is more socially acceptable than hostile sexism, it can contribute to gender inequality (Cassidy & Krendi, 2019; Glick & Fiske, 2012). For example, studies show that people who hold attitudes of benevolent sexism tend to support the hiring of women in traditionally feminine jobs that tend to have lower pay and prestige and tend to oppose the hiring of women in traditionally masculine positions (Hideg & Ferris, 2016).

What about gender-role stereotypes in other cultures? In a survey of more than 25 cultures, psychologists John Williams and his colleagues (1999) and Deborah Best (2001) discovered a high degree of agreement on the characteristics associated with each sex.

Recent research has highlighted that gender stereotypes can change over time. The researchers analyzed over 70 years of survey data for more than 30,000 people in the United States (Eagly et al., 2019). They found a shift in gender stereotypes toward a perception of equality in many areas, including competence and intelligence. The researchers attribute the shift to women's changing roles in the workplace, an indication that cultural change can lead to changes in stereotypes.

Differences Related to Sex and Gender

Are men and women radically different? It's a common theme in some self-help books, such as the series of books inspired by *Men Are from Mars, Women Are from Venus* (Gray, 2012).

When psychologists scientifically investigate the issue of gender differences, what do they find? *Are* men and women fundamentally different in *all* areas of their lives, as is often claimed in the popular media? Not really. In many aspects of behavior, including social, personality, and cognitive aspects, men and women, across cultures and generations, are very similar (Gerber, 2009; Guimond, 2008; Hyde, 2014; Zell et al., 2015). Janet Hyde and colleagues (2019) prefer to talk about the "psychological gender mosaic." The idea is that most women and men have some characteristics perceived as stereotypically male *and* some as stereotypically female. These researchers describe a study in which participants indicated their engagement in 10 "highly

sex Biologically determined physical characteristics, such as differences in genetic composition and reproductive anatomy and function.

gender The cultural, social, and psychological meanings that are associated with masculinity and femininity.

gender roles The behaviors, attitudes, and personality traits that are designated as either masculine or feminine in a given culture.

gender identity A person's psychological sense of self as male or female.

sexual orientation The direction of a person's emotional and erotic attraction whether toward members of the opposite sex, the same sex, both sexes, or neither sex.

gender-role stereotypes The beliefs and expectations people hold about the typical characteristics, preferences, and behavior of men and women.

Nelly George/Alamy Stock Photo

⌃ **How Accurate Are Gender-Role Stereotypes?** First Lieutenant Candice Bowen is the first female infantry officer in the National Guard of the state of Virginia. When the National Guard is deployed, infantry officers lead soldiers in combat. Yet, U.S. women were once barred from all combat duty. In January 2013, the U.S. defense secretary announced that the ban against women in combat would be phased out by 2016. Yet, even when women were still barred from infantry and other land-based combat units, dozens of female soldiers were killed by military attacks on the ground in Iraq and Afghanistan. How does the active participation of women in the military violate traditional gender-role stereotypes?

THINK LIKE A SCIENTIST

Are you more likely to associate men with science? Go to Achieve Resources to **Think Like a Scientist** about **Gender Stereotypes.**

Achieve

MYTH ◀ SCIENCE

Is it true that most gender differences are caused by biological factors?

gendered" activities—such as playing video games, scrapbooking, taking a bath, and watching porn. There were gender differences for all of these activities, but not even 1 percent of students endorsed only feminine or only masculine activities.

Relatedly, there *are* some significant differences between women and men, even beyond anatomical differences and physiological diversity (Eagly et al., 2004; Wood & Eagly, 2010). However, many psychologists (including many of those who write textbooks) are reluctant to point out the gender differences that have been substantiated. Why? Basically, because some people are quick to equate a gender *difference* with a gender *deficiency*. For example, women's differences from men have historically been used to suggest that women are inferior to men (Moradi et al., 2010; Nutt, 2010). But because men and women are different does not mean that one gender is, as a group, better or worse than another gender.

We've already noted some gender differences in previous chapters, such as male–female differences in friendship patterns (Chapter 9). But before we note other differences, two important qualifications need to be stressed. First, the differences between men and women are *average* differences, not absolute differences. As with other generalizations in psychology, no single finding will apply to *all* men and *all* women. For example, consider the general finding that men tend to think about sex more often than do women (King et al., 2009; Tiegs et al., 2007). In fact, *some* women (19 percent) think about sex more often than almost half the male population. Moreover, in one study, researchers observed that men were more likely than women to think about sex, but they were also more likely than women to think about other biological needs—sleep and food (T. Fisher et al., 2012). The point here is that we tend to focus on the gender differences that fit our expectations. For any given gender difference, there is a wide range of individual variation within each group. There is also quite a bit of overlap between the two groups.

Second, finding that a gender difference exists is one matter. Explaining what *caused* that difference is another matter altogether. For instance, consider the observation that women are more likely than men to wear earrings. This finding says nothing about the *cause* of that difference. Acknowledging that a gender difference exists does not automatically mean that such differences are "natural," "inevitable," or "unchangeable." It is a myth that most gender differences are biologically based.

Bearing these qualifications in mind, let's look at three areas of gender differences: personality, emotionality, and cognitive abilities. Although some differences do exist in these areas, men and women are more similar than they are different (Hyde, 2007, 2014).

Personality Differences For *most* personality characteristics, there are *no* significant average differences between men and women. For example, women and men are, on average, very similar on such characteristics as impulsiveness and orderliness. However, men and women consistently differ on two personality dimensions. The first is that women tend to be more *nurturant* than men. The second is that men tend to be more *assertive* than women (Palomares, 2009; Schmitt et al., 2008).

Summarizing several studies, including cross-cultural research, psychologist Richard Lippa (2010) found that women tended to be more "people-oriented" and less "thing-oriented" than men. As psychologist Alice Eagly (1995) observed, "In general, women tend to manifest behaviors that can be described as socially sensitive, friendly, and concerned with others' welfare, whereas men tend to manifest behaviors that can be described as dominant, controlling, and independent."

Differences in Emotionality Many people also believe that women are much more emotional than men. One of our culture's most pervasive gender stereotypes is that women express their emotions more frequently and intensely than men do. In contrast, men supposedly are calmer and possess greater emotional control (Vigil, 2009). Studies have shown that *both* men and women view women as the more emotional sex

(Barrett & Bliss-Moreau, 2009). But do such widely held stereotypes reflect actual gender differences in emotional experience?

Like so many stereotypes, the gender stereotypes of emotions are not completely accurate. It is a myth that women are more emotional than men. In fact, research suggests that women and men are fairly similar in the *experience* of emotions, although they do differ somewhat in the *expression* of emotions (Chaplin, 2015). For example, researchers have found that women sometimes are more emotionally expressive than men, even when women and men do not differ in the self-ratings of emotions that they experience (Kring & Gordon, 1998; Thunberg & Dimberg, 2000). Women tend to both smile and cry more than men, for example (Fischer & LaFrance, 2015). On the other hand, women and men do not seem to differ in all types of emotional expressions, and in some cases, such as the tendency to furrow their brows when angry, men are more expressive (McDuff et al., 2017).

For both men and women, the expression of emotions is also strongly influenced by *culturally determined display rules,* or societal norms of appropriate behavior in different situations. In many cultures, including the United States, women are allowed a wider range of emotional expressiveness and responsiveness than men. For men, it's considered "unmasculine" to be too open in expressing certain emotions. Crying is especially taboo (Warner & Shields, 2007). Thus, there are strong cultural and gender-role expectations concerning emotional expressiveness and sensitivity.

Culturally determined social norms likely contribute to a phenomenon called "toxic masculinity," a concept propelled into the mainstream by a viral ad for Gillette, the U.S. razor company. "Boys will be boys," the ad proclaimed, but then portrayed men calling out other men on sexist behavior such as catcalling women, or men stopping boys from bullying each other. Many saw the ad as uplifting, but others perceived it as an affront against masculinity (Smith, 2019). Research, however, suggests that toxic masculinity is harmful. In one study, men who adhered to traditional gender roles related to power and domination, particularly over women, tended to have decreased psychological well-being (Kaya et al., 2019). Another report found many boys in the United States felt pressure to adhere to masculine stereotypes, even when they didn't want to (PLAN International, 2018). For example, one-third of boys said they felt pressure to dominate other people. (And, of course, this is not just a U.S. issue.)

The Gillette ad haters missed the point, though. These same researchers identified other aspects of masculinity that are associated with *increased* psychological well-being, including a focus on personal success and achievement (Kaya et al., 2019). Gillette wasn't against masculinity per se, just the aspects that are unhealthy for men and detrimental to women. The "American Psychological Association Guidelines for Psychological Practice with Boys and Men" (2018) echo the findings of these researchers. Based on decades of research, the APA guidelines outline aspects of masculinity, including restricting emotion, that are harmful, and outline ways, such as embracing their roles as fathers, that can help men to thrive.

Some men are now embracing other models of masculinity. As just one example, the 20-something British performer Sam Fender talked about the influence of toxic masculinity on his songwriting. As a response to suicides by young British men, he lamented "a world where men don't feel they can talk about their problems, no matter how bad they are." Fender explained that he "started to question all the archaic ideas of what a bloke is supposed to be" (Farber, 2019). As the Gillette ad concludes, "It's only by challenging ourselves to do more that we can get closer to our best."

Does women's higher emotional expressivity clash with a high-powered career? You may have heard the stereotype that women's tendency toward greater emotional expressiveness translates into an inability to be a strong leader. A *Harvard Business Review* (2013) headline, for example, read: "Emotional, bossy, too nice: The biases that still hold female leaders back." Yet, there is research linking effective leadership with the ability to express emotions (Ilies et al., 2013; Riggio & Reicherd, 2008). And successful leadership styles seem to be shifting, with an increasing value placed on a combination of stereotypically masculine *and* stereotypically feminine traits (Koenig et al., 2011).

MYTH ◄ SCIENCE
Is it true that most women are more emotional than men?

▲ **"A Sign of Weakness"** Many psychological scientists have studied "toxic masculinity," which refers to a sometimes-extreme adherence to cultural norms of masculinity, often to a degree that is harmful to women and constrains men's choices. One example of toxic masculinity was the choice, by some men, not to wear a mask at he height of the pandemic to protect them and others from COVID-19, despite overwhelming evidence that masks help. Researcher Peter Glick (2020) points out that some men perceive that wearing a mask "makes them look weak, and avoiding that is evidently more important to them than demonstrating responsible behavior." Relatedly, in one study (not yet peer-reviewed), men were more likely than women to say that wearing a mask is "not cool" and "a sign of weakness" (Capraro & Barcelo, 2020).

CRITICAL THINKING

Gender Differences: Women in Science, Technology, Engineering, and Mathematics Fields

In recent years, the research on gender differences in cognitive abilities, particularly those related to math, has focused on the disproportionately low numbers of women in science, technology, engineering, and mathematics (STEM) fields. At each level of education and career, there are fewer and fewer women (Goulden et al., 2011).

A number of psychology researchers have examined the reasons for this gender imbalance. As we learned in this chapter, research exploring possible gender differences in cognitive abilities has largely dismissed this as a primary influence (Hyde, 2014). In fact, research has demonstrated that scientists from underrepresented groups, including women and people from minoritized racial groups, are more likely than others to develop innovative ideas (Hofstra et al., 2020). Unfortunately, people from marginalized groups also are less likely to be rewarded for their scientific creativity.

Many researchers have explored the impacts of discrimination and implicit bias that may directly or indirectly drive women's choices and opportunities (Moss-Racusin et al., 2012; Raymond, 2013). For example, Asia Eaton and her colleagues (2020) had U.S. science professors rate resumes of recent Ph.D. graduates. The resumes were identical except for the names, which were chosen to indicate gender and race (Black, Latino/Latina, Asian, or White)—Bradley Miller for a White man and Shanice Banks for a Black woman, for example. The science professors generally rated the male applicants higher than the female applicants in competence and the likelihood that they would get hired. Further, the

Bloomberg/Getty Images

Pursuing Equality in Science An international study found no overall difference in science abilities between boys and girls (OECD, 2010). Nevertheless, fewer women than men pursue careers in science. Scientist Hayat Sindi is working to change that. Born in Saudi Arabia, Sindi earned a doctorate in biotechnology in the United Kingdom. She co-founded a company, Diagnostics for All, to introduce inexpensive technologies to diagnose diseases in the developing world. And she works for gender equality, particularly in Arab countries, in her role as a Goodwill Ambassador for the United Nations Educational, Scientific and Cultural Organization (UNESCO; Almutawakel, 2018).

science professors generally rated the White and Asian applicants higher than the Black and Latino/Latina applicants. These findings highlight the particular challenges faced by women of color in STEM fields.

Kyodo News/TAINAN/Taiwan/Newscom

Women in Power As successful leadership styles shift, value is increasingly placed on both stereotypically masculine and feminine qualities. This shift might lead to more women, like Tsai Ing-wen, the first female President of Taiwan, in top leadership positions. During the pandemic, President Tsai received praise for her leadership in Taiwan, which led the world both in prevention measures like quarantining and testing and in outcome, with fewer than 800 cases in 2020 (Frieden, 2021).

Cognitive Differences Is one sex smarter, more logical, or more creative than the other? No. For *most* cognitive abilities, there are *no* significant differences between males and females (Buss, 1995b; Hyde, 2007, 2016). In fact, psychologists have been questioning the idea that there are cognitive differences for 100 years. *Leta Hollingworth* (1886–1939), whom we introduced in the chapter on Thinking, Language, and Intelligence as the originator of the word *gifted* with respect to intelligence, was perhaps the first psychologist to question cognitive gender differences. She pushed back against the idea, common at the time, that males were more variable than females on any given physical or psychological trait—meaning that females were "doomed to mediocrity." Hollingworth believed that any differences were cultural or societal rather than either innate or based on physical differences. In one study, she measured the skulls of 1,000 infant boys and 1,000 infant girls. She found that boys' skulls were a little larger than girls' skulls, on average, but there seemed to be more variability in girls' skulls.

Hollingworth's assertion of gender equality with respect to cognitive skills has been backed by more recent research. However, once again, some limited differences do exist in this area. Here are some of the best-substantiated gender-related cognitive differences:

- **Verbal, reading, and writing skills.** Females consistently score slightly higher than males on tests of verbal fluency, but there doesn't seem to be a gender difference on other skills such as reading comprehension, vocabulary, and essay writing (Hyde, 2016).

- **Spatial skills.** Males outscore females on some, but not all, tests of spatial skills (Stancey & Turner, 2010). For example, males consistently outperform females on

In another study, more than 500,000 people from 34 countries completed an Implicit Association Test (IAT), a test that measures unconscious associations. (Go to Achieve to try an IAT on gender stereotypes in the Think Like a Scientist feature.) More than 70 percent of participants in this study unconsciously viewed science as more of a masculine than a feminine pursuit (Nosek et al., 2009). A more recent study, however, found that female STEM students, as compared with male STEM students and all students in other fields, exhibited an implicit bias *toward* women in STEM (Farrell & McHugh, 2017).

There also is some evidence that women are *choosing* not to pursue STEM careers. Some blame the lack of female mentors and role models or the perception that the STEM fields are biased against women for this choice (Moss-Racusin et al., 2018; Rosser 2012). Others report that girls who are particularly good at math might be even better at reading, making them less likely to pursue math (Breda & Napp, 2019). Still others cite the effects of deeply rooted gender norms. For example, Lisa DiDonato and JoNell Strough (2013) found that college students tended to prefer gender stereotypical majors and careers for themselves.

Researchers and policy makers have identified a number of solutions to the problem of gender imbalance in STEM fields. First, it may help to explore ways to remove the potential for bias. In one study, contributions by female software coders were accepted more so than those by their male peers, but only if their gender was hidden; otherwise, contributions by male coders were accepted more often (Terrell et al., 2017). So, when possible, the identities of scientists might be withheld prior to judgments of their work. Similarly, Eaton and her colleagues (2020) suggest that professors writing letters of recommendation should be careful not to divulge information indicating an applicant's gender or race.

Second, researchers suggest providing girls, as well as boys, with early STEM experiences and exposure to a broader representation of people in STEM to counter prevailing gender stereotypes (Cheryan et al., 2015, 2017). Third, formal recruitment and retention practices should be established to increase the numbers of women (National Academy of Sciences, 2007). Fourth, researchers and policy groups have questioned the inherently rigid structure of many STEM careers—for example, the large amount of time spent on campus to conduct laboratory experiments. The National Academy of Sciences (2007) pointed out that "anyone lacking the work and family support traditionally provided by a 'wife' is at a serious disadvantage." But, the NAS observed, men were more likely than women to have a spouse at home to provide family support. Moreover, the gender gap in STEM achievement was greater between women and men with children than between women and men without children (Goulden et al., 2009). These researchers encouraged structural changes in STEM fields, like flexible hours and child care, that would benefit both women and men. Psychological science is helping both to explain gender disparities in STEM and to identify solutions.

CRITICAL THINKING QUESTIONS

- Have you or your friends ever felt pressure to like or to dislike a certain academic discipline based on your gender?
- What institutional structures and policy changes might make a career in STEM more hospitable to both women and men who want families?

---

tests measuring the ability to mentally rotate three-dimensional figures (Jansen & Heil, 2010). However, both males and females can improve their spatial skills with experience, so some researchers have encouraged the inclusion of spatial skills in the school curriculum (Hyde, 2016; Verdine et al., 2017). And women are significantly better than men at remembering the location of objects (Spiers et al., 2008; Voyer et al., 2007).

- **Math skills.** Previous research indicated that, on *average,* males do slightly better than females on tests of advanced mathematical ability (see Halpern et al., 2011). However, more recent research indicates that in countries in which girls take as much math as boys, such as the United States, there no longer seems to be a gender difference (Hyde, 2016).

The recent apparent lack of a difference in math skills deserves more comment. One widely believed stereotype is that males are much better than females at math, but science does not back this myth (Schmader et al., 2004). Over the past several decades, the so-called gender gap in mathematics has steadily narrowed in the United States. Moreover, culture seems to play a role. In a study of more than 12,000 children of immigrants, gender differences in math were lower among those whose parents were from countries with higher gender equality (Nollenberger et al., 2014). However, it is true that more males than females score in the very highest range in advanced math achievement tests (D. Reilly et al., 2015). One possible explanation is that very advanced mathematics draws heavily upon spatial abilities (Halpern et al., 2007). We explore gender differences in science and mathematics further in the Critical Thinking box.

Is it true that girls score just as highly as boys on national tests of math skills?

Gender Development

■ KEY THEME

Gender roles are the behaviors, attitudes, and traits that a given culture associates with masculinity and femininity.

⹂ KEY QUESTIONS

• What gender differences develop during childhood?
• What are the major theories that explain gender development?

Being male or female does make a vast difference in most societies. In the United States, newborn babies are often "color-coded" within moments of their birth—girls swaddled in pink and boys in blue. That, of course, is just the beginning of life in a world strongly influenced by sex and gender (see Denny & Pittman, 2007). Many parents may try to raise their children in a "gender-neutral" fashion. However, research shows that even one-year-olds are already sensitive to subtle gender differences in behavior and mannerisms (Poulin-Dubois & Serbin, 2006).

Gender Differences in Childhood Behavior: Spider-Man Versus Barbie

Most toddlers begin using gender labels between the ages of 18 and 21 months. And, roughly between the ages of 2 and 3, children can identify themselves and other children as boys or girls, although the details are still a bit fuzzy to them (Zosuls et al., 2009). Preschoolers don't yet understand that sex is determined by physical characteristics. This is not surprising, considering that the biologically defining sex characteristics—the genitals—are hidden from view most of the time. Instead, young children identify the sexes in terms of external attributes, such as hairstyle, clothing, and activities. This is what most people understand as gender expression.

From about the age of 18 months to the age of two years, sex differences in behavior begin to emerge (Miller et al., 2006). These differences become more pronounced throughout early childhood. Toddler girls play more with soft toys and dolls, and ask for help from adults more than toddler boys do. Toddler boys play more with blocks and transportation toys, such as trucks and wagons. They also play more actively than do girls (see Ruble et al., 2006).

Research suggests that these choices may be in part innate, but they also are due to socialization (see Todd et al., 2017). We know that children are treated differently based on their gender from the time they are born. One study, for example, found that fathers were more likely to engage in "rough-and-tumble" play and to use achievement-related words like *win* with their sons than with their daughters (Mascaro et al., 2017). And the presence of gendered toys in the home also seems to shape children's preferences (Boe & Woods, 2018).

Roughly between the ages of 2 and 3, preschoolers start acquiring gender stereotypes for toys, clothing, household objects, games, and work. Indeed, children categorize jobs by age 5. Valentina Cartei and her colleagues (2020) asked 5- to 10-year-old children to talk in the voice of people in gender-stereotypical jobs. When asked to "imagine how a mechanic sounds," children used more masculine voices, including lower pitch, for the stereotypically masculine profession. When asked to "imagine how a nurse sounds," children used more feminine voices, including higher pitch, for the stereotypically feminine profession.

By the age of 3, children have developed a clear preference for toys that are associated with their own sex. This tendency continues throughout childhood (Berenbaum et al., 2008; Freeman, 2007). An exception to this pattern is seen in many transgender children. For example, James, whom you met in the Prologue, always identified as a boy. He described having a "split wardrobe" as a child. This included the girls' clothing that others expected him to wear and the boys' clothing he preferred.

"I don't see liking trucks as a boy thing. I see it as a liking-trucks thing."

Liza Donnelly The New Yorker Collection/The Cartoon Bank

Paul Bradbury/Getty Images

Stuart Fox/Getty Images

∧ **Separate Worlds?** In early childhood, boys tend to play in groups and favor competitive games and team sports. In contrast, girls tend to establish close relationships with one or two other girls and to cement their friendships by sharing thoughts and feelings (Beal, 1994; Martin & Ruble, 2010). How might such gender differences affect intimate relationships in adolescence and adulthood?

Children are far more rigid than adults in their beliefs in gender stereotypes. Children's strong adherence to gender stereotypes may be a necessary step in developing a gender identity (Halim & Ruble, 2009). Boys are far more rigid than girls in their preferences for toys associated with their own sex. Their attitudes about the sexes are also more rigid than are those held by girls. As girls grow older, they become even more flexible in their views of sex-appropriate activities and attributes, but boys become even less flexible (Schmalz & Kerstetter, 2006).

Girls' more flexible attitude toward gender roles may reflect society's greater tolerance of girls who cross gender lines in attire and behavior. A girl who plays with boys, or who plays with boys' toys, may develop the grudging respect of both sexes. But a boy who plays with girls or with girls' toys may be ostracized by both sexes. Girls are often proud to be labeled a "tomboy," but for many boys, being called a "sissy" is still the ultimate insult (Thorne, 1993). This helps to explain why James's parents were fine with him calling himself a *tomboy*, a socially acceptable term for girls.

James has observed others' expectations from the vantage point of having lived as both female and male at different points in his life. In his turning point story in the Prologue, the boy in the community garden took James's shovel so "she" wouldn't get "her" hands dirty. As a guy, James frequently fields questions about why he is not into stereotypically masculine activities, such as weight lifting. James explains that he hates stereotypes, noting, "I'm not the geek/nerd *stereotype*. But, if you are going to stick me in a category, I'm that one. I'm not a jock." And he hates expectations about how he should dress: "Like you are not allowed to wear bright colors anymore because you're a man?"

As we've seen, contrary to many people's perceptions, there are very few significant differences between the sexes in either personality traits or intellectual abilities. Yet in many ways, children's behavior mirrors the gender-role stereotypes that are predominant in our culture.

Achieve

Barcroft Media/boclips

How does socialization affect children's gender development? Go to **Achieve** and **Video: Gender Neutral Parenting: Why Can't Our Sons Wear Dresses?**

Explaining Gender Differences: Contemporary Theories

Many theories have been proposed to explain the differing patterns of male and female behavior in our culture and in other cultures (see Reid et al., 2008). (Let's face it, you probably have a few opinions on the issue yourself.) We won't even attempt to cover the full range of ideas. Instead, we'll describe three categories of influential psychological theories.

Historically, Alice Eagly and Wendy Wood (2013) observed, most psychologists have explained gender differences with a focus primarily on sociocultural explanations or primarily on biological explanations. Eagly and Wood argue that *both* viewpoints are important. Based on Eagly and Wood's premise, we will discuss some explanations based primarily on sociocultural factors, including social learning theory and gender

Are Males More Interested in Sports than Females Are? Anyone who's watched a closely contested girls' basketball game can attest to the fact that girls can be just as competitive in sports as boys. Contrary to what some people think, there is no evidence to support the notion that girls are inherently less interested in sports than boys. During the middle childhood years, from ages 6 to 10, boys and girls are equally interested in sports (Women's Sports Foundation, 2007). Participating in sports enhances the self-esteem of girls as much as it does boys, especially during adolescence (Slutzky & Simpkins, 2009).

social learning theory of gender development The theory that gender roles are acquired through the basic processes of learning, including reinforcement, punishment, and modeling.

gender schema theory The theory that gender development is influenced by the formation of schemas, or mental representations, of masculinity and femininity.

schema theory, some explanations based primarily on biological factors including evolutionary theory, and interactionist theories that combine both approaches. In the chapter on personality, we will discuss Freud's ideas on the development of gender roles.

Social Learning Theory: Learning Gender Roles

Based on the principles of learning, the **social learning theory of gender-role development** (also called cognitive social learning theory) is *the theory that gender roles are acquired through the basic processes of learning, including reinforcement, punishment, and modeling* (Bussey & Bandura, 2004; Hyde, 2014). According to this theory, from a very young age, children are reinforced or rewarded when they display gender-appropriate behavior and punished when they do not. A little boy may be praised for not crying when he's hurt, while a little girl is comforted if she does.

How do children acquire their understanding of gender norms? Children, for example, learn gender differences through *modeling*. They are exposed to many sources of information about gender roles, including television, video games, books, films, and observation of same-sex adult role models. They observe and then imitate the sex-typed behavior that they observe (Bronstein, 2006; Leaper & Friedman, 2007). By observing and imitating such models—whether it's Mom cooking, Dad fixing things around the house, or a male superhero rescuing a helpless woman in a movie—children come to understand that certain activities and attributes are considered more appropriate for one sex than for the other (Martin & Ruble, 2010).

Gender Schema Theory: Constructing Gender Categories

Gender schema theory, developed by **Sandra Bem** (1944–2014), incorporates some aspects of social learning theory (Martin et al., 2004; Renk et al., 2006). However, Bem (1981) approached gender-role development from a more strongly cognitive perspective. **Gender schema theory** is *the theory that gender development is influenced by the formation of schemas, or mental representations, of masculinity and femininity* (Martin & Ruble, 2004). That is, children actively create gender categories. Saying that "trucks are for boys and dolls are for girls" is an example of a gender schema. Gender schemas influence how people pay attention to, perceive, interpret, and remember gender-relevant behavior. The role of gender schemas in children's behavior was highlighted in a study that found that children who more strongly believed in gender schemas were more likely to choose gendered toys than were children who did not strongly believe in gender schemas (Weisgram, 2016).

Children readily assimilate new information into their existing gender schemas (Miller et al., 2006). In a classic study, four- to nine-year-olds were given boxes of gender-neutral gadgets, such as hole punches (Bradbard et al., 1986). But some gadgets were labeled as "girl toys" and some as "boy toys." The boys played more with the "boy" gadgets, and the girls played more with the "girl" gadgets. A week later, the children easily remembered which gadgets went with each sex. They also remembered more information about the gadgets that were associated with their own sex. Simply labeling the objects as belonging to boys or to girls had powerful consequences for the children's behavior and memory—evidence of the importance of gender schemas in learning and remembering new information.

Gender schemas are pervasive. For example, research has documented differences in line with gender roles in children's Halloween costumes, dolls, action figures, valentines, and television ads for toys (Murnen et al., 2016; Smith, 2015). There have been some changes; major retailers including Target, Disney, and Amazon no longer categorize products such as toys and Halloween costumes as "boy" and "girl" (Tabuchi, 2015). But gender schemas are unlikely to disappear anytime soon.

Evolutionary Theories Some researchers use primarily biological explanations to explain gender differences in behavior and personality. Perhaps the most prominent of

Randy Faris/Getty Images

the biological explanations are those that cite evolution as the primary cause of many gender differences. According to the evolutionary approach, gender differences are the result of generations of the dual forces of sexual selection and parental investment (Hyde, 2014). Physical and psychological characteristics—related to either the choice of a mate or the investment in raising one's children—that increased the likelihood of reproductive success tend to become more common. According to evolutionary psychology, behavior and traits are adaptive to the degree that they further the transmission of one's genes to the next generation and beyond.

Evolutionary explanations have been explored for gender differences in a number of areas, including cognitive skills (see Cosmides & Tooby, 2013). For example, women seem to be better than men at spatial skills when the target is edible plants. Evolutionary researchers attribute this gender difference to a need for women to have foraging expertise in generations past (New et al., 2007).

However, the topic of mate preferences has received more research attention by evolutionary psychologists (Schmitt et al., 2012). To investigate mate preferences, psychologist David Buss (1994, 2009) coordinated a large-scale survey of more than 10,000 people in 37 different cultures. Across all cultures, Buss found, men were more likely than women to value youth and physical attractiveness in a potential mate. In contrast, women were more likely than men to value financial security, access to material resources, high status and education, and good financial prospects.

Buss (1995a, 2009, 2011), an evolutionary psychologist, interprets these gender differences as reflecting the different "mating strategies" of men and women. He contends that men and women face very different "adaptive problems" in selecting a mate. According to Buss (1995b, 1996), the adaptive problem for men is to identify and mate with women who are likely to be successful at bearing their children. Thus, men are more likely to place a high value on youth, because it is associated with fertility, and physical attractiveness, because it signals that the woman is probably physically healthy and has high-quality genes. Women also seek "good" genes, and thus they value men who are healthy and attractive. But women, on the other hand, have a more pressing need: making sure that the children they do bear survive to carry their genes into future generations (Buss, 2011). Thus, they seek men who possess the resources that the women and their offspring will need to survive.

The evolutionary explanation of sex differences, whether in mate preferences or other areas, is controversial (Confer et al., 2010). Some psychologists argue that it is overly deterministic and does not sufficiently acknowledge the role of culture, gender-role socialization, and other social factors (Eagly & Wood, 2011; Pedersen et al., 2010). A re-analysis of some of Buss's data, for example, found that the importance women place on a potential mate's resources is lower in cultures with more gender equality (Eagly & Wood, 1999).

With respect to his research on mate preferences, Buss (2011) reported that his extensive survey also found that men and women across 37 cultures agreed that the *most* important factor in choosing a mate was mutual attraction and love. And both sexes rated kindness, intelligence, emotional stability, health, and a pleasing personality as more important than a prospective mate's financial resources or good looks.

Buss also flatly states that explaining some of the reasons that might underlie sexual inequality does *not* mean that sexual inequality is natural, correct, or justified. Rather, evolutionary psychologists believe that we must understand the conditions that foster sexual inequality in order to overcome or change those conditions (Buss & Schmitt, 2011).

Interactionist Theories Eagly and Wood (2013) point out that there are many areas of agreement between those who favor sociocultural explanations and those who favor biological explanations. They encourage the development of interactionist theories that explain a given observation using a combination of explanations.

Let's look at one example highlighted by Eagly and Wood (2013)—the division of labor along gender lines. Eagly and Wood observe that men tend to be physically larger and stronger than women and that women are biologically responsible for reproduction.

⌃ **Gendered Toys** Children's toys continue to reinforce gender stereotypes, not only in subtle ways but also in obvious ways as in these Lego displays. One study analyzed the language and themes used in the marketing and packaging of the LEGO Friends line, which is marketed to girls, and the LEGO City line, which is marketed to boys (Reich et al., 2018). The researchers found that the Friends line emphasized "hobbies, being domestic, caring for others, socializing, being amateurs, and appreciating and striving for beauty," whereas the City line emphasized "skilled professions, heroism, and expertise" (p. 285).

Laurence Griffiths/Getty Images

⌃ Challenging Expectations What makes weight lifting a "male" activity? Sarah Robles, a world champion weight lifter from the United States, engages in athletic pursuits that many might not expect for a woman. Are biological constraints a factor here?

These biological differences mean that it can be more efficient for men to be responsible for some activities—say, those that involve heavy lifting—and women to be responsible for others—say, those that involve nurturing an infant. Eagly and Wood (2013) also point out that there are social and psychological factors that create expectations in society that make the "division of labor seem natural and inevitable."

For example, since James began living as a man, several people have wondered why he does not engage in masculine athletic feats. "You should lift weights," he's been told as a man, but not as a woman. This suggestion draws on gender role beliefs about what women and men *should* do, rather than on examining James's biological abilities—or his preferences! Indeed, James's biological abilities just before and after his transition to living as a man would have been the same. Conversely, you may have seen women scoop crying babies from their husbands' arms because the men were thought biologically incapable of soothing the baby.

Biology plays a role in what women and men do, but both women and men might be prevented from taking part in certain activities for reasons other than biological or physical limitations. Psychological and socially driven beliefs about talents and abilities can also limit opportunities and choices. From the interactionist perspective, it is the interplay of biological constraints and psychological and social constraints that drives the division of labor.

Eagly and Wood (2013) admit that it is challenging to incorporate the many biological and sociocultural influences that might drive any given behavior. However, they see attempts at integrating explanations from the two categories as essential to gaining a fuller understanding of the psychology of sex and gender. For more on the role of culture in the expression of gender, see the Culture and Human Behavior box, "The Outward Display of Gender."

Beyond Male and Female: Variations in Sex Development and Gender Identity

So far in this chapter, we have explored gender differences and explanations of the development of gender roles. As we have seen, men and women are different, but they are not polar opposites. Instead, there is a great deal of overlap between them. Despite that, most people develop a clear sense of gender identity as either male *or* female. For most people, their sense of gender identity is consistent with their physical anatomy.

But for a significant minority of people, including James, gender identity and biological sex are not consistent. In other cases, biological factors blur the distinctions between male and female cells and body structures. During the course of prenatal development, chromosomal anomalies or atypical hormonal levels can affect the development of genitals or reproductive organs. The result is that there are other variations in gender identity beyond the typical categories of male or female.

Intersex People **Intersex** is a *condition in which a person's biological sex is ambiguous, often combining aspects of both male and female anatomy and physiology.* According to DSM-5, intersex people are diagnosed as having a disorder of sex development. However, many object to the designation of intersex people as having a disorder (see Kraus, 2015). Psychologists point to the biological diversity of sex and note that people who are intersex do not necessarily need medical treatment or exhibit a related mental illness (Carpenter, 2020; Kraus, 2015). Elizabeth Reis (2007) introduced the term *divergence of sex development* as a way to capture the experience of people who are intersex without stigmatizing or medicalizing the condition. And many intersex people have embraced "the language of identity, human rights, and pride" (Caplan-Bricker, 2017).

In most cases, up until six or seven weeks of gestation, the genital tissue is identical in male and female fetuses. Typically, after this point, the Y chromosome spurs the development of male genitalia. In the absence of the Y chromosome, female genitalia develop. But sometimes, this process is disrupted, which can cause a wide range of combinations of sex chromosomes and sex anatomy (Ainsworth, 2015). With a disorder of sex development, reproductive structures may be partly male and partly female, tissues may be insensitive to the effects of hormones, or tissues may be exposed to hormone levels that are inconsistent with the person's genetic sex (Pasterski, 2008).

intersex Condition in which a person's biological sex is ambiguous, often combining aspects of both male and female anatomy and physiology.

Until recently, there was little general awareness of the condition. What is most likely the first U.S. birth certificate listing "intersex" instead of "male" or "female" was only granted in 2016, to 55-year-old Sara Kelly Keenan (O'Hara, 2016). Adding an official third gender to account for intersex people and others who do not identify as either male or female is becoming a trend with U.S. states, countries, airlines, and other organizations (Harmon, 2019). Germany, for example, created a third-gender category in 2017 (Eddy & Bennett, 2017). The Culture and Human Behavior box discusses India's introduction of a third gender.

In past years, most infants who were born with ambiguous genitals were surgically "corrected" so as to have the appearance of one sex or the other. In some cases, the gender labels imposed at birth eventually conflicted with the adolescents' developing gender identities. And people who are intersex are not always identified at birth (Lindahl, 2019). In a high-profile example, several women were discovered to be intersex only when they were challenged as elite athletes with masculine appearances (Padawer, 2016). The humiliating examinations that followed these challenges led some women to stage legal fights. One woman successfully argued that the practice is unfairly discriminatory.

Today, some intersex advocacy groups, such as the InterACT Advocates for Intersex Youth (interactadvocates.org), oppose surgical and other interventions in infancy. Intersex advocacy organizations believe that the stigma associated with the condition is the biggest problem faced by people who are intersex (Chase, 2003, 2006). Such organizations recommend that parents and doctors should assign a gender to the newborn infant but should not perform irreversible surgery. Rather, surgery and hormone treatments, if needed, should be offered when the person is mature enough to provide informed consent—and after the intersex person's gender identity has been formed.

Transgender People **Transgender** is a *condition in which a person's psychological gender identity conflicts with their biological sex.* For transgender people, the sex they are assigned at birth—male or female—is in conflict with their gender identity—who they know themselves to be (Sohn & Bosinski, 2007). A *transgender man*, such as James, is someone assigned female at birth who identifies and lives as a man. A *transgender woman* is someone assigned male at birth who identifies and lives as a woman. A *cisgender man* or *woman* refers to someone who is assigned a sex at birth that matches their gender identity, such as a person assigned female at birth who identifies and lives as a woman. Because this situation is viewed as the norm, the term is infrequently used. Beyond cisgender and transgender, some people are non-binary, neither exclusively male nor exclusively female. Non-binary people, as well as some other people, often use "they" and "them" as their personal pronouns.

What percentage of people identify as transgender? Across multiple countries, about 0.5 percent of people describe themselves as transgender (Collin et al., 2016). In the United States, that translates into about 1.4 million transgender people (Flores et al., 2016). Data suggest that this rate has been constant for decades (Herman et al., 2017). So, despite increased media focus on transgender people, being transgender is not something new. In fact, historical records indicate the presence of varying gender identities, including being transgender, for hundreds of years (Diavolo, 2017). In Italy in the 1700s, for example, *il femminiello* referred to a person who was assigned male at birth, but dressed and acted as a woman and identified as a third gender (Mauriello, 2017). In North America, prior to colonization, there were multiple genders among many indigenous groups, including the Navajo, Lakota, and Zuni people (Reis, 2004). Many North American indigenous people have reclaimed these historical identities, adopting the term *two-spirit* not just for transgender people, but for all who identify as LGBT (Robinson, 2019). (See the Culture and Human Behavior box for additional examples—people who identify as Muxes in Mexico and as hijra in India.)

Researchers are not yet certain what causes people to be transgender. But most researchers point to biological factors, in part because transgender people's brains seem to be neither completely like those of cisgender women nor like those of cisgender men in terms of structure and processes (Kranz et al., 2014; Smith et al., 2015).

Like James, the typical transgender person has the strong feeling, often present since childhood, of having been born in the body of the wrong sex (Cohen-Kettenis &

The Washington Post/Getty Images

▲ **Intersex Activist** A growing number of intersex activists are speaking out, asking that their communities consider their being intersex as a sexual identity rather than a medical condition. Among them is Anastasia von Buskirk who told a reporter that "In ninth or 10th grade, we were learning about — I don't think they used the word 'intersex' — but intersex conditions, and I was reading the descriptions, trying to figure out which one I was. I went to my teacher and said, 'I think I'm one of these,' and my teacher basically said, 'If you are, you shouldn't tell anyone'" (Caplan-Bricker, 2017). Anastasia was able to ignore that message, and now the activist work she is doing alongside her intersex peers is helping to educate their communities about biological diversity and to change perceptions about intersex people.

transgender Condition in which a person's psychological gender identity conflicts with their biological sex.

CULTURE AND HUMAN BEHAVIOR

The Outward Display of Gender

We have outlined the differences based on biological sex, as well as some based on gender. We have also emphasized the remarkable diversity among individual people of a given biological sex or gender identity. Is there also diversity in the expression of gender across cultures and not just across individual people? In the United States, for example, there are fewer constraints on girls' and women's attire than there are on boys' and men's attire. Blue jeans on a girl are perfectly acceptable, but a skirt on a boy may raise a few eyebrows.

This gender-based rigidity for men may be, in part, culture-based. There are cultures that promote flexibility, at least in some circumstances. Some Zulu men and boys in South Africa belong to a Baptist church and participate in a ceremonial retreat twice a year (Yablonsky, 2013). During these month-long festivals, male church members wear "feminine" clothes, including skirts and headbands adorned with pompoms. South African artist Zwelethu Mthethwa told a reporter, "Zulu culture is all about being macho, and I like the way they flip that."

In other cultures, gender roles are rigidly defined, but it is sometimes acceptable for either a man or a woman to occupy the role of a man. In parts of southeastern Europe, households were traditionally headed by men, and women were considered part of the property. When there was no male heir, a female heir often would be recruited to become a "sworn virgin" (or "kollovar") and head the household (A. Young, 2000). In this role, she made decisions for her extended family on matters ranging from education to marriage. She also represented the family at village meetings.

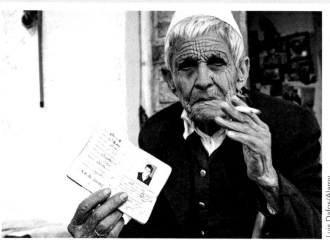

Luis Dafos/Alamy

▲ **Sworn Virgin** In 2008, the BBC interviewed 88-year-old Qamile Stema of Albania, shown here, one of the last of the sworn virgins. She had accepted the male role when her father died, leaving no male heirs, and she discovered that she enjoyed it. Stema listed the privileges she enjoyed that were denied to other women: She could work, smoke, pray with the men at the mosque, and carry a weapon. Stema concluded, "I've had a good life."

Of course, for most women, the decision to become a sworn virgin was not based on gender identity, but rather on protection of the family's assets. Nonetheless, in this very traditional society and era, sworn

---

Is it true that transgender people are lesbians or gay men?

Pfafflin, 2010; Zucker & Cohen-Kettenis, 2008). It is a myth that all transgender people are lesbians or gay men. Gender identity is distinct from sexual orientation. A transgender person may be gay, lesbian, bisexual, heterosexual, or asexual. James, for example, identifies as a straight man and is romantically interested in women.

Some transgender people choose to undergo *gender confirmation surgery* (formerly referred to as sex reassignment surgery), hormone replacement therapy, or both to bring their sex assigned at birth into alignment with their gender identity. This process is unique to each person and is called *transition.* Even before making these decisions, some transgender people undergo a "social transition" during which they may change their name, pronouns, and clothing styles (Turban, 2017).

Younger transgender people may also choose to take puberty blockers, a drug that prevents the changes that occur during puberty until they can begin hormone replacement therapy (Lopez et al., 2018). Research suggests that young transgender people who undergo a social transition and take puberty blockers have better psychological and social outcomes than their peers who do not (de Vries et al., 2014; Durwood et al., 2017). Researchers continue to conduct longitudinal studies that follow young transgender people to learn what transition practices lead to the best outcomes (Olson-Kennedy et al., 2019). In general, however, transition seems to have positive outcomes. A research project at Cornell University reviewed more than 70 studies and concluded that medical treatments such as hormone therapy and surgeries tend to increase the psychological well-being of transgender people (What We Know, 2018).

Is being transgender a psychological disorder? A diagnosis of *gender dysphoria* is made only when a transgender person experiences intense distress or problems

Nicola 'Okin' Frioli/Anzenberg/Redux

⌃ **A Third Gender** The Muxes are men in the indigenous Zapotec community of southern Mexico who dress like women and take on a female gender role in their society. For hundreds of years, the Muxes have existed as a third gender, one respected by their community more readily than gay men and other gender nonconforming men.

In other cultures, the range of acceptable gender roles is broadened for some people. In India, the hijra are considered a "third sex"—"neither man nor woman" (Nanda, 1999). The hijra include transgender women, intersex people, and men who cross-dress without taking additional steps to become female (Hossain, 2012). Unlike many transgender people in other parts of the world, many hijra make no attempt to appear female (Nanda, 1999).

Beyond the identification as hijra by individual men, groups of hijra form a subculture within Indian society, often living as a community under the leadership of a guru often called a "mother" or "grandmother" (Barry, 2016; Kalra, 2012). Some hijra earn money by performing at ritual events such as births or marriages (Nanda, 1999). Hijra tend to be accepted and even respected for their "other-worldliness," to a much larger extent than transgender people who are not part of these communities or who live in other parts of the world (Nanda, 1999). In 2014, India's Supreme Court created a legal "third gender" that includes transgender people and hijra. There have been similar traditions of an accepted third gender, including the wakashu until the late 1800s in Japan and the Muxes today in Mexico (Chira, 2017; Mirandé, 2014).

Although these examples are striking ones, they underline the role that culture plays for all of us in our gender expression—whether as a young girl who dresses as a tomboy in a Western culture or as a man who wears a kilt and headband as part of a Baptist tradition in Zulu cultures. Cultural expectations can constrain or broaden our gender-related choices.

virgins lived as men, adopting the attire and hairstyles typical for men—sometimes even a traditionally male name. More importantly, they were accepted as men, routinely socializing and interacting with men on an equal basis. In exchange for the respect accorded a man, sworn virgins renounced any sexual or romantic relationships.

functioning at work, in relationships, or in other areas (American Psychiatric Association, 2013). Previously called *gender identity disorder,* the language was recently changed to emphasize that it is the feeling of *distress,* and not the discrepancy, that is considered to be a psychological disorder. Most professionals today, as well as most transgender people, disagree with classifying gender-variant behaviors, attitudes, and feelings as a mental illness (Ashley, 2019; Davies & Davies, 2020; Johnson, 2019).

Intersex and transgender people, including James, continue to face discrimination and prejudice in many aspects of their lives (Elischberger et al., 2016; Norton & Herek, 2013). Such discrimination can have profound consequences. Transgender people in the United States are twice as likely to be living in poverty and three times as likely to be unemployed as the general population (James et al., 2016). More disturbing, a survey of almost 6,500 transgender people found that those who had been denied access to bathrooms or on-campus housing that matched their gender identity were more likely than other transgender people to have attempted suicide (Seelman, 2016). Many intersex people have the additional challenge of growing up in ignorance of their medical background. But some would argue that their lives are not all that different from those of cisgender people. In line with that thought, Jim Costich (2003)—writer, activist, father, and self-identified gay intersex man—explained:

> Ultimately every single person is confined, conflicted, marginalized, and minimalized in some way by the arbitrary, unreasonable, and impossible artificial gender expectations of our society. This is no less true for [cisgender people] than for [intersex people]. Whenever we show them how parts of their story are like parts of our story, and vice versa, we knock another brick out of the gender wall.

George Tames/The New York Times. Redux

▲ **Pioneers of Sex Research: William Masters (1915–2001) and Virginia Johnson (1925–2013)** In 1966 Masters and Johnson, shown here interviewing a couple, broke new ground in the scientific study of sexual behavior when they published *Human Sexual Response*. In that book they provided the first extensive laboratory data on the anatomy and physiology of the male and female sexual response. Although intended for clinicians, the book became a best-seller that was translated into over 30 languages. Some critics felt the Masters and Johnson research had violated "sacred ground" and dehumanized sexuality. But others applauded *Human Sexual Response* for advancing the understanding of human sexuality and dispelling misconceptions. The techniques they developed are still widely used in sex therapy today.

MYTH ◀ SCIENCE

Is it true that once they are in their 70s and 80s, very few adults are sexually active?

❯ **Intimacy in Middle Adulthood** Marriage is the mainstay of middle adulthood. Among those in the age group of 45 to 54 years, more than two-thirds are married (U.S. Census Bureau, 2008a). Although middle-aged marriage is often depicted as boring in the media, studies consistently show that marital quality improves from young adulthood to middle adulthood. As children are successfully launched into the world, couples have more time for each other and the activities that interest them. It is in this context—the marital relationship—that middle-aged adults realize the most satisfying affectionate, sexual, and emotional experiences (Gorchoff et al., 2008; Henry et al., 2007; Rosen & Bachmann, 2008).

There's growing recognition of the need for laws that might help lead to reduced discrimination and stigma based on sexual orientation and gender identity. The Yogyakarta Principles (yogyakartaprinciples.org), developed by international human rights experts and most recently updated in 2017, provide an important blueprint for activists and policy makers (Carpenter, 2020; Grinspan et al., 2017).

Human Sexuality

■ **KEY THEME**
Multiple factors are involved in understanding human sexuality.

⹀ **KEY QUESTIONS**
- What are the four stages of human sexual response?
- How does sexual motivation differ among animal species?
- What biological factors are involved in sexual motivation?

Psychologists consider the drive to have sex a basic human motive. But what exactly motivates that drive? Obviously, there are differences between sex and other basic motives, such as hunger. Engaging in sexual intercourse is essential to the survival of the human species, but it is not essential to the survival of any specific person. In other words, you'll die if you don't eat, but you won't die if you don't have sex.

First Things First: The Stages of Human Sexual Response

The human sexual response cycle was first mapped by sex research pioneers **William Masters** and **Virginia Johnson** during the 1950s and 1960s. Masters and Johnson observed hundreds of people engage in more than 10,000 episodes of sexual activity in their laboratory. Their findings, published in 1966, indicated that the human sexual response could be described as a cycle with four stages: excitement, plateau, orgasm, and resolution.

Which Americans have the most active sex lives? Although you might guess young, single adults, the fact is that, at least among heterosexual people, married or cohabiting couples have the most active sex lives (Herbenick et al., 2010; Reece et al., 2010). And most people enjoy their sex lives.

Contrary to myth, for many people, sexual activity continues across the lifespan. More than half of heterosexual people aged 60 to 85 years old are sexually active. In fact, about one-third of 75- to 85-year-olds remain sexually active (Lindau & Gavrilova, 2010). There is less research on aging and sexuality among lesbians and gay men, but the research suggest that many lesbian and gay people also remain sexually active later in life. Unlike the heterosexual population, however, members of the current older generation of gay and lesbian people may be less likely to initiate new sexual relationships because of the higher levels of stigma they have experienced across their lifetimes (DeLamater & Koepsel, 2015).

Thomas Barwick/Getty Images

What Motivates Sexual Behavior?

In most animals, sexual behavior is biologically determined and triggered by hormonal changes in the female. During the cyclical period known as *estrus*, a female animal is fertile and receptive to male sexual advances. The female animal will often actively signal her willingness to engage in sexual activity—as any owner of an unspayed female cat or dog that's "in heat" can testify. In many, but not all, species, sexual activity takes place only when the female is in estrus.

As you go up the evolutionary scale, moving from relatively simple to more sophisticated animals, sexual behavior becomes less biologically determined and more subject to learning and environmental influences. For example, in some primate species, such as monkeys and apes, sexual activity can occur at any time, not just when the female is fertile. In these species, sexual interaction serves important social functions, defining and cementing relationships among the members of the primate group.

One rare species of chimplike apes, the bonobos of the Democratic Republic of the Congo, exhibits varied sexual behavior that seems to serve important social functions (de Waal, 2007; Parish & de Waal, 2000). Although most nonhuman animals *copulate,* or have sex, with the male mounting the female from behind, bonobos often copulate face-to-face. Bonobos also engage in oral sex and intense tongue kissing. Among the bonobos, sexual interaction is used to increase group cohesion, avoid conflict, and decrease tension that might be caused by competition for food.

In humans, of course, sexual behavior is not limited to a woman's fertile period. And, motives for sexual behavior are not limited to reproduction. Even when a woman's ovaries, which produce the female sex hormone *estrogen,* are surgically removed or stop functioning during menopause, there is little or no drop in sexual interest.

In male animals, removal of the testes (castration) typically causes a steep drop in sexual activity and interest. Castration causes a significant decrease in levels of *testosterone,* the hormone responsible for male sexual development.

Of course, sexual behavior is greatly influenced by many different factors—social, cultural, and more. Could evolution have played a role?

Sexual Orientation: The Elusive Search for an Explanation

■ KEY THEME
Sexual orientation refers to whether a person is sexually attracted to members of a different sex, the same sex, both sexes, or neither sex.

⹂ KEY QUESTIONS
- Why is sexual orientation sometimes difficult to identify?
- What factors have been associated with sexual orientation?

Given that biological factors seem to play an important role in motivating sexual desire, it seems only reasonable to ask whether biological factors also play a role in sexual orientation. Sexual orientation refers to whether a person is sexually aroused by members of the same sex, a different sex, both sexes, or neither sex. A *heterosexual* person is sexually attracted to people of the other sex, a *homosexual* person to people of the same sex, and a *bisexual* person to people of the same and different sexes. Technically, the term *homosexual* can be applied to either men or women. However, homosexual women are usually called *lesbians.* Homosexual men typically use the term *gay* to describe their sexual orientation. And, people who are *asexual* are not sexually attracted to people of any sex, regardless of their actual sexual behavior (Bogaert, 2006). Asexual people may or may not have romantic attractions, so some asexual people identify as romantic asexual people and some as aromantic asexual people (Antonsen et al., 2020). (The term *allosexual* is increasingly used to refer to all people who are *not* asexual.)

Sexual orientation is not nearly as cut and dried as many people believe. Some people *are* exclusively heterosexual or homosexual, but others are less easy to categorize. Some people explicitly identify as "mostly," but not exclusively, heterosexual or homosexual (Savin-Williams, 2016; Vrangalova & Savin-Williams, 2012). Some people who consider themselves heterosexual have had a homosexual experience at some point in their lives. In the same vein, many people who identify as homosexual have had heterosexual experiences (Malcolm, 2008; Rieger et al., 2005). Other people consider themselves to be homosexual but have been involved in long-term, committed heterosexual relationships. The key points are that there is a range of sexual orientations and there

▲ **The Bonobos of the Congo** Bonobos demonstrate a wide variety of sexual interactions, including face-to-face copulation, kissing, and sexual interaction among same-sex pairs (Fruth & Hohmann, 2006; Parish & de Waal, 2000). Sexual behavior is not limited to reproduction; it seems to play an important role in maintaining peaceful relations among members of the bonobo group. As Frans de Waal (1995) wrote, "For these animals, sexual behavior is indistinguishable from social behavior."

REUTERS/Alamy

FIGURE 10.1 The Increase in Bisexuality Among Women The overall percentage of the U.S. population who identify as LGBTQ has increased in recent years, primarily because of increases in people who identify as bisexual (Bridges, 2017). In particular, the percentage of women who identified as bisexual increased from just over 3 percent in 2008 to about 8 percent in 2016. More recent data suggest that these trends are continuing (Compton & Bridges, 2019). And there are racial differences in these numbers. In one survey, 23 percent of young Black women identified as bisexual (Bridges & Moore, 2019).

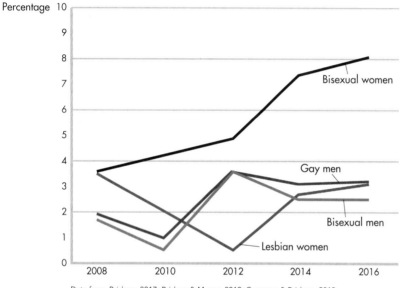

Data from: Bridges, 2017; Bridges & Moore, 2019; Compton & Bridges, 2019.

is not always a perfect correspondence between a particular person's sexual identity, sexual desires, and sexual behaviors. As bisexual journalist Charles Blow (2015) writes, "Attraction is attraction, and it doesn't always wear a label."

Determining the number of people who are homosexual, heterosexual, bisexual, or asexual is challenging. First, survey results vary depending on how the researchers define the terms *homosexual, heterosexual, bisexual,* and *asexual* (Bogaert, 2006; Savin-Williams, 2009). Where the survey is conducted, how survey participants are selected, and how the survey questions are worded also affect the results.

Depending upon how sexual orientation is defined, estimates of the prevalence rate of homosexuality in the general population range from 1 percent to 21 percent (Savin-Williams, 2006). More important than the exact number of gay and lesbian people is the recognition that gay and lesbian people constitute a significant segment of the adult population. According to recent estimates, about 7 percent of women and 5 percent of men in the United States report having ever engaged in homosexual behavior (F. Xu et al., 2010a, 2010b). Worldwide, researchers estimate that less than 5 percent of the population is homosexual, with no evidence that rates have changed over time or are different across cultures (Bailey et al., 2016).

Overall, the percentage of the U.S. population who identify as LGBTQ is growing. The increase is due, in large part, to increases in the numbers of people who identify as bisexual (see **Figure 10.1**). Approximately 3 percent of the U.S. population identify as bisexual, a rate about double that for those who identify as lesbian or gay (Bridges, 2017). The increase is particularly high among young people, and particularly among young Black women (Mishel et al., 2018). In a recent U.S. survey, 23 percent of Black women between the ages of 18 and 34 identified as bisexual (Bridges & Moore, 2019).

Asexuality has been studied much less than other sexual orientations. However, one study of over 18,000 people living in the United Kingdom found that about 1 percent of people reported no sexual attraction to other people (Bogaert, 2004). In addition to a lack of sexual attraction to other people, asexual people were less likely than other people to report that they masturbated and had sexual fantasies (Yule et al., 2017). Yet, many asexual people report difficulties in convincing people that asexuality is real (Robbins et al., 2016). One young asexual person expressed relief when she found a support group for people like her (Kaletsky, 2015). As 22-year-old Anna Goshua (2018) wrote about her asexual orientation, "While romance and sex are an important part of growing up for many, these experiences do not constitute a universal rite of passage. They don't define our maturity or our ability to form fulfilling relationships, and they certainly don't diminish our humanity."

What Determines Sexual Orientation? Despite considerable research on this question, psychologists don't know what determines sexual orientation. Still, research on sexual orientation has pointed toward several general conclusions, especially with regard to homosexuality. For one, there is more evidence in support of non-environmental causes such as genetics than of environmental causes such as cultural acceptance of varying sexual orientations (Bailey et al., 2016).

Evidence from multiple studies shows that genetics plays a role in determining sexual orientation (Rodriguez-Larralde & Paradisi, 2009). But it's not just a single gene, or even a few, that drive sexual orientation. Researcher Andrea Ganna and his colleagues (2019) examined genetic material from about 0.5 million people using data sets from companies like 23andMe and found that multiple genes are responsible for sexual orientation. They also concluded that about a third of the variability related to sexual orientation is due to genetic differences among people. But most genetic studies compare the incidence of homosexuality among pairs of identical twins (who have identical genes), fraternal twins (who are genetically as similar as any two nontwin siblings), and nontwin siblings. In both men and women, research has shown that the closer the degree of genetic relationship, the more likely it is that when one sibling is homosexual, the other would also be homosexual. Moreover, genetics contributes to same-sex orientation in both men and women, but it contributes to a much lesser degree in women than men (Alanko et al., 2010; Långström et al., 2010).

For example, one intriguing finding is that the more older brothers a man has, the more likely he is to be gay (Blanchard, 2008; Blanchard & Lippa, 2008). Could a same-sex orientation be due to psychological factors, such as younger brothers being bullied or indulged by older male siblings? Or being treated differently by their parents, or some other family dynamic?

No. Collecting data on men who grew up in adoptive or blended families, Anthony Bogaert (2007a) found that only the number of biologically related older brothers predicted same-sex orientation. Living with older brothers who were *not* biologically related had no effect at all. As Anthony Bogaert (2007b) explains, "It's not the brothers you lived with; it's the environment within the same womb—sharing the same mom." Researchers don't have an explanation for the effect, which has been replicated in multiple studies (see Bogaert, 2007a). One suggestion is that carrying successive male children might trigger some sort of immune response in the mother that, in turn, influences brain development in the male fetus (James, 2006).

In general, the only conclusion we can draw from these studies is that some biological factors are *correlated* with a same-sex orientation (Mustanski et al., 2002). As we've stressed, correlation does not necessarily indicate causality, only that two factors *seem* to occur together. So stronger conclusions about the role of genetic and biological factors in determining sexual orientation await more definitive research findings.

Several researchers now believe that sexual orientation is established as early as age 6 (Strickland, 1995). Do children who later grow up to be homosexual differ from children who later grow up to be heterosexual? In at least one respect, there seems to be a difference.

Typically, boys and girls differ in their choice of toys, playmates, and activities from early childhood. However, studies that ask gay men and lesbians about their childhoods have found that gay men and lesbians across many different cultures are less likely to have followed the typical pattern of gender-specific behaviors in childhood (Bailey et al., 2016; Lippa, 2008; Rieger et al., 2008). Compared to heterosexual men, gay men recall engaging in more cross-sex-typed behavior during childhood. For example, they remembered playing more with girls than with other boys, preferring girls' toys over boys' toys, and disliking rough-and-tumble play. Lesbians are also more likely to recall cross-gender behavior in childhood. One study suggests that lesbians show an even greater degree of gender nonconformity than gay men (Lippa, 2008).

Once sexual orientation is established, whether heterosexual or homosexual, it is highly resistant to change (Drescher & Zucker, 2006). The vast majority of homosexual people would be unable to change their orientation even if they wished to, just as the majority of heterosexual people would be unable to change their orientation if *they* wished to. Thus, it's a mistake to assume that people who are homosexual have deliberately chosen their sexual orientation any more than people who are heterosexual have. In fact, researcher J. Michael Bailey and his colleagues (2016) push back against the whole question of choice with regard to sexual orientation: "It makes sense to say that people choose their sexual partners, but it doesn't make sense to say that they choose their desires."

The bottom line is that whether we are homosexual, bisexual, heterosexual, or asexual, changing our sexual orientation is generally not possible, although recent

Hyoung Chang/MediaNews Group/The Denver Post via Getty Images/Getty Images

▲ **Colorado Governor Jared Polis** Jared Polis, the first openly gay governor in the U.S., has worked to expand the rights of the LGBTQ community, signing groundbreaking bills banning conversion therapy and allowing transgender and intersex people to change the sex on their birth certificate (Osborne, 2019). His work also benefits Coloradans more broadly, including with respect to education and the pandemic. Polis is just one of the growing number of leaders of government around the world who are LGBTQ.

Joshua Lott/The New York Times/Redux

▲ **Same-Sex Couples and Their Children** Research on same-sex couples in committed, long-term relationships shows that their relationships are quite similar to those of heterosexual couples in most ways (Balsam et al., 2008). One exception: Lesbian couples were better than heterosexual or gay couples at harmonious problem solving (Roisman et al., 2008). What about their children? Research consistently has shown that the children of same-sex parents are very similar to the children of heterosexual parents (Farr, 2017; Patterson, 2006, 2008). And, contrary to popular belief, teenagers with same-sex parents have peer relationships and friendships that are much like those of teenagers with heterosexual or single parents (Wainwright & Patterson, 2008; Rivers et al., 2008).

Gene Fischer

❯ **James and Karma** Since James first told his story for the Prologue, his life has seen a lot of changes. James is now married. Having left New York because of anti-transgender sentiment in his community, James, his wife Misty, and their three cats now live on the West Coast of the United States. (James is pictured here with his late cat, Karma.) He is still hoping to have transition surgery, but he and Misty prioritized buying a house first. James is trying to figure out a new career path, but the pandemic slowed down his search. In the meantime, while Misty works, James is focused on fixing up their house and property—doing some construction and landscaping—and doing most of the cooking. Life, James reports, has only gotten better.

research suggests that some people do experience shifts in sexual orientation over time or across situations, something called sexual fluidity (e.g., Diamond, 2016).

Homosexuality has not been considered a sexual disorder by clinical psychologists or psychiatrists since 1973 (American Psychiatric Association, 1994; Silverstein, 2009). Many research studies have also found that homosexual people who are comfortable with their sexual orientation are just as well adjusted as are heterosexual people (see Strickland, 1995). Indeed, both the American Psychological Association (2009) and the World Psychiatric Association (Bhugra et al., 2016) have issued statements noting that there is no evidence to support therapies that aim to change sexual orientation. (Sexual fluidity is something that occurs naturally, not by forcing a change.) Further, it has been found that such therapies can lead to serious psychological outcomes for some people (Shidlo & Schroeder, 2002). As a result, in the United States, some states have banned such therapies through the legal system (Eckholm, 2013).

Nevertheless, discrimination and prejudice against gay, lesbian, and bisexual people continues to exist. A survey of almost 16,000 U.S. high school students found that gay, lesbian, and bisexual students were more likely than heterosexual students to be depressed or to be a victim of bullying or violence (Kann et al., 2016). Violence against LGBTQ people has increased in recent years in the United States (National Coalition of Anti-Violence Programs, 2017). Worldwide, there is a wide disparity in perceptions of homosexuality, although acceptance of gay and lesbian people is generally increasing (Poushter & Kent, 2020). Despite this, hate crimes based on sexual orientation and gender identity are common globally (Ghafoori et al., 2019). In the United States and Canada, 15 to 20 percent of hate crimes are based on these identities.

Closing Thoughts

From birth, each of us is profoundly influenced by the biological, social, cultural, and psychological forces that shape our gender identity and expression of sexuality. As you've seen in this chapter, a person's gender identity is firmly entrenched by late childhood and adolescence.

Throughout adulthood, the expression of sexuality centers on stable interpersonal relationships that are based not only on physical intimacy but also on emotional and psychological intimacy. Even in old age, the need for physical, emotional, and psychological intimacy remains strong.

Over the course of life, much of who we are is defined by our gender and sexual identities. Often without our awareness, those identities shape the activities we are drawn to, the relationships we form, and how we react in many situations. Most people develop a conventional sense of gender identity and sexual orientation and form sexual relationships that follow the predominant patterns endorsed by society. But other people, like James, are faced with the challenge of accepting themselves in a society that is often not very tolerant of gender diversity.

We hope that in reading this chapter, you've developed not only a greater appreciation of your own gender and sexual identities but also a better understanding of people whose gender identity or sexual orientation is different from your own. In Psych for Your Life, we'll change gears a bit, providing suggestions for strengthening intimate relationships.

Strengthening Intimate Relationships

Building strong interpersonal relationships, particularly in long-term relationships, can lead to a happier, more fulfilling life. This might be particularly true of marriage. According to psychologist Eli Finkel, many modern partnerships reflect an "all-or-nothing marriage." People want their partners to fulfill a range of roles, and provide everything from friendship to sex to self-esteem to personal growth (Finkel et al., 2015). Such high expectations can lead a marriage to fail—or can lead people to avoid getting married in the first place. But, as Finkel (2017) explains, "the best marriages today . . . are the best marriages the world has ever known." His research suggests that all intimate relationships can grow stronger if they adopt the best practices of strong marriages.

Even in a strong relationship, the demands and hassles of maintaining a household make occasional conflict inevitable. Despite what many people think, the happiest long-term relationships are not conflict free. After studying hundreds of married couples, psychologists John Gottman and Julie Schwartz Gottman discovered that resolving conflict plays a key role in strengthening relationships and marital happiness (Gottman, 2002, 2011; Gottman et al., 2006, 2007). This is part of why long-term partnerships are such hard work.

Finkel (2017) agrees and has compiled a great deal of research findings that address the big-ticket items that make a marriage work. These typically involve hard work, including building strong communication skills and working toward equality—gender equality, in particular, for different-sex couples. But Finkel also outlines the research on what he calls "lovehacks," small changes that people can make to strengthen their relationship. Here is a summary of Finkel's eight lovehacks—four that address weaknesses in a relationship and four that build on existing relationship strengths.

Lovehacks That Address Weaknesses

1. *Change your attributions:* In the chapter on social psychology, you'll learn about attributions—our explanations for others' behavior. Too often, we attribute the behavior of others to something about that person (an internal attribution) rather than something about the environment (an external attribution). Yet, we routinely give ourselves the benefit of the doubt. "You forgot my birthday because you don't care, but I forgot yours because my mother was in the hospital." When you're upset by your partner's behavior, take a minute to come up with some possible external attributions about the situation or environment.

2. *Change your perspective on conflict:* When you're having an argument, try to view the argument from an outsider's perspective. Finkel and his colleagues (2013) suggest the following exercise: "Think about this disagreement with your partner from the perspective of a neutral third party who wants the best for all involved … How might this person think about the disagreement?" If you find it difficult to imagine a neutral perspective, ask yourself why—even in the middle of an argument, if possible.

3. *Fight back against insecurity:* When your partner compliments you, think about that compliment as a general compliment rather than a specific one. So, if your partner comments on your new haircut, don't think, "My partner didn't like how I looked previously." Rather, think, "My partner likes how I look!"

4. *Think in terms of growth, not destiny:* Some people think of relationships as "meant to be," whereas others think relationships can grow stronger with effort. Research shows that those who believe in relationship destiny are less likely to put in the hard work necessary when times are tough. It's helpful to remind yourself that simply believing that your relationship can grow stronger is correlated with the relationship actually growing stronger.

Lovehacks That Build on Strengths

1. *Attributions again:* This lovehack is the flip side of the first lovehack, which focused on weaknesses. Just as we develop explanations for negative behavior, we also develop explanations for positive behavior. So, when your partner does something nice, don't think, "They must want something." Rather, think, "Wow, they're so nice!"

2. *Practice gratitude:* Make a point to think about the ways in which you are grateful for your partner's contributions to the relationship. Consider making this a habit—spending a couple minutes at the end of every day. The best part, according to research, is that practicing gratitude can increase our partners' kindness toward us. The effect is even stronger if you tell your partner about your gratitude.

3. *Celebrate:* When something good happens to your partner, make a point of celebrating. Rather than quiet acknowledgment, show enthusiasm and share in your partner's happiness.

4. *Touch your partner:* "Affectionate touch"—holding hands, touching an arm, and so on—tends to increase feelings of security and trust in relationships.

It's important to remember that these lovehacks are based on evidence from psychological research from multiple studies. And research has shown that gay and lesbian couples are more likely to naturally use some of these tactics than straight couples (Garcia & Umberson, 2019; Gottman et al., 2003). For example, gay and lesbian couples are more likely to approach a conflict in a positive way than in a negative way, and are more likely to inject humor and affection into a difficult discussion.

With all this talk about marriage and other long-term intimate relationships, it's important not to ignore the increasing population of single people. As psychologist Bella DePaulo (2014, 2017) points out, the ranks of single people who are not interested in marriage and divorced people who do not end up remarrying are growing. She observes that more U.S. households are now composed of single people living solo than of married couples with children. DePaulo (2014) wants marriage researchers to expand their focus—"not how can a person achieve the best marriage possible but how can people achieve the best life possible?"

Regardless of your relationship status, you can use many of these lovehacks to nurture the most important relationships in your life, whether with a spouse, a best friend, or a sibling. You don't even need both partners to sign on—or even be aware you're doing them—to make these lovehacks work. Give one (or more) a try—and maybe recruit your partner, too. After all, a strong social support network is psychologically protective for all of us (Werner-Seidler et al., 2017).

CHAPTER REVIEW

Gender and Sexuality

Achieve, Macmillan Learning's online study platform, features the full e-book of *Discovering Psychology,* the **LearningCurve** adaptive quizzing system, videos, and a variety of activities to boost your learning. Visit **Achieve** at macmillanlearning.com.

KEY PEOPLE

Sandra Bem, p. 348   Virginia Johnson, p. 354   William Masters, p. 354

KEY TERMS

sex, p. 340

gender, p. 340

gender roles, p. 340

gender identity, p. 340

sexual orientation, p. 340

gender-role stereotypes, p. 341

social learning theory of gender-role development, p. 348

gender schema theory, p. 348

intersex, p. 350

transgender, p. 351

Gender and Sexuality

Sex: biologically determined characteristics
Gender: cultural, social, and psychological meanings of maleness and femaleness
Gender roles: culturally designated behaviors, attitudes, and traits associated with gender
Gender identity: a person's psychological sense of self as male or female
Sexual orientation: the direction of a person's emotional and erotic attraction

Kyodo News/TAINAN/Taiwan/Newscom

Gender stereotypes and gender roles:
Gender stereotypes: the beliefs people have about typical characteristics and behaviors of each sex
Differences related to sex and gender:
- More gender similarities than differences
- Much overlap between sexes

Gender Development

Explaining gender differences:
- **Gender schema theory,** developed by **Sandra Bem** (1944–2014), and **social learning theory** cite sociocultural explanations.
- Evolutionary theories cite sexual selection and parental investment.
- Interactionist theories combine sociocultural and biological explanations.

Sun xinming/AP Images

The Washington Post/Getty Images

Variations in gender identity:
- **Intersex** people have ambiguous biological sex.
- For **transgender** people, **gender identity** conflicts with biological sex.
- For **cisgender** people, gender identity matches biological sex.
- *Transition* is the process in which a transgender person chooses to undergo *gender confirmation surgery*, hormone replacement therapy, or both to bring their sex assigned at birth into alignment with their gender identity.

Human Sexuality

Stages of human sexual response identified by **Virginia Johnson** (1925–2013) and **William Masters** (1915–2001):
- Excitement, plateau, orgasm, resolution

In nonhuman animals, sexual behavior is biologically determined, typically triggered by hormonal changes in the female.

REUTERS/Alamy

Sexual orientation:
- Variations include *homosexual* (gay and lesbian), *heterosexual, bisexual,* and *asexual.*
- Not easily categorized
- Causes are unknown
- Develops at an early age and is resistant to change
- Homosexual orientation associated with gender-atypical play in childhood

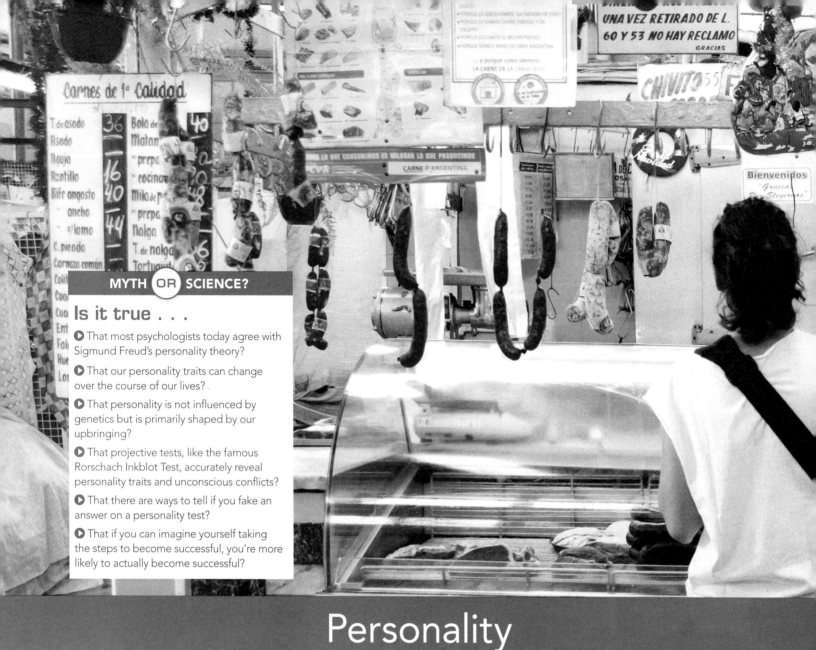

MYTH OR SCIENCE?

Is it true . . .

▶ That most psychologists today agree with Sigmund Freud's personality theory?

▶ That our personality traits can change over the course of our lives? .

▶ That personality is not influenced by genetics but is primarily shaped by our upbringing?

▶ That projective tests, like the famous Rorschach Inkblot Test, accurately reveal personality traits and unconscious conflicts?

▶ That there are ways to tell if you fake an answer on a personality test?

▶ That if you can imagine yourself taking the steps to become successful, you're more likely to actually become successful?

Personality

PROLOGUE

Identical Twins?

A young woman in Bogotá, Colombia, was startled to see an engineer from her firm working behind the butcher counter at a local store. She called out, but he acted as if he didn't know her. When they spoke, she learned that he wasn't her co-worker, Jorge, but rather a young man named William who looked exactly like Jorge (Dominus, 2015)!

Back at work, Jorge was amused by his friend's story and shocked by the photo she later showed him (Cosoy, 2016). Intrigued, Jorge sought out William's Facebook page. In photo after photo, Jorge saw uncanny similarities. Strangest of all were the photos

of William's brother, Wilber. In nearly every detail, from his posture to the shape of his lips, Wilber was the very image of Jorge's own fraternal twin, Carlos! So, a second pair of brothers—William and Wilber—looked exactly like Jorge and his twin brother, Carlos.

In a remarkable series of discoveries, Jorge learned that the two sets of brothers were born at the same time, and at one point, one twin in each pair received care at the same hospital in Bogotá (Dominus, 2015). That was when William and Carlos were mistakenly swapped at the hospital, a conclusion later supported by DNA testing. All four men currently live in Bogotá, but William and Wilber were raised in a rural area, leaving school at a young age to work in the sugar cane fields.

For social scientists, the discovery led to a once-in-a-lifetime opportunity, the chance to study a situation that they could never plan. Each of the Bogotá twins is an identical twin, but was raised with a supposed fraternal twin. To researchers' knowledge, this is the only situation in which so many twin relationships exist among just four people.

The brothers agreed to work with psychology researchers Yesika Montoya from Colombia and Nancy Segal from the United States. Dr. Segal explained that "studying twins reared apart separates genetic and environmental effects on behavior better than any research design I know" (Dominus, 2015).

Psychologists are intrigued by the extent to which the identical twins are similar. Despite growing up together, Jorge and

Design Pics Inc/Alamy Stock Photo

Carlos had always known that they were very different (Llenas, 2015); Jorge is the joker with the sunny personality, whereas Carlos is more serious-minded. And supposed fraternal twins William and Wilber had noticed differences, too. When comparing identical twin pairs, however, these characteristics match up: William and Jorge are both outgoing and like to make people laugh, and Wilber's darker moods mirror Carlos's.

But there also were several differences between the identical twins, perhaps because of where they grew up (Dominus, 2015). The most obvious difference is physical: The boys raised in the city are taller than their rural counterparts. In terms of personality, Carlos, raised in the city with a comfortable lifestyle and university education, is more cynical than

his rural identical twin, Wilber. And Jorge, also raised in the city, is more optimistic than his rural identical twin. Dr. Segal anticipated that the identical twins would be similar on most traits and was surprised to find a number of differences in her preliminary testing. Segal reported that she "came away with a real respect for the effect of an extremely different environment"—in this case, a big city versus rural Colombia (Dominus, 2015).

All four men are now very close and call themselves "four brothers" (Cosoy, 2016). Their willingness to share their story helps us understand the fundamental differences in people's personalities—both across and within families. We'll return to the story of the brothers from Bogotá throughout the chapter. 〜

⊙ **IN THIS CHAPTER:**

personality An individual's unique and relatively consistent patterns of thinking, feeling, and behaving.

personality theory A theory that attempts to describe and explain similarities and differences in people's patterns of thinking, feeling, and behaving.

Introduction: What Is Personality?

■ KEY THEME

Personality is defined as an individual's unique and relatively consistent patterns of thinking, feeling, and behaving.

≡ KEY QUESTIONS

• What are the four major theoretical perspectives on personality?

That you already have an intuitive understanding of the word *personality* is easy to demonstrate. When reading this chapter's Prologue, it probably made sense to you that the brothers had similar personalities in many respects. Indeed, we frequently toss around the word *personality* in everyday conversations. "He's very competent, but he has an abrasive personality." "She's got such a delightful personality, you can't help liking her."

Your intuitive understanding of personality is probably very similar to the way that psychologists define the concept. **Personality** is defined as *an individual's unique and relatively consistent patterns of thinking, feeling, and behaving.* There are many different ways—or theories—to understand personality. A **personality theory** is *a theory that attempts to describe and explain similarities and differences in people's patterns of thinking, feeling, and behaving.* In short, a personality theory tries to explain the *whole person*. It's important to stress that no single theory can explain all the aspects of human personality. Every personality theory has its unique strengths and limitations.

There are many personality theories, but they can be roughly grouped under four basic perspectives: the psychoanalytic, humanistic, social cognitive, and trait perspectives. In a nutshell, here's what each perspective emphasizes:

• The *psychoanalytic perspective* emphasizes the importance of unconscious processes and the influence of early childhood experience.

• The *humanistic perspective* represents an optimistic look at human nature, emphasizing the self and the fulfillment of a person's unique potential.

• The *social cognitive perspective* emphasizes learning and conscious cognitive processes, including the importance of beliefs about the self, goal setting, and self-regulation.

• The *trait perspective* emphasizes the description and measurement of specific personality differences among individuals.

❯ **Explaining Personality** Some people are outgoing, expressive, and fun-loving. Other people consistently display the opposite qualities. Are such personality differences due to early childhood experiences? Genetics? Social environment? Personality theories attempt to account for the individual differences that make each one of us unique. The unusual situation of the twins switched at birth provides a way for researchers to make multiple comparisons based on both genetics and the environment.

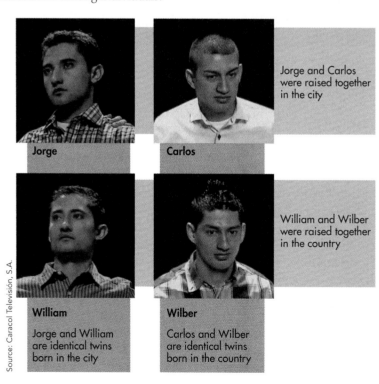

Jorge

Carlos

Jorge and Carlos were raised together in the city

William

Wilber

William and Wilber were raised together in the country

Jorge and William are identical twins born in the city

Carlos and Wilber are identical twins born in the country

Source: Caracol Television, S.A.

After examining some of the major personality theories that reflect each perspective, we'll consider a closely related topic—how personality is measured and evaluated. And yes, we'll talk about the famous inkblots. But for the inkblots to make sense, we need to trace the evolution of modern personality theories. We'll begin with the tale of a bearded, cigar-smoking gentleman from Vienna of whom you just may have heard—Sigmund Freud.

The Psychoanalytic Perspective on Personality

■ **KEY THEME**
Freud's psychoanalysis stresses the importance of unconscious forces, sexual and aggressive instincts, and early childhood experience.

≡ KEY QUESTIONS
- What were the key influences on Sigmund Freud's thinking?
- How are unconscious influences revealed?
- What are the three basic structures of personality, and what are the defense mechanisms?

Sigmund Freud, one of the most influential figures of the twentieth century, was the founder of psychoanalysis. **Psychoanalysis** is *Freud's theory of personality that stresses the influence of unconscious mental processes, the importance of sexual and aggressive instincts, and the enduring effects of early childhood experience on later personality development.* Although many of Freud's ideas have not held up under research scrutiny, his ideas have become part of our common culture. So, it is difficult to imagine just how radical he seemed to his contemporaries. The following biographical sketch highlights some of the important influences that shaped Freud's ideas and theory.

The Life of Sigmund Freud

Sigmund Freud was born in 1856 in what is today Příbor, Czech Republic. When he was four years old, his family moved to Vienna, where he lived for most of his life.

Freud was extremely intelligent and intensely ambitious. He studied medicine, became a physician, and then proved himself to be an outstanding physiological researcher. Early in his career, Freud was among the first investigators of a new drug that had anesthetic and mood-altering properties—cocaine. But his enthusiasm for the medical potential of cocaine quickly faded when he recognized that the drug was addictive (Fancher, 1973; Gay, 2006).

Prospects for an academic career in scientific research were poor, especially for a Jew in Vienna, which was intensely anti-Semitic at that time. So Freud reluctantly gave up physiological research for a private practice in neurology. One of Freud's daughters, the youngest of his six children, **Anna Freud** (1895–1982), later became an important psychoanalytic theorist.

Influences in the Development of Freud's Ideas Freud's theory evolved gradually during decades of self-analysis as well as observation of patients in his private practice. Early on, Freud embraced the technique of hypnosis to help patients talk freely and express pent-up emotions. But not all patients could be hypnotized. Eventually, Freud developed **free association**, *a psychoanalytic technique in which the patient spontaneously reports all thoughts, feelings, and mental images that arise, revealing unconscious thoughts and emotions.*

In 1900, Freud published what many consider his most important work, *The Interpretation of Dreams.* By the early 1900s, Freud had developed the basic tenets of his psychoanalytic theory and was gaining international recognition and developing a following. Freud continued to refine his theory throughout his life, publishing many books, articles, and lectures.

psychoanalysis (in personality) Freud's theory of personality that stresses the influence of unconscious mental processes, the importance of sexual and aggressive instincts, and the enduring effects of early childhood experiences on later personality development.

free association A psychoanalytic technique in which the patient spontaneously reports all thoughts, feelings, and mental images that arise, revealing unconscious thoughts and emotions.

Photo by Time Life Pictures/Mansell/The LIFE Picture Collection/Getty Images

⌃ **Freud the Outsider** Sigmund Freud (1856–1939) was influential during his life, and continues to be influential even now. He developed a theory of personality called psychoanalysis, which emphasizes unconscious mental processes and the influence of early childhood experience. Although many of his ideas have not been supported by research, his then-revolutionary ideas laid the groundwork for many current ideas in psychology.

unconscious Freud's term to describe thoughts, feelings, wishes, and drives that are operating below the level of conscious awareness.

Freud's final decades were filled with tragedy. As the Nazis came to power, Freud fled to London with some family members; there he lived until dying from cancer in 1939. But four of his sisters died in extermination camps. Today, Freud's legacy continues to influence psychology, philosophy, literature, art, and psychotherapy (Merlino et al., 2008; O'Roark, 2007).

Freud's Dynamic Theory of Personality

Freud (1940) saw personality and behavior as the result of a constant interplay among conflicting psychological forces. He believed that these psychological forces operate at three different levels of awareness: the conscious, the preconscious, and the unconscious. All the thoughts, feelings, and sensations that you're aware of at this particular moment represent the *conscious* level. The *preconscious* contains information that you're not currently aware of but can easily bring to conscious awareness, such as memories of recent events or your street address.

However, the conscious and preconscious are merely the visible tip of the iceberg of the mind. The bulk of this psychological iceberg is made up of the **unconscious**, *Freud's term to describe thoughts, feelings, wishes, and drives that are operating below the level of conscious awareness* (see **Figure 11.1**). According to Freud's theories, you're not directly aware of these submerged thoughts and drives, but the unconscious exerts an enormous influence on your conscious thoughts and behavior.

Although it is not directly accessible, Freud (1904) believed that unconscious material often seeps through to the conscious level in distorted, disguised, or symbolic forms. For example, Freud thought that unconscious wishes and conflicts can be discovered in dreams and free associations. He also believed that the unconscious can be revealed in unintentional actions, such as accidents, mistakes, instances of forgetting, and inadvertent slips of the tongue (1904, 1933). These slips of the tongue, such as saying the name of an ex-partner in a romantic situation with a new partner, are often referred to as "Freudian slips."

FIGURE 11.1 Freud's Beliefs about Levels of Awareness and the Structure of Personality Freud believed that personality is composed of three psychological components—the id, the ego, and the superego—that operate at different levels of awareness. If you think of personality as being like an iceberg, the bulk of this psychological iceberg is represented by the irrational, impulsive id, which lies beneath the waterline of consciousness. Unlike the entirely unconscious id, the rational ego and the moralistic superego are at least partially conscious.

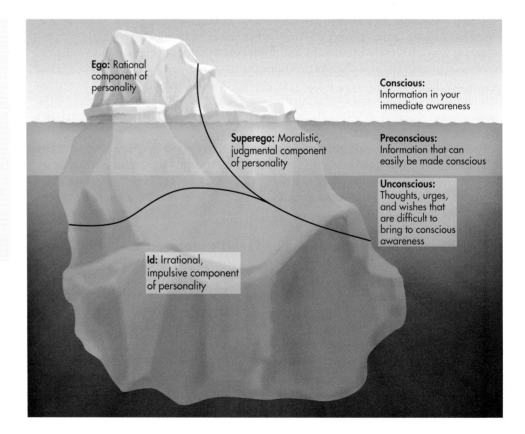

Ego: Rational component of personality

Superego: Moralistic, judgmental component of personality

Id: Irrational, impulsive component of personality

Conscious: Information in your immediate awareness

Preconscious: Information that can easily be made conscious

Unconscious: Thoughts, urges, and wishes that are difficult to bring to conscious awareness

The Structure of Personality Freud (1933) believed that there are three basic structures of personality—the id, the ego, and the superego (see Figure 11.1). Understand that Freud did not see these as separate identities or brain structures. Rather, they are distinct psychological processes.

The **id,** *in Freud's theory, is the completely unconscious irrational component of personality that seeks immediate satisfaction of instinctual urges and drives.* The id is connected to the biological urges that perpetuate the existence of the individual and the species—hunger, thirst, physical comfort, and, most important, sexuality. It is immune to logic, morality, and the demands of the outside world.

The id is ruled by the **pleasure principle**—*the fundamental human motive to obtain pleasure and avoid tension or discomfort* (Freud, 1920). Thus, the id strives to increase pleasure, reduce tension, and avoid pain. Equipped only with the id, Freud believed that the newborn infant is completely driven by the pleasure principle and wants their needs addressed immediately. However, the external world can't or won't always immediately satisfy those needs.

Thus, the *ego* is a new dimension of personality that develops from part of the id. The **ego** *in Freud's theory, is the partly conscious rational component of personality that regulates thoughts and behavior, and is most in touch with the demands of the external world* (Freud, 1933). As the mediator between the id's instinctual demands and the restrictions of the outer world, the ego operates on the reality principle. According to Freud, the **reality principle** is *the capacity to postpone gratification until the appropriate time or circumstances exist in the external world* (Freud, 1940). For example, a child may learn, perhaps after being scolded by their parent, to wait their turn rather than pushing another child off a playground swing.

In early childhood, the ego must deal with external parental demands and limitations. Implicit in those demands are the parents' values and morals, their ideas of the right and wrong ways to think, act, and feel. Eventually, the child encounters other advocates of society's values, such as teachers and religious and legal authorities (Freud, 1926). Gradually, these social values move from being externally imposed demands to being *internalized* rules and values.

By about age five or six, the young child has developed an internal, parental voice that is partly conscious. The **superego** is, *in Freud's theory, the partly conscious, self-evaluative, moralistic component of personality that is formed through the internalization of parental and societal rules.* The superego evaluates the acceptability of behavior and thoughts, then praises or admonishes. Put simply, your superego represents your conscience, issuing demands "like a strict father with a child" (Freud, 1926).

The Ego Defense Mechanisms: Unconscious Self-Deceptions
The ego has a difficult task. It must be strong, flexible, and resourceful to mediate conflicts among the instinctual demands of the id, the moral authority of the superego, and external restrictions. According to Freud (1923), everyone experiences an ongoing daily battle among these three warring personality processes.

When the demands of the id or superego threaten to overwhelm the ego, *anxiety* results (Freud, 1915b). If a realistic solution or compromise is not possible, the ego may use what Freud called **defense mechanisms**, *largely unconscious distortions of thoughts or perceptions that act to reduce anxiety* (A. Freud, 1946; Freud, 1915c). By resorting to defense mechanisms, the ego can maintain an integrated sense of self while searching for a more acceptable and realistic solution to a conflict between the id and superego.

The most fundamental defense mechanism is **repression**, *the unconscious exclusion of anxiety-provoking thoughts, feelings, and memories from conscious awareness* (Freud, 1915a, 1936). In simple terms, repression is unconscious forgetting. Common examples include traumatic events, embarrassments, disappointments, episodes of physical pain or illness, and unacceptable urges.

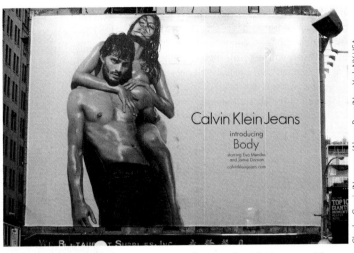

Appealing to the Id How would Freud explain the appeal of this billboard? In Freud's theory, the id is ruled by the pleasure principle—the instinctual drive to increase pleasure, reduce tension, and avoid pain.

id In Freud's theory, the completely unconscious, irrational component of personality that seeks immediate satisfaction of instinctual urges and drives.

pleasure principle The fundamental human motive to obtain pleasure and avoid tension or discomfort.

ego In Freud's theory, the partly conscious rational component of personality that regulates thoughts and behavior, and is most in touch with the demands of the external world.

reality principle The capacity to postpone gratification until the appropriate time or circumstances exist in the external world.

superego In Freud's theory, the partly conscious, self-evaluative, moralistic component of personality that is formed through the internalization of parental and societal rules.

defense mechanisms Largely unconscious distortions of thoughts or perceptions that act to reduce anxiety.

repression (in psychoanalytic theory of personality and psychotherapy) The unconscious exclusion of anxiety-provoking thoughts, feelings, and memories from conscious awareness.

> **Sublimation** In Freud's view, creative or productive behaviors represent the rechanneling of sexual energy—a form of displacement he termed *sublimation*. Freud believed that civilization's greatest achievements are the result of the sublimation of instinctual energy into socially acceptable activities, like the work of this artist. Later personality theorists criticized Freud's refusal to consider creativity a drive in its own right.

H. Mark Weidman Photography/Alamy Stock Photo

Repression, however, is not an all-or-nothing psychological process. As Freud (1939) explained, "The repressed material retains its impetus to penetrate into consciousness." In other words, if you encounter a situation that is similar to one you've repressed, bits and pieces of memories of the previous situation may begin to resurface. In such instances, the ego may employ other defense mechanisms that allow the urge or information to remain only partially conscious.

This is what occurs with **displacement**, *the defense mechanism that involves unconsciously shifting the target of an emotional urge to a substitute target that is less threatening or dangerous* (A. Freud, 1946). For example, an employee angered by a supervisor's unfair treatment may displace their hostility onto family members when they come home from work. The employee consciously experiences anger but directs it toward someone other than its true target, which remains unconscious.

Some major defense mechanisms are summarized in **Table 11.1**. The use of defense mechanisms is common, and they can be helpful on a short-term basis. But, in Freud's view, the drawback to using any defense mechanism is that maintaining these self-deceptions requires psychological energy. Freud (1936) pointed out that this "continuous expenditure of effort" depletes psychological energy that is needed to cope effectively with the demands of daily life.

TABLE 11.1

Major Ego Defense Mechanisms

Defense	Description	Example
Repression	Exclusion from consciousness of anxiety-producing thoughts or feelings; the most basic defense mechanism	Three years after being in a traumatic car accident, a person can remember only vague details about the event.
Displacement	The redirection of emotional impulses toward a less-threatening substitute person or object	Angered by a neighbor's hateful comment, a mother spanks her daughter for accidentally spilling her milk.
Sublimation	A form of displacement in which sexual urges are rechanneled into productive, nonsexual activities	A graduate student works on her thesis 14 hours a day while her husband is on an extended business trip.
Rationalization	Justifying one's actions or feelings with socially acceptable explanations rather than consciously acknowledging one's true motives or desires	After being rejected by a prestigious university, a student explains that he is glad because he would be happier at a smaller, less competitive school.
Projection	The attribution of one's own unacceptable urges or qualities to others	A married woman who is sexually attracted to a co-worker accuses him of flirting with her.
Reaction formation	Thinking or behaving in a way that is the extreme opposite of unacceptable urges or impulses	Threatened by his sexual attraction to girls, an adolescent boy teases and torments adolescent girls.
Denial	The failure to recognize or acknowledge the existence of anxiety-provoking information	Despite having multiple drinks every night, a man says he is not an alcoholic because he never drinks before 5 P.M.
Regression	Retreating to a behavior pattern characteristic of an earlier stage of development	After her parents' bitter divorce, a 10-year-old girl refuses to sleep alone, crawling into bed with her mother.

Personality Development: The Psychosexual Stages

■ KEY THEME
The psychosexual stages are age-related developmental periods, and each stage represents a different focus of the id's sexual energies.

≡ KEY QUESTIONS
- What are the five psychosexual stages, and what are the core conflicts of each stage?
- What is the consequence of fixation?
- What role does the Oedipus complex play in personality development?

According to Freud (1905), people progress through five psychosexual stages of development. The foundations of adult personality are established during the first five years of life, as the child progresses through the *oral, anal,* and *phallic* psychosexual stages. The *latency stage* occurs during late childhood, and the fifth and final stage, the *genital stage,* begins in adolescence. Freud believed that each psychosexual stage represents a different focus of the id's sexual energies.

It is important to point out that Freud was *not* saying that an infant experiences sexual urges in the same way that an adult does. Instead, Freud believed that the infant or young child expresses primitive sexual urges by seeking sensual pleasure from different areas of the body. Thus, the **psychosexual stages** are, *in Freud's theory, age-related developmental periods in which the child's sexual impulses are focused on different body areas and are expressed through the activities associated with those areas.*

Fixation: Unresolved Developmental Conflicts
At each psychosexual stage, Freud (1905) believed, the infant or young child is faced with a developmental conflict that must be successfully resolved in order to move on to the next stage. The heart of this conflict is the degree to which parents either frustrate or overindulge the child's expression of pleasurable feelings. In Freud's theory, a healthy personality and sense of sexuality result when conflicts are successfully resolved at each stage of psychosexual development.

The result of an unresolved developmental conflict is fixation at a particular stage. The person continues to seek pleasure through behaviors that are similar to those associated with that psychosexual stage. For example, Freud might say that the adult who constantly chews gum, smokes, or bites their fingernails has unresolved oral psychosexual conflicts.

The Oedipus Complex: A Psychosexual Drama
The most critical conflict that the child must successfully resolve for healthy personality and sexual development occurs during the phallic stage (Freud, 1923, 1940). As the child becomes more aware of pleasure derived from the genital area, Freud believed, the child develops a sexual attraction to the opposite-sex parent and hostility toward the same-sex parent. This is the famous **Oedipus complex**, *in Freud's theory, a child's unconscious sexual desire for the opposite-sex parent, usually accompanied by hostile feelings toward the same-sex parent.* The complex is named after Oedipus, the protagonist of a Greek myth. Abandoned at birth, Oedipus does not know the identity of his parents. As an adult, he unknowingly kills his father and marries his mother.

According to Freud, this attraction to the opposite-sex parent plays out as a sexual drama in the child's mind. For boys, the Oedipus complex unfolds as a confrontation with the father for the affections of the mother. To resolve the Oedipus complex and these anxieties, the little boy ultimately joins forces with his former enemy by resorting to **identification**, *a defense mechanism that involves reducing anxiety by imitating the behavior and characteristics of another person.* That is, he imitates and internalizes his father's values, attitudes, and mannerisms.

displacement The defense mechanism that involves unconsciously shifting the target of an emotional urge to a substitute target that is less threatening or dangerous.

psychosexual stages In Freud's theory, age-related developmental periods in which the child's sexual impulses are focused on different body areas and are expressed through the activities associated with those areas.

Oedipus complex In Freud's theory, a child's unconscious sexual desire for the opposite-sex parent, usually accompanied by hostile feelings toward the same-sex parent.

identification A defense mechanism that involves reducing anxiety by imitating the behavior and characteristics of another person.

"He has a few things to work through, but we're good together."

Tom Cheney/The New Yorker Collection/The Cartoon Bank

∧ Competing with Mom for Dad?
According to Freud, the child identifies with the same-sex parent as a way of resolving sexual attraction toward the opposite-sex parent—the Oedipus complex. Freud believed that imitating the same-sex parent also plays an important role in the development of gender identity and, ultimately, of healthy sexual maturity.

According to Freud, girls also ultimately resolve the Oedipus complex by identifying with the same-sex parent. But the underlying sexual drama in girls follows different themes. The little girl discovers that little boys have a penis and that she does not. She feels a sense of deprivation and loss that Freud termed *penis envy.*

Freud felt that because of the intense anxiety associated with the Oedipus complex, the sexual urges of boys and girls become repressed during the latency stage in late childhood. Outwardly, children in the latency stage express a strong desire to associate with same-sex peers, a preference that strengthens the child's sexual identity.

Freud believed that the incestuous urges of the Oedipus complex start to resurface in adolescence, during the genital stage, but they are prohibited by the moral ideals of the superego as well as by societal restrictions. Thus, the person directs sexual urges toward socially acceptable substitutes, who often resemble the person's opposite-sex parent (Freud, 1905).

Freud's views on female sexuality, particularly the concept of penis envy, are among his most severely criticized ideas. Perhaps recognizing that his explanation of female psychosexual development rested on shaky ground, Freud (1926) admitted, "We know less about the sexual life of little girls than of boys. But we need not feel ashamed of this distinction. After all, the sexual life of adult women is a 'dark continent' for psychology."

The Neo-Freudians: Freud's Descendants and Dissenters

■ KEY THEME
The neo-Freudians followed Freud in stressing the importance of the unconscious and early childhood, but they developed their own personality theories.

≡ KEY QUESTIONS
- How did the neo-Freudians generally depart from Freud's ideas?
- What were the key ideas of Jung, Horney, and Adler?
- What are three key criticisms of Freud's theory and of the psychoanalytic perspective?

Freud's ideas were always controversial. But by the early 1900s, he had attracted a number of followers, many of whom went to Vienna to study with him. These early followers developed their own personality theories, but they kept the foundations that Freud had established. Hence, these theorists are often called *neo-Freudians* (the prefix *neo* means "new"). The neo-Freudians and their theories are considered part of the psychoanalytic perspective on personality.

In general, the neo-Freudians disagreed with Freud on three key points. First, they took issue with Freud's belief that behavior was primarily motivated by sexual urges. Second, they disagreed with Freud's contention that personality is fundamentally determined by early childhood experiences. Instead, the neo-Freudians believed that personality can also be influenced by experiences throughout the lifespan. Third, the neo-Freudian theorists departed from Freud's generally pessimistic view of human nature and society.

In the chapter on lifespan development, we described the psychosocial theory of one famous neo-Freudian, Erik Erikson. In this chapter, we'll look at the basic ideas of three other important neo-Freudians: Carl Jung, Karen Horney, and Alfred Adler.

Carl Jung: Archetypes and the Collective Unconscious
Born in a small town in Switzerland, **Carl Jung** (1875–1961) was fascinated by the myths, folktales, and religions of his own and other cultures. After studying medicine, Jung was drawn to the relatively new field of psychiatry because he believed it could provide deeper insights into the human mind (Jung, 1963).

Intrigued by Freud's ideas, Jung corresponded with him at great length. But ultimately, Jung rejected Freud's belief that human behavior is fueled by the instinctual drives of sex and aggression. Instead, Jung believed that people are motivated by a

JGI/Jamie Grill/Getty Images

more general psychological energy that pushes them to achieve psychological growth, self-realization, and psychic wholeness and harmony.

Jung (1936) believed that the deepest part of the individual psyche is the *collective unconscious*. The **collective unconscious**, *in Jung's theory, is the hypothesized part of the unconscious mind that is inherited from previous generations and that contains universally shared ancestral experiences and ideas.* He described the collective unconscious as containing "the whole spiritual heritage of mankind's evolution, born anew in the brain structure of every individual" (Jung, 1931). Contained in the collective unconscious are the *archetypes,* mental images of universal human themes and experiences.

Not surprisingly, Jung's concepts of the collective unconscious and shared archetypes have been criticized as being unscientific or mystical. As far as we know, individual experiences cannot be genetically passed down from one generation to the next. Regardless, Jung's ideas make more sense if you think of the collective unconscious as reflecting shared human experiences.

Karen Horney: Basic Anxiety and "Womb Envy"

Trained as a Freudian psychoanalyst, **Karen Horney** (1885–1952) (pronounced HORN-eye) emigrated from Germany to the United States during the Great Depression in the 1930s. While Freud traced psychological problems to sexual conflicts, Horney found that her U.S. patients were much more worried about their jobs and economic problems than their sex lives. Thus, Horney came to stress the importance of cultural and social factors in personality development — matters that Freud had largely ignored (Horney, 1945). Ultimately, Horney believed in the potential of humans to change and grow throughout their lives.

Horney stressed the importance of social relationships, especially the parent–child relationship, in the development of personality. She believed that disturbances in human relationships, not sexual conflicts, were the cause of psychological problems. Such problems arise from the attempt to deal with basic anxiety, which Horney (1945) described as "the feeling a child has of being isolated and helpless in a potentially hostile world."

Horney also sharply disagreed with Freud's interpretation of female development, especially his notion that women suffer from penis envy. What women envy in men, Horney (1926) claimed, is not their penis, but their superior status in society. In fact, Horney contended that men often suffer *womb envy,* envying women's capacity to bear children. Neatly standing Freud's view of feminine psychology on its head, Horney argued that *men* compensate for their relatively minor role in reproduction by constantly striving to make creative achievements in their work (Gilman, 2001).

Horney's departure from Freud's theories led to anger among her peers at the New York Psychoanalytic Institute, where she had been teaching longer than any of them (Quinn, 2019). She refused to back down, however, so they demoted her. Horney quit in protest. Although others followed her lead and joined her in forming a new institute, it never achieved national recognition and her work was long overlooked. Yet, one of her strongest critics later praised her work, noting that Horney was "ahead of her time in recognizing psychoanalysis as a humanity rather than a rigid science" (Quinn, 2019).

Alfred Adler: Feelings of Inferiority and Striving for Superiority

Born in Vienna, **Alfred Adler** (1870–1937) was an extremely sickly child, but he overcame his physical weaknesses through determination and hard work. After studying medicine, he became associated with Freud. But from the beginning of Adler's interest in psychoanalysis, he disagreed with Freud on several issues. In particular, Adler placed much more emphasis on the importance of conscious thought processes and social motives (West & Bubenzer, 2012). Eventually, Adler broke away from Freud to establish his own theory of personality.

Adler (1933b) believed that the most fundamental human motive is *striving for superiority* — the desire to improve oneself, master challenges, and move toward

Allstar Picture Library Limited/Alamy Stock Photo

▲ Archetypes in Popular Culture
According to Jung, archetypal images are often found in popular myths, novels, and even films. Consider the universal themes portrayed in the film *The Black Panther*. Several characters represent the archetype of the hero in the film, including King T'Challa, center, who is going through a classic coming-of-age story arc (Dennison, 2018). Other heroes include Nakia, on the left, who also represents wisdom; Okoye, who also represents loyalty; Queen Ramonda, who also represents strength; and Shuri, on the right, who also represents intelligence. On the other hand, Killmonger represents the archetype of the anti-hero or villain.

Bettmann/Getty Images

▲ Karen Horney and Human Potential
Karen Horney shared Jung's belief that people are not doomed to psychological conflict and problems. Also like Jung, Horney believed that the drive to grow psychologically and achieve one's potential is a basic human motive. Horney (1945) said, "I believe that man can change and go on changing as long as he lives."

collective unconscious In Jung's theory, the hypothesized part of the unconscious mind that is inherited from previous generations and that contains universally shared ancestral experiences and ideas.

self-perfection and self-realization. Striving toward superiority arises from universal feelings of inferiority that are experienced during infancy and childhood, when the child is helpless and dependent on others. These feelings motivate people to *compensate* for their real or imagined weaknesses by emphasizing their talents and abilities and by working hard to improve themselves (R. Watts, 2012). Hence, Adler (1933a) saw the universal human feelings of inferiority as ultimately constructive and valuable.

Like Horney, Adler believed that humans were motivated to grow and achieve their personal goals. And, like Horney, Adler emphasized the importance of cultural influences and social relationships (Carlson et al., 2008; West & Bubenzer, 2012). Adler's ideas about the benefits of goals for learning and achievement, and the central role of culture and social relationships, are still important today (Bettner, 2020).

Evaluating Freud and the Psychoanalytic Perspective on Personality

Sigmund Freud's ideas have had a profound and lasting impact on our culture and on our understanding of human nature (see Merlino et al., 2008). Despite his contributions, however, there are several valid criticisms of Freud's theory and, more generally, of the psychoanalytic perspective. As one critic said, "Step by step, we are learning that Freud has been the most overrated figure in the entire history of science and medicine — one who wrought immense harm through the propagation of false etiologies, mistaken diagnoses, and fruitless lines of inquiry" (Crews, 2006). We'll discuss three of the most important problems next.

Inadequacy of Evidence Freud's theory relies wholly on data derived from his relatively small number of patients and from self-analysis. Most of Freud's patients were well-educated members of the middle and upper classes in Vienna at the beginning of the twentieth century. Any way you look at it, this is a small and rather skewed sample from which to draw sweeping generalizations about human nature.

Furthermore, it is impossible to objectively assess Freud's "data." Freud did not take notes during his private therapy sessions. And, of course, when Freud did report a case in detail, it was still his own interpretation of the case that was recorded. Was Freud imposing his own ideas onto his patients, seeing only what he expected to see? Some critics think so (see Grünbaum, 2006, 2007).

Lack of Testability Many psychoanalytic concepts are so vague and ambiguous that they are impossible to objectively measure or confirm (Crews, 2006; Grünbaum, 2006). For example, how might you go about proving the existence of the id or the superego?

Psychoanalytic "proof" often has a "heads I win, tails you lose" style to it. In other words, psychoanalytic concepts are often impossible to disprove because even seemingly contradictory information can be used to support Freud's theory. For example, if your memory of childhood doesn't jibe with Freud's description of the psychosexual stages or the Oedipus complex, well, that's because you've repressed it.

As Freud acknowledged, psychoanalysis is better at explaining *past* behavior than at predicting future behavior (Gay, 1989). Indeed, psychoanalytic interpretations are so flexible that a given behavior can be explained by any number of completely different motives. For example, a man who is extremely affectionate toward his wife might be exhibiting displacement of a repressed incestuous urge (he is displacing his repressed affection for his mother onto his wife), reaction formation (he actually hates his wife intensely, so he compensates by being overly affectionate), or fixation at the oral stage (he is overly dependent on his wife).

Nonetheless, several key psychoanalytic ideas have been substantiated by empirical research (Cogan et al., 2007; Westen, 1990, 1998). Among these are the ideas that: (1) much of mental life is unconscious; (2) early childhood experiences have a critical influence on interpersonal relationships and psychological adjustment; and (3) people differ significantly in the degree to which they regulate their impulses, emotions, and thoughts toward adaptive and socially acceptable ends.

⌃ A Century of Influence One indicator of Freud's influence is his continuing presence in popular culture. He appeared on the cover of *Time* magazine four different times, and has been featured as a character in dozens of films and even television shows — from *Saturday Night Live* to *Star Trek*. You can even buy a "Yo Mama" T-shirt that plays on Freud's focus on young boys' supposed obsession with their mothers — the Oedipus complex.

BustedTees

Sexism Many people feel that Freud's theories reflect a sexist view of women. Because penis envy produces feelings of shame and inferiority, Freud (1925) claimed, women are more vain, masochistic, and jealous than men. He also believed that women are more influenced by their emotions and have a lesser ethical and moral sense than men.

As Horney and other female psychoanalysts have pointed out, Freud's theory uses male psychology as a prototype. Women are essentially viewed as a deviation from the norm of masculinity (Horney, 1926; Thompson, 1950). Perhaps, Horney suggested, psychoanalysis would have evolved an entirely different view of women if it were not dominated by the male point of view. Similarly, **Melanie Klein** (1882–1960), one of the most influential psychoanalysts in history, expanded Freud's ideas to include the points of view of mothers and children (Crann, 2010).

To Freud's credit, women were quite active in the early psychoanalytic movement. Several female analysts became close colleagues of Freud (Freeman & Strean, 1987; Roazen, 1999, 2000). And, it was Freud's daughter Anna, rather than any of his sons, who followed in his footsteps as an eminent psychoanalyst (Smirle, 2012). Ultimately, Anna Freud became her father's successor as leader of the international psychoanalytic movement, like Klein, bringing his work to the study of children. In fact, Melanie Klein and Anna Freud clashed after they had both moved to London. Their debates were eventually published as the *Freud-Klein Controversies 1941–45* (Crann, 2010). Both are remembered as pioneers in psychoanalysis. Anna Freud's obituary noted that she "virtually invented the systematic study of the emotional and mental life of the child" (Reuters, 1982).

The weaknesses in Freud's theory and in the psychoanalytic approach to personality are not minor problems. As you'll see in the chapter on therapies, very few psychologists practice Freudian psychoanalysis today. All the same, Freud made some lasting contributions to modern psychological thinking. Most important, he drew attention to the existence and influence of mental processes that occur outside conscious awareness, an idea that continues to be actively investigated by today's psychological researchers.

▲ **Anna Freud (1895–1982)** Freud's youngest daughter, Anna, became his chief disciple and was herself the founder of a psychoanalytic school. Expanding on her father's theory, she applied psychoanalysis to therapy with children. She is shown here addressing a debate on psychoanalysis at the Sorbonne University in Paris in 1950.

Bettmann/Getty Images

MYTH ◄ SCIENCE

Is it true that most psychologists today agree with Sigmund Freud's personality theory?

The Humanistic Perspective on Personality

■ KEY THEME
The humanistic perspective emphasizes free will, self-awareness, and psychological growth.

⹀ KEY QUESTIONS
- What roles do the self-concept, the actualizing tendency, and unconditional positive regard play in Rogers's personality theory?
- What are key strengths and weaknesses of the humanistic perspective?

By the 1950s, the field of personality was dominated by two completely different perspectives: Freudian psychoanalysis and B. F. Skinner's brand of behaviorism (see the chapter on learning). While Freud's theory of personality proposed elaborate and complex internal states, Skinner believed that psychologists should focus on observable behaviors and on the environmental factors that shape and maintain those behaviors (see Rogers & Skinner, 1956).

The Emergence of the "Third Force"

Another group of psychologists had a fundamentally different view of human nature. In opposition to both psychoanalysis and behaviorism, they championed a "third force" in psychology, which they called *humanistic psychology*. **Humanistic psychology** is *the view of personality that emphasizes the inherent goodness of people, human potential, self-actualization, the self-concept, and healthy personality development* (Cain, 2002).

humanistic psychology (theory of personality) The view of personality that generally emphasizes the inherent goodness of people, human potential, self-actualization, the self-concept, and healthy personality development.

Everett Collection/Newscom

⋀ Carl Rogers, Humanistic Psychologist
Carl Rogers is perhaps the best-known humanistic psychologist. His fundamentally optimistic perspective focused on the human capacity for growth. At bottom, Rogers (1961) believed, each person is asking, "Who am I, really? How can I get in touch with this real self, underlying all my surface behavior? How can I become myself?"

In contrast to Freud's pessimistic view of people as being motivated by unconscious sexual and destructive instincts, the humanistic psychologists saw people as being innately good. Humanistic psychologists also differed from psychoanalytic theorists by their focus on the *healthy* personality rather than on psychologically troubled people.

In contrast to the behaviorist view that human and animal behavior is due largely to environmental reinforcement and punishment, the humanistic psychologists believed that people are motivated by the need to grow psychologically. They also doubted that laboratory research with rats and pigeons accurately reflected the essence of human nature, as the behaviorists claimed. Instead, humanistic psychologists contended that the most important factor in personality is the individual's *conscious, subjective perception of their self* (Purkey & Stanley, 2002).

The two most important contributors to the humanistic perspective were Carl Rogers and Abraham Maslow. In the chapter on motivation, we discussed **Abraham Maslow's** famous *hierarchy of needs* and his concept of self-actualization. Like Maslow, Rogers emphasized the tendency of human beings to strive to fulfill their potential and capabilities (Kirschenbaum, 2004; Kirschenbaum & Jourdan, 2005).

Carl Rogers: On Becoming a Person

Carl Rogers (1902–1987) grew up in a large, close-knit family in a suburb of Chicago. After dismissing a career as a minister, Rogers turned to the study of psychology, ultimately enjoying a long, distinguished career as a psychotherapist, writer, and university professor.

Like Freud, Rogers developed his personality theory from his clinical experiences. Rogers referred to his patients as "clients" to emphasize their voluntary participation in therapy. In marked contrast to Freud, Rogers was continually impressed by his clients' drive to develop their potential.

These observations convinced Rogers that the most basic human motive is the *actualizing tendency*. The **actualizing tendency** is, *in Roger's theory, the innate drive to maintain and enhance the human organism* (Bohart, 2007; Bozarth & Wang, 2008). According to Rogers, all other human motives, whether biological or social, are secondary. He compared the actualizing tendency to a child's drive to learn to walk despite early frustration and falls.

The Self-Concept   Rogers (1959) was struck by how frequently his clients in therapy said, "I'm not really sure who I am," or "I just don't feel like myself." This observation helped form the cornerstone of Rogers's personality theory: the idea of the self-concept. The **self-concept** is *the set of perceptions and beliefs that you hold about yourself.* These include your nature, your personal qualities, and your typical behavior.

The self-concept begins evolving early in life. As children develop greater self-awareness, there is an increasing need for positive regard. *Positive regard* is the sense of being loved and valued by other people, especially one's parents (Bozarth, 2007; Farber & Doolin, 2011).

Rogers (1959) maintained that most parents provide their children with conditional positive regard. **Conditional positive regard** is, *in Rogers's theory, the sense that the child is valued and loved only when they behave in a way that is acceptable to others.* The problem with conditional positive regard is that it causes the child to learn to deny or distort their genuine feelings. For example, if little Amy's parents scold and reject her when she expresses angry feelings, her strong need for positive regard will cause her to deny her anger, even when it's justified or appropriate.

Rogers believed that people deny feelings because they contradict the self-concept. In this case, people are in a state of *incongruence:* Their self-concept conflicts with their actual experience (Rogers, 1959). As this process continues over time, a person progressively becomes more "out of touch" with their true feelings and their essential self, often experiencing psychological problems as a result.

How is incongruence to be avoided? In the ideal situation, a child experiences a great deal of unconditional positive regard from parents and other authority figures.

actualizing tendency In Rogers's theory, the innate drive to maintain and enhance the human organism.

self-concept The set of perceptions and beliefs that you hold about yourself.

conditional positive regard In Rogers's theory, the sense that the child is valued and loved only if they behave in a way that is acceptable to others.

Ellen B. Senisi

‹ Unconditional Positive Regard
Rogers contended that healthy personality development is the result of being unconditionally valued and loved as a person (Bozarth, 2007). He advised parents and teachers to control a child's inappropriate behavior without rejecting the child himself. Such a style of discipline teaches acceptable behaviors without diminishing the child's sense of self-worth.

Unconditional positive regard is, *in Rogers's theory, the child's sense that they will be valued and loved even if they don't conform to the standards and expectations of others.* In this way, the child's actualizing tendency is allowed its fullest expression. However, Rogers did *not* advocate permissive parenting. Instead, he maintained that parents can discipline their child without undermining the child's sense of self-worth.

For example, parents can disapprove of a child's specific *behavior* without completely rejecting the *child themself.* In effect, the parent's message should be: "I do not value your behavior right now, but I still love and value *you.*" In this way, according to Rogers, the child's essential sense of self-worth can remain intact.

Rogers (1957b) believed that the *fully functioning person* has a flexible, constantly evolving self-concept. They experience *congruence:* Their sense of self is consistent with their emotions and experiences (Farber, 2007). Therefore, they are capable of changing in response to new experiences.

Evaluating the Humanistic Perspective on Personality

The humanistic perspective has been criticized on two particular points. First, humanistic theories are hard to validate or test scientifically. For example, concepts like the self-concept, unconditional positive regard, and the actualizing tendency are difficult to define or measure objectively.

Second, many psychologists believe that humanistic psychology's view of human nature is too optimistic (Bohart, 2013). For example, if self-actualization is a universal human motive, why are self-actualized people so hard to find? And, can we really account for all the evil in the world by attributing it to a restrictive upbringing or society?

The influence of humanistic psychology has waned since the 1960s and early 1970s (Cain, 2003). Nevertheless, it has made lasting contributions, especially in the realms of psychotherapy, education, and parenting (Farber, 2007; Joseph & Murphy, 2013).

The Social Cognitive Perspective on Personality

■ KEY THEME
The social cognitive perspective stresses conscious thought processes, self-regulation, and the importance of situational influences.

≡ KEY QUESTIONS
- What is the principle of reciprocal determination?
- What is the role of self-efficacy beliefs in personality?
- What are the key strengths and weaknesses of the social cognitive perspective?

unconditional positive regard In Rogers's theory, the child's sense that they will be valued and loved even if they don't conform to the standards and expectations of others.

social cognitive theory Bandura's theory of personality, which emphasizes the importance of conscious cognitive processes, social experiences, self-efficacy beliefs, and reciprocal determinism.

reciprocal determinism A model proposed by Bandura that explains human functioning and personality as caused by the interaction of behavioral, cognitive, and environmental factors.

self-efficacy The beliefs that people have about their ability to meet the demands of a specific situation; feelings of self-confidence.

Have you ever noticed how different your behavior and sense of self can be in different situations? Consider this example: You feel pretty confident as you enter your college statistics class. After all, you're pulling an A, and your instructor nods approvingly every time you participate in class, which you do frequently. In contrast, your English composition class is a disaster. You're worried about passing the course, and you're afraid to even ask a question, much less participate in class. Even a casual observer would notice how differently you behave in the two different situations.

The idea that a person's conscious thought processes in different situations strongly influence their actions is one important characteristic of the *social cognitive perspective* on personality (Cervone et al., 2011). According to the social cognitive perspective, people actively process information from their social experiences. This information influences their goals, expectations, beliefs, and behavior, as well as the specific environments they choose.

The social cognitive perspective differs from psychoanalytic and humanistic perspectives in several ways. First, rather than basing their approach on self-analysis or insights derived from psychotherapy, social cognitive personality theorists rely heavily on experimental findings. Second, the social cognitive perspective emphasizes conscious, self-regulated behavior rather than unconscious mental influences and instinctual drives. And third, as in our statistics-versus-English-class example, the social cognitive approach emphasizes that our sense of self can vary, depending on our thoughts, feelings, and behaviors in a given situation.

Albert Bandura and Social Cognitive Theory

Several contemporary personality theorists have embraced the social cognitive approach to explaining personality, but the most influential is **Albert Bandura** (1925–2021). We examined Bandura's classic research on *observational learning* in the chapter on learning. In the chapter on motivation, we encountered Bandura's more recent research on self-efficacy. Here, you'll see how Bandura's ideas on both these topics are reflected in his personality theory, called social cognitive theory. **Social cognitive theory** is *Bandura's theory of personality, which emphasizes the importance of conscious cognitive processes, social experiences, self-efficacy beliefs, and reciprocal determinism* (Bandura, 2004b, 2006).

As Bandura's early research demonstrated, we learn many behaviors by observing, and then imitating, the behavior of other people. But, as Bandura (1997) has pointed out, we don't merely observe people's actions. We also observe the consequences that follow people's actions, the *rules* and *standards* that apply to behavior in specific situations, and the ways in which people *regulate their own behavior*. Thus, environmental influences are important, but conscious, self-generated goals and standards also exert considerable control over thoughts, feelings, and actions (Bandura, 2001, 2018).

For example, consider your own goal of getting a university education. No doubt many social and environmental factors influenced your decision. In turn, your conscious decision to attend a university determines many aspects of your current behavior, thoughts, and emotions. And your goal of attending university classes determines which environments you choose.

Reciprocal determinism is *Bandura's model that explains human functioning and personality as caused by the interaction of behavioral, cognitive, and environmental factors* (Bandura, 1986, 1997; see **Figure 11.2**). According to this principle, each factor both influences the other factors and is influenced by the other factors.

⌃ **Albert Bandura and Social Cognitive Theory** Albert Bandura emphasizes the importance of conscious cognitive processes in the development of personality. Bandura (2001) explained that "Unless people believe they can produce desired results and forestall detrimental ones by their actions, they have little incentive to act or persevere in the face of difficulties."

Beliefs of Self-Efficacy Collectively, a person's cognitive skills, abilities, and attitudes represent the person's *self-system.* According to Bandura (2001), our self-system guides how we perceive, evaluate, and control our behavior in different situations. Bandura (2004b) has found that the most critical elements influencing the self-system are our beliefs of self-efficacy. **Self-efficacy** refers to *the beliefs that people have about their ability to meet the demands of a specific situation; feelings of self-confidence.*

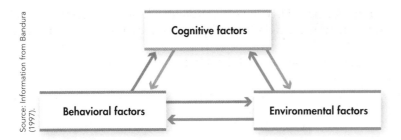

Source: Information from Bandura (1997).

FIGURE 11.2 Reciprocal Determinism
Reciprocal determinism explains human functioning and personality as caused by the interaction of behavioral, cognitive, and environmental factors. Each factor both influences the other factors and is influenced by the other factors.

Self-efficacy is different from self-esteem, which is our belief in our own worth rather than our confidence that we can do something in particular.

For example, suppose you were faced with the problem of applying for financial aid. Your sense of self-efficacy about finances and forms would affect your behavior and your fears of failure or hopes of success (Bandura, 1992; Ozer & Bandura, 1990). If you completely lacked a sense of self-efficacy in this arena, you might even quit, regardless of whether you were actually capable of completing the task. Bandura's concept of self-efficacy makes it easier to understand why people often fail to perform optimally at certain tasks, even though they possess the necessary skills.

From early in life, children develop feelings of self-efficacy from their experiences in dealing with different situations, such as athletic, social, and academic activities (Bandura et al., 2003). Feelings of self-efficacy strengthen when we perform a task successfully, and weaken when we fail. As Bandura (1992) has pointed out, developing self-efficacy begins in childhood, but it is a lifelong process.

Evaluating the Social Cognitive Perspective on Personality

A key strength of the social cognitive perspective on personality is its grounding in empirical laboratory research (Bandura, 2004a). Unlike vague psychoanalytic and humanistic concepts, the concepts of social cognitive theory are scientifically testable—that is, they can be operationally defined and measured. For example, psychologists can study beliefs of self-efficacy by comparing participants who are low in self-efficacy in a given situation with participants who are high in self-efficacy (see Ozer & Bandura, 1990). Not surprisingly, then, the social cognitive perspective has had a major impact on the study of personality.

However, some psychologists feel that the social cognitive approach to personality applies *best* to laboratory research. In the typical laboratory study, the relationships among a limited number of very specific variables are studied. In everyday life, situations are far more complex, with multiple factors converging to affect behavior and personality. Thus, an argument can be made that clinical data, rather than laboratory data, may be more reflective of human personality.

The social cognitive perspective also ignores unconscious influences, emotions, and conflicts. Thus, it seems to lack the richness of psychoanalytic and humanistic theories, which strive to explain the whole person, including the unconscious, irrational, and emotional aspects of personality (McAdams & Pals, 2006; Westen, 1990). Comparing the psychoanalytic, humanistic, and social cognitive approaches to personality provides very different views of human nature. To better understand the differences among these views, see the Critical Thinking box on the next page.

Nevertheless, by emphasizing the reciprocal interaction of mental, behavioral, and situational factors, the social cognitive perspective recognizes the complex combination of factors that influence our everyday behavior. By emphasizing the important role of learning, especially observational learning, the social cognitive perspective offers a developmental explanation of human functioning that persists throughout one's lifetime. Finally, by emphasizing the self-regulation of behavior, the social cognitive perspective places most of the responsibility for our behavior—and for the consequences we experience—squarely on our own shoulders.

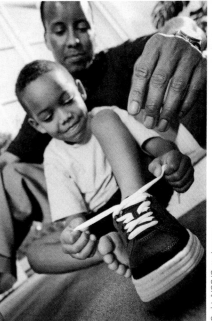

Corbis/VCG/Getty Images

▲ **Self-Efficacy** As Albert Bandura (2004b), explained, "The most effective way of developing a strong sense of efficacy is through mastery experiences. Successes build a robust belief in one's efficacy." By encouraging his son and helping him learn how to tie his shoes, this father is fostering the young boy's sense of self-efficacy.

CRITICAL THINKING

Freud, Rogers, and Bandura: Contrasting Views on Human Nature

Freud's view of human nature was deeply pessimistic. He believed that human aggression was part of the unconscious—an innate, persistent, and pervasive instinct. Were it not for internal super-ego restraints and external societal restraints, civilization as we know it would collapse. As Freud (1930) wrote in *Civilization and Its Discontents:*

> Men are not gentle creatures who want to be loved, and who at the most can defend themselves if they are attacked; they are, on the contrary, creatures among whose instinctual endowments is to be reckoned a powerful share of aggressiveness. . . . *Man is a wolf to man.*

In Freud's view, then, the essence of human nature is both unconscious and destructive. If you follow current events, you may find it hard to disagree. People *are* often exceedingly cruel and selfish. Control of these instincts is necessary. Yet societal, cultural, religious, and moral restraints also make people frustrated, neurotic, and unhappy. When "good" or "moral" behavior occurs, Freud would argue, it is only when our true nature is restrained through superego control, displacement, and so forth. A pretty gloomy picture, isn't it?

But is this truly the essence of human nature? Carl Rogers disagreed strongly. "I do not discover man to be well characterized in his basic nature by such terms as *fundamentally hostile, antisocial, destructive, evil,*" Rogers (1957a) wrote. Instead, Rogers believed that people are more accurately described as "positive, forward-moving, constructive, realistic, trustworthy."

If this is so, how can Rogers account for the evil and cruelty in the world? In sharp contrast to Freud, Rogers (1981) attributed the existence of evil to cultural factors, such as "the injustice of our distribution of wealth" and "cultivated prejudices." Insisting that people are innately good, Rogers (1964) said we should *trust* the human organism:

> I dare to believe that when the human being is inwardly free to choose whatever he deeply values, he tends to value those objects, experiences, and goals that will make for his own survival, growth, and development, and for the survival and development of others.

Social cognitive theorists also disagree with Freud, although their reasons are different from those of Rogers. They discount the importance of unconscious instincts, instead emphasizing that behavior is driven by conscious goals and motives. Like Rogers, Albert Bandura has taken issue with Freud's explanation of war and cruelty as being caused by a failure to control the id's destructive impulses. However, unlike Rogers, Bandura's response has not been about an unconscious, human instinct at all. Bandura (1986) noted that some of the most horrifying examples of human cruelty have instead involved conscious, *rational* behavior:

> People frequently engage in destructive activities, not because of reduced self-control, but because their cognitive skills and self-control are too well enlisted through moral justification and

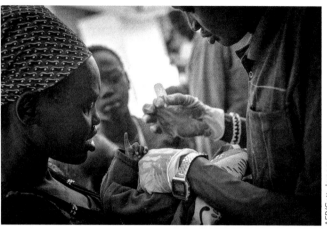

AFP/Getty Images

Are People Innately Good or Innately Evil? A member of Doctors Without Borders administers polio vaccines to children who are among the tens of thousands of refugees fleeing civil war in South Sudan. Doctors Without Borders is an international group of medical workers that won the Nobel Peace Prize for its work in helping the victims of violence and disasters all over the world.

On one hand, violence motivated by political or ethnic hatred seems to support Freud's contentions about human nature. On the other hand, the selfless behavior of those who help others, often at a considerable cost to themselves, seems to support Rogers's view. Or do these viewpoints ignore the role of conscious, rational behaviors in such events?

self-exonerative devices in the service of destructive causes. The infamous extermination procedures of Nazi concentration camps were perfected in laboratories using human victims. . . . The massive threats to human welfare are generally brought about by deliberate acts of principle, rather than unrestrained acts of impulse.

Given the differing views of Freud, Rogers, and Bandura, what is your opinion about human nature?

CRITICAL THINKING QUESTIONS

- In your opinion, which theorist's explanation seems most accurate? Are people inherently driven by aggressive instincts, as Freud claimed; naturally good, as Rogers claimed; or driven primarily by conscious goals and motives, as Bandura claimed?

- Consider a contemporary conflict or atrocity. How would Freud, Rogers, and Bandura explain people's behavior?

- In what ways do you see these theorists' views about human nature reflected in their ideas, such as Freud's concept of defense mechanisms, Rogers's emphasis on the importance of unconditional positive regard, and Bandura's concern with developing a sense of self-efficacy?

The Trait Perspective on Personality

■ KEY THEME

Trait theories of personality focus on identifying, describing, and measuring individual differences.

≡ KEY QUESTIONS

- What are traits, and how do surface traits and source traits differ?
- What are three influential trait theories, and how might heredity affect personality?
- What are the key strengths and weaknesses of trait theories of personality?

Suppose we asked you to describe the personality of a close friend. How would you begin? Would you describe their personality in terms of their unconscious conflicts, the congruence of their self-concept, or their level of self-efficacy? Probably not. Instead, you'd probably generate a list of their personal characteristics, such as "outgoing," "cheerful," and "generous." This rather commonsense approach to personality is shared by the trait theories. The trait approach to personality is very different from the theories we have encountered so far. The psychoanalytic, humanistic, and social cognitive theories emphasize the *similarities* among people. They focus on discovering the universal processes of motivation and development that explain human personality (Revelle, 1995, 2007). Although these theories do deal with individual differences, they do so only indirectly. In contrast, the trait approach to personality *focuses primarily on describing individual differences* (Funder & Fast, 2010).

"Oh, God! Here comes little Miss Perky."

Lee Lorenz/The New Yorker Collection/The Cartoon Bank

Trait theorists view the person as being a unique combination of personality characteristics or attributes, called *traits*. A **trait** is formally defined as a *relatively stable, enduring predisposition to consistently behave in a certain way*. **Trait theory** is *a theory of personality that focuses on identifying, describing, and measuring individual differences in behavioral predispositions*. Think back to our story of the four brothers in the chapter Prologue. While growing up in Bogotá, supposed fraternal twins Jorge and Carlos noticed differences they identified in terms of personality traits: Jorge was sunny, while Carlos was serious. People do tend to describe others in terms of traits. Participants in a study in Germany were asked to describe people they knew (Leising et al., 2014). Across all participants, 624 adjectives were generated. Among these, the adjectives most frequently used were those that were more "traitlike," such as extraverted and honest. It seems that it's natural for us to think in this way.

People possess traits to different degrees. For example, a person might be extremely shy, somewhat shy, or not shy at all. Hence, a trait is typically described in terms of a range from one extreme to its opposite. Most people fall in the middle of the range (average shyness), while fewer people fall at opposite poles (extremely shy or extremely outgoing).

Surface Traits and Source Traits

Most of the terms that we use to describe people are **surface traits**—*personality characteristics or attributes that can be easily inferred from observable behaviors*. Examples of surface traits include attributes like "happy," "exuberant," "spacey," and "gloomy." The list of potential surface traits is extremely long. Personality researcher Gordon Allport combed through an English-language dictionary and discovered more than 4,000 words that described specific personality traits (Allport & Odbert, 1936). (Studying personality structures based on language has since been named the lexical approach, which we'll discuss in more detail later [Ashton & Lee, 2005].)

trait A relatively stable, enduring predisposition to consistently behave in a certain way.

trait theory A theory of personality that focuses on identifying, describing, and measuring individual differences in behavioral predispositions.

surface traits Personality characteristics or attributes that can be easily inferred from observable behavior.

The most fundamental dimensions of personality are **source traits**, *the broad, basic traits that are hypothesized to be universal and relatively few in number.* Some personality researchers have argued that source traits have stronger genetic links and are more stable than surface traits, although others disagree with these distinctions (Kandler et al., 2014). Regardless, as the most basic dimension of personality, a source trait can potentially give rise to a vast number of surface traits. Trait theorists believe that there are relatively few source traits. Thus, one goal of trait theorists has been to identify the most basic set of universal source traits that can be used to describe all individual differences (Pervin, 1994).

Two Representative Trait Theories: Raymond Cattell and Hans Eysenck

How many source traits are there? Not surprisingly, trait theorists differ in their answers. Pioneer trait theorist **Raymond Cattell** reduced Allport's list of 4,000 terms to about 171 characteristics by eliminating terms that seemed to be redundant or uncommon (see John, 1990). Cattell collected data on a large sample of people, who were rated on each of the 171 terms. He then used a statistical technique called *factor analysis* to identify the traits that were most closely related to one another. After further research, Cattell reduced his list to 16 key personality factors, which are listed in **Table 11.2**.

An even simpler model of universal source traits was proposed by British psychologist **Hans Eysenck** (1916–1997). Eysenck's methods were similar to Cattell's, but his conception of personality includes just three dimensions. The first dimension is *introversion–extraversion,* which is the degree to which a person directs their energies outward toward the environment and other people versus inward toward their inner and self-focused experiences. A person who is high on the dimension of *introversion* might be quiet, solitary, and reserved, avoiding new experiences. A person high on the *extraversion* scale would be outgoing and sociable, enjoying new experiences and stimulating environments.

Eysenck's second major dimension is *neuroticism–emotional stability. Neuroticism* refers to a person's predisposition to become emotionally upset, while stability reflects a person's predisposition to be emotionally even. Surface traits associated with neuroticism are anxiety, tension, depression, and guilt. At the opposite end, emotional stability is associated with the surface traits of being calm, relaxed, and even-tempered.

Eysenck believed that by combining these two dimensions, people can be classified into four basic types: introverted–neurotic, introverted–stable, extraverted–neurotic, and extraverted–stable. Each basic type is associated with a different combination of surface traits, as shown in **Figure 11.3**. For example, the outgoing, joke-loving twins Jorge and William, whom you met in the chapter Prologue, would likely be classified as extraverted–stable. Carlos and Wilber, with their darker, serious moods, might be classified as introverted–neurotic. However, Carlos and Wilber were also known as "big flirts" who were easy to anger (Dominus, 2015). Could they actually be extraverted–neurotic?

In later research, Eysenck identified a third personality dimension, called *psychoticism* (Eysenck, 1990; Eysenck & Eysenck, 1975). A person high on this trait is antisocial, cold, hostile, and unconcerned about others. A person who is low on psychoticism is warm and caring toward others.

Eysenck (1990) believed that individual differences in personality are due to biological differences among people. For example, Eysenck proposed that an introvert's nervous system is more easily aroused than is an extravert's nervous system. Assuming that people tend to seek out an optimal level of arousal (see

TABLE 11.2

Cattell's 16 Personality Factors

1 Reserved, unsociable	↔	Outgoing, sociable
2 Less intelligent, concrete	↔	More intelligent, abstract
3 Affected by feelings	↔	Emotionally stable
4 Submissive, humble	↔	Dominant, assertive
5 Serious	↔	Happy-go-lucky
6 Expedient	↔	Conscientious
7 Timid	↔	Venturesome
8 Tough-minded	↔	Sensitive
9 Trusting	↔	Suspicious
10 Practical	↔	Imaginative
11 Forthright	↔	Shrewd, calculating
12 Self-assured	↔	Apprehensive
13 Conservative	↔	Experimenting
14 Group-dependent	↔	Self-sufficient
15 Undisciplined	↔	Controlled
16 Relaxed	↔	Tense

Raymond Cattell believed that personality could be described in terms of 16 source traits, or basic personality factors. Each factor represents a dimension that ranges between two extremes.

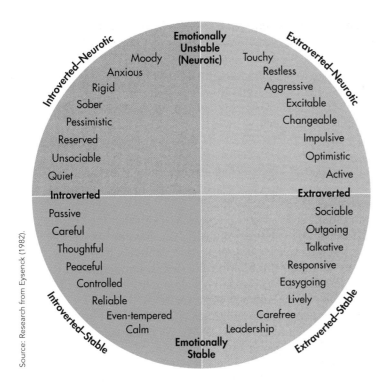

Source: Research from Eysenck (1982).

FIGURE 11.3 Eysenck's Theory of Personality Types Hans Eysenck's representation of the four basic personality types. Each type represents a combination of two basic personality dimensions: extraversion–introversion and neuroticism–emotional stability. Note the different surface traits in each quadrant that are associated with each basic personality type.

the chapter on motivation and emotion), extraverts would seek stimulation from their environment more than introverts would. And, because introverts would be more uncomfortable than extraverts in a highly stimulating environment, introverts would be much less likely to seek out stimulation.

Do introverts and extraverts actually prefer different environments? One study found that extraverted students tended to study in a relatively noisy, open area of a university library, whereas introverted students preferred to study in a quiet section of the library (Campbell & Hawley, 1982). More recently, researchers found that extraverted people preferred to visit flat, open areas like the beach, where you're out in the open among people, and introverts preferred wooded, secluded areas (Oishi et al., 2015). As Eysenck's theory predicts, the extraverts preferred environments that provided stimulation, while the introverts preferred environments that minimized stimulation.

It's important to mention that Eysenck—both as a person and with respect to his work—has attracted controversy. He has been accused of being a racist, a proponent of eugenics, and of manipulating his data (O'Grady, 2020). Indeed, Cattell has also been accused of being a eugenicist (Tucker, 2009). Yet, several prominent psychologists disagree with these conclusions. As introductory psychology authors who are trying to accurately portray the history of our field, while promoting diversity, equity, and inclusion, we will continue to follow and report on the historians of psychology who are investigating their work.

Sixteen Are Too Many, Three Are Too Few: The Five-Factor Model

Many trait theorists felt that Cattell's trait model was too complex and that his 16 personality factors could be reduced to a smaller, more basic set of traits. Yet Eysenck's three-dimensional trait theory seemed too limited, failing to capture other important dimensions of human personality (see Block, 1995).

Today, the consensus among many trait researchers is that the essential building blocks of personality can be described in terms of five basic personality dimensions, which are sometimes called "the Big Five" (Funder, 2001). The **five-factor model of personality**, is *a trait theory of personality that identifies extraversion, neuroticism, agreeableness, conscientiousness, and openness to experience as the fundamental building blocks of personality.* These five dimensions represent the structural organization of personality traits (McCrae & Costa, 1996, 2003).

Creativalmages/Getty Images

To see the differences among the five basic personality dimensions, go to **Achieve** and try **Concept Practice: The "Big Five" Personality Traits.**

five-factor model of personality A trait theory of personality that identifies extraversion, neuroticism, agreeableness, conscientiousness, and openness to experience as the fundamental building blocks of personality.

TABLE 11.3

The Five-Factor Model of Personality

Low	⟷	High
Factor 1: Openness to Experience		
Down-to-earth		Imaginative
Conventional, uncreative		Original, creative
Prefer routine		Prefer variety
Factor 2: Conscientiousness		
Lazy		Hardworking
Aimless		Ambitious
Quitting		Persevering
Factor 3: Extraversion		
Reserved		Affectionate
Loner		Joiner
Quiet		Talkative
Factor 4: Agreeableness		
Antagonistic		Acquiescent
Ruthless		Softhearted
Suspicious		Trusting
Factor 5: Neuroticism		
Calm		Worrying
Even-tempered, unemotional		Temperamental, emotional
Hardy		Vulnerable

Source: Research from McCrae & Costa (1990).

This table shows the five major personality factors, according to Big Five theorists Robert McCrae and Paul Costa, Jr. You can use the acronym OCEAN to help you remember the five factors. Listed below each major personality factor are surface traits that are associated with it. Note that each factor represents a dimension or range between two extreme poles. Most people will fall somewhere in the middle between the two opposing poles.

Different trait researchers describe the five basic traits somewhat differently. However, the most commonly accepted five factors are openness to experience, conscientiousness, extraversion, agreeableness, and neuroticism. (The first letter of each spells OCEAN, a helpful tool to remember them.) **Table 11.3** summarizes the Big Five traits as defined by personality theorists Robert McCrae and Paul Costa, Jr. Note that Factor 1, neuroticism, and Factor 2, extraversion, are essentially the same as Eysenck's first two personality dimensions.

Does the five-factor model describe the universal structure of human personality? The answer appears to be yes. Several international studies have found that people across countries and cultures had personality traits that fit, for the most part, within the overall Big Five personality structure (McCrae et al., 2005; Rossier et al., 2005; Tackett et al., 2012).

Based on abundant cross-cultural research, trait theorists Jüri Allik and Robert McCrae (2002, 2004, 2013) believe that the Big Five personality traits are basic features of the human species, universal, and probably biologically based. Some theorists have even linked the biologically driven temperament we're born with (as discussed in the chapter on lifespan development) to our later personality traits (Rothbart et al., 2000; Slobodskaya & Kozlova, 2016). Relatedly, many psychologists think that traits may be associated with specific patterns of brain activity or structure (Canli, 2004, 2006; Sampaio et al., 2014). We discuss an attempt to investigate that relationship in the Focus on Neuroscience box, "The Neuroscience of Personality: Brain Structure and the Big Five" on page 385.

Some personality researchers, however, are unconvinced, pointing out that there are culturally specific patterns of behavior that do not easily fit the five-factor model (Carlo et al., 2014; Gurven et al., 2013, 2014). Some research has not found the Big 5 to apply to non-WEIRD cultures—that is, it may not apply to culture that are not Western, educated, industrialized, rich, and democratic (Laajaj et al., 2020). So, although the Big Five remains the dominant trait model of personality, another model may better represent personality traits cross-culturally. Some research supports a particular model, one with six factors.

Based on international and cross-cultural research, Michael Ashton and Kibeom Lee (2007) proposed a six-factor model, an expansion of the Big Five. Ashton and Lee (2005) are supporters of what's called the lexical approach to understanding the structure of personality. ("Lexical" refers to the vocabulary of a language.) As Ashton and Lee (2005) explain, the lexical approach is based on the idea that "the major dimensions of personality should be represented [with the] common . . . adjectives of natural languages." That is, if a particular trait is important enough to notice, then a word will be invented for it. By studying a language, you can learn about a particular culture's understanding of personality.

The Big Five was developed in English, but as we noted, doesn't seem to apply in other cultures and languages. Ashton and Lee wondered about researcher bias: Were researchers simply finding what they were looking for? Based on additional lexical research, Ashton and Lee realized that if you let the language, not expectations about personality factors, drive the research, a sixth factor, honesty–humility, turned up. Later lexical research in English supported the presence of this sixth factor as well. Ashton and Lee (2007) called their new model *HEXACO*.

HEXACO stands for (H)onesty–humility, (E)motionality, e(X)traversion, (A)greeableness, (C)onscientiousness, and (O)penness to experience. **Table 11.4** lists the characteristics associated with each of these factors, as well as comparisons with their Big Five counterparts. There are two main differences between the Big Five and HEXACO. First, there is the new honesty–humility factor, some characteristics of which fall under agreeableness in the Big Five. Second, anger-related characteristics have shifted from the Big Five neuroticism factor (called emotionality in HEXACO) to the HEXACO agreeableness factor.

Despite the past dominance of the Big Five, the HEXACO model is becoming increasingly popular (Zettler et al., 2020). And HEXACO might be a more useful

TABLE 11.4

The HEXACO Model of Personality

HEXACO factor	Characteristics	Relation to the Big Five
Honesty–humility	Sincere, fair, modest vs. sly, boastful	Not in the Big Five
Emotionality	Emotional, fearful vs. stable, brave	Like neuroticism, but does not include anger for those with high scores
eXtraversion	Outgoing, talkative vs. shy, quiet	Very similar
Agreeableness	Patient, gentle vs. ill-tempered, stubborn	Like agreeableness, but includes anger for those with low scores
Conscientiousness	Organized, careful vs. sloppy, irresponsible	Very similar
Openness to experience	Creative, unconventional vs. shallow, unimaginative	Similar, but more emphasis on unconventionality

Source: Research from Ashton & Lee (2007)

This table shows the six HEXACO factors according to personality theorists Michael Ashton and Kibeom Lee. Each factor represents a dimension or range between two extreme poles, represented by the adjectives in the middle column. The righthand column shows how each of these factors matches up with the Big Five.

model than the Big Five for some personality research (Anglim & O'Connor, 2019; Ashton et al., 2014; Lee & Ashton, 2019). For example, the HEXACO model is a better predictor of psychological well-being than the Big Five (Aghababaei & Arji, 2014).

The HEXACO model also helps us understand the *dark triad*, a cluster of three personality traits that characterize people who are more likely than others to cause harm and create societal problems (Paulhus & Williams, 2002). The dark triad has been linked with the concept of "evil," with traits that include Machiavellianism, which is a tendency to manipulate others; low-level narcissism, which includes a sense of entitlement; and low-level psychopathy, which combines impulsivity with a lack of empathy (Book et al., 2015). Think Darth Vader from *Star Wars* or Killmonger from *Black Panther*. Some researchers have added a fourth dark trait to form a dark tetrad—sadism, or the desire to cause suffering in others (Book et al., 2016).

Understanding the dark triad (or tetrad) might help us to prevent harm to society, including by leaders of governments, corporations, and other organizations. But these dark traits are not a great fit with the Big Five, correlating to varying degrees with three of the five factors. The HEXACO model is more directly useful, with scores on the dark-triad (and dark-tetrad) characteristics negatively correlating with scores on the honesty–humility factor: People higher on dark traits tend to be lower on honesty–humility (Aghababaei et al., 2014; Book et al., 2016).

But don't worry! There's a light triad, too, which centers on valuing the worth of every person (Kaufman et al., 2019). The light triad is exemplified by many movie heroes, from the Jedi Rey in *Star Wars* to Wonder Woman. And it turns out that the light triad positively correlates with the honesty–humility factor.

The HEXACO model may one day become more commonly used than the Big Five. Or personality research may uncover new models. For example, some researchers argue that there still only is true support for three personality factors—extraversion, agreeableness, and conscientiousness—across languages (De Raad et al., 2010). In the meantime, let's turn back to the ever-popular, and widely researched, Big Five.

Tetra Images/Getty Images

▲ **Situational Personality?** Social expectations for a given situation can alter the expression of our underlying personality traits. The woman in this photo may typically be extremely outgoing, but when visiting a quiet museum, she'll likely rein in her extraversion.

MYTH ▶ SCIENCE

Is it true that our personality traits can change over the course of our lives?

For the most part, the Big Five structure of personality seems to apply across the lifespan. The one exception may be in childhood, during which, researchers have observed, there is a sixth personality trait, called "activity," that appears to be independent of any of the Big Five traits (Shiner & DeYoung, 2013). Described as a "sixth fundamental factor," activity assesses a child's overall levels of energy, motion, and physical activity (De Pauw, 2016). In a study of thousands of children, researchers documented all of the Big Five factors, plus activity (Soto & John, 2014; Soto & Tackett, 2015). This expanded structure is sometimes referred to as the Little Six, both as a nod to the Big Five but also to indicate that it applies to children. Human personality structure seems to drop the "activity" factor by late adolescence, and it's striking that the "adult" personality structure seems to exist at all ages.

Personality psychologists have long been interested in whether personality traits are consistent from one situation to another. In fact, personality theorists have long engaged in something called the "person-situation debate," arguing whether our personality or the context is the stronger predictor of behavior (Donnellan et al., 2009; Furr & Funder, 2021). Consider someone who is very conscientious with respect to their studies, but the opposite at a part-time job they hate. Is that apparent inconsistency an actual shift in personality from one situation to the other? Or is it just a difference in how personality traits are expressed? Situations in which our behavior is limited by social "rules" or expectations may limit the expression of personality characteristics even as those traits remain stable. For example, even the most extraverted person may be subdued at a funeral. In general, behavior is most likely to reflect the underlying personality traits in familiar, informal, or private situations with few social rules or expectations (A. H. Buss, 1989, 2001).

Even when situational influences like social rules lead to inconsistencies in how other people express their personality traits, differences based on personalities remain. The person and the situation are both important (e.g., Furr & Funder, 2021). For example, a shy person and an outgoing person may both be quieter in a library than at a party, but the shy person is likely to be quieter than the outgoing person in *both* situations. In addition, we tend to experience other people in the same types of situations — our instructors in classes and our friends in social situations. As a result, we tend to experience the expression of others' personalities as consistent (Mischel & Shoda, 1995; Mischel et al., 2002).

So, personality traits seem to be relatively stable across situations. What about over time? The consensus among personality psychologists has also been that personality traits are relatively stable over time. Researchers have long believed that a young adult who is very extraverted and relatively open to new experiences, for example, is likely to grow into an older adult who could be described in much the same way (Edmonds et al., 2013; McCrae & Costa, 2006). But more and more, researchers are calling this assumption into question (Roberts et al., 2005, 2017).

Specifically, researchers have observed that some personality traits do change over the lifespan (Harris et al., 2016; Wagner et al., 2020). People tend to experience a slight decline in neuroticism. But most people become more agreeable, conscientious, and emotionally stable as they mature psychologically (Caspi et al., 2005; Roberts et al., 2006). These shifts are most evident in early and late adulthood (Milojev & Sibley, 2014).

Why might these shifts occur? One reason is that personality traits sometimes change in response to experiences, including our emotional ones. For example, people who reported higher levels of overall happiness were more likely to later experience increases in extraversion, agreeableness, and conscientiousness (Soto, 2014). And they also were more likely to experience decreases in neuroticism. The same pattern of long-term changes in personality traits seems to occur among those who mature through experiencing new responsibilities, such as getting married, starting a new job, or having a child (Golle et al., 2018; Roberts et al., 2005; Specht et al., 2012). There are even some suggestions that the COVID lockdown may have shifted some people's personalities (Jarrett, 2020). And some new research suggests that those who

@ FOCUS ON NEUROSCIENCE

The Neuroscience of Personality: Brain Structure and the Big Five

Many personality theorists, like Hans Eysenck, believed that personality traits are associated with characteristic biological differences among people (DeYoung & Gray, 2009). Some studies have confirmed this belief, identifying distinct patterns of brain activity associated with different personality traits (Canli, 2004, 2006). For example, brain imaging studies showed that people who were high in extraversion showed higher levels of brain activation in response to positive images than people who were low in extraversion. Similarly, people who score high on neuroticism show more activation in response to negative images than people who score low on neuroticism (Canli et al., 2001).

Are personality traits also associated with brain structure? Psychologist Colin DeYoung and his colleagues (2010) had over 100 participants undergo MRI scans and also take the *NEO-Personality Inventory*, a personality test that is used to measure the Big Five. The researchers then compared the brain scans and the personality test results. They found the following:

- *Extraversion* was associated with larger brain tissue volume in the *medial orbitofrontal cortex*, a brain region that is associated with sensitivity to rewarding stimuli.
- *Agreeableness* was associated with increased volume in the *posterior cingulate cortex*, a brain region associated with understanding the beliefs of others (Saxe & Powell, 2006).
- *Conscientiousness* was associated with a large region of the frontal cortex called the *middle frontal gyrus*, which is known to be involved in planning, working memory, and self-regulation.

But not all personality traits had such clear correlations. *Neuroticism* was associated with a mixed pattern of brain structure differences. And DeYoung and his colleagues (2010) found no significant pattern of brain differences associated with openness to experience.

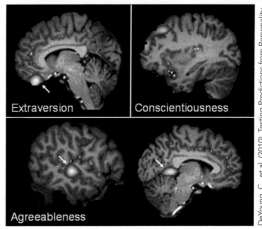

Personality Traits and the Brain Red and yellow highlight regions where brain volume was significantly associated with specific personality traits. The lighter the color, the stronger the association (DeYoung et al., 2010).

Are such studies merely phrenology with a modern face? These findings, while still preliminary, do suggest that there are biological influences on personality. It's important to note, though, that the findings are *correlational*. It's entirely possible that the brain differences are caused by different patterns of behavior rather than the other way around.

Further, both brain differences and personality traits are shaped by the complex interaction of environmental, genetic, and biological influences. As DeYoung (2010) says, the ultimate goal is to use the methods of neuroscience to help generate a new theory of personality—one in which personality is seen as a "system of dynamic, interacting elements that generates the ongoing flux of behavior and experience."

undergo "personality growth"—that is, increases in extraversion and conscientiousness and decreases in neuroticism—tend to experience better career outcomes (Hoff et al., 2020).

The new understanding that our personality traits are not necessarily stable raises an important question: Can we choose to change our personalities? It turns out that most of us would like to do so. In one study, 87 percent of people surveyed wanted to be more extraverted, and 97 percent wanted to be more conscientious (Hudson & Roberts, 2014). Tracking people who wanted to change, researchers found that they did change, at least to a small degree (Hudson & Fraley, 2015). In a recent study, participants were randomly assigned to be either extraverted or introverted for a week (Margolis & Lyubomirsky, 2019). To be an extravert, participants acted as "talkative, assertive, and spontaneous" as they could. To be an introvert, they acted as "deliberate, quiet, and reserved" as they could. The randomly assigned extraverts reported higher levels of psychological well-being than did those assigned to be introverts, an indication that we can both change our personality-related behaviors and reap the rewards of those changes.

behavioral genetics An interdisciplinary field that studies the effects of genes and heredity on behavior.

Findings about our potential to change our personalities are an important direction in personality research. In the words of researchers Danielle Dick and Richard Rose (2002), "genes confer dispositions, not destinies."

Personality Traits and Behavioral Genetics: Just a Chip off the Old Block?

Do personality traits run in families? Are personality traits determined by genetics? Many trait theorists, such as Raymond Cattell and Hans Eysenck, believed that traits are at least partially genetic in origin. For example, Sandy's daughter, Laura, has always been outgoing and sociable, traits that she shares with both her parents. But is she outgoing because she inherited that trait? Or is she outgoing because outgoing behavior was modeled and reinforced? Is it even possible to sort out the relative influence that genetics and environmental experiences have on personality traits?

Behavioral genetics is *an interdisciplinary field that studies the effects of genes and heredity on behavior.* Most behavioral genetics studies on humans involve measuring similarities and differences among members of a large group of people who are genetically related to different degrees. The basic research strategy is to compare the degree of difference among participants to their degree of genetic relatedness. If a trait is genetically influenced, then the more closely two people are genetically related, the more you would expect them to be similar on that trait (see the chapter on thinking, learning, and intelligence).

Such studies may involve comparisons between identical twins and fraternal twins or comparisons between identical twins reared apart and identical twins reared together. Even though it involves just four people, the research involving Jorge, Carlos, William, and Wilber allows for all these types of comparisons. Adoption studies, in which adopted children are compared to their biological and adoptive relatives, are also used in behavioral genetics.

Evidence from twin studies and adoption studies shows that certain personality traits *are* substantially influenced by genetics (Amin et al., 2011; McCrae et al., 2010). The evidence for genetic influence is particularly strong for extraversion and neuroticism, two of the Big Five personality traits (Plomin et al., 1994, 2001; Weiss et al., 2008). Twin studies have also found that openness to experience, conscientiousness, and agreeableness are also influenced by genetics, although to a lesser extent (Bouchard, 2004; Harris et al., 2007).

Is it true that personality is not influenced by genetics, but is primarily shaped by our upbringing?

So is personality completely determined by genetics? Not at all. As behavioral geneticists Robert Plomin and Essi Colledge (2001) explain, "Individual differences in complex psychological traits are due at least as much to environmental influences as they are to genetic influences." In other words, the influence of environmental factors on personality traits is at least equal to the influence of genetic factors (Rowe, 2003). For example, identical twins are most alike in early life. As the twins grow up, leave home, and encounter different experiences and environments, their personalities become more different (Bouchard, 2004; Polderman et al., 2015).

Do Animals Have Personality Traits?

If you've ever owned a pet, you're probably already convinced that animals have personalities. But what does the science say? Is there a sort of Big Five for animals?

Australian researchers analyzed owners' ratings of behaviors for almost 3,000 pet cats (Brulliard, 2016; Roetman et al., 2017). Rated behaviors included the degree to which a cat is "vigilant," meaning watchful or observant, and "inventive," or likely to do new things, such as climbing into bags or boxes (Gartner et al., 2014).

The research team identified clusters of statistically related behaviors to outline a feline Big Five: skittishness, outgoingness, dominance, spontaneity, and friendliness. Skittishness relates to neuroticism in humans; outgoingness relates to extraversion; and friendliness relates to agreeableness. **Figure 11.4** shows the ratings for your author Susan's cat Milla, which match Susan's observations of Milla's shy but sweet nature.

Many other studies also have found that animals exhibit personality traits, defined as groups of behaviors that: (1) tend to cluster together, (2) remain relatively stable across time and situations, and (3) vary among the individuals in a species (Walton & Toth, 2016). Did

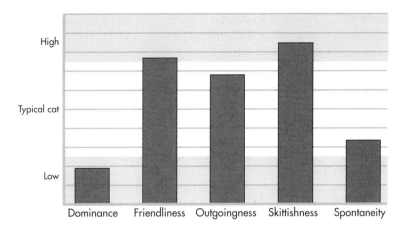

FIGURE 11.4 Big Five for Cats Your author Susan completed a personality test for her cat, Milla, rating the degree to which Milla exhibits 52 behaviors. Susan was not surprised to see that Milla was very high in friendliness and outgoingness. Susan also was not surprised that Milla, a former street kitten abandoned by her mother, was also high in skittishness.

you notice that the definition for animal personality is more restrictive than the definition for human personality, which also refers to thinking and feeling? Because we can't know what animals are thinking and feeling, researchers must rely on behaviors, which can be assessed either through ratings as in the cat study or by coding behaviors as they occur.

Animal personalities have been documented in more than 200 species—from insects to birds to mammals (Byrnes & Brown, 2016). These measures are about as reliable and valid as human personality measures (Carere & Locurto, 2011). This means measures of animal personalities seem to have consistent results over time and among different raters, and the ratings seem to match up with other, related behaviors (Locurto, 2007).

The idea that animals have personalities is not new. Ivan Pavlov, who demonstrated classical conditioning in dogs (see the chapter on learning), described four personality types for dogs—excitable, lively, quiet, and inhibited (Locurto, 2007). In fact, Pavlov's research formed the basis for Eysenck's work on human personality, which originally had two dimensions and four personality types (see Figure 11.3 earlier in the chapter).

Research on nonhuman animal personalities is not simply a fascinating topic for animal owners and researchers. It also teaches us about human personality. Given the fact that both animal and human behavior is driven by evolution, it's not surprising that we see similarities in animal and human traits. But it's useful to be able to observe the entire life of an organism, including its reproductive success. So lifespan data—which are easier to collect for nonhuman animals than humans—can help us better understand the evolutionary role of personality. As in humans, personality traits in animals emerge early in life and are, at least in part, genetic (Byrnes & Brown, 2016; Locurto, 2007). But it's easier to observe personality patterns and related behaviors over the lifetime of a nonhuman animal (Walton & Toth, 2016).

Further, like humans, animals vary on specific traits like liveliness or extraversion. Why would it be adaptive for individuals to vary on a given trait, rather than just all evolving to have the same, ideal level of that trait? Research on nonhuman animal personalities provides one possible answer. A meta-analysis documented the benefits of variation across animal species, at least for some traits (Smith & Blumstein, 2008). For

Quentin Jones.jonesphoto.com.au

△ **Sharks with Personalities** Australian researcher Culum Brown studied whether Port Jackson sharks had personalities (Byrnes & Brown, 2016). Each shark in the study was released from a closed box into an unknown habitat four separate times. Some sharks were quick to emerge, an indication of boldness, whereas others were more timid. Each shark's degree of boldness tended to be the same across all four trials, an indication of a stable personality.

Source: Caracol Televisión S.A.

❮ **Heredity or Environment?** Along with sharing common genes, many identical twins share common interests and personality characteristics. Here, all four brothers introduced in the Prologue sit together; from left are identical twins William and Jorge, then identical twins Wilber and Carlos. Similarities between the identical twins are evident even though they were raised separately in very different environments. When interviewed, family members readily identified their shared characteristics: "Who were the crybabies of the family? Carlos and Wilber! Who had sweet temperaments? Jorge and William! Who were more organized? Carlos and Wilber! Who were the girl chasers? Carlos and Wilber! Who were the strongest? Jorge and William!" (Dominus, 2015). Because the identical twins were reared apart, it's likely that at least some of their similarities are due to genetic influences.

example, bold animals tend to fare better than timid animals in terms of mating, but they are more likely to die young. So, a full range of personality traits may allow a species, including our own, to survive across a range of contexts.

Evaluating the Trait Perspective on Personality

Although psychologists continue to disagree on how many basic traits exist in human personality, they do generally agree that people can be described and compared in terms of basic personality traits. But like the other personality theories, the trait approach has its weaknesses.

One criticism is that trait theories don't really explain human personality (Epstein, 2010; Pervin, 1994). Instead, they simply label general predispositions to behave in a certain way. Second, trait theorists don't attempt to explain how or why individual differences develop (Boyle, 2008). After all, saying that trait differences are due partly to genetics and partly to environmental influences isn't saying much.

A third criticism is that trait approaches generally fail to address other important personality issues, such as the basic motives that drive human personality or how psychological change and growth occur (Block, 2010; McAdams & Walden, 2010). Conspicuously absent are the grand conclusions about the essence of human nature that characterize the psychoanalytic and humanistic theories. So, although trait theories are useful in describing individual differences and predicting behavior, they have limitations.

On the other hand, personality traits are, from a statistical perspective, impressive predictors of a variety of pretty major life outcomes (Roberts et al., 2007). Our personality traits seem to be just as strong of a predictor—with respect to important relationship, career, and lifespan outcomes—as are our socioeconomic status and cognitive ability, typically measured via IQ scores. Understanding one's personality is clearly important to understanding one's life more generally.

As you've seen, each of the major perspectives on personality has contributed to our understanding of human personality. The four perspectives are summarized in **Table 11.5**. In the next section, we'll briefly survey the tests that are used in personality assessment.

TABLE 11.5

The Major Personality Perspectives

Perspective	Key Theorists	Key Themes and Ideas
Psychoanalytic	Sigmund Freud	Influence of unconscious psychological processes; importance of sexual and aggressive instincts
	Carl Jung	The collective unconscious and archetypes
	Karen Horney	Parent–child relationship, womb envy
	Alfred Adler	Striving for superiority, compensating for inferiority
Humanistic	Carl Rogers	Emphasis on the self-concept and psychological growth
	Abraham Maslow	Hierarchy of needs and self-actualization
Social Cognitive	Albert Bandura	Emphasis on conscious thoughts, self-efficacy beliefs, self-regulation, and goal setting
Trait	Raymond Cattell	16 source traits of personality
	Hans Eysenck	Three basic dimensions introversion–extraversion, neuroticism–emotional stability, and psychoticism
	Robert McCrae, Paul Costa, Jr.	Five-factor model: neuroticism, extraversion, openness to experience, agreeableness, and conscientiousness
	Michael Ashton, Kibeom Lee	Six-factor HEXACO model that adds an honesty–humility trait to the Big 5

Assessing Personality: Psychological Tests

■ KEY THEME
Tests to measure and evaluate personality fall into two basic categories: projective tests and self-report inventories.

≡ KEY QUESTIONS
- What are the most widely used personality tests, and how are they administered and interpreted?
- What are some key strengths and weaknesses of projective tests and self-report inventories?

When we discussed intelligence tests in the chapter on thinking, language, and intelligence, we described the characteristics of a good psychological test. Beyond intelligence tests, there are hundreds of different psychological tests. A **psychological test** is *a test that assesses a person's abilities, aptitudes, interests, or personality on the basis of a systematically obtained sample of behavior* (Spies et al., 2010). Any psychological test is useful insofar as it achieves two basic goals:

1. It accurately and consistently reflects a person's characteristics on some dimension.

2. It predicts a person's future psychological functioning or behavior.

In this section, we'll look at the very different approaches used in the two basic types of personality tests—projective tests and self-report inventories. We'll then evaluate the strengths and weaknesses of each approach.

Projective Tests: Like Seeing Things in the Clouds

A **projective test** is *a type of personality test that involves a person's interpreting an ambiguous image.* In the most commonly used projective tests, a person is presented with a vague image, such as an inkblot or an ambiguous scene, and then is asked to describe what they "see" in the image. The person's response is thought to be a projection of their unconscious conflicts, motives, psychological defenses, and personality traits. Notice that this idea is related to the defense mechanism of *projection*, which was described in Table 11.1 earlier in the chapter. The famous **Rorschach Inkblot Test** is *a projective test using inkblots, developed by Swiss psychiatrist Hermann Rorschach in 1921* (Hertz, 1992).

The Rorschach test consists of 10 cards, 5 that show black-and-white inkblots and 5 that depict colored inkblots. One card at a time, the person describes whatever they see in the inkblot. The examiner records the person's responses verbatim and also observes their behavior, gestures, and reactions.

Numerous scoring systems exist for the Rorschach. Interpretation is based on such criteria as whether the person reports seeing humans or animals, perceives movement, or deals with the whole blot or just fragments of it (Exner, 2007; Exner & Erdberg, 2005).

The **Thematic Apperception Test**, abbreviated **TAT**, is *a projective personality test, developed by Henry Murray and colleagues, that involves creating stories about ambiguous scenes.* The person is asked to create a story about the ambiguous scene, including what the characters are feeling and how the story turns out. The stories are scored for the motives, needs, anxieties, and conflicts of the main character (Bellak, 1993; Langan-Fox & Grant, 2006; Moretti & Rossini, 2004). As with the Rorschach, interpreting the TAT involves the subjective judgment of the examiner.

Strengths and Limitations of Projective Tests
Projective tests are mainly used in psychotherapy. According to many clinicians, the primary strength of projective tests is that they provide a wealth of qualitative information about an individual's psychological functioning, information that can be explored further in psychotherapy.

However, there are several drawbacks to projective tests. Most importantly, the scoring of projective tests is highly subjective, requiring the examiner to make numerous

psychological test A test that assesses a person's abilities, aptitudes, interests, or personality on the basis of a systematically obtained sample of behavior.

projective test A type of personality test that involves a person's interpreting an ambiguous image.

Rorschach Inkblot Test A projective test using inkblots, developed by Swiss psychiatrist Hermann Rorschach in 1921.

Thematic Apperception Test (TAT) A projective personality test, developed by Henry Murray and colleagues, that involves creating stories about ambiguous scenes.

GRANGER - Historical Picture Archive

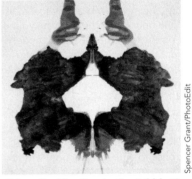

Spencer Grant/PhotoEdit

⌃ What Do You See in the Inkblot?
Intrigued by Freud's and Jung's theories, Swiss psychiatrist Hermann Rorschach (1884–1922) set out to develop a test that would reveal the contents of the unconscious. Rorschach believed that people were more likely to expose their unconscious conflicts, motives, and defenses in their descriptions of the ambiguous inkblots than they would be if the same topics were directly addressed. Rorschach published a series of 10 inkblots with an accompanying manual in 1921. Because he died the following year, Rorschach never knew how popular his projective test would become. Although the validity of the test is questionable, the Rorschach Inkblot Test is still the icon most synonymous with psychological testing in the popular media.

MYTH ◄ SCIENCE

Is it true that projective tests, like the famous Rorschach Inkblot Test, accurately reveal personality traits and unconscious conflicts?

▲ **The Thematic Apperception Test**
Developed by psychologists Christiana Morgan and Henry Murray (1935), the TAT involves creating a story about a highly evocative, ambiguous scene, like the one on the card held by the young boy on the left. The person is thought to project their own motives, conflicts, and other personality characteristics into the story they create. According to Murray (1943), "Before he knows it, he has said things about an invented character that apply to himself, things which he would have been reluctant to confess in response to a direct question."

self-report inventory A type of psychological test in which a person's responses to standardized questions are compared to established norms.

Minnesota Multiphasic Personality Inventory (MMPI) A self-report inventory that assesses personality characteristics and psychological disorders; used to assess both normal and disturbed populations.

judgments about the person's responses. Consequently, two examiners may test the same individual and arrive at different conclusions. In addition, projective tests are poor at predicting future behavior.

The bottom line? It is a myth that the Rorschach Inkblot Test accurately reveals personality traits and unconscious conflicts. Despite their widespread use, hundreds of studies of projective tests seriously question their *validity*—that the tests measure what they purport to measure—and their *reliability*—the consistency of test results (Hunsley et al., 2015; Lilienfeld et al., 2012; Weiner & Meyer, 2009). Nonetheless, projective tests remain very popular, especially among clinical, counseling, and school psychologists (Leichtman, 2004; Lilienfeld et al., 2012).

Self-Report Inventories

A **self-report inventory** is *a type of psychological test in which a person's responses to standardized questions are compared to established norms.* These inventories typically use a paper-and-pencil format and take a direct, structured approach to assessing personality. People answer specific questions or rate themselves on various dimensions of behavior or psychological functioning. Often called *objective personality tests,* self-report inventories contain items that have been shown by previous research to differentiate among people on a particular personality characteristic. In fact, self-report personality inventories were among the measures that the researchers asked Jorge, Carlos, William, and Wilber to complete to learn more about their similarities and differences (Dominus, 2015). Unlike projective tests, self-report inventories are objectively scored by comparing a person's answers to standardized norms collected on large groups of people.

The most widely used test in this category is the **Minnesota Multiphasic Personality Inventory**, abbreviated **MMPI**, *a self-report inventory that assesses personality characteristics and psychological disorders; used to assess both normal and disturbed populations* (Butcher, 2010). First published in the 1940s and revised in the 1980s, the most widely used version is referred to as the MMPI-2. The MMPI consists of over 500 statements. The person responds to each statement with "True," "False," or "Cannot say." Topics include social, political, religious, and sexual attitudes; physical and psychological health; interpersonal relationships; and abnormal thoughts and behaviors (Delman et al., 2008; Graham, 1993; McDermut & Zimmerman, 2008). Items similar to those used in the MMPI are shown in **Table 11.6**.

Although the MMPI-2 is the most widely used version, the shorter MMPI-2-RF ("RF" stands for restructured form) has rapidly gained in popularity (Selbom,

TABLE 11.6

Simulated MMPI-2 Items

Most people will use somewhat unfair means to gain profit or an advantage rather than lose it.

I am often very tense on the job.

The things that run through my head sometimes are horrible.

Sometimes there is a feeling like something is pressing in on my head.

Sometimes I think so fast I can't keep up.

I am worried about sex.

I believe I am being plotted against.

I wish I could do over some of the things I have done.

Source: MMPI-2®.

2019). The MMPI-2-RF seems to do a better job at differentiating between clusters of symptoms and seems to be less biased with respect to gender and ethnicity (Whitman et al., 2019). But the MMPI-3, published in 2020, may soon overtake its predecessors (Ben-Porath & Tellegen, 2020). The MMPI-3 was developed using a sample that was representative of the current U.S. population, so the group to which test-takers are compared is far more diverse than the previous versions. In addition, a separate Spanish-language version was developed using a sample composed of Spanish speakers in the United States, so Spanish-speaking test-takers are now compared with other Spanish speakers.

The MMPI is widely used by clinical psychologists and psychiatrists to assess patients. It is also used to evaluate the mental health of candidates for such occupations as police officers, doctors, nurses, and professional pilots. What keeps people from simply answering items in a way that makes them look psychologically healthy? Like many other self-report inventories, the MMPI has special scales to detect whether a person is answering honestly and consistently (Butcher, 2010; Pope et al., 2006). For example, if someone responds "True" to items such as "I *never* put off until tomorrow what I should do today" and "I *always* pick up after myself," it's probably a safe bet that they are inadvertently or intentionally distorting their other responses.

The MMPI was originally designed to assess mental health and detect psychological symptoms. In contrast, the **California Psychological Inventory (CPI)** is *a self-report inventory that assesses personality characteristics in normal populations* (Boer et al., 2008; Megargee, 2009). Of the over 400 true–false items on the long version of the CPI, nearly half are drawn from the MMPI. The CPI provides measures on such characteristics as interpersonal effectiveness, self-control, independence, and empathy. Profiles generated by the CPI are used to predict such things as high school and college grades, delinquency, and job performance (see Crites & Taber, 2002).

Another widely used personality test is the *Myers–Briggs Type Indicator* (abbreviated *MBTI*). The MBTI was developed by Isabel Briggs Myers and Katharine Cook Briggs (see Gladwell, 2004; Quenk, 2009). Myers and Briggs were intrigued by Carl Jung's personality theory and his proposal that people could be categorized into discrete personality "types." The Myers–Briggs test differs from other self-report tests in that it is designed to assess personality *types* rather than measure personality *traits*.

The notion of personality types is fundamentally different from personality traits. Measures of traits, like the CPI, give us scores along a continuum—for example, from low to high with respect to self-control. However, measures of types, like the MBTI, place us into distinct categories that don't overlap (Arnau et al., 2003; Wilde, 2011).

The MBTI arrives at personality type by measuring a person's *preferred* way of dealing with information, making decisions, and interacting with others, and categorizes them into one of 16 different personality types.

Despite the MBTI's widespread use in business, counseling, and career guidance settings, research has pointed to several problems with the MBTI. One problem is *reliability*—people can receive different MBTI results on different test-taking occasions. Equally problematic is the issue of *validity*. For example, research does not support the claim of a relationship between MBTI personality types and occupational success (Pittenger, 2005). More troubling is the lack of evidence supporting the existence of 16 distinctly different personality types (Hunsley et al., 2003). Despite its unscientific nature, it may be popular because, according to a recent history of tests and measures, it focuses on positive rather than negative aspects of personality, so it "flatters those who take it" (Kindley, 2016). The author continued, "Of all the personality tests developed in the 20th century . . . the MBTI is the closest to the language of pop psychology and self-help."

Thus, most researchers in the field of psychological testing advise that caution be exercised in interpreting MBTI results, especially in applying them to vocational choices or predictions of occupational success (see Pittenger, 2005).

Although the MBTI is not likely valid, personality researchers have used statistical methods to identify personality types based on patterns of responses to measures of the Big Five. One study used several datasets of more than 1.5 million participants to identify four patterns of personality traits—or types (Gerlach et al.,

California Psychological Inventory (CPI)
A self-report inventory that assesses personality characteristics in normal populations.

Is it true that there are ways to tell if you fake an answer on a personality test?

THINK LIKE A SCIENTIST
Can an assessment of your personality predict job success? Go to Achieve: Resources to **Think Like a Scientist** about **Employment-Related Personality Tests.**

 Achieve

AzmanL/Getty Images

^ Self-Report Inventories and Selfies
According to one study, self-report ratings of personality traits match aspects of the selfies that people post online (Qiu et al., 2015). For example, people higher in conscientiousness were less likely than others to post selfies taken in private locations, like inside their homes, and people higher in neuroticism were more likely than others to show a duckface pose (shown here).

2018). First, the average type scored close to the mean on all Big Five traits. Second, the self-centered type was high in extraversion but low on other traits, including agreeableness and conscientiousness. Third, the reserved type includes those particularly low in openness to experience. And fourth, the role model type is low in neuroticism and higher in everything else—extraversion, openness, agreeableness, and conscientiousness. Unlike the MBTI, these types might never become popular, because everyone would want to be the role model! But research continues to support the potential use of personality measures as predictors in a range of contexts, from vocational to social to health (Bliedorn et al., 2019). Perhaps personality types will become a useful predictive tool.

Strengths and Limitations of Self-Report Inventories The two most important strengths of self-report inventories are their *standardization* and their *use of established norms* (see Chapter 7). Each person receives the same instructions and responds to the same items. The results of self-report inventories are objectively scored and compared to norms established by previous research. In fact, both the MMPI and the CPI can be scored by computer.

As a general rule, the reliability and validity of self-report inventories are far greater than those of projective tests. Thousands of studies have demonstrated that the MMPI, the CPI, and similar tests provide accurate, consistent results that can be used to generally predict behavior (Anastasi & Urbina, 1997; Archer & Smith, 2014; Hamby et al., 2015). Moreover, these measures have also been shown to predict characteristics such as goals, interests, and attitudes (Kandler et al., 2014).

It turns out that self-report inventories predict a wide range of specific behaviors. For example, results from self-report inventories are related to some aspects of student behaviors and student choices such as academic majors (Vedel et al., 2015).

Self-report ratings have also been shown to match up with online behaviors, such as our tendency to "like" things on social media. As Wu Youyou and his colleagues (2015) report, "Participants with high openness to experience tend to like Salvador Dali, meditation, or TED talks; participants with high extraversion tend to like partying, Snookie (reality show star), or dancing."

But it's not just your social media that tells the world about you. Your "digital footprint," which also includes things like your location, your Internet searches, and which Wi-Fi networks you join, more accurately predicts your scores on the Big Five traits than do other people's observations (Hinds & Joinson, 2019).

If your online behavior "knows" your personality better than actual people do, then maybe self-report inventories are suspect. And they do have several limitations. First, despite the inclusion of items designed to detect deliberate deception, there is considerable evidence that people can still successfully fake responses and answer in socially desirable ways (Anastasi & Urbina, 1997; Holden, 2008). Second, some people are prone to responding in a set way. They may consistently pick the first alternative or answer "True" whether the item is true for them or not. And some tests, such as the MMPI and CPI, include hundreds of items. Taking these tests can become quite tedious, and people may lose interest in carefully choosing the most appropriate response.

Third, people are not always accurate judges of their own behavior, attitudes, or attributes. And some people defensively deny their true feelings, needs, and attitudes, even to themselves (Cousineau & Shedler, 2006; Shedler et al., 1993). For example, a person might indicate that they enjoy parties, even though they actually avoid social gatherings whenever possible.

To sum up, personality tests are generally useful strategies that can provide insights about the psychological makeup of people. But no personality test, by itself, is likely to provide a definitive description of a given individual. In practice, psychologists and other mental health professionals, including the psychologists who studied the four brothers in Bogotá, usually combine personality test results with behavioral observations and background information, including interviews with family members, co-workers, or other significant people in the person's life.

Closing Thoughts

Over the course of this chapter, you've encountered firsthand some of the most influential contributors to modern psychological thought. As you'll see in the chapter on therapies, the major personality perspectives provide the basis for many forms of psychotherapy. Clearly, the psychoanalytic, humanistic, social cognitive, and trait perspectives each provide a fundamentally different way of conceptualizing personality. That each perspective has strengths and limitations underscores the point that no single perspective can explain all aspects of human personality. Indeed, no one personality theory could explain all the similarities and differences among the four brothers from Bogotá or the ways in which their personalities drove their changing relationships. The four young men are now friends, and they have forged connections with each other's families. As Wilber said to William, the brother with whom he was raised, "So we were swapped. . . . You're my brother, and you'll be my brother until the day I die" (Dominus, 2015). Given the complex factors involved in human personality, it's doubtful that any single theory ever will capture the essence of human personality in its entirety. Even so, each perspective has made important and lasting contributions to the understanding of human personality.

 PSYCH FOR YOUR LIFE

Possible Selves: Imagine the Possibilities

Some psychologists believe that a person's self-concept is not a singular mental self-image, as Carl Rogers proposed, but a *multifaceted system* of related images and ideas (Hermans, 1996; Markus & Kunda, 1986). This collection of related images about yourself reflects your goals, values, emotions, and relationships (Markus & Cross, 1990; Markus & Wurf, 1987; Unemori et al., 2004).

According to psychologist Hazel Markus and her colleagues, your **possible selves** is *the aspect of the self-concept that includes images of the selves that you hope, fear, or expect to become in the future.* As Markus and co-researcher Paula Nurius (1986) wrote, "The possible selves that are hoped for might include the successful self, the creative self, the rich self, the thin self, or the loved and admired self, whereas the dreaded possible selves could be the alone self, the depressed self, the incompetent self, the alcoholic self, the unemployed self, or the bag lady self."

The Influence of Hoped-for and Dreaded Possible Selves

Possible selves are more than just idle daydreams or wishful fantasies. In fact, possible selves influence our behavior in important ways (Destin et al., 2018; Markus & Nurius, 1986). We're often not aware of the possible selves that we have incorporated into our self-concepts. Nevertheless, they can serve as powerful forces that either activate or stall our efforts to reach important goals. Your incentive, drive, and motivation are greatly influenced by your possible selves, and so are your decisions and choices about future behavior (Hoyle & Sherrill, 2006; Robinson et al., 2003). Our hoped-for possible selves can even influence how we feel about our lives. People have the deepest regrets when their actual selves are quite different from their "ideal selves" (Davidai & Gilovich, 2018).

Imagine that you harbor a hoped-for possible self of becoming a successful musician. You would probably practice with greater regularity and intensity than someone who does not hold a vivid mental picture of attaining TikTok viral status or being named Best New Artist at the MTV Video Music Awards.

Hoped-for possible selves can influence behavior even when they are not realistic. For example, in the Prologue you read about William, the twin who was switched at birth and raised in rural Colombia. While in the military, William had visions of a possible self as an officer. His superiors nominated him for officer training because of his

possible selves The aspect of the self-concept that includes images of the selves that you hope, fear, or expect to become in the future.

obvious effort and intelligence. Unfortunately, he was ineligible because he lacked a high school education. Although he would never become an officer, the idea motivated him to finish high school after he left the military. His drive contributed to his success as a butcher, and he was quickly promoted to manager.

Possible Selves, Self-Efficacy Beliefs, and Motivation

Self-efficacy beliefs are closely connected to the idea of possible selves. Performing virtually any task involves the construction of a possible self that is capable of and competent in performing the action required (Ruvolo & Markus, 1992).

Thus, people who vividly imagine possible selves as "successful because of hard work" persist longer and expend more effort on tasks than do people who imagine themselves as "unsuccessful despite hard work" (Ruvolo & Markus, 1992). One study found that imagining a future successful self led to improved academic performance among at-risk students—young women from lower-income families (Destin et al., 2018). It is true that the motivation to achieve academically increases when your possible selves include a future self who is successful because of academic achievement (Oyserman & James, 2011; Oyserman et al., 2015). To be most effective, possible selves should incorporate concrete strategies for attaining goals. For example, students who visualized themselves taking specific steps to improve their grades—such as doing homework daily or signing up for tutoring—were more successful than students who simply imagined themselves doing better in school (Oyserman et al., 2004).

Applying the Research: Assessing Your Possible Selves

How can you apply these research findings to *your* life? First, it's important to stress again that we're often unaware of how the possible selves we've mentally constructed influence our beliefs, actions, and self-evaluations. Thus, the first step is to consciously assess the role that your possible selves play in your life (Oyserman & James, 2011).

Take a few moments and jot down the "possible selves" that are active in your working self-concept. To help you in this task, write three responses to each of the following questions:

1. Next year, I expect to be . . .

2. Next year, I am afraid that I will be . . .

3. Next year, I want to avoid becoming . . .

After focusing on the short-term future, take these same questions and extend them to 5 years from now or even 10 years from now. Most likely, certain themes and goals will consistently emerge. Now the critical questions:

- How are your possible selves affecting your current *motivation*, goals, feelings, and decisions?
- Are your possible selves even remotely plausible?
- Are they pessimistic and limiting?
- Are they unrealistically optimistic?

Finally, ask yourself honestly: What realistic strategies are you using to try to become the self that you want to become? To avoid becoming the selves that you dread?

How can you improve the likelihood that you will achieve some of your possible selves? One approach is to link your expectations and hopes to concrete strategies about how to behave to reach your desired possible self (Oyserman et al., 2004).

These questions should help you gain some insight into whether your possible selves are influencing your behavior in productive, constructive ways. If they are not, now is an excellent time to think about replacing or modifying the possible selves that operate most powerfully in your own self-concept. Why is this so important? Because to a large extent, who we become is guided by who we imagine we'll become. Just imagine the possibilities of who *you* could become!

MYTH ▶ SCIENCE

Is it true that if you can imagine yourself taking the steps to become successful, you're more likely to actually become successful?

CHAPTER REVIEW

Personality

 Achieve

Achieve, Macmillan Learning's online study platform, features the full e-book of *Discovering Psychology,* the **LearningCurve** adaptive quizzing system, videos, and a variety of activities to boost your learning. Visit **Achieve** at macmillanlearning.com.

KEY PEOPLE

Alfred Adler, p. 371

Albert Bandura, p. 376

Raymond Cattell, p. 380

Hans Eysenck, p. 380

Anna Freud, p. 365

Sigmund Freud, p. 365

Karen Horney, p. 371

Carl Jung, p. 370

Melanie Klein, p. 373

Abraham Maslow, p. 374

Carl Rogers, p. 374

KEY TERMS

personality, p. 364

personality theory, p. 364

psychoanalysis (in personality), p. 365

free association, p. 365

unconscious, p. 366

id, p. 367

pleasure principle, p. 367

ego, p. 367

reality principle, p. 367

superego, p. 367

defense mechanisms, p. 367

repression (in psychoanalytic theory of personality and psychotherapy), p. 367

displacement, p. 368

psychosexual stages, p. 369

Oedipus complex, p. 369

identification, p. 369

collective unconscious, p. 371

humanistic psychology (theory of personality), p. 373

actualizing tendency, p. 374

self-concept, p. 374

conditional positive regard, p. 374

unconditional positive regard, p. 375

social cognitive theory, p. 376

reciprocal determinism, p. 376

self-efficacy, p. 376

trait, p. 379

trait theory, p. 379

surface traits, p. 379

source traits, p. 380

five-factor model of personality, p. 381

behavioral genetics, p. 386

psychological test, p. 389

projective test, p. 389

Rorschach Inkblot Test, p. 389

Thematic Apperception Test (TAT), p. 389

self-report inventory, p. 390

Minnesota Multiphasic Personality Inventory (MMPI), p. 390

California Personality Inventory (CPI), p. 391

possible selves, p. 393

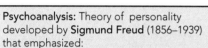

Personality

An individual's unique and relatively consistent patterns of thinking, feeling, and behaving

Personality theories explain how people are similar or different in these patterns.

Photo by Time Life Pictures/Mansell/ The LIFE Picture Collection/Getty Images

Psychoanalytic Perspective

Psychoanalysis: Theory of personality developed by **Sigmund Freud** (1856–1939) that emphasized:

- Using the technique of **free association** to uncover **unconscious** determinants of behavior and personality
- Enduring effects of early childhood experiences on later personality development

Freud contended that personality consists of three conflicting psychological forces:

- The **id**—irrational, impulsive personality dimension ruled by the **pleasure principle**
- The **ego**—rational, mediating personality dimension that operates according to the **reality principle**
- The **superego**—moralistic, self-evaluative personality component consisting of internalized parental and societal values and rules

Defense mechanisms: Unconscious distortions of reality that temporarily reduce anxiety, including:

- **Repression**
- Sublimation
- Projection
- Denial
- Regression
- **Displacement**
- Rationalization
- Reaction formation

Psychosexual stages: Freud's five age-related developmental periods in which sexual impulses are expressed through different bodily zones: oral, anal, phallic, latency, and genital

- During phallic stage, child must resolve **Oedipus complex** through **identification** with same-sex parent.
- Fixation at a particular stage may result if the developmental conflicts are not successfully resolved.

The Neo-Freudians:
Carl Jung (1875–1961)

- Emphasized psychological growth and proposed the existence of the **collective unconscious** and archetypes

Karen Horney (1885–1952)

- Emphasized role of social relationships in protecting against anxiety

Alfred Adler (1870–1937)

- Believed the most fundamental human motive was to strive for superiority

Anna Freud (1882–1960)

Melanie Klein (1895–1982)

Allstar Picture Library Limited/Alamy Stock Photo

Humanistic Perspective

Humanistic psychology emphasizes:

- Inherent goodness of people
- **Self-concept,** self-awareness, and free will
- Human potential and psychological growth
- Healthy personality development

Carl Rogers (1902–1987) proposed that:

- The **actualizing tendency** is the inborn drive to maintain and enhance the organism.
- People are motivated to maintain a consistent **self-concept.**
- **Conditional positive regard** by parents leads to incongruence so that self-concept conflicts with experience.
- **Unconditional positive regard** by parents leads to congruence.

Abraham Maslow (1908–1970) contended that:

- People are motivated by hierarchy of needs.
- People strive for self-actualization.

AFP/Getty Images

Social Cognitive Perspective

Albert Bandura (1925–2021), **social cognitive theory:**
- Active processing of information from social experiences
- Conscious self-generated goals and self-regulation
- Development of a self-system based on a person's skills, abilities, and attitudes

Reciprocal determinism is the interaction of behavioral, cognitive, and environmental factors in the self-regulation of behavior.

Self-efficacy:
- Beliefs in a particular situation influence a person's motivation, behavior, performance, and persistence.

Corbis/VCG/Getty Images

Trait Perspective

Trait theories identify, describe, and measure individual differences in traits.
- **Surface traits** can be inferred from easily observable behaviors.
- **Source traits** are the most basic dimensions of personality.

Source: Caracol Televisión S.A.

Behavioral genetics studies the effects of genes and heredity on behavior and traits.

Raymond Cattell (1905–1998)
- Identified 16 personality factors

Hans Eysenck (1916–1997)
- Proposed three basic personality dimensions: introversion–extraversion, neuroticism–emotional stability, and psychoticism

Five-factor model of personality identified five source traits:
- Neuroticism
- Extraversion
- Openness to experience
- Agreeableness
- Conscientiousness

HEXACO model of personality identified six source traits:
- (H)onesty–humility
- (E)motionality
- e(X)traversion
- (A)greeableness
- (C)onscientiousness
- (O)penness to experience

Assessing Personality

Psychological tests should:
- Be valid and reliable
- Accurately reflect a person's characteristics
- Predict future psychological and behavioral functioning

Spencer Grant/PhotoEdit

Projective tests:
- Based on psychoanalytic perspective
- Person responds to vague stimulus
- Subjectively scored
- Include **Rorschach Inkblot Test** and **Thematic Apperception Test (TAT)**

Self-report inventories:
- Use standardized question-and-answer formats
- Are objectively scored with results compared to established norms
- Include the **Minnesota Multiphasic Personality Inventory (MMPI)** and **California Personality Inventory (CPI)**

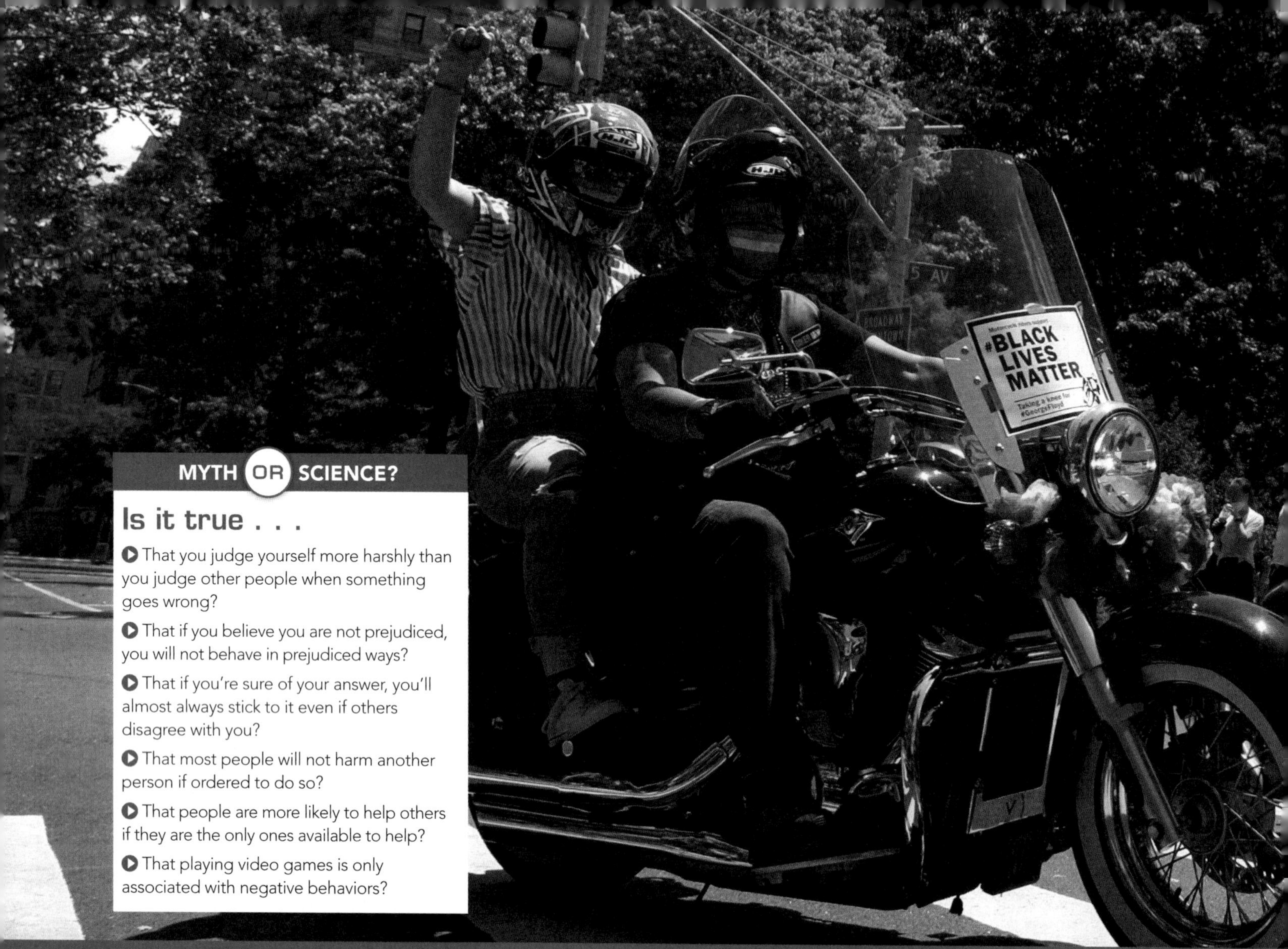
#BLACK
LIVES
MATTER

MYTH OR SCIENCE?

Is it true . . .

- That you judge yourself more harshly than you judge other people when something goes wrong?
- That if you believe you are not prejudiced, you will not behave in prejudiced ways?
- That if you're sure of your answer, you'll almost always stick to it even if others disagree with you?
- That most people will not harm another person if ordered to do so?
- That people are more likely to help others if they are the only ones available to help?
- That playing video games is only associated with negative behaviors?

Social Psychology

PROLOGUE

The Sirens Women's Motorcycle Club

The Sirens Women's Motorcycle Club of New York City was founded in 1986 as an antidote to the male-dominated motorcycle clubs that frequently discriminated against female riders. Jen Baquial joined the Sirens in 2010, and became its president six years later. Baquial avoided motorcycle clubs before finding the Sirens because "they're mostly men only" (J. Baquial, personal communication, July 26, 2017). She explained, "Women are not allowed to ride with them unless they're on the back seat. The culture was . . . really not for me." She describes finding the Sirens as finding her "family."

Other than limiting themselves to female members, the Sirens represent the remarkable diversity of New York City: "beautifully diverse in age, race, profession, sexual orientation and personal style" (Bologna, 2016). Their diversity helps the Sirens to break down stereotypes. For example, one Siren, Molly, is a welder, a male-dominated job, but her signature look includes bright red lipstick. Another club member, AJ, is a lawyer with five children; AJ got her own motorcycle at age 18 after a revelation, wondering why she'd been riding on the back of her boyfriend's bike when she could just ride on her own (Vogt & Goldman, 2016a, 2016b). More actively, members of the Sirens, regardless of their sexual orientation, have been riding in New York City's Pride March since 1986, and have been leading the march since 1987.

Beyond their demographics and diversity efforts, the Sirens are not an ordinary motorcycle club. They are involved in an ongoing volunteer effort to help women and children. The Sirens are the primary delivery people for the New York Milk Bank, a nonprofit organization that collects breast milk from women who produce more than they can use and then distributes it to babies in need. For example, for a number of infants who have health problems or were born too early,

CHAPTER **12**

breast milk increases their chances of survival, yet not all mothers produce it. The collaboration began when Julie Bouchet-Horwitz, the executive director of the Milk Bank, observed the handling ability of motorcyclists quickly weaving through traffic. Donated breast milk, a highly perishable substance, needs to be transported quickly. Bouchet-Horwitz realized that the Sirens could help, and that was the beginning of a wonderful collaboration (Bologna, 2016). As Baquial explained, "We started brainstorming about how we could get this done. She had a need. We have bikes" (J. Baquial, personal communication, July 26, 2017).

Now, the Milk Bank sends out alerts to a WhatsApp group of volunteer Sirens.

An available rider picks up the breast milk from one of more than 20 collection sites across New York State where breastfeeding mothers can drop off donated milk. The Siren then delivers it to a processing center where it's pasteurized for safety (Vogt & Goldman, 2016b). WhatsApp alerts also recruit motorcyclists who pick up the processed milk and deliver it to the homes of mothers who cannot produce breast milk and to hospital maternity wards.

Are you surprised that members of a motorcycle club would donate so much of their time? The Milk Bank pays for the riders' tolls and mileage, but not their time. Why would the riders volunteer? As Baquial explained, "Because we're helping babies. That's kind of it." She talked about the bonds they form with some of the mothers, and the joy in watching babies grow healthier because of the milk they deliver. Basically, Baqual says, she and her fellow Sirens volunteer because "there's a real person at the end of it."

When you see a photo of the Sirens, do you make a judgment about what members of a motorcycle club might be like? Does that judgment change when you learn more about them? Were you surprised at their volunteer efforts? Like the Sirens, we all engage with our social environments in a variety of ways. As we navigate the world, we both conform to social norms and break stereotypes. We both perform selfless acts and judge others' behavior. And, like the Sirens, sometimes we behave in unexpected ways. In this chapter, we will look at how we interpret our social environment, including how we form impressions of other people and explain their behavior. We'll explore how our own behavior, including the likelihood that we will help or harm others, is influenced by the social environment and other people. In the process, we'll come back to the story of the Sirens to illustrate several important concepts. ∿

Introduction: What Is Social Psychology?

Social psychology is *a branch of psychology that investigates how a person's thoughts, feelings, and behavior are influenced by the presence of other people and by the social and physical environment.* The social situations can include being alone, in the presence of others, or in front of a crowd of onlookers.

Like other psychology specialty areas, social psychology emphasizes certain concepts. For example, one important social psychology concept is that of your *self.* Your **sense of self** is *your sense of who you are in relation to other people, a unique sense of identity that has been influenced by the presence of other people and by your social, cultural, and psychological experiences.* Your sense of self plays a key role in how you perceive and react to others.

The role of culture in shaping our behaviors has been a recurring theme throughout this book, but is particularly relevant for social psychology. We'll explore the ways in which our thoughts, feelings, and behavior in social situations are influenced by many aspects of culture, including by race and ethnicity. A number of psychologists have been leaders in addressing the importance of culture, race, and ethnicity. *Hector Betancourt* and *Steven Regeser Lopez* (1993) wrote a groundbreaking article, *The Study of Culture, Ethnicity, and Race in American Psychology*, that emphasized the need to understand how these factors affect people from marginalized groups, and people from majority groups, too. They argued that a full understanding of psychology requires attention to culture, ethnicity, and race, and that research in these areas should not be "segregated from mainstream psychology." A few years later, *Stanley Sue* (1999) argued that psychological science did not place sufficient value on research with members of racial and ethnic minority groups.

One of the pioneers of the study of race and ethnicity was **James Jackson** (1944–2020), a social psychologist who founded the landmark Program for Research on Black Americans at the University of Michigan (APS, 2020). Through the program, Jackson launched the National Survey of Black Americans (NSBA), a database that has been used by many researchers and has led to hundreds of research papers. Jackson's work centered on the experiences of Black people in the United States, rather than comparing them with White people, as had historically been done. His colleague, Robert Taylor, described his legacy: "James Jackson would always say that the main contribution of the N.S.B.A. was the understanding that not all Black people are alike" (Genzlinger, 2020).

Social psychology research focuses on many different topics. In this chapter, we'll focus on two key research areas in social psychology. **Social cognition** refers to *the mental processes people use to make sense of their social environments.* Researchers investigate how we form impressions of other people, how we interpret the meaning of other people's behavior, and how our behavior is affected by our attitudes (Bodenhausen et al., 2003; Frith & Frith, 2012).

Social influence focuses on *the effect of situational factors and other people on an individual's behavior.* The study of social influence includes such questions as why we conform to group norms, what compels us to obey an authority figure, under what circumstances we will help a stranger, and what leads us to behave in ways that intentionally harm other people.

social psychology Branch of psychology that studies how a person's thoughts, feelings, and behavior are influenced by the presence of other people and by the social and physical environment.

sense of self Your sense of who you are in relation to other people, a unique sense of identity that has been influenced by your social, cultural, and psychological experiences.

social cognition The mental processes people use to make sense of their social environments.

social influence The effect of situational factors and other people on an individual's behavior.

Person Perception: Forming Impressions of Other People

Person perception refers to the mental processes we use to form judgments about other people.

- How do context and social norms affect person perception?
- How do social categorization, implicit personality theories, and physical attractiveness affect person perception?

Consider the following scenario. You're attending college in a big city and you commute from your apartment to campus via the subway. If you want to sit down, you'll have to sit next to another passenger. In a matter of seconds, you must decide which stranger you'll share your ride home with, elbow to elbow, thigh to thigh. How will you decide?

Whether it's a seat on the subway or in a crowded movie theater, this is a task that most of us confront almost every day: On the basis of very limited information, we must quickly draw conclusions about the nature and likely behavior of people who are complete strangers to us.

Person perception refers to *the mental processes used to form judgments and draw conclusions about the characteristics and motives of other people*. Person perception is an active, subjective process that always occurs in some *interpersonal context*—situations that involve interactions between two or more people (Quadflieg & Penton-Voak, 2017; Smith & Collins, 2009).

In the interpersonal context of a subway car, you evaluate people based on minimal interaction. In a mere tenth of a second, you evaluate the other person's attractiveness, likeability, competence, trustworthiness, and aggressiveness (Willis & Todorov, 2006). These first impressions then guide your reactions to others. On the subway, you may quickly choose not to sit next to a big guy with a scowl on his face. Why? Because you perceive him as threatening. Of course, he could be a florist who's surly because he's getting home late.

We also evaluate people in terms of how we expect them to act in a particular context. We pay attention to whether they violate **social norms**—*the unwritten "rules," or expectations, for appropriate behavior in a particular social situation* (Legros & Cislaghi, 2020; Milgram, 1992). For example, sitting next to someone on a subway when there are empty seats available is a violation of a social norm.

How does person perception play out in the online world of social media? Social psychologists have turned their attention to person perception in online contexts. For example, a profile photograph is more important than written text in creating our perceptions of a new acquaintance. Even a comment about enjoying time with a big group of friends doesn't outweigh a photo depicting a loner on a park bench, who generally would be perceived as introverted (Van Der Heide et al., 2012). Even subtle characteristics of a profile photo can influence the way someone is perceived. For example, women photographed from a downward angle are perceived as smaller, more submissive, and more attractive (Makhanova et al., 2017).

On a short subway ride or after a quick glance at a social media profile, you'll probably never learn whether your first impressions were accurate or not. But first impressions are often wrong (Olivola & Todorov, 2010). Even if we have more encounters with a person, it takes a while for our first impressions to change. Our first impression can color our overall impression of a person, something called the *halo effect* (Nisbett & Wilson, 1977). Initial information tends to create a "halo" around a person, and it becomes harder to notice new information that might conflict with the initial judgment. Thus, many professors grade work anonymously—they don't want their previous impressions of you affecting their evaluation of your current work (Malouff et al., 2013).

Fortunately, in situations that involve long-term relationships with other people, such as in a classroom or at work, we do start to fine-tune our impressions as we acquire additional information about the people we come to know (Smith & Collins, 2009). And there are even some situations in which first impressions can be changed quite rapidly, such as when we're provided with evidence that shows why are first impressions were misguided

The New York Milk Bank, Inc.

˄ Making Split-Second Decisions About Strangers This is Jen Baquial, president of The Sirens Women's Motorcycle Club. Based on her motorcycle and gear, would you expect her to be a volunteer for an organization that delivers breast milk to babies? As she observed, laughing: "I think people try to stereotype motorcycle riders as the rough, tough criminal type" (J. Baquial, personal communication, July 26, 2017). In contrast to the stereotype, since the late 1980s, the club has worked to support initiatives related to women's health. Baquial added, "[The Milk Bank] is perfect for us. It's exactly what we focus on to help women."

person perception The mental processes used to form judgments and draw conclusions about the characteristics and motives of other people.

social norms The unwritten "rules," or expectations, for appropriate behavior in a particular social situation.

social categorization The mental process of classifying people into groups on the basis of their shared characteristics.

explicit cognition Deliberate, conscious mental processes involved in perceptions, judgments, decisions, and reasoning.

implicit cognition Automatic, nonconscious mental processes that influence perceptions, judgments, decisions, and reasoning.

implicit personality theory A network of assumptions or beliefs about the relationships among various types of people, traits, and behaviors.

THINK LIKE A **SCIENTIST**

What factors in an online dating profile make you want to meet someone? Go to Achieve: Resources to **Think Like a Scientist** about **Online Dating**.

Achieve

(Ferguson et al., 2019). For example, in one study, impressions of a bald man as belonging to a White supremacist group were quickly changed when participants learned he was a cancer patient (Wyer, 2010).

Social Categorization: Using Mental Shortcuts in Person Perception

Along with person perception, the subway scenario illustrates our natural tendency to group people into categories. **Social categorization** is *the mental process of classifying people into groups on the basis of common characteristics.*

So how do you socially categorize people who are complete strangers, such as the other passengers on the subway? To a certain extent, you consciously focus on easily observable features, such as the other person's gender, age, or clothing (Kinzler et al., 2010; Miron & Branscomben, 2008). With a quick glance, you might socially categorize someone as "Asian male, 20-something, fraternity sweatshirt, probably a college student." Social psychologists use the term **explicit cognition** to refer to these *deliberate, conscious mental processes involved in perceptions, judgments, decisions, and reasoning.*

However, your social perceptions are not always completely conscious considerations. In many situations, you react to another person automatically. Social psychologists use the term **implicit cognition** to describe the *automatic, nonconscious mental processes that influence perceptions, judgments, decisions, and reasoning* (Gawronski & Payne, 2010).

Implicit personality theory is *a network of assumptions or beliefs about the relationships among various types of people, traits, and behaviors.* Different models exist to explain how implicit personality theories develop and function (see Critcher & Dunning, 2009; Ybarra, 2002). But in general terms, your previous social and cultural experiences influence the cognitive *schemas,* or mental frameworks, you hold about the traits and behaviors associated with different "types" of people (see Uleman et al., 2008).

Physical appearance cues play an important role in person perception and social categorization (Olivola & Todorov, 2010). Particularly influential is the implicit personality theory that most people have for physically attractive people, particularly with respect to their faces (see Lemay et al., 2010; Todorov et al., 2015). Starting in childhood, we are bombarded with the cultural message that "what is beautiful is good." As a result of such conditioning, most people have an implicit personality theory that associates physical attractiveness with a wide range of desirable characteristics.

Decades of research have shown that good-looking people are perceived as being more intelligent, happier, and better adjusted than other people (Eagly et al., 1991; Lorenzo et al., 2010). Several studies, using ratings of both women and men, have even found differences among the same people before and after plastic surgery (M. Reilly et al., 2015). After evaluating photos, participants judged women to be more attractive, likeable, and socially skilled after plastic surgery than they were before plastic surgery (Lu et al., 2018; Parsa et al., 2019; M. Reilly et al., 2015).

But are beautiful people *actually* happier, smarter, or more successful than the rest of us? Economists Daniel Hamermesh and Jason Abrevaya (2011) analyzed data from surveys conducted in four countries and concluded that more attractive people *do* tend to be happier, primarily because they also tended to have improved economic outcomes, such as higher salaries and more successful spouses.

Some studies have found that attractive people also tend to have higher self-esteem, intelligence, and other desirable personality traits than people of more average appearance (Langlois et al., 2000; Sheppard et al., 2011). Why? One possibility is that, throughout their lives, they receive more favorable treatment from other people, such as parents, teachers, employers, and peers (Hernández-Julián & Peters, 2015; Sheppard et al., 2011). The Focus on Neuroscience on the next page discusses evidence demonstrating that there may also be a brain-based reason for the greater social success of beautiful people.

Travel Pictures/Alamy

▲ **Using Social Categories** We often use superficial cues such as clothing and context to assign people to social categories and draw conclusions about their behavior. What sorts of social categories are evident here?

Obviously, the social categorization process has both advantages and disadvantages. Relegating someone to a social category on the basis of superficial information ignores that person's unique qualities. Sometimes these conclusions are wrong, as may have occurred initially between members of the Sirens motorcycle club and volunteers at the New York Milk Bank. As Jen Baquial notes, "I think people have a picture of what a biker is, right? We're not that. We're all really nice people that just ride together. Professional women" (J. Baquial, personal communication, July 26, 2017).

On the other hand, relying on social categories is a natural, adaptive, and efficient cognitive process. Social categories provide us with considerable basic information about other people. From an evolutionary perspective, the ability to make rapid judgments about strangers is probably an evolved characteristic that conferred survival value in our evolutionary past.

Disney XD /Marvel Entertainment© ABC/Getty Images

Disney XD /Marvel Entertainment© ABC/Getty Images

⟨ What Is Beautiful Is Good We are culturally conditioned to associate beauty with goodness and evil with ugliness—an implicit personality theory that has been dubbed the "what is beautiful is good" myth (Sheppard et al., 2011). For example, in the Marvel Universe, it's often easy to distinguish between the heroes and the villains. Here, the brightly dressed Ms. Marvel (Kamala Khan) with her beautifully inked dark hair is a force of good—not to mention that she is the first Muslim superhero in the Marvel Universe to appear on the big screen. And Ultron's intimidating animation and coloring suggest that he is a force of chaos and evil.

🧠 FOCUS ON NEUROSCIENCE

Does Ingroup Bias Help Us Ignore Our Friends' Bad Behavior, but Not Strangers'?

Does ingroup bias help us maintain friendships? Ingroup bias leads us to form more positive impressions of people in our ingroup than of people in an outgroup. Researchers BoKyung Park and Liane Young (2020) wondered whether impressions of ingroup members, including our friends, extend to giving them a pass for bad behavior.

Park and Young conducted a study in which they asked participants to bring a friend. During the study, participants were told that they would play a game that involved giving and taking money with their friend, and then separately, with a stranger. The participants played the game in a different room from their playing partners—while also being scanned using functional magnetic resonance imaging (fMRI)—but the participants weren't actually playing anyone. Unknown to the participants, the experimenters had predetermined the behaviors of the other players.

Before they started, participants rated how close they felt to the other players—their friend and the stranger. They gave closeness ratings again after their playing partner either gave money to or took money from them. The researchers found that the participants tended to downgrade how close they felt to the stranger more so than their friend when they took money from them. In effect, they ignored their friend's bad behavior, but not the stranger's.

This difference was reflected by the fMRI as well. There was less activity in a part of the brain between the temporal and parietal lobes, the right temporo-parietal junction (RTPJ), when the participant discounted their friend's bad behavior than when they discounted the stranger's bad behavior. The RTPJ is a part of the brain involved in processing information, including information we use to make moral judgments (see Young et al., 2007). As the graph shows, the lower the RTPJ activity, the more of a pass that participants gave friends' bad behavior (Park & Young, 2020). Interestingly, the participants who showed this RTPJ activity pattern the most—that is, those who gave their friends a pass for their bad behavior—tended to report actually having more friends.

The researchers believe that their findings demonstrate "the potential benefits of ingroup bias," including maintaining close interpersonal relationships. The researchers "are optimistic that future work may uncover ways to apply these findings to enhancing intergroup cooperation and negotiation."

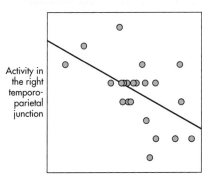

Activity in the right temporo-parietal junction

Preference given to friend vs. stranger

attribution The mental process of inferring the cause of someone's behavior, including one's own.

fundamental attribution error The tendency to attribute the behavior of others to internal, personal characteristics, while ignoring or underestimating the effects of external, situational factors.

blaming the victim The tendency to blame an innocent victim of misfortune for having somehow caused the problem or for not having taken steps to avoid or prevent it.

hindsight bias The tendency, after an event has occurred, to overestimate one's ability to have foreseen or predicted the outcome of an event.

just-world hypothesis The assumption that the world is fair and that therefore people get what they deserve and deserve what they get.

self-serving bias The tendency to attribute successful outcomes of one's own behavior to internal causes and unsuccessful outcomes to external, situational causes.

MYTH ◀ **SCIENCE**

Is it true that you judge yourself more harshly than you judge other people when something goes wrong?

> **Blaming the Victim** At age 14, Elizabeth Smart was kidnapped at knifepoint from her bedroom and held captive for nine months. She was deprived of food and raped multiple times every day. After she was rescued, many people asked why she hadn't done more to escape. After all, they pointed out, her captor often brought a veiled Smart out in public. Smart has become an activist for victim's rights and has worked with the U.S. Justice Department (Tinwala, 2021). She has explained that she was terrified by her captor's threats against her family: "You can never judge a child or a victim of any crime on what they should have done, because you weren't there and you don't know" (Serrano, 2013). Why do people often "blame the victim" after crimes, accidents, or other tragedies?

Attribution: Explaining Behavior

■ KEY THEME
Attribution refers to the process of explaining your own behavior and the behavior of other people.

≡ KEY QUESTIONS
- What are the fundamental attribution error and the self-serving bias?
- How do attributional biases affect our judgments about the causes of behavior?
- How does culture affect attributional processes?

On the first day of class, you sit down and turn to say hi to the classmate next to you. She ignores you and focuses on her phone. You think to yourself, "What a jerk."

Why did you arrive at that conclusion? After all, it's completely possible that your classmate is having a bad day and just doesn't feel up to talking or is responding to an urgent text message.

Attribution is *the mental process of inferring the cause of someone's behavior, including one's own*. Psychologists also use the word *attribution* to refer to the explanation you make for a particular behavior. The attributions you make strongly influence your thoughts and feelings about other people.

If your explanation for the silent classmate is that she is just an unpleasant, unfriendly person, you demonstrated a common cognitive bias. The **fundamental attribution error** is *the tendency to attribute the behavior of others to internal, personal characteristics, while ignoring or underestimating the role of external, situational factors* (Ross, 1977). Even though it's entirely possible that situational forces were behind another person's behavior, we tend to automatically assume that the cause is an internal, personal characteristic (Bauman & Skitka, 2010; Zimbardo, 2007).

The fundamental attribution error plays a role in **blaming the victim**, *the tendency to blame an innocent victim of misfortune for having somehow caused the problem or for not having taken steps to avoid or prevent it*. For example, many people blame the poor for their dire straits, the sick for bringing on their illnesses, and victims of domestic violence or rape for somehow "provoking" their attackers.

The blaming the victim explanatory pattern is reinforced by another common cognitive bias. **Hindsight bias** is *the tendency, after an event has occurred, to overestimate one's ability to have foreseen or predicted the outcome* (Roese & Vohs, 2012). In everyday conversations, this is the person who confidently proclaims *after* the event,

Jim Urquhart/AP Images

"I could have told you that would happen." In the case of blaming the victim, hindsight bias makes it seem as if the victim should have predicted—and prevented—what happened (Goldinger et al., 2003).

Why do people often resort to blaming the victim? Social psychologist Melvin Lerner (1980) calls this the **just-world hypothesis** *the assumption that the world is fair and that therefore people get what they deserve and deserve what they get*. Blaming the victim reflects the belief that, because the world is just, the victim must have done something to deserve their fate (Maes et al., 2012). Collectively, these cognitive biases and explanatory patterns help psychologically insulate us from the uncomfortable thought "It could have just as easily been me" (Alves & Correia, 2008; IJzerman & Van Prooijen, 2008).

The Self-Serving Bias: Using Explanations to Meet Our Needs

Have you ever listened to other students react to their grades on an important exam? If so, you've probably heard an example of the **self-serving bias**, *the tendency to attribute successful outcomes of one's own behavior to internal causes and unsuccessful outcomes to external, situational causes.* When students do well on a test, they tend to congratulate themselves and to attribute their success to how hard they studied, their intelligence, and so forth—all *internal* attributions. But when a student bombs a test, the *external* attributions fly left and right: "They were all trick questions!""I couldn't concentrate because the guy behind me kept coughing" (Kruger & Gilovich, 2004).

In a wide range of situations, people tend to credit themselves for their success and to blame their failures on external circumstances (Allen et al., 2020; Mezulis et al., 2004). Psychologists explain the self-serving bias as resulting from an attempt to save face and protect self-esteem in the face of failure (Kurman, 2010; Kwan et al., 2008). Some evolutionary psychologists argue that the self-serving bias leads people to feel and appear more confident than might be justified in a particular situation (von Hippel & Trivers, 2011). If others then perceive us as more confident, we may have more access to resources that allow us to survive and pass on our genes. Although common in many societies, the self-serving bias is far from universal, as cross-cultural psychologists have discovered (see the Culture and Human Behavior box).

Jamie Squire/Getty Images

∧ **Explaining Misfortune: The Self-Serving Bias** Given the self-serving bias, are these NASCAR drivers—including Dale Earnhardt, Jr., in car #88—likely to explain their accident by listing internal factors such as their own carelessness or recklessness? Or are they more likely to blame external factors, such as another driver's poor handling of their vehicle or slick conditions on the Daytona International Speedway?

CULTURE AND HUMAN BEHAVIOR

Explaining Failure and Murder: Culture and Attributional Biases

The self-serving bias is common in individualistic cultures such as Australia and the United States, but it is far from universal. In many collectivistic cultures, an opposite attributional bias is often demonstrated (Dean & Koenig, 2019; Mezulis et al., 2004). Called the *self-effacing bias* or *modesty bias*, it involves blaming failure on internal, personal factors, while attributing success to external, situational factors.

For example, compared to U.S. students, Japanese and Chinese students are more likely to attribute academic failure to personal factors, such as lack of effort, instead of situational factors (Dornbusch et al., 1996). Thus, a Japanese student who does poorly on an exam is likely to say, "I didn't study hard enough." In contrast, Japanese and Chinese students tend to attribute academic *success* to *situational factors.* For example, they might say, "The exam was very easy" or "There was very little competition this year" (Stevenson et al., 1986).

One study asked participants to rate people who were answering questions about their achievements (Chen & Jing, 2012). Collectivistic participants tended to prefer the people who gave modest answers, whereas individualistic participants tended to like people who boasted in their answers.

Cross-cultural differences are also evident with the fundamental attribution error. In general, members of collectivistic cultures are less likely to commit the fundamental attribution error than are

members of individualistic cultures (R. Bond & Smith, 1996; Dean & Koenig, 2019). That is, collectivists are more likely to attribute the causes of another person's behavior to external, situational factors rather than to internal, personal factors—the exact *opposite* of the attributional bias that is demonstrated in individualistic cultures (Uskul & Kitayama, 2011).

To test this idea in a naturally occurring context, psychologists Michael Morris and Kaiping Peng (1994) compared articles reporting the same mass murders in Chinese-language and English-language newspapers. In one case, the murderer was a Chinese graduate student attending a U.S. university. In the other case, the murderer was a U.S. postal worker. Whether the murderer was American or Chinese, the news accounts were fundamentally different depending on whether the *reporter* was American or Chinese.

The U.S. reporters were more likely to explain the killings by making personal internal attributions. For example, U.S. reporters emphasized the postal worker's "history of being mentally unstable." In contrast, the Chinese reporters emphasized situational factors, such as the fact that the postal worker had recently been fired from his job.

Clearly, then, how we account for our successes and failures, as well as how we account for the actions of others, is yet another example of how human behavior is influenced by cultural conditioning.

attitude A learned tendency to evaluate some object, person, or issue in a particular way.

The Social Psychology of Attitudes

■ KEY THEME
An attitude is a learned tendency to evaluate objects, people, or issues in a particular way.

≡ KEY QUESTIONS
- What are the three components of an attitude?
- Under what conditions are attitudes most likely to determine behavior?
- What is cognitive dissonance?

Should high school graduation requirements include a class on basic sex education, birth control methods, and safe sex? Should COVID vaccines be mandated by workplaces? Should the government be doing more to prepare for climate change?

On these and many other subjects, you've probably formed an attitude. Psychologists formally define an **attitude** as *a learned tendency to evaluate some object, person, or issue in a particular way* (Banaji & Heiphetz, 2010; Bohner & Dickel, 2011). Attitudes are typically positive or negative, but they can also be *ambivalent,* as when you have mixed feelings about an issue, person, or group (Costarelli, 2011).

As shown in **Figure 12.1**, attitudes can include three components. First, an attitude may have a *cognitive component:* your thoughts about a given topic or object. Second, an attitude may have an *emotional component.* Finally, an attitude may have a *behavioral component,* in which attitudes are reflected in action.

Along with forming attitudes toward objects, ideas, or political campaigns, we also form attitudes about people. The In Focus box on the next page, "Interpersonal Attraction and Liking," discusses some of the factors that affect the thoughts and feelings that we develop about other people.

The Effect of Attitudes on Behavior

Most people assume that their attitudes tend to guide their behavior. But social psychologists have consistently found that people don't always act in accordance with their attitudes. For example, you might disapprove of cheating yet find yourself peeking at a classmate's exam paper when the opportunity presents itself.

FIGURE 12.1 The Components of Attitudes An attitude is a positive or negative evaluation of an object, person, or idea. An attitude may have cognitive, emotional, and behavioral components.

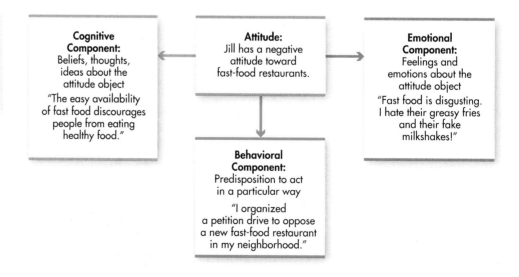

Cognitive Component: Beliefs, thoughts, ideas about the attitude object
"The easy availability of fast food discourages people from eating healthy food."

Attitude: Jill has a negative attitude toward fast-food restaurants.

Emotional Component: Feelings and emotions about the attitude object
"Fast food is disgusting. I hate their greasy fries and their fake milkshakes!"

Behavioral Component: Predisposition to act in a particular way
"I organized a petition drive to oppose a new fast-food restaurant in my neighborhood."

● IN FOCUS

Interpersonal Attraction and Liking

In psychology, *attraction* refers to feeling drawn to other people—having positive thoughts and feelings about them. Often, attraction motivates us to interact with or develop a relationship with the attractive person.

What makes one person more attractive than another? Personal characteristics such as warmth and trustworthiness, adventurousness, and social status influence judgments of attractiveness (Finkel & Baumeister, 2010; Sprecher & Felmlee, 2008). But physical features, especially facial features, are probably the most significant factor in attractions.

Physical features include a preference for specific body proportions among women that is consistent across cultures (Singh et al.,

2010). Whether heavy or thin, a woman with a waist that is a good deal smaller than her hips seems to be universally viewed as attractive. This is true even among men who are blind; without ever having seen images of women considered beautiful, they preferred this proportion when they felt female mannequins (Karremans et al., 2010). Why? This body proportion has been shown to predict both lower risk for a range of diseases and increased reproductive success (Bovet, 2019; Singh & Singh, 2011). Evolutionary researchers suggest that this preference makes perfect sense, as a healthy reproductive partner increases the chance of genes being passed on.

Some aspects of attraction are *interpersonal*. For example, especially in Western cultures we are more attracted to people whom we perceive as being like us—in physical characteristics, personality traits, attitudes, and even psychological health (Finkel & Baumeister, 2010).

Familiarity is another predictor of attraction and liking. In general, the more we interact with a person, the more we tend to like that person. Why? One explanation is that *most* interactions with other people are relatively pleasant (Reis et al., 2011). So, unless a person is particularly obnoxious or *unpleasant*, frequent interactions lead to more feelings of mutual pleasure.

The situations in which we interact with people also affect attraction. When happy, intoxicated, or physically aroused by exercise or exertion, we are more likely to rate others as attractive (Finkel & Baumeister, 2010). And, if we anticipate that attractive people are likely to be attracted to or like *us*, we're more likely to be attracted to them, and to like them (Stinson et al., 2009).

Finally, feelings of attraction can be influenced by the socioeconomic and cultural environment. For example, men in societies in which food and resources are in short supply tend to prefer heavier women (Swami & Tovée, 2006; Tovée et al., 2006). Conversely, a preference for thinner women is more common in societies where resources are abundant (Swami et al., 2010).

▲ **Ideals of Beauty Around the World** Large eyes, a wide smile, and full lips are attractive in cultures around the world. The beautiful smiles of a Hmong woman from Thailand and a man from the Omo Delta in East Africa would be considered attractive by any cultural standard.

When are your attitudes likely to influence or determine your behavior? Social psychologists have found that you're most likely to behave in accordance with your attitudes when:

- you anticipate a favorable outcome or response from others for behaving that way.
- your attitudes are extreme or are frequently expressed (Ajzen, 2001).
- you are very knowledgeable about the subject (Fabrigar & Wegener, 2010).
- you have a vested interest in the subject and personally stand to gain or lose something on a specific issue (Thornton & Tizard, 2010).

Clearly, your attitudes do influence your behavior in many instances. Now, consider the opposite question: Can your behavior influence your attitudes?

The Effect of Behavior on Attitudes: Fried Grasshoppers for Lunch?!

Suppose you have volunteered to participate in a psychology experiment. At the lab, a friendly experimenter asks you to indicate your degree of preference for a variety of

Fried Grasshoppers: Tasty or Disgusting? Most Americans do not rate fried grasshoppers as one of their favorite foods. Suppose you agreed to eat a handful of grasshoppers after being asked to do so by a rude, unfriendly experimenter. Do you think your attitude toward fried grasshoppers would improve more than that of a person who ate grasshoppers after being asked to do so by a friendly, polite experimenter? Why or why not?

> **Attitudes and Behavior** These student protesters in Madrid, Spain, are denouncing changes in their country's education laws, which include increases in the cost of higher education. People who hold strong opinions and express them openly, like these protestors, are most likely to behave in ways that are consistent with their attitudes.

cognitive dissonance An unpleasant state of psychological tension (*dissonance*) that occurs when two thoughts or perceptions (*cognitions*) are inconsistent.

foods, including fried grasshoppers, which you rank pretty low on the list. During the experiment, the experimenter instructs you to eat some fried grasshoppers. You manage to swallow three of the crispy critters. At the end of the experiment, your attitudes toward grasshoppers as a food source are surveyed again.

Later in the day, you talk to a friend who also participated in the experiment. You mention how friendly and polite you thought the experimenter was. But your friend had a different experience. They thought the experimenter was an arrogant, rude jerk.

Here's the critical question: Whose attitude toward eating fried grasshoppers is more likely to change in a positive direction? Given that you interacted with a friendly experimenter, most people assume that *your* feelings about fried grasshoppers are more likely to have improved than your friend's attitude. In fact, it is your friend—who encountered the obnoxious experimenter—who is much more likely to hold a more positive attitude toward eating fried grasshoppers than you.

At first glance, this finding seems to go against the grain of common sense. So how can we explain this outcome? The fried grasshoppers story represents the basic design of a classic experiment by social psychologist *Philip Zimbardo* and his colleagues (1965). Zimbardo's experiment underscored the importance of cognitive dissonance, a phenomenon first identified by social psychologists Leon Festinger and J. Merrill Carlsmith (1959). **Cognitive dissonance** is *an unpleasant state of psychological tension (dissonance) that occurs when two thoughts or perceptions (cognitions) are inconsistent.* This state of dissonance, which results from our awareness that our attitudes and behavior conflict, is so unpleasant that we are strongly motivated to reduce it (Festinger, 1957, 1962; Gawronski, 2012). We want to point out here that cognitive dissonance is a term that is often used incorrectly. You'll hear people use the term when, for instance, when there are mixed messages and they have to decide which one to believe. But cognitive dissonance really does refer to the specific situation in which thoughts and behaviors conflict.

Cognitive dissonance commonly occurs in situations in which you become uncomfortably aware that your behavior and your attitudes are in conflict (Cooper, 2012). If your behavior *cannot* be easily justified, how can you resolve the contradiction and eliminate the unpleasant state of dissonance? Since you can't go back and change the behavior, *you change your attitude to make it consistent with your behavior.*

Let's take another look at the results of the grasshopper study, this time from the perspective of cognitive dissonance theory. Your attitude toward eating grasshoppers did *not* change. Why? Because you could easily rationalize the conflict between your attitude ("Eating grasshoppers is disgusting") and your behavior (eating three grasshoppers). You probably justified your behavior by saying something like, "I ate the grasshoppers because I wanted to help out the nice experimenter." However, your friend, who encountered the rude experimenter, can't use that rationalization. Thus, they experienced an uncomfortable state of cognitive dissonance. Since they can't go back and change their behavior, they are left with the only part of the equation that can be changed—their attitude. "You know, eating those grasshoppers wasn't *that* bad," your friend comments. "In fact, they were kind of crunchy." Notice how their change in attitude reduces the dissonance between their previous attitude and their behavior. And they might not have even realized that their attitude had changed.

This response to cognitive dissonance does not seem to be unique to humans. Louisa Egan and her colleagues (2007) reported cognitive dissonance among capuchin monkeys who were forced to choose between two colors of M&Ms that they previously liked equally. After choosing one, the monkeys preferred the chosen M&M color from then on. It was not just that they were familiar with chosen M&M. Even when the researchers made the choice, the monkeys preferred the M&M color over the other options.

Attitude change due to cognitive dissonance is quite common in everyday life. For instance, researchers have found that people who quit smoking offered fewer rationalizations for smoking. But if they started smoking again, they started rationalizing again. For example, some said, "You've got to die of something, so why not enjoy yourself and smoke" (Fotuhi et al., 2013). Similarly, during the pandemic, numerous people justified their risky actions, such as going to a bar and drinking unmasked, by rationalizing. They decided, falsely, that COVID is not that serious or that masks don't actually work. Psychologists Elliot Aronson and Carol Tavris (2020) encourage us to pay attention when we feel the discomfort caused by a mismatch between our beliefs and actions. They urge us to ask ourselves "Why am I believing this? Why am I behaving this way? Have I thought it through or am I simply taking a short cut, following the party line, or justifying the effort I put into joining the group?"

Cognitive Dissonance Attitude change due to cognitive dissonance is common in everyday life. When you are out shopping, have you ever rationalized an impulsive purchase you couldn't really afford, saying, "This is too good a bargain to pass up"?

Understanding Prejudice

■ KEY THEME
Prejudice refers to a negative attitude toward people who belong to a specific social group, while stereotypes are clusters of characteristics that are attributed to people who belong to specific social categories.

≡ KEY QUESTIONS
- What is the function of stereotypes, and how do they relate to prejudice?
- What are ingroups and outgroups, and how do they influence social judgments?
- What are implicit attitudes, and how are they measured?

In this section, you'll see how person perception, attribution, and attitudes come together in explaining **prejudice**—*a negative attitude toward people who belong to a specific social group.*

Prejudice is ultimately based on the exaggerated notion that members of other social groups are very different from members of our own social group. So as you read this discussion, it's important to keep two well-established points in mind. First, *people from different groups, such as from different racial and ethnic groups, are far more alike than they are different* (Mallett & Wilson, 2010; Wagner et al., 2011). Second, any differences that may exist *between* members of different groups are far smaller than differences *among* various members of the same group (Bodenhausen & Richeson, 2010).

It also is important to observe that conversations about prejudice often focus on race and ethnicity. But prejudice can occur with respect to many different kinds of social groups, and can vary across cultures (Fiske, 2017). There can be prejudice based on sexual orientation, gender identity, religion, or age. There can also be prejudice based on a person's identification with multiple groups, a phenomenon that is often referred to as intersectionality (Bowleg, 2017; Hester et al., 2020; Kang & Bodenhausen, 2015).

Intersectionality refers to *the ways in which a person's different group identities combine to influence their experience in the world,* including prejudice and discrimination. For example, Amanda Gorman, the 22-year-old poet who performed her work at the 2021 U.S. presidential inauguration, talked about her experiences balancing coursework, activism, and her duties as the first U.S. National Youth Poet Laureate: "I'm navigating all that while also being a young Black woman navigating the intersectionality of my identity" (Hawgood, 2017).

prejudice A negative attitude toward people who belong to a specific social group.

intersectionality The ways in which a person's different group identities combine to influence their experiece in the world.

stereotype A cluster of characteristics that are associated with all members of a specific social group, often including qualities unrelated to the objective criteria that define the group.

From Stereotypes to Prejudice: Ingroups and Outgroups

As we noted earlier, using social categories to organize information about other people seems to be a natural cognitive tendency. Many social categories can be defined by relatively objective characteristics, such as age, language, religion, and skin color. A specific kind of social category is a **stereotype**—*a cluster of characteristics that are associated with all members of a specific social group, often including qualities unrelated to the objective criteria that define the group*. Stereotypes are based on the assumption that people have certain characteristics *because* of their membership in a particular group.

Stereotypes typically include qualities unrelated to the objective criteria that define a given category (Crawford et al., 2011). For example, we can objectively sort people into different categories by age. But our stereotypes for different age groups may include qualities that have little or nothing to do with "number of years since birth." Association of "boring and conservative" with middle-aged adults is an example of associating unrelated qualities with age groups—that is, stereotyping.

Like our use of other social categories, our tendency to stereotype social groups seems to be a natural cognitive process. Stereotypes simplify social information so that we can sort out, process, and remember information about other people more easily (Bodenhausen & Richeson, 2010; Martin et al., 2014). But like other mental shortcuts we've discussed in this chapter, relying on stereotypes can cause problems. Attributing a stereotypic cause for an outcome or event can blind us to the true causes of events (Johnston & Miles, 2007). For example, a parent who assumes that a girl's poor computer skills are due to her gender rather than a lack of instruction might never encourage her to overcome her problem.

> **The Power of Stereotypes** U.S. movies have made the image of the cowboy almost universally recognizable. What kinds of qualities are associated with the stereotype of the cowboy? You might have thought of a straight White man who is macho and rugged, a loner who is interested in the outdoors, but not interested in the trappings of wealth. How might that stereotype be an inaccurate portrayal of a person working on a cattle ranch today?

Design Pics/Carson Ganci/Getty Images

Some stereotypes are positive (Czopp et al., 2015). For example, Asian Americans are often stereotyped as highly intelligent, and women are viewed as nurturing. Although there are some benefits from positive stereotypes, there are also downsides, including that people can feel depersonalized and can feel that their choices are constrained.

Once stereotypes are formed, they are hard to shake. Sometimes stereotypes have a kernel of truth, making them easy to confirm, especially when you see only what you expect to see (Jussim et al., 2015). Even so, there's a vast difference between a kernel and the cornfield. When stereotypic beliefs become expectations that are applied to *all* members of a given group, stereotypes can be both misleading and damaging (Dovidio & Gaertner, 2010).

Consider the stereotype that men are more assertive than women and that women are more nurturing than men. This stereotype does have evidence to support it, but only in terms of the *average* difference between men and women (Wood & Eagly, 2010). Thus, it would be unfair and often inaccurate to automatically apply this stereotype to every individual man and woman.

Equally important, when confronted by evidence that contradicts a stereotype, people tend to discount that information in a variety of ways (Phelan & Rudman, 2010; Rudman & Fairchild, 2004). For example, suppose you grew up in Boston as a fan of the Red Sox baseball team and are convinced that all fans of the archrival team, the New York Yankees, are obnoxious jerks. (Of course, Yankees fans think the same thing about Sox fans!) At a neighborhood event, you meet someone in a Yankees cap and have a friendly conversation about baseball. Will this experience change your stereotype of Yankees fans? Probably not. It's more likely that you'll conclude that this individual Yankees fan is an *exception* to the stereotype. If you run into more than one friendly Yankees fan, you may create a mental subgroup for individuals who belong to the larger group but depart from the stereotype in some way (Queller & Mason, 2008; Sherman et al., 2005). By creating a subcategory of "friendly Yankees fans," you can still maintain your more general stereotype of Yankees fans as obnoxious jerks.

Creating exceptions allows people to maintain stereotypes in the face of contradictory evidence. Typical of this exception-that-proves-the-rule approach is the Bostonian who says, "Hey, I'm not prejudiced! In fact, I've got a couple of good friends who are Yankees fans."

Stereotypes are closely related to another tendency in person perception. People have a strong tendency to perceive others in terms of two basic social categories: "us" and "them." More precisely, the **ingroup** ("us") refers to *a social group to which one belongs*. The **outgroup** ("them") refers to *a social group to which one does not belong*. Preferences for the ingroup start early (Rhodes & Chalik, 2013; Wynn et al., 2018). One study conducted in the United States and in Taiwan found that as soon as the children in the racial majority could categorize people according to race, preferences for their own race emerged (Dunham et al., 2013). Among children as young as three and four years old, [W]hite Americans preferred [W]hite faces over [B]lack or Asian faces, and Asians in Taiwan preferred Asian faces over [W]hite faces.

Ingroups and outgroups aren't necessarily limited to racial, ethnic, or religious boundaries. Virtually any characteristic can be used to make ingroup and outgroup distinctions: Mac versus PC users, hip-hop versus country music fans, and even, it seems, graham cracker lovers versus green bean lovers. Both 9-month-old and 14-month-old infants liked a rabbit puppet better when it shared their preference for either graham crackers or green beans (Hamlin et al., 2013).

Two important patterns characterize our views of ingroups versus outgroups. First, when we describe the members of our *ingroup*, we typically see them as being quite varied, despite having enough features in common to belong to the same group. In other words, we notice the diversity within our own group.

Second, *the tendency to see members of outgroups as very similar to one another* is called the **outgroup homogeneity effect**. (The word *homogeneity* means "similarity" or "uniformity.") For example, what qualities do you associate with the category of "engineering major"? If you're *not* an engineering major, you're likely to see engineering majors as a rather similar crew: male, logical, analytical, conservative, and so forth. However, if you *are* an engineering major, you're much more likely to see your ingroup as quite *heterogeneous*, or varied (Dovidio & Gaertner, 2010).

Ingroup bias is *the tendency to judge the behavior of our ingroup members favorably and outgroup members unfavorably*. We succeeded because we worked hard; they succeeded because they lucked out. We failed because of circumstances beyond our control; they failed because they're stupid and incompetent. We're thrifty; they're stingy. And so on.

In combination, stereotypes and ingroup/outgroup bias form the *cognitive* basis for prejudicial attitudes. But, as with many attitudes, prejudice also has a strong *emotional* component (Jackson, 2011). In the case of prejudice, the emotions are intensely negative — and evident in brain scans. In one study, participants viewing images of low-status people — such as homeless people or people who abuse substances — showed increased activity in the amygdala and insula, an indication of disgust (Harris & Fiske, 2006). The same researchers examined participants' responses to images of people often stereotyped as incompetent, such as people who are elderly or disabled. Participants viewing these images showed increased activity in the prefrontal

ingroup A social group to which one belongs.

outgroup A social group to which one does not belong.

outgroup homogeneity effect The tendency to see members of outgroups as very similar to one another.

ingroup bias The tendency to judge the behavior of ingroup members favorably and outgroup members unfavorably.

Jack Taylor/Getty Images

▲ **Overcoming and Combating Prejudice** In an unexpected victory, Sadiq Khan, the son of immigrants from Pakistan, was elected mayor of London in 2016. He is the first Muslim to be elected mayor of any capital city in the European Union. Khan has talked about his own experience with prejudice and has made unity among Londoners a central feature of his role as mayor. He wrote an article against anti-Semitism for a Jewish newspaper in which he said, "I am proud that London is a city where, the vast majority of the time, Jewish people, Christians, Muslims, Sikhs, Buddhists, those who are not members of an organized faith, [B]lack, [W]hite, rich, young, gay, lesbian — don't simply tolerate each other, but respect, embrace and celebrate each other" (Khan, 2016).

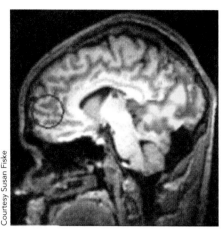

Courtesy Susan Fiske

▲ **Emotions and Prejudice** Psychologists Lasana Harris and Susan Fiske (2006) examined the link between prejudice and negative emotions. They used fMRI to examine the brains of participants viewing images of people often stereotyped as incompetent, such as the elderly or disabled. Participants who viewed these images showed higher levels of activity in the prefrontal cortex, as indicated here by the orange spot circled in red. This is a pattern associated with the experience of pity.

Is it true that if you believe you are not prejudiced, you will not behave in prejudiced ways?

implicit attitudes Preferences and biases toward particular groups that are automatic, spontaneous, unintentional, and often unconscious.

cortex, activity that accompanies pity (see photo to the left). *Behaviorally,* prejudice can be displayed in some form of *discrimination* — behaviors ranging from sneering at to physically attacking members of an outgroup (Dovidio & Gaertner, 2010). Online gamers, for example, were more likely to cheat when playing with strangers than with members of a group with whom they identified (Chen & Wu, 2015).

How can we account for the extreme emotions that often characterize prejudice against outgroup members? One theory holds that prejudice and intergroup hostility increase when different groups are competing for scarce resources, whether jobs, acreage, oil, water, or political power (see Pratto & Glasford, 2008). Prejudice and intergroup hostility are also likely to increase during times of social change (Brewer, 1994; Staub, 1996). However, policies that promote diversity can *decrease* prejudice, even when groups are in conflict (Guimond et al., 2013).

But prejudice often exists in the absence of direct competition for resources, changing social conditions, or even contact with members of a particular outgroup. What accounts for prejudice in such situations? One explanation is that people are often prejudiced against groups that are perceived as threatening to important ingroup norms and values (Esses et al., 2005; Louis et al., 2013). For example, a person might be extremely prejudiced against gay and lesbian people because they feel that the others threaten their ingroup's cherished values, such as a strong commitment to traditional sex roles and family structure. This explanation is supported by several neuroscience studies that observed increased activity in the amygdala when participants viewed someone of a different race (Cikara & Van Bavel, 2014). The amygdala is associated with responses related to fear.

Implicit Attitudes Most people today agree that prejudice and racism are wrong. Blatant displays of racist, sexist, or homophobic speech or behavior are no longer socially acceptable. However, some psychologists now believe that overt forms of prejudice have been replaced by more subtle forms of prejudice (Hewstone et al., 2002; Sritharan & Gawronski, 2010). These types of subtle, biased responses are often called *microaggressions* (Sue, 2010). Definitions vary, but in general microaggresssions refer to often unintentional behaviors that slight members of a group, and can have harmful psychological consequences (Seaton et al., 2010; Sue, 2017; Williams, 2020a, 2020b). Not surprisingly, prejudice is linked with microaggressions. Research found that White people in the United States who score higher on measures of racial prejudice also tend to report a higher likelihood that they would engage in microaggressions (Kanter et al., 2017).

Sometimes people who are not *consciously* prejudiced against particular groups nevertheless respond in prejudiced ways (Plant & Devine, 2009). For example, a man who consciously strives to be nonsexist may be reluctant to consult a female surgeon, or when he hears a news story that mentions a police officer, he may assume the officer is a man. Such biased responses can sometimes affect behavior in ways that we neither intend nor realize (Devine, 2001; Stanley et al., 2011). And many of these effects can be harmful. For Black Americans, for example, implicit attitudes about race have been linked to difficulties getting hired or receiving lifesaving medical treatment, to higher rates of discipline in school, and to an increased likelihood of being the victim of police violence (Hetey & Eberhardt, 2018; Kraus et al., 2019; Okonofua & Eberhardt, 2015; Richardson, 2015).

How can such responses be explained? In contrast to *explicit* attitudes, of which you are consciously aware, **implicit attitudes** are *preferences and biases toward particular groups that are automatic, spontaneous, unintentional, and often unconscious* (Bohner & Dickel, 2011). They are sometimes, but not always, unconscious (Sritharan & Gawronski, 2010).

Our implicit attitudes often differ from our explicit attitudes, especially when social and cultural norms prohibit negative attitudes regarding race, gender, or sexual orientation (Bodenhausen & Richeson, 2010). If people won't admit or aren't consciously aware of implicit attitudes, how can they be detected and measured? The most widely used test to measure implicit attitudes and preferences is the *Implicit Association Test,* or *IAT,* developed by psychologist Anthony Greenwald and his colleagues (1998).

The IAT is a computer-based test that measures the degree to which you associate particular groups of people with specific characteristics or attributes. The IAT is based on the assumption that people can sort images and words more easily when concepts seem to "match" or go together. So, for example, the Age IAT measures the speed with which you classify pairings of "good" or "bad" words with photographs of people of different ages. Other IATs measure implicit attitudes toward sexual orientation, weight, disability, and racial and ethnic groups. Visit implicit.harvard.edu to try the IAT yourself.

The IAT has been completed by over 20 million people around the world (Axt, 2018). The results suggest that implicit preferences are quite pervasive. As Brian Nosek and his colleagues (2007) concluded, "Social preferences are not possessed exclusively by a privileged few—they are a general characteristic of human social cognition." There also is research that suggests that IAT scores can be useful, predicting voting behavior, for example (Jost, 2019).

Although in wide use, the IAT is controversial (see Amodio & Mendoza, 2010; Gawronski, 2019). For example, some researchers argue that the ease with which certain associations are made may reflect familiarity with cultural stereotypes rather than personal bias or prejudice (Blanton et al., 2009). Other researchers have demonstrated that brief training can reduce prejudice as measured by the IAT (Calanchini et al., 2013). And, the degree to which *implicit* attitudes affect *actual* behavior is still an open question, although some studies suggest that they do (see Greenwald et al., 2009; Stanley et al., 2011).

Despite controversies about the IAT, there is evidence that implicit attitudes can be changed. Psychologists agree that becoming *aware* of our biased attitudes, whether implicit or explicit, is an important step toward overcoming them (Devine et al., 2012; Paluck & Green, 2009). For example, after research findings of racial bias among referees in the National Basketball Association league were widely publicized in the media, the racial bias decreased markedly (Pope et al., 2013). Also, mindfulness meditation, introduced in the chapter on consciousness, has been shown to reduce implicit bias based on both age and race (Lueke & Gibson, 2015). And there is evidence that the environment can affect implicit bias within a community. On U.S. university campuses, both faculty diversity as well as the absence of public monuments to the Confederacy were associated with lower mean levels of implicit bias against Black people (Vuletich & Payne, 2019). We turn to the topic of overcoming prejudice in the next section.

Overcoming Prejudice

■ KEY THEME
Prejudice can be overcome when people cooperate to achieve a common goal.

⹂ KEY QUESTIONS
- How has this finding been applied in the educational system?
- What other conditions are essential to reducing tension between groups?

How can prejudice be combated? A classic series of studies conducted by Turkish-born U.S. psychologist **Muzafer Sherif** (1906–1988) and his wife and colleague, U.S. social psychologist **Carolyn Wood Sherif** (1922–1982), helped clarify the conditions that produce intergroup conflict *and* harmony. Sherif, Wood Sherif, and their colleagues (1961) studied a group of 11-year-old boys in an unlikely setting for a scientific experiment: a summer camp located at Robbers Cave State Park in Oklahoma.

It is important to note that Carolyn Wood Sherif's work on this study and many other important social psychology studies, including her solo work on gender and social power, was long overlooked (Sherif et al., 1961; Wood Sherif, 1982). As Wood Sherif pointed out about her work with her husband, "A careful historian will recognize that both of us were involved in everything published under the name of Sherif after 1945. In several instances, when Muzafer asked me to appear as co-author, instead of in footnote or preface, I declined, a tendency that persisted into the 1960s. I would not do so again. I now believe that the world which viewed me as a wife who probably typed her husband's papers (which I did not) defined me to myself more than I realized" (Wood Sherif, 1983, pp. 285–286).

Pretending to be camp counselors and staff, the researchers randomly assigned the campers to two groups and arranged for them to meet in a series of competitive games. A fierce rivalry quickly developed, demonstrating the ease with which mutually hostile groups could be created. The rivalry intensified until the two groups began vandalizing each others' property, alarming the researchers. But simply increasing peaceful contact did not mitigate the antagonism between the groups. Sherif, Wood Sherif, and their fellow researchers only overcame the hostility by creating situations in which the two groups *cooperated to achieve a common goal* (Sherif, 1956; Sherif et al., 1961).

It is important to point out that later investigations into Sherif and Wood Sherif's study have found discrepancies between what they reported and what actually happened (Perry, 2018; Shariatmadari, 2018). First, the reported experiment was a repeat of an earlier version that failed to achieve the desired results. In that earlier camp, the two groups, the Pythons and Panthers, didn't take the researchers' bait to war with each other. Second, the researchers manipulated the situation—they "egged the boys on, providing them with the means to provoke one another." And third, from an ethical perspective, there was no informed consent; neither the boys nor their parents knew they were signing up for anything other than a typical summer camp.

Even if the results hold up, others researchers have questioned whether these results would apply to other intergroup situations. After all, these boys were homogeneous: White, middle class, Protestant, healthy, and well adjusted (Fiske & Ruscher, 1993; Sherif, 1966). There were no *intrinsic* differences between the two groups. Yet, recent research suggests that intergroup cooperation might work to produce similar results in other settings (Hein et al., 2016). When people of Swiss descent received help from people of Balkan descent, an outgroup about which many Swiss people hold negative stereotypes, researchers observed an increase in empathy toward other members of that outgroup.

> **Overcoming Group Conflict** To decrease hostility between the two groups at Robbers Cave, the researchers created situations that required the joint efforts of both groups to achieve a common goal, such as fixing the water supply. These cooperative tasks helped the boys recognize their common interests and become friends.

The Drs. Nicholas and Dorothy Cummings Center for the History of Psychology, The University of Akron

Social psychologist Elliot Aronson (1990, 1992) adapted the results of the Robbers Cave experiments to a different group situation—a newly integrated elementary school. Aronson and his colleagues developed the *jigsaw classroom technique,* which stressed cooperative, rather than competitive, learning situations (see Aronson, 1990; Aronson & Bridgeman, 1979). This approach brought together students in small, ethnically diverse groups to work on a mutual project. Like the pieces of a jigsaw puzzle, each student became an expert on one aspect of the overall project and had to teach it to the other members of the group.

The results? Children in the jigsaw classrooms had higher self-esteem and a greater liking for children in other ethnic groups than did children in traditional classrooms. They also demonstrated a lessening of negative stereotypes and prejudice, and a reduction in intergroup hostility (see Aronson, 1987, 1995; Aronson & Bridgeman, 1979).

Lessons from Robbers Cave and the jigsaw classroom have been used to reduce prejudice and conflict among racial, ethnic, and religious groups around the world (Aboud et al., 2012; Craig et al., 2017). For example, a number of programs have been developed to promote cooperation between Israelis and Palestinians through joint projects in which members of both groups work together to stage a play, conduct scientific studies, or play on a soccer team (Maoz, 2012) or of financially supporting a charitable organization that benefited both Christians and Muslims. It remains for future research to explore programs that might reduce discrimination in ways that generalize more broadly.

It also is important to recognize that discrimination grows not only out of individual prejudice, but also out of longstanding and entrenched cultural and institutional structures (Salter et al., 2018). Psychological interventions must target legal, health, educational, and other structures as well as prejudice at the individual level. For example, researchers Phia Salter and Glenn Adams (2016) examined Black History Month displays in U.S. high schools (Salter & Adams, 2016). They found that displays in majority-White schools tended to focus on individual accomplishments and racial diversity, whereas those in majority-Black schools embedded these topics in a deeper discussion of historical racism and barriers. Further, the types of displays that were more common in Black than in White schools "were more effective at promoting support for anti-racism policies," and perhaps might be adopted more widely across schools.

conformity Adjusting opinions, judgments, or behaviors so that they match those of other people, or the norms of a social group or situation.

Conformity: Following the Crowd

■ KEY THEME
Social influence involves the study of how behavior is influenced by other people and by the social environment.

≡ KEY QUESTIONS
- What factors influence the degree to which people will conform?
- Why do people conform?
- How does culture affect conformity?

As we noted earlier, *social influence* is the psychological study of how our behavior is influenced by the social environment and other people. For example, in a class where no one asks questions, maybe you feel uncomfortable raising your hand.

If you change your behavior to mesh with that of your classmates, you demonstrate conformity. **Conformity** refers to *adjusting opinions, judgments, or behaviors so that they match those of other people, or the norms of a social group or situation* (Hogg, 2010).

There's no question that all of us conform to group or situational norms to some degree. The more critical issue is *how far* we'll go to adjust our perceptions and opinions so that they're in sync with the majority opinion—an issue that intrigued social psychologist **Solomon Asch** (1907–1996). Asch (1951) posed a straightforward question: Would people still conform to the group if the group opinion was clearly wrong?

To study this question experimentally, Asch (1955) chose a simple task with an obvious answer (**Figure 12.2**). A group of people sat at a table and looked at a series of cards. On one side of each card was a standard line. On the other side were three comparison lines. All each person had to do was publicly indicate which comparison line was the same length as the standard line.

Asch's experiment had a hidden catch. All the people sitting around the table were actually coordinating with the experimenter, except for one—the real participant. Had you been the real participant in Asch's (1956) experiment, here's what you would have experienced. The first card is shown, and the five people ahead of you respond, one at a time, with the obvious answer: "Line B." Now it's your turn, and you respond the same. The second card is put up. Again, the answer is obvious and the group is unanimous. So far, so good.

Then the third card is shown, and the correct answer is just as obvious: Line C. But the first person confidently says, "Line A." And so does everyone else, one by one. Now it's your turn. To you it's clear that the correct answer is Line C. But the five people ahead of you have already publicly chosen Line A. How do you respond? You hesitate. Do you go with the flow or with what you know?

The real participant was faced with the uncomfortable situation of disagreeing with a unanimous majority on 12 of 18 trials in Asch's experiment.

FIGURE 12.2 The Line Judgment Task Used in the Asch Conformity Studies In Asch's classic studies on conformity, participants were asked to pick the comparison line that matched the standard line.

Standard line

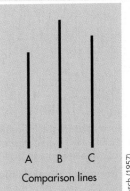
A B C
Comparison lines

Asch (1957).

MYTH ◄ SCIENCE

Is it true that if you're sure of your answer, you'll almost always stick to it even if others disagree with you?

Notice, there was no direct pressure to conform—just the implicit, unspoken pressure of answering differently from the rest of the group.

Over 100 participants experienced Asch's experimental dilemma. Not surprisingly, participants differed in their degree of conformity. Nonetheless, the majority of Asch's participants (76 percent) conformed with the group judgment on at least one of the critical trials. When the data for all participants were combined, the participants followed the majority and gave the wrong answer on *37 percent* of the critical trials (Asch, 1955, 1957). In comparison, a control group of participants who responded alone instead of in a group accurately chose the matching line 99 percent of the time.

Although the majority opinion clearly exerted a strong influence, it's also important to stress the flip side of Asch's results. On almost two-thirds of the trials in which the majority named the wrong line, the participants stuck to their guns and gave the correct answer, despite being in the minority (see Friend et al., 1990; Hodges & Geyer, 2006). And 95 percent defied the majority and gave the correct response at least once. In fact, some researchers argue that these results show more independence than conformity (Griggs, 2015a).

Factors Influencing Conformity

The basic model of Asch's classic experiment has been used in hundreds of studies exploring the dynamics of conformity (Bond, 2005). It's even been examined in online contexts, where people are making decisions based on the responses of anonymous, unseen others (Rosander & Eriksson, 2012; Zhu et al., 2012). Why do we sometimes find ourselves conforming to the larger group? There are two basic reasons.

First, *behavior motivated by the desire to gain social acceptance and approval* is referred to as **normative social influence.** Second *behavior that is motivated by the desire to be correct* is called **informational social influence** (Turner, 2010).

Asch and other researchers identified several conditions that promote conformity, which are summarized in **Table 12.1**. But Asch also discovered that conformity *decreased* under certain circumstances. For example, having an ally seemed to counteract the social influence of the majority. Participants were more likely to go against the majority view if just one other participant did so, even if the other person's dissenting opinion was wrong (Allen & Levine, 1969; Packer, 2008b). Conformity also lessens even if the other dissenter's competence is questionable, as in the case of a dissenter who wore thick glasses and complained that he could not see the lines very well (Allen & Levine, 1971; Turner, 2010).

▲ **Peer Groups and Conformity** Conformity to group norms peaks in early adolescence, but continues into adulthood as illustrated by the similarities in attire among these three women on the golf course. Think about your own group of friends or other groups at your school. How important is it for adolescents and young adults to fit in with others in their age range, especially those in their peer group?

Culture and Conformity

Patterns of conformity vary widely across cultures. For example, conformity is generally higher in collectivistic cultures than in individualistic cultures (R. Bond & Smith, 1996).

normative social influence Behavior that is motivated by the desire to gain social acceptance and approval.

informational social influence Behavior that is motivated by the desire to be correct.

TABLE 12.1

Factors That Promote Conformity

You're more likely to conform to group norms when:

- You are facing a unanimous group of at least four or five people

- You must give your response in front of the group

- You have not already expressed commitment to a different idea or opinion

- You find the task to be ambiguous or difficult

- You doubt your abilities or knowledge in the situation

- You are strongly attracted to a group and want to be a member of it

Sources: Asch (1955); Campbell & Fairey (1989); Deutsch & Gerard (1955); Gerard et al., (1968); Tanford & Penrod (1984).

Because individualistic cultures tend to emphasize independence, self-expression, and standing out from the crowd, the whole notion of conformity tends to carry a negative connotation.

In collectivistic cultures, however, publicly conforming while privately disagreeing tends to be regarded as socially appropriate tact or sensitivity. Publicly challenging the judgments of others, particularly the judgment of members of one's ingroup, would be considered rude, tactless, and insensitive to the feelings of others. In one study, participants in individualistic and collectivistic cultures read one of two descriptions of a person entering a business meeting (Stamkou et al., 2019). In the nonconformity condition, the person arrived late, disrupted the meeting to get a cup of coffee, and interrupted others. At the end he said, "Rules are there to be broken." In the conformity condition, the person arrived on time, let others speak before he did, and got coffee after the meeting. He said, "Rules are there for a reason." Participants in collectivist cultures viewed the nonconformist as less powerful and expressed moral outrage toward him. Those in individualistic cultures viewed him as more powerful and expressed less moral outrage about the norm violations.

Obedience: Just Following Orders

■ KEY THEME
Stanley Milgram conducted a series of controversial studies on obedience, which is behavior performed in direct response to the orders of an authority.

≡ KEY QUESTIONS
- What were the results of Milgram's original obedience experiments?
- What experimental factors were shown to increase the level of obedience?
- What experimental factors were shown to decrease the level of obedience?

One of social psychology's most creative and influential researchers, **Stanley Milgram** is best known for his experimental investigations of obedience. **Obedience** is *the performance of a behavior in response to a direct command.* Typically, an authority figure or a person of higher status, such as a teacher or supervisor, gives the command.

Milgram was intrigued by Asch's discovery of how easily people could be swayed by group pressure. But Milgram wanted to investigate behavior that had greater personal significance than simply judging line lengths on a card (Milgram, 1963). Thus, Milgram posed what he saw as the most critical question: Could a person be pressured by others into committing an immoral act, some action that violated his or her own conscience, such as hurting a stranger? In his efforts to answer that question, Milgram embarked on one of the most systematic and controversial investigations in the history of psychology: to determine how and why people obey the destructive commands of an authority figure (Blass, 2009; Russell, 2011).

Milgram's Original Obedience Experiment

Milgram was only 28 years old and a new faculty member at Yale University when he conducted his first obedience experiments. Milgram's all-male participants represented a wide range of occupational and educational backgrounds. Postal workers, high school teachers, white-collar workers, engineers, and laborers participated in the study.

Outwardly, it appeared that two participants showed up at the same time at Yale University to take part in the psychology experiment, but the second participant was actually an accomplice working with Milgram. When both participants arrived, the experimenter, wearing a white lab coat, greeted them and gave them a plausible explanation of the study's purpose: to examine the effects of punishment on learning.

Both participants drew slips of paper to determine who would be the "teacher" and who the "learner." However, the drawing was rigged so that the real participant was always the teacher and the accomplice was always the learner. Assigned to the role of the teacher, the real participant would be responsible for "punishing" the learner's mistakes by administering electric shocks.

▲ **Obedience in Sports and Medicine** Gymnast Maggie Nichols was the first to speak out about serial sexual abuser Larry Nasser, the physician for USA Gymnastics (Connor & Fitzpatrick, 2018). Nichols and her fellow gymnasts obeyed the directions of Nasser, even when his actions were sexually abusive, as an authority figure who was backed by other authority figures within USA Gymnastics. Even though Nichols was concerned about what happened during her visits with Nasser, she said, "I accepted what he was doing because I was told by adults that he was the best doctor and he could help relieve my pain." Nichols's initial unquestioning obedience of an authority figure, as we'll see, is a common human tendency. Her courage in speaking up first is what is uncommon.

obedience The performance of a behavior in response to a direct command.

⌃ Milgram's "Shock Generator"
A young Stanley Milgram sits next to his "shock generator." Milgram went to great lengths to make the shock generator look as authentic as possible. The front panel of the bogus shock generator had been engraved by professional industrial engravers. Whenever the teacher pressed a shock switch, the red light above the switch went on, a buzzing and clicking sound was heard, and the needle on the voltage meter swung to the right.

MYTH ◄ SCIENCE

Is it true that most people will not harm another person if ordered to do so?

After the drawing, the teacher and learner were taken to separate rooms where they could not see each other. Speaking into a microphone, the teacher tested the learner on a simple word-pair memory task. The learner's response was registered in an answer box positioned on top of the "shock generator" in front of the teacher. Each time the learner answered incorrectly, the teacher was to deliver an electric shock.

Just in case there was any lingering doubt in the teacher's mind about the legitimacy of the shock generator, the *teacher* was given a sample jolt using the switch marked 45 volts. In fact, this sample shock was the only real shock given during the course of the staged experiment.

The first time the learner answered incorrectly, the teacher was to deliver an electric shock at the 15-volt level. With each subsequent error, the teacher was told to progress to the next level on the shock generator. The teacher was also told to announce the voltage level to the learner before delivering the shock.

At predetermined voltage levels, the learner vocalized first his discomfort, then his pain, and, finally, agonized screams. At 210 volts, the learner responded: "Ugh!! Experimenter! Get me out of here. I've had enough. I *won't* be in the experiment any more" (Milgram, 1974). At 330 volts, the learner responded, in part, with an intense and prolonged agonized scream and the words "Let me out of here. Let me out of here. My heart's bothering me. Let me out, I tell you" (Milgram, 1974). After 330 volts, the learner's script called for him to fall silent. If the teacher protested that he wished to stop or that he was worried about the learner's safety, the experimenter would say, "The experiment requires that you continue" or "You have no other choice, you *must* continue."

According to the script, the experiment would be halted when the teacher refused to obey the experimenter's orders to continue. Alternatively, if the teacher obeyed the experimenter, the experiment would be halted once the teacher had progressed all the way to the maximum shock level of 450 volts.

Either way, Milgram indicated that after the experiment, it should be explained to the teacher that the learner had not actually received dangerous shocks. To underscore this point, a "friendly reconciliation" would be planned between the teacher and the learner, and the true purpose of the study would be explained to the participant. As you'll see, participants were not always debriefed right away.

The Results of Milgram's Original Experiment

Can you predict how Milgram's participants behaved? Of the 40 participants, how many obeyed the experimenter and went to the full 450-volt level? On a more personal level, how do you think *you* would have behaved had you been one of Milgram's participants?

Milgram himself asked psychiatrists, college students, and middle-class adults to predict how participants would behave (see Milgram, 1974). *None* of those surveyed thought that any of Milgram's participants would go to the full 450 volts.

As it turned out, they were all wrong. *Two-thirds of Milgram's participants—26 of the 40—were fully compliant and went to the full 450-volt level.* And of those who defied the experimenter, *not one stopped before the 300-volt level.* **Table 12.2** shows the results of Milgram's original obedience study.

Surprised? Milgram himself was stunned by the results, never expecting that the majority of participants would administer the maximum voltage. Were his results a fluke? The answer to both these questions is no. Milgram's obedience study has been repeated many times in the United States and other countries (see Blass, 2000, 2012). And, in fact, Milgram (1974) replicated his own study on numerous occasions, using variations of his basic experimental procedure.

In one replication, for instance, Milgram's participants were 40 women. The results were identical. Confirming Milgram's results since then, eight other studies also found no sex differences in obedience to an authority figure (see Blass, 2000, 2004; Burger, 2009).

Perhaps Milgram's participants saw through his elaborate experimental hoax, as some critics have suggested (Orne & Holland, 1968). Was it possible that the participants did not believe that they were really harming the learner? Milgram (1965) himself reported that only 56.1 percent of participants "fully believed the learner was getting painful shocks." And unpublished data from Milgram's studies do suggest that participants were more likely to obey if they did *not* believe the learner was actually receiving shocks (Perry, 2013). But many of Milgram's participants seemed totally convinced that the situation was authentic. And they did not behave in a cold-blooded, unfeeling way. Far from it. As the experiment progressed, many participants showed signs of extreme tension and conflict.

In describing the reaction of one participant, Milgram (1963) wrote, "I observed a mature and initially poised businessman enter the laboratory smiling and confident. Within 20 minutes he was reduced to a twitching, stuttering wreck, who was rapidly approaching a point of nervous collapse." Extreme reactions like this one have led people to question the ethics of Milgram's experiment (Baumrind, 1964; Perry, 2013).

Milgram, along with other researchers, identified several aspects of the experimental situation that had a strong impact on the participants (see Blass, 1992, 2000; Milgram, 1965). Overall, he demonstrated that the rate of obedience rose or fell depending upon the situational variables the participants experienced (Zimbardo, 2007). Here are some of the forces that influenced participants to continue obeying the experimenter's orders:

- **The situation, or context, in which the obedience occurred.** The participants were familiar with the basic nature of scientific investigation, and believed that scientific research was worthwhile (Milgram, 1974).

- **A previously well-established mental framework to obey.** Participants arrived at the lab with the mental expectation that they would obediently follow the directions of the experimenter.

- **The gradual, repetitive escalation of the task.** The shocks, like the learner's protests, escalated only gradually.

- **The experimenter's behavior and reassurances.** Participants were continually reassured that the *experimenter* was responsible for the learner's well-being.

- **The physical and psychological separation from the learner.** First, the learner was in a separate room and not visible.

- **Confidence that the learner was actually receiving shocks.** At least some of Milgram's participants suspected that the learner was not receiving shocks (Milgram, 1965; Perry, 2013).

Conditions That Undermine Obedience: Variations on a Theme

In a lengthy series of experiments, Milgram systematically varied the basic obedience paradigm. To give you some sense of the enormity of Milgram's undertaking, approximately *1,000* participants, each tested individually, experienced some variation of Milgram's obedience experiment.

By varying his experiments, Milgram identified several conditions that decreased the likelihood of destructive obedience, which are summarized in **Figure 12.3**. For example, when teachers were allowed to act as their own authority and freely choose the shock level, 95 percent of them did not venture beyond 150 volts—the first point at which the learner protested.

TABLE 12.2

The Results of Milgram's Original Study

Shock Level	Switch Labels and Voltage Levels	Number of Participants Who Refused to Administer a Higher Voltage Level
	Slight Shock	
1	15	
2	30	
3	45	
4	60	
	Moderate Shock	
5	75	
6	90	
7	105	
8	120	
	Strong Shock	
9	135	
10	150	
11	165	
12	180	
	Very Strong Shock	
13	195	
14	210	
15	225	
16	240	
	Intense Shock	
17	255	
18	270	
19	285	
20	300	5
	Extreme Intensity Shock	
21	315	4
22	330	2
23	345	1
24	360	1
	Danger: Severe Shock	
25	375	1
26	390	
27	405	
28	420	
	XXX	
29	435	
30	450	26

Contrary to what psychiatrists, college students, and middle-class adults predicted, the majority of Milgram's participants did not refuse to obey by the 150-volt level of shock. As this table shows, 14 of Milgram's 40 participants (35 percent) refused to continue at some point after administering 300 volts to the learner. However, 26 of the 40 participants (65 percent) remained obedient to the very end, administering the full 450 volts to the learner.

Source: Data from Milgram (1974).

Experimental Variations

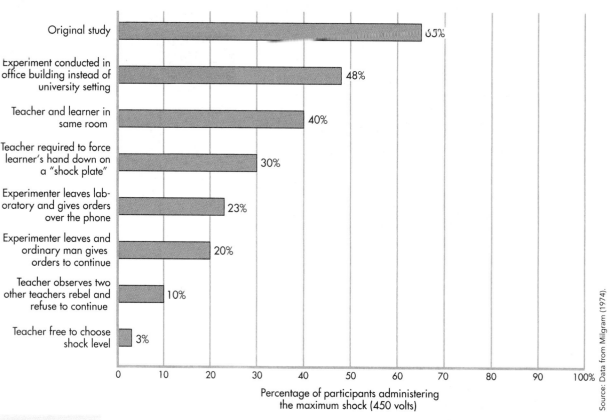

Original study	65%
Experiment conducted in office building instead of university setting	48%
Teacher and learner in same room	40%
Teacher required to force learner's hand down on a "shock plate"	30%
Experimenter leaves laboratory and gives orders over the phone	23%
Experimenter leaves and ordinary man gives orders to continue	20%
Teacher observes two other teachers rebel and refuse to continue	10%
Teacher free to choose shock level	3%

Percentage of participants administering
the maximum shock (450 volts)

Source: Data from Milgram (1974).

FIGURE 12.3 Factors That Decrease Destructive Obedience By systematically varying his basic experimental design, Milgram identified several factors that diminish the likelihood of destructive obedience. In this graph, you can see the percentage of participants who administered the maximum shock in different experimental variations.

> **The Game of Death** The French television show *Game of Death*, a 2010 recreation of Stanley Milgram's experiment, demonstrated that high levels of obedience still can occur. Here, the host (left) is shown with a "contestant" seated before an array of levers. Eighty-one percent of the contestants on *Game of Death* obeyed the host's order to shock another contestant who had answered a question incorrectly. In an interview, *Game of Death* producer Christophe Nick explained, "Most of us think we have free thinking and so we are responsible for our acts. This experience shows that in certain circumstances, a power—the TV in this case—is able to make you do something you don't want to do." One contestant agreed with Nick's assertion. He said, "I wanted to stop the whole time, but I just couldn't. I didn't have the will to do it. And that goes against my nature. I haven't really figured out why I did it" (Beardsley, 2010).

LE JEU DE LA MORT (2009)

Many people wonder whether Milgram would get the same results if his experiments were repeated today. Are people still as likely to obey an authority figure? There have been several replications or partial replications in recent years, including several by entertainment or news media (BBC News, 2008; Burger, 2009; Doliński et al., 2017; Lowry, 2011; Perry, 2013). For example, using methods similar to Milgram's, French researchers found high levels of obedience in a game-show setting in a TV studio where participants obeyed a television host (Beauvois et al., 2012). In the show, called *Game of Death,* the researchers used all the trappings of a television production to convince participants that the situation was real.

The researchers recruited 76 participants from Paris, having excluded anyone who was aware of Milgram's research. Participants were asked to shock another "contestant" every time he answered a question incorrectly. (As in Milgram's study, the "contestant" was an actor who was not actually receiving shocks.) So, what do you think happened? Eighty-one percent of participants obeyed, a result statistically similar to Milgram's findings. Importantly, unlike in Milgram's era, there was an immediate international outcry about the ethics of putting unwitting participants in such a situation.

Milgram's research is not without critics. Called a "contentious classic," psychologists today question Milgram's ethics, methodology, and conclusions (Griggs & Whitehead, 2015; Tavris, 2014). With respect to ethics, we now know that Milgram did not tell about 600 participants that they were *not* actually shocking the learner until about a year later (Perry, 2013). And Milgram's methodology was sometimes sloppy; the experimenter often veered far from the script when prodding participants to continue (Gibson, 2017).

Despite these criticisms, more than 50 years after the publication of Milgram's research, the moral issues that his findings highlighted are still with us.

Asch, Milgram, and the Real World: Implications of the Classic Social Influence Studies

The scientific study of conformity and obedience has produced some important insights. The first is the degree to which our behavior is influenced by situational factors (see Benjamin & Simpson, 2009; Zimbardo, 2007). Being at odds with the majority or with authority figures is uncomfortable for most people—enough so that our judgment and perceptions can be distorted and we may act in ways that violate our conscience.

More important, perhaps, is the insight that each of us *does* have the capacity to resist group or authority pressure (Bocchiaro & Zimbardo, 2010). Because the central findings of these studies are so dramatic, it's easy to overlook the fact that some participants refused to conform or obey despite considerable social and situational pressure (Packer, 2008a). Consider the response of a participant in one of Milgram's later studies (Milgram, 1974). A 32-year-old industrial engineer named Jan Rensaleer protested when he was commanded to continue at the 255-volt level:

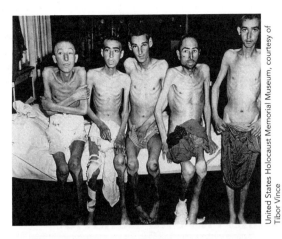

United States Holocaust Memorial Museum, courtesy of Tibor Vince

Jerome Delay/AP Images

‹ Destructive Obedience and Prejudice Blind obedience to authority combined with ethnic prejudice in Germany during World War II led to the slaughter of millions of Jews in concentration camps. When questioned after the war, Nazi officials and soldiers claimed that they were "just following orders." In the decades since the end of World War II, genocide, ethnic cleansing, and politically inspired mass killings have occurred in Cambodia, Bosnia and Herzegovina, Rwanda, and the Sudanese Darfur. As of 2021, in the Central African Republic, thousands of people had been killed and hundreds of thousands of people had been displaced from their homes (Human Rights Watch, 2020a; UNHCR, 2015). The United Nations only formally started supporting the return of refugees in 2018 (africanews, 2018).

> *Experimenter:* It is absolutely essential that you continue.
>
> *Mr. Rensaleer:* Well, I won't—not with the man screaming to get out.
>
> *Experimenter:* You have no other choice.
>
> *Mr. Rensaleer:* I do have a choice. *(Incredulous and indignant)* Why don't I have a choice? I came here on my own free will. I thought I could help in a research project. But if I have to hurt somebody to do that, or if I was in his place, too, I wouldn't stay there. I can't continue. I'm very sorry. I think I've gone too far already, probably.

Like some of the other participants in the obedience and conformity studies, Rensaleer effectively resisted the situational and social pressures that pushed him to obey. **Table 12.3** summarizes several strategies that can help people resist the pressure to conform or obey in a destructive, dangerous, or morally questionable situation.

How are such people different from those who conform or obey? Unfortunately, there's no satisfying answer to that question. No specific personality trait consistently predicts conformity or obedience in experimental situations such as those Asch and Milgram created (see Blass,

---

TABLE 12.3

Resisting an Authority's Unacceptable Orders

- Verify your own discomfort by asking yourself, "Is this something I would do if I were controlling the situation?"

- Express your discomfort. It can be as simple as saying, "I'm really not comfortable with this."

- Resist even slightly objectionable commands so that the situation doesn't escalate into increasingly immoral or destructive obedience.

- If you realize you've already done something unacceptable, stop at that point rather than continuing to comply.

- Find or create an excuse to get out of the situation and validate your concerns with someone who is not involved with the situation.

- Question the legitimacy of the authority. Most authorities have legitimacy only in specific situations. If authorities are out of their legitimate context, they have no more authority in the situation than you do.

- If it is a group situation, find an ally who also feels uncomfortable with the authority's orders. Two people expressing dissent in harmony can effectively resist conforming to the group's actions.

Sources: Information from American Psychological Association (2004); Asch (1956, 1957); Blass (1991, 2004); Haney et al. (1973); Migram (1963, 1974); Zimbardo (2000, 2004, 2007).

2000, 2004; Burger, 2009). In other words, the social influences that Asch and Milgram created in their experimental situations can be compelling even to people who are normally quite independent.

Finally, we need to emphasize that conformity and obedience are not completely bad in and of themselves. Quite the contrary. Conformity and obedience are necessary for an orderly society, which is why such behaviors were instilled in all of us as children. The critical issue is not so much whether people conform or obey, because we all do so every day of our lives. Rather, the critical issue is whether the norms we conform to, or the orders we obey, reflect values that respect the rights, well-being, and dignity of others.

Altruism and Aggression: Helping and Hurting Behavior

■ KEY THEME
Prosocial behavior describes any behavior that helps another person, including altruistic acts. Aggression describes behavior that is intended to harm another person.

⚌ KEY QUESTIONS
- What factors increase the likelihood that people will help a stranger?
- What factors decrease the likelihood that people will help a stranger?
- How can the lack of bystander response in the Genovese murder case be explained in light of psychological research on helping behavior?
- What factors increase the likelihood that people will harm another person?

It was about 3:20 A.M. on Friday, March 13, 1964, when 28-year-old Kitty Genovese returned home from her job managing a bar.

As she got out of her car, she noticed a man at the end of the parking lot, about 100 feet from the entrance to her apartment, where she lived with her girlfriend, Mary Ann Zielonko (Roberts, 2020). When the man moved in her direction, she began walking toward a nearby police call box, which was under a streetlight in front of a bookstore. On the opposite side of the street was a 10-story apartment building. As she neared the streetlight, the man grabbed her and she screamed. Across the street, lights went on in the apartment building. "Oh, my God! He stabbed me! Please help me! Please help me!" she screamed.

"Let that girl alone!" a man yelled from one of the upper apartment windows. The attacker looked up, then walked off, leaving Kitty on the ground, bleeding. The street became quiet. Minutes passed. One by one, lights went off. Struggling to her feet, Kitty made her way toward her apartment. As she rounded the corner of the building moments later, her assailant returned, stabbing her again. "I'm dying! I'm dying!" she screamed.

Again, lights went on. Windows opened and people looked out. This time, the assailant got into his car and drove off. It was now 3:35 A.M. Fifteen minutes had passed since Kitty's first screams for help. Staggering, then crawling, Kitty moved toward the entrance of her apartment. She never made it. Her attacker returned, searching the apartment entrance doors. At the second apartment entrance, he found her, slumped at the foot of the steps. This time, he stabbed her to death.

There is evidence that one person called the police after the first attack, although the police did not respond (Griggs, 2015b). No one else called until 3:50 A.M. The police took just two minutes to arrive at the scene after this second call. About half an hour later, an ambulance carried Kitty Genovese's body away. Only then did people come out of their apartments to talk to the police.

Over the next two weeks, police investigators learned that anywhere from 6 to 38 people had seen or heard Kitty's murder—a murder that involved three separate attacks over a period of about 30 minutes. Why didn't anyone try to help her? Why did only one person call the police when she first screamed for help?

When *The New York Times* interviewed various experts, they seemed baffled, although one expert said it was a "typical" reaction (Mohr, 1964). If there was a common theme in

⌃ **Kitty Genovese (1935–1964)** Kitty Genovese had grown up in Brooklyn. As a young woman, she managed a sports bar in Queens, shown here. The story of her murder, perhaps witnessed by as many as 38 people, kicked off decades of research on when people intervene to help others.

New York Daily News Archive/Getty Images

their explanations, it seemed to be "apathy." The occurrence was simply representative of the alienation and depersonalization of life in a big city, people said (see Rosenthal, 1964a, 1964b).

Not everyone bought this pat explanation. In the first place, it isn't true. For one, Kitty Genovese's brother Bill later reported that he talked "to the man who shouted down at [her killer] through a window that night, a woman who insisted that she had called the police, and a friend of Kitty's who came downstairs and held her as she died. In his view, the apathetic bystander is a false narrative of what happened" (Kassin, 2017). Indeed, by several accounts Kitty's friend and neighbor Sophia Farrar rushed downstairs and comforted her as she died (Roberts, 2020).

In addition, there is evidence of bystanders intervening beyond Kitty Genovese's murder. One study examined video footage from three countries—the Netherlands, South Africa, and the United Kingdom—where public cameras are common (Philpot et al., 2020). The researchers examined footage of public conflicts ranging from heated verbal disagreements to physical fights. Ninety percent of the time, at least one bystander intervened. Ironically, Kitty Genovese's killer was eventually caught when two bystanders intervened when he was committing a burglary five days after her murder (Kassin, 2017). As social psychologists **Bibb Latané** (b. 1937) and **John Darley** (b. 1938) (1970) later pointed out in their landmark book, *The Unresponsive Bystander: Why Doesn't He Help?*:

> People often help others, even at great personal risk to themselves. For every "apathy" story, one of outright heroism could be cited. . . . People sometimes help and sometimes don't. What determines when help will be given?

That's the critical question, of course. When do people help others? And why do people help others?

Altruism refers to *helping another person with no expectation of personal benefit* (Batson et al., 2011). An altruistic act is fundamentally selfless—the individual is motivated purely by the desire to help someone in need. Everyday life is filled with little acts of altruistic kindness, such as the stranger who thoughtfully holds a door open for you as you juggle an armful of packages, and bigger ones, such as the members of the Sirens motorcycle club delivering milk to babies in need.

Altruistic actions fall under the broader heading of **prosocial behavior**, which describes *any behavior that helps another person, whether the underlying motive is self-serving or selfless*. Note that prosocial behaviors are not necessarily altruistic. Sometimes we help others out of guilt. And, sometimes we help others in order to gain something, such as recognition, rewards, increased self-esteem, or having the favor returned (Batson et al., 2011). Whatever the reason, there is evidence from neuroscience research that some forms of prosocial behavior lead to activation in the brain structures associated with rewards (Kurzban et al., 2015). This might explain why people who engage in prosocial behaviors tend to be

▲ **Prosocial Behavior in Action** Many people volunteer their time and energy to help others. In northeastern Japan, high school student volunteers cleared homes of mud deposited by a destructive typhoon.

Kyodo News/Getty Images

TPG/AP Images

⟨ **Coming to the Aid of a Stranger** Everyday life is filled with examples of people who come to the aid of a stranger in distress, like the man shown here in Ningbo, China. He bravely scaled three stories of a building to save a three-year-old boy. The boy was dangling dangerously in the air, his head stuck between security bars over his window. The man climbed up to the boy and held him until he could be rescued by firefighters.

altruism Helping another person with no expectation of personal reward or benefit.

prosocial behavior Any behavior that helps another, whether the underlying motive is self-serving or selfless.

happier than those who do not (Nelson et al., 2016). And other research demonstrates a link between altruism and increased mating success, such as being more attractive to sexual partners and having more sexual partners (Arnocky et al., 2016). Researchers suggest that such findings highlight possible evolutionary causes for altruistic behavior. And finally, highlighting another benefit of diversity, a large international study found that people living in more racially diverse neighborhoods tended to exhibit more prosocial behaviors than those not living in such neighborhoods (Nai et al., 2018).

Factors That Increase the Likelihood of Bystanders Helping

Kitty Genovese's death triggered hundreds of investigations into the conditions under which people will help others (Dovidio, 1984; Dovidio et al., 2006). Those studies began in the 1960s with the pioneering efforts of Bibb Latané and John Darley, who conducted a series of ingenious experiments in which it appears that help is needed. For example, in one study, participants believed they were overhearing an epileptic seizure (Darley & Latané, 1968). In another study, participants were in a room that started to fill with smoke (Latané & Darley, 1968). Based on these studies, Latané and Darley concluded that people must pass through three stages before they offer help. First, they must notice an emergency situation. Second, they must interpret it as a situation that actually requires help. Third, they must decide that it is their responsibility to offer help (Latané & Darley, 1968).

Other researchers joined the effort to understand what factors influence a person's decision to help another (see Fischer et al., 2011; Zaki & Mitchell, 2013). Some of the most significant factors that increase the likelihood of helping include:

- **Personality factors.** In real-life situations such as cyberbullying or when a fallen bicyclist appeared to need help, people with higher levels of empathy were more likely to intervene (Bethlehem et al., 2016; Machakova, 2020).

- **The "feel good, do good" effect.** People who feel happy or fortunate are more likely to decide to help others (see Forgas et al., 2008; C. Miller, 2009).

- **Feeling guilty.** People tend to be more helpful when feeling guilty, such as after telling a lie (Basil et al., 2006; T. Cohen et al., 2012; de Hooge et al., 2011).

- **Seeing others who are willing to help.** We're more likely to decide to help if we observe others do the same (Fischer et al., 2011). This is true even when we are the recipient of help (Tsvetkova & Macy, 2014).

- **Perceiving the other person as deserving help.** We're more likely to decide to help people who are in need of help through no fault of their own, such as when their wallet has been stolen (Burn, 2009; Latané & Darley, 1970).

- **Knowing how to help.** Knowing what to do and being physically capable of helping contributes greatly to the decision to help someone else (Fischer et al., 2011; Steg & de Groot, 2010). In line with this, U.S. universities are required to provide bystander training to give students skills to intervene, for example, to prevent a sexual assault (Coker et al., 2016). A meta-analysis found that students who participated in these training programs were more likely to intervene than those who did not receive the training (Jouriles et al., 2018).

- **A personalized relationship.** Whether online or in real life, when people have any sort of personal relationship with another person, they're more likely to decide to help that person (Brody & Vangelisti, 2015; Vrugt & Vet, 2009). For example, when online interactions are *not* anonymous, a personal relationship makes people more likely to help, such as in cyberbullying situations (Macháčková et al., 2013; Machakova, 2020).

- **A dangerous situation.** People also are more likely to decide to help in dangerous situations, such as those that are clearly an emergency and those when the perpetrator is present (Fischer et al., 2011). Even in an online context, bystanders are more likely to intervene in cyberbullying when it is more severe (Bastiaensens et al., 2014; Machakova, 2020).

Factors That Decrease the Likelihood of Bystanders Helping

Unfortunately, instances in which bystanders fail to intervene are still regularly reported. For example, 18-year-old Tyler Flach fatally stabbed 16-year-old Yaseen Morris during an after-school fight while 50 to 70 other students watched, taking mobile phone videos of the attack and uploading them to social media, but failing to call for help (Romo, 2019). People also fail to help online. Dozens of people watched a Facebook Live stream of the sexual assault of a 15-year-old girl by six assailants (Reynolds, 2017). None of the viewers reported the crime.

Given examples like these and many others, it's important to consider influences that decrease the likelihood of helping behavior. As we look at some of the key findings, we'll also note how each factor might have played a role in the death of Kitty Genovese.

- **The presence of other people.** In general, it is true that people are much more likely to decide to help when they are alone (Fischer et al., 2011; Latané & Nida, 1981). The **bystander effect** is *a phenomenon in which the greater the number of people present, the less likely each individual is to help someone in distress* (Brody & Vangelisti, 2016).

There seem to be two major reasons for the bystander effect. First, the **diffusion of responsibility** is *a phenomenon in which the presence of other people makes it less likely that any individual will help someone in distress because the obligation to intervene is shared among all the onlookers.* Ironically, the sheer number of bystanders seemed to be the most significant factor working against Kitty Genovese. Remember that when she first screamed, a man yelled down, "Let that girl alone!" With that, each observer instantly knew that they were not the only one watching the events on the street below. Hence, no single individual felt the full responsibility to help.

Second, the bystander effect seems to occur because each of us is motivated to some extent by the desire to behave in a socially acceptable way (*normative social influence*). In the case of Kitty Genovese, the lack of intervention by any of the witnesses may have signaled the others that intervention was not appropriate, wanted, or needed.

- **Being in a big city or a very small town.** Kitty Genovese was attacked late at night in one of the biggest cities in the world. Research by Robert Levine and his colleagues (2008) confirmed that people are less likely to decide to help strangers in big cities, but other aspects of city life, like crowding and economic status, also affect helping. On the other hand, people are *also* less likely to help a stranger in towns with populations under 5,000 (Steblay, 1987).

- **Vague or ambiguous situations.** When situations are ambiguous and people are not certain that help is needed, they're less likely to decide to offer help (Machakova, 2020; Solomon et al., 1978). The ambiguity of the situation may also have worked against Kitty Genovese. The people in the apartment building saw a man and a woman struggling on the street below but had no way of knowing whether the two were acquainted. "We thought it was a lovers' quarrel," some of the witnesses later said (Gansberg, 1964).

- **When the personal costs for helping outweigh the benefits.** If the potential costs of helping outweigh the benefits, it's less likely that people will help (Fischer et al., 2006, 2011). The witnesses in the Genovese case may have felt that the benefits of helping Genovese were outweighed by the potential hassles and danger of becoming involved in the situation.

On a small yet universal scale, the murder of Kitty Genovese dramatically underscores the power of situational and social influences to affect our behavior. Social psychological research has provided insights about the factors that influenced the behavior of those who witnessed the Genovese murder but that is not, a justification for the inaction of the bystanders. After

△ The Bystander Effect: What Would You Do? What would you do if you came across a man lying crumpled on the ground on a college campus? Would you stop to help him, call campus security, or look away and hurry past? What factors in the scene shown in the photograph make it more or less likely that the woman will stop to try to help a stranger?

MYTH ▶ SCIENCE

Is it true that people are more likely to help others if they are the only ones available to help?

bystander effect A phenomenon in which the greater the number of people present, the less likely each individual is to help someone in distress.

diffusion of responsibility A phenomenon in which the presence of other people makes it less likely that any individual will help someone in distress because the obligation to intervene is shared among all the onlookers.

A

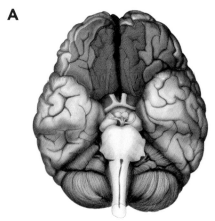

B

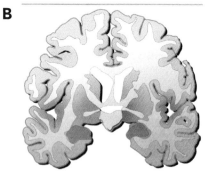

⌃ **Aggression and the Brain** Some researchers offer a biological explanation for aggression. They suggest that aggression occurs when people have trouble regulating their emotions. In fact, some of the brain patterns that researchers observe for aggression are similar to those that they observe for the regulation of emotion. The colored parts of the brain in this figure are involved in both emotion regulation and aggression. Psychologist Richard Davidson and his colleagues (2000) saw similar activity for both emotion regulation and aggression in parts of the prefrontal cortex (A) and the amygdala (B).

> **Bar Fights** The rate of violence tends to be higher among people who have consumed alcohol. Research conducted in bars found a positive correlation between levels of intoxication and the frequency and intensity of violent incidents (Graham et al., 2006).

aggression Verbal or physical behavior intended to cause harm to other people.

all, Kitty Genovese's death probably could have been prevented had more people intervened. If we understand the factors that decrease helping behavior, we can recognize and overcome those obstacles when we encounter someone who needs assistance.

Aggression: Hurting Behavior

The flip side of helping behavior is hurting behavior, or **aggression**—*verbal or physical behavior intended to cause harm to other people.* To be classified as aggression, the aggressor must believe that their behavior is harmful to the other person, and the other person must not wish to be harmed (Anderson & Bushman, 2002). A child who hits their little brother, a mugger who threatens their victim, a boss who screams at their subordinates, or a terrorist who fires shots in a crowded mall—all are engaged in acts of aggression. But the doctor who knowingly inflicts pain while setting a broken arm is not.

Have you ever wondered about the wide variation in aggressive tendencies? Why does one friend threaten a fistfight when provoked, while another calmly walks away? Like helping behavior, hurting behavior is driven by a range of factors—biological, psychological, and sociocultural.

The Influence of Biology on Aggression   Researchers have long thought that our tendency to behave aggressively has a biological component. Biological theories of aggression include genetic, structural, and biochemical explanations.

The Influence of Genes and Brain Structure   When someone behaves aggressively, it appears that may be driven, at least in part, by inborn personality characteristics. One study found that identical twins had similar aggressive tendencies whether or not they were raised together. Because identical twins share 100 percent of their genes, this finding indicates a strong genetic influence on aggressive behavior (Bouchard et al., 1990; Segal, 2012). Two meta-analyses that explored studies on heredity and aggression concluded that genetics played a significant role in people's levels of aggressiveness (Ferguson, 2010; Miles & Carey, 1997). Evolutionary theorists assert that a genetic predisposition toward aggression can help people to acquire or secure resources for themselves and for those who share their genes (Buss & Duntley, 2006; Ferguson & Beaver, 2009).

Another biological explanation for aggression points to differences in the parts of the brain that regulate emotion, including the amygdala, the prefrontal cortex, and the limbic system (Bobes et al., 2013; Davidson et al., 2000; Meyer-Lindenberg et al., 2006). For example, researchers have observed differences in the prefrontal cortex of people who are prone to aggressive and angry outbursts (Best et al., 2002).

Biochemical Influences   Biochemical influences on aggression include the hormone testosterone and alcohol abuse (Geniole, 2019). For example, Irene van Bokhoven and her colleagues (2006) followed 96 boys from kindergarten through age 21. They found that boys who had higher levels of testosterone over this period were more likely to have criminal records as adults. Links between aggression and higher levels of testosterone have also been found in women (Banks & Dabbs, 1996; Dabbs & Hargrove, 1997).

However, it's important not to overstate the link between testosterone and aggression. In a meta-analysis of 45 studies, Angela Book and her colleagues (2001) found only a weak relationship between the two. Further, some researchers point out that high testosterone can also have positive effects. For example, it may be linked to good negotiation and leadership skills (Yildirim & Derksen, 2012).

Matt Cardy/Getty Images

Although most people who consume alcohol are not violent, the rate of violence is higher among those under the influence of alcohol than among those who have not consumed alcohol (Page et al., 2016; Pedersen et al., 2014). This effect has been established in both laboratory and everyday settings (Chermack & Taylor, 1995; Exum, 2006; Graham et al., 2006). One research team bravely spent over 1,000 nights in over 100 bars in Toronto, Canada, and logged more than 1,000 violent incidents. As the crowd became more intoxicated, aggressive incidents were more likely to occur. And, the aggressive person's level of intoxication was generally related to the severity of the violent act (Graham et al., 2006).

Psychological Influences on Aggression   While it's clear that there are biological influences on aggression, there also are psychological influences. For example, a great deal of aggressive behavior is learned. In addition, there are situational factors that can increase people's tendency to be aggressive.

Learning   People who are violent are often mimicking behavior they have seen, a form of observational learning. For example, in the chapter on learning, you read about Albert Bandura's classic Bobo doll experiments in which children learned to behave aggressively toward a large balloon doll by watching a brief video in which an adult did the same. Exposure to violence may also lead to aggression over the longer term. Researchers have found that both women and men exposed to violence in their families while growing up were more likely to abuse their partners and their children as adults (Heyman & Smith Slep, 2002). But a higher likelihood is not a guarantee that the family pattern of violence will be repeated. In fact, most people who were exposed to violence as children *do not* grow up to be abusers themselves.

In the learning chapter's Critical Thinking box, "Does Exposure to Media Violence *Cause* Aggressive Behavior?" you read about the considerable disagreement among scientists as to whether viewing media violence is related to aggressive behavior (see Bushman et al., 2009; Ferguson & Konijn, 2015). Much of the research connecting media violence to actual aggressive behavior is correlational. Remember from the chapter on research methods that correlational studies cannot tell us whether one variable, such as viewing violence, causes another, such as aggression. The research that is experimental and could show causal links is primarily in artificial situations, and does not predict behavior long-term (Ferguson, 2018; Ferguson & Wang, 2019; Hilgard et al., 2019). And it's a myth that media—whether video games, songs, or films—only lead to negative behavior. Some media actually lead to increases in prosocial behavior (Ng, 2016).

Frustration   Aggression can also be driven by situational factors that are annoying or frustrating. For example, researchers have identified high temperatures as a source for frustration-linked aggression (Anderson & Bushman, 2002). Violence in Minneapolis increased as nighttime temperatures increased (Bushman et al., 2005). Even exposure to words associated with hotter temperatures—*sunburn* or *sweats*, for example—leads to increased hostility as compared with neutral or colder words (DeWall & Bushman, 2009). Temperature is also linked to violence on a global scale (Van Lange et al., 2016). As climate change leads to warmer temperatures globally, increased rates of conflict between individuals and between groups are being reported (Hsiang et al., 2013).

When's the last time you got really frustrated or angry? If you drive, it might have been behind the wheel. About one-third of us admit to having been the aggressor in a road rage situation, and that's particularly true of younger drivers and male drivers (Smart et al. 2003). Road rage results from a number of factors, especially frustration — the frustration that results when we perceive

MYTH ◀ **-SCIENCE-**

Is it true that playing video games is only associated with negative behaviors?

Stuart Pearce/AGE Fotostock

❮ **Road Rage** Aggression can result from the frustration we feel in a stressful situation. For example, "road rage" can stem from frustration experienced while driving, perhaps because we have been cut off by another driver or have encountered an unexpected detour.

inappropriate or reckless driving behavior, when there is heavy traffic, or when we're running late (Wickens et al., 2013). These factors are even more frustrating—and even more likely to lead to aggression—when we're already stressed out for other reasons (Wickens et al., 2013).

Gender, Culture, and Aggression Quick—which gender do you think is more likely to engage in aggressive behavior? In this case, the stereotype that males are the more aggressive gender is true, on average. (But just on average. As with every psychology finding, there are lots of exceptions.) Psychologist John Archer (2004) conducted a meta-analysis of aggression in real-world settings. He concluded that "Direct, especially physical, aggression was more common in males than females at all ages sampled, was consistent across cultures, and occurred from early childhood on, showing a peak between 20 and 30 years." And violence was particularly pronounced among men who perceived themselves as being less masculine than they desired to be, perhaps because they are attempting to demonstrate their masculinity (Reidy et al., 2016). Research suggests, however, that girls and women are just as aggressive as boys in *indirect* aggression, which refers to aggression related to interactions, such as gossiping and spreading rumors (Archer & Coyne, 2005).

Why are men more likely than women to behave in physically aggressive ways? There may be biological reasons. Evolutionary theorists suggest that aggressive men are more likely to have resources, which attract desirable mating partners (Buss & Duntley, 2006). In addition, men are more likely to use aggression in the context of mating. For example, in an experiment, men who thought about sexual topics were more likely to behave aggressively than men who thought about topics related to happiness (Ainsworth & Maner, 2012).

But there also are environmental explanations. The ways in which girls and boys exhibit aggression are influenced by the reactions of others. Girls and boys learn different aggression-related scripts—or guides for how they should act—by responding to input from peers and teachers, parents and other family members, and the media (Ostrov & Godleski, 2010).

Cultural factors also influence aggression. For example, there are regional and national differences in certain types of aggression based on the concept of a culture of honor (Vandello et al., 2008). A *culture of honor* is one in which actions perceived as damaging your reputation must be addressed (Vandello & Cohen, 2004). In some countries, such as Turkey, the culture of honor is focused on offenses against one's family (Cihangir, 2013; van Osch et al., 2013).

In the Americas, especially the southern United States and Latin America, aggression tends to be based on a culture of masculine honor. In such cultures, violence that is seen as helping a man restore his reputation for masculinity is more acceptable. For example, if a man is mocked at a sporting event, a violent response might be seen as reasonable or even admirable (Vandello & Cohen, 2003).

Cultures with significant income inequality also have higher rates of aggression, particularly murder (Elgar & Aitken, 2010; Nivette, 2011; Wilkinson & Pickett, 2009). The high correlation between these two measures, shown in **Figure 12.4**, demonstrates that sociocultural factors, in addition to biological and psychological factors, are important predictors of aggression.

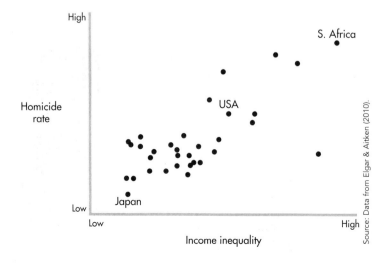

FIGURE 12.4 Income Inequality and Murder A study of 33 countries found a very strong link between the level of income inequality in a country and the homicide rate (Elgar & Aitken, 2010). As you can see in this graph, many countries, such as Japan, are low in both inequality and homicide, whereas others, such as South Africa, are very high in both. The United States is above average for both measures.

Source: Data from Elgar & Aitken (2010).

The Influence of Groups on Individual Behavior

social loafing The tendency to expend less effort on a task when it is a group effort.

■ KEY THEME
Individual behavior can be strongly influenced by the presence of others.

∷ KEY QUESTIONS
- What are social loafing and social striving?
- What are social facilitation and deindividuation?

In our discussions of conformity, obedience, and altruism, we have touched on a variety of ways in which the presence of other people influences an individual's thoughts and behavior. In this section, we'll focus directly on how the behavior of individuals can be affected by being part of a group. As you'll see, the diffusion of responsibility that can occur when a group of people observes someone who needs help also contributes to other aspects of group behavior.

Social Loafing: When Individual Effort Is "Lost in The Crowd"

The performance and motivation of individuals who are part of a group can be influenced by many different factors (Hogg, 2010). *The tendency to expend less effort on a task when it is a group effort* is a phenomenon called **social loafing**. You may have experienced social loafing when you participated in a group project for school. Have you ever felt the frustration when your group earned an A, but one of your group members did almost nothing to deserve that grade? Social loafing is especially pronounced when it's difficult or impossible to assess each individual's contribution to the collective effort. As a general rule, the greater the number of people involved in a collective effort, the lower each individual's output (Karau & Williams, 1993).

Social loafing is reduced or eliminated when (1) the group is composed of people we know, (2) we are members of a highly valued group, or (3) the task is meaningful or unique. Interestingly, women are generally less likely to engage in social loafing than are men (Karau & Williams, 1993).

Why does social loafing occur? Like the diffusion of responsibility that occurs when a group witnesses someone who needs help, a similar diffusion of responsibility seems to occur among group members working on a collective task. The responsibility for attaining the group goal is spread across all the group members, resulting in reduced effort by each individual group member (Latané, 1981). Social loafing can also occur because people expect other group members to slack off. To keep the situation equal, people reduce their efforts to match the level of effort they expect other group members to display (see Kerr & Tindale, 2004).

Cultural Variations: Social Striving Social loafing is a common phenomenon in individualistic cultures. However, cross-cultural psychologists have found that social loafing is not only absent but *reversed* in many collectivistic cultures, including in China, Israel, and Japan (M. Bond & Smith, 1996; Hong et al., 2008). That is, individuals worked *harder* when they were in groups than when they were alone — a pattern referred to as *social striving.*

Why is social loafing less pronounced or even absent in collectivistic cultures? In collectivistic cultures, group success tends to be more highly valued than individual success. Moreover, the social norms in collectivistic cultures encourage a sense of social responsibility and hard work within groups (Karau & Williams, 1993).

Social Facilitation: Individual Performance in the Presence of Others

When your individual efforts go undetected and are "lost in the crowd," individual performance may drop. But what if your individual efforts are *not* lost in the crowd but, instead, are the focus of the crowd's attention? Would your performance then be the same in the presence of others as it would be if you were working alone?

∨ Social Loafing You've probably worked on a group project for at least one of your classes. Did all of your classmates contribute equally to the project? Or were there students who just coasted, letting everyone else do most of the work? Many students dislike group projects because they fear social loafing. But it doesn't always take place. When people know the other members of their group, social loafing is less likely to occur. What other factors make social loafing less likely?

Jacob Ammentorp Lund/Getty Images

REUTERS/Jason Cairnduff

˄ Social Facilitation As the crowd watches and applauds their performance, these elite athletes are likely to turn in some of their best times. When does the presence of other people facilitate the performance of a task? When does it work against us?

Partly, it depends on the complexity of the task that you're trying to perform. When a task is relatively simple or well rehearsed, there is a pattern called **social facilitation**, *the tendency for the presence of other people to enhance individual performance.* So, In your new job as a cook, if others are watching you perform simple tasks like weighing an ingredient, your individual performance tends to improve. However, if the task is complex or poorly learned, such as flipping an omelet or throwing dough to create a perfectly sized pizza crust, the opposite effect can occur: The presence of other people is likely to *hinder* performance (Allport, 1920, 1924; Travis, 1925).

How can this be explained? Several factors are involved (Geen, 1995; Guerin, 2003). When a task is simple or well learned, increased motivation, spurred on by the anticipation of being positively evaluated, seems to work to our benefit. Hence, a well-trained athlete is likely to perform better when others are present than when alone (Guerin, 1986).

However, when the task is complex or poorly learned, arousal coupled with apprehension about being negatively evaluated tends to work against us. For example, the apprehensive actor who is not well rehearsed may end up flubbing lines in front of the opening night audience.

Deindividuation: When Group Members Feel Anonymous

What happens when you combine the increased arousal due to the presence of others with the diffusion of responsibility that characterizes social loafing and the bystander effect? In combination, increased arousal and a diminished sense of responsibility can lead to deindividuation. **Deindividuation** refers to *the reduction of self-awareness and inhibitions that can occur when a person is part of a group whose members feel anonymous* (Zimbardo, 2004).

Under these conditions, people may do things that they wouldn't do if they were alone or identifiable. For example, deindividuation can help explain adolescent acts of vandalism on Halloween. Succumbing to the feeling of anonymity provided by darkness and Halloween masks, groups of otherwise law-abiding teenagers may commit minor acts of vandalism, such as smashing pumpkins.

The deindividuation people experience when they interact anonymously in online contexts also can lead them to engage in antisocial behavior. Examples include cheating in online games, trolling, and online aggression, often called cyberbullying (Chen & Wu, 2015; Sticca & Perren, 2012).

Serious consequences can result from deindividuation in person, as well as online. For example, during a mob or a riot, the large crowd of people and general social chaos heighten both arousal and the sense of anonymity. This volatile combination can lead to mobs of rioting people who smash windows, steal, and injure innocent bystanders. Deindivuation is also an important factor in the rise of cyberbullying, due to the anonymity people feel when online (Chan et al., 2021; Wang & Sek-yum Ngai, 2020).

˅ Breaking Stereotypes and Exhibiting Altruism The Sirens are an all-women motorcycle club whose members break stereotypes and show altruism in their prosocial work delivering breast milk to babies in need. A number of the Sirens are shown here, along with several members of the New York Milk Bank, the organization with which they partner for their volunteer work.

Sirens Women's Motorcycle Club of NYC

How can deindividuation be counteracted? An important element of deindividuation is the reduced sense of self-awareness (Diener, 1980; Mullen et al., 2003). Thus, one way to counteract deindividuation is to heighten self-awareness. For example, when a mirror was placed above a bowl of Halloween candy, unattended trick-or-treaters were less likely to take more candy than they were told they could take (Beaman et al., 1979). Simply seeing their own faces in the mirror increased personal self-awareness and reduced impulsive, dishonest actions. In contrast, trick-or-treaters who did not see their faces in a mirror were more likely to take more candy than they were supposed to.

Closing Thoughts

We began this chapter with a prologue about an all-women motorcycle club, the Sirens, who break stereotypes and exhibit altruism in their work delivering milk to babies in need. The story of the Sirens underscores a theme that was repeatedly echoed throughout our subsequent discussions of person perception, attribution, and attitudes. Our subjective impressions, whether they are accurate or not, play a pivotal role in how we perceive and think about other people.

A different theme emerged in our later discussions of conformity, obedience, helping behavior, and hurting behavior. Social and situational factors, especially the behavior of others in the same situation, can have powerful effects on how we act at a given moment. Each of us has the freedom to choose how we respond in a given situation. When we're aware of the social forces that influence us, it can be easier for us to choose wisely.

In the final analysis, we are social animals who often influence one another's thoughts, perceptions, and actions, sometimes in profound ways. In the following Psych for Your Life section, we'll look at some of the ways that social psychological insights have been applied by professional persuaders—and how you can counteract attempts to persuade you.

social facilitation The tendency for the presence of other people to enhance individual performance.

deindividuation The reduction of self-awareness and inhibitions that can occur when a person is a part of a group whose members feel anonymous.

persuasion The deliberate attempt to influence the attitudes or behavior of another person in a situation in which that person has some freedom of choice.

PSYCH FOR YOUR LIFE

The Persuasion Game

"We must all be public health professionals now," physician Lawrence Bonchek (2020) stated, emphasizing the importance of persuasion in a pandemic. Bonchek noted that, despite scientific evidence supporting mask wearing to protect ourselves and others, some people refused to wear them, even when they were mandatory. Their refusal was particularly concerning in closed spaces like stores, buses, or airplanes. American Airlines flight attendant Allie Malis echoed this concern, noting that "Enforcing mask compliance has been one of the most difficult parts of our job" (Kaur & Osipova, 2021). As a society, we can, of course, use mandates and penalties to encourage mask wearing when warranted. But it's probably better to use persuasion, too. A study by the State of Illinois found that more than half of people who wore masks said they did so to protect themselves or others, and only 14 percent because it was a requirement (Wittenberg, 2020). The persuasive goal, then, was to convince people that masks are protective.

The State of Illinois study tested a number of different messages. Many didn't seem to work, but messages that compared masks to sports helmets or seat belts increased the percentages of people who said they were likely to wear masks from 89 percent to 92 percent. This is a small effect, but it could be quite meaningful in a pandemic. We might use this finding to persuade those in our own lives. **Persuasion** is *the deliberate attempt to influence the attitudes or behavior of another person in a situation in which that person has some freedom of choice.*

Professional persuaders often manipulate people's attitudes and behavior using techniques based on two fundamental social norms: the rule of reciprocity and the rule of commitment (Cialdini & Sagarin, 2005). Here we'll provide you with some practical suggestions to avoid being taken in by persuasion techniques.

The Rule of Reciprocity

The *rule of reciprocity* is a simple but powerful social norm (Burger et al., 2009; Melamed et al., 2020; Shen et al., 2011). If someone gives you something or does you a favor, you feel obligated to return the favor. So after a classmate lets you copy their lecture notes for the class session you missed, you feel obligated to return a favor when they ask for one.

The "favor" can be almost anything freely given, such as a free food sample in a grocery store or a free gardening workshop at your local hardware store. The rule of reciprocity is part of the sales strategy used by companies like Hulu and Netflix that offer

Richard B. Levine/Newscom

▲ **The Rule of Reciprocity** It's not altruism that prompted Panda Express to give away samples of their popular "Orange Chicken" dish at an event in New York City. Many companies employ marketing representatives, often university students, to host promotional events at music festivals, on campus, or wherever people congregate, hoping to inspire brand loyalty. U.S. businesses spend an estimated $20 billion a year on promotional products, hoping that the "rule of reciprocity" will make recipients feel obligated to respond by purchasing their brands in the future.

"free" trials of their streaming services. It's also why department stores that sell expensive cosmetics offer "free" makeovers. Technically, you are under "no obligation" to buy anything, but you do feel pressured to reciprocate by buying the product (Cialdini, 2009).

One strategy that uses the rule of reciprocity is called the *door-in-the-face technique* (Turner et al., 2007). First, the persuader makes a large request that you're certain to refuse. For example, Joe asks to borrow $500. You figuratively "slam the door in his face" by quickly turning him down. But then Joe, apologetic, appears to back off and makes a much smaller request—to borrow $20. From your perspective, it appears that Joe has made a concession to you and is trying to be reasonable. This puts you in the position of reciprocating with a concession of your own. "Well, I can't lend you $500," you grumble, "but I guess I could lend you 20 bucks." Of course, the persuader's real goal was to persuade you to comply with the second, smaller request.

The Rule of Commitment

Another powerful social norm is the *rule of commitment.* Once you make a public commitment, there is psychological and interpersonal pressure on you to behave consistently with your earlier commitment. The *foot-in-the-door technique* is one strategy that capitalizes on the rule of commitment (Guéguen et al., 2008; Rodafinos et al., 2005). Here's how it works.

First, the persuader makes a small request that you're likely to agree to. For example, they might stop you on the street and ask you to sign a petition supporting some social cause. By agreeing to do so, you've made a small *commitment* to the social cause. At that point, they have gotten their "foot in the door." Next, the persuader asks you to comply with a second, larger request, such as making a donation to the group they represent. Because of your earlier commitment, you feel psychologically pressured to behave consistently by now agreeing to the larger commitment (Cialdini, 2009).

Defending Against Persuasion Techniques

It is increasingly important to be aware that persuasive messages can impact your attitudes and behavior. For several years now, online advertisers have targeted messages directly to you based on your online behavior, such as your browsing history or "likes" on social media (Ur et al., 2012). But they may now also be targeting you based on your personality.

Some of your personality traits, such as how outgoing or anxious you are, can be predicted from your social media profile (Bachrach et al., 2012). And ads might be more persuasive when they were matched to personality (Hirsh et al., 2012). Specifically, for an ad for a mobile phone, outgoing people responded best when they were promised "you'll always be where the excitement is," and anxious people responded best when they were told that the phone would help them "stay safe and secure."

So, in a world where you are increasingly targeted, how can you reduce the likelihood that you'll be manipulated into making a decision that may not be in your best interest? Here are three practical suggestions.

1. Sleep on it.

Persuasive transactions typically occur quickly. Part of this is our own doing. We've finally decided to go look at a new laptop, automobile, or whatever, so we're psychologically primed to buy the product. The persuader uses this psychological momentum to help coax you into signing on the dotted line right then and there before you can have second thoughts. So when you think you've got the deal you want, tell the persuader that you always sleep on important decisions before making a final commitment.

The sleep-on-it rule often provides an opportunity to discover whether the persuader is deliberately trying to pressure or manipulate you. If the persuader responds to your sleep-on-it suggestion by saying something like "This offer is good for today only," then it's likely that they are afraid that your commitment to the deal will crumble if you think about it too carefully or look elsewhere.

2. Play devil's advocate.

List all of the reasons why you should *not* buy the product or make a particular commitment (Albarracín & Vargas, 2010; Crano & Prislin, 2006). Arguing *against* the decision will help activate your critical thinking skills. It's also helpful to discuss important decisions with a friend, who might point out disadvantages that you have overlooked.

3. When in doubt, do nothing.

Learn to trust your gut feelings when something doesn't feel quite right. If you feel that you're being psychologically pressured or cornered, you probably are. As a general rule, if you feel any sense of hesitation, lean toward the conservative side and do nothing. If you take the time to think things over, you'll probably identify the source of your reluctance.

⟨ CHAPTER REVIEW

Social Psychology

 **Achieve,** Macmillan Learning's online study platform, features the full e-book of *Discovering Psychology,* the **LearningCurve** adaptive quizzing system, videos, and a variety of activities to boost your learning. Visit **Achieve** at macmillanlearning.com.

KEY PEOPLE

Solomon Asch, p. 415

John Darley, p. 423

James Jackson, p. 400

Bibb Latané, p. 423

Stanley Milgram, p. 417

Muzafer Sherif, p. 413

Carolyn Wood Sherif, p. 413

KEY TERMS

social psychology, p. 400

sense of self, p. 400

social cognition, p. 400

social influence, p. 400

person perception, p. 401

social norms, p. 401

social categorization, p. 402

explicit cognition, p. 402

implicit cognition, p. 402

implicit personality theory, p. 402

attribution, p. 404

fundamental attribution error, p. 404

blaming the victim, p. 404

hindsight bias, p. 404

just-world hypothesis, p. 404

self-serving bias, p. 405

attitude, p. 406

cognitive dissonance, p. 408

prejudice, p. 409

intersectionality, p. 409

stereotype, p. 410

ingroup, p. 411

outgroup, p. 411

outgroup homogeneity effect, p. 411

ingroup bias, p. 411

implicit attitudes, p. 412

conformity, p. 415

normative social influence, p. 416

informational social influence, p. 416

obedience, p. 417

altruism, p. 423

prosocial behavior, p. 423

bystander effect, p. 425

diffusion of responsibility, p. 425

aggression, p. 426

social loafing, p. 429

social facilitation, p. 430

deindividuation, p. 430

persuasion, p. 431

Social Psychology

Studies how your thoughts, feelings, and behavior are influenced by the presence of other people and by the social and physical environment.

↓

An understanding of culture is particularly important for social psychology, although it has been long overlooked. Social psychologist **James Jackson** (1944–2020) was a leader in psychology research on Black people in the United States.

The New York Milk Bank, Inc.

Design Pics/Carson Ganci/Getty Images

Social Cognition

↓

Studies how we form impressions of others, how we interpret the meaning of other people's behavior, and how our behavior is affected by our attitudes.

Person Perception

Active process that occurs in an interpersonal context; influenced by:
- **Sense of self**
- Subjective perceptions
- **Social norms**
- Personal goals
- Self-perception

↓

Person perception can involve mental shortcuts:
- **Social categorization**
- **Explicit cognition**
- **Implicit cognition**
- **Implicit personality theories**

Attribution

Explaining the behavior of others can be affected by:
- **Fundamental attribution error**
- **Blaming the victim**
- **Hindsight bias**
- **Self-serving bias**
- **Self-effacing bias**
- **Just-world hypothesis**

Attitudes

- A learned tendency to evaluate an object, person, or issue in a particular way
- Can have cognitive, emotional, and behavioral components
- Although attitudes typically influence behavior, sometimes behavior influences our attitudes.

↓

When behavior conflicts with attitudes, **cognitive dissonance** may result.

Prejudice

A negative attitude toward people who belong to a specific group

Stereotypes:
- Form of social categorization in which characteristics are attributed to all members of a group
- Fostered by **ingroup** and **outgroup** thinking, and the **outgroup homogeneity effect.**
- **Ingroup bias** occurs when we attribute positive qualities to members of our own group.
- **Implicit attitudes** are evaluations that are automatic and unintentional.

Muzafer Sherif (1906–1988) and **Carolyn Wood Sherif** (1922–1982) Robbers Cave experiment; intergroup conflict can be decreased when groups engage in a cooperative effort.

Disney XD /Marvel Entertainment© ABC/ Getty Images

p.studio66/Shutterstock

Disney XD /Marvel Entertainment© ABC/ Getty Images

Social Influence

Social psychology research area that investigates how our behavior is affected by situational factors and other people

Conformity

When you adjust your opinions, judgments, or behavior in response to real or imagined group pressure, **normative social influence,** or **informational social influence**

Solomon Asch (1907–1996) Showed that people will conform to the majority opinion even when they know it is objectively wrong

Obedience

Performing a behavior in response to a direct command by an authority figure or person of higher status

Stanley Milgram (1933–1984) Studied obedience of destructive orders

Factors influencing obedience:
- Mental framework favoring obedience
- Situation or context
- Escalation of the task
- Experimenter's behavior
- Separation from victim
- Presence of others who resist

Altruism and Aggression

Prosocial behavior: Behavior that helps others
Altruism: Helping behavior with no expectation of personal gain or benefit

Bibb Latané (b. 1937) and **John Darley** (b. 1938) Studied the factors that influence whether people will help a stranger

Factors *increasing* helping behavior include the "feel good, do good" effect, guilt, and seeing others help. Factors *decreasing* helping behavior include the **bystander effect** and **diffusion of responsibility.**

Aggression: Verbal or physical behavior intended to cause harm to others

"Influence of Groups"

Social loafing: The tendency to expend less effort on a task when it is a group effort.

Social facilitation: The tendency for the presence of other people to enhance individual performance.

Deindividuation: The reduction of self awareness and inhibitions that can occur when a person is a part of a group whose members feel anonymous.

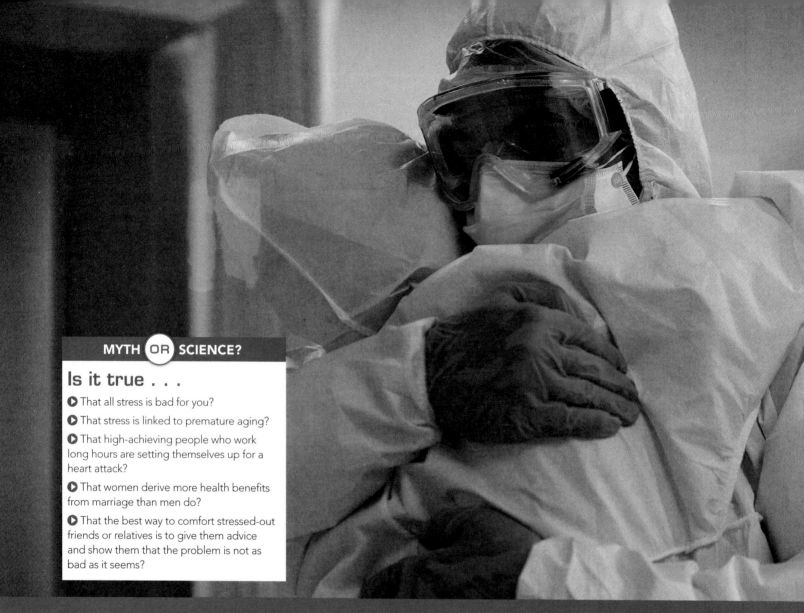

Stress, Health, and Coping

PROLOGUE

Stress and Health in the Time of COVID

In the early days of 2020, people in the United States began to hear news reports about a highly contagious, potentially lethal virus, first in China and then Italy. There had been similar reports of a "super virus" in 2013, but it didn't have a significant impact in the United States. Early 2020 was an entirely different scenario, though, starting on January 21 when the U.S. Centers for Disease Control and Prevention (2021b) confirmed that a case of COVID had been detected. Coronaviruses are a group of

highly contagious viruses that cause respiratory tract infections in humans. We will never know if it was the 2013 false alarm, restricted information flow, delayed governmental response, or even widespread disbelief of the existence of the virus among U.S. citizens, but the U.S. health care system, along with those of a number of other countries around the world, was woefully underprepared for the spread of this virus. The toll has been devastating. By the May, there had been well over 30 million cases in the United States and about 160 million globally (*The New York Times*, 2021a, 2021b). More than 550,000 had died in the United States, with the death count surpassing 3 million globally.

COVID has killed more people in the United States than the 418,500 soldiers and civilians who died during World War II, the (National World War II Museum, n.d.). Comparing the casualties of war to victims of a disease is unfortunately appropriate in the case of COVID. In the last year, frontline health care workers have been be forced into roles that bear a closer resemblance to battlefield medics than doctors and nurses who have been trained to deal with individual deaths. It had been years since most doctors and nurses were trained for a "multiple casualty" scenario in which they wouldn't have enough medical equipment required to treat people in need. They were not prepared for the

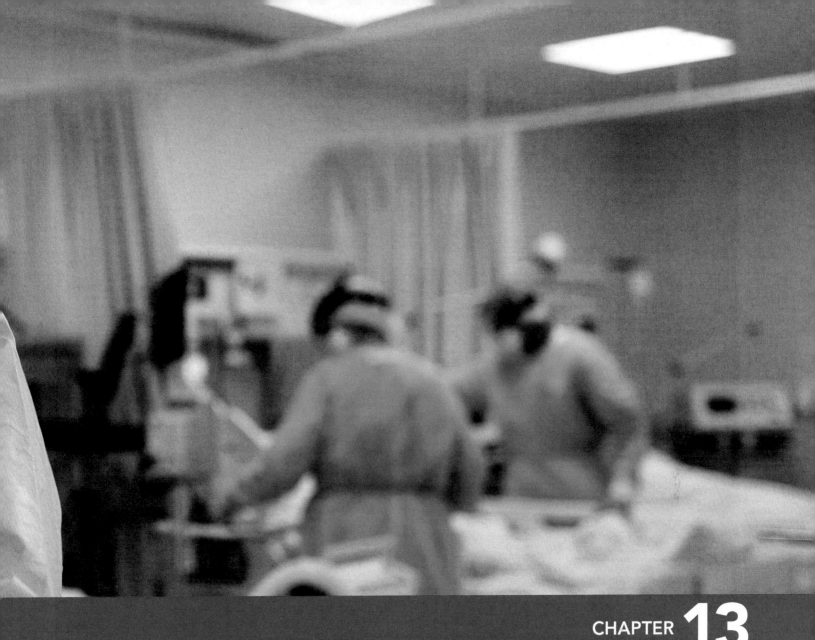
Tempura/Getty Images

makeshift treatment centers in hotels or the temporary morgues in refrigerator trucks. These medical professionals placed themselves in harm's way on a daily basis because of a highly contagious airborne virus. At the same time, they needed to protect themselves and the lives of their loved ones. The health concerns are obvious, but it is also a tremendous amount of stress to manage.

The nature of this virus meant that patients needed to be kept isolated from family members—even as they took their last breaths. Often, this left nurses in the position of sitting with dying patients and holding a smartphone while their family members said their remote goodbyes to their loved one, who was often unconscious and on a respirator.

Besides all that, doctors and nurses have been asked to take double and triple shifts—an attempt to care for more patients than the U.S. health care system is designed to treat. Again and again, comparisons were made to battlefield medics. And if there is one thing psychology has contributed to our understanding of soldiers, it is the fact that the experience of war is a uniquely intense and often traumatic type of psychological stress. In fact, we have even defined a constellation of symptoms that are now termed posttraumatic stress disorder (PTSD), which we will learn more

- INTRODUCTION: Stress and Health Psychology
- Physical Effects of Stress: The Mind–Body Connection
- Individual Factors That Influence the Response to Stress
- Coping: How People Deal with Stress
- Closing Thoughts
- PSYCH FOR YOUR LIFE: Minimizing the Effects of Stress

about in the next chapter. What is relevant to our frontline health care workers is the awareness that when the disease itself is under control, we will need to help our frontline workers cope with the long-lasting traumatic impact of the stress they have endured. There will be valuable lessons to be learned about how to train future health care workers for these types of scenarios.

In this chapter, we will examine how stress impacts humans physical and psychological health. Then we will discuss how important this understanding is for developing coping strategies that minimize the often long and dark shadow of disproportionate stress and trauma. ∿

Introduction: Stress and Health Psychology

■ KEY THEME
When events are perceived as exceeding your ability to cope with them, you experience an unpleasant emotional and physical state called stress.

⁼ KEY QUESTIONS
- What is health psychology, and what is the biopsychosocial model?
- How do life events, traumatic events, daily hassles, and burnout contribute to stress?
- What are some social and cultural sources of stress?

Most sources of stress are more mundane than a contagious and deadly virus. As a college student, you are no doubt familiar with feeling "stressed out." Juggling the demands of classes, work, friends, and family can be challenging. In fact, many of us have reported steadily increasing levels of stress in recent years, even before the pandemic (APA, 2019).

It will not surprise you to know that people in the United States experienced a significant increase in stress during the pandemic. In their annual *Stress in America*™ survey, the American Psychological Association asked 3,013 people to rate their level of stress on a scale of 1 to 10, where 1 meant "little to no stress" and 10 meant "a great deal of stress." In the pre-pandemic 2019 survey (APA, 2019), the average stress level in the United States was 4.9, already a worrisome level. But in the COVID-era 2020 survey (APA, 2020), the average stress level was 5.4, and when asked about their stress level related to the pandemic, the average stress level was 5.9. These are substantial one-year increases, and the numbers are even higher among parents of children ages 18 and younger—an alarming stress level of 6.7. Parents reported stress related to financial issues, their children's education, health care, and even "missing out on major milestones" like graduations.

In the United States and many other countries, **stress** is generally defined as *a negative emotional state occurring in response to events that are perceived as taxing or exceeding a person's resources or ability to cope.* This definition emphasizes the important role played by a person's evaluation, or *appraisal,* of events in the experience of stress. Developed by **Richard Lazarus** (1922–2002), the **cognitive appraisal model** is *a model of stress that emphasizes the role of an individual's evaluation (appraisal) of events and situations and of the resources that they have available to deal with the event or situation* (Lazarus & Folkman, 1984; Smith & Kirby, 2011).

If we think that we have adequate resources to deal with a situation, it will probably create little or no stress in our lives. But if we perceive our resources as being inadequate to deal with a situation we see as threatening, challenging, or even harmful, we'll experience the effects of stress. If our coping efforts are effective, stress will decrease. If they are ineffective, stress will increase. For example, you may have a month when you have unexpected expenses, but you regulate your stress response (as you know you have enough savings to cover the increased expenses). If you do not have enough savings to cover your monthly expenses, then you will likely experience stress. You might then look for other ways to deal with your money shortage, such as asking family members for help and/or working with bill collectors to reduce the amount they are asking for each month. Depending on how these (or other possible coping) attempts work, you will

stress A negative emotional state occurring in response to events that are perceived as taxing or exceeding a person's resources or ability to cope.

cognitive appraisal model of stress A model of stress that emphasizes the role of an individual's evaluation (appraisal) of events and situations and of the resources that they have available to deal with the event or situation.

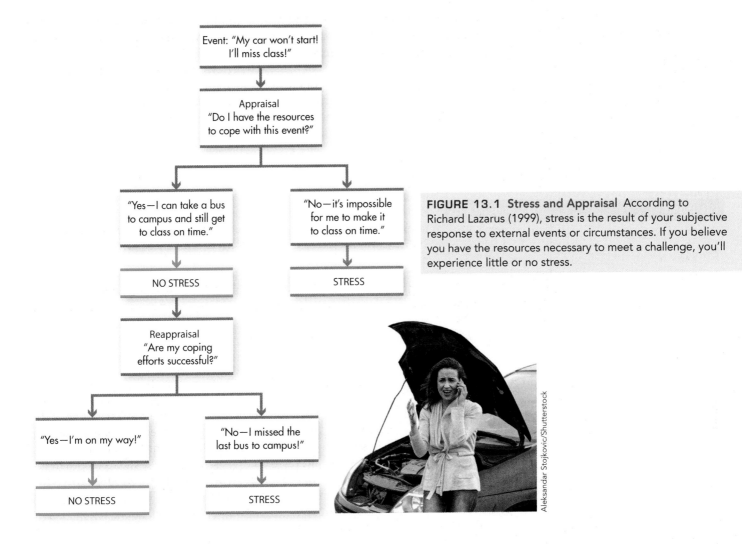

FIGURE 13.1 Stress and Appraisal According to Richard Lazarus (1999), stress is the result of your subjective response to external events or circumstances. If you believe you have the resources necessary to meet a challenge, you'll experience little or no stress.

likely feel increased or decreased stress. **Figure 13.1** depicts the relationship between stress and appraisal.

In this chapter, we'll take a close look at stress and its effects. **Health psychology** is *the branch of psychology that studies how biological, behavioral, and social factors influence health, illness, medical treatment, and health-related behaviors.* Health psychologists work with many different health care professionals, including physicians, nurses, social workers, and occupational and physical therapists. In both research and clinical practice, health psychologists are guided by the **biopsychosocial model**, which is *the belief that physical health and illness are determined by the complex interaction of biological, psychological, and social factors* (G. E. Miller et al., 2009). In this chapter, we'll look closely at the roles that different biological, psychological, and social factors play in our experience of health and illness.

Sources of Stress

Life is filled with potential **stressors**—*events or situations that are perceived as harmful, threatening, or challenging.* Virtually any event or situation can be a stressor if you question your ability or resources to deal effectively with it (Cooper & Dewe, 2007; Lazarus & Folkman, 1984). In this section, we'll survey some of the most important and common stressors.

Life Events and Change: Is *Any* Change Stressful? Early stress researchers Thomas Holmes and Richard Rahe (1967) believed that any change

health psychology The branch of psychology that studies how biological, behavioral, and social factors influence health, illness, medical treatment, and health-related behaviors.

biopsychosocial model The belief that physical health and illness are determined by the complex interaction of biological, psychological, and social factors.

stressors Events or situations that are perceived as harmful, threatening, or challenging.

that required you to adjust your behavior and lifestyle would cause stress. In an attempt to measure the amount of stress people experienced, they developed the *Social Readjustment Rating Scale (SRRS)*. The scale included 43 life events that are likely to require some level of change. Each life event was assigned a numerical rating of its relative impact, ranging from 11 to 100 *life change units* (see **Table 13.1**). Cross-cultural studies have shown that people in many different cultures tend to rank the magnitude of stressful events in a similar way (McAndrew et al., 1998; Noone, 2017; Wong & Wong, 2006).

According to the life events approach, *any* change, whether positive or negative, produces stress. Holmes and Rahe found that people who had accumulated more than 150 life change units within a calendar year had an increased rate of physical or psychological illness (Holmes & Masuda, 1974; Rahe, 1972). Some research has suggested that life events perceived as more unpleasant have a greater negative impact on health (Hatch & Dohrenwend, 2007). Currently, most researchers agree with these findings, and further note the importance of considering individual differences that can make any change a source of significant life stress itself (Kagan, 2016). As many psychologists have emphasized, it is the often the unexpected nature of life changes, or the uncertainty related to them, that causes some individuals stress (Brosschot et al., 2016).

The original life events scale has been revised and updated so that it better weighs the influences of gender, age, marital status, and other individual characteristics (Hobson & Delunas, 2001). New scales have also been developed for specific groups (Dohrenwend, 2006). For instance, the College Student Stress Scale measures unique experiences of college student life that contribute to stress, such as "flunking a class" and "difficulties with parents" (Feldt, 2008). Most recently, life events scales have also taken cross-cultural factors such as race and ethnicity into account. These factors are important to consider because they have been shown to increase stressful life events in and of themselves (Jean-Baptiste et al., 2020a, 2020b; 2021). Finally, it is worth noting that the type of stressful life events included here do not reflect the smaller, cumulative "daily hassles" that we will discuss shortly.

It is important to keep in mind the amount of stress an event produces might vary widely from one person to another. For example, if you are in a marriage filled with conflict, getting divorced (73 life change units) might be significantly less stressful than remaining married.

Traumatic Events One category of life events deserves special mention. *Traumatic events* are events or situations that are negative, severe, and far beyond our normal expectations for everyday life or life events (Magruder et al., 2017; Robinson & Larson, 2010). Witnessing or surviving a violent attack, being in a serious accident, and having experiences associated with combat, war, or major disasters are examples having of events that are typically considered to be traumatic. Due to the COVID pandemic, frontline health care workers are now in a higher-risk category for PTSD than before the pandemic.

Traumatic events are surprisingly common, especially among young adults. One large survey of university students found that 85 percent reported living through a traumatic event (Frazier et al., 2009). The most common traumatic events experienced by college students were the unexpected death of a loved one, sexual assault, and family violence.

Traumatic events, even relatively mild ones like a minor car accident, can be stressful. When traumas are intense or repeated, some psychologically vulnerable people may develop *posttraumatic stress disorder* (abbreviated *PTSD*). As we will see in the chapter on psychological disorders, PTSD is a disorder that involves intrusive thoughts of the traumatic

TABLE 13.1

The Social Readjustment Rating Scale: Sample Items

Life Event	Life Change Units
Death of spouse	100
Divorce	73
Marital separation	65
Death of close family member	63
Major personal injury or illness	53
Marriage	50
Fired at work	47
Retirement	45
Pregnancy	40
Change in financial state	38
Death of close friend	37
Change to different line of work	36
Mortgage or loan for major purchase	31
Foreclosure on mortgage or loan	30
Change in work responsibilities	29
Outstanding personal achievement	28
Begin or end school	26
Trouble with boss	23
Change in work hours or conditions	20
Change in residence	20
Change in social activities	18
Change in sleeping habits	16
Vacation	13
Christmas	12
Minor violations of the law	11

Source: Holmes & Rahe (1967).

The Social Readjustment Rating Scale, developed by Thomas Holmes and Richard Rahe (1967), was an early attempt to quantify the amount of stress experienced by people in a wide range of situations.

event, emotional numbness, and symptoms of anxiety, such as nervousness, sleep disturbances, and irritability. However, it's important to note that *most* people recover from traumatic events without ever developing PTSD (Howlett & Stein, 2016). For example, research shows that fewer than 10 percent of those exposed to traumatic events go on to develop PTSD, although the rate is much higher for victims of rape and violent assault (Breslau, 2012). Most people are remarkably resilient—a topic we discuss next.

Developing Resilience There's a famous saying that "whatever doesn't kill you makes you stronger." Psychologist Mark Seery and his colleagues (2010) set out to test that hypothesis in a multi-year, longitudinal study of the relationship between well-being and negative life events. They carefully measured health outcomes and the total amount of negative events experienced over a lifetime in a large, representative sample of U.S. adults.

Seery and his colleagues (2010) found that, as expected, *high* levels of total lifetime adversity were associated with poor health outcomes. But, it turned out, so were very *low* levels of adversity. As shown in **Figure 13.2**, faring best of all were people with a *moderate* level of adversity. They were not only healthier, but coped better with recent misfortune than people who had experienced either very low or high levels of adversity. Experiencing *some* stress was healthier than experiencing no stress at all.

Why might experiencing some adversity be healthier, in the long run, than living a charmed, stress-free life? Seery argues that people who are *never* exposed to stressful, difficult events don't develop the ability to cope with adversity when it does occur—as it eventually does. So, even minor setbacks can be perceived as overwhelming.

In contrast, people who have had to cope with a moderate level of adversity develop *resilience*—the ability to cope with stress and adversity, to adapt to negative or unforeseen circumstances, and to rebound after negative experiences. Just as moderate exercise builds muscle and aerobic capacity, leading to physical fitness, moderate experience of adversity builds resilience. Perhaps it's not surprising, then, that later research found that people with a moderate history of adverse life events coped better with two laboratory stressors than people with either a low or a high level of negative life events (Seery et al., 2013). They had a higher tolerance for physical pain and were less reactive to the psychological stress of taking a difficult test.

Daily Hassles What made you feel "stressed out" in the past week? Chances are, it was not a major life event. Instead, it was probably some unexpected but minor

▲ **Major Life Events and Stress** Would the birth of a child or losing your home in a fire both produce damaging levels of stress? According to the life events approach, any event that required you to change or adjust your lifestyle would produce significant stress—whether the event was positive or negative, planned or unexpected. How was the life events approach modified by later research?

MYTH ◀ SCIENCE

Is it true that all stress is bad for you?

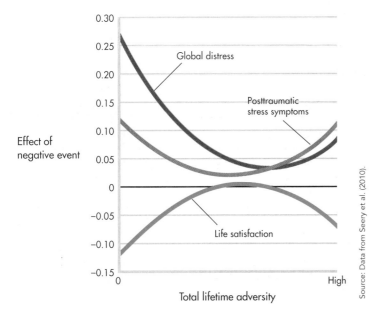

FIGURE 13.2 Whatever Doesn't Kill You Makes You Stronger Psychologist Mark Seery and his colleagues (2010) found that people who had experienced *some* adversity in their lives handled new stressors better than people who had experienced either a high level of adversity or none at all. After experiencing a significant negative event, they were less distressed (the purple line) and experienced fewer posttraumatic stress symptoms (the orange line). Even more important, they were generally happier with their lives (the green line) than people whose lives had been either very hard or relatively carefree.

Effect of negative event

Global distress

Posttraumatic stress symptoms

Life satisfaction

Total lifetime adversity

Source: Data from Seery et al. (2010).

daily hassles Everyday minor events that annoy and upset people.

TABLE 13.2

Examples of Daily Hassles

Daily Hassles Scale

- Concern about weight
- Concern about health of family member
- Not enough money for housing
- Too many things to do
- Misplacing or losing things
- Too many interruptions
- Don't like current work duties
- Traffic
- Car repairs or transportation problems

College Daily Hassles Scale

- Increased class workload
- Troubling thoughts about your future
- Fight with boyfriend/girlfriend
- Concerns about meeting high standards
- Wasting time
- Computer problems
- Concerns about failing a course
- Concerns about money

Acculturative Daily Hassles for Children

- It bothers me when people force me to be like everyone else.
- Because of the group I'm in, I don't get the grades I deserve.
- I don't feel at home here in the United States.
- People think I'm shy, when I really just have trouble speaking English.
- I think a lot about my group and its culture.

Sources: Research from Blankstein & Flett (1992); Kanner et al. (1981); Ross et al. (1999); Staats et al. (2007); Suarez-Morales et al. (2007).

Arguing that "daily hassles" could be just as stress-inducing as major life events, Richard Lazarus and his colleagues constructed a 117-item Daily Hassles Scale. Later, other researchers developed daily hassles scales for specific groups.

annoyance, such as splotching ketchup on your new T-shirt, misplacing your keys, or getting into an argument with your roommate.

Stress researcher Richard Lazarus and his colleagues suspected that such ordinary irritations in daily life might be an important source of stress. To explore this idea, they developed a scale measuring **daily hassles**—*everyday minor events that annoy and upset people* (DeLongis et al., 1982; Kanner et al., 1981). **Table 13.2** lists examples from the original Daily Hassles Scale and from other scales developed for specific populations.

The frequency of daily hassles, as well as a tendency to react more negatively to hassles, are linked to mental and physical illness, unhealthy behaviors, and decreased well-being (Charles et al., 2013; O'Connor et al., 2008). Some researchers have found that the number of daily hassles people experience is a better predictor of physical illness and symptoms than is the number of major life events experienced (Almeida et al., 2005).

Why do daily hassles take such a toll? One explanation is that such minor stressors are *cumulative* (Asselmann et al., 2017; Grzywacz & Almeida, 2008). Each hassle may be relatively unimportant in itself, but after a day or two filled with minor hassles, the effects add up. People feel drained, grumpy, and stressed out.

Daily hassles also contribute to the stress produced by major life events. Any major life change can create a ripple effect, generating a host of new daily hassles (Maybery et al., 2007). For example, although the COVID pandemic has been a source of large life stressors, it has also caused daily hassles on a smaller scale. During the pandemic, people were asked to wear masks, keep six feet of social distance from other people in public, and wash their hands or use hand sanitizer multiple times per day (giving many people dry, cracked skin). And don't forget the the hassle of sourcing suddenly hard-to-find products like masks and hand sanitizer—and, early in the pandemic, toilet paper!

▲ **Major Life Events, Daily Hassles, and Stress: The COVID Pandemic** After the world was consumed with COVID, a highly contagious and potentially lethal virus, people were forced to make significant changes to their everyday lives. Before vaccines were available, people were asked to wear medical face masks when outside of their own homes and to avoid close contact with large groups. It was also recommended by the Centers for Disease Control that individuals avoid close contact like hugging, kissing, or even handshaking with anyone outside of those with whom they lived. Here, two school children engage in an "elbow bump" something that came about to cope with the stress of social isolation and affirm social relationships. The daily hassles created by the pandemic added to the high levels of stress felt by all those affected.

Are there gender differences in the experience of daily hassles? Interpersonal conflict is the most common source of daily stress for *both* men and women (Almeida et al., 2005). However, women are more likely to report daily stress that is associated with friends and family, while men are more likely to feel hassled by stressors that are school- or work-related (Zwicker & DeLongis, 2010). For both sexes, stress at work or school tends to affect home life (Asselmann et al., 2017; Bodenmann et al., 2010). For women, daily stress tends to spill over into their interactions with their partners. Men, on the other hand, are more likely to simply withdraw. In fact, one study found that the most likely place to find a father after a stressful day at work was sitting alone in a room (Repetti et al., 2009).

Work Stress and Burnout: Is It Quitting Time Yet? Whether due to concerns about job security, unpleasant working conditions, difficult supervisors, or unreasonable demands and deadlines, *work stress* can produce a pressure cooker environment that takes a significant toll on your physical health (Nakao, 2010). Even before the pandemic, work stress could increase the likelihood of unhealthy behaviors.

Burnout is *an unhealthy condition caused by chronic, prolonged work stress that is characterized by exhaustion, cynicism, and a sense of failure or inadequacy*. In essence, burnout develops when job demands exceed job resources (Bakker & Demerouti, 2017; Demerouti et al., 2010). There are three key components of burnout (Maslach & Leiter, 2005, 2008). First, people feel *exhausted,* as if they've used up all of their emotional and physical resources. Second, people experience feelings of *cynicism,* demonstrating negative or overly detached attitudes toward the job or work environment. People also often feel unappreciated (Demerouti et al., 2010). Third, people feel a sense of *failure or inadequacy.* They may feel incompetent and unproductive and have a sharply reduced sense of accomplishment. In fact, some researchers have observed a great deal of overlap between the symptoms of burnout and the symptoms of major depressive disorder (Bianchi et al., 2015).

One workplace condition that commonly produces burnout is work *overload,* when the demands of the job exceed the worker's ability to meet them (Maslach & Leiter, 2008). A second is *lack of control.* Generally, the more control you have over your work and work environment, the less stressful it is (Q. Wang et al., 2010). Complex, demanding jobs are much less likely to produce feelings of overload, burnout, or stress when workers have control over how they perform those jobs (Chung-Yan, 2010). Burnout was particularly pronounced during the pandemic among women, many of whom had increased workloads at home, and among frontline workers (e.g., Aldossari & Chaudhry, 2020; White et al., 2021).

However, even in high-stress occupations or demanding work environments, burnout can be prevented. Burnout is least likely to occur when there is a sense of *community* in the workplace (Maslach & Leiter, 2008; Woodhead et al., 2014). Supportive coworkers, a sense of teamwork, and a positive work environment can all buffer workplace stress and prevent burnout. So, too, can *job crafting*—a term used to describe actions employees take to proactively change either the demands of the job or their personal resources (Bakker & Demerouti, 2017; Tims et al., 2013). Examples might be seeking to learn new skills, assuming more (or fewer) responsibilities, or finding ways to make your job more personally meaningful, such as mentally reframing a sales job as "helping customers" rather than "selling products."

Social and Cultural Sources of Stress For disadvantaged groups exposed to crime, poverty, substandard housing, and pollution and other forms of environmental degradation, including disproportionate levels of police brutality, everyday living conditions can be a significant source of stress (Haushofer & Fehr, 2014; King & Ogle, 2014). People who live under difficult or unpleasant conditions often experience *chronic* stress, which means it is ongoing (Adler & Rehkopf, 2008; Destin, 2019). This is of particular concern among Black Americans,

burnout An unhealthy condition caused by chronic, prolonged work stress that is characterized by exhaustion, cynicism, and a sense of failure or inadequacy.

FIGURE 13.3 Subjective Socioeconomic Status and Health The *objective* socioeconomic status of a group of volunteers was assessed in terms of income level and education. The volunteers' *subjective* social status was assessed them to indicate where they thought they stood relative to other people in the United States in terms of income, education, and occupation. All the volunteers were then exposed to a cold virus. Even after controlling for factors such as smoking and other risk factors, Sheldon Cohen and his colleagues (2008) found that subjective, rather than objective, social status was associated with susceptibility to infection. Regardless of their objective socioeconomic status, participants who perceived themselves as being lower in social status were more susceptible to infection than those who did not.

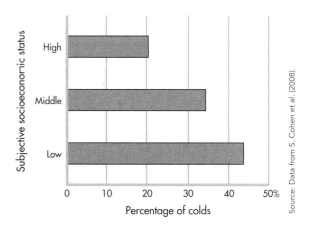

Source: Data from S. Cohen et al. (2008).

who face disproportionate levels of violence and police brutality, which have significant and long-lasting negative effects on physical and psychological health (Rivara et al., 2019).

Chronic stress is also associated with lower *socioeconomic status* (SES), which is a measure of overall status in society (Chandola & Marmot, 2011). The core components of SES are income, education, and occupation. One finding that has been consistent over time and across multiple cultures is the strong association of physical health and longevity with SES (Adler, 2009).

People in lower SES groups tend to experience more negative life events *and* more daily hassles than people in more privileged groups (Hatch & Dohrenwend, 2007). People in less privileged groups also tend to have fewer resources to help them cope with the stressors that they do experience. Thus, it's not surprising that people in the lowest socioeconomic levels tend to have the highest levels of psychological distress, illness, and premature death (Bale & Jovanovic, 2020; Braveman et al., 2010).

Beyond these external factors, low social status is in itself highly stressful (Hackman et al., 2010). Many studies have shown that perceiving yourself as being of low social status is associated with poorer physical health—*regardless* of your objective social status as measured by traditional SES measures (Adler, 2009; Derry et al., 2013; Goodman et al., 2015; Rahal et al., 2020).

The powerful effects of perceived social status were demonstrated in a study by Sheldon Cohen and his colleagues (Cohen, 2016; Cohen et al., 2008). Volunteers were exposed to a cold virus (see **Figure 13.3**). The volunteers who saw themselves as being low on a measure of social status relative to others social status had higher rates of infection than volunteers who *objectively* matched them on social status measures but *subjectively* did not see themselves as being of low status.

Racism and discrimination, including on the basis of religion, sexual orientation, or gender identity, are other important sources of chronic stress for many people (Brondolo et al., 2011; Ong et al., 2009; Rivara et al., 2019). In one survey, for example, more than three-quarters of Black adolescents reported being treated as incompetent or dangerous—or both—because of their race (Sellers et al., 2006). Such subtle instances of racism, called *microaggressions,* take a cumulative toll (Schmitt et al., 2014; Sue et al., 2008). Whether it's subtle or blatant, racism significantly contributes to the chronic stress often experienced by members of minoritized groups. Racism can also increase the risk for stress-related health problems such as hypertension (Churchwell et al., 2020; Hicken et al., 2014; Rivara et al., 2020; Serchen et al., 2020).

Stress can also result when cultures clash. For refugees, immigrants, and their children, adapting to a new culture can be extremely stressful (Berry, 2003; Jamil et al., 2007). The Culture and Human Behavior box "The Stress of Adapting to a New Culture" describes factors that influence the degree of stress experienced by people encountering a new culture.

acculturative stress (uh-CUL-chur-uh-tiv) The stress that results from the pressure of adapting to a new culture.

CULTURE AND HUMAN BEHAVIOR

The Stress of Adapting to a New Culture

Refugees, immigrants, and even international students are often unprepared for the dramatically different values, language, food, customs, and climate that await them in their new land. The process of changing one's values and customs as a result of contact with another culture is referred to as *acculturation*. **Acculturative stress** is *the stress that results from the pressure of adapting to a new culture* (Sam & Berry, 2010).

Cross-cultural psychologist John Berry (2003, 2006) has found that a person's attitudes are important in determining how much acculturative stress is experienced (Sam & Berry, 2010). When people encounter a new cultural environment, they are faced with two questions: (1) Should I seek positive relations with the dominant society? (2) Is my original cultural identity of value to me, and should I try to maintain it?

The answers produce one of four possible patterns of acculturation: integration, assimilation, separation, or marginalization (see the diagram). Each pattern represents a different way of coping with the stress of adapting to a new culture (Berry, 1994, 2003).

Integrated individuals continue to value their original cultural customs but also seek to become part of the dominant society. They embrace a *bicultural* identity (Huynh et al., 2011). Biculturalism is associated with higher self-esteem and lower levels of depression, anxiety, and stress, on average, suggesting that the bicultural identity may be the most adaptive acculturation pattern (Schwartz et al., 2010). In fact, a meta-analysis of 83 studies showed that biculturalism had the strongest association with psychological and social adjustment (Nguyen & Benet-Martínez, 2013). The successfully integrated individual's level of acculturative stress will be low (Y. Lee, 2010).

Assimilated individuals give up their old cultural identity and try to become part of the new society. They adopt the customs and social values of the new environment, and abandon their original cultural traditions.

Assimilation usually involves a moderate level of stress, partly because it involves a psychological loss—one's previous cultural identity. People who follow this pattern also face the possibility of being rejected either by members of the majority culture or by members of their original culture (Schwartz et al., 2010). The process of learning new behaviors and suppressing old behaviors can also be moderately stressful.

Individuals who follow the pattern of *separation* maintain their cultural identity and avoid contact with the new culture. They may refuse to learn the new language, live in a neighborhood that is

Sean Gallup/Getty Images

▲ **Acculturative Stress** Acculturative stress can be reduced when immigrants learn the language and customs of their newly adopted home. Here, students from countries as diverse as Afghanistan, Iran, Chechnya, and Somalia attend government-sponsored language classes in Potsdam, Germany.

primarily populated by others of the same ethnic background, and socialize only with members of their own ethnic group.

In some cases, separation is not voluntary but is due to the dominant society's unwillingness to accept the new immigrants. Thus, it can be the result of discrimination. Whether voluntary or involuntary, the level of acculturative stress associated with separation tends to be high.

Finally, *marginalized* people lack cultural and psychological contact with *both* their traditional cultural group and the culture of their new society. Marginalization leads to the loss of important features of their traditional culture without replacing them with a new cultural identity.

Although rare, the path of marginalization is associated with the greatest degree of acculturative stress. Marginalized individuals are stuck in an unresolved conflict between their traditional culture and the new society, and may feel as if they don't really belong anywhere. Fortunately, only a small percentage of immigrants fall into this category (Schwartz et al., 2010).

Source: Research from Sam & Berry (2010).

		Question 1: Should I seek positive relations with the dominant society?	
		Yes	**No**
Question 2: Is my original cultural identity of value to me, and should I try to maintain it?	**Yes**	Integration	Separation
	No	Assimilation	Marginalization

‹ **Patterns of Adapting to a New Culture** According to cross-cultural psychologist John Berry, there are four basic patterns of adapting to a new culture (Sam & Berry, 2010). Which pattern is followed depends on how the person responds to the two key questions shown.

Physical Effects of Stress: The Mind–Body Connection

■ KEY THEME

Stress affects physical health through its effects on the endocrine system, the immune system, and chromosomes.

≡ KEY QUESTIONS

- What endocrine pathways are involved in the fight-or-flight response and the general adaptation syndrome?
- What are telomeres, and how are they affected by acute and chronic stress?
- What is psychoneuroimmunology, and how does the immune system interact with the nervous system?

From headaches to heart attacks, stress contributes to a wide range of disorders, especially when it is long-term, or chronic. Basically, stress appears to undermine physical well-being in two ways: indirectly and directly.

First, stress can *indirectly* affect a person's health by prompting behaviors that jeopardize physical well-being, such as not eating or sleeping properly or failing to get enough exercise (Habhab et al., 2009; Mezick et al., 2009; Stults-Kolehmainen & Sinha, 2014). High levels of stress can also interfere with cognitive abilities, such as attention, concentration, memory, and decision making (McNeil & Morgan, 2010; Thompson, 2010). In turn, such cognitive disruptions can increase the likelihood of accidents and injuries.

Second, stress can *directly* affect physical health by altering body functions, leading to physical symptoms, illness, or disease (Zachariae, 2009). For example, people who are under a great deal of stress often tighten their neck and head muscles, resulting in tension headaches. Even stress experienced early in life is associated with cancer or diabetes later in life (Fagundes & Way, 2014). But exactly how do stressful events influence bodily processes, such as muscle contractions?

Stress and the Endocrine System

To explain the connection between stress and health, researchers have focused on how the nervous system, including the brain, interacts with two other important body systems: the endocrine and immune systems. We'll first consider the role of the endocrine system in our response to stressful events and then look at the connections between stress and the immune system.

Walter Cannon: Stress and the Fight-or-Flight Response

Any kind of immediate threat to your well-being is a stress-producing experience that triggers a cascade of changes in your body. As we've noted in previous chapters, this *rapidly occurring chain of internal physical reactions that prepare people to either fight or take flight from an immediate threat* is called the **fight-or-flight response**.

The fight-or-flight response was first described by American physiologist **Walter Cannon** (1875–1945), one of the earliest contributors to stress research. Cannon (1932) found that the fight-or-flight response involved both the sympathetic nervous system and the endocrine system (see the chapter on neuroscience and behavior).

With the perception of a threat, the hypothalamus and lower brain structures activate the fight or flight response, which in turn, stimulates the sympathetic nervous system (see left side of **Figure 13.4**). The sympathetic nervous system then triggers the adrenal glands to secrete **catecholamines**, which are *hormones secreted by the adrenal medulla that cause rapid physiological arousal and include adrenaline and noradrenaline.* Circulating through the blood, these hormones trigger the rapid and intense bodily changes associated with the survival-related aspects of the fight-or-flight response. Once the threat is removed, the high level of bodily arousal subsides gradually, usually within about 20 to 60 minutes.

As a short-term reaction, the fight-or-flight response helps ensure survival by swiftly mobilizing internal physical resources to defensively attack or flee an immediate threat. Without question, the fight-or-flight response is useful if you're suddenly faced with a life-threatening situation. However, if exposure to a threat is prolonged, the intense arousal

fight-or-flight response Rapidly occurring chain of internal physical reactions that prepare people to either fight or take flight from an immediate threat.

catecholamines (cat-uh-COLE-uh-meenz) Hormones secreted by the adrenal medulla that cause rapid physiological arousal and include adrenaline and noradrenaline.

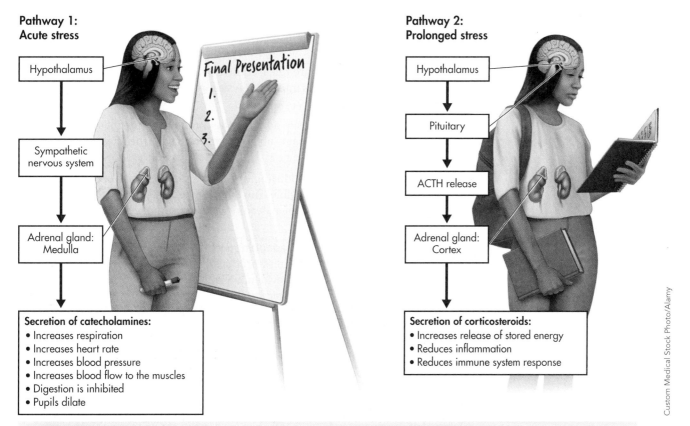

Pathway 1: Acute stress

Hypothalamus → Sympathetic nervous system → Adrenal gland: Medulla →

Secretion of catecholamines:
- Increases respiration
- Increases heart rate
- Increases blood pressure
- Increases blood flow to the muscles
- Digestion is inhibited
- Pupils dilate

Final Presentation
1.
2.
3.

Pathway 2: Prolonged stress

Hypothalamus → Pituitary → ACTH release → Adrenal gland: Cortex →

Secretion of corticosteroids:
- Increases release of stored energy
- Reduces inflammation
- Reduces immune system response

Custom Medical Stock Photo/Alamy

FIGURE 13.4 Endocrine System Pathways in Stress Two different endocrine system pathways are involved in the response to stress (Joëls & Baram, 2009). Walter Cannon identified the endocrine pathway shown on the left side of this diagram. This is the pathway involved in the fight-or-flight response to immediate threats. Hans Selye identified the endocrine pathway shown on the right. This second endocrine pathway plays an important role in dealing with prolonged, or chronic, stressors.

of the fight-or-flight response can also become prolonged. Part of the human experience often involves intense and prolonged stress even in situations that are not life-threatening. As neuroscientist Robert Sapolsky (2008) points out, "No zebra on earth, running for its life, would understand why fear of speaking in public would cause you to secrete the same hormones that it's doing at that point to save its life." Under these conditions, Cannon believed, a prolonged fight-or-flight response could prove harmful to physical health.

Hans Selye: Stress and the General Adaptation Syndrome Cannon's suggestion that prolonged stress could be physically harmful was confirmed by Canadian endocrinologist **Hans Selye**. Selye found that rats exposed to prolonged stressors exhibited a similar pattern of physiological changes. Their adrenal glands became enlarged while immune system glands shrank, and they lost weight and developed ulcers. Selye believed that these distinct physical changes represented the essential effects of stress—the body's response to any demand placed on it.

Selye (1956, 1976) found that prolonged stress activates a second endocrine pathway (see Figure 13.4) that involves the hypothalamus, the pituitary gland, and the adrenal cortex. In response to a stressor, the hypothalamus signals the pituitary gland to secrete a hormone called *adrenocorticotropic hormone*, abbreviated *ACTH*. In turn, ACTH stimulates the adrenal cortex to release *corticosteroids*, the most important of which are the *glucocorticoids*, including cortisol. **Corticosteroids** are *hormones released by the adrenal cortex that play a key role in the body's response to long-term stressors.*

In the short run, the stress hormones provide several benefits, helping protect the body against the harm caused by stressors. For example, cortisol reduces inflammation of body tissues and enhances muscle tone in the heart and blood vessels. However, unlike the effects of adrenaline and noradrenaline, which tend to diminish rather quickly, cortisol may have long-lasting effects. If a stressor is prolonged, continued high levels of cortisol can weaken important body systems, lowering immunity and increasing susceptibility to physical symptoms of illness.

John Olson/Getty Images

▲ **A Pioneer in Stress Research** With his tie off and his feet up, Canadian endocrinologist Hans Selye (1907–1982) looks the picture of relaxation. Selye documented the physical effects of exposure to prolonged stress. His popular book *The Stress of Life* (1956) helped make *stress* a household word.

corticosteroids (core-tick-oh-STER-oydz) Hormones released by the adrenal cortex that play a key role in the body's response to long-term stressors.

general adaptation syndrome Hans Selye's term for the three-stage progression of physical changes that occur when an organism is exposed to intense and prolonged stress. The three stages are alarm, resistance, and exhaustion.

telomeres Repeated, duplicate DNA sequences that are found at the very tips of chromosomes and that protect the chromosomes' genetic data during cell division.

immune system Body system that produces specialized white blood cells that protect the body from viruses, bacteria, and tumor cells.

psychoneuroimmunology The scientific study of the connections among psychological processes (psycho-), the nervous system (-neuro-), and the immune system (-immunology).

The **general adaptation syndrome** is *Hans Selye's term for the three-stage progression of physical changes that occur when an organism is exposed to intense and prolonged stress. The three stages are alarm, resistance, and exhaustion.*

1. *Alarm stage:* Catecholamines are released by the adrenal medulla. Intense arousal occurs, and the body mobilizes internal physical resources to meet the demands of the stress-producing event.

2. *Resistance stage:* As the body tries to adapt to the continuing stressful situation, physiological arousal lessens but remains above normal. Because the stress response system is already taxed, resistance to new stressors is impaired.

3. *Exhaustion stage:* If the stress-producing event persists, the symptoms of the alarm stage reappear, only now irreversibly. The body's energy reserves become depleted and adaptation begins to break down, leading to exhaustion, physical disorders, and, potentially, death.

Selye's description of the general adaptation syndrome firmly established some of the critical biological links between stress-producing events and their potential impact on physical health. There is mounting evidence that chronic stress can lead to increased vulnerability to acute and chronic physical diseases, as well as psychological problems (Biggs et al., 2017; Hammen, 2005; G. E. Miller et al., 2009). And, as we'll see in the next section, there is new evidence explaining the link between chronic stress and premature aging.

Stress, Chromosomes, and Aging: The Telomere Story

Diseases associated with aging and even premature aging itself have long been associated with chronic stress (Epel, 2009a; Kiecolt-Glaser & Glaser, 2010). But how might psychological stress affect physical aging?

One part of the answer may ultimately be found in the chromosomes. **Telomeres** are *repeated, duplicate DNA sequences that are found at the very tips of chromosomes and that protect the chromosomes' genetic data during cell division* (see **Figure 13.5**). Like the plastic tips that protect shoelaces from fraying, telomeres protect the genetic data in the chromosomes from being broken or scrambled during cell division. With each cell division, the string of telomeres gets shorter. When telomeres become too short, the cell can no longer divide and may die or atrophy, causing tissue damage or loss. It is true that stress is linked to premature aging. A growing body of literature has linked shorter telomeres with aging, age-related diseases, and mortality (see Blackburn & Epel, 2017).

Although telomere length is roughly reflective of a cell's age, the story is not that simple. Surprisingly, telomeres can also *lengthen* in response to physiological changes (Epel, 2009b). An enzyme called *telomerase* has the capacity to add DNA to shortened telomeres, rebuilding and extending the length of telomeres (Epel et al., 2010).

Could telomeres be implicated in the link between stress and premature aging? The tentative answer seems to be *yes*. First, several studies have linked elevated levels of stress hormones to shorter telomeres (see Epel, 2009b). Second, researchers have

MYTH ▶ SCIENCE

Is it true that stress is linked to premature aging?

FIGURE 13.5 Telomeres As shown in the drawing, *telomeres* are short, repeated DNA sequences that are found at the very pink tips of chromosomes (Epel, 2009b). In the photo, the telomeres are the fluorescent pink tips on the blue-stained human chromosomes. As we age, cells divide and telomeres get progressively shorter. However, an enzyme called *telomerase* can protect and even lengthen telomeres. Psychologists are actively studying the environmental factors that affect telomere length, including behavioral interventions that increase telomerase activity (Blackburn & Epel, 2012, 2017; Jacobs et al., 2011).

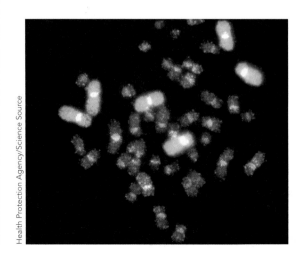

Health Protection Agency/Science Source

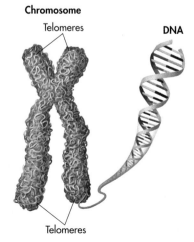

Chromosome
Telomeres
DNA
Telomeres

discovered that people who are under chronic stress tend to have shortened telomeres (Schutte & Malouff, 2014). For example, 9-year-old boys living in a stressful family environment had telomeres that were, on average, 40 percent shorter than those in 9-year-old boys living in nurturing family environments (Mitchell et al., 2014). Shortened telomeres have also been found among Black women who report experiencing institutional racism, and feel unable to seek out social support from others (Lu et al., 2019).

Although research on telomeres and telomerase activity is still in its infancy, new findings suggest potential interventions that might someday be used to target telomeres to improve health and prevent age-related degenerative diseases. For example, research suggests that engaging in healthy behaviors—such as eating well, exercising, and getting enough sleep—helps protect telomeres from the effects of stress (Puterman et al., 2010, 2015). Researchers are also actively investigating the impact of factors like stress management, meditation, social support, and diet on telomeres (see Blackburn & Epel, 2017; Lu et al., 2019).

Stress and the Immune System

The **immune system** is the *body system that produces specialized white blood cells that protect the body from viruses, bacteria, and tumor cells.* Your immune system comprises several organs, including bone marrow, the spleen, the thymus, and the lymph nodes (see **Figure 13.6**). The most important elements of the immune system are *lymphocytes*—the specialized white blood cells that fight bacteria, viruses, and other foreign invaders. Lymphocytes are initially manufactured in the bone marrow. From the bone marrow, they migrate to other immune system organs, such as the thymus and spleen, where they develop more fully and are stored until needed.

Psychoneuroimmunology   Until the 1970s, the immune system was thought to be completely independent of other body systems, including the nervous and endocrine systems. Thus, most scientists believed that psychological processes could not influence the immune system response.

However, research in a new interdisciplinary field called *psychoneuroimmunology* helped establish that there are many interconnections among these systems, including the brain (Ader, 1993). **Psychoneuroimmunology** is *the scientific study of the connections among psychological processes* (psycho-), *the nervous system* (-neuro-), *and the immune system* (-immunology).

First, the central nervous system and the immune system are *directly* linked via sympathetic nervous system fibers, which influence the production and functioning of lymphocytes.

Second, the surfaces of lymphocytes contain receptor sites for neurotransmitters and hormones, including catecholamines and cortisol. Thus, rather than operating independently, the activities of lymphocytes and the immune system are directly influenced by neurotransmitters, hormones, and other chemical messengers from the nervous and endocrine systems.

Third, psychoneuroimmunologists have discovered that lymphocytes themselves *produce* neurotransmitters and hormones. These neurotransmitters and hormones, in turn, influence the nervous and endocrine systems. In other words, there is ongoing interaction and communication among the nervous system, the endocrine system, and the immune system (Kendall-Tackett, 2010). Each system influences *and* is influenced by the other systems (Kiecolt-Glaser, 2009).

Stressors That Can Influence the Immune System   When researchers began studying how stress affects the immune system, they initially focused on extremely stressful events, such as the reentry of returning astronauts or being forced to stay awake for days (see Kiecolt-Glaser & Glaser, 1993). These highly stressful events, it turned out, were associated with reduced immune system functioning.

Further research found that immune system functioning was also affected by more common stresses. For example, the stress caused by the end or disruption of important interpersonal relationships impairs immune function, putting people at greater risk for health problems (Kiecolt-Glaser et al., 2009; Wright & Loving, 2011). And perhaps not surprisingly, chronic stressors that continue for years, such as caring for a family member with Alzheimer's disease, also diminish immune system functioning (Jeckel et al., 2010). Even

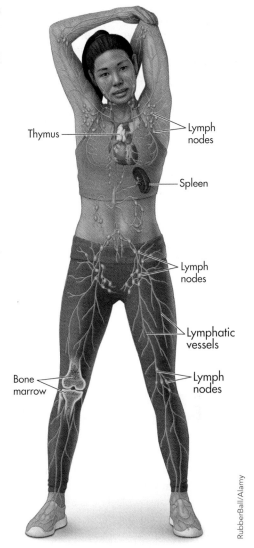

FIGURE 13.6 The Immune System Your immune system battles bacteria, viruses, and other foreign invaders that try to set up housekeeping in your body. The specialized white blood cells that fight infection are manufactured in the bone marrow and are stored in the thymus, spleen, and lymph nodes until needed.

RubberBall/Alamy

FIGURE 13.7 Stress and the Common Cold Are you more likely to catch a cold if you're under a great deal of stress? In a classic series of studies, Sheldon Cohen and his colleagues (1991, 1993) measured levels of psychological stress in healthy volunteers, then exposed them to a cold virus. They found an almost perfect relationship between the level of stress and the rate of infection. The higher the volunteers' psychological stress level, the higher the rate of respiratory infection.

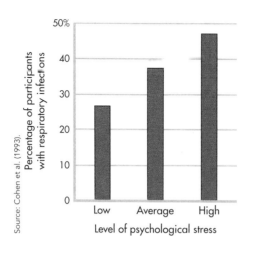

Source: Cohen et al. (1993).

ordinary stressors, such as marital arguments or the pressure of exams, can adversely affect the immune system (Lester et al., 2010).

What are the practical implications of reduced immune system functioning? One consistent finding is that psychological stress increases the length of time it takes for a wound to heal. In one study, dental students volunteered to receive two small puncture wounds on the roofs of their mouths (Marucha et al., 1998). To compare the impact of stress on wound healing, the students received the first wound when they were on summer vacation and the second wound three days before their first major exam during the fall term. The results? The wounds inflicted before the major test healed an average of 40 percent more slowly—an extra three days—than the wounds inflicted on the same volunteers during summer vacation. Other studies have shown similar findings (Glaser & Kiecolt-Glaser, 2005; Gouin & Kiecolt-Glaser, 2012).

What about the relationship between stress and infection? In a series of carefully controlled studies, psychologist Sheldon Cohen and his colleagues (2006, 2012) demonstrated that people who are experiencing high levels of stress are more susceptible to infection by a cold virus than people who are not under stress (see **Figure 13.7**).

🧠 FOCUS ON NEUROSCIENCE

The Mysterious Placebo Effect

The placebo effect is perhaps one of the most dramatic examples of how cognitive activity—in this case, beliefs—influences physiological responses. A placebo is an inactive substance with no known effects, such as a sugar pill or an injection of sterile water. Placebos are often used in biomedical research to help gauge the effectiveness of an actual medication or treatment. But after being given a placebo, many research participants, including those suffering from pain or diseases, experience benefits from the placebo treatment (Klinger et al., 2014). How can this be explained?

One possible way that placebos might reduce pain is by activating the brain's own natural painkillers—the *endorphins*. (The endorphins are structurally similar to opioid painkillers, like morphine.) One reason for believing this is that a drug called *naloxone*, which blocks the brain's endorphin response, also blocks the painkilling effects of placebos (Price et al., 2008). Might placebos reduce pain by activating the brain's natural opioid network?

A brain imaging study by Swedish neuroscientist Predrag Petrovic and his colleagues (2002) tackled this question. In the study, painfully hot metal was placed on the back of each volunteer's hand. Each volunteer was then given an injection of either an actual opioid painkiller or a saline solution placebo. About 30 seconds later, positron emission tomography (PET) was used to scan the participants' brain activity.

Both the volunteers who received the painkilling drug *and* the volunteers who received the placebo treatment reported that the injection provided pain relief. In the two PET scans shown here, you can see that the genuine painkilling drug (left) and the placebo (right) activated the same brain area, called the *anterior cingulate cortex* (marked by the cross). The anterior cingulate cortex is known to

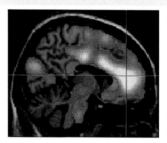 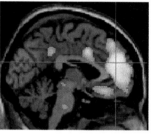

Received opioid painkiller   **Received placebo**

Republished with permission of American Association for the Advancement of Science, (Left) Figure 1b (Right) Figure 3a from Petrovic, Predrag; Kalso, Eija; Petersson, Karl M.; & Ingvar, Martin. (2002). Placebo and opioid analgesia—Imaging a shared neuronal network. *Science, 295*(5560), 1737–1740. https://doi.org/10.1126/science.1067176. Permission conveyed through Copyright Clearance Center, Inc.

contain many opioid receptors. Interestingly, the level of brain activity was directly correlated with the participants' perception of pain relief. The PET scan on the right shows the brain activity of those participants who had strong placebo responses.

Many questions remain about exactly how placebos work, but studies by Petrovic (2010) and others have substantiated the biological reality of the placebo effect. For example, Jon-Kar Zubieta and his colleagues (2005) showed that a placebo treatment activated opioid receptors in several brain regions associated with pain. Further, the greater the activation, the higher the level of pain individual volunteers tolerated. As these studies show, cognitive expectations, learned associations, and emotional responses can have a profound effect on the perception of pain. Research has also demonstrated that placebos produce measurable effects on other types of brain processes, including those of people experiencing Parkinson's disease or major depressive disorder (de la Fuente-Fernández, 2009; Hunter et al., 2009).

Participants who experienced *chronic* stressors that lasted a month or longer were *most* likely to develop colds after being exposed to a cold virus. One reason may be that chronic stress triggers the secretion of corticosteroids, which affect immune system functioning. Other research has shown that stress interferes with the effectiveness of influenza vaccinations (Pedersen et al., 2009).

Health psychologists have found that a wide variety of stressors are associated with diminished immune system functioning, increasing the risk of health problems and slowing recovery times (see Kiecolt-Glaser, 2009). However, while stress-related decreases in immune system functioning may heighten our susceptibility to health problems, exposure to stressors does not automatically translate into poorer health.

First, although prolonged, chronic stress impairs immune functioning, remember that acute, short-term stress actually enhances immune functioning (Dhabhar, 2011; Groer et al., 2010). Second, physical health is affected by the interaction of many factors, including heredity, nutrition, health-related habits, and access to medical care. Of course, your level of exposure to bacteria, viruses, and other sources of infection or disease will also influence your likelihood of becoming sick.

Finally, the simple fact is that some people are more vulnerable to the negative effects of stress than others. Why? As you'll see in the next section, researchers have found that a wide variety of psychological factors can influence people's reactions to stressors (Pedersen et al., 2011).

Individual Factors That Influence the Response to Stress

■ KEY THEME
Psychologists have identified several psychological factors that can modify an individual's response to stress and affect physical health.

≡ KEY QUESTIONS
- How do feelings of control, explanatory style, and negative emotions influence stress and health?
- What is Type A behavior, and what role does hostility play in the relationship between Type A behavior and health?

People vary a great deal in the way they respond to a distressing event, whether it's a parking ticket or a bad grade on a crucial exam. In part, individual differences in reacting to stressors result from how people appraise an event and their resources for coping with the event. However, psychologists and other researchers have identified several factors that influence an individual's response to stressful events. In this section, we'll take a look at some of the most important psychological and social factors that seem to affect an individual's response to stress.

Psychological Factors

It's easy to demonstrate the importance of psychological factors in the response to stressors. For example, the next time you are waiting in line for something, watch how differently people react to news of delays. Some people take the news calmly, while others become enraged and indignant. Psychologists have confirmed what common sense suggests: Psychological processes play a key role in determining the level of stress experienced.

Personal Control Whether it be a wildfire threatening your home or a paperwork snafu in your college financial aid office, situations that you perceive as being beyond your control are highly stressful. In contrast, having a sense of

⌄ Uncontrollable Events During 2020, many people from around the world saw an unprecedented number of social stressors, including a worldwide pandemic, political upheaval, and economic instability (uncertainty). People were subjected to a constantly and rapidly changing day-to-day existence. As a result, many people began to more frequently check news sources as a means to help cope with the uncertainty of daily life. Psychological research has shown that events and situations that are perceived as being beyond your control are especially likely to cause stress (Heth & Somer, 2002). Given that, how might you be able to lessen the stressful impact of such situations?

LeoPatrizi/Getty Images

optimistic explanatory style External, unstable, and specific explanations for negative events.

pessimistic explanatory style Internal, stable, and global explanations for negative events.

control over a stressful situation *reduces* the impact of stressors and decreases feelings of anxiety and depression (Dulin et al., 2013; Thompson, 2009). People who can control a stress-producing event often show no more psychological distress or physical arousal than people who are not exposed to the stressor at all.

Psychologists Judith Rodin and Ellen Langer (1977) first demonstrated the importance of a sense of control in a classic series of studies with nursing home residents. One group of residents — the "high-control" group — was given the opportunity to make choices about their daily activities and to exercise control over their environment. In contrast, residents assigned to the "low-control" group had little control over their daily activities. Decisions were made for them by the nursing home staff. Eighteen months later, the high-control residents were more active, alert, sociable, and healthier, on average, than the low-control residents. And, twice as many of the low-control residents had died (Langer & Rodin, 1976; Rodin & Langer, 1977).

How does a sense of control affect health? If you feel that you can control a stressor by taking steps to minimize or avoid it, you will experience less stress, both psychologically and physiologically (Heth & Somer, 2002; Heth et al., 2004). Having a sense of personal control also enhances positive emotions, such as self-confidence and feelings of self-efficacy, autonomy, and self-reliance. In contrast, feeling a lack of control over events produces all the hallmarks of the stress response. Levels of catecholamines and corticosteroids increase, and the effectiveness of immune system functioning decreases (see Maier & Watkins, 2000).

Further, not everyone benefits from feelings of enhanced personal control. Cross-cultural studies have shown that a sense of control is more highly valued in individualistic, Western cultures than in collectivistic, Eastern cultures (Thompson, 2009). Comparing Japanese and British participants, Darryl O'Connor and Mikiko Shimizu (2002) found that a heightened sense of personal control *was* associated with a lower level of perceived stress — but *only* among the British participants.

Explanatory Style: Optimism Versus Pessimism We all experience failure, rejection, or defeat at some point in our lives. Yet despite repeated failures, rejections, or defeats, some people persist in their efforts. In contrast, some people give up in the face of failure and setbacks — the essence of *learned helplessness*, which we discussed in the chapter on learning. What distinguishes between those who persist and those who give up?

According to psychologist **Martin Seligman** (1990, 1992), how people explain their failures and defeats makes the difference. People who have an **optimistic explanatory style** tend to use *external, unstable, and specific explanations for negative events*. In contrast, people who have a **pessimistic explanatory style** use *internal, stable, and global explanations for negative events*. Pessimists are also inclined to believe that no amount of personal effort will improve their situation. Not surprisingly, pessimists tend to experience more stress than optimists.

Let's look at these two explanatory styles in action. Optimistic Olive sees an attractive guy at a party and starts across the room to introduce herself and strike up a conversation. As she approaches him, the guy glances at her, then abruptly turns away. Hurt by the obvious snub, Optimistic Olive retreats to the bar. At the same party, Pessimistic Pete sees an attractive woman across the room and approaches her. He, too, gets a cold shoulder. Standing at opposite ends of the bar, here is what each of them is thinking:

> OPTIMISTIC OLIVE: *What's* his *problem?* (External explanation: The optimist blames other people or external circumstances.)
>
> PESSIMISTIC PETE: *I must have said the wrong thing. She probably saw me spill my drink.* (Internal explanation: The pessimist blames themself.)
>
> OPTIMISTIC OLIVE: *I'm really not looking my best tonight. I've just got to get more sleep.* (Unstable, temporary explanation)
>
> PESSIMISTIC PETE: *Let's face it, I'm a pretty boring guy and really not very good-looking.* (Stable, permanent explanation)
>
> OPTIMISTIC OLIVE: *He looks pretty preoccupied. Maybe he's waiting for his date to arrive.* (Specific explanation)

How Do You Explain Your Setbacks and Failures? No one is thrilled to receive a failing grade on an important paper or exam. However, everyone experiences setbacks, rejection, and failure at some point. The way you explain your setbacks has a significant impact on motivation and on mental and physical health.

mediaphotos/Getty Images

PESSIMISTIC PETE: Women never give me a second look, probably because I dress like a nerd and I never know what to say to them. (Global, pervasive explanation)

OPTIMISTIC OLIVE: Whoa! Who's that guy over there?! Okay, Olive, turn on the charm! Here goes! (Perseverance after a rejection)

PESSIMISTIC PETE: Maybe I'll just hold down this corner of the room or go home and play some video games. (Passivity and withdrawal after a rejection)

Most people, of course, are neither as completely optimistic as Olive nor as totally pessimistic as Pete. Instead, they fall somewhere along the spectrum of optimism and pessimism. Further, explanatory style may vary somewhat in different situations (Fosnaugh et al., 2009). Even so, a person's characteristic explanatory style, particularly for negative events, is relatively stable across the lifespan (Abela et al., 2008).

Explanatory style is linked to health consequences (Brummett et al., 2006; Wise & Rosqvist, 2006). For example, men with an optimistic explanatory style at age 25 were significantly healthier, on average, at age 50 than men with a pessimistic explanatory style (Peterson & Park, 2007). Other studies have shown that a pessimistic explanatory style is associated with poorer physical health (Peterson & Steen, 2009). For example, first-year law school students who had an optimistic, confident, and generally positive outlook had significantly higher levels of lymphocytes, T cells, and helper T cells. Explaining the positive relationship between optimism and good health, Suzanne Segerstrom and her colleagues (2003) suggest that optimists are more inclined to persevere in their efforts to overcome obstacles and challenges. Optimism has even been shown to help people cope with pain (Boselie et al., 2014; Goodin & Bulls, 2013). In particular, positive expectations—that the situation will improve—seem to buffer the effects of stressful events (Kleiman et al., 2017).

Chronic Negative Emotions Some people seem to have been born with a sunny, cheerful disposition. But other people almost always seem to be generally unhappy—they frequently experience bad moods and negative emotions like anger, irritability, worry, or sadness (D. J. Miller et al., 2009). Are people who are prone to chronic negative emotions more likely to suffer health problems?

Many studies have found a strong link between negative emotions and poor health (see Lahey, 2009). For example, a meta-analysis of more than 100 studies found that people who are habitually anxious, depressed, angry, or hostile *are* more likely to develop a chronic disease such as arthritis or heart disease (Friedman & Booth-Kewley, 2003).

This effect is even evident in communities. Johannes Eichstaedt and his colleagues (2015, 2018a) studied Twitter feeds in over 1,000 counties in the United States. They found that counties where tweets were more likely to include negative emotions, such as hostility, relationship tensions, or boredom, tended to have higher death rates from heart disease.

It is also important to consider the role of culture. For example, although expressing anger is predictive of ill health, such as heart disease, among people in the United States, expressing anger actually seems to be protective among Japanese people (Kitayama et al., 2015). The researchers suspect that this cultural difference is because the expression of anger indicates the presence of stressful experiences among people in the United States. But in Japan, anger is more commonly related to power and a sense of control, because most Japanese people do not feel free to openly express anger.

Positive Emotions If negative emotions are associated with poor health, are positive emotions associated with good health? First, positive emotions are *not* just the absence of negative emotions (Larsen et al., 2009). The health benefits of experiencing positive emotions go beyond merely dampening or eliminating negative emotions (Stellar et al., 2015).

Research has shown that positive emotions are associated with increased resistance to infection, decreased illnesses, fewer reports of illness symptoms, less pain, and increased longevity (Pressman & Cohen, 2005; Steptoe et al., 2009). One large Canadian study found that people who experienced high levels of positive emotion

Type A behavior pattern A behavioral and emotional style characterized by a sense of time urgency, hostility, and competitiveness.

MYTH ◄ SCIENCE

Is it true that high-achieving people who work long hours are setting themselves up for a heart attack?

⌄ The Type A Behavior Pattern The Type A behavior pattern includes hostility, ambition, and a sense of time urgency. Type A people hate wasting time and often try to do two or more things at once. But research has shown that hostility, anger, and cynicism are more damaging to physical health than ambition or time urgency (Suls & Bunde, 2005).

were less likely to develop heart disease than people who reported low levels of positive emotions (Davidson et al., 2010).

Like negative emotions, positive emotions also seem to be predictive of health in social media studies. In the Twitter study described previously, counties where tweets more often contained positive emotions, like optimism, tended to have lower death rates from heart disease (Eichstaedt et al., 2015, 2018a). This effect was found at an international level as well. Countries whose residents reported higher levels of positive emotions also tended to have higher reported levels of physical health (Pressman et al., 2013). This was true among wealthier countries like Ireland, as well as among lower-income countries like Haiti.

How might positive emotions affect health? First, positive emotions bring calming and health protective effects to the cardiovascular, endocrine, and immune systems (Brummett et al., 2009). Second, positive emotions are associated with health-promoting behaviors, such as regular exercise, eating a healthy diet, and not smoking. Finally, individuals who frequently experience positive emotions tend to have more friends and stronger social networks than people who don't (Steptoe et al., 2009).

Type A Behavior and Hostility The concept of Type A behavior originated over 40 years ago, when two cardiologists, Meyer Friedman and Ray Rosenman (1974), noticed that many of their patients shared certain traits. **Type A behavior pattern** is *a behavioral and emotional style characterized by a sense of time urgency, hostility, and competitiveness*. In contrast, people who were more relaxed and laid back were classified as displaying the *Type B behavior pattern*. After tracking the health of more than 3,000 middle-aged, healthy men, researchers found that those classified as Type A were twice as likely to develop heart disease as those classified as Type B. This held true even when the Type A men did not display other known risk factors for heart disease, such as smoking, high blood pressure, and elevated levels of cholesterol in their blood.

Although early results linking the Type A behavior pattern to heart disease were impressive, studies soon began to appear in which Type A behavior did *not* reliably predict the development of heart disease (see Krantz & McCeney, 2002; Myrtek, 2007). These findings led researchers to question whether the different components of the Type A behavior pattern were equally hazardous to health. After all, many people thrive on hard work, especially when they enjoy their jobs. And, high achievers don't necessarily suffer from health problems.

When researchers focused on the association between heart disease and each separate component of the Type A behavior pattern—time urgency, hostility, and achievement striving—an important distinction began to emerge. Feeling a sense of time urgency and being competitive or achievement oriented did *not* seem to be associated with the development of heart disease. Instead, the critical component that emerged as the strongest predictor of cardiac disease was *hostility*—the tendency to feel angry, annoyed, resentful, and contemptuous (Chida & Steptoe, 2009; J. E. Williams, 2010). Hostile people are much more likely than other people to develop heart disease, even when other risk factors are taken into account (Lohse et al., 2017; Niaura et al., 2002; J. E. Williams, 2010). These findings fit with the research we talked about in the previous section describing a link between negative emotions like hostility and poor health outcomes across counties and countries.

Hostile Type As tend to react more intensely to a stressor than other people do (Chida & Hamer, 2008). They tend to experience greater increases in blood pressure and heart rate. Because of their attitudes and behavior, hostile men and women also tend to *create* more stress in their own lives (Suls & Bunde, 2005). They also tend to experience more frequent, and more severe, negative life events and daily hassles than other people.

In general, the research evidence demonstrating the role of personality factors in the development of stress-related disease is impressive. Nevertheless, it's important to keep this evidence in perspective: Personality characteristics are just *some* of the many factors involved in the overall picture of health and disease. We look at this issue in more detail in the Critical Thinking box on the next page. And, in Psych for Your Life, at the end of this chapter, we describe some of the steps you can take to help you minimize the effects of stress on your health.

Do Personality Factors Cause Disease?

- You overhear a co-worker saying, "I'm not surprised he had a heart attack—the guy is a workaholic!"
- An acquaintance casually remarks, "She's been so depressed since her divorce. No wonder she got cancer."
- A tabloid headline hails, "New Scientific Findings: Use Your Mind to Cure Cancer!"

Statements like these make health psychologists, psychoneuroimmunologists, and physicians extremely uneasy. Why? Throughout this chapter, we've presented scientific evidence that emotional states can affect the functioning of the endocrine system and the immune system. Both systems play a significant role in the development of various physical disorders. We've also shown that personality factors, such as hostility and pessimism, are associated with an increased likelihood of developing poor health. But saying that "emotions affect the immune system" is a far cry from making such claims as "a positive attitude can cure cancer."

Psychologists and other scientists are cautious in the statements they make about the connections between personality and health for several reasons. First, many studies investigating the role of psychological factors in disease are *correlational*. That is, researchers have statistical evidence that two factors happen together so often that the presence of one factor reliably predicts the occurrence of the other. However, correlation does not necessarily indicate causality—it indicates only that two factors occur together. It's completely possible that some third, unidentified factor may have caused the other two factors to occur.

Second, personality factors might indirectly lead to disease via poor health habits. Low conscientiousness, high sensation seeking, and high extraversion are each associated with poor health habits (Atherton et al., 2014; Lodi-Smith et al., 2010; Miller & Quick, 2010). In turn, poor health habits are associated with higher rates of illness. That's why psychologists who study the role of personality factors in disease are typically careful to measure and consider the possible influence of the participants' health practices.

Third, it may be that the disease influences a person's emotions, rather than the other way around (Spezzaferri et al., 2009). After being diagnosed with advanced cancer or heart disease, most people would probably find it difficult to feel cheerful, optimistic, or in control of their lives.

One way that researchers try to disentangle the relationship between personality and health is to conduct carefully controlled prospective studies. A *prospective study* starts by assessing an initially healthy group

agf photo/SuperStock. Licensed material is being used for illustrative purposes only; person depicted in the licensed material is a model.

▲ **Personality and Health** Some personality factors, such as pessimism, are associated with poorer health.

of participants on variables thought to be risk factors, such as certain personality traits. Then the researchers track the health, personal habits, health habits, and other important dimensions of the participants' lives over a period of months, years, or decades. In analyzing the results, researchers can determine the extent to which each risk factor contributed to the health or illness of the participants. Thus, prospective studies provide more compelling evidence than do studies that are based on people who are already in poor health. Researchers will need to examine the intersection of personality traits with socioeconomic status, racial and ethnic identities, and biological aspects of sex and gender into account in order to truly understand how personality interacts with models of disease within different contexts (Lehman et al., 2017).

CRITICAL THINKING QUESTIONS

- Given that health professionals frequently advise people to change their health-related behaviors to improve physical health, should they also advise people to change their psychological attitudes, traits, and emotions? Why or why not?
- What are the advantages and disadvantages of correlational studies? Prospective studies?

Social Factors: A Little Help from Your Friends

■ KEY THEME
Social support refers to the resources provided by other people.

⹅ KEY QUESTIONS
- How has social support been shown to benefit health?
- How can relationships and social connections sometimes increase stress?
- What gender differences have been found in social support and its effects?

social support The resources provided by other people in times of need.

Psychologists have become increasingly aware of the importance that close relationships play in our ability to deal with stressors and, ultimately, in our physical health (Uchino & Birmingham, 2011). Consider the following research evidence:

- Analyzing 148 studies that included over 300,000 participants, Julianne Holt-Lunstad and her colleagues (2010) found that people who were socially isolated were twice as likely to die over a given period than were people with strong social relationships—a risk factor that is roughly equivalent to smoking 15 cigarettes a day.

- In a study begun in the 1950s, college students rated their parents' level of love and caring. A half-century later, 87 percent of those who had rated their parents as being "low" in love and caring had been diagnosed with a serious physical disease. In contrast, only 25 percent of those who had rated their parents as being "high" in love and caring had been diagnosed with a serious physical disease (Shaw et al., 2004).

- Social isolation in nonhuman animals seems to have similar consequences as those for loneliness in humans, possibly because isolated individuals need to maintain heightened vigilance to increase their chances of survival (Cacioppo et al., 2015b). This focus on self-preservation may cause stress and worsened physical and mental health.

These are just a few of the hundreds of studies exploring how interpersonal relationships influence our health and ability to tolerate stress (Cohen, 2004; Uchino, 2009). To investigate the role played by personal relationships in stress and health, psychologists measure the level of **social support**—*the resources provided by other people in times of need.*

Decades of psychological research have shown that socially isolated people have poorer health and higher death rates than people who have many social contacts or relationships (Holt-Lunstad et al., 2015). In fact, social isolation seems to be as potent a health risk as smoking, alcohol abuse, obesity, or physical inactivity (Holt-Lunstad et al., 2010; Steptoe et al., 2013). Social isolation was a particular risk factor for mental health during the pandemic (e.g., Usher et al., 2020).

Beyond social isolation, researchers have found that the more *diverse* your social network, the more pronounced the health benefits (Cohen & Janicki-Deverts, 2009). That is, prospective studies have shown that the people who live longest are those who have more *different types* of relationships—such as being married; having close relationships with family members, friends, and neighbors; and belonging to social, political, or religious groups (Berkman & Glass, 2000; Ellwardt et al., 2015b). In fact, researchers have found that people who live in such diverse social networks have:

- greater resistance to upper respiratory infections (Cohen, 2005).

- lower incidence of stroke and cardiovascular disease among women in a high-risk group (Rutledge et al., 2004, 2008).

- lower incidence of dementia and cognitive loss in old age (Desai et al., 2010; Ellwardt et al., 2015a).

▲ **The Benefits of Social Support**
Social support from your community can buffer the effects of stress, especially during natural disasters. Here, young Nepali volunteers work together to help clear the rubble from homes in their neighborhood after a 7.9-magnitude earthquake struck Nepal in April 2015.

▲ **Pets as a Source of Social Support**
Pets can provide both companionship and social support, especially for people with limited social contact. Studies have found that the presence of a pet cat or dog can lower blood pressure and lessen the cardiovascular response to acute stress (Allen et al., 2002).

How Social Support Benefits Health Social support may benefit our health and improve our ability to cope with stressors in several ways (Feeney & Collins, 2014; Uchino, 2009). First, the social support of friends and relatives can modify our appraisal of a stressor's significance, including the degree to which we perceive it as threatening or harmful. Simply knowing that support and assistance are readily available may make the situation seem less threatening.

Second, the presence of supportive others seems to decrease the intensity of physical reactions to a stressor (Uchino et al., 2010). Thus, when faced with a painful medical procedure or some other stressful situation, many people find the presence of a supportive friend to be calming.

Third, social support can influence our health by making us less likely to experience negative emotions (Cohen, 2004). Given the well-established link between chronic negative emotions and poor health, a strong social support network can promote positive moods and emotions, enhance self-esteem, and increase feelings of personal control. In contrast, loneliness and depression are unpleasant emotional states that increase levels of stress hormones and adversely affect immune system functioning (Cacioppo et al., 2015a; Irwin & Miller, 2007).

The flip side of the coin is that relationships with others can also be a significant *source* of stress (Lund et al., 2014; Rook et al., 2011). In fact, negative interactions with other people are sometimes more effective at creating psychological distress than positive interactions are at improving well-being (Rafaeli et al., 2008). And, although married people tend to be healthier than unmarried people overall, marital conflict has been shown to have adverse effects on physical health, especially for women (Robles, 2014; Whisman et al., 2010).

Clearly, the quality of interpersonal relationships is an important determinant of whether those relationships help or hinder our ability to cope with stressful events (Rook, 2015). When other people are perceived as being judgmental, their presence may increase the individual's physical reaction to a stressor. In two clever studies, psychologist Karen Allen and her colleagues (1991, 2002) demonstrated that the presence of a favorite dog or cat was more effective than the presence of a spouse or friend in lowering reactivity to a stressor. Why? Perhaps because the pet was perceived as being nonjudgmental, non-evaluative, and unconditionally supportive. Unfortunately, the same is not always true of friends, family members, and partners.

Stress may also increase when well-meaning friends or family members offer unwanted or inappropriate social support. The In Focus box on the next page offers some suggestions on how to provide helpful social support and avoid inappropriate support behaviors.

RICH ADDICKS/The New York Times/Redux

⌃ The Health Benefits of Companionship
Marteen and Wiley Blankenship celebrated their 48th wedding anniversary by working as volunteers in Alabama, helping people in a small town devastated by a violent tornado. Many studies have shown that couples and married people tend to live longer than people who are single, divorced, or widowed. In fact, adults who never marry are about 58 percent more likely to die early than those who are married and living with their spouse (Kaplan & Kronick, 2006).

Gender Differences in the Effects of Social Support
Who do you turn to when you are in need of help? In general, men tend to rely heavily on a close relationship with their spouse or partner. Women, in contrast, are more likely to list close friends along with their spouse as confidants (Ackerman et al., 2007; Coventry et al., 2004). Because men tend to have a much smaller network of intimate others, they may be particularly vulnerable to social isolation, especially if their spouse dies. That may be one reason that the health benefits of being married are more pronounced for men than for women (Zwicker & DeLongis, 2010). It is a myth that women derive more health benefits from marriage than men do.

When stressful events strike, women tend to reach out to one another for support and comfort (Taylor & Master, 2011). For example, given that approximately 80 percent of health care workers who are on the front lines of the COVID pandemic are women, we may have to consider the critical importance of social support in preventing and treating stress-related conditions.

Throughout their lives, women tend to mobilize social support—especially from other women—in times of stress (Zwicker & DeLongis, 2010). Psychologist Shelley Taylor (2006, 2012) suggests an evolutionary explanation for this gender difference in coping with threats or stressful circumstances. She points out that neither fighting nor fleeing is likely to be an adaptive response for females who are pregnant, nursing, or caring for their offspring. Instead, female animals "tend and befriend." That is, they take cover and "tend" to their offspring, protecting them from harm, and they seek out and "befriend" allies from social networks to provide help during stressful conditions (Taylor & Master, 2011).

MYTH ◂ SCIENCE

Is it true that women derive more health benefits from marriage than men do?

IN FOCUS

Providing Effective Social Support

A close friend turns to you for help in a time of crisis or personal tragedy. What should you do or say? Appropriate social support can help people weather crises and can significantly reduce the amount of distress that they feel. Inappropriate support, in contrast, may only make matters worse (Uchino, 2009).

Researchers generally agree that there are several broad categories of social support. Three are most commonly studied: emotional, tangible, and informational. Each provides different beneficial functions (Lett et al., 2009).

Emotional support includes expressions of concern, empathy, and positive regard. *Tangible support* involves direct assistance, such as providing transportation, lending money, or helping with meals, child care, or household tasks. When people offer helpful suggestions, advice, or possible resources, they are providing *informational support*.

It's possible that all three kinds of social support might be provided by the same person, such as a relative, spouse, or very close friend. More commonly, we turn to different people for different kinds of support (Masters et al., 2007).

Psychologists have identified several support behaviors that are typically perceived as helpful by people under stress (Goldsmith, 2004; Hobfoll et al., 1992). In a nutshell, you're most likely to be perceived as helpful if you:

- are a good listener and show concern and interest.
- ask questions that encourage the person under stress to express their feelings and emotions.
- express understanding about why the person is upset.
- express affection for the person, whether with a warm hug or simply a pat on the arm.
- are willing to invest time and attention in helping.
- can help the person with practical tasks, such as housework, transportation, or responsibilities at work or school.

NicolasMcComber/Getty Images

MYTH ◄ ~~SCIENCE~~

Is it true that the best way to comfort stressed-out friends or relatives is to give them advice and show them that the problem is not as bad as it seems?

Just as important is knowing what *not* to do or say. It is a myth that the best way to comfort stressed-out friends or relatives is to give them advice and show them that the problem is not as bad as it seems. Here are several behaviors that, however well intentioned, are often perceived as unhelpful:

- Giving advice that the person under stress has not requested
- Telling the person, "I know exactly how you feel." It's a mistake to think that you have experienced distress identical to what the other person is experiencing.

- Talking about yourself or your own problems
- Minimizing the importance of the person's problem by saying things like "Hey, don't make such a big deal out of it," "It could be a lot worse," or "Don't worry, everything will turn out okay."
- Joking or acting overly cheerful
- Offering your philosophical or religious interpretation of the stressful event by saying things like, "It's fate," "It's God's will," or "It's your karma."
- Making a big deal out of the support and help you do provide, which may make the recipient feel even more anxious or vulnerable. In fact, "invisible support," in which the recipient isn't aware of your help, is one of the most effective forms of social support (Bolger & Amarel, 2007; Howland & Simpson, 2010). For example, asking a question in class because you know that a classmate doesn't understand the material would be an example of invisible support.

Finally, remember that although social support is helpful, it is *not* a substitute for counseling or psychotherapy. If a friend seems overwhelmed by problems or emotions, or is having serious difficulty handling the demands of everyday life, you should encourage them to seek professional help. Most university campuses have a counseling center or a health clinic that can provide referrals to qualified mental health workers. Sliding fee schedules, based on ability to pay, are usually available, and many campus counseling centers are free of charge for students. Thus, you can assure the person that cost need not be an obstacle to getting help—or an additional source of stress!

Why do women "tend and befriend" rather than "fight or flee," as men do? Taylor (2006, 2012) points to the effects of the hormone oxytocin. Present in higher amounts in females than in males, oxytocin is associated with maternal behaviors in all female mammals, including humans. Some studies have found that women are more apt to seek out social support when given the hormone oxytocin (Cardoso et al., 2016). But in general, research on the effects of oxytocin are mixed (see page 54). And research has shown that men, too, sometimes befriend, or seek allies under stressful conditions, so the tend-and-befriend behavior pattern may not be limited to women (Berger et al., 2016).

Although women are more likely to seek and provide social support, they are also more vulnerable to some of its problematic aspects. First, women are more likely than men to serve as *providers* of support, which can be a stressful role (Ekwall & Hallberg, 2007).

Second, women may be more likely to suffer from the *stress contagion effect,* becoming upset about negative life events that happen to other people whom they care about (Dalgard et al., 2006). Since women tend to have larger and more intimate social networks than men, they have more opportunities to become distressed by what happens to people who are close to them. And women are more likely than men to be upset about negative events that happen to their relatives and friends. In contrast, men are more likely to be distressed only by negative events that happen to their immediate family—their spouses and children (Rosenfield & Smith, 2010).

Coping: How People Deal with Stress

■ KEY THEME
Coping refers to the ways in which we try to change circumstances, or our interpretation of circumstances, to make them less threatening.

≡ KEY QUESTIONS
- What are the two basic forms of coping, and when is each form typically used?
- What are some of the most common coping strategies?
- How does culture affect coping style?

Imagine that you discovered that you weren't allowed to register for classes because the financial aid office had lost your paperwork. How would you react? What would you do? The strategies that you use to deal with distressing events are examples of coping. **Coping** refers to *the ways in which we try to change circumstances, or our interpretation of circumstances, to make them more favorable and less threatening* (Folkman, 2009).

When coping is effective, we adapt to the situation and stress is reduced. Unfortunately, coping efforts do not always help us adapt. Maladaptive coping can involve thoughts and behaviors that intensify or prolong distress, or that produce self-defeating outcomes (Thompson et al., 2010). The rejected lover who continually dwells on their former companion, passing up opportunities to form new relationships and letting their studies slide, is demonstrating maladaptive coping. Maladaptive coping can also include maladaptive behaviors. People of all ages sometimes engage in unhealthy coping behaviors. But one survey found that millennials are significantly more likely than those of other generations to cope by eating more or by becoming a couch potato—for example, playing video games or spending too much time online (APA, 2013).

Adaptive coping responses serve many functions (Folkman, 2009; Folkman & Moskowitz, 2007). Most important, adaptive coping involves realistically evaluating the situation and determining what can be done to minimize the impact of the stressor. But adaptive coping also involves dealing with the emotional aspects of the situation. In other words, adaptive coping often includes developing emotional tolerance for negative life events, maintaining self-esteem, and keeping emotions in balance. Finally, adaptive coping efforts are directed toward preserving important relationships.

Traditionally, coping has been broken down into two major categories: *problem-focused* and *emotion-focused* (Folkman & Moskowitz, 2004). As you'll see in the next sections, each type of coping serves a different purpose. However, people are flexible in the coping styles they adopt, often relying on different coping strategies for different stressors (Bonanno & Burton, 2013; Kammeyer-Mueller et al., 2009).

▲ **Ways of Coping** Like the stress response itself, adaptive coping is a dynamic and complex process. Imagine that your landlord told you that you had to move in 10 days. What types of coping strategies might prove most helpful?

coping The ways in which we try to change circumstances, or our interpretation of circumstances, to make them more favorable and less threatening.

Ziv Koren/Polaris Images/Kathmandu/Nepal/Newscom

▲ Problem-Focused and Emotion-Focused Coping Strategies Dealing with the devastation that follows major disasters requires multiple coping strategies. Thousands of people were killed and hundreds of thousands of homes destroyed or damaged in the major earthquake that hit Nepal in April 2015. Along with coping with the emotional impact of losing homes, friends, and family members, people must also call upon problem-focused strategies to deal with the challenges of rebuilding shattered communities. This woman is sifting through the rubble of her home in historic Durbar Square in Kathmandu, searching for whatever belongings she can salvage.

THINK LIKE A **SCIENTIST**

Can you reduce your stress level by watching cute animal videos? Go to Achieve: Resources to **Think Like a Scientist** about **Coping with Stress.**

  Achieve

problem-focused coping Coping efforts primarily aimed at directly changing or managing a threatening or harmful stressor.

emotion-focused coping Coping efforts primarily aimed at relieving or regulating the emotional impact of a stressful situation.

Problem-Focused Coping Strategies: Changing the Stressor

Problem-focused coping is *coping efforts primarily aimed at directly changing or managing* a threatening or harmful stressor. Problem-focused coping strategies tend to be most effective when you can exercise some control over the stressful situation or circumstances (Kammeyer-Mueller et al., 2009; Park et al., 2004).

Planful problem solving involves efforts to rationally analyze the situation, identify potential solutions, and then implement them. In effect, you take the attitude that the stressor represents a problem to be solved. Once you assume that mental stance, you follow the basic steps of problem solving (see the chapter on thinking, language, and intelligence).

When people tackle a problem head on, they engage in *confrontive coping.* Ideally, confrontive coping is direct and assertive but not hostile or angry. When it is hostile or aggressive, confrontive coping may well generate negative emotions in the people being confronted, damaging future relations with them (Folkman & Lazarus, 1991). However, if you recall our earlier discussion of hostility, then you won't be surprised to find that hostile individuals often engage in confrontive coping (Vandervoort, 2006).

Emotion-Focused Coping Strategies: Changing Your Reaction to the Stressor

When the stressor is one over which we can exert little or no control, we often focus on the aspect of the situation that we *can* control — the emotional impact of the stressor on us. When people think that nothing can be done to alter a situation, they tend to rely on **emotion-focused coping**, *coping efforts primarily aimed at relieving or regulating the emotional impact of a stressful situation.* They direct their efforts toward relieving or regulating the emotional impact of the stressful situation (Scott et al., 2010). Although emotion-focused coping doesn't change the problem, it can help you feel better about it. For example, in the early days of the COVID pandemic, New Yorkers would open their windows, or step out onto their balconies, and cheer, bang pots and pans, sing, and make as much noise as possible to acknowledge the 7 P.M. shift change at New York City hospitals. When exhausted health care workers emerged from hospitals each night, they were greeted with impossible-to-miss sounds of acknowledgment and gratitude.

When you shift your attention away from the stressor and toward other activities, you're engaging in the emotion-focused coping strategy called *escape–avoidance.* As the name implies, the basic goal is to escape or avoid the stressor and neutralize distressing emotions. Excessive sleeping and the use of drugs and alcohol are maladaptive forms of escape–avoidance, as are escaping into fantasy or wishful thinking. More constructive escape–avoidance strategies include exercising or immersing yourself in your studies, hobbies, or work.

Because you are focusing your attention on something other than the stressor, escape–avoidance tactics provide emotional relief in the short run. Thus, avoidance strategies can be helpful when you are facing a stressor that is brief and has limited consequences. But avoidance strategies such as wishful thinking tend to be counterproductive when the stressor is a severe or long-lasting one, like a serious or chronic disease (Wolf & Mori, 2009).

In the long run, escape–avoidance tactics are associated with poor adjustment and feelings of depression and anxiety (Murberg & Bru, 2005; Woodhead et al., 2013). That's not surprising if you think about it. After all, the problem *is* still there. And if the problem is one that needs to be dealt with promptly, such as academic problems, the delays caused by escape–avoidance strategies can make the stressful situation worse.

Seeking social support is the coping strategy that involves turning to friends, relatives, or other people for emotional, tangible, or informational support. As we discussed earlier in the chapter, having a strong network of social support can help buffer the impact of stressors (Uchino, 2009). Confiding in a trusted friend gives you an opportunity to vent your emotions and better understand the stressful situation.

When you acknowledge the stressor but attempt to minimize or eliminate its emotional impact, you're engaging in the coping strategy called *distancing.* Having an attitude of joy and lightheartedness in daily life, and finding the humor in life's absurdities or ironies, is a constructive form of distancing (Kuhn et al., 2010; McGraw et al., 2013). Sometimes people emotionally distance themselves from a stressor by discussing it in a detached, depersonalized, or intellectual way.

In certain high-stress occupations, distancing can help workers cope with painful human problems. Clinical psychologists, social workers, rescue workers, police officers, and medical personnel often use distancing to some degree to help them deal with distressing situations without falling apart emotionally themselves.

In contrast to distancing, *denial* is a refusal to acknowledge that the problem even exists. Like escape–avoidance strategies, denial can compound problems in situations that require immediate attention.

Perhaps the most constructive emotion-focused coping strategy is *positive reappraisal.* When we use positive reappraisal, we try not only to minimize the negative emotional aspects of the situation but also to create positive meaning by focusing on personal growth (Folkman, 2009). Even in the midst of deeply disturbing situations, positive reappraisal can help people experience positive emotions and minimize the potential for negative aftereffects (Nowlan et al., 2015; Weiss & Berger, 2010).

Some people turn to their religious or spiritual beliefs to help them cope with stress. *Positive religious coping* includes seeking comfort or reassurance in prayer or from a religious community, or believing that your personal experience is spiritually meaningful. Positive religious coping is generally associated with lower levels of stress and anxiety, improved mental and physical health, and enhanced well-being (Ano & Vasconcelles, 2005).

On the other hand, religious beliefs can also lead to a less positive outcome. Individuals who respond with *negative religious coping,* in which they become angry, question their religious beliefs, or believe that they are being punished, tend to experience increased levels of distress, poorer health, and decreased well-being (Ano & Vasconcelles, 2005; Smith et al., 2005).

For many people, religious coping offers a sense of control or certainty during stressful events or circumstances (Hogg et al., 2010; Kay et al., 2010). For example, some people find strength in the notion that adversity is a test of their religious faith or that they have been given a particular challenge in order to fulfill a higher moral purpose. Thus, religious or spiritual beliefs can increase resilience, optimism, and personal growth during times of stress and adversity (Pargament & Cummings, 2010).

Finally, it's important to note that there is no single "best" coping strategy. In general, the most effective coping is flexible, meaning that we fine-tune our coping strategies to meet the demands of a particular stressor (Carver, 2011; Cheng, 2009). And, people often use multiple coping strategies, combining problem-focused and emotion-focused forms of coping. In the initial stages of a stressful experience, we may rely on emotion-focused strategies to help us step back emotionally from a problem. Once we've regained our equilibrium, we may use problem-focused coping strategies to identify potential solutions.

Although it's virtually inevitable that you'll encounter stressful circumstances, there are coping strategies that can help you minimize their health effects. We suggest several techniques in the Psych for Your Life section at the end of the chapter.

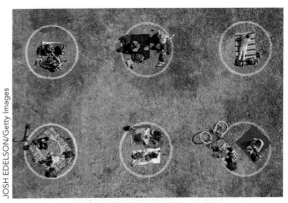

JOSH EDELSON/Getty Images

▲ **Coping During a Pandemic** Pictured above you see people taking advantage of being outdoors while still trying to maintain a safe distance from one another. The California park depicted here used painted circles six feet apart in the grass to encourage social distancing. These circles were also thought to help people cope with the stress of social isolation by enabling people to spend time away from their homes, enjoying fresh air, in the presence of others.

⌄ **Positive Reappraisal: Transcending Tragedy** Arno Michaelis (left) reached out to Pardeep Kaleka six weeks after Kaleka's father was killed in the 2012 attack on a Sikh temple by a white supremacist in Milwaukee. Michaelis himself once belonged to a white supremacist organization, but had long since renounced the racist movement. Together, Michaelis and Kaleka formed a new group, Serve2Unite, which travels to schools and community organizations to combat hate groups and promote a message of love and understanding (Terry, 2013). About their unlikely partnership, Kaleka (2013) said, "We were both hoping . . . we could take something tragic and turn it into something positive—a learning experience for the entire community." A bullet hole still marks the doorway of the temple where Kaleka's father was killed.

Morry Gash/AP Images

Wang xiwei cd/AP Images

∧ **Culture and Coping** This young boy lost his legs in a devastating earthquake that killed almost 100,000 people in southwest China. Do coping strategies differ across cultures? According to some researchers, people in China, Japan, and other Asian cultures are more likely to rely on emotional coping strategies than people in individualistic cultures (Heppner, 2008; Yeh et al., 2006).

∨ **Coping Amid Tragedy** For almost twelve months, and after over 300,000 deaths, there was very little for frontline health care workers to celebrate. When it was announced that a vaccine was going to be distributed, health care workers at a hospital in Boston were quick to "dance it out." A group of health care workers got together outside their hospital to symbolically shake off the stress of extra long hours, lost patients, and seemingly hopeless conditions under which they had been working. The clip went viral as it seemed to capture a nation's collective hope following the announcement of the first COVID vaccine.

Culture and Coping Strategies

Culture can influence the choice of coping strategies (Chun et al., 2006). People in the United States and other members of individualistic cultures tend to emphasize personal autonomy and personal responsibility in dealing with problems. Thus, they are *less* likely to seek social support in stressful situations than are members of collectivistic cultures, such as Asian cultures (Wong & Wong, 2006). Members of collectivistic cultures tend to be more oriented toward their social group, family, or community and toward seeking help with their problems (Kuo, 2013).

Individualists also tend to emphasize the importance and value of exerting control over their circumstances, especially circumstances that are threatening or stressful (O'Connor & Shimizu, 2002). Thus, they favor problem-focused strategies, such as confrontive coping and planful problem solving. These strategies involve directly changing the situation to achieve a better fit with their wishes or goals (Wong & Wong, 2006).

In collectivistic cultures, however, a greater emphasis is placed on controlling your personal reactions to a stressful situation rather than trying to control the situation itself (Zhou et al., 2012). According to some researchers, people in China, Japan, and other Asian cultures are more likely to rely on emotional coping strategies than people in individualistic cultures. Coping strategies that are particularly valued in collectivistic cultures include emotional self-control, gracefully accepting one's fate and making the best of a bad situation, and maintaining harmonious relationships with family members (Heppner, 2008; Yeh et al., 2006). This emotion-focused coping style emphasizes gaining control over inner feelings by accepting and accommodating yourself to existing realities (O'Connor & Shimizu, 2002).

For example, people in Japan emphasize accepting difficult situations with maturity, serenity, and flexibility (Gross, 2007). Common sayings in Japan are "The true tolerance is to tolerate the intolerable" and "Flexibility can control rigidity." Along with controlling inner feelings, many Asian cultures also stress the goal of controlling the outward expression of emotions, however distressing the situation (Park, 2010).

These cultural differences in coping underscore the point that there is no formula for effective coping in all situations. That we use multiple coping strategies throughout almost every stressful situation reflects our efforts to identify what will work best at a given moment in time. To the extent that any coping strategy helps us identify realistic alternatives, manage our emotions, and maintain important relationships, it is adaptive and effective.

Closing Thoughts

From disasters and major life events to the minor hassles and annoyances of daily life, stressors come in all sizes and shapes. Stress is an unavoidable part of life. If prolonged or intense, stress can adversely affect both our physical and psychological well-being. Fortunately, most of the time people deal effectively with the stresses in their lives. But effective coping can minimize the effects of even the most intense stressors, like living through a global pandemic.

Ultimately, the level of stress that we experience is due to a complex interaction of psychological, biological, and social factors. We hope that reading this chapter has given you a better understanding of how stress affects *your* life and how you can reduce its impact on your physical and psychological well-being. In Psych for Your Life, we'll suggest some concrete steps you can take to minimize the harmful impact of stress in *your* life.

PSYCH FOR YOUR LIFE

Minimizing the Effects of Stress

Sometimes stressful situations persist despite our best efforts to resolve them. Knowing that chronic stress can jeopardize your health, what can you do to minimize the adverse impact of stress on your physical well-being? Here are four practical suggestions.

Suggestion 1: Avoid or Minimize the Use of Stimulants

When dealing with stressful situations, people often turn to stimulants to help keep them going, such as coffee or caffeinated energy drinks. If you know someone who smokes, you've probably observed that most smokers react to stress by increasing their smoking (Ng & Jeffery, 2003; Todd, 2004). The problem is that common stimulants like caffeine and nicotine actually work *against* you in coping with stress. They increase the physiological effects of stress by raising heart rate and blood pressure. In effect, users of stimulants are already primed to respond with greater reactivity, exaggerating the physiological consequences of stress (Klein et al., 2010).

The best advice? Avoid stimulants altogether. If that's not possible, make a conscious effort to monitor your use of stimulants, especially when you're under stress. You'll find it easier to deal with stressors when your nervous system is not already in high gear because of caffeine, nicotine, or other stimulants. Minimizing your use of stimulants will also make it easier for you to implement the next suggestion.

Suggestion 2: Exercise Regularly

Numerous studies all point to the same conclusion: Regular exercise, particularly aerobic exercise like walking, swimming, or running, is one of the best ways to reduce the impact of stress (Edenfield & Blumenthal, 2011; Thøgersen-Ntoumani et al., 2015). The key word here is *regular*. Try walking briskly for 20 minutes four or five times a week. It will improve your physical health and help you cope with stress. In fact, just about any kind of physical exercise helps buffer the negative effects of stress. (Rapidly clicking your computer mouse doesn't count.) Compared to sofa slugs, physically fit people are less physiologically reactive to stressors and produce lower levels of stress hormones (Hamer et al., 2006). Psychologically, regular exercise reduces anxiety and depressed feelings, and increases self-confidence and self-esteem.

Westend61/Getty Images

Suggestion 3: Get Enough Sleep

With the ongoing push to get more and more done, people often stretch their days by short-changing themselves on sleep. But sleep deprivation just adds to your feelings of stress. "Without sufficient sleep it is more difficult to concentrate, make careful decisions, and follow instructions," explains researcher Mark Rosekind (2003). "You are more likely to make mistakes or errors, and are more prone to being impatient and lethargic. And, your attention, memory and reaction time are all adversely affected."

The stress–sleep connection also has the potential to become a vicious cycle. School, work, or family-related pressures contribute to reduced or disturbed sleep, leaving you less than adequately rested and making efforts to deal with the situation all the more taxing and distressing (Akerstedt et al., 2009). And inadequate sleep, even for just a few nights, takes a physical toll on the body, leaving us more prone to health problems (Cohen et al., 2009).

Fortunately, research indicates that the opposite is also true: Getting adequate sleep promotes resistance and helps buffer the effects of stress (Lange et al., 2010). For some suggestions to help promote a good night's sleep, see the Psych for Your Life section in the chapter on consciousness.

Suggestion 4: Practice a Relaxation or Meditation Technique

You can significantly reduce stress-related symptoms by regularly using any one of a variety of relaxation techniques (Benson, 2010). *Meditation* is one effective stress reduction strategy. As discussed in the chapter on consciousness, there are many different meditation techniques, but they all involve focusing mental attention, heightening awareness, and quieting internal chatter. Most meditation techniques are practiced while sitting quietly, but others involve movement, such as yoga and walking meditation. Many studies have demonstrated the physical and psychological benefits of meditation, including lessening the effects of stress (Chiesa & Serretti, 2009; Ludwig & Kabat-Zinn, 2008).

One form of meditation that has been receiving a great deal of attention in psychology is called *mindfulness meditation.* Mindfulness techniques were developed as a Buddhist practice more than 2,000 years ago, but modern psychologists and other health practitioners have adapted these practices for use in a secular context (Didonna, 2008). Mindfulness practice has been shown to be helpful in both preventing and relieving stress (Creswell & Lindsay, 2014; Jha et al., 2010; Weinstein et al., 2009).

Definitions of mindfulness are as varied as the practices associated with it. It's important to note, also, that strictly speaking, *mindfulness* refers to an approach to everyday life as well as a formal meditation technique (Shapiro & Carlson, 2009). However, for our purposes, **mindfulness meditation** can be defined as *a technique in which practitioners focus* awareness *on* present experience *with* acceptance (Siegel et al., 2008).

Advocates of mindfulness practice believe that most psychological distress is caused by our *reactions* to events and circumstances—our emotions, thoughts, and judgments. As psychologist Mark Williams points out, "We are always explaining the world to ourselves, and we react emotionally to these explanations rather than to the facts. . . . Thoughts are not facts" (Williams et al., 2007). Mindfulness practice is a way to correct that habitual perspective, clearing and calming the mind in the process. David Ludwig and Jon Kabat-Zinn (2008) explain:

> Mindfulness can be considered a universal human capacity proposed to foster clear thinking and open-heartedness. As such, this form of meditation requires no particular religious or cultural belief system. The goal of mindfulness is to maintain awareness moment by moment, disengaging oneself from strong attachment to beliefs, thoughts, or emotions, thereby developing a greater sense of emotional balance and well-being.

In other words, mindfulness meditation involves paying attention to your ongoing mental experience in a nonjudgmental, nonreactive manner (Ludwig & Kabat-Zinn, 2008; Shapiro & Carlson, 2009). The *mindfulness of breathing* technique is a simple mindfulness practice that is often recommended for beginners.

Mindfulness of Breathing

- Find a comfortable place to sit quietly. Assume a sitting posture that is relaxed yet upright and alert. Close your eyes and allow the muscles in your face, neck, and shoulders to slowly relax.

- Focus on your breath as your primary object of attention, feeling the breathing in and breathing out, the rise and fall of your abdomen, the sensation of air moving across your upper lip and in your nostrils, and so forth.

- Whenever some other phenomenon arises in the field of awareness, note it, and then gently bring the mind back to the breathing. As thoughts, feelings, or images arise in your mind, simply note their presence and go back to focusing your attention on the physical sensation of breathing.

mindfulness meditation A technique in which practitioners focus *awareness* on *present experience* with *acceptance.*

- To maintain attention on your breathing, it's sometimes helpful to count your breaths. Inhale gently, exhale, and then speak the word one in your mind. Inhale gently, exhale, and mentally speak the word two. Do the same up until the count of four, and then start over again. Remember, focus on the physical sensation of breathing, such as the feeling of air moving across your nostrils and upper lip, the movement of your chest and abdomen, and so forth.

How long should you meditate? Many meditation teachers advise that you begin with a short, easily attainable goal, such as meditating for five minutes without taking a break. As you become more comfortable in your practice, gradually work your way up to longer periods of time, ideally 20 to 30 minutes per session.

Sources: Shapiro & Carlson (2009); Wallace (2009); Williams et al. (2007).

CHAPTER REVIEW

Stress, Health, and Coping

 **Achieve,** Macmillan Learning's online study platform, features the full e-book of *Discovering Psychology,* the **LearningCurve** adaptive quizzing system, videos, and a variety of activities to boost your learning. Visit **Achieve** at macmillanlearning.com.

KEY PEOPLE

Walter Cannon, p. 446   Richard Lazarus, p. 438   Martin Seligman, p. 452   Hans Selye, p. 447

KEY TERMS

stress, p. 438

cognitive appraisal model, p. 438

health psychology, p. 439

biopsychosocial model, p. 439

stressors, p. 439

daily hassles, p. 442

burnout, p. 443

acculturative stress, p. 445

fight-or-flight response, p. 446

catecholamines, p. 446

corticosteroids, p. 447

general adaptation syndrome, p. 448

telomeres, p. 448

immune system, p. 449

psychoneuroimmunology, p. 449

optimistic explanatory style, p. 452

pessimistic explanatory style, p. 452

Type A behavior pattern, p. 454

social support, p. 456

coping, p. 459

problem-focused coping, p. 460

emotion-focused coping, p. 460

mindfulness meditation, p. 464

Stress

Negative emotional state in response to events appraised as taxing or exceeding a person's resources

Health psychologists:
- Study stress and other factors that influence health, illness, and treatment
- Are guided by the **biopsychosocial model**

Stressors: Events or situations that produce stress

Richard Lazarus (1922–2002)
- Developed **cognitive appraisal model** of stress
- Established importance of daily hassles

Aleksandar Stojkovic/Shutterstock

Life events and change:
- Life events approach: Stressors are any events that require adaptation.
- Social Readjustment Rating Scale measures impact of life events.

Social and cultural sources of stress:
- Poverty, low social status, racism, and discrimination can cause chronic stress.
- **Acculturative stress** results from the pressure of adapting to a new culture.

Tempura/Getty Images

- **Daily hassles:** Minor, everyday events that annoy and upset people
- **Burnout:** State of exhaustion, cynicism, and feelings of inadequacy caused by prolonged work stress

Custom Medical Stock Photo/Alamy

Physical Effects of Stress

Walter Cannon (1871–1945)
- Identified endocrine pathway involved in **fight-or-flight response** to acute stress
- Noted roles of sympathetic nervous system and release of **catecholamines** by the adrenal medulla

Hans Selye (1907–1982)
- Identified endocrine pathway in three-stage **general adaptation syndrome** response to prolonged stress
- Noted roles of hypothalamus, pituitary gland, and release of **corticosteroids** by the adrenal cortex

Chronic stress may produce premature aging and disease by shortening the length of **telomeres,** the protective caps found on the ends of chromosomes.

Psychoneuroimmunology studies interconnections of psychological processes, nervous and endocrine systems, and **immune system.**

Catchlight Visual Services/Alamy Stock Photo

Type A behavior pattern:
- Predicts heart disease
- Hostility is most important health-compromising component

Chronic negative emotions:
- Produce more stress
- Contribute to development of some chronic diseases

Individual Factors That Influence the Response to Stress

Personal control: Impact of stressors reduced when people feel sense of control over situation

Social support:
- Improves health and ability to deal with stressors
- May increase stress when inappropriate
- Women are more likely to provide social support but are also more vulnerable to the stress contagion effect.
- Men are less likely to be upset by negative events outside their immediate family.

Explanatory style:
- **Optimistic explanatory style** uses external, unstable, specific explanations for negative events.
- **Pessimistic explanatory style** uses internal, stable, global explanations for negative events.

NicolasMcComber/Getty Images

Coping

The ways in which people change circumstances or their interpretations of circumstances to make them more favorable and less threatening

Morry Gash/AP Photo

Cultural influences on coping:
- Individualistic cultures favor problem-focused coping strategies.
- Collectivistic cultures emphasize emotion-focused strategies.

Emotion-focused coping:
- Involves changing emotional reactions to the stressor
- Includes escape–avoidance, seeking social support, distancing, denial, and positive reappraisal

Problem-focused coping:
- Attempts to change stressful situation
- Includes confrontive coping and planful problem solving

Wang xiwei cd/AP Images

MYTH **OR** SCIENCE?

Is it true . . .

▶ That most people with a psychological disorder are violent?

▶ That psychological disorders are rare?

▶ That the less anxiety you have, the better?

▶ That people who are perfectionists probably have obsessive–compulsive disorder?

▶ That many psychological disorders run in families?

▶ That the types of psychological disorders are pretty much the same in every culture?

▶ That people with schizophrenia have a "split personality"?

Psychological Disorders

PROLOGUE

"I'm Flying! I've Escaped!"

During her first semester of college, Elyn Saks became increasingly anxious. When a stranger came to stay overnight in her dorm, a high school student considering the school, Elyn's agitation spiked. And she snapped. With no warning, Elyn ran into the wintry night, darting around the snowy campus, and extending her arms as if in flight. She shouted, "I'm flying! I've escaped!" (Saks, 2008).

This wasn't the first time Elyn lost touch with reality or behaved irrationally. One

night, she swallowed a whole bottle of aspirin and her friends rushed her to the emergency room. Other times, she would go days without eating, sleeping, or bathing. And she couldn't always distinguish what was real from what was not. After a tumultuous first year of university, Elyn asked her parents to help her find a therapist. Eventually, she was diagnosed with *schizophrenia*, a serious psychological disorder in which sufferers are often disconnected from the world around them.

Elyn's episodes in college were early indicators of psychotic breaks she would eventually suffer. Over the years, she experienced delusional beliefs, such as thinking that her therapist wanted to kill her. And she frequently had

hallucinations—for example, hearing her name being called when she was alone.

Over many difficult years, Elyn struggled with her condition and tried a number of different treatments. She sometimes lost touch with reality for months at a time and spent extended periods in inpatient psychiatric hospitals, which predicted a grim future. Elyn was told she would never live and work on her own.

Throughout these struggles, however, Elyn actively sought treatment for her symptoms and continued to work hard in school. With help from skilled clinicians, she graduated from Vanderbilt University first in her class, then went on to earn a master's at Oxford University and a law degree at Yale University. Today, Elyn's schizophrenia is

well controlled by medication and therapy, treatments you'll learn about in the chapter on therapies. Elyn describes her emergence from her symptoms of schizophrenia as "daylight dawning after a long night."

Elyn is now happily married and is a successful professor. In 2009, Elyn won a MacArthur Foundation "Genius Grant" and used the MacArthur funding to found an institute that studies mental health and ethics.

In her memoir, Elyn shares that she will always need treatment to control the symptoms of her illness. But she is hopeful that the story of her success will spur mental health professionals to reconsider the assumption that people with schizophrenia are unlikely to ever live productive, successful lives.

In this chapter, you'll learn about the symptoms that characterize some of the most common psychological disorders. The symptoms of many psychological disorders are not as easily seen as those that Elyn experienced. And there is a wide range of psychological disorders that differ in symptoms, severity, and prognosis. But whether the psychological symptoms are obvious or not, they can impair a person's ability to function. You'll also learn about some of the underlying causes of psychological disorders—including biological, psychological, and environmental factors that have been implicated as contributing to many psychological disorders. Later in the chapter, we'll come back to Elyn's story. ◠

Introduction: Understanding Psychological Disorders

■ KEY THEME

Understanding psychological disorders includes considerations of their origins, symptoms, and development, as well as how behavior relates to cultural and social norms.

⯇ KEY QUESTIONS

- What is a psychological disorder, and what differentiates abnormal behavior from normal behavior?
- What is DSM-5, and how was it developed?
- How prevalent are psychological disorders?

Have you ever seen someone walking alone talking to themselves? Does this seem like typical behavior to you? It depends. Take a moment to consider how you would decide whether or not the person's behavior seems "typical," "quirky," or even "disturbing." Most people, consciously or not, tend to be relatively judgmental when it comes to understanding behaviors that appear unusual. This response often reflects common misconceptions about psychological disorders that we hope to dispel in this chapter.

First, when we encounter people whose behavior strikes us as weird, unpredictable, or baffling, it's easy to dismiss them. Even if a person's behavior is seriously disturbed, labeling that person as "crazy" tells us nothing meaningful. What are the person's specific symptoms? What might be the cause of the symptoms? How did they develop? How long can they be expected to last? And how might the person be helped?

The area of psychology and medicine that focuses on these questions is called **psychopathology**—*the scientific study of the origins, symptoms, and development of psychological disorders*. In this chapter and the next, we'll take a closer look at psychological disorders and their treatment.

Second, there's the belief that "crazy" or "abnormal" behavior is very different from "normal" behavior. Granted, sometimes it is, but the line that divides "normal" from "abnormal" behavior is often not as sharply defined as most people think. In many instances, the difference between normal and abnormal behavior is a matter of degree. For example, as you leave your apartment or house, it's normal to check or even double-check that the door is securely locked. However, if you feel compelled to go back and check the lock 50 times, it would be considered abnormal behavior.

The dividing line between normal and abnormal behavior is often determined by the social or cultural context in which a particular behavior occurs. For example, among traditional Hindus in India, certain dietary restrictions are followed as part of the mourning process. It would be a serious breach of social norms if an Indian widow ate fish, meat, onions, garlic, or any other "hot" foods within six months after her husband's death. A Catholic widow in the United States would not worry about these food restrictions.

Finally, there is still a strong social stigma attached to suffering from a psychological disorder (Pingani et al., 2016; Tucker et al., 2013). Studies have found that people with a major mental illness belong to the most stigmatized group in modern society (Hinshaw & Stier, 2008; Schomerus et al., 2012). The stigma associated with psychological disorders varies culturally. For example, in the United States, stigma is higher in Black and Latino/Latina communities (DeFreitas et al., 2018; Givens, 2020). Stigma is also higher in Asian countries than in other parts of the world, and among Asian people in non-Asian countries (Krendl & Pescosolido, 2020).

Particularly in popular media, people with psychological disorders, regardless of race and ethnicity, are portrayed in highly negative, stereotyped ways (Klin & Lemish, 2008; Nairn et al., 2011). One stereotype is that of the mentally disturbed person as a helpless victim; another is that of the mentally ill person as an evil villain who is unpredictable, dangerous, and violent (Camp et al., 2010; Sowislo et al., 2017). But *are* people with psychological disorders more violent than other people?

⯅ A Voice for People with Mental Illnesses Elyn Saks, whose story is featured in this chapter's prologue, directs the Saks Institute for Mental Health Law, Policy, and Ethics, which she founded at the University of Southern California. The institute works to inform policy decisions related to mental health. "Our objective is to help people with mental illness lead fulfilling and productive lives," Saks writes (2018).

Courtesy of USC Gould School of Law

psychopathology The scientific study of the origins, symptoms, and development of psychological disorders.

First, it is a myth that most people with a psychological disorder are violent. Researchers estimate that only 4 percent of all violent acts are committed by people with a mental illness (Varshney et al., 2016). Second, there is some evidence of *slightly* higher rates of violence among people with severe mental illnesses if they are experiencing extreme psychological symptoms, such as paranoid delusional ideas and auditory hallucinations, like hearing voices (Bucci et al., 2013; Skeem et al., 2015). However, a person with a mental illness who is *not* suffering from such extreme symptoms is no more likely than others to be involved in violent or illegal behavior (Peterson et al., 2014). And other research has found that rates of violence among people with severe mental illnesses were only elevated if they were also abusing alcohol or drugs (Elbogen & Johnson, 2009).

Often, the incidence of violent behavior among people who suffer from mental health issues is exaggerated in media portrayals. In turn, the exaggerated fear of violence from people with a psychological disorder contributes to the stigma of mental illness (Fazel et al., 2009).

The social stigma that can be associated with psychological disorders often makes people reluctant to seek the help of mental health professionals (Bathje & Pryor, 2011; Corrigan et al., 2014). Some researchers believe we should use alternative means, such as social media, to reach people who may need help. To learn more, read the Critical Thinking box, "Should Social Media Help to Diagnose Disorders?"

What Is a Psychological Disorder?

What exactly are we talking about when we say that someone has a psychological disorder? A **psychological disorder** is *a pattern of behavioral or psychological symptoms that causes significant personal distress, impairs the ability to function in one or more important areas of life* (e.g., work or schooling), *or both* (DSM-5, 2013). An important qualification is that the pattern of behavioral or psychological symptoms must represent a serious departure from the prevailing social and cultural norms. Hence, the behavior of a traditional Hindu woman who refuses to eat onions, garlic, or other "hot" foods following the death of her husband is typical behavior because that norm is part of the Hindu culture.

What determines whether a given pattern of symptoms or behaviors qualifies as a psychological disorder? Throughout this chapter, you'll notice numerous references to DSM-5. **DSM-5** is *the abbreviation for the Diagnostic and Statistical Manual of Mental Disorders, Fifth Edition, which describes the symptoms of a disorder and diagnostic guidelines*. It was published in 2013 by the American Psychiatric Association.

The first edition of the *Diagnostic and Statistical Manual* was published in 1952. With each new edition, the number of distinct disorders has increased—from fewer than a hundred in the first edition to more than three times that number in recent editions, including DSM-5 (Frances & Widiger, 2012; Houts, 2002). Some disorders that are relatively well known today, such as eating disorders, attention-deficit/hyperactivity disorder, and social anxiety disorder, were added only in more recent editions. And, some behavior patterns that were categorized as "disorders" in early editions, such as homosexuality, have been dropped because we now understand that sexual orientation is not pathological.

DSM-5 describes more than 260 specific psychological disorders, plus numerous additional conditions, like child physical abuse and educational problems—a grand total of 541 diagnostic categories (Blashfield et al., 2014). It provides codes for each disorder and includes the symptoms, the criteria that must be met to make a diagnosis, as well as the frequency, typical course, and risk factors for each disorder. It also includes issues related to gender and culture for each disorder. DSM-5 provides mental health professionals with both a common language for labeling disorders and comprehensive guidelines for diagnosing them.

DSM-5 increasingly matches the disorders outlined in a similar manual, the World Health Organization's *International Classification of Diseases (ICD)*. The ICD is the international standard for diagnostic classifications, and mental health clinicians in the United States are now required to reference its diagnostic codes when seeking reimbursement through health insurance companies (Chamberlin, 2014).

MYTH ◄ **SCIENCE**

Is it true that most people with a psychological disorder are violent?

MBI/Alamy Stock Photo

⌃ **The Stigmatizing Language of Abnormal Behavior** If you saw this person talking to themselves, what word might you use to describe them? "Abnormal"? Or even "crazy"? These words help to create a stigma about a behavior that is atypical. And that stigma can have harmful consequences for the psychological well-being of the person with the stigmatized condition. You might also be wrong. Perhaps this person is talking on the phone with earbuds that aren't visible. It also turns out that talking out loud to ourselves is fairly common (Mari-Beffa, 2017).

psychological disorder A pattern of behavioral and psychological symptoms that causes significant personal distress, impairs the ability to function in one or more important areas of life, or both.

DSM-5 The abbreviation for the *Diagnostic and Statistical Manual of Mental Disorders*, Fifth Edition, which describes the symptoms of a disorder and diagnostic guidelines.

CRITICAL THINKING

Should Social Media Help to Diagnose Disorders?

Can your online behavior provide a window into your mind? Some researchers think so. One study found differences between the Instagram photos of depressed and nondepressed people (Reece & Danforth, 2016). Depressed people, for example, were more likely to use the "Inkwell" filter that made their photos black and white. Similarly, the mention of symptoms of depression, such as sadness or loneliness, on Facebook or Twitter predicted future episodes of depression, even several months before a diagnosis (Eichstaedt et al., 2018b; Reece et al., 2017). And analyses of the language used in text messages (e.g., degree of positive emotion and anger) and Google Searches (e.g., "how to kill yourself") are able to predict, statistically, who is at high risk for attempting suicide (Glenn et al., 2020; Ma-Kellams et al., 2016).

Social media can shed light on patterns of psychopathology at the group level as well as at the individual level. One study found positive correlations between the numbers of tweets related to depression or schizophrenia and the numbers of "crisis episodes," such as admissions to inpatient units, reported by London mental health centers (Kolliakou et al., 2020). Could tweets help mental health centers prepare for an increase in cases or help to identify categories of people who are most at risk for a crisis?

Some researchers believe that information about online behavior could be harnessed to help identify people who may be struggling with psychological disorders and who could benefit from referrals or formal diagnoses. But there also are ethical concerns (Inkster et al., 2016). What if someone is identified as having psychological problems because of a false or exaggerated posting? Could such an identification violate someone's privacy in a way that is upsetting? Should organizations be required to gain consent before reviewing someone's social media for diagnostic purposes? One study in the United Kingdom found that just 15 percent of people were comfortable with the analysis of their social media posts for depression without their consent (Ford et al., 2019). And it wasn't an effect of age; the percentage was just barely higher—20 percent—among 16–24-year-olds.

These kinds of concerns led to a short life for one Twitter app (N. Lee, 2014). Called *Samaritans Radar*, the app monitored friends' tweets. If a tweet included certain phrases—like "tired of being alone" or "hate myself"—Samaritans Radar would alert the user and offer guidance on how to provide help (D. Lee, 2014). Despite the public nature of the original tweets, critics had privacy concerns, worrying that the alerts would embolden "stalkers and bullies." The app was suspended after just nine days.

These concerns are serious ones. But social media are widely used, produce enormous amounts of data, and can offer accurate

Buena Vista Images/Getty Images

▲ **Social Media and Diagnosis** Is using Instagram's "Inkwell" filter to make photos black and white a sign that someone might be depressed?

information about people's thoughts and experiences. Some researchers believe their use could eventually "revolutionise mental healthcare" (Inkster et al., 2016). But first, ethical guidelines must be developed. How can psychologists ensure confidentiality for people whose information is gathered online? What requirements should guide the reporting of worrisome posts? And how can psychologists address the public's privacy concerns (Inkster et al., 2016)?

Until widely accepted ethical guidelines are developed, researchers suggest using online tools only for research with participants who give consent (Eichstaedt et al., 2018b; Inkster et al., 2016). Adding a human step to the process may help, too. Both Instagram and Facebook have introduced new tools to help people who are suicidal, but they are triggered only when a friend, rather than a computer algorithm, raises an alert (Rogers, 2016; Singer, 2018).

CRITICAL THINKING QUESTIONS

- Are there situations in which a need for intervention could outweigh privacy concerns?

- If your online activity suggests that you may have a serious psychological disorder, would you want the social media platform to communicate this to you? Would you want the social media platform to notify your friends?

- You notice that your friend has been sounding very depressed in their comments on Instagram. How is this observation different from data gathered by researchers looking at Instagram?

It's important to understand that DSM-5 was not written by a single person or even a small group of experts. Rather, DSM-5 represents the *consensus* of hundreds of mental health professionals, mostly psychiatrists and clinical psychologists, as well as scientists who study psychopathology, representing many different organizations and perspectives. The American Psychiatric Association also developed a Web site to allow both professionals and the public to provide feedback (Blashfield et al., 2014).

Despite these efforts, DSM-5 has many critics (see Frances & Widiger, 2012; Wakefield, 2013a; G. Watts, 2012). More specifically, it has been criticized for:

- inclusion of some conditions that are too typical to be considered disorders, such as extreme sadness related to bereavement (Maj, 2012; Zachar et al., 2017).

- use of arbitrary cutoffs to draw the line between people with and without a particular disorder, and even between different diagnoses (Allsopp et al., 2019; Caspi et al., 2014; Insel, 2013; Laceulle et al., 2015).

- gender bias for some diagnoses (Marecek & Gavey, 2013; Yonkers & Clarke, 2011); for example, the criteria for autism spectrum disorder tend to emphasize symptoms that boys experience more than girls, so girls are more likely to be undiagnosed (Haney, 2016).

- possible bias resulting from the financial ties of many DSM-5 authors to the pharmaceutical industry, which might benefit from the expansion of mental illness categories (Cosgrove & Krimsky, 2012).

Despite its flaws, DSM-5 is the most comprehensive and authoritative set of guidelines available for diagnosing psychological disorders. Thus, we'll refer to the DSM often in this chapter.

Although DSM and its categories form the most accepted diagnostic model right now, there are other ways to understand psychological disorders (Clark et al., 2017). Some researchers are using biological findings to understand what psychological disorders have in common rather than what makes them different (Cuthbert & Insel, 2013; Lang et al., 2016). The U.S. National Institute of Mental Health (NIMH) is leading long-term efforts to develop a new diagnostic system based on these common factors rather than on traditional categories. Called Research Domain Criteria, or RDoC for short, this system provides a framework for researchers to understand both environmental and neurological underpinnings of psychological disorders (NIMH, n.d.). One feature of this initiative is that it approaches symptoms of mental illness as dimensions, rather than as strict categories. With dimensions, someone can be low, high, or in the middle.

In line with RDoC, researchers have taken several approaches to understanding general aspects shared by all psychological disorders (Del Giudice, 2016). Some have identified similar genetic risk factors and similar changes in the brain (Gandal et al., 2018; Goodkind et al., 2015; Plomin et al., 2016). Others have identified a general p factor that incorporates the wide array of symptoms underlying all forms of mental illness (Caspi et al., 2014). The p factor provides a measure of the overall severity of psychological disorders, and it relates to a cluster of risk factors including a family history of mental illness and early neurological problems, such as with language development.

Although they disagree about the specifics, these theorists agree that there is some set of general, shared characteristics of psychological disorders (Del Giudice, 2016; Hofmann et al., 2016; Laceulle et al., 2015). These new approaches are an exciting development that may change the diagnosis, and even the treatment, of mental illness. Researchers warn, however, that these new approaches are unlikely to replace the DSM in the near future (Kraemer, 2015).

The Prevalence of Psychological Disorders: A 50–50 Chance?

Just how common are psychological disorders? To investigate that question, researcher Ronald Kessler and his colleagues (2005a, 2005b) conducted a nationally representative survey of more than 9,000 Americans, ages 18 and older. Called the National Comorbidity Survey Replication (NCS-R), the survey involved more than two years of face-to-face interviews throughout the country. Participants were asked if they had experienced specific symptoms of psychological disorders: (1) during the previous 12 months and (2) at any point in their lives.

The NCS-R results reconfirmed many of the findings of previous national surveys, including the finding that psychological disorders are much more prevalent than many people believe (Kessler et al., 2005c). Specifically, the NCS-R found that one out of four respondents (26 percent) reported experiencing the symptoms of a psychological

MYTH ◀ SCIENCE

Is it true that psychological disorders are rare?

Massimo Pizzotti/AGE Fotostock

▲ How Prevalent Are Psychological Disorders? Psychological disorders are far more common than most people think. According to the National Institute of Mental Health (2021a), about one in five U.S. adults has experienced the symptoms of some type of psychological disorder during the previous year. And almost half will experience a mental illness at some point during their lives (Kessler et al., 2005b). Although these rates may seem disturbing, researcher Ronald Kessler (2003) puts it into perspective: "It wouldn't surprise anyone if I said that 99.9% of the population had been physically ill at some time in their life. Why, then, should it surprise anyone that 50% of the population has been mentally ill at some time in their life?"

THINK LIKE A SCIENTIST

Tracking the incidence of mental health problems is challenging. Can Internet searches reveal trends? Go to Achieve: Resources to **Think Like a Scientist** about **Tracking Mental Illness Online.**

  Achieve

disorder during the previous year (Kessler et al., 2005b). And almost one in two adults (46 percent) had experienced the symptoms of a psychological disorder at some point in their lives. The NCS-R and other surveys like it also reveal a high degree of comorbidity, which means that people diagnosed with one disorder are also frequently diagnosed with an additional disorder. In fact, about 46 percent of people with a mental illness have at least two at the same time. **Figure 14.1** shows the lifetime prevalence of some of the major categories of psychological disorders.

Recent numbers back the findings of the NCS-R. In 2019, approximately 50 million adults in the United States had a psychological disorder (SAMHSA, 2020). About one in five have had a mental illness in the past year (NIMH, 2021a). And rates of mental illness are high not just in the United States but also globally. In a large-scale study conducted in conjunction with the World Health Organization, researchers surveyed about 85,000 people in 17 countries from almost every continent (Kessler et al., 2007). On average, the lifetime rate of mental illness was found to be about one in three.

Recent research found that a quarter of people in the United States with a mental illness reported that they did not have access to treatment in 2019 (SAMSHA, 2020). This trend is shared globally, with several factors contributing to this unmet need for treatment, including lack of insurance, low income, and lack of access to mental health care (Santiago et al., 2013; Wang et al., 2011). Some people also fail to seek treatment because of lack of awareness, fear of stigmatization, or a belief that treatment would not help (Clement et al., 2015; Knettel, 2016). Indian-born psychiatrist *Shekhar Saxena* perceives the lack of mental health care as an enormous problem even in countries with economic resources: "When it comes to mental health, all countries are developing countries" (Davies, 2018). The current Director of the Department of Mental Health and Substance Abuse at the World Health Organization (WHO), Saxena has been described as "a giant in the world of mental health." His work focuses on reducing stigma and expanding access to treatment. This work will be particularly relevant given the increase in psychological disorders during the pandemic (Wu et al., 2021).

Even without treatment, though, it seems clear that most people manage to weather psychological symptoms without becoming completely debilitated and needing professional intervention (Mojtabai et al., 2011). One explanation for this is that the symptoms of many psychological disorders, especially those involving mild to moderate symptoms, diminish with the simple passage of time or with improvements in the person's overall situation. Nevertheless, many effective treatments available for psychological disorders can produce improvements that occur much more quickly and endure longer. We'll look at the different types of therapies used to treat psychological disorders in the next chapter.

For the remainder of this chapter, we'll focus on psychological disorders in six DSM-5 categories: anxiety, posttraumatic stress, and obsessive–compulsive disorders; depressive and bipolar disorders; eating disorders; personality disorders; dissociative disorders; and schizophrenia. Along with being some of the most common disorders encountered by mental health professionals, they're also the ones that our students ask

FIGURE 14.1 The Lifetime Prevalence of Psychological Disorders This graph shows the lifetime prevalence for some of the major categories of psychological disorders based on findings from the National Comorbidity Survey Replication (NCS-R). The NCS-R reconfirmed that the lifetime prevalence of experiencing a psychological disorder is almost one out of two.

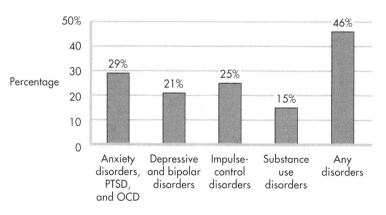

Lifetime prevalence estimates

TABLE 14.1

Some Additional Diagnostic Categories in DSM-5

Diagnostic Category	Core Features	Examples of Specific Disorders
Neurodevelopmental disorders	Wide range of developmental, behavioral, learning, and communication disorders that are usually first diagnosed in infancy, childhood, or adolescence. Symptoms of a particular disorder may vary depending on a child's age and development level.	**Autism spectrum disorder:** Onset of symptoms prior to age of 3. Characterized by: (1) deficits in social communication and social interaction and (2) restricted, repetitive behaviors, interests, and activities; diagnosed according to level of symptom of severity, ranging from "requiring support" to "requiring very substantial support." **Tourette's disorder:** Onset prior to age of 18. Characterized by motor tics, such as recurring spasmodic movements of the head or arms, and vocal tics, such as recurring and sudden clicking, grunting, or snorting sounds. Sometimes involves uncontrollable utterances of profane or obscene words.
Substance-related and addictive disorders (see the chapter Consciousness and Its Variations)	Cluster of cognitive, behavioral, and physiological symptoms indicating that the individual continues using the substance or engaging in the behavior despite significant problems.	**Substance use disorder:** Recurrent substance use that involves impaired control, disruption of social, occupational, and interpersonal functioning, and the development of craving, tolerance, and withdrawal symptoms. **Gambling disorder:** Persistent gambling that disrupts personal, family, and/or vocational pursuits.
Somatic symptoms and related disorders	Persistent, recurring complaints of bodily (or *somatic*) symptoms that are accompanied by abnormal thoughts, feelings, and behaviors in response to these symptoms.	**Somatic symptom disorder:** Characterized by excessive worry or distress that is out of proportion to the seriousness of physical symptoms that are present. **Illness anxiety disorder:** Excessive preoccupation with one's health and worry about illness despite the absence of serious physical symptoms.
Disruptive, impulse-control, and conduct disorders	Problems in the self-control of emotions and behaviors as manifested in behaviors that harm or violate the rights of others.	**Kleptomania:** The recurrent failure to resist impulses to steal items that are not needed for personal use or for their monetary value. **Pyromania:** Deliberately setting fires on more than one occasion, accompanied by pleasure, gratification, or relief of tension.

Source: American Psychiatric Association (2013).

This table includes some of the main diagnostic categories that are *not* covered in this chapter. We cover the major classes of psychological disorders in this chapter. Other important, but less common, diagnostic categories are shown here.

about most often. To help you distinguish between typical and maladaptive behaviors, we'll start the discussion of each mental illness category by describing behavior that falls within the typical range of psychological functioning, such as common feelings of anxiety or normal variations in mood.

Table 14.1 describes other categories of psychological disorders contained in the DSM-5. Some of these disorders have been discussed in previous chapters. In the Psych for Your Life section at the end of this chapter, we'll look at what you can do to help prevent one of the most disturbing consequences of psychological problems—suicide.

Anxiety Disorders, Posttraumatic Stress Disorder, and Obsessive–Compulsive Disorder

■ KEY THEME

Intense anxiety that disrupts normal functioning is an essential feature of the anxiety disorders, posttraumatic stress disorder, and obsessive–compulsive disorder.

≡ KEY QUESTIONS

• How does pathological anxiety differ from normal anxiety?

• What characterizes generalized anxiety disorder and panic disorder?

• What are the phobias, and how have they been explained?

anxiety An unpleasant emotional state characterized by physical arousal and feelings of tension, apprehension, and worry.

anxiety disorders A category of psychological disorders in which extreme anxiety is the main diagnostic feature and causes significant disruptions in the person's cognitive, behavioral, or interpersonal functioning.

generalized anxiety disorder (GAD) An anxiety disorder characterized by excessive, global, and persistent symptoms of anxiety.

MYTH ◄ SCIENCE

Is it true that the less anxiety you have, the better?

▲ **Adele and Anxiety Disorders** Singer Adele has long suffered from debilitating anxiety while touring. She described having regular "anxiety attacks" that limit how often she plays to large audiences. She told a reporter, "One show in Amsterdam I was so nervous I escaped out the fire exit. I've thrown up a couple of times. . . . I have anxiety attacks a lot" (Touré, 2011).

The emotion is familiar to all of us. **Anxiety** is *an unpleasant emotional state characterized by physical arousal and feelings of tension, apprehension, and worry*. Although it is unpleasant, anxiety is sometimes helpful. Think of anxiety as your personal internal alarm system that tells you that something is not quite right. When it alerts you to a realistic threat, anxiety is adaptive and helpful. For example, anxiety about your grades may motivate you to study harder.

Anxiety has both physical and mental effects. As your internal alarm system, anxiety puts you on *physical alert,* preparing you to defensively "fight" or "flee" potential dangers. Anxiety also puts you on *mental alert,* making you focus your attention squarely on the threatening situation. You become extremely vigilant, scanning the environment for potential threats. When the threat has passed, your alarm system shuts off and you calm down. But even if the problem persists, you can normally put your anxious thoughts aside temporarily and attend to other matters.

Anxiety disorders are *a category of psychological disorders in which extreme anxiety is the main diagnostic feature and causes significant disruptions in the person's cognitive, behavioral, or interpersonal functioning.* It's as if you've triggered a faulty car alarm that activates at the slightest touch and has a broken "off " switch. Three features distinguish typical anxiety from pathological anxiety. First, pathological anxiety is *irrational.* The anxiety is provoked by perceived threats that are exaggerated or nonexistent, and the anxiety response is out of proportion to the actual importance of the situation. Second, pathological anxiety is *uncontrollable.* The person can't shut off the alarm reaction, even when they know it's unrealistic. And third, pathological anxiety is *disruptive.* It interferes with relationships, job or academic performance, or everyday activities. In short, pathological anxiety is unreasonably intense, frequent, persistent, and disruptive (Beidel & Stipelman, 2007; Woo & Keatinge, 2008).

As a symptom, anxiety occurs in many different psychological disorders. In the anxiety disorders, however, anxiety is the *main* symptom, although it is manifested differently in each of the disorders. Other disorders are not technically anxiety disorders, although they include anxiety as a symptom. These include posttraumatic stress disorder (PTSD) and obsessive–compulsive disorder (OCD). In this section, we'll talk about anxiety disorders, PTSD, and OCD, but we'll first focus on the anxiety disorders.

Disorders that include anxiety—the anxiety disorders, PTSD, and OCD—are among the most common of all psychological disorders. According to some estimates, they will affect about one in four people in the United States during their lifetimes (Kessler et al., 2005b; McGregor, 2009). Globally, more than 250 million people around the world, or about 4 percent of the population, experience an anxiety disorder in any given year (WHO, 2017). Evidence of disabling anxiety has been found in virtually every culture studied, although symptoms may vary from one cultural group to another (Chentsova-Dutton & Tsai, 2007; WHO, 2017). Most of these disorders are much more common in women than in men (McLean et al., 2011; WHO, 2017).

Generalized Anxiety Disorder: Worrying About Anything and Everything

Generalized anxiety disorder (GAD) is *an anxiety disorder characterized by excessive, global, and persistent symptoms of anxiety.* People with this disorder are regularly tense and anxious, and their anxiety is pervasive. They feel anxious about a wide range of life circumstances, sometimes with little or no apparent justification (Craske & Waters, 2005; Sanfelippo, 2006). The more issues about which a person worries excessively, the more likely it is that they suffer from generalized anxiety disorder (DSM-5, 2013). U.S. singer–songwriter Charlie Puth has talked about his struggles with this kind of constant anxiety; he explains, "I'm already a very in-my-head anxious person. I don't really do well when I'm alone a lot because I'm alone with my thoughts which is not good. It gets very freaky" (Caramanica, 2018).

Normally, anxiety quickly dissipates when a threatening situation is resolved. In generalized anxiety disorder, however, when one source of worry is removed, another quickly moves in to take its place. The anxiety can be attached to virtually any object or to none at all.

Explaining Generalized Anxiety Disorder   What causes generalized anxiety disorder? As is true with most psychological disorders, environmental, psychological, and genetic as well as other biological factors are probably involved in GAD (Moreno-Peral et al., 2014; Payne et al., 2014). For example, a brain that is "wired" for anxiety can give a person a head start toward developing GAD in later life, but problematic relationships and stressful experiences can make the possibility more likely. Signs of problematic anxiety can be evident from a very early age, such as in the example of a child with a very shy temperament who consistently feels overwhelming anxiety in new situations or when separated from their parents. In some cases, such children develop anxiety disorders such as GAD in adulthood (Creswell & O'Connor, 2011; Weems & Silverman, 2008).

Panic Attacks and Panic Disorders: Sudden Episodes of Extreme Anxiety

Generalized anxiety disorder is like the dull ache of a sore tooth—a constant, ongoing sense of uneasiness, distress, and apprehension. In contrast, a **panic attack** is *a sudden episode of extreme anxiety that rapidly escalates in intensity.* The most common symptoms of a panic attack are a pounding heart, rapid breathing, breathlessness, and a choking sensation. Accompanying the intense, escalating surge of physical arousal are feelings of terror and the belief that one is about to die, go crazy, or completely lose control. A panic attack typically peaks within 10 minutes of onset and then gradually subsides. Nevertheless, the physical symptoms of a panic attack are so severe and frightening that it's not unusual for people to rush to an emergency room, convinced they are having a heart attack, stroke, or seizure (Buccelletti et al., 2013; Craske & Barlow, 2008).

Sometimes panic attacks occur after a stressful experience, such as an injury or illness, or during a stressful period of life, such as while changing jobs or during a period of marital conflict (Conway et al., 2016; Moitra et al., 2011). In other cases, however, panic attacks seem to come from nowhere.

A **panic disorder** is *an anxiety disorder in which the person experiences frequent and unexpected panic attacks.* One person may have panic attacks several times a month. Another person may go for months without an attack and then experience panic attacks for several days in a row. Understandably, people with panic disorder are quite apprehensive about when and where the next panic attack will hit (Craske & Waters, 2005; Good & Hinton, 2009).

Some panic disorder sufferers go on to develop agoraphobia. **Agoraphobia** is *an anxiety disorder involving extreme fear of suffering a panic attack or other embarrassing or incapacitating symptoms in a public situation where escape is impossible and help is unavailable* (DSM-5, 2013). For example, crowds, stores, elevators, public transportation, or even traveling in a car may be avoided. Many people with agoraphobia, imprisoned by their fears, never leave their homes. For some, this was worsened by the pandemic.

For example, Anya, a 32-year-old accountant, experienced infrequent but intense attacks of anxiety and fearfulness. Heart pounding and perspiring heavily, she felt as though she couldn't breathe. More than once, Anya called an ambulance because she was convinced she was having a heart attack. As her panic attacks increased in frequency and severity, Anya quit her job, fearful that she might have a panic attack while driving to work, riding the elevator to her office, or meeting with clients.

Explaining Panic Disorder   People with panic disorder are often hypersensitive to the signs of physical arousal (Schmidt & Keough, 2010). The fluttering heartbeat or momentary dizziness that the average person barely notices signals disaster to the panic-prone. Researchers have suggested that this oversensitivity to physical arousal is one of three important factors in the development of panic disorder. This *triple vulnerabilities model* of panic states that a biological predisposition toward anxiety, a low sense of control over potentially life-threatening events, and an oversensitivity to physical sensations combine to make a person vulnerable to panic attacks (Bentley et al., 2013; Craske & Barlow, 2008; McGinn et al., 2015).

panic attack   A sudden episode of extreme anxiety that rapidly escalates in intensity.

panic disorder   An anxiety disorder in which the person experiences frequent and unexpected panic attacks.

agoraphobia   An anxiety disorder involving extreme fear of suffering a panic attack or other embarrassing or incapacitating symptoms in a public situation where escape is impossible and help is unavailable.

PeopleImages/Getty Images. Licensed material is being used for illustrative purposes only; person depicted in the licensed material is a model.

^ Agoraphobia   People with agoraphobia fear suffering a panic attack if stuck in an enclosed place, like an elevator. People with agoraphobia often avoid situations in which they feel they cannot escape. Some never leave their homes.

IN FOCUS

Mental Health During the Pandemic

What if everyone in the world experienced a traumatic event at the same time? What sounded like a mere thought experiment as recently as 2019 became reality when the pandemic led to long lockdowns in many parts of the world. Millions of people became gravely ill or died, lost a loved one, lost a job, went hungry, or experienced profound social isolation.

The effects of the pandemic were exacerbated by longstanding racial disparities. Because the pandemic was first identified in Wuhan, China, there was a rise in anti-Asian sentiment and even violence against Asian people in many countries (Cheng, 2021; Human Rights Watch, 2020b). Then, in May 2020, George Floyd, a Black man, died while handcuffed, lying facedown under the knee of a Minneapolis police officer, who was later convicted of his murder. The murder of George Floyd, the latest in a string of killings of Black people at the hands of police, led to a reckoning about race, and a burgeoning antiracism movement, in the United States and many other places around the world.

The pandemic, most likely in combination with the rising racial tensions and xenophobia, led to an increase in psychological disorders. Surveys in countries around the world have documented startling elevations in perceived stress, depression, and anxiety (e.g., Limcaoco et al., 2020; Mazza et al., 2020; Robillard et al., 2020; Torales et al., 2020). A meta-analysis of 50 studies documented that about half of the general public experienced pandemic-related psychological consequences including sleep problems, anxiety, and depression (Krishnamoorthy et al., 2020). These rates were higher among health care workers, and even higher among those who were sick with COVID-19. Another meta-analysis of more than 60 studies found that global rates of depression and anxiety went from around 10 percent before the pandemic to around 30 percent during the pandemic (Wu et al., 2021).

We also have witnessed vast inequalities during the pandemic, and these are true for mental health as well. As author Dana Givens (2020) wrote, "between the disproportionate toll of the coronavirus on Black and Hispanic people and the social unrest associated with the Black Lives Matter movement, Black people have a new set of stresses. Even Michelle Obama has said she's been dealing with 'low-grade depression.'" Research shows that members of marginalized racial and ethnic groups face increased risk for mental illness due to ongoing structural inequalities that have been exacerbated during the pandemic, including higher rates of working in essential jobs and lack of access to mental health care (Loeb et al., 2020).

Women also face greater psychological risks during the pandemic due to their disproportionate numbers in essential jobs and the intensified pandemic burdens of child care and other household duties, often while employed (Thibaut & van Wijngaarden-Cremers, 2020). So do the elderly, who are more likely to be socially isolated and therefore at higher risk for psychological disorders (Armitage & Nellums, 2020). And young people in the LGBT community have been cut off from their social support systems and may be spending more time at home, sometimes with families who do not accept them (Gonzales et al., 2020).

There have been anecdotal reports that some people with psychological disorders are doing better during the pandemic, perhaps because they have developed coping skills through therapy or because their lives have slowed down (Jarral, 2020). Daniel, a university instructor in his 40s, who has long suffered from depressive and anxiety disorders, describes the relief he has experienced during the pandemic: "My usual life feels like a pinball machine. You're whacking the buttons and the paddles are flailing around,

phobia A persistent and irrational fear of a specific object, situation, or activity.

specific phobia An excessive, intense, and irrational fear of a specific object, situation, or activity that is actively avoided or endured with marked anxiety.

People with panic disorder may also be victims of their own maladaptive thinking. According to the *catastrophic cognitions theory,* people with panic disorder are not only oversensitive to physical sensations, they also tend to *catastrophize* the meaning of their experience (Hinton & Hinton, 2009; Sandin et al., 2015). A few moments of increased heart rate after climbing a flight of stairs is misinterpreted as the warning signs of a heart attack. Such catastrophic misinterpretations simply add to the physiological arousal, creating a vicious circle in which the frightening symptoms intensify.

Classical conditioning, which we read about in the chapter on learning, plays a role in both of these models of panic disorder (Lissek et al., 2010). For example, a person may experience panic attacks following a neutral stimulus such as an increase in heart rate. Eventually, they might be conditioned to associate the increased heart rate with panic attacks. The increased heart rate is then a conditioned stimulus that leads to the conditioned response of panic. So, classical conditioning adds fuel to the vicious circle of panic disorder.

Syndromes resembling panic disorder have been reported in many cultures (Chentsova-Dutton & Tsai, 2007; Hinton & Hinton, 2009). For example, the Spanish phrase *ataque de nervios* literally means "attack of nerves." It's a disorder reported in many Latin American cultures, including in Puerto Rico and among many other Latinos/Latinas in the United States. *Ataque de nervios* has many symptoms in common with panic disorder—heart palpitations, dizziness, and the fear of dying, going crazy, or losing control. However, the person experiencing *ataque de nervios* also becomes hysterical. They may scream, swear, strike out at others, sometimes not even making contact, and it just doesn't feel like that any more" (Jarral, 2020). Similarly, film critic Juan Barquín, who has suffered from major depressive disorder, explains, "Not having those expectations of what you have to do on a regular basis is just so refreshing by comparison to having all those established norms" (Bradley, 2020). (Of course, those who are unemployed, essential workers, or juggling a job and children at home may be less likely to have such experiences.) Psychologist Anthony Mancini (2020), who researches trauma and loss, speculates that future research will show uneven responses to the pandemic, and that some people may indeed do better, perhaps because of increased connections and cooperation with their communities and social network. And some people might experience posttraumatic growth, positive change following a trauma, that we discuss in the section on posttraumatic stress disorder.

One silver lining of the combination of the need for social distancing and rising rates of psychological disorders is that telehealth and other forms of eHealth have—finally—been legalized, expanding access to mental health care. (We'll explore these changes more in the chapter on therapies.) Unfortunately, the sheer number of people in need of treatment has overwhelmed clinicians, and the waiting lists for psychotherapy

Gary Dineen/Getty Images

Paul George's Lockdown Paul George, a professional basketball player for the Los Angeles Clippers in the U.S. National Basketball Association (NBA), entered the pandemic bubble, which required isolation, including from family (Youngmisuk, 2020). George soon found himself in what he described as "a dark place" and became the first NBA player to shoot below 25 percent for three games in a row, the worst NBA playoff performance over a three-game stretch since 1960. "I underestimated mental health, honestly. I had anxiety. A little bit of depression. Just being locked in here. I just wasn't there. I checked out." George bounced back, crediting his turnaround to sessions with a team mental health professional and the social support of his teammates, "the camaraderie, the brotherhood. I can't thank this squad enough" (Esnaashari, 2020). George's experience during the pandemic is not uncommon. Even with the enormous resources of the NBA, lockdown is isolating—and difficult.

increased during the pandemic. Perhaps, when the pandemic ends and our lives return to some semblance of "normal," the expansion of platforms through which people might seek psychotherapy will be among the good things that came out of the pandemic.

and break things. Funerals, accidents, or family conflicts often trigger such attacks. Because *ataque de nervios* tends to elicit immediate social support from others, it seems to be a culturally shaped, acceptable way to respond to severe stress.

The Phobias: Fear and Loathing

A **phobia** is *a persistent and irrational fear of a specific object, situation, or activity.* In the general population, *mild* irrational fears that don't significantly interfere with a person's ability to function are very common. Many people are fearful of certain animals, such as dogs or snakes, or are moderately uncomfortable in particular situations, such as flying in a plane or riding in a glass elevator. Nonetheless, many people cope with such fears without being overwhelmed with anxiety. As long as the fear doesn't interfere with their daily functioning, they would not be diagnosed with a psychological disorder.

In comparison, a **specific phobia** is *an excessive, intense, and irrational fear of a specific object, situation, or activity that is actively avoided or endured with marked anxiety.* In some people, encountering the feared situation or object can provoke a full-fledged panic attack. Importantly, the incapacitating terror and anxiety interfere with the person's ability to function in daily life. Consider the case of Armand Dávila, who has a phobia of needles (Rosenwald, 2020). He hyperventilates when he even sees a needle and avoids injections unless absolutely necessary. He understands his phobia could have an impact on his health, especially with COVID vaccines. "At some point, you really do need to

Vassiliy Vishnevskiy/iStockphoto

Yuck! It's hard to suppress a shudder of disgust at the sight of a slug sliming its way across the sidewalk. Instinctively, it seems, many people find such creatures repulsive, possibly because they are associated with disease, infection, or filth. Such phobias may reflect a fear of contamination or infection that is also based on human evolutionary history (Cisler et al., 2007).

TABLE 14.2

Some Unusual Phobias

Amathophobia	Fear of dust
Anemophobia	Fear of wind
Aphephobia	Fear of being touched by another person
Bibliophobia	Fear of books
Catotrophobia	Fear of breaking a mirror
Ergophobia	Fear of work or responsibility
Erythrophobia	Fear of red objects
Gamophobia	Fear of marriage
Hypertrichophobia	Fear of growing excessive amounts of body hair
Levophobia	Fear of things being on the left side of your body
Phobophobia	Fear of acquiring a phobia
Phonophobia	Fear of the sound of your own voice
Triskaidekaphobia	Fear of the number 13

▲ **Social Anxiety Disorder** About one out of eight adults in the United States has experienced social anxiety disorder at some point in their life (Kessler et al., 2005a). Social anxiety disorder is far more debilitating than everyday shyness. People with social anxiety disorder are intensely fearful of being watched or judged by others. Even ordinary activities, such as eating lunch in a public café, can cause unbearable anxiety.

ask: What am I more afraid of? COVID or the needle? It's COVID." He plans to get the shot while distracting himself: "You have to put on your big boy pants, close your eyes and wear your headphones."

Globally, about 7 percent of the population experiences a specific phobia at some time in their lives (Wardenaar et al., 2017). More than twice as many women as men suffer from specific phobia, and the rates are higher in higher-income countries. For example, more than 12 percent of the U.S. population experiences a specific phobia at some time in their lives. Occasionally, people have unusual phobias. (See **Table 14.2**.) Oprah Winfrey, for example, has been afraid of chewing gum since she was a child, when her grandmother left used gum around the house. In an interview with Jamie Foxx, she told him, "When I saw you chewing on Oscar night, I freaked out" (*O Magazine*, 2005). Generally, the objects or situations that produce specific phobias tend to fall into four categories:

- Fear of particular situations, such as flying, driving, crowds, or enclosed places
- Fear of features of the natural environment, such as heights or lightning
- Fear of injury or blood, including fear of injections or dental procedures
- Fear of animals and insects, such as snakes, spiders, dogs, cats, slugs, or bats

Social Anxiety Disorder: Fear of Being Judged in Social Situations A second type of phobia also deserves additional comment. **Social anxiety disorder** is *an anxiety disorder involving the extreme and irrational fear of being embarrassed, judged, or scrutinized by others in social situations*. It is one of the most common psychological disorders and is more prevalent among women than men (Altemus, 2006; Kessler et al., 2005b). Social anxiety disorder goes well beyond the shyness that everyone sometimes feels at social gatherings. Rather, the person with social anxiety disorder is paralyzed by fear of social situations in which they may be judged by others. Eating a meal in public, making small talk at a party, or using a public restroom can be agonizing.

The core of social anxiety disorder seems to be an irrational fear of being critically evaluated by others. This fear is fed by an exaggerated tendency to pay attention to negative information in social settings, such as noticing one person's unhappy expression rather than others' happy expressions (Grafton & MacLeod, 2016). Some, but not all, people with social anxiety disorder recognize that their fear is excessive and irrational. Even so, they approach social situations with tremendous dread and anxiety (Kashdan et al., 2013). In severe cases, they may even suffer a panic attack in social situations.

As with panic attacks, cultural influences can add some novel twists to social anxiety disorder. Consider *taijin kyofusho,* a disorder that usually affects young Japanese men. It has several features in common with social anxiety disorder, including extreme social anxiety and avoidance of social situations. However, the person with *taijin kyofusho* is not worried about being embarrassed. Rather, reflecting the cultural emphasis of concern for others, the person with *taijin kyofusho* fears that their appearance, smell, or body language will offend, insult, or embarrass other people (Iwamasa, 1997; Norasakkunkit et al., 2012).

Explaining Phobias: Learning Theories The development of some phobias can be explained in terms of basic learning principles (Craske & Waters, 2005). *Classical conditioning* may well be involved in the development of a specific phobia that can be traced back to some sort of traumatic event. In the chapter on learning, we saw how psychologist John Watson classically conditioned "Little Albert" to fear a tame lab rat that had been paired with loud noise. Following the conditioning, the infant's fear generalized to other furry objects.

More recently, researchers demonstrated the role of classical conditioning in the development of phobias by pairing something new, like an invented cartoon character named Spardi, with something frightening, like a picture of a woman being mugged at knifepoint. Participants rated Spardi as more frightening in this circumstance than when the character was paired with something pleasant, like a picture of a sunset (Vriends et al., 2012).

ilovezion/Shutterstock

John Arnold/Shutterstock

‹ An Evolutionary Fear of Holes Some people are afraid of a certain pattern of holes like those you might see in a chocolate bar, in soap bubbles, or on a lotus seed head like the one shown here. This condition is called trypophobia. Researchers Geoff Cole and Arnold Wilkins (2013) found striking similarities between the visual pattern that triggers fear in trypophobics and the markings on poisonous animals, like certain snakes or the poison dart frog shown here. They speculate that an ability to quickly notice a poisonous creature gave people an evolutionary advantage, even if it sometimes led them to fear harmless objects.

Operant conditioning can also be involved in the avoidance behavior that characterizes phobias. A person who is afraid of dogs might quickly learn that they could reduce their anxiety and fear by avoiding dogs altogether. To use operant conditioning terms, their *operant response* of avoiding dogs is *negatively reinforced* by the relief from anxiety and fear that they experience.

Observational learning can also be involved in the development of phobias. Some people learn to be phobic of certain objects or situations by observing the fearful reactions of someone else who acts as a *model* in the situation. The child who observes a parent react with sheer panic to the sight of a spider or mouse may imitate the same behavioral response. People can also develop phobias from observing vivid media accounts of disasters, as when some people become afraid to fly after watching graphic TV coverage of a plane crash.

We also noted in the chapter on learning that humans seem *biologically prepared* to acquire fears of certain animals or situations, such as snakes or heights, which were survival threats in human evolutionary history (Workman & Reader, 2008).

Posttraumatic Stress Disorder and Obsessive–Compulsive Disorder: Anxiety and Intrusive Thoughts

■ KEY THEME
Extreme anxiety and intrusive thoughts are symptoms of both posttraumatic stress disorder (PTSD) and obsessive–compulsive disorder (OCD).

≡ KEY QUESTIONS
- What is PTSD, and what causes it?
- What is obsessive–compulsive disorder?
- What are the most common types of obsessions and compulsions?

Posttraumatic stress disorder (PTSD) is *a disorder triggered by extreme trauma that results in intrusive memories; avoidance of stimuli; negative changes in thoughts and emotions; and a persistent state of heightened physical arousal.* Extreme traumas are events that produce intense feelings of horror and helplessness, such as a serious physical injury or threat of injury to yourself or to loved ones. Although not classified as an anxiety disorder, some of the same patterns of emotion, cognition, and behavior mark both PTSD and anxiety disorders.

Originally, PTSD was primarily associated with military combat. Veterans of military conflict in Afghanistan and Iraq, like veterans of earlier wars, have a higher prevalence of PTSD than nonveterans (E. Cohen et al., 2011). However, it's now known that PTSD can *also* develop among nonmilitary personnel exposed to violent conflicts and that PTSD is common among refugees (Yuval et al., 2016). And it can develop in survivors of other sorts of extreme traumas, such as natural disasters, physical or sexual assault, or terrorist attacks (McNally, 2003). Relief workers and emergency service personnel, such as people working in Greece with refugees fleeing war in other countries, can also develop PTSD symptoms (Berger et al., 2012; Sifaki-Pistolla et al., 2016). Simply

▼ Invisible Wounds: PTSD Among U.S. Veterans Marine veteran Charles Gerard served in Afghanistan, where he witnessed fellow Marines wounded in an ambush that he survived. He was later treated for PTSD (Philipps, 2015). Like Gerard, some 300,000 veterans have been diagnosed with PTSD or major depressive disorder (Tanielian, 2008). The high rate of PTSD and suicide may be related to unique aspects of the Iraq and Afghanistan conflicts. As Veterans Affairs physician Karen Seal and her colleagues (2008) observed, "The majority of military personnel experience high-intensity guerrilla warfare and the chronic threat of roadside bombs and improvised explosive devices. Some soldiers endure multiple tours of duty, many experience traumatic injury, and more of the wounded survive than ever before."

TODD HEISLER/The New York Times/Redux

social anxiety disorder An anxiety disorder involving the extreme and irrational fear of being embarrassed, judged, or scrutinized by others in social situations.

posttraumatic stress disorder (PTSD) A disorder triggered by extreme trauma that results in intrusive memories; avoidance of stimuli; negative changes in thoughts and emotions; and a persistent state of heightened physical arousal.

STEPHEN MORRISON/European Pressphoto Agency/Newscom

▲ **The Ravages of War: Child Soldiers**
An estimated quarter-million children serve as unwilling combatants in wars today, most of them kidnapped from their families and forced to serve as soldiers. Child soldiers not only suffer torture and violence, they are also often forced to commit atrocities against others. Not surprisingly, these children suffer from very high rates of post-traumatic stress disorder (Klasen et al., 2015; Kohrt et al., 2008). One survey of former child soldiers in refugee camps in Uganda found that 97 percent of the children suffered from PTSD symptoms (see J. Dawson, 2007; Derluyn et al., 2004). Rehabilitation centers have been established throughout Uganda and the Democratic Republic of Congo, where many of these children live, but more assistance is desperately needed (Ursano & Shaw, 2007; Winkler et al., 2015). This girl hides her eyes during a role-playing game at a rehabilitation center. Role-playing is used to help children cope with the trauma of the violence that they saw or took part in.

obsessive–compulsive disorder (OCD)
A disorder characterized by intrusive, repetitive, and unwanted thoughts (obsessions) and repetitive behaviors or mental acts that an individual feels driven to perform (compulsions).

obsessions Repeated, intrusive, and uncontrollable irrational thoughts or mental images that cause extreme anxiety and distress.

compulsions Repetitive behaviors or mental acts that a person feels driven to perform in order to prevent or reduce anxiety and distress or to prevent a dreaded event or situation.

witnessing the injury or death of others can be sufficiently traumatic for PTSD to occur. And some researchers have documented PTSD symptoms in people who were exposed to trauma in the media, such as graphic images related to terrorism, war, or natural disasters (Holman et al., 2020; Yeung et al., 2016).

In any given year, it's estimated that more than 5 million U.S. adults experience PTSD. There is also a significant gender difference—more than twice as many women as men experience PTSD after exposure to trauma (Olff et al., 2007). Children can also experience the symptoms of PTSD. For example, PTSD has been observed in children living in a war zone in the Middle East and children living in New Orleans after Hurricane Katrina (Fasfous et al., 2013; Langley et al., 2014).

Four core clusters of symptoms characterize PTSD (DSM-5, 2013). First, the person *frequently recalls the event,* replaying it in their mind. Such recollections are often *intrusive,* meaning that they are unwanted and interfere with normal thoughts. Recollections can even be triggered by unrelated events. After the Boston Marathon bombings in 2013, almost 40 percent of a sample of military veterans in Boston who already suffered from PTSD reported increased emotional distress (Miller et al., 2013). Second, the person *avoids stimuli or situations* that tend to trigger memories of the experience. Third, they may experience *negative alterations in thinking, moods, and emotions.* One person described the "sinking feeling that I'd always be a downer, always on guard, never able to relax" (Bethea, 2016). Fourth, the person experiences *increased physical arousal.* They may be easily startled, experience sleep disturbances, have problems concentrating and remembering, and be prone to irritability or angry outbursts (DSM-5, 2013).

Posttraumatic stress disorder is somewhat unusual in that the source of the disorder is the traumatic event itself, rather than a cause that lies within the individual. Even well-adjusted and psychologically healthy people may develop PTSD when exposed to an extremely traumatic event (Ozer et al., 2003). Terrorist attacks, because of their suddenness and intensity, are particularly likely to produce posttraumatic stress disorder in survivors, rescue workers and observers (Neria et al., 2011). For example, five years after the 9/11 terrorist attacks, more than 11 percent of rescue and recovery workers met formal criteria for PTSD—a rate comparable to that of soldiers returning from active duty in Iraq and Afghanistan (Stellman et al., 2008). Among people who had directly witnessed the attacks, over 16 percent had PTSD symptoms four years after the attacks (Farfel et al., 2008; Jayasinghe et al., 2008).

We know that exposure to a trauma is necessary for the development of PTSD. However, it's also important to note that no stressor, no matter how extreme, produces posttraumatic stress disorder in everyone. Many people are remarkably resilient in the face of trauma. As worries grew about the ramifications of pandemic-related trauma, psychiatrist Denise Sloan pointed out that "the most common response to trauma is resilience" (Taitz, 2020). Most people who experience trauma never develop PTSD. And some even experience an outcome known as *posttraumatic growth* (Calhoun & Tedeschi, 2014; Fletcher & Sarkar, 2013). Posttraumatic growth occurs when people experience positive change, rather than negative outcomes, after experiencing a trauma. Positive changes can include stronger relationships with loved ones, an enhanced appreciation for life, or a deeper sense of religion or spirituality. Some research suggests that posttraumatic growth can occur at the same time as posttraumatic stress (Blix et al., 2016). So, someone who experiences a negative response to stress or trauma may also experience positive psychological outcomes in the long term.

Why is it that some people develop PTSD while others don't? Several factors influence the likelihood of developing posttraumatic stress disorder. First, there are biological predispositions. A vulnerability to PTSD can be inherited (Wilker & Kolassa, 2013). Second, people with a personal or family history of psychological disorders are more likely to develop PTSD when exposed to an extreme trauma (Amstadter et al., 2009; Koenen et al., 2008). Third, the magnitude of the trauma plays an important role. More extreme stressors are more likely to produce PTSD. Frequency of exposure is a factor as well. When people undergo *multiple* traumas, the incidence of PTSD can be quite high. One study even observed PTSD symptoms among journalists who never left the newsroom but were frequently exposed to traumatic images (Feinstein et al., 2014).

Obsessive–Compulsive Disorder

When you finish making dinner, you probably check to make sure the stove is off. You may even double-check just to be on the safe side. But once you're confident that the stove is off, you don't think about it again. Some people trivialize the term "obsessive–compulsive disorder" or "OCD," saying, "I'm so OCD," to describe this behavior or a tendency to be extremely neat (Pavelko & Myrick, 2015). But most people who say this probably do not have an actual diagnosis. Some people with an actual diagnosis of OCD find the casual use of the term offensive, including author Alison Dotson, who points out, "OCD isn't cute" (Tipu, 2015).

Here's a sense of what OCD is really like. Imagine you've checked the stove *30* times. Yet you're still not quite sure that the stove is really off. You know the feeling is irrational, but you feel compelled to check again and again. Imagine you've *also* had to repeatedly check that the coffeepot was unplugged, that the door was locked. Finally, imagine that you got only 10 minutes into an after-dinner movie before you felt compelled to return to the kitchen and check *again*—because you still were not certain.

Sound agonizing? This is the psychological world of the person who suffers from one form of obsessive–compulsive disorder. **Obsessive–compulsive disorder (OCD)** is *a disorder characterized by intrusive, repetitive, and unwanted thoughts (obsessions) and repetitive behaviors or mental acts that an individual feels driven to perform (compulsions).* Like PTSD, OCD is not classified as an anxiety disorder, but shares similar symptom patterns.

Obsessions are *repeated, intrusive, uncontrollable irrational thoughts or mental images that cause extreme anxiety and distress.* Obsessions are not the same as everyday worries. Normal worries typically have some sort of factual basis, even if they're somewhat exaggerated. In contrast, obsessions have little or no basis in reality and are often extremely far-fetched. One common theme is pathological doubt about having accomplished a simple task, such as shutting off appliances (Antony et al., 2007; Renshaw et al., 2010). Another common obsession is an irrational fear of dirt, germs, and other forms of contamination.

Compulsions are *repetitive behaviors or mental acts that a person feels driven to perform in order to prevent or reduce anxiety and distress or to prevent a dreaded event or situation.* Typically, compulsions are ritual behaviors that must be carried out in a certain pattern or sequence. Compulsions may be *overt physical behaviors,* such as repeatedly washing your hands, checking doors or windows, or entering and reentering a doorway until you walk through exactly in the middle. Or they may be *covert mental behaviors,* such as counting or reciting certain phrases to yourself. But note that the person does not compulsively wash their hands because the enjoy being clean. Rather, they wash their hands because to *not* do so causes extreme anxiety. Writer Mike Sacks, who suffers from OCD, says that he has "a murky sense that something bad will happen" if he gets dirty. He explains that, with his actions, including compulsive handwashing, he's also trying to protect family and friends from contamination (Sacks, 2016).

Interestingly, obsessions and compulsions take a similar shape in different cultures around the world. However, the *content* of the obsessions and compulsions tends to mirror the particular culture's concerns and beliefs. In the United States, compulsive washers are typically preoccupied with obsessional fears of germs and infection. But in rural Nigeria and rural India, compulsive washers are more likely to have obsessional concerns about religious purity rather than germs (Rapoport, 1989; Rego, 2009).

Explaining Obsessive–Compulsive Disorder

Once someone develops an anxious response, conditioning can reinforce it. The unpleasant feeling of anxiety can be temporarily relieved by giving in to compulsive behaviors, like Mike Sacks's handwashing (Cavedini et al., 2006). Although it provides only short-term relief, the compulsive behavior is likely to be repeated because reinforcement has occurred.

Evidence suggests that biological factors are also involved in obsessive–compulsive disorder (Chamberlain & Fineberg, 2013). For example, OCD has been linked with broad deficits in the ability to manage cognitive processes such as attention (Snyder

MYTH ◄ **SCIENCE**

Is is true that people who are perfectionists probably have obsessive–compulsive disorder?

Ellen Brait

▲ **A Mission to Help Others** Jenny Jaffe, a woman in her 20s, suffered from obsessive–compulsive disorder for years. "I just was miserable living in my own head. And I had all of these horrible, intrusive thoughts," Jaffe told a reporter (Brait, 2015). Years of therapy helped Jaffe improve, and she wanted to help reduce the stigma of mental illness and give others the hope she didn't have when she was in her teens. She founded Project UROK (pronounced "you are OK"), which creates "funny, meaningful videos . . . made by people who have been there before" and distributes them on social media (projecturok.org). Jaffe explains, "I wish I could go back and tell my teenage self how cool life got and this is sort of my way of doing that."

^ Obsessions and Compulsions
Before his successful treatment, writer
Mike Sacks experienced obsessions as
well as compulsions, including a compul-
sion to wash his hands up to 25 times a
day. In reference to his obsessions, he
writes, with a dry sense of humor, that
he "can once again use a kitchen knife
without thinking it may one day be used
to stab someone, which is great news but
not something to brag about on a dating
profile" (Sacks, 2016).

Marie Warsh

TABLE 14.3

Disorders Involving Intense Anxiety

Generalized Anxiety Disorder

- Persistent, chronic, unreasonable worry and anxiety
- General symptoms of anxiety, including persistent physical arousal

Panic Disorder

- Frequent and unexpected panic attacks, with no specific or identifiable trigger

Specific Phobia

- Intense anxiety triggered by a specific object or situation
- Persistent avoidance of feared object or situation

Social Anxiety Disorder

- Irrational anxiety related to being embarrassed, judged, or scrutinized in social situations.

Posttraumatic Stress Disorder (PTSD)

- Anxiety triggered by intrusive, recurrent memories of a highly traumatic experience

Obsessive–Compulsive Disorder (OCD)

- Anxiety caused by uncontrollable, persistent, recurring thoughts (obsessions) and/or urges to perform certain actions (compulsions)

et al., 2014). This may, in turn, be linked to dysfunction in specific brain areas, such as those involved in the fight-or-flight response, and in the frontal lobes, which play a key role in our ability to think and plan ahead (Anderson & Savage, 2004; Pujol et al., 2011).

Deficiencies in the neurotransmitters norepinephrine and serotonin have also been implicated in OCD. When treated with drugs that increase the availability of these substances in the brain, many patients with OCD experience a marked decrease in symptoms. Excess of the neurotransmitter glutamate has also been found to be associated with OCD symptoms (Maia & Cano-Colino, 2015).

The anxiety, posttraumatic stress, and obsessive–compulsive disorders are summarized in **Table 14.3**.

Depressive and Bipolar Disorders: Disordered Moods and Emotions

■ KEY THEME

In the depressive and the bipolar disorders, disturbed emotions cause psychological distress and impair daily functioning.

≡ KEY QUESTIONS

- What are the symptoms and course of major depressive disorder, persistent depressive disorder, bipolar disorder, and cyclothymic disorder?
- How prevalent are depressive and bipolar disorders?
- What factors contribute to the development of depressive and bipolar disorders?

Let's face it, we all have our ups and downs. When things are going well, we feel cheerful and optimistic. When events take a more negative turn, our mood can sour. We feel miserable and pessimistic. Either way, the intensity and duration of our moods are usually in proportion to the events going on in our lives. That's completely normal.

In the depressive disorders and the bipolar and related disorders, however, emotions violate the criteria of typical moods. In quality, intensity, and duration, a person's emotional state does not seem to reflect what's going on in their life. A person may feel a pervasive sadness despite the best of circumstances. Or a person may be extremely energetic and overconfident with no apparent justification. These mood changes persist much longer than the normal fluctuations in moods that we all experience.

Because disturbed moods and emotions are core symptoms in both the depressive and bipolar disorders, they are sometimes called *mood disorders* or *affective disorders*. The word "affect" is synonymous with "emotion" or "feelings." In DSM-5, depressive disorders and bipolar disorders are given their own distinct categories rather than grouped together. In this section, we'll look at depressive disorders first and then turn to bipolar disorders.

Major Depressive Disorder: More Than Ordinary Sadness

Major depressive disorder is *a mood disorder characterized by extreme and persistent feelings of despondency, worthlessness, and hopelessness, causing impaired emotional, cognitive, behavioral, and physical functioning.* It is hard to convey to those who have never experienced it. One person with depression, Ravi, explained to researchers, "You get into a state I think mentally where, you're just like out on an island. And . . . you can see from that island another shore and all these people are there, but there's no way that you can get across" (Smith & Rhodes, 2015). Another wrote of her experience, "For me, depression can feel like the worst flu ever, with no end in sight" (Petrow, 2016).

The Symptoms of Major Depressive Disorder The quotes above give you a feeling for how the symptoms of depression affect the whole person—emotionally, cognitively, behaviorally, and physically. Emotional symptoms include feelings of sadness, guilt, or worthlessness. Cognitive symptoms include difficulty thinking, concentrating, and remembering. Behavioral symptoms include crying and withdrawal from social activities. And physical symptoms include changes in appetite and weight, sleep difficulties (sleeping too much or too little), and diminished sexual interest. Depression is also often accompanied by the physical symptoms of anxiety (Andover et al., 2011). Some depressed people experience a sense of physical restlessness or nervousness, demonstrated by fidgeting or aimless pacing.

Suicide is always a potential risk in major depressive disorder (Brådvik & Berglund, 2010). Thoughts become globally pessimistic and negative about the self, the world, and the future (Beck et al., 1979; Everaert et al., 2018). Approximately 10 percent of those suffering from major depressive disorder attempt suicide (McGirr et al., 2007).

To be diagnosed with major depressive disorder, a person must display most of the symptoms described for two weeks or longer (DSM-5, 2013). In many cases, there doesn't seem to be any external reason for the persistent feeling of depression. In other cases, a person's downward emotional spiral has been triggered by a negative life event, stressful situation, or chronic stress (Gutman & Nemeroff, 2011).

One significant negative event deserves special mention: the death of a loved one. Previous editions of the *Diagnostic and Statistical Manual* stated that depression-like symptoms that might accompany grieving did not qualify as major depression unless those symptoms persisted for two months, rather than two weeks. The DSM-5 removes that special treatment for bereavement, based on the reasoning that bereavement is like any other psychosocial event that might trigger a depressive episode. Although it is common to feel a sense of loss and deep sadness when a close friend or family member dies, feelings of worthlessness, self-loathing, and the inability to anticipate happiness or pleasure may indicate that major depressive disorder may be present (DSM-5, 2013).

Although major depressive disorder can occur at any time, some people experience symptoms that intensify at certain times of the year. For people with *seasonal affective disorder (SAD)*, repeated episodes of major depressive disorder are as predictable as the changing seasons, especially the onset of autumn and winter, when there is the least amount of sunlight. The evidence for the existence of SAD is contradictory. Some observe that SAD is more common among women and among people who live in the northern latitudes (Partonen & Pandi-Perumal, 2010). Others question the existence of SAD, citing evidence that "depression is unrelated to latitude, season, or sunlight" (Traffanstedt et al., 2016).

major depressive disorder A mood disorder characterized by extreme and persistent feelings of despondency, worthlessness, and hopelessness, causing impaired emotional, cognitive, behavioral, and physical functioning.

Kevin Winter/Getty Images

▲ **Sarah Silverman** Sarah Silverman has been outspoken about her struggles with mental illness in interviews and in her work (Winkelman, 2019). In the dramatic film *I Smile Back*, comedian Sarah Silverman played a woman who was profoundly depressed. Silverman likes using her performances "to open minds or change minds or get information out" (Gross, 2015). This role allowed Silverman to share the experience of major depressive disorder, something she herself began suffering as a teenager. She described the symptoms as coming on quickly: "Like, you ever just sit? And you're just sitting there, and you're fine. And then you just—the next moment you just go, oh, Jesus, I have the flu. You know, like, it just—it's that fast." With ongoing treatment, she now manages her depression. "I feel like I can live life," Silverman says.

∧ Kristen Bell and Depression Actor Kristen Bell has been open about the fact that she has grappled with anxiety and depression for several years. "Everyone thinks there's some shame in it," she explained to an interviewer (Gariano, 2019). But she wants people to see beyond the supposed "glitter" of her life. "I am someone who takes a medication for her anxiety and depression. I am someone who has to check myself and sometimes—if I'm feeling really low—make a checklist of good and bad things in my life to see if it's my mental state or if we really have a problem." By speaking out, Bell hopes to reduce the stigma associated with mental illness.

bipolar disorder A mood disorder involving periods of incapacitating depression alternating with periods of extreme euphoria and excitement; formerly called *manic depression*.

manic episode A sudden, rapidly escalating emotional state characterized by extreme euphoria, excitement, physical energy, and rapid thoughts and speech.

Some people experience a chronic form of depression called *persistent depressive disorder* that is often less severe than major depressive disorder. Persistent depressive disorder may develop after some stressful event or trauma, such as the death of a parent in childhood (DSM-5, 2013). Although the person functions adequately, they have a chronic case of "the blues" that can continue for years.

The Prevalence and Course of Major Depressive Disorder Major depressive disorder is often called "the common cold" of psychological disorders, and for good reason: It is among the most prevalent psychological disorders. And in terms of its physical, psychological, and economic impact, it's one of the most devastating of *any* illness worldwide (Ledford, 2014; World Health Organization, 2017). In any given year, about 20 million adults in the United States and 300 million people around the world are affected by major depressive disorder (SAMHSA, 2020; WHO, 2017). In terms of lifetime prevalence, many researchers have estimated that about 15 percent of Americans will be affected by major depressive disorder at some point in their lives. However, some researchers suspect that number is too low. In a longitudinal study following more than 800 people for 30 years—from childhood through adulthood—about half the sample experienced an episode of major depressive disorder at some point (Rohde et al., 2013). That number is likely to rise given the marked increase in cases of depression during the pandemic (Krishnamoorthy et al., 2020).

Women are about twice as likely as men to be diagnosed with major depressive disorder (Hyde et al., 2008; Kuehner, 2017). Why the striking gender difference? Research suggests one reason that women are more vulnerable to depression. It may be because women experience a greater degree of chronic stress in daily life combined with a lesser sense of personal control than men (Kuehner, 2017; Nolen-Hoeksema, 2001). The interaction of these factors creates a vicious circle that intensifies and perpetuates depressed feelings in women (Nolen-Hoeksema & Hilt, 2009; Nolen-Hoeksema et al., 2007). Some researchers, however, suggest that there may not actually be a gender difference in the prevalence of major depressive disorder. Rather, there may be a gender difference in how depression is expressed: Men often experience different symptoms—anger, substance abuse, and risk-taking—that aren't counted toward the diagnosis (Martin et al., 2013).

There also are cultural differences related to major depressive disorder. Although depression occurs globally with similar symptom presentation across different countries, people often talk about it differently (Ferrari et al., 2013; Simon et al., 2002). For example, people in Cambodia refer to their experience with depression as "the water in my heart has fallen" (Singh, 2015). And the Haitian word for depression translates to "thinking too much" (Singh, 2015). Such differences in the language and understanding of depression must be taken into account when diagnosing and treating this disorder.

Many people who experience major depressive disorder try to cope with the symptoms without seeking professional help (Edlund et al., 2008; Farmer et al., 2012). Left untreated, the symptoms of major depressive disorder can easily last six months or longer. When not treated, depression may become a recurring mental illness that becomes progressively more severe (Hammen, 2005; Roca et al., 2011). However, it's important to note that several effective treatments for depression are available. We will describe many of these treatments in the next chapter.

Bipolar Disorder: An Emotional Roller Coaster

Henry, a therapy client in his fifties, was being treated for depression. After several months of appointments, he failed to show up for two weekly appointments in a row. When he returned, he greeted everyone in the waiting room and at the front desk as if they were old friends. Henry entered his therapist's office grinning, his eyes wild.

Henry's new mood was not just a decrease in his symptoms of depression. It was a swing in the opposite direction. Henry excitedly told his therapist that he had quit his job and was putting his savings into an investment scheme. He soon changed topics. "I won't be here next week because I'm going to Mexico! I'm staying at a famous resort in Tulum!" He explained that he would connect with Hollywood stars there, and would soon be working on a movie project.

Henry spoke loudly and so rapidly that his words often got tangled up with each other. His grinning, rapid-fire speech was punctuated with grand, sweeping gestures and exaggerated facial expressions. Before his therapist could get a word in edgewise and long before the scheduled end of the therapy session, Henry left, explaining that he had to go shopping for new hunting gear.

The Symptoms of Bipolar Disorder Henry displayed classic symptoms of the psychological disorder that used to be called *manic depression* and is today called **bipolar disorder,** *a mood disorder involving periods of incapacitating depression alternating with periods of extreme euphoria and excitement; formerly called manic depression.* In contrast to major depressive disorder, bipolar disorder almost always involves extreme moods at *both* ends of the emotional spectrum. A **manic episode** is *a sudden, rapidly escalating emotional state characterized by extreme euphoria, excitement, physical energy, and rapid thoughts and speech.* For the vast majority of people with bipolar disorder, a manic episode immediately precedes or follows a bout with major depressive disorder. However, a small percentage of people with bipolar disorder experience only manic episodes (DSM-5, 2013).

Many people use the term "manic" informally to describe people who are in a more energetic mood than normal. But a true manic episode is much more extreme than what we often mean in casual conversation. Manic episodes typically begin suddenly, and symptoms escalate rapidly. During a manic episode, people are uncharacteristically euphoric, expansive, and excited for several days or longer. Although they sleep very little, they have boundless energy. Often, they have grandiose plans for obtaining wealth, power, and fame (Carlson & Meyer, 2006; Miklowitz, 2008). Sometimes the grandiose ideas represent *delusional,* or false, beliefs. Henry's belief that he would make movies with Hollywood stars whom he would meet in Mexico was delusional.

Henry's fast-forward speech was loud and virtually impossible to interrupt. During a manic episode, words are spoken so rapidly, they're often slurred as the person tries to keep up with his own racing thought processes. Attention is easily distracted by virtually anything, triggering a *flight of ideas,* in which thoughts rapidly and loosely shift from topic to topic.

Not surprisingly, the ability to function during a manic episode is severely impaired. Hospitalization is usually required, partly to protect people from the potential consequences of their inappropriate decisions and behaviors. During manic episodes, people can also run up a mountain of bills, disappear for weeks at a time, become sexually promiscuous, or commit illegal acts. Very commonly, the person becomes agitated or verbally abusive when others question their grandiose claims (Miklowitz & Johnson, 2007).

Some people experience a milder but chronic form of bipolar disorder called cyclothymic disorder. In *cyclothymic disorder,* people experience moderate but frequent mood swings for two years or longer. These mood swings are not severe enough to qualify as either bipolar disorder or major depressive disorder.

The Prevalence and Course of Bipolar Disorder The onset of bipolar disorder typically occurs in the person's early 20s. The extreme mood swings of bipolar disorder tend to start and stop much more abruptly than the mood changes of major depressive disorder. And while an episode of major depression can easily last for six months or longer, the manic and depressive episodes of bipolar disorder tend to be much shorter—lasting anywhere from a few days to a couple of months (Fagiolini et al., 2013; Solomon et al., 2010). But contrary to what many people think, the cycling between manic and depressive episodes does not occur in minutes, or even hours.

Bipolar disorder is far less common than major depressive disorder. Among people who have had at least one depressive episode, only about 9 percent eventually are

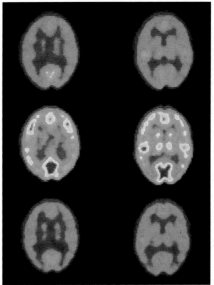

Courtesy of Dr. Lew Baxter and Dr. Michael Phelps, University of California, Los Angeles

Brain Activity During the Extremes of Bipolar Disorder These PET scans record the brain activity of an individual with bipolar disorder as they cycled rapidly from depression to mania and back to depression over a 10-day period. In the top and bottom PET scans, the blue and green colors clearly show the sharp reduction in overall brain activity that coincided with the episodes of depression. In the center PET scans, the bright red, orange, and yellow colors indicate high levels of activity in diverse brain regions during the intervening episodes of mania.

Source: Lewis Baxter and Michael E. Phelps, UCLA School of Medicine.

Emma McIntyre/AMA2019/Getty Images

Selena Gomez and Bipolar Disorder Singer Selena Gomez talked with her friend, singer Miley Cyrus, on Cyrus's Instagram livestream about the solace Gomez found in getting diagnosed with bipolar disorder (Bennett, 2020). "When I have more information, it actually helps me, it doesn't scare me once I know it … I wanted to know everything about it and it took the fear away."

Based on a person's history and current symptoms, are you able to determine what their diagnosis might be? Go to **Achieve** and try **Concept Practice: Types of Mood Disorders.**

MYTH ▶ SCIENCE

Is it true that many psychological disorders run in families?

△ **Creativity, Depressive Disorders, and Bipolar Disorders** Does mental illness fuel creativity? There have been scores of examples of the troubled "creative genius" — from writer Mark Twain and poet Sylvia Plath, both of whom suffered from severe bouts of depression, to performer and rapper Kanye West and singer-songwriter Amy Winehouse, both of whom were diagnosed with bipolar disorder. (Plath and Winehouse died by suicide.) Research on the connection between creativity and depression is mixed (Taylor, 2017). But research does support a genetic connection between creativity and bipolar symptoms (Greenwood, 2020). The story, however, is more complicated. The most creative people are actually the family members who are related to those with bipolar disorder but either do not suffer from bipolar disorder or have mild symptoms. For those with more severe symptoms, creativity is typically impeded. And research suggests that a belief in the connection between creativity and mania, in particular, may lead people with bipolar disorder to avoid necessary treatment (S. Johnson et al., 2012).

diagnosed with bipolar disorder (Bukh et al., 2016). Unlike major depressive disorder, there are no differences between the sexes in the rate at which bipolar disorder occurs. For both men and women, the lifetime risk of developing bipolar disorder is about 1 percent (Merikangas et al., 2007; Moreira et al., 2017). Bipolar disorder is rarely diagnosed in childhood.

In the vast majority of cases, bipolar disorder is a recurring psychological disorder (Jones & Tarrier, 2005). Often, bipolar disorder recurs when the individual stops taking *lithium,* a medication that helps control the disorder which, it turned out, was what had happened with Henry.

Explaining Depressive Disorders and Bipolar Disorders

Multiple factors appear to be involved in the development of depressive and bipolar disorders. First, family, twin, and adoption studies suggest that some people inherit a *genetic predisposition,* or a greater vulnerability, to depressive and bipolar disorders (Kendler et al., 2006; Levinson, 2009; Smoller & Finn, 2003). Researchers have consistently found that both major depressive disorder and bipolar disorder, like most psychological disorders, tend to run in families, although bipolar disorder has much stronger genetic roots than major depressive disorder (Moore et al., 2013; Sullivan et al., 2012).

A second factor that has been implicated in the development of depressive and bipolar disorders is differences in the activation of structures in the brain. For example, one study found that people who were depressed showed increased activation in certain parts of the brain when trying to get rid of negative words in their working memory (Foland-Ross et al., 2013). People who were not depressed showed similar activation, an indication of effort, when getting rid of positive words.

Another important factor is disruptions in brain chemistry. Since the 1960s, several medications, called *antidepressants,* have been developed to treat major depressive disorder. Some researchers believe that increased levels in the brain of some neurotransmitters, such as norepinephrine and serotonin, accompany an improvement in the symptoms of depression among people taking antidepressants. Antidepressant medications will be discussed in more detail in the chapter on therapies.

Abnormal levels of another neurotransmitter may also be involved in bipolar disorder. For decades, it's been known that the drug lithium effectively alleviates symptoms of both mania and depression. Lithium works in complex ways, but the main way is by regulating the availability of a neurotransmitter called *glutamate,* which acts as an excitatory neurotransmitter in many brain areas (Dixon & Hokin, 1998; Malhi & Outhred, 2016; Vosahlkova & Svoboda, 2016). By normalizing glutamate levels, lithium helps prevent both the excesses that may cause mania and the deficits that may cause depression.

Stress is also implicated in the development of depressive and bipolar disorders (Quinn & Joormann, 2015). First, major depressive disorder and chronic stress lead to remarkably similar changes in the neurochemistry of the brain (Hill et al., 2012). Second, major depressive disorder is often triggered by traumatic and stressful events (Gutman & Nemeroff, 2011). Exposure to recent stressful events is one of the best predictors of episodes of major depressive disorder (Muscatell et al., 2009; Vrshek-Schallhorn et al., 2013).

In summary, considerable evidence points to the role of genetic factors, biochemical factors, and stressful life events in the development of both depressive disorders and bipolar disorders (Feliciano & Areàn, 2007). However, exactly how these factors interact to cause these disorders is still being investigated. **Table 14.4** summarizes the symptoms of the most important depressive disorders and bipolar disorders.

TABLE 14.4

Depressive Disorders and Bipolar Disorders

Major Depressive Disorder	
• Loss of interest or pleasure in almost all activities	• Difficulty sleeping or excessive sleeping
• Despondent mood; feelings of emptiness, worthlessness, or guilt	• Diminished ability to think, concentrate, or make decisions
• Preoccupation with death or suicidal thoughts	• Diminished appetite and significant weight loss

Persistent Depressive Disorder
• Chronic depressed feelings that are often less severe than those that accompany major depressive disorder

Seasonal Affective Disorder (SAD)
• Recurring depressive episodes that follow a seasonal pattern, typically occurring in the fall and winter and subsiding in the spring and summer

Bipolar Disorder
• One or more manic episodes characterized by euphoria, high energy, grandiose ideas, inappropriate self-confidence, and decreased need for sleep
• Usually one or more major depressive episodes
• In some cases, may rapidly alternate between symptoms of mania and major depressive disorder

Cyclothymic Disorder
• Moderate, recurring mood swings that are not severe enough to qualify as major depressive disorder or bipolar disorder

Eating Disorders: Anorexia, Bulimia, and Binge-Eating Disorder

■ **KEY THEME**

Anorexia nervosa, bulimia nervosa, and binge-eating disorder are psychological disorders characterized by severely disturbed, maladaptive eating behaviors.

▬ **KEY QUESTIONS**
- What are the symptoms, characteristics, and causes of anorexia nervosa?
- What are the symptoms, characteristics, and causes of bulimia nervosa?
- What are the symptoms, characteristics, and causes of binge-eating disorder?

Eating disorders are a *category of psychological disorders characterized by severe disturbances in eating behavior.* Eating disorders can include extreme reduction of food intake, severe bouts of overeating, and obsessive concerns about body shape or weight (DSM-5, 2013). The three main types of eating disorders are *anorexia nervosa, bulimia nervosa,* and *binge-eating disorder,* which usually begin during adolescence or early adulthood (see **Table 14.5**). Of the people who experience an eating disorder, 90 to 95 percent are female (Støving et al., 2011). Despite the 10-to-1 female-to-male ratio, the central features of eating disorders are similar for males and females.

Anorexia Nervosa: Life-Threatening Weight Loss **Anorexia nervosa** is *an eating disorder characterized by excessive weight loss, an irrational fear of gaining weight, and distorted body self-perception.* First, the person refuses to maintain a minimally normal body weight, usually through restricting calories by eating very little food, but also often by burning calories, such as with excessive exercise. Second, despite being dangerously underweight, the person with anorexia is intensely afraid of gaining weight or becoming fat. Third, they have a distorted perception about the size of their body. Although emaciated, they look in the mirror and see themselves as fat or obese, denying the seriousness of their weight loss (DSM-5, 2013).

eating disorder Category of psychological disorders characterized by severe disturbances in eating behavior.

anorexia nervosa An eating disorder characterized by excessive weight loss, an irrational fear of gaining weight, and distorted body self-perception.

bulimia nervosa An eating disorder characterized by binges of extreme overeating followed by self-induced vomiting, misuse of laxatives, or other methods to purge excess food and prevent weight gain.

John Shearer/AMA2019/Getty Images

⌃ **Taylor Swift: Praise, Punishment, and Eating Behaviors** Singer-songwriter Taylor Swift recently opened up about her history of disordered eating, explaining that "my relationship with food was exactly the same psychology that I applied to everything else in my life: If I was given a pat on the head, I registered that as good. If I was given a punishment, I registered that as bad" (Stump, 2020). Swift responded both to praise for being thin and to criticism for supposed imperfections by dieting to the point that she sometimes felt like she would pass out when she performed. "Now I realize," Swift says, "if you eat food, have energy, get stronger, you can do all these shows and not feel [exhausted]."

TABLE 14.5

Eating Disorders

Anorexia Nervosa
• Severe and extreme disturbance in eating habits and calorie intake
• Body weight that is significantly less than what would be considered normal for the person's age, height, and gender, and refusal to maintain a normal body weight
• Intense fear of gaining weight or becoming fat
• Distorted perceptions about the severity of weight loss and a distorted self-image, such that even an extremely emaciated person may perceive themselves as fat

Bulimia Nervosa
• Recurring episodes of binge eating, which is defined as an excessive amount of calories within a two-hour period
• The inability to control or stop the excessive eating behavior
• Recurrent episodes of purging, which is defined as using laxatives, diuretics, self-induced vomiting, or other methods to prevent weight gain

Binge-Eating Disorder
• Recurring episodes of binge eating
• The inability to control or stop the excessive eating behavior
• Not associated with recurrent episodes of purging or other methods to prevent weight gain

The severe malnutrition caused by anorexia disrupts body chemistry in ways that are very similar to those caused by starvation. Basal metabolic rate decreases, as do blood levels of glucose, insulin, and leptin. Other hormonal levels drop, including the level of reproductive hormones. In women, reduced estrogen may result in the menstrual cycle stopping. In men, decreased testosterone disrupts sex drive and sexual function (Pinheiro et al., 2010).

Bulimia Nervosa and Binge-Eating Disorder **Bulimia nervosa** is *an eating disorder characterized by binges of extreme overeating followed by self-induced vomiting, misuse of laxatives, or other methods to purge excess food and prevent weight gain.* Like people with anorexia, people with bulimia nervosa fear gaining weight. Intense preoccupation and dissatisfaction with their bodies are also apparent. However, people with bulimia typically stay within a normal weight range or may even be slightly overweight. Another difference is that people with bulimia usually recognize that they have an eating disorder.

People with bulimia nervosa experience extreme periods of binge eating, consuming as many as 50,000 calories on a single binge. Binges typically occur twice a week and are often triggered by negative feelings or hunger. During the binge, the person usually consumes sweet, high-calorie foods that can be swallowed quickly, such as ice cream, cake, and candy. Binges typically occur in secrecy, leaving the person feeling ashamed, guilty, and disgusted by their own behavior. After bingeing, they compensate by purging themselves of the excessive food by self-induced vomiting or by misuse of laxatives or enemas. Once they purge, they often feel psychologically relieved. Some people with bulimia don't purge themselves of the excess food. Rather, they use fasting and excessive exercise to keep their body weight within the normal range (DSM-5, 2013).

Like anorexia nervosa, bulimia nervosa can take a serious physical toll on the body. Repeated purging disrupts the body's electrolyte balance, leading to muscle cramps, irregular heartbeat, and other cardiac problems, some potentially fatal. Stomach acids from self-induced vomiting erode tooth enamel, causing tooth decay and damage to the gastrointestinal tract (Powers, 2009).

Like people with bulimia, people with *binge-eating disorder* engage in bingeing behaviors (DSM-5, 2013). Unlike people with bulimia, they do not engage in purging or other behaviors that rid their bodies of the excess food. People with binge-eating disorder experience the same feelings of distress, lack of control, and shame that people with bulimia experience.

Causes of Eating Disorders: A Complex Picture Anorexia, bulimia, and binge-eating disorder involve decreases in brain activity of the neurotransmitter *serotonin* (Bailer & Kaye, 2011; Kuikka et al., 2001). Disrupted brain chemistry may also contribute to the fact that eating disorders frequently co-occur with other psychiatric disorders, such as major depressive disorder, substance abuse disorder, personality disorders, obsessive–compulsive disorder, and anxiety disorders (Thompson et al., 2007; Swanson et al., 2011).

Family interaction patterns may also contribute to eating disorders. For example, critical comments by parents or siblings about a child's weight, or parental modeling of disordered eating, may increase the odds that an individual develops an eating disorder (Quiles Marcos et al., 2013; Thompson et al., 2007). There also is evidence that other psychological characteristics may be risk factors. For example, having negative beliefs about oneself is associated with having an eating disorder (Yiend et al., 2014). Also, researchers have found that a tendency toward perfectionism in childhood—traits like needing to complete schoolwork perfectly and feeling a need to obey rules without question—was associated with a later diagnosis of anorexia (Halmi et al., 2012).

Although cases of eating disorders have been documented for at least 150 years, contemporary Western cultural attitudes toward thinness and dieting probably contribute to the increased incidence of eating disorders today. This seems to be especially true with anorexia, which occurs predominantly in Western or "westernized" countries (Anderson-Fye, 2009). We discuss this issue and the more general topic of culture's effects on psychological disorders in the Culture and Human Behavior box "Culture-Bound Syndromes."

> **personality disorder** Inflexible, maladaptive, and stable patterns of thoughts, emotions, behavior, and interpersonal functioning that deviate from the expectations of the individual's culture.

Personality Disorders: Maladaptive Traits

■ **KEY THEME**

The personality disorders are characterized by inflexible, maladaptive patterns of thoughts, emotions, behavior, and interpersonal functioning.

⹀ **KEY QUESTIONS**

- How do people with a personality disorder differ from people who are psychologically well adjusted?
- What behaviors and personality characteristics are associated with antisocial and borderline personality disorders?

Like every other person, you have your own unique *personality*—the consistent and enduring patterns of thinking, feeling, and behaving that characterize you as an individual. As we explained in the chapter on personality, your personality can be described as a specific collection of traits. Your *personality traits* are relatively stable predispositions to behave or react in certain ways. But the psychologically well-adjusted person possesses a fair degree of flexibility and adaptiveness. Based on our experiences with others, we modify how we display our personality traits so that we can think, feel, and behave in healthier and more appropriate ways.

In contrast, the characteristics of a **personality disorder** involve *inflexible, maladaptive, and stable patterns of thoughts, emotions, behavior, and interpersonal functioning that deviate from the expectations of the individual's culture.* However, the behavior of people with personality disorders goes well beyond that of a more typical individual who occasionally experiences an emotional meltdown or who is grumpier, more aloof, or more self-centered than most people.

⌃ **Mental Health Awareness** Originally from Colombia, Angie Sweeney now lives in Florida, where she runs a mental health support group for Latinos. Sweeney, who has been diagnosed with both bipolar disorder and borderline personality disorder, has been working to raise mental health awareness in the Latino community.

CULTURE AND HUMAN BEHAVIOR

Culture-Bound Syndromes

At several points in this chapter, we've noted ways in which culture shapes the symptoms of psychological disorders. Psychological disorders do not always look the same in every culture. And further, some disorders, called *culture-specific disorders* or *culture-bound syndromes*, appear to be found only in a single culture.

 MYTH ◀ SCIENCE

Is it true that the types of psychological disorders are pretty much the same in every culture?

For example, *hikikomori* is a syndrome first identified in Japan that involves a pattern of extreme social withdrawal (Teo, 2010). People suffering from *hikikomori*, usually young men, become virtual recluses, often confining themselves to a single room in their parents' home, sometimes for years. They refuse all engagement with the outside world and, in some cases, do not speak even to family members who care for them. They spend their time alone in their room, preoccupied with watching television, playing video games, or surfing the Internet. People suffering from *hikikomori* are more likely than the general population to have other psychological disorders and are at increased risk for suicide (Yong & Nomura, 2019). Once rare, *hikikomori* has become a social phenomenon. Some estimates are that a million or more young people in Japan live as *hikikomori* (Watts, 2002).

Hikikomori has symptoms in common with several Western disorders, including social anxiety disorder and agoraphobia. However, its specific features are uniquely Japanese, reflecting social pressures to succeed in school and to conform to social expectations (Teo, 2010; Teo & Gaw, 2010). Also implicated is the close, almost symbiotic relationship that is encouraged between mothers and children, especially sons, in Japan (Wong & Ying, 2006).

Societal shifts, however, may have led to the spread of *hikikomori* symptoms to other cultures. As the Internet allows for more people to stay at home and as more young people live at home into

▲ **Shutting Themselves In** Nineteen-year-old Dai Hasebe has lived as a hikikomori or shut-in since he was 11 years old, rarely leaving his family's Tokyo apartment. Like other *hikikomori*, he does not attend school or hold a job.

adulthood, *hikikomori* symptoms have been observed in a number of other countries including Hong Kong, Oman, and Spain (Kato et al., 2018). One study found a correlation between *hikikomori* symptoms and symptoms of Internet Gaming Disorder (IGD) in players of Massive Multiplayer Online (MMO) games (Stavropolous et al., 2019). (IGD, a condition listed in DSM-5 as being studied, involves an excessive amount of time playing online games coupled with high levels of distress.) Those who played MMO games the most were more likely to live at home with their parents and to be socially isolated.

Western cultures have culture-bound syndromes, too. Consider the case of anorexia nervosa. Its incidence is highest in the United

The personality disorders involve pervasive patterns of perceiving, relating to and thinking about the self, other people, and the environment that interfere with long-term functioning (Oltmanns & Balsis, 2011). And, these maladaptive behaviors are not restricted to isolated episodes or specific circumstances. Rather, these maladaptive patterns of emotions, thought processes, and behavior tend to be very stable over time. Personality disorders, which occur in about 10 percent of the general population, usually become evident during adolescence or early adulthood (Lenzenweger, 2008).

Many researchers believe that personality disorders reflect conditions in which "normal" personality traits are taken to an abnormal extreme (Samuel et al., 2010; Trull & Widiger, 2008). For example, it's normal to feel uneasy or sad when separated from a loved one. In a personality disorder, however, these responses reach pathological extremes. Rather than uneasiness, a person might experience intense feelings of desperation and intense anxiety. And rather than sadness, the person might experience unbearably intense feelings of abandonment and emptiness.

Despite the fact that the maladaptive personality traits consistently cause personal or social turmoil, people with personality disorders often blame others for their difficulties.

States, Western Europe, and other "westernized" cultures, where an unnaturally slender physique is the cultural ideal (Anderson-Fye, 2009). In these cultures, self-starvation is associated with an intense fear of becoming fat (DSM-5, 2013). Similar to *hikikomori*, however, anorexia has been spreading to other cultures. In this case, global transmission of information about psychological disorders may be contributing to the spread of syndromes that were once culture bound.

For example, Chinese psychiatrist Sing Lee only learned about eating disorders during his training in the United Kingdom in the 1980s. Upon his return home to Hong Kong, he combed through hospital records and interviewed colleagues but could find very few occurrences of anorexia nervosa or other eating disorders in his native country (S. Lee et al., 1993).

But that all changed in 1994, when 14-year-old schoolgirl Charlene Hsu Chi-Ying, emaciated and weighing only 75 pounds, collapsed and died on a busy street in the heart of Hong Kong (Watters, 2010). The dramatic nature of her death led to breathless media coverage. "Girl Who Died in Street Was a Walking Skeleton" read one headline. Within hours, many people in Hong Kong read about anorexia nervosa for the first time. With no traditional framework for understanding why an honor student would deliberately starve herself to death, the Hong Kong media sought out Western explanations, blaming images of women in the media and the fashion industry. Over the next decade, eating disorders in Hong Kong, Japan, and other Asian countries skyrocketed, and patients were much more likely to report a fear of being fat (S. Lee et al., 2010; Pike & Borovoy, 2004).

Many questions about culture-bound syndromes remain unanswered. For example, it is not clear whether culture-bound syndromes like *hikikomori* are distinct disorders, or whether they represent a culturally influenced expression of some more universal

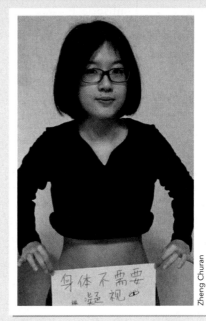

#A4Waist In a recent trend, many young women in China aimed to lose weight until their waist could be hidden by a sheet of A4 standard letter paper, which is about 8 inches wide (Tatlow, 2016). They posted these photos on social media with the hashtag #A4Waist. Not everyone was on board with the trend. Zheng Churan posted this photo with a piece of A4 paper turned the long way. The message she wrote on the paper translates to "Bodies don't need eyes staring at them."

underlying pathology—one that, in the case of *hikikomori*, we're now seeing in other countries. And when a disorder like anorexia nervosa appears to spread across cultures, is the increased incidence actually *caused* by media coverage? Or does it simply reflect an increase in the diagnosis of cases that already existed? These questions are complex and unlikely to have simple answers. As we've seen throughout this chapter, psychological disorders reflect the complex interaction of biological predispositions and psychological factors and are always expressed within a particular social and cultural context.

Even if they are aware of their maladaptive personality patterns, they typically don't think there's anything wrong with them. Consequently, people with personality disorders often don't seek help.

DSM-5 identifies 10 distinct personality disorders, summarized in **Table 14.6**. These disorders are organized into three basic clusters: odd, eccentric personality disorders; dramatic, emotional, erratic personality disorders; and anxious, fearful personality disorders. However, this classification system is problematic (American Psychiatric Association, 2012a, 2012b). For example, many people display the characteristics of more than one personality disorder, making diagnosis difficult. Also, some of the names can be confusing. For example, obsessive–compulsive personality disorder does not have OCD's characteristic obsessions and compulsions. Similarly, schizoid and schizotypal personality disorders lack the psychotic features of schizophrenia.

In this section, we'll focus our discussion on two of the more serious personality disorders, antisocial personality disorder and borderline personality disorder. These two disorders are also among the most thoroughly researched.

Personality Disorders

Odd, Eccentric Cluster	Dramatic, Emotional, Erratic Cluster	Anxious, Fearful Cluster
Paranoid Personality Disorder • Pervasive but unwarranted distrust and suspiciousness; assumes that other people intend to deceive, exploit, or harm them. **Schizoid Personality Disorder** • Pervasive detachment from social relationships; emotionally cold and flat; indifferent to praise or criticism from others; preference for solitary activities; lacking in close friends. **Schizotypal Personality Disorder** • Odd thoughts, speech, emotional reactions, mannerisms, and appearance; impaired social and interpersonal functioning; often superstitious.	**Antisocial Personality Disorder** • Blatantly disregards or violates the rights of others; impulsive, irresponsible, deceitful, manipulative, and lacking in guilt or remorse. **Borderline Personality Disorder** • Intense, unstable relationships, emotions, and self-image; impulsive; desperate efforts to avoid real or imagined abandonment; feelings of emptiness; self-destructive tendencies. **Histrionic Personality Disorder** • Exaggerated, dramatic expression of emotions and attention-seeking behavior that often includes sexually seductive or provocative behaviors. **Narcissistic Personality Disorder** • Grandiose sense of self-importance; exaggerates abilities and accomplishments; excessive need for admiration; boastful, pretentious; lacking in empathy.	**Avoidant Personality Disorder** • Extreme social inhibition and social avoidance due to feelings of inadequacy, and hypersensitivity to criticism, rejection, or disapproval. **Dependent Personality Disorder** • Excessive need to be taken care of, leading to submissive, clinging behaviors; fears of separation; and the inability to assume responsibility. **Obsessive–Compulsive Personality Disorder** • Rigid preoccupation with orderliness, personal control, rules, or schedules that interferes with completing tasks; unreasonable perfectionism.

Source: Information from DSM-5 (2013).

Antisocial Personality Disorder: Violating the Rights of Others—Without Guilt or Remorse

Antisocial personality disorder is *a personality disorder characterized by a pervasive pattern of disregarding and violating the rights of others*. Often referred to as a *psychopath* or *sociopath,* the individual with antisocial personality disorder has the ability to lie, cheat, steal, and otherwise manipulate and harm other people. And when caught, the person shows little or no remorse for having caused pain, damage, or loss to others (Patrick, 2007). It's as though the person has no conscience or sense of guilt. This pattern of blatantly disregarding and violating the rights of others is the central feature of antisocial personality disorder (DSM-5, 2013). Although many people associate violence with antisocial personality disorder, a history of violence is not necessary for the diagnosis (DSM-5, 2013). In fact, there is a wide range of behaviors associated with antisocial personality disorder (Baskin-Sommers, 2016). There is even evidence that some psychopaths succeed in high-status, competitive professions such as in business or politics where a ruthless personality might be useful (Boddy et al., 2010; Lilienfeld et al., 2015). One woman who had been diagnosed as a psychopath, an alternative term for antisocial personality disorder, explained, "People believe that if you have a lack of empathy, that automatically opens a floodgate of antisocial behavior. That's not really how it works. I may not care, I may not have an emotional reaction to someone's pain, but that doesn't mean that I'm going out of my way to *cause* pain. It just means that I don't have that emotional response" (Heaney, 2018). Researchers have also noted a relative lack of anxiety in these individuals, especially those most likely to harm others for their own benefit (De Brito & Hodgins, 2009; Neumann et al., 2013). Approximately 4 percent of the general population displays the characteristics of antisocial personality disorder, with men far outnumbering women (Grant et al., 2004).

Evidence of the maladaptive personality patterns associated with antisocial personality disorder is often seen in childhood or early adolescence (Diamantopoulou et al., 2010; Hiatt & Dishion, 2008). In many cases, the child has repeated run-ins with the law or school authorities. Behaviors that draw the attention of authorities can include cruelty to animals, attacking or harming adults or other children, theft, setting fires, and destroying property. During childhood and adolescence, this pattern of behavior is typically diagnosed as *conduct disorder.* The habitual failure to conform to social norms and rules often becomes the person's predominant life theme, which continues into adulthood (Patrick, 2007).

antisocial personality disorder A personality disorder characterized by a pervasive pattern of disregarding and violating the rights of others.

Deceiving and manipulating others for their own personal gain is another hallmark of individuals with antisocial personality disorder. With an uncanny ability to look you directly in the eye and speak with complete confidence and sincerity, they will lie in order to gain money, sex, or whatever their goal may be. Often, they are contemptuous about the feelings or rights of others, blaming the victim for their stupidity. This quality makes antisocial personality disorder especially difficult to treat because clients often manipulate and lie to their therapists, too (McMurran & Howard, 2009).

Because they are consistently irresponsible, individuals with antisocial personality disorder often end up in the criminal justice system, develop alcoholism, or have difficulties holding a job (Hasin et al., 2011; Fridell et al., 2008). However, by middle to late adulthood, the antisocial tendencies of such individuals tend to diminish.

Borderline Personality Disorder: Chaos and Emptiness

> Borderline individuals are the psychological equivalent of third-degree-burn patients. They simply have no emotional skin. Even the slightest touch or movement can create immense suffering.

This is how psychologist Marsha Linehan (2009) describes the chaotic, unstable world of people with **borderline personality disorder (BPD)**, *a personality disorder characterized by instability of interpersonal relationships, self-image, and emotions, and marked impulsivity.* BPD, more common in women than men, is characterized by impulsiveness and chronically unstable emotions, relationships, and self-image. Moods and emotions are intense, fluctuating, and extreme, often vastly out of proportion to the triggering incident, and seemingly uncontrollable (Southward & Cheavens, 2018). The person with BPD unpredictably swings from one mood extreme to another. Inappropriate, intense, and often uncontrollable episodes of anger are another hallmark of this disorder (Berenson et al., 2011).

Relationships with others are as chaotic and unstable as the person's moods. The person with BPD has a chronic, pervasive sense of emptiness. Desperately afraid of abandonment, they alternately cling to others and push them away. Because their sense of identity is so fragile, they constantly seek reassurance and self-definition from others. When it is not forthcoming, they may erupt in furious anger or abject despair.

Relationships careen out of control as the person shifts from inappropriately idealizing the newfound lover or friend to viewing them with complete contempt or hostility. They see themselves, and everyone else, as absolutes: ecstatic or miserable, perfect or worthless (Arntz & ten Haaf, 2012; de Montigny-Malenfant et al., 2013). Writer Sarah Haufrect (2016) described how her mother's BPD destroyed her relationships. Her mother divorced twice and alienated all of her friends "over bizarre arguments of which I'd only hear the murky details, or they'd been driven away by my mom's general operating procedures: a consistent pattern of destruction to herself and others."

Often, the deep despair and inner emptiness that people with BPD experience are outwardly expressed in self-destructive behavior (Linehan & Dexter-Mazza, 2008). "Cutting" or other acts of self-mutilation, threats of suicide, and suicide attempts are common, especially in response to perceived rejection or abandonment. Underscoring the seriousness of BPD is a grim statistic: As many as 10 percent of those who meet the BPD criteria eventually die by suicide, an extremely high percentage that is about *50 times* the suicide rate for the general population (American Psychiatric Association, 2001; Qin, 2011).

Along with being among the most severe of the personality disorders, borderline personality disorder is also the most commonly diagnosed. One survey found that BPD was more prevalent than previously thought. Estimates suggest that BPD affects about 6 percent of the U.S. population, or possibly some 18 million people (Grant et al., 2008).

What Causes Borderline Personality Disorder?
As with the other personality disorders, multiple factors have been implicated. A comprehensive theory, called the *biosocial developmental theory of borderline personality disorder,* has been proposed by Marsha Linehan (1993; Crowell et al., 2009). According to this view, BPD is the outcome

borderline personality disorder (BPD) A personality disorder characterized by instability of interpersonal relationships, self-image, and emotions, and marked impulsivity.

Pete Davidson and Borderline Personality Disorder *Saturday Night Live* cast member Pete Davidson was diagnosed with borderline personality disorder a few years ago. He spoke about his confusion prior to his diagnosis (Juneau, 2021). "[I] just thought something was wrong and didn't know how to deal with it. Then, when somebody finally tells you, the weight of the world feels lifted off your shoulders. You feel so much better."

dissociative experience A break or disruption in consciousness during which awareness, memory, and personal identity become separated or divided.

dissociative disorders A category of psychological disorders in which extreme and frequent disruptions of awareness, memory, and personal identity impair the ability to function.

of a unique combination of biological, psychological, and environmental factors. Some children are born with a biological temperament that is characterized by extreme emotional sensitivity, a tendency to be impulsive, and the tendency to experience negative emotions. Linehan believes that BPD results when such biologically vulnerable children are raised by caregivers who do not teach them how to control their impulses or help them learn how to understand, regulate, and appropriately express their emotions (Crowell et al., 2009).

In some cases, Linehan believes, parents or caregivers actually shape and reinforce the child's pattern of frequent, intense emotional displays by their own behavior. For example, they may sometimes ignore a child's emotional outbursts and sometimes reinforce them. In Linehan's theory, a history of abuse and neglect may be present but is not a necessary ingredient in the toxic mix that produces BPD. Despite the difficulties faced by people suffering from BPD, treatments developed by Linehan and her colleagues have been shown to help patients to manage this mental illness (see Bohus et al., 2000).

The Dissociative Disorders: Fragmentation of the Self

■ KEY THEME
In the dissociative disorders, disruptions in awareness, memory, and identity interfere with the ability to function in everyday life.

≡ KEY QUESTIONS
- What is dissociation, and how do normal dissociative experiences differ from the symptoms of dissociative disorders?
- What are dissociative amnesia, dissociative amnesia with dissociative fugue, and dissociative identity disorder (DID)?
- What is thought to cause DID?

Despite the many changes you've experienced throughout your lifetime, you have a pretty consistent sense of identity. You're aware of your surroundings and can easily recall memories from the recent and distant past. In other words, a typical personality is one in which *awareness, memory,* and *personal identity* are associated and well integrated.

In contrast, a **dissociative experience** is *a break or disruption in consciousness during which awareness, memory, and personal identity become separated or divided.* Although that may sound unusual, dissociative experiences are not inherently pathological. Mild dissociative experiences are quite common and completely normal (Dalenberg et al., 2009; Wieland, 2011). For example, you become so absorbed in a book or movie that you lose all track of time. Or, while driving your usual route to school, you may become so preoccupied with your thoughts—maybe about class that day—that when you arrive on campus, much of the trip is a blur. In each of these cases, you've experienced a temporary "break" or "separation" in your memory or awareness—a temporary, mild dissociative experience. They might even be adaptive in some traumatic circumstances. U.S. gymnast Laurie Hernandez, an Olympic champion, described a dissociative response to the emotional abuse she experienced from her coach, Maggie Haney (Macur, 2020): "As soon as Maggie raised her voice past a certain point, that space in my brain would pull the parachute and I couldn't hear her. As soon as practice was over, it was like my brain was a computer and I wiped out everything."

Clearly, then, dissociative experiences are not necessarily pathological. **Dissociative disorders** are *a category of psychological disorders in which extreme and frequent disruptions of awareness, memory, and personal identity impair the ability to function.* That is the dissociative experiences are much more extreme or more frequent, and they severely disrupt everyday functioning. Awareness, or recognition of familiar surroundings, may be completely obstructed. Memories of pertinent personal information may be unavailable to consciousness. Identity may be lost, confused, or fragmented (Dell & O'Neil, 2009).

⌃ Dissociation and Possession A member of the Dongria Kondh people in eastern India dances in a trance during a ceremony on top of Niyamgiri Mountain, which the community regards as sacred. Such dissociative trance and possession states are common in religions around the world (Krippner, 1994; Maraldi et al., 2021). When dissociative experiences take place within a religious ritual context, they are not considered abnormal. In fact, such experiences may be highly valued (Mulhern, 1991).

The category of dissociative disorders consists of two basic disorders: (1) *dissociative amnesia,* which can occur either with or without *dissociative fugue,* and (2) *dissociative identity disorder,* which was previously called *multiple personality disorder.* Until recently, the dissociative disorders were thought to be extremely rare. How rare? An extensive review conducted in the 1940s uncovered a grand total of 76 reported cases of dissociative disorders since the beginnings of modern medicine in the 1700s (Taylor & Martin, 1944). The clinical picture changed dramatically in the 1970s, when a surge of dissociative disorder diagnoses occurred (Kihlstrom, 2005). Later in this discussion, we'll explore some of the possible reasons as well as the controversy surrounding the "epidemic" of dissociative disorders that began in the 1970s.

Dissociative Amnesia and Dissociative Fugue: Forgetting and Wandering

Dissociative amnesia is a *dissociative disorder involving the partial or total inability to recall important information.* Dissociative amnesia is not due to a medical condition, such as an illness, an injury, or a drug. Usually the person develops amnesia for personal events and information, rather than for general knowledge or skills. That is, the person may not be able to remember their spouse's name but does remember how to read and who Martin Luther King, Jr., was. In most cases, dissociative amnesia is a response to stress, trauma, or an extremely distressing situation, such as combat, marital problems, or physical abuse (McLewin & Muller, 2006).

Some cases of dissociative amnesia involve a **dissociative fugue,** a *type of dissociative amnesia involving sudden and unexpected travel away from home, extensive amnesia, and identity confusion.* In amnesia with dissociative fugue, the person outwardly appears completely normal. However, the person is confused about their identity. While in the fugue state, they suddenly and inexplicably travel away from their home, wandering to other cities or even countries. In some cases, people in a fugue state adopt a completely new identity.

As is true with other cases of amnesia, dissociative fugues are thought to be associated with traumatic events or stressful periods. However, it's unclear as to *how* a fugue state develops or *why* a person experiences a fugue state rather than other sorts of symptoms, such as simple anxiety or depression. Interestingly, when the person "awakens" from the fugue state, they may remember their past history but have amnesia for what occurred *during* the fugue state (DSM-5, 2013).

Dissociative Identity Disorder: Multiple Personalities

Among the dissociative disorders, none is more fascinating—or controversial—than dissociative identity disorder, formerly known as *multiple personality disorder.* **Dissociative identity disorder (DID)** is *a dissociative disorder involving extensive memory disruptions for personal information along with the presence of two or more distinct identities, or "personalities," within a single person.*

Typically, each personality has their own name and is experienced as if they have their own personal history and self-image. These alternate personalities, often called *alters* or *alter egos,* may be of widely varying ages and different genders. Alters are not really separate people. Rather, they constitute a "system of mind" (Courtois & Ford, 2009). That is, the alters seem to embody different aspects of the individual's personality that, for some reason, cannot be integrated into the primary personality. The alternate personalities hold memories, emotions, and motives that are not admissible to the individual's conscious mind. At different times, different alter egos take control of the person's experience, thoughts, and behavior. Typically, the primary personality is unaware of the existence of the alternate personalities. However, the alter egos may have knowledge of each other's existence and share memories (see Kong et al., 2008). Sometimes the experiences of one alter are accessible to another alter but not vice versa.

Symptoms of amnesia and memory problems are reported in virtually all cases of DID (Dorahy et al., 2014). There are frequent gaps in memory for both recent and childhood experiences. Commonly, those with DID "lose time" and are unable to recall their behavior or whereabouts during specific time periods. In addition to their memory problems,

dissociative amnesia Dissociative disorder involving the partial or total inability to recall important personal information.

dissociative fugue (fyoog) Type of dissociative amnesia involving sudden and unexpected travel away from home, extensive amnesia, and identity confusion.

dissociative identity disorder (DID) A dissociative disorder involving extensive memory disruptions for personal information along with the presence of two or more distinct identities, or "personalities" within a single person.

Nicole Bengiveno/The New York Times/Redux

▲ Dissociative Fugue: "Who Am I Now?" Just before a new school year, 23-year-old teacher Hannah Upp disappeared. Intensive search efforts produced nothing, but then Hannah was seen at a Manhattan Apple store and, later, at a Starbucks. Hannah was finally rescued when a Staten Island Ferry crew saw her swimming almost a mile from shore—three weeks after she initially disappeared. Hannah had no memories of the events following her disappearance and was disturbed by her amnesia and flight. In an interview, she said, "It's not your fault, but it's still somehow you. So it's definitely made me reconsider everything. Who was I before? Who was I then—is that part of me? Who am I now?" (Marx & Didziulis, 2009). Although psychologists don't understand what causes dissociative amnesia with dissociative fugue, stressful events are often implicated. Sadly, Hannah went missing again in September 2017 from the Virgin Island of St. Thomas, where she was working as a teacher (Aviv, 2018). She has not been found (Fitzsimons, 2020).

people with DID typically have numerous psychiatric and physical symptoms, along with a chaotic personal history (Cardeña & Gleaves, 2007; Rodewald et al., 2011).

Not all mental health professionals are convinced that DID is a genuine psychological disorder (Cardeña & Gleaves, 2007; Lynn et al., 2006). One reason for skepticism is that reported cases sharply increased in the early 1970s, shortly after books, films, and television dramas about what was then called multiple personality disorder became popular. Not only the number of cases but also the number of "alters" showed a dramatic increase (Kihlstrom, 2005). To some psychologists, such findings suggest that patients with DID learned "how to behave like a multiple" from media portrayals of sensational cases or by responding to their therapists' suggestions (Gee et al., 2003; Lynn et al., 2012). People with another mental illness or other vulnerability might be particularly susceptible to such influences (Lynn et al., 2012). And there is research to support this conclusion. Guy Boysen and Alexandra VanBergen (2014) reviewed many studies of people with dissociative identity disorder, and concluded that "in terms of key symptoms of the disorder, people taught to simulate DID are largely indistinguishable from people actually diagnosed with DID."

On the other hand, DID is not the only psychological disorder for which prevalence rates have increased over time. For example, rates of obsessive–compulsive disorder and PTSD have also increased over the past few decades, primarily because mental health professionals have become more aware of these disorders and more likely to screen for symptoms. The dissociative disorders are summarized in **Table 14.7**.

Explaining Dissociative Identity Disorder According to one explanation, dissociative identity disorder represents an extreme form of dissociative coping (Moskowitz et al., 2009). A very high percentage of patients with DID report having suffered extreme physical or sexual abuse in childhood—over 90 percent in most surveys (Foote et al., 2006; Sar et al., 2007). According to this explanation, to cope with the trauma, the child "dissociates" themselves from it, creating alternate personalities to experience the trauma.

Over time, alternate personalities are created to deal with the memories and emotions associated with intolerably painful experiences. In effect, dissociation becomes a pathological defense mechanism that the person uses to cope with overwhelming experiences.

Although widely accepted among therapists who work with patients with DID, the dissociative coping theory is difficult to test empirically. One problem is that memories of childhood are notoriously unreliable. Because DID is usually diagnosed in adulthood, it is difficult, and often impossible, to determine whether the reports of childhood abuse are real or imaginary.

Another problem with the "traumatic memory" explanation of dissociative identity disorder is that just the *opposite* effect occurs to most trauma victims—they are bothered by recurring and intrusive memories of the traumatic event. For example, in a study by Gail Goodman

TABLE 14.7

Dissociative Disorders

Dissociative Amnesia
- Inability to remember important personal information, too extensive to be explained by ordinary forgetfulness

Dissociative Amnesia with Dissociative Fugue
- Sudden, unexpected travel away from home

Confusion about personal identity or assumption of new identity

Dissociative Identity Disorder
- Presence of two or more distinct identities, each with consistent personality traits and behavior
- Behavior that is controlled by two or more distinct recurring identities
- Amnesia; frequent memory gaps

and her colleagues (2003), more than 80 percent of young adults with a documented history of childhood sexual abuse remembered the abuse. Of those who didn't report the abuse, reluctance to disclose the abuse and being too young to remember the abuse seemed to be the most likely explanations. Although the scientific debate about the validity of the dissociative disorders is likely to continue for some time, the dissociative disorders are fundamentally different from the last major category of disorders we'll consider—schizophrenia.

Schizophrenia: A Different Reality

■ KEY THEME
One of the most serious psychological disorders is schizophrenia, which involves severely distorted beliefs, perceptions, and thought processes.

≡ KEY QUESTIONS
- What are the major symptoms of schizophrenia, and how do positive and negative symptoms differ?
- How does culture affect the symptoms of schizophrenia?
- What factors have been implicated in the development of schizophrenia?

Normally, you've got a pretty good grip on reality. You can easily distinguish between external reality and the different kinds of mental states that you routinely experience, such as dreams or daydreams.

If any psychological disorder demonstrates the potential for losing touch with reality, it's schizophrenia. **Schizophrenia** is *a psychological disorder in which the ability to function is impaired by severely distorted beliefs, perceptions, and thought processes*. In media accounts and casual conversation, a person with schizophrenia is often mistakenly described as having a "split personality." But Elyn Saks (2008), whom you met in the Prologue, explains that "the schizophrenic mind is not split, but shattered." During a schizophrenic episode, people lose their grip on reality. Like Elyn screaming, "I'm flying! I've escaped!" as she raced around campus, people become engulfed in an entirely different inner world, one that is often characterized by mental chaos, disorientation, and frustration.

Symptoms of Schizophrenia

The characteristic symptoms of schizophrenia can be described in terms of two broad categories: positive and negative symptoms. **Positive symptoms** reflect *an excess or distortion of normal functioning including delusions, hallucinations, and disorganized thoughts and behavior*. In contrast, **negative symptoms** reflect *defects or deficits in normal functioning, including flat affect.*

According to DSM-5, schizophrenia is diagnosed when two or more of these characteristic symptoms are actively present for a month or longer. At least one symptom must be delusions, hallucinations, or disorganized speech. Usually, schizophrenia also involves a longer personal history, typically six months or more, of odd behaviors, beliefs, perceptual experiences, and other less severe signs of mental disturbance (Keshavan et al., 2011). In Elyn's case, her symptoms lasted for years (Saks, 2008).

Schizophrenia may be diagnosed either with or without catatonia (DSM-5, 2013). *Catatonia* includes symptoms that reflect highly disturbed movements or actions. These may include bizarre postures or grimaces, complete immobility, no speech or very little speech, or extremely agitated behavior.

Positive Symptoms: Delusions, Hallucinations, and Disturbances in Sensation, Thinking, and Speech
A **delusion** is *a false belief that persists despite compelling contradictory evidence*. Schizophrenic delusions are not simply unconventional or inaccurate beliefs. Rather, they are bizarre and far-fetched notions. At times, Elyn believed that she was an evil person who was capable of committing terrible violent acts, including killing children (Saks, 2008). The delusional person often becomes preoccupied with their erroneous beliefs and ignores any evidence that contradicts them.

schizophrenia A psychological disorder in which the ability to function is impaired by severely distorted beliefs, perceptions, and thought processes.

positive symptoms An excess or distortion of normal functioning including delusions, hallucinations, and disorganized thoughts and behavior.

negative symptoms Defects or deficits in normal functioning, including flat affect.

delusion A false belief that persists despite compelling contradictory evidence.

MYTH ◄ SCIENCE

Is it true that people with schizophrenia have a "split personality"?

Glimpses of Schizophrenia Artist Karen Sorenson, who manages her schizophrenia with medication, painted *Electricity Makes You Float* shortly after the 9/11 World Trade Center attacks. The painting, she says, grew out of a "psychotic fantasy . . . I thought that I could shoot rays of energy from the palms of my hands and blow up buildings. Somehow I identified with murderers. Making this picture helped free me of the obsessiveness of the idea . . . [by] putting it out there into the brilliance of daylight" (Sorenson, 2011).

hallucination A false or distorted perception that seems vividly real to the person experiencing it.

Certain themes consistently appear in schizophrenic delusions. *Delusions of reference* reflect the person's false conviction that other people's behavior and ordinary events are somehow personally related to them. For example, they are certain that billboards and advertisements are about them or contain cryptic messages directed at them. In contrast, *delusions of grandeur* involve the belief that the person is extremely powerful, important, or wealthy. In *delusions of persecution,* the basic theme is that others are plotting against or trying to harm the person or someone close to them. *Delusions of being controlled* involve the belief that outside forces—aliens, the government, or random people, for example—are trying to exert control on the individual. Delusional thinking may lead to dangerous behaviors, as when a person responds to their delusional ideas by hurting themselves or attacking others.

One of the most disturbing experiences in schizophrenia is a **hallucination**, *a false or distorted perception that seems vividly real to the person experiencing it.* The content of hallucinations is often tied to the person's delusional beliefs. For example, if they harbor delusions of grandeur, hallucinated voices may reinforce their grandiose ideas by communicating instructions from God, the devil, or angels.

When a schizophrenic episode is severe, hallucinations can be virtually impossible to distinguish from objective reality. When symptoms are less severe, the person may recognize that the hallucination is a product of their own mind. As Elyn reported, she knew that she had to try to control her psychotic thoughts at school and was sometimes able to do so. To learn more about why auditory hallucinations are so hard to distinguish from actual sounds, read the Focus on Neuroscience on page 501.

Along with sensory distortions, the person may experience severely disorganized thinking. It becomes enormously difficult to concentrate, remember, and integrate important information while ignoring irrelevant information (Barch, 2005). Such disorganized thinking is often reflected in the person's speech (Badcock et al., 2011). Ideas, words, and images are sometimes strung together in ways that seem nonsensical to the listener.

Negative Symptoms: Deficits in Normal Functioning
Negative symptoms consist of marked deficits or decreases in behavioral or emotional functioning. One commonly seen negative symptom is referred to as *diminished emotional expression* or flat affect. Emotional responsiveness and facial expressions are reduced, and speech is slow and monotonous.

Negative symptoms also include the inability to initiate or persist in even simple forms of goal-directed behaviors, such as bathing or engaging in social activities. Instead, the person seems to be completely apathetic, sometimes sitting still for hours at a time. In combination, the negative symptoms accentuate the isolation of the person with schizophrenia, who may appear uncommunicative and completely disconnected from his or her environment. Not everyone with schizophrenia experiences negative symptoms. Elyn Saks wrote of feeling lucky to have escaped experiencing most negative symptoms (Saks, 2008).

Schizophrenia Symptoms and Culture
Symptoms of schizophrenia often vary across cultures. For example, researchers found that people in the United States were more likely to experience auditory hallucinations that were dark and sometimes vicious, whereas people in Ghana and India were more likely to report having a positive relationship with their voices (Luhrmann et al., 2015). As one Indian participant explained while laughing, "I have a companion to talk to" (Khazan, 2014).

There are also cultural differences in delusions. For example, some themes that would be considered to be delusional in one culture might be widely held beliefs in another culture. The International Study on Psychotic Symptoms examined data from over 1,000 people with schizophrenia in seven countries: Austria, Georgia, Ghana, Lithuania, Nigeria, Pakistan, and Poland (Stompe et al., 2006). About 17 percent of the delusions that were experienced were culturally specific. For example, in Nigeria and

A Truly Modern Delusion With the rise of reality television, the "Truman Show" delusion—the belief that your life is being filmed as a show—is increasingly common (Fuchs, 2020; Gold & Gold, 2012). *The Truman Show* is a 1998 hit movie about an insurance salesperson who discovered that his entire life was secretly being filmed for broadcast. Patients themselves refer to "Truman Show" symptoms—or sometimes to "Matrix" symptoms, referring to the 1999 film that imagines a future in which the global population is trapped inside a game-like simulation but believe that it is the real world. While experiencing the Truman Show delusion, Ohio college student Nick Lotz even took an acting course to improve his "performance." He believed that the goal of his delusional reality show was to join the cast of *Saturday Night Live*—a truly culturally specific modern delusion (Marantz, 2013).

©Paramount Pictures/courtesy Everett Collection

Hearing and Seeing Within Your Own Mind

Most of us talk to ourselves, but we usually don't talk to ourselves out loud so others can hear us. We often engage in what is called internal speech, silent thinking that resembles speech (Alderson-Day et al., 2017). In fact, most of you reading this may even be reading it out loud, but within your mind. Because that may not be true for all of you, try this: read the following "out loud," but silently within your mind: "I see a pink sheep." You might feel a little weird now that you're paying attention to that internal voice. Did you picture a pink sheep in your mind, even though you likely never saw a pink sheep in the real world? Seeing something in your "mind's eye" that you have never actually seen and hearing something in your "mind's ear" that you have never actually heard are among the amazing things the human brain can do. But what makes this ability truly exceptional is that the internal picture of a pink sheep was a product of your own brain activity.

Brain research demonstrates that when we use our mind's eye, or internal speech, brain activity looks nearly identical to actually seeing something or hearing something. When we engage in internal speech, for example, many of the same regions in the auditory cortex (found in the temporal lobe) show nearly as much brain activity as when we hear actual speech (Pernet et al., 2015). And when we create mental images, we show nearly as much brain activity in the occipital cortex as when we see things in the real world (Ganis et al., 2004). Now imagine that you don't know it's actually your own brain producing that speech or that image. It would be frightening, and the experience would be similar to having actual hallucinations.

As you have read, one of the positive symptoms of schizophrenia is hallucinations, usually hearing voices. People suffering from schizophrenia are often plagued by disorganized thinking, so it can be hard to know whether brain imaging captures actual hallucinations. Different research techniques, however, provide consistent results that show brain activity of auditory processing during auditory hallucinations (e.g., Leroy et al., 2017; Shergill et al., 2000). The difference between auditory hallucinations and your own internal speech

The Hallucinating Brain Researcher David Silbersweig and his colleagues (1995) used PET scans to take a "snapshot" of brain activity during schizophrenic hallucinations. The scan shown here was recorded at the exact instant a person with schizophrenia hallucinated disembodied heads yelling orders at him. The bright orange areas reveal activity in the left auditory and visual areas of his brain but not in the frontal lobe, which normally is involved in organized thought processes.

points to the difference between internal speech among typical people and auditory hallucinations, such as those experienced by people with psychotic disorders like schizophrenia. Typical people are aware that their brain is responsible for the "voice" inside their head, and there is a pattern of brain activity that shows this (Pernet et al., 2015).

People who experience auditory hallucinations show deficits in brain regions that are consistently associated with self-awareness (Stephane et al., 2006). Brain imaging also reveals that people with schizophrenia may demonstrate reduced brain activity in the prefrontal cortex along with increased brain activity in the limbic system (Escarti et al., 2010). Together, this pattern of brain activity shows an inability to recognize the self-based nature of inner speech, which may represent the neurological underpinnings of distressing auditory hallucinations (Ford et al., 2009; Stephane et al., 2006).

Ghana there were relatively high rates of delusions that involved "being an angel or a prophet," concepts that are integral parts of these cultures.

Even within a single culture, the content of delusions changes as the culture shifts. A study of delusions in U.S. inpatient psychiatric patients found that delusions have changed over time. During World War II, delusions tended to center on Nazi soldiers. Recently, delusions are more likely to involve technology and media (Cannon & Kramer, 2012). The *Truman Show* photo illustrates a modern spin on delusions involving surveillance.

The Prevalence and Course of Schizophrenia

Every year, approximately 1 million Americans are treated for schizophrenia. Worldwide, no society or culture is immune to this psychological disorder. One study found a global prevalence rate of less than 1 percent, with an estimated 21 million people

What is it like to live with schizophrenia? Go to **Achieve** and watch **Video: Schizophrenia** to hear Mo's story.

Esmé Weijun Wang and the Stereotypes of Severe Mental Illness Esmé Weijun Wang is a Taiwanese-American writer who has won awards for her work. She also has a diagnosis of schizoaffective disorder, a disorder that combines the symptoms of a psychotic disorder like schizophrenia with the symptoms of a mood disorder. On the *Unladylike* podcast, Wang spoke eloquently about the expectations faced by people with a severe mental illness, especially those without her impressive academic degrees and stylishness (Conger & Ervin, 2020). "I'm always really cognizant of passing as high functioning, and at the same time I wrestle with whether that's something that I, you know, should take advantage of and how I use that. How much do I use that privilege of being high functioning? The phrase high functioning is really looked at with a lot of caution in the disability rights community, which makes a lot of sense because it does not make sense to treat people who are so-called high functioning better than it is to treat people who are not. And yet that's very much the case."

with schizophrenia worldwide (Charlson et al., 2018). But another comprehensive review of almost 200 studies concluded that global rate of schizophrenia was close to 4 percent, meaning that schizophrenia may be far more widespread than was once believed (Saha et al., 2005).

The onset of schizophrenia typically occurs during young adulthood, as it did with Elyn (Gogtay et al., 2011). The good news is that about one-quarter of those who experience an episode of schizophrenia recover completely and never experience another episode. Another one-quarter experience recurrent episodes of schizophrenia but often with only minimal impairment in their ability to function.

Now the bad news. For the rest of those who have experienced an episode of schizophrenia—about one-half of the total—schizophrenia becomes a chronic mental illness, and the ability to function may be severely impaired. The people in this last category face the prospect of repeated hospitalizations and extended treatment. Thus, chronic schizophrenia places a heavy emotional, financial, and psychological burden on people with the disorder, their families, and society (Combs & Mueser, 2007). Yet, as Elyn's story shows, a diagnosis of schizophrenia does not mean that a person cannot be successful in their career and personal life.

Cultural factors also seem to affect the outcome of schizophrenia. Despite less access to mental health care, people with schizophrenia often have a better outcome in the developing world than in the developed world (Haro et al., 2011; World Health Organization, 1998). For example, the World Health Organization (WHO) found that full recovery after a single episode of psychosis occurred in just 3 percent of cases in the United States but in 54 percent of cases in India. The WHO (1998) suggests that people in the developing world might be more accepting of mental illness and are more likely to have extended family support systems than people in the developed world. However, other studies have qualified these findings. For example, for people with schizophrenia living in the developing world, the decline in symptoms did not necessarily coincide with improved life functioning (Haro et al., 2011).

Explaining Schizophrenia

Schizophrenia is an extremely complex disorder. There is enormous individual variability in the onset, symptoms, and duration of and recovery from schizophrenia. So it shouldn't come as a surprise that the causes of schizophrenia seem to be equally complex. In this section, we'll survey some of the factors that have been implicated in the development of schizophrenia.

Genetic Factors: Family, Twin, Adoption, and Gene Studies Studies of families, twins, and adopted individuals have firmly established that genetic factors play a significant role in many cases of schizophrenia (Pogue-Geile & Yokley, 2010). First, family studies have consistently shown that schizophrenia tends to cluster in certain families (Choi et al., 2007; Helenius et al., 2012). Second, family and twin studies have consistently shown that the more closely related a person is to someone who has schizophrenia, the greater the risk that they will be diagnosed with schizophrenia at some point in their lifetime (see **Figure 14.2**). Third, adoption studies have consistently shown that if either *biological* parent of an adopted individual had schizophrenia, the adopted individual is at greater risk to develop schizophrenia (Wynne et al., 2006). And fourth, by studying families that display a high rate of schizophrenia, researchers have consistently found that the presence of certain genetic variations seems to increase susceptibility to the disorder (Fanous et al., 2005; Williams et al., 2005).

Ironically, some of the best evidence that points to genetic involvement in schizophrenia—the almost 50 percent risk rate for a person whose identical twin has schizophrenia—is the same evidence that underscores the importance of environmental factors (Gejman et al., 2010; Oh & Petronis, 2008). If schizophrenia were purely a matter of inherited maladaptive genes, then you would expect a risk rate much closer to 100 percent

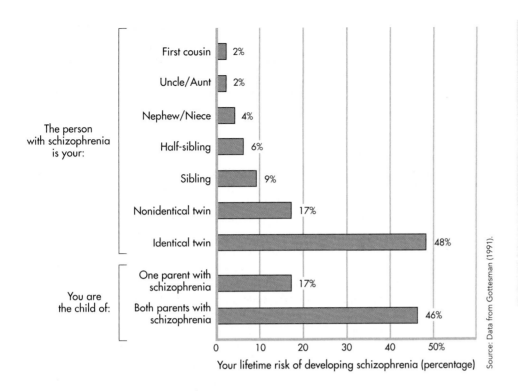

The person with schizophrenia is your:

- First cousin — 2%
- Uncle/Aunt — 2%
- Nephew/Niece — 4%
- Half-sibling — 6%
- Sibling — 9%
- Nonidentical twin — 17%
- Identical twin — 48%

You are the child of:

- One parent with schizophrenia — 17%
- Both parents with schizophrenia — 46%

Your lifetime risk of developing schizophrenia (percentage)

Source: Data from Gottesman (1991).

FIGURE 14.2 The Risk of Developing Schizophrenia Among Blood Relatives The risk percentages shown here reflect the collective results of about 40 studies investigating the likelihood of developing schizophrenia among blood relatives. As you can see, the greatest risk occurs if you have an identical twin who has schizophrenia (48 percent lifetime risk) or if both of your biological parents have schizophrenia (46 percent lifetime risk). Some research suggests that the rates may be even higher than the ones in this figure if one or both of your parents have schizophrenia (Sørensen et al., 2014). However, environmental factors are also involved in the development of schizophrenia.

for identical twins. Obviously, nongenetic factors must play a role in explaining why half of identical twins who have a twin who has schizophrenia do *not* develop schizophrenia.

The Immune System: The Viral Infection Theory

Some researchers have theorized that schizophrenia might be caused by exposure to an influenza virus or other viral infection during prenatal development or shortly after birth (Arias et al., 2012; Yudofsky, 2009). A virus might seem an unlikely cause of a serious mental illness, but viruses *can* spread to the brain and spinal cord by traveling along nerves. According to this theory, exposure to a viral infection during prenatal development or early infancy affects the developing brain, producing changes that make the individual more vulnerable to schizophrenia later in life.

There is growing evidence to support the viral infection theory. In one compelling study, researchers compared stored blood samples of 64 mothers of people who later developed schizophrenia with a matched set of blood samples from women whose children did not develop schizophrenia (Brown et al., 2004). The blood samples had been collected years earlier during the women's pregnancies. The women who had been exposed to the flu virus during the first trimester had a sevenfold increased risk of bearing a child who later developed schizophrenia. In a similar study, researchers examined medical records from about 1.5 million births in Denmark between 1977 and 2002 (Nielsen et al., 2016). Children whose mothers were hospitalized for an infection during pregnancy were about 30 percent more likely than other children to develop schizophrenia years later. A related finding is that schizophrenia and related symptoms occur more often in people who were born in the winter and spring months, when upper respiratory infections are most common (Konrath et al., 2016; Torrey et al., 1996). Researchers are just beginning to explore whether children born to mothers who had COVID-19 while pregnant might be at risk to develop schizophrenia later in life (Zimmer et al., 2021).

Abnormal Brain Structures: Loss of Gray Matter

Researchers have found that about half of the people with schizophrenia show abnormalities in brain structure or function (Bernard & Mittal, 2015; Haut et al., 2014). The most consistent finding has been the enlargement of the fluid-filled cavities, called *ventricles,* located deep within

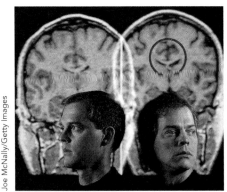

Identical Twins but Not Identical Brains David and Steven Elmore are identical twins, but they differ in one important respect—Steven (right) has schizophrenia. Behind each is a CT scan, which reveals that Steven's brain is slightly smaller, with less area devoted to the cortex at the top of the brain. Steven also has larger fluid-filled ventricles, which are circled in red on his brain scan. As researcher Daniel Weinberger (1995) commented, "The part of the cortex that Steven is missing serves as perhaps the most evolved part of the human brain. It performs complicated tasks such as thinking organized thoughts. This might help explain why paranoid delusions and hallucinations are characteristic of schizophrenia."

the brain (Kempton et al., 2010; Meduri et al., 2010). However, researchers are not certain how enlarged ventricles might be related to schizophrenia.

Other differences that have been found are a loss of gray matter tissue and lower overall volume of the brain (Hajima et al., 2013; Vita et al., 2012). Researchers also have observed particular patterns of connections among brain structures in people with schizophrenia. For example, researchers found that people with schizophrenia as well as people at high risk for developing schizophrenia showed lower levels of connectivity between: (1) regions of the temporal lobes that are responsible for learning and memory, and (2) the parts of the brain responsible for hearing, language, and processing images (Haut et al., 2014). This pattern of decreased connectivity may account for the memory problems often experienced by people with schizophrenia.

Although there is evidence that brain abnormalities are found in schizophrenia, such findings do not prove that brain abnormalities are the sole cause of schizophrenia. First, some people with schizophrenia do *not* show brain abnormalities. Second, the evidence is correlational. Researchers are still investigating whether differences in brain structures and activity are the cause or the consequence of schizophrenia. Third, the kinds of brain abnormalities seen in schizophrenia are also seen in other mental illnesses. Rather than specifically causing schizophrenia, it's quite possible that brain abnormalities might contribute to psychological disorders in general.

Abnormal Brain Chemistry: Hypotheses Related to Neurotransmitters

There are several hypotheses that attribute schizophrenia to imbalances in neurotransmitters. The oldest of these is the dopamine hypothesis, which attributes schizophrenia to excessive activity of the neurotransmitter dopamine in the brain. Two pieces of indirect evidence support this notion. First, antipsychotic drugs, such as Haldol, Thorazine, and Stelazine, *reduce or block dopamine activity in the brain.* These drugs reduce schizophrenic symptoms, especially positive symptoms, in many people. Second, drugs that enhance dopamine activity in the brain, such as amphetamines and cocaine, can produce schizophrenia-like symptoms in adults who do not have schizophrenia or increase symptoms in people who already have schizophrenia.

However, there is also evidence that contradicts the dopamine hypothesis (Jucaite & Nyberg, 2012). For example, not all individuals who have schizophrenia experience a reduction of symptoms in response to the antipsychotic drugs that reduce dopamine activity in the brain. And for many patients, these drugs reduce some but not all schizophrenic symptoms, and tend to reduce positive symptoms more than negative symptoms (Kendler & Schaffner, 2011). One new theory is that some parts of the brain, such as the limbic system, may have too much dopamine, while other parts of the brain, such as the cortex, may have too little (Combs & Mueser, 2007; Kendler & Schaffner, 2011). There also is increasing evidence that imbalances in other neurotransmitters—glutamate and adenosine—are related to schizophrenia (Boison et al., 2012; Lau et al., 2013). Thus, the connection between neurotransmitters and schizophrenia symptoms remains unclear.

Psychological Factors: Unhealthy Families No single psychological factor seems to emerge consistently as causing schizophrenia. Rather, it seems that those who are genetically predisposed to develop schizophrenia may be more vulnerable to the effects of disturbed family environments (Tienari & Wahlberg, 2008).

Strong support for this view came from a landmark study conducted by Finnish psychiatrist Pekka Tienari and his colleagues (1987, 1994). In the Finnish Adoptive Family Study of Schizophrenia, researchers followed about 150 adopted individuals whose biological mothers had schizophrenia. The study also included a control group of about 180 adopted individuals whose biological mothers did *not* have schizophrenia.

Tienari and his colleagues (1994, 2006; Wynne et al., 2006) found that adopted children whose biological mothers had schizophrenia had a much higher rate of

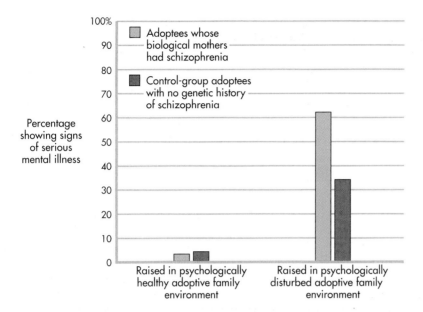

FIGURE 14.3 The Finnish Adoptive Family Study of Schizophrenia In the Finnish Adoptive Family Study, psychiatrist Pekka Tienari and his colleagues (1994, 2006) tracked the mental health of two groups of adopted individuals: one group with biological mothers who had schizophrenia and a control group whose biological mothers did not have schizophrenia. This graph shows the strong influence of the adoptive family environment on the development of serious mental illnesses.

schizophrenia than did the children in the control group. However, this was true *only* when the children were raised in an adoptive home that included psychologically disturbed members. As you can see in **Figure 14.3**, when children with a genetic background of schizophrenia were raised in a psychologically healthy adoptive family, they were *no more likely* than the control-group children to develop schizophrenia.

Put simply, a healthy psychological environment may counteract a person's inherited vulnerability for schizophrenia. Conversely, a psychologically unhealthy family environment can act as a catalyst for the onset of schizophrenia, especially for those individuals with a genetic history of schizophrenia (Tienari & Wahlberg, 2008).

After more than a century of intensive research, schizophrenia remains a baffling disorder. Thus far, no single biological, psychological, or social factor has emerged as the causal agent in schizophrenia. And it's virtually impossible to know what caused schizophrenia in any single individual like Elyn. Nevertheless, researchers are expressing greater confidence that the pieces of the schizophrenia puzzle are beginning to form a more coherent picture.

Closing Thoughts

In this chapter, we've looked at the symptoms and causes of several psychological disorders. We've seen that some of the symptoms of psychological disorders represent a sharp break from normal experience. The behavior of Elyn Saks in the Prologue is an example of the severely disrupted functioning characteristic of schizophrenia. In contrast, the symptoms of other psychological disorders, such as the anxiety disorders and depressive disorders, differ from normal experience primarily in their degree, intensity, and duration.

Psychologists are only beginning to understand the causes of many psychological disorders. The broad picture that emerges reflects a familiar theme: Biological, psychological, and social factors all contribute to the development of psychological disorders. In the next chapter, we'll look at how psychological disorders are treated.

In the final section, Psych for Your Life, we'll explore one of the most serious consequences of psychological problems—suicide. Because people who are contemplating suicide often turn to their friends before they seek help from a mental health professional, we'll also suggest several ways in which you can help a friend who expresses suicidal intentions.

PSYCH FOR YOUR LIFE

Understanding and Helping to Prevent Suicide

Who Dies by Suicide?

Suicide and attempted suicide are all too common. Each year almost 800,000 people around the world take their own lives, including almost 50,000 in the United States (World Health Organization, 2019). For every death by suicide, it's estimated that more than 25 people have attempted suicide — a total of about 1.4 million attempts a year in the United States alone (NIMH, 2021b).

Although the rate of suicide decreased around the world by about 30 percent between 1990 and 2016, the reverse has been true in the United States (Naghavi, 2018). Between 1999 and 2018, the suicide rate in the United States increased by about 35 percent (Hedegaard et al., 2020). This was true regarldess of gender or age.

On average, someone dies by suicide in the United States every 10 minutes. It is estimated that each suicide affects the lives of at least six other people.

Most people don't realize that about two and a half times as many people in the United States die each year from suicide as from homicide (Centers for Disease Control and Prevention, 2021a). The global numbers are equally surprising. The World Health Organization (2019) reported that there are "more deaths due to suicide than to malaria, breast cancer, or war and homicide."

In the United States and other high-income countries, women outnumber men by almost two to one in the number of suicide attempts (NIMH, 2021b). However, men outnumber women by almost four to one in suicide deaths, primarily because men tend to use more lethal methods, such as shooting and hanging (Hedegaard et al., 2020). Rates in the United States are also higher in rural areas than in urban areas. Globally, the suicide rate for men is twice that for women (World Health Organization, 2019).

Suicide is the second leading cause of death for young people ages 15 to 34 (Centers for Disease Control and Prevention, 2015c). Worldwide, suicide is a leading cause of death among people ages 15 to 29, second only to traffic fatalities (World Health Organization, 2019). And although the rates in the United States are highest for Native American people followed by White people, rates are growing fastest among young Black people, especially boys and men between the ages of 15 and 24 (Curtin & Hedegaard, 2019; Jones-Eversley et al., 2020). Although data related to suicides in young people tend to receive more media attention, those rates are still below that of older adults. In fact, the highest suicide rate consistently occurs in the oldest segments of our population — among those aged 75 and above (NIMH, 2021b).

What Risk Factors Are Associated with Suicidal Behavior?

Hundreds of studies have identified psychosocial and environmental factors associated with an increased risk of suicidal behavior (see Hawton et al., 2012; Joiner et al., 2005; Lieb et al., 2005; Nock et al., 2013, 2018). Factors that increase the risk of suicidal behavior are listed here. We have **bolded** the ones that were higher for many people during the pandemic (Zalsman et al., 2020).

- **Feelings of hopelessness and social isolation**
- **Recent relationship problems (including from being cooped up together during the pandemic) or a lack of significant relationships**
- Poor coping and problem-solving skills
- Poor impulse control and impaired judgment

- Rigid thinking or irrational beliefs
- **A major psychological disorder, especially major depressive disorder, bipolar disorder, or schizophrenia, especially if untreated**
- **Alcohol or other substance abuse**
- Childhood physical or sexual abuse
- Prior self-destructive behavior
- A family history of suicide
- Presence of a firearm in the home
- Exposure to bullying, including cyberbullying (H. Fisher et al., 2012)
- **Unemployment and financial hardship**
- **Worry and uncertainty about the future**

Why Do People Become Suicidal?

The suicidal person's view of life has become progressively more pessimistic and negative. At the same time, their view of self-inflicted death as an alternative to life becomes progressively more acceptable and positive (Shneidman, 1998, 2004).

Some people choose suicide to escape the pain of a chronic illness or the slow, agonizing death of a terminal disease (Rogers et al., 2020). Others attempt suicide because of feelings of hopelessness, depression, guilt, rejection, failure, or shame (Lester, 1997, 2010). The common denominator is that they see suicide as the only escape from their unbearably painful emotions (Lester, 2010).

When faced with a dilemma, the average person tends to see a range of possible solutions, accepting the fact that none of the solutions may be ideal. In contrast, the suicidal person's thinking has become rigid and constricted. They can see only two ways to solve their problems: a magical resolution or suicide. Often, death seems to be the only logical option (Shneidman, 1998, 2004).

How Can You Help Prevent Suicide?

If someone is truly intent on taking their own life, it may be impossible to prevent them from doing so. But that does not mean that you can't try to help a friend who is expressing suicidal intentions. People often turn to their friends rather than to mental health professionals. If a friend confides that they are feeling hopeless and suicidal, these guidelines may help you help your friend.

It's important to stress, however, that these guidelines are meant only to help you provide "psychological first aid" in a crisis situation. They do not qualify you as a suicide prevention expert. Your goal is to help your friend through the immediate crisis so that they can be directed to a mental health professional. But it's important not to avoid or ignore a friend in crisis. Ultimate Fighting Championship star Ronda Rousey lost her father and grandfather to suicide and has admitted to having suicidal thoughts herself. She explains, "I feel like there's been an overly negative light on [discussing suicidal thoughts]. It's something real people are going through, not something like a weakness that we should condemn" (TMZ, 2016). These guidelines might help toward decreasing the stigma of suicidal thoughts and helping people find help.

Guideline 1: Actively listen as the person talks and vents their feelings.
About half of those who die by suicide had communicated their intentions to friends or family members (Pompili et al., 2016). Research suggests that sharing such intentions is a risk factor and should be taken seriously. When a friend is despondent and desperate, you can help by listening, expressing your understanding and compassion, and, if necessary, referring them to a professional counselor or suicide prevention specialist.

The suicidal person often feels isolated or lonely, with few sources of social support (Joiner, 2010). Let the person talk, and try to genuinely empathize with your friend's feelings. An understanding friend who is willing to take the time to listen patiently without passing judgment may provide just the support the person needs to overcome the immediate suicidal feelings.

Guideline 2: Don't deny or minimize the person's suicidal intentions.

Brushing aside suicidal statements with platitudes, like "Don't be silly, you've got everything to live for," or clichés, like "Every cloud has a silver lining," is not helpful. This is not the time to be patronizing or superficial. Instead, ask your friend if they want to talk about their feelings. Try to be matter-of-fact and confirm that they are seriously suicidal, rather than exaggerating their frustration or disappointment.

How can you confirm that the person is suicidal? Simply ask, "Are you really thinking about killing yourself?" Talking about specific suicide plans (how, when, and where), giving away valued possessions, and putting one's affairs in order are some indications that a person's suicidal intentions are serious.

Guideline 3: Identify other potential solutions.

The suicidal person is operating with psychological blinders that prevent them from seeing alternative courses of action or other ways of looking at their problems. How can you remove those blinders? Simply saying "Here are some options you may not have thought about" is a good starting point. You might list alternative solutions to the person's problems, helping them to understand that other potential solutions do exist, even though none may be perfect (Shneidman, 1998).

Guideline 4: Ask the person to delay their decision.

Most suicidal people are ambivalent about wanting to die. If your friend did not have mixed feelings about attempting suicide, they probably wouldn't be talking to you. If they are still intent on suicide after talking about other alternatives, ask them to *delay* their decision. Even a few days' delay may give the person enough time to psychologically regroup, consider alternatives, or seek help.

Guideline 5: Encourage the person to seek professional help.

If the person is seriously suicidal and may harm themselves in the near future, do *not* leave them alone. The most important thing you can do is help to get the person referred to a mental health professional for evaluation and treatment. If you don't feel you can do this alone, find another person to help you.

There are any number of resources you can suggest, including local suicide hotlines or mental health associations, the university counseling service, and the person's family doctor or religious adviser. In the United States you can also suggest calling 1-800-SUICIDE (1-800-784-2433), which will connect you with a crisis center in your area. If you prefer to text, the Crisis Text Line (crisistextline.org) is available in the United States and Canada (text 741741), the United Kingdom (85258), and Ireland (50808). And for those in the LGBT community, the Trevor Project (thetrevorproject.org, or 866-488-7386) is an excellent suicide prevention resource. Outside of the United States and the other countries listed above, you can find the nearest crisis center on the Web site of the International Association for Suicide Prevention (https://www.iasp.info/crisis-centres-helplines/).

∨ **Learning to Be a Supportive Friend** University students contemplating suicide often turn first to a friend or roommate rather than seeking professional help or confiding in an adult (Drum et al., 2009). Many colleges and universities have trained students to help other students who seem to be in distress (e.g., Bauer-Wolf, 2019). If a friend is despondent, you can help by listening empathically, expressing your understanding and compassion, and, if necessary, referring them to a counselor or suicide prevention resource.

Gretchen Ertl/NYTimes/Redux

CHAPTER REVIEW

Psychological Disorders

 **Achieve,** Macmillan Learning's online study platform, features the full e-book of *Discovering Psychology,* the **LearningCurve** adaptive quizzing system, videos, and a variety of activities to boost your learning. Visit **Achieve** at macmillanlearning.com.

KEY TERMS

psychopathology, p. 470

psychological disorder (mental illness), p. 471

DSM-5, p. 471

anxiety, p. 476

anxiety disorders, p. 476

generalized anxiety disorder (GAD), p. 476

panic attack, p. 477

panic disorder, p. 477

agoraphobia, p. 477

phobia, p. 479

specific phobia, p. 479

social anxiety disorder, p. 480

posttraumatic stress disorder (PTSD), p. 481

obsessive–compulsive disorder (OCD), p. 483

obsessions, p. 483

compulsions, p. 483

major depressive disorder, p. 485

bipolar disorder, p. 487

manic episode, p. 487

eating disorder, p. 489

anorexia nervosa, p. 489

bulimia nervosa, p. 490

personality disorder, p. 491

antisocial personality disorder, p. 494

borderline personality disorder (BPD), p. 495

dissociative experience, p. 496

dissociative disorders, p. 496

dissociative amnesia, p. 497

dissociative fugue, p. 497

dissociative identity disorder (DID), p. 497

schizophrenia, p. 499

positive symptoms, p. 499

negative symptoms, p. 499

delusion, p. 499

hallucination, p. 500

Psychological Disorders or Mental Illnesses

→ Patterns of behavioral and psychological symptoms that cause significant personal distress and/or impair a person's ability to function

Psychopathology: Scientific study of the origins, symptoms, and development of psychological disorders

Diagnostic and Statistical Manual of Mental Disorders (DSM): Contains information and specific diagnostic criteria for over 260 different psychological disorders

Disorders Related to Anxiety

Generalized anxiety disorder (GAD): Chronic global feelings of unreasonable anxiety

Panic disorder: Sudden unpredictable episodes of **panic attacks**

Phobias:
- Intense, irrational fear and avoidance of an object or situation
- Types include **specific phobia, social anxiety disorder,** and **agoraphobia.**

Obsessive–compulsive disorder (OCD):
- Persistent anxiety caused by intrusive repetitive thoughts (**obsessions**)
- Anxiety reduced by performing repetitive behaviors (**compulsions**)

Ellen Brait

Posttraumatic stress disorder (PTSD):
- Reaction to psychological or physical trauma
- Frequent intrusive trauma memories
- Avoidance of trigger situations
- Emotional numbness
- Heightened physical arousal and anxiety

Depressive and Bipolar Disorders

Serious, persistent emotional disruptions that cause psychological discomfort and impair ability to function

Bipolar disorder:
- Bouts of **manic episodes** that usually alternate with incapacitating periods of major depressive disorder
- Some experience only manic episodes.
- Inappropriate euphoria, excitement, flight of ideas, and high energy during mania
- Previously called *manic depression*

Emma McIntyre/AMA2019/ Getty Images

Cyclothymic disorder:
- Frequent, unpredictable mood swings
- Not severe enough to be bipolar disorder or major depressive disorder

Major depressive disorder:
- Emotional symptoms: despondency, helplessness, worthlessness
- Behavioral symptoms: slowed movements, dejected expressions
- Cognitive symptoms: difficulty thinking, concentrating, and suicidal thoughts
- Physical symptoms: loss of physical and mental energy, appetite and sleep changes

Seasonal affective disorder (SAD):
- Recurring episodes of major depressive disorder during fall and winter months
- Associated with reduced sunlight exposure

Persistent depressive disorder:
- Chronic, low-grade depressed feelings
- Ability to function not seriously impaired

Eating Disorders

Severe, maladaptive disturbances in eating behavior

Anorexia nervosa:
- Severe restriction of food intake
- Body weight significantly lower than normal
- Irrational fear of gaining weight
- Distorted self-image

Bulimia nervosa:
- Recurring episodes of binge eating
- Recurring episodes of purging food

Binge-eating disorder:
- Recurring, uncontrollable episodes of binge eating
- Not associated with methods to control weight

Personality Disorders

Personality traits characterized by inflexible, maladaptive patterns of thoughts, emotions, behavior, and interpersonal functioning

FilmMagic/Getty Images

Antisocial personality disorder:
- Recurring pattern of blatant lying, cheating, manipulating, and harming others
- No sense of conscience, guilt, or remorse

Borderline personality disorder:
- Unstable self-image, emotional control, and interpersonal relationships
- Mood swings, impulsiveness, substance abuse, and self-destructive tendencies
- Extreme fear of abandonment

Dissociative Disorders

Extreme **dissociative experiences** that disrupt the normal integration of awareness, memory, and personal identity

Dissociative amnesia: Inability to recall important personal information that is not due to a medical condition, drug, or ordinary forgetfulness

Dissociative fugue:
- Identity confusion combined with sudden, unexplained wandering away from home
- Post-fugue amnesia for event

Dissociative identity disorder (DID):
- Memory disruptions of personal identity combined with presence of two or more distinct identities termed alters
- Controversial psychological disorder of which many clinicians are skeptical
- Previously called *multiple personality disorder*

Karen Robinson/Guardian/eyevine/Redux

Schizophrenia

Severely distorted thought processes, beliefs, and perceptions that impair functioning

Positive symptoms: Excesses or distortions of normal functioning
- **Delusions:** False beliefs
- **Hallucinations:** False perceptions
- Severely disorganized thoughts, speech, and behavior

Negative symptoms: Deficits in normal functioning
- **Flat affect:** Emotionally blunted reactions

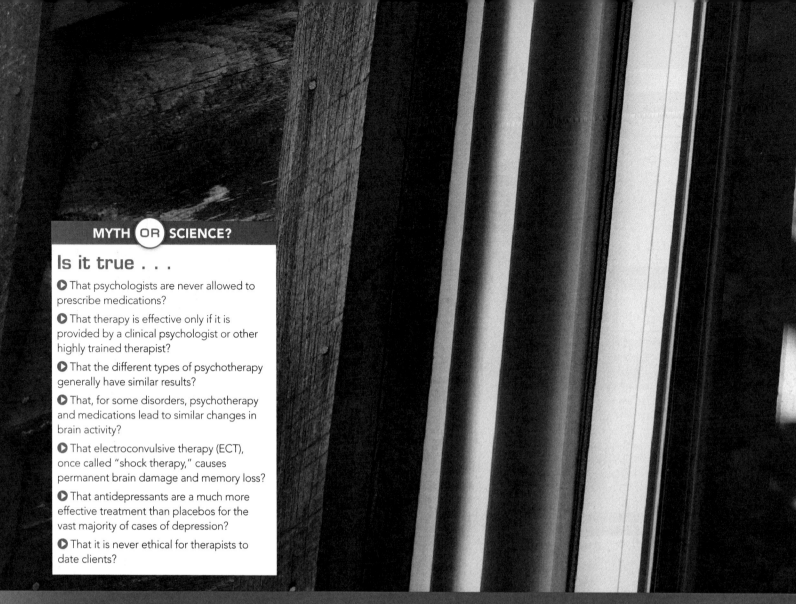

MYTH (OR) SCIENCE?

Is it true . . .

▶ That psychologists are never allowed to prescribe medications?

▶ That therapy is effective only if it is provided by a clinical psychologist or other highly trained therapist?

▶ That the different types of psychotherapy generally have similar results?

▶ That, for some disorders, psychotherapy and medications lead to similar changes in brain activity?

▶ That electroconvulsive therapy (ECT), once called "shock therapy," causes permanent brain damage and memory loss?

▶ That antidepressants are a much more effective treatment than placebos for the vast majority of cases of depression?

▶ That it is never ethical for therapists to date clients?

Therapies

PROLOGUE

"A Clear Sense of Being Heard . . ."

Marcia is an extraordinarily kind, intelligent woman with a ready laugh. She's happily married, has a good job as a feature writer for a newspaper, and has two young children, who only occasionally drive her crazy. If Marcia has a flaw, it's that she blames herself when anything goes wrong.

Juggling a full-time career, marriage, and parenting is a challenge for anyone, but Marcia makes it look easy. Outwardly,

Marcia appears to have it all. But a few years ago, she began to experience a pervasive sense of dread and unease—feelings that gradually escalated into a full-scale depressive episode. Marcia describes the onset of her feelings in this way:

> Physically, I began to feel as if I were fraying around the edges. I had a constant sense of anxiety and a recurring sense of being a failure. . . . I started worrying constantly about my children. Are they safe? Are they sick? What's going to happen? . . . It finally struck me that my worrying and my anxiety and my feelings of being a failure were not going to go away on their own.

Marcia decided to seek therapy. Marcia summarizes her therapy experience this way:

> How has therapy helped me? I invariably feel great relief. I feel a sense of being understood by someone who knows me but who is detached from me. I have a clear sense of being heard, as though my therapist has given me a gift of listening and of allowing me to see myself as the worthwhile and capable person I am. It is as though therapy allows me to see more clearly into a mirror that my problems have obscured.

Over the course of several months, Marcia gradually began to feel better. Today, Marcia is calmer, more confident,

Adam Weiss/Gallery Stock

CHAPTER **15**

and feels much more in control of her emotions and her life. As Marcia's mental health improved, so did her relationships with her children and her husband.

Psychotherapy has enabled me to become more resilient after some emotional conflict. It has had a preventive effect in helping me to ignore or manage situations that might under certain circumstances trigger depression, anxiety, or obsessive worry. And it makes me a better parent and marriage partner.

Marcia's experience with psychotherapy reflects many of the themes we will touch on in this chapter. We'll look at different forms of therapy that psychologists and other mental health professionals use to help people cope with psychological problems. We'll also consider the popularity of newer ways to deliver mental health care — including self-help groups and technology-based treatments — and how they differ from more traditional forms of therapy. Toward the end of the chapter, we'll discuss biomedical approaches to the treatment of psychological disorders. Over the course of the chapter, we'll come back to Marcia's story. ∿

↑ Seeking Help People enter psychotherapy for many different reasons. Some people seek to overcome severe psychological disorders, while others want to learn how to cope better with everyday challenges or relationship problems. And, for some people, the goal of therapy is to attain greater self-knowledge or personal fulfillment.

Is it true that psychologists are never allowed to prescribe medications?

psychotherapy Treatment of emotional, behavioral, and interpersonal problems through psychological techniques that promote understanding of problems and modify troubling feelings, behaviors, or relationships.

biomedical therapies Use of medications, electroconvulsive therapy, or other medical treatments to treat the symptoms associated with psychological disorders.

Introduction: Psychotherapy and Biomedical Therapy

■ KEY THEME
Two forms of therapy are used to treat psychological disorders and personal problems—psychotherapy and biomedical therapies.

☰ KEY QUESTIONS
- What is psychotherapy, and what is its basic assumption?
- What is biomedical therapy, and how does it differ from psychotherapy?

People seek help from mental health professionals for a variety of reasons. Like Marcia, many people seek help because they are suffering from some form of a *psychological disorder*—troubling thoughts, feelings, or behaviors that cause psychological discomfort or interfere with a person's ability to function.

But not everyone who seeks professional help is suffering from a psychological disorder. Many people seek help in dealing with troubled relationships, adjusting to life's transitions, coping with stress, and so on.

In this chapter, we'll look at the two broad forms of treatment that mental health professionals use to help people: *psychotherapy* and *biomedical therapy*. **Psychotherapy** refers to the *treatment of emotional, behavioral, and interpersonal problems through psychological techniques that promote understanding of problems and modify troubling feelings, behaviors, or relationships*. **Table 15.1** summarizes the diverse range of mental health professionals who use psychotherapy techniques to help people.

In contrast to psychotherapy, the **biomedical therapies** involve the *use of medications, electroconvulsive therapy, or other medical treatments to treat the symptoms associated with psychological disorders*. Drugs that are used to treat psychological disorders are termed *psychotropic medications*. The biomedical therapies are based on the assumption that the symptoms of many psychological disorders involve biological factors, such as abnormal brain chemistry. As we saw in the chapter on disorders, the involvement of biological factors in many psychological disorders is well documented. Treating psychological disorders with a combination of psychotherapy and biomedical therapy, especially psychotropic medications, has become increasingly common (Cuijpers et al., 2009; Sudak, 2011).

Until recently, only licensed physicians were legally allowed to prescribe psychotropic medications. However, that tradition may be changing. Since the 1990s, a movement to allow specially trained psychologists to prescribe has achieved some success. At this time, only a limited number of psychologists prescribe medications. And, the idea remains controversial (Linda & McGrath, 2017). However, the pandemic has highlighted the lack of psychiatrists in many parts of the United States, leading some to argue that extending prescribing privileges to more psychologists might help address the lack of access (Gaeta, 2020). And an increasing number of clinical psychologists *are* involved in medication treatment decisions or have clients who are taking psychotropic medications. Recognizing this trend, the American Psychological Association (2011) released guidelines for psychologists regarding prescription medications. Among other points, the guidelines stress that psychologists who are involved in medication decisions should educate themselves about potential benefits and side effects of any medication.

We'll begin this chapter by surveying some of the most influential approaches in psychotherapy: psychoanalytic, humanistic, behavioral, and cognitive. Each approach is based on different assumptions about the underlying causes of psychological problems. And each approach uses different strategies to produce beneficial changes in the way a person thinks, feels, and behaves—the ultimate goal of all forms of psychotherapy. After discussing the effectiveness of psychotherapy, we'll look at the most commonly used biomedical treatments for psychological disorders.

TABLE 15.1

Who's Who Among Mental Health Professionals in the United States

Clinical psychologist	Holds an academic doctorate (Ph.D., Psy.D., or Ed.D.) and is required to be licensed to practice. Assesses and treats mental, emotional, and behavioral disorders. Has expertise in psychological testing and evaluation, diagnosis, psychotherapy, research, and prevention of mental and emotional disorders.
Counseling psychologist	Holds an academic doctorate and must be licensed to practice. Assesses and treats mental, emotional, and behavioral problems and disorders. Historically treated disorders of lesser severity, but now there is less distinction between the practices of clinical and counseling psychologists.
Psychiatrist	Holds a medical degree (M.D. or D.O.) and is required to be licensed to practice. Has expertise in the diagnosis, treatment, and prevention of mental and emotional disorders. Often has training in psychotherapy. May prescribe medications and medical procedures.
Psychoanalyst	Usually a psychiatrist or clinical psychologist who has received additional training in the specific techniques of psychoanalysis, the form of psychotherapy originated by Sigmund Freud.
Licensed professional counselor	Holds at least a master's degree in counseling, with supervised training in assessment and therapy techniques. May be certified in specialty areas. Most states require licensure or certification.
Psychiatric social worker	Holds a master's degree in social work (M.S.W.). Training includes an internship in a social service agency or mental health center. Usually has certification or licensing. May have training in psychotherapy.
Marriage and family therapist	Usually holds a master's degree, with extensive supervised experience in couple or family therapy. May also have training in individual therapy. Many states require licensing.
Psychiatric nurse	Holds an R.N. degree and has selected psychiatry or mental health nursing as a specialty. May or may not have training in psychotherapy.

psychoanalysis (in psychotherapy) A type of psychotherapy originated by Sigmund Freud in which free association and transference are used to explore repressed or unconscious impulses, anxieties, and internal conflicts.

⌄ **The Varied Workplaces of Psychologists** Clinical and counseling psychologists work in a wide variety of venues. Prison psychologist Tamara Russell, pictured here, oversees a staff of clinicians at the Washington State Penitentiary in Walla Walla, Washington. She received an award from the American Psychological Association for her innovative and effective work. The creative programming she introduced includes "Kittens in the Klink," a way for inmates to learn altruism by being paired with motherless kittens that they feed and socialize until the kittens are old enough to be adopted. As Russell explains, "A lot of guys never realized they could do something for others" (Hagar, 2013).

Psychoanalytic Therapy

◼ KEY THEME
Psychoanalysis is a form of therapy developed by Sigmund Freud and is based on his theory of personality.

⹀ KEY QUESTIONS
- What are the key assumptions and techniques of psychoanalytic therapy?
- How do short-term dynamic therapies differ from psychoanalysis, and what is interpersonal therapy?

When cartoonists portray a psychotherapy session, they often draw a person lying on a couch and talking while a bearded man sits behind the patient, passively listening. This stereotype reflects some of the key ingredients of traditional **psychoanalysis**, *a type of psychotherapy originated by* **Sigmund Freud** *in which free association and transference are used to explore repressed or unconscious impulses, anxieties, and internal conflicts.* Although psychoanalysis was developed over a century ago, its assumptions and techniques continue to influence many psychotherapies today (Borden, 2009; Lerner, 2008; Luborsky & Barrett, 2006).

GREG LEHMAN/AP Images

free association Psychoanalytic technique in which the patient spontaneously reports all thoughts, feelings, and mental images that arise, revealing unconscious thoughts and emotions.

resistance The patient's unconscious attempts to block the revelation of repressed memories and conflicts.

interpretation Psychoanalytic technique in which the psychoanalyst offers carefully timed explanations of the patient's dreams, feelings, or behaviors to help explore unconscious conflicts or motivations.

transference The process by which emotions and desires associated with a significant person in the patient's life, such as a parent, are unconsciously transferred onto the psychoanalyst.

Sigmund Freud and Psychoanalysis

As a therapy, traditional psychoanalysis is closely interwoven with Freud's theory of personality. As you may recall from the chapter on personality, Freud stressed that early childhood experiences provided the foundation for later personality development. When early experiences result in unresolved conflicts and frustrated urges, these emotionally charged memories are *repressed,* or pushed out of conscious awareness. Although unconscious, these repressed conflicts continue to influence a person's thoughts and behavior, including the dynamics of their relationships with others.

Psychoanalysis is designed to help unearth unconscious conflicts so that the patient attains *insight* into the real source of their problems. Through the intense relationship that develops between the psychoanalyst and the patient, long-standing psychological conflicts are recognized and reexperienced. If the analytic treatment is successful, the conflicts are resolved.

Freud developed several techniques to coax long-repressed memories, impulses, and conflicts to a patient's consciousness (Liff, 1992). **Free association** is a *psychoanalytic technique in which the patient spontaneously reports all thoughts, feelings, and mental images that arise, revealing unconscious thoughts and emotions.*

Blocks in free association, such as a sudden silence or an abrupt change of topic, were thought to be signs of resistance. **Resistance** is *the patient's conscious or unconscious attempts to block the process of revealing repressed memories and conflicts* (Luborsky & Barrett, 2006).

The psychoanalyst sometimes makes an **interpretation**, a *psychoanalytic technique in which the psychoanalyst offers carefully timed explanations of the patient's dreams, feelings, or behaviors to help explore unconscious conflicts or motivations.* The timing of such interpretations is important. If an interpretation is offered before the patient is psychologically ready, they may reject the interpretation or respond defensively, increasing resistance (Prochaska & Norcross, 2014).

One of the most important processes that occurs in the relationship between the patient and the psychoanalyst is called transference. **Transference** is *the process by which emotions and desires associated with a significant person in the patient's life, such as a parent, are unconsciously transferred onto the psychoanalyst.* The psychoanalyst encourages transference by purposely remaining as neutral as possible. This therapeutic neutrality is designed to produce "optimal frustration" so that the patient transfers and projects unresolved conflicts onto the psychoanalyst (Magnavita, 2008). These conflicts are then relived and played out in the context of the relationship between the psychoanalyst and the patient. As these conflicts are resolved, maladaptive behavior patterns that were previously driven by unconscious conflicts can be replaced with more adaptive emotional and behavioral responses.

Melanie Klein (1882–1960), who was introduced in the chapter on personality, developed play theory as a means to treat children with psychoanalysis (Crann, 2010; Klein, 1955). Klein viewed play as a means of free association for children, who do not have the verbal ability of adults. Through play, Klein believed, the therapist could understand a child's unconscious conflicts, and interpret these conflicts and any transference that results (Donaldson, 1996). Klein's work led to new techniques that have informed play therapy with children today (Pehrsson & Aguilera, 2007; Sherwin-White, 2018). The traditional psychoanalyst sees the patient three times a week or more, often for years. This has been true even for child patients. Obviously, traditional psychoanalysis is a slow, expensive process that few people can afford. For those who have the time and the money, traditional psychoanalysis is still available.

Freud's Famous Couch During psychoanalytic sessions, Freud's patients would lie on this couch. Freud himself sat at the head of the couch, out of the patient's view. Freud believed that this arrangement encouraged the patient's free flow of thoughts, feelings, and images. Although some traditional psychoanalysts still have the patient lie on a couch, many psychoanalysts today favor comfortable chairs on which analyst and patient sit, facing each other.

AP Photo

Short-Term Dynamic Therapies

Most people entering psychotherapy today are not seeking the kind of major personality overhaul that traditional psychoanalysis claims to produce. Instead, people come to therapy expecting help with specific problems. People also expect therapy to provide beneficial changes in a matter of weeks or months, not years.

Short-term dynamic therapy is a *type of psychotherapy based on psychoanalytic theory but differing in that it is time-limited, has specific goals, and involves an active, rather than neutral, role for the therapist* (Levenson, 2010, 2011). These short-term dynamic therapies have several features in common. Therapeutic contact lasts for no more than a few months. The patient's problems are quickly assessed at the beginning of therapy. The therapist and patient agree on specific, concrete, and attainable goals. In the actual sessions, most psychodynamic therapists are more directive than are traditional psychoanalysts, actively engaging the patient in a dialogue.

One particularly influential short-term psychodynamic therapy is **interpersonal therapy**, abbreviated **IPT**, *a brief psychodynamic psychotherapy that focuses on current relationships and is based on the assumption that symptoms are caused and maintained by interpersonal problems.* It was originally developed as a brief treatment for major depressive disorder (Gunlicks-Stoessel & Weissman, 2011). During treatment, the therapist helps the person understand their particular interpersonal problem and develop strategies to resolve it.

Interpersonal therapy may be brief or long-term, but it is highly structured (Blanco et al., 2006; Teyber, 2009). IPT is used to treat eating disorders and substance use disorders as well as major depressive disorder. It is also effective in helping people deal with interpersonal problems, such as marital conflict, parenting issues, and conflicts at work (Bleiberg & Markowitz, 2008). In one innovative application, IPT was successfully used to treat symptoms of major depressive disorder in villagers in Uganda, demonstrating its effectiveness in a non-Western culture (Bolton et al., 2003).

Even though traditional, lengthy psychoanalysis is uncommon today, Freud's basic assumptions and techniques continue to be influential. Contemporary research has challenged many of Freud's original ideas. However, modern researchers continue to study the specific factors that seem to influence the effectiveness of basic Freudian techniques, such as interpretation, transference, and the role of insight in reducing psychological symptoms (Glucksman & Kramer, 2004; Luborsky & Barrett, 2006).

Humanistic Therapy

■ KEY THEME
The most influential humanistic psychotherapy is client-centered therapy, which was developed by Carl Rogers.

≡ KEY QUESTIONS
- What are the key assumptions of humanistic therapy, including client-centered therapy?
- What therapeutic techniques and conditions are important in client-centered therapy?
- How do client-centered therapy and psychoanalysis differ?

The *humanistic perspective* in psychology emphasizes human potential, self-awareness, and freedom of choice (see the chapter on personality). Humanistic psychologists contend that the most important factor in personality is the individual's conscious, subjective perception of their self. They see people as being innately good and motivated by the need to grow psychologically. If people are raised in a genuinely accepting atmosphere and given freedom to make choices, they will develop healthy self-concepts and strive to fulfill their unique potential as human beings (Kirschenbaum & Jourdan, 2005; Pos et al., 2008).

short-term dynamic therapy Type of psychotherapy based on psychoanalytic theory but differing in that it is time-limited, has specific goals, and involves an active, rather than neutral, role for the therapist.

interpersonal therapy (IPT) A brief psychodynamic psychotherapy that focuses on current relationships and is based on the assumption that symptoms are caused and maintained by interpersonal problems.

Rich Fury/Getty Images

⌃ Tiffany Haddish: "Just Have a Conversation" Comedian and actor Tiffany Haddish is known for being funny and unrelentingly positive. So, people are often surprised that she has overcome so many challenges (Kennedy, 2018). When a reporter asked if she had sought therapy, Haddish answered "Girl, yes! Years, years, years of therapy! . . . Now, I go every month. If I'm not home, I Skype with my therapist." Haddish also notes that Black people in the United States are less likely than White people to get treated for mental illnesses. "From my experience, the [B]lack community thinks [therapy is] going to hurt you, or they'll do experiments on you, or whatever . . . the [B]lack community is afraid, . . . I'm always like: 'Hey. You can go to a counselor and just talk. . . . Just have a conversation'" (Kennedy, 2018).

Carl Rogers and Client-Centered Therapy

The humanistic perspective has exerted a strong influence on psychotherapy (Cain, 2002, 2003; Schneider & Krug, 2009). Probably the most influential of the humanistic psychotherapies was developed by **Carl Rogers** (1902–1987). **Client-centered therapy** is a *type of psychotherapy in which the therapist is nondirective and reflective, and the client directs the focus of each therapy session*. In naming his therapy, Rogers (1951) deliberately used the word *client* rather than *patient*. He believed that the medical term *patient* implied that people in therapy were "sick" and were seeking treatment from an all-knowing authority figure who could "heal" or "cure" them. Instead of stressing the therapist's expertise or perceptions of the patient, client-centered therapy emphasizes the *client's* subjective perception of themselves and their environment (Cain, 2002; Raskin & Rogers, 2005).

Like Freud, Rogers saw the therapeutic relationship as the catalyst that leads to insight and lasting personality change. But Rogers viewed the nature of this relationship very differently from Freud. According to Rogers (1977), the therapist should not exert power by offering carefully timed "interpretations" of the patient's unconscious conflicts. Advocating just the opposite, Rogers believed that the therapist should be *nondirective*. The therapist's role is to create the conditions that allow the client, not the therapist, to direct the focus of therapy (Bozarth et al., 2002).

What are the therapeutic conditions that promote self-awareness, psychological growth, and self-directed change? Rogers (1957c, 1980) believed that three qualities of the therapist are necessary: *genuineness, unconditional positive regard,* and *empathic understanding.* First, *genuineness* means that the therapist honestly and openly shares their thoughts and feelings with the client. By modeling genuineness, the therapist indirectly encourages the client to exercise this capability more fully in themselves.

Second, the therapist must value, accept, and care for the client, whatever their problems or behavior. Rogers called this quality *unconditional positive regard* (Bozarth & Wang, 2008). Rogers believed that people develop psychological problems largely because they have consistently experienced only *conditional acceptance.* That is, parents, teachers, and others have communicated this message to the client: "I will accept you *only if* you conform to my expectations." The therapist who successfully creates a climate of unconditional positive regard fosters the person's natural tendency to move toward self-fulfilling decisions without fear of evaluation or rejection.

Third, the therapist must communicate *empathic understanding* by reflecting the content and personal meaning of the feelings being experienced by the client. In effect, the therapist creates a psychological mirror, to help the client begin to see themselves, and their problems, more clearly (Freire, 2007).

Rogers believed that when the therapeutic atmosphere contains genuineness, unconditional positive regard, and empathic understanding, change is more likely to occur. Such conditions foster feelings of being psychologically safe, accepted, and valued. In effect, the client is moving in the direction of *self-actualization*—the realization of their unique potentials and talents.

▲ **Group Therapy Session with Carl Rogers** Rogers filmed many of his therapy sessions as part of an ongoing research program to identify the most helpful aspects of client-centered therapy. Shown on the far right, Rogers contended that human potential would flourish in an atmosphere of genuineness, unconditional positive regard, and empathic understanding.

Michael Rougier/Getty Images

Motivational Interviewing: Helping Clients Commit to Change Like psychoanalysis, client-centered therapy has evolved and adapted to changing times. Of particular note has been the development of motivational interviewing (Miller & Rollnick, 2012). *Motivational interviewing (MI)* is a technique designed to help clients overcome the mixed feelings or reluctance they might have about committing to change. MI is used for a range of psychological problems, but has most frequently been applied to addictions, such as substance use disorders or gambling, or to techniques to improve health, such as through diet or exercise (Lundahl et al., 2010; Morton et al., 2015). Usually lasting only a session or two, MI is more directive

client-centered therapy Type of psychotherapy in which the therapist is nondirective and reflective, and the client directs the focus of each therapy session; also called *person-centered therapy*.

TABLE 15.2

Comparing Psychodynamic and Humanistic Therapies

Type of Therapy	Founder	Source of Problems	Treatment Techniques	Goals of Therapy
Psychoanalysis	Sigmund Freud	Repressed, unconscious conflicts stemming from early childhood experiences	Free association and transference	To recognize, work through, and resolve long-standing conflicts
Client-centered therapy	Carl Rogers	Conditional acceptance that causes the person to develop a distorted self-concept and worldview	Nondirective; unconditional positive regard, genuineness, and empathic understanding	To develop self-awareness, self-acceptance, and self-determination

than the techniques used in traditional client-centered therapy (Arkowitz et al., 2007; Hettema et al., 2005).

The main goal of MI is to encourage and strengthen the client's self-motivating statements, or "change talk" (Hayes et al., 2011; Magill et al., 2018). These are expressions of the client's need, desire, and reasons for change. Using a client-centered approach, the therapist responds with empathic understanding and reflective listening, helping the client explore their own values and motivations for change.

Along with being influential in individual psychotherapy, the client-centered approach has been applied to group therapy, marital counseling, parenting, education, business, health behaviors, and even community and international relations (Chen et al., 2011; Frost et al., 2018; Henderson et al., 2007; Wagner & Ingersoll, 2012). **Table 15.2** compares some aspects of psychoanalysis and client-centered therapy.

Behavior Therapy

■ KEY THEME
Behavior therapy uses learning principles to directly change problem behaviors.

⹀ KEY QUESTIONS
- What are the key assumptions of behavior therapy?
- What therapeutic techniques are based on classical conditioning, and how are they used to treat psychological disorders and problems?
- What therapy treatments are based on operant conditioning, and how are they used to treat psychological disorders and problems?

Psychoanalysis, client-centered therapy, and other insight-oriented therapies maintain that the road to psychologically healthier behavior is through increased self-understanding of motives and conflicts. As insights are acquired through therapy, problem behaviors and feelings presumably will give way to more adaptive behaviors and emotional reactions.

However, gaining insight into the source of problems does not necessarily result in desired changes in behavior and emotions. You may fully understand *why* you are behaving in counterproductive ways, but your maladaptive behaviors may continue. For instance, an adult who is extremely anxious about public speaking may understand that they feel that way because they were raised by a critical and demanding parent. But having this insight into the underlying cause of their anxiety may do little, if anything, to reduce their anxiety or change their avoidance of public speaking.

Behavior therapy is a *type of psychotherapy that focuses on directly changing maladaptive behavior patterns by using basic learning principles and techniques; also called behavior modification.* Behavior therapists assume that maladaptive behaviors are *learned*, just as adaptive behaviors are. Thus, the basic strategy in behavior therapy involves reducing the frequency of maladaptive behaviors and learning more adaptive behaviors in their place. Behavior therapists employ techniques that are based on the learning principles of classical conditioning, operant conditioning, and observational learning.

Chris Rout/Alamy

⌃ **Behavior Therapy—From Bad Habits to Severe Psychological Disorders** Nail biting and cigarette smoking are examples of the kinds of everyday maladaptive behaviors that can be successfully treated with behavior therapy. Behavioral techniques can also be used to treat more severe psychological problems, such as phobias, and to improve functioning in people with severe mental illnesses such as schizophrenia and autism spectrum disorder.

behavior therapy Type of psychotherapy that focuses on directly changing maladaptive behavior patterns by using basic learning principles and techniques; also called *behavior modification*.

Mary Cover Jones (1896–1987) This photograph, taken around 1919, shows Mary Cover Jones as a college student in her early 20s. Although Jones pioneered the use of behavioral techniques in therapy and is widely regarded as the first behavior therapist, she did not consider herself a "behaviorist" and ultimately came to disagree with many of Watson's views. Fifty years after she treated Peter, Jones (1975) wrote, "Now I would be less satisfied to treat the fears of a three-year-old . . . in isolation from him as a tantalizingly complex person with unique potentials for stability and change."

counterconditioning Behavior therapy technique that involves learning a new response that is incompatible with a previously learned response.

exposure therapy Behavioral therapy for phobias, panic disorder, PTSD, or related anxiety disorders in which the person is repeatedly exposed to the disturbing object or situation under controlled conditions.

systematic desensitization Type of behavior therapy that involves learning a new conditioned response (relaxation) that is incompatible with or inhibits the old conditioned response (fear and anxiety).

Techniques Based on Classical Conditioning

Just as Pavlov's dogs learned to salivate to a ticking metronome that had become associated with food, learned associations can be at the core of some maladaptive behaviors, including strong negative emotional reactions. In the 1920s, psychologists John Watson and Rosalie Rayner demonstrated this phenomenon with their famous "Little Albert" study. In the chapter on learning, we described how Watson and Rayner classically conditioned an infant known as Little Albert to fear a tame lab rat by repeatedly pairing the rat with a loud clanging sound. Over time, Albert's conditioned fear generalized to other furry objects.

Mary Cover Jones: The First Behavior Therapist

Watson and Rayner never tried to eliminate Little Albert's fears. But their research inspired psychologist **Mary Cover Jones** to explore ways of reversing conditioned fears. With Watson acting as a consultant, Jones (1924a) treated a three-year-old named Peter who was fearful of various furry objects, including a tame rabbit. Jones used a procedure that has come to be known as **counterconditioning**—a *behavior therapy technique that involves learning a new conditioned response that is incompatible with a previously learned response.*

Jones's procedure was very simple (Jones, 1924b; Watson, 1924). The caged rabbit was brought into Peter's view but kept far enough away to avoid eliciting fear (the original conditioned response). With the rabbit visible at a tolerable distance, Peter happily munched his favorite snack, milk and crackers. Peter's favorite food was used because, presumably, the enjoyment of eating would naturally elicit a positive response (the desired conditioned response). Such a positive response would be incompatible with the negative response of fear.

Every day for almost two months, the rabbit was inched closer and closer to Peter as he ate his milk and crackers. As Peter's tolerance for the rabbit's presence gradually increased, he was eventually able to hold the rabbit in his lap, petting it with one hand while happily eating with his other hand (Jones, 1924a, 1924b). Not only was Peter's fear of the rabbit eliminated, but he also stopped being afraid of other furry objects (Watson, 1924).

Systematic Desensitization and Exposure Therapies

Mary Cover Jones's pioneering studies in treating children's fears laid the groundwork for the later development of more standardized procedures to treat phobias and other anxiety disorders. **Exposure therapy** is *behavioral therapy for phobias, panic disorder, PTSD, or related anxiety disorders in which the person is repeatedly exposed to the disturbing object or situation under controlled conditions.* A person gradually and repeatedly relives a frightening experience under controlled conditions to help them overcome their fear of the dreaded object or situation.

One widely used type of exposure therapy, called *systematic desensitization,* was developed in the 1950s (Wolpe, 1958, 1982). Based on the same premise as counterconditioning, **systematic desensitization** is a *type of behavior therapy that involves learning a new conditioned response (relaxation) that is incompatible with or inhibits the old conditioned response (fear and anxiety).*

Three basic steps are involved in systematic desensitization. First, the patient learns *progressive relaxation,* which involves successively relaxing one muscle group after another until a deep state of relaxation is achieved. Second, the behavior therapist helps the patient construct an *anxiety hierarchy,* sometimes called an *exposure hierarchy,* which is a list of anxiety-provoking images associated with the feared situation, arranged in a hierarchy from least to most anxiety-producing (see the left side of **Figure 15.1**). The third step involves the actual process of desensitization through exposure to feared experiences. While deeply relaxed, the patient imagines the least-threatening scene on the anxiety hierarchy. After they can maintain complete relaxation while imagining this scene, they move to the next. If the patient begins to feel anxiety, the therapist guides them back to imagining the previous scene. If necessary, the therapist helps the patient relax again, using the progressive relaxation technique.

Over several sessions, the patient gradually and systematically works their way up the hierarchy, imagining each scene while maintaining complete relaxation. Once mastered with mental images, the desensitization procedure may be continued with exposure to the actual feared situation, which is called *in vivo systematic desensitization.* If the technique is successful, the feared situation no longer produces a conditioned response of fear and anxiety. The In Focus box "Using Virtual Reality to Treat Phobia and Posttraumatic Stress Disorder" describes systematic desensitization using a "virtual reality" version of the actual feared situation.

In practice, systematic desensitization is often combined with other techniques, such as *observational learning* (Bandura, 2004b). For example, in addition to using an anxiety hierarchy, a behavior therapist's treatment of someone afraid of flying on airplanes could include showing them videos of people calmly boarding and riding on airplanes.

Researchers initially believed that exposure therapy works through a process called *habituation,* in which the fear response to a particular situation diminishes as the patient acclimates to it through exposure. But, more recent research supports the importance of *inhibitory learning,* a process through which the patient develops new connections between the feared situation and safety cues that block out the original connections between that situation and danger (Weisman & Rodebaugh, 2018). Some have referred to this process as "safety learning" because the patient begins to associate a wide variety of safety cues with the feared situation (Knowles & Olatunji, 2019). Exposure therapy that focuses on habituation rather than inhibitory learning may not be sufficient to create safety learning and the real-world outcomes the patient desires, such as decreasing overall anxiety levels and reducing avoidance behavior (Craske et al., 2008).

To be clear, there is a great deal of evidence that exposure therapy is effective, but the importance of inhibitory learning has been increasingly documented (and it doesn't always happen). Often, a patient's fear decreases during exposure because they associate specific safety signals—such as the presence of the therapist, a friend, or even their mobile phone—with a reduction in fear (Craske et al., 2008, 2014). So, the fear reduction experienced during therapeutic exposure may not generalize to the real-world situations that lead to a patient's anxiety where those cues do not exist—such as social situations, elevators, or the dentist's office. Clients need a wider variety of safety cues, given that they can't take their therapist everywhere.

But research suggests ways to increase inhibitory learning. In particular, variability within exposure therapy can make a difference. Rather than directly ascending the hierarchy of systematic desensitization, the therapist might mix it up. For example, the therapist

A Traditional Systematic Desensitization Hierarchy (habituation process)	A Variable Exposure Sequence (inhibitory learning process)
1. Ask a barista how they're doing as you order coffee at your favorite spot.	8. Volunteer to make phone calls on behalf of a cause you support.
2. Email a professor to ask a question about the upcoming test.	1. Ask a barista how they're doing as you order coffee at your favorite spot.
3. Call a store on the phone to ask if they carry a particular item.	4. Post a message asking a question in the courseware for your course.
4. Post a message asking a question in the courseware for your course.	7. Volunteer to send text messages on behalf of a cause you support.
5. Ask a stranger for directions.	10. Ask someone out on a date.
6. Ask classmates if they want to form a study group.	6. Ask classmates if they want to form a study group.
7. Volunteer to send text messages on behalf of a cause you support.	2. Email a professor to ask a question about the upcoming test.
8. Volunteer to make phone calls on behalf of a cause you support.	3. Call a store on the phone to ask if they carry a particular item.
9. Ask strangers in your university dining hall if you can join them.	9. Ask strangers in your university dining hall if you can join them.
10. Ask someone out on a date.	5. Ask a stranger for directions.

FIGURE 15.1 Examples of Traditional Systematic Desensitization and Variable Exposure Sequences As part of in vivo systematic desensitization, the therapist helps the client develop an anxiety hierarchy. The sample anxiety hierarchy shown here illustrates the kinds of situations that might be listed by a person who has social anxiety disorder. Traditionally, the patient would work through the hierarchy on the left, starting with the least scary activity, and then move up step by step. More recent research suggests that a strict hierarchy may not work as well as a more varied sequence of exposure, such as in the list on the right (e.g., Sewart & Craske, 2020).

Fuse/Getty Images

could expose a client who fears heights to a variety of situations in no particular order, "such as 8th floor, 2nd floor, 10th floor and 3rd floor balconies in more than one situation (e.g., inside versus outside stairwell) and [approaching] the precipice in different ways (e.g., looking out versus down)" (Craske et al., 2008). (See Figure 15.1 for an example of a traditional hierarchy alongside a variable hierarchy.) Therapists can also introduce exposure without the usual safety signals, for example, having a client ride an elevator alone in the therapist's building, without a therapist or mobile phone. When the exposure experiences are not as predictable, it becomes easier for the client to build connections with a wide range of safety signals that generalize more easily to new situations.

Aversive Conditioning The psychologist John Garcia first demonstrated how taste aversions could be classically conditioned (see the chapter on learning). After rats drank a

🔍 IN FOCUS

Using Virtual Reality to Treat Phobia and Posttraumatic Stress Disorder

Virtual reality (VR) therapy consists of computer-generated scenes that you view wearing goggles and a special motion-sensitive headset.

VR technology was first used in the treatment of specific phobias, including fear of flying, heights, spiders, driving, and enclosed places (Côté & Bouchard, 2008). In the virtual reality scene, patients are progressively exposed to the feared object or situation. For example, psychologist Ralph Lamson used virtual reality as a form of computer-assisted systematic desensitization to help more than 60 patients conquer their fear of heights. Once the goggles are donned, patients begin a 40-minute journey that starts in a café and progresses to a narrow wooden plank that leads to a bridge.

Although computer-generated and cartoonlike, the scenes of being high above the ground on the plank or bridge are realistic enough to trigger the physiological indicators of anxiety. Lamson encourages the person to stay in the same spot until the anxiety diminishes. Once relaxed, the person continues the VR journey. After virtual reality therapy, over 90 percent of Lamson's patients successfully rode a glass elevator up to the 15th floor.

Once experimental, virtual reality therapy has become an accepted treatment for specific phobias and is now being extended to other disorders, including other anxiety disorders, substance-related disorders, schizophrenia, and eating disorders, often working best as an addition to more traditional treatments (Cieślik et al., 2020; Freeman et al., 2017). One innovative application of VR therapy is in the treatment of posttraumatic stress disorder (PTSD) in war veterans (McLay et al., 2011). Marine veteran Joshua Musser was treated with virtual reality therapy after fighting in Iraq and developing PTSD. Musser told CNN (2011), "It put you back in Iraq where you kind of have one foot here and one foot there. The only thing outside of Iraq that you hear is [the clinical psychologist's] voice, and so when she sees that I'm really starting to stress out . . . she would be in my ear and be pulling me back."

VR therapy is easier and less expensive to administer than graduated exposure to the actual feared object or situation. Another advantage is that the availability of VR may make people who are extremely phobic more willing to seek treatment. And, research suggests that patients will be less likely to refuse treatment or drop out of treatment with virtual exposure than with real-world exposure (Meyerbröker & Emmelkamp, 2010).

NICoE photo by Linsey Pizzulo

⌃ Virtual Reality Navy researcher Jena McLellan is shown here demonstrating the use of a Computer-Assisted Rehabilitation Environment, a virtual reality system used to treat war veterans who have posttraumatic stress disorder. The technology creates the very realistic sensation of being immersed in a feared environment to help veterans overcome their trauma-related anxieties. Once experimental, virtual reality treatment has been shown to be effective in treating specific phobias and other disorders, including posttraumatic stress disorder in combat veterans and in victims of terrorist attacks (Freedman et al., 2010; Opriş et al., 2012; Shiban et al., 2016).

sweet-flavored water, Garcia injected them with a drug that made them ill. The rats developed a strong taste aversion for the sweet-flavored water, avoiding it altogether (Garcia et al., 1966). In much the same way, **aversive conditioning** is *a relatively ineffective type of behavior therapy that involves repeatedly pairing an aversive stimulus with the occurrence of undesirable behaviors or thoughts*. For substance use disorder and addiction, nausea-inducing drugs can be used to create taste aversions. For example, a medication called *Antabuse* is used in aversion therapy for alcoholism (Ellis & Dronsfield, 2013). Consuming alcohol while taking Anatabuse produces bouts of extreme, highly unpleasant nausea.

Aversive conditioning techniques have been applied to a wide variety of problem behaviors (Cain & LeDoux, 2008). However, mental health professionals are typically very cautious about the use of such techniques, partly because of their potential to harm or produce discomfort for clients (C. B. Fisher, 2009; Francis, 2009). In addition, aversive techniques are generally not very effective (Emmelkamp, 2004).

Techniques Based on Operant Conditioning

B.F. Skinner's *operant conditioning* model of learning is based on the simple principle that behavior is shaped and maintained by its consequences (see the chapter on learning). Behavior therapists have developed several treatment techniques that are derived from operant conditioning. *Shaping* involves reinforcing successive approximations of a desired behavior. Shaping is often used to teach appropriate behaviors to patients who have difficulties due to autism spectrum disorder, intellectual disability, or severe mental illness. For example, shaping has been used to increase the attention span of hospitalized patients with severe schizophrenia (Combs et al., 2011; Mueser et al., 2013).

Other operant conditioning techniques involve controlling the consequences that follow behaviors. *Positive* and *negative reinforcement* are used to increase the incidence of desired behaviors. *Extinction,* or the absence of reinforcement, is used to reduce the occurrence of undesired behaviors.

Let's illustrate how operant techniques are used in therapy by describing a behavioral program to treat a four-year-old girl's sleeping problems (Ronen, 1991). The first step in the treatment program was to identify specific problem behaviors and determine their *baseline rate,* or how often each problem occurred before treatment began (see **Figure 15.2**). The baseline rate allowed the therapist to objectively measure the

aversive conditioning A relatively ineffective type of behavior therapy that involves repeatedly pairing an aversive stimulus with the occurrence of undesirable behaviors or thoughts.

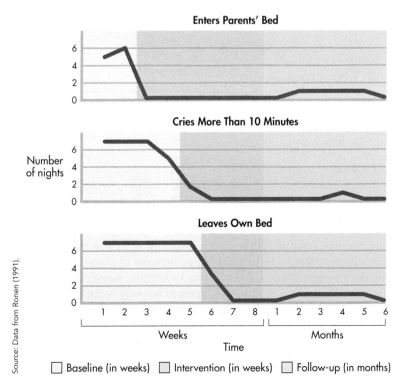

Source: Data from Ronen (1991).

FIGURE 15.2 The Effect of Operant Conditioning Techniques These graphs depict the changes in three specific sleep-related problem behaviors of a four-year-old girl over the course of behavioral therapy. The intervention for each problem behavior was introduced separately over several weeks. As you can see, behavior therapy produced a rapid reduction in the rate of each problem behavior. The green area shows the maintenance of desired behavior changes over a six-month follow-up.

Taesam Do/Getty Images

TABLE 15.3

Behavior Therapy

Type of Therapy	Founder	Source of Problems	Treatment Techniques	Goals of Therapy
Behavior therapy	Based on classical conditioning, operant conditioning, and observational learning	Learned maladaptive behavior patterns	Systematic desensitization, virtual reality, aversive conditioning, reinforcement and extinction, token economy, observational learning	To unlearn maladaptive behaviors and replace them with adaptive, appropriate behaviors

child's progress. The parents next identified several very specific behavioral goals for their daughter. These goals included not crying when she was put to bed, not crying if she woke up in the night, not getting into her parents' bed, and staying in her own bed throughout the night.

The parents were taught operant techniques to decrease the undesirable behaviors and increase desirable ones. For example, to *extinguish* the girl's screaming and crying, the parents were taught to ignore the behavior rather than continue to reinforce it with parental attention. In contrast, desirable behaviors were to be *positively reinforced* with abundant praise, encouragement, social attention, and other rewards. Figure 15.2 shows the little girl's progress for three specific problem behaviors.

Reinforcement techniques have been applied to many different kinds of psychological problems, from habit and weight control to helping children with autism spectrum disorder learn to speak and behave more adaptively.

The **token economy** is a *form of behavior therapy in which the therapeutic environment is structured to reward desired behaviors with tokens or points that may eventually be exchanged for tangible rewards*. Basically, tokens or points are awarded as positive reinforcers for desirable behaviors and withheld or taken away for undesirable behaviors. The tokens can be exchanged for other reinforcers, such as special privileges.

Token economies have been most successful in controlled environments in which the behavior of the client is under ongoing surveillance or supervision. Thus, token economies have been used in classrooms, inpatient psychiatric units, and group homes (Field et al., 2004; Kamps et al., 2011; Kokaridas et al., 2013). Although effective, token economies are difficult to implement, especially in community-based outpatient clinics, so they are not in wide use today (R. P. Lieberman, 2000).

Table 15.3 summarizes key points about behavior therapy.

Cognitive Therapies

■ KEY THEME
Cognitive therapies are based on the assumption that psychological problems are due to maladaptive thinking.

☰ KEY QUESTIONS
- What are rational-emotive behavior therapy and cognitive therapy, and how do they differ?
- What are cognitive-behavioral therapy and mindfulness-based therapies?

While behavior therapy assumes that faulty learning is at the core of problem behaviors and emotions, the cognitive therapies assume that the culprit is *faulty thinking*. **Cognitive therapies** are a *group of psychotherapies based on the assumption that psychological problems are due to illogical patterns of thinking; techniques focus on recognizing and altering unhealthy thinking patterns*. The key assumption of the cognitive therapies could be put like this: Most people blame their unhappiness and problems on external events and situations, but the real cause of unhappiness is the way the

token economy Form of behavior therapy in which the therapeutic environment is structured to reward desired behaviors with tokens or points that may eventually be exchanged for tangible rewards.

cognitive therapies Group of psychotherapies based on the assumption that psychological problems are due to illogical patterns of thinking; techniques focus on recognizing and altering unhealthy thinking patterns.

person *thinks* about the events, not the events themselves. Thus, cognitive therapists zero in on the faulty, irrational patterns of thinking that they believe are causing the psychological problems. Once faulty, irrational patterns of thinking have been identified, the next step is to *change* them to more adaptive, healthy patterns of thinking. In this section, we'll look at how this change is accomplished in two influential forms of cognitive therapy: Ellis's *rational-emotive behavior therapy* (REBT) and Beck's *cognitive therapy* (CT).

Albert Ellis and Rational-Emotive Behavior Therapy

Albert Ellis (1913–2007) succinctly summarized the role of cognition in mental health: "You largely feel the way you think." As a practicing psychoanalyst, Ellis became increasingly disappointed with the psychoanalytic approach to solving human problems. Psychoanalysis simply didn't seem to work: His patients would have insight after insight, yet never get any better.

In the 1950s, Ellis began to take a more active, directive role in his therapy sessions. He developed **rational-emotive behavior therapy**, abbreviated as **REBT**, a *type of cognitive therapy that focuses on changing the client's irrational beliefs*. The key premise of REBT is that people's difficulties are caused by their faulty expectations and irrational beliefs (Ellis, 1991; Ellis & Ellis, 2011; Ellis, 2013).

Ellis pointed out that most people mistakenly believe that they become upset and unhappy because of external events. But Ellis (1993; Ellis & Ellis, 2011) would argue that it's not external events that make people miserable — it's their *interpretation* of those events. In rational-emotive behavior therapy, psychological problems are explained by the "ABC" model, as shown in **Figure 15.3**. According to this model, when an *Activating event* (**A**) occurs, it is the person's *Beliefs* (**B**) about the event that cause emotional *Consequences* (**C**).

Identifying the core irrational beliefs that underlie personal distress is the first step in rational-emotive behavior therapy. Often, irrational beliefs reflect "shoulds" that are absolutes, such as the notion that "I should be competent at everything I do." The consequences of such thinking are unhealthy emotions and responses that interfere with constructive attempts to change disturbing situations (Ellis & Ellis, 2011). Other common irrational beliefs are listed in **Table 15.4**.

The next step in REBT is for the therapist to vigorously *dispute the irrational beliefs*. In doing so, rational-emotive behavior therapists tend to be very direct and even confrontational (Ellis & Ellis, 2011). The long-term therapeutic goal is to teach clients to recognize and dispute their own irrational beliefs in a wide range of situations. However, responding "rationally" to unpleasant situations does not mean denying

rational-emotive behavior therapy (REBT) Type of cognitive therapy that focuses on changing the client's irrational beliefs.

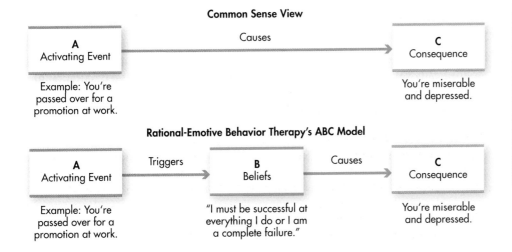

Common Sense View

A
Activating Event → Causes → C
Consequence

Example: You're passed over for a promotion at work.

You're miserable and depressed.

Rational-Emotive Behavior Therapy's ABC Model

A
Activating Event → Triggers → B
Beliefs → Causes → C
Consequence

Example: You're passed over for a promotion at work.

"I must be successful at everything I do or I am a complete failure."

You're miserable and depressed.

FIGURE 15.3 The "ABC" Model in Rational-Emotive Behavior Therapy Common sense tells us that unhappiness and other unpleasant emotions are caused by unpleasant or disturbing events. This view is shown in the top part of the figure. But Albert Ellis (1993) points out that it is really our *beliefs* about the events, not the events themselves, that make us miserable, as diagrammed in the bottom part of the figure.

According to rational-emotive behavior therapy, unhappiness and psychological problems can often be traced to people's irrational beliefs. Becoming aware of these irrational beliefs is the first step toward replacing them with more rational alternatives. Some of the most common irrational beliefs are listed to the right.

TABLE 15.4

Irrational Beliefs

1. You must be loved or approved of by virtually everyone in your community.

2. You must be thoroughly competent, adequate, and achieving in all possible respects.

3. Certain people are wicked or villainous, and they should be blamed and punished. You should become extremely upset over other people's wrongdoings.

4. It is easier to avoid than to face difficulties and responsibilities. Avoiding difficulties whenever possible is more likely to lead to happiness than facing difficulties.

5. You need to rely on someone stronger than yourself.

6. Your past history is an all-important determinant of your present behavior. Because something once strongly affected your life, it should indefinitely have a similar effect.

Source: Information from Ellis (1991).

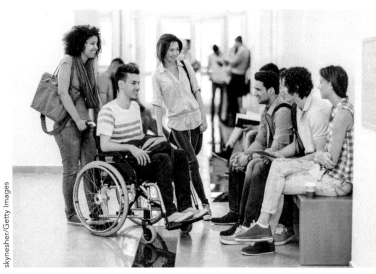

▲ **Unknown Thoughts** In any particular group, there can be many unknown thoughts going on beneath the surface for each person. The person in the wheelchair probably has different thoughts than the person pushing the wheelchair. And the people sitting on the bench are probably thinking different things than the people in front of them. Each person grapples with their own thoughts and issues. We can't know what somebody else is thinking.

cognitive therapy (CT) Therapy developed by Aaron T. Beck that focuses on changing the client's unrealistic and maladaptive beliefs.

your feelings (Dryden 2009; Ellis & Bernard, 1985). Ellis believes that it is perfectly appropriate and rational to feel sad when you are rejected or regretful when you make a mistake. Appropriate emotions are the consequences of rational beliefs, such as "I would prefer that everyone like me, but that's not likely to happen."

Rational-emotive behavior therapy is a popular approach in clinical practice, partly because it is straightforward and simple. It has been shown to be generally effective in the treatment of major depressive disorder, social anxiety disorder, and certain other anxiety disorders. Rational-emotive behavior therapy is also useful in helping people overcome self-defeating behaviors, such as an excessive need for approval, extreme shyness, and chronic procrastination (David et al., 2009; Ellis, 2013).

Ellis's wife, Australian psychologist *Debbie Joffe Ellis* (b. 1956), has carried on her husband's work since his death. She co-authored his final book on REBT, which was published after his death and which she has since revised (Ellis & Ellis, 2011, 2019). Joffe Ellis continues to lecture and teach widely about REBT. And research continues to support the effectiveness of the therapy (David et al., 2017).

Aaron Beck and Cognitive Therapy

Cognitive therapy, abbreviated **CT**, is a *therapy developed by Aaron T. Beck that focuses on changing the client's unrealistic and maladaptive beliefs*. It grew out of his research on depression (Beck, 2004; Beck et al., 1979). Like Albert Ellis, psychiatrist **Aaron T. Beck** (b. 1921) was initially trained as a psychoanalyst. Seeking to scientifically validate the psychoanalytic assumption that depressed patients "have a need to suffer," Beck began collecting data on the free associations and dreams of his depressed patients. What he found, however, was that depressed people have an extremely negative view of the past, present, and future (Beck et al., 1979). Rather than realistically evaluating their situation, depressed patients have developed a *negative cognitive bias*, consistently distorting their experiences in a negative way. Their negative perceptions of events and situations are shaped by deep-seated, self-deprecating beliefs, such as "I can't do anything right," "I'm worthless," or "I'm unlovable" (Beck, 1991). Beck's cognitive therapy essentially focuses on correcting the cognitive biases that underlie major depressive disorder and other psychological disorders (see **Table 15.5** on the next page).

TABLE 15.5

Cognitive Biases in Depression

Cognitive Bias (Error)	Description	Example
Arbitrary inference	Drawing a negative conclusion when there is little or no evidence to support it	When Jena cancels lunch with her friend Paige, Paige assumes that Jena doesn't like her anymore.
Selective abstraction	Focusing on a single negative detail taken out of context and ignoring the more important aspects of the situation	During Kaori's annual review, her manager praises her job performance but notes that she could be a little more confident when she deals with customers. Kaori decides that her manager is on the verge of firing her because of her poor customer relations skills.
Overgeneralization	Drawing a sweeping, global conclusion based on an isolated incident and applying that conclusion to other unrelated areas of life	Raj confidently answers a question in class, but it's wrong and he is quickly corrected by the instructor. Raj concludes that he is not smart enough to succeed in a professional career.
Personalization	Taking responsibility, blaming oneself, or applying external events to oneself when there is no basis or evidence for making the connection	Andrei becomes extremely upset when his instructor warns the class about plagiarism. He thinks the instructor's warning was aimed at him, and he concludes that the instructor suspects him of plagiarizing.

Source: Information from Beck et al. (1979).

According to Aaron Beck, people with major depressive disorder perceive and interpret experiences in very negative terms. They are prone to systematic errors in logic, or cognitive biases, which shape their negative interpretation of events. This table shows some of the most common cognitive biases in major depressive disorder.

Beck's CT has much in common with Ellis's rational-emotive behavior therapy. Like Ellis, Beck believes that what people think creates their moods and emotions. And like REBT, CT involves helping clients identify faulty thinking and replace unhealthy patterns of thinking with healthier ones.

But in contrast with Ellis's emphasis on "irrational" thinking, Beck believes that major depressive disorder and other psychological problems are caused by *distorted thinking* and *unrealistic beliefs* (Hollon & Beck, 2004; Wright et al., 2011). Rather than logically debating the "irrationality" of a client's beliefs, the CT therapist encourages the client to *empirically test the accuracy of their assumptions and beliefs* (Hollon & Beck, 2004; Wills, 2009). Let's look at how this occurs in Beck's CT.

The first step in CT is to help the client learn to recognize and monitor the automatic thoughts that occur without conscious effort or control. What's an automatic thought? Imagine that you knock your coffee off your desk. What first comes to mind? Something adaptive like, "Not a great start to the day, but things happen," or "what a clumsy idiot I am"? Because their perceptions are shaped by their negative cognitive biases, depressed people usually have automatic thoughts that reflect very negative interpretations of experience, like the maladaptive thought that you're a "clumsy idiot."

In the second step of CT, the therapist helps the client learn how to *empirically test* the reality of the automatic thoughts that are so upsetting. For example, to test the belief that "I always say the wrong thing," the therapist might assign the person the task of

TABLE 15.6

Comparing Cognitive Therapies

Type of Therapy	Founder	Source of Problems	Treatment Techniques	Goals of Therapy
Rational-emotive behavior therapy (REBT)	Albert Ellis	Irrational beliefs	Very directive: Identify, logically dispute, and challenge irrational beliefs.	Surrender of irrational beliefs and absolutist demands
Cognitive therapy (CT)	Aaron T. Beck	Unrealistic, distorted perceptions and interpretations of events due to cognitive biases	Directive collaboration: Teach client to monitor automatic thoughts; test accuracy of conclusions; correct distorted thinking and perception.	Accurate and realistic perception of self, others, and external events

initiating a conversation with three acquaintances and noting how often they actually said the wrong thing.

Initially, the CT therapist models techniques for evaluating the accuracy of automatic thoughts, hoping to eventually teach the client to do the same on their own. The CT therapist also strives to create a therapeutic climate of *collaboration* that encourages the client to contribute to the evaluation of the logic and accuracy of automatic thoughts (Beck et al., 1979). This approach contrasts with the confrontational approach used by the REBT therapist, who directly challenges the client's thoughts and beliefs.

Beck's cognitive therapy has been shown to be effective in treating major depressive disorder and other psychological disorders, including anxiety disorders, borderline personality disorders, eating disorders, posttraumatic stress disorder, and relationship problems (Beck & Dozois, 2011; Butler et al., 2006; Dobson & Dobson, 2009; Gaudiano, 2008). Along with effectively treating major depressive disorder, cognitive therapy may also help *prevent* it from recurring, especially if clients learn and then use the skills they have learned in therapy (Beck & Alford, 2009).

Aaron Beck's work continues through the many psychologists around the world who have been trained in cognitive therapy. But his work is most directly carried on by his daughter, U.S. psychologist *Judith Beck* (b. 1954), who has frequently published with her father. Judith Beck is currently president of the Beck Institute for Cognitive Behavior Therapy in Philadelphia, her father's former position.

Table 15.6 summarizes the key characteristics of Ellis's rational-emotive behavior therapy and Beck's cognitive therapy.

Cognitive-Behavioral Therapy and Mindfulness-Based Therapies

Although we've presented cognitive and behavioral therapies in separate sections, it's important to note that cognitive and behavioral techniques are often combined in therapy. **Cognitive-behavioral therapy** (abbreviated **CBT**) is *therapy that integrates cognitive and behavioral techniques and that is based on the assumption that thoughts, moods, and behaviors are interrelated* (Hollon & Beck, 2004). Along with challenging maladaptive beliefs and substituting more adaptive cognitions, the therapist uses behavior modification, shaping, reinforcement, and modeling to teach problem solving and to change unhealthy behavior patterns.

The hallmark of cognitive-behavioral therapy is its pragmatic approach. Therapists design an integrated treatment plan, combining techniques from the behavioral and the cognitive approaches that are most appropriate for specific problems.

Cognitive-behavioral therapy has been used in the treatment of children, adolescents, and the elderly (Dautovich & Gum, 2011; Kazdin, 2004; Weisz & Kazdin, 2010).

cognitive-behavioral therapy (CBT) Therapy that integrates cognitive and behavioral techniques and that is based on the assumption that thoughts, moods, and behaviors are interrelated.

Studies have shown that CBT is a very effective treatment for many disorders, including major depressive disorder, eating disorders, substance use disorders, and anxiety disorders (Sheldon, 2011). CBT has even been used to help people coping with stress, anxiety, or depression while hospitalized for COVID-19 (Ferrario et al., 2021).

Cognitive-behavioral therapy can also help decrease the incidence of positive symptoms, such as delusions and hallucinations, in patients with schizophrenia and psychotic symptoms by teaching them how to test the reality of their mistaken beliefs and perceptions (Morrison et al., 2014; Wright et al., 2009). CBT also offers flexibility. It can be adapted for use in different cultures (Naeem et al., 2015). Outcomes seem to be similar when therapists provide CBT via the Internet (Andersson et al., 2014; Hedman et al., 2012). And it can even be used to prevent the onset of mental illness in people determined to be at risk (Brent et al., 2015).

One exciting development in CBT is its growing use as a *transdiagnostic therapy*. This means that specific CBT techniques can be effective across multiple diagnoses (Schaeuffele et al., 2021). In fact, CBT started out as a set of techniques that could be used with multiple psychological disorders. However, shortly after its inception, researchers outlined specific techniques for individual disorders. Now researchers are increasingly realizing the high comorbidity among psychological disorders—about 40 percent of people with a mental illness meet diagnostic criteria for more than one—as well as the likelihood that there are universal factors that contribute to many different disorders. So, CBT is returning to its roots, and treatments (including those delivered via the Internet) that address multiple disorders at the same time (Schaeuffele et al., 2021). Sometimes, transdiagnostic CBT takes the form of "one size fits all" with techniques addressing multiple issues, and sometimes it takes the form of "my size fits me" with CBT tailored to address a specific patient's multiple issues (Scheuffele et al., 2021, p. 90).

An emerging approach in cognitive-behavioral therapy involves the use of mindfulness techniques. These new therapies are called *mindfulness-based interventions, mindfulness-based therapies,* or *mindfulness and acceptance therapies* (Chiesa & Malinowski, 2011; Cullen, 2011). As discussed in the chapters on consciousness and stress, health, and coping, *mindfulness* is a meditation technique that involves *present-centered awareness without judgment* (Hölzel et al., 2011). Contemporary mindfulness practices are based on Buddhist meditation techniques that originated over 2,000 years ago.

Mindfulness-based stress reduction (MBSR) was the first mindfulness-based therapy to earn broad acceptance. Developed by Jon Kabat-Zinn (2003, 2013), MBSR involves a structured program of mindfulness meditation, yoga and mindful body practices, and group discussion. The success of MBSR in the treatment of stress and anxiety helped spark the development of other mindfulness-based therapies targeted to specific disorders. For example, *mindfulness-based cognitive therapy (MBCT)* was developed to treat major depressive disorder, although it has been expanded to include other disorders (Coelho et al., 2013; Khoury et al., 2013; Schaeuffele et al., 2021).

Although a relatively new approach, the mindfulness-based therapies show promise (Khoury et al., 2013; Schaeuffele et al., 2021). Two meta-analyses found that mindfulness-based approaches were effective treatments for depressive disorders, although results were mixed for anxiety disorders (Barnhofer et al., 2016; Strauss et al., 2014). And, one large, carefully controlled study found that MBCT was as effective as antidepressant medications in preventing relapse after an acute episode of major depressive disorder (Bieling et al., 2012; Segal et al., 2010).

Mindfulness-Based Stress Reduction Yoga is one of many mindfulness-based activities that can reduce stress. These employees of a New York-based Armani store are participating in a yoga session. An increasing number of employers provide yoga or other stress-management programs to their employees.

Marilynn K. Yee/The New York Times/Redux

group therapy Form of psychotherapy that involves one or more therapists working simultaneously with a small group of clients.

Group and Family Therapy

■ KEY THEME
Group therapy involves one or more therapists working with several clients simultaneously.

■ KEY QUESTIONS
• What are some key advantages of group therapy?
• What is family therapy, and how do its assumptions and techniques differ from those of individual therapy?

Individual psychotherapy offers a personal relationship between a client and a therapist, one that is focused on a single client's problems, thoughts, and emotions. But individual psychotherapy has certain limitations that group and family therapy can help overcome (Norcross et al., 2005; Schachter, 2011).

Group Therapy

Group therapy is a *form of psychotherapy that involves one or more therapists working simultaneously with a small group of clients.* Virtually any approach—psychodynamic, client-centered, behavioral, or cognitive—can be used in group therapy (Free, 2008; Tasca et al., 2011). And just about any problem that can be handled individually can be dealt with in group therapy (Garvin, 2011).

Group therapy has a number of advantages over individual psychotherapy. First, because a single therapist can work simultaneously with several people, it is less expensive for the client and less time-consuming for the therapist. Second, rather than relying on a client's self-perceptions about how they relate to other people, the therapist can observe their actual interactions with others (Burlingame et al., 2004; Yalom, 2005).

Third, the support and encouragement provided by the other group members may help a person feel less alone and understand that other people struggle with similar problems. For example, a team of family therapists set up group meetings with family members and co-workers of people who had died in the attacks on the World Trade Center (Boss et al., 2003). One woman, who had lost dozens of co-workers, some of them close friends, explained the impact of the group sessions in this way:

> As I saw the widows dealing with their loss, and believing it a bit more, it helped me to accept it even more. It was easier with sharing together. Strength in numbers. It makes you feel less alone.

A Couple Therapy Session Couple therapists typically work with both members of a couple at the same time. The couple therapist can then directly observe how the partners interact, resolve differences, and exert control over one another. As unhealthy patterns of couple interactions are identified, they can often be replaced with new patterns that promote the psychological well-being of the couple as a unit, as well as of each individual partner.

Group therapies in the aftermath of other disasters, including Hurricane Katrina, have provided similar support (Salloum et al., 2009). And group therapy—well, the online version—has been an essential tool during the pandemic, when the increased demand for psychotherapy outstripped supply (Caron, 2021; Marmarosh et al., 2020).

Group therapy is typically conducted by a mental health professional. In contrast, *self-help groups* and *support groups* are typically conducted by nonprofessionals. Self-help groups and support groups have become increasingly popular in the United States and other countries, and can be very helpful. During the increased demand for mental health care during the pandemic, support groups provided a valuable option that was typically free (Caron, 2021). As discussed in the In Focus box on page 532, "Increasing Access During the Pandemic: Meeting the Need for Mental Health Care," the potential of these groups to promote mental health should not be underestimated.

fstop123/Getty Images

Family, Network, and Couple Therapy

Most forms of psychotherapy tend to see a person's problems—and the solutions to those problems—as primarily originating within the each individual. **Family therapy** is a *form of psychotherapy that is based on the assumption that the family is a system and that treats the family as a unit.* The major goal of family therapy is to alter and improve the ongoing interactions among family members.

The family is seen as a dynamic structure in which each member plays a unique role. According to this view, every family has certain unspoken "rules" of interaction and communication. Some of these tacit rules revolve around issues such as which family members exercise power and how, who keeps the peace, and what kinds of alliances members have formed among themselves. As such issues are explored, unhealthy patterns of family interaction can be identified and replaced with new "rules" that promote the psychological health of the family as a unit.

Family therapy is often used to enhance the effectiveness of individual psychotherapy. For example, patients with schizophrenia are less likely to experience relapses when family members are involved in therapy (Kopelowicz et al., 2007; O'Brien et al., 2014).

One variation on family therapy, *network therapy*, might be described as kind of an extended-family therapy, including a wider range of a patient's community in their treatment. One of the pioneers of network therapy was **Carolyn Attneave** (1920–1992), who has been described as "undoubtedly the most well-known psychologist of American Indian background" (LaFromboise & Trimble, 1996). Attneave observed that people's broad networks of family and friends (not just an inner circle of immediate family members) form a core of social support for most of us, and were not included in most family therapy. Along with her colleague Ross Speck, Attneave introduced network therapy in indigenous communities in the United States, referring to the idea of a "'Clan' or 'Tribal Unit'" (Attneave, 1969). In indigenous communities, network therapy has often been conducted in homes, sometimes with dozens of people. Sessions can last for hours, with the therapist often taking the role of a participant alongside the client and the people in their network (Attneave, 1969).

Attneave (1969) emphasized the importance of network therapy in indigenous communities: "While close-knit extended family ties are not unique to American Indians, or even universal among them, extended families are often seen as viable social units" (p. 192). But she also advocated for the use of network therapy more broadly. Her work was influential not just in American Indian communities, but also in other communities—nationally and internationally (La Fromboise & Trimble, 1996). Moreover, Attneave documented the effectiveness of network therapy, even for those with serious mental illnesses (Attneave, 1969). For example, Attneave demonstrated that network therapy often reduced the likelihood of hospitalization for people with schizophrenia (LaFromboise & Trimble, 1996).

Beyond indigenous communities, network therapy is most commonly used for people with addictions (Galanter, 2020). In fact, Attneave (1990) wrote about this model, and she was among the earliest clinicians to refer to such network sessions as "interventions" for people who are addicted. In an intervention, a person's social network comes together to persuade that person they need help for their addiction. Other network-based treatment models for addiction combine individual and network therapy, involving the client's family and peer network in therapy—not every time but on a regular and recurring basis—to support the client's recovery (Galanter & Brook, 2001).

Many family therapists also provide *marital* or *couple therapy* (Bischoff, 2011). As is the case with family therapy, there are many different approaches to couple therapy (Lebow, 2008; Snyder & Balderrama-Durbin, 2012). For example, *behavioral couple therapy* is based on the assumption that couples are satisfied when they experience more reinforcement than punishment in their relationship. Thus, it focuses on increasing caring behaviors and teaching couples how to constructively resolve conflicts and problems. In general, most couple therapies have the goal of improving communication, reducing negative communication, and increasing intimacy between the pair. (For more evidence-based advice on improving relationships, romantic and otherwise, see the Psych for Your Life in Chapter 10 on reducing relationship conflict.)

⌃ Carolyn Attneave and Network Therapy Carolyn Attneave was one of the pioneers of network therapy, and was "internationally renowned for her expertise in cross-cultural topics in counseling and psychotherapy" (LaFromboise & Trimble, 1996). The key to network therapy, as Attneave observed, is that a person's broad network of family and friends (not just their inner circle of immediate family) form a core of social support. Often, this wider network of people has not been included in family therapy.

family therapy Form of psychotherapy that is based on the assumption that the family is a system and that treats the family as a unit.

IN FOCUS

Increasing Access During the Pandemic: Meeting the Need for Mental Health Care

Even before the pandemic, in the United States, more than two-thirds of people with mental illnesses in the general population went untreated, with even higher rates for Black and Latino people and for those with more severe psychological disorders (Creedon & Lê Cook, 2016; Kazdin & Blase, 2011; Weissman et al., 2017). And historically, people have been even less likely to get treatment in many other countries, particularly developing countries, where there are far fewer mental health clinicians (Kohn, 2014; Pillard, 2017; Wang et al., 2011). The lack of mental health care, and the inequity in its availability, have been even more dramatic since the pandemic began, in the United States and around the world (Altiraifi & Rapfogel, 2020; Moreno et al., 2020; WHO, 2020a). Psychologists, other mental health clinicians, and policy makers have been working to address this problem. Indeed, the pandemic has highlighted the roles that policy makers—for example, government employees and decision makers—play in the management of mental health care at a scaled-up level (Ornell et al., 2020). Some of the most interesting innovations in increasing access involve the use of clinicians without traditional training, and technology-driven solutions (Zhou et al., 2020).

MYTH ◀ SCIENCE

Is it true that therapy is effective only if it is provided by a clinical psychologist or other highly trained therapist?

Paraprofessionals and Lay Counselors

Clinicians who have not received traditional academic training are increasingly delivering mental health care, including during the pandemic (Kola, 2020). Community health workers, paraprofessionals without extensive medical or psychological training, provide education and raise awareness about mental health, teach coping skills, and provide some psychological treatments—often in community settings such as schools or homes (Kohrt et al., 2018; Rotheram-Borus et al., 2012). Paraprofessionals typically have some kind of training and may earn a certificate in their field, but they do not earn the licensure that a professional, such as a psychologist or licensed clinical social worker, has.

Lay counselors have even less training than paraprofessionals. For example, in a refugee camp in Uganda, Somali and Rwandan refugees with as little as a primary school education received brief training as lay counselors to serve other refugees with PTSD (Neuner et al., 2008). Following treatment, about 30 percent of their fellow refugees met the criteria for PTSD, as compared with more than 60 percent of those who were not treated.

The United States has relatively few mental health paraprofessionals (Rotheram-Borus et al., 2012). A lay counselor model exists, however, in many Latino communities in the United States, which deploy minimally trained mental health care workers called *promotoras* into neighborhoods (Tran et al., 2014). Lay counselors are also used in the United States to provide online or telephone support—"hotlines"—for people who are thinking of suicide, have been sexually assaulted, or are trying to quit smoking.

Self-Help Groups

Self-help groups have long offered another venue for mental health care delivery by nonprofessionals. Among the best-known self-help groups are Alcoholics Anonymous (AA), Narcotics Anonymous (NA), and Self-Management and Recovery Training (SMART Recovery), all free of charge. AA and NA follow a 12-step structure that includes themes of admitting that you have a problem, seeking help from a "higher power," and helping other people who have the same problem. SMART Recovery is not grounded in religion, and is based on cognitive-behavioral principles. AA, NA, SMART Recovery, and other self-help groups aimed at a variety of diagnoses are found in many different countries.

Just how helpful are self-help groups? Research has shown that self-help groups can be as effective as therapy provided by a mental health professional, at least for some psychological problems (Harwood & L'Abate, 2010). During the pandemic, many self-groups quickly adapted and held online group sessions or developed phone networks for one-on-one support (Liese & Monley, 2020). In this way, they likely provided support for people who could not access mental health care in more traditional ways.

Paul Burke/Aristide Foundation

▲ **Lay Mental Health Workers** In a refugee camp in Port-au-Prince, Haiti, a lay mental health worker teaches relaxation techniques to people who have been displaced from their homes. Studies suggest that people treated by lay mental health workers have better mental health outcomes than people who receive no care (see Neuner et al., 2008).

Technology-Based Solutions

Research also supports the use of technological solutions to deliver mental and physical health care to underserved areas (Ben-Zeev, 2012; Moreno et al., 2020; Teachman, 2014). When the technology involves computers or smartphones, this innovation is often called *eHealth*. Psychotherapy delivered via Internet technology, such as Skype, is about as effective as face-to-face psychotherapy, and its use skyrocketed during the pandemic (Di Carlo et al., 2020; Moreno et al., 2020). Many governments around the world, including in the United States, loosened legal restrictions on eHealth during the pandemic, changes that many hope will persist and even expand, helping to reduce inequities in mental health care access. For example, during the pandemic, eHealth was broadly available in 80 percent of high-income countries, but not even in 50 percent of low-income countries (WHO, 2020).

During the pandemic, access also increased by using technology that allows the delivery of mental health treatment without the need for a therapist (Kola, 2020; Walk-Morris, 2016). For example, supportive emails or text messages, sent automatically, have been used for conditions ranging from smoking addiction to eating disorders (Bauer et al., 2003; Lenert et al., 2004). In one case, people with schizophrenia were sent more than 800 automatic text messages over several months (Granholm et al., 2012). For example, a text might ask, "What do you do to help cope with voices?" Patients who received these messages were more likely to take their medication regularly, had more social interactions, and had less severe hallucinations than those who did not receive the messages. Moreover, automated programs offer cost-effective means of delivering treatment in multiple languages.

Research has also supported the effectiveness of self-administered cognitive-behavioral therapies that use technology (Ebert et al., 2015). A treatment technique called cognitive bias modification (CBM) targets anxiety and depression (Hertel et al., 2017; Lau & Pile, 2015; Teachman, 2014). In one variation aimed at reducing anxiety, patients play a game in which players learn to direct their attention to nonthreatening target (see image; Dennis & O'Toole, 2014; MacLeod & Mathews, 2012). Repeated play has been demonstrated to lead to decreases in symptoms of anxiety. One meta-analysis found that self-guided therapy might also help people with depression (Cuijpers et al., 2011). For example, in two different studies, people randomly assigned to use a free app based on cognitive-behavioral strategies were compared to people in control groups (Birney et al., 2016; Roepke et al., 2015). Those who used one of the apps, MoodHacker or SuperBetter, showed a greater decrease in symptoms of depression than did those in the control groups. Also, while not quite an app, exergames (online games that involve physical exercise) showed promise during the isolation of the pandemic (Viana & de Lina, 2020).

Although apps seem like an ideal solution to the lack of access to mental health care, especially during the pandemic, it's important to examine the research. Many apps have been subjected to experimental validation, but the vast majority have not (Schueller & Torous, 2020). Anyone can launch an app and claim it helps people with depression, anxiety, eating disorders, or any other psychological problem, but few app developers have gathered the data that creators of apps like MoodHacker or Super Better have (Marshall et al., 2020). Be cautious when downloading an app and ask good questions. Was it developed by a psychologist or other mental health professional? Do they provide data on this particular app? Did they publish their data?

Increased and equitable access to mental health care is an important goal. However, as the use of unconventional resources to deliver treatment increases, the field of psychology will face new challenges. First, just because treatment is available does not mean people in need will use it or that it will be effective (Kazdin & Rabbitt, 2013; Zulfic et al., 2020). And, new ethical and legal considerations have arisen, including some related to confidentiality and privacy (Lustgarten & Colbow, 2017; Moreno et al., 2020; Novotney, 2017). Grappling with the logistical and ethical issues of innovative ways to provide treatment is worth it, however, if access to much-needed care is expanded in an equitable way (Bashshur et al., 2020). The expansion of these innovations in mental-health delivery might be a silver lining of the pandemic.

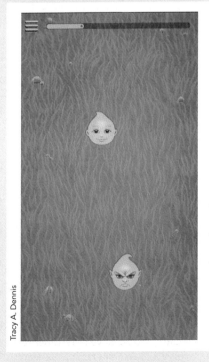

An Anxiety-Reducing Game Psychologists Tracy Dennis and Laura O'Toole (2014) found that playing a video game based on a treatment called *cognitive bias modification* resulted in a decrease in symptoms of anxiety. People earn points when they direct their attention away from anxiety-provoking targets, like the scary cartoon character, and toward the friendly-looking characters.

Tracy A. Dennis

Evaluating the Effectiveness of Psychotherapy

■ KEY THEME
Decades of research demonstrate that psychotherapy is effective in helping people with psychological disorders.

⩵ KEY QUESTIONS
• What are the common factors that contribute to successful outcomes in psychotherapy?
• Why is it important to consider culture in psychotherapy?
• What is eclecticism?

Let's start with a simple fact: Most people with psychological symptoms do *not* seek help from mental health professionals (Jagdeo et al., 2009; WHO World Mental Health Survey Consortium, 2004). Some people may be reluctant to seek treatment because of the stigma that is still associated with psychological problems (Pescosolido et al., 2013; Wahl, 2012). And, of course, not everyone has access to professional treatment (Kazdin & Blase, 2011; Weissman et al., 2017). But many people eventually weather their psychological problems without professional intervention, sometimes seeking help and support from friends and family. Does psychotherapy offer significant benefits over just waiting for symptoms to subside?

The basic strategy for investigating this issue is to compare people who enter psychotherapy with a carefully selected, matched control group of people who do not receive psychotherapy (Freeman & Power, 2007; Nezu & Nezu, 2008). During the past half-century, hundreds of such studies have investigated the effectiveness of the major forms of psychotherapy (Cooper, 2008; Nathan & Gorman, 2007). To combine and interpret the results of such large numbers of studies, researchers have used a statistical technique called *meta-analysis.* Meta-analysis involves pooling the results of multiple studies into a single analysis, essentially creating one large study that can reveal overall trends in the data.

When meta-analysis is used to summarize studies that compare people who receive psychotherapy treatment to no-treatment controls, researchers consistently arrive at the same conclusion: *Psychotherapy is significantly more effective than no treatment.* On average, the person who completes psychotherapy treatment is better off than about 80 percent of those in the untreated control group (Cooper, 2008; Lambert & Ogles, 2004).

The benefits of psychotherapy usually become apparent in a relatively short time. As shown in **Figure 15.4**, approximately 50 percent of people show significant improvement

FIGURE 15.4 Psychotherapy Versus No Treatment This graph depicts the rates of improvement for more than 2,000 people in weekly psychotherapy and for 500 people who did not receive psychotherapy. As you can see, after only eight weekly sessions, more than 50 percent of participants receiving psychotherapy improved significantly. After the same length of time, only 4 percent of participants not receiving psychotherapy showed "spontaneous remission" of symptoms. Clearly, psychotherapy accelerates both the rate and degree of improvement for those experiencing psychological problems.

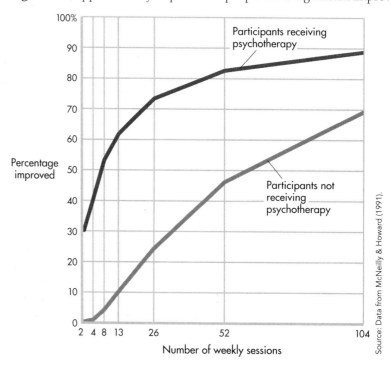

Source: Data from McNeilly & Howard (1991).

by the eighth weekly session of psychotherapy. By the end of six months of weekly psychotherapy sessions, about 75 percent are significantly improved (Baldwin et al., 2009; Lambert et al., 2001).

The gains that people make as a result of psychotherapy also tend to endure long after the therapy has ended, sometimes for years (Lambert & Ogles, 2004; Shedler, 2010). And, multiple meta-analyses have found that individual and group therapy are equally effective in producing significant gains in psychological functioning (Burlingame et al., 2004; Cuijpers et al., 2008).

Brain imaging technologies provide another line of evidence demonstrating the impact of psychotherapy for people with many psychological disorders (Barsaglini et al., 2014; Karlsson, 2011). In one study, PET scans were used to measure brain activity before and after 10 weeks of therapy for obsessive–compulsive disorder (Schwartz et al., 1996; Schwartz & Begley, 2002). The psychotherapy patients who improved showed the same changes in brain function that are associated with effective drug therapy for this disorder.

Nevertheless, it's important to note that psychotherapy is *not* a miracle cure. Some people who enter psychotherapy improve only slightly or not at all. Others drop out early, presumably because therapy wasn't working as they had hoped (Barrett et al., 2008). And in some cases, people get worse despite therapeutic intervention (Crawford et al., 2016; Linden, 2013).

Is One Form of Psychotherapy Superior?

Given that the major types of psychotherapy use different assumptions and techniques, does one type of psychotherapy stand out as more effective than the others? In some cases, one type of psychotherapy *is* more effective than another in treating a particular problem (Barlow et al., 2013; Budd & Hughes, 2009). For example, cognitive, cognitive-behavioral, and behavior therapies tend to be more successful than insight-oriented therapies in helping people who are experiencing panic disorder, obsessive–compulsive disorder, phobias, and posttraumatic stress disorder (Clark et al., 2003; Craske & Barlow, 2008; Foa et al., 2013). Some have argued that cognitive-behavioral therapies (CBT) are "the gold standard in psychotherapy," observing that CBT has been researched more than any other psychotherapy; in head-to-head match-ups, CBT usually fares better than other therapies; and the ways in which CBT is said to work fit best with current research on the brain and behavior (David et al., 2018).

Others have pushed back against CBT as "the gold standard," pointing out researcher bias toward CBT, and calling for more research (Leichsenring & Steinert, 2017). And, when meta-analyses are used to assess the collective results of treatment outcome studies, a surprising but consistent finding emerges: *In general, there is little or no difference in the effectiveness of different psychotherapies.* Despite sometimes dramatic differences in psychotherapy techniques, all the standard psychotherapies have very similar success rates (Cooper, 2008; Luborsky et al., 2002). For example, one meta-analysis examined seven different types of psychotherapy for depression (Barth et al., 2013). All seven were more effective than a control group in which patients received no therapy, and the seven were fairly similar in their effectiveness in reducing symptoms of depression. More recent research suggests that some therapies work well across a wide range of psychological disorders (Schaeuffele et al., 2021).

One important qualification must be made at this point. In this chapter, we've devoted considerable time to explaining the major approaches to therapy. Although distinct, all of these psychotherapy approaches have in common the fact that they are *empirically supported treatments.* In other words, they are based on known psychological principles, have been subjected to controlled scientific trials, and have demonstrated their effectiveness in helping people with psychological problems (David & Montgomery, 2011).

In contrast, one ongoing issue in contemporary psychotherapy is the proliferation of *untested* psychotherapies (Barlow et al., 2013). The fact that there is little difference in outcome among the empirically supported therapies does *not* mean that any and every form of psychotherapy is equally effective (Dimidjian & Hollon, 2010; Herbert et al., 2000). Too often, untested therapy techniques are heavily marketed and promoted,

MYTH ▶ SCIENCE

Is it true that the different types of psychotherapy generally have similar results?

Spencer Grant/PhotoEdit

⌃ **Therapeutic Sensitivity to Cultural Differences** A therapist's sensitivity to a client's cultural values can affect the ability to form a good working relationship and, ultimately, the success of psychotherapy (Qureshi, 2020; Thompson et al., 2004). Thus, some clients prefer to see therapists who are from the same ethnic or cultural background, as is the case with the Black therapist and client shown here. In general, therapists have become more attuned to the important role played by culture in effective psychotherapy.

promising miraculous cures with little or no empirical research to back up their claims (Lazarus, 2000; Lilienfeld, 2007). The problem of untested treatments is particularly true in the growing but unregulated market for mental health technologies, such as mobile apps (Neary & Schueller, 2018).

Psychologist James Herbert and colleagues (2000) argue that before being put into widespread use, new therapies should provide empirically based answers to the following questions:

- Does the treatment work better than no treatment?
- Does the treatment work better than a placebo?
- Does the treatment work better than standard treatments?
- Does the treatment work through the processes that its proponents claim?

Often, "revolutionary" new therapies are developed, advertised, and marketed directly to the public—and to therapists—*before* controlled scientific studies of their effectiveness have been conducted (Lazarus, 2000). Many of the untested therapies are ineffective or are no more effective than established therapies (Lilienfeld, 2011; Lohr et al., 2003).

Of course, the goal of any psychological therapy is to help people in need. See **Table 15.7** for the basics of psychological first aid, guidance often used by people working with international and disaster relief organizations.

TABLE 15.7

Psychological First Aid

LOOK: It's important to determine...	
	... the general situation.
	... who needs help.
	... any risks.
	... any needs.
LISTEN: It's important to...	
	... ask people if they need help.
	... listen attentively.
	... avoid judgment.
	... stay calm.
	... ask what they need.
LINK: Help them...	
	... get the information they need.
	... connect with their social support system.
	... problem-solve.
	... find the specific services they need, such as professional mental health services.

People working with international and disaster relief organizations have long promoted psychological first aid (PFA), the cousin of the physical first aid that we all know (for example, bandages and CPR). For either version of first aid, the goal is to provide everyone, and not just trained emergency personnel, with the tools to help people in our communities. After all, there aren't always trained people available during emergencies. The need for PFA has only increased during the pandemic as so many more people have experienced trauma. "While it is not intended as a long-term solution, this method of care is valuable and timely during an emergency, such as the current COVID-19 pandemic" (Minihan et al., 2020). This table lays out the basics of psychological first aid based on guidance from the International Federation of Red Cross and Red Crescent Societies (2020), which emphasizes that much of this work can be done remotely (phone or online) during the pandemic or other situations during which in-person help is not possible. So, the next time you talk with a friend in distress, try these steps, but also consider helping them connect with professional help. For more information on psychotherapy, see the Psych for Your Life at the end of the chapter, which includes a section about finding a therapist.

CULTURE AND HUMAN BEHAVIOR

Cultural Values and Psychotherapy

The goals and techniques of many established approaches to psychotherapy tend to reflect European and North American cultural values (McGoldrick et al., 2005; Mutiso et al., 2014; T. B. Smith et al., 2011). Even viewing psychotherapy as an option is not universal. Writer Melody Moezzi, the U.S.-born child of Iranian immigrants, explained that "my people don't do psychotherapy. We have friends. We have families. We have pharmacies. Paying strangers to listen to our problems isn't our style" (2015). Moezzi eventually did seek therapy. In this box, we'll look at how European and North American cultural values can clash with the values of clients from other cultures, diminishing the effectiveness of psychotherapy.

A Focus on the Individual Versus the Group

In Western psychotherapy, the client is usually encouraged to become more assertive, more self-sufficient, and less dependent on others in making decisions. Problems are assumed to have an internal cause and are expected to be solved by the client alone. Therapy emphasizes meeting the client's individual needs, even if those needs conflict with the demands of significant others. In collectivistic cultures, however, the needs of the individual are much more strongly identified with the needs of the group to which they belong (Brewer & Chen, 2007; Pedersen et al., 2008; D. Sue & D. M. Sue, 2008; D. W. Sue & D. Sue, 2008).

For example, traditional American Indians are less likely than European Americans to believe that personal problems are due to a cause within the individual (Garrett, 2008). Instead, one person's problems may be seen as a problem for the entire community to resolve. Network therapy—which you learned about in the section on family, network, and couple therapy—is often used in American Indian communities (Dueck et al., 2018).

Latino cultures, too, emphasize interdependence over independence. In particular, they stress the value of *familismo*—the importance of the extended family network. Because the sense of family is so central to Latino culture, some psychologists recommend that members of the client's extended family, such as grandparents and in-laws, be actively involved in psychological treatment (Garza & Watts, 2010).

Many collectivistic Asian cultures also emphasize a respect for the needs of others (Lee & Mock, 2005). According to Japanese *Naikan therapy*, being self-absorbed is the surest path to psychological suffering. Thus, the goal of Naikan therapy is to replace the focus on the self with a sense of gratitude and obligation toward others. Rather than talking about how their own needs were not met by family members, the Naikan client is asked to meditate on how they have failed to meet the needs of others.

The Importance of Insight Versus Avoidance

Psychodynamic, humanistic, and cognitive therapies all stress the importance of insight or awareness of an individual's thoughts and feelings. But many cultures do *not* emphasize the importance of exploring painful thoughts and feelings in resolving psychological problems. For example, Asian cultures stress that mental health is enhanced by the avoidance of negative thinking. Hence, a depressed or anxious person in China and many other Asian countries would be encouraged to *avoid* focusing on upsetting thoughts (Kim & Park, 2008).

The Degree of Intimate Disclosure Between Therapist and Client

Many Western psychotherapies are based on the assumption that the clients will disclose their deepest feelings and most private thoughts to their therapists. But in some cultures, intimate details of one's personal life would never be discussed with a stranger. For example, a Vietnamese student vowed never to return to see a psychologist she had consulted about her struggles with depression. The counselor, she complained, was too "nosy" and asked too many personal questions. In many cultures, people are far more likely to turn to family members or friends than they are to mental health professionals (Leung & Boehnlein, 2005).

Recognizing the need for psychotherapists to become more culturally sensitive, the American Psychological Association (APA) recommends formal training in multicultural awareness for all psychologists. The APA (2017b) has also published extensive guidelines for psychologists who provide psychological help to culturally diverse populations. Interested students can download a copy of the APA guidelines at apa.org /about/policy/multicultural-guidelines

Lezlie Sterling/Tribune News Service/Newscom

∧ **Drumming Therapy** At the Sacramento Native American Health Center in California, several people of American Indian descent participate in a healing ritual that involves drumming on traditional instruments. For many Native Americans, healing practices involve the community.

eclecticism (ih-KLEK-tih-siz-um) The pragmatic and integrated use of techniques from different psychotherapies.

What Factors Contribute to Effective Psychotherapy?

How can we explain the fact that different forms of psychotherapy are basically equivalent in producing positive results? One possible explanation is that the factors that are crucial to producing improvement are present in *all* effective therapies. Researchers have identified a number of *common factors* that are related to a positive therapy outcome (Bjornsson, 2011; Laska et al., 2014; Wampold, 2015).

First and most important is the quality of the *therapeutic relationship* (Cooper, 2008; Norcross & Lambert, 2011; Norcross & Wampold, 2011). When psychotherapy is helpful, the therapist–client relationship is characterized by mutual respect, trust, hope, and common goals.

Second, certain *therapist characteristics* are associated with successful therapy. Helpful therapists have a caring attitude and the ability to listen empathically. They are genuinely committed to their clients' welfare (Aveline, 2005).

Effective therapists are also sensitive to the *cultural differences* that may exist between themselves and their clients (Qureshi, 2020; D. W. Sue & D. Sue, 2008). As described in the Culture and Human Behavior box, cultural differences can be a barrier to effective psychotherapy. Increasingly, training in cultural sensitivity and multicultural issues is being incorporated into psychological training programs (Qureshi, 2020; Sammons & Speight, 2008).

Martha Bernal (1931–2001), the Texas-born daughter of Mexican immigrants to the United States, was the first U.S. Latina psychologist and a vocal proponent of *multicultural training* for psychologists. *Melba Vasquez* (b. 1951), the first Latina president of the American Psychological Association (APA), said of Bernal that "she helped to advance a multicultural psychology—one that recognizes the importance of diversity in training, recruitment, and research" (2010). Bernal was an early adherent of behavioral principles, but she soon shifted her focus (Bernal et al., 1980). Bernal "was horrified to learn that over time, she had adopted racist ideas without her conscious awareness" (p. 363; Vasquez & Lopez, 2002). This realization led Bernal to turn her attention to promoting multicultural training, particularly the training of psychologists from marginalized ethnic and racial groups (Bernal & Castro, 1994; Quintana & Bernal, 1995; Vasquez & Lopez, 2002).

Bernal was also a leader in psychology professional organizations, roles that were an important part of her advocacy for multicultural training (Vasquez, 2010). Bernal served on the APA's Board of Ethnic Minority Affairs; in the National Latino/a Psychological Association; and on the Committee on Gay, Lesbian, and Bisexual Affairs. Her groundbreaking work has not always received the attention it warrants, but it lives on. Although she is not specifically cited in the current multicultural guidelines of the American Psychological Association, her imprint is evident in its ideas and values (Clauss-Ehlers et al., 2019; Sue, 2009).

Increasingly, a personalized approach to therapy is being facilitated by the movement of mental health professionals toward **eclecticism**—*the pragmatic and integrated use of techniques from different psychotherapies* (Hollanders, 2007; Lambert et al., 2004). (A very similar approach is called *integrative* psychotherapy.) The eclectic approach is built on the concept that common factors underlie most types of psychotherapy, so tailored combinations of techniques can be effective (Wachtel et al., 2020). Today, therapists identify themselves as eclectic more often than any other approach (Norcross et al., 2005; Lambert & Ogles, 2004). *Eclectic psychotherapists* might, for example, integrate insight-oriented techniques with specific behavioral techniques to help someone suffering from extreme shyness.

Biomedical Therapies

■ KEY THEME

The biomedical therapies are medical treatments for the symptoms of psychological disorders and include medication and electroconvulsive therapy.

⹀ KEY QUESTIONS

- What medications are used to treat the symptoms of schizophrenia, anxiety, bipolar disorder, and major depressive disorder, and how do they achieve their effects?

- What is electroconvulsive therapy, and what are its advantages and disadvantages?

Medical treatments for psychological disorders actually predate modern psychotherapy by hundreds of years. In past centuries, patients were whirled, soothed, drenched, restrained, and isolated—all in an attempt to alleviate symptoms of psychological disorders. Today, such "treatments" seem cruel, inhumane, and useless. Keep in mind, however, that these early treatments were based on the limited medical knowledge of the time. As you'll see in this section, some of the early efforts to treat psychological disorders did eventually evolve into treatments that are widely used today.

For the most part, it was not until the twentieth century that effective biomedical therapies were developed to treat the symptoms of psychological disorders. Today, the most common biomedical therapy is the use of **psychotropic medications**—*prescription drugs that alter mental functions, alleviate psychological symptoms, and are used to treat psychological disorders.* You can see how medications affect neurotransmitter functioning in the synapses between neurons in Figure 2.6 on page 49. Although often used alone, psychotropic medications are increasingly combined with psychotherapy (Cuijpers et al., 2020; Sudak, 2011).

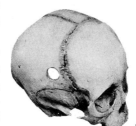

GRANGER - Historical Picture Archive

Bettmann/Getty Images

⌃ **Historical Treatments for Mental Illness** (Left) Found in Peru, this pre-Columbian skull shows the results of primitive surgery on the brain, called *trephining,* presumably as a treatment to allow evil spirits to leave the body. (Right) A "tranquilizing chair" was developed in the early 1800s to restrain and sedate unmanageable patients.

Antipsychotic Medications

For more than 2,000 years, traditional practitioners of medicine in India used an herb derived from the snakeroot plant to diminish the psychotic symptoms commonly associated with schizophrenia: hallucinations, delusions, and disordered thought processes (Bhatara et al., 1997). In the 1930s, Indian physicians discovered that the herb was also helpful in the treatment of high blood pressure. They developed a synthetic version of the herb's active ingredient, called *reserpine.* Reserpine was later used to treat schizophrenia.

During the 1950s French scientists began investigating the psychoactive properties of another drug, called *chlorpromazine.* Like reserpine, chlorpromazine diminished the psychotic symptoms commonly seen in schizophrenia. Therefore, reserpine and chlorpromazine were dubbed **antipsychotic medications**, *prescription drugs that are used to reduce psychotic symptoms; frequently used in the treatment of schizophrenia; also called neuroleptics.* Because chlorpromazine had fewer side effects than reserpine, it nudged out reserpine as the preferred medication for treating schizophrenia-related symptoms. Since then, chlorpromazine has been better known by its trade name, *Thorazine,* and is still used to treat psychotic symptoms.

How do these drugs diminish psychotic symptoms? Reserpine and chlorpromazine act differently on the brain, but both drugs reduce levels of the neurotransmitter called *dopamine.* Since their development, more than 30 other antipsychotic medications have been developed, all of which act on dopamine receptors in the brain (Abi-Dargham, 2004; Laruelle et al., 2003; Richtand et al., 2007).

The first antipsychotics effectively reduced the *positive symptoms* of schizophrenia—hallucinations, delusions, and disordered thinking (see the chapter on disorders). This therapeutic effect had a revolutionary impact on the number of people hospitalized for schizophrenia. Until the 1950s, patients with schizophrenia were thought to be incurable. These chronic patients formed the bulk of the population in the "back wards" of psychiatric hospitals. With the introduction of the antipsychotic medications, however, the number of patients in mental hospitals decreased dramatically in much of the world (see **Figure 15.5**). Patients in some parts of the world—including Venezuela since its economic crisis and parts

psychotropic medications (sy-ko-TRO-pick) Prescription drugs that alter mental functions, alleviate psychological symptoms, and are used to treat psychological disorders.

antipsychotic medications (an-tee-sy-KAHT-ick or an-ty-sy-KAHT-ick) Prescription drugs that are used to reduce psychotic symptoms; frequently used in the treatment of schizophrenia; also called *neuroleptics.*

FIGURE 15.5 Change in the Number of Patients Hospitalized for Psychological Disorders, 1946–1983 When the first antipsychotic drugs came into wide use in the late 1950s, the number of people hospitalized for psychological disorders began to drop dramatically (Julien, 2011). The numbers have remained relatively stable since then. More recent data suggest that there are just under 200,000 people in inpatient treatment for psychological disorders at any time (Lutterman et al., 2017). These numbers, however, may underestimate how many people actually need treatment. There was a shortage of inpatient beds during the pandemic (Rapoport, 2020).

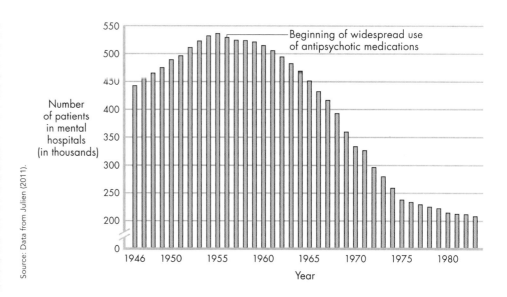

Source: Data from Julien (2011).

▲ **A Psychiatric Crisis** As Venezuela's economy collapsed, the country ran out of many common psychotropic medications, and when they were available, people often could not afford them (Krygier & Faiola, 2019). Accel and Gerardo Simeone were among the victims of this crisis. Both men have schizophrenia, and without antipsychotic medications, their symptoms, including severe auditory hallucinations, have returned. Many psychiatric institutions have released the patients they are now unable to treat. Like Accel and Gerardo, these patients often end up being cared for by their families. Here, the brothers share a meal with their parents, Mario and Evelin. Evelin has had to give up her job to care for them and told a reporter, "I am tired. This is too much sometimes" (Casey, 2016).

MERIDITH KOHUT/The New York Times/Redux

of West Africa—don't have regular access to antipsychotic medications (Krygier & Faiola, 2019). As a result, antiquated treatments, like chaining people who are psychotic, continue (Casey, 2016; Human Rights Watch, 2020c).

Drawbacks of Antipsychotic Medications Even though the early antipsychotic drugs allowed thousands of patients to be discharged from hospitals, these drugs had a number of drawbacks. First, they didn't actually *cure* schizophrenia. Psychotic symptoms often returned if a person stopped taking the medication. Second, the early antipsychotic medications were not very effective in eliminating *negative symptoms*—social withdrawal, apathy, and lack of emotional expressiveness. In some cases, the drugs even made negative symptoms worse. Third, the antipsychotics often produced unwanted side effects, such as dry mouth, weight gain, constipation, sleepiness, and poor concentration (Stahl, 2009).

Fourth, the fact that the early antipsychotics *globally* altered brain levels of dopamine turned out to be a double-edged sword. Dopamine pathways in the brain are involved not only in psychotic symptoms but also in typical motor movements. Consequently, the early antipsychotic medications could produce motor-related side effects—muscle tremors, rigid movements, and a masklike facial expression. Even more disturbing, the long-term use of antipsychotic medications causes a small percentage of people to develop a potentially irreversible motor disorder called *tardive dyskinesia*. Tardive dyskinesia is characterized by severe, uncontrollable facial tics and grimaces.

Closely tied to the various side effects of the first antipsychotic drugs is a fifth problem: the "revolving door" pattern of hospitalization, discharge, and rehospitalization. People with schizophrenia, once stabilized by antipsychotic medication, were released from hospitals into the community. But because of either the medication's unpleasant side effects or inadequate medical follow-up, or both, many patients eventually stopped taking the medication. When psychotic symptoms returned, the patients were rehospitalized.

The Atypical Antipsychotics Beginning around 1990, a second generation of antipsychotic drugs began to be introduced. **Atypical antipsychotic medications** are *newer antipsychotic medications that block dopamine receptors in brain regions associated with psychotic symptoms rather than more globally throughout the brain, decreasing side effects*. These drugs affect brain levels of dopamine and *serotonin*. The atypical antipsychotics have several advantages over the older antipsychotic drugs (Advokat et al., 2019). First, the new drugs are less likely to cause movement-related side effects. That's because they do not block dopamine receptors in the movement areas of the brain. Instead, they more selectively target dopamine receptors in brain areas associated with psychotic symptoms. The atypical antipsychotics are also much more effective in treating the negative symptoms of schizophrenia (Woo et al., 2009).

The atypical antipsychotic medications sparked considerable hope for better therapeutic effects, fewer adverse reactions, and greater patient compliance. Although they were less likely to cause movement-related side effects, the second-generation antipsychotics caused some of the same side effects as the first-generation antipsychotics, including weight gain and cardiac problems. Equally important, large-scale studies have demonstrated that the newer antipsychotic medications do *not* produce greater improvements than the older ones (Crossley et al., 2010). The effectiveness of antipsychotics in general is enhanced when patients also have access to individual psychotherapy, family therapy, and support with respect to pursuing education and employment (Kane et al., 2015).

Antianxiety Medications

Anxiety that is intense and persistent can be disabling, interfering with a person's ability to eat, sleep, and function. **Antianxiety medications** are *prescription drugs that are used to alleviate the symptoms of anxiety.* They are prescribed to help people deal with the problems and symptoms associated with pathological anxiety.

The best-known antianxiety drugs are the *benzodiazepines,* which include the trade-name drugs *Valium* and *Xanax.* These antianxiety medications calm jittery feelings, relax the muscles, and promote sleep. In general, the benzodiazepines produce their effects by increasing the level of *GABA,* a neurotransmitter that inhibits the transmission of nerve impulses in the brain and slows brain activity (see the chapter on neuroscience).

Taken for a week or two, and in therapeutic doses, the benzodiazepines can effectively reduce anxiety levels. However, the benzodiazepines have several potentially dangerous side effects. First, they can reduce coordination, alertness, and reaction time. Second, their effects can be intensified when they are combined with alcohol and many other drugs, including over-the-counter antihistamines. Such a combination can produce severe drug intoxication and even death.

Third, the benzodiazepines can be physically addictive if taken in large quantities or over a long period of time. Because of their addictive potential, the benzodiazepines are less widely prescribed today, although some experts believe they are still overprescribed (Lader, 2008).

An antianxiety drug, buspirone, has fewer side effects. Buspirone, often prescribed for anxiety along with an antidepressant, is not a benzodiazepine, and it does not affect the neurotransmitter GABA. It is believed to affect brain dopamine and serotonin levels (Davidson et al., 2009). Buspirone relieves anxiety while allowing the individual to maintain normal alertness. And buspirone seems to have a very low risk of dependency and physical addiction.

However, buspirone has one major drawback: It must be taken for two to three *weeks* before anxiety is reduced. While this decreases buspirone's potential for abuse, it also decreases its effectiveness for treating acute anxiety.

A newer medication that has been explored as a treatment for anxiety disorders and posttraumatic stress disorder is MDMA, short for methylenedioxymethamphetamine (Baldwin et al., 2014 ; Chi & Gold, 2020). MDMA is often called "ecstasy" when used as a recreational drug. There is growing evidence that a few doses of MDMA, prescribed and monitored by a physician, can improve the outcome for people undergoing psychotherapy for these and other disorders (Gill et al., 2020; Mitchell et al., 2021; Mithoefer et al., 2016). MDMA use can lead to dangerous or unpleasant side effects and has the potential for abuse (Chi & Gold, 2020). It is typically taken only a few times, however, diminishing the likelihood that this will occur (Meyer, 2013; Oehen et al., 2013). Despite the availability of newer treatment options for immediate, short-term relief from anxiety, the benzodiazepines are still regarded as the most effective medications currently available.

atypical antipsychotic medications Newer antipsychotic medications that block dopamine receptors in brain regions associated with psychotic symptoms rather than more globally throughout the brain, decreasing side effects.

antianxiety medications Prescription drugs that are used to alleviate the symptoms of anxiety.

▲ **Lady Gaga: "I'm Not Ashamed"** Flamboyant performing artist Lady Gaga has been outspoken about her battles with mental illness, which include eating disorders, posttraumatic stress disorder, and depression. Lady Gaga told a reporter, "I'm not ashamed to talk about it." She said that she wanted her fans to "stop acting like we should be embarrassed" to talk about mental health and seeking treatment (Blistein, 2017; CTV News, 2013). She also has talked about taking antipsychotic medication, a common treatment for people with a variety of psychological disorders—not just psychotic disorders, but also bipolar disorder, depression, posttraumatic stress disorder, and obsessive compulsive disorder. Although antipsychotic medications are commonly prescribed, their use remains stigmatized, more so than most other treatments. Lady Gaga's openness is valuable in combating stigma. She told a reporter that she experienced an enormous benefit from taking antipsychotic medication. She said that without this treatment, she would "spiral very frequently." She added, "Medicine really helped me. A lot of people are afraid of medicine for their brains to help them. I really want to erase the stigma around this" (López, 2020)

lithium A naturally occurring substance that is used in the treatment of bipolar disorder.

antidepressant medications Prescription drugs that are used to reduce the symptoms associated with major depressive disorder.

selective serotonin reuptake inhibitors (SSRIs) Class of antidepressant medications that increase the availability of serotonin in the brain and cause fewer side effects than earlier antidepressants

Lithium

In the chapter on psychological disorders, we described *bipolar disorder*, previously known as *manic depression*. The medication most commonly used to treat bipolar disorder is **lithium**, *a naturally occurring substance that is used in the treatment of bipolar disorder*. Lithium counteracts manic symptoms, and to a lesser degree depressive symptoms (Malhi et al., 2017; Nivoli et al., 2012). Its effectiveness in treating bipolar disorder has been well established since the 1960s (Preston et al., 2008).

As a treatment for bipolar disorder, lithium can prevent acute manic episodes over the course of a week or two. Once an acute manic episode is under control, the long-term use of lithium can help prevent relapses into either mania or major depressive disorder. The majority of patients with bipolar disorder respond well to lithium therapy. However, some people on lithium therapy experience relapses (Severus et al., 2009).

Like all other medications, lithium has potential side effects. If the lithium level is too low, manic symptoms persist. If it is too high, lithium poisoning may occur, with symptoms such as vomiting, muscle weakness, and reduced muscle coordination. Consequently, the patient's lithium blood level must be carefully monitored.

Bipolar disorder can also be treated with an anticonvulsant medicine called *Depakote*. Originally used to prevent epileptic seizures, Depakote seems to be especially helpful in treating those who rapidly cycle through bouts of bipolar disorder several times a year. Regardless of whether lithium or Depakote is used to treat someone with bipolar disorder, additional treatment with individual or family therapy tends to increase the likelihood that a patient will take their medication as prescribed and experience reduced symptoms (Oud et al., 2016).

Antidepressant Medications

The **antidepressant medications** are *prescription drugs that are used to reduce the symptoms associated with major depressive disorder*. They counteract the classic symptoms of major depressive disorder—hopelessness, guilt, difficulty concentrating, and disruptions in sleep, energy, appetite, and sexual desire. The first generation of antidepressants consists of two classes of drugs, called *tricyclics* and *MAO inhibitors*. Tricyclics and MAO inhibitors affect multiple neurotransmitter pathways in the brain. Evidence suggests that these medications alleviate major depressive disorder by increasing the availability of two key brain neurotransmitters, *norepinephrine* and *serotonin*. However, it can take up to six *weeks* before depressive symptoms begin to lift (Thase & Denko, 2008).

Tricyclics and MAO inhibitors can be effective in reducing depressive symptoms, but they can also produce numerous side effects (Holsboer, 2009). Tricyclics can cause weight gain, dizziness, dry mouth and eyes, and sedation. And, because tricyclics affect the cardiovascular system, an overdose can be fatal. As for the MAO inhibitors, they can interact with a chemical found in many foods, including cheese, smoked meats, and red wine. Eating or drinking these while taking an MAO inhibitor can result in dangerously high blood pressure, leading to stroke or even death.

The search for antidepressants with fewer side effects led to the development of the second generation of antidepressants, which include *trazodone* and *bupropion*, trade name *Wellbutrin*. Although chemically different from the tricyclics, the second-generation antidepressants were generally no more effective than the first-generation ones, and they turned out to have many of the same side effects.

In 1987, the picture changed dramatically with the introduction of a third group of antidepressants. **Selective serotonin reuptake inhibitors**, abbreviated **SSRIs**, are a *class of antidepressant medications that increase the availability of serotonin in the brain and cause fewer side effects than earlier antidepressants*. Compared with the earlier antidepressants, the new antidepressants act much more selectively in targeting specific serotonin pathways in the brain. The first SSRI to be released was *fluoxetine*, which is better known by its trade name, *Prozac*. Prozac was quickly followed by its chemical cousins, *Zoloft* and *Paxil*.

Michael Hickey/Getty Images

⌃ **A Ragin' Violent Storm** Kid Cudi has written on social media about his decision to seek professional treatment for depression: "If I didn't come [for treatment], I would've done something to myself. . . . There's a ragin' violent storm inside of my heart at all times." Cudi is open about his treatment and has rapped about taking the SSRI Lexapro. His openness has led to a hashtag—#YouGoodMan—aimed at reducing the stigma associated with depression among Black people (Harris, 2016). Cudi explains, "It took me a while to get to this place of commitment, to say I'm gonna get through this. To know that we can take our pain and turn it into something" (Murdock, 2020).

Prozac was specifically designed to alleviate depressive symptoms with fewer side effects than earlier antidepressants. It achieved that goal with considerable success. Although no more effective than tricyclics or MAO inhibitors, Prozac and the other SSRI antidepressants tend to produce fewer, and milder, side effects. But no medication is risk-free. Among Prozac's potential side effects are headaches, nervousness, difficulty sleeping, loss of appetite, and sexual dysfunction (Bresee et al., 2009).

One promising new treatment is an experimental drug called ketamine (Kryst et al., 2020; Loo, 2018; Singh et al., 2017). As discussed in the chapter on consciousness, ketamine is used in high doses as an anesthetic and called Special K when sold as a street drug. In one study, 71 percent of severely depressed patients who received intravenous ketamine saw a decrease in depressive symptoms within just one day, as compared with 0 percent of those taking placebo (Zarate et al., 2006). There were some serious side effects from ketamine, such as hallucinations. Although none lasted more than two hours, the side effects have spurred researchers to search for safer alternatives that act in similar ways to ketamine (Gerhard et al., 2016; Malinow, 2016; Zanos et al., 2016).

Despite its impressive effectiveness, ketamine is likely to be used only in emergency situations, in large part because its effects tend to last no more than a week. However, ketamine's fast response time means that seriously depressed people who visit the ER might be able to forgo inpatient treatment. During the time it takes for ketamine to wear off, more traditional antidepressants and psychotherapy might have time to start working. There also is evidence that the use of ketamine reduces suicide rates (DiazGranados et al., 2010).

Antidepressants are often used in the treatment of disorders other than depression, sometimes in combination with other drugs. For example, the SSRIs are commonly prescribed to treat anxiety disorders, obsessive–compulsive disorder, and eating disorders (Davidson et al., 2009; Lissemore et al., 2014; Mitchell et al., 2013). Wellbutrin is also used to treat a number of other disorders, including anxiety, obesity, and adult attention-deficit/hyperactivity disorder (Ahima, 2011; K.-U. Lee et al., 2009). Under the name Zyban, Wellbutrin is also prescribed to help people stop smoking.

Many researchers believe that genetic differences, and other biological differences including in patterns of brain connectivity, may explain why people respond so differently to antidepressants and other psychotropic medications (Alhajji & Nemeroff, 2015; Crisafulli et al., 2011). The new field of *pharmacogenetics* is the study of how genes influence an individual's response to drugs (Corponi et al., 2018; Nurnberger, 2009). As this field advances, it may help overcome the trial-and-error nature of prescribing not only antidepressants but other psychotropic medications as well.

How do antidepressants and psychotherapy compare in their effectiveness? Several large-scale studies have found that both cognitive therapy and interpersonal therapy are just as effective as antidepressant medication in producing remission from depressive symptoms (Amick et al., 2015; Imel et al., 2008). Brain imaging studies are just beginning to show how such treatments might change brain activity—a topic that we showcase in the Focus on Neuroscience box on the next page. Despite these findings, more people with depression are treated with antidepressants than with psychotherapy (Marcus & Olfson, 2010).

Electroconvulsive Therapy

As we have just seen, millions of prescriptions are written for antidepressant medications every year. In contrast, a much smaller number of patients receive **electroconvulsive therapy**, or **ECT**, a *biomedical therapy used primarily in the treatment of major depressive disorder that involves electrically inducing a brief brain seizure; also called electroshock therapy.* ECT is a relatively simple and quick medical procedure, usually performed in a hospital. The patient lies on a table. Electrodes are placed on one or both of the patient's temples, and the patient is given a short-term, light anesthetic and muscle-relaxing drugs.

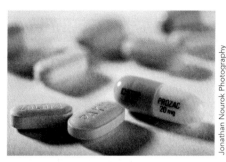

^ **The Most Commonly Prescribed Class of Medication** The number of people treated with antidepressant medication more than doubled from 13 million people in 1996 to 27 million people in 2005 (Olfson & Marcus, 2009). That number climbed to 37 million by 2019 (Read & Davies, 2019). Partially fueling the increase is the rise in the number of prescriptions written by physicians who do *not* give the patient a psychiatric diagnosis (Mojtabai & Olfson, 2011).

THINK LIKE A **SCIENTIST**

How would a "party drug" end up being prescribed for depression? Go to Achieve Resources to **Think Like a Scientist** about **Ketamine**.

Achieve

electroconvulsive therapy (ECT) Biomedical therapy used primarily in the treatment of major depressive disorder that involves electrically inducing a brief brain seizure; also called *electroshock therapy.*

Psychotherapy and the Brain

Major depressive disorder is characterized by a variety of physical symptoms and includes changes in brain activity (Abler et al., 2007; Kempton et al., 2011). Antidepressants are assumed to work by changing brain chemistry and activity. Does psychotherapy have the same effect?

To address this question, fMRI scans were done on 27 people with major depressive disorder and compared to a matched group of 25 participants who were *not* depressed (Siegle et al., 2007). Compared with the nondepressed adults, the depressed individuals showed altered brain activity following an emotional task and a cognitive task. These tasks were chosen because major depressive disorder tends to affect both people's emotional responses and their thought processes.

For the emotional task, both groups were asked to briefly view negative emotional words that they perceived to be relevant for them personally. The depressed people showed increased activity in the *amygdala*. The control group, made up of people who were not depressed, did not exhibit activity in the amygdala following this task. In addition, after completing a cognitive task in which they were asked to mentally sort a short list of numbers, depressed people showed less activity in the *prefrontal cortex* than did those in the control group.

A sample of nine of the depressed people in this study then completed 14 weeks of cognitive therapy (DeRubeis et al., 2008). After treatment, the brain activity of the people treated for depression resembled that of the control group. The posttreatment brain scan shown here displays the activity in the amygdala in response to viewing the negative emotional word "ugly" for people in the control group or for people treated for depression. The graph highlights the differences among these two groups and a third group, people who have not yet been treated for depression. People who do not suffer from depression are indicated in green; people with depression who have been treated with cognitive therapy are indicated in purple; and people with depression who have not been treated are indicated in dark red. There is increased brain activation only among the third group, the depressed people before treatment.

MYTH ▶ SCIENCE

Is it true that, for some disorders, psychotherapy and medications lead to similar changes in brain activity?

Interestingly, the changes in brain activation that result from psychotherapy are similar to changes that result from medications. For example, in a study of people with major depressive disorder, PET scans revealed that patients who took the antidepressant Paxil and patients who completed interpersonal therapy (discussed earlier in this chapter) showed a trend toward more typical brain functioning (Brody et al., 2001). Activity declined significantly in brain regions that had shown unusually high activity before treatment began.

As these findings emphasize, psychotherapy—and not just antidepressant medication—affects brain chemistry and functioning. Such effects are not limited to depression. Similar changes toward a more typical pattern of brain functioning have also been found in people with panic disorder, posttraumatic stress disorder, obsessive–compulsive disorder, phobias, and other anxiety disorders after psychotherapy treatment (Barsaglini et al., 2014; Karlsson, 2011; Straube et al., 2006).

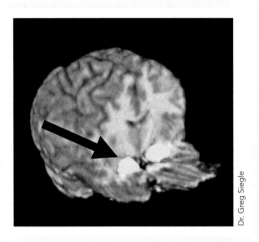

Dr. Greg Siegle

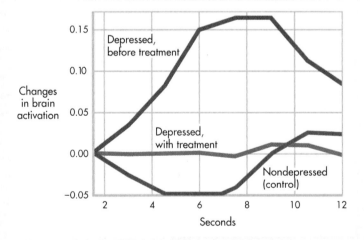

Changes in brain activation — Seconds

Depressed, before treatment
Depressed, with treatment
Nondepressed (control)

While the patient is unconscious, a split-second burst of electricity induces a brief seizure. After the anesthesia wears off and the patient wakes up, confusion and disorientation may be present for a few hours. To treat major depressive disorder, the patient typically receives two to three treatments per week for two to seven weeks, with less frequent follow-up treatments for several additional months (Fink, 2009; van Dierman et al., 2018).

In the short term, ECT is a very effective treatment for severe cases of major depressive disorder: About 80 percent of patients improve (Rasmussen, 2009). ECT also relieves the symptoms of depression very quickly, typically within days. Author Donald Antrim once described his experience with ECT as "the color came back on" (Sullivan, 2014). And as the symptoms of depression decrease, ECT patients' quality of life tends to increase to a level similar to that in people without depression (McCall et al., 2013).

Typically, ECT is used only after other forms of treatment, including psychotherapy and medication, have failed, especially when depressive symptoms are severe. For some people, such as elderly individuals, ECT may be less dangerous than antidepressant drugs. In general, the complication rate from ECT is very low.

Nevertheless, inducing a brain seizure is not a matter to be taken lightly. ECT has potential dangers. Serious cognitive impairments can occur, such as extensive amnesia and disturbances in language and verbal abilities. However, fears that ECT might produce brain damage have not been confirmed by research (Eschweiler et al., 2007; McDonald et al., 2009).

Perhaps ECT's biggest drawback is that its antidepressive effects can be short-lived. Relapses within four months are relatively common (Glass, 2001). About half the patients treated for major depressive disorder experience a relapse within six months. Today, patients are often treated with long-term antidepressant medication following ECT, which reduces the relapse rate (McCall et al., 2011). In severe, recurrent cases of major depressive disorder, ECT may also be periodically readministered to prevent the return of depressive symptoms.

At this point, you may be wondering why ECT is not in wider use. The reason is that ECT is considered controversial (Dukart et al., 2014; Shorter, 2009). Not everyone agrees that ECT is either safe or effective. Nevertheless, ECT is now available in most major metropolitan areas in the United States (Shorter, 2009).

How does ECT work? Despite many decades of research, it's still not known exactly why electrically inducing a convulsion relieves the symptoms of depression (Michael, 2009). One theory is that ECT seizures may somehow "reboot" the brain by depleting and then replacing neurotransmitters (Swartz, 2009).

Some new, experimental treatments suggest that those seizures may not actually be necessary. That is, it may be possible to provide lower levels of electrical current to the brain than traditional ECT delivers and still reduce severe symptoms of depression and other mental illnesses. For example, *transcranial direct current stimulation (tDCS)* is similar to ECT, but uses a small fraction of the electricity (Brunoni et al., 2012; Shiozawa et al., 2014). Another, related treatment is *transcranial magnetic stimulation (TMS)*, which involves stimulation of certain regions of the brain with magnetic pulses of various frequencies. Unlike ECT, both tDCS and TMS require no anesthetic, induce no seizures, and can be conducted in a private doctor's office rather than a hospital (Dell'Osso & Altamura, 2014; Rosenberg & Dannon, 2009).

Yet another experimental treatment, *vagus nerve stimulation (VNS)*, involves the surgical implantation of a device about the size of a pacemaker into the left chest wall. The device provides brief, intermittent electrical stimulation to the left vagus nerve, which runs through the neck and connects to the brain stem (Fang et al., 2016; McClintock et al., 2009). Finally, *deep brain stimulation (DBS)* utilizes electrodes surgically implanted in the brain and a battery-powered neurostimulator surgically implanted in the chest. Wires under the skin connect the two implants, and the neurostimulator sends electrical signals to the brain (Fink, 2009; Schläpfer & Bewernick, 2009).

Keep in mind that tDCS, TMS, VNS, and DBS are still experimental, and some of the research findings are mixed (Papageorgiou et al., 2017). And like ECT, the specific mechanisms by which they may work are not entirely clear. Still, researchers are hopeful that these techniques will provide additional viable treatment options for people suffering from severe psychological symptoms (McDonald et al., 2009; Nguyen & Gordon, 2015).

MYTH ◄ SCIENCE

Is it true that electroconvulsive therapy (ECT), once called "shock therapy," causes permanent brain damage and memory loss?

CRITICAL THINKING

Do Antidepressants Work Better Than Placebos?

Are antidepressants just fancy placebos? Consider this statement by psychologist Irving Kirsch on a 2012 episode of the TV news show *60 Minutes*: "The difference between the effect of the placebo and the effect of an antidepressant is minimal for most people."

Kirsch's surprising statement is based on meta-analyses (Fournier et al., 2010; Kirsch et al., 2008) that included all studies, published and unpublished, that had been submitted to the U.S. Food and Drug Administration during the process of approval for new antidepressants.

Kirsch and his colleagues found that most patients improved with *either* antidepressants or placebos (see graph on next page). Antidepressants were found to work better than placebos for some patients—but only those with very high levels of depression, the area shown in blue. Except in that area, the difference between the lines could have simply occurred by chance. Overall, according to Kirsch and his colleagues, about 80 percent of the improvement from antidepressants seems to be due to a placebo effect. And other researchers have reported similar findings (Khan & Brown, 2015).

The placebo effect has been well documented and is not limited to psychological disorders. Placebos have been demonstrated to lead to improvements in a range of health problems, including the management of pain and the treatment of symptoms related to the gastrointestinal, endocrine, cardiovascular, respiratory, and immune systems (Atlas & Wager, 2014; Price et al., 2008). What causes the placebo effect? It is most likely a combination of patients' expectations that a pill will help combined with the benefits of receiving treatment in a supportive environment (Furukuwa et al., 2016; Rutherford et al., 2014).

You may now be thinking that the placebo effect means that any improvements are just imaginary. But as described in the chapter on stress and health, brain imaging shows that placebos lead to real biological changes (Meissner et al., 2011). In response to a placebo, patients with Parkinson's disease experience increased dopamine activation, pain patients saw less neural activity in the parts of the brain associated with pain, and depressed patients experienced metabolic increases in the same parts of the brain that respond to antidepressants (Price et al., 2008). And, these improvements tend to come without the side effects and potentially high costs of "real" medication.

Kirsch (2014a) argues that we should question whether it's worth the risk of giving a "real" drug when a placebo is just as effective for some people. But this may be a hard sell to physicians and patients who believe that antidepressants are the most effective treatment for depression. Other researchers view the pharmaceutical industry, which has immense resources, as contributing to exaggerated reports of the effects of medications (Cuijpers et al., 2010). Pharmaceutical companies have billions of dollars at stake in convincing physicians and patients that their medications are effective, and they spend more than $25 billion each year just in the United States marketing their drugs (Kornfield et al., 2013).

MYTH ◄ SCIENCE

Is it true that antidepressants are a much more effective treatment than placebos for the vast majority of cases of depression?

While acknowledging concerns about the influence of the pharmaceutical industry, other researchers have found that antidepressants are superior to placebos. Using different statistical methods, several researchers identified a subset of about 20 percent of patients who benefited from antidepressants over placebos at all levels of depression severity (Horder et al., 2011; Thase et al., 2011). But even these researchers don't entirely dispute Kirsch's findings.

Closing Thoughts

As you've seen throughout this chapter, a wide range of therapies is available to help people who are troubled by psychological symptoms and disorders. Like our friend Marcia, whose story we told in the Prologue, many people benefit psychologically from psychotherapy. As the first part of the chapter showed, psychotherapy can help people by providing insight, developing more effective behaviors and coping strategies, and changing thought patterns.

The biomedical therapies, discussed in the second part of the chapter, can also help people with psychological problems. This was also true in Marcia's case, when she reluctantly agreed to try an antidepressant medication. For almost a year, Marcia took a low dose of one of the SSRI antidepressant medications. It helped in the short term, lessening the feelings of depression and anxiety and giving her time to work through various issues in therapy and develop greater psychological resilience. Today, people are increasingly being helped by a combination of psychotherapy and one of the psychotropic medications.

As our discussion of the effectiveness of psychotherapy has shown, characteristics of both the therapist and the client are important to the success of psychotherapy. In the Psych for Your Life section at the end of this chapter, we describe the attitudes that should be brought to the therapeutic relationship, discuss some general ground rules of psychotherapy, and dispel some common misunderstandings.

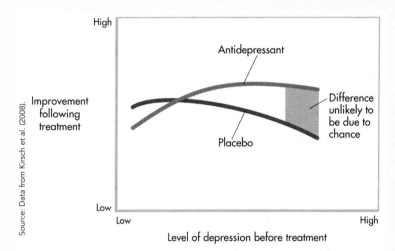

Source: Data from Kirsch et al. (2008).

▲ **Placebo Versus Antidepressant** This graph shows improvement for depressed people with varying starting levels of depression—from low depression on the left to high depression on the right. The green line shows improvement for depressed people taking antidepressant medication. The red line shows improvement for depressed people taking placebos. Antidepressants did produce greater improvement for some people, but these differences were only substantial enough to be considered "real" in people with the highest levels of initial depression (area indicated by blue shading).

As more is known about the effects of placebos, there is more discussion about how to harness their power. For example, patients who observe others improve after taking a medication often experience greater improvement themselves, likely because the expectation that the medication will work is enhanced (Faasse & Petrie, 2016). And researchers also suggest that clinicians should receive training on ethical ways to openly and successfully prescribe placebos by educating patients about their effectiveness (Brody & Miller, 2011). In the past, clinicians believed that successful treatment with placebos required that the patients believe the placebo was real, but some now question this premise. One study on irritable bowel syndrome (IBS) observed improvement in patients even after they were told they were receiving "placebo pills made of an inert substance, like sugar pills, that have been shown in clinical studies to produce significant improvement in IBS symptoms through mind–body self-healing processes" (Kaptchuk et al., 2010).

Research on the placebo effect continues to accumulate. However, despite Kirsch's argument, it's important to remember that many people have been and continue to be helped by antidepressant medication. Other treatment options, such as psychotherapy, may be unavailable. So, if antidepressants are helping you, you should continue to take them as directed by your physician. It can be dangerous to stop taking antidepressant medications without guidance from a physician.

CRITICAL THINKING QUESTIONS

- What is the ethical problem with giving a patient a placebo and saying it is an antidepressant?
- Why might placebos work even if people know they've been given a placebo?
- Why might simply giving a patient a placebo openly not work without additional education?

 PSYCH FOR YOUR LIFE

What to Expect in Psychotherapy

The cornerstone of psychotherapy is the relationship between the therapist and the person seeking help. But the therapy relationship is different from all other close relationships. On one hand, the therapist–client relationship is characterized by intimacy and the disclosure of very private, personal experiences. On the other hand, there are distinct boundaries to the therapist–client relationship. To a therapy client, especially one who is undertaking psychotherapy for the first time, the therapy relationship may sometimes seem confusing and contradictory.

The following guidelines should help you understand the special nature of the therapy relationship and develop realistic expectations about the process of psychotherapy.

1. Find a competent, qualified psychotherapist.

Where should you go for help? Most universities have a student counseling center or health clinic where you can ask to see a counselor or request a referral to a qualified therapist. You can also ask family members, friends, your family doctor, or a religious leader for suggestions.

If possible, learn more about the therapist before your first visit (APA Help Center, 2021; apa.org/helpcenter). What are their qualifications? Do they have experience with treating problems like yours? What approach do they take to treatment? Is the approach evidence-based? If you still have questions, you can do your own research. The U.S. government's Substance Abuse and Mental Health Services Administration (SAMHSA) publishes a well-vetted compilation of resources on evidence-based treatments: samhsa.gov/resource-search/ebp

Along with professional background, personal qualities are also important. When psychotherapists were asked how they chose their own therapists, openness, warmth, and caring were among the top criteria (Nordal, 2010).

Perhaps most important, you should feel comfortable with your therapist. Many psychotherapists offer a free initial consultation. So if you don't feel comfortable with the first psychotherapist you meet, don't hesitate to try out a couple of therapists before making your decision (Amada, 2011).

2. Strengthen your commitment to change.

Therapy is not about maintaining the status quo. It is about making changes in terms of how you think, feel, act, and respond. For many people, the idea of change produces mixed feelings. You can increase the likelihood of achieving your goals in therapy by thinking about the reasons you want to change and reminding yourself of your commitment to change (Hettema et al., 2005; Miller & Rose, 2009).

3. Therapy is a collaborative effort.

Don't expect your therapist to do all the work for you. Therapy is a two-way street (APA Help Center, 2012). If you are going to benefit from psychotherapy, you must actively participate in the therapeutic process. Often, therapy requires effort not only during the therapy sessions but also *outside* them. Many therapists assign "homework" to be completed between sessions. You may be asked to keep a diary of your thoughts and behaviors, read assigned material, rehearse skills that you've learned in therapy, and so forth.

4. Don't expect your therapist to make decisions for you.

One of the most common misunderstandings about psychotherapy is that your therapist is going to tell you how to run your life. Not so. Your therapist won't make your decisions for you, but they *will* help you explore your feelings about important decisions—including ambivalence or fear. Some people find this frustrating because they want the therapist to tell them what to do. But if your therapist made decisions for you, it would only foster dependency and undermine your ability to be responsible for your own life (Amada, 2011).

5. Expect therapy to challenge how you think and act.

As you confront issues that you've never discussed before or even admitted to yourself, you may find therapy very anxiety-provoking. Moments of psychological discomfort are a normal, even expected, part of the therapy process.

Think of therapy as a psychological magnifying glass. Therapy tends to magnify both your strengths and your weaknesses. Such intense self-scrutiny is not always flattering. Examining how you habitually deal with failure and success, conflict and resolution, and disappointment and joy can be disturbing. You may have to acknowledge your own immature, maladaptive, or destructive behavior patterns. Although it can be painful, becoming aware that changes are needed is a necessary step toward developing healthier forms of thinking and behavior.

6. Your therapist is not a substitute friend.

Unlike friendship, which is characterized by a mutual give-and-take, psychotherapy is focused solely on *you*. Rather than thinking of your therapist as a friend, think of them as an expert consultant—someone you've hired to help you deal better with your problems. The fact that your therapist is not socially or personally involved with you allows them to respond objectively and honestly. Part of what allows you to trust your therapist and "open up" emotionally is the knowledge that your therapist is ethically and legally bound to safeguard the confidentiality of what you say.

▲ **Active Minds** With more than 400 chapters on U.S. campuses, members of the student organization Active Minds (activeminds.org) promote awareness of mental health, work to reduce stigma, and encourage their fellow students to seek treatment. Perhaps there's a chapter on your campus. Here, University of Pennsylvania student Kathryn DeWitt talks with members of her Active Minds chapter about her own experiences with depression.

MARK MAKELA/The New York Times/Redux

7. Therapeutic intimacy does not include sexual intimacy.

It's common for clients to have strong feelings of affection, love, and even sexual attraction toward their therapists (Martin et al., 2011; Pope & Tabachnick, 1993). After all, the most effective therapists tend to be warm, empathic people who are genuinely caring and supportive (Beutler et al., 2004). However, *it is never ethical or appropriate for a therapist to have any form of sexual contact with a client.* There are *no* exceptions to that statement. Sexual contact between a therapist and a client violates the ethical standards of *all* mental health professionals. A psychotherapist who engages in sexual behavior with a client risks losing their license to practice psychotherapy.

Rather than exploiting a client's feelings of sexual attraction, an ethical therapist will help the client understand and work through such feelings. Therapy should ultimately help you develop closer, more loving relationships with other people—but *not* with your therapist.

MYTH ▶ SCIENCE

Is it true that it is never ethical for therapists to date clients?

8. Don't expect change to happen overnight.

Change occurs in psychotherapy at different rates for different people. How quickly change occurs depends on many factors, such as the seriousness of your problems, the degree to which you are psychologically ready to make needed changes, and the therapist's skill in helping you implement those changes. As a general rule, most people make significant progress in a few months of weekly therapy sessions (Harnett et al., 2010). You can help create the climate for change by choosing a therapist you feel comfortable working with and by genuinely investing yourself in the therapy process.

🔲 CHAPTER REVIEW

Therapies

 Achieve

Achieve, Macmillan Learning's online study platform, features the full e-book of *Discovering Psychology,* the **LearningCurve** adaptive quizzing system, videos, and a variety of activities to boost your learning. Visit **Achieve** at macmillanlearning.com.

KEY PEOPLE

Carolyn Attneave, p. 531	Martha Bernal, p. 538	Sigmund Freud, p. 515	Carl Rogers, p. 518
Aaron T. Beck, p. 526	Albert Ellis, p. 525	Mary Cover Jones, p. 520	

KEY TERMS

psychotherapy, p. 514	interpersonal therapy (IPT), p. 517	rational-emotive behavior therapy (REBT), p. 525	antipsychotic medications, p. 539
biomedical therapies, p. 514	client-centered therapy, p. 518	cognitive therapy (CT), p. 526	atypical antipsychotic medications, p. 540
psychoanalysis (in psychotherapy), p. 515	behavior therapy, p. 519	cognitive-behavioral therapy (CBT), p. 528	antianxiety medications, p. 541
free association, p. 516	counterconditioning, p. 520	group therapy, p. 530	lithium, p. 542
resistance, p. 516	exposure therapy, p. 520	family therapy, p. 531	antidepressant medications, p. 542
interpretation, p. 516	systematic desensitization, p. 520	eclecticism, p. 538	selective serotonin reuptake inhibitors (SSRIs), p. 542
transference, p. 516	aversive conditioning, p. 523	psychotropic medications, p. 539	electroconvulsive therapy (ECT), p. 543
short-term dynamic therapies, p. 517	token economy, p. 524		
	cognitive therapies, p. 524		

Psychotherapy

The treatment of emotional, behavioral, and interpersonal problems with psychological techniques

AP Photo

Psychoanalysis

- Developed by **Sigmund Freud** (1856–1939)
- Goal is to unearth repressed conflicts and resolve them in therapy

Techniques and processes include:
- **Free association**
- **Resistance**
- **Interpretation**
- **Transference**

Short-term dynamic therapies:
- More problem-focused and of shorter duration than traditional psychoanalysis
- Therapists are more directive.
- **Interpersonal therapy (IPT)** focuses on current relationships.

Behavior Therapy

- Assumes maladaptive behaviors are learned and uses learning principles to directly change problem behaviors
- **Mary Cover Jones** (1896–1987) was first behavior therapist, using **counterconditioning** to extinguish phobic behavior.

Classical conditioning principles seen in use of:
- **Exposure therapies**
- **Systematic desensitization**
- **Aversive conditioning**

Operant conditioning techniques:
- **Positive and negative reinforcement**
- **Extinction**
- **Token economies**

Cognitive Therapies

Assume psychological problems are caused by maladaptive patterns of thinking

Rational-emotive behavior therapy (REBT):
- Developed by **Albert Ellis** (1913–2007)
- Involves identifying and challenging core irrational beliefs

Cognitive therapy (CT):
- Developed by **Aaron T. Beck** (b. 1921)
- Involves teaching the client to recognize negative automatic thoughts and cognitive biases

- **Cognitive-behavioral therapy (CBT)** combines cognitive and behavioral techniques.
- Mindfulness and acceptance-based therapies incorporate mindfulness techniques into therapy, teaching clients to change their relationship to maladaptive thoughts and emotions.

University of Washington Libraries, Special Collections, [UW 39802] Access. No. 3308-002, Box 12 Carolyn L. Attneave Papers

Humanistic Therapy

Client-centered therapy:
- Developed by **Carl Rogers** (1902–1987)
- Client directs the focus of therapy sessions.
- Therapist is genuine, demonstrates unconditional positive regard, and communicates empathic understanding.

Group and Family Therapy

- **Group therapy** is cost-effective.
- Therapists can observe clients interacting with other group members.
- Clients benefit from support of other group members.
- Clients can try out new behaviors in a safe environment.
- **Family therapy** assumes the family is an inter-dependent system.
- *Network therapy*, pioneered by **Carolyn Attneave** (1920–1992), includes people from the client's support network beyond their immediate family.
- Marital or couple therapy seeks to improve communication, problem-solving skills, and intimacy.

Evauating the Effectiveness of Psychotherapy

Psychotherapy is significantly more effective than no treatment.
- Some therapies are more effective for specific disorders.
- Empirically supported treatments have demonstrated their effectiveness in controlled scientific trials.

Spencer Grant/PhotoEdit

Factors that contribute to effective psychotherapy:
- Quality of the therapeutic relationship
- Caring, empathic, responsive therapist
- Motivated, optimistic client
- Supportive family and stable living situation
- Culturally sensitive therapist
- A good match between client and therapy techniques

Multicultural training, pioneered by **Martha Bernal** (1931–2001), is now required of psychologists in the United States and many other countries.

Most psychotherapists take an eclectic approach; **eclecticism** refers to the pragmatic and integrated use of techniques from different psychotherapies.

MERIDITH KOHUT/The New York Times/Redux

Antipsychotic medications:
- Reserpine
- Chlorpromazine
- **Atypical antipsychotics**

Psychotropic medications:
Prescription drugs that alter mental functions, alleviate psychological symptoms, and are used to treat psychological disorders

Lithium treats bipolar disorder.

Antianxiety medications:
- Benzodiazepines
- Buspirone

Biomedical Therapies

Antidepressant medications:
- Tricyclics
- MAO inhibitors
- Second-generation antidepressants
- **Selective serotonin reuptake inhibitors (SSRIs)**
- Dual-action antidepressants

Electroconvulsive therapy (ECT):
Involves delivering a brief electric shock to the brain
Newer, experimental treatments:
- Transcranial direct current stimulation (tDCS)
- Transcranial magnetic stimulation (TMS)
- Vagus nerve stimulation (VNS)
- Deep brain stimulation (DBS)

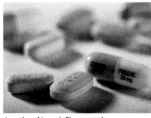

Jonathan Nourok Photography

Statistics: Understanding Data

The (Supposed) Power of a Hot Coffee

PROLOGUE

In October 2008, a U.S. psychology study made international news. Headlines promised that "Warm coffee can melt hearts" (CBC News, 2008) and "Hot drinks encourage warmer feelings" (Sample, 2008). The suggestion was that holding a hot coffee can make people perceive others (maybe you?) as a warmer person. Should you be handing out hot beverages at a job interview? On a first date? Or is this finding too good to be true?

In your introductory psychology class, you may have participated in research studies, much like the hot-coffee experiment that Lawrence Williams and John Bargh (2008) conducted. They recruited 41 undergraduate students to determine if the independent variable, coffee temperature, had an effect on the dependent variable, ratings of the warmth of another person's personality. Arriving participants were met by a member of the research team, a confederate, in the lobby. The confederate was carrying multiple items, including a coffee and a clipboard, and asked the participant to briefly hold the cup of coffee while she wrote down some information. Half of the participants were randomly assigned to be handed a cup of *hot* coffee and half were randomly assigned to be handed a cup of *iced* coffee.

Soon after, participants rated the personality of a target person, a fictional "Person A," on a measure of interpersonal warmth with scores ranging from 1 (cold) to 7 (warm). Williams and Bargh (2008) conducted a statistical analysis of their data, and found that participants who held the hot coffee rated Person A as warmer, on average, than did participants who held the iced coffee. They did a separate study with 53 participants using hot packs (think hand warmers) and cold packs, and found similar results with respect to participants' later altruistic behavior. The researchers concluded that holding the warm beverage or the hot pack primed participants to perceive others as having a warm personality or to act in ways consistent with a warmer personality. Williams and Bargh published their findings in a journal, but not just any journal. They published in *Science*, one of the most prestigious academic journals in the world! And that led to the international headlines.

But that's not the end of the story. Some psychologists wondered how such brief interventions could lead to these effects, especially with just 41 and 53 participants. Could these findings have been simply a chance occurrence? By that point, there had been a growing number of studies that used similar priming techniques in social situations, many with results that sounded too good to be true. A revolution in psychological science soon emerged, one that you learned about in Chapter 1. The *open-science movement* urged transparency

hxyume/Getty Images

about research protocols and analyses so that others can assess and even replicate earlier work (Vazire, 2018; Wagenmakers et al., 2018). *Replication*—repeating other researchers' studies to see if the same statistical results occur—became an important part of the movement. As replication became increasingly common, a so-called *replication crisis* emerged. Many highly publicized studies were failing to replicate.

Williams and Bargh's studies were obvious choices for replication. These were surprising results based on a brief intervention with relatively few participants. Dermot Lynott and his colleagues (2014) conducted "three high-powered, independent replications" of the hot pack versus ice pack study in the United States and the United Kingdom. In other words, they conducted three separate studies, each of which had a lot of what statisticians call *power*, something that increases with larger and larger samples. Compared to the 53 participants in the original hot-pack study, the three replications had a total of 861 participants. Individual analyses of each study, as well as a larger analysis of all 861 participants, failed to replicate Williams and Bargh's findings. So, save your money on your next first date or job interview. There just doesn't seem to be evidence that offering a hot coffee will make a difference.

The open science movement has uncovered other findings, like those of Williams and Bargh, that were likely not real in the first place. But it has also supported a great deal of research, including some related to social priming. And it has strengthened the field of psychological science. These new practices allow researchers to more readily figure out which findings are likely due to chance and which are likely real. Open science can help us "look forward to building a more robust . . . psychology for the future" (Lynott et al., 2014).

We'll use this study to help you understand **statistics**, *a branch of mathematics used by researchers to organize, summarize,* *and interpret data.* The job of assessing what conclusions can be drawn from the research findings is the domain of *inferential statistics,* which we'll discuss later in this appendix. We'll begin by exploring how research findings can be summarized in ways that are brief yet meaningful and easy to understand. For this, researchers use *descriptive statistics.* We'll also explore some of the new challenges and exciting advances in statistics! ∿

Descriptive Statistics

Both the original studies investigating the effect of warm objects and cold objects on interpersonal warmth, as well as the failed replication of one of those studies, **generated a large amount of data. How did the researchers make sense of such a mass of information? How did they summarize it in meaningful ways? The answer lies in descriptive statistics. **descriptive statistics**, *mathematical methods used to organize and summarize data.* Descriptive statistics do just what their name suggests—describe data. There are many ways to describe information. This appendix will examine four of the most common: frequency distributions, measures of central tendency, measures of variability, and measures of relationships between variables. Since we don't have access to all the data that these researchers gathered, we'll use hypothetical numbers to illustrate these statistical concepts.

Frequency Distribution

Here are hypothetical data for the 41 people in the first study by Williams and Bargh (2008). We created data that matched the actual means from this study:

6, 6, 1, 2, 6, 4, 6, 5, 5, 5, 4, 5, 6, 5, 6, 4, 6, 4, 7, 3, 3,
3, 6, 4, 2, 4, 4, 4, 6, 5, 6, 3, 4, 5, 3, 3, 3, 3, 5, 5, 7

Even with only 41 participants, it is difficult to make much sense of these data. Researchers need a way to organize such *raw scores* so that the information makes sense at a glance. One way to organize the data is to determine how many participants gave a rating of 1 on the 1–7 scale, how many gave a rating of 2, and so on, until all of the possible ratings are accounted for. If the data were put into a table, the table would look like **Table A.1**.

This table is one way of presenting a **frequency distribution**—*a summary of how often various scores occur in a sample of scores; score values are arranged in order of magnitude, and the number of times each score occurs is recorded.* Categories are set up (in this case, ratings of interpersonal warmth from 1 to 7), and occurrences of each category are tallied to give the frequency of each one.

What information can be gathered from this frequency distribution table? We know immediately that most of the participants gave ratings of 4, 5, or 6, toward the warmer end of the scale.

A table like this is one way of presenting a frequency distribution. It shows at a glance that most of the people in our hypothetical data set gave ratings of 4, 5, or 6, closer to the maximum of 7 (warm) for ratings of interpersonal warmth (Williams & Bargh, 2008). (These fictional data represent the actual sample size and means for this study.) The distribution includes numbers of participants who responded with each rating for their perception of the interpersonal warmth of the experimenter who handed them a cup of coffee—from 1 (cold) to 7 (warm). For example, 10 participants rated the experimenter a 6 in terms of warmth. This distribution shows the numbers for everyone—those who were handed an iced coffee and those who were handed a hot coffee. Unfortunately, this study did not replicate.

TABLE A.1

A Frequency Distribution Table

Rating of Researcher from Cold to Warm	Frequency
1	1
2	2
3	8
4	9
5	9
6	10
7	2
Total	41

Some frequency distribution tables include an extra column that shows the percentage of cases in each category. For example, what percentage of participants gave an interpersonal warmth rating of 3? The percentage is calculated by dividing the category frequency (8) by the total number of people (41), which yields about 0.195, or 19.5 percent.

Although a table is good for summarizing data, it is often useful to present a frequency distribution visually, with graphs. One type of graph is the **histogram**, *a way of graphically representing a frequency distribution; a type of bar chart using vertical bars that touch.* Categories (in our example, the different ratings of interpersonal warmth) are placed on the *x*-axis (horizontal), and the *y*-axis (vertical) shows the frequency of each category. **Figure A.1** depicts a histogram for the participants who were handed a cold beverage. The resulting graph looks something like a city skyline, with buildings of different heights. For more guidance on creating a helpful graph, see **Table A.2**.

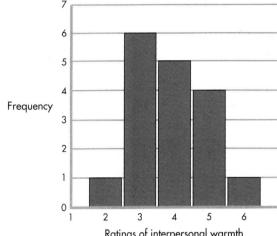

Histograms are helpful for getting a sense of the shape of a distribution. The histogram in Figure A.1 rises sharply over the lower categories, peaking at 3, and gradually diminishing from there. Such a distribution is a **skewed distribution,** *an asymmetrical distribution: In a positively skewed distribution, most of the scores are low scores; in a negatively skewed distribution, most of the scores are high scores.* This means that if we drew a line through the middle of the *x*-axis (at a rating of 4), more scores would be piled up on one side of the line than on the other. More specifically, the histogram in Figure A.1 represents a *positively skewed* distribution, indicating that most people had low scores. The "tail" of the distribution extends in a positive direction. A *negatively skewed* distribution would have mostly high scores, with fewer scores at the low end of the distribution. In this case, the tail of the distribution would extend in a negative direction. With these hypothetical data, the pattern for the participants who held a hot beverage is a negatively skewed distribution. There is a peak toward the higher end of the distribution, with the tail extending in a negative direction. You can see this in **Figure A.2**—a distribution with a slight negative skew.

In contrast to skewed distributions, a **symmetrical distribution** is *a distribution in which scores fall equally on both sides of the graph; the normal curve is an example of a symmetrical distribution.* A special case of a symmetrical distribution, the normal curve, is discussed in a later section.

FIGURE A.1 A Histogram (Positive Skew) This histogram is another way of presenting the hypothetical data given in Table A.1. The histogram shows that, for participants who held a cold beverage, most people gave lower ratings, with a peak around three. This is immediately clear from the fact that the highest bars on the chart are on the left, where the interpersonal warmth ratings are lowest.

TABLE A.2

Creating a Clear Graph

A well-designed graph should make the data easier to understand. But a poorly designed graph often just leads to confusion. When you encounter a graph or when you're creating one, ask yourself the seven questions in this checklist.

Does the graph have a clear, specific title?

Are both axes labeled with the names of the variables? Do all labels read left to right—even the one on the y-axis?

Are all terms on the graph the same terms that are used in the text that the graph is to accompany? Have all unnecessary abbreviations been eliminated?

Are the units of measurement (e.g., minutes, percentages) included in the labels?

Do the values on the axes either go down to 0 or have cut marks (double slashes) to indicate that they do not go down to 0?

Are colors used in a simple, clear way?

Has all *chartjunk*, anything decorative that detracts from the data, been eliminated?

Source: Nolan & Heinzen (2021).

statistics A branch of mathematics used by researchers to organize, summarize, and interpret data.

descriptive statistics Mathematical methods used to organize and summarize data.

frequency distribution A summary of how often various scores occur in a sample of scores; score values are arranged in order of magnitude, and the number of times each score occurs is recorded.

histogram A way of graphically representing a frequency distribution; a type of bar chart that uses vertical bars that touch.

skewed distribution An asymmetrical distribution: In a *positively skewed* distribution, most of the scores are low scores; in a *negatively skewed* distribution, most of the scores are high scores.

symmetrical distribution A distribution in which scores fall equally on both sides of the graph; the normal curve is an example of a symmetrical distribution.

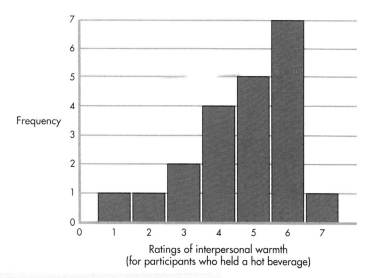

FIGURE A.2 A Histogram (Negative Skew) When more scores fall at the high end of a distribution than at the low end, the distribution is said to be negatively skewed. We see a negatively skewed distribution for these hypothetical data, which matches the actual mean, for the interpersonal warmth ratings from participants who held a hot beverage.

measure of central tendency A single number that presents some information about the "center" of a frequency distribution.

mode The most frequently occurring score in a distribution.

median The score that divides a frequency distribution exactly in half so that the same number of scores lie on each side of it.

mean The sum of a set of scores in a distribution divided by the number of scores; the mean is usually the most representative measure of central tendency.

Measures of Central Tendency

Frequency distributions can be used to organize a set of data and tell us how scores are generally distributed. But researchers often want to put this information into a more compact form. They want to be able to summarize a distribution with a single score that is "typical." To do this, they use a **measure of central tendency**, *a single number that presents some information about the "center" of a frequency distribution.*

The Mode The **mode** is *the most frequently occurring score in a distribution.* The mode in the histogram shown in Figure A.1 (based on hypothetical data) is 3. More participants who were handed a cold beverage gave a rating of 3 for the interpersonal warmth of the experimenter than any other rating category. What is the mode for the histogram shown in Figure A.2? Did you guess 6? Yes, more participants who were handed a hot beverage gave a rating of 6 to the experimenter than any other rating category. In these examples, the mode is a fairly accurate representation of central tendency, but this is not always the case. In the distribution 1, 1, 1, 10, 20, 30, the mode is 1, yet half the scores are 10 and above. This type of distortion is the reason measures of central tendency other than the mode are needed.

The Median Another way of describing central tendency is to determine the **median,** *the score that divides a frequency distribution exactly in half so that the same number of scores lie on each side of it.* If the (hypothetical) interpersonal warmth rating scores for the 20 participants who held a cold beverage were laid out from lowest to highest, they would look like this:

2, 3, 3, 3, 3, 3, 3, 4, 4, 4, 4, 4, 5, 5, 5, 5, 6, 6, 6, 7

↑

What would the middle score be? Since there are 20 scores, look for the point that divides the distribution in half, with 10 scores on each side of this point. The median can be found between the 10th and 11th scores (indicated by the arrow). In this distribution, the answer is easy: The median is 4, very similar to the mode of 3. (The median for those who were handed a hot beverage was 5, also similar to the mode for this distribution of 6.)

The Mean A problem with the mode and the median is that both measures reflect only one score in the distribution. For the mode, the score of importance is the most frequent one; for the median, it is the middle score. A better measure of central tendency is usually one that reflects *all* scores. For this reason, the most commonly used measure of central tendency is the mean, or arithmetic average. The **mean** is *the sum of a set of scores in a distribution divided by the number of scores; the mean is usually the most representative measure of central tendency.* You have calculated the mean many times. It is computed by summing a set of scores and then dividing by the number of scores that went into the sum. In the example we used to calculate the median for those handed a cold beverage, adding together the participants' ratings gives a total of 85; the number of scores is 20, and 85 divided by 20 gives a mean of 4.25. (The mean for those handed a hot beverage, calculated in the same way, was 4.71. These are the actual means in the study.)

Formulas are used to express how a statistic is calculated. The formula for the mean is

$$\overline{X} = \frac{\sum X}{N}$$

In this formula, each letter and symbol has a specific meaning:

$\overline{X}$ is the symbol for the mean. (It's pronounced "X-bar." Sometimes you'll see M used as the symbol of the mean instead.)

Σ is sigma, the Greek letter for capital S, and it stands for "sum." (Taking a course in statistics is one way to learn the Greek alphabet!)

X represents the scores in the distribution, so the numerator of the equation says, "Sum up all the scores."

N is the total number of scores in the distribution. Therefore, the formula says, "The mean equals the sum of all the scores divided by the total number of scores."

Although the mean is usually the most representative measure of central tendency because each score in a distribution enters into its computation, it is particularly susceptible to the effect of extreme scores. Any unusually high or low score will pull the mean in its direction. Suppose, for example, that in our frequency distribution for interpersonal warmth ratings by those handed an iced coffee, one participant mistakenly gave a rating of 70 instead of 7 and we didn't notice this error. The mean ratings for interpersonal warmth would jump from 4.25 to 7.4. This new mean is deceptively high, given that most of the scores in the distribution cluster around 3. Because of just that one extreme score, the mean has become less representative of the distribution. When the mean is not representative of the scores, it is usually better to use the median. In our example, the median would still be 4, despite the extreme score of 70. Frequency tables and graphs are important tools for helping us identify extreme scores, or even inaccurate scores, *before* we start computing statistics.

Measures of Variability

In addition to identifying the central tendency in a distribution, researchers may want to know how much the scores in that distribution differ from one another. Are they grouped closely together or widely spread out? To answer this question, we need some **measure of variability**, *a single number that presents information about the spread of scores in a distribution.* **Figure A.3** shows two distributions with the same mean but with different variability.

The **range** is *a simple measure of variability, which is computed by subtracting the highest score in the distribution from the lowest score.* For the 20 participants who were handed an iced coffee, the lowest rating of interpersonal warmth was 2 and the highest was 7. The range of rating scores in this group would be $7 - 2 = 5$.

As a measure of variability, the range provides a limited amount of information because it depends on only the two most extreme scores in a distribution (the highest and lowest scores). A more useful measure of variability would give some idea of the average amount of variation in a distribution. But variation from what? The most common way to measure variability is to determine how far scores in a distribution vary from the distribution's mean. We saw earlier that the mean is usually the best way to represent the "center" of the distribution, so the mean seems like an appropriate reference point.

What if we subtract the mean from each score in a distribution to get a general idea of how far each score is from the center? When the mean is subtracted from a score, the result is a *deviation* from the mean. Scores that are above the mean would have positive deviations, and scores that are below the mean would have negative deviations. To get an average deviation, we would need to sum the deviations and divide by the number of deviations that went into the sum. There is a problem with this procedure, however. If deviations from the mean are added together, the sum will be 0 because the negative and positive deviations will cancel each other out. In fact, the real definition of the mean is "the only point in a distribution where all the scores' deviations from it add up to 0."

When we need to "get rid of" the negative deviations in mathematics, the problem is solved by squaring. If a negative number is squared, it becomes positive. So instead of simply adding up the deviations and dividing by the number of scores (N), we first square each deviation and then add together

measure of variability A single number that presents information about the spread of scores in a distribution.

range A simple measure of variability, which is computed by subtracting the highest score in a distribution from the lowest score.

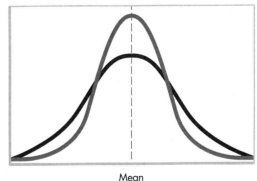

FIGURE A.3 Distributions with Different Variability Two distributions with the same mean can have very different variability, or spread, as shown in these two curves. Notice how one is more spread out than the other; its scores are distributed more widely.

Mean

standard deviation A measure of variability; expressed as the square root of the sum of the squared deviations around the mean divided by the number of scores in the distribution.

the *squared* deviations and divide by N. Finally, we need to compensate for the squaring operation. To do this, we take the square root of the number just calculated. This leaves us with the **standard deviation,** *a measure of variability that is expressed as the square root of the sum of the squared deviations around the mean divided by the number of scores in the distribution.* The larger the standard deviation, the more spread out are the scores in a distribution.

Let's look at an example to make this clearer. **Table A.3** lists the ratings of interpersonal warmth for the 20 participants who were handed an iced coffee. The mean, which is the sum of the ratings divided by 20, is calculated to be 4.25, as shown at the bottom of the left-hand column. The first step in computing the standard deviation is to subtract the mean from each score, which gives that score's deviation from the mean. These deviations are listed in the third column of the table. The next step is to square each of the deviations (done in the fourth column), add the squared deviations ($\Sigma(X - \bar{X})^2 = 33.75$), and divide that total by the number of participants ($N = 20$). Finally, we take the square root to obtain the standard deviation ($SD = 1.299$). The formula for the standard deviation (SD) incorporates these instructions:

$$SD = \sqrt{\frac{\Sigma(X - \bar{X})^2}{N}} = \sqrt{\frac{33.75}{20}} = 1.299$$

To calculate the standard deviation, you simply add all the scores in a distribution (the left-hand column in this example) and divide by the total number of scores to get the mean. Then you subtract the mean from each score (second column) to get a list of deviations from the mean (third column). Next you square each deviation (fourth column), add the squared deviations together, divide by the total number of cases, and take the square root.

TABLE A.3

Calculating the Standard Deviation

Rating X	Mean X̄	Rating Minus Mean X – X̄	(Rating Minus Mean) Squared (X – X̄)²
3	4.25	−1.25	1.5625
6	4.25	1.75	3.0625
4	4.25	−0.25	0.0625
2	4.25	−2.25	5.0625
4	4.25	−0.25	0.0625
4	4.25	−0.25	0.0625
4	4.25	−0.25	0.0625
6	4.25	1.75	3.0625
5	4.25	0.75	0.5625
6	4.25	1.75	3.0625
3	4.25	−1.25	1.5625
4	4.25	−0.25	0.0625
5	4.25	0.75	0.5625
3	4.25	−1.25	1.5625
3	4.25	−1.25	1.5625
3	4.25	−1.25	1.5625
3	4.25	−1.25	1.5625
5	4.25	0.75	0.5625
5	4.25	0.75	0.5625
7	4.25	2.75	7.5625
Mean = 4.25		Sum = 0	Sum = 33.75

$$SD = \sqrt{\frac{\Sigma(X - \bar{X})^2}{N}} = \sqrt{\frac{33.75}{20}} = 1.299$$

When scores have large deviations from the mean, the *standard deviation* is also large, and when scores have small deviations from the mean, the *standard deviation* is also small.

z-Scores and the Normal Curve

The mean and the standard deviation provide useful descriptive information about an entire set of scores. But researchers can also describe the relative position of any individual score in a distribution. To give us this information, we use a statistic called a **z-score**, *a number, expressed in standard deviation units, that shows a score's deviation from the mean*:

$$z = \frac{X - \overline{X}}{SD}$$

This equation says that to compute a z-score, we subtract the mean from the score we are interested in (that is, we calculate its deviation from the mean) and divide this quantity by the standard deviation. A positive z-score indicates that the score is above the mean, and a negative z-score shows that the score is below the mean. The larger the z-score, the farther away from the mean the score is.

Let's take an example from the distribution for interpersonal warmth scores for those handed an iced coffee. What is the z-score of a rating of 6? To find out, you simply subtract the mean from 6 and divide by the standard deviation.

$$z = \frac{6 - 4.25}{1.299} = 1.35$$

A z-score of +1.35 tells us that a person who gave an interpersonal warmth rating of 6 falls about one and a third standard deviations above the mean. In contrast, a person who gave a rating of 2 falls below the mean and would have a negative z-score. If you calculate this z-score, you will find it is −1.73. This means that a rating of 2 is almost two standard deviations below the mean.

Some variables, such as height, weight, and IQ, if graphed for large numbers of people, fall into a characteristic pattern. **Figure A.4** shows this pattern of the **standard normal curve** or the **standard normal distribution,** *a symmetrical distribution forming a bell-shaped curve in which the mean, median, and mode are all equal and fall in the exact middle.* The x-axis of Figure A.4 is marked off in standard deviation units, which, conveniently, are also z-scores. Notice that most of the cases fall between −1 and +1 SDs, with the number of cases sharply tapering off at either end. This pattern is the reason the normal curve is often described as "bell shaped."

The great thing about the normal curve is that we know exactly what percentage of the distribution falls between any two points on the curve. Figure A.4 shows the percentages of cases between major standard deviation units. For example, 34 percent of the distribution falls between 0 and +1. That means that 84 percent of the distribution falls below one standard deviation (the 34 percent that is between 0 and +1, plus the 50 percent that falls below 0). A person who obtains a z-score of +1 on some normally distributed variable has scored better than 84 percent of the other people in the distribution. If a variable is normally distributed (that is, if it has the standard bell-shaped pattern), a person's z-score can tell us exactly where that person stands relative to everyone else in the distribution.

z-score A number, expressed in standard deviation units, that shows a score's deviation from the mean.

standard normal curve or **standard normal distribution** A symmetrical distribution forming a bell-shaped curve in which the mean, median, and mode are all equal and fall in the exact middle.

FIGURE A.4 The Standard Normal Curve The standard normal curve has several characteristics. Most apparent is its symmetrical bell shape. On such a curve, the mean, the median, and the mode all fall at the same point. But not every curve that is shaped roughly like a bell is a standard normal curve. With a normal curve, specific percentages of the distribution fall within each standard deviation unit from the mean. These percentages are shown on the graph. (Because of rounding, percentages add up to more than 100 percent.)

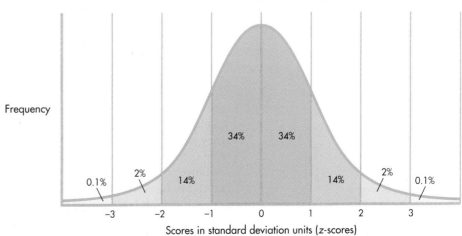

correlation The relationship between two variables.

correlation coefficient A numerical indication of the magnitude and direction of the relationship (the correlation) between two variables.

positive correlation A finding that two factors vary systematically in the same direction, increasing or decreasing together.

negative correlation A finding that two factors vary systematically in opposite directions, one increasing as the other decreases.

scatter diagram or **scatter plot** A graph that represents the relationship between two variables.

Correlation

So far, the statistical techniques we've looked at focus on one variable at a time, such as ratings of interpersonal warmth. **Correlation,** allows statisticians to look at *the relationship between two variables*. Statistically, the relationship between two variables can be expressed by a single number called a **correlation coefficient,** *a numerical indication of the magnitude and direction of the relationship (the correlation) between two variables*.

To compute a correlation coefficient, we need two sets of measurements from the same individuals. To take a simple example, let's determine the correlation between height (we'll call this the x variable) and weight (the y variable). We start by obtaining height and weight measurements for each individual in a group. The idea is to combine all these measurements into one number that expresses something about the relationship between the two variables, height and weight. However, we are immediately confronted with a problem: The two variables are measured in different ways. Height is measured in inches (or centimeters), and weight is measured in pounds (or kilograms). We need some way to place both variables on a single scale.

Think back to our discussion of the normal curve and z-scores. What do z-scores do? They take data of any form and put them into a standard scale. Remember, too, that a high score in a distribution always has a positive z-score, and a low score in a distribution always has a negative z-score. To compute a correlation coefficient, the data from both variables of interest can be converted to z-scores. So, each individual will have two z-scores: one for height (the x variable) and one for weight (the y variable).

Then, to compute the correlation coefficient, each person's two z-scores are multiplied together. All these "cross-products" are added up, and this sum is divided by the number of individuals. In other words, a correlation coefficient is the average (or mean) of the z-score cross-products of the two variables being studied:

$$\text{correlation coefficient} = \frac{\sum z_x z_y}{N}$$

A correlation coefficient can range from +1.00 to −1.00. The exact number provides two pieces of information: It tells us about the magnitude of the relationship being measured, and it tells us about its *direction*. The *magnitude,* or strength, of the relationship is indicated by the size of the number. A number close to 1 (whether positive or negative) indicates a strong relationship, while a number close to 0 indicates a weak relationship. The sign (+ or −) of the correlation coefficient tells us about the relationship's direction.

A **positive correlation** is *a finding that two factors vary systematically in the same direction, increasing or decreasing together*. It means that as one variable increases in size, the second variable also increases. For example, height and weight are positively correlated: As height increases, weight tends to increase also. In terms of z-scores, a positive correlation means that high z-scores on one variable tend to be multiplied by high z-scores on the other variable and that low z-scores on one variable tend to be multiplied by low z-scores on the other. Remember that just as two positive numbers multiplied together result in a positive number, so two negative numbers multiplied together also result in a positive number. When the cross-products are added together, the sum in both cases is positive.

A **negative correlation** is *a finding that two factors vary systematically in opposite directions, one increasing as the other decreases*. It in contrast, means that two variables are *inversely* related. As one variable increases in size, the other variable decreases. For example, instructors like to believe that the more hours students study, the fewer errors they will make on exams. In z-score language, high z-scores (which are positive) on one variable (more hours of study) tend to be multiplied by low z-scores (which are negative) on the other variable (fewer errors on exams), and vice versa, making negative cross-products. When the cross-products are summed and divided by the number of cases, the result is a negative correlation coefficient.

An easy way to show different correlations is with graphs. *A graph that represents the relationship between two variables* is a **scatter diagram** or **scatter plot.** The scatter plots in Figures A.5, A.6, and A.7 show the relationships between different measures of stress and psychological well-being (Schiffrin & Nelson, 2010). Although the correlations are from the actual study, the dots in the figures are hypothetical; they represent the correlation but are not the actual data points.

Figure A.5 shows a moderately strong positive relationship between a measure of satisfaction with life and a measure of happiness, two similar concepts. The pattern of the data points generally forms a line running from the lower left to the upper right. When calculated, this particular correlation coefficient is +.65, which indicates a correlation roughly in the middle between 0 and +1.00. In other words, people who report that they are happier also tend to report a higher satisfaction with their lives. The "tended to" part is important. Some people who reported being happy did not also report satisfaction with life, while the reverse was also true. A +1.00 correlation, or a *perfect* positive correlation, would indicate that self-reported happiness was *always* accompanied by high reports of life satisfaction, and vice versa. What would a scatter diagram of a perfect +1.00 correlation look like? It would be a straight diagonal line starting in the lower left-hand corner of the graph and progressing to the upper right-hand corner.

The study also found some negative correlations. **Figure A.6** illustrates a *negative* correlation between reported stress levels and reported levels of happiness. This correlation coefficient is −.58. Note that the data points fall in the opposite direction from those in Figure A.5, indicating that as levels of reported stress increased, levels of reported happiness decreased. The pattern of points in Figure A.6 is also not a perfect relationship. A *perfect* negative relationship would be illustrated by a straight diagonal line starting in the upper left-hand corner of the graph and ending at the lower right-hand corner.

Finally, **Figure A.7** shows two variables that are not related to each other. The hypothetical correlation coefficient between reported happiness levels and scores on a measure of memory is +.03, barely above 0. In the scatter diagram, data points form no particular pattern. From a *z*-score point of view, when two variables are not related, the cross-products are mixed—that is, some are positive and some are negative. Sometimes high *z*-scores on one variable go with high *z*-scores on the other, and low *z*-scores on one variable go with low *z*-scores on the other. In both cases, positive cross-products result. In other pairs of scores, high *z*-scores on one variable go with low *z*-scores on the other variable (and vice versa), producing negative cross-products. When the cross-products for the two variables are summed, the positive and negative numbers cancel each other out, resulting in a 0 (or close to 0) correlation.

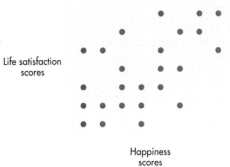

Life satisfaction scores

Happiness scores

FIGURE A.5 Scatter Plot of a Positive Correlation A correlation (or the lack of one) can be clearly shown on a scatter plot. This one shows a moderately strong positive correlation between participants' scores on a happiness measure and on a measure of life satisfaction (Schiffrin & Nelson, 2010). It's not surprising that these scales would be related. The positive direction of the correlation is indicated by the upward-sloping pattern of the dots, from bottom left to top right. This means that if one variable is high, the other tends to be high, too, and vice versa. That the strength of the relationship is only moderate is indicated by the fact that the data points (each indicating an individual participant's score) are not all positioned along a straight diagonal line.

Happiness scores

FIGURE A.6 Scatter Plot of a Negative Correlation In general, people who report higher levels of stress tend to report lower levels of happiness. This negative correlation is indicated by the downward-sloping pattern of dots, from upper left to lower right.

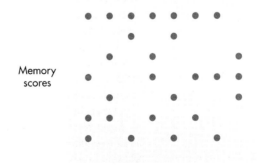

Memory scores

Happiness scores

FIGURE A.7 Scatter Plot of No Correlation This is a completely made-up correlation between happiness and memory in which the variables are not related. This scatter plot shows that lack of relationship. The points show no particular pattern or trend, thus indicating the likely absence of a correlation.

In addition to describing the relationship between two variables, correlation coefficients are useful for another purpose: prediction. If we know a person's score on one of two related variables, we can predict how they will perform on the other variable. For example, there are a number of online tools that claim to predict how long you will live. You enter information about your gender, education level, current stressful circumstances, health-related problems and behaviors, and many other variables. The Web site uses these factors to predict a single dependent variable, how long you are likely to live. Statistical techniques are used to determine the relative importance of each of these factors and to calculate the points that should be assigned to each level of a factor. Combining these factors provides a better prediction than any single factor because none of the individual factors correlates perfectly with how long you're likely to live.

One thing you cannot conclude from a correlation coefficient is *causality*. In other words, the fact that two variables are highly correlated does not necessarily mean that one variable directly causes the other. Take the stress and happiness correlation. This negative correlation tells us that people in the study who reported more stress tended to also report less happiness. It's possible that a stressful life had a direct effect on perceived happiness, but it is also possible that someone who tends to be a less happy person experiences life as more stressful. It also is possible that one or more other variables affected both stress and happiness. For example, perhaps difficult life circumstances both caused people to experience more stress and less happiness. As discussed in the chapter on research methods, the *experimental method* is the only method that can provide compelling scientific evidence of a cause-and-effect relationship between two or more variables. Can you think of a way to test the hypothesis that increased stress causes a decrease in happiness? As you may be thinking right now, such an experiment—one in which you randomly assign some people to experience stressful life events and others not to—is likely unethical to carry out.

Inferential Statistics

Earlier we reported the actual means from the Williams and Bargh (2008) study in which participants rated the interpersonal warmth of a researcher. Participants who were handed a hot coffee gave higher ratings of interpersonal warmth—a mean of 4.71—than did those handed an iced coffee—a mean of 4.25. So, the means indicated that holding the hot coffee led to perceptions of the experimenter as warmer than holding the iced coffee. But this may or may not be a meaningful result. We would expect the average rating scores to be somewhat different for the two groups because each group consisted of different people. Any difference could be due simply to chance. But are the differences in the average ratings scores between the two groups large enough *not* to be due to chance alone? If other researchers conducted the same study with different participants, would they be likely to get the same general pattern of results? To answer such questions, we turn to **inferential statistics**, *mathematical methods used to determine how likely it is that a study's outcome is due to chance and whether the outcome can be legitimately generalized to a larger population.*

Depending on the data, different inferential statistics can be used to answer questions such as the ones raised in the preceding paragraph. For example, a ***t*-test** is *a test used to establish whether the means of two groups are statistically different from each other.* Researchers could use a *t*-test, for instance, to compare average energy level at the end of the study in the traditional and alternative groups. Another *t*-test could compare the average energy level at the beginning and end of the study within the alternative group.

The findings analyzed with a *t*-test can be displayed in a visual depiction of data called a *bar graph,* where the height of each bar represents the average level for each group. In a bar graph, unlike in a histogram, the bars do not touch.

We can get a sense of the difference between groups by looking at the means or from a bar graph, but we need an inferential statistic, like a *t*-test, to determine how likely a particular finding is to have occurred as a matter of nothing more than chance or random variation. If the inferential statistic indicates that the odds of a particular finding

inferential statistics Mathematical methods used to determine how likely it is that a study's outcome is due to chance and whether the outcome can be legitimately generalized to a larger population.

t-test Test used to establish whether the means of two groups are statistically different from each other.

occurring are considerably greater than mere chance, we can conclude that our results are *statistically significant*. In other words, we can conclude with a high degree of confidence that the manipulation of the independent variable, rather than simply chance, is the reason for the results.

To see how this works, let's go back to the normal curve for a moment. Remember that we know exactly what percentage of a normal curve falls between any two z-scores. If we choose one person at random out of a normal distribution, what is the chance that this person's z-score is above +2? If you look back at Figure A.4 (on page A-7), you will see that about 2.1 percent of the curve lies above a z-score (or standard deviation unit) of +2. Therefore, the chance, or *probability,* that the person we choose will have a z-score above +2 is .021 (or 2.1 chances out of 100). That's a pretty small chance. If you study the normal curve, you will see that the majority of cases (about 96 percent) fall between −2 and +2 SDs, so a person chosen at random is not likely to fall above a z-score of +2.

When researchers test for statistical significance, they usually employ statistics other than z-scores, and they may use distributions that differ in shape from the normal curve. The logic, however, is the same. They compute some kind of inferential statistic that they compare to the appropriate distribution. This comparison tells them the likelihood of obtaining their results if chance alone is operating.

The problem is that no test exists that will tell us for sure whether our intervention or manipulation "worked"; we always have to deal with probabilities, not certainties. Researchers have developed some conventions to guide them in their decisions about whether or not their study results are statistically significant. Generally, when the probability of obtaining a particular result if random factors alone are operating is less than .05 (5 chances out of 100), the results are considered statistically significant. Researchers who want to be even more sure set their probability value at .01 (1 chance out of 100).

Because researchers deal with probabilities, there is a possibility of an *erroneous conclusion that study results are significant*, called a **Type I error**. The results of one study, therefore, should never be completely trusted. For researchers to have greater confidence in a particular effect or result, the study should be *repeated,* or replicated. If the same results are obtained in different studies, then we can be more certain that our conclusions about a particular intervention or effect are correct.

The second decision error that can be made is a **Type II error**, a *failure to find a significant effect that does, in fact, exist.* This is when a researcher fails to find a significant effect, yet that significant effect really exists. A Type II error results when a study does not have enough *power;* in a sense, the study is not strong enough to find the effect the researcher is looking for. Higher power may be achieved by improving the research design and measuring instruments, or by increasing the number of participants being studied.

Type I errors, in particular, have become a problem in psychology research. As noted in the chapter that covered research methods, as well as in the prologue for this appendix, *replication* is an important part of the scientific method. Researchers are more confident that their results are accurate when a study is conducted repeatedly yielding the same basic research results. Efforts to replicate — or reproduce — a number of findings have failed. In one study, an international team of more than 100 researchers found that 64 percent of a sample of important studies failed to replicate (Open Science Collaboration, 2015). And we know from the prologue of this appendix that the results of Williams and Bargh's (2008) original study did not replicate in additional studies with many more participants (Lynott et al., 2014). This may sound bad for psychological science, but there's a silver lining. These failures have fueled an "open science" movement, in which researchers share their data as they work to build a foundation of accepted science (Alter & Gonzalez, 2018; Gilmore et al., 2018).

The increasing awareness of just how widespread Type I errors are has also highlighted a second problem. Many people downplay the fact that inferential statistics are based on probability. When we say a finding is significant, this means that there is a low probability that the result is due to chance. But a significant finding doesn't give us a sense of how large or important a finding is. Inferential statistics, then, can lead people to focus on whether a finding is significant, with little consideration of what that

Type I error Erroneous conclusion that study results are significant.

Type II error Failure to find a significant effect that does, in fact, exist.

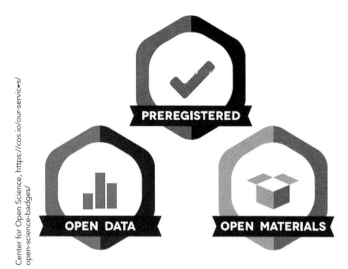

Center for Open Science, https://cos.io/our-services/open-science-badges/

▲ **Open Science Badges** Open science badges are awarded to published research for three reasons. The "Preregistered" badge is awarded when researchers posted their research design and data analyses online before they collected their data. The "open data" and "open materials" badges are awarded when researchers share their data and their research materials, often on an open Web site that is shared in the article. As more and more journals adopted the badge system, science grew increasingly transparent. In one major journal, the percentage of researchers sharing their data grew from 3% before the badges existed to 39% not long after (Kidwell et al., 2016).

finding actually means (Nuzzo, 2014). So, alongside the "open science" movement is the "new statistics" movement (Cumming, 2013). This movement refers primarily to two statistics that, ideally, are reported in addition to or instead of inferential statistics.

The first new statistic, *effect size,* gives us a sense of how large a finding is, not just whether or not it is statistically significant. A statistically significant but small difference may not be worth paying attention to. It may, for example, indicate a change that isn't even noticeable. For example, in the Williams and Bargh (2008) study, the researchers did find a significant difference between the ratings of participants handed a cold coffee and participants handed a hot coffee. They did not report an effect size, but we estimated an effect size based on their means, using a few different sets of data, and their finding seems to have been a small effect. So, even if the study had replicated, we may not have wanted to waste our money buying hot coffees to hand to everyone we meet. On the other hand, *if* the study had replicated *and if* it were a large effect, it might have been worth the money and effort to try to influence potential employers, first dates, or even instructors.

The second statistic, the *confidence interval,* gives us a sense of the range of plausible variables for each group mean. We traditionally calculate means for the groups in a study as estimates of the true means in the population. But we could calculate confidence intervals instead. For example, instead of calculating a mean of, say, 15, we might calculate a confidence interval of 12 to 18—that is, it is plausible that the true mean is anywhere from 12 to 18. Intervals highlight the uncertainty behind statistics. When we report a single number, it can imply that that must be the real number. The interval estimate makes it clearer that we're not all that sure. In fact, researchers who interpreted data based *only* on an interval estimate tended to be more accurate than researchers who also took inferential statistics into account (Coulson et al., 2010). Psychology researchers continue to use inferential statistics, which is why it is still helpful to learn them. But the field is shifting, so it is also important to learn the new statistics.

 PSYCH FOR YOUR LIFE

Five Questions to Ask When You Read a Study in the News

During the pandemic, we all became hyperaware of research findings as they were released in real time. We cared deeply about avoiding COVID and getting vaccines. There will always be scientific headlines, including those about psychological research, to care about. For example, an article in the *Harvard Business Review* described a study that compared the effects on stress of (1) a workshop that taught breathing exercises and (2) a workshop that introduced cognitive stress-reduction techniques (Seppälä et al., 2020). Each participant was randomly assigned to one of the workshops. Researchers told participants that they would experience a stressful situation "akin to presenting at a business meeting," and then measured several markers of stress.

From this appendix, you now have a foundation for understanding the statistics that underlie any scientific finding you see in the news, such as the one about breathing techniques versus cognitive techniques to inoculate yourself against stress. When you read about a scientific finding like this, ask yourself the following five questions.

1. *What type of statistic?* Was this study experimental (comparing groups and using an inferential statistic for groups, such as a *t*-test) or was it correlational (calculating a correlation coefficient)? Remember that a study that uses a correlation coefficient doesn't tell us what variable causes another.

   In this case, the article describes a comparison of two groups, so an inferential statistic such as a t-test might have been used to determine whether there was a statistically significant difference between groups. And remember from the chapter on research methods that when we use random assignment, we can draw conclusions about one variable causing another.

2. *What is the difference?* For studies that demonstrate a difference, does the article report means? What does the difference indicate?

   The article did not report means, but it did report a difference—the breathing workshop "was more beneficial in terms of immediate impact on stress."

3. *How much variability is there?* Some articles will discuss variable outcomes. If each group has a lot of variability, it is more difficult to know if this intervention is likely to work for any individual person. You can also look for a graph. Data visualizations are increasingly used by the media, and some articles will include a graph that lets you see the distribution.

   The article did not provide any information on variability, so we can't say how much overlap there was between groups. That is, we know there was a difference between the means, but there still may be many people who don't fit the overall pattern. We would still want to pick the breathing workshop if we could, though.

4. *What is the effect size?* A news article is not likely to report an effect size, but you can still get a sense of how large or meaningful the finding is. Do they provide any numbers or use any language that gives a sense of how large the effect is? Does it seem like an important enough difference that people should make a change in their lives?

   The article did not report an effect size, but they said that "these effects were even stronger when measured three months later." Of course, stronger is relative, and may not mean a strong, or large, effect, but it's a good sign.

5. *Has it been replicated?* Is this a single study, or one of many that have largely reported the same findings? Flashy findings, like the hot coffee study, get attention, but may have been a Type I error (occurring just by chance). Before you change your life because of a study, wait for the replication.

   The article on stress management referred first to "two recently published studies" and then described a third study conducted with "veterans from Iraq and Afghanistan who struggled with trauma" that led to similar results. Of course, we can always have more replications, but it's a good sign that three studies have supported this finding.

A basic understanding of research methods and statistics can make you an educated consumer of information, including about psychological science.

↖ APPENDIX REVIEW

KEY TERMS

statistics, p. A-2	measure of central tendency, p. A-4	standard deviation, p. A-6	negative correlation, p. A-8
descriptive statistics, p. A-2	mode, p. A-4	z-score, p. A-7	scatter diagram (scatter plot), p. A-8
frequency distribution, p. A-2	median, p. A-4	standard normal curve (standard normal distribution), p. A-7	inferential statistics, p. A-10
histogram, p. A-3	mean, p. A-4	correlation, p. A-8	*t*-test, p. A-10
skewed distribution, p. A-3	measure of variability, p. A-5	correlation coefficient, p. A-8	Type I error, p. A-11
symmetrical distribution, p. A-3	range, p. A-5	positive correlation, p. A-8	Type II error, p. A-11

Statistics
A branch of mathematics that researchers use to organize and interpret data

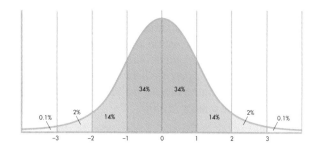

Descriptive Statistics
Summaries of data that make the data meaningful and easy to understand

Frequency distribution:
- Summary of how often various scores occur in a sample of scores
- Can be presented in the form of a table or a graph such as a **histogram**
- Can be **symmetrical distribution** or asymmetrical **(skewed distribution)**
- **Standard normal curve:** A symmetrical distribution forming a bell-shaped curve in which the mean, the median, and the mode are all equal and fall in the exact middle

Measures of variability show how closely scores in a distribution are grouped.
- **Range:** The highest score minus the lowest score
- **Standard deviation:** The square root of the sum of the squared deviations around the mean divided by the number of scores; eliminates the problem of negative deviations
- **z-score:** Shows how far away from the mean a score is in terms of standard deviation units

Measures of central tendency of a distribution:
- **Mode:** Most frequent score
- **Median:** Middle score in the distribution
- **Mean:** Arithmetic average of scores; usually the best overall representation of central tendency, but influenced by very high or very low scores

Correlation refers to the relationship between two variables.
- **Correlation coefficient:** A numerical indication of the magnitude and direction of the relationship between two variables.

- **Positive correlation:** As one variable increases in size, the second variable also increases.
- **Negative correlation:** As one variable increases in size, the second variable decreases.
- A correlational relationship is not necessarily a causal relationship.
- Correlation can be presented visually in a **scatter diagram** or **scatter plot.**

hxyume/Getty Images

Inferential Statistics
- Used to determine whether a study's outcomes can be generalized to a larger population
- Provide information about whether a study's findings are statistically significant

t-test: Technique used to compare the means of two groups
Incorrect *t*-test results could reflect:
- **Type I error:** Researcher erroneously concluded study results were significant, or
- **Type II error:** Researcher failed to find significant effect that does, in fact, exist.

Movements developing due to problems with inferential statistics:
- Open science: researchers share data
- New statistics: researchers report effect sizes and confidence intervals

Industrial/Organizational Psychology

Weird Kid

PROLOGUE

"[M]y name is Brittany. And I'm here today because I was a weird kid." Brittany Graziosi, a bright millennial with a killer work ethic, is also a single mom. Like many of her generation, Brittany has worked at a number of jobs. She's waited tables, tended bar, booked bands, driven for ride services, and managed a flea market. For a while, she worked in sales, traveling New Jersey doing retail training for a marketing firm. At the time, she thought her sales position was the "best job I was ever going to get for someone without a formal education." But, she confesses with a smile, "Thankfully, I got fired."

Freed from this more traditional position, Brittany pursued her passion, creating jewelry that combined her love of art, science, and nature. She makes earrings from animal bones, for example. "I became an artist," she explained, "because that is what weird kids do." But Brittany is also a natural leader. She took her project further, reaching out to artists who shared her sensibility for unusual creations like "taxidermy and horror art, Halloween art." Her entrepreneurial instincts kicked in, and she soon founded the Jersey City Oddities Market.

Skilled at social media, Brittany individually promoted each of the 43 vendors who signed up for the first market, which

▲ **A Revolution in How We Work** The career trajectory of Brittany, an entrepreneurial millennial, captures many of the changes that have occurred in the workplace. Shown here at one of her pop-up markets, Brittany has held multiple jobs and even founded her own company. She now has a storefront, Cooper & Bay, where she sells her own science-based art as well as that of many other artists and makers. Her online presence is at baycuriosities.com. Brittany's storefront has space for retail, art and maker studios, and classes. She recently taught a class for budding jewelry makers on how to solder. Like Brittany, many members of the Millennial and Gen Z cohorts will have to be more creative and flexible in their careers than previous generations.

garnered over $18,000 in sales! Her community of artists quickly grew on Facebook and Instagram, and she organized additional markets. Ultimately, she entered the Start Something Challenge, a statewide competition for entrepreneurs that attracted 112 entries. Over several months, the contestants were narrowed down to

semifinalists and then finalists. After her compelling pitch about being a weird kid, Brittany was awarded first prize, a $10,000 business grant.

Brittany used her business grant to fuel the opening of a brick-and-mortar location that serves as an "oddities incubator," a co-working space for artists and makers. Artists can use her space to lower their production costs — for example, renting her equipment to make screen prints. They can also sell their wares in the adjacent store and use the space to teach art classes. Brittany also continues to sell her own art and that of her colleagues in an online store and in larger pop-up markets.

As she built her business, Brittany noticed the lack of racial and ethnic diversity and the lack of inclusion in the oddities community. So, she began actively recruiting to expand diversity among the vendors she represents, removed the word "oddities" from her market, and rebranded as Cooper & Bay. Brittany also promotes inclusion, working to bring more art forms related to science, such as taxidermy classes and nature-based jewelry classes, to the diverse and lower-income communities in which she has always lived. She plans to offer "scholarships" for students to take the workshops. For that reason, she has ignored advice to move her business to a community where it might be more lucrative. She'd rather be a part of a community where she can make a difference.

Brittany's career trajectory exemplifies that of many people in the current workforce. She has hopped from job to job, harnessed the Internet and social media, honed her leadership skills in atypical work environments, envisioned a new twist on co-working, embraced diversity and inclusion initiatives, and balanced her work with caring for her young son. In this appendix, we'll highlight the changing nature of employment, including during the pandemic. We'll also introduce you to the many benefits of bringing psychology to the workforce—wherever that is. As we explore the field of industrial and organizational psychology, we'll return to Brittany's story. ∿

What Is Industrial/Organizational Psychology?

Industrial/organizational (I/O) psychology is *the branch of psychology that focuses on the study of human behavior in the workplace*. The "industrial," or "I," side of I/O psychology focuses on measuring human characteristics and matching those characteristics to particular jobs. This process involves applying psychological research findings to personnel functions such as pre-employment testing, placement, training and development, and performance management. This specialty, often called **personnel psychology**, *a subarea of I/O psychology that focuses on matching people's characteristics to job requirements, accurately measuring job performance, and assessing employee training needs*.

In contrast, the "organizational," or "O," side focuses on the workplace culture and its influence on employee behavior. Organizational psychology helps companies develop a culture that fulfills organizational goals while addressing employee needs. Organizational psychologists, then, apply psychological findings to areas such as leadership development, team building, motivation, ethics training, and wellness planning. **Organizational behavior** is *a subarea of I/O psychology that focuses on the workplace culture and its influence on employee behavior*. In their research and work, I/O psychologists generally concentrate on these content areas:

1. **JOB ANALYSIS.** Job analysts must determine the duties of a particular position, as well as the personal characteristics that best match those duties.

Michael L. Abramson/Getty Images

⌃ **Designing for People** The ergonomics subarea of industrial/organizational psychology is concerned with the human factors involved in the use of workplace procedures and equipment. For example, this factory's procedure for tightening bolts on the wheel of a log skidder requires the mechanic to kneel and heft a heavy wrench—a tiring, painful position. The employer installed a counterbalanced tool that allows the operator to sit level with the wheel and work with his legs and back relaxed.

2. **SELECTION AND PLACEMENT.** This area includes the development of assessment techniques to help select job applicants most likely to be successful in a given job or organization.

3. **TRAINING AND DEVELOPMENT.** Psychologists in this field may design customized training programs and evaluate the effectiveness of those programs.

4. **PERFORMANCE MANAGEMENT AND EVALUATION.** Companies are often concerned with ways to improve their performance evaluation systems. Performance management systems include teaching managers how to collect evaluation data, how to avoid evaluation errors, and how to communicate the results.

5. **ORGANIZATIONAL DEVELOPMENT.** The goal of organizational development (OD) is to bring about positive change in an organization, through assessment of the organizational social environment and culture.

6. **LEADERSHIP DEVELOPMENT.** Leadership research strives to identify the traits, behaviors, and skills that great leaders have in common. One goal is matching an organization's mission with the optimal leadership profile.

7. **TEAM BUILDING.** Team membership and successful team design are critical to the needs of today's organizations.

This appendix benefits from previous contributions from Claudia Cochran-Miller, *El Paso Community College*, and Marie Waung, *University of Michigan, Dearborn*.

8. **QUALITY OF WORK LIFE.** Psychologists in this area study the factors that contribute to a productive and healthy workforce, such as benefits packages and employee-centered policies.

9. **ERGONOMICS (OR HUMAN FACTORS).** The focus of ergonomics is the design of equipment and the development of work procedures based on human capabilities and limitations. Ergonomics helps employers provide healthier and safer workplaces.

History of I/O Psychology

Although I/O psychology is often misperceived as a new field in psychology, it is actually more than a century old. In the chapter Introduction and Research Methods, you learned about Wilhelm Wundt, generally credited as the founder of psychology. Wundt's first research assistant, James McKeen Cattell (1890), broke new ground in the field of mental testing, thus influencing the job application process in subsequent decades. Today, pre-employment testing has become a basic step for screening job applicants, helping many organizations with their hiring decisions.

Another pioneer in the field of I/O psychology is Hugo Münsterberg. Also one of Wundt's students, he published the field's first textbook, *Psychology and Industrial Efficiency* (1913). Here, Münsterberg explained the benefits of matching the job to the worker. He believed that successful matches had benefits for both the employee and the employer, including increased job satisfaction and higher worker productivity.

Just one year after Münsterberg's textbook was published, psychologist and engineer **Lillian Moller Gilbreth** (1878–1972) published her pioneering doctoral dissertation, "The Psychology of Management," which applied principles of psychology to the workplace. Gilbreth frequently collaborated with her husband, industrial engineer Frank Gilbreth, but the couple's publishers decided to omit her name from their publications so that readers would not discount work co-authored by a woman, even though Lillian had earned a Ph.D. and Frank had not even attended university. The Gilbreths developed innovations in workplace efficiency, such as improved lighting and regular breaks, as well as innovations in workplace psychological well-being, such as suggestion boxes and free books (Graham, 1999). Gilbreth also applied her interest in scientific management to the home, where she had long employed full-time help. Because of her work, once-novel home improvements—including pedals to open trash can lids, shelves in refrigerator doors, and wall-mounted light controls—are now standard.

Gilbreth first earned fame for her parenting, and then for her home improvements. But she eventually achieved notice for the sheer breadth of her achievements. She has been described as having "achieved an astounding number of 'firsts'" (APS, 2017). These include being the first woman to be elected to the National Academy of Engineering, the first female psychologist to be featured on a U.S. postage stamp, and many more. But she always looked to the future. She encouraged the world to "always be on the lookout for new leaders, for young people with a new slant on things"—in other words, to look for new Lillian Gilbreths (APS, 2017).

∧ **Lillian Moller Gilbreth** Pioneering organizational psychologist Lillian Gilbreth, shown here on the far right, was described in the 1940s as "a genius in the art of living" (Kennedy, 2012). The film *Cheaper by the Dozen* was based on the best-selling book that 2 of her 12 children, 11 of whom are shown here, wrote about their childhood. Gilbreth's home doubled as a sort of real-world laboratory that tested her and her husband Frank's ideas about efficiency. Frank is shown here on the far left.

Industrial (Personnel) Psychology

Personnel psychologists have three major goals: selecting the best applicants for jobs, training employees so that they perform their jobs effectively, and accurately evaluating employee performance. The first step in attaining each of these goals is to perform a job analysis.

industrial/organizational (I/O) psychology The branch of psychology that focuses on the study of human behavior in the workplace.

personnel psychology A subarea of I/O psychology that focuses on matching people's characteristics to job requirements, accurately measuring job performance, and assessing employee training needs.

organizational behavior A subarea of I/O psychology that focuses on the workplace culture and its influence on employee behavior.

job analysis A technique to identify the major responsibilities of a job, along with the human characteristics needed to fill it.

Job Analysis

When job descriptions are lacking or inaccurate, employers and employees may experience frustration as tasks are confused and positions are misunderstood or even duplicated. Consequently, I/O psychologists are called upon to conduct job analyses that result in accurate job descriptions, benefiting everyone involved. Outdated or inflated job descriptions may land organizations in legal hot water. In the United States, a job description that indicates more knowledge, skill, or ability than is actually needed to perform well in a job could violate the Americans with Disabilities Act. For example, sewing straight seams may be determined solely by touch; thus, if a garment manufacturer required sewing machine operators to have perfect vision, then people with visual impairments—some of whom may be able to sew perfect seams—would be excluded from employment unfairly. The U.S. Equal Employment Opportunity Commission (EEOC), the U.S. Department of Labor (DOL), and the Americans with Disabilities Act (ADA) all endorse job analysis as a precautionary method to avoid legal problems (U.S. DOL, 2017; U.S. EEOC, 2017).

Job analysis is *a technique to identify the major responsibilities of a job, along with the human characteristics needed to fill it.* Someone performing a job analysis may observe employees at work, interview them, or ask them to complete surveys regarding major job duties and tasks. This information is then used to create or revise job descriptions. Sometimes this information can even be used to restructure an organization. Why should an employer invest in this process? Systems built on job analysis have a better chance of reducing turnover and improving productivity and morale (Breaugh, 2017; Felsberg, 2004).

Job analysis is also important for designing effective training programs. In 2019, U.S. organizations spent $83 billion on training programs for their employees (*Training*, 2019). U.S. occupational definitions are outlined on a website called O*NET online (onetonline.org). O*NET provides summary reports for each job that include the various titles that might be given to that job, the duties expected of people in that position, and the education, abilities, and skills (including technology skills) that are necessary. It also includes information on trends for the growth and salary of that occupation. And it shares related links, such as to professional organizations that might be helpful to job seekers in that area. You can even click through to job openings. We encourage you to take a few minutes now and check out your chosen career!

I/O psychologists can assist organizations in creating customized and effective training programs that integrate job analysis data with organizational goals. Modern training programs should include collaborative and on-demand methods, such as e-learning, virtual classrooms, and podcasts, so as to maximize training success. The best training results are achieved not only through effective delivery methods but also when the training objectives are directly linked to performance outcomes.

Finally, job analysis is useful in designing performance appraisal systems. Job analysis defines and clarifies job competencies so that performance appraisal instruments may be developed and training results can be assessed. This process helps managers make their expectations and ratings easy to understand. As more companies realize the benefits of job analysis, they will call upon I/O psychologists to design customized performance management systems to better track and communicate employee performance.

A Closer Look at Personnel Selection

"What was the last costume you wore?" "If you were an animal, which animal would you be?" Yes, these are actual questions asked on job interviews. The first question was asked by David Gilboa, the cofounder of the trendy eyeglasses company Warby Parker. The second one was asked by Stormy Simon; she is the former president of Overstock (Gillett & Cain, 2017). But, as fun as the questions are, they are not likely to yield useful responses for hiring. In fact, research suggests that interviews lead to worse decisions than concrete information about past performance (e.g., Dana et al., 2013).

How, then, should we approach the hiring process? Whether you are looking for a job or trying to fill a position at your company, it's helpful to understand the personnel selection process. The more you know about how selection decisions are made, the

▲ **Matching Job and Applicant** A job analysis helps to pinpoint the qualities a person must have to succeed at a particular job. Not everyone has the special combination of compassion and toughness needed to be an effective physical therapist, for instance.

more likely you are to find a job that fits your needs, skills, and interests—and this benefits employers and employees alike.

The goal in personnel selection is to hire only those applicants who will perform the job effectively. There are many selection devices available for the screening process, including psychological tests, work samples, selection interviews, and even computerized algorithms. With so many devices available, each with strengths and weaknesses, personnel psychologists are often called upon to recommend those devices that might best be used in a particular selection process. Consequently, they must consider **selection device validity**, *the extent to which a selection device is successful in distinguishing between those applicants who will become high performers at a certain job and those who will not.*

Psychological Tests

Psychological tests are frequently used in the selection process to help recruiters quickly, inexpensively, and accurately identify whether an applicant's aptitudes and personality traits match the position requirements (Wonderlic, 2005). Common types of psychological tests are integrity/honesty tests, cognitive ability tests, mechanical aptitude tests, motor and sensory ability tests, and personality tests. A survey of Fortune 1000 firms found that 28 percent of employer respondents use honesty/integrity tests, 22 percent screen for violence potential, and 20 percent screen for personality (Piotrowski & Armstrong, 2006).

Let's first examine the popularity of *integrity tests,* which came about largely because of legislation limiting the use of polygraph tests in the workplace. According to the 2015 National Retail Security Survey (National Retail Federation, 2015), employee theft accounted for $15 billion, more than one-third of all retail losses in the United States. Unfortunately, integrity tests are plagued with concerns about validity, reliability, fairness, and privacy (Fine & Pirak, 2016; Karren & Zacharias, 2007; Van Iddekinge et al., 2012). Despite these problems, several million integrity tests are administered in the United States every year (Wanek et al., 2003).

Cognitive ability tests measure general intelligence or specific cognitive skills, such as mathematical or verbal ability. Sample items from two cognitive ability tests are presented in **Figure B.1**. *Mechanical ability tests* measure mechanical reasoning and may

selection device validity The extent to which a personnel selection device is successful in distinguishing between those applicants who will become high performers at a certain job and those who will not.

(a) 1. RESENT/RESERVE—Do these words
1 have similar meanings
2 have contradictory meanings
3 mean neither the same nor opposite
2. Paper sells for 21 cents per pad. What will 4 pads cost?

(b)

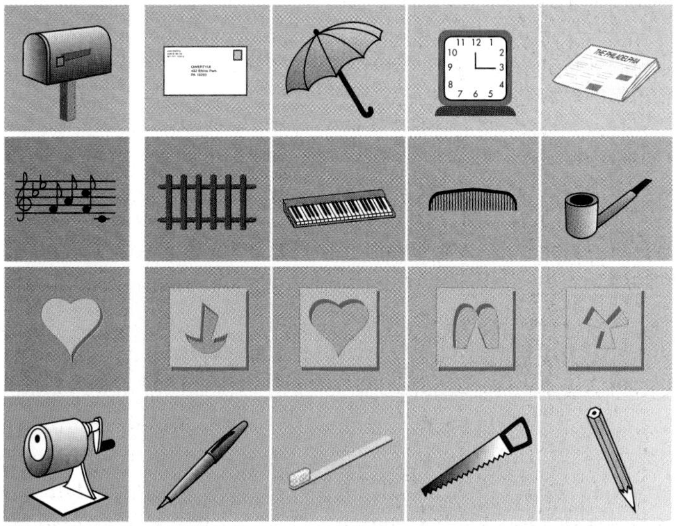

For each item find the picture that goes best with the picture in the first box. Draw a dark line from the upper right corner to the lower left corner in the proper box to show the right answer.

Sources: Corsini (1958); Wonderlic (1998).

FIGURE B.1 Sample Items from Two Cognitive Ability Tests Cognitive ability tests can measure either general intelligence or specific cognitive skills, such as mathematical ability. (a) These two items are from the Wonderlic Personnel Test, which is designed to assess general cognitive ability. Employers assume that people who cannot answer most questions correctly would not be good candidates for jobs that require general knowledge and reasoning skills. The first answer is "3," that "resent/reserve" mean neither the same nor opposite. The second answer is 84 cents. (b) The chart is from the Nonverbal Reasoning Test. It assesses reasoning skills apart from the potentially confounding factor of skill with the English language. The four answers, in order, are envelope, keyboard, heart shape, and pencil.

FIGURE B.2 Sample Items from a Mechanical Ability Test Questions such as these from the Resource Associates Mechanical Reasoning Test are designed to assess a person's ability to figure out the physical properties of things. Such a test might be used to predict job performance for carpenters or assembly-line workers. The answer to the first question is that the piston is moving in "Direction A." The answer to the second question is "same" (gravity acts on both in the same way).

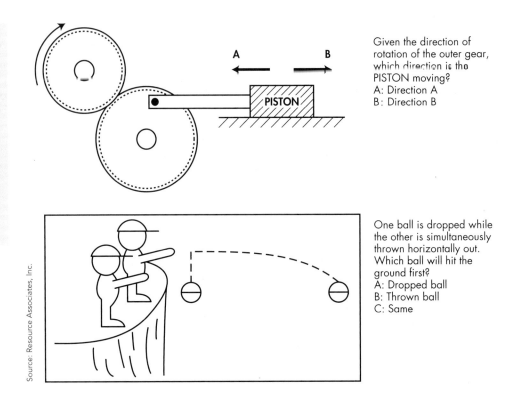

Source: Resource Associates, Inc.

be used to predict job performance for engineering, carpentry, and assembly work. **Figure B.2** presents sample items from the Resource Associates Mechanical Reasoning Test. *Motor ability tests* include measures of fine dexterity in fingers and hands, accuracy and speed of arm and hand movements, and eye–hand coordination. *Sensory ability tests* include measures of visual acuity, color vision, and hearing.

Personality tests are designed to measure personality characteristics. An assessment of personality characteristics, such as depressive symptoms, might be appropriate for selecting people for sensitive jobs, such as nuclear power plant operator, police officer, or airline pilot (Hoffmann & Hoffmann, 2017). Tests designed to measure typical personality traits, however, are more popular for the selection of employees (Bates, 2002). Tests based on the Big Five Model, described in detail in the chapter on personality, allow employers to identify traits such as conscientiousness, extraversion, and agreeableness (Bates, 2002; Judge et al., 2013). This information can also be used to understand employee motivation and enhance team building and team selection. However, researchers warn of two problems with personality tests in hiring. Employers can't prevent people from faking their answers to personality tests, and the tests just aren't that good at predicting job success (Morgeson et al., 2007). One of the most commonly administered workplace personality tests is the Myers-Briggs Personality Inventory (MBTI). Despite its popularity, there is little evidence to support its validity. In many ways, it's considered pseudoscientific. (For a longer discussion of the problematic nature of the MBTI, see p. 391 in the chapter on personality.)

Work Samples and Situational Exercises

Two other kinds of personnel selection devices are work samples and situational exercises. Work samples are typically used for jobs involving the manipulation of objects, whereas situational exercises are usually used for jobs involving managerial or professional skills. Work samples have been called "high-fidelity simulations" in that they require applicants to complete tasks as if they were on the job (Motowidlo et al., 1997). Companies like Toyota, Quest Diagnostics, and SunTrust Bank have been using interactive job simulations in their selection process. At Toyota, for example, applicants must demonstrate their ability to read dials and gauges and spot safety problems in a virtual setting as a part of their "Computer Assembler Audition."

Work samples and situational exercises can also be used to assess candidates' potential for success in training programs. For decisions on hiring surgical trainees, for example, researchers are exploring the use of situational exercises that assess leadership, interpersonal skills, and decision making (Gardner et al., 2016). Whether for training programs or regular employment, hiring-related situational exercises have benefits. These simulations are perceived as enjoyable by candidates, reduce legal challenges by those who are not hired, and help to reduce turnover among those who are hired, given that they offer candidates a realistic understanding of the job (Earnest et al., 2011; Hausknecht et al., 2004; Winkler, 2006).

Selection Interviews

Great news! You passed the pre-employment test and have been called in for an interview. Now it's just a matter of sailing through the objective interview, right? Wrong! Chances are that the company's interviewing methods are subjective, outdated, and non-research-based. The Society for Human Resource Management (SHRM) has found that as many as 40 percent of companies continue to use unstructured interviews, ignoring research that supports objective selection strategies (Dana et al., 2013). Furthermore, only 24 percent of companies actually used scoring scales to rate the interviewee responses, fostering even greater subjectivity.

In contrast to unstructured interviews, *structured behavioral interviews,* if developed and conducted properly, are adequate predictors of job performance. A structured interview should be based on a job analysis, prepared in advance, standardized for all applicants, and evaluated by a panel of interviewers trained to record and rate the applicant's responses using a numeric rating scale (Levashina et al., 2014). When these criteria are met, the interview is likely to be an effective selection tool (Krohe, 2006).

Technology in Hiring

Hiring is increasingly technology-driven. Many of these selection techniques can be delivered using technology—a virtual interview, for example, or an online gamified version of personality testing (McCord et al., 2019). Technology also offers entirely new ways to assess potential employees.

For example, companies are increasingly turning to social media, with more than 40 percent using social networking sites to screen job candidates (SHRM, 2016). Companies may choose to rely on social media as a screening tool because it is seen as an accurate representation of a candidate's personality. One study found that strangers' ratings of Facebook profiles were better predictors of job performance than were traditional personality tests (Kluemper et al., 2012). So, your online presence may be a hiring criterion. Do you think you're immune because you set your social media sites to private? Think again. Several of our students have reported being asked to log in to their social media profiles during job interviews. On the other hand, employers should be careful. Research suggests that applicants perceive companies in a more negative light when they use social media for hiring (Jeske & Schultz, 2019; Stoughton et al., 2015).

A number of companies have taken technology-driven hiring a step further by automating the entire process (Miller, 2015; Wisenberg Brin, 2019). Software implements an algorithm, a set of objective formulas aimed at choosing the employees most likely to be successful. If the algorithms are designed well, they can eliminate bias and over time can help companies—including Google, Uber, and Marriott—identify the characteristics that best predict success (Mainka, 2019). In one prominent example, Google asks candidates for information on behaviors, personality, and attitudes, including how old they were when they first became excited about computers (Hansell, 2007). Google's algorithm, described by one management professor as "breathtaking" in its innovation, has helped Google sort top prospects from among the more than 1 million applications they receive every year (Sullivan, 2013). Google's own research has shown its algorithm's ability to both choose excellent employees and decrease the time spent in making hiring decisions.

Algorithms offer enormous promise for more efficient hiring, but it is not yet clear that they are effective on their own in eliminating bias (Ajunwa et al., 2016; Raghavan et al., 2020). Moreover, there isn't sufficient research to know whether algorithms lead to successful hires. In the United States, for example, two-thirds of employers don't even gather data to see if employees hired via algorithms worked out (Cappelli, 2019). For example, imagine that an algorithm includes a seemingly objective measure like commuting distance. In the United States, commuting distance has been shown to be associated with race as a result of a long history of housing segregation (Tufekci, 2016). We need I/O psychologists to help us understand how to maximize the efficiency of algorithm-based hiring while reducing the possibility of bias.

The bottom line on hiring? "The advice on selection is straightforward: Test for skills. Ask [those assessing candidates] to show evidence that they can actually predict who the good employees will be. Do fewer, more-consistent interviews" (Cappelli, 2019).

Organizational Behavior

Organizational behavior (OB) focuses on how the organization and the social environment in which people work affect their attitudes and behaviors. Job satisfaction is the attitude most thoroughly researched by I/O psychologists, with tens of thousands of studies to date. The impact of leadership on attitudes and behaviors is another well-researched OB topic. We will examine both of these topics here.

Job Satisfaction

Rania and Lucy are both engineers who work in the same department of the same company. Rania is almost always eager to get to work in the morning. She feels that her work is interesting and that she has plenty of opportunities to learn new skills. In contrast, Lucy is unhappy because she feels that she doesn't get the recognition she deserves at work. She also complains that the company doesn't give enough vacation time to employees and that it provides inadequate benefits. Lucy can't think of many good things about her job. She's even beginning to feel that her job is negatively affecting her personal life.

Fortunately, Rania is more typical of U.S. workers than Lucy is. Before the pandemic, research found that 89 percent of U.S. workers were satisfied with their jobs, the highest rate in 10 years (SHRM, 2017). Survey research since the pandemic found an increase in employee engagement, a characteristic that includes job satisfaction—the highest rate in the last 20 years (Tyler, 2020). This trend may be a result of layoffs during the pandemic leaving only the most engaged employees or "the result of improved communication between employees and their leaders."

Several approaches have been used to explain differences in job satisfaction. The **discrepancy hypothesis** is an *approach to explaining job satisfaction that focuses on the discrepancy, if any, between what a person wants from a job and how that person evaluates what is actually experienced at work.* The approach consists of three ideas: (1) that people differ in what they want from a job, (2) that people differ in how they evaluate what they experience at work, and (3) that job satisfaction is based on the difference between what is desired and what is experienced (Lawler, 1973; Locke, 1976). Rania and Lucy, for instance, may not only want different things from their jobs; they may also make different assessments of the same events at work. Although their supervisor may treat them in the same encouraging manner, Rania may see the boss's encouragement as supportive while Lucy may view it as condescending. As a result, one perceives a discrepancy between desires and experiences, whereas the other does not.

discrepancy hypothesis Approach to explaining job satisfaction that focuses on the discrepancy, if any, between what a person wants from a job and how that person evaluates what is actually experienced at work.

Other factors have also been identified as contributing to job satisfaction. The 2017 SHRM Job Satisfaction Survey, for example, found that respect from employers was rated as an important factor in employee job satisfaction by the largest percentage of respondents.

Leadership

I/O psychologists have invested extensive energy searching for the formula for a great leader. *Leaders* are those who have the ability to direct groups toward the attainment of organizational goals. There are several classic theories that shaped our early views of leadership. The **trait approach to leader effectiveness** is an *approach to determining what makes an effective leader that focuses on the personal characteristics displayed by successful leaders*. One of the earliest theories, it was based on the idea that great leaders are *born,* not made. This approach assumed that leaders possess certain qualities or characteristics resulting in natural abilities to lead others. A large number of traits—such as height, physical attractiveness, dominance, resourcefulness, and intelligence—were examined. However, researchers found little connection between personal traits and leader effectiveness (Hollander & Julian, 1969; Stogdill, 1948).

Consequently, the emphasis turned to another explanation for effective leadership. Could leaders be *made*? Could they be taught "leadership behaviors" that would make them more effective? The **behavioral theories of leader effectiveness** are *theories of leader effectiveness that focus on differences in the behaviors of effective and ineffective leaders* (e.g., McGregor, 1960). For example, was management's role to focus on the job, pressuring employees toward greater productivity? Or was management's role to focus on people, cultivating employees' inherent self-motivation? Research found that ineffective managers focused only on one or the other: If your boss cared only about production, then your job satisfaction and morale might decline. But if your boss was "all heart" and held no production expectations, your job satisfaction might be high but your productivity low (Bass, 1981; Locke & Schweiger, 1979). The most effective leaders focus on both.

Next to evolve were **situational (or contingency) theories of leadership**, *leadership theories claiming that various situational factors influence a leader's effectiveness*. The idea was that there was no one "best" way to manage *every* employee (Miner, 2005). These theories claimed that the best leaders are those who utilize the leadership style most appropriate for the employee and the situation at hand. These theories tended to be complicated, but they did a better job of explaining leader effectiveness than either the trait approach or behavioral theories.

Much of the research on leadership emphasized the impact of leaders on followers, ignoring the fact that followers also influence leaders. In contrast, the **leader–member exchange model** *emphasizes that the quality of the interactions between supervisors and subordinates varies depending on the unique characteristics of both* (Bauer & Erdogan, 2015). Positive leader–member relationships are characterized by mutual trust, respect, and liking. These relationships have numerous benefits, including higher job satisfaction and goal commitment, improved work climate, and lower turnover rates (Gerstner & Day, 1997; Gomez & Rosen, 2001). Although the leader–member exchange model has been criticized for being overly broad (Gottfredson et al., 2020), it is still used by researchers who study leadership.

More recently, leadership research has focused on topics such as transformational versus transactional leadership, charismatic leadership, shared leadership, and servant leadership, which is highlighted in the In Focus box, "Servant Leadership: When It's Not All About You." Although researchers have yet to find the formula for a perfect leader, they have shed a bright light on the optimal conditions for leadership development.

trait approach to leader effectiveness Approach to determining what makes an effective leader that focuses on the personal characteristics displayed by successful leaders.

behavioral theories of leader effectiveness Theories of leader effectiveness that focus on differences in the behaviors of effective and ineffective leaders.

situational (contingency) theories of leadership Leadership theories claiming that various situational factors influence a leader's effectiveness.

leader–member exchange model Emphasizes that the quality of the interactions between supervisors and subordinates varies depending on the unique characteristics of both.

∧ **"You Have to Speak Up"** Rosalind Brewer, who goes by Roz, was formerly the chief operating officer of Starbucks. In 2021, she became the chief executive officer (CEO) of Walgreens (Lucas et al., 2021). She is the only Black female CEO of a Fortune 500 company. The youngest of five children from parents who were Detroit factory workers, Brewer is a graduate of Spelman College, a historically Black college and university (HBCU). Brewer emphasizes diversity in her leadership roles: "Every now and then you have to nudge your partners. You have to speak up and speak out. And I try to use my platform for that" (Alcorn, 2021).

Workplace Trends and Issues

The Society for Human Resource Management (Doheny, 2021) annually identifies the top challenges facing companies, although the typical issues that employers face have changed during the pandemic. These are among the top pandemic-related challenges (also from Brooks & Ling, 2020; Knifflin et al., 2021):

1. Maintaining the culture of the organization

2. Managing the challenges, including those related to communication, of having so many people working remotely (many for the first time)

3. Addressing concerns about employees' mental health, including the stress of the pandemic, loneliness among remote workers, and burnout among workers in general

4. Supporting workers faced with the added burdens of managing child care and supporting at-home learning

During the pandemic, every basic assumption about how we work has been questioned. Even for essential workers whose specific work requirements have not changed, so many aspects of their jobs, particularly those related to safety, have been upended. Based on these trends, the workplace of the future is expected to become more dynamic, diversified, flexible, health- and safety-conscious, and responsive. Organizations and their employees will need to adapt to the ever-changing world of work, complete with resource limitations and technological innovations. In the next sections, we'll look at some of these trends in the workplace, as well as how they have been impacted by the pandemic.

Workforce Diversity: Recruiting and Retaining Diverse Talent

Changing workforce demographics and expectations often require employers to adapt their workplace practices, including related to diversity, equity, and inclusion. These expectations often grow out of large-scale societal changes. For example, the #MeToo movement, which built on social media posts by activist Tarana Burke in 2006, became a global phenomenon in 2017. #MeToo calls for an end to sexual harassment and sexual assault, particularly in the workplace. Similarly, the global antiracist movement that emerged in the summer of 2020 has accelerated a movement toward increased diversity, equity, and inclusion, including in workplaces.

Diverse employees have diverse needs, interests, and expectations. Perhaps because of these diverse needs, companies have a tendency to want to hire people who match the existing workplace culture, rather than work to diversify the culture (Corritore et al., 2020). The pressure to adapt can be challenging, but diverse employees can also help organizations be more successful (Woolley et al., 2015). Work teams, just like individuals, have varying levels of cognitive ability, and the smartest teams seem to be those that are the most diverse (Cooke, 2015). A range of studies have shown the positive effects of teams that are diverse in culture, ethnicity, and gender, as well as in the approach to work, such as in communication styles. For example, diverse teams are more likely to accurately value stocks, develop novel products, and introduce innovative ideas (Díaz-García et al., 2013; Levine et al., 2014; Nathan & Lee, 2013). Moreover, both racial and gender diversity are linked with increases in sales, numbers of customers, and profits (Herring, 2009; Hunt et al., 2015).

Importantly, adaptability predicts success among employees more than fit. Researchers analyzed more than 10 million internal emails of employees of a technology company. They found that employees who shifted their communication style to the match the company's culture as it shifted over time "were more successful than employees who exhibited high cultural fit when first hired" (Corritore et al., 2020). One study looked at marital diversity and found more success in the workplace—and in rock bands—that had a mix of single and partnered members (Jehn & Conlon, 2018).

Q IN FOCUS

Servant Leadership: When It's Not All About You

What do Jeffrey Skilling, Martin Shkreli, and Rupert Stadler have in common? They were all entrusted with leadership positions for corporate giants, in these cases Enron, Turing Pharmaceuticals, and Audi. They also failed miserably in their posts as leaders. Former CEO of the now-defunct Enron, Jeffrey Skilling, for example, went to federal prison having been found guilty of fraud and insider trading in one of the United States' most notorious cases of corporate corruption.

There's a growing body of research that suggests that an organization's culture is a reflection of its leader (Oreg & Berson, 2018). In the examples we just described, all three of these individuals are what some researchers call narcissistic leaders. What does that mean for their organizations? Some degree of narcissism can help leaders to be more charismatic and effective (Fatfouta, 2019; Grijalva et al., 2015). But research on selfish leadership demonstrates that leaders who are high in narcissism display certain behaviors that make them more likely to take self-serving risks, inconsiderate of the role of stewardship placed upon them as leaders. One study found that such CEOs focus on themselves at the expense of organizational awareness (Chatterjee & Hambrick, 2007; Galvin et al., 2015). By featuring their pictures, their names, and their stories on organizational literature, these CEOs demand all the attention, instead of sharing the spotlight with the hardworking "stagehands" behind the scenes. As Jeffrey Skilling famously said, "I am Enron" (McLean & Elkind, 2003).

Enter the servant leader. In 1970, Robert Greenleaf, a retired AT&T corporate executive, was the first to use the term servant leader. He defined a servant leader as one who makes service to others, including one's employees, the foremost leadership objective. Greenleaf believed that servant leaders are successful because of their sincere commitment to helping their followers succeed. They invert the organizational chart, placing employee needs above their own (Zandy, 2007). Employee-centeredness, where the leader's focus is on employee concerns, allows leaders to roll up their sleeves during crunch times. Most important, servant leaders' humility allows them to recognize their employees as emerging leaders who need organizational support to reach their potential (Roberts, 2019). Humility is the servant leader's most prominent trait, unlike the narcissistic leader's self-promotion.

Warren Buffett, one of the richest men in the world, exemplifies servant leadership. Buffett's financial success often overshadows his generous spirit and humble demeanor; he has pledged to give 99 percent of his $89 billion fortune to charity. Buffett was reported to have said, "If you're in the luckiest 1 percent of humanity, you owe it to the rest of humanity to think about the other 99 percent" (Schwantes, 2018). As a leader, he values the development of his staff and colleagues, often acknowledging his own mistakes before announcing their successes. His ethical transparency allows

everything to be disclosed. Buffett says, "You don't need to play outside the lines. You can make a lot of money hitting the ball down the middle" (George, 2006). If only Skilling, Shkreli, and Stadler had followed his lead.

Mike Coppola/Getty Images

⌃ **Why Were You Not Part of This?** Hamdi Ulukaya (wearing glasses in this photo), a Turkish-Kurdish immigrant to the United States, is the billionaire founder of Chobani, the company that makes the best-selling Greek-style yogurt. He's also well known for his generosity: Ulukaya has implemented a policy to hire refugees at his Chobani manufacturing plants in the United States. He has also joined Warren Buffett and others in pledging to donate a large percentage of his wealth. In Ulukaya's case, the wealth will go to a charity he founded that works with businesses to support refugees, including by hiring them (tent.org). Ulukaya is now working with companies in Colombia to help refugees from Venezuela by providing jobs. "It's good for the companies to be a part of this," Ulukaya said during a trip to Colombia. "Because people 5 years or 10 years from now are going to question, 'What did you do about this? Why were you not part of this?'" (Fieser, 2019).

A news headline about the study proclaimed: "Rock Bands Need a Married Square as Much as They Do the Wild Bachelor" (Jacobs, 2018).

When there are managers or task forces explicitly responsible for developing and promoting programs to increase diversity, equity, and inclusion within a company, outcomes have been found to be more successful than when other tactics, including affirmative action initiatives and diversity training, are used (Dobbin & Kalev, 2015). Why? Some believe it's because they introduce a layer of accountability and oversight that encourages everyone in the organization to consider diversity in hiring decisions.

Technology in the Workplace: Data, Big and Small

Increasingly, companies are using technology to more effectively and efficiently manage the people who work for them. (We'll address the enormous changes related to video-conferencing in the next section.) For example, we know that immediate feedback is helpful in the classroom (Hattie & Yates, 2014); some companies think it might help in the workplace, too. General Electric developed a smartphone app that allows managers to give immediate feedback — say, quick notes after a meeting (Streitfeld, 2015). And Amazon has a tool called "Anytime Feedback" to allow employees to send positive or negative comments to management.

Not all technology feels friendly, however. For example, technology designed to monitor employees can feel intrusive. When a money-transfer company called Intermax required regional salespeople to download a tracking app that was on 24 hours a day, some employees complained (Streitfeld, 2015). One woman reported her manager joking that "he knew how fast she was driving at all times." In the office, many companies use the Internet for employee surveillance to root out illegal behaviors, to ensure that company information is not being shared, and to reduce "time theft" through nonwork Internet use (Rosenblat et al., 2014). Although employees may understand that monitoring is meant to increase efficiency, many have "a gut feeling that monitoring is invasive or sinister" (Rosenblat et al., 2014). During the pandemic, the rise of remote work led to monitoring-related concerns among about 60 percent of UK workers, with more than a third of employees saying they would quit if such surveillance were implemented (OWLLabs, 2020b).

These digital trends seem likely to increase, despite worker concerns. In the words of Khiv Singh, vice president of an India-based company that develops these kinds of workplace technologies, "We have pedometers to measure how far we walk, apps to monitor our blood pressure, stress level, the calories we're taking in, the calories we're burning. But the office is where we spend the majority of time, and we don't measure our work" (Steitfeld, 2015). I/O psychologists are helping to change that, and they can help us understand the impact of assessment on workers, too. Almost certainly, the expansion of remote work during the pandemic will contribute to the conversation.

∧ Co-Working Spaces Pre-pandemic, co-working spaces offered an alternative to the social and professional isolation of remote work and freelance, gig-economy jobs. Austin-based co-working space owner Felicity Maxwell (personal communication, March 25, 2021) described the changes that occurred during the pandemic when the very survival of her business was in jeopardy. "Good news is that many coworking communities continued to thrive by shifting to virtual events and reworking their existing space to accommodate new health and safety concerns. Thankfully, humans continue to crave social interaction, which is why the flexibility offered by coworking is perfect as we transition to a new work/professional paradigm." Maxwell predicts that the networking central to co-working spaces will continue, although the networking tools will likely change.

Remote Work: The Best Retention Tool

Before the pandemic, about half of U.S. workers held jobs that could be performed at home by telecommuting, often called working remotely, at least part of the time (GlobalWorkplaceAnalytics, 2019). Remote workers are defined as those who work for an employer who permits them to work off-site, rather than those who are self-employed. For professional jobs, the percentage of employers who allow at least some employees to work remotely had been increasing rapidly even before the pandemic. In 2018, for example, 56 percent of companies worldwide permitted remote work, with that number even higher in the United States—85 percent (OWLLabs, 2018). Worldwide, 16 percent of companies were fully remote, with all employees working remotely.

An international team of researchers documented the changes in work patterns during the pandemic (Knifflin et al., 2021). These changes included an enormous shift to remote work, a shift that these researchers expect will last well beyond the pandemic. In the United States, close to 70 percent of full-time employees and, in the United Kingdom, close to half of full-time employees are working fully at home (OWLLabs, 2020a, 2020b). Expectations related to working from home changed along with these trends. Most workers said that they prefer working from home. In the United States, half said they would quit if they could not continue to work remotely after the pandemic, and almost a quarter would accept a pay cut if they could work from home at least part of the time (OWLLabs, 2020a). These percentages were also high in the United Kingdom—about 40 percent and 45 percent, respectively. Why is remote work so popular? Remote work offers advantages such as flexible work schedules, more freedom at work, and less time wasted commuting.

As with any major change in the workplace, remote working poses new challenges to organizations. There are drawbacks to working from home, such as the potential for feeling socially and professionally isolated. (And during the pandemic, work from home was combined with child care and oversight of remote learning for many parents.)

Another drawback of remote work involves the negative emotions and mental exhaustion that define what is often called "Zoom fatigue." During the pandemic, the use of videoconferencing programs skyrocketed. With Zoom alone, the number of users grew from 10 million in 2019 to 300 million just by April 2020 (Wiederhold, 2020). Why is videoconferencing so draining? Some research blames the almost imperceptible but constant delay during videoconferencing that "[disrupts] our normal intricate human communication methods that have been finely tuned over centuries to help humans survive" (Wiederhold, 2020). Several researchers offer suggestions on how to fight the fatigue (Fosslien & Duffy, 2020; OWLLabs, 2020a; Widerhold, 2020). Have one no-meeting day every week. Build in breaks, scheduling a 25- or 50-minute meeting rather than a half hour or an hour. Refrain from multitasking, as hard as that is, because it reduces productivity and attention, and drains your alertness. And finally, consider going old-school and using audio only when meeting with small groups or skipping meetings altogether when issues could be resolved via email or a Slack message.

However, research suggests that working remotely has predominantly positive effects for both employees and employers, particularly when remote work is not full-time. Employees who work remotely some of the time tend to be more satisfied, productive, and loyal to the employer, and organizations that permit remote working tend to have increased profits and productivity (Allen et al., 2015; Gajendran & Harrison, 2007; OWLLabs, 2020a). In addition, some groups have particularly benefited from remote work during the pandemic. These include parents (particularly women who have taken on a disproportionate amount of extra work) and people with some disabilities, who have demonstrated increased productivity outside of the "long hours, rigid schedules, and uninterrupted, in-person performance at a centralized workspace" (Travis, 2020). I/O psychologists guide employers to implement remote work options in ways that are beneficial for both employer and employee—many of which harness the lessons learned during COVID.

The Gig Economy: The Changing Nature of Work

Beyond remote workers, there's another class of workers who enjoy flexibility, but lack the security and benefits that many employers provide. Self-employed workers, often called freelancers or independent contractors, are part of what is termed "the gig economy." Paid for individual projects, or gigs, some work as freelancers in versions of traditional full-time jobs like editors, accountants, and electricians. Others work on demand through app-based start-ups like ride-sharing sites or Web sites like Amazon's

The Gig Economy The gig economy encompasses a wide range of jobs, but many are unskilled and short term. Internet-based companies have developed to connect people looking for freelance work with people who need a specific job done. Through one such company, TaskRabbit, so-called taskers sign up to help with odd jobs such as moving, cleaning, furniture assembly, and errands. Each one-time gig can be as short as a single hour. Here, "taskers" are packing boxes for a company that supplies clients with environmentally sustainable products.

Peter Bohler/Redux Pictures

Mechanical Turk that match people with time for a quick job with people who need to get small tasks done. Brittany, whom we featured in the prologue, was among these workers, driving on and off for ride services over several years.

This category of workers is growing. As of 2020, close to 60 million Americans worked as freelancers—more than 60 percent of them by choice (FinancesOnline, 2021; Lesonsky, 2019). Some people do gig work to supplement their income from another job (Rothwell, 2019). And some people just prefer gig work to traditional jobs. Between projects, filmmaker Tykecia Hayes picks up gigs working as a personal assistant. "I'm able to work when I need money and take off when I need to," Hayes explains. "That's the beauty of it" (Torpey & Hogan, 2016). But others complain about the need to balance multiple jobs, the inconsistent nature of the work, and the lack of benefits (Torpey & Hogan, 2016). Low pay is another issue (Dilawar, 2018). In 2016, 92 percent of U.S. workers contracting jobs through Amazon's Mechanical Turk platform reported earning far less than minimum wage (Hitlin, 2016). One Mechanical Turker reported that they were "lucky to get $5 a day" (Mehrotra, 2020).

For all its promise and problems, the gig economy is not going away. it has already replaced many traditional jobs. In some cases, on-demand services like food delivery replace full-time jobs like hotel room-service cooks; in other cases, big corporations are hiring temporary workers and contractors in increasing numbers (Kim, 2020; Wakabayashi, 2019). As these disruptions continue to occur, especially during the pandemic, I/O psychologists can help employers manage the impact on workers and customers when converting traditional jobs into gig work. I/O psychologists can also help guide policies that promote the benefits of the gig economy while protecting this class of workers.

Emotional Labor: Smile—or Else!

The specialty grocery company Trader Joe's made headlines when an employee filed a complaint with the U.S. National Labor Relations Board (NLRB) about unfair practices (Scheiber, 2016). He was fired, he said, for not having the "positive attitude" that was, in fact, a Trader Joe's job requirement. Throughout the service industry in the United States and in many countries worldwide, employees have long been required to project a happy demeanor to customers, a practice called "emotional labor" (Kramer, 2013).

I/O psychologist Alicia Grandey's (2000; Grandey & Sayre, 2019) research on emotional labor, which she calls "managing emotions for pay," demonstrates that the practice contributes to stress and burnout, both of which are discussed in more detail in the chapter on stress, health, and coping. She and her colleagues have also found evidence that those who engage in emotional labor drink more alcohol than others (Grandey et al., 2019). Grandey and her colleagues (2015) propose that employers banish "service with a smile" rules, focusing instead on creating a company culture that is genuinely positive. The NLRB may have listened. For example, they ordered the telecommunications giant T-Mobile to remove a rule that required employees "to maintain a positive work environment" (Scheiber, 2016).

Work–Life Balance: Engaging and Retaining Employees

Juggling the demands of both career and family can lead to many conflicts, but there are workplace interventions, including informal ones, that can reduce these conflicts (French & Shockley, 2020). This struggle, often called *work–family conflict* or *work–life balance,* results in higher absenteeism, lower morale, and higher turnover in the workplace. The problem is particularly common in the United States, and was exacerbated everywhere during the pandemic. In the Prologue, we heard about Brittany's balance between her various jobs and raising her young son. An Organisation for Economic

Co-operation and Development (OECD) report ranked the United States 29th in work–life balance out of the 40 countries it studied (OECD, n.d.). The OECD noted that the United States lacks many family-friendly policies. In particular, it's the only country in their study that does not have a national policy requiring paid leave for new parents. Research shows that "[workplace] policies for families in the U.S. are weaker than those of *all* high-income countries and even many middle- and low-income countries" (Heymann, 2007). Thibaut and van Wijngaarden-Cremers (2020) have documented the particular perils of these policies for women during the pandemic. Because women have been bearing a disproportionate amount of child care and homemaking duties during the pandemic, as compared to men, they are also experiencing a disproportionate amount of psychological consequences.

Some researchers have reframed the work–family conflict in positive terms: work–family engagement (Crain & Hammer, 2013). And during the pandemic, many employees valued the time with their families that remote work permitted (OWLLabs, 2020a). Results from a meta-analysis of 38 studies found that employee perceptions of family-friendly work culture, along with supportive bosses and spouses, can reduce work–family conflict (Mesmer-Magnus & Viswesvaran, 2006). Another study found that a company's emphasis on workplace flexibility led to higher job satisfaction among employees (Daniel & Sonnentag, 2016). Therefore, it makes good business sense to help working parents balance the demands of work and family life.

To keep pace with evolving challenges such as the workplace trends and issues we have described, I/O psychologists constantly need to adjust the focus of their research and its applications. This is only more true during and after the pandemic. In the future, I/O psychologists will continue to have a significant role in and around the workplace.

Single Mom, Artist, and Versatile Worker Like many millennials, Brittany has held a range of jobs and also has been entrepreneurial, founding her own art-and-science-based business. Brittany juggles her work with caring for her young son, Lucian. Sometimes that means bringing him to work. Lucian likes to paint while she's in her art studio and "always breaks something" when he accompanies her to estate sales and thrift stores to seek out materials for her art. The pandemic blurred boundaries between work and childcare for many people, particularly for women, and may lead to lasting changes in work-life balance.

APPENDIX REVIEW

KEY PEOPLE

Lillian Moller Gilbreth, p. B-3

KEY TERMS

industrial/organizational (I/O) psychology, p. B-2

personnel psychology, p. B-2

organizational behavior, p. B-2

job analysis, p. B-4

selection device validity, p. B-5

discrepancy hypothesis, p. B-8

trait approach to leader effectiveness, p. B-9

behavioral theories of leader effectiveness, p. B-9

situational (contingency) theories of leadership, p. B-9

leader–member exchange model, p. B-9

Industrial/Organizational Psychology

The study of human behavior in the workplace

Lillian Moller Gilbreth (1878–1972): Pioneer of industrial/organizational (I/O) psychology who applied I/O principles to the workplace and home

Personnel Psychology

A subarea of I/O psychology that focuses on matching people's characteristics to job requirements, accurately measuring job performance, and assessing employee training needs

Allison Shelley/Getty Images

- A **job analysis** helps determine the major responsibilities of a job and the human characteristics needed to fill it.
- **Selection device validity** is the extent to which a device such as an interview or work sample helps distinguish applicants who will become high performers.
- Psychological tests used in the selection process include integrity tests, cognitive ability tests, and personality tests.

Workplace Trends and Issues

- Workforce diversity
- Technology in the workplace
- Telework and telecommuting
- The gig economy
- Emotional labor
- Work–life balance

Organizational Behavior

A subarea of I/O psychology that focuses on the workplace culture and its influence on employee behavior

- Job satisfaction is studied by examining the **discrepancy hypothesis,** which looks at the gaps between what a person wants from a job and what that person actually experiences.
- Leadership effectiveness has been studied through the **trait approach, behavioral theories,** and most effectively, through **situational (contingency) theories.** The **leader–member exchange model** is used for describing relationships between leaders and employers.

Peter Bohler/Redux Pictures

GLOSSARY

A

absolute threshold The smallest possible strength of a stimulus that can be detected half the time.

accommodation The process by which the lens changes shape to focus incoming light so that it falls on the retina.

acculturative stress (uh-CUL-chur-uh-tiv) The stress that results from the pressure of adapting to a new culture.

acetylcholine (uh-seet-ull-KO-leen) A neurotransmitter that is the chemical means by which neurons communicate with muscles.

achievement motivation The desire to direct your behavior toward excelling, succeeding, or outperforming others at some task.

achievement test A test designed to measure a person's level of knowledge, skill, or accomplishment in a particular area.

action potential A brief electrical impulse that transmits information along the axon of a neuron.

activation–synthesis model of dreaming The theory that brain activity during sleep produces dream images (*activation*), which are combined by the brain into a dream story (*synthesis*).

activity theory of aging The psychosocial theory that life satisfaction in late adulthood is highest when people maintain the level of activity they displayed earlier in life.

actualizing tendency In Rogers's theory, the innate drive to maintain and enhance the human organism.

adolescence The transitional stage between late childhood and the beginning of adulthood, during which sexual maturity is reached.

adolescent growth spurt The period of accelerated growth during puberty, involving rapid increases in height and weight.

adrenal glands A pair of endocrine glands that produce hormones involved in the human stress response and play a key role in the fight-or-flight response.

aggression Verbal or physical behavior intended to cause harm to other people.

agoraphobia An anxiety disorder involving extreme fear of suffering a panic attack or other embarrassing or incapacitating symptoms in a public situation where escape is impossible and help is unavailable.

algorithm A problem-solving strategy that involves following a specific rule, procedure, or method that inevitably produces the correct solution.

alpha brain waves Brain-wave pattern associated with relaxed wakefulness and drowsiness.

altruism Helping another person with no expectation of personal reward or benefit.

Alzheimer's disease (AD) A progressive disease that destroys the brain's neurons, gradually impairing memory, thinking, language, and other cognitive functions, resulting in the complete inability to care for oneself.

amnesia (am-NEE-zha) Severe memory loss.

amphetamines (am-FET-uh-meenz) A class of stimulant drugs that arouse the central nervous system and suppress appetite.

amygdala (uh-MIG-dull-uh) An almond-shaped cluster of neurons at the base of the temporal lobe.

animal cognition or **comparative cognition** The study of animal learning, memory, thinking, and language.

anorexia nervosa An eating disorder characterized by excessive weight loss, an irrational fear of gaining weight, and distorted body self-perception.

anterograde amnesia Loss of memory caused by the inability to store new memories.

anthropomorphism The attribution of human traits, motives, emotions, or behaviors to nonhuman animals or inanimate objects.

antianxiety medications Prescription drugs that are used to alleviate the symptoms of anxiety.

antidepressant medications Prescription drugs that are used to reduce the symptoms associated with major depressive disorder.

antipsychotic medications (an-tee-sy-KAHT-ick or an-ty-sy-KAHT-ick) Prescription drugs that are used to reduce psychotic symptoms; frequently used in the treatment of schizophrenia; also called *neuroleptics*

antisocial personality disorder A personality disorder characterized by a pervasive pattern of disregarding and violating the rights of others.

anxiety An unpleasant emotional state characterized by physical arousal and feelings of tension, apprehension, and worry.

anxiety disorders A category of psychological disorders in which extreme anxiety is the main diagnostic feature and causes significant disruptions in the person's cognitive, behavioral, or interpersonal functioning.

aphasia (uh-FAYZH-yuh) The partial or complete inability to articulate ideas or understand spoken or written language because of brain injury or damage.

aptitude test A test designed to assess a person's capacity to benefit from education or training.

arousal theory The view that people are motivated to maintain a level of arousal that is optimal—neither too high nor too low.

attachment The emotional bond that forms between an infant and caregiver(s), especially their parents.

attention The capacity to selectively focus awareness on particular stimuli in your external environment or on your internal thoughts or sensations.

attitude A learned tendency to evaluate some object, person, or issue in a particular way.

attribution The mental process of inferring the cause of someone's behavior, including one's own.

atypical antipsychotic medications Newer antipsychotic medications that block dopamine receptors in brain regions associated with psychotic symptoms rather than more globally throughout the brain, decreasing side effects.

audition The scientific term for the sense of hearing.

authoritarian parenting style Parenting style in which parents are demanding and unresponsive toward their children's needs or wishes.

authoritative parenting style Parenting style in which parents set clear standards for their children's behavior but are also responsive to their children's needs and wishes.

autonomic nervous system (aw-toe-NAHM-ick) The subdivision of the peripheral nervous system that regulates *involuntary* functions, such as heartbeat, blood pressure, breathing, and digestion.

availability heuristic A strategy in which the likelihood of an event is estimated on the basis of how readily available other instances of the event are in memory.

aversive conditioning A relatively ineffective type of behavior therapy that involves repeatedly pairing an aversive stimulus with the occurrence of undesirable behaviors or thoughts.

axon The part of the neuron that carries information *from* the neuron *to* other cells in the body, including other neurons, glands, and muscles.

axon terminals Small branches at the end of the axon.

B

barbiturates (barb-ITCH-yer-its) A category of depressant drugs that reduce anxiety and produce sleepiness.

basic emotions The most fundamental set of emotion categories, which are biologically innate, evolutionarily determined, and culturally universal.

basilar membrane (BAZ-uh-ler or BAYZuh-ler) The membrane within the cochlea of the ear that contains the hair cells.

behavior modification   The application of learning principles to help people develop more effective or adaptive behaviors.

behavior therapy   Type of psychotherapy that focuses on directly changing maladaptive behavior patterns by using basic learning principles and techniques; also called *behavior modification*.

behavioral genetics   An interdisciplinary field that studies the effects of genes and heredity on behavior.

behavioral theories of leader effectiveness   Theories of leader effectiveness that focus on differences in the behaviors of effective and ineffective leaders.

behaviorism   School of psychology and theoretical viewpoint that emphasizes the study of observable behaviors, especially as they pertain to the process of learning.

beta brain waves   Brain-wave pattern associated with alert wakefulness.

bilingualism   Fluency in two or more languages.

binocular cues   (by-NOCK-you-ler) Distance or depth cues that require the use of both eyes.

biological preparedness   The idea that an organism is innately predisposed to form associations between certain stimuli and responses.

biological psychology   The scientific study of the biological bases of behavior and mental processes.

biomedical therapies   Use of medications, electroconvulsive therapy, or other medical treatments to treat the symptoms associated with psychological disorders.

biopsychosocial model   The belief that physical health and illness are determined by the complex interaction of biological, psychological, and social factors.

bipolar disorder   A mood disorder involving periods of incapacitating depression alternating with periods of extreme euphoria and excitement; formerly called *manic depression*.

blaming the victim   The tendency to blame an innocent victim of misfortune for having somehow caused the problem or for not having taken steps to avoid or prevent it.

blind spot   The point at which the optic nerve leaves the eye, producing a small gap in the field of vision.

body mass index (BMI)   A numerical measure of body fat and weight status based on height and weight.

borderline personality disorder (BPD)   A personality disorder characterized by instability of interpersonal relationships, self-image, and emotions, and marked impulsivity.

bottom-up processing   Emphasizes sensory receptors in detecting the basic features of a stimulus; attention focuses on the parts of the pattern before moving to the whole.

brainstem   A region of the brain made up of the hindbrain and the midbrain.

Broca's area   A brain region in the frontal lobe of the dominant hemisphere, usually the left, that is critical for speech production.

bulimia nervosa   An eating disorder characterized by binges of extreme overeating followed by self-induced vomiting, misuse of laxatives, or other methods to purge excess food and prevent weight gain.

burnout   An unhealthy condition caused by chronic, prolonged work stress that is characterized by exhaustion, cynicism, and a sense of failure or inadequacy.

bystander effect   A phenomenon in which the greater the number of people present, the less likely each individual is to help someone in distress.

C

caffeine   (kaff-EEN) A stimulant drug found in coffee, tea, cola drinks, chocolate, and many over-the-counter medications.

California Psychological inventory (CPI)   A self-report inventory that assesses personality characteristics in normal populations.

case study   An intensive, in-depth investigation of an individual, a family, or some other social unit.

catecholamines   (cat-uh-COLE-uh-meenz) Hormones secreted by the adrenal medulla that cause rapid physiological arousal and include adrenaline and noradrenaline.

cell body   The part of a neuron that contains structures that process nutrients, providing the energy the neuron needs to function; also called the *soma*.

central nervous system (CNS)   The division of the nervous system that consists of the brain and spinal cord.

centration   The tendency to focus, or *center*, on only one aspect of a situation and ignore other important aspects of the situation.

cerebellum   (sair-uh-BELL-um) A large, two-sided hindbrain structure at the back of the brain that is responsible for muscle coordination and equilibrium.

cerebral cortex   (suh-REE-brull or SAIRuh-brull) The wrinkled outer portion of the forebrain, which contains the most sophisticated brain centers.

cerebral hemispheres   The nearly symmetrical left and right halves of the cerebral cortex.

chromosome   A long, threadlike structure composed of twisted parallel strands of DNA.

chunking   Increasing the amount of information that can be held in short-term memory by grouping related items together into a single unit, or *chunk*.

circadian rhythm   (ser-KADE-ee-en) A roughly 24-hour-long cycle of fluctuations in biological and psychological processes.

classical conditioning   The basic learning process that involves repeatedly pairing a neutral stimulus with a response-producing stimulus until the neutral stimulus elicits the same response.

client-centered therapy   Type of psychotherapy in which the therapist is nondirective and reflective, and the client directs the focus of each therapy session; also called *person-centered therapy*

clustering   Organizing items into related groups, or clusters, during recall from long-term memory.

cocaine   An illegal stimulant derived from the leaves of the coca plant, which is found in South America.

cochlea   (COKE-lee-uh or COCK-lee-uh) The coiled, fluid-filled inner-ear structure that contains the basilar membrane and hair cells.

cognition   The mental activities involved in acquiring, retaining, and using knowledge.

cognitive appraisal model of stress   A model of stress that emphasizes the role of an individual's evaluation (appraisal) of events and situations and of the resources that they have available to deal with the event or situation.

cognitive appraisal theory of emotion   The theory that emotional responses are triggered by a cognitive evaluation.

cognitive dissonance   An unpleasant state of psychological tension (*dissonance*) that occurs when two thoughts or perceptions (*cognitions*) are inconsistent.

cognitive map   Tolman's term for the mental representation of the layout of a familiar environment.

cognitive therapies   Group of psychotherapies based on the assumption that psychological problems are due to illogical patterns of thinking; techniques focus on recognizing and altering unhealthy thinking patterns.

cognitive therapy (CT)   Therapy developed by Aaron T. Beck that focuses on changing the client's unrealistic and maladaptive beliefs.

cognitive-behavioral therapy (CBT)   Therapy that integrates cognitive and behavioral techniques and that is based on the assumption that thoughts, moods, and behaviors are interrelated.

collective unconscious   In Jung's theory, the hypothesized part of the unconscious mind that is inherited from previous generations and that contains universally shared ancestral experiences and ideas.

collectivistic cultures   Cultures that emphasize the needs and goals of the group over the needs and goals of the individual.

color   The perceptual experience of different wavelengths of light, involving hue, saturation (purity), and brightness (intensity).

comparative psychology   The branch of psychology that studies the behavior of nonhuman animals.

comprehension vocabulary   The words that are understood by an infant or child.

compulsions   Repetitive behaviors or mental acts that a person feels driven to perform in order to prevent or reduce anxiety and distress or to prevent a dreaded event or situation.

concept   A mental category of objects or ideas based on properties they share.

concrete operational stage   The third stage of cognitive development, which lasts from about age 7 to adolescence and is characterized by the ability to think logically about concrete objects and situations.

conditional positive regard   In Rogers's theory, the sense that the child is valued and loved only if they behave in a way that is acceptable to others.

conditioned reinforcer   A stimulus or event that has acquired reinforcing value by being associated with a primary reinforcer; also called a secondary reinforcer.

conditioned response (CR) The learned, reflexive response to a previously neutral stimulus.

conditioned stimulus (CS) A formerly neutral stimulus that acquires the capacity to elicit a reflexive response.

conditioning The process of learning associations between environmental events and behavioral responses.

cones The short, thick, pointed sensory receptors of the eye that detect color.

confirmation bias The tendency to seek out evidence that confirms an existing belief while ignoring evidence that might contradict or undermine that belief.

conformity Adjusting opinions, judgments, or behaviors so that they match those of other people, or the norms of a social group or situation.

confounding variable Extraneous variables that are not the focus of the experiment but could affect the outcome of an experiment.

consciousness Personal awareness of mental activities, internal sensations, and the external environment.

conservation The understanding that two equal quantities remain equal even if the form or appearance is rearranged, as long as nothing is added or subtracted.

context effect The tendency to recover information more easily when the retrieval occurs in the same setting as the original learning of the information.

continuous reinforcement A schedule of reinforcement in which every occurrence of a particular response is followed by a reinforcer.

control group Group of participants exposed to the control condition of the independent variable; also called *control condition*.

coping The ways in which we try to change circumstances, or our interpretation of circumstances, to make them more favorable and less threatening.

corpus callosum A thick band of axons that connects the two cerebral hemispheres and acts as a communication link between them.

correlation The relationship between two variables.

correlation coefficient A numerical indication of the magnitude and direction of the relationship (the *correlation*) between two variables.

correlational study A study that examines how strongly two variables are related to, or associated with, each other.

cortical localization The idea that particular brain areas are associated with specific functions.

corticosteroids (core-tick-oh-STER-oydz) Hormones released by the adrenal cortex that play a key role in the body's response to long-term stressors.

counterconditioning Behavior therapy technique that involves learning a new response that is incompatible with a previously learned response.

creativity A group of cognitive processes used to generate useful, original, and novel ideas or solutions to problems.

critical thinking Actively questioning statements rather than blindly accepting them.

cross-sectional design Research strategy for studying a variable or set of variables among a group of participants at a single point in time.

cued recall A test of long-term memory that involves remembering an item of information in response to a retrieval cue.

culture The attitudes, values, beliefs, and behaviors shared by a group of people and communicated from one generation to another.

D

daily hassles Everyday minor events that annoy and upset people.

decay theory The view that forgetting is due to normal brain processes that occur over time.

defense mechanisms Largely unconscious distortions of thoughts or perceptions that act to reduce anxiety.

deindividuation The reduction of self-awareness and inhibitions that can occur when a person is a part of a group whose members feel anonymous.

delusion A false belief that persists despite compelling contradictory evidence.

demand characteristics In a research study, subtle cues or signals expressed by the researcher that communicate the kind of response or behavior that is expected from the participant.

dementia Progressive deterioration and impairment of memory, reasoning, language, and other cognitive functions as the result of disease, injury, or substance abuse.

dendrites The part of the neuron that *receives* messages from other neurons.

deoxyribonucleic acid (DNA) The double-stranded molecule that encodes genetic instructions.

dependent variable The factor that is observed and measured for change in an experiment; also called the *outcome variable*.

depressants A category of psychoactive drugs that depress or inhibit brain activity.

depth perception The use of visual cues to perceive the distance or the three-dimensional characteristics of an object.

descriptive research Research that uses scientific procedures for systematically observing and describing behavior.

descriptive statistics Mathematical methods used to organize and summarize data.

developmental psychology The study of how people change physically, cognitively, and socially throughout the lifespan.

difference threshold The smallest possible difference between two stimuli that can be detected half the time; also called *just noticeable difference*.

diffusion MRI (dMRI) An imaging technique that maps neural connections in the brain by tracking the movement of water molecules along myelinated axons.

diffusion of responsibility A phenomenon in which the presence of other people makes it less likely that any individual will help someone in distress because the obligation to intervene is shared among all the onlookers.

discrepancy hypothesis Approach to explaining job satisfaction that focuses on the discrepancy, if any, between what a person wants from a job and how that person evaluates what is actually experienced at work.

discriminative stimulus A specific stimulus that increases the likelihood of a particular response because it indicates that reinforcement is likely to occur.

displacement The defense mechanism that involves unconsciously shifting the target of an emotional urge to a substitute target that is less threatening or dangerous.

display rules Social and cultural regulations governing emotional expression, especially facial expressions.

dissociation The splitting of consciousness into two or more simultaneous streams of mental activity.

dissociative amnesia Dissociative disorder involving the partial or total inability to recall important personal information.

dissociative anesthetics Class of drugs that reduce sensitivity to pain and produce feelings of detachment and dissociation, rather than actual hallucinations; includes the club drugs phencyclidine (PCP) and ketamine.

dissociative disorders A category of psychological disorders in which extreme and frequent disruptions of awareness, memory, and personal identity impair the ability to function.

dissociative experience A break or disruption in consciousness during which awareness, memory, and personal identity become separated or divided.

dissociative fugue (fyoog) Type of dissociative amnesia involving sudden and unexpected travel away from home, extensive amnesia, and identity confusion.

dissociative identity disorder (DID) A dissociative disorder involving extensive memory disruptions for personal information along with the presence of two or more distinct identities, or "personalities" within a single person.

dopamine (DOPE-uh-meen) A neurotransmitter involved in movement, attention, learning, and pleasurable or rewarding sensations.

double-blind technique An experimental control in which both the participants and the researchers are "blind," or unaware of the treatment or condition to which the participants have been assigned.

dream An unfolding sequence of thoughts, perceptions, and emotions that typically occurs during REM sleep and is experienced as a series of real-life events.

drive A need or internal motivational state that activates behavior to reduce the need and restore homeostasis.

drive theories The view that behavior is motivated by the desire to reduce internal tension caused by unmet biological needs.

drug abuse (formally called *substance use disorder*) Recurrent substance use that involves impaired control, disruption of social, occupational, and interpersonal functioning, and the development of craving, tolerance, and withdrawal symptoms.

drug tolerance　A condition in which increasing amounts of a physically addictive drug are needed to produce the original, desired effect.

DSM-5　The abbreviation for the *Diagnostic and Statistical Manual of Mental Disorders*, Fifth Edition, which describes the symptoms of a disorder and diagnostic guidelines.

E

eardrum　A tightly stretched membrane that vibrates when hit by sound waves.

eating disorder　Category of psychological disorders characterized by severe disturbances in eating behavior.

eclecticism　(ih-KLEK-tih-siz-um) The pragmatic and integrated use of techniques from different psychotherapies.

effect size　A statistic that tells us, in general terms, whether a particular finding is small, medium, or large.

ego　In Freud's theory, the partly conscious rational component of personality that regulates thoughts and behavior, and is most in touch with the demands of the external world.

egocentrism　The inability to take another person's perspective or point of view.

elaborative rehearsal　Rehearsal that involves focusing on the meaning of information to help encode and transfer it to long-term memory.

electroconvulsive therapy (ECT)　Biomedical therapy used primarily in the treatment of major depressive disorder that involves electrically inducing a brief brain seizure; also called *electroshock therapy*.

electroencephalograph　(e-lec-tro-en-SEFF-uh-low-graph) An instrument that uses electrodes placed on the scalp to measure and record the brain's rhythmical electrical activity.

embryonic period　The second period of prenatal development, extending from the third week through the eighth week.

emerging adulthood　In industrialized countries, the distinct stage of the lifespan from the late teens through the 20s, characterized by exploration and flexibility in social roles, vocational choices, and relationships.

emotion　A complex psychological state that involves three distinct but related components: a cognitive experience, a physiological response, and a behavioral or expressive response.

emotion-focused coping　Coping efforts primarily aimed at relieving or regulating the emotional impact of a stressful situation.

empirical evidence　Verifiable evidence that is based upon objective observation, measurement, and/or experimentation.

encoding　The process of transforming information into a form that can be entered into and retained by the memory system.

encoding failure　The inability to recall specific information because of insufficient encoding of the information for storage in long-term memory.

encoding specificity principle　The principle that retrieval is more likely to be successful when the conditions of information retrieval are similar to the conditions of information encoding.

endocrine system　(EN-doe-krin) The system of glands, located throughout the body, that secrete hormones into the bloodstream.

endorphins　A class of neurotransmitter that is produced by the brain and released in response to pain and stress.

epigenetics　The study of the cellular mechanisms that control gene expression and of the ways that gene expression impacts health and behavior.

episodic memory　Category of long-term memory that includes memories of particular events, including the time and place that they occurred.

ESP (extrasensory perception)　Perception of information by some means other than through the normal processes of sensation.

ethnocentrism　The belief that one's own culture or ethnic group is superior to all others and the related tendency to use one's own culture as a standard by which to judge other cultures.

exemplars　Individual instances of a concept or category, held in memory.

experimental group　Group of participants who are exposed to all experimental conditions, including the treatment condition of the independent variable; also called *experimental condition*.

experimental research　A method of investigation used to demonstrate cause-and-effect relationships by purposely manipulating one factor thought to produce change in another factor.

explicit cognition　Deliberate, conscious mental processes involved in perceptions, judgments, decisions, and reasoning.

explicit memory　Information or knowledge that can be consciously recollected; also called *declarative memory*.

exposure therapy　Behavioral therapy for phobias, panic disorder, PTSD, or related anxiety disorders in which the person is repeatedly exposed to the disturbing object or situation under controlled conditions.

extinction (in classical conditioning)　The gradual weakening and apparent disappearance of conditioned behavior.

extinction (in operant conditioning)　A phenomenon that occurs when a learned response no longer results in reinforcement, and the likelihood of the behavior's being repeated gradually declines.

extrinsic motivation　External factors or influences on behavior, such as rewards, consequences, or social expectations.

F

facial feedback hypothesis　The view that expressing a specific emotion, especially facially, causes the subjective experience of that emotion.

false memory　A distorted or fabricated recollection of something that did not actually occur.

family therapy　Form of psychotherapy that is based on the assumption that the family is a system and that treats the family as a unit.

fetal period　The third and longest period of prenatal development, extending from the ninth week until birth.

fight-or-flight response　Rapidly occurring chain of internal physical reactions that prepare people to either fight or take flight from an immediate threat.

figure–ground relationship　Gestalt principle stating that a perception is automatically separated into the *figure*, which is the main element of the scene, and the *ground*, which is its background.

five-factor model of personality　A trait theory of personality that identifies extraversion, neuroticism, agreeableness, conscientiousness, and openness to experience as the fundamental building blocks of personality.

flashbulb memory　The recall of very specific images or details surrounding a vivid, rare, or significant personal event; details may or may not be accurate.

forebrain　The largest and most complex brain region, which contains centers for complex behaviors and mental processes; also called the *cerebrum*.

forgetting　The inability to recall information that was previously available.

formal operational stage　The fourth stage of cognitive development, which lasts from adolescence through adulthood and is characterized by thinking logically about abstract principles and hypothetical situations.

fovea　(FOE-vee-uh) A small area in the center of the retina, composed entirely of cones, where visual information is most sharply focused.

free association　A psychoanalytic technique in which the patient spontaneously reports all thoughts, feelings, and mental images that arise, revealing unconscious thoughts and emotions.

frequency　The rate of vibration, or the number of sound waves per second.

frequency distribution　A summary of how often various scores occur in a sample of scores; score values are arranged in order of magnitude, and the number of times each score occurs is recorded.

frequency theory　The view that the basilar membrane vibrates at the same frequency as the sound wave.

frontal lobe　The largest lobe of each cerebral hemisphere; it processes voluntary muscle movements and is involved in thinking, planning, and emotional control.

functional fixedness　The tendency to view objects as functioning only in their usual or customary way.

functional magnetic resonance imaging (fMRI)　An imaging technique that uses magnetic fields to map brain activity by measuring changes in the brain's blood flow and oxygen levels.

functional plasticity　The brain's ability to shift functions from damaged to undamaged brain areas.

functionalism　Early school of psychology that emphasized studying the purpose, or function, of behavior and mental experiences.

fundamental attribution error The tendency to attribute the behavior of others to internal, personal characteristics, while ignoring or underestimating the effects of external, situational factors.

G

g **factor or general intelligence** The notion that a general intelligence factor is responsible for a person's overall performance on tests of mental ability.

GABA (gamma-aminobutyric acid) A neurotransmitter that communicates *inhibitory* messages.

gate-control theory of pain Theory that physiological and psychological factors cause spinal gates to open and relay to the brain patterns of stimulation that are perceived as pain.

gender The cultural, social, and psychological meanings that are associated with masculinity and femininity.

gender identity A person's psychological sense of self as male or female.

gender-role stereotypes The beliefs and expectations people hold about the typical characteristics, preferences, and behavior of men and women.

gender roles The behaviors, attitudes, and personality traits that are designated as either masculine or feminine in a given culture.

gender schema theory The theory that gender development is influenced by the formation of schemas, or mental representations, of masculinity and femininity.

gene A unit of DNA on a chromosome that encodes instructions for making a particular protein molecule.

general adaptation syndrome Hans Selye's term for the three-stage progression of physical changes that occur when an organism is exposed to intense and prolonged stress. The three stages are alarm, resistance, and exhaustion.

generalized anxiety disorder (GAD) An anxiety disorder characterized by excessive, global, and persistent symptoms of anxiety.

genotype (JEEN-oh-type) The genetic makeup of an individual organism.

germinal period The first two weeks of prenatal development.

Gestalt psychology (geh-SHTALT) School of psychology that maintained sensations are actively processed according to consistent perceptual rules, producing meaningful whole perceptions, or *gestalts*.

glial cells (glia) (GLEE-ull) Cells that provide the structural and functional support for neurons throughout the nervous system.

glutamate A neurotransmitter that conveys excitatory messages.

group therapy Form of psychotherapy that involves one or more therapists working simultaneously with a small group of clients.

gustation Scientific name for the sense of taste.

H

hair cells The hair-like sensory receptors for sound, which are embedded in the basilar membrane.

hallucination A false or distorted perception that seems vividly real to the person experiencing it.

health psychology The branch of psychology that studies how biological, behavioral, and social factors influence health, illness, medical treatment, and health-related behaviors.

heritability The percentage of variation within a given population that is due to heredity.

heuristic A problem-solving strategy that involves following a general rule of thumb to reduce the number of possible solutions.

hierarchy of needs Maslow's levels of motivation that progress from basic physical needs to psychological needs to self-fulfillment needs.

higher order conditioning Procedure in which a conditioned stimulus from one learning trial functions as the unconditioned stimulus in a new conditioning trial; also called *second order conditioning*.

hindbrain A region at the base of the brain containing several structures that regulate basic life functions.

hindsight bias The tendency, after an event has occurred, to overestimate one's ability to have foreseen or predicted the outcome of an event.

hippocampus A large forebrain structure that is part of the limbic system and embedded in the temporal lobe in each cerebral hemisphere.

histogram A way of graphically representing a frequency distribution; a type of bar chart that uses vertical bars that touch.

homeostasis (home-ee-oh-STAY-sis) The idea that the body monitors and maintains internal states, such as energy supplies, at relatively constant levels.

hormones Chemical messengers secreted into the bloodstream primarily.

humanistic psychology School of psychology that emphasizes each person's unique potential for psychological growth and self-direction.

humanistic psychology (theory of personality) The view of personality that generally emphasizes the inherent goodness of people, human potential, self-actualization, the self-concept, and healthy personality development.

humanistic theories of motivation The view that emphasizes the importance of psychological and cognitive factors in motivation, especially the notion that people are motivated to realize their personal potential.

hypnosis (hip-NO-sis) A cooperative social interaction in which the hypnotized person responds to the hypnotist's suggestions with changes in perception, memory, thoughts, and behavior

hypothalamus (hi-poe-THAL-uh-muss) A complex structure that is found just beneath the thalamus (where its name comes from); it is the direct link between the endocrine system and the nervous system via the pituitary gland.

hypothesis (high-POTH-uh-sis) A tentative statement that describes the relationship between two or more variables.

I

id In Freud's theory, the completely unconscious, irrational component of personality that seeks immediate satisfaction of instinctual urges and drives.

identification A defense mechanism that involves reducing anxiety by imitating the behavior and characteristics of another person.

identity A person's sense of self, including their memories, experiences, and the values and beliefs that guide their behavior.

imagination inflation A memory phenomenon in which vividly imagining an event markedly increases confidence that the event actually occurred.

immune system Body system that produces specialized white blood cells that protect the body from viruses, bacteria, and tumor cells.

implicit attitudes Preferences and biases toward particular groups that are automatic, spontaneous, unintentional, and often unconscious.

implicit cognition Automatic, nonconscious mental processes that influence perceptions, judgments, decisions, and reasoning.

implicit memory Information or knowledge that affects behavior or task performance but cannot be consciously recollected; also called *nondeclarative memory*.

implicit personality theory A network of assumptions or beliefs about the relationships among various types of people, traits, and behaviors.

incentive theories The view that behavior is motivated by the pull of external goals, such as rewards.

independent variable A factor that is purposely manipulated to produce change in an experiment; also called a *predictor variable*.

individualistic cultures Cultures that emphasize the needs and goals of the individual over the needs and goals of the group.

induction A discipline technique that combines parental control with explaining why a behavior is prohibited.

industrial/organizational (I/O) psychology The branch of psychology that focuses on the study of human behavior in the workplace.

inferential statistics Mathematical methods used to determine how likely it is that a study's outcome is due to chance and whether the outcome can be legitimately generalized to a larger population.

informational social influence Behavior that is motivated by the desire to be correct.

information-processing model of cognitive development Model that views cognitive development as a process that is continuous over the lifespan and that studies the development of basic mental processes such as attention, memory, and problem solving.

ingroup   A social group to which one belongs.

ingroup bias   The tendency to judge the behavior of ingroup members favorably and outgroup members unfavorably.

inner ear   The part of the ear where sound is transduced into neural impulses; it consists of the cochlea and semicircular canals.

insight   The sudden realization of how a problem can be solved.

insomnia   A condition in which a person regularly experiences an inability to fall asleep, to stay asleep, or to feel adequately rested by sleep.

instinct theories   The view that certain human behaviors are innate and due to evolutionary programming.

instinctive drift   The tendency of an animal to revert to instinctive behaviors that can interfere with the performance of an operantly conditioned response.

intellectual disability   Neurodevelopmental disorder in which deficits in mental abilities impair functioning such that standards of personal independence are not met (formerly called *mental retardation*).

intellectual giftedness   A condition in which individuals have an IQ of 130 or higher and exceptional abilities in areas related to intelligence.

intelligence   The global capacity to think rationally, act purposefully, and deal effectively with the environment.

intelligence quotient (IQ)   A measure of general intelligence derived by comparing an individual's score with the scores of others in the same age group.

interference theory   The theory that forgetting is caused by one memory competing with or replacing another memory

interneuron   A type of neuron that communicates information between neurons.

interpersonal engagement   Emotion dimension reflecting the degree to which emotions involve a relationship with another person or other people.

interpersonal therapy (IPT)   A brief psychodynamic psychotherapy that focuses on current relationships and is based on the assumption that symptoms are caused and maintained by interpersonal problems.

interpretation   Psychoanalytic technique in which the psychoanalyst offers carefully timed explanations of the patient's dreams, feelings, or behaviors to help explore unconscious conflicts or motivations.

intersectionality   The ways in which a person's different group identities combine to influence their experience in the world.

intersex   Condition in which a person's biological sex is ambiguous, often combining aspects of both male and female anatomy and physiology.

intrinsic motivation   The desire to engage in tasks that are inherently satisfying and enjoyable, novel, or optimally challenging.

irreversibility   The inability to mentally reverse a sequence of events or logical operations.

J

James–Lange theory of emotion   The theory that emotions arise from the perception of body changes.

job analysis   A technique to identify the major responsibilities of a job, along with the human characteristics needed to fill it.

just-world hypothesis   The assumption that the world is fair and that therefore people get what they deserve and deserve what they get.

L

language   A system for combining arbitrary symbols to produce an infinite number of meaningful statements.

latent learning   Tolman's term for learning that occurs in the absence of reinforcement but is not behaviorally demonstrated until a reinforcer becomes available.

lateralization of function   The notion that specific psychological or cognitive functions are processed primarily on one side of the brain.

law of effect   Learning principle in which responses followed by satisfying effects are strengthened (more likely to occur again), but responses followed by dissatisfying effects are weakened (less likely to occur again).

leader–member exchange model   Emphasizes that the quality of the interactions between supervisors and subordinates varies depending on the unique characteristics of both.

learned helplessness   A phenomenon in which exposure to inescapable and uncontrollable aversive events produces passive behavior.

learning   A process that produces a relatively enduring change in behavior or knowledge as a result of an individual's experience.

learning styles   The idea, not supported by research, that people differ with regard to what mode of instruction is most effective for them.

lens   A transparent structure, located behind the pupil, that actively focuses, or bends, light as it enters the eye.

leptin   Hormone produced by fat cells that signals the hypothalamus, regulating hunger and eating behavior

limbic system   A group of forebrain structures that form a border around the brainstem and are involved in emotion, motivation, learning, and memory.

linguistic relativity hypothesis   The hypothesis that differences among languages cause differences in the thoughts of their speakers; also called the *Whorfian hypothesis*.

lithium   A naturally occurring substance that is used in the treatment of bipolar disorder.

longitudinal design   Research strategy that tracks a particular variable or set of variables in the same group of participants over time, sometimes for years.

long-term memory   The stage of memory that represents the long-term storage of information.

long-term potentiation   A long-lasting increase in synaptic strength between two neurons.

LSD   (lysergic acid diethyl-amide) A powerful synthetic psychedelic drug.

M

magnetic resonance imaging (MRI)   An imaging technique that produces highly detailed images of the body's structures and tissues, using electromagnetic signals generated by the body in response to magnetic fields.

maintenance rehearsal   The mental or verbal repetition of information in order to maintain it beyond the usual 20-second duration of short-term memory.

major depressive disorder   A mood disorder characterized by extreme and persistent feelings of despondency, worthlessness, and hopelessness, causing impaired emotional, cognitive, behavioral, and physical functioning.

manic episode   A sudden, rapidly escalating emotional state characterized by extreme euphoria, excitement, physical energy, and rapid thoughts and speech.

marijuana   A psychoactive drug derived from the hemp plant.

MDMA or ecstasy   Synthetic club drug that combines stimulant and mild psychedelic effects.

mean   The sum of a set of scores in a distribution divided by the number of scores; the mean is usually the most representative measure of central tendency.

measure of central tendency   A single number that presents some information about the "center" of a frequency distribution.

measure of variability   A single number that presents information about the spread of scores in a distribution.

median   The score that divides a frequency distribution exactly in half so that the same number of scores lie on each side of it.

meditation   A group of techniques that induce an altered state of focused attention and heightened awareness.

medulla   (muh-DOOL-uh) A hindbrain structure that controls vital life functions.

memory   The mental processes that enable you to encode, retain, and retrieve information over time.

memory consolidation   The gradual, physical process of converting new long-term memories to stable, enduring memory codes.

memory trace or engram   The hypothetical brain changes associated with a particular stored memory.

menarche   (meh-NAR-kee) A female's first menstrual period, which occurs during puberty.

menopause   The natural cessation of menstruation and the end of reproductive capacity in women.

mental age   A measurement of intelligence in which an individual's mental level is expressed in terms of the average abilities of a given age group.

mental image   A mental representation of objects or events that are not physically present.

mental set   The tendency to persist in solving problems with solutions that have worked in the past.

mescaline   (MESS-kuh-lin) A psychedelic drug derived from the peyote cactus.

meta-analysis   A statistical technique that involves pooling the effect sizes of several research studies into a single analysis.

midbrain   An important relay station that contains centers involved in the processing of auditory and visual sensory information.

middle ear   The part of the ear that amplifies sound wave; it consists of three small bones: the hammer, the anvil, and the stirrup.

mindfulness meditation   A technique in which practitioners focus *awareness* on *present experience* with *acceptance*.

Minnesota Multiphasic Personality inventory (MMPI)   A self-report inventory that assesses personality characteristics and psychological disorders; used to assess both normal and disturbed populations.

mirror neurons   Brain cells that become activated both when individuals perform a motor act and when they observe the same motor act done by another individual.

misinformation effect   A memory-distortion phenomenon in which your existing memories can be altered if you are exposed to misleading information.

mode   The most frequently occurring score in a distribution.

monocular cues   (mah-NOCK-you-ler) Distance or depth cues that can be processed by either eye alone.

mood congruence   An encoding specificity phenomenon in which a given mood tends to evoke memories that are consistent with that mood.

moon illusion   A visual illusion involving the misperception that the moon is larger when it is on the horizon than when it is directly overhead.

moral reasoning   The aspect of cognitive development that has to do with how an individual reasons about moral decisions.

motivation   The biological, emotional, cognitive, or social forces that activate and direct behavior.

motor neuron   A type of neuron that communicates information to the muscles and glands of the body.

Müller-Lyer illusion   A famous visual illusion involving the misperception of the identical length of two lines, one with arrows pointed inward, one with arrows pointed outward.

myelin sheath   (MY-eh-lin) A white, fatty covering wrapped around the axons of some, but not all, neurons in the brain.

N

narcolepsy   (NAR-ko-lep-see) A sleep disorder characterized by excessive daytime sleepiness and brief lapses into episodes of sleep throughout the day.

natural experiment   A study investigating the effects of a naturally occurring event on the research participants.

naturalistic observation   The systematic observation and recording of behaviors as they occur in their natural setting.

negative correlation   A finding that two factors vary systematically in opposite directions, one increasing as the other decreases.

negative punishment   A situation in which an operant is followed by the removal or subtraction of a reinforcing stimulus; also called *punishment by removal.*

negative reinforcement   A situation in which a response results in the removal of, avoidance of, or escape from an aversive, or undesired, stimulus, increasing the likelihood that the response will be repeated in similar situations.

negative symptoms   Defects or deficits in normal functioning, including flat affect.

nerves   Large bundles of neuron axons that carry information in the peripheral nervous system.

nervous system   A system of up to 1 *trillion linked* neurons throughout your body in a complex, organized communication network.

neurocognitive model of dreaming   Model that emphasizes the continuity between waking and dreaming cognition.

neurogenesis   The development of new neurons.

neurons   Cells that are highly specialized to receive and transmit information from one part of the body to another.

neuroscience   The study of the nervous system, especially the brain.

neurotransmitters   Chemical messengers manufactured by a neuron.

nicotine   A potent and addictive stimulant drug found in all tobacco products, including smokeless tobacco.

nightmare   A vivid and frightening or unpleasant anxiety dream that occurs during REM sleep.

norepinephrine   (nor-ep-in-EF-rin) A neurotransmitter implicated in the activation of neurons throughout the brain and helps the body gear up in the face of danger or threat.

normal curve or **normal distribution**   A bell-shaped distribution of individual differences in a normal population in which most scores cluster around the average score.

normative social influence   Behavior that is motivated by the desire to gain social acceptance and approval.

NREM sleep   Quiet, typically dreamless sleep in which rapid eye movements are absent.

O

obedience   The performance of a behavior in response to a direct command.

obesity   Condition characterized by excessive body fat and a body mass index equal to or greater than 30.0.

object permanence   The understanding that an object continues to exist even when it can no longer be seen.

observational learning   Learning that occurs through observing the actions of others.

obsessions   Repeated, intrusive, and uncontrollable irrational thoughts or mental images that cause extreme anxiety and distress.

obsessive–compulsive disorder (OCD)   A disorder characterized by intrusive, repetitive, and unwanted thoughts (obsessions) and repetitive behaviors or mental acts that an individual feels driven to perform (compulsions).

obstructive sleep apnea (OSA)   (APP-nee-uh) A sleep disorder in which the person repeatedly stops breathing during sleep.

occipital lobe   (ock-SIP-it-ull) An area at the back of each cerebral hemisphere that is the primary receiving area for visual information.

oedipus complex   In Freud's theory, a child's unconscious sexual desire for the opposite-sex parent, usually accompanied by hostile feelings toward the same-sex parent.

olfaction   Scientific name for the sense of smell.

olfactory bulb   (ole-FACK-tuh-ree) The enlarged ending of the olfactory cortex at the front of the brain where the sensation of smell is registered.

open science   The use of transparent research practices, including sharing the procedures of a study, the specifics of how the statistics were calculated, and the research data.

operant   Any "active behavior that operates upon the environment to generate consequences" (Skinner, 1953).

operant chamber or **Skinner box**   B. F. Skinner invented this experimental apparatus to scientifically study the relationship between environmental events and active behaviors.

operant conditioning   The basic learning process that involves changing the probability that a response will be repeated by manipulating the consequences of that response.

operational definition   A precise description of how the variables in a study will be measured, manipulated, or changed.

opioids   (OH-pee-oidz) A category of psychoactive drugs that are chemically similar to morphine and have strong pain relieving properties; also called *opiates* or *narcotics.*

opponent-process theory of color vision   Theory that color vision is the product of opposing pairs of color receptors: red–green, blue–yellow, and black–white; when one member of a pair is stimulated, the other is inhibited.

optic chiasm   (KY-az-uhm) The point in the brain where the optic nerve fibers from each eye meet and partly cross over to the opposite side of the brain.

optic nerve   The thick nerve that exits from the back of the eye and carries visual information to the visual cortex in the brain.

optimistic explanatory style   External, unstable, and specific explanations for negative events.

organizational behavior   A subarea of I/O psychology that focuses on the workplace culture and its influence on employee behavior.

outer ear   The part of the ear that collects sound waves; includes the pinna, the ear canal, and the eardrum.

outgroup   A social group to which one does not belong.

outgroup homogeneity effect   The tendency to see members of outgroups as very similar to one another.

oxytocin   A hormone involved in reproduction, social motivation, and social behavior that is produced by the hypothalamus and released into the bloodstream by the pituitary gland.

P

pain   The unpleasant sensory and emotional experience associated with actual or potential bodily damage.

panic attack   A sudden episode of extreme anxiety that rapidly escalates in intensity.

panic disorder   An anxiety disorder in which the person experiences frequent and unexpected panic attacks.

parapsychology   The scientific investigation of claims of paranormal phenomena and abilities.

parasomnias   (pare-uh-SOM-nee-uz) Category of sleep disorders characterized by undesirable physical arousal, behaviors, or events during sleep or sleep transitions; includes *sleepwalking, sleep terrors, sleepsex,* and *sleep-related eating disorder*.

parasympathetic nervous system   The branch of the autonomic nervous system that conserves and maintains your physical resources.

partial reinforcement   A situation in which the occurrence of a particular response is only sometimes followed by a reinforcer

partial reinforcement effect   The phenomenon in which behaviors that are conditioned using partial reinforcement are more resistant to extinction than behaviors that are conditioned using continuous reinforcement.

perception   The process of integrating, organizing, and interpreting sensations.

perceptual constancy   The tendency to perceive objects, especially familiar objects, as constant and unchanging despite changes in sensory input.

perceptual illusion   The misperception of the true characteristics of an object or an image.

perceptual set   The tendency to perceive objects or situations from a particular frame of reference.

parietal lobe   (puh-RYE-ut-ull) An area on each hemisphere of the cerebral cortex, located above the temporal lobe, that processes the body's sensations.

peripheral nervous system   (per-IF-er-ull) The division of the nervous system that includes all the nerves lying outside the central nervous system.

permissive parenting style   Parenting style in which parents are extremely tolerant and not demanding; permissive-indulgent parents are responsive to their children, while permissive-indifferent parents are unresponsive.

person perception   The mental processes used to form judgments and draw conclusions about the characteristics and motives of other people.

personality   An individual's unique and relatively consistent patterns of thinking, feeling, and behaving.

personality disorder   Inflexible, maladaptive, and stable patterns of thoughts, emotions, behavior, and interpersonal functioning that deviate from the expectations of the individual's culture.

personality theory   A theory that attempts to describe and explain similarities and differences in people's patterns of thinking, feeling, and behaving.

personnel psychology   A subarea of I/O psychology that focuses on matching people's characteristics to job requirements, accurately measuring job performance, and assessing employee training needs.

persuasion   The deliberate attempt to influence the attitudes or behavior of another person in a situation in which that person has some freedom of choice.

pessimistic explanatory style   Internal, stable, and global explanations for negative events.

phenotype   (FEEN-oh-type) The observable traits or characteristics of an organism as determined by the interaction of genetics and environmental factors.

pheromones   Chemical signals that have evolved for communication with other members of the same species; also called *chemosignals*.

phobia   A persistent and irrational fear of a specific object, situation, or activity.

physical dependence   A condition in which a person has physically adapted to a drug so that they must take it regularly in order to avoid withdrawal symptoms.

pitch   The relative highness or lowness of a sound, determined by the frequency of a sound wave.

pituitary gland   (pih-TOO-ih-tare-ee) A pea-sized gland just under the brain that regulates the production of other hormones by many of the glands in the endocrine system.

place theory   The view that different frequencies cause larger vibrations at different locations along the basilar membrane.

placebo   A fake substance, treatment, or procedure that has no known direct effects.

placebo effect   Any change attributed to a person's beliefs and expectations rather than to an actual drug, treatment, or procedure.

placebo response   An individual's psychological and physiological response to what is actually a fake treatment or drug; also called *placebo effect*.

pleasure principle   The fundamental human motive to obtain pleasure and avoid tension or discomfort.

pons   A hindbrain structure that connects the medulla to the two sides of the cerebellum and helps coordinate and integrate movements on each side of the body.

positive correlation   A finding that two factors vary systematically in the same direction, increasing or decreasing together.

positive punishment   A situation in which an operant is followed by the presentation or addition of an aversive stimulus; also called *punishment by application*.

positive reinforcement   A situation in which a response is followed by the addition of a reinforcing stimulus, increasing the likelihood that the response will be repeated in similar situations.

positive symptoms   An excess or distortion of normal functioning including delusions, hallucinations, and disorganized thoughts and behavior.

positron-emission tomography (PET)   An imaging technique that provides color coded images of brain activity by tracking the brain's use of a radioactively tagged compound, such as glucose, oxygen, or a drug.

possible selves   The aspect of the self-concept that includes images of the selves that you hope, fear, or expect to become in the future.

posthypnotic suggestion   An instruction given during hypnosis asking a person to carry out a specific behavior following the hypnotic session.

posttraumatic stress disorder (PTSD)   A disorder triggered by extreme trauma that results in intrusive memories; avoidance of stimuli; negative changes in thoughts and emotions; and a persistent state of heightened physical arousal.

prejudice   A negative attitude toward people who belong to a specific social group.

prenatal stage   The stage of development before birth that is divided into the germinal, embryonic, and fetal periods.

preoperational stage   The second stage of cognitive development, which lasts from about age 2 to age 7, and is characterized by increasing use of symbols and prelogical thought processes.

primary reinforcer   A stimulus or event that is naturally or inherently reinforcing for a given species.

primary sex characteristics   Sex organs that are directly involved in reproduction.

proactive interference   Forward-acting memory interference in which an old memory interferes with remembering a new memory.

problem solving   Thinking and behavior directed toward attaining a goal that is not readily available.

problem-focused coping   Coping efforts primarily aimed at directly changing or managing a threatening or harmful stressor.

procedural memory   Category of longterm memory that includes memories of different skills, operations, and actions.

production vocabulary   The words that an infant or child understands and can speak.

projective test   A type of personality test that involves a person's interpreting an ambiguous image.

proprioception   The sense of body movement and position.

prosocial behavior   Any behavior that helps another, whether the underlying motive is self-serving or selfless.

prospective memory   Remembering to do something in the future.

prototype   The most typical instance of a particular concept.

psychedelic drugs   (sy-kuh-DEL-ick) A category of psychoactive drugs that create sensory and perceptual distortions, alter mood, and affect thinking.

psychiatry   Medical specialty focused on the diagnosis, treatment, causes, and prevention of mental and behavioral disorders.

psychoactive drug   A chemical substance that affects brain function and alters consciousness, perception, mood, or behavior. physical

psychoanalysis   Personality theory and form of psychotherapy that emphasizes the role of unconscious factors in determining personality and behavior.

psychoanalysis (in personality)   Freud's theory of personality that stresses the influence of unconscious mental processes, the importance of sexual and aggressive instincts, and the enduring effects of early childhood experiences on later personality development.

psychoanalysis (in psychotherapy)   A type of psychotherapy originated by Sigmund Freud in which free association and transference are used to explore repressed or unconscious impulses, anxieties, and internal conflicts.

psychological disorder   A pattern of behavioral and psychological symptoms that causes significant personal distress, impairs the ability to function in one or more important areas of life, or both.

psychological test   A test that assesses a person's abilities, aptitudes, interests, or personality on the basis of a systematically obtained sample of behavior.

psychology   The scientific study of behavior and mental processes.

psychoneuroimmunology   The scientific study of the connections among psychological processes (psycho-), the nervous system (-neuro-), and the immune system (-immunology).

psychopathology   The scientific study of the origins, symptoms, and development of psychological disorders.

psychosexual stages   In Freud's theory, age-related developmental periods in which the child's sexual impulses are focused on different body areas and are expressed through the activities associated with those areas.

psychotherapy   Treatment of emotional, behavioral, and interpersonal problems through psychological techniques that promote understanding of problems and modify troubling feelings, behaviors, or relationships.

psychotropic medications   (sy-ko-TRO-pick) Prescription drugs that alter mental functions, alleviate psychological symptoms, and are used to treat psychological disorders.

puberty   The stage of adolescence in which an individual reaches sexual maturity and becomes physiologically capable of sexual reproduction.

punishment   The presentation of a stimulus or event following a behavior that acts to decrease the likelihood of the behavior being repeated.

pupil   The opening in the middle of the iris that changes size to let in different amounts of light.

R

random assignment   The process of assigning participants to experimental conditions so that all participants have an equal chance of being assigned to any of the conditions or groups in the study.

random selection   Process by which every member of the larger group has an equal chance of being selected for inclusion in the sample.

range   A simple measure of variability, which is computed by subtracting the highest score in a distribution from the lowest score.

rational-emotive behavior therapy (REBT)   Type of cognitive therapy that focuses on changing the client's irrational beliefs.

reality principle   The capacity to postpone gratification until the appropriate time or circumstances exist in the external world.

recall   A test of long-term memory that involves retrieving information without the aid of retrieval cues; also called *free recall*.

reciprocal determinism   A model proposed by Bandura that explains human functioning and personality as caused by the interaction of behavioral, cognitive, and environmental factors.

recognition   A test of long-term memory that involves identifying correct information out of several possible choices.

reinforcement   The occurrence of a stimulus or event following a response that increases the likelihood of that response being repeated.

reliability   The ability of a test to produce consistent results when administered on repeated occasions under similar conditions.

REM sleep   Type of sleep during which rapid eye movements (REM) and dreaming usually occur and voluntary muscle activity is suppressed.

replicate   To repeat a study in order to increase confidence in the validity of the original findings.

representative sample   A selected segment that very closely parallels the larger population being studied on relevant characteristics.

representativeness heuristic   A strategy in which the likelihood of an event is estimated by comparing how similar it is to the prototype of the event.

repression   Motivated forgetting that occurs unconsciously, a memory that is blocked and unavailable to consciousness.

repression (in psychoanalytic theory of personality and psychotherapy)   The unconscious exclusion of anxiety-provoking thoughts, feelings, and memories from conscious awareness.

resistance   The patient's unconscious attempts to block the revelation of repressed memories and conflicts.

resting potential   The state in which a neuron is prepared to activate and communicate its message if it receives sufficient stimulation.

reticular formation   (reh-TICK-you-ler) A network of nerve fibers located in the center of the medulla that helps regulate attention, arousal, and sleep; also called the *reticular activating system.*

retina   (RET-in-uh) A thin, light-sensitive membrane located at the back of the eye, which contains the sensory receptors for vision.

retrieval cue   A clue, prompt, or hint that helps trigger recall of a given piece of information stored in long-term memory.

retrieval cue failure   The inability to recall long-term memories because of inadequate or missing retrieval cues.

retrieval   The process of recovering information stored in memory so that we are consciously aware of it.

retroactive interference   Backward acting memory interference in which a new memory interferes with remembering an old memory.

retrograde amnesia   Loss of memory, especially for episodic information of recent events.

reuptake   The process by which neurotransmitter molecules detach from the receptor and are reabsorbed by the presynaptic neuron so they can be recycled and used again.

rods   The long, thin, blunt sensory receptors of the eye that are highly sensitive to light, but not to color.

Rorschach inkblot Test   A projective test using inkblots, developed by Swiss psychiatrist Hermann Rorschach in 1921.

S

sample   A selected segment of the population used to represent the group that is being studied.

scatter diagram or **scatter plot**   A graph that represents the relationship between two variables.

schedule of reinforcement   The delivery of a reinforcer according to a preset pattern based on the number of responses or the time interval between responses.

schemas   (SKEE-muh) Organized clusters of information about particular topics.

schizophrenia   A psychological disorder in which the ability to function is impaired by severely distorted beliefs, perceptions, and thought processes.

scientific method   A set of assumptions, attitudes, and procedures that guides researchers in creating questions to investigate, in generating evidence, and in drawing conclusions.

secondary sex characteristics   Sexual characteristics that develop during puberty and are not directly involved in reproduction but differentiate between the sexes.

selection device validity   The extent to which a personnel selection device is successful in distinguishing between those applicants who will become high performers at a certain job and those who will not.

selective serotonin reuptake inhibitors (SSRIs)   Class of antidepressant medications that increase the availability of serotonin in the brain and cause fewer side effects than earlier antidepressants

self-concept   The set of perceptions and beliefs that you hold about yourself.

self-determination theory (SDT)   Deci and Ryan's theory that optimal human functioning can occur only if the psychological needs for autonomy, competence, and relatedness are satisfied.

self-efficacy   The beliefs that people have about their ability to meet the demands of a specific situation; feelings of self-confidence.

self-report inventory   A type of psychological test in which a person's responses to standardized questions are compared to established norms.

self-serving bias   The tendency to attribute successful outcomes of one's own behavior to internal causes and unsuccessful outcomes to external, situational causes.

semantic memory   Category of long-term memory that includes memories of general knowledge, concepts, facts, and names.

semantic network model   A model that describes units of information in long-term memory as being organized in a complex network of associations.

sensation seeking   The degree to which an individual is motivated to experience high levels of sensory and physical arousal associated with varied and novel activities.

sensation   The process of detecting a physical stimulus, such as light, sound, heat, or pressure.

sense of self   Your sense of who you are in relation to other people, a unique sense of identity that has been influenced by your social, cultural, and psychological experiences.

sensorimotor stage   The first stage of cognitive development, from birth to about age 2, the period during which infants acquire knowledge through sensing and manipulating objects.

sensory adaptation   The gradual decline in sensitivity to a constant stimulus.

sensory memory   The stage of memory that registers information from the environment and holds it for a very brief period of time.

sensory neuron   A type of neuron that conveys information about the environment, such as light or sound, from specialized receptor cells in the sense organs to the brain.

sensory receptors   Specialized cells unique to each sense organ that respond to a particular form of sensory stimulation.

serial position effect   The tendency to retrieve information more easily from the beginning and the end of a list rather than from the middle.

serotonin   (ser-uh-TONE-in) A neurotransmitter involved in sleep, sensory perceptions, moods, and emotional states.

set-point theory   Theory that humans and other animals have a natural body weight, called the *set-point weight*, that the body maintains.

sex   Biologically determined physical characteristics, such as differences in genetic composition and reproductive anatomy and function.

sex chromosomes   Chromosomes, designated as X or Y, that determine biological sex; the 23rd pair of chromosomes in humans.

sexual orientation   The direction of a person's emotional and erotic attraction whether toward members of the opposite sex, the same sex, both sexes, or neither sex.

shape constancy   The perception that a familiar object remains the same shape regardless of the image produced on the retina.

shaping   The operant conditioning procedure of selectively reinforcing successively closer approximations of a goal behavior until the goal behavior is displayed.

short-term dynamic therapy   Type of psychotherapy based on psychoanalytic theory but differing in that it is time-limited, has specific goals, and involves an active, rather than neutral, role for the therapist.

short-term memory   The active stage of memory in which information is stored for up to about 20 seconds.

situational (contingency) theories of leadership   Leadership theories claiming that various situational factors influence a leader's effectiveness.

size constancy   The perception that a familiar object remains the same shape regardless of the image produced on our retinas.

skewed distribution   An asymmetrical distribution: In a *positively* skewed distribution, most of the scores are low scores; in a *negatively skewed* distribution, most of the scores are high scores.

sleep disorder   A serious and consistent sleep disturbance that interferes with daytime functioning and causes subjective distress.

sleep paralysis   A temporary condition in which a person is unable to move upon awakening in the morning or during the night.

sleep terrors   Sleep disturbance involving an episode of increased physiological arousal, panic, frightening hallucinations, and no recall of the episode; also called *night terrors*.

sleepwalking   A sleep disturbance characterized by an episode of walking or performing other actions during stage 3 NREM sleep.

social anxiety disorder   An anxiety disorder involving the extreme and irrational fear of

being embarrassed, judged, or scrutinized by others in social situations.

social categorization   The mental process of classifying people into groups on the basis of their shared characteristics.

social cognition   The mental processes people use to make sense of their social environments.

social cognitive theory   Bandura's theory of personality, which emphasizes the importance of conscious cognitive processes, social experiences, self-efficacy beliefs, and reciprocal determinism.

social facilitation   The tendency for the presence of other people to enhance individual performance.

social influence   The effect of situational factors and other people on an individual's behavior.

social learning theory of gender development   The theory that gender roles are acquired through the basic processes of learning, including reinforcement, punishment, and modeling.

social loafing   The tendency to expend less effort on a task when it is a group effort.

social norms   The unwritten "rules," or expectations, for appropriate behavior in a particular social situation.

social psychology   Branch of psychology that studies how a person's thoughts, feelings, and behavior are influenced by the presence of other people and by the social and physical environment.

social support   The resources provided by other people in times of need.

somatic nervous system   The subdivision of the peripheral nervous system that communicates sensory information received by sensory receptors along sensory nerves *to* the central nervous system.

source confusion   A memory distortion that occurs when the true source of the memory is forgotten.

source traits   The broad, basic traits that are hypothesized to be universal and relatively few in number.

specific phobia   An excessive, intense, and irrational fear of a specific object, situation, or activity that is actively avoided or endured with marked anxiety.

spinal reflexes   Simple, automatic behaviors that occur without any brain involvement.

spontaneous recovery   The reappearance of a previously extinguished conditioned response after a period of time without exposure to the conditioned stimulus

stage model of memory   A model describing memory as consisting of three distinct stages: sensory memory, short-term memory, and long-term memory.

standard deviation   A measure of variability; expressed as the square root of the sum of the squared deviations around the mean divided by the number of scores in the distribution.

standard normal curve or **standard normal distribution**   A symmetrical distribution forming a bell-shaped curve in which the mean, median, and mode are all equal and fall in the exact middle.

standardization The administration of a test to a large, representative sample of people under uniform conditions for the purpose of establishing norms.

statistically significant A mathematical indication that research results are not very likely to have occurred by chance if there truly isn't anything to be found.

statistics A branch of mathematics used by researchers to analyze, summarize, and interpret the data they have collected.

stem cells Cells that can divide indefinitely, renew themselves, and give rise to a variety of other types of cells.

stereotype A cluster of characteristics that are associated with all members of a specific social group, often including qualities unrelated to the objective criteria that define the group.

stereotype threat A psychological predicament in which fear that you will be evaluated in terms of a negative stereotype about a group to which you belong creates anxiety and self-doubt, lowering performance.

stimulants A category of psychoactive drugs that increase brain activity, arouse behavior, and increase mental alertness.

stimulus control therapy Insomnia treatment involving specific guidelines to create a strict association between the bedroom and rapid sleep onset.

stimulus discrimination The occurrence of a learned response to a specific stimulus but not to other, similar stimuli.

stimulus generalization The occurrence of a learned response not only to the original stimulus but to other, similar stimuli as well.

stimulus threshold The minimum level of stimulation required to activate a particular neuron.

storage The process of retaining information in memory so that it can be used at a later time.

stress A negative emotional state occurring in response to events that are perceived as taxing or exceeding a person's resources or ability to cope.

stressors Events or situations that are perceived as harmful, threatening, or challenging.

structural plasticity The brain's ability to change its physical structure in response to learning, active practice, or environmental influences.

Structuralism Early school of psychology holding that even our most complex conscious experiences could be broken down into elemental "*structures*," or component parts, of sensations and feelings.

superego In Freud's theory, the partly conscious, self-evaluative, moralistic component of personality that is formed through the internalization of parental and societal rules.

suppression Motivated forgetting that occurs consciously, a deliberate attempt to not think about and remember specific information.

surface traits Personality characteristics or attributes that can be easily inferred from observable behavior.

survey A structured set of questions designed to investigate the opinions, behaviors, or characteristics of a particular group.

symbolic thought The ability to use words, images, and symbols to represent the world.

symmetrical distribution A distribution in which scores fall equally on both sides of the graph; the normal curve is an example of a symmetrical distribution.

sympathetic nervous system The branch of the autonomic nervous system that is the body's emergency system, rapidly activating bodily systems to meet threats or emergencies.

synapse (SIN-aps) The point of communication between two neurons.

synaptic gap (sin-AP-tick) A tiny fluid-filled space between the presynaptic and postsynaptic neurons.

synaptic transmission (sin-AP-tick) The entire process of transmitting information at the synapse.

synaptic vesicles (sin-AP-tick VESS-ick-ullz) Tiny sacs in the axon terminal.

systematic desensitization Type of behavior therapy that involves learning a new conditioned response (relaxation) that is incompatible with or inhibits the old conditioned response (fear and anxiety).

T

t-test Test used to establish whether the means of two groups are statistically different from each other.

taste aversion A classically conditioned dislike for and avoidance of a particular food that develops when an organism becomes ill after eating the food.

taste buds The specialized sensory receptors for taste that are located on the tongue and inside the mouth and throat pain.

telomeres Repeated, duplicate DNA sequences that are found at the very tips of chromosomes and that protect the chromosomes' genetic data during cell division.

temperament Inborn predispositions to consistently behave and react in a certain way.

temporal lobe An area on each hemisphere of the cerebral cortex, near the temples, that is the primary receiving area for auditory information.

teratogens Agents or substances that can potentially harm the developing fetus.

testing effect The finding that practicing retrieval of information from memory produces better retention than restudying the same information for an equivalent amount of time.

thalamus (THAL-uh-muss) A rounded forebrain structure located within each cerebral hemisphere that processes sensory information (except smell).

the need to belong The drive to form and maintain lasting positive relationships that are characterized by mutual concern and caring.

Thematic Apperception Test (TAT) A projective personality test, developed by Henry Murray and colleagues, that involves creating stories about ambiguous scenes.

theory A tentative explanation that tries to integrate and account for the relationship of diverse findings on the same topic.

thinking The manipulation of mental representations of information in order to draw inferences and conclusions.

tip-of-the-tongue (ToT) experience A memory phenomenon that involves the sensation of knowing that specific information is stored in long-term memory, but being temporarily unable to retrieve it.

token economy Form of behavior therapy in which the therapeutic environment is structured to reward desired behaviors with tokens or points that may eventually be exchanged for tangible rewards.

top-down processing Emphasizes the observer's experience in arriving at meaningful perceptions; attention moves from the whole to part of the pattern.

trait A relatively stable, enduring predisposition to consistently behave in a certain way.

trait approach to leader effectiveness Approach to determining what makes an effective leader that focuses on the personal characteristics displayed by successful leaders.

trait theory A theory of personality that focuses on identifying, describing, and measuring individual differences in behavioral predispositions.

transduction The process by which physical energy is converted into a coded neural signal that can be processed by the nervous system.

transference The process by which emotions and desires associated with a significant person in the patient's life, such as a parent, are unconsciously transferred onto the psychoanalyst.

transgender Condition in which a person's psychological gender identity conflicts with their biological sex.

trial and error A problem-solving strategy that involves attempting different solutions and eliminating those that do not work.

triarchic theory of intelligence Robert Sternberg's theory that there are three distinct forms of intelligence: analytic, creative, and practical.

trichromatic theory of color vision Theory that the sensation of color results because cones are especially sensitive to red light (long wavelengths), green light (medium wavelengths), or blue light (short wavelengths).

two-factor theory of emotion Schachter and Singer's theory that emotion is the interaction of physiological arousal and the cognitive label that we apply to explain the arousal.

Type A behavior pattern A behavioral and emotional style characterized by a sense of time urgency, hostility, and competitiveness.

Type I error Erroneous conclusion that study results are significant.

Type II error Failure to find a significant effect that does, in fact, exist.

U

unconditional positive regard   In Rogers's theory, the child's sense that they will be valued and loved even if they don't conform to the standards and expectations of others.

unconditioned response (UCR)   The unlearned, reflexive response that is elicited by an unconditioned stimulus.

unconditioned stimulus (UCS)   The natural stimulus that reflexively elicits a response without the need for prior learning.

unconscious   Freud's term to describe thoughts, feelings, wishes, and drives that are operating below the level of conscious awareness.

V

validity   The ability of a test to measure what it is intended to measure.

variable   A factor that can vary, or change, in ways that can be observed, measured, and verified.

W

wavelength   The distance from one wave peak to another.

Wernicke's area   A brain region in the left temporal lobe of the dominant hemisphere, usually the left, that is crucial for the comprehension of language.

working memory   The temporary storage and active, conscious manipulation of information needed for complex cognitive tasks, such as reasoning, learning, and problem solving.

Z

z-score   A number, expressed in standard deviation units, that shows a score's deviation from the mean.

zone of proximal development   Vygotsky's theory about the gap between what children can accomplish on their own and what they can accomplish with the help of others who are more competent.

zygote   The single cell formed at conception from the union of the egg cell and sperm cell.

REFERENCES

Abel, Ted; Havekes, Robbert; Saletin, Jared M.; & Walker, Matthew P. (2013). Sleep, plasticity and memory from molecules to whole-brain networks. *Current Biology, 23*, R774–R788. https://doi.org/10.1016/j.cub.2013.07.0

Abela, John R. Z.; Auerbach, Randy P.; & Seligman, Martin E. P. (2008). Dispositional pessimism across the lifespan. In Keith S. Dobson & David J. A. Dozois (Eds.), *Risk factors in depression*. Elsevier Academic Press.

Abi-Dargham, Anissa. (2004). Do we still believe in the dopamine hypothesis? New data bring new evidence. *International Journal of Neuropsychopharmacology, 7*(Suppl. 1), S1–S5.

Abler, Birgit; Erk, Susanne; & Herwig, Uwe. (2007). Anticipation of aversive stimuli activates extended amygdala in unipolar depression. *Journal of Psychiatric Research, 41*(6), 511–522.

Aboud, Frances, E.; Tredoux, Colin; Tropp, Linda R.; Brown, Christia S.; Niens, Ulrike; & Noor, Noraini M. (2012). Interventions to reduce prejudice and enhance inclusion and respect for ethnic differences in early childhood: A systematic review. *Developmental Review, 32*, 307–226.

Abramson, Charles H. (2003a). *Charles Henry Turner—A timeline*. Oklahoma State Psychology Museum & Resource Center. https://psychology.okstate.edu/museum/turner/turnertime.html

Abramson, Charles H. (2003b). Charles Henry Turner: Contributions of a forgotten African American to honey bee research. *American Bee Journal, 143*, 643–644.

Ackerman, Joshua M.; Kenrick, Douglas T.; & Schaller, Mark. (2007). Is friendship akin to kinship? *Evolution and Human Behavior, 28*(5), 365–374.

Ackerman, Phillip L. (2014). Adolescent and adult intellectual development. *Current Directions in Psychological Science, 23*, 246–251. https://doi.org/10.1177/0963721414534960

Ackerman, Phillip L. (2017). Adult intelligence: The construct and the criterion problem. *Perspectives on Psychological Science, 12*(6), 987–998. https://doi.org/10.1177/174569161770343

Adachi, Tomonori; Fujino, Haruo; Nakae, Aya; Mashimo, Takashi; & Sasaki, Jun. (2014). A meta-analysis of hypnosis for chronic pain problems: A comparison between hypnosis, standard care, and other psychological interventions. *International Journal of Clinical and Experimental Hypnosis, 62*, 1–28. https://doi.org/10.1080/00207144.2013.841471

Adair, Linda S., & Gordon-Larsen, Penny. (2001). Maturational timing and overweight prevalence in US adolescent girls. *American Journal of Public Health, 91*, 642–644. https://doi.org/10.2105/AJPH.91.4.642

Aday, Jacob S.; Mitzkovitz, Cayla M.; Bloesch, Emily K.; Davoli, Christopher C.; & Davis, Alan K. (2020). Long-term effects of psychedelic drugs: A systematic review. *Neuroscience and Biobehavioral Reviews, 113*, 179–189. https://doi.org/10.1016/j.neubiorev.2020.03.017

Ader, Robert. (1993). Conditioned responses. In Bill Moyers & Betty Sue Flowers (Eds.), *Healing and the mind*. Doubleday.

Adler, Alfred. (1933a). Advantages and disadvantages of the inferiority feeling. In Heinz L. Ansbacher & Rowena R. Ansbacher (Eds.), *Superiority and social interest: A collection of later writings*. Norton.

Adler, Alfred. (1933b). On the origin of the striving for superiority and of social interest. In Heinz L. Ansbacher & Rowena R. Ansbacher (Eds.), *Superiority and social interest: A collection of later writings*. Norton.

Adler, Nancy E. (2009). Health disparities through a psychological lens. *American Psychologist, 64*(8), 663–673.

Adler, Nancy E., & Rehkopf, David H. (2008). U.S. disparities in health: Descriptions, causes, and mechanisms. *Annual Review of Public Health, 29*, 235–252.

Adolphs, Ralph. (2010). Conceptual challenges and directions for social neuroscience. *Neuron, 65*(6), 752–767. https://doi.org/10.1016/j.neuron.2010.03.006

Adolphs, Ralph; Tranel, Daniel; & Damasio, Antonio R. (1998). The human amygdala in social judgment. *Nature, 393*, 470–474.

Adriaanse, Marieke A.; Gollwitzer, Peter M.; De Ridder, Denise T. D.; de Wit, John B. F.; & Kroese, Floor M. (2011). Breaking habits with implementation intentions: A test of underlying processes. *Personality and Social Psychology Bulletin, 37*, 502–513. https://doi.org/10.1177/0146167211399102

Advokat, Claire D.; Comaty, Joseph E.; & Julien, Robert M. (2014). *Julien's primer of drug action: A comprehensive guide to the actions, uses, and side effects of psychoactive drugs* (13th ed.). Worth Publishers.

Advokat, Claire D.; Comaty, Joseph E.; & Julien, Robert M. (2019). *Julien's primer of drug action: A comprehensive guide to the actions, uses, and side effects of psychoactive drugs* (14th ed.). Worth Publishers.

africanews. (April 10, 2018). UNHCR begins repatriation of Central African Republic refugees from Congo. *africanews*. http://www.africanews.com/2018/04/10/unhcr-begins-repatriation-of-central-african-republic-refugees-from-congo//

Aghababaei, Naser, & Arji, Akram. (2014). Well-being and the HEXACO model of personality. *Personality and Individual Differences, 56*, 139–142. https://doi.org/10.1016/j.paid.2013.08.037

Aghababaei, Naser; Mohammadtabar, Somayeh; & Saffarinia, Majid. (2014). Dirty dozen vs. the H factor: Comparison of the dark triad and honesty-humility in prosociality, religiosity, and happiness. *Personality and Individual Differences, 67*, 6–10. https://doi.org/10.1016/j.paid.2014.03.026

Ahima, Rexford S. (2011). Principles of obesity therapy. In Rexford S. Ahima (Ed.), *Metabolic basis of obesity* (pp. 359–379). Springer.

Aiken, Lewis R. (1997). *Psychological testing and assessment* (9th ed.) Allyn & Bacon.

Ainslie, George. (1975). Specious reward: A behavioral theory of impulsiveness and impulse control. *Psychological Bulletin, 82*, 463–496.

Ainslie, George. (1992). *Picoeconomics: The strategic interaction of successive motivational states within the person*. Cambridge, England: Cambridge University Press.

Ainsworth, Claire. (2015, February 18). Sex redefined: The idea of two sexes is simplistic. Biologists now think there is a wider spectrum than that. *Nature, 518*, 288–291. http://www.nature.com/news/sex-redefined-1.16943

Ainsworth, Mary D. Salter. (1979). Attachment as related to mother–infant interaction. In Jay S. Rosenblatt, Robert A. Hinde, Colin Beer, & Marie Busnel (Eds.), *Advances in the study of behavior* (Vol. 9). Academic Press.

Ainsworth, Mary D. Salter; Blehar, Mary C.; Waters, Everett; & Wall, Sally. (1978). *Patterns of attachment: A psychological study of the Strange Situation*. Erlbaum.

Ainsworth, Sarah E., & Maner, Jon. K. (2012). Sex begets violence: Mating motives, social dominance, and physical aggression in men. *Journal of Personality and Social Psychology, 103*(5), 819–829. https://doi.org/10.1037/a0029428

Ajina, Sara, & Bridge, Holly. (2017). Blindsight and unconscious vision: What they teach us about the human visual system. *The Neuroscientist, 23*, 529–541. https://doi.org/10.1177/1073858416673817

Ajunwa, Ifeoma; Friedler, Sorelle; Scheidegger, Carlos; & Venkatasubramanian, Suresh. (2016). Hiring by algorithm: Predicting and preventing disparate impact. *SSRN Electronic Journal,*1–29. https://doi.org/10.2139/ssrn.2746078

Ajzen, Icek. (2001). Nature and operations of attitudes. *Annual Review of Psychology, 52*(1), 27–58.

Akerstedt, Torbjörn; Nilsson, Peter M.; & Kecklund, Gören. (2009). Sleep and recovery. In Sabine Sonnetag, Pamela L. Perrewé, and Daniel Ganster (Eds.), *Current perspectives on job-stress recovery.*JAI Press/Emerald Group.

Aksglaede, Lise; Juul, Anders; Olsen, Lina W.; & Sorensen, Thorkild I. (2009). Age at puberty and the emerging obesity epidemic. *PLOS ONE, 4*(12), e8450. https://doi.org/10.1371/journal.pone.0008450

Alanko, Katarina; Santtila, Pekka; Harlaar, N.; Witting, Katarina; Varjonen, Markus; Jern, Patrik; Johansson, Ada; von der Pahlen, Bettina; & Sandnabba, N. Kenneth. (2010). Common genetic effects of gender atypical behavior in childhood and sexual orientation in adulthood: A study of Finnish twins. *Archives of Sexual Behavior, 39*, 81–92.

Albarracín, Dolores, & Vargas, Patrick. (2010). Attitudes and persuasion: From biology to social responses to persuasive intent. In S. T. Fiske, D. T. Gilbert & G. Lindzey (Eds.), *Handbook of social psychology* (Vol. 1, pp. 394–427). Wiley.

Albert, Dustin; Chein, Jason; & Steinberg, Laurence. (2013). The teenage brain: Peer influences on adolescent decision making. *Current Directions in Psychological Science, 22*,114–120. https://doi.org/10.1177/0963721412471347

Albuquerque, David; Manco; & Nóbrega, Clévio. (2016). Genetics of human obesity. In Samin I. Ahmad & Syed Khalid Imam (Eds.), *Obesity: A practical guide.* Springer International Publishing.

Alcorn, Chauncey. (2021, March 15). Rosalind Brewer officially takes the helm at Walgreens, becoming the only Black woman Fortune 500 CEO. *WRAL.com*. https://www.wral.com/rosalind-brewer-officially-takes-the-helm-at-walgreens-becoming-the-only-black-woman-fortune-500-ceo/19576620/

Alderson-Day, Ben; Bernini, Marco; & Fernyhough, Charles. (2017). Uncharted features and dynamics of reading: Voices, characters, and crossing of experiences. *Consciousness and Cognition, 49,* 98–109. https://doi.org/10.1016/j.concog.2017.01.003

Aldossari, Maryam, & Chaudhry, Sara. (2020). Women and burnout in the context of a pandemic. *Gender, Work & Organization, 28*(2), 826–834. https://doi.org/10.1111/gwao.12567

Aldridge, Jerry, & Christensen, Lois M. (Eds.). (2013). Mamie Phipps Clark (1917–1983). *In stealing from the mother: The marginalization of women in education and psychology from 1900–2010* (pp. 105–112). Rowman & Littlefield Education.

Alexander, Charles N.; Robinson, Pat; Orme-Johnson, David W.; &Schneider, Robert H. (1994). The effects of transcendental meditation compared to other methods of relaxation and meditation in reducing risk factors, morbidity, and mortality. *Homeostasis in Health and Disease, 35,* 243–263.

Alhajji, Lujain, & Nemeroff, Charles. (2015). Personalized medicine and mood disorders. *Psychiatric Clinics of North America, 38,* 395–403. https://doi.org/10.1016/j.psc.2015.05.003

Alladi, Suvarna; Bak, Thomas H.; Duggirala, Vasanta; Surampudi, Bapiraju; Shailaja, Mekala; Shukla, Anuj Kumar; Chaudhuri, Jaydip Ray; & Kaul, Subhash S. (2013). Bilingualism delays age at onset of dementia, independent of education and immigration status. *Neurology, 81,* 1938–1944. https://doi.org/10.1212/01.wnl.0000436620.33155.a4

Allen, Daniel N.; Strauss, Gregory P.; Kemtes, Karen A.; & Goldstein, Gerald. (2007). Hemispheric contributions to nonverbal abstract reasoning and problem solving. *Neuropsychology, 21,* 713–720.

Allen, Gayle. (2015, November 9). CM 006: Mick Ebeling on how to achieve the impossible. *Curious Minds: Innovation in Life and Work.* Podcast http://www.gayleallen.net/cm-006-mick-ebeling-on-how-to-achieve-the-impossible/

Allen, Jenny; Weinrich, Mason; Hoppitt, Will; & Rendell, Luke. (2013). Network-based diffusion analysis reveals cultural transmission of lobtail feeding in humpback whales. *Science, 340,* 485–488. https://doi.org/10.1126/science.1231976

Allen, Jon G. (2005). *Coping with trauma: Hope through understanding* (2nd ed.). C215American Psychological Association.

Allen, Karen M.; Blascovich, Jim; & Mendes, Wendy B. (2002). Cardiovascular reactivity and the presence of pets, friends, and spouses: The truth about cats and dogs. *Psychosomatic Medicine, 64,* 727–739.

Allen, Karen M.; Blascovich, Jim; Tomaka, Joe; & Kelsey, Robert M. (1991). Presence of human friends and pet dogs as moderators of autonomic responses to stress in women. *Journal of Personality and Social Psychology, 61,* 582–589.

Allen, Laura B.; McHugh, R. Kathryn; & Barlow, David H. (2008). Emotional disorders: A unified protocol. In David H. Barlow (Ed.), *Clinical handbook of psychological disorders* (4th ed., pp. 216–249). Guilford.

Allen, Mark S.; Robson, Davina A.; Martin, Luc J.; & Laborde, Sylvain. (2020). Systematic review and meta-analysis of self-serving attribution biases in the competitive context of organized sport. *Personality and Social Psychology Bulletin, 46*(7), 1027–1043. https://doi.org/10.1177/0146167219893995

Allen, Tammy; Golden, Timothy; & Shockley, Kristen. (2015). How effective is telecommuting? Assessing the status of our scientific findings. *Psychological Science in the Public Interest, 16,* 40–68. https://doi.org/10.1177/1529100615593273

Allen, Vernon L., & Levine, John M. (1969). Consensus and conformity. *Journal of Experimental Social Psychology, 5,* 389–399.

Allen, Vernon L., & Levine, John M. (1971). Social support and conformity: The role of independent assessment of reality. *Journal of Experimental Social Psychology, 7,* 48–58.

Allik, Jüri, & McCrae, Robert R. (2002). A five-factor theory perspective. In Robert R. McCrae & Jüri Allik (Eds.), *The five-factor model of personality across cultures.* Kluwer Academic/Plenum.

Allik, Jüri, & McCrae, Robert R. (2004). Toward a geography of personality traits: Patterns of profiles across 36 cultures. *Journal of Cross-Cultural Psychology, 35,* 13–28.

Allik, Jüri, & McCrae, Robert R. (2013). Universality of the five-factor model of personality. In Paul T. Costa; & Thomas A. Widiger (Eds.), *Personality disorders and the Five Factor Model of Personality.* American Psychological Association.

Allport, Floyd H. (1920). The influence of the group upon association and thought. *Journal of Experimental Psychology, 3,* 159–182.

Allport, Gordon W. (1924). The study of the undivided personality. *Journal of Abnormal & Social Psychology, 19,* 132–141.

Allport, Gordon W., & Odbert, Harold S. (1936). Trait-names: A psycholexical study. *Psychological Monographs, 47*(211).

Allsopp, Kate; Read, John; Corcoran, Rhiannon; & Kinderman, Peter. (2019). Heterogeneity in psychiatric diagnostic classification. *Psychiatry Research, 279,* 15–22. https://doi.org/10.1016/j.psychres.2019.07.005

Almeida, David M.; Neupert, Shevaun D.; Banks, Sean R.; & Serido, Joyce. (2005). Do daily stress processes account for socioeconomic health disparities? *Journal of Gerontology: Series B, 60B,* 34–39.

Almutawakel, Boushra Yahya. (2018). Meet the 9 Arabs Included in BBC's 100 Women List for 2018. *About Her.* https://www.abouther.com/node/15431/people/leading-ladies/meet-9-arabs-included-bbc%E2%80%99s-100-women-list-2018

Al-Shawaf, Laith; Lewis, David M.G.; Wehbe, Yzar S.; & Buss, David M. (2019). Context, Environment, and Learning in Evolutionary Psychology. In Todd. K Shackelford & Viviana A. Weekes-Shackleford (Eds.) *Encyclopedia of Evolutionary Psychological Science* (Living Edition). Springer Nature Switzerland AG. https://doi.org/10.1007/978-3-319-16999-6_227-1

Altemus, Margaret. (2006). Sex differences in depression and anxiety disorders: Potential biological determinants. *Hormones and Behavior, 50*(4), 534–538. https://doi.org/10.1016/j.yhbeh.2006.06.031

Alter, George, & Gonzalez, Richard. (2018). Responsible practices for data sharing. *American Psychologist, 73,* 146–156. https://doi.org/10.1037/amp0000258.

Altiraifi, Azza, & Rapfogel, Nicole. (2020). *Mental health care was severely inequitable, then came the coronavirus crisis.* Center for American Progress. https://www.americanprogress.org/issues/disability/reports/2020/09/10/490221/mental-health-care-severely-inequitable-came-coronavirus-crisis/

Altmann, Erik M. (2009). Evidence for temporal decay in short-term episodic memory. *Trends in Cognitive Sciences, 13*(7), 279.

Alves, Hélder, & Correia, Isabel. (2008). On the normativity of expressing the belief in a just world: Empirical evidence. *Social Justice Research, 21,* 106–118.

Alwin, Duane F. (2009). History, cohorts, and patterns of cognitive aging. In Hayden B. Bosworth and Christopher Hertzog (Eds.), *Aging and cognition: Research methodologies and empirical advances* (pp. 9–38). American Psychological Association.

Alzheimer's Association. (2016). Alzheimer's disease facts and figures. *Alzheimer's & Dementia, 12.* http://www.alz.org/facts/overview.asp

Amabile, Teresa M. (1996). *Creativity in context.* Westview Press.

Amabile, Teresa M. (2001). Beyond talent: John Irving and the passionate craft of creativity. *American Psychologist, 56,* 333–336.

Amada, Gerald. (2011). *A guide to psychotherapy.* Evans.

Ambady, Nalini; Chiao, Joan Y.; & Chiu, Pearl. (2006). Race and emotion: Insights from a social neuroscience perspective. In John T. Cacioppo, Penny S. Visser, & Cynthia L. Pickett (Eds.), *Social neuroscience: People thinking about thinking people.* MIT Press.

American Association on Intellectual and Developmental Disabilities. (2010). Frequently asked questions on intellectual disability. https://aaidd.org/intellectual-disability/definition/faqs-on-intellectual-disability

American Psychiatric Association. (1994). *Diagnostic and statistical manual of mental disorders* (4th ed.).

American Psychiatric Association. (2001). Practice guideline for the treatment of patients with borderline personality disorder. *American Journal of Psychiatry, 158*(Suppl10), 1–52.

American Psychiatric Association. (2012a). *Personality disorders.* http://www.dsm5.org/proposedrevision/pages/personalitydisorders.aspx

American Psychiatric Association. (2012b). *Rationale for the proposed changes to the personality disorders classification in DSM-5.* http://www.dsm5.org/Documents/Personality%20Disorders/Rationale20for%20the%20Proposed%20changes%20to%20the%20Personality%20Disorders%20in%20DSM-5%205-1-12.pdf

American Psychiatric Association. (2013). *Diagnostic and statistical manual of mental disorders* (5th ed.).

American Psychological Association (APA). (2002). Ethical principles of psychologists and code of conduct. *American Psychologist, 57,* 1060–1073. Retrieved from http://www.apa.org/ethics/code/index.aspx

American Psychological Association (APA). (2004). Obeying and resisting malevolent orders. http://www.apa.org/research/action/order.aspx

American Psychological Association (APA). (2005). New definition: Hypnosis. Division 30, Society for Psychological Hypnosis. http://www.apa.org/divisions/div30/define_hypnosis.html

American Psychological Association (APA). (2007). Guidelines for psychological practice with girls and women. *American Psychologist, 62,* 949–979.

American Psychological Association (APA). (2009). Resolution on appropriate affirmative responses to sexual orientation distress and change efforts. http://www.apa.org/about/policy/sexual-orientation.aspx

American Psychological Association (APA). (2010). Ethical principles of psychologists and code of conduct: 2010 Amendments. Retrieved from http://www.apa.org/ethics/code/index.aspx

American Psychological Association (APA). (2011). Practice guidelines regarding psychologists' involvement in pharmacological issues. *American Psychologist, 66*(9), 835–849. https://doi.org/10.1037/a0025890

American Psychological Association (APA). (2012). Guidelines for Ethical Conduct in the Care and Use of Animals. https://www.apa.org/science/leadership/care/guidelines

American Psychological Association (APA). (2013). *Stress in America: Missing the health care connection.*

American Psychological Association (APA). (2017a). Ethical principles of psychologists and code of conduct: 2017 Amendments. https://www.apa.org/ethics/code

American Psychological Association (APA). (2017b). *Multicultural guidelines: An ecological approach to context, identity, and intersectionality, 2017.* https://www.apa.org/about/policy/multicultural-guidelines

American Psychological Association (APA). (2018). *APA guidelines for psychological practice with boys and men.* Retrieved from http://www.apa.org/about/policy/psychological-practice-boys-men-guidelines.pdf

American Psychological Association (APA). (2019). *Stress in America: Stress and Current Events.* Stress in America™ Survey. https://www.apa.org/news/press/releases/stress/2019/stress-america-2019.pdf

American Psychological Association (APA). (2020). *Stress in America™ 2020: A national mental health crisis.* Stress in America™ Survey. https://www.apa.org/news/press/releases/stress/2020/sia-mental-health-crisis.pdf

American Psychological Association Working Group on Investigation of Memories of Childhood Abuse. (1998). Final conclusions of the American Psychological Association Working Group on Investigation of Memories of Childhood Abuse. *Psychology, Public Policy, and Law, 4,* 933–940.

Amick, Halle; Gartlehner, Gerald; Gaynes, Bradley; Forneris, Catherine; Asher, Gary; Morgan, Laura; Coker-Schwimmer, Emmanuel; Boland; Lux, Linda J.; Gaylord, Susan; Bann, Carla; Pierl, Christiane Barbara; & Lohr, Kathleen. (2015). Comparative benefits and harms of second generation antidepressants and cognitive behavioral therapies in initial treatment of major depressive disorder: Systematic review and meta-analysis. *British Medical Journal, 351.* https://doi.org/10.1136/bmj.h6019

Amin, N.; Schuur, M.; Gusareva, E. S.; Isaacs, A.; Aulchenko, Y. S.; Kirichenko, A. V.; Zorkoltseva, I. V.; Axenovich, T. I.; Oostra, B. A.; Janssens A. C. J. W.; & van Duijn, C. M. (2011). A genome-wide linkage study of individuals with high scores on NEO personality traits. *Molecular Psychiatry.* https://doi.org/10.1038/mp.2011.97

Amodio, David M., & Mendoza, Saaid A. (2010). Implicit intergroup bias: Cognitive, affective, and motivational underpinnings. In Bertram Gawronski & B. Keith Payne (Eds.), *Handbook of implicit social cognition: Measurement, theory, and applications.* Guilford.

Amstadter, Ananda B.; Nugent, Nicole R.; & Koenen, Karestan C. (2009). Genetics of PTSD: Fear conditioning as a model for future research. *Psychiatric Annals, 39*(6), 358–367. https://doi.org/10.3928/00485713-20090526-01

Anastasi, Anne, & Urbina, Susana. (1997). *Psychological testing* (7th ed.). Prentice Hall.

Anderson, Craig A., & Bushman, Brad J. (2002). Human aggression. *Annual Review of Psychology, 53*(1), 27–51. https://doi.org/10.1146/annurev.psych.53.100901.135231

Anderson, Craig A.; Shibuya, Akik; Ihori, Nobuko; Swing, Edward L.; Bushman, Brad J.; Sakamoto, Akira; Rothstein, Hannah R.; & Saleem, Muniba. (2010). Violent video game effects on aggression, empathy, and prosocial behavior in Eastern and Western countries: A meta-analytic review. *Psychological Bulletin, 136*(2), 151–173. https://doi.org/10.1037/a0018251

Anderson, Karen E., & Savage, Cary R. (2004). Cognitive and neurobiological findings in obsessive-compulsive disorder. *Psychiatric Clinics of North America, 27*(1), 37–47. https://doi.org/10.1016/S0193-953X(03)00107-2

Anderson, Michael C.; Reinholz, Julia; Kuhl, Brice A.; & Mayr, Ulrich. (2011). Intentional suppression of unwanted memories grows more difficult as we age. *Psychology and Aging, 26,* 397–405.

Anderson, Norman B. (2012, January). 120 years strong. *Monitor on Psychology, 43,* 9.

Anderson-Fye, Eileen. (2009). Cross-cultural issues in body image among children and adolescents. In Linda Smolak & J. Kevin Thompson (Eds.), *Body image, eating disorders, and obesity in youth: Assessment, prevention, and treatment* (2nd ed., pp. 113–133). American Psychological Association.

Andersson, Gerhard; Cuijpers, Pim; Carlbring, Per; Riper, Heleen; & Hedman, Erik. (2014). Guided internet-based vs. face-to-face cognitive behavior therapy for psychiatric and somatic disorders: A systematic review and meta-analysis. *World Psychiatry, 13,* 288–295. https://doi.org/10.1002/wps.20151

Andics, Attila; Gábor, Anna; Gácsi, Márta; Faragó, Tamás; Szabo, Dora; & Miklosi, Adam. (2016). Neural mechanisms for lexical processing in dogs. *Science, 353*(6303), 1030–1032. https://doi.org/10.1126/science.aaf3777

Andover, Margaret S.; Izzo, Genevieve N.; & Kelly, Chris A. (2011). Comorbid and secondary depression. In Dean McKay & Eric A. Storch (Eds.), *Handbook of child and adolescent anxiety disorders* (pp. 135–153). Springer Science + Business Media.

Anglim, Jeromy, & O'Connor, Peter. (2019). Measurement and research using the big five, HEXACO, and narrow traits: A primer for researchers and practitioners. *Australian Journal of Psychology, 71,* 16–25. https://doi.org/10.1111/ajpy.12202

Anguera, Joaquin A.; Boccanfuso, Jacqueline L.; Rintoul, Jean L.; Al-Hashimi, Omar; Faraji, Farshid; Janowich, Jacki; Kong, E.; Larraburo, Y.; Rolle, C.; Johnston, E.; & Gazzaley, Adam. (2013). Video game training enhances cognitive control in older adults. *Nature, 501,* 97–101. https://doi.org/10.1038/nature12486

Annese, Jacopo; Schenker-Ahmed, Natalie M.; Bartsch, Hauke; Maechler, Paul; Sheh, Colleen; Thomas, Natasha; Kayano, Junya; Ghatan, Alexander; Bresler, Noah; Frosch, Matthew P.; Klaming, Ruth; & Corkin, Suzanne. (2014). Postmortem examination of patient H.M.'s brain based on histological sectioning and digital 3D reconstruction. *Nature Communications, 5,* Article 3122. https://doi.org/10.1038/ncomms4122

Ano, Gene G., & Vasconcelles, Erin B. (2005). Religious coping and psychological adjustment to stress: A meta-analysis. *Journal of Clinical Psychology, 61,* 461–480.

Antonsen, Amy N.; Zdaniuk, Bozena; Yule, Morag; & Brotto, Lori A. (2020). Ace and aro: Understanding differences in romantic attractions among persons identifying as asexual. *Archives of Sexual Behavior, 49,* 1615–1630. https://doi.org/10.1007/s10508-019-01600-1

Antony, Martin M.; Purdon, Christine; & Summerfeldt, Laura J. (2007). *Psychological treatment of obsessive compulsive disorders: Fundamentals and beyond.* American Psychological Association.

APA Help Center. (2021). *Psychology help center.* https://www.apa.org/helpcenter

APA Help Center. (2012). *How to find help through seeing a psychologist.* http://www.apa.org/helpcenter/therapy.aspx

Arar, Sara. (2017, October 26). Crown Prince inaugurates tech event for youth. *The Jordan Times.* http://www.jordantimes.com/news/local/crown-prince-inaugurates-tech-event-youth

Arch, Joanna J., & Landy, Lauren N. (2015). Emotional benefits of mindfulness. In Kirk Warren Brown, J. David Creswell, & Richard M. Ryan (Eds.), *Handbook of mindfulness: Theory, research, and practice.* Guilford.

Archbold, Georgina E. B.; Bouton, Mark E.; & Nader, Karim (2010). Evidence for the persistence of contextual fear memories following immediate extinction. *European Journal of Neuroscience, 31*(7), 1303–1311.

Archer, John. (2004). Sex differences in aggression in real-world settings: A meta-analytic review. *Review of General Psychology, 8*(4), 291–322. https://doi.org/10.1037/1089-2680.8.4.291

Archer, John, & Coyne, Sarah M. (2005). An integrated review of indirect, relational, and social aggression. *Personality and Social Psychology Review, 9*(3), 212–230.

Archer, Robert P., & Smith, Steven R. (2014). *Personality assessment* (2nd ed.). Routledge.

Arden, Rosalind; Bensky, Miles; & Adams, Mark. (2016). A review of cognitive abilities in dogs, 1911 through 2016: More individual differences, please! *Current Directions in Psychological Science, 25,* 307–12. https://doi.org/10.1177/0963721416667718

Arendt, Josephine; Stone, Barbara; & Skene, Debra J. (2005). Sleep disruption in jet lag and circadian rhythm-related disorders. In Meir H. Kryger, Thomas Roth, & William C. Dement (Eds.), *Principles and practice of sleep medicine* (4th ed.). Elsevier Saunders.

Arias, Elizabeth. (2016). Changes in life expectancy by race and Hispanic origin in the United States, 2013–2014. *NCHS Data Brief, no. 244.* National Center for Health Statistics.

Arias, Isabel; Sorlozano, Antonio; Villegas, Enrique; Luna, Juan de Dios; Mckenney, Kathryn; Cervilla, Jorge; Gutierrez, Blanca; & Gutierrez, Jose. (2012). Infectious agents associated with schizophrenia: A meta-analysis. *Schizophrenia Research, 136,* 128–136. https://doi.org/10.1016/j.schres.2011.10.026

Arkowitz, Hal; Westra, Henny A.; Miller, William R.; & Rollnick, Stephen. (Eds.). (2007). *Motivational interviewing in the treatment of psychological problems.* Guilford Press.

Armitage, Richard, & Nellums, Laura B. (2020, March 19). COVID-19 and the consequences of isolating the elderly. *The Lancet Public Health.* https://doi.org/10.1016/S2468-2667(20)30061-X

Arnau, Randolph C.; Green, Bradley A.; Rosen, David H.; Gleaves, David H.; & Melancon, Janet G. (2003). Are Jungian preferences really categorical? An empirical investigation using taxometric analysis. *Personality and Individual Differences, 34,* 233–251.

Arnett, Jeffrey Jensen. (2000). Emerging adulthood: A theory of development from the late teens through the twenties. *American Psychologist, 55,* 469–480. https://doi.org/10.1037/0003-066X.55.5.469

Arnett, Jeffrey Jensen. (2004). *Emerging adulthood: The winding road from the late teens through the twenties.* Oxford University Press.

Arnett, Jeffrey Jensen. (2010). Oh, grow up! Generational grumbling and the new life stage of emerging adulthood—Commentary on Trzesniewski & Donnellan (2010). *Perspectives on Psychological Science, 5,* 89–92. https://doi.org/10.1177/1745691609357016

Arnett, Jeffrey Jensen. (2011). Emerging adulthood(s): The cultural psychology of a new life stage. In Lene Arnett Jensen (Ed.), *Bridging cultural and developmental approaches to psychology: New syntheses in theory, research, and policy.* Oxford University Press.

Arnocky, Steven; Piché, Tina; Albert, Graham; Ouellette, Danielle; & Barclay, Pat. (2016). Altruism predicts mating success in humans. *British Journal of Psychology, 108,* 416–435. https://doi.org/10.1111/bjop.12208

Arnott, David, & Gao, Shijia. (2019). Behavioral economics for decision support systems researchers. *Decision Support Systems, 122.* https://doi.org/10.1016/j.dss.2019.05.003

Arntz, Arnoud, & ten Haaf, José. (2012). Social cognition in borderline personality disorder: Evidence for dichotomous thinking but no evidence for less complex attributions. *Behaviour Research and Therapy, 50*(11), 707–718. https://doi.org/10.1016/j.brat.2012.07.002

Aronson, Elliot. (1987). Teaching students what they think they already know about prejudice and desegregation. In Vivian Parker Makosky (Ed.), *G. Stanley Hall Lecture Series* (Vol. 7). American Psychological Association.

Aronson, Elliot. (1990). Applying social psychology to desegregation and energy conservation. *Personality and Social Psychology Bulletin, 16,* 118–132.

Aronson, Elliot. (1992). The return of the repressed: Dissonance theory makes a comeback. *Psychological Inquiry, 3,* 303–311.

Aronson, Elliot. (1995). *The social animal* (7th ed.).Freeman.

Aronson, Elliot, & Bridgeman, Diane. (1979). Jigsaw groups and the desegregated classroom: In pursuit of common goals. *Personality and Social Psychology Bulletin, 5,* 438–466.

Aronson, Elliot, & Tavris, Carol. (2020, July 12). The role of cognitive dissonance in the pandemic. *The Atlantic.* https://www.theatlantic.com/ideas/archive/2020/07/role-cognitive-dissonance-pandemic/614074/

Asch, Solomon E. (1951). Effects of group pressure upon the modification and distortion of judgments. In Harold S. Guetzkow (Ed.), *Groups, leadership, and men: Research in human relations. Reports on research sponsored by the Human Relations and Morale Branch of the Office of Naval Research, 1945–1950.* Carnegie Press.

Asch, Solomon E. (1955, November). Opinions and social pressure. *Scientific American, 193,* 31–35.

Asch, Solomon E. (1956). Studies of independence and conformity: A minority of one against a unanimous majority. *Psychological Monographs, 70*(9, Whole No. 416).

Asch, Solomon E. (1957). An experimental investigation of group influence. In *Symposium on preventive and social psychiatry.* U.S. Government Printing Office, Walter Reed Army Institute of Research.

Ashcraft, Mark H. (1994). *Human memory and cognition* (2nd ed.). HarperCollins.

Ashley, Florence. (2019). The misuse of gender dysphoria: Toward greater conceptual clarity in transgender health. *Perspectives on Psychological Science,* 1–6. https://doi.org/10.1177/1745691619872987

Ashton, Michael C., & Lee, Kibeom. (2005). A defence of the lexical approach to the study of personality structure. *European Journal of Personality: Published for the European Association of Personality Psychology, 19*(1), 5–24. https://doi.org/10.1002/per.541

Ashton, Michael C., & Lee, Kibeom. (2007). Empirical, theoretical, and practical advantages of the HEXACO model of personality structure. *Personality and Social Psychology Review, 11*(2), 150–166. https://doi.org/10.1177/1088868306294907

Ashton, Michael; Lee, Kibeom; & de Vries, Reinout E. (2014). The HEXACO honesty-humility, agreeableness, and emotionality factors: A review of research and theory. *Personality and Social Psychology Review, 18*(2), 139–152. https://doi.org/10.1177/1088868314523838

Asken, Breton Michael; DeKosky, Steven T.; Clugston, James R.; Jaffee, Michael S.; & Bauer, Russell M. (2018). Diffusion tensor imaging (DTI) findings in adult civilian, military, and sport-related mild traumatic brain injury (mTBI): A systematic critical review. *Brain Imaging and Behavior, 12,* 585–612. https://doi.org/10.1007/x11682-017-9708-9

Asselmann, Eva; Wittchen, Hans-Ulrich; Lieb, Roselind; & Beesdo-Baum, Katja. (2017). A 10-year prospective-longitudinal study of daily hassles and incident psychopathology among adolescents and young adults: Interactions with gender, perceived coping efficacy, and negative life events. *Social Psychiatry and Psychiatric Epidemiology, 52,* 1353–1362. https://doi.org/10.1007/s00127-017-1436-3

Association for Psychological Science (APS). (2017, September 19). "A genius in the art of living": Industrial psychology pioneer Lillian Gilbreth. https://www.psychologicalscience.org/publications/observer/obsonline/a-genius-in-the-art-of-living-lillian-moller-gilbreth-industrial-psychology-pioneer.html

Association for Psychological Science (APS). (2020, November 30). Remembering James S. Jackson (1944-–2020). Association for Psychological Science. https://www.psychologicalscience.org/observer/james-jackson-tribute

Atherton, Olivia; Robins, Richard; Rentfrow, P. Jason; & Lamb, Michael. (2014). Personality correlates of risky health outcomes: Findings from a large Internet study. *Journal of Research in Personality, 50,* 56–60. https://doi.org/10.1016/j.jrp.2014.03.002

Atkinson, Richard C., & Shiffrin, Richard M. (1968). Human memory: A proposed system and its control processes. In Kenneth W. Spence & Janet T. Spence (Eds.), *The psychology of learning and motivation: Advances in research and theory* (Vol. 2). Academic Press.

Atlas, Lauren, & Wager, Tor. (2014). A meta-analysis of brain mechanisms of placebo analgesia: Consistent findings and unanswered questions. In Benedetti, Fabrizio, Enck, Paul, Frisaldi, Elisa, & Schedlowski, Manfred (Eds.). *Handbook of experimental pharmacology*(Vol. 225, pp. 37–69). Springer-Verlag.

Ator, Nancy A. (2005). Conducting behavioral research: Methodological and laboratory animal welfare issues. In Chana K. Akins, Sangeeta Panicker, & Christopher L. Cunningham (Eds.), *Laboratory animals in research and teaching: Ethics, care, and methods.* American Psychological Association.

Attneave, Carolyn L. (1969). Therapy in tribal settings and urban network intervention. *Family Process, 8*(2), 192–210. https://doi.org/10.1111/j.1545-5300.1969.00192.x

Attneave, Carolyn L. (1990). Core network intervention: An emerging paradigm. *Journal of Strategic and Systemic Therapies, 9*(1), 3–10. https://doi.org/10.1521/jsst.1990.9.1.3

Au, Raymond C. P.; Watkins, David A.; & Hattie, John A. C. (2010). Academic risk factors and deficits of learned hopelessness: A longitudinal study of Hong Kong secondary school students. *Educational Psychology, 30*(2), 125–138.

Auld, M. Christopher., & Powell, Lisa M. (2009). Economics of food energy density and adolescent body weight. *Economica, 76*(304), 719–740. https://doi.org/10.1111/j.1468-0335.2008.00709.x

Austin, James H. (2009). *Selfless insight: Zen and the meditative transformations of consciousness.* MIT Press.

Aveline, Mark. (2005). The person of the therapist. *Psychotherapy Research, 15*(3), 155–164.

Ayins, Andrew L. (2012). Needling the status quo: Comment on "Acupuncture for Chronic Pain." *Archives of Internal Medicine, 172*(19), 1–2. https://doi.org/10.1001/archinternmed.2012.4198

Aviv, Rachel. (2018, April 2). How a young woman lost her identity. *The New Yorker.* https://www.newyorker.com/magazine/2018/04/02/how-a-young-woman-lost-her-identity

Axelrod, Vadim, & Yovel, Galit. (2015). Successful decoding of famous faces in the fusiform face area. *PLOS ONE, 10,* 1–20. https://doi.org/10.1371/journal.pone.011712

Axt, Jordan. (2018, May 30). Tracking the use of Project Implicit data. *Project Implicit Blog.* https://implicit.harvard.edu/implicit/user/jaxt/blogposts/piblogpost020.html

Azevedo, Frederico A. C.; Carvalho, Ludmila R. B.; Grinberg, Lea T.; Farfel, José M., Ferretti, Renata E. P.; Leite, R. E., Filho, Wilson J.; Lent, Robert; & Herculano-Houzel, Suzana. (2009). Equal numbers of neuronal and nonneuronal cells make the human brain an isometrically scaled-up primate brain. *Journal of Comparative Neurology, 513,* 532–541. https://doi.org/10.1002/cne.21974

Aziz-Zadeh, Lisa; S.-L. Liew, Sook-Lei; & Dandekar, Francesco. (2013). Exploring the neural correlates of visual creativity. *Social Cognitive and Affective Neuroscience, 8,* 475–480. https://doi.org/10.1093/scan/nss021

Baars, Barnard. (2005). Consciousness eclipsed: Jacques Loeb, Ivan P. Pavlov, and the rise of reductionistic biology after 1900. *Consciousness and Cognition, 14,* 219–230.

Babel, Przemysław. (2019). Classical conditioning as a distinct mechanism of placebo effects. *Frontiers in Psychology, 10,* 1–6. https://doi.org/10.3389/fpsyt.2019.00449

Bachhuber, Marcus A.; Saloner, Brendan; Cunningham, Chinazo O.; & Barry, Colleen L. (2014). Medical cannabis laws and opioid analgesic overdose mortality in the United States, 1999-2010. *JAMA Internal Medicine.* https://doi.org/:10.1001/jamainternmed.2014.4005

Bachrach, Yoram; Kosinski, Michal; Graepel, Thore; Kohli, Pushmeet; & Stillwell, David. (2012, June). Personality and patterns of Facebook usage. In *Proceedings of the 3rd Annual ACM Web Science Conference* (pp. 24–32). Evanston, IL, June 22–24, 2012.

Badcock, Johanna C.; Dragovic, Milan; Garrett, Coleman; & Jablensky, Assen (2011). Action (verb) fluency in schizophrenia: Getting a grip on odd speech. *Schizophrenia Research, 126*(1–3), 138–143. https://doi.org/10.1016/j.schres.2010.11.004

Baddeley, Alan D. (1992, January 31). Working memory. *Science, 255*(5044), 556–559. https://doi.org/10.1126/science.1736359

Baddeley, Alan D. (2002). Is working memory still working? *European Psychologist, 7,* 85–97. https://doi.org/10.1027/1016-9040.7.2.85

Baddeley, Alan D. (2007). *Working memory, thought, and action.* Oxford University Press.

Baddeley, Alan D. (2010). Working memory. *Current Biology, 20*(4), R136–R140. https://doi.org/10.1016/j.cub.2009.12.014

Baddeley, Alan D.; Bäckman, Lars; & Nyberg, Lars. (2010). Long-term and working memory: How do they interact? *Memory, aging and the brain: A Festschrift in honour of Lars-Göran Nilsson* (pp. 7–23). Psychology Press.

Baddeley, Alan D.; Eysenck, Michael W.; & Anderson, Michael C. (2009). *Memory.* Psychology Press.

Bader, Alan P., & Phillips, Roger D. (2002). Fathers' recognition of their newborns by visual-facial and olfactory cues. *Psychology of Men and Masculinity, 3,* 79–84.

Bae, Christine L.; Therriault, David J.; & Redifer, Jenni L. (2019). Investigating the testing effect: Retrieval as a characteristic of effective study strategies. *Learning and Instruction, 60,* 206–214. https://doi.org/10.1016/j.learninstruc.2017.12.008

Baer, John. (1993). *Creativity and divergent thinking: A task-specific approach.* Erlbaum.

Baer, Ruth; Crane, Catherine; Miller, Edward; & Kuyken, Willem. (2019). Doing no harm in mindfulness-based programs: Conceptual issues and empirical findings. *Clinical Psychology Review, 71,* 101–114. https://doi.org/10.1016/j.cpr.2019.01.001

Bailer, U. F., & Kaye, W. H. (2011). Serotonin: Imaging findings in eating disorders. *Current Topics in Behavioral Neuroscience, 6,* 59–79. https://doi.org/10.1007/7854_2010_78

Bailey, J. Michael; Vasey, Paul; Diamond, Lisa; Breedlove, S. Marc; Vilain, Eric; & Epprecht, Marc. (2016). Sexual orientation, controversy, and science. *Psychological Science in the Public Interest, 17,* 45–101. https://doi.org/10.1177/1529100616637616

Bailey, Marian Breland, & Bailey, Robert E. (1993). "Misbehavior": A case history. *American Psychologist, 48,* 1157–1158.

Baillargeon, Renée. (2004). Infants' physical world. *Current Directions in Psychological Science, 13,* 89–94.

Baillargeon, Renée. & DeVos, Julie. (1991). Object permanence in young infants: Further evidence. *Child Development, 62,* 1227–1246.

Baillargeon, Renée; Li, Jie; Gertner, Yael; & Wu, Di. (2011). How do infants reason about physical events? In Usha Goswami (Ed.), *The Wiley-Blackwell Handbook of Childhood and Cognitive Development* (2nd ed.). Wiley-Blackwell.

Baillargeon, Renée; Stavans, Maayan; Wu, Di; Gertner, Yael; Setoh, Peipei; Kittredge, Audrey K.; & Bernard, Amélie. (2012). Object individuation and physical reasoning in infancy: An integrative account. *Language Learning and Development, 8,* 4–46. https://doi.org/10.1080/15475441.2012.630610

Baird, Abigail A. (2007). Moral reasoning in adolescence: The integration of emotion and cognition. In Walter Sinnott-Armstrong (Ed.), *Moral psychology* (Vol. 3): *The neuroscience of morality: Emotion, disease, and development* (pp. 323–342). MIT Press.

Baird, Abigail A.; Kagan, Jerome; Gaudette, Thomas; Walz, Kathryn A.; Hershlag, Natalie; & Boas, David A. (2002). Frontal lobe activation during object permanence: Data from near-infrared spectroscopy. *NeuroImage, 16,* 1120–1126. https://doi.org/10.1006/nimg.2002.1170

Baird, Abigail A., & Roellke, Emma V. (2015). Girl Uninterrupted: The neural basis of moral development among adolescent females. In Jean Decety & Thalia Wheatly (Eds.), *The moral brain: A multidisciplinary perspective* (pp. 157–179). MIT Press.

Baird, Benjamin; Mrazek, Michael D.; Phillips, Dawa T.; & Schooler, Jonathan W. (2014). Domain-specific enhancement of metacognitive ability following meditation training. *Journal of Experimental Psychology: General.* Advance online publication. https://doi.org/10.1037/a0036882

Bakker, Arnold B., & Demerouti, Evangelia. (2017). Job demands-resources theory: Taking stock and looking forward. *Journal of Occupational Health Psychology, 22,* 273–285. https://doi.org/10.1037/ocp0000056

Bakker, Arnold B.; Demerouti, Evangelia; & Dollard, Maureen F. (2008). How job demands affect partners' experience of exhaustion: Integrating work-family conflict and crossover theory. *Journal of Applied Psychology, 93*(4), 901–911.

Bakoyiannis, Ioannis; Gkioka, Eleana; Pergialiotis, Vasileios; Mastroleon, Ioanna; Prodromidou, Anastasia; Vlachos, Georgios D.; & Perrea, Despina. (2014). Fetal alcohol spectrum disorders and cognitive functions of young children. *Reviews in the Neurosciences, 25,* 631–639. https://doi.org/10.1515/revneuro-2014-0029

Balbo, Marcella; Leproult, Rachel; & Van Cauter, Eve. (2010). Impact of sleep and its disturbances on hypothalamo-pituitary-adrenal axis activity. *International Journal of Endocrinology.* https://doi.org/10.1155/2010/759234

Baldwin, David S.; Anderson, Ian M.; Nutt, David J.; Allgulander, Christer; Bandelow, Borwin; den Boer, Johan A.; Christmas, David M.; Davies, Simon; Fineberg, Naomi; Lidbetter, Nicky; Malizia, Andrea; McCrone, Paul; Nabarro, Daniel; O'Neill, Catherine; Scott, Jan; van der Wee, Nic; & Wittchen, Hans-Ulrich. (2014). Evidence-based pharmacological treatment of anxiety disorders, post-traumatic stress disorder and obsessive-compulsive disorder: A revision of the 2005 guidelines from the British Association for Psychopharmacology. *Journal of Psychopharmacology, 28*(5), 1–37. https://doi.org/10.1177/0269881114525674

Baldwin, Scott A.; Berkelion, Arjan; Atkins, David C.; Olsen, Joseph A.; & Nielsen, Stevan L. (2009, April). Rates of change in naturalistic psychotherapy: Contrasting dose-effect and good-enough level models of change. *Journal of Consulting and Clinical Psychology, 77*(2), 203–211.

Bale, Tracy L., & Jovanovic, Tanja. (2020). The critical importance in identifying the biological mechanisms underlying the effects of racism on mental health. *Neuropsychopharmacology, 46,* 233. https://doi.org/10.1038/s41386-020-00801-w

Ballard, Clive; Gauthier, Serge; Corbett, Anne; Brayne, Carol; Aarsland, Dag; Baudry, Michel; Bi, Xiaoning; Gall, Christine; & Lynch, Gary. (2011). The biochemistry of memory: The 26 year journey of a 'new and specific hypothesis.' *Neurobiology of Learning and Memory, 95*(2), 125–133.

Ballesteros, Soledad; Voelcker-Rehage, Claudia; & Bherer, Louis. (2018). Editorial: Cognitive and brain plasticity induced by physical exercise, cognitive training, video games, and combined interventions. *Frontiers in Human Neuroscience, 12,* 169. https://doi.org/10.3389/fnhum.2018.00169

Balsam, Kimberly F.; Beauchaine, Theodore P.; Rothblum, Esther D.; & Solomon, Sondra F. (2008). Three-year follow-up of same-sex couples who had civil unions in Vermont, same-sex couples not in civil unions, and heterosexual married couples. *Developmental Psychology, 44,* 102–116.

Bamford, Nigel S.; Zhang, Hui; Joyce, John A.; Scarlis, Christine A.; Hanan, Whitney; Wu, Nan-Ping; André, Véronique M.; Cohen, Rachel; Cepeda, Carlos; Levine, Michael S.; Harleton, Erin; & Sulzer, David. (2008). Repeated exposure to methamphetamine causes long-lasting presynaptic corticostriatal depression that is renormalized with drug readministration. *Neuron, 58*(1), 89–103. https://doi.org/10.1016/j.neuron.2008.01.033

Banaji, Mahzarin R., & Heiphetz, Larisa. (2010). Attitudes. In S. T. Fiske, D. T. Gilbert & G. Lindzey (Eds.), *Handbook of social psychology, Vol. 1,* (pp. 353–393). Wiley.

Bandura, Albert. (1965). Influence of models' reinforcement contingencies on the acquisition of imitative behaviors. *Journal of Personality and Social Psychology, 1,* 589–595.

Bandura, Albert. (1974). Behavior theory and the models of man. *American Psychologist, 29,* 859–869.

Bandura, Albert. (1977). *Social learning theory.* Prentice Hall.

Bandura, Albert. (1986). *Social foundations of thought and action: A social cognitive theory.* Prentice Hall.

Bandura, Albert. (1990). Conclusion: Reflections on nonability determinants of competence. In Robert J. Sternberg & John Kolligian, Jr. (Eds.), *Competence considered.* Yale University Press.

Bandura, Albert. (1991). Self-regulation of motivation through anticipatory and self-reactive mechanisms. In Richard Dienstbier (Ed.), *Nebraska Symposium on Motivation 1990* (Vol. 38). University of Nebraska Press.

Bandura, Albert. (1992). Exercise of personal agency through the self-efficacy mechanism. In Ralf Schwarzer (Ed.), *Self-efficacy: Thought control of action.* Hemisphere.

Bandura, Albert. (1997). *Self-efficacy: The exercise of control.* Freeman.

Bandura, Albert. (2001). Social cognitive theory: An agentic perspective. *Annual Review of Psychology, 52,* 1–26. https://doi.org/10.1146/annurev.psych.52.1.1

Bandura, Albert. (2002). Environmental sustainability by sociocognitive deceleration of population growth. In Peter Schmuck & Wesley P. Schultz (Eds.), *The psychology of sustainable development.* Kluwer.

Bandura, Albert. (2004a). Health promotion by social cognitive means. *Health Education & Behavior, 31*(2), 143–164. https://doi.org/10.1177/1090198104263660

Bandura, Albert. (2004b). Swimming against the mainstream: The early years from chilly tributary to transformative mainstream. *Behaviour Research and Therapy, 42,* 613–630. https://doi.org/10.1016/j.brat.2004.02.001

Bandura, Albert. (2006). Towards a psychology of human agency. *Perspectives on Psychological Science, 1,* 164–180.

Bandura, Albert. (2008). An agentic perspective on positive psychology. In Shane J. Lopez (Ed.), *Positive psychology: Exploring the best in people.* Greenwood.

Bandura, Albert. (2018). Toward a psychology of human agency: Pathways and reflections. *Perspectives on Psychological Science, 13*(2), 130–136. https://doi.org/10.1177/17456916176992

Bandura, Albert; Caprara, Gian Vittorio; Barbaranelli, Claudio; Gerbino, Maria; & Pastorelli, Concetta. (2003). Role of affective self-regulatory efficacy in diverse spheres of psychosocial functioning. *Child Development, 74,* 769–782.

Bandura, Albert; Ross, Dorothea; & Ross, Sheila A. (1963). Imitation of film-mediated aggressive models. *Journal of Abnormal and Social Psychology, 66,* 3–11.

Banerjee, Abhijit; La Ferrara, Elianna; & Orozco-Olvera, Victor H. (2019). The entertaining way to behavioral change: Fighting HIV with MTV. *National Bureau of Economic Research Working Paper Series, 26029,* 1–45. https://doi.org/10.3386/w26096

Banks, Terry, & Dabbs, J. M. (1996). Salivary testosterone and cortisol in a deliquent and violent urban subculture. *Journal of Social Psychology, 136*(1), 49–56.

Bansal, Agam; Garg, Chandan; Pakhare, Abhijith; & Gupta, Samiksha. (2018). Selfies: A boom or bane? *Journal of Family Medicine and Primary Care, 7*(4), 828–831. https://doi.org/10.4103/jfmpc.jfmpc_109_18

Baptista, Johann; Derakhshani, Max; & Tressoldi, Patrizio E. (2015). Explicit anomalous cognition: A review of the best evidence in ganzfeld, forced choice, remote viewing and dream studies. In Etzel Cardeña, John Palmer, & David Marcusson-Clavertz (Eds.). *Parapsychology: A handbook for the 21st century.* McFarland.

Baranski, Erica. (2015, January 22). It's all happening: The future of crowdsourcing science. Open Science Collaboration. http://osc.centerforopenscience.org/2015/01/22/crowdsourcing-science/

Barch, Deanna M. (2005). The cognitive neuroscience of schizophrenia. *Annual Review of Clinical Psychology, 1,* 321–353. https://doi.org/10.1146/annurev.clinpsy.1.102803.143959

Barlow, David H.; Bullis, Jacqueline R.; Comer, Jonathan S.; & Ametaj, Amantia A. (2013). Evidence-based psychological treatments: An update and a way forward. *Annual Review of Clinical Psychology, 9,* 1–27. https://doi.org/10.1146/annurev-clinpsy-050212-185629

Barlow, Jon; Ebeling, Caskey; Ebeling, Mick (Producers); & Ebeling, Caskey (Director). (2012). Getting up: The Tempt One story [Documentary Film]. United States: Ebeling Group. https://www.reelhouse.org/gettingup/gettingtemptonestory/gettingtemptonestorytrailer

Barnes, Edward. (1973). IQ testing and minority school children: Imperatives for change. *Journal of Non-White Concerns in Personnel and Guidance, 2*(1), 4–20. https://doi.org/10.1002/j.2164-4950.1973.tb00324.x

Barnes, Jo; Dong, Christine Y.; McRobbie, Hayden; Walker, Natalie; Mehta, Monaz; & Stead, Lindsay F. (2010). Hypnotherapy for smoking cessation. *Cochrane Database of Systematic Reviews, 2010*(10), No. CD001008. https://doi.org/10.1002/14651858.CD001008.pub2

Barnhofer, Thorsten; Huntenburg, Julia; Lifshitz, Michael; Wild, Jennifer; Antonova, Elena; & Margulies, Daniel. (2016). How mindfulness training may help to reduce vulnerability for recurrent depression: A neuroscience perspective. *Clinical Psychological Science, 4,* 328–343. https://doi.org/10.1177/2167702615595036

Barrett, Lisa F. (2015, September 1). Psychology is not in crisis. *The New York Times.* http://www.nytimes.com/2015/09/01/opinion/psychology-is-not-in-crisis.html

Barrett, Lisa F., & Bliss-Moreau, Eliza. (2009). She's emotional. He's having a bad day: Attributional explanations for emotion stereotypes. *Emotion, 9,* 649–658.

Barrett, Marna S.; Chua, Wee-Jhong; Crits-Christoph, Paul; Gibbons, Mary Beth; & Thompson, Don. (2008, June). Early withdrawal from mental health treatment: Implications for psychotherapy practice. *Psychotherapy: Theory, Research, Practice, Training, 45*(2), 247–267.

Barrow, Karen. (2018, March 27). Patient voices: narcolepsy. *The New York Times.* https://www.nytimes.com/interactive/2018/well/patient-voices-narcolepsy.html

Barry, Elaine S. (2019). Co-sleeping as a proximal context for infant development: The importance of physical touch. *Infant Behavior and Development, 57.* https://doi.org/10.1016/j.infbeh.2019.101385

Barry, Ellen. (2016). Mortal to divine and back: India's transgender goddesses. *The New York Times.* https://www.nytimes.com/2016/07/25/world/asia/india-transgender.html

Barsaglini, Alessio; Sartori, Guiseppe; Benetti, Stefania; Pettersson-Yeo, William; & Mechelli, Andrea. (2014). The effects of psychotherapy on brain function: A systematic and critical review. *Progress in Neurobiology, 114,* 1–14. https://doi.org/10.1016/j.pneurobio.2013.10.006

Barth, Jürgen; Munder, Thomas; Gerger, Heike; Nüesch, Eveline; Trelle, Sven; Znoj, Hansjörg; Jüni, Peter; & Cuijpers, Pim. (2013). Comparative efficacy of seven psychotherapeutic interventions for patients with depression: A network meta-analysis. *PLOS Medicine, 10*(5), e1001454. https://doi.org/10.1371/journal.pmed.1001454

Bartlett, Frederic C. (1932). *Remembering.* Cambridge University Press.

Bartz, Jennifer; Simeon, Daphne; Hamilton, Holly; Kim, Suah; Crystal, Sarah; Braun, Ashley; Vicens, Victor; & Hollander, Eric. (2011). Social effects of oxytocin in humans: Context and person matter. *Trends in Cognitive Science, 15,* 301–309.

Barušs, Imants, & Rabier, Vanille. (2014). Failure to replicate retrocausal recall. *Psychology of Consciousness: Theory, Research, and Practice, 1,* 82–91. https://doi.org/10.1037/cns0000005

Bas-Hoogendam, Janna Marie; van Steenbergen, Henk; van der Wee, Nic J. A.; & Westenberg, P. Michiel. (2020). Amygdala hyperreactivity to faces conditioned with a social-evaluative meaning–a multiplex, multigenerational fMRI study on social anxiety endophenotypes, *NeuroImage: Clinical, 26.* https://doi.org/10.1016/j.nicl.2020.102247

Bashore, Theodore R., & Rapp, Paul E. (1993). Are there alternatives to traditional polygraph procedures? *Psychological Bulletin, 113,* 3–22.

Bashshur, Rashid L.; Doarn, Charles R.; Frenk, Julio M.; Kvedar, Joseph C.; Shannon, Gary W.; & Woolliscroft, James O. (2020). Beyond the COVID pandemic, telemedicine, and health care. *Telemedicine and e-Health, 26*(11), 1310–1313. https://doi.org/10.1089/tmj.2020.0328

Basil, Debra Z.; Ridgway, Nancy M.; & Basil, Michael D. (2006). Guilt appeals: The mediating effect of responsibility. *Psychology & Marketing, 23*(12), 1035–1054.

Baskin-Sommers, Arielle R. (2016). Dissecting antisocial behavior: The impact of neural, genetic, and environmental factors. *Clinical Psychological Science, 4*(3), 500–510. https://doi.org/10.1177/2167702615626904

Bass, Bernard M. (1981). *Stogdill's handbook of leadership.* Free Press.

Bass, Ellen, & Davis, Linda. (1994). *The courage to heal* (3rd ed.). HarperPerennial.

Basso, Olga. (2007). Right or wrong? On the difficult relationship between epidemiologists and handedness. *Epidemiology, 18,* 191–193.

Bastardi, Anthony; Uhlmann, Eric L.; & Ross, Lee. (2011). Wishful thinking: Belief, desire, and the motivated evaluation of scientific evidence. *Psychological Science, 22,* 731–732.

Bastiaanssen, Thomaz; Cussotto, Sofia; Claesson, Marcus J.; Clarke, Gerard; Dinan, Timothy G.; & Cryan, John F. (2020). Gutted! Unraveling the role of the microbiome in major depressive disorder. *Harvard Review of Psychiatry, 28*(1), 26–39. https://doi.org/10.1097/HRP.0000000000000243

Bastiaensens, Sara; Vandebosch, Heidi; Poels, Karolien; Van Cleemput, Katrien; DeSmet, Ann; & De Bourdeaudhuij, Ilse. (2014). Cyberbullying on social network sites: An experimental study into bystanders' behavioural intentions to help the victim or reinforce the bully. *Computers in Human Behavior, 31,* 259–271. https://doi.org/10.1016/j.chb.2013.10.036

Bates, Steve. (2002, February). Personality counts. *HR Magazine, 47,* 28.

Bathje, Geoff J., & Pryor, John B. (2011). The relationships of public and self-stigma to seeking mental health services. *Journal of Mental Health Counseling, 33*(2), 161–177. https://doi.org/10.17744/mehc.33.2.g6320392741604l1

Batsell, W. Robert, Jr.; Perry, Jennifer L.; Hanley, Elizabeth; & Hostetter, Autumn B. (2017). Ecological validity of the testing effect: The use of daily quizzes in introductory psychology. *Teaching of Psychology, 44,* 18–23. https://doi.org/10.1177/0098628316677492

Batson, C. Daniel; Ahmad, Nadia; & Stocks, E. L. (2011). Four forms of prosocial motivation: Egoism, altruism, collectivism, and principalism. In David Dunning (Ed.), *Social motivation* (pp. 103–126). Psychology Press.

Baudry, Michel; Bi, Xiaoning; Gall, Christine; & Lynch, Gary. (2011). The biochemistry of memory: The 26 year journey of a 'new and specific hypothesis.' *Neurobiology of Learning and Memory, 95*(2), 125–133.

Bauer, Patricia J.; Tasdemir-Ozdes, Aylin; & Larkina, Marina (2014). Adults' reports of their earliest memories: Consistency in events, ages, and narrative characteristics over time. *Consciousness and Cognition: An International Journal, 27,* 76–88. https://doi.org/10.1016/j.concog.2014.04.008

Bauer, Stephanie; Percevic, Robert; Okon, Eberhard; Meermann, Rolf U.; & Kordy, Hans. (2003). Use of text messaging in the aftercare of patients with bulimia nervosa. *European Eating Disorders Review, 11*(3), 279–290.

Bauer, Talya, & Erdogan, Berrin. (2015). Leader–member exchange (LMX) theory. *Oxford Handbooks Online.* https://doi.org/10.1093/oxfordhb/9780199326174.013.0002

Bauer-Wolf, Jeremy. (2019, May 7). Suicide-prevention training for all. *Inside Higher Ed.* https://www.insidehighered.com/news/2019/05/07/u-iowa-requiring-suicide-prevention-training-all-students#disqus_thread

Bauman, Christopher W., & Skitka, Linda J. (2010). Making attributions for behaviors: The prevalence of correspondence bias in the general population. *Basic and Applied Social Psychology, 32*(3), 269–277.

Baumeister, Roy F., & Leary, Mark R. (1995). The need to belong: Desire for human attachments as a fundamental human motivation. *Psychological Bulletin, 117*(3), 497–529. https://doi.org/10.1037/0033-2909.117.3.497

Baumeister, Roy F., & Masicampo, E. J. (2010). Conscious thought is for facilitating social and cultural interactions: How mental simulations serve the animal–culture interface. *Psychological Review, 117*(3), 945–971. https://doi.org/10.1037/a0019393

Baumeister, Roy F.; Masicampo, E. J.; & Vohs, Kathleen D. (2011). Do conscious thoughts cause behavior? *Annual Review of Psychology, 62,* 331–361. https://doi.org/10.1146/annurev.psych.093008.131126

Baumrind, Diana. (1964). Some thoughts on ethics of research: After reading Milgram's "Behavioral Study of Obedience." *American Psychologist, 19,* 421–423.

Baumrind, Diana. (1971). Current patterns of parental authority. *Developmental Psychology Monographs, 4,* 1–103.

Baumrind, Diana. (1991). The influence of parenting style on adolescent competence and substance abuse. *Journal of Early Adolescence, 11,* 56–95.

Baumrind, Diana. (2005). Patterns of parental authority and adolescent autonomy. *New Directions for Child & Adolescent Development, 2005*(108), 61–69.

Bayer, Ute C., & Gollwitzer, Peter M. (2007). Boosting scholastic test scores by willpower: The role of implementation intentions. *Self and Identity, 6,* 1–19.

Bayley, Peter J., & Squire, Larry R. (2002). Medial temporal lobe amnesia: Gradual acquisition of factual information by nondeclarative memory. *Journal of Neuroscience, 22,* 5741–5748.

BBC News. (2008, December 19). People 'still willing to torture.' *BBC News.* http://news.bbc.co.uk/2/hi/7791278.stm

Beal, Carole R. (1994). *Boys and girls: The development of gender roles.* McGraw-Hill.

Beaman, Arthur L.; Klentz, Bonnel; Diener, Edward; & Svanum, Soren. (1979). Self-awareness and transgression in children: Two field studies. *Journal of Personality and Social Psychology, 37,* 1835–1846.

Beardsley, Eleanor. (2010, March 18). Fake TV game show 'tortures' man, shocks France. *NPR.* http://www.npr.org/templates/story/story.php?storyId=124838091

Beauvois, Jean-Léon; Courbet, Didier; & Oberlé, Dominque. (2012). The prescriptive power of the television host: A transposition of Milgram's obedience paradigm to the context of TV game show. *Revue Européenne de Psychologie Appliquée, 62,* 111–119.

Beck, Aaron T. (1991). Cognitive therapy: A 30-year retrospective. *American Psychologist, 46,* 368–375.

Beck, Aaron T. (2004, March). Quoted in Anita Bowles, "Beck in action." *APS Observer, 17*(3), 7–8.

Beck, Aaron T., & Alford, Brad A. (2009). *Depression: Causes and treatment.* Philadelphia, PA: University of Pennsylvania Press.

Beck, Aaron T., & Dozois, David J. A. (2011). Cognitive therapy: Current status and future directions. *Annual Review of Medicine, 62*(1), 397–409. https://doi.org/10.1146/annurev-med-052209-100032

Beck, Aaron T.; Rush, A. John; Shaw, Brian F.; & Emery, Gary. (1979). *Cognitive therapy of depression.* Guilford.

Beck, Diane M. (2010). The appeal of the brain in the popular press. *Perspectives on Psychological Science, 5,* 762–766. https://doi.org/10.1177/1745691610388779

Beck, Hall P.; Levinson, Sharman; & Irons, Gary. (2009). Finding Little Albert: A journey to John B. Watson's infant laboratory. *American Psychologist, 64*(7), 605–614.

Beck, Hall P.; Levinson, Sharman; & Irons, Gary. (2010). The evidence supports Douglas Merritte as Little Albert. *American Psychologist, 65,* 301–303. https://doi.org/10.1037/a0019444

Bedi, Gillinder; Hyman, David; & de Wit, Harriet. (2010). Is ecstasy an "empathogen"? Effects of ±3,4-methylenedioxymethamphetamine on prosocial feelings and identification of emotional states in others. *Biological Psychiatry, 68,* 1134–1140. https://doi.org/10.1016/j.biopsych.2010.08.003

Behrmann, Marlene, & Plaut, David C. (2015). A vision of graded hemispheric specialization. *Annals of the New York Academy of Sciences, 1359,* 30–46. https://doi.org/10.1111/nyas.12833

Beidel, Deborah C., & Stipelman, Brooke. (2007). Anxiety disorders. In Michel Hersen, Samuel M. Turner, & Deborah C. Beidel (Eds.), *Adult psychopathology and diagnosis* (5th ed., pp. 349–409). Wiley.

Beins, Bernard C. (2011). Methodological and conceptual issues in crosscultural research. In K. D. Keith (Ed.), *Cross-cultural psychology: Contemporary themes and perspectives* (pp. 37–55). Wiley-Blackwell.

Bekoff, Marc. (2007). *The emotional lives of animals.* New World Library.

Belgrave, Faye Z., & Allison, Kevin W. (2010). *African American psychology: From Africa to America.* Sage.

Bell, Martha Ann, & Fox, Nathan A. (1992). The relations between frontal brain electrical activity and cognitive development during infancy. *Child Development, 63*(5), 1142–1163. https://doi.org/10.2307/1131523

Bellak, Leopold. (1993). *The Thematic Apperception Test, the Children's Apperception Test, and the Senior Apperception Technique in Clinical Use* (5th ed.). Allyn & Bacon.

Bellander, Martin; Berggren, Rasmus; Mårtensson, Johan; Brehmer, Yvonne; Wenger, Elisabeth; Li, Tie-Qiang; Bodammer, Nils C; Shing, Yee-Lee;

Werkle-Bergner, Markus; & Lövdén, Martin. (2016). Behavioral correlates of changes in hippocampal gray matter structure during acquisition of foreign vocabulary. *NeuroImage, 131,* 205–213. https://doi.org/10.1016/j.neuroimage.2015.10.020

Belsky, Jay. (1992). Consequences of child care for children's development: A deconstructionist view. In Alan Booth (Ed.), *Child care in the 1990s: Trends and consequences.* Erlbaum.

Belsky, Jay. (2001). Emanuel Miller Lecture: Developmental risks (still) associated with early child care. *Journal of Child Psychology, Psychiatry and Allied Disciplines, 42,* 845–859.

Belsky, Jay. (2002). Quantity counts: Amount of child care and children's socioemotional development. *Journal of Development & Behavioral Pediatrics, 23,* 167–170.

Belsky, Jay. (2006). Determinants and consequences of infant-parent attachment. In Catherine Susan Tamis-LeMonda (Ed.), *Child psychology: A handbook of contemporary issues* (2nd ed., pp. 53–77). Psychology Press.

Belsky, Jay. (2009). Classroom composition, childcare history and social development: Are childcare effects disappearing or spreading? *Social Development, 18*(1), 230–238.

Belsky, Jay; Steinberg, Laurence; Houts, Renate M.; & Halpern-Felsher, Bonnie L. (2010). The development of reproductive strategy in females: Early maternal harshness → earlier menarche → increased sexual risk taking. *Developmental Psychology, 46*(1), 120–128.

Belsky, Jay; Vandell, D. L.; Burchinal, M.; Clarke-Stewart, K. A.; McCartney, K.; & Owen, M. T. (2007). Are there long-term effects of early child care? *Child Development, 78*(2), 681–701.

Bem, Daryl J. (2011). Feeling the future: Experimental evidence for anomalous retroactive influences on cognition and affect. *Journal of Personality and Social Psychology, 100,* 407–425.

Bem, Daryl. (2016). Evaluating the evidence for paranormal psychology [Review of the book *Parapsychology: A handbook for the 21st century,* by Etzel Cardeña, John Palmer, and David Marcusson-Clavertz (Eds.)]. *PsycCRITIQUES, 61*(22), article 1. https://doi.org/10.1037/a0040324

Bem, Daryl; Tressoldi, Patrizio; Rabeyron, Thomas; & Duggan, Michael. (2015). Feeling the future: A meta-analysis of 90 experiments on the anomalous anticipation of random future events. *F1000 Research, 4,* 1188. https//doi.org/10.12688/f1000research.7177.1

Bem, Sandra L. (1981). Gender schema theory: A cognitive account of sex typing. *Psychological Review, 88,* 354–364.

Ben Haim, Lucile, & Rowitch, David H. (2017). Functional diversity of astrocytes in neural circuit regulation. *Nature Reviews Neuroscience, 18,* 31–41. https://doi.org/10.1038/nrn.2016.159

Benedetti, Fabrizio; Carlino, Elisa; & Pollo, Antonella. (2010). How placebos change the patient's brain. *Neuropsychopharmacology, 36,* 339–354. https://doi.org/10.1038/npp.2010.81

Benedetti, Fabrizio; Frisaldi, Elisa; Carlino, Elisa; Giudetti, Lucia; Pampallona, Alan; Zibetti, Maurizio; Lanotte, Michele; & Lopiano, Leonardo. (2016). Teaching neurons to respond to placebos. *Journal of Physiology, 594,* 5647–5660. https://doi.org/10.1113/JP271322

Ben-Hamou, Monsif; Marshall, Nathaniel S.; Grunstein, Ronald R.; Saini, Bandana; & Fois, Romano A. (2011). Spontaneous adverse event reports associated with zolpidem in Australia 2001–2008. *Journal of Sleep Research, 20,* 559–568. https://doi.org/10.1111/j.1365-2869.2011.00919.x

Benjamin, Ludy T., Jr., & Simpson, Jeffry A. (2009). The power of the situation: The impact of Milgram's obedience studies on personality and social psychology. *American Psychologist, 64*(1), 12–19. https://doi.org/10.1037/a0014077

Bennett, Craig M., & Baird, Abigail A. (2006). Anatomical changes in the emerging adult brain: A Voxel-based morphometry study. *Human Brain Mapping, 27*(9), 766–777. https://doi.org/10.1002/hbm.20218

Bennett, Dalton; Brown, Emma; Mirza, Atthar; Cahlan, Sarah; Lee, Joyce Sohyun; Kelly, Meg; Samuels, Elyse; & Swaine, Jon. (2021, January 16). 41 minutes of fear: A video timeline from inside the Capitol siege. *The Washington Post.* https://www.washingtonpost.com/investigations/2021/01/16/video-timeline-capitol-siege/?arc404=true

Bennett, Jessica. (2020, April 3). Selena Gomez reveals bipolar diagnosis during Miley Cyrus live stream. *Page Six.* https://pagesix.com/2020/04/03/selena-gomez-reveals-bipolar-diagnosis-during-miley-cyrus-live-stream/

Benningfield, Margaret M., & Cowan, Ronald L. (2013). Brain serotonin function in MDMA (ecstasy) users: Evidence for persisting neurotoxicity. *Neuropsychopharmacology, 38,* 253–255. https://doi.org/10.1038/npp.2012.178

Ben-Porath, Yossef S., & Tellgen, A. (2020). *Minnesota Multiphasic Personality Inventory-3.* Pearson.

Bensafi, M.; Tsutsui, T.; Khan, R.; Levenson, R. W.; & Sobel, N. (2004). Sniffing a human sex-steroid derived compound affects mood and autonomic arousal in a dose-dependent manner. *Psychoneuroendocrinology, 29,* 1290–1299. https://doi.org/10.1016/j.psyneuen.2004.03.007

Benson, Herbert. (2010). *Relaxation revolution: The science and genetics of mind body healing.* Scribner.

Benson, Nicholas; Beaujean, A. Alexander; & Taub, Gordon E. (2015). Using score equating and measurement invariance to examine the Flynn effect in the Wechsler Adult Intelligence Scale. *Multivariate Behavioral Research, 50*(4), 398-415. https://doi.org/10.1080/00273171.2015.1022642

Bentley, Kate H.; Gallagher, Matthew W.; Boswell, James F.; Gorman, Jack M.; Shear, Katherine M.; Woods, Scott W.; & Barlow, David H. (2013). The interactive contributions of perceived control and anxiety sensitivity in panic disorder: A triple vulnerabilities perspective. *Journal of Psychopathology and Behavioral Assessment, 35,* 57–64. https://doi.org/10.1007/s10862-012-9311-8

Ben-Zeev, Dror. (2012). Mobile technologies in the study, assessment, and treatment of schizophrenia. *Schizophrenia Bulletin.* Advance online publication. https://doi.org/10.1093/schbul/sbr179

Berenbaum, Sheri A.; Martin, Carol L.; Hanish, Laura D.; Briggs, Philip T.; & Fabes, Richard A. (2008). Sex differences in children's play. In Jill B. Becker, Karen J. Berkley, Nori Geary, Elizabeth Hampson, James P. Herman, & Elizabeth A. Young (Eds.), *Sex differences in the brain: From genes to behavior.* Oxford University Press.

Berenson, Kathy R.; Downey, Geraldine; Rafaeli, Eshkol; Coifman, Karin G.; & Paquin, Nina Leventhal. (2011). The rejection–rage contingency in borderline personality disorder. *Journal of Abnormal Psychology, 120*(3), 681–690. https://doi.org/10.1037/a0023335

Berger, Justus; Heinrichs, Markus; von Dawans, Bernadette; Way, Baldwin M.; & Chen, Frances S. (2016). Cortisol modulates men's affiliative responses to acute social stress. *Psychoneuroendocrinology, 63,* 1–9. https://doi.org/10.1016/j.psyneuen.2015.09.004

Berger, William; Evandro, Silvia F.; Figueira, Ivan; Marques-Portella, Carla; Luz, Mariana P.; Neylan, Thomas C.; Marmar, Charles R.; & Mendlowics, Mauro V. (2012). Rescuers at risk: A systematic review and meta-regression analysis of the worldwide current prevalence and correlates of PTSD in rescue workers. *Social Psychiatry and Psychiatric Epidemiology, 47,* 1001–1011. https://doi.org/10.1007/s00127-011-0408-2

Berkman, Lisa F., & Glass, Thomas. (2000). Social integration, social networks, social support, and health. In Lisa F. Berkman & Ichir Kawachi (Eds.), *Social epidemiology* (pp. 137–173). Oxford University Press.

Berlyne, Daniel E. (1960). *Conflict, arousal, and curiosity.* McGraw-Hill.

Berlyne, Daniel E. (1971). *Aesthetics and psychobiology.* Appleton-Century-Crofts.

Berman, David, & Lyons, William. (2007). The first modern battle for consciousness: J. B. Watson's rejection of mental images. *Journal of Consciousness Studies, 14,* 5–26.

Berna, Chantal; Leknes, Siri; Holmes, Emily A.; Edwards, Robert R.; Goodwin, Guy M.; & Tracey, Irene. (2010). Induction of depressed mood disrupts emotion regulation neurocircuitry and enhances pain unpleasantness. *Biological Psychiatry, 67,* 1083–1090. https://doi.org/10.1073/pnas.0505210102

Bernal, Martha E.; & Castro, Felipe G. (1994). Are clinical psychologists prepared for service and research with ethnic minorities? *American Psychologist, 49*(9), 797–805. https://doi.org/10.1037/0003-066X.49.9.797

Bernal, Martha E.; Klinnert, Mary D.; & Schultz, Leola A. (1980). Outcome evaluation of behavioral parent training and client-centered parent counseling for children with conduct problems. *Journal of Applied Behavior Analysis, 13*(4), 677–691. https://doi.org/10.1901/jaba.1980.13-677

Bernard, Jessica A., & Mittal, Vijay A. (2015). Dysfunctional activation of the cerebellum in s+B598chizophrenia: A functional neuroimaging meta-analysis. *Clinical Psychological Science, 3*(4), 545–566. https://doi.org/10.1177/2167702614542463

Bernard, Luther L. (1924). *Instinct: A study in social psychology.* Holt.

Bernstein, Daniel M., & Loftus, Elizabeth F. (2009). How to tell if a particular memory is true or false. *Perspectives on Psychological Science 4,* 370–374.

Bernstein, Robert. (2010). Census bureau reports families with children increasingly face unemployment. Retrieved from http://www.census.gov/Press-Release/www/releases/archives/families_households/014540.html

Berry, John W. (1994). Acculturative stress. In Walter J. Lonner & Roy Malpass (Eds.), *Psychology and culture.* Allyn & Bacon.

Berry, John W. (2003). Conceptual approaches to acculturation. In Kevin M. Chun, Pamela Balls Organista, & Gerardo Marín (Eds.), *Acculturation: Advances in theory, measurement and applied research.* American Psychological Association.

Berry, John W. (2006). Acculturative stress. In Paul T. P. Wong & C. J. Lilian Wong (Eds.), *Handbook of multicultural perspectives on stress and coping* (pp. 287–298). Spring.

Berwick, Robert; Friederici, Angela; Chomsky, Noam; & Bolhuis, Johan. (2013). Evolution, brain, and the nature of language. *Trends in Cognitive Science, 17,* 89–98. https://doi.org/10.1016/j.tics.2012.12.002

Bessesen, D. H. (2011). Regulation of body weight: What is the regulated parameter? *Physiology and Behavior, 104,* 599–607.

Best, Deborah L. (2001). Gender concepts: Convergence in cross-cultural research and methodology. *Cross-Cultural Research: Journal of Comparative Social Science, 35,* 23–43. https://doi.org/10.1177/106939710103500102

Best, Mary; Williams, J. Michael; & Coccaro, Emil F. (2002). Evidence for a dysfunctional prefrontal circuit in patients with an impulsive aggressive disorder. *Proceedings of the National Academy of Sciences, 99*(12), 8448–8453.

Betancourt, Hector, & Lopez, Steven R. (1993). The study of culture, ethnicity, and race in American psychology. *American Psychologist, 48*(6), 629–637.

Bethea, Nate (2016, January 22). Sarah Palin, this is what PTSD is really like. *The New York Times.* http://nyti.ms/1REktqG

bethlehem, Richard; Allison, Carrie; van Andel, Emma; Coles, Alexander; Neil, Kimberley; & Baron-Cohen, Simon. (2016). Does empathy predict altruism in the wild? *Social Neuroscience,* https://doi.org/10.1080/17470919.2016.124994

Bettner, Betty Lou. (2020). Are Alfred Adler and Rudolf Dreikurs relevant for parents today? *The Journal of Individual Psychology, 76*(1), 70–78. https://doi.org/10.1353/jip.2020.0018

Beutler, Larry E.; Malik, Mary; Alimohamed, Shabia; Harwood, T. Mark; Talebi, Hani; Noble, Sharon; & Wong, Eunice. (2004). Therapist variables. In Michael J. Lambert (Ed.), *Bergin and Garfield's handbook of psychotherapy and behavior change* (5th ed.). iley.

Bhatara, Vinod S.; Sharma, J. N.; Gupta, Sanjay; & Gupta, Y. K. (1997). *Rauwolfia serpentina:* The first herbal antipsychotic. *American Journal of Psychiatry, 154,* 894.

Bhugra, Dinesh; Eckstrand, Kristen; Levounis, Petros; Kar, Anindya; & Javate, Kenneth. (2016). WPA position statement on gender identity and same-sex orientation, attraction, and behaviours. *World Psychiatric Association.* Retrieved from https://www.ncbi.nlm.nih.gov/pmc/articles/PMC5032493/

Bialystok, Ellen. (2011). Reshaping the mind: The benefits of bilingualism. *Canadian Journal of Experimental Psychology, 65,* 229–235. https://doi.org/10.1037/a0025406

Bialystok, Ellen; Craik, Fergus I. M.; Green, David W.; & Gollan, Tamar H. (2009). Bilingual minds. *Psychological Science in the Public Interest, 10,* 89–129. https://doi.org/10.1177/1529100610387084

Bialystok, Ellen; Craik, Fergus I. M.; & Luk, Gigi. (2012). Bilingualism: Consequences for mind and brain. Trends in Cognitive Sciences, 16, 240–250. https://doi.org/10.1016/j.tics.2012.03.001

Bianchi, Renzo; Schonfeld, Irvin; & Laurent, Eric. (2015). Burnout and depression overlap: A review. *Clinical Psychology Review, 36,* 28–41. https://doi.org/10.1016/j.cpr.2015.01.004

Bieling, Peter J.; Hawley, Lance L.; Bloch, Richard T.; Corcoran, Kathleen M.; Levitan, Robert D.; Young, L. Trevor; MacQueen, Glenda M.; & Segal, Zindel V. (2012). Treatment-specific changes in decentering following mindfulness-based cognitive therapy versus antidepressant medication or placebo for prevention of depressive relapse. *Journal of Consulting and Clinical Psychology, 80*(3), 365–372. https://doi.org/10.1037/a0027483

Biggs, Amanda; Brough, Paula; & Drummond, Suzie. (2017). Lazarus and Folkman's psychological stress and coping theory. In Cary L. Cooper & James Campbell Quick (Eds.), *The handbook of stress and health: A guide to research and practice,* first edition. John Wiley & Sons, Ltd. https://doi.org/10.1002/9781118993811.ch21

Bihm, Elson M.; Gillaspy, J. Arthur, Jr.; Abbott, Hannah J.; & Lammers, William J. (2010a). More misbehavior of organisms: A Psi Chi lecture by Marian and Robert Bailey. *The Psychological Record, 60*(3), 505–522.

Bihm, Elson M.; Gillaspy, J. Arthur, Jr.; Lammers, William J.; & Huffman, Stephanie P. (2010b). IQ zoo and teaching operant concepts. *The Psychological Record, 60*(3), 523–526.

Bilalić, Merim; McLeod, Peter; & Gobet, Fernand. (2008). Inflexibility of experts—Reality or myth? Quantifying the Einstellung effect in chess masters. *Cognitive Psychology, 56,* 73–102.

Binet, Alfred, & Simon, Théodore. (1905). New methods for the diagnosis of the intellectual level of subnormals. *L'Année Psychologique, 11,* 191–244.

Birks, Jacqueline, & Grimley Evans, John. (2009). Ginkgo biloba for cognitive impairment and dementia. *Cochrane Database Systematic Reviews.* https://doi.org/10.1002/14651858.CD003120.pub3

Birney, Amelia; Gunn Rebecca; Russell, Jeremy; & Ary, Dennis. (2016). MoodHacker mobile web app with email for adults to self-manage mild-to-moderate depression: Randomized controlled trial. *Journal of Medical Internet Research: Mobile and Ubiquitous Health, 4*(1), e8. https://doi.org/10.2196/mhealth.4231

Biro, Frank M.; Pajak, Ashley; Wolff, Mary S.; Pinney, Susan M.; Windham, Gayle C.; Galvez, Maida P.; Greenspan, Louise C.; Kushi, Larry H.; & Teitelbaum, Susan L. (2018). Age of menarche in a longitudinal US cohort. *Journal of Pediatric & Adolescent Gynecology, 31*(4), 339–345. https://doi.org/10.1016/j.jpag.2018.05.002

Bischoff, Richard J. (2011). The state of couple therapy. In Joseph L. Wetchler (Ed.), *Handbook of clinical issues in couple therapy.* Routledge.

Bisson, Melissa, & Levine, Timothy. (2009). Negotiating a friends with benefits relationship. *Archives of Sexual Behavior, 38*(1), 66–73. https://doi.org/10.1007/s10508-007-9211-2

Bitterman, M. E. (2006). Classical conditioning since Pavlov. *Review of General Psychology, 10,* 365–376.

Bizumic, Boris; Duckitt, John; Popadic, Dragan; Dru, Vincent; & Krauss, Stephen. (2009). A cross-cultural investigation into a reconceptualization of ethnocentrism. *European Journal of Social Psychology, 39*(6), 871–899.

Bjork, Robert A.; Dunlosky, John; & Kornell, Nate (2013). Self-regulated learning: Beliefs, techniques, and illusions. *Annual Review of Psychology, 64,* 417–444. https://doi.org/10.1146/annurev-psych-113011-143823

Bjorklund, Barbara R. (1995). Language development and cognition. In David F. Bjorklund (Ed.), *Children's thinking: Developmental function and individual differences* (2nd ed.). Brooks/Cole.

Bjornsson, Andri S. (2011). Beyond the "psychological placebo": Specifying the nonspecific in psychotherapy. *Clinical Psychology: Science and Practice, 18*(2), 113–118.

Blackburn, Elizabeth, & Epel, Elissa S. (2012). Too toxic to ignore. *Nature, 490,* 169–171. https://doi.org/10.1038/490169a

Blackburn, Elizabeth, & Epel, Elissa. (2017). *The telomere effect.* Grand Central Publishing.

Blanchard, Ray. (2008). Sex ratio of older siblings in heterosexual and homosexual, right-handed and non-right-handed men. *Archives of Sexual Behavior, 37*(6), 977–981.

Blanchard, Ray, & Lippa, Richard A. (2008). The sex ratio of older siblings in non-right-handed homosexual men. *Archives of Sexual Behavior, 37*(6), 970–976.

Blanco, Carlos; Clougherty, Kathleen F.; & Lipsitz, W. Joshua. (2006). Homework in interpersonal psychotherapy (IPT): Rationale and practice. *Journal of Psychotherapy Integration, 16*(2), 201–218. https://doi.org/10.1037/1053-0479.16.2.201

Blankstein, Kirk R., & Flett, Gordon L. (1992). Specificity in the assessment of daily hassles: Hassles, locus of control, and adjustment in college students. *Canadian Journal of Behavioural Science, 24,* 382–398.

Blanton, Hart; Klick, Jonathan; Mitchell, Gregory; Jaccard, Jacques; Mellers, Barbara; & Tetlock, Philip E. (2009). Strong claims and weak evidence: Reassessing the predictive validity of the IAT. *Journal of Applied Psychology, 94,* 567–582.

Blashfield, Roger K.; Keeley, Jared W.; Flanagan, Elizabeth H.; & Miles, Shannon R. (2014). The cycle of classification: DSM-I through DSM-5. *Annual Review of Clinical Psychology, 10,* 25–51. https://doi.org/10.1146/annurev-clinpsy-032813-153639

Blass, Thomas. (1991). Understanding behavior in the Milgram obedience experiment. *Journal of Personality and Social Psychology, 60,* 398–413.

Blass, Thomas. (1992). The social psychology of Stanley Milgram. In Mark P. Zanna (Ed.), *Advances in experimental social psychology* (Vol. 25). Academic Press.

Blass, Thomas. (2000). The Milgram Paradigm after 35 years. Some things we now know about obedience to authority. In Thomas Blass (Ed.), *Obedience to authority: Current perspectives on the Milgram paradigm* (pp. 35–59). Erlbaum.

Blass, Thomas. (2004). *The man who shocked the world: The life and legacy of Stanley Milgram.* Basic Books.

Blass, Thomas. (2009). From New Haven to Santa Clara: A historical perspective on the Milgram obedience experiments. *American Psychologist, 64,* 37–45. https://doi.org/10.1037/a0014434

Blass, Thomas. (2012). A cross-cultural comparison of studies of obedience using the Milgram paradigm: A review: Cross-cultural comparison of studies of obedience. *Social and Personality Psychology Compass, 6*(2), 196–205. https://doi.org/10.1111/j.1751-9004.2011.00417.x

Bleiberg, Kathryn L., & Markowitz, John C. (2008). Interpersonal psychotherapy for depression. In David H. Barlow (Ed.), *Clinical handbook of psychological disorders: A step-by-step treatment manual* (4th ed.). Guilford.

Blevins, Jason. (2016). Avalanche educators grapple with social media's influence on backcountry travelers' decision making. *The Denver Post.* http://www.denverpost.com/2016/10/10/colorado-avalanches-backcountry-skiing-snowboarding-social-media/

Bliedorn, Wiebke; Hill, Patrick L.; Back, Mitja D.; Denissen, Jaap J. A.; Hennecke, Marie; Hopwood, Christopher J.; Jokela, Markus; Kandler, Christian; Lucas, Richard E.; Luhmann, Maike; Orth, Ulrich; Wagner, Jenny; Wrzus, Cornelia; Zimmermann, Johannes; & Roberts, Brent. (2019). The policy relevance of personality traits. *American Psychologist, 74*(9), 1056–1067. https://doi.org/10.1037/amp0000503

Blistein, Jon. (2017, April 18). Watch Lady Gaga, Prince William discuss mental health stigma. *Rolling Stone.* http://www.rollingstone.com/culture/news/watch-lady-gaga-prince-william-discuss-mental-health-w477421

Blix, Ines; Birkeland, Marianne S.; Hansen, Marianne B.; & Heir, Trond. (2016). Posttraumatic growth—An antecedent and outcome of posttraumatic stress: Cross-lagged associations among individuals exposed to terrorism. *Clinical Psychological Science, 4,* 620–628. https://doi.org/10.1177/2167702615615866

Block, Jack. (1995). A contrarian view of the five-factor approach to personality description. *Psychological Bulletin, 117,* 187–215.

Block, Jack. (2010). The five-factor framing of personality and beyond: Some ruminations. *Psychological Inquiry, 21*(1), 2–25.

Blow, Charles. (2015, September 7). Sexual attraction and fluidity. *The New York Times.* https://www.nytimes.com/2015/09/07/opinion/charles-m-blow-sexual-attraction-and-fluidity.html

Blüher, Matthias. (2019). Obesity: Global epidemiology and pathogenesis. *Nature Reviews Endocrinology, 15,* 288–298. https://doi.org/10.1038/s41574-019-0176-8

Blumstein, Daniel T., & Fernandez-Juricic, Esteban. (2010). *A primer of conservation behavior.* Sinauer Associates.

Bobes, Maria A.; Ostrosky, Feggy; Diaz, Karla; Romero, Cesar; Borja, Karina; Santos, Yusniel; & Valdés-Sosa, Mitchell. (2013). Linkage of functional and structural anomalies in the left amygdala of reactive-aggressive men. *Social Cognitive and Affective Neuroscience, 8,* 928–936.

Bocchiaro, Piero, & Zimbardo, Philip G. (2010). Defying unjust authority: An exploratory study. *Current Psychology: A Journal for Diverse Perspectives on Diverse Psychological Issues, 29*(2), 155–170.

Boddy, Clive R.; Ladyshewsky, Richard; & Galvin, Peter. (2010). Leaders without ethics in global business: Corporate psychopaths. *Journal of Public Affairs, 10*(3), 121–138. https://doi.org/10.1002/pa.352

Bodenhausen, Galen V., & Richeson, Jennifer A. (2010). Prejudice, stereotyping, and discrimination. In R. F. Baumeister & E. J. Finkel (Eds.), *Advanced social psychology: The state of the science* (pp. 341–383). Oxford University Press.

Bodenhausen, Galen V.; Macrae, C. Neil; & Hugenberg, Kurt. (2003). Social cognition. In T. Million & M. J. Lerner (Eds.), *Handbook of psychology: Personality and social psychology, 5*, 257–282. Wiley.

Bodenmann, Guy; Atkins, David C.; Schär, Marcel; & Poffet, Valérie. (2010). The association between daily stress and sexual activity. *Journal of Family Psychology, 24*(3), 271–279.

Boduroglu, Aysecan; Shah, Priti; & Nisbett, Richard E. (2009). Cultural differences in allocation of attention in visual information processing. *Journal of Cross-Cultural Psychology, 40*(3), 349–360. https://doi.org/10.1177/0022022108331005

Boe, Josh L., & Woods, Rebecca J. (2018). Parents' influence on infants' gender-typed toy preferences. *Sex Roles, 79*, 358–373. https://doi.org/10.1007/s11199-017-0858-4

Boer, Douglas P.; Starkey, Nicola J.; & Hodgetts, Andrea M. (2008). The California Psychological Inventory—434- and 260-item editions. In Gregory J. Boyle, Gerald Matthews, & Donald H. Saklofske (Eds.), *The SAGE Handbook of personality theory and assessment, Vol. 2. Personality measurement and testing.* Sage.

Boeree, C. George. (2006). Jean Piaget. *Personality theories.* Retrieved from http://www.ship.edu/~cgboeree/piaget.html

Bogaert, Anthony F. (2004). Asexuality: Prevalence and associated factors in a national probability sample. *Journal of Sex Research, 41*(3), 279–287. https://doi.org/10.1080/00224490409552235

Bogaert, Anthony F. (2005). Age at puberty and father absence in a national probability sample. *Journal of Adolescence, 28*, 541–546.

Bogaert, Anthony F. (2006). Toward a conceptual understanding of asexuality. *Review of General Psychology, 10*(3), 241–250. https://doi.org/10.1037/1089-2680.10.3.241

Bogaert, Anthony F. (2007a). Extreme right-handedness, older brothers, and sexual orientation in men. *Neuropsychology, 21*, 141–148.

Bogaert, Anthony F. (2007b, June 5). Quoted in Michael Abrams, "The real story on gay genes." *Discover*, 424.

Bogaert, Anthony F. (2008). Menarche and father absence in a national probability sample. *Journal of Biosocial Science, 40*, 623–636. https://doi.org/10.1017/S0021932007002386

Bohart, Arthur C. (2007). The actualizing person. In Mick Cooper, Maureen O'Hara, Peter F. Schmid, & Gill Wyatt (Eds.), *The handbook of person-centered psychotherapy and counselling.* Palgrave Macmillan.

Bohart, Arthur C. (2013). Darth Vader, Carl Rogers, and self-organizing wisdom. In Arthur C. Bohart, Barbara S. Held, Eward Mendelowitz, & Kirk J. Schneider (Eds.), *Humanity's dark side: Evil, destructive experience, and psychotherapy.* American Psychological Association. https://doi.org/10.1037/13941-003

Bohlmeijer, Ernst; Roemer, Marte; & Cuijpers, Pim. (2007). The effects of reminiscence on psychological well-being in older adults: A meta-analysis. *Aging & Mental Health, 11*(3), 291–300.

Bohn, Annette, & Berntsen, Dorthe. (2008). Life story development in childhood: The development of life story abilities and the acquisition of cultural life scripts from late middle childhood to adolescence. *Developmental Psychology, 44*(4), 1135–1147.

Bohner, Gerd, & Dickel, Nina. (2011). Attitudes and attitude change. *Annual Review of Psychology, 62*, 391–417.

Bohus, Martin; Haaf, Brigitte; Stiglmayr, Christian; Pohl, Ulrike; Boehme, Renate; & Linehan, Marsha. (2000). Evaluation of inpatient dialectical-behavioral therapy for borderline personality disorder—A prospective study. *Behaviour Research and Therapy, 38*(9), 875–887. https://doi.org/10.1016/S0005-7967(99)00103-5

Boison, Detlev; Singer, Philipp; Shen, Hae-Ying; Feldon, Joram; & Yee, Benjamin K. (2012). Adenosine hypothesis of schizophrenia–opportunities for pharmacotherapy. *Neuropharmacology, 62*(3), 1527–1543. https://doi.org/10.1016/j.neuropharm.2011.01.048

Boland, Julie E.; Chua, Hannah Faye; Nisbett, Richard E. (2008). How we see it: Culturally different eye movement patterns over visual scenes. In Keith Rayner, Deli Shen, Xuejun Bai, & Guoli Yan (Eds.), *Cognitive and cultural influences on eye movements* (pp. 363–378). Tianjin People's Publishing House.

Bolger, Niall, & Amarel, David. (2007). Effects of social support visibility on adjustment to stress: Experimental evidence. *Journal of Personality and Social Psychology, 92*(3), 458–475.

Bolles, Robert C. (1985). The slaying of Goliath: What happened to reinforcement theory? In Timothy D. Johnston & Alexandra T. Pietrewicz (Eds.), *Issues in the ecological study of learning.* Erlbaum.

Bologna, Caroline. (2016, December 1). These badass women motorcyclists are delivering breast milk to babies in need. *HuffPost*. https://www.huffpost.com/entry/these-badass-women-motorcyclists-are-delivering-breast-milk-to-babies-in-need_n_583dcdf3e4b06539a78aa43f?guccounter=1

Bolton, Paul; Bass, Judith; Neugebauer, Richard; Verdeli, Helen; Clougherty, Kathleen F.; Wickramaratne, Priya; Speelman, Liesbeth; Ndogoni, Lincoln; & Weissman, Myrna. (2003). Group interpersonal psychotherapy for depression in rural Uganda: A randomized controlled trial. *Journal of the American Medical Association, 289*(23), 3117–3124. https://doi.org/10.1001/jama.289.23.3117

Bonanno, George, & Burton, Charles. (2013). Regulatory flexibility: An individual differences perspective on coping and emotion regulation. *Perspectives on Psychological Science, 8*(6), 591–612. https://doi.org/10.1177/1745691613504116

Bonchek, Lawrence I. (2020). We are all public health professionals now. *The Journal of Lancaster General Hospital, 15*(3), 65–66.

Bond, Charles F. (2008). A few can catch a liar, sometimes. *Applied Cognitive Psychology, 22*, 1298–1300.

Bond, Michael Harris. (1986). *The psychology of the Chinese people.* Oxford University Press.

Bond, Michael Harris, & Smith, Peter B. (1996). Cross-cultural social and organizational psychology. *Annual Review of Psychology, 47*, 205–235.

Bond, Rod (2005). Group size and conformity. *Group Processes & Intergroup Relations, 8*(4), 331–354.

Bond, Rod, & Smith, Peter B. (1996). Culture and conformity: A meta-analysis of studies using Asch's (1952b, 1956) line judgment task. *Psychological Bulletin, 119*, 111–137.

Bond, Rod, & Smith, Peter B. (1996). Culture and conformity: A meta-analysis of studies using Asch's (1952b, 1956) line judgment task. *Psychological Bulletin, 119*, 111–137.

Bonnet, Michael H. (2005). Acute sleep deprivation. In Meir H. Kryger, Thomas Roth, & William C. Dement (Eds.), *Principles and practice of sleep medicine* (4th ed.). Elsevier Saunders.

Book, Angela S.; Starzyk, Katherine B.; & Quinsey, Vernon L. (2001). The relationship between testosterone and aggression: A meta-analysis. *Aggression and Violent Behavior, 6*(6), 579–599.

Book, Angela; Visser, Beth A.; Blais, Julie; Hosker-Field, Ashley; Methot-Jones, Tabatha; Gauthier, Nathalie Y.; Volk, Anthony; Holden, Ronald R.; & D'Agata, Madeleine T. (2016). Unpacking more "evil": What is at the core of the dark tetrad? *Personality and Individual Differences, 90*, 269–272. https://doi.org/10.1016/j.paid.2015.11.009

Book, Angela; Visser, Beth A.; & Volk, Anthony A. (2015). Unpacking "evil": Claiming the core of the Dark Triad. *Personality and Individual Differences, 73*, 29–38. https://doi.org/10.1016/j.paid.2014.09.016

Bootzin, Richard R., & Epstein, Dana R. (2011). Understanding and treating insomnia. *Annual Review of Clinical Psychology, 7*, 435–458.

Borbély, Alexander A., & Achermann, Peter. (2005). Sleep homeostasis and models of sleep regulation. In Meir H. Kryger, Thomas Roth, & William C. Dement (Eds.), *Principles and practice of sleep medicine* (4th ed.). Elsevier Saunders.

Borden, William. (2009). *Contemporary psychodynamic theory and practice.* Lyceum Books.

Borghans, Lex; Golsteyn, Bart H. H.; Jeckman, James J.; & Humphries, John Eric. (2016). What grades and achievement tests measure. *Proceedings of the National Academy of Science, 113*, 13354–13359. https://doi.org/10.1073/pnas.1601135113

Bornstein, Marc H. (2014). Human infancy . . . and the rest of the lifespan. *Annual Review of Psychology, 65*, 121–158.

Borst, Jelmer P.; Taatgen, Niels A.; & van Rijn, Hedderik. (2010). The problem state: A cognitive bottleneck in multitasking. *Journal of Experimental Psychology: Learning, Memory, and Cognition, 26*, 363–382.

Bosch, Jos A., & Cano, Annmarie. (2013) Health Psychology special section on disparities in pain. *Health Psychology, 32*, 1115–1116. https://doi.org/10.1037/hea0000041

Boselie, Jantine; Vancleef, Linda; Smeets, Tom; & Peters, Madelon. (2014). Increasing optimism abolishes pain-induced impairments in executive task performance. Pain, *155*(2), 334–340. https://doi.org/10.1016/j.pain.2013.10.014

Boss, Pauline; Beaulieu, Lorraine; Wieling, Elizabeth; Turner, William; & LaCruz, Shulaika. (2003). Healing loss, ambiguity, and trauma: A community-based intervention with families of union workers missing after the 9/11 attack in New York, NY City. *Journal of Marital and Family Therapy, 29*, 455–467.

Bouchard, Geneviève. (2014). How do parents react when their children leave home? An integrative review. *Journal of Adult Development, 21*, 69–79. https://doi.org/10.1007/s10804-013-9180-8

Bouchard, Thomas J., Jr. (2004). Genetic influence on human psychological traits. *Psychological Science, 13*, 148–151.

Bouchard, Thomas J.; Lykken, David T.; McGue, Matthew; Segal, Nancy L.; & Tellegen, Auke. (1990). Sources of human psychological differences: The Minnesota study of twins reared apart. *Science, 250*(4978), 223–228.

Boudry, Maarten; Blancke, Stefaan; & Pigliucci, Massimo. (2015). What makes weird beliefs thrive? The epidemiology of pseudoscience. *Philosophical Psychology, 28*, 1177–1198. https://doi.org/10.1080/09515089.2014.971946

Bouton, Mark E. (2007). *Learning and behavior: A contemporary synthesis.* Sinauer.

Bovet, Jeanne. (2019). Evolutionary theories and men's preferences for women's waist-to-hip ratio: Which hypotheses remain? A systematic review. *Frontiers in Psychology, 10*, 1–20. https://doi.org/10.3389/fpsyg.2019.01221

Bowen, Sarah; Vieten, Cassandra; Witkiewitz, Katie; & Carroll, Haley. (2015). A mindfulness-based approach to addiction. In Kirk Warren Brown, J. David Creswell, & Richard M. Ryan. *Handbook of mindfulness: Theory, research, and practice.* Guilford.

Bowlby, John. (1969). *Attachment and Loss: Vol. 1. Attachment.* Basic Books.

Bowlby, John. (1988). *A secure base.* Basic Books.

Bowleg, Lisa. (2017). Intersectionality: An underutilized but essential theoretical framework for social psychology. In Keith, Kenneth D. (Eds), *The Palgrave handbook of critical social psychology* (pp. 507–529). Palgrave Macmillan. https://doi.org/10.1057/970 1 137-51018-1_29

Boyke, Janina; Driemeyer, Joenna; Gaser, Christian; Büchel, Christian; & May, Arne. (2008). Training-induced brain structure changes in the elderly. *Journal of Neuroscience, 28,* 7031–7035.

Boyle, Gregory J. (2008). Critique of the five-factor model of personality. In Gregory J. Boyle, Gerald Matthews, & Donald H. Saklofske (Eds.), *The SAGE handbook of personality theory and assessment, Vol. 1. Personality theories and models.* Sage.

Boysen, Guy A., & VanBergen, Alexandra. (2014). Simulation of multiple personalities: A review of research comparing diagnosed and simulated dissociative identity disorder. *Clinical Psychology Review, 34*(1), 14–28. https://doi.org/10.1016/j.cpr.2013.10.008

Bozarth, Jerold D. (2007). Unconditional positive regard. In Mick Cooper, Maureen O'Hara, Peter F. Schmid, & Gill Wyatt (Eds.), *The handbook of person-centered psychotherapy and counselling.* Palgrave Macmillan.

Bozarth, Jerold D., & Wang, Chun-Chuan. (2008). The "unitary actualizing tendency" and congruence in client-centered therapy. In Brian E. Levitt (Ed.), *Reflections on human potential: Bridging the person-centered approach and positive psychology.* PCCS Books.

Bozarth, Jerold D.; Zimring, Fred M.; & Tausch, Reinhard. (2002). Client-centered therapy: The evolution of a revolution. In David J. Cain & Julius Seeman (Eds.), *Humanistic psychotherapies: Handbook of research and practice.* American Psychological Association.

Bradbard, Marilyn R.; Martin, Carol L.; Endsley, Richard C.; & Halverson, Charles F. (1986). Influence of sex stereotypes on children's exploration and memory: A competence versus performance distinction. *Developmental Psychology, 22,* 481–486.

Bradley, Laura. (2020, April 5). The coronavirus pandemic is a devastating mass trauma—but some people with anxiety and depression have seen their symptoms improve. *The Daily Beast.* https://www.thedailybeast.com/coronavirus-is-making-a-lot-of-people-anxious-and-depressed-but-some-sufferers-actually-feel-better-now

Bradshaw, G. A.; Schore, Allan N.; Brown, Janine L.; Poole, Joyce H.; & Moss, Cynthia J. (2005). Elephant breakdown. Social trauma: Early disruption of attachment can affect the physiology, behaviour, and culture of animals and humans over generations. *Nature, 433,* 807.

Brådvik, Louise, & Berglund, Mats. (2010). Depressive episodes with suicide attempts in severe depression: Suicides and controls differ only in the later episodes of unipolar depression. *Archives of Suicide Research, 14*(4), 363–367. https://doi.org/10.1080/13811118.2010.524068

Braffman, Wayne, & Kirsch, Irving. (1999). Imaginative suggestibility and hypnotizability: An empirical analysis. *Journal of Personality and Social Psychology, 77,* 578–587.

Brait, Ellen. (2015, March 13). Coming to the rescue of troubled teens. *NY City Lens.* http://nycitylens.com/2015/03/coming-to-the-rescue-of-troubled-teens/

Branje, Susan. (2018). Development of parent-adolescent relationships: Conflict interactions as a mechanism of change. *Child Development Perspectives, 12*(3), 171–176. https://doi.org/10.1111/cdep.12278

Bransford, John D., & Stein, Barry S. (1993). *The IDEAL problem solver: A guide for improving thinking, learning, and creativity* (2nd ed.). Worth Publishers

Braun, Stephen. (2001, Spring). Ecstasy on trial: Seeking insight by prescription. *Cerebrum, 3,* 10–21.

Braunstein, Laura Martin; Gross, James J.; & Ochsner, Kevin N. (2017). Explicit and implicit emotion regulation: A multi-level framework. *Social Cognitive and Affective Neuroscience, 12*(10), 1545–1557. https://doi.org/10.1093/scan/nsx096

Braveman, Paula A.; Cubbin, Catherine; Egerter, Susan; Williams, David R.; & Pamuk, Elsie. (2010). Socioeconomic disparities in health in the United States: What the patterns tell us. *American Journal of Public Health, 100*(S1), S186–S196.

Bray, Emily E.; MacLean, Evan L; & Hare, Brian A. (2014). Context specificity of inhibitory control in dogs. *Animal Cognition, 17,* 15–31. https://doi.org/10.1007/s10071-013-0633-z

Brazelton, T. Berry, & Cramer, Bertrand G. (1990). *The earliest relationship: Parents, infants, and the drama of early attachment.* Addison-Wesley Publishing.

Breakspear, Michael. (2017). Dynamic models of large-scale brain activity. *Nature Neuroscience, 20,* 340–352. https://doi.org/10.1038/nn.4497

Breaugh, James A. (2017). The contribution of job analysis to recruitment. In Harold W. Goldstein, Elaine D. Pulakos, Jonathan Passmore, & Carla Semedo (Eds.), *The Wiley Blackwell handbook of the psychology of recruitment, selection and employee retention* (pp. 12–28). Wiley Blackwell.

Breck, John; Bohr, Adam; Poddar, Sourav; McQueen, Matthew B.; & Casault, Tracy. (2019). Characteristics and incidence of concussion among a US collegiate undergraduate population. *JAMA Network Open, 2*(12): e1917626. https://doi.org/10.1001/jamanetworkopen.2019.17626

Breda, Thomas, & Napp, Clotilde. (2019). Girls' comparative advantage in reading can largely explain the gender gap in math-related fields. *Proceedings of the National Academy of Sciences, 116*(31), 15435–15440. https://doi.org/10.1073/pnas.1905779116

Breinbauer, Hayo A.; Anabalón, Jose L.; Gutierrez, Daniela; Cárcamo, Rodrigo; Olivares, Carla; & Caro, Jorge. (2012). Output capabilities of personal music players and assessment of preferred listening levels of test subjects: Outlining recommendations for preventing music-induced hearing loss. *Laryngoscope, 122,* 2549–2556. https://doi.org/10.1002/lary.23596

Brennen, Tim; Vikan, Anne; & Dybdahl, Ragnhild. (2007). Are tip-of-the-tongue states universal? Evidence from the speakers of an unwritten language. *Memory, 15*(2), 167–176.

Brenning, Katrijn; Soenens, Bart; Mabbe, Elien; & Vansteenkiste, Maarten. (2019). Ups and downs in the joy of motherhood: Maternal well-being as a function of psychological needs, personality, and infant temperament. *Journal of Happiness Studies, 20,* 229–250. https://doi.org/10.1007/s10902-017-9936-0

Brent, David; Brunwasser, Steven; Hollon, Steven; Weersing, Robin; Clarke, Gregory; Dickerson, John; . . . & Garber, Judy. (2015). Effect of a cognitive-behavioral prevention program on depression 6 years after implementation among at-risk adolescents: A randomized clinical trial. *Journal of the American Medical Association: Psychiatry, 72,* 1110–1118. https://doi.org/10.1001/jamapsychiatry.2015.1559

Brescoll, Victoria, & Uhlmann, Eric. (2005). Attitudes toward traditional and nontraditional parents. *Psychology of Women Quarterly, 29,* 436–445. https://doi.org/10.1111/j.1471-6402.2005.00244.x

Bresee, Catherine; Gotto, Jennifer; & Rapaport, Mark H. (2009). Treatment of depression. In Alan F. Schatzberg & Charles B. Nemeroff (Eds.), *The American Psychiatric Publishing textbook of psychopharmacology* (4th ed., pp. 1081–1111). American Psychiatric Publishing.

Breslau, Naomi. (2012). Epidemiology of posttraumatic stress disorder in adults. In J. Gayle Beck & Denise M. Sloan (Eds.), The Oxford handbook of traumatic stress disorders. Oxford University Press.

Breslin, Paul A. S. (2013). An evolutionary perspective on food and human taste. *Current Biology, 23,* R409–R418. https://doi.org/10.1016/j.cub.2013.04.010

Bretherton, Inge, & Main, Mary. (2000). Mary Dinsmore Salter Ainsworth (1913–1999). *American Psychologist, 55,* 1148–1149.

Brewer, Marilynn B. (1994). The social psychology of prejudice: Getting it all together. In Mark P. Zanna & James M. Olson (Eds.), *The psychology of prejudice: The Ontario Symposium* (Vol. 7). Erlbaum.

Brewer, Marilynn B., & Chen, Ya-Ru. (2007). Where (who) are collectives in collectivism? Toward conceptual clarification of individualism and collectivism. *Psychological Review, 114*(1), 133–151.

Brewer, Neil, & Wells, Gary L. (2011). Eyewitness identification. *Current Directions in Psychological Science 20,* 24–27. https://doi.org/10.1177/0963721410389169

Bridges, Tristan. (2017, May 31). 2016 GSS Update on the U.S. LGB population 2.0. *Inequality by (Interior) Design.* https://inequalitybyinteriordesign.wordpress.com/2017/05/31/2016-gss-update-on-the-u-s-lgb-population-2-0/

Bridges, Tristan, & Moore, Mignon R. (2019, June 11). 23% of young Black women now identify as bisexual. *Medical Xpress.* https://medicalxpress.com/news/2019-06-young-black-women-bisexual.html

Bridgman, Todd; Cummings, Stephen; & Ballard, John. (2019). Who built Maslow's pyramid? A history of the creation of management studies' most famous symbol and its implications for management education. *Academy of Management Learning & Education, 18*(1), 81–98. https://doi.org/10.5465/amle.2017.0351

Britz, Juliane; Hernàndez, Laura Díaz; Ro, Tony; & Michel, Christoph M. (2014). EEG-microstate dependent emergence of perceptual awareness. *Frontiers in Behavioral Neuroscience 8,* 2–10. https://doi.org/10.3389/fnbeh.2014.00163

Brody, Arthur L.; Saxena, Sajaya; Stoessel, Paula; Gillies, Laurie; Fairbanks, Lynn A.; Alborzian, Shervin; Phelps, Michael E.; Huang, Sung-Cheng; Wu, Hsiao-Ming; Ho, Matthew L.; Ho, Mai K.; Au, Scott C.; Maidment, Karron; & Baxter, Lewis R. (2001). Regional brain metabolic changes in patients with major depression treated with either paroxetine or interpersonal therapy. *Archives of General Psychiatry, 58*(7), 631–640. https://doi.org/10.1001/archpsyc.58.7.631

Brody, Howard, & Miller, Franklin G. (2011). Lessons from recent research about the placebo effect—From art to science. *Journal of the American Medical Association, 306*(23), 2612–2613. https://doi.org/10.1001/jama.2011.1850

Brody, Nathan. (2003). Construct validation of the Sternberg Triarchic abilities test: Comment and reanalysis. *Intelligence, 31*(4), 319–329. https://doi.org/10.1016/S0160-2896(01)00087-3

Brody, Nicholas, & Vangelisti, Anita. (2015). Bystander intervention in cyberbullying. *Communication Monographs.* https://doi.org/10.1080/03637751.2015.1044256

Brondolo, Elizabeth; ver Halen, Nisha Brady; Libby, Daniel; & Pencille, Melissa. (2011). Racism as a psychosocial stressor. In Richard J. Contrada & Andrew Baum (Eds.), *The handbook of stress science: Biology, psychology, and health.* Springer.

Bronstein, Phyllis. (2006). The family environment: Where gender role socialization begins. In Judith Worell & Carol D. Goodheart (Eds.), *Handbook of girls' and women's psychological health: Gender and well-being across the lifespan* (pp. 262–271). Oxford University Press.

Brooks, C. Darren, & Ling, Jeff. (2020). "Are we doing enough": An examination of the utilization of Employee Assistance Programs to support the mental health needs of employees during the COVID-19 pandemic. *Journal of Insurance Regulation, 39*(8), 1–34.

Brooks-Gunn, Jeanne. (1988). Antecedents and consequences of variations of girls' maturational timing. In Melvin D. Levine & Elizabeth R. McAnarney (Eds.), *Early adolescent transitions.* Lexington Books.

Brooks-Gunn, Jeanne, & Reiter, Edward O. (1990). The role of pubertal processes. In S. Shirley Feldman & Glen R. Elliott (Eds.), *At the threshold: The developing adolescent.* Harvard University Press.

Brosschot, Jos F.; Verkuil, Bart; & Thayer, Julian F. (2016). The default response to uncertainty and the importance of perceived safety in anxiety and stress: An evolution-theoretical perspective. *Journal of Anxiety Disorders, 41,* 22–34. https://doi.org/10.1016/j.janxdis.2016.04.012

Brown, Alan S.; Begg, Melissa D.; Gravenstein, Stefan; Schaefer, Catherine A.; Wyatt, Richard J.; Bresnahan, Michaeline; Babulas, Vicki P.; & Susser, Ezra S. (2004). Serological evidence of prenatal influenza in the etiology of schizophrenia. *Archives of General Psychiatry, 61*(8), 774–780. https://doi.org/10.1001/archpsyc.61.8.774

Brown, Geoffrey L.; Mangelsdorf, Sarah C.; & Neff, Cynthia. (2012). Father involvement, paternal sensitivity, and father–child attachment security in the first 3 years. *Journal of Family Psychology, 26,* 421–430. https://doi.org/10.1037/a0027836

Brown, Roger, & Kulik, James. (1982). Flashbulb memories. In Ulric Neisser (Ed.), *Memory observed: Remembering in natural contexts.* Freeman.

Bruchey, Aleksandra K.; Jones, Carolyn E.; & Monfils, Marie-H. (2010). Fear conditioning by-proxy: Social transmission of fear during memory retrieval. *Behavioural Brain Research, 214*(1), 80–84.

Brulliard, Karin. (2016). Your cat is a lot deeper than you think. *Washington Post.* https://www.washingtonpost.com/news/animalia/wp/2016/03/18/your-cat-is-a-lot-deeper-than-you-think/

Brummett, Beverly H.; Boyle, Stephen H.; Kuhn, Cynthia M.; Siegler, Ilene C.; & Williams, Redford B. (2009). Positive affect is associated with cardiovascular reactivity, norepinephrine level, and morning rise in salivary cortisol. *Psychophysiology, 46*(4), 862–869.

Brummett, Beverly H.; Helms, Michael J.; Dahlstrom, W. Grant; & Siegler, Ilene C. (2006). Prediction of all-cause mortality by the Minnesota Multiphasic Personality Inventory Optimism-Pessimism Scale scores: Study of a college sample during a 40-year follow-up period. *Mayo Clinic Proceedings, 81*(12), 1541–1544.

Brunoni, Andre R.; Nitsche, Michael A.; Bolognini, N.; Bikson, M.; Wagner, T.; Merabet, L.; Edwards, Dylan J.; Valero-Cabre, Antoni; Rotenberg, Alexander; Pascual-Leone, Alvaro; Ferrucci, Roberta; Priori, Alberto; Boggio, Paulo Sergio; & Fregni, Felipe. (2012). Clinical research with transcranial direct current stimulation (tDCS): Challenges and future directions. *Brain Stimulation: Basic, Translational, and Clinical Research in Neuromodulation, 5*(3), 175–195. https://doi.org/10.1016/j.brs.2011.03.002

Brunton, Elizabeth; Bolin, Jessica; Leon, Javier; & Burnett, Scott. (2019). Fright or flight? Behavioural responses of kangaroos to drone-based monitoring. *Drones, 3*(2). https://doi.org/10.3390/drones3020041

Bryant, Gregory A., & Barrett, H. Clark. (2007). Recognizing intentions in infant-directed speech: Evidence for universals. *Psychological Science, 18,* 746–751.

Bryant, Gregory A.; Lienard, Pierre; & Barrett, H. Clark. (2012). Recognizing infant-directed speech across distant cultures: Evidence from Africa. *Journal of Evolutionary Psychology, 10,* 47–59. https://doi.org/10.1556/jep.10.2012.2.1

Buccelletti, Francesco; Ojetti, Veronica; Carroccia, Annarita; Marsiliani, Davide; Mangiola, F.; Calabro, G.; Iacomini, P.; Zuccala, Giuseppe; & Franceschi, Francesco. (2013). Recurrent use of the emergency department in patients with anxiety disorder. *European Review for Medical and Pharmacological Sciences, 17,* 100–106.

Bucci, Sandra; Birchwood, Max; Twist, Laura; Tarrier, Nicholas; Emsley, Richard; & Haddock, Gillian. (2013). Predicting compliance with command hallucinations: Anger, impulsivity and appraisals of voices' power and intent. *Schizophrenia Research, 147*(1), 163–168. https://doi.org/10.1016/j.schres.2013.02.037

Buckley, Kerry W. (1982). The selling of a psychologist: John Broadus Watson and the application of behavioral techniques to advertising. *Journal of the History of the Behavioral Sciences, 18,* 207–221.

Buckley, Kerry W. (1989). *Mechanical man: John Broadus Watson and the beginnings of behaviorism.* Guilford.

Bucur, Barbara; Madden, David J.; Spaniol, Julia; Provenzale, James M.; Cabeza, Roberto; White, Leonard E.; & Huettel, Scott A. (2008). Age-related slowing of memory retrieval: Contributions of perceptual speed and cerebral white matter integrity. *Neurobiology of Aging, 29*(7), 1070–1079.

Budd, Rick, & Hughes, Ian. (2009). The dodo bird verdict—Controversial, inevitable and important: A commentary on 30 years of meta-analyses. *Clinical Psychology & Psychotherapy, 16*(6), 510–522.

Budnik, Alicja & Henneberg, Maciej. (2017). Worldwide increase of obesity is related to the reduced opportunity for natural selection. *PLoS ONE, 12*(1). https://doi.org/10.1371/journal.pone.0170098

Buil, Alfonso; Brown, Andrew; Lappalainen, Tuuli; Viñuela, Ana; Davies, Matthew; Zheng, Hou-Feng; . . . & Dermitzakis, Emmanouil. (2015). Gene-gene and gene-environment interactions detected by transcriptome sequence analysis in twins. *Nature Genetics, 47,* 88–91. https://doi.org/10.1038/ng.3162

Bukh, Jens D.; Andersen, Per K.; & Kessing, Lars V. (2016). Rates and predictors of remission, recurrence and conversion to bipolar disorder after the first lifetime episode of depression—a prospective 5-year follow-up study. *Psychological Medicine, 46,* 1151–1161. https://doi.org/10.1017/s0033291715002676

Burger, Jerry M. (2009). Replicating Milgram: Would people still obey today? *American Psychologist, 64*(1), 1–11.

Burger, Jerry M.; Sanchez, Jackeline; Imberi, Jenny E.; & Grande, Lucia R. (2009). The norm of reciprocity as an internalized social norm: Returning favors even when no one finds out. *Social Influence, 4*(1), 11–17. https://doi.org/10.1080/15534510802131004

Buri, John R.; Louiselle, Peggy A.; Misukanis, Thomas M.; & Mueller, Rebecca A. (1988). Effects of parental authoritarianism and authoritativeness on self-esteem. *Personality and Social Psychology Bulletin, 14,* 271–282.

Burkley, Melissa. (2018, December 12). The hour between dog and wolf: Harnessing the power of hypnogogia. *The Literary Life,* Jan/Feb 2019, 25–31. https://www.pw.org/content/the_hour_between_dog_and_wolf_harnessing_the_power_of_hypnagogia

Burlingame, Gary M.; MacKenzie, K. Roy; & Strauss, Bernhard. (2004). Small group treatment: Evidence for effectiveness and mechanisms of change. In Michael J. Lambert (Ed.), *Bergin and Garfield's handbook of psychotherapy and behavior change* (5th ed.). Wiley.

Burn, Shawn Meghan. (2009). A situational model of sexual assault prevention through bystander intervention. *Sex Roles, 60*(11–12), 779–792.

Bushman, Brad J., & Anderson, Craig A. (2007). Measuring the effect of violent media on aggression. *American Psychologist, 62,* 253–254.

Bushman, Brad J.; Gollwitzer, Mario; & Cruz, Carlos. (2014). There is broad consensus: Media researchers agree that violent media increase aggression in children, and pediatricians and parents concur. *Psychology of Popular Media Culture.* https://doi.org/10.1037/ppm0000046

Bushman, Brad J.; Huesmann, L. Rowell; & Whitaker, Jodi L. (2009). Violent media effects. In R. L. Nabi & M. B. Oliver (Eds.), *Media processes and effects* (pp. 361–376). Sage.

Bushman, Brad J.; Wang, Morgan C.; & Anderson, Craig A. (2005). Is the curve relating temperature to aggression linear or curvilinear? Assaults and temperature in Minneapolis reexamined. *Journal of Personality and Social Psychology, 89*(1), 62–66. https://doi.org/10.1037/0022-3514.89.1.62

Bushnell, I. W. R. (2001). Mother's face recognition in newborn infants: Learning and memory. *Infant and Child Development, 10,* 67–74.

Buss, Arnold H. (1989). Personality as traits. *American Psychologist, 44,* 1378–1388.

Buss, Arnold H. (2001). *Psychological dimensions of the self.* Sage.

Buss, David M. (1994). *The evolution of desire: Strategies of human mating.* Basic Books.

Buss, David M. (1995a). Evolutionary psychology: A new paradigm for psychological science. *Psychological Inquiry, 6,* 1–31.

Buss, David M. (1995b). Psychological sex differences: Origins through sexual selection. *American Psychologist, 50,* 164–168.

Buss, David M. (1996). Sexual conflict: Evolutionary insights into feminism and into feminism and the "Battle of the Sexes." In David M. Buss & Neil M. Malamuth (Eds.), *Sex, power, conflict: Evolutionary and feminist perspectives.* Oxford University Press.

Buss, David M. (2009). The great struggles of life: Darwin and the emergence of evolutionary psychology. *American Psychologist, 64,* 140–148.

Buss, David M. (2011). *Evolutionary psychology: The new science of the mind* (4th ed.). Pearson.

Buss, David M., & Duntley, Joshua D. (2006). The evolution of aggression. In Mark Schaller, Jeffry. A. Simpson, & Douglas. T. Kenrick (Eds.), *Evolution and social psychology* (pp. 263–286). Psychology Press.

Buss, David M., & Schmitt, David P. (2011). Evolutionary psychology and feminism. *Sex Roles, 64*(9–10), 768–787.

Bussey, Kay, & Bandura, Albert. (2004). Social cognitive theory of gender development and functioning. In Alice H. Eagly, Anne E. Beall, & Robert J. Sternberg (Eds.), *The psychology of gender* (2nd ed.). Guilford.

Butcher, James N. (2010). Personality assessment from the nineteenth to the early twenty-first century: Past achievements and contemporary challenges. *Annual Review of Clinical Psychology, 6,* 1–20.

Butler, Andrew C.; Chapman, Jason E.; Forman, Evan M.; & Beck, Aaron T. (2006, January). The empirical status of cognitive-behavioral therapy: A review of meta-analyses. *Clinical Psychology Review, 26*(1), 17–31.

Byrnes, Evan E., & Brown, Chris. (2016). Individual personality differences in Port Jackson sharks *Heterodontus portusjacksoni. Journal of Fish Biology, 89,* 1142–1157. https://doi.org/10.1111/jfb.12993

Bystron, Irina; Blakemore, Colin; & Rakic, Pasko. (2008). Development of the human cerebral cortex: Boulder Committee revisited. *National Review Neuroscience, 9*(2), 110–122. https://doi.org/10.1038/nrn2252

Cacioppo, John; Cacioppo, Stephanie; Capitanio, John; & Cole, Steven. (2015a). The neuroendocrinology of social isolation. *Annual Review of Psychology, 66,* 733–767. https://doi.org/10.1146/annurev-psych-010814-015240

Cacioppo, John; Cacioppo, Stephanie; Cole, Steven; Capitanio, John; Goossens, Luc; & Boomsma, Dorret. (2015b). Loneliness across phylogeny and a call for comparative studies and animal models. *Perspectives on Psychological Science, 10,* 202–212. https://doi.org/10.1177/1745691614564876

..., Christopher K., & LeDoux, Joseph E. (2008). Brain mechanisms of Pavlovian and instrumental aversive conditioning. In Robert J. Blanchard, D. Caroline Blanchard, Guy Griebel, & David Nutt (Eds.), *Handbook of Behavioral Neuroscience* (Vol. 17): *Handbook of Anxiety and Fear* (pp. 103–124). Elsevier. https://doi.org/10.1016/S1569 -7339(07)00007-0

Cain, David J. (2002). Defining characteristics, history, and evolution of humanistic psychotherapies. In David J. Cain & Julius Seeman (Eds.), *Humanistic psychotherapies: Handbook of research and practice*. American Psychological Association.

Cain, David J. (2003). Advancing humanistic psychology and psychotherapy: Some challenges and proposed solutions. *Journal of Humanistic Psychology, 43*(3), 10–41. https://doi.org/10.1177/0022167803043003003

Calanchini, Jimmy; Gonsalkorale, Karen; Sherman, Jeffrey W.; & Klauer, Karl C. (2013). Counter-prejudicial training reduces activation of biased associations and enhances response monitoring. *European Journal of Social Psychology, 43*, 321–325.

Calero-García, M. D.; Navarro-González, E.; & Muñoz-Manzano, L. (2007). Influence of level of activity on cognitive performance and cognitive plasticity in elderly persons. *Archives of Gerontology and Geriatrics, 45*, 307–318.

Calhoun, Lawrence G., & Tedeschi, Richard G. (2014). *Handbook of posttraumatic growth: Research and practice*. Psychology Press.

Calvert, Sandra L.; Appelbaum, Mark; Dodge, Kenneth A.; Graham, Sandra; Nagayama Hall, Gordon C.; Hamby, Sherry; Fasig-Caldwell, Lauren G.; Citkowicz, Martyna; Galloway, Daniel P.; & Hedges, Larry V. (2017). The American Psychological Association Task Force assessment of violent video games: Science in the service of public interest. *American Psychologist, 72*(2), 126–143. https://doi.org/10.1037/a0040413

Camp, Mary E.; Webster, Cecil R.; Coverdale, Thomas R.; Coverdale, John H.; & Nairn, Ray. (2010). The Joker: A dark night for depictions of mental illness. *Academic Psychiatry, 34*, 145–149. https://doi.org/10.1176/appi.ap.34.2.145

Campbell, Jennifer D., & Fairey, Patricia J. (1989). Informational and normative routes to conformity: The effect of faction size as a function of norm extremity and attention to the stimulus. *Journal of Personality and Social Psychology, 57*, 457–458.

Campbell, John B., & Hawley, Charles W. (1982). Study habits and Eysenck's theory of extraversion-introversion. *Journal of Research in Personality, 16*, 139–146.

Campbell, MacGregor. (2011). Game on: When work becomes play. *New Scientist*, issue 2794.

Campbell, Matthew W., & de Waal, Frans B. M. (2011). Ingroup-outgroup bias in contagious yawning by chimpanzees supports link to empathy. *PLOS ONE, 6*(4), 10.1371/journal.pone.0018283

Campbell, Matthew W.; Carter, J. Devyn; Proctor, Darby; Eisenberg, Michelle L.; & de Waal, Frans B. M. (2009, September 9). Computer animations stimulate contagious yawning in chimpanzees. *Proceedings of the Royal Society, Biological Sciences*. https://doi.org/10.1098/rspb.2009.1087

Campbell, Megan E., & Cunnington, Ross. (2017). More than an imitation game: Top-down modulation of the human mirror system. *Neuroscience & Biobehavioral Reviews, 75*, 195–202. https://doi.org/10.1016/j.neubiorev.2017.01.035

Canivez, Gary L., & Youngstrom, Eric A. (2019). Challenges to the Cattell-Horn-Carroll theory: Empirical, clinical, and policy implications. *Applied Measurement in Education, 32*(3), 232–248. https://doi.org/10.1080/08957347.2019.1619562

Canli, Turhan. (2004). Functional brain-mapping of extraversion and neuroticism: Learning from individual differences in emotion processing. *Journal of Personality, 72*, 1105–1132.

Canli, Turhan. (2006) *Biology of personality and individual differences*. Guilford.

Canli, Turhan; Zhao, Zuo; Desmond, John E.; Kang, Eunjoo; Gross, James; & Gabrieli, John D. E. (2001). An fMRI study of personality influences on brain reactivity to emotional stimuli. *Behavioral Neuroscience, 115*, 33–42.

Cannon, Brooke J., & Kramer, Lorraine Masinos. (2012). Delusion content across the 20th century in an American psychiatric hospital. *International Journal of Social Psychiatry, 58*(3),323–327.

Cannon, Walter B. (1927). The James-Lange theory of emotion: A critical examination and an alternative theory. *American Journal of Psychology, 39*, 106–124.

Cannon, Walter B. (1932). *The wisdom of the body*. Norton.

Cant, Jonathan S., & Goodale, Melvyn A. (2011). Scratching beneath the surface: New insights into the functional properties of the lateral occipital area and parahippocampal place area. *Journal of Neuroscience, 31*(22), 8248–8258. https://doi.org/10.1523 /jneurosci.6113-10.2011

Caplan-Bricker, Nora. (2017, Oct. 5). THEIR TIME After generations in the shadows, the intersex rights movement has a message for the world: We aren't disordered and we aren't ashamed. *The Washington Post.* https://www.washingtonpost.com/sf/style /2017/10/05/the-intersex-rights-movement-is-ready-for-its-moment/?utm_term =.e4645a4f89a2

Cappelli, Peter. (2019, April 23). Viewpoint: Your approach to hiring is all wrong. *SHRM.* https://www.shrm.org/resourcesandtools/hr-topics/talent-acquisition/pages /viewpoint-your-approach-to-hiring-is-all-wrong.aspx

Capraro, Valerio, & Barcelo, Hélène. (2020). The effect of messaging and gender on intentions to wear a face covering to slow down COVID-19 transmission. *PsyArXiv.* https://doi.org/10.31234/osf.io/tg7vz

Caramanica, Jon. (2018, May 16). Charlie Puth got famous. Then he got good. *The New York Times.* https://www.nytimes.com/2018/05/16/arts/music/charlie-puth-voicenotes -interview.html

Cardeña, Etzel, & Gleaves, David H. (2007). Dissociative disorders. In Michel Hersen, Samuel M. Turner, & Deborah C. Beidel (Eds.), *Adult psychopathology and diagnosis* (5th ed.). Wiley.

Cardeña, Etzel. (2018, May 24). The experimental evidence for parapsychological phenomena: A review. *American Psychologist.* https://doi.org/10.1037/amp0000236

Cardeña, Etzel; Palmer, John; & Marcusson-Clavertz, David (Eds). (2015). *Parapsychology: A handbook for the 21st century.* McFarland. https://doi.org/10.1016 /j.psyneuen.2004.03.007

Cardoso, Christopher; Valkanas, Helen; Serravalle, Lisa; & Ellenbogen, Mark A. (2016). Oxytocin and social context moderate social support seeking in women during negative memory recall. *Psychoneuroendocrinology, 70*, 63–69. https://doi.org/10.1016/j .psyneuen.2016.05.001

Carere, Claudio, & Locurto, Charles. (2011). Interaction between animal personality and animal cognition. *Current Zoology,57*, 491–498. https://doi.org/10.1093/czoolo/57.4.491

Carhart-Harris, Robin; Kaelen, Mendel; & Nutt, David (2014). How do hallucinogens work on the brain? *The Psychologist, 27*, 662-665.

Carlo, Gustavo; Knight, George P.; Roesch, Scott C.; Opal, Deanna; & Davis, Alexandra. (2014). Personality across cultures: A critical analysis of Big Five research and current directions. In Frederick T. L. Leong, Lillia Comas-Díaz, Gordon C. Nagayama Hall, Vonnie C. McLoyd, & Joseph E. Trimble (Eds.), *APA Handbook of Multicultural Psychology, Vol. 1: Theory and research.* American Psychological Association. https://doi.org/10.1037/14189-015

Carlson, Gabrielle A., & Meyer, Stephanie E. (2006). Phenomenology and diagnosis of bipolar disorder in children, adolescents, and adults: Complexities and developmental issues. *Development and Psychopathology, 18*(4), 939–969. https://doi.org/10.1017 /S0954579406060470

Carlson, Jon; Watts, Richard; & Maniacci, Michael. (2008). *Adlerian therapy: Theory and practice.* American Psychological Association.

Carmody, James. (2015). Reconceptualizing mindfulness: The psychological principles of attending in mindfulness practice and their role in well-being. In Kirk Warren Brown, J. David Creswell, & Richard M. Ryan (Eds.), *Handbook of mindfulness: Theory, research, and practice.* Guilford.

Carney, Dana R.; Cuddy, Amy; & Yap, Andy J. (2010). Power posing: Brief nonverbal displays affect neuroendocrine levels and risk tolerance. *Psychological Science, 21*, 1363–1368. https://doi.org/10.1177/0956797610383437

Caron, Christina. (2021, February 17). "Nobody has openings": Mental health providers struggle to meet demand. *The New York Times.* https://www.nytimes.com/2021/02/17 /well/mind/therapy-appointments-shortages-pandemic.html

Carpenter, Morgan. (2020). Intersex human rights, sexual orientation, gender identity, sex characteristics and the Yogyakarta principles plus 10. *Culture, Health, & Sexuality*, 1–16. https://doi.org/10.1080/13691058.2020.1781262

Carpenter, Shana K.; Cepeda, Nicholas J.; Rohrer, Doug; Kang, Sean H. K; & Pashler, Harold. (2012). Using spacing to enhance diverse forms of learning: Review of recent research and implications for instruction. *Educational Psychology Review, 24*, 369–378. https://doi.org/10.1007/s10648-012-9205-z

Carpenter, Siri. (2012). That gut feeling. *Monitor on Psychology: American Psychological Association, 43*(8). https://www.apa.org/monitor/2012/09/gut-feeling

Carpintero, Helio. (2004). Watson's behaviorism: A comparison of the two editions (1925 and 1930). *History of Psychology, 7*(2), 183–202.

Carr, Katelyn A., & Epstein, Leonard. (2011). Relationship between food habituation and reinforcing efficacy of food. *Learning and Motivation, 42*, 165–172.

Carretti, Barbara; Borella, Erika; & De Beni, Rossana. (2007). Does strategic memory training improve the working memory performance of younger and older adults? *Experimental Psychology, 54*, 311–320.

Carroll, John B. (1997). The three-stratum theory of cognitive abilities. In Dawn P. Flanagan, Judy L. Genshaft, & Patti L. Harrison (Eds.), *Contemporary intellectual assessment: Theories, tests, and issues* (pp. 122–130). Guilford Press.

Carroll, Joseph; Baraas, Rigmor C.; Wagner-Schuman, Melissa; Rha, Jungtae; Siebe, Cory A.; Sloan, Christina; Tait, Diane M.; Thompson, Summer; Morgan, Jessica I. W.; Neitz, Jay; Williams, David R.; Foster, David H.; & Neitz, Maureen. (2009). Cone photoreceptor mosaic disruption associated with Cys203Arg mutation in the M-cone opsin. *Proceedings of the National Academy of Sciences, 106*, 20948–20953.

Carskadon, Mary A., & Dement, William C. (2005). Normal human sleep: An overview. In Meir H. Kryger, Thomas Roth, & William C. Dement (Eds.), *Principles and practice of sleep medicine* (4th ed.). Elsevier Saunders.

Carskadon, Mary A., & Rechtschaffen, Allan. (2005). Monitoring and staging human sleep. In Meir H. Kryger, Thomas Roth, & William C. Dement (Eds.), *Principles and practice of sleep medicine* (4th ed.). Elsevier Saunders.

Cartei, Valentina; Oakhill, Jane; Garnham, Alan; Banerjee, Robin; & Reby, David. (2020). "This is what a mechanic sounds like": Children's vocal control reveals implicit occupational stereotypes. *Psychological Science*, 1–11. https://doi.org/10.1177 /0956797620929297

Carter, C. Sue. (2014). Oxytocin pathways and the evolution of human behavior. *Annual Review of Psychology, 65*, 17–39. https://doi.org/10.1146/annurev-psych-010213-115110

Cartwright, Rosalind D. (2004). Sleepwalking violence: A sleep disorder, a legal dilemma, and a psychological challenge. *American Journal of Psychiatry, 161*, 1149–1158.

Cartwright, Rosalind D. (2007). Response to M. Pressman: Factors that predispose, prime, and precipitate NREM parasomnias in adults: Clinical and forensic implications. *Sleep Medicine Review, 11*, 5–30.

Cartwright, Rosalind D. (2010). *The twenty-four hour mind: The role of sleep and dreaming in our emotional lives.* Oxford University Press.

Carver, Charles S. (2011). Coping. In Richard J. Contrada & Andrew Baum (Eds.), *The handbook of stress science: Biology, psychology, and health.* Springer.

Casey, B. J. (2013). The teenage brain: An overview. *Current Directions in Psychological Science, 22*, 80–81. https://doi.org/10.1177/0963721413486971

Casey, B. J. (2015). Beyond simple models of self-control to circuit-based accounts of adolescent behavior. *Annual Review of Psychology, 66*, 295–319. https://doi.org/10.1146/annurev-psych-010814-015156

Casey, B. J., & Caudle, Kristina. (2013). The teenage brain: Self control. *Current Directions in Psychological Science, 22*, 82–87. https://doi.org/10.1177/0963721413480170

Casey, Nicholas. (2016). At a loss for meds, Venezuela's mentally ill spiral downward. *The New York Times.* https://www.nytimes.com/2016/10/02/world/americas/venezuela-mental-health-medicine-shortages.html

Caspi, Avshalom; Houts, Renate M.; Belsky, Daniel W.; Goldman-Mellor, Sidra J.; Harrington, HonaLee; Israel, Salomon; Meier, Madeline H.; Ramrakha, Sandhya; Shalev, Idan; Poulton, Richie; & Moffitt, Terrie E. (2014). The p factor: One general psychopathology factor in the structure of psychiatric disorders? *Clinical Psychological Science, 2*(2), 119–137. https://doi.org/10.1177/2167702613497473

Caspi, Avshalom; Roberts, Brent W.; & Shiner, Rebecca L. (2005). Personality development: Stability and change. *Annual Review of Psychology, 56*, 453–484.

Cassidy, Brittany S., & Krendl, Anne C. (2019). A crisis of competence: Benevolent sexism affects evaluations of women's competence. *Sex Roles, 81*, 505–520. https://doi.org/10.1007/s11199-019-1011-3

Catala, Amélie; Grandgeorge, Marine; Schaff, Jean-Luc; Cousillas, Hugo; Hausberger, Martine; & Cattet, Jennifer. (2019). Dogs demonstrate the existence of an epileptic seizure odour in humans. *Nature, 9.* https://doi.org/10.1038/s41598-019-40721-4

Caton, Hiram. (2007). Getting our history right: Six errors about Darwin and his influence. *Evolutionary Psychology, 5*, 52–69.

Cattaneo, Zaira, & Vecchi, Tomaso. (2008). Supramodality effects in visual and haptic spatial processes. *Journal of Experimental Psychology: Learning, Memory, and Cognition, 34*, 631–642.

Cattell, James McKeen. (1890). Mental tests and measurements. *Mind, 15*, 373–381.

Cavedini, Paolo; Gorini, Alessandra; & Bellodi, Laura. (2006). Understanding obsessive–compulsive disorder: Focus on decision making. *Neuropsychology Review, 16*, 3–15. https://doi.org/10.1007/s11065-006-9001-y

CBC News. (2008, October 23). *Warm coffee can melt hearts, researchers say.* https://www.cbc.ca/news/technology/warm-coffee-can-melt-hearts-researchers-say-1.736446?ref=rss

Ceci, Stephen J., & Williams, Wendy M. (2009). Should scientists study race and IQ? Yes: The scientific truth must be pursued. *Nature, 457*, 788–789.

Celesia, Gastone G. (2010). Visual perception and awareness: A modular system. *Journal of Psychophysiology, 24*(2), 62–67.

Centers for Disease Control and Prevention. (2015a, January 6). Alcohol poisoning kills six people in the US each day. http://www.cdc.gov/media/releases/2015/p0106-alcohol-poisoning.html

Centers for Disease Control and Prevention. (2015b). National Vital Statistics System mortality data. Retrieved from http://www.cdc.gov/nchs/deaths.htm

Centers for Disease Control and Prevention. (2015c). *Suicide: Facts at a glance* [Brochure]. Retrieved from https://www.cdc.gov/violenceprevention

Centers for Disease Control and Prevention. (2019a, February 12). *Concussion signs and symptoms.* Heads up. https://www.cdc.gov/headsup/basics/concussion_symptoms.html

Centers for Disease Control and Prevention. (2019b, February 12). *Recovery from concussion.* Heads up. https://www.cdc.gov/headsup/basics/concussion_recovery.html

Centers for Disease Control and Prevention. (2020, March 19). Fentanyl. https://www.cdc.gov/drugoverdose/opioids/fentanyl.html

Centers for Disease Control and Prevention. (2021a). *Assault or homicide.* U.S. Department of Health and Human Services. https://www.cdc.gov/nchs/fastats/homicide.htm

Centers for Disease Control and Prevention. (2021b). *First travel-related case of 2019 novel coronavirus detected in United States.* https://www.cdc.gov/media/releases/2020/p0121-novel-coronavirus-travel-case.html

Cervone, Daniel; Mor, Nilly; Orom, Heather; Shadel, William G.; & Scott, Walter D. (2011). Self-efficacy beliefs and the architecture of personality: On knowledge, appraisal, and self-regulation. In Kathleen D. Vohs & Roy F. Baumeister (Eds.), *Handbook of self-regulation: Research, theory, and applications.* Guilford.

Chabris, Christopher, & Simons, Daniel. (2010). *The invisible gorilla: And other ways our intuitions deceive us.* Crown Publishers/Random House.

Chamberlain, Samuel R., & Fineberg, Naomi, A. (2013). The neurobiology of obsessive-compulsive disorder. In Kevin Oscsner & Stephen M. Kosslyn (Eds.), *The Oxford handbook of cognitive neuroscience. The cutting edges* (pp. 463–473). Oxford University Press.

Chamberlin, Jamie. (2014, June). New law moves ICD-10-CM implementation to 2015. *Monitor on Psychology, 45*(6), 12. http://www.apa.org/monitor/2014/06/upfront-icd.aspx

Champagne, Frances A. (2010). Early adversity and developmental outcomes: Interaction between genetics, epigenetics, and social experiences across the life span. *Perspectives on Psychological Science, 5*, 564–574. https://doi.org/10.1177/1745691610383494

Champagne, Frances A., & Mashoodh, Robin. (2009). Genes in context: Gene–environment interplay and the origins of individual differences in behavior. *Current Directions in Psychological Science, 18*, 127–131.

Chan, Tommy K.H.; Cheung, Christy M.K.; & Lee, Zach W.Y. (2021). Cyberbullying on social network sites: A literature review and future research directions. *Information & Management, 58*, 1–16. https://doi.org/10.1016/j.im.2020.103411

Chance, Paul. (1999). Thorndike's puzzle boxes and the origins of the experimental analysis of behavior. *Journal of the Experimental Analysis of Behavior, 72*, 433–440.

Chandola, Tarani & Marmot, Michael G. (2011). Socioeconomic status and stress. In Richard J. Contrada & Andrew Baum (Eds.), *The handbook of stress science: Biology, psychology, and health.* Springer.

Chandrashekar, Jayaram; Hoon, Mark A.; Ryba, Nichola Mays J. P.; & Zuker, Charles S. (2006). The receptors and cells for mammalian taste. *Nature, 444*, 288–294.

Chang, Anne-Marie; Aeschbach, Daniel; Duffy, Jeanne F.; & Czeisler, Charles A. (2015). Evening use of light-emitting eReaders negatively affects sleep, circadian timing, and next-morning alertness. *Proceedings of the National Academy of Sciences, 112*, 1232–1237. https://doi.org/10.1073/pnas.1418490112

Chaplin, Tara. (2015). Gender and emotion expression: A development contextual perspective. *Emotion Review, 7*, 14–21. https://doi.org/10.1177/1754073914544408

Chaput, Jeanne-Paul, & Tremblay, Angelo. (2009). Obesity and physical inactivity: The relevance of reconsidering the notion of sedentariness. *Obesity Facts, 2*, 249–254.

Charles, Susan T., & Carstensen, Laura L. (2010). Social and emotional aging. *Annual Review of Psychology, 61*, 383–409.

Charles, Susan; Piazza, Jennifer; Mogle, Jaqueline; Sliwinski, Martin; & Almeida, David. (2013). The wear and tear of daily stressors on mental health. *Psychological Science, 24*, 733–741. https://doi.org/10.1177/0956797612462222

Charlson, Fiona J.; Ferrari, Alize J.; Santomauro, Damian F.; Diminic, Sandra; Stockings, Emily; Scott, James G.; McGrath, John J.; & Whiteford, Harvey A. (2018). Global epidemiology and burden of schizophrenia: Findings from the global burden of disease study 2016. *Schizophrenia Bulletin, 44*(6), 1195–1203. https://doi.org/10.1093/schbul/sby058

Chase, Cheryl. (2003). What is the agenda of the intersex patient advocacy movement? *Endocrinologist, 13*, 240–242. http://www.isna.org/drupal/agenda.

Chase, Cheryl. (2006). Successes of the Chicago conference. DSD Symposium, October 2006. *Intersex Society of North America.* http://www.isna.org/agenda

Chatterjee, Arijit & Hambrick, Donald C. (2007). It's all about me: Narcissistic chief executive officers and their effects on company strategy and performance. *Administrative Science Quarterly, 52*, 351–386.

Chaudhari, Nirupa; Landin, Ana Marie; & Roper, Stephen D. (2000). A metabotropic glutamate receptor variant functions as a taste receptor. *Nature Neuroscience, 3*, 113–119.

Chen, Fang Fang, & Jing, Yiming. (2012). The impact of individualistic and collectivistic orientation on the judgement of self-presentation. *European Journal of Social Psychology, 42*, 470–481. https://doi.org/10.1002/ejsp.1872

Chen, Vivian Hsueh Hua, & Wu, Yuehua. (2015). Group identification as a mediator of the effect of players' anonymity on cheating in online games. *Behaviour and Information Technology, 34*(7), 658–667. https://doi.org/10.1080/0144929X.2013.843721

Chen, Xinguang; Murphy, Debra A.; Naar-King, Sylvie; & Parsons, Jeffery T. (2011). A clinic-based motivational intervention improves condom use among subgroups of youth living with HIV. *Journal of Adolescent Health, 49*(2), 193–198. https://doi.org/10.1016/j.jadohealth.2010.11.252

Cheng, Anne Anlin. (2021, February 21). What this wave of anti-Asian violence reveals about America. *The New York Times.* https://www.nytimes.com/2021/02/21/opinion/anti-asian-violence.html

Cheng, C. (2009). Dialectical thinking and coping flexibility: A multimethod approach. *Journal of Personality, 77*(2), 471–494.

Cheng, Guo; Buyken, Anette E.; Shi, Lijie; Karaolis-Danckert, Nadina; Kroke Anja; Wudy, Stefan A.; Degen, Gisela H.; & Remer, Thomas. (2012). Beyond overweight: Nutrition as an important lifestyle factor influencing timing of puberty. *Nutrition Reviews, 70*, 133–152. https://doi.org/10.1111/j.1753-4887.2011.00461.x

Chentsova-Dutton, Yulia E., & Tsai, Jeanne L. (2007). Cultural factors influence the expression of psychopathology. In Scott O. Lilienfeld & William T. O'Donohue (Eds.), *The great ideas of clinical science* (pp. 375–396). Routledge.

..ack, Stephen T., & Taylor, Stuart P. (1995). Alcohol and human physical aggression: Pharmacological versus expectancy effects. *Journal of Studies on Alcohol and Drugs, 56*(4), 449–456.

Cheryan, Sapna; Master, Allison; & Meltzoff, Andrew. (2015). Cultural stereotypes as gatekeepers: Increasing girls' interest in computer science and engineering by diversifying stereotypes. *Frontiers in Psychology, 6*, 1–8. https://doi.org/10.3389/fpsyg.2015.00049

Cheryan, Sapna; Ziegler, Sianna; & Montoya, Amanda. (2017). Why are some STEM fields more gender balanced than others? *Psychological Bulletin, 143*, 1–35. https://doi.org/10.1037/bul0000052

Chi, Kelly Rae. (2014, November). White's the matter. *The Scientist, 28*(11), 67.

Chi, Tingying; & Gold, Jessica A. (2020). A review of emerging therapeutic potential of psychedelic drugs in the treatment of psychiatric illnesses. *Journal of the Neurological Sciences, 411*, 116715. https://doi.org/10.1016/j.jns.2020.116715

Chida, Yoichi, & Hamer, Mark. (2008). Chronic psychosocial factors and acute physiological responses to laboratory-induced stress in healthy populations: A quantitative review of 30 years of investigations. *Psychological Bulletin, 134*(6), 829–885.

Chida, Yoichi, & Steptoe, Andrew. (2009). The association of anger and hostility with future coronary heart disease: A meta-analytic review of prospective evidence. *Journal of the American College of Cardiology, 53*(11), 936–946.

Chiesa, Alberto, & Malinowski, Peter. (2011). Mindfulness based approaches: Are they all the same? *Journal of Clinical Psychology, 67*, 1–21. https://doi.org/10.1002/jclp.20776

Chiesa, Alberto, & Serretti, Alessandro. (2009). Mindfulness-based stress reduction for stress management in healthy people: A review and meta-analysis. *Journal of Alternative and Complementary Medicine, 15*(5), 593–600.

Chira, Susan. (2017, March 10). When Japan had a third gender. *The New York Times.* https://www.nytimes.com/2017/03/10/arts/design/when-japan-had-a-third-gender.html

Choi, Kyeong-Sook; Jeon, Hyun Ok; & Lee, Yu-Sang (2007). Familial B515association of schizophrenia symptoms retrospectively measured on a lifetime basis. *Psychiatric Genetics, 17*(2), 103–107. https://doi.org/10.1097/YPG.0b013e328012.a3b0

Chomsky, Noam. (1965). *Aspects of a theory of syntax.* MIT Press.

Chooi, Yu Chung; Ding, Cherlyn; & Magkos, Faidon. (2019). The epidemiology of obesity. *Metabolism Clinical and Experimental, 92*, 6–10. https://doi.org/10.1016/j.metabol.2018.09.005

Christensen, Garret; Wang, Z., Levy Paluck, E., Swanson, N., Birke, D., Miguel, E., & Littman, R. (2020). Open science practices are on the rise: The State of Social Science (3S) Survey. https://escholarship.org/uc/item/0hx0207r

Christiani, David C. (2019). Vaping-induced lung injury. *New England Journal of Medicine.* https://doi.org/10.1056/NEJMe1912032

Christidis, Peggy; Lin, Luona; Conroy, Jessica; & Stamm, Karen. (2019). 2008-17: Psychology master's and doctoral degrees awarded by subfield, institution type, gender and race/ethnicity. American Psychological Association Center for Workforce Studies. https://www.apa.org/workforce/publications/2017-postsecondary-data/report.pdf

Chrysikou, Evangelia G. (2006). When shoes become hammers: Goal-derived categorization training enhances problem-solving performance. *Journal of Experimental Psychology: Learning, Memory, and Cognition, 32*, 935–942.

Chua, Hannah Faye; Boland, Julie E.; & Nisbett, Richard E. (2005). Cultural variation in eye movements during scene perception. *Proceedings of the National Academy of Sciences, 102*, 12629–12633.

Chun, Chi-Ah; Moos, Rudolf H.; & Cronkite, Ruth C. (2006). Culture: A fundamental context for the stress and coping paradigm. In Paul T. P. Wong, Lilian Chui Jan Wong, and Walter J. Lonner (Eds.), *Handbook of multicultural perspectives on stress and coping.* Spring.

Chun, Marvin M.; Golomb, Julie D.; & Turk-Browne, Nicholas B. (2011). A taxonomy of external and internal attention. *Annual Review of Psychology, 62*, 73–101. https://doi.org/10.1146/annurev.psych.093008.100427

Chung-Yan, Greg A. (2010). The nonlinear effects of job complexity and autonomy on job satisfaction, turnover, and psychological well-being. *Journal of Occupational Health Psychology, 15*(3), 237–251.

Churchwell, Keith; Elkind, Mitchell S. V.; Benjamin, Regina M.; Carson, April P.; Chang, Edward K.; Lawrence, Willie; Mills, Andrew; Odom, Tanya M.; Rodriguez, Carlos J.; Rodriguez, Fatima; Sanchez, Eduardo; Sharrief, Anjail Z.; Sims, Mario; & Williams, Olajide. (2020). Call to action: Structural racism as a fundamental driver of health disparities: A presidential advisory from the American Heart Association. *Circulation, 142*, e454–e468. https://doi.org/10.1161/CIR.0000000000000936

Cialdini, Robert B. (2009). Compliance. In D. Sander & K. Scherer (Eds.), *The Oxford companion to emotion and the affective sciences.* Oxford University Press.

Cialdini, Robert B., & Sagarin, Brad J. (2005). Principles of interpersonal influence. In T. C. Brock & M. C. Green (Eds.), *Persuasion: Psychological insights and perspectives* (pp. 143–169). Sage.

Cieślik, Błazej; Mazurek, Justyna; Rutkowski, Sebastian; Kiper, Paweł; Turolla, Andrea; & Szczepańska-Gieracha, Joanna. (2020). Virtual reality in psychiatric disorders: A systematic review of reviews. *Complementary Therapies in Medicine, 52,* 102480. https://doi.org/10.1016/j.ctim.2020.102480

Cihangir, Sezgin. (2013). Gender specific honor codes and cultural change. *Group Processes & Intergroup Relations, 16*(3), 319–333. https://doi.org/10.1177/1368430212463453

Cikara, Mina, & Van Bavel, Jay J. (2014). The neuroscience of intergroup relations: An integrative review. *Perspectives on Psychological Science, 9*, 245–274. https://doi.org/10.1177/1745691614527464

Cinamon, Rachel Gali; Weisel, Amatzia; & Tzuk, Kineret. (2007). Work-family conflict within the family: Crossover effects, perceived parent–child interaction quality, parental self-efficacy, and life role attributions. *Journal of Career Development, 34*, 79–100.

Cisler, Josh M.; Reardon, John M.; & Williams, Nathan L. (2007). Anxiety sensitivity and disgust sensitivity interact to predict contamination fears. *Personality and Individual Differences, 42*(6), 935–946. https://doi.org/10.1016/j.paid.2006.09.004

Clark, David M.; Ehlers, Anke; McManus, Freda; Hackman, Ann; Fennell, Melanie; Campbell, Helen; Flower, Teresa; Davenport, Clare; & Louis, Beverly. (2003). Cognitive therapy versus fluoxetine in generalized social phobia: A randomized placebo-controlled trial. *Journal of Counseling and Clinical Psychology, 71*, 1058–1067.

Clark, Graeme M.; Clark, Jonathan C. M.; & Furness, John B. (2013). The evolving science of cochlear implants. *Journal of the American Medical Association, 310*, 1225–1226. https://doi.org/10.1001/jama.2013.278142

Clark, Lee Anna; Cuthbert, Bruce; Lewis-Fernández, Roberto; Narrow, William E.; & Reed, Geoffrey M. (2017). Three approaches to understanding and classifying mental disorder: ICD-11, DSM-5, and the National Institute of Mental Health's research domain criteria (RDoC). *Psychological Science in the Public Interest, 18*(2), 72–145. https://doi.org/10.1177/1529100617727266

Clark, Ruth C. (2019). *Evidence-based training methods: A guide for training professionals* (3rd ed.). ADT Press.

Clauss-Ehlers, Caroline S.; Chiriboga, David A.; Hunter, Scott J.; Roysircar, Gargi; & Tummala-Narra, Pratyusha. (2019). APA Multicultural Guidelines executive summary: Ecological approach to context, identity, and intersectionality. *American Psychologist, 74*(2), 232–244. https://doi.org/10.1037/amp0000382

Clay, Rebecca. (2003, April). Researchers replace midlife myths with facts. *Monitor on Psychology, 34*, 38–39. https://doi.org/10.1037/e300092003-024

Clayton, Nicola S.; Bussey, Timothy J.; & Dickinson, Anthony. (2003). Can animals recall the past and plan for the future? *Nature Reviews Neuroscience, 4*(8), 685–691. https://doi.org/10.1038/nrn1180

Clement, Sarah; Schauman, Oliver; Graham, Tanesha; Maggioni, Francesca; Evans-Lacko, Sara; Bezborodovs, Nikita; Morgan, C.; Rüsch, N.; Brown, J. S. L.; & Thornicroft, G. (2015). What is the impact of mental health-related stigma on help-seeking? A systematic review of quantitative and qualitative studies. *Psychological Medicine, 45*(1), 11–27. https://doi.org/10.1017/s0033291714000129

Clifasefi, Seema L.; Garry, Maryanne; & Loftus, Elizabeth. (2007). Setting the record (or video camera) straight on memory: The video camera model of memory and other memory myths. In Sergio Della Sala (Ed.), *Tall tales about the mind and brain: Separating fact from fiction.* Oxford University Press.

CNN (Producer). (2011). *Virtual reality battles PTSD* [Video]. Available from https://www.cnn.com/videos/tech/2011/09/23/virtual-reality-battles.cnn

Coelho, Carlos M., & Purkis, Helena. (2009). The origins of specific phobias: Influential theories and current perspectives. *Review of General Psychology, 13*(4), 335–348.

Coelho, Helen F.; Canter, Peter H.; & Ernst, E. (2013). Mindfulness-based cognitive therapy: Evaluating current evidence and informing future research. *Psychology of Consciousness: Theory, Research, and Practice, 1*(S), 97–107. https://doi.org/10.1037/2326-5523.1.S.97

Coffee, Pete; Rees, Tim; & Haslam, S. Alexander. (2009). Bouncing back from failure: The interactive impact of perceived controllability and stability on self-efficacy beliefs and future task performance. *Journal of Sports Sciences, 27*, 1117–1124.

Cogan, Rosemary; Cochran, Bradley S.; & Velarde, Luis C. (2007). Sexual fantasies, sexual functioning, and hysteria among women: A test of Freud's (1905) hypothesis. *Psychoanalytic Psychology, 24*(4), 697–700.

Cohen, Adam B. (2009). Many forms of culture. *American Psychologist, 64*(3), 194–204.

Cohen, Adam B. (2010). Just how many different forms of culture are there? *American Psychologist, 65*(1), 59–61.

Cohen, Alexandra; Breiner, Kaitlyn; Steinberg, Laurence; Bonnie, Richard; Scott, Elizabeth; Taylor-Thompson, Kim; Rudolph, Marc D.; Chein, Jason; Richeson, Jennifer A.; Heller, Aaron S.; Silverman, Melanie R.; Dellarco, Danielle V.; Fair, Damien A.; Galván, Adriana; & Casey, B. J. (2016). When is an adolescent an adult? Assessing cognitive control in emotional and nonemotional contexts. *Psychological Science, 27*(4), 549–562. https://doi.org/10.1177/0956797615627625

Cohen, Estee; Zerach, Gadi; & Solomon, Zahava. (2011). The implication of combat-induced stress reaction, PTSD, and attachment in parenting among war veterans. *Journal of Family Psychology, 25*(2), 688–698. https://doi.org/10.1037/a0024065.

Cohen, Geoffrey L.; Purdie-Vaughns, Valerie; & Garcia, Julio. (2012). An identity threat perspective on intervention. In Michael Inzlicht & Toni Schmader (Eds.), *Stereotype threat: Theory, process, and application.* Oxford University Press.

Cohen, Koby; Weizman, Abraham; & Weinstein, Aviv. (2019). Positive and negative effects of cannabis and cannabinoids on health. *Clinical Pharmacology & Therapeutics, 105*. https://doi.org/10.1002/cpt.1381

Cohen, Sheldon. (2004). Social relationships and health. *American Psychologist, 59,* 676–684, 547.

Cohen, Sheldon. (2005). Keynote Presentation at the Eight International Congress of Behavioral Medicine: The Pittsburgh common cold studies: Psychosocial predictors of susceptibility to respiratory infectious illness. *International Journal of Behavioral Medicine, 12*(3), 123–131.

Cohen, Sheldon. (2016). Psychological stress, immunity, and physical disease. In Robert Sternberg, Susan Fiske, & Donald Foss (Eds.), *Scientists making a difference: One hundred eminent behavioral and brain scientists talk about their most important contributions* (pp. 419–23). Cambridge University Press.

Cohen, Sheldon; Alper, Cuneyt M.; & Doyle, William J. (2006). Positive emotional style predicts resistance to illness after experimental exposure to rhinovirus or influenza A virus. *Psychosomatic Medicine, 68*(6), 809–815.

Cohen, Sheldon; Doyle, William J.; Alper, Cuneyt M.; Janicki-Deverts, Denise; & Turner, Ronald B. (2009). Sleep habits and susceptibility to the common cold. *Archives of Internal Medicine, 169*(1), 62–67.

Cohen, Sheldon, & Janicki-Deverts, Denise. (2009). Can we improve our physical health by altering our social networks? *Perspectives on Psychological Science, 4,* 375–378.

Cohen, Sheldon; Janicki-Deverts, Denise; Doyle, William; Miller, Gregory; Frank, Ellen; Rabin, Bruce; & Turner, Ronald. (2012). Chronic stress, glucocorticoid receptor resistance, inflammation, and disease risk. *Proceedings of the National Academy of Sciences,109*(16), 5995–5999. https://doi.org/10.1073/pnas.1118355109

Cohen, Sheldon; Alper, Cuneyt M.; Doyle, William J.; Adler, Nancy; Treanor, John J.; & Turner, Ronald B. (2008). Objective and subjective socioeconomic status and susceptibility to the common cold. *Health Psychology, 27,* 268–274. https://doi.org/10.1037 /0278-6133.27.2.268

Cohen, Sheldon; Tyrrell, David A. J.; & Smith, Andrew P. (1991). Psychological stress and susceptibility to the common cold. *New England Journal of Medicine, 325,* 606–612.

Cohen, Sheldon; Tyrrell, David A. J.; & Smith, Andrew P. (1993). Negative life events, perceived stress, negative affect, and susceptibility to the common cold. *Journal of Personality and Social Psychology, 64,* 131–140.

Cohen, Taya R.; Panter, Abigail T.; & Turan, Nazli. (2012). Guilt proneness and moral character. *Current Directions in Psychological Science, 21*(5), 355–359. https://doi.org /10.1177/0963721412454874

Cohen-Kettenis, Peggy T., & Pfafflin, Friedemann. (2010). The DSM diagnostic criteria for gender identity disorder in adolescents and adults. *Archives of Sexual Behavior, 39*(2), 499–513.

Coker, Ann L.; Bush, Heather M.; Fisher, Bonnie S.; Swan, Suzanne C.; Williams, Corrine M.; Clear, Emily R.; & DeGue, Sarah. (2016). Multi-college bystander intervention evaluation for violence prevention. *American Journal of Preventative Medicine, 50*(3), 295–302. https://doi.org/10.1016/j.amepre.2015.08.034

Colangelo, James J. (2007). Recovered memory debate revisited: Practice implications for mental health counselors. *Journal of Mental Health Counseling, 29*(2), 93–120.

Colby, Anne, & Kohlberg, Lawrence. (1984). Invariant sequence and internal consistency in moral judgment stages. In William M. Kurtines & Jacob L. Gewirtz (Eds.), *Morality, moral behavior, and moral development.* Wiley.

Colby, Anne; Kohlberg, Lawrence; Gibbs, John; & Lieberman, Marcus. (1983). A longitudinal study of moral judgment. *Monographs of the Society for Research in Child Development, 48,* (1–2), 1–124.

Cole, Geoff G., & Wilkins, Arnold J. (2013). Fear of holes. *Psychological Science, 24*(10), 1–6. https://doi.org/10.1177/0956797613484937

Cole, Michael, & Packer, Martin. (2011). Culture and cognition. In Kenneth D. Keith (Ed.), *Cross-cultural psychology: Contemporary themes and perspectives.* Wiley-Blackwell.

Collerton, Joanna.; Davies, Karen; Jagger, Carol; Kingston, Andrew; Bond, John; Eccles, Martin P.; Robinson, Louise A.; Martin-Ruiz, Carmen; von Zglinicki, Thomas; James, Oliver F. W.; & Kirkwood, Thomas B. L. (2009). Health and disease in 85 year olds: Baseline findings from the Newcastle 85 + cohort study. *BMJ, 339,* b4904. https://doi.org/10.1136/bmj.b4904

Collin, Lindsay; Reisner, Sari; Tangpricha, Vin; & Goodman, Michael. (2016). Prevalence of transgender depends on the "case" definition: A systematic review. *Journal of Sexual Medicine, 13,* 613–626. https://doi.org/10.1016/j.jsxm.2016.02.001

Collins, Allan M., & Loftus, Elizabeth F. (1975). A spreading activation theory of semantic processing. *Psychological Review, 82,* 407–428.

Collins, W. Andrew. (2003). More than myth: The developmental significance of romantic relationships during adolescence. *Journal of Research on Adolescence, 13,* 1–24.

Colrain, Ian M., & Baker, Fiona C. (2011). Changes in sleep as a function of adolescent development. *Neuropsychology Review, 21,* 5–21. https://doi.org/10.1007/s11065-010-9155-5

Coltheart, Max, & McArthur, Genevieve. (2012). Neuroscience, educationand educational efficacy research. In Sergio Della Sala & Mike Anderson (Eds.), *Neuroscience in education: The good, the bad, and the ugly.* Oxford University Press.

Colwell, Christopher S. (2011). Neuroscience: Sleepy neurons? *Nature, 472,* 427–428. https://doi.org/10.1038/472427a

Combs, Dennis R., & Mueser, Kim T. (2007). Schizophrenia. In Michel Hersen, Samuel M. Turner, & Deborah C. Beidel (Eds.), *Adult psychopathology and diagnosis* (5th ed., pp. 234–285). Wiley.

Combs, Dennis R.; Chapman, Dustin; Waguspack, Jace; Basso, Michael R.; & Penn, David L. (2011). Attention shaping as a means to improve emotion perception deficits in outpatients with schizophrenia and impaired controls. *Schizophrenia Research, 127*(1–3), 151–156.

Compton, D'Lane, & Bridges, Tristan. (April 12, 2019). 2018 GSS update on the U.S. LGB population. *Inequality by (Interior) Design.* https://inequalitybyinteriordesign.word-press.com/2019/04/12/2018-gss-update-on-the-u-s-lgb-population/

Compton, William C. (2018). Self-actualization myths: What did Maslow really say? *Journal of Humanistic Psychology.* https://doi.org/10.1177/0022167818761929

Confer, Jaime C.; Easton, Judith A.; Fleischman, Diana S.; Goetz, Cari D.; Lewis, David M. G.; Perilloux, Carin; & Buss, David M. (2010). Evolutionary psychology: Controversies, questions, prospects, and limitations. *American Psychologist, 65,* 110–126. https://doi.org/10.1037/a0018413

Conger, Cristen; & Ervin, Caroline (Hosts). (2020, February 18). How to Mind Mental Illness with Esmé Weijun Wang (No. 77) [Audio podcast transcript]. In *Unladylike.* Unladylike Media. https://unladylike.co/transcripts/episode-77

Conley, Colleen S., & Rudolph, Karen D. (2009). The emerging sex difference in adolescent depression: Interacting contributions of puberty and peer stress. *Development Psychopathology, 21*(2), 593–620. https://doi.org/10.1017/ S0954579409000327

Connell, Lauren C.; Porensky, Lauren M.; Chalfoun, Anna D.; & Scasta, John D. (2019). Black-tailed prairie dog, Cynomys ludovicianus (Sciuridae), metapopulation response to novel sourced conspecific signals. *Animal Behaviour, 150,* 189–199. https://doi.org/10.1016/j.anbehav.2019.02.004

Connolly, J. A., & McIsaac, C. (2009). Romantic relationships in adolescence. In R. M. Lerner & L. Steinberg (Eds.), *Handbook of Adolescent Psychology, Vol. 2: Contextual influences on adolescent development* (3rd ed., pp. 104–151). Wiley.

Connor, Tracy; & Fitzpatrick, Sarah. (2018, January 9). Gymnast Maggie Nichols was first to report abuse by Larry Nassar. *NBC News.* https://www.nbcnews.com/news /us-news/gymnast-maggie-nichols-was-first-report-abuse-larry-nassar-n836046

Conroy, David E. (2017). Achievement motives. In Andrew J. Elliot, Carol S. Dweck, & David S. Yeager, Eds. *Handbook of competence and motivation: Theory and application* (2nd ed.). Guilford.

Conway, Christopher; Rutter, Lauren; & Brown, Timothy. (2016). Chronic environmental stress and the temporal course of depression and panic disorder: A trait-state-occasion modeling approach. *Journal of Abnormal Psychology,125,* 53–63. https://doi.org/10.1037/abn0000122

Conway, Martin A.; & Holmes, Alison. (2004). Psychosocial stages and the accessibility of autobiographical memories across the life cycle. *Journal of Personality, 72,* 461–480. https://doi.org/10.1111/j.0022-3506.2004.00269.x

Conway, Martin A.; Meares, Kevin; & Standart, Sally. (2004). Images and goals. *Memory, 12*(4), 525–531. https://doi.org/10.1080/09658210444000151

Cook, Emily C.; Buehler, Cheryl; & Henson, Robert. (2009). Parents and peers as social influences to deter antisocial behavior. *Journal of Youth and Adolescence, 38*(9), 1240–1252.

Cook, Thomas D.; Deng, Yingding; & Morgano, Emily. (2007). Friendship influences during early adolescence: The special role of friends' grade point average. *Journal of Research on Adolescence, 17*(2), 325–356.

Cook, Travis A. R.; Luczak, Susan E.; Shea, Shoshana H.; Ehlers, Cindy L.; Carr, Lucinda G.; & Wall, Tamara L. (2005). Associations of ALDH2 and ADH1B genotypes with response to alcohol in Asian Americans. *Journal of Studies on Alcohol, 66,* 196–204.

Cooke, Nancy. (2015). Team cognition as interaction. *Current Directions in Psychological Science, 24,* 415–419. https://doi.org/10.1177/0963721415602474

Cooke, Richard; French, David P.; & Sniehotta, Falko F. (2010). Wide variation in understanding about what constitutes 'binge-drinking.' *Drugs: Education, Prevention & Policy, 17*(6), 762–775. https://doi.org/10.3109/09687630903246457

Cooper, Cary L., & Dewe, Philip. (2007). Stress: A brief history from the 1950s to Richard Lazarus. In Alan Monat, Richard S. Lazarus, & Gretchen Reevy (Eds.), *The Praeger handbook on stress and coping: Vol. 1.* Praeger/Greenwood.

Cooper, Joel. (2012). Cognitive dissonance theory. In Paul A. M. Van Lange, Arie W. Kruglanski, & E. Tory Higgins (Eds.), *Handbook of theories of social psychology* (Vol. 1). Sage.

Cooper, Mick. (2008). *Essential research findings in counseling and psychotherapy.* Sage.

Copeland, William E.; Worthman, Carol; Shanahan, Lilly; Costello, E. Jane; & Angold, Adrian. (2019). Early pubertal timing and testosterone associated with higher levels of adolescent depression in girls. *Journal of the American Academy of Child & Adolescent Psychiatry, 58*(12), 1197–1206. https://doi.org/10.1016/j.jaac.2019.02.007

Corbett, Jennifer E. (2017). The whole warps the sum of its parts: Gestalt-defined-group mean size biases memory for individual objects. *Psychological Science, 28,* 12–22. https://doi.org/10.1177/0956797616671524

Corkin, Suzanne. (2002). What's new with the amnesic patient H.M.? *Nature Reviews Neuroscience, 3,* 153–160.

Corkin, Suzanne. (2013). *Present tense: The unforgettable life of the amnesic patient, H. M.* Basic Books.

Corponi, Filippo; Fabbri, Chiara; & Serretti, Alessandro. (2018). Pharmacogenetics in psychiatry. In Kim Brosen & Per Damkier (Eds.), *Advances in pharmacology, 83,* 297–331. Academic Press. https://doi.org/10.1016/bs.apha.2018.03.003

...igan, Patrick W.; Druss, Benjamin G.; & Perlick, Deborah A. (2014). The impact of mental illness stigma on seeking and participating in mental health care. *Psychological Science in the Public Interest, 15*(2), 37–70. https://doi.org/10.1177/1529100614531398

Corritore, Matthew; Goldberg, Amir; & Srivastava, Sameer B. (2020). The new analytics of culture. *Harvard Business Review.* https://hbr.org/2020/01/the-new-analytics-of-culture

Corsini, Raymond J. (1958). *The Nonverbal Reasoning Test: To measure the capacity to reason logically as indicated by solutions to pictorial problems.* Pearson Performance Solutions.

Cosgrove, Lisa, & Krimsky, Sheldon. (2012). A comparison of DSM-IV and DSM-5 panel members' financial associations with industry: A pernicious problem persists. *PLOS Medicine, 9*(3), e1001190. https://doi.org/10.1371/journal.pmed.1001190

Cosmides, Leda, & Tooby, John. (2013). Evolutionary psychology: New perspectives on cognition and motivation. *Annual Review of Psychology, 64,* 201–209.

Cosoy, Natalio. (2016). Brotherly love: Colombian switched twins pull together. *BBC News.* http://www.bbc.co.uk/news/world-latin-america-35220779

Costa, Albert, & Sebastián-Gallés, Núria. (2014). How does the bilingual experience sculpt the brain? *Nature Reviews Neuroscience, 15,* 336–345.

Costarelli, Sandro. (2011). Seeming ambivalent, being prejudiced: The moderating role of attitude basis on experienced affect. *Group Dynamics: Theory, Research, and Practice, 15*(1), 49–59.

Costich, Jim. (2003). *An intersex primer: Our lives.* http://www.bodieslikeours.org/stories.html

Cote, Kimberly A.; Lustig, Kari A.; & MacDonald, Kevin J. (2019). The role of sleep in processing emotional information. *Handbook of Sleep Research, 30.* https://doi.org/10.1016/B978-0-12-813743-7.00033-5

Côté, Sophie, & Bouchard, Stéphane. (2008). Virtual reality exposure's efficacy in the treatment of specific phobias: A critical review. *Journal of CyberTherapy and Rehabilitation, 1*(1), 75–91.

Coulson, Melissa; Healey, Michelle; Fidler, Fiona; & Cumming, Geoff. (2010). Confidence intervals permit, but do not guarantee, better inference than statistical significance testing. *Frontiers in Psychology: Quantitative Psychology and Measurement, 1,* 1–9. https://doi.org/10.3389/fpsyg.2010.00026

Courage, Mary L., & Howe, Mark L. (2002). From infant to child: The dynamics of cognitive change in the second year of life. *Psychological Bulletin, 128,* 250–277.

Courtois, Christine A., & Ford, Julian D. (Eds.). (2009). *Treating complex traumatic stress disorders: An evidence-based guide.* Guilford.

Cousineau, Tara McKee, & Shedler, Jonathan. (2006). Predicting physical health: Implicit mental health measures versus self-report scales. *Journal of Nervous and Mental Disease, 194*(6), 427–432.

Coventry, Will L.; Gillespie, Nathan A.; Heath, A. C.; & Martin, N. G. (2004). Perceived social support in a large community sample—age and sex differences. *Social Psychiatry and Psychiatric Epidemiology, 39*(8), 625–636.

Covington, Taylor. (2020, September 1). Drowsy driving statistics. *The Zebra.* https://www.thezebra.com/research/drowsy-driving-statistics/

Cowan, Nelson. (2001). The magical number 4 in short-term memory: A reconsideration of mental storage capacity. *Behavioral and Brain Sciences, 24,* 87–185.

Cowan, Nelson. (2005). *Working memory capacity: Essays in cognitive psychology.* Psychology Press.

Cowan, Nelson. (2010). The magical mystery four: How is working memory capacity limited, and why? *Current Directions in Psychological Science, 19*(1), 51–57.

Cowan, Nelson. (2015). George Miller's magical number of immediate memory in retrospect: Observations on the faltering progression of science. *Psychological Review, 122,* 536–541. https://doi.org/10.1037/a0039035

Cowan, Nelson; Chen, Zhijian; & Rouder, Jeffrey N. (2004). Constant capacity in an immediate serial-recall task: A logical sequel to Miller (1956). *Psychological Science, 15,* 634–640.

Cowan, Nelson; Morey, Candice C.; & Chen, Zhijian. (2007). The legend of the magical number seven. In Sergio Della Sala (Ed.), *Tall tales about the mind and brain: Separating fact from fiction.* Oxford University Press.

Cowen, Phil J., & Browning, Michael. (2015). What has serotonin to do with depression? *World Psychiatry, 14*(2): 158–160. https://doi.org/10.1002/wps.20229

Cowen, Tyler. (2016). Conversations with Tyler: Margalit Fox on life, death, and the best job in journalism. *Medium.* https://medium.com/conversations-with-tyler/margalit-fox-obituary-writer-new-york-times-f4169ede40

Coyle, Emily F.; Van Leer, Elizabeth; Schroeder, Kingsley, M.; & Fulcher, Megan. (2015). Planning to have it all: Emerging adults' expectations of future work-family conflict. *Sex Roles, 72,* 547–557. https://doi.org/10.1007/s11199-015-0492-y

Craig, Maureen A.; Rucker, Julian M.; & Richeson, Jennifer A. (2018). The pitfalls and promise of increasing racial diversity: Threat, contact, and race relations in the 21st century. *Current Directions in Psychological Science, 27*(3), 188–193. https://doi.org/10.1177/0963721417727086

Craik, Fergus I. M.; & Bialystok, Ellen. (2006). Cognition through the lifespan: Mechanisms of change. *Trends in Cognitive Sciences, 10,* 131–138.

Craik, Fergus I. M.; Govoni, Richard; Naveh-Benjamin, Moshe; & Anderson, Nicole D. (1996). The effects of divided attention on encoding and retrieval processes in human memory. *Journal of Experimental Psychology: General, 125,* 159–180.

Crain, Tori; & Hammer, Leslie. (2013). Work-family enrichment: A systematic review of antecedents, outcomes, and mechanisms. In Arnold Bakker (Ed.), *Advances in positive organizational psychology* (pp. 303–328), Emerald Group.

Cramblet Alvarez, Leslie D.; Jones, K. Nicole; Walljasper-Schuyler, Chelsea; Trujillo, Marissa; Weiser, Mikayla A.; Rodriguez, Jerome L.; Ringler, Rachael L.; & Leach, Jonah L. (2019). Psychology's Hidden Figures: Undergraduate psychology majors' (in)ability to recognize our diverse pioneers. *Psi Chi Journal of Psychological Research, 24*(2), 84–96. https://doi.org/10.24839/2325-7342.JN24.2.84

Crann, Sara. (2010). Profile of Melanie Klein. In A. Rutherford (Ed.), *Psychology's Feminist Voices Multimedia Internet Archive.* https://feministvoices.com/profiles/melanie-klein

Crano, William D., & Prislin, R. (2006). Attitudes and persuasion. *Annual Review of Psychology, 57,* 345–374.

Craske, Michelle G., & Barlow, David H. (2008). Panic disorder and agoraphobia. In David H. Barlow (Ed.), *Clinical handbook of psychological disorders* (4th ed., pp. 1–64). Guilford.

Craske, Michelle G., & Waters, Allison M. (2005). Panic disorder, phobias, and generalized anxiety disorder. *Annual Review of Clinical Psychology, 1,* 197–225. https://doi.org/10.1146/annurev.clinpsy.1.102803.143857

Craske, Michelle G.; Kircanski, Katharina; Zelikowski, Moriel; Mystkowski, Jayson; Chowdhury, Najwa; & Baker, Aaron. (2008). Optimizing inhibitory learning during exposure therapy. *Behavior Research and Therapy, 46*(1), 5–27. https://doi.org/10.1016/j.brat.2007.10.003

Craske, Michelle G.; Treanor, Michael; Conway, Christopher C.; & Zbozinek, Tomislav. (2014). Maximizing exposure therapy: An inhibitory learning approach. *Behaviour Research and Therapy, 58,* 10–23. https://doi.org/10.1016/j.brat.2014.04.006

Crawford, Jarret T.; Jussim, Lee; Madon, Stephanie; Cain, Thomas R.; & Stevens, Sean T. (2011). The use of stereotypes and individuating information in political person perception. *Personality and Social Psychology Bulletin.* https://doi.org/10.1177/0146167211399473

Crawford, Mike; Thana, Lavanya; Farquharson, Lorna; Palmer, Lucy; Hancock, Elizabeth; Bassett, Paul; Clarke, Jeremy; & Parry, Glenys. (2016). Patient experience of negative effects of psychological treatment: Results of a national survey. *British Journal of Psychiatry, 208,* 260–265. https://doi.org/10.1192/bjp.bp.114.162628

Creamer, MeLisa R.; Wang, Teresa W.; Babb, Stephen; Cullen, Karen A.; Day, Hannah; Willis, Gordon; Jamal, Ahmed; & Neff, Linda. (2019). Tobacco product use and cessation indicators among adults—United States, 2018. *Morbidity and Mortality Weekly Report, 68*(45), 1013–1019. https://doi.org/10.15585/mmwr.mm6845a2

Creedon, Timothy; & Lê Cook, Benjamin. (2016). Access to mental health care increased but not for substance use, while disparities remain. *Health Affairs, 35,* 1017–1021. https://doi.org/10.1377/hlthaff.2016.0098

Creswell, Cathy, & O'Connor, Thomas G. (2011). Interpretation bias and anxiety in childhood: Stability, specificity and longitudinal associations. *Behavioural and Cognitive Psychotherapy, 39*(2), 191–204.

Creswell, J. David. (2017). Mindfulness interventions. *Annual Review of Psychology, 68,* 491–516. https://doi.org/10.1146/annurev-psych-042716-051139

Creswell, J. David, & Lindsay, Emily. (2014). How does mindfulness training affect health? A mindfulness stress suffering account. *Current Directions in Psychological Science, 23,* 401–407. https://doi.org/10.1177/0963721414547415

Crews, Frederick. (2006). The unknown Freud. In Frederick Crews (Ed.), *Follies of the wise: Dissenting essays.* Shoemaker & Hoard.

Crisafulli, C.; Fabbri, C.; Porcelli, S.; Drago, A.; Spina, E.; De Ronchi, D.; & Serretti, A. (2011). Pharmacogenetics of antidepressants. *Frontiers in Pharmacology, 2,* 6. https://doi.org/10.3389/fphar.2011.00006

Critcher, Clayton R., & Dunning, David. (2009). Egocentric pattern projection: How implicit personality theories recapitulate the geography of the self. *Journal of Personality and Social Psychology, 97*(1), 1–16. https://doi.org/10.1037/a0015670

Crites, John O., & Taber, Brian J. (2002). Appraising adults' career capabilities: Ability, interest, and personality. In Spencer G. Niles (Ed.), *Adult career development: Concepts, issues and practices* (3rd ed., pp. 120–138). National Career Development Association.

Crossley, Nicolas A.; Constante, Miguel; McGuire, Philip; Power, Paddy. (2010). Efficacy of atypical v. typical antipsychotics in the treatment of early psychosis: Meta-analysis. *British Journal of Psychiatry, 196,* 434–439.

Crowell, Sheila E.; Beauchaine, Theodore P.; & Linehan, Marsha M. (2009). A biosocial developmental model of borderline personality disorder: Elaborating and extending Linehan's theory. *Psychological Bulletin, 135*(3), 495–510. https://doi.org/10.1037/a0015616

Csikszentmihalyi, Mihaly, & Nakamura, Jeanne. (2011). Positive psychology: Where did it come from, where is it going? In Kennon M. Sheldon, Todd B. Kashdan, & Michael F. Steger (Eds.), *Designing positive psychology: Taking stock and moving forward.* Oxford University Press. https://doi.org/10.1093/acprof:oso/9780195373585.003.0001

CTV News. (2013, November 10). Lady Gaga used therapy to cope with fame. *CTV News.* http://www.ctvnews.ca/entertainment/lady-gaga-used-therapy-to-cope-with-fame-1.1536107

Cuddy, Amy. (2012). Your body language may shape who you are. *TED.* TEDGlobal 2012, Edinburgh, Scotland. https://www.ted.com/talks/amy_cuddy_your_body_language_shapes_who_you_are

Cuddy, Amy J.; Schultz. S. Jack; & Fosse, Nathan E. (2018). P-curving a more comprehensive body of research on postural feedback reveals clear evidential value for power-posing effects: Reply to Simmons and Simonsohn (2017). *Psychological Science,* 1–11. https://doi.org/10.1177/0956797617746749

Cuijpers, Pim; Donker, Tara; Johansson, Robert; Mohr, David; Straten, Annemieke; & Andersson, Gerhard. (2011). Self-guided psychological treatment for depressive symptoms: A meta-analysis. *PLOS ONE, 6,* e21274. https://doi.org/10.1371/journal.pone.0021274

Cuijpers, Pim; Noma, Hisashi; Karyotaki, Eirini; Vinkers, Christiaan H.; Cipriani, Andrea; & Furukawa, Toshi A. (2020). A network meta-analysis of the effects of psychotherapies, pharmacotherapies and their combination in the treatment of adult depression. *World Psychiatry, 19*(1), 92–107. https://doi.org/10.1002/wps.20701

Cuijpers, Pim; Smit, Filip; Bohlmeijer, Ernst; Hollon, Steven D.; & Andersson, Gerhard. (2010). Efficacy of cognitive-behavioural therapy and other psychological treatments for adult depression: Meta-analytic study of publication bias. *British Journal of Psychiatry, 196,* 173–178. https://doi.org/10.1192/bjp.bp.109.066001

Cuijpers, Pim; van Straten, Annemieke; Andersson, Gerhard; & van Oppen, Patricia. (2008). Psychotherapy for depression in adults: A metaanalysis of comparative outcome studies. *Journal of Consulting and Clinical Psychology, 76*(6), 909–922.

Cuijpers, Pim; van Straten, Annemieke; Warmerdam, Lisanne; & Andersson, Gerhard. (2009). Psychotherapy versus the combination of psychotherapy and pharma-cotherapy in the treatment of depression: A meta-analysis. *Depression & Anxiety, 26*(3), 279–288. https://doi.org/10.1002/da.20519

Cullen, Karen A.; Gentzke, Andrea S.; Sawdey, Michael D.; Chang, Joanne T.; Anic, Gabriella M.; Wang, Teresa W.; Creamer, MeLisa R.; Jamal, Ahmed; Ambrose, Bridget K.; & King, Brian A. (2019). E-cigarette use among youth in the United States, 2019. *Journal of the American Medical Association, 322,* 2095–2103. https://doi.org/10.1001/jama.2019.18387

Cullen, Margaret. (2011). Mindfulness-based interventions: An emerging phenome-non. *Mindfulness, Mindfulness, 2,* 186–193. https://doi.org/10.1007/s12671-011-0058-1

Cullen, Michael J.; Hardison, Chaitra M.; & Sackett, Paul R. (2004). Using SAT–grade and ability–job performance relationships to test predictions derived from stereo-type threat theory. *Journal of Applied Psychology, 89*(2), 220–230. https://doi.org/10.1037/0021-9010.89.2.220

Cumming, Geoff. (2013). The new statistics: Why and how. *Psychological Science, 27,* 7–29. https://doi.org/10.1177/0956797613504966

Cunningham, Jacqueline L. (1997). Alfred Binet and the quest for testing higher men-tal functioning. In Wolfgang G. Bringmann, Helmut E. Lück, Rudolf Miller, & Charles E. Early (Eds.), *A pictorial history of psychology.* Quintessence.

Cunningham, William A., & Brosch, Tobias. (2012). Motivational salience: Amygdala tuning from traits, needs, values, and goals. *Current Directions in Psychological Science 21,* 54–59. https://doi.org/10.1177/0963721411430832

Curtin, Sally C.; & Hedegaard, Holly. (2019). *Suicide rates for females and males by race and ethnicity: United States, 1999 and 2017.* National Center for Health Statistics. https://www.cdc.gov/nchs/data/hestat/suicide/rates_1999_2017.htm

Cushen, P. J., Hackathorn, J., Vázquez Brown, M. D., Rife, S. C., Joyce, A. W., Smith, E. D., Bordieri, M. J., Anderson, P. W., Karlsson, M. E., & Daniels, J. (2019). "What's on the Test?": The Impact of Giving Students a Concept-List Study Guide. *Teaching of Psychology, 46*(2), 109-114. https://doi.org/10.1177/0098628319834171

Custers, Eugene J. F. M., & ten Cate, Olle T. J. (2011). Very long-term retention of basic science knowledge in doctors after graduation. *Medical Education, 45*(4), 422–430. https://doi.org/10.1111/j.1365-2923.2010.03889.x

Cuthbert, Bruce N.; & Insel, Thomas R. (2013). Toward the future of psychiatric diag-nosis: The seven pillars of RDoC. *BMC Medicine, 11,* 126. https://doi.org/10.1186/1741-7015-11-126

Cytowic, R. E. (1995). Synesthesia: Phenomenology and neuropsychology. *Psyche, 2*(10), 2-10.

Cytowic, Richard, & Eagleman, David M. (2009). *Wednesday is indigo blue: Discover-ing the brain of synesthesia.* MIT Press.

Czeisler, Charles A., & Gooley, Joshua J. (2007). Sleep and circadian rhythms in humans. Cold Spring Harbor Symposia on *Quantitative Biology, 72,* 579–597. https://doi.org/10.1101/sqb.2007.72.064

Czopp, Alexander; Kay, Aaron; & Cheryan, Sapna. (2015). Positive stereotypes are pervasive and powerful. *Perspectives on Psychological Science, 10,* 451–463. https://doi.org/10.1177/1745691615588091

D'Angelo, Maria, & Humphreys, Karin. (2015). Tip-of-the-tongue states reoccur because of implicit learning, but resolving them helps. *Cognition, 142,* 166–190. https://doi.org/10.1016/j.cognition.2015.05.019

D'Esposito, Mark, & Postle, Bradley R. (2015). The cognitive neuroscience of work-ing memory. *Annual Review of Psychology, 66,* 115–141. https://doi.org/10.1146/annurev-psych-010814-015031

Dabbs, James M.; & Hargrove, Marian F. (1997). Age, testosterone, and behavior among female prison inmates. *Psychosomatic Medicine, 59*(5), 477–480.

Daffner, Kirk R. (2010). Promoting successful cognitive aging: A comprehensive review. *Journal of Alzheimers Disease, 19*(4), 1101–1122. https://doi.org/10.3233/0T1L4201H5104272/JAD-2010-1306

Dagnall, Neil; Parker, Andrew; & Munley, Gary. (2007). Paranormal belief and rea-soning. *Personality and Individual Differences, 43*(6), 1406–1415.

Dalenberg, Constance J.; Paulson, Kelsey; Dell, Paul F.; & O'Neil, John A. (2009). The case for the study of 'normal' dissociation processes. In Paul F. Dell & John A. O'Neill (Eds.), *Dissociation and the dissociative disorders: DSM-V and beyond* (pp. 145–154). Routledge/Taylor & Francis Group.

Dalgard, Odd Steffen; Dowrick, Christopher; Lehtinen, Ville; Vazquez- Barquero, Jose Luis; Casey, Patricia; Wilkinson, Greg; Ayuso-Mateos, Jose Luis; Page, Helen; Dunn, Graham; & ODIN Group. (2006). Negative life events, social support and gender difference in depression: A multinational community survey with data from the ODIN study. *Social Psychiatry and Psychiatric Epidemiology, 41*(6), 444–451. https://doi.org/10.1007/s00127-006-0051-5

Damasio, Antonio R., & Carvalho, Gil B. (2013). The nature of feelings: Evolutionary and neurobiological origins. *Nature Reviews Neuroscience 14,* 143–152. https://doi.org/10.1038/nrn3403

Damasio, Hanna; Grabowski, T.; Frank, Randall; Galaburda, A. M.; & Damasio, A. R. (1994). The return of Phineas Gage: Clues about the brain from the skull of a famous patient. *Science, 264,* 1102–1105.

Damisch, Lysann; Stoberock, Barbara; & Mussweiler, Thomas. (2010). Keep your fingers crossed! How superstition improves performance. *Psychological Science, 21,* 1014–1020. https://doi.org/10.1177/0956797610372631

Dana, Jason; Dawes, Robyn; & Peterson, Nathanial. (2013). Belief in the unstruc-tured interview: The persistence of an illusion. *Judgment and Decision Making, 8*(5), 512–520.

Daniel, Stefanie; & Sonnentag, Sabine. (2016). Crossing the borders: The relation-ship between boundary management, work–family enrichment and job satisfaction. *International Journal of Human Resource Management, 27,* 407–426. https://doi.org/10.1080/09585192.2015.1020826

Darley, John. M., & Latané, Bibb. (1968). Bystander intervention in emergencies: Diffusion of responsibility. *Journal of Personality and Social Psychology, 8*(4p1), 377.

Dar-Nimrod, Ilan, & Heine, Steven J. (2011). Genetic essentialism: On the deceptive determinism of DNA. *Psychological Bulletin, 137,* 800–818. https://doi.org/10.1037/a0021860

Darwin, Charles R. (1859/1998). *On the origin of species by means of natural selection.* Modern Library.

Darwin, Charles R. (1871). *The descent of man, and selection in relation to sex* (Introduc-tions by John T. Bonner and Robert M. May). Princeton University Press.

Darwin, Charles R. (1872/1998). *The expression of the emotions in man and animals* (3rd ed.). Appleton.

Dause, Tyler J., & Kirby, Elizabeth D. (2019). Aging gracefully: Social engagement joins exercise and enrichment as a key lifestyle factor in resistance to age-related cognitive decline. *Neural Regeneration Research, 14*(1), 39–42. https://doi.org/10.4103/1673-5374.243698

Dautovich, Natalie D., & Gum, Amber M. (2011). Cognitive behavioral therapy for late-life depression and comorbid psychiatric conditions. In Kristen Sorocco, Kristen Hilliard, & Sean Lauderdale (Eds.), *Cognitive behavior therapy with older adults: Innova-tions across care settings.* Springer.

David, Daniel; Cotet, Carmen; Matu, Silviu; Mogoase, Cristina; & Stefan, Simona. (2017). 50 years of rational-emotive and cognitive-behavioral therapy: A systematic review and meta-analysis. *Journal of Clinical Psychology, 74*(3), 304–318. https://doi.org/10.1002/jclp.22514

David, Daniel; Cristea, Ioana; & Hofmann, Stefan G. (2018). Why cognitive behav-ioral therapy is the current gold standard of psychotherapy. *Frontiers in Psychiatry, 9,* 4. https://doi.org/10.3389/fpsyt.2018.00004

David, Daniel; Lynn, Steven Jay; & Ellis, Albert. (Eds.). (2009). *Rational and irratio-nal beliefs: Research, theory, and clinical practice.* Oxford University Press.

David, Daniel, & Montgomery, Guy H. (2011). The scientific status of psychother-apies: A new evaluative framework for evidence-based psychosocial interventions. *Clinical Psychology: Science and Practice, 18*(2), 89–99.

Davidai, Shai, & Gilovich, Thomas. (2018). The ideal road not taken: The self-discrepancies involved in people's most enduring regrets. *Emotion, 18*(3), 439–452. https://doi.org/10.1037/emo0000326

Davidson, Jonathan R. T.; Connor, Kathryn M.; & Zhang, Wei. (2009). Treatment of anxiety disorders. In Alan F. Schatzberg & Charles B. Nemeroff (Eds.), *The American Psychiatric Publishing textbook of psychopharmacology* (4th ed., pp. 1171–1199). American Psychiatric Publishing.

Davidson, Karina; Mostofsky, Elizabeth; & Whang, William. (2010). Don't worry, be happy: Positive affect and reduced 10-year incident coronary heart disease: The Canadian Nova Scotia Health Survey. *European Heart Journal, 31,* 1065–1070.

Davidson, Louise & Davenport, Richard. (2016, March). Exploding head syndrome. *Pulse.* http://www.pulsetoday.co.uk/clinical/clinical-specialties/neurology/obscure-diagnosis-exploding-head-syndrome/20031281.article

Davidson, Richard J., & Dahl, Cortland J. (2018). Outstanding challenges in scientific research on mindfulness and meditation. *Perspectives on Psychological Science, 13,* 62–65. https://doi.org/10.1177/1745691617718358

REFERENCES

...son, Richard J., & Kaszniak, Alfred W. (2015). Conceptual and methodological issues in research on mindfulness and meditation. *American Psychologist, 70*, 581–592. https://doi.org/10.1037/a0039512

Davidson, Richard J.; Ekman, Paul; Frijda, Nico H.; Goldsmith, H. H.; Kagan, Jerome; Lazarus, Richard; Panksepp, Jaak; Watson, David; & Clark, Lee Anna. (1994). How are emotions distinguished from moods, temperament, and other related affective constructs? In P. Ekman & R. J. Davidson (Eds.), *Series in affective science. The nature of emotion: Fundamental questions*, 49–96. Oxford University Press.

Davidson, Richard J.; Putnam, Katherine M.; & Larson, Christine L. (2000). Dysfunction in the neural circuitry of emotion regulation—a possible prelude to violence. *Science, 289*(5479), 591–594.

Davidson, Richard R. (2010). Commentary: Empirical explorations of mindfulness: Conceptual and methodological conundrums. *Emotion, 10*, 8–11.

Davies, Claire L., & Miron, Veronique E. (2018). Distinct origins, gene expression and function of microglia and monocyte-derived macrophages in CNS myelin injury and regeneration. *Clinical Immunology, 189*, 57–62. https://doi.org/10.1016/j.clim.2016.06.016

Davies, Rachael. (2018). Shekhar Saxena: making mental health a development priority. *The Lancet, 392*(10157), P1509. https://doi.org/10.1016/S0140-6736(18)32476-0

Davies, Robert D., & Davies, Madeline E. (2020). The (slow) depathologizing of gender incongruence. *The Journal of Nervous and Mental Disease, 208*(2), 152–154. https://doi.org/10.1097/NMD.0000000000001119

Davis, Catherine M., & Riley, Anthony L. (2010). Conditioned taste aversion learning. *Annals of the New York Academy of Sciences, 1187*(1), 247–275.

Davis, Deborah, & Loftus, Elizabeth F. (2007). Internal and external sources of misinformation in adult witness memory. In Michael P. Toglia, J. Don Read, & R. C. L. Lindsay (Eds.), *The handbook of eyewitness psychology. Vol. I: Memory for events.* Erlbaum.

Davis, Deborah, & Loftus, Elizabeth. (2009). The scientific status of "repressed" and "recovered" memories of sexual abuse. In J. L. Skeem, K. S. Douglas & S. O. Lilienfeld (Eds.), *Psychological science in the courtroom: Consensus and controversy* (pp. 55–79). Guilford.

Davis, J. I.; Senghas, A.; Brandt, F.; & Ochsner, K. N. (2010). The effects of BOTOX injections on emotional experience. *Emotion, 10*(3), 433–440. https://doi.org/10.1037/a0018690

Davis, Jake H., & Thompson, Evan. (2015). Developing attention and decreasing affective bias: Toward a cross-cultural cognitive science of mindfulness. In Kirk Warren Brown, J. David Creswell, & Richard M. Ryan (Eds.), *Handbook of mindfulness: Theory, research, and practice.* Guilford.

Dawkins, Lynne, & Corcoran, Olivia. (2014). Acute electronic cigarette use: Nicotine delivery and subjective effects in regular users. *Psychopharmacology, 231*, 401–407. https://doi.org/10.1007/s00213-013-3249-8

Dawson, Jennifer A. (2007). African conceptualisations of posttraumatic stress disorder and the impact of introducing Western concepts. *Psychology, Psychiatry, and Mental Health Monographs, 2*, 101–112.

De Brito, Stéphane A., & Hodgins, Sheilagh. (2009). Antisocial personality disorder. In Mary McMurran & Richard Howard (Eds.), *Personality, personality disorder and violence* (pp. 133–153). Wiley-Blackwell.

de Dreu, Carsten K. W.; Greer, Lindred L.; Van Kleef, Gerben A.; Shalvi, Shaul; & Michel J. J. Handgraaf. (2011). Oxytocin promotes human ethnocentrism. *Proceedings of the National Academy of Sciences, 8*, 1262–1266. https://doi.org/10.1073/pnas.1015316108

de Groot, Jasper H. B.; Semin, Gün R.; & Smeets, Monique A. M. (2014). I can see, hear, and smell your fear: Comparing olfactory and audiovisual media in fear communication. *Journal of Experimental Psychology: General, 143*(2), 825–834. https://doi.org/10.1037/a0033731

de Hooge, Ilona E.; Nelissen, Rob M. A.; Breugelmans, Seger M.; & Zeelenberg, Marcel. (2011). What is moral about guilt? Acting 'prosocially' at the disadvantage of others. *Journal of Personality and Social Psychology, 100*(3), 462–473.

de la Fuente-Fernández, Raúl. (2009). The placebo-reward hypothesis: Dopamine and the placebo effect. *Parkinsonism & Related Disorders, 15*(Suppl. 3), S72–S74.

de Montigny-Malenfant, Béatrice; Santerre, Marie-Ève; Bouchard, Sébastien; Sabourin, Stéphane; Lazaridès, Ariane; & Bélanger, Claude. (2013). Couples' negative interaction behaviors and borderline personality disorder. *American Journal of Family Therapy, 41*(3), 259–271. https://doi.org/10.1080/01926187.2012.688006

De Pauw, Sarah. (2016). Childhood personality and temperament. *Oxford Handbooks Online.* https://doi.org/10.1093/oxfordhb/9780199352487.013.21

De Raad, Boele; Barelds, Dick P. H.; Mlacic, Boris; Church, A. Timothy; Katigbak, Marcia S.; Ostendorf, Fritz; Hrebícková, Martina; Di Blas, Lisa; & Szirmák, Zsófia. (2010). Only three personality factors are fully replicable across languages: Reply to Ashton and Lee. *Journal of Research in Personality, 44*, 442–445. https://doi.org/10.1016/j.jrp.2010.05.005

De Vries, Annelou, L. C.; McGuire, Jennifer K.; Steensma, Thomas D.; Wagenaar, Eva C. F.; Doreleijers, Theo A. H.; & Cohen-Kettenis, Peggy T. (2014). Young adult psychological outcome after puberty suppression and gender reassignment. *Pediatrics, 134*(4), 696–704. https://doi.org/10.1542/peds.2013-2958

de Waal, Frans B. M. (1995, March). Bonobo sex and society. *Scientific American, 271*, 82–88.

de Waal, Frans B. M. (2007). Bonobos, left and right. *Skeptic, 13*(3), 64–66, 3p; (AN 27214210).

de Waal, Frans B. M. (2011). What is an animal emotion? *Annals of the New York Academy of Science, 1224, The Year In Cognitive Neuroscience,* 191–206. https://doi.org/10.1111/j.1749-6632.2010.05912.x

de Waal, Frans B. M., & Ferrari, Pier Francesco. (2010). Towards a bottom-up perspective on animal and human cognition. *Trends in Cognitive Sciences, (14)*5, 201–207. https://doi.org/10.1016/j.tics.2010.03.003

de Waal, Frans B. M., & Preston, Stephanie D. (2017). Mammalian empathy: Behavioural manifestations and neural basis. *Nature Reviews Neuroscience, 18*(8), 498–509. https://doi.org/10.1038/nrn.2017.72

Deal, David T., & Chartrand, Tanya L. (2011). Embodied emotion perception: Amplifying and dampening facial feedback modulates emotion perception accuracy. *Social Psychological and Personality Science, 2*, 673–678. https://doi.org/10.1177/1948550611406138

Dean, Kristy K.; & Koenig, Anne M. (2019). Cross-cultural differences and similarities in attribution. In Keith, Kenneth D. (Eds), *Cross-Cultural psychology: Contemporary themes and perspectives* (2nd ed., pp. 575–597). John Wiley & Sons. https://doi.org/10.1002/9781119519348.ch28

Deary, Ian J.; Johnson, Wendy; & Houlihan, Lorna M. (2009). Genetic foundations of human intelligence. *Human Genetics, 126*(1), 215–232.

Decety, Jean, & Cacioppo, John. (2010). Frontiers in human neuroscience: The golden triangle and beyond. *Perspectives on Psychological Science, 5*, 767–771. https://doi.org/10.1177/1745691610388780

Deci, Edward L., & Ryan, Richard M. (2000). The "what" and "why" of goal pursuits: Human needs and the self-determination of behavior. *Psychological Inquiry, 11*, 227–268.

Deci, Edward L., & Ryan, Richard M. (2012a). Motivation, personality, and development within embedded social contexts: An overview of self-determination theory. In Richard M. Ryan (Ed.), *The Oxford handbook of human motivation.* Oxford University Press.

Deci, Edward L., & Ryan, Richard M. (2012b). Self-determination theory. In Paul A. M. Van Lange, Arie Kruglanski, & E. Tory Higgins (Eds.), *Handbook of theories of social psychology* (Vol. 1). Sage.

Deffler, Samantha A.; Fox, Cassidy; Ogle, Christin M.; & Rubin, David C. (2016). All my children: The roles of semantic category and phonetic similarity in the misnaming of familiar individuals. *Memory and Cognition, 44*, 989–999. https://doi.org/10.3758/s13421-016-0613-z.

DeFreitas, Stacie Craft; Crone, Travis; DeLeon, Martha; & Ajayi, Anna. (2018). Perceived and personal mental health stigma in Latino and African American college students. *Frontiers in Public Health, 6*, 49. https://doi.org/10.3389/fpubh.2018.00049

DeKeyser, Robert (2000). The robustness of critical period effect in second language acquisition. *SSLA, 22*, 499–533.

Dekker, Sanne; Lee, Nikki C.; Howard-Jones, Paul; & Jolles, Jelle. (2012). Neuromyths in education: Prevalence and predictors of misconceptions among teachers. *Frontiers in Psychology, 3*, article 429. https://doi.org/10.3389/fpsyg.2012.00429

Del Giudice, Marco. (2016). The life history model of psychopathology explains the structure of psychiatric disorders and the emergence of the p factor: A simulation study. *Clinical Psychological Science, 4*(2), 299–311. https://doi.org/10.1177/2167702615583628

DeLamater, John, & Koepsel, Erica. (2014). Relationships and sexual expression in later life: A biopsychosocial perspective. *Sexual and Relationship Therapy, 30,* 37–59. https://doi.org/10.1080/14681994.2014.939506

DeLisi, Richard, & Staudt, Joanne. (1980). Individual differences in college students' performance on formal operations tasks. *Journal of Applied Developmental Psychology, 1*, 163–174.

Dell, Paul F., & O'Neil, John Allison (Eds.). (2009). *Dissociation and the dissociative disorders: DSM-V and beyond.* Routledge.

Dell'Osso, Bernardo; & Altamura, A. Carlo. (2014). Transcranial brain stimulation techniques for major depression: Should we extend TMS lessons to tDCS? *Clinical Practice & Epidemiology in Mental Health, 10*, 92–93.

Delman, Howard M.; Robinson, Delbert G.; & Kimmelblatt, Craig A. (2008). General psychiatric symptoms measures. In A. John Rush, Jr., Michael B. First, & Deborah Blacker (Eds.), *Handbook of psychiatric measures* (2nd ed., pp. 61–82). American Psychiatric Publishing.

Delmas, P.; Hao, J.; & Rodat-Despoix, L. (2011). Molecular mechanisms of mechanotransduction in mammalian sensory neurons. *Nature Reviews Neuroscience, 12*(3), 139–153.

DeLoache, Judy S., & LoBue, Vanessa. (2009). The narrow fellow in the grass: Human infants associate snakes and fear. *Developmental Science, 12*(1), 201–207. https://doi.org/10.1111/j.1467-7687.2008.00753.x

DeLongis, Anita; Coyne, James C.; Dakof, C.; Folkman, Susan; & Lazarus, Richard S. (1982). Relationship of daily hassles, uplifts, and major life events to health status. *Health Psychology, 1*, 119–136.

Demb, Jonathan B., & Brainard, David H. (2010). Neurons show their true colors. *Nature, 467*, 670–671.

Demerouti, Evangelia; Mostert, Karina; & Bakker, Arnold B. (2010). Burnout and work engagement: A thorough investigation of the independency of both constructs. *Journal of Occupational Health Psychology, 15*(3), 209–222.

Deneris, Evan S., & Wyler, Steven C. (2012). Serotonergic transcriptional networks and potential importance to mental health. *Nature Neuroscience, 15(4),* 519–27. https://doi.org/10.1038/nn.3039

Deng, Yaling; Chang, Lei; Yang, Meng; Huo, Meng; & Zhou, Renlai. (2016). Gender differences in emotional response: Inconsistency between experience and expressivity. *PLoS ONE, 11*(6). https://doi.org/10.1371/journal.pone.0158666

Denk, Franziska; McMahon, Stephen B.; & Tracey, Irene. (2014). Pain vulnerability: A neurobiological perspective. *Nature Neuroscience, 17,* 192–200. https://doi.org/10.1038/nn.3628

Dennis, J. Michael, & Li, Rick. (2007, October 10). More honest answers to Web surveys? A study of data collection mode effects. *Journal of Online Research10(7),* 1–15.

Dennis, Nancy A., & Cabeza, Roberto. (2008). Neuroimaging of healthy cognitive aging. In F. I. M. Craik and T. A. Salthouse (Eds.), *The handbook of aging and cognition* (pp. 1–54). Erlbaum.

Dennis, Tracy A., & O'Toole, Laura J. (2014). Mental health on the go: Effects of a gamified attention-bias modification mobile application in trait-anxious adults. *Clinical Psychological Science, 2*(5), 576–590. https://doi.org/10.1177/2167702614522228

Dennison, Kara. (2018, March 19). Growing up king: Coming-of-age in Black Panther. *The Sartorial Geek.* http://sartorialgeek.com/growing-up-king-coming-of-age-in-black -panther/

Denny, Dallas, & Pittman, Cathy. (2007). Gender identity: From dualism to diversity. In Mitchell S. Tepper & Annette Fuglsang Owens (Eds.). *Sexual Health. Vol 1: Psychological foundations. Praeger perspectives: Sex, love, and psychology.* Praeger/Greenwood.

DePaulo, Bella. (2014). A singles studies perspective on mount marriage. *Psychological Inquiry, 25*(1), 64-68. https://doi.org/10.1080/1047840X.2014.878173

DePaulo, Bella. (2017). Toward a positive psychology of single life. In D. S. Dunn (Ed.), *Positive Psychology: Established and Emerging Issues* (p. 251). Routledge/Taylor & Francis Group.

Derluyn, Ilse; Broekaert, Eric; Schuyten, Gilberte; & De Temmerman, Els. (2004). Post-traumatic stress in former Ugandan child soldiers. *Lancet, 363*(9412), 861–863. https://doi.org/10.1016/S0140-6736(04)15734-6

Derry, Heather; Fagundes, Christopher; Andridge, Rebecca; Glaser, Ronald; Malarkey, William; & Kiecolt-Glaser, Janice. (2013). Lower subjective social status exaggerates interleukin-6 responses to a laboratory stressor. *Psychoneuroendocrinology, 38,* 2676–2685. https://doi.org/10.1016/j.psyneuen.2013.06.026

DeRubeis, Robert J.; Siegle, Greg J.; & Hollon, Steven D. (2008). Cognitive therapy versus medication: Treatment outcomes and neural mechanisms. *Nature Reviews Neuroscience, 9*(10), 788–796. https://doi.org/10.1038/nrn2345

Desai, Abhilash K.; Grossberg, George T.; & Chibnall, John T. (2010). Healthy brain aging: A road map. *Clinics in Geriatric Medicine, 26*(1), 1–16.

Destin, Mesmin. (2019). Socioeconomic mobility, identity, and health: Experiences that influence immunology and implications for intervention. *American Psychologist, 74*(2), 207–217. https://doi.org/10.1037/amp0000297

Destin, Mesmin; Manzo, Vida M.; & Townsend, Sarah S. M. (2018). Thoughts about a successful future encourage action in the face of challenge. *Motivation and Emotion, 42,* 321–333. https://doi.org/10.1007/s11031-017-9664-0

Deutsch, Morton, & Gerard, Harold B. (1955). A study of normative and informational social influence upon individual judgment. *Journal of Abnormal and Social Psychology, 51,* 629–636.

DeValois, Russell L., & DeValois, Karen K. (1975). Neural coding of color. In Edward C. Carterette & Morton P. Friedman (Eds.), *Handbook of perception* (Vol. 5). Academic Press.

Devine, Patricia G. (2001). Implicit prejudice and stereotyping: How automatic are they? Introduction to the special section. *Journal of Personality and Social Psychology, 81,* 757–759.

Devine, Patricia, G.; Forscher, Patrick S.; Austin, Anthony J.; & Cox, William T.L. (2012). Long-term reduction in implicit race bias: A prejudice habit-breaking intervention. *Journal of Experimental Social Psychology, 48,* 1267–1278. https://doi.org/10.1016/j.jesp .2012.06.003

DeVos, George Alphonse. (1992). *Social cohesion and alienation: Minorities in the United States and Japan.* Westview Press.

DeVos, George Alphonse; & Wagatsuma, Hiroshi. (1967). *Japan's invisible race: Caste in culture and personality.* University of California Press.

Devulapalli, Krishnasastri K.; Talbott, Jason F.; Narvid, Jared; Gean, Alisa; Rehani, Bhavya; Manley, Geoffrey; Uzelac, Alan; Yuh, Esther; & Huang, Michael C. (2018). Utility of repeat head CT in patients with blunt traumatic brain injury presenting with small isolated falcine or tentorial subdural hematomas. *American Journal of Neuroradiology, 39*(4): 654–657. https://doi.org/10.3174/ajnr.A5557

DeWall, Nathan C., & Bushman, Brad J. (2009). Hot under the collar in a lukewarm environment: Words associated with hot temperature increase aggressive thoughts and hostile perceptions. *Journal of Experimental Social Psychology, 45*(4), 1045–1047. https://doi.org/10.1016/j.jesp.2009.05.003

DeYoung, Colin G. (2010). Toward a theory of the Big Five. *Psychological Inquiry, 21,* 26–33.

DeYoung, Colin G., & Gray, Jeremy R. (2009). Personality neuroscience: Explaining individual differences in affect, behavior, and cognition. In P. J. Corr & G. Matthews (Eds.), *Cambridge handbook of personality* (pp. 323–346). Cambridge University Press.

DeYoung, Colin G.; Hirsh, Jacob B.; Shane, Matthew S.; Papademetris, Xenophon; Rajeevan, Nallakkandi; & Gray, Jeremy R. (2010). Testing predictions from personality neuroscience: Brain structure and the big five. *Psychological Science, 21*(6), 820–828.

Dhabhar, Firdaus S. (2011). Effects of stress on immune function: Implications for immunoprotection and immunopathology. In Richard J. Contrada & Andrew Baum (Eds.), *The handbook of stress science: Biology, psychology, and health.* Springer.

Di Carlo, Francesco; Sociali, Antonella; Picutti, Elena; Pettorruso, Mauro; Vellante, Federica; Verrastr, Valeria; Martinotti, Giovanni; & di Giannantonio, Massimo. (2020). Telepsychiatry and other cutting-edge technologies in COVID-19 pandemic: Bridging the distance in mental health assistance. *The International Journal of Clinical Practice, 75*(1), e13716.. https://doi.org/10.1111/ijcp.13716

Diamantopoulou, Sofia; Verhulst, Frank C.; & van der Ende, Jan. (2010). Testing developmental pathways to antisocial personality problems. *Journal of Abnormal Child Psychology: An official publication of the International Society for Research in Child and Adolescent Psychopathology, 38*(1), 91–103. https://doi.org/10.1007/s10802-009-9348-7

Diamond, Adele. (2009). The interplay of biology and the environment broadly defined. *Developmental Psychology, 45,* 1–8, 361.

Diamond, Lisa M. (2016). Sexual fluidity in male and females. *Current Sexual Health Reports, 8,* 249–256. https://doi.org/10.1007/s11930-016-0092-z

Diamond, Solomon. (2001). Wundt before Leipzig. In Robert W. Rieber & David K. Robinson (Eds.), *Wilhelm Wundt in history: The making of a scientific psychology.* Kluwer Academic/Plenum Publishers.

Diano, Matteo; Tamietto, Marco; Celeghin, Aalessia; Weiskrantz, Lawrence; Tatu, Mona-Karina; Bagnis, Arianna; Duca, Sergio; Geminiani, Giuliano; Cauda, Franco; & Costa, Tommaso. (2017). Dynamic changes in amygdala psychophysiological connectivity reveal distinct neural networks for facial expressions of basic emotions. *Scientific Reports, 7,* 45260. https://doi.org/10.1038/srep45260

Diavolo, Lucy. (2017). Gender variance around the world over time. teenVOGUE. Retrieved from https://www.teenvogue.com/story/gender-variance-around-the-world

Díaz-García, Cristina; González-Moreno, Angela; & Sáez-Martínez, Francisco. (2013). Gender diversity within R&D teams: Its impact on radicalness of innovation. *Innovation: Management, Policy & Practice, 15,* 149–160. https://doi.org/10.5172/impp.2013.15.2.149

DiazGranados, Nancy; Ibrahim, Lobna; Brutsche, Nancy; Ameli, Rezvan; Henter, Ioline, D.; Luckenbaugh, David A.; Machado-Vieira, Rodrigo; & Zarate, Carlos A. (2010). Rapid resolution of suicidal ideation after a single infusion of an NMDA antagonist in patients with treatment-resistant major depressive disorder. *Journal of Clinical Psychiatry, 71*(12), 1605–1611. https://doi.org/10.4088/JCP.09m05327blu

Dick, Danielle M., & Rose, Richard J. (2002). Behavior genetics: What's new? What's next? *Current Directions in Psychological Science, 11,* 70–74.

Dick, Danielle M.; Agrawal, Arpana; Keller, Matthew C.; Adkins, Amy; Aliev, Fazil; Monroe, Scott; Hewitt, John K.; Kendler, Kenneth S.; & Sher, Kenneth J. (2015). Candidate gene–environment interaction research: Reflections and recommendations. *Perspectives on Psychological Science, 10,* 37–59. https://doi.org/10.1177/1745691614556682

Dickinson, Anthony, & Balleine, Bernard W. (2000). Causal cognition and goal-directed action. In Cecilia Heyes & Ludwig Huber (Eds.), *The evolution of cognition.* MIT Press.

DiDonato, Lisa, & Strough, JoNell. (2013). Do college students' gender-typed attitudes about occupations predict their real-world decisions? *Sex Roles, 68,* 536–549. https://doi.org/10.1007/s11199-013-0275-2

Didonna, Fabrizio. (Ed.). (2008). *Clinical handbook of mindfulness.* Springer.

Diener, Ed. (1980). Deindividuation: The absence of self-awareness and self-regulation in group members. In Paul B. Paulus (Ed.), *Psychology of group influence.* Erlbaum.

DiFeliceantonio, Alexandra G., & Small, Dana M. (2019). Dopamine and diet-induced obesity. *Nature Neuroscience, 22,* 1–2. https://doi.org/10.1038/s41593-018 -0304-0

Dijk, Derk-Jan; Duffy, Jeanne F.; Silva, Edward J.; Shanahan, Therasa L.; Boivin, Diane B.; & Czeisler, Charles A. (2012). Amplitude reduction and phase shifts of melatonin, cortisol and other circadian rhythms after a gradual advance of sleep and light exposure in humans. *PLOS ONE, 7,* Article e30037. https://doi.org/10.1371/journal. pone.0030037

Dijksterhuis, Ap, & Aarts, Henk. (2010). Goals, attention, and (un)consciousness. *Annual Review of Psychology, 61,* 467–90. https://doi.org10.1146/annurev.psych.093008 .100445

Dilawar, Arvind. (2018, October 26). Here's why UberEats couriers went on strike in the U.K. this month. *Pacific Standard.* https://psmag.com/news/uk-workers-challenge -uber-with-nationwide-strike

Dimidjian, Sona, & Hollon, Steven D. (2010). How would we know if psychotherapy were harmful? *American Psychologist, 65*(1), 21–33.

Dinsmoor, James A. (1992). Setting the record straight: The social views of B. F. Skinner. *American Psychologist, 47,* 1454–1463.

Dishion, Thomas J., & Tipsord, Jessica M. (2011). Peer contagion in child and adolescent social and emotional development. *Annual Review of Psychology, 62,* 189–214. https://doi.org/10.1146/annurev.psych.093008.100412

[...]an F., & Hokin, Lowell E. (1998, July 7). Lithium acutely inhibits and chronically up-regulates and stabilizes glutamate by presynaptic nerve endings in mouse cerebral cortex. *Proceedings of the National Academy of Sciences, 95*(14), 8363–8368. https://doi.org/10.1073/pnas.95.14.8363

Dobbin, Frank; & Kalev, Alexandra. (2015). Why firms need diversity managers and task forces. In Massimo Pilati, Hina Sheikh, Francesca Sperotti, & Chris Tilly (Eds.), *How global migration changes the workforce diversity equation* (pp. 170–198). Cambridge Scholars.

Dobson, Deborah, & Dobson, Keith. (2009). *Evidence-based practice of cognitive-behavioral therapy.* Guilford.

Doheny, Kathleen. (2021, February 6). Top challenges for managers in 2020. *SHRM. https://www.shrm.org/ResourcesAndTools/hr-topics/people-managers/pages/top-challenges-for-managers-in-2020.aspx*

Dohrenwend, Bruce P. (2006). Inventorying stressful life events as risk factors for psychopathology: Toward resolution of the problem of intracategory variability. *Psychological Bulletin, 132*(3), 477–495.

Doliński, Dariusz; Grzyb, Tomasz; Folwarczny, Michał; Grzybała, Patrycja; Kryzszycha, Karolina; Martynowska, Karolina; & Trojanowski, Jakub. (2017). Would you deliver an electric shock in 2015? Obedience in the experimental paradigm developed by Stanley Milgram in the 50 years following the original studies. *Social Psychological and Personality Science,* 1–7. https://doi.org/10.1177/1948550617693060

Domhoff, G. William. (2003). *The scientific study of dreams: Neural networks, cognitive development, and content analysis.* American Psychological Association.

Domhoff, G. William. (2005a). Refocusing the neurocognitive approach to dreams: A critique of the Hobson versus Solms debate. *Dreaming, 15,* 3–20.

Domhoff, G. William. (2005b). The content of dreams: Methodologic and theoretical implications. In Meir H. Kryger, Thomas Roth, & William C. Dement (Eds.), *Principles and practice of sleep medicine* (4th ed.). Elsevier Saunders.

Domhoff, G. William. (2007). Realistic simulation and bizarreness in dream content: Past findings and suggestions for future research. In Deirdre Barrett & Patrick McNamara (Eds.), *The new science of dreaming: Content, recall, and personality characteristics* (Vol. 2). Praeger Press.

Domhoff, G. William. (2010). The case for a cognitive theory of dreams. https://dreams.ucsc.edu/Library/domhoff_2010a.html

Domhoff, G. William. (2011). The neural substrate for dreaming: Is it a subsystem of the default network? *Consciousness and Cognition, 20*(4), 1163–1174. https://doi.org/10.1016/j.concog.2011.03.001

Dominus, Susan. (2015). The mixed-up brothers of Bogotá. *The New York Times.* http://www.nytimes.com/2015/07/12/magazine/the-mixed-up-brothers-of-bogota.html

Donaldson, Gail. (1996). Between practice and theory: Melanie Klein, Anna Freud and the development of child analysis. *Journal of the History of the Behavioral Sciences, 32*(2), 160–176. https://doi.org/10.1002/(SICI)1520-6696(199604)32:2<160::AID-JHBS4>3.0.CO;2-%23

Donnellan, M. Brent; Lucas, Richard E.; & Fleeson, William. (2009). Introduction to personality and assessment at age 40: Reflections on the legacy of the person-situation debate and the future of person-situation integration. *Journal of Research in Personality, 43,* 117–119. https://doi.org/10.1016/j.jrp.2009.02.010

Dorahy, Martin J.; Brand, Bethany L.; Sar, Vedat; Kruger, Christa; Stavropoulos, Pam; Martinez-Taboas, Alfonso; Lewis-Fernández, Roberto; & Middleton, Warwick. (2014). Dissociative identity disorder: An empirical overview. *Australian and New Zealand Journal of Psychiatry, 48*(5), 402–417. https://doi.org/10.1177/0004867414527523

Dornbusch, Sanford M.; Glasgow, Kristan L.; & Lin, I-Chun. (1996). The social structure of schooling. *Annual Review of Psychology, 47,* 401–429.

Doss, Brian D.; Rhoades, Galena K.; Stanley, Scott M.; & Markman, Howard J. (2009). The effect of the transition to parenthood on relationship quality: An 8-year prospective study. *Journal of Personality and Social Psychology, 96*(3), 601–619.

Doty, Richard L. (2014). Human pheromones: Do they exist? In Carla Mucignat-Caretta (Ed.). *Neurobiology of chemical communication.* CRC Press/Taylor & Francis.

Dovern, Anna; Fink, Gereon R.; Fromme, A. Christina B.; Wohlschläger, Afra M.; Weiss, Peter H.; & Riedl, Valentin. (2012). Intrinsic network connectivity reflects consistency of synesthetic experiences. Journal of *Neuroscience, 32,* 7614–7621. https://doi.org/10.1523/JNEUROSCI.5401-11.2012

Dovidio, John F. (1984). Helping behavior and altruism: An empirical and conceptual overview. *Advances in Experimental Social Psychology, 17,* 361–427.

Dovidio, John F., & Gaertner, Samuel L. (2010). Intergroup bias. In S. T. Fiske, D. T. Gilbert & G. Lindzey (Eds.), *Handbook of social psychology,* (Vol. 2, pp. 1084–1121). Wiley.

Dovidio, John F.; Piliavin, Jane Allyn; & Schroeder, David A. (2006). *The social psychology of prosocial behavior.* Erlbaum.

Drea, Christine M. (2015). D'scent of man: A comparative survey of primate chemosignaling in relation to sex. *Hormones and Behavior, 68,* 117–133. https://doi.org/10.1016/j.yhbeh.2014.08.001

Drescher, Jack, & Zucker, Kenneth J. (2006). *Position statement on therapies focused on attempts to change sexual orientation (reparative or conversion therapies).* Harrington Park/Haworth Press.

Drews, Frank A.; Pasupathi, Monisha; & Strayer, David L. (2008). Passenger and cell phone conversations in simulated driving. *Journal of Experimental Psychology: Applied, 14,* 398–400.

Driemeyer, Joenna; Boyke, Janina; Gaser, Christian; Büchel, Christian; & May, Arne. (2008). Changes in gray matter induced by learning—Revisited. *PLOS ONE, 3,* e2669.

Drimalla, Hanna; Landwehr, Niels; Hess, Ursula; & Dziobek, Isabel. (2019). From face to face: The contribution of facial mimicry to cognitive and emotional empathy. *Cognition and Emotion, 33*(8), 1672–1686. https://doi.org/10.1080/02699931.2019.1596068

Dror, Otniel E. (2014). The Cannon–Bard thalamic theory of emotions: A brief genealogy and reappraisal. Emotion Review, 6, 13–20. https://doi.org/10.1177/1754073913494898

Drouyer, Elise; Rieux, Camille; Hut, Roelof A.; & Cooper, Howard M. (2007). Responses of suprachiasmatic nucleus neurons to light and dark adaptation: Relative contributions of melanopsin and rod–cone inputs. *Journal of Neuroscience, 27*(36), 9623–9631.

Drum, David J.; Brownson, Chris; Denmark, Adryon Burton; & Smith, Shanna E. (2009). New data on the nature of suicidal crises in college students: Shifting the paradigm. *Professional Psychology: Research and Practice, 40,* 213-222. https://doi.org/10.1037/a00014465

Dryden, Windy. (2009). *How to think and intervene like an REBT therapist.* Routledge.

DSM-5. (2013). *Diagnostic and statistical manual of mental disorders* (Fifth edition). American Psychiatric Association.

Dubol, Manon; Trichard, Christian; Leroy, Claire; Sandu, Anca-Larisa; Rahim, Mehdi; Granger, Bernard; Tzavara, Eleni; Karila, Laurent; Martinot, Jean-Luc; & Artiges, Eric. (2018). Dopamine transporter and reward anticipation in a dimensional perspective: A multimodal brain imaging study. *Neuropsychopharmacology, 43,* 820–827. https://doi.org/10.1038/npp.2017.183

Duckworth, Angela L.; Gendler, Tamar Szabó; & Gross, James J. (2016). Situational strategies for self-control. *Perspectives on Psychological Science, 11,* 35–55. https://doi.org/10.1177/1745691615623247

Dudai, Yadin. (2004). The neurobiology of consolidations, or, How stable is the engram? *Annual Review of Psychology, 55,* 51–86.

Dudai, Yadin; Nalbantian, Suzanne; Matthews, Paul M.; & McClelland, James L. (2011). The Engram revisited: On the elusive permanence of memory. *The memory process: Neuroscientific and humanistic perspectives* (pp. 29–40). MIT Press.

Dueck, Al; Muchemi, Sheila; & Ng, Ed. (2018). Indigenous psychotherapies and religion: Moral vision and embodied communities. *Pastoral Psychology, 67,* 235–265 https://doi.org/10.1007/s11089-018-0802-8

Dufner, Michael; Arslan, Ruben C.; Hagemeyer, Birk; Schönbrodt, Felix D.; & Denissen, Jaap J. A. (2015). Affective contingencies in the affiliative domain: Physiological assessment, associations with the affiliation motive, and prediction of behavior. *Journal of Personality and Social Psychology, 109,* 662–676. https://doi10.1037/pspp0000025

Dukart, Juergen; Regen, Francesca; Kherif, Ferath; Colla, Michael; Bajbouj, Malek; Heuser, Isabella; Frackowiak, Richard S.; & Draganski, Bogdan. (2014). Electroconvulsive therapy-induced brain plasticity determines therapeutic outcome in mood disorders. *Proceedings of the National Academy of Sciences (PNAS),111*(3), 1156–1161. https://doi.org/10.1073/pnas.1321399111

Dulin, Patrick; Hanson, Bridget; & King, Diane. (2013). Perceived control as a longitudinal moderator of late-life stressors on depressive symptoms. *Aging & Mental Health, 17,* 718–723. https://doi.org/10.1080/13607863.2013.784956

Duman, Ronald S. (2018, March). The dazzling promise of ketamine. *Cerebrum,* 1–13. http://www.dana.org/Cerebrum/2018/The_Dazzling_Promise_of_Ketamine/

Duncker, Karl. (1945). On problem solving. *Psychological Monographs, 58*(Whole No. 270).

Dunham, Yarrow; Chen, Eva E.; & Banaji, Mahzarin R. (2013). Two signatures of implicit intergroup attitudes: Developmental invariance and early enculturation. *Psychological Science, 24*(6), 860–868.

Dunkel Schetter, Christine. (2011). Psychological science on pregnancy: Stress processes, biopsychosocial models, and emerging research issues. *Annual Review of Psychology, 62,* 531–58. https://doi.org/10.1146/annurev.psych.031809.130727

Dunlap, Glen; Iovannone, Rose; Wilson, Kelly J.; Kincaid, Donald K.; & Strain, Phillip. (2010). Prevent-teach-reinforce: A standardized model of school-based behavioral intervention. *Journal of Positive Behavior Interventions, 12*(1), 9–22.

Dunlosky, John; Rawson, Katherine A.; Marsh, Elizabeth J.; Nathan, Mitchell J.; & Willingham, Daniel T. (2013). Improving students' learning with effective learning techniques: Promising directions from cognitive and educational psychology. *Psychological Science in the Public Interest, 14*(1), 4–58. https://doi.org/10.1177/1529100612453266

Duque, Alvaro, & Spector, Reynold. (2019). A balanced evaluation of the evidence for adult neurogenesis in humans: implication for neuropsychiatric disorders. *Brain Structure and Function,* 224: 2281–2295. https://doi.org/10.1007/x00429-019-01917-6

Durwood, Lily; McLaughlin, Katie A.; & Olson, Kristina R. (2017). Mental health and self-worth in socially transitioned transgender youth. *Journal of the American Academy of Child and Adolescent Psychiatry, 56*(2), 116–123. https://doi.org/10.1016/j.jaac.2016.10.016

Dweck, Carol S., & Grant, H. (2008) Self-theories, goals, and meaning J. Shah (Ed.), *Handbook of motivation science* (pp. 405–416). Guilford.

Dweck, Carol S., & Leggett, Ellen L. (1988). A social-cognitive approach to motivation and personality. *Psychological Review, 95,* 256–273.

Eagly, Alice H. (1995). The science and politics of comparing women and men. *American Psychologist, 50,* 145–158.

Eagly, Alice H.; Ashmore, Richard. D.; Makhijani, Mona G.; & Longo, Laura C. (1991). What is beautiful is good, but . . . : A meta-analytic review of research on the physical attractiveness stereotype. *Psychological Bulletin, 110,* 109–128.

Eagly, Alice H.; Beall, Anne E.; & Sternberg, Robert J. (2004). *The psychology of gender* (2nd ed.). Guilford.

Eagly, Alice H; Nater, Christina; Miller, David I.; Kaufmann, Michèle; & Sczesny, Sabine. (2019). Gender stereotypes have changed: A cross-temporal meta-analysis of U.S. public opinion polls from 1946 to 2018. *American Psychologist, 75,* 301–315. https://doi.org/10.1037/amp0000494

Eagly, Alice H., & Wood, Wendy. (1999). The origins of sex differences in human behavior: Evolved dispositions versus social roles. *American Psychologist, 54*(6), 408–423. https://doi.org/10.1037/0003-066X.54.6.408

Eagly, Alice H.; & Wood, Wendy. (2011). Feminism and the evolution of sex differences and similarities. *Sex Roles, 64,* 758–767. https://doi.org/10.1007/s11199-011-9949-9

Eagly, Alice H., & Wood, Wendy. (2013). The nature–nurture debates: 25 years of challenges in understanding the psychology of gender. *Perspectives on Psychological Science, 8*(3), 340–357.

Earnest, David; Allen, David; & Landis, Ronald. (2011). Mechanisms linking realistic job previews with turnover: A meta-analytic path analysis. *Personnel Psychology, 64,* 865–897. https://doi.org/10.1111/j.1744-6570.2011.01230.x

Easton, Caroline J.; Mandel, Dolores; & Babuscio, Theresa. (2007). Differences in treatment outcome between male alcohol dependent offenders of domestic violence with and without positive drug screens. *Addictive Behaviors, 32,* 2151–2163.

Eatock, Ruth Anne, & Songer, Jocelyn E. (2011) Vestibular hair cells and afferents: Two channels for head motion signals. *Annual Review of Neuroscience. 34,* 501–534. https://doi.org/10.1146/annurev-neuro-061010-113710

Eaton, Asia A.; Saunders, Jessica F.; Jacobson, Ryan, K.; & West, Keon. (2020). How gender and race stereotypes impact the advancement of scholars in STEM: Professors' biased evaluations of physics and biology post-doctoral candidates. *Sex Roles, 82,*127–141. https://doi.org/10.1007/s11199-019-01052-w

Ebbinghaus, Hermann. (1885/1987). *Memory: A contribution to experimental psychology* (Henry A. Ruger & Clara E. Bussenius, Trans.). Dover.

Ebert, David; Zarski, Anna-Carlotta; Christensen, Helen; Stikkelbroek, Yvonne; Cuijpers, Pim; Berking, Matthias; & Riper, Heleen. (2015). Internet and computer-based cognitive behavioral therapy for anxiety and depression in youth: A meta-analysis of randomized controlled outcome trials. *PLOS ONE, 10,* e0119895. https://doi.org/10.1371/journal.pone.0119895

Eckholm, E. (2013). Court hears gay "conversion therapy" arguments. *The New York Times.* http://www.nytimes.com/2013/04/18/us/day-in-court-for-california-law-banning-conversion-therapy.html

Eddy, Melissa, & Bennett, Jessica. (2017). Germany must allow third gender category, court rules. *The New York Times.* https://www.nytimes.com/2017/11/08/world/europe/germany-third-gender-category-vanja.html

Edenfield, Teresa M., & Blumenthal, James A. (2011). Exercise and stress reduction. In Richard J. Contrada & Andrew Baum (Eds.), *The handbook of stress science: Biology, psychology, and health.* Springer.

Edlund, Mark J.; Fortney John C.; Reaves, Christina M.; Pyne, Jeffrey M.; & Mittal, Dinesh. (2008). Beliefs about depression and depression treatment among depressed veterans. *Medical Care, 46*(6), 581–589. https://doi.org/10.1097/MLR.0b013e3181648e46

Edmonds, Grant W.; Goldberg, Lewis R.; Hampson, Sarah E.; & Barckley, Maureen. (2013). Personality stability from childhood to midlife: Relating teachers' assessments in elementary school to observer- and self-ratings 40 years later. *Journal of Research in Personality, 47,* 505–513. https://doi.org/10.1016/j.jrp.2013.05.003

Edwards, Robert R.; Campbell, Claudia; Jamison, Robert N.; & Wiech, Katja. (2009). The neurobiological underpinnings of coping with pain. *Current Directions in Psychological Science, 18,* 237–241. https://doi.org/10.1111/j.1467-8721.2009.01643.x

Edwards, Timothy L.; Browne, Clare M.; Schoon, Adee; Cox, Christophe; & Poling, Alan. (2017). Animal olfactory detection of human diseases: Guidelines and systematic review. *Journal of Veterinary Behavior, 20,* 59–73. https://doi.org/10.1016/j.jveb.2017.05.002

Egan, Louisa C.; Santos, Laurie R.; & Bloom, Paul. (2007). The origins of cognitive dissonance: Evidence from children and monkeys. *Psychological Science, 18*(11), 978–983. https://doi.org/10.1111/j.1467-9280.2007.02012.x

Egan, Susan K., & Perry, David G. (2001). Gender identity: A multi-dimensional analysis with implications for psychosocial adjustment. *Developmental Psychology, 37,* 451–463.

Eichstaedt, Johannes C.; Schwartz, H. Andrew; Giorgi, Salvatore; Kern, Margaret L.; Park, Gregory; Sap, Maarten; Labarthe, Darwin R.; Larson, Emily E.; Seligman, Martin E. P.; & Ungar, Lyle H. (2018a, March 15). More evidence that Twitter language predicts heart disease: A response and replication. *PsyArXiv Preprints.* Retrieved from psyarxiv.com/p75ku. https://doi.org/10.17605/OSF.IO/P75KU

Eichstaedt, Johannes C.; Schwartz, Hansen A.; Kern, Margaret L.; Park, Gregory; Labarthe, Darwin R.; Merchant, Raina M.; Jha, Sneha; Agrawal, Megha; Dziurzynski, Lukasz; Sap, Maarten; Weeg, Christopher; Larson, Emily E.; Ungar Lyle H.; & Seligman, Martin E. P. (2015). Psychological language on Twitter predicts county-level heart disease mortality. *Psychological Science, 26,* 159–169. https://doi.org/10.1177/0956797614557867

Eichstaedt, Johannes C.; Smith, Robert J.; Merchant, Raina M.; Ungar, Lyle H.; Crutchley, Patrick; Preoṭiuc-Pietro, Daniel; Asch, David A.; & Schwartz, H. Andrew. (2018b). Facebook language predicts depression in medical records. *Proceedings of the National Academy of the United States of America, 115*(44), 11203–11208. https://doi.org/10.1073/pnas.1802331115

Eickenberg, Michael; Gramfort, Alexandre; Varoquaux, Gaël & Thiriona, Bertrand. (2017). Seeing it all: Convolutional network layers map the function of the human visual system. *Neuroimage, 152,* 184–194. https://hal.inria.fr/hal-01389809

Eisenberger, Naomi I. (2015). Social pain and the brain: Controversies, questions, and where to go from here. *Annual Review of Psychology, 66,* 601–629. https://doi.org/10.1146/annurev-psych-010213-115146

Eisenberger, Robert; Armeli, Stephen; & Pretz, Jean. (1998). Can the promise of reward increase creativity? *Journal of Personality and Social Psychology, 74,* 704–714.

Eisenstein, Michael. (2010). Taste: More than meets the mouth. *Nature, 468*(7327), S18–S19.

Ekman, Paul. (1980). *The face of man.* Garland.

Ekman, Paul. (1982). *Emotion in the human face* (2nd ed.). Cambridge University Press.

Ekman, Paul. (1992). Facial expressions of emotion: New findings, new questions. *Psychological Science, 3,* 34–38.

Ekman, Paul. (1993). Facial expression and emotion. *American Psychologist, 48,* 384–392.

Ekman, Paul. (1998). Afterword. In Charles Darwin (1872), *The expression of the emotions in man and animals.* Oxford University Press.

Ekman, Paul. (2003). *Emotions revealed: Recognizing faces and feelings to improve communication and emotional life.* Holt.

Ekman, Paul, & Cordaro, Daniel. (2011). What is meant by calling emotions basic? *Emotion Review, 3,* 364–370. https://doi.org/10.1177/1754073911410740

Ekman, Paul, & Davidson, Richard J. (1993). Voluntary smiling changes regional brain activity. *Psychological Science, 4,* 342–345.

Ekman, Paul, & Davidson, Richard J. (Eds.). (1994). Series in affective science. *The nature of emotion: Fundamental questions.* Oxford University Press.

Ekman, Paul, & Friesen, Wallace V. (1978). *Facial action coding system: A technique for the measurement of facial movement.* Consulting Psychologists Press.

Ekman, Paul; Friesen, Wallace V.; O'Sullivan, Maureen; Chan, Anthony; Diacoyanni-Tarlatzis, Irene; Heider, Karl; Krause, Rainer; LeCompte, William; Ayhan Pitcairn, Tom; Ricci-Bitti, Pio E.; Scherer, Klaus; Tomita, Masatoshi; & Tzavaras, Athanase. (1987). Universal and cultural differences in the judgments of facial expressions of emotion. *Journal of Personality and Social Psychology, 53*(4), 712–717. https://doi.org/10.1037/0022-3514.53.4.712

Ekman, Paul, & O'Sullivan, Maureen. (2006). From flawed self-assessment to blatant whoppers: The utility of voluntary and involuntary behavior in detecting deception. *Behavioral Sciences and the Law, 24,* 673–686.

Ekman, Paul; O'Sullivan, Maureen; & Frank, Mark G. (1999). A few can catch a liar. *Psychological Science, 10,* 263–266.

Ekwall, Anna Kristensson, & Hallberg, Ingalill Rahm. (2007). The association between caregiving satisfaction, difficulties and coping among older family caregivers. *Journal of Clinical Nursing, 16*(5), 832–844.

Elbogen, Eric B., & Johnson, Sally C. (2009). The intricate link between violence and mental disorder: Results from the national epidemiologic survey on alcohol and related conditions. *Archives of General Psychiatry, 66*(2),152–161. https://doi.org/10.1001/archgenpsychiatry.2008.537

Elfenbein, Hillary A., & Ambady, Nalini. (2002). On the universality and cultural specificity of emotion recognition: A meta-analysis. *Psychological Bulletin, 128*(2), 203–235. https://doi.org/10.1037/0033-2909.128.2.203

Elgar, Frank J., & Aitken, Nicole. (2010). Income inequality, trust and homicide in 33 countries. *European Journal of Public Health, 21*(2), 241–246. https://doi.org/10.1093/eurpub/ckq068

Elhai, Jon D.; Levine, Jason C.; & Hall, Brian J. (2019). The relationship between anxiety symptom severity and problematic smartphone use: A review of the literature and conceptual frameworks. *Journal of Anxiety Disorders, 62,* 45–52. https://doi.org/10.1016/j.janxdis.2018.11.005

Elischberger, Holger; Glazier, Jessica; Hill, Eric; & Verduzco-Baker, Lynn. (2016). "Boys don't cry"—or do they? Adult attitudes toward and beliefs about transgender youth. *Sex Roles, 75,* 197–214. https://do.org/10.1007/s11199-016-0609-y

Elkins, Gary; Marcus, Joel; & Bates, Jeff. (2006). Intensive hypnotherapy for smoking cessation: A prospective study. *International Journal of Clinical and Experimental Hypnosis, 54,* 303–315.

Elliot, Andrew J., & Dweck, Carol S. (1988). "Goals: An approach to motivation and achievement", *Journal of Personality and Social Psychology, 54,* 5–12.

Elliott, Robert, & Farber, Barry A. (2010). Carl Rogers: Idealistic pragmatist and psychotherapy research pioneer. In Louis G. Castonguay, Christopher J. Muran, Lynne Angus, Jeffrey A. Hayes, Nicholas Ladany, & Timothy Anderson (Eds.), *Bringing psychotherapy research to life: Understanding change through the work of leading clinical researchers* (pp. 17–27). American Psychological Association.

Ellis Island Museum. (1914). Immigrant intelligence testing example [Exhibit].

Ellis, Albert. (1991). *Reason and emotion in psychotherapy.* Carol.

Ellis, Albert. (1993). Reflections on rational-emotive therapy. *Journal of Consulting and Clinical Psychology, 61,* 199–201.

Ellis, Albert. (2013). *Better, deeper and more enduring brief therapy: The rational emotive behavior therapy approach.* Routledge.

Ellis, Albert, & Bernard, Michael E. (1985). What is rational-emotive therapy (RET)? In Albert Ellis & Michael E. Bernard (Eds.), *Clinical applications of rational-emotive therapy.* Plenum Press.

Ellis, Albert, & Ellis, Debbie Joffe. (2011). *Rational emotive therapy.* American Psychological Association.

Ellis, Albert; & Ellis, Debbie Joffe. (2019). *Rational emotive behavior therapy.* American Psychological Association.

Ellis, Bruce J. (2004). Timing of pubertal maturation in girls: An integrated life history approach. *Psychological Bulletin, 130,* 920–958.

Ellis, Bruce J., & Essex, Marilyn J. (2007). Family environments, adrenarche, and sexual maturation: A longitudinal test of a life history model. *Child Development, 78,* 1799–1817.

Ellis, Pete M., & Dronsfield, Alan T. (2013). Antabuse's diamond anniversary: Still sparkling on? *Drug and Alcohol Review, 32*(4), 342–344. https://doi.org/10.1111/dar.12018

Ellwardt, Lea; Van Tilburg, Theo; & Aartsen, Marja. (2015a). The mix matters: Complex personal networks relate to higher cognitive functioning in old age. *Social Science & Medicine, 125,* 107–115. https://doi.org/10.1016/j.socscimed.2014.05.007

Ellwardt, Lea; van Tilburg, Theo; Aartsen, Marja; Wittek, Rafael; & Steverink, Nardi. (2015b). Personal networks and mortality risk in older adults: A twenty-year longitudinal study. *PLOS ONE,10*(3), 11–13. https://doi.org/10.1371/journal.pone.0116731

Elson, Malte, & Ferguson, Christopher J. (2014a). Does https://doing media violence research make one aggressive? The ideological rigidity of social-cognitive theories of media violence and a response to Bushman and Huesmann (2013), Krahé (2013), and Warburton (2013). *European Psychologist, 19,* 68–75. https://doi.org/10.1027/1016-9040/a000185

Elson, Malte, & Ferguson, Christopher J. (2014b). Twenty-five years of research on violence in digital games and aggression: Empirical evidence, perspectives, and a debate gone astray. *European Psychologist, 19,* 33–46. https://doi.org/10.1027/1016-9040/a000147

Emmelkamp, Paul M. G. (2004). Behavior therapy with adults. In Michael J. Lambert (Ed.), *Bergin and Garfield's handbook of psychotherapy and behavior change* (5th ed.). Wiley.

Empson, Jacob. (2002). *Sleep and dreaming* (3rd ed.). Palgrave/St. Martin's Press.

Engber, Daniel. (2019). Unexpected clues emerge about why diets fail. *Nature Medicine, 25,* 1637–1639. https://doi.org/10.1038/s41591-019-0632-y

Enriori, Pablo J.; Evans, Anne E.; Sinnayah, Puspha; & Cowley, Michael A. (2006). Leptin resistance and obesity. *Obesity, 14*(Suppl. 5), 254S–258S.

Epel, Elissa S. (2009a). Psychological and metabolic stress: A recipe for accelerated cellular aging? *Hormones, 8,* 7–22.

Epel, Elissa S. (2009b). Telomeres in a life-span perspective: A new "psychobiomarker"? *Current Directions in Psychological Science, 18,* 6–10.

Epel, Elissa S.; Lin, Jue; Dhabhar, Firdaus S.; Wolkowitz, Owen M.; Puterman, E.; Karan, Lori; & Blackburn, Elizabeth H. (2010). Dynamics of telomerase activity in response to acute psychological stress. *Brain, Behavior, and Immunity, 24,* 531–539. https://doi.org/10.1016/j.bbi.2009.11.018

Epstein, Russell, & Kanwisher, Nancy. (1998). A cortical representation of the local visual environment. *Nature, 392,* 598–601. https://doi.org/10.1038/33402

Epstein, Seymour. (2010). The big five model: Grandiose ideas about surface traits as the foundation of a general theory of personality. *Psychological Inquiry, 21*(1), 34–39.

Erdelyi, Matthew Hugh. (2006a). The unified theory of repression. *Behavioral and Brain Sciences, 29,* 499–551. https://doi.org/10.1017/S0140525X06009113

Erdelyi, Matthew Hugh. (2006b). The return of the repressed. *Behavioral and Brain Sciences, 29*(5), 535–551. https://doi.org/10.1017/S0140525X06479115

Erdelyi, Matthew Hugh. (2010). The ups and downs of memory. *American Psychologist, 65,* 623–633.

Erickson, Kirk I.; Voss, Michelle W.; Prakash, Ruchika S.; Basak, Chandramallika; Szabo, Amanda; Chaddock, Laura; Kim, Jennifer S.; Heo, Susie; Alves, Heloisa; White, Siobhan M.; Wojcicki, Thomas R.; Mailey, Emily; Vieira, Victoria J.; Martin, Stephen A.; Pence, Brandt D.; Woods, Jeffrey A.; McAuley, Edward; & Kramer, Arthur F. (2011). Exercise training increases size of hippocampus and improves memory. *Proceedings of the National Academy of Sciences, 108*(7), 3017–3022. https://doi.org/10.1073/pnas.1015950108

Erikson, Erik H. (1964a). *Childhood and society* (Rev. ed.). Norton.

Erikson, Erik H. (1964b). *Insight and responsibility.* Norton.

Erikson, Erik H. (1968). *Identity: Youth and crisis.* Norton.

Erikson, Erik H.; Erikson, Joan M.; & Kivnick, Helen Q. (1986). *Vital involvement in old age: The experience of old age in our time.* Norton.

Eriksson, Peter S.; Perfilieva, Ekaterina; Björk-Eriksson, Thomas; Alborn, Ann-Marie; Nordborg, Claes; Peterson, Daniel A.; & Gage, Fred H. (1998). Neurogenesis in the adult hippocampus. *Nature Medicine, 4,* 1313–1317.

Eroglu, Cagla, & Barres, Ben A. (2010). Regulation of synaptic connectivity by glia. *Nature 468,* 223–231. https://doi.org/10.1038/nature09612

Ersoy, Betul; Balkan, C.; & Gunnay, T. (2005). The factors affecting the relation between the menarcheal age of mother and daughter. *Child: Care, Health and Development, 31,* 303–308.

Escartí, María Jose; de la Iglesia-Vayá, Mari; Martí-Bonmatí, Luis; Robles, Montserrat; Carbonell, Jose; Lull, Juan Jose; García-Martí, Gracián; Manjón, Jose Vicente; Aguilar, Eduardo Jesús; Aleman, André; & Sanjuán, Julio. (2010). Increased amygdala and parahippocampal gyrus activation in schizophrenic patients with auditory hallucinations: An fMRI study using independent component analysis. *Schizophrenia Research, 117,* 31–41. https://doi.org/10.1016/j.schres.2009.12.028

Eschweiler, Gerhard W.; Vonthein, Reinhard; & Bode, Ruediger. (2007). Clinical efficacy and cognitive side effects of bifrontal versus right unilateral electroconvulsive therapy (ECT): A short-term randomised controlled trial in pharmaco-resistant major depression. *Journal of Affective Disorders, 101*(1–3), 149–157. https://doi.org/10.1016/j.jad.2006.11.012

Esnaashari, Farbod. (2020, August 26). Paul George reveals he was dealing with depression in NBA bubble. *SI.* https://www.si.com/nba/clippers/news/paul-george-reveals-depression-and-anxiety-issues

Esses, Victoria M.; Jackson, Lynne M.; & Dovidio, John F. (2005). Instrumental relations among groups: Group competition, conflict, and prejudice. In John F. Dovidio, John, Peter Glick, & Laurie A. Rudman (Eds.), *On the nature of prejudice: Fifty years after Allport* (pp. 227–243). Blackwell.

Estes, William K., & Skinner, B. F. (1941). Some quantitative properties of anxiety. *Journal of Experimental Psychology, 29,* 390–400.

Evans, Carol, & Waring, Michael. (2012). Applications of styles in educational instruction and assessment. In Li-fang Zhang, Robert J. Sternberg, & Stephen Rayner (Eds.). *Handbook of intellectual styles: Preferences in cognition, learning, and thinking.* Springer.

Evans, Rand B. (1991). E. B. Titchener on scientific psychology and technology. In Gregory A. Kimble, Michael Wertheimer, & Charlotte White (Eds.), *Portraits of pioneers in psychology* (Vol. 1). American Psychological Association.

Evans, Rand B., & Rilling, Mark. (2000). How the challenge of explaining learning influenced the origins and development of John B. Watson's behaviorism. *American Journal of Psychology, 113,* 275–301.

Everaert, Jonas; Bronstein, Michael V.; Cannon, Tyrone D.; & Joormann, Jutta. (2018). Looking through tinted glasses: Depression and social anxiety are related to both interpretation biases and inflexible negative interpretations. *Clinical Psychological Science, 6*(4), 517–528. https://doi.org/10.1177/2167702617747968

Everett, Daniel L. (2005). Cultural constraints on grammar and cognition in Pirahã: Another look at the design features of human language. *Current Anthropology, 46,* 621–646.

Everett, Daniel L. (2008, January 19). Quoted in Liz Else & Lucy Middleton. "Interview: Out on a limb over language." *New Scientist, 2639,* 42–44.

Exner, John E., Jr. (2007). A new U.S. adult nonpatient sample. *Journal of Personality Assessment, 89*(Suppl. 1), S154–S158.

Exner, John E., Jr., & Erdberg, Philip. (2005). *The Rorschach: A comprehensive system* (3rd ed.). Wiley.

Exum, M. Lyn. (2006). Alcohol and aggression: An integration of findings from experimental studies. *Journal of Criminal Justice, 34*(2), 131–145.

Eysenck, Hans J. (1982). *Personality, genetics, and behavior.* Praeger.

Eysenck, Hans J. (1990). Biological dimensions of personality. In Lawrence A. Pervin (Ed.), *Handbook of personality: Theory and research.* Guilford.

Eysenck, Hans J., & Eysenck, Sybil B. G. (1975). *Psychoticism as a dimension of personality.* Hodder & Stoughton.

Faasse, Kate, & Petrie, Keith. (2016). From me to you: The effect of social modeling on treatment outcomes. *Current Directions in Psychological Science, 25,* 438–443. https://doi.org/10.1177/0963721416657316

Fabrigar, Leandre R., & Wegener, Duane T. (2010). Attitude structure. In R. F. Baumeister & E. J. Finkel (Eds.), *Advanced social psychology: The state of the science* (pp. 177–216). Oxford University Press.

Fagiolini, Andrea.; Forgione, Rocco; Maccari, Mauro; Cuomo, Alessandro; Morana, Benedetto; Dell'Osso, Mario C.; Pellegrini, Francesca; & Rossi, Alessandro. (2013). Prevalence, chronicity, burden, and borders of bipolar disorder. *Journal of Affective Disorders,148,* 161–169. https://doi.org/10.1016/j.jad.2013.02.001

Fagundes, Christopher, & Way, Baldwin. (2014). Early-life stress and adult inflammation. *Current Directions in Psychological Science, 23,* 277–283. https://doi.org/10.1177/0963721414535603

Fahs, Breanne. (2007). Second shifts and political awakenings: Divorce and the political socialization of middle-aged women. *Journal of Divorce & Remarriage, 47*(3–4), 43–66.

Fairchild, Amy L., & Bayer, Ronald. (2015). Smoke and fire over e-cigarettes. *Science, 347,* 375–376. https://doi.org/10.1126/science.126071

Fancher, Raymond E. (1973). *Psychoanalytic psychology: The development of Freud's thought.* Norton.

Fancher, Raymond E. (1996). *Pioneers of psychology* (3rd ed.). Norton.

Fang, Jiliang; Egorova, Natalia; Rong, Peijing; Liu, Jun; Hong, Yang; Fan, Yangyang; . . . & Kong, Jian. (2016). Early cortical biomarkers of longitudinal transcutaneous vagus nerve stimulation treatment success in depression. *NeuroImage: Clinical, 14,* 105–111. https://doi.org/10.1016/j.nicl.2016.12.016

Fanous, Ayman H.; van den Oord, Edwin J.; Riley, Brien P.; Aggen, Steven H.; Neale, Michael C.; O'Neill, F. Anthony; Walsh, Dermot; & Kendler, Kenneth S. (2005). Relationships between a high-risk haplotype in the *DTNBP1* (dysbindin) gene and clinical features of schizophrenia. *American Journal of Psychiatry, 162,* 1824–1832. https://doi.org/10.1176/appi.ajp.162.10.1824

Fantz, Robert L. (1961, May). The origin of form perception. *Scientific American, 204,* 66–72.

Fantz, Robert L.; Ordy, J. M.; & Udelf, M. S. (1962). Maturation of pattern vision in infants during the first six months. *Journal of Comparative and Physiological Psychology, 55,* 907–917.

Farb, Norman A. S.; Anderson, Adam K.; Mayberg, Helen; Bean, Jim; McKeon, Deborah; & Segal, Zindel V. (2010). Minding one's emotions: Mindfulness training alters the neural expression of sadness. *Emotion, 10*(1), 25–33. https://doi.org/10.1037/a0017151.supp

Farber, Barry A. (2007). On the enduring and substantial influence of Carl Rogers' not-quite necessary nor sufficient conditions. *Psychotherapy: Theory, Research, Practice, Training, 44,* 289–294.

Farber, Barry A., & Doolin, Erin M. (2011). Positive regard. *Psychotherapy, 48*(1), 58–64.

Farber, Jim. (2019). The new angry young men: Rockers who rail against 'toxic masculinity.' *The New York Times.* https://www.nytimes.com/2019/01/11/style/rock-masculinity-men-emotions.html

Farfel, Mark; DiGrande, Laura; Brackbill, Robert; Prann, Angela; Cone, James; Friedman, Stephen; Walker, Deborah J.; Pezeshki, Grant; Thomas, Pauline; Galea, Sandro; Williamson, David; Frieden, Thomas R.; & Thorpe, Lorna. (2008). An overview of 9/11 experiences and respiratory and mental health conditions among World Trade Center Health Registry enrollees. *Journal of Urban Health, 85*(6), 880–909. https://doi.org/10.1007/s11524-008-9317-4

Farmer, Caroline; Farrand, Paul; & O'Mahen, Heather. (2012). 'I am not a depressed person': How identity conflict affects help-seeking rates for major depressive disorder. *BMC Psychiatry, 12,* 164. https://doi.org/10.1186/1471-244X-12-164

Farr, Rachel. (2017). Does parental sexual orientation matter? A longitudinal follow-up of adoptive families with school-age children. *Developmental Psychology, 53,* 252–264. https://doi.org/10.1037/dev0000228

Farrell, Lynn; & McHugh, Louise. (2017). Examining gender-STEM bias among STEM and non-STEM students using the Implicit Relational Assessment Procedure (IRAP). *Journal of Contextual Behavioral Science, 6,* 80–90. https://doi.org/10.1016/j.jcbs.2017.02.001

Farrell, Meagan T., & Abrams, Lise. (2011). Tip-of-the-tongue states reveal age differences in the syllable frequency effect. *Journal of Experimental Psychology: Learning, Memory, and Cognition, 37*(1), 277–285.

Farris-Trimble, Ashley; McMurray, Bob; Cigrand, Nicole; Tomblin, J. Bruce. (2014). The process of spoken word recognition in the face of signal degradation. *Journal of Experimental Psychology: Human Perception and Performance, 40,* 308–327. https://doi.org/10.1037/a0034353

Fasfous, Ahmed F.; Peralta-Ramirez, Isabel; & Pérez-Garcia, Miguel. (2013). Symptoms of PTSD among children living in war zones in same cultural context and different situations. *Journal of Muslim Mental Health, 7*(2), 47–61. https://doi.org/10.3998/jmmh.10381607.0007.203

Fatfouta, Ramzi. (2019). Facets of narcissism and leadership: A tale of Dr. Jekyll and Mr. Hyde? *Human Resource Management Review, 29,* 1-12. https://doi.org/10.1016/j.hrmr.2018.10.002

Fausey, Caitlin M.; Long, Bria L.; Inamori, A.; & Boroditsky, L. (2010). Constructing agency: The role of language. *Frontiers in Psychology,1,* 162. https://doi.org/10.3389/fpsyg.2010.00162

Fazel, Seena; Langstrom, Niklas; Hjern, Anders; Grann, Martin; & Lichtenstein, Paul. (2009). Schizophrenia, substance abuse, and violent crime. *Journal of the American Medical Association, 301*(19), 2016–2023. https://doi.org/10.1001/jama.2009.675

Feeney, Brooke, & Collins, Nancy. (2014). A new look at social support: A theoretical perspective on thriving through relationships. *Personality and Social Psychology Review,19*(2), 113–147. https://doi.org/10.1177/1088868314544222

Feinstein, Anthony; Audet, Blair; & Waknine, Elizabeth. (2014). Witnessing images of extreme violence: A psychological study of journalists in the newsroom. *Journal of the Royal Society of Medicine Open, 5*(8), 1–7. https://doi.org/10.1177/2054270414533323

Feldman Barrett, Lisa, & Russell, James A. (1999). The structure of current affect: Controversies and emerging consensus. *Current Directions in Psychological Science, 8,* 10–14.

Feldt, Ronald C. (2008). Development of a brief measure of college stress: The College Student Stress Scale. *Psychological Reports, 102,* 855–860.

Feliciano, Leilani, & Areán, Patricia A. (2007). Mood disorders: Depressive disorders. In Michel Hersen, Samuel M. Turner, & Deborah C. Beidel (Eds.), *Adult psychopathology and diagnosis* (5th ed., pp. 286–316). Wiley.

Felsberg, Eric J. (2004). Conducting job analyses and drafting lawful job descriptions under the Americans with Disabilities Act. *Employment Relations Today, 31,* 91–93.

Ferguson, Christopher J. (2010). Genetic contributions to antisocial personality and behavior: A meta-analytic review from an evolutionary perspective. *Journal of Social Psychology,150*(2), 160–180.

Ferguson, Christopher J. (2014). Is video game violence bad? *The Psychologist, 27,* 324–327.

Ferguson, Christopher J. (2018). Violent video games, sexist video games, and the law: Why can't we find effects? Annual Review of Law and Social Science, 14, 411-426. https://doi.org/10.1146/annurev-lawsocsci-101317-031036

Ferguson, Christopher J., & Beaver, Kevin M. (2009). Natural born killers: The genetic origins of extreme violence. *Aggression and Violent Behavior, 14,* 286–294. https://doi.org/10.1016/j.avb.2009.03.005

Ferguson, Christopher J., & Kilbourn, John. (2009). The public health risks of media violence: A meta-analytic review. *Journal of Pediatrics, 154,* 759–763.

Ferguson, Christopher J., & Konijn, Elly A. (2015, January 19). She said/he said: A peaceful debate on video game violence. *Psychology of Popular Media Culture.* https://doi.org/10.1037/ppm0000064

Ferguson, Christopher J., & Wang, John C. K. (2019). Aggressive video games are not a risk factor for future aggression in youth: A longitudinal study. *Journal of Youth and Adolescence, 48,* 1439–1456. https://doi.org/10.1007/s10964-019-01069-0

Ferguson, Melissa J.; Mann, Thomas C.; Cone, Jeremy; & Shen, Xi. (2019). When and how implicit first impressions can be updated. *Current Directions in Psychological Science, 28*(4), 331–336. https://doi.org/10.1177/096372141983520

Ferrari, Alize J.; Somerville, Adele J.; Baxter, Amanda J.; Norman, Rosana; Patten, Scott B.; Vos, Theo; & Whiteford, Harvey A. (2013). Global variation in the prevalence and incidence of major depressive disorder: A systematic review of the epidemiological literature. *Psychological Medicine, 43,* 471–481. https://doi.org/10.1017/S0033291712001511

Ferrario, Silvia R.; Panzeri, Anna; Cerutti, Paola; & Sacco, Daniela. (2021). The psychological experience and intervention in post-acute COVID-19 inpatients. *Neuropsychiatric Disease and Treatment, 17,* 413–422. https://doi.org/10.2147/NDT.S283558

Feshbach, Seymour, & Tangney, June. (2008). Television viewing and aggression:Some alternative perspectives. *Perspectives on Psychological Sciences, 3,* 387–389.

Festinger, Leon. (1957). *A theory of cognitive dissonance.* Stanford University Press.

Festinger, Leon. (1962). Cognitive dissonance. *Scientific American, 207,* 93–99. (Reprinted in *Contemporary psychology: readings from* Scientific American, 1971, Freeman.)

Festinger, Leon, & Carlsmith, J. Merrill. (1959). Cognitive consequences of forced compliance. *Journal of Abnormal and Social Psychology, 58,* 203–210.

Fezehai, Malin. (2019, May 30). In Turkey, keeping a language of whistles alive. *The New York Times.* https://www.nytimes.com/2019/05/30/arts/in-turkey-keeping-alive-a-language-of-whistles.html?smid=nytcore-ios-share

Field, Clinton E.; Nash, Heather M.; Handwerk, Michael L.; & Friman, Patrick C. (2004). A modification of the token economy for nonresponsive youth in family-style residential care. *Behavior Modification, 28,* 438–457.

Field, Tiffany. (2009). *Complementary and alternative therapies research.* American Psychological Association.

Fielder, Robyn L., & Carey, Michael P. (2010). Prevalence and characteristics of sexual hookups among first-semester female college students. *Journal of Sex & Marital Therapy, 36*(4), 346–359.

Fields, R. Douglas. (2013). Map the other brain. *Nature, 501,* 25–27.

Fieser, Ezra. (2019, August 28). Yogurt billionaire's solution to world refugee crisis: Hire them. *Bloomberg.* https://www.bloomberg.com/news/articles/2019-08-28/yogurt-billionaire-s-solution-to-world-refugee-crisis-hire-them

Filippello, Pina; Buzzai, Caterina; Costa, Sebastino; Orecchio Susanna; & Sorrenti, Luana. (2018). Teaching style and academic achievement: The mediating role of learned helplessness and mastery orientation. *Psychology in the Schools, 57*(1), 5–16. https://doi.org/10.1002/pits.22315

FinancesOnline. (2021). Number of freelancers in the US 2021/2022: Demographics, platforms, and trends. https://financesonline.com/number-of-freelancers-in-the-us/

Fine, Ione. (2002). Quoted in *The man who learnt to see.* BB2 Documentary.

Fine, Saul, & Pirak, Merav. (2016). Faking fast and slow: Within-person response time latencies for measuring faking in personnel testing. *Journal of Business Psychology, 31,* 51–64. https://doi.org/10.1007/s10869-015-9398-5

Finger, Stanley. (2010). The birth of localization theory. *Handbook of Clinical Neurology, 95,* 117–128. https://doi.org/10.1016/S0072-9752(08)02110-6

Fink, Max. (2009). *Electroconvulsive therapy: A guide for professionals & their patients.* Oxford University Press.

Finkel, Eli J. (2017). *The all-or-nothing marriage: How the best marriages work.* Random House.

Finkel, Eli J., & Baumeister, Roy F. (2010). Attraction and rejection. In R. F. Baumeister & E. J. Finkel (Eds.), *Advanced social psychology: The state of the science.* Oxford University Press.

Finkel, Eli J.; Cheung, Elaine O.; Emery, Lydia F.; Carswell, Kathleen L.; & Larson, Grace M. (2015). The suffocation model: Why marriage in America is becoming an all-or-nothing institution. *Current Directions in Psychological Science, 24*(3), 238-244. https://doi.org/10.1177/0963721415569274

Finkel, Eli J.; Slotter, Erica B.; Luchies, Laura B.; Walton, Gregory M.; & Gross, James J. (2013). A brief intervention to promote conflict reappraisal preserves marital quality over time. *Psychological Science, 24,* 1595–1601. https://doi.org/10.1177/0956797612474938

Finley, Jason R.; Benjamin, Aaron S.; & McCarley, Jason S. (2014). Metacognition of multitasking: How well do we predict the costs of divided attention? *Journal of Experimental Psychology: Applied, 20,* 158–165. https://doi.org/10.1037/xap0000010

Finnigan, Katherine M., & Corker, Katherine S. (2016). Do performance avoidance goals moderate the effect of different types of stereotype threat on women's math performance? *Journal of Research in Personality, 63,* 36–43. https://doi.org/10.1016/j.jrp.2016.05.009

Fischer, Agneta, & LaFrance, Marianne. (2015). What drives the smile and the tear: Why women are more emotionally expressive than men. *Emotion Review, 7,* 22–29. https://doi.org/10.1177/1754073914544406

Fischer, Agneta H.; Rodriguez-Mosquera, Patricia M.; van Vianen, Annelies E. M.; & Manstead, Antony S. R. (2004). Gender and culture differences in emotion. *Emotion, 4,* 87–94.

Fischer, Peter; Greitemeyer, Tobias; Pollozek, Fabian; & Frey, Dieter. (2006). The unresponsive bystander: Are bystanders more responsive in dangerous emergencies? *European Journal of Social Psychology, 36*(2), 267–278.

Fischer, Peter; Krueger, Joachim I.; Greitemeyer, Tobias; Vogrincic, Claudia; Kastenmüller, Andreas; Frey, Dieter; Heene, Moritz; Wicher, Magdalena; & Kainbacher, Martina. (2011). The bystander-effect: A meta-analytic review on bystander intervention in dangerous and non-dangerous emergencies. *Psychological Bulletin, 137*(4), 517–537. https://doi.org/10.1037/a0023304

Fishbach, Ayelet, & Converse, Benjamin A. (2010). Walking the line between goals and temptations: Asymmetric effects of counteractive control. In Ran R. Hassin, Kevin N. Ochsner, & Yaacov Trope (Eds.), *Self control in society, mind, and brain* (pp. 389–407). Oxford University Press.

Fisher, Celia B. (2009). *Decoding the ethics code: A practical guide for psychologists* (2nd ed.). Sage.

Fisher, Celia B., & Vacanti-Shova, Karyn. (2012). The responsible conduct of psychological research: An overview of ethical principles, APA Ethics Code standards, and federal regulations. In Samuel J. Knapp, Michael C. Gottlieb, Mitchell M. Handelsman, Leon D. VandeCreek (Eds.), *APA handbook of ethics in psychology, Vol 2: Practice, teaching, and research.* American Psychological Association. https://doi.org/10.1037/13272-016

Fisher, Helen L.; Moffitt, Terrie; Houts, Renate M.; Belsky, Daniel W.; Arseneault, Louise; & Caspi, Avshalom. (2012). Bullying victimization and risk of self harm in early adolescence: Longitude cohort study. *British Medical Journal, 344,* 1–9. https://doi.org/10.1136/bmj.e2683

Fisher, Terri D.; Moore, Zachary T.; & Pittenger, Mary-Jo. (2012). Sex on the brain? An examination of frequency of sexual cognitions as a function of gender, erotophilia, and social desirability. *Journal of Sex Research, 49*(1), 69–77.

Fiske, Susan T. (2017). Prejudices in cultural contexts: Shared stereotypes (gender, age) versus variable stereotypes (race, ethnicity, religion). *Perspectives on Psychological Science, 12,* 791–799. https://doi.org/10.1177/1745691617708204

Fiske, Susan T., & Ruscher, Janet B. (1993). Negative interdependence and prejudice: Whence the affect? In Diane M. Mackie & David L. Hamilton (Eds.), *Affect, cognition, and stereotyping: Interactive processes in group perception.* Academic Press.

Fitzsimons, Billi. (2020, March 5). The haunting true story of Hannah Upp, the woman who disappeared three times. *MSN.* https://www.msn.com/en-nz/news/world/the-haunting-true-story-of-hannah-upp-the-woman-who-disappeared-three-times/ar-BB13wi5K

Fivush, Robyn. (2011). The development of autobiographical memory. *Annual Review of Psychology, 62*(1), 559–582. https://doi.org/10.1146/annurev.psych.121208.131702

Fletcher, David, & Sarkar, Mustafa. (2013). Psychological resilience: A review and critique of definitions, concepts and theory. *European Psychologist,18,* 12–23. https://doi.org/10.1027/1016-9040/a000124

Flor, Herta. (2014). Psychological pain interventions and neurophysiology: Implications for a mechanism-based approach. *American Psychologist, 69,* 188–196. https://doi.org/10.1037/a0035254

Flore, Paulette C.; Mulder, Joris; & Wicherts, Jelte M. (2019). The influence of gender stereotype threat on mathematics test scores of Dutch high school students: A registered report. *Comprehensive Results in Social Psychology, 3*(2), 140-174. https://doi.org/10.1080/23743603.2018.1559647

Flore, Paulette C., & Wicherts, Jelte M. (2015). Does stereotype threat influence performance of girls in stereotyped domains? A meta-analysis. *Journal of School Psychology, 53,* 25–44. https://doi.org/10.1016/j.jsp.2014.10.002

Flores, Andrew; Herman, Jody; Gates, Gary; & Brown, Taylor. (2016). *How many adults identify as transgender in the United States?* The Williams Institute. Retrieved from https://williamsinstitute.law.ucla.edu/publications/trans-adults-united-states/

Flynn, James R. (2007a). Solving the IQ puzzle. *Scientific American Mind, 18,* 24–31.

Flynn, James R. (2007b). What lies behind g(I) and g(ID). *European Journal of Personality, 21,* 722–724.

Flynn, James R. (2009). *What is intelligence? Beyond the Flynn effect.* Cambridge University Press.

Foa, Edna B.; Gillihan, Seth J.; & Bryant, Richard A. (2013). Challenges and successes in dissemination of evidence-based treatments for posttraumatic stress: Lessons learned from prolonged exposure therapy for PTSD. *Psychological Science in the Public Interest, 14*(2), 65–111. https://doi.org/10.1177/1529100612468841

Foer, Joshua. (2011). *Moonwalking with Einstein: The art and science of remembering everything.* Penguin.

Foland-Ross, Lara C.; Hamilton, Paul; Joormann, Jutta; Berman, Marc G.; Jonides, John; & Gotlib, Ian H. (2013). The neural basis of difficulties disengaging from negative irrelevant material in major depression. *Psychological Science, 24*(3), 334–44. https://doi.org/10.1177/0956797612457380

Folkman, Susan, & Lazarus, Richard S. (1991). Coping and emotion. In Alan Monat & Richard S. Lazarus (Eds.), *Stress and coping: An anthology* (3rd ed.). Columbia University Press.

Folkman, Susan, & Moskowitz, Judith Tedlie. (2004). Coping: Pitfalls and promise. *Annual Review of Psychology, 55,* 745–774.

Folkman, Susan, & Moskowitz, Judith Tedlie. (2007). Positive affect and meaning-focused coping during significant psychological stress. In Miles Hewstone, Henk A. W. Schut, John B. F. De Wit, Kees Van Den Bos, & Margaret S. Stroebe (Eds.), *The scope of social psychology: Theory and applications* (pp. 193–208). Psychology Press.

Folkman, Susan. (2009). Commentary on the special section "Theory-based approaches to stress and coping": Questions, answers, issues, and next steps in stress and coping research. *European Psychologist, 14*(1), 72–77.

Fontanella, Lara; Maretti, Mara; & Sarra, Annalina. (2014). Gender fluidity across the world: A multilevel item response theory approach. *Quality and Quantity, 48,* 2553–2568. https://doi.org/10.1007/s11135-013-9907-4

Foote, Brad; Smolin, Yvette; & Kaplan, Margaret. (2006). Prevalence of dissociative disorders in psychiatric outpatients. *American Journal of Psychiatry, 163*(4), 623–629. https://doi.org/10.1176/appi.ajp.163.4.623

Ford, Elizabeth; Curlewis, Keegan; Wongkoblap, Akkapon; & Curcin, Vasa. (2019). Public opinions on using social media content to identify users with depression and target mental health care advertising: mixed methods survey. *JMIR Mental Health, 6*(11) e12942. https://doi.org/10.2196/12942

Ford, Judith M.; Roach, Brian J.; Jorgensen, Kasper W.; Turner, Jessica A.; Brown, Gregory G.; Notestine, Randy; Bischoff-Grethe, Amanda; Greve, Douglas; Wible, Cynthia; Lauriello, John; Belger, Aysenil; Mueller, Byron A.; Calhoun, Vincent; Preda, A.; Keator, David; O'Leary, Daniel S.; Lim, Kelvin O.; Glover, Gary; Potkin, Steven G.; & Mathalon, Daniel H. (2009). Tuning in to the voices: A multisite fMRI study of auditory hallucinations. *Schizophrenia Bulletin, 35*(1), 58–66. https://doi.org/10.1093/schbul/sbn140

Forgas, Joseph P.; Dunn, Elizabeth; & Granland, Stacey. (2008). Are you being served . . . ? An unobtrusive experiment of affective influences on helping in a department store. *European Journal of Social Psychology, 38,* 333–342.

Foschi, Renato, & Cicciola, Elisabetta. (2006). Politics and naturalism in the 20th century psychology of Alfred Binet. *History of Psychology, 9,* 267–289.

Fosco, Gregory M.; Stormshak, Elizabeth A.; Dishion, Thomas J.; & Winter, Charlotte. (2012). Family relationships and parental monitoring during middle school as predictors of early adolescent problem behavior. *Journal of Clinical Child and Adolescent Psychology, 41,* 202–213. https://doi.org/10.1080/15374416.2012.651989

Fosnaugh, Jessica; Geers, Andrew L.; & Wellman, Justin A. (2009). Giving off a rosy glow: The manipulation of an optimistic orientation. *Journal of Social Psychology, 149*(3), 249–263.

Fosslien, Liz, & Duffy, Molly W. (2020, April 29). How to combat Zoom fatigue. *Harvard Business Review.* https://hbr.org/2020/04/how-to-combat-zoom-fatigue

Fotuhi, Omid; Fong, Geoffrey T.; Zanna, Mark P.; Borland, Ron; Yong, Hua H.; & Cummings, K. Michael. (2013). Patterns of cognitive dissonance-reducing beliefs among smokers: A longitudinal analysis from the International Tobacco Control (ITC) Four Country Survey. *Tobacco Control, 22,* 52–58.

Fougnie, Daryl; Zughni, Samir; Godwin, Douglass; & Marois, René. (2015). Working memory storage is intrinsically domain specific. *Journal of Experimental Psychology: General, 144,* 30–47. https://doi.org/10.1037/a0038211

Foulkes, David, & Domhoff, G. William. (2014). Bottom-up or top-down in dream neuroscience? A top-down critique of two bottom-up studies. *Consciousness and Cognition: An International Journal, 27,* 168–171. https://doi.org/10.1016/j.concog.2014.05.002

Fournier, Jay C.; DeRubeis, Robert J.; Hollon, Steven D.; Dimidjian, Sona; Amsterdam, Jay D.; Shelton, Richard C.; & Fawcett, Jan. (2010). Antidepressant drug effects and depression severity: A patient-level meta-analysis. *Journal of the American Medical Association, 303*(1), 47–53. https://doi.org/10.1001/jama.2009.1943

Fowler, Robert L., & Barker, Anne S. (1974). Effectiveness of highlighting for retention of text material. *Journal of Applied Psychology, 59*(3), 358–364. https://doi.org/10.1037/h0036750

Fox, Margalit. (2008). *Talking hands: What sign language reveals about the mind.* Simon & Schuster.

Fox, Margalit. (2018a). Dovey Johnson Roundtree, barrier-breaking lawyer, dies at 104. *The New York Times.* https://www.nytimes.com/2018/05/21/obituaries/dovey-johnson-roundtree-dead.html

Fox, Margalit. (2018b). She knows how to make an exit. You're reading it. *The New York Times.* https://www.nytimes.com/2018/06/28/insider/obituary-writer-margalit-fox-retires.html

Fox, William M. (1982). Why we should abandon Maslow's need hierarchy theory. *Journal of Humanistic Education and Development, 21,* 29–32.

Fraga, Mario F.; Ballestar, Esteban; Paz, Maria F.; Ropero, Santiago; Setien, Fernando; Ballestar, Maria L.; Heine-Suñer, Damia; Cigudosa, Juan C.; Urioste, Miguel; Benitez, Javier; Boix-Chornet, Manuel; Sanchez-Aguilera, Abel; Ling, Charlotte; Carlsson, Emma; Poulsen, Pernille; Vaag, Allan; Stephan, Zarko; Spector, Tim D.; Wu, Yue-Zhong; Plass, Christoph; & Manel Esteller. (2005). Epigenetic differences arise during the lifetime of monozygotic twins. *Proceedings of the National Academy of Sciences, 102*(30), 10604–10609. https://doi.org/10.1073/pnas.0500398102

Fram, Alan. (2007). That's the spirit: One-third of people believe in ghosts—and some report seeing one. *Associated Press Archive,* Record No. d8SGT3CG0. Associated Press.

Frances, Allen J., & Widiger, Thomas. (2012). Psychiatric diagnosis: lessons from the DSM-IV past and cautions for the DSM-5 future. *Annual Review of Clinical Psychology, 8,* 109–130. https://doi.org/10.1146/annurev-clinpsy-032511-143102.

Francis, Ronald D. (2009). *Ethics for psychologists* (2nd ed.). Wiley-Blackwell.

Frank, Beatrice; Glikman, Jenny A.; & Marchini, Silvio. (Eds.). (2019). *Human–wildlife interactions: Turning conflict into coexistence* (vol. 23). Cambridge University Press.

Frank, Marcos G., & Heller, H. Craig. (2019). The function(s) of sleep. In Hans-Peter Landolt & Derk-Jan Dijk (Eds.), *Sleep-Wake Neurobiology and Pharmacology* (pp. 3–34). Springer.

Frank, Mark G., & Stennett, Janine. (2001). The forced-choice paradigm and the perception of facial expressions of emotion. *Journal of Personality and Social Psychology, 80,* 75–85.

Frank, Michael C.; Everett, Daniel L.; Fedorenko, Evelina; & Gibson, Edward. (2008). Number as a cognitive technology: Evidence from Piraha language and cognition. *Cognition, 108,* 819–824.

Franklin, Lu Ann. (2016, December 26). New Life for Old Bags project to create sleeping mats for homeless vets really takes off. *NWI Times.* http://www.nwitimes.com/lifestyles/new-life-for-old-bags-project-to-create-sleeping-mats/article_d8ba3f52-5635-580b-a9fe-6a19ee3cc52d.html

Frazier, Patricia; Anders, Samantha; Perera, Sulani; Tomich, Patricia; Tennen, Howard; Park, Crystal; & Tashiro, Ty. (2009). Traumatic events among undergraduate students: Prevalence and associated symptoms. *Journal of Counseling Psychology, 56,* 450–460.

Free, Michael L. (2008). *Cognitive therapy in groups: Guidelines and resources for practice* (2nd ed.). Wiley.

Freedman, Sara A.; Hoffman, Hunter G.; Garcia-Palacios, Azucena; Weiss, Patrice L. (Tamar); Avitzour, Sara; & Josman, Naomi. (2010). Prolonged exposure and virtual reality–enhanced imaginal exposure for PTSD following a terrorist bulldozer attack: A case study. *Cyberpsychology, Behavior, and Social Networking, 13*(1), 95–101. https://doi.org/10.1089/cyber.2009.0271.

Freeman, Chris, & Power, Mick. (2007). *Handbook of evidence-based psychotherapies: A guide for research and practice.* Wiley.

Freeman, Daniel; Reeve, Sarah; Robinson, A.; Ehlers, Anke; Clark, David; Spanlang, Bernhard; & Slater, Mel. (2017). Virtual reality in the assessment, understanding, and treatment of mental health disorders. *Psychological Medicine,* 1–8. https://doi.org/10.1017/S003329171700040X

Freeman, Ellen W. (2010). Associations of depression with the transition to menopause. *Menopause, 17,* 823–827. https://doi.org/10.1097/gme.0b013e3181db9f8b

Freeman, Kevin B., & Riley, Anthony L. (2009). The origins of conditioned taste aversion learning: A historical analysis. In S. Reilly & T. Schachtman (Eds.), *Conditioned taste aversion: Behavioral and neural processes* (pp. 9–36). Oxford University Press.

Freeman, Lucy, & Strean, Herbert S. (1987). *Freud and women.* Continuum.

Freeman, Nancy K. (2007). Preschoolers' perceptions of gender appropriate toys and their parents' beliefs about genderized behaviors: Miscommunication, mixed messages, or hidden truths? *Early Childhood Education Journal, 3,* 357–366.

Freidel, Paul; Young, Bruce; & van Hemmen, J. Leo. (2008). Auditory localization of ground-borne vibrations in snakes. *Physical Review Letters, 100,* 048701.

Freire, Elizabeth S. (2007). Empathy. In Mick Cooper, Maureen O'Hara, Peter F. Schmid, & Gill Wyatt (Eds.), *The handbook of person-centered psychotherapy and counseling.* Palgrave Macmillan.

French, Kimberly A.; & Shockley, Kristen M. (2020). Formal and informal supports for managing work and family. *Current Directions in Psychological Science, 29*(2), 207–216. https://doi.org/10.1177/0963721420906218

Frenda, Steven J.; Knowles, Eric D.; Saletan, William; Loftus, Elizabeth F. (2013). False memories of fabricated political events. *Journal of Experimental Social Psychology, 49,* 280–286. https://doi.org/10.1016/j.jesp.2012.10.013

Frenda, Steven J.; Nichols, Rebecca M.; & Loftus, Elizabeth F. (2011). Current issues and advances in misinformation research. *Current Directions in Psychological Science, 20*(1), 20–23. https://doi.org/10.1177/0963721410396620

Frenzel, Stefan; Wittfeld, Katharina; Habes, Mohamad; Klinger-König, Johanna; Bülow, Robin; Völzke, Henry; & Grabe, Hans Jörgen. (2020). A biomarker for Alzheimer's disease based on patterns of regional brain atrophy. *Frontiers in Psychiatry, 10.* https://doi.org/10.3389/fpsyt.2019.00953

Freud, Anna. (1946). *The ego and mechanisms of defence* (Cecil Baines, Trans.). International Universities Press.

Freud, Sigmund. (1904/1965). *The psychopathology of everyday life* (Alan Tyson, Trans., & James Strachey, Ed.). Norton.

Freud, Sigmund. (1905). *Three essays on the theory of sexuality* (James Strachey, Ed.). Basic Books.

Freud, Sigmund. (1911). On dreams. In Peter Gay (Ed.), *The Freud reader.* Norton.

Freud, Sigmund. (1915a). Repression. In Joan Riviere (Trans.), *Collected Papers: Vol. 4. Papers on metapsychology and applied psychoanalysis.* Hogarth.

Freud, Sigmund. (1915b). Analysis, terminable and interminable. In Joan Riviere (Trans.), *Collected Papers: Vol. 5. Miscellaneous papers* (2nd ed.). Hogarth.

Freud, Sigmund. (1915c). Libido theory. In Joan Riviere (Trans.), *Collected papers: Vol. 5. Miscellaneous papers* (2nd ed.). Hogarth.

Freud, Sigmund. (1920). *Beyond the pleasure principle* (James Strachey, Ed.). Norton.

Freud, Sigmund. (1923). *The ego and the id* (Joan Riviere, Trans., & James Strachey, Ed.). Norton.

Freud, Sigmund. (1925). Some psychical consequences of the anatomical distinction between the sexes. In Peter Gay (Ed.), *The Freud reader.* Norton.

Freud, Sigmund. (1926). *The question of lay analysis: An introduction to psychoanalysis* (Nancy Proctor-Gregg, Trans.). Imago.

Freud, Sigmund. (1930/1961). *Civilization and its discontents* (James Strachey, Ed. & Trans.). Norton.

Freud, Sigmund. (1933). *New introductory lectures on psychoanalysis* (W. J. H. Sprott, Trans.). Norton.

Freud, Sigmund. (1936). *The problem of anxiety* (Henry Alden Bunker, Trans.). The Psychoanalytic Quarterly Press and Norton.

Freud, Sigmund. (1939). *Moses and monotheism* (Katherine Jones, Trans.). Vintage Books.

Freud, Sigmund. (1940). *An outline of psychoanalysis* (James Strachey, Trans.). Norton.

Fridell, Mats; Hesse, Morten; Jæger, Mads Meier; & Kühlhorn, Eckart. (2008). Antisocial personality disorder as a predictor of criminal behaviour in a longitudinal study of a cohort of abusers of several classes of drugs: Relation to type of substance and type of crime. *Addictive Behaviors, 33*(6), 799–811. https://doi.org/10.1016/j.addbeh.2008.01.001

Frieden, Tom. (2021, January 1). Which countries have responded best to Covid-19? *Wall Street Journal.* Retrieved from https://www.wsj.com/articles/which-countries-have-responded-best-to-covid-19-11609516800

Friedman, Howard S., & Booth-Kewley, Stephanie. (2003). The 'disease-prone personality': A meta-analytic view of the construct. In Peter Salovey & Alexander J. Rothman (Eds.), *Social psychology of health.* Psychology Press.

Friedman, Jeffrey M. (2009). Causes and control of excess body fat. *Nature, 459,* 340–342.

Friedman, Meyer, & Rosenman, Ray H. (1974). *Type A behavior and your heart.* Knopf.

Friend, Ronald; Rafferty, Yvonne; & Bramel, Dana. (1990). A puzzling misinterpretation of the Asch "conformity" study. *European Journal of Social Psychology, 20,* 29–44.

Friesen, Wallace V. (1972). Cultural differences in facial expressions in a social situation: An experimental test of the concept of display rules. Unpublished doctoral dissertation, University of California, San Francisco.

Frijns, C. J. M.; Laman, D. M.; van Duijn, M. A. J.; & van Duijn, H. (1997). Normal values of patellar and ankle tendon reflex latencies. *Clinical Neurology and Neurosurgery, 99*(1), 31–36. https://doi.org/10.1016/s0303-8467(96)00593-8

Frith, Chris D., & Frith, Uta. (2012). Mechanisms of social cognition. *Annual Review of Psychology, 63*(1), 287–313. https://doi.org/10.1146/annurev-psych-120710-100449

Frost, Helen; Campbell, Pauline; Maxwell, Margaret; O'Carroll, Ronan E.; Dombrowski, Stephan U.; Williams, Brian; Cheyne, Helen; Coles, Emma; & Pollock, Alex. (2018). Effectiveness of motivational interviewing on adult behavior change in health and social care settings: A systematic review of reviews. *PLoS ONE, 13*(10), e0204890. https://doi.org/10.1371/journal.pone.0204890

Fruth, Barbara, & Hohmann, Gottfried. (2006). Social grease for females? Same-sex genital contacts in wild bonobos. In Volker Sommer & Paul L. Vasey (Eds.), *Homosexual behaviour in animals: An evolutionary perspective.* Cambridge University Press.

Fuchs, Thomas. (2020). Delusion, reality, and intersubjectivity: A phenomenological and enactive analysis. *Philosophy, Psychiatry, & Psychology, 27*(1), 61–79. https://doi.org/10.1353/ppp.2020.0009

Fujita, Kentaro, & Roberts, Joseph C. (2010). Promoting prospective self-control through abstraction. *Journal of Experimental Social Psychology, 46,* 1049–1054.

Fullana, Miguel A.; Harrison, Benjamin J.; Soriano-Mas, Carles; Vervliet, Bram; Cardoner, Narcis; Àvila-Parcet, Avila; & Radua, Joaquim. (2015). Neural signatures of human fear conditioning: An updated and extended meta-analysis of fMRI studies. *Molecular Psychiatry, 21,* 1–9. https://doi.org/10.1038/mp.2015.88

Fuller, Patrick M.; Gooley, Joshua J.; & Saper, Clifford B. (2006). Neurobiology of the sleep-wake cycle: Sleep architecture, circadian regulation, and regulatory feedback. *Journal of Biological Rhythms, 21,* 482–493.

Funder, David C. (2001). Personality. *Annual Review of Psychology, 52,* 197–221.

Funder, David C., & Fast, Lisa A. (2010). Personality in social psychology. In Susan T. Fiske, Daniel T. Gilbert, & Gardner Lindzey (Eds.), *Handbook of social psychology,* (Vol. 1). Wiley.

Furman, Wyndol, & Simon, Valerie A. (2004). Concordance in attachment states of mind and styles with respect to fathers and mothers. *Developmental Psychology, 40,* 1239–1247.

Furnham, Adam. (2008). *Personality and intelligence at work: Exploring and explaining individual differences at work.* Routledge.

Furr, R. Michael, & Funder, David C. (2021). Persons, situations, and person–situation interactions. In Oliver P. John & Richard W. Robins (Eds.), *Handbook of personality: Theory and research,* (pp. 667–685). Guilford.

Furukawa, Toshi; Cipriani, Andrea; Atkinson, Lauren Z.; Leucht, Stefan; Ogawa, Usuke; Takeshima, Nozomi; Hayasaka, Yu; Chaimani, Anna; & Salanti, Georgia. (2016). Placebo response rates in antidepressant trials: A systematic review of published and unpublished double-blind randomized controlled studies. *The Lancet Psychiatry, 3,* 1059–1066. https://doi.org/10.1016/S2215-0366(16)30307-8

Gable, Shelly L.; Hopper, Elizabeth A.; & Schooler, Jonathan W. (2019). When the muses strike: Creative ideas of physicists and writers routinely occur during mind wandering. *Psychological Science, 30*(3), 396–404. https://doi.org/10.1177/0956797618820626

Gaeta, Christopher. (2020). The advent of psychologists receiving prescription privileges: Implications from the COVID-19 global pandemic. *Journal of Health Care Finance, 47*(2), 1–5.

Gage, Fred. (2019). Adult neurogenesis in mammals: Neurogenesis in adulthood has implications for sense of self, memory, and disease. *Science, 364*(6443), 827–828. https://doi.org/10.1126/science.aav6885

Gagne, Jeffrey R.; Vendlinski, Matthew K.; & Goldsmith, H. Hill. (2009). The genetics of childhood temperament. In Yong-Kyu Kim (Ed.), *Handbook of behavior genetics* (pp. 251–267). Springer Science + Business Media.

Gajendran, Raji V., & Harrison, David A. (2007). The good, the bad, and the unknown about telecommuting: Meta-analysis of psychological mediators and individual consequences. *Journal of Applied Psychology, 92,* 1524–1541.

Galak, Jeff; LeBoeuf, Robyn A.; Nelson, Leif D.; & Simmons, Joseph P. (2012). Correcting the past: Failures to replicate psi. *Journal of Personality and Social Psychology, 103,* 933–948. https://doi.org/10.1037/a0029709

Galambos, Nancy L.; Barker, Erin T.; & Krahn, Harvey J. (2006). Depression, self-esteem, and anger in emerging adulthood: Seven-year trajectories. *Developmental Psychology, 42,* 350-365. https://doi.org/10.1037/0012-1649.42.2.350

Galanter, Eugene. (1962). Contemporary psychophysics. In Roger Brown, Eugene Galanter, Eckhard H. Hess, & George Mandler (Eds.), *New directions in psychology.* Holt, Rinehart & Winston.

Galanter, Marc. (2021) Network Therapy. In Nady el-Guebaly; Giuseppe Carrà; Marc Galanter; & Alexander M. Baldacchino (Eds.), *Textbook of Addiction Treatment* (pp. 459–473). Springer. https://doi.org/10.1007/978-3-030-36391-8_32

Galanter, Marc, & Brook, D. (2001). Network therapy for addiction: Bringing family and peer support into office practice. *International Journal of Group Psychotherapy, 51,* 101–22. https://doi.org/10.1521/ijgp.51.1.101.49734

Galati, Dario; Scherer, Klaus B.; & Ricci-Bitti, Pio E. (1997). Voluntary facial expression of emotion: Comparing congenitally blind with normally sighted encoders. *Journal of Personality and Social Psychology, 73,* 1363–1379.

Galati, Dario; Sini, Barbara; Schmidt, Susanne; & Tinti, Carla. (2003). Spontaneous facial expressions in congenitally blind and sighted children aged 8–11. *Journal of Visual Impairment and Blindness, 97,* 418–428.

Galla, Brian M., & Duckworth, Angela L. (2015). More than resisting temptation: Beneficial habits mediate the relationship between self-control and positive life outcomes. *Journal of Personality and Social Psychology, 109,* 508–525. https://doi.org/10.1037/pspp0000026

Gallo, David A., & Wheeler, Mark E. (2013). Episodic memory. In Daniel Reisberg (Ed.), *The Oxford handbook of cognitive psychology.* Oxford University Press.

Galván, Adriana. (2020). The need for sleep in the adolescent brain. *Trends in Cognitive Sciences, 24,* 79–89. https://doi.org/10.1016/j.tics.2019.11.002

Galvin, Benjamin; Lange, Donald; & Ashforth, Blake. (2015). Narcissistic organizational identification: Seeing oneself as central to the organization's identity. *Academy of Management Review, 40,* 163–181. https://doi.org/10.5465/amr.2013.0103

Gaml-Sørensen, Anne; Brix, Nis; Ernst, Andreas; Lunddorf, Lea Lykke Harrits; & Ramlau-Hansen, Cecilia Høst. (2021). Father absence in pregnancy or during childhood and pubertal development in girls and boys: A population-based cohort study. *Child Development.* https://doi.org/10.1111/cdev.13488

Gandal, Michael J.; Haney, Jillian R.; Parikshak, Neelroop N.; Leppa, Virpi; Ramaswami, Gokul; Hartl, Chris; Schork, Andrew J.; Appadurai, Vivek; Buil, Alfonso; Werge, Thomas M.; Liu, Chunyu; White, Kevin P.; CommonMind Consortium; PsychENCODE Consortium; iPSYCH-BROAD Working Group; Horvath, Steve; & Geschwind, Daniel H. (2018). Shared molecular neuropathology across major psychiatric disorders parallels polygenic overlap. *Science, 359*(6376), 693–697. https://doi.org/10.1126/science.aad6469

Gangl, Markus, & Ziefle, Andrea. (2009). Motherhood, labor force behavior, and women's careers: An empirical assessment of the wage penalty for motherhood in Britain, Germany, and the United States. *Demography, 46,* 341–369.

Ganis, Giorgio; Thompson, William L.; & Kosslyn, Stephen M. (2004) Brain areas underlying visual mental imagery and visual perception: An fMRI study. *Cognitive Brain Research, 20*(2), 226–241. https://doi.org/10.1016/j.cogbrainres.2004.02.012

Ganley, Colleen M.; Mingle, Leigh A.; Ryan, Allison M.; Ryan, Katherine; Vasilyeva, Marina; & Perry, Michelle. (2013). An examination of stereotype threat effects on girls' mathematics performance. *Developmental Psychology, 49*(10), 1886–1897. https://doi.org/10.1037/a0031412

Ganna, Andrea; Verweij, Karin J. H.; Nivard, Michel G.; Maier, Robert; Wedow, Robbee; Busch, Alexander S.; Abdellaoui, Abdel; Guo, Shengru; Sathirapongsasuti, J. Fah; 23andMe Research Team; Lichenstein, Paul; Lundström, Sebastian; Långström, Niklas; Auton, Adam; Harris, Kathleen M.; Beecham, Gary W.; Martin, Eden R.; Sanders, Alan R.; Perry, John R. B...; & Zietsch, Brendan P. (2019). Large-scale GWAS reveals insights into the genetic architecture of same-sex sexual behavior. *Science, 365*(6456), 1–22. https://doi.org/10.1126/science.aat7693

Gansberg, Martin. (1964, March 27). 37 who saw murder didn't call the police. *The New York Times,* pp. 1, 38.

García, Eugene E., & Náñez, José E., Sr. (2011). *Bilingualism and cognition: Informing research, pedagogy, and policy.* American Psychological Association.

Garcia, Fernando, & Gracia, Enrique. (2009). Is always authoritative the optimum parenting style? Evidence from Spanish families. *Family Therapy, 36*(1), 17–47.

Garcia, John. (1981). Tilting at the paper mills of academe. *American Psychologist, 36,* 149–158.

Garcia, John. (1997). Foreword by Robert C. Bolles: From mathematics to motivation. In Mark E. Bouton & Michael S. Fanselow (Eds.), *Learning, motivation, and cognition: The functional behaviorism of Robert C. Bolles.* American Psychological Association.

Garcia, John. (2003). Psychology is not an enclave. In Robert J. Sternberg (Ed.), *Psychologists defying the crowd: Stories of those who battled the establishment and won.* American Psychological Association.

Garcia, John; Ervin, Frank R.; & Koelling, Robert A. (1966). Learning with prolonged delay of reinforcement. *Psychonomic Science, 5,* 121–122. https://doi.org/10.3758/BF03328311

Garcia, John, & Koelling, Robert A. (1966). Relation of cue to consequence in avoidance learning. *Psychonomic Science, 4,* 123–124.

Garcia, Michael A., & Umberson, Debra. (2019). Marital strain and psychological distress in same-sex and different-sex couples. *Journal of Marriage and Family, 81,* 1253–1268. https://doi.org/10.1111/jomf.12582

Gardner, Aimee; Ritter, Matthew; Paige, John; Ahmed, Rami; Fernandez, Gladys; & Dunkin, Brian. (2016). Simulation-based selection of surgical trainees: Considerations, challenges, and opportunities. *Journal of American College of Surgeons, 223,* 530–536. https://doi.org/10.1016/j.jamcollsurg.2016.05.021

Gardner, Howard. (1993). *Frames of mind: The theory of multiple intelligences* (2nd ed.). Basic Books.

Gardner, Howard. (1998a). Are there additional intelligences? The case for naturalist, spiritual, and existential intelligences. In J. Kane (Ed.), *Education, information, and transformation.* Prentice Hall.

Gardner, Howard. (1998b, Winter). A multiplicity of intelligences. *Scientific American Presents: Exploring Intelligence, 9,* 18–23.

Gardner, Howard. (2003). Three distinct meanings of intelligence. In Robert Sternberg, Jacques Lautrey, & Todd I. Lubert (Eds.), *Models of intelligence: International perspectives.* American Psychological Association.

Gardner, Michael K. (2011). Theories of intelligence. In M. A. Bray & T. J. Kehle (Eds.), *The Oxford handbook of school psychology* (pp. 79–100). Oxford University Press.

Gardony, Aaron L.; Taylor, Holly A.; & Brunyé, Tad T. (2014). What does physical rotation reveal about mental rotation? *Psychological Science, 25,* 605–612. https://doi.org/10.1177/0956797613503174

Garger, John; Vracheva, Veselina P.; & Jacques, Paul. (2020). A tipping point analysis of service-learning hours and student outcomes. *Education and Training, 62*(4), 413–425. https://doi.org/10.1108/ET-09-2019-0210

Gariano, Francesca. (2019, November 24). Kristen Bell gets candid about how she deals with her anxiety and depression. *Today.* https://www.today.com/health/kristen-bell-interview-frozen-2-star-talks-anxiety-depression-t168179

Garrett, Brandon L. (2011). *Convicting the innocent.* Harvard University Press.

Garrett, Michael T. (2008). Native Americans. In Garrett McAuliffe (Ed.), *Culturally alert counseling: A comprehensive introduction* (pp. 220–254). Sage.

Garrison, Katie E.; Tang, David; & Schmeichel, Brandon J. (2016). Embodying power: A preregistered replication and extension of the power pose effect. *Social Psychological and Personality Science, 7,* 623–630. https://doi.org/10.1177/1948550616652209

Garry, Maryanne; Hope, Lorraine; Zajac, Rachel; Verrall, Ayesha J.; & Robertson, Jamie M. (2021). Contact tracing: A memory task with consequences for public health. *Perspectives on Psychological Science, 16*(1), 175–187. https://doi.org/10.1177/1745691620978205

Garry, Maryanne, & Polaschek, Devon L. L. (2000). Imagination and memory. *Current Directions in Psychological Science, 9*(1), 6–10. https://doi.org/10.1111/1467-8721.00048

Gartner, Marieke C.; Powell, David M.; & Weiss, Alexander. (2014). Personality structure in the domestic cat (Felis silvestris catus), Scottish wildcat (Felis silvestris grampia), clouded leopard (Neofelis nebulosa), snow leopard (Panthera uncia), and African lion (Panthera leo): A comparative study. *Journal of Comparative Psychology,128,* 414–426. https://doi.org/10.1037/a0037104

Garvin, Charles. (2011). Group work with people who suffer from serious mental illness. In Geoffrey L. Greif & Paul H. Ephross (Eds.), *Group work with populations at risk.* Oxford University Press.

Garza, Yvonne, & Watts, Richard E. (2010). Filial therapy and Hispanic values: Common ground for culturally sensitive helping. *Journal of Counseling & Development, 88*(1), 108–113.

Gatchel, Robert J.; Howard, Krista; & Haggard, Rob. (2011). Pain: The biopsychosocial perspective. In R. J. Contrada & A. Baum (Eds.), *The handbook of stress science: Biology, psychology, and health* (pp. 461–473). Springer.

Gaudiano, Brandon A. (2008). Cognitive-behavioural therapies: Achievements and challenges. *Evidence-Based Mental Health, 11,* 5–7.

Gawronski, Bertram. (2012). Back to the future of dissonance theory: Cognitive consistency as a core motive. *Social Cognition, 30*(6), 652–668.

Gawronski, Bertram. (2019). Six lessons for a cogent science of implicit bias and its criticism. *Perspectives on Psychological Science, 14*(4), 574–595. https://doi.org/10.1177/17456916198260

Gawronski, Bertram, & Payne, B. Keith. (2010). *Handbook of implicit social cognition: Measurement, theory, and applications.* Guilford.

Gay, Peter. (Ed.). (1989). *The Freud reader.* Norton.

Gay, Peter. (2006). *Freud: A life for our time.* Norton.

Gazzaniga, Michael S. (2005). Forty-five years of split-brain research and still going strong. *Nature Reviews Neuroscience, 6,* 653–659. https://doi.org/10.1038/nrn1723

Ge, Xiaojia; Kim, Irene J.; Brody, Gene H.; Conger, Rand D.; Simons, Ronald L.; Gibbons, Frederick X.; & Cutrona, Carolyn E. (2003). It's about timing and change: Pubertal transition effects on symptoms of major depression among African American youths. *Developmental Psychology, 39*(3), 430–439. https://doi.org/10.1037/0012-1649.39.3.430

Geary, Nori. (2020). Control-theory models of body-weight regulation and body-weight- regulatory appetite. *Appetite, 144.* https://doi.org/10.1016/j.appet.2019.104440

Gee, Travis; Allen, Kelly; & Powell, Russell A. (2003). Questioning premorbid dissociative symptomatology in dissociative identity disorder: Comment on Gleaves, Hernandez, and Warner (1999). *Professional Psychology: Research and Practice, 34*(1), 114–116. https://doi.org/10.1037/0735-7028.34.1.114

Geen, Russell G. (1995). Human motivation: A social psychological approach. Brooks/Cole.

Gejman, Pablo; Sanders, Alan; & Duan, Jubao. (2010). The role of genetics in the etiology of schizophrenia. *Psychiatric Clinics of North America, 33,* 35–66. https://doi.org/10.1016/j.psc.2009.12.003

Geldard, Frank A. (1972). *The human senses* (2nd ed.). Wiley.

Gendolla, Guido H. E. (2000). On the impact of mood on behavior: An integrative theory and a review. *Review of General Psychology, 4,* 378–408.

Gendolla, Guido H. E. (2017). Comment: Do emotions influence action? – Of course, they are hypo-phenomena of motivation. *Emotion Review, 9*(4), 348–350. https://doi.org/10.1177/1754073916673211

Geniole, Shawn N.; Procyshyn, Tanya L.; Marley, Nicole; Ortiz, Triana L.; Bird, Brian M.; Marcellus, Ashley L.; Welker, Kevin M.; Bonin, Pierre L.; Goldfarb, Bernard; & Carré, Justin M. (2019). Using a psychopharmacogenetic approach to identify the pathways through which—and the people for whom—testosterone promotes aggression. *Psychological Science, 30*(4), 481-494. https://doi.org/10.1177/0956797619826970

Gentile, Barbara F., & Miller, Benjamin O. (2009). *Foundations of psychological thought: A history of psychology.*Sage.

Gentilucci, Maurizio, & Dalla Volta, Riccardo. (2007). The motor system and the relationships between speech and gesture. *Gesture, 7,* 159–177.

Genzlinger, Neil. (2020, September 11). James Jackson, who changed the study of Black America, dies at 76. *The New York Times.* https://www.nytimes.com/2020/09/11/us/james-jackson-dead.html

George, Alice Lloyd. (2018, January 1). A conversation with Dean Kamen on the myth of "Eureka!" *TechCrunch.* https://techcrunch.com/2018/01/01/a-conversation-with-dean-kamen-on-the-myth-of-eureka/

George, Bill. (2006, October 30). The master gives it back. *U.S. News & World Report,* 66–68.

Georgopoulos, Neoklis A.; Markou, Kostas B.; Theodoropoulou, Anastasia; Vagenakis, George A.; Mylonas, Panagiotis; & Vagenakis, Apostolos G. (2004). Growth, pubertal development, skeletal maturation and bone mass acquisition in athletes. *Hormones (Athens), 3*(4), 233–243.

Geraci, Lisa, & Manzano, Isabel. (2010). Distinctive items are salient during encoding: Delayed judgements of learning predict the isolation effect. *Quarterly Journal of Experimental Psychology, 63*(1), 50–64.

Gerard, Harold B.; Wilhelmy, Roland A.; & Conolley, Edward S. (1968). Conformity and group size. *Journal of Personality and Social Psychology, 8,* 79–82.

Gerber, Andrew J.; Peterson, Bradley S.; Giedd, Jay N.; Lalonde, F. M.; Celano, M. J.; White, S. L.; Wallace, G. L.; Lee, N. R.; & Lenroot, R. K. (2009). Anatomical brain magnetic resonance imaging of typically developing children and adolescents. *Journal of the American Academy of Child and Adolescent Psychiatry, 48*(5), 465–470. https://doi.org/10.1097/CHI.0b013e31819f2715

Gerber, Gwendolyn L. (2009). Status and the gender stereotyped personality traits: Toward an integration. *Sex Roles, 61,* 297–316.

Gerhard, Danielle; Wohleb, Eric; & Duman, Ronald. (2016). Emerging treatment mechanisms for depression: Focus on glutamate and synaptic plasticity. *Drug Discovery Today, 21,* 454–464. https://doi.org/10.1016/j.drudis.2016.01.016

Gerlach, Martin; Farb, Beatrice; Revelle, William; & Nunes Amaral, Luis A. (2018). A robust data-driven approach identifies four personality types across four large datasets. *Nature Human Behavior, 2,* 735–742. https://doi.org/10.1038/s41562-018-0419-z

Gerrie, Matthew P.; Garry, Maryanne; & Loftus, Elizabeth F. (2004). False memories. In Neil Brewer & Kip Williams (Eds.), *Psychology and law: An empirical perspective.* Guilford.

Gershoff, Elizabeth Thompson. (2002). Corporal punishment by parents and associated child behavior and experiences: A meta-analytic and theoretical review. *Psychological Bulletin, 128*(4), 539–579. https://doi.org/10.1037/0033-2909.128.4.539

Gershoff, Elizabeth T., & Grogan-Kaylor, Andrew. (2016). Spanking and child outcomes: Old controversies and new meta-analyses. *Journal of Family Psychology, 30*(4), 453-469. https://doi.org/10.1037/fam0000191

Gershoff, Elizabeth Thompson; Grogan-Kaylor, A.; Lansford, J. E.; Chang, L.; Zelli, A.; Deater-Deckard, K.; & Dodge, K. A. (2010). Parent discipline practices in an International sample: Associations with child behaviors and moderation by perceived normativeness. *Child Development, 81*(2), 487–502. https://doi.org/10.1111/j.1467-8624.2009.01409.x

Gerstner, Charlotte R., & Day, David V. (1997, December). Metaanalytic review of leader-member exchange theory: Correlates and construct issues. *Journal of Applied Psychology, 82,* 827–844.

Gesselman, Amanda N.; Ta, Vivan P.; & Garcia, Justin R. (2019). Worth a thousand interpersonal words: Emoji as affective signals for relationship-oriented digital communication. *PLoS ONE 14*(8). https://doi.org/10.1371/journal.pone.0221297

Gesser-Edelsburg, Anat; Guttman, Nurit; & Israelashvili, Moshe. (2010). An entertainment-education study of secondary delegitimization in the Israeli-Palestinian conflict. *Peace and Conflict: Journal of Peace Psychology, 16*(3), 253–274.

Ghafoori, Bita; Caspi, Yael; Salgado, Carolina; Allwood, Maureen; Kreither, Johanna; Hunt, Tanya; Waelde, Lynn C.; Slobodin, Ortal; Failey, Mieko; Gilberg, Porter; Larrondo, Paulina; Ramos, Nadia; von Haumeder, Anna; & Nadal, Kevin. (2019). Global perspectives on the trauma of hate-based violence: An International Society for Traumatic Stress Studies briefing paper. *International Society for Traumatic Stress Studies.* www.istss.org/hate-based-violence

Gibbs, John C. (2003). Moral development and reality: Beyond the theories of Kohlberg and Hoffman. Sage.

Gibson, Stephen. (2017). Developing psychology's archival sensibilities: Revisiting Milgram's "obedience" experiments. *Qualitative Psychology, 4,* 73–89. https://doi.org/10.1037/qup0000040

Giedd, Jay N. (2008). The teen brain: Insights from neuroimaging. *Journal of Adolescent Health, 42*(4), 335–343. https://doi.org/10.1016/j.jadohealth.2008.01.007

Giedd, Jay N. (2009, January/February). The teen brain: Primed to learn, primed to take risks. *Cerebrum.* http://www.dana.org/news/cerebrum/detail.aspx?id=19620

Gigerenzer, Gerd, & Gaissmaier, Wolfgang. (2011). Heuristic decision making. *Annual Review of Psychology, 62,* 451–458. https://doi.org/10.1146/annurev-psych-120709-14534

Gigerenzer, Gerd, & Goldstein, Daniel G. (2011). The recognition heuristic: A decade of research. *Judgment and Decision Making, 6*(1), 100–121.

Gilhooly, Kenneth (2016). Incubation and intuition in creative problem solving. *Hypothesis and Theory, 7,* 1–9.

Gill, Hartej; Gill, Barjot; Chen-Li, David; El-Halabi, Sabine; Rodrigues, Nelson B.; Cha, Danielle S.; Lipsitz, Orly; Lee, Yena; Rosenblat, Joshua D.; Majeed, Amna; Mansur, Rodrigo B.; Nasri, Flora; Ho, Roger; & McIntyre, Roger S. (2020). The emerging role of psilocybin and MDMA in the treatment of mental illness. *Expert Review of Neurotherapeutics, 20*(12), 1263–1273. https://doi.org/10.1080/14737175.2020.1826931

Gillett, Rachel, & Cain, Áine. (2017, January 8). 5 wacky interview questions you'll hear at companies like Zappos, Slack, and WarbyParker. *Business Insider.* https://www.businessinsider.com/wacky-interview-questions-successful-bosses-2017-1

Gilligan, Carol A. (1982). *In a different voice: Psychological theory and women's development.* Harvard University Press.

Gilman, Sander L. (2001). Images in psychiatry: Karen Horney, M.D., 1885–1952. *American Journal of Psychiatry, 158,* 1205.

Gilmore, Rick O.; Kennedy, Joy Lorenzo; & Adolph, Karen E. (2018). Practical solutions for sharing data and materials from psychological research. *Advances in Methods and Practices in Psychological Science.* https://doi.org/10.1177/2515245917746500

Gilovich, Thomas. (1997, March/April). Some systematic biases of everyday judgment. *Skeptical Inquirer, 21,* 31–35.

Gilson, Lucy L., & Madjar, Nora. (2011). Radical and incremental creativity: Antecedents and processes. *Psychology of Aesthetics, Creativity, and the Arts,* 5, 21–28.

Gioia G. A., Collins M., & Isquith P. K. (2008). Improving identification and diagnosis of mild traumatic brain injury with evidence: Psychometric support for the acute concussion evaluation. *Journal of Head Trauma Rehabilitation, 23*(4), 230–242. https://doi.org/10.1097/01.HTR.0000327255.38881.ca

Gire, James T. (2011). Cultural variations in perceptions of aging. In Kenneth D. Keith (Ed.), *Cross-cultural psychology: Contemporary themes and perspectives.*Wiley-Blackwell.

Givens, Dana. (2020). The extra stigma of mental illness for African-American. *The New York Times.* https://www.nytimes.com/2020/08/25/well/mind/black-mental-health.html

Gladwell, Malcolm. (2004, September 20). Annals of psychology: Personality plus. *The New Yorker,* 42–48.

Glaser, Ronald, & Kiecolt-Glaser, Janice K. (2005). Stress-induced immune dysfunction: Implications for health. *Nature Reviews Immunology, 5,* 243–250. https://doi.org /10.1038/nri1571

Glass, Arnold L., & Kang, Mengxue. (2019). Dividing attention in the classroom reduces exam performance. *Educational Psychology, 39*(3), 395–408. https://doi.org /10.1080/01443410.2018.1489046

Glass, Richard M. (2001). Electroconvulsive therapy: Time to bring it out of the shadows. *Journal of the American Medical Association, 285,* 1346–1348. https://doi.org/10.1001 /jama.285.10.1346

Glasser, Matthew F.; Smith, Stephen M.; Marcus, Daniel S.; Andersson, Jesper L. R.; Auerbach, Edward J.; Behrens, Timothy E.; Coalson, Timothy S.; Harms, Michael P.; Jenkinson, Mark; Moeller, Steen; Robinson, Emma C.; Sotiropoulos, Stamatios N.; Xu, Junqian; Yacoub, Essa; Ugurbil, Kamil; & Van Essen, David C (2016). The human connectome project's neuroimaging approach. *Nature Neuroscience, 19,* 1175–1187. https://doi.org/10.1038/nn.4361

Gleaves, David H.; Smith, Steven M.; Butler, Lisa D.; & Spiegel, David. (2004). False and recovered memories in the laboratory and clinic: A review of experimental and clinical evidence. *Clinical Psychology: Science and Practice, 11,* 3–28.

Gleitman, Henry. (1991). Edward Chace Tolman: A life of scientific and social purpose. In Gregory A. Kimble, Michael Wertheimer, & Charlotte White (Eds.), *Portraits of pioneers in psychology.* American Psychological Association/Erlbaum.

Glenn, Jeffrey J.; Nobles, Alicia L.; Barnes, Laura E.; & Teachman, Bethany A. (2020). Can text messages identify suicide risk in real time? A within-subjects pilot examination of temporally sensitive markers of suicide risk. *Clinical Psychological Science, 8*(4), 704–722. https://doi.org/10.1177/2167702620906146

Glick, Peter. (2020, April 30). Masks and emasculation: Why some men refuse to take safety precautions. *Scientific American.* https://blogs.scientificamerican.com/observations /masks-and-emasculation-why-some-men-refuse-to-take-safety-precautions/

Glick, Peter, & Fiske, Susan T. (2001). An ambivalent alliance: Hostile and benevolent sexism as complementary justifications for gender inequality. *American Psychologist, 56,* 109–118. https://doi.org/10.1037/0003-066X.56.2.109

Glick, Peter, & Fiske, Susan T. (2003). An ambivalent alliance: Hostile and benevolent sexism as complementary justifications for gender inequality. In: Scott Plous (Ed.), Understanding prejudice and discrimination (pp. 225–236). McGraw-Hill.

Glick, Peter, & Fiske, Susan T. (2012). An ambivalent alliance: Hostile and benevolent sexism as complementary justifications for gender inequality. In Dixon, John; & Levine, Mark (Eds.). *Beyond prejudice: Extending the social psychology of conflict, inequality and social change* (pp. 70–89). Cambridge University Press.

Glicksohn, Arit, & Cohen, Asher. (2011). The role of Gestalt grouping principles in visual statistical learning. *Attention, Perception, & Psychophysics, 73*(3), 708–713. https://doi.org/10.3758/s13414-010-0084-4

GlobalWorkplaceAnalytics. (2019). Latest telecommuting/mobile work/remote work statistics. https://globalworkplaceanalytics.com/telecommuting-statistics

Glucksman, Myron L., & Kramer, Milton. (2004). Using dreams to assess clinical change during treatment. *Journal of the American Academy of Psychoanalysis and Dynamic Psychiatry, 32*(2), 345–358. https://doi.org/10.1521/jaap.32.2.345.35276

Glynn, Shawn M.; Aultman, Lori Price; & Owens, Ashley M. (2005). Motivation to learn in general education programs. *Journal of General Education, 54*(2), 150–170.

Goel, Lakshmi, & Schnusenberg, Oliver. (2019). Why some people multitask better than others: Predicting learning. *Information Systems Management, 36*(1), 15–23. https://doi.org/10.1080/10580530.2018.1553646

Gogtay, Nitin; Giedd, Jay N.; Lusk, Leslie; Hayashi, Kiralee M.; Greenstein, Deanna; Vaituzis, A. Catherine; Nugent, Tom F., III; Herman, David H.; Clasen, Liv S.; Toga, Arthur W.; Rapoport, Judith L.; & Thompson, Paul M. (2004, May 25). Dynamic mapping of human cortical development during childhood through early adulthood. *Proceedings of the National Academy of Sciences, 101*(21), 8174–8179. https://doi.org/10.1073/pnas.0402680101

Gogtay, Nitin; Vyas, Nora S.; Testa, Renee; Wood, Stephen J.; & Pantelis, Christos. (2011). Age of onset of schizophrenia: Perspectives from structural neuroimaging studies. *Schizophrenia Bulletin, 37*(3), 504–513. https://doi.org/10.1093/schbul/sbr030

Goh, Joshua O.; Tan, Jiat C.; & Park, Denise C. (2009). Culture modulates eye-movements to visual novelty. *PLOS ONE, 4*(12), e8238. https://doi.org/10.1371 /journal.pone.0008238

Gold, Joel, & Gold, Ian. (2012). The "Truman Show" delusion: Psychosis in the global village. *Cognitive Neuropsychiatry, 17*(6),455–472. https://doi.org/10.1080/13546805.2012.666113

Goldinger, Stephen D.; Kleider, Heather M.; Azuma, Tamiko; & Beike, Denise R. (2003). "Blame the victim" under memory load. *Psychological Science, 14*(1), 81–85.

Goldsmith, D. J. (2004). *Communicating social support.* Cambridge University Press.

Golle, Jessika; Rose, Norman; & Göllner, Richard. (2018). School or work? The choice may change your personality. *Psychological Science, 30*(1), 32–42. https://doi.org /10.1177/0956797618806298

Gollwitzer, Peter M. (1999). Implementation intentions: Strong effects of simple plans. *American Psychologist, 54,* 493–503.

Gollwitzer, Peter M. (2014). Weakness of the will: Is a quick fix possible? *Motivation and Emotion, 38,* 305–322. https://doi.org/10.1007/s11031-014-9416-3

Gollwitzer, Peter M.; Gawrilow, Caterina; & Oettingen, Gabriele. (2010). The power of planning: Self-control by effective goal-striving. In R. R. Hassin, K. N. Ochsner, & Y. Trope (Eds.), Self control in society, mind, and brain (pp. 279–296). Oxford University Press.

Gollwitzer, Peter M.; Parks-Stamm, Elizabeth J.; Jaudas, Alexander; & Sheeran, Paschal. (2008). Flexible tenacity in goal pursuit. In James Y. Shah & Wendi L. Gardner (Eds.), *Handbook of motivation science.* Guilford.

Gomez, C., & Rosen, B. (2001, December). The leader-member exchange as a link between managerial trust and employee empowerment. *Group & Organization Management, 26,* 512.

Gonzales, Gilbert; Loret de Mola, Emilio; Gavulic, Kyle A.; McKay, Tara; & Purcell, Christopher. (2020). Mental health needs among lesbian, gay, bisexual, and transgender college students during the COVID-19 pandemic. *Journal of Adolescent Health, 67*(5), 645–648. https://doi.org/10.1016/j.jadohealth.2020.08.006

Good, Byron J., & Hinton, Devon E. (2009). Introduction: Panic disorder in cross-cultural and historical perspective. In Devon E. Hinton & Byron J. Good (Eds.), *Culture and panic disorder* (pp. 1–28). Stanford University Press.

Good, Catherine; Aronson, Joshua; & Harder, Jayne Ann. (2008). Problems in the pipeline: Stereotype threat and women's achievement in high-level math courses. *Journal of Applied Developmental Psychology, 29,* 17–28.

Goodenough, Florence. (1932). The expression of emotion in a blind-deaf child. *Journal of Abnormal Social Psychology, 27,* 328–333.

Goodhines, Patricia A.; Gellis. Les A.; Ansell, Emily B.; & Park, Aesoon. (2019). Cannabis and alcohol use for sleep aid: A daily diary investigation. *Health Psychology.* http://doi.org/10.1037/hea0000765

Goodin, Burel, & Bulls, Hailey. (2013). Optimism and the experience of pain: Benefits of seeing the glass as half full. *Current Pain and Headache Reports,17*(5). https://doi.org/10.1007/s11916-013-0329-8.

Goodkind, Madeleine; Eickhoff, Simon; Oathes, Desmond; Jiang, Ying; Chang, Andrew; Jones-Hagata, Laura; Ortega, Brissa N.; Zaiko, Yevgeniya V.; Roach, Erika L.; Korgaonkar, Mayuresh S.; Grieve, Stuart M.; Galatzer-Levy, Isaac; Fox, Peter T.; & Etkin, Amit. (2015). Identification of a common neurobiological substrate for mental illness. *JAMA Psychiatry, 72*(4), 305–315. https://doi.org/10.1001 /jamapsychiatry.2014.2206

Goodman, Elizabeth; Maxwell, Sarah; Malspeis, Susan; & Adler, Nancy. (2015). Developmental trajectories of subjective social status. *Pediatrics, 136*(3), e633–e640. https://doi.org/10.1542/peds.2015-1300

Goodman, Gail S.; Ghetti, Simona; Quas, Jodi A.; Edelstein, Robin S.; Alexander, Kristen Weede; Redlich, Allison D.; Cordon, Ingrid M.; & Jones, David P. H. (2003). A prospective study of memory for child sexual abuse: New findings relevant to the repressed-memory controversy. *Psychological Science, 14*(2), 113–118. https://doi.org /10.1111/1467-9280.01428

Gorchoff, Sara M.; John, Oliver P.; & Helson, Ravenna. (2008). Contextualizing change in marital satisfaction during middle age: An 18-year longitudinal study. *Psychological Science, 19*(11), 1194–1200. https://doi.org/10.1111/j.1467-9280.2008.02222.x

Gordon, Barry. (2008, February 7). Quoted in Robynne Boyd, "Do people only use 10 percent of their brains?" *Scientific American.* Retrieved from http://www.scientificamerican .com/article/people-only-use-10-percent-of-brain

Gordon, Peter. (2004, October 15). Numerical cognition without words: Evidence from Amazonia. *Science, 306,* 496–499.

Goshua, Anna. (2018, October 26). It's time to start treating asexual and aromatic people like the adults we are. *Slate.* https://slate.com/human-interest/2018/10 /asexuality-awareness-week-infantilization-phase.html

Goswami, Usha. (2006). Neuroscience and education: From research to practice? *Nature Reviews Neuroscience, 7,* 2–7.

Gottesman, Irving I. (1991). *Schizophrenia genesis: The origins of madness.* Freeman.

Gottfredson, Linda S. (1998, winter). The general intelligence factor. *Scientific American Presents: Exploring Intelligence, 9,* 24–29.

Gottfredson, Linda S. (2003). Dissecting practical intelligence theory: Its claims and evidence. *Intelligence, 31*(4), 343-397. https://doi.org/10.1016/S0160-2896(02)00085-5

Gottfredson, Ryan K.; Wright, Sarah L.; & Heaphy, Emily D. (2020). A critique of the Leader-Member Exchange construct: Back to square one. *The Leadership Quarterly, 31*(6), 101385. https://doi.org/10.1016/j.leaqua.2020.101385

Gottfried, Jay. (2010). Central mechanisms of odour object perception. *Nature Reviews Neuroscience 11*, 628–641. https://doi.org/10.1038/nrn2883

Gottman, John M. (2002). A multidimensional approach to couples. In Florence W. Kaslow & Terence Patterson (Eds.), *Comprehensive handbook of psychotherapy: Cognitive-behavioral approaches.* Wiley.

Gottman, John M. (2011). *The science of trust.* Norton.

Gottman, John M.; Gottman, Julie S.; & DeClaire, Joan. (2006). *10 lessons to transform your marriage.* Three Rivers Press.

Gottman, John M.; Gottman, Julie S.; & DeClaire, Joan. (2007). *Ten lessons to transform your marriage: America's love lab experts share their strategies for strengthening your relationship.* Harmony.

Gottman, John Mordechai; Levenson, Robert W.; Gross, James; Frederickson, Barbara L.; McCoy, Kim, Rosenthal, Leah; Ruef, Anna; & Yoshimoto, Dan. (2003). Correlates of gay and lesbian couples' relationship satisfaction and relationship dissolution. *Journal of Homosexuality, 45*(1), 23-43. https://doi.org/10.1300/J082v45n01_02

Gouin, Jean-Philippe, & Kiecolt-Glaser, Janice. (2012). The impact of psychological stress on wound healing: Methods and mechanisms. *Immunology and Allergy Clinics of North America,31*(1), 81–93. https://doi.org/10.1016/j.iac.2010.09.010

Goulart, Vinícius D.; Azevedo, Pedro G.; van de Schepop, Joanna A.; Teixeira, Camila P.; Barçante, Luciana; Azevedo, Cristiano S.; & Young, Robert J. (2009). GAPs in the study of zoo and wild animal welfare. *Zoo Biology, 28*(6), 561–573.

Gould, Stephen Jay. (1993). *The mismeasure of man* (2nd ed.). Norton.

Goulden, Marc; Frasch, Karie; & Mason, Mary Ann. (2009). *Staying competitive: Patching America's leaky pipeline in the sciences.* Center for American Progress. http://americanprogress.org/issues/technology/report/2009/11/10/6979/staying-competitive/

Goulden, Marc; Mason, Mary Ann; & Frasch, Karie. (2011). Keeping women in the science pipeline. *Annals of the American Academy of Political and Social Science, 638,* 141–162. https://doi.org/10.1177/0002716211416925

Grabe, Shelly; Ward, L. Monique; & Hyde, Janet Shibley. (2008). The role of the media in body image concerns among women: A metaanalysis of experimental and correlational studies. *Psychological Bulletin, 134,* 460–476.

Graf, Nikki. (2019, November 6). Key findings on marriage and cohabitation in the U.S. *Pew Research Center.* https://www.pewresearch.org/fact-tank/2019/11/06/key-findings-on-marriage-and-cohabitation-in-the-u-s/

Grafton, Ben; & Macleod, Colin. (2016). Engaging with the wrong people: The basis of selective attention to negative faces in social anxiety. *Clinical Psychological Science,4,* 793–804. https://doi.org/10.1177/2167702615616344

Graham, Jesse; Nosek, Brian A.; Haidt, Jonathan; Iyer, Ravi; Koleva; Spassena; & Ditto, Peter H. (2011). Mapping the moral domain. *Journal of Personality and Social Psychology.* https://doi.org/10.1037/a0021847

Graham, John R. (1993). *MMPI-2: Assessing personality and psychopathology* (2nd ed.). Oxford University Press.

Graham, Kathryn D.; Osgood, D. Wayne.; Wells, Samantha.; & Stockwell, Tim. (2006). To what extent is intoxication associated with aggression in bars? A multilevel analysis. *Journal of Studies on Alcohol and Drugs, 67,* 382–390.

Graham, Laurel. (1999). Domesticating efficiency: Lillian Gilbreth's scientific management of homemakers. 1924-1930. Signs, 24, 633–675. http://www.jstor.org/stable/3175321

Graham, William K., & Balloun, Joe (1973). An empirical test of Maslow's need hierarchy theory. *Journal of Humanistic Psychology, 13,* 97–108.

Grandey, Alicia A. (2000). Emotional regulation in the workplace: A new way to conceptualize emotional labor. *Journal of Occupational Health Psychology, 5*(1), 95–110. https://doi.org/10.1037/1076-8998.5.1.95

Grandey, Alicia A.; Frone, Michael R.; Melloy, Robert C.; & Sayre, Gordon M. (2019). When are fakers also drinkers? A self-control view of emotional labor and alcohol consumption among U.S. service workers. *Journal of Occupational Health Psychology, 24*(3), 482–497. https://doi.org/10.1037/ocp0000147

Grandey, Alicia A.; Rupp, Deborah; & Brice, William N. (2015). Emotional labor threatens decent work: A proposal to eradicate emotional display rules. *Journal of Organizational Behavior, 36,* 770–785. https://doi.org/10.1002/job.2020

Grandey, Alicia A.; & Sayre, Gordon M. (2019). Emotional labor: Regulating emotions for a wage. *Current Directions in Psychological Science, 28*(2), 131–137. https://doi.org/10.1177/0963721418812771

Granholm, Eric; Ben-Zeev, Dror; Link, Peter C.; Bradshaw, Kristen R.; & Holden, Jason L. (2012). Mobile assessment and treatment for schizophrenia (MATS): A pilot trial of an interactive text-messaging intervention for medication adherence, socialization, and auditory hallucinations. *Schizophrenia Bulletin, 38*(3), 414–425. https://doi.org/10.1093/schbul/sbr155

Grant, Bob. (2014, September). On the other hand. *The Scientist, 28.* Retrieved from http://www.the-scientist.com/?articles.view/articleNo/40868/title/On-the-Other-Hand

Grant, Bridget F.; Chou, S. Patricia; Goldstein, Risë B.; Huang, Boji; Stinson, Frederick S.; Saha, Tulshi D.; Smith, Sharon M.; Dawson, Deborah A.; Pulay, Attila J.; Pickering, Roger P.; & Ruan, W. June. (2008, April). Prevalence, correlates, disability, and comorbidity of DSM-IV borderline personality disorder: Results from the Wave 2 National Epidemiologic Survey on Alcohol and Related Conditions. *Journal of Clinical Psychiatry, 69*(4), 533–545. https:/doi.org/10.4088/jcp.v69n0404

Grant, Bridget F.; Hasin, Deborah S.; Stinson, Frederick S.; Dawson, Deborah A.; Chou, S. Patricia; Ruan, W. June; & Pickering, Roger P. (2004). Prevalence, correlates, and disability of personality disorders in the United States: Results from the National Epidemiologic Survey on Alcohol and Related Conditions. *Journal of Clinical Psychiatry, 65*(7), 948–958. https://doi.org/10.4088/jcp.v65n0711

Grant, Joshua A.; Courtemanche, Jérôme; Duerden, Emma G.; Duncan, Gary H.; & Rainville, Pierre. (2010). Cortical thickness and pain sensitivity in zen meditators. *Emotion, 10*(1), 43–53. https://doi.org/10.1037/a0018334

Grant, Joshua A.; Courtemanche, Jérôme; & Rainville, Pierre. (2011). A non-elaborative mental stance and decoupling of executive and pain-related cortices predicts low pain sensitivity in Zen meditators. *Pain, 152,* 150–156. https://doi.org/10.1016/j.pain.2010.10.006

Gray, John. (2012). *Men are from Mars, women are from Venus: The classic guide to understanding the opposite sex.* Harper. (Originally published 1992.)

Green, Joseph P.; Lynn, Steven Jay; & Montgomery, Guy H. (2006). A meta-analysis of gender, smoking cessation, and hypnosis: A brief communication. *International Journal of Clinical and Experimental Hypnosis, 54,* 224–233.

Greenberg, Daniel L., & Rubin, David C. (2003). The neuropsychology of autobiographical memory. *Cortex, 39,* 687–728.

Greenfield, Patricia M. (1997). You can't take it with you: Why ability assessments don't cross cultures. *American Psychologist, 52,* 1115–1124.

Greenfield, Patricia M. (2003, February). Quoted in Benson, Etienne. "Intelligence across cultures." *APA Monitor on Psychology, 34,* 56.

Greenwald, Anthony G.; McGhee, Debbie E.; & Schwartz, Jordan L. K. (1998). Measuring individual differences in implicit cognition: The implicit association test. *Journal of Personality and Social Psychology, 74,* 1464–1480.

Greenwald, Anthony G.; Poehlman, T. Andrew; Uhlmann, Eric; & Banaji, Mahzarin R. (2009). Understanding and using the Implicit Association Test: III. Meta-analysis of predictive validity. *Journal of Personality and Social Psychology, 97,* 17–41.

Greenwood, Tiffany A. (2020, February 10). Creativity and bipolar disorder: A shared genetic vulnerability. *Annual Review of Clinical Psychology, 16,* 239–264. https://doi.org/10.1146/annurev-clinpsy-050718-095449

Greer, Stephanie M.; Goldstein, Andrea N.; & Walker, Matthew P. (2013). The impact of sleep deprivation on food desire in the human brain. *Nature Communications, 4,* Article No, 2259. https://doi.org/10.1038/ncomms3259

Gregory, Richard L. (1968, November). Visual illusions. *Scientific American, 212,* 66–76.

Griffiths, Roland R.; Johnson, Matthew W.; Carducci, Michael A.; Umbricht, Annie; Richards, William A.; Richards, Brian D.; Cosimano, Mary P.; & Klinedinst, Margaret A. (2016). Psilocybin produces substantial and sustained decreases in depression and anxiety in patients with life-threatening cancer: A randomized double-blind trial. *Journal of Psychopharmacology, 30,* 1181–1197. https://doi.org/10.1177/0269881116675513

Grigg-Damberger, Madeleine; Gozal, David; Marcus, Carole L.; Quan, Stuart F.; Rosen, Carol L.; Chervin, Ronald D.; Wise, Merill; Picchietti, Daniel L.; Sheldon, Stephan H.; & Iber, Conrad. (2007). Visual scoring of sleep and arousal in infants and children. *Journal of Clinical Sleep Medicine, 3,* 201–240.

Griggs, Richard A. (2014). The continuing saga of Little Albert in introductory psychology textbooks. *Teaching of Psychology, 41*(4), 309–317. https://doi.org/10.1177/0098628314549702

Griggs, Richard A. (2015a). The disappearance of independence in textbook coverage of Asch's social pressure experiments. *Teaching of Psychology, 42,* 137–142. https://doi.org/10.1177/0098628315569939

Griggs, Richard A. (2015b). The Kitty Genovese story in introductory psychology textbooks: Fifty years later. *Teachings of Psychology, 42,* 149–152. https://doi.org/10.1177/0098628315573138

Griggs, Richard A., & Whitehead, George I. (2015). Coverage of Milgram's obedience experiments in social psychology textbooks: Where have all the criticisms gone? *Teaching of Psychology, 42*(4), 315–322. https://doi.org/10.1177/0098628315603065

Grijalva, Emily; Harms, Peter; Newman, Daniel; Gaddis, Blaine; & Fraley, Chris. (2015). Narcissism and leadership: A meta-analytic review of linear and nonlinear relationships. *Personnel Psychology, 68,* 1–47. https://doi.org/10.1111/peps.12072

Grinspan, Mauro C.; Carpenter, Morgan; Ehrt, Julia; Kara, Sheherezade; Narrain, Arvind; Patel, Pooja; Sidoti, Chris; & Tabengwa, Monica. (2017). The Yogyakarta Principles plus 10: Additional principles and state obligations on the application of international human rights law in relation to sexual orientation, gender identity, gender expression and sex characteristics to complement the Yogyakarta principles. *Yogyakarta Principles.* http://yogyakartaprinciples.org/wp-content/uploads/2017/11/A5_yogyakartaWEB-2.pdf

Groer, Maureen; Meagher, Mary W.; & Kendall-Tackett, Kathleen. (2010). An overview of stress and immunity. In Kathleen Kendall-Tackett (Ed.), *The psychoneuroimmunology of chronic disease: Exploring the links between inflammation, stress, and illness.* American Psychological Association.

Groh, Ashley; Fearson, Pasco; IJzendoorn, Marinus; Bakermans-Kranenburg, Marian; & Roisman, Glenn. (2016). Attachment in the early life course: Meta-analytic evidence for its role in socioemotional development. *Child Development Perspectives, 11,* 70–76. https://doi.org/10.1111/cdep.12213

Grolnick, Wendy S.; Kurowski, Carolyn O.; McMenamy, Jannette M.; Rivkin, Inna; & Bridges, Lisa J. (1998). Mothers' strategies for regulating their toddlers' distress. *Infant Behavior and Development, 21,* 437–450. http://doi.org/10.1016/S0163-6383(98)90018-2

Gross, Garrett G.; Junge, Jason A.; Mora, Rudy J.; Kwon, Hyung-Bae; Olson, C. Anders; Takahashi, Terry T.; Liman, Emily R.; Ellis-Davies, Graham C.R.; Ellis-Davies, Graham C.R.; McGee, Aaron W.; Sabatini, Bernardo L.; Roberts, Richard W.; & Arnold, Don B. (2013). Recombinant probes for visualizing endogenous synaptic proteins in living neurons. *Neuron 78,* 971–985. https://doi.org/10.1016/j.neuron.2013.04.017

Gross, James J. (2007). The cultural regulation of emotions. In James J. Gross (Ed.), *Handbook of emotion regulation* (pp. 486–503). Guilford

Gross, Terry. (2015, October 22). Sarah Silverman opens up about depression, comedy and troublemaking [Interview]. http://www.npr.org/templates/transcript/transcript.php?storyId=450830121

Grower, Petal; Ward, L. Monique; & Beltz, Adriene M. (2019). Downstream consequences of pubertal timing for young women's body beliefs. *Journal of Adolescence, 72,* 162–166. https://doi.org/10.1016/j.adolescence.2019.02.012

Grubin, Don. (2010). Polygraphy. In Jennifer M. Brown & Elizabeth A. Campbell, (Eds.), *The Cambridge handbook of forensic psychology.* Cambridge University Press.

Grünbaum, Adolf. (2006). Is Sigmund Freud's psychoanalytic edifice relevant to the 21st century? *Psychoanalytic Psychology, 23,* 257–284.

Grünbaum, Adolf. (2007). The reception of my Freud-critique in the psychoanalytic literature. *Psychoanalytic Psychology, 24,* 545–576.

Grunstein, Ronald. (2005). Continuous positive airway pressure treatment for obstructive sleep apnea-hypopnea syndrome. In Meir H. Kryger, Thomas Roth, & William C. Dement (Eds.), *Principles and practice of sleep medicine* (4th ed.). Elsevier Saunders.

Grusec, Joan E. (2011). Socialization processes in the family: Social and emotional development. *Annual Review of Psychology, 62,* 243–69. https://doi.org/10.1146/annurev.psych.121208.131650

Grussu, Pietro; Quatraro, Rosa M.; & Nasta, Maria T. (2005). Profile of mood states and parental attitudes in motherhood: Comparing women with planned and unplanned pregnancies. *Birth: Issues in Perinatal Care, 2,* 107–114.

Grzywacz, Joseph G., & Almeida, David M. (2008). Stress and binge drinking: A daily process examination of stressor pile-up and socioeconomic status in affect regulation. *International Journal of Stress Management, 15*(4), 364–380.

Gu, Simeng; Wang, Fushun; Cao, Caiyun; Wu, Erxi; Tang, Yi-Yuan; & Huang, Jason H. (2019). An integrative way for studying neural basis of basic emotions with fMRI. *Frontiers in Neuroscience, 13,* 628. https://doi.org/10.3389/fnins.2019.00628

Guay, Julie A.; Lebretore, Brittany M.; Main, Jesse M.; DeGrangesco, Katelyn E.; Taylor, Jessica L.; & Amedoro, Sarah M. (2016). The era of sport concussion: Evolution of knowledge, practice, and the role of psychology. *American Psychologist, 71,* 875–887. https//doi.org/10.1037/a0040430

Guéguen, Nicolas; Marchand, Marie; Pascual, Alexandre; & Lourel, Marcel. (2008). Foot-in-the-door technique using a courtship request: A field experiment. *Psychological Reports, 103*(2), 529–534.

Guerin, Bernard. (1986). Mere presence effects in humans: A review. *Journal of Experimental Social Psychology, 22,* 38–77.

Guerin, Bernard. (2003). Social behaviors as determined by different arrangements of social consequences: Diffusion of responsibility effects with competition. *Journal of Social Psychology, 143,* 313–329. https://doi.org/10.1080/00224540309598447

Guimond, Serge. (2008). Psychological similarities and differences between women and men across cultures. *Social and Personality Psychology Compass, 2,* 494–510.

Guimond, Serge; Crisp, Richard J.; De Oliveira, Pierre; Kamiejski, Rodolphe; Kteily, Nour; Kuepper, Beate; Lalonde, Richard N.; Levin, Shana; Pratto, Felicia; Tougas, Francine; Sidanius, Jim; & Zick, Andreas. (2013). Diversity policy, social dominance, and intergroup relations: Predicting prejudice in changing social and political contexts. *Journal of Personality and Social Psychology, 104*(6), 941–958. https://doi.org/10.1037/a0032069

Guindon, José, & Hohmann, Andrea. (2009). Pain: Mechanisms and measurement. In Gary G. Berntson & John T. Cacioppo (Eds.), *Handbook of neuroscience in the behavioral sciences.* Wiley.

Gujar, Ninad; Yoo, Seung-Schik; Hu, Peter; & Walker, Matthew P. (2011). Sleep deprivation amplifies reactivity of brain reward networks, biasing the appraisal of positive emotional experiences. *Journal of Neuroscience, 31*(12): 4466–4474. https://doi.org/10.1523/jneurosci.3220-10.2011

Gunlicks-Stoessel, Meredith & Weissman, Myrna M. (2011). Interpersonal psychotherapy (IPT). In Leonard M. Horowitz & Stephen Strack (Eds.), *Handbook of interpersonal psychology: Theory, research, assessment, and therapeutic interventions* (pp. 533–544). Wiley.

Gurven, Michael; von Rueden, Christopher; Massenkoff, Maxim; Kaplan, Hillard; & Lero Vie, Marino. (2013). How universal is the Big Five? Testing the five-factor model of personality variation among forager–farmers in the Bolivian Amazon. *Journal of Personality and Social Psychology, 104,* 354–370. https://doi.org/10.1037/a0030841

Gurven, Michael; von Rueden, Christopher; Stieglitz, Jonathan; Kaplan, Hillard; & Rodriguez, Daniel E. (2014). The evolutionary fitness of personality traits in a small-scale subsistence society. *Evolution and Human Behavior, 35,* 17–25. https://doi.org/10.1016/j.evolhumbehav.2013.09.002

Guthrie, Robert V. (1976). *Even the rat was white: A historical view of psychology.* Harper & Row

Guthrie, Robert V. (2000). Francis Cecil Sumner: The first African American pioneer in psychology. In Gregory A. Kimble & Michael Wertheimer (Eds.), *Portraits of pioneers in psychology* (Vol. 4, pp. 180–193). American Psychological Association.

Guthrie, Robert V. (2004). *Even the rat was white: A historical view of psychology.* Pearson Education.

Gutman, David A., & Nemeroff, Charles B. (2011). Stress and depression. In Richard J. Contrada & Andrew Baum (Eds.), *The handbook of stress science: Biology, psychology, and health* (pp. 345–357). Springer.

Guyer, Amanda E.; Monk, Christopher S.; McClure-Tone, Erin B.; Nelson, Eric E.; Roberson-Nay, Roxann; Adler, Abby D.; Fromm, Stephen J.; Leibenluft, Ellen; Pine, Daniel S.; & Ernst, Monique. (2008). A developmental examination of amygdala response to facial expressions. *Journal of Cognitive Neuroscience, 20*(9), 1565–1582. https://doi.org/10.1162/jocn.2008.20114

Häberling, Isabelle S.; Corballis, Paul M.; & Corballis, Michael C. (2016). Language, gesture, and handedness: Evidence for independent lateralized networks. *Cortex, 82,* 72–85. https://doi.org/10.1016/j.cortex.2016.06.003

Habhab, Summar; Sheldon, Jane P; & Loeb, Roger C. (2009). The relationship between stress, dietary restraint, and food preferences in women. *Appetite, 52*(2), 437–444.

Hacker, Carl D.; Roland, Jarod L.; Kim, Albert H.; Shimony, Joshua S. & Leuthardt, Eric C. (2019). Resting-state network mapping in neurosurgical practice: A review. *Neurosurgical Focus, 47*(6), E15. https://doi.org/10.3171/2019.9.focus19656

Hackett, Troy A., & Kaas, Jon H. (2009). Audition. In Gary G. Berntson & John T. Cacioppo (Eds.), *Handbook of neuroscience in the behavioral sciences.* Wiley.

Hackman, Daniel A.; Farah, Martha J.; Meaney, Michael J. (2010). Socioeconomic status and the brain: Mechanistic insights from human and animal research. *Nature Reviews Neuroscience, 11,* 651–659.

Hadhazy, A. (2010). Think twice: How the gut's "second brain" influences mood and well-being. *Scientific American,* February 12. https://www.scientificamerican.com/article/gut-second-brain/

Hadid, Diaa. (2020, May 21). All-girl robotics team in Afghanistan works on low-cost ventilator . . . with car parts. *Goats and Soda.* https://www.npr.org/sections/goatsandsoda/2020/05/21/858087604/all-girl-robotics-team-in-afghanistan-works-on-low-cost-ventilator-with-car-part

Hagar, Sheila. (2013, September 19). Washington State Penitentiary psychologist earns national acclaim for programs. *Union-Bulletin.* https://www.union-bulletin.com/news/washington-state-penitentiary-psychologist-earns-national-acclaim-for-programs/article_268be76b-2e7d-5172-a2b6-51786802fa5e.html

Haggard, Patrick; Clark, Sam; & Kalogeras, Jeri. (2002). Voluntary action and conscious awareness. *Nature Neuroscience, 5,* 382–385. https://doi.org/10.1038/nn827

Haidt, Jonathan. (2007). The new synthesis in moral *psychology. Science, 316,* 998–1002.

Haidt, Jonathan. (2010). Moral psychology must not be based on faith and hope: Commentary on Narvaez (2010). *Perspectives on Psychological Science, 5,* 182–184.

Hajima, Sander; Haren, Neeltje; Cahn, Wiepke; Koolschijn, Cédric; Pol, Hilleke; & Kahn, René. S. (2012). Brain volumes in schizophrenia: A meta-analysis in over 18 000 subjects. *Schizophrenia Bulletin, 39*(5), 1129–1138. https://doi.org/10.1093/schbul/sbs118

Hakuta, Kenji; Bialystok, Ellen; & Wiley, Edward (2003). A test of the critical period hypothesis for second language acquisition. *Psychological Science, 14,* 31–38.

Halbrook, Yemaya J.; O'Donnell, Aisling T.; & Msetfi, Rachel M. (2019). When and how video games can be good: A review of the positive effects of video games on well-being. *Perspectives on Psychological Science, 14*(6), 1096–1104. https://doi.org/10.1177/1745691619986380

Halim, May; Ruble, Dianne; Tamis-LeMonda, Catherine; Shrout, Patrick; & Amodio, David. (2017). Gender attitudes in early childhood: Behavioral consequences and cognitive antecedents. *Child Development, 88,* 882–899. https://doi.org/10.1111/cdev.12642

Hall, Gordon C. Nagayama; Yip, Tiffany; & Zárate, Michael A. (2016). On becoming multicultural in a monocultural research world: A conceptual approach to studying ethnocultural diversity. *American Psychologist, 71,* 40–51. https://doi.org/10.1037/a0039734

Haller, Jozsef. (2018). The role of central and medial amygdala in normal and abnormal aggression: A review of classical approaches. *Neuroscience and Biobehavioral Reviews, 85,* 34–43. https://doi.org/10.1016/j.neubiorev.2017.09.017

Halmi, Katherine A.; Bellace, Dara; Berthod, Samantha; Gosh, Samiran; Berrettini, Wade; Brandt, Harry A.; Bulik, Cynthia M.; Crawford, Steve; Fichter, Manfred M.; Johnson, Craig L.; Kaplan, Allan; Kaye, Walter H.; Thornton, Laura; Treasure, Janet; Woodside, D. Blake; & Strober, Michael. (2012). An examination of early childhood perfectionism across anorexia nervosa subtypes. *International Journal of Eating Disorders, 45*(6), 800–807. https://doi.org/10.1002/eat.22019

Halpern, Diane F.; Benbow, Camilla P.; Geary, David C.; Gur, Ruben C.; Hyde, Janet Shibley; & Gernsbacher, Morton Ann. (2007). The science of sex differences in science and mathematics. *Psychological Science in the Public Interest, 8*(1), 1–51. https://doi.org/10.1111/j.1529-1006.2007.00032.x

Halpern, Diane F.; Beninger, Anna S.; & Straight, Carli A. (2011). Sex differences in intelligence. In Robert J. Sternberg & Scott Barry Kaufman (Eds.), *The Cambridge handbook of intelligence* (pp. 253–270). Cambridge University Press.

Halpern, John H.; Sherwood, Andrea R.; Hudson, James I.; Yurgelun-Todd, Deborah; & Pope, Harrison G. (2005). Psychological and cognitive effects of long-term peyote use among Native Americans. *Biological Psychiatry, 58,* 624–631.

Hamann, Stephan. (2009). The human amygdala and memory. In P. J. Whalen & E. A. Phelps (Eds.), *The human amygdala* (pp. 177–203). Guilford.

Hamby, Tyler; Taylor, Wyn; Snowden, Audrey; & Peterson, Robert. (2015). A meta-analysis of the reliability of free and for-pay Big Five scales. *Journal of Psychology,150,* 422–430. https://doi.org/10.1080/00223980.2015.1060186

Hamer, Mark; Taylor, Adrian H.; & Steptoe, Andrew. (2006). The effect of acute aerobic exercise on stress related blood pressure responses: A systematic review and meta-analysis. *Biological Psychology, 71*(2), 183–190.

Hamermesh, Daniel S., & Abrevaya, Jason. (2011). Beauty is the promise of happiness? (Discussion Paper No. 5600). The Institute for the Study of Labor (IZA).

Hamilton, S., & Hamilton, M.A. (2006). School, work, and emerging adulthood. In J. J. Arnett & J. L. Tanner (Eds.), *Emerging adults in America: Coming of age in the 21st century.* American Psychological Association.

Hamlin, J. Kiley; Mahajan, Neha; Liberman, Zoe; & Wynn, Karen. (2013). Not like me = bad: Infants prefer those who harm dissimilar others. *Psychological Science, 24*(4), 589–594. https://doi.org/10.1177/0956797612457785

Hammen, Constance. (2005). Stress and depression. *Annual Review of Clinical Psychology, 1,* 293–319. https://doi.org/10.1146/annurev.clinpsy.1.102803.143938

Haney, Craig; Banks, Curtis; & Zimbardo, Philip. (1973). Interpersonal dynamics in a simulated prison. *International Journal of Criminology and Penology, 1,* 69–97.

Haney, Jolynn. (2016). Autism, females, and the DSM-5: Gender bias in autism diagnosis. *Social Work in Mental Health, 14*(4), 396–407. https://doi.org/10.1080/15332985.2015.1031858

Hansell, Saul. (2007). Google answer to filling jobs is an algorithm. *The New York Times.* http://nyti.ms/1YhkyEJ

Hardman, Kyle O.; & Cowan, Nelson. (2016). Reasoning and memory: People make varied use of the information available in working memory. *Journal of Experimental Psychology: Learning, Memory, and Cognition,42,* 700–722. https://doi.org/10.1037/xlm0000197

Hardt, Oliver; Wang, Szu-Han; & Nader, Karim. (2010). Storage or retrieval deficit: The yin and yang of amnesia. *Learning and Memory, 16,* 224–230.

Hardy, Sam A.; Bhattacharjee, Amit; Reed, Americus, II; & Aquino, Karl. (2010). Moral identity and psychological distance: The case of adolescent parental socialization. *Journal of Adolescence, 33*(1), 111–123.

Harlow, Harry F. (1958) The nature of love. *American Psychologist, 13,* 673–685.

Harlow, John M. (1869). Recovery from passage of an iron bar through the head. (Read before the Massachusetts Medical Society, June 3, 1868.) David Clapp & Son Medical and Special Journal Office.

Harman, S. Mitchell. (2005). Testosterone in older men after the Institute of Medicine Report: Where do we go from here? *Climacteric, 8,* 124–135.

Harmon, Amy. (2019). Which box to you check? Some states are offering a nonbinary option. *The New York Times.* https://www.nytimes.com/2019/05/29/us/nonbinary-drivers-licenses.html?smid=nytcore-ios-share

Harnett, Paul; O'Donovan, Analise; & Lambert, Michael J. (2010). The dose response relationship in psychotherapy: Implications for social policy. *Clinical Psychologist, 14*(2), 39–44.

Haro, Josep M.; Novick, Diego; Bertsch, Jordan; Karagiania, Jamie; Dossenbach, Martin; & Jones, Peter B. (2011). Cross-national clinical and functional remission rates: Worldwide schizophrenia outpatient health outcomes (W-SOHO) study. *British Journal of Psychiatry, 199,* 194–201. https://doi.org/10.1192/bjp.bp.110.082065

Harper, Sarah. (2014). Economic and social implications of aging societies. *Science, 346,* 587–592.

Harris, Aisha. (2016, October 5). Kid Cudi's candid revelation about struggling with depression and suicidal thoughts could help others. *Slate.* http://www.slate.com/blogs/browbeat/2016/10/05/kid_cudi_reveals_he_suffers_from_depression_and_suicidal_urges_in_a_remarkably.html

Harris, Ben. (1979). Whatever happened to Little Albert? *American Psychologist, 34,* 151–160.

Harris, Ben. (2011). Letting go of Little Albert: Disciplinary memory, history, and the uses of myth. *Journal of the History of the Behavioral Sciences, 47,* 1–17. https://doi.org/10.1002/jhbs.20470

Harris, Julie Aitken; Vernon, Philip A.; & Jang, Kerry L. (2007, January). Rated personality and measured intelligence in young twin children. *Personality and Individual Differences, 42*(1), 75–86.

Harris, Julie M.; Nefs, Harold T.; & Grafton, Catherine E. (2008). Binocular vision and motion-in-depth. *Spatial Vision, 21*(6), 531–547. https://doi.org/10.1163/156856808786451462

Harris, Lasana T., & Fiske, Susan T. (2006). Dehumanizing the lowest of the low. *Psychological Science, 17*(10), 847–853.

Harris, Matthew A.; Brett, Caroline E.; Johnson, Wendy; & Deary, Ian J. (2016). Personality stability from age 14 to age 77 years. *Psychology and Aging, 31*(8), 862–874. https://doi.org/10.1037/pag0000133

Harrison, Robert V. (2012, December 13). The prevention of noise-induced hearing loss in children. *International Journal of Pediatrics, 2012,* 473–541. https://doi.org/10.1155/2012/473541

Hart, Dan. (2005). The development of moral identity. In G. Carlo & C. P. Edwards (Eds.), *Moral motivation through the life span* (pp. 165–196). University of Nebraska Press.

Harter, Susan. (1990). Self and identity development. In S. Shirley Feldman & Glen R. Elliott (Eds.), *At the threshold: The developing adolescent.* Harvard University Press.

Hartshorne, Joshua K., & Germine, Laura T. (2015). When does cognitive functioning peak? The asynchronous rise and fall of different cognitive abilities across the life span. *Psychological Science, 26,* 433–443. https://doi.org/10.1177/0956797614567339

Hartwig, Marissa K., & Dunlosky, John. (2012). Study strategies of college students: Are self-testing and scheduling related to achievement? *Psychonomic Bulletin & Review, 19*(1), 126–134. https://doi.org/10.3758/s13423-011-0181-y

Harvard Business Review. (2013, September). Harvard Business Publishing.

Harvey, Allison G. (2011). Sleep and circadian functioning: Critical mechanisms in the mood disorders? *Annual Review of Clinical Psychology, 7,* 297–319. https://doi.org/10.1146/annurev-clinpsy-032210-104550

Harvey, Megan A.; Sellman, John D.; Porter, Richard J.; & Frampton, Christopher M. (2007). The relationship between non-acute adolescent cannabis use and cognition. *Drug & Alcohol Review, 26,* 309–319.

Harvey, Nigel. (2007, February). Use of heuristics: Insights from forecasting research. *Thinking & Reasoning, 13*(1), 5–24.

Harwood, T. M., & L'Abate, L. (2010). *Self-help in mental health: A critical review.* Springer Science Business Media.

Hashash, Mahmoud; Zeid, Maya Abou; & Moacdieh, Nadine Marie. (2019). Social media browsing while driving: Effects on driver performance and attention allocation. *Transportation Research Part F, 63,* 67–82. https://doi.org/10.1016/j.trf.2019.03.021

Hasin, Deborah; Fenton, Miriam C.; Skodol, Andrew; Krueger, Rorbert; Keyes, Katherine; Geier, Timothy; Greenstein, Eliana; Blanco, Carlos; & Grant, Bridget. (2011). Personality disorders and the 3-year course of alcohol, drug, and nicotine use disorders. *Archives of General Psychiatry, 68*(11), 1158–1167. https://doi.org/10.1001/archgenpsychiatry.2011.136

Hatch, Stephani L., & Dohrenwend, Bruce P. (2007). Distribution of traumatic and other stressful life events by race/ethnicity, gender, SES, and age: A review of the research. *American Journal of Community Psychology, 40,* 313–332.

Hattie, John, & Yates, Gregory. (2014). Using feedback to promote learning. In Benassi, Victor; Overson, Catherine; & Hakala, Christopher (Eds.), *Applying science of learning in education: Infusing psychological science into the curriculum.* Society for the Teaching of Psychology. http://teachpsych.org/ebooks/asle2014/index.php

Hatton, Holly; Conger, Rand D.; Larsen-Rife, Dannelle; & Ontai, Lenna. (2010). An integrative and developmental perspective for understanding romantic relationship quality during the transition to parenthood. In M. S. Schulz, M. K. Pruett, P. K. Kerig & R. D. Parke (Eds.), *Strengthening couple relationships for optimal child development: Lessons from research and intervention* (pp. 115–129). American Psychological Association.

Haufrect, Sarah. (2016). I loved, lived with, and lost my mother to borderline personality disorder. *Salon.* http://www.salon.com/2016/02/28/i_loved_lived_with_and_lost_my_mother_to_borderline_personality_disorder/

Hauser, Marc D. (2000). *Wild minds: What animals really think.* Holt.

Haushofer, Johannes, & Fehr, Ernst. (2014). On the psychology of poverty. *Science, 344,* 862–867. https://doi.org/10.1126/science.1232491

Hausknecht, John; Day, David; & Thomas, Scott. (2004). Applicant reactions to selection procedures: An updated model and meta-analysis. *Cornell University, ILR School.* http://digitalcommons.ilr.cornell.edu/articles/125

Haut, Kristen; Erp, Theo; Knowlton, Barbara; Bearden, Carrie; Subotnik, Kenneth; Ventura, Joseph; Nuechterlein, Keith; & Cannon, Tyrone. (2014). Contributions of feature binding during encoding and functional connectivity of the medial temporal lobe structures to episodic memory deficits across the prodromal and first-episode phases of schizophrenia. *Clinical Psychological Science, 3*(2), 159–174. https://doi.org/10.1177/2167702614533949

Havas, David A.; Glenberg, Arthur M.; Gutowski, Karol A.; Lucarelli, Mark J.; & Davidson, Richard J. (2010). Cosmetic use of botulinum toxin-A affects processing of emotional language. *Psychological Science, 21,* 895–900. https://doi.org/10.1177/0956797610374742

Havermans, Remco C.; Janssen, Tim; Giesen, Janneke, C.A.H.; Roefs, Anne; & Jansen, Anita. (2009) Food liking, food wanting, and sensory-specific satiety. *Appetite, 52,* 222–225.

Hawgood, Alex. (2017, November 3). Meet Amanda Gorman, America's first youth poet laureate. *The New York Times.* https://www.nytimes.com/2017/11/03/style/amanda-gorman-first-youth-poet-laureate.html

Hawton, Keith; Saunders, Kate E. A.; & O'Connor, Rory C. (2012). Suicide 1: Self-harm and suicide in adolescents. *Lancet, 379,* 2373–2382.

Hay, Jennifer; Johnson, Victoria E.; Smith, Douglas H.; & Stewart, William. (2016). Chronic traumatic encephalopathy: The neuropathological legacy of traumatic brain injury. *Annual Review of Pathology: Mechanisms of Disease, 11*, 21–45. https//doi.org/10.1146/annurev-pathol-012615-044116

Hayatbakhsh, Muhammad R.; Najman, Jake M.; McGee, Tara R.; Bor, William; & O'Callaghan, Michael J. (2009). Early pubertal maturation in the prediction of early adult substance use: A prospective study. *Addiction, 104*(1), 59–66.

Hayes, Steven C.; Villatte, Matthieu; Levin, Michael; & Hildebrandt, Mikaela. (2011). Open, aware, and active: Contextual approaches as an emerging trend in the behavioral and cognitive therapies. *Annual Review of Clinical Psychology, 7*, 141–168. https://doi.org/10.1146/annurev-clinpsy-032210-104449

Hayne, Harlene; Garry, Maryanne; & Loftus, Elizabeth F. (2006). On the continuing lack of scientific evidence for repression. *Behavioral and Brain Sciences, 29*, 521–522. https://doi.org/10.1017/S0140525X06319115

He, Wan; Goodkind, Daniel; & Kowal, Paul. (2016). An aging world: 2015: International population reports, P95/16-1. *U.S. Census Bureau*. U.S. Government Printing Office.

Heaney, Katie. (2018, August 10). My life as a psychopath. *The Cut*. https://www.thecut.com/2018/08/my-life-as-a-psychopath.html

Heaps, Christopher M., & Nash, Michael. (2001). Comparing recollective experience in true and false autobiographical memories. *Journal of Experimental Psychology: Learning, Memory, and Cognition, 27*, 920–930.

Hearst, Eliot. (1999). After the puzzle boxes: Thorndike in the 20th century. *Journal of the Experimental Analysis of Behavior, 72*, 441–446.

Heaven, Patrick, & Ciarrochi, Joseph. (2008). Parental styles, gender and the development of hope and self-esteem. *European Journal of Personality, 22*(8), 707–724.

Heavey, Christopher L.; Lefforge, Noelle L.; Lapping-Carr, Leiszle; & Hurlburt, Russell T. (2017). Mixed emotions: Toward a phenomenology of blended and multiple feelings. *Emotion Review, 9*, 105–110. https://doi.org/10.1177/1754073916639661

Hebb, Donald O. (1955). Drives and the C. N. S. (central nervous system). *Psychological Review, 62*, 243–254.

Hedegaard, Holly; Curtin, Sally C., & Warner, Margaret. (2020, April). *Increase in suicide mortality in the United States, 1999–2018*. National Center for Health Statistics. https://www.cdc.gov/nchs/products/databriefs/db330.htm

Hedman, Erik; Ljótsson, Brjánn; & Lindefors, Nils. (2012). Cognitive behavior therapy via the internet: A systematic review of applications, clinical efficacy and cost-effectiveness. *Expert Review of Pharmacoeconomics & Outcomes Research, 12*, 745–764. https://doi.org/10.1586/erp.12.67

Heerey, Erin A., & Crossley, Helen M. (2013). Predictive and reactive mechanisms in smile reciprocity. *Psychological Science, 24*, 1446–1455. https://doi.org/10.1177/0956797612472203

Heider, Eleanor Rosch, & Olivier, Donald C. (1972). The structure of the color space in naming and memory for two languages. *Cognitive Psychology, 3*, 337–354.

Hein, Grit; Engelmann, Jan; Vollberg, Marius; & Tobler, Philippe. (2016). How learning shapes the empathic brain. *Proceedings of the National Academy of Sciences, 113*, 80–85. https://doi.org/10.1073/pnas.1514539112

Heine, Steven J.; & Norenzayan, Ara. (2006). Toward a psychological science for a cultural species. *Perspectives on Psychological Science, 1*, 251–269.

Held, Lisa. (2010). Profile of Leta Hollingworth. In A. Rutherford (Ed.), *Psychology's Feminist Voices Multimedia Internet Archive*. http://www.feministvoices.com/leta-hollingworth

Helenius, Dorte; Munk-Jorgensen, Povl; & Steinhausen, Hans-Christoph. (2012). Family load estimates of schizophrenia and associated risk factors in a nation-wide population study of former child and adolescent patients up to forty years of age. *Schizophrenia Research, 139*(1–3), 183–188. https://doi.org/10.1016/j.schres.2012.05.014

Henderson, Valerie Land; O'Hara, Maureen; Barfield, Gay Leah; & Rogers, Natalie. (2007). Applications beyond the therapeutic context. In Mick Cooper, Maureen O'Hara, Peter F. Schmid, & Gill Wyatt (Eds.), *The handbook of person-centred psychotherapy and counselling*. Palgrave Macmillan.

Hennessey, Beth A. (2010). The creativity-motivation connection. In J. C. Kaufman & R. J. Sternberg (Eds.), *The Cambridge handbook of creativity* (pp. 342–365). Cambridge University Press.

Hennessey, Beth A., & Amabile, Teresa M. (2010). Creativity. *Annual Review of Psychology, 61*, 569–598. https://doi.org/10.1146/annurev.psych.093008.100416

Henrich, Joseph. (2014). Rice, psychology, and innovation. *Science, 344*, 593–594. https://doi.org/10.1126/science.1253815

Henrich, Joseph; Heine, Steven J.; & Norenzayan, Ara. (2010). The weirdest people in the world? *The Behavioral and Brain Sciences, 33*, 61–83. https://doi.org/10.1017/S0140525X0999152X

Henry, Nancy J. M.; Berg, Cynthia A.; Smith, Timothy W.; & Florsheim, Paul. (2007). Positive and negative characteristics of marital interaction and their association with marital satisfaction in middle-aged and older couples. *Psychology and Aging, 22*, 428–441.

Heppner, Puncky Paul. (2008). Expanding the conceptualization and measurement of applied problem solving and coping: From stages and dimensions to the almost forgotten cultural context. *American Psychologist, 63*, 805–816.

Herbenick, Debby; Reece, Michael; Schick, Vanessa; Sanders, Stephanie A; Dodge, Brian; Fortenberry J. Dennis. (2010). Sexual behavior in the United States: Results from a national probability sample of men and women ages 14–91. *Journal of Sexual Medicine, 7*(Suppl. 5), 255–265. https://doi.org/10.1111/j.1743-6109/2010.02012.x

Herbert, James D.; Lilienfeld, Scott O.; Lohr, Jeffrey M.; Montgomery, Robert W.; O'Donohue, William T.; Rosen, Gerald M.; & Tolin, David F. (2000). Science and pseudoscience in the development of eye movement desensitization and reprocessing: Implications for clinical psychology. *Clinical Psychology Review, 20*, 945–971.

Herculano-Houzel, Suzana. (2009). The human brain in numbers: A linearly scaled-up primate brain. *Frontiers in Human Neuroscience, 3*, 31. https://doi.org/10.3389/neuro.09.031.2009

Herholz, Sibylle C.; Halpern, Andrea R.; & Zatorre, Robert J. (2012). Neuronal correlates of perception, imagery, and memory for familiar tunes. *Journal of Cognitive Neuroscience, 24*, 1382–1397. https://doi.org/10.1162/jocn_a_00216

Herman, Jody; Flores, Andrew; Brown, Taylor; Wilson, Bianca; & Conron, Kerith. (2017). *Age of individuals who identify as transgender in the United States*. Williams Institute, UCLA School of Law.

Herman, Louis M. (2002). Exploring the cognitive world of the bottlenosed dolphin. In Marc Bekoff, Colin Allen, & Gordon M. Burghardt (Eds.), *The cognitive animal: Empirical and theoretical perspectives on animal cognition*. MIT Press.

Hermans, Hubert J. M. (1996). Voicing the self: From information processing to dialogical interchange. *Psychological Bulletin, 119*, 31–50.

Hernández-Julián, Rey, & Peters, Christina (2015). Student appearance and academic performance. *Journal of Human Capital, 11*, 247–262.

Herndon, Phillip; Myers, Bryan; Mitchell, Katherine; Kehn, Andre; & Henry, Sarah. (2014). False memories for highly aversive early childhood events: Effects of guided imagery and group influence. *Psychology of Consciousness: Theory, Research, and Practice, 1*, 20–31. https://doi.org/10.1037/cns0000011

Herring, Cedric. (2009). Does diversity pay? Race, gender, and the business case for diversity. *American Sociological Review, 74*, 208–224. https://doi.org/10.1177/000312240907400203

Hertel, Paula; Maydon, Amaris; Cottle, Julia; & Vrijsen, Janna. (2017). Cognitive bias modification: Retrieval practice to simulate and oppose ruminative memory biases. *Clinical Psychological Science, 5*, 122–130. https://doi.org/10.1177/2167702616649366

Hertz, Marguerite R. (1992). Rorschach-bound: A 50-year memoir. *Professional Psychology: Research and Practice, 23*, 168–171.

Hertzog, Christopher; Kramer, Arthur F.; Wilson, Robert S.; & Ulman, Lindenberger (2009). Enrichment effects on adult cognitive development: Can the functional capacity of older adults be preserved and enhanced? *Psychological Science in the Public Interest, 9*, 1–65.

Hester, Neil; Payne, Keith; Brown-Iannuzzi, Jasmin; & Gray, Kurt. (2020). On intersectionality: How complex patterns of discrimination can emerge from simple stereotypes. *Psychological Science, 31*(8), 1013–1024. https://doi.org/10.1177/0956797620929979

Hetey, Rebecca C.; & Eberhardt, Jennifer L. (2018). The numbers don't speak for themselves: Racial disparities and the persistence of inequality in the criminal justice system. *Current Directions in Psychological Science, 27*(3), 183–187. https://doi.org/10.1177/09637214187639

Heth, Josephine Todrank; Schapira, Daniel; & Nahir, A. Menachim. (2004). Controllability awareness, perceived stress and tolerating chronic illness. In Serge P. Shohov (Ed.), *Advances in psychology research* (Vol. 28). Nova Science.

Heth, Josephine Todrank, & Somer, Eli. (2002). Characterizing stress tolerance" "Controllability awareness" and its relationship to perceived stress and reported health. *Personality and Individual Differences, 33*, 883–895.

Hettema, Jennifer; Steele, Julie; & Miller, William R. (2005). Motivational interviewing. *Annual Review of Clinical Psychology, 1*, 91–111. https://doi.org/10.1146/annurev.clinpsy.1.102803.143833

Hewstone, Miles; Rubin, Mark; & Willis, Hazel (2002). Intergroup bias. *Annual Review of Psychology, 53*, 575–604.

Heyes, Cecilia. (2020). Psychological mechanisms forged by cultural evolution. *Current Directions in Psychological Science, 29*(4), 399–404. https://doi.org/10.1177/0963721420917736

Heyman, Richard E., & Smith Slep, Amy M. (2002). Do child abuse and interparental violence lead to adulthood family violence? *Journal of Marriage and Family, 64*, 864–870.

Heymann, Jody. (2007, February). The healthy families act: The importance to Americans' livelihoods, families, and health. Written testimony submitted to the U.S. Senate Committee on Health, Education, Labor, and Pensions. https://www.worldpolicycenter.org/sites/default/files/Healthy%20Families%20Act-U.S.Senate%20Comm.%20Test-2007.pdf

Hiatt, Kristina D., & Dishion, Thomas J. (2008). Antisocial personality development. In Theodore P. Beauchaine & Stephen P. Hinshaw (Eds.), *Child and adolescent psychopathology* (pp. 370–404). Wiley.

Hicken, Margaret; Lee, Hedwig; Morenoff, Jeffrey; House, James; & Williams, David. (2014). Racial/ethnic disparities in hypertension prevalence: Reconsidering the role of chronic stress. *American Journal of Public Health, 104*(1), 117–123. https:/doi.org/10.2105/ajph.2013.301395

Hickok, Gregory; Bellugi, Ursula; & Klima, Edward S. (2001, June). Sign language in the brain. *Scientific American, 184,* 58–65.

Hideg, Ivona, & Ferris, D. Lance. (2016). The compassionate sexist? How benevolent sexism promotes and undermines gender equality in the workplace. *Journal of Personality and Social Psychology, 111,* 706–727. https://doi.org/10.1037/pspi0000072

Higgins, E. Tory (2004). Making a theory useful: Lessons handed down. *Personality and Social Psychology Review, 8*(2), 138–145.

Hilgard, Ernest R. (1986a). *Divided consciousness: Multiple controls in human thought and action.* Wiley.

Hilgard, Ernest R. (1986b, January). A study in hypnosis. *Psychology Today, 20,* 23–27.

Hilgard, Ernest R. (1991). A neodissociation interpretation of hypnosis. In Steven J. Lynn & J. Rhue (Eds.), *Theories of hypnosis: Current models and perspectives.* Guilford.

Hilgard, Ernest R. (1992). Divided consciousness and dissociation. *Consciousness and Cognition, 1,* 16–32.

Hilgard, Ernest R.; Hilgard, Josephine R.; & Barber, Joseph. (1994). *Hypnosis in the relief of pain* (Rev. ed.). Brunner/Mazel.

Hilgard, Ernest R., & Marquis, Donald G. (1940). *Conditioning and learning.* Appleton-Century-Crofts.

Hilgard, Joseph; Engelhardt, Christopher R.; Rouder, Jeffrey N.; Segert, Ines L.; & Bartholow, Bruce D. (2019). Null effects of game violence, game difficulty, and 2D:4D digit ratio on aggressive behavior. *Psychological Science, 30*(4), 606–616. https://doi.org/10.1177/095679761982968

Hilgard, Joseph; Engelhardt, Christopher R.; Rouder, Jeffrey N.; Segert, Ines L.; & Bartholow, Bruce D. (2019). Null effects of game violence, game difficulty, and 2D:4D digit ratio on aggressive behavior. *Psychological Science, 30*(4), 606–616. https://doi.org/10.1177/0956797619829688

Hill, Kevin T., & Miller, Lee M. (2010). Auditory attentional control and selection during cocktail party listening. *Cerebral Cortex, 20*(3), 583–590. https://doi.org/10.1093/cercor/bhp124

Hill, Matthew N.; Hellemans, Kim G. C.; Verma, Pamela; Gorzalka, Boris B.; & Weinberg, Joanne. (2012). Neurobiology of chronic mild stress: Parallels to major depression. *Neuroscience and Biobehavioral Reviews, 36*(9), 2085–2117. https://doi.org/10.1016/j.neubiorev.2012.07.001

Hillberg, Tanja; Hamilton-Giachritsis, Catherine; & Dixon, Louise. (2011). Review of meta-analyses on the association between child sexual abuse and adult mental health difficulties: A systematic approach. *Trauma, Violence, & Abuse, 12*(1), 38–49. https://doi.org/10.1177/1524838010386812

Hinds, Joanne, & Joinson, Adam. (2019). Human and computer personality prediction from digital footprints. *Current Directions of Psychological Science, 28*(2), 204–211. https://doi.org/10.1177/0963721419827849

Hines, Terence M. (2003). *Pseudoscience and the paranormal: A critical examination of the evidence* (2nd ed.). Prometheus.

Hinshaw, Stephen P., & Stier, Andrea. (2008). Stigma as related to mental disorders. *Annual Review of Psychology, 4,* 67–93. https://doi.org/10.1146/annurev.clinpsy.4.022007.141245

Hinton, Devon E., & Hinton, Susan D. (2009). Twentieth-century theories of panic in the United States. In Devon E. Hinton & Byron J. Good (Eds.), *Culture and panic disorder* (pp. 113–131). Stanford University Press.

Hirsh, Jacob B.; Kang, Sonia K.; & Bodenhausen, Galen V. (2012). Personalized persuasion tailoring persuasive appeals to recipients' personality traits. *Psychological Science, 23*(6), 578–581. https://doi.org/10.1177/0956797611436349

Hirst, William, & Phelps, Elizabeth A. (2016). Flashbulb memories. *Current Directions in Psychological Science, 25,* 36–41. https://doi.org/10.1177/0963721415622487

Hirst, William; Phelps, Elizabeth A.; Meksin, Robert; Vaidya, Chandan J.; Johnson, Marcia K.; Mitchell, Karen J.; Buckner, Randy L.; Budson, Andrew E.; Gabrieli, John D. E.; Lustig, Cindy; Mather, Mara; Ochsner, Kevin N.; Schacter, Daniel; Simons, Jon S.; Lyle, Keith B.; Cuc, Alexandru F.; & Olsson, Andreas. (2015). A ten-year follow-up of a study of memory for the attack of September 11, 2001: Flashbulb memories and memories for flashbulb events. *Journal of Experimental Psychology: General, 144*(3), 604–623. https://doi.org/10.1037/xge0000055

Hitlin, Paul. (2016, July 11). Research in the crowdsourcing age, a case study. *Pew Research Center.* http://pewrsr.ch/29HfTs2

Hobfoll, Stevan E.; Lilly, Roy S.; & Jackson, Anita P. (1992). Conservation of social resources and the self. In Hans O. F. Veiel & Urs Baumann (Eds.), *The meaning and measurement of social support.* Hemisphere.

Hobson, Charles, J., & Delunas, Linda. (2001). National norms and life-event frequencies for the revised Social Readjustment Rating Scale. *International Journal of Stress Management, 8,* 299–314.

Hobson, J. Allan. (2005, October 27). Sleep is of the brain, by the brain and for the brain. *Nature, 437,* 1254–1264.

Hobson, J. Allan. (2017). Stages of consciousness: Waking, sleeping, and dreaming. In Susan Schneider & Max Weidner (Eds.). *The Blackwell Companion to Consciousness* (2nd ed.). Wiley.

Hobson, J. Allan; Sangsanguan, Suchada; Arantes, Henry; & Kahn, David. (2011). Dream logic—The inferential reasoning paradigm. *Dreaming, 21*(1), 1–15. https://doi.org/10.1037/a0022860

Hobson, J. Allan; Stickgold, Robert; & Pace-Schott, Edward F. (1998). The neuropsychology of REM sleep dreaming. *NeuroReport, 9*(3), R1–R14.

Hochreiter, W. W.; Ackermann, D. K.; & Brütsch, H. P. (2005). [Andropause]. *Ther Umsch, 62*(12), 821–826.

Hodges, Bert H., & Geyer, Anne L. (2006). A nonconformist account of the Asch experiments: Values, pragmatics, and moral dilemmas. *Personality and Social Psychology Review, 10*(1), 2–19.

Hoff, Kevin A.; Einarsdóttir, Sif; Chu, Chu; Briley, Daniel A.; & Rounds, James. (2020). Personality changes predict early career outcomes: Discovery and replication in 12-year longitudinal studies. *Psychological Science,* 1–16. https://doi.org/10.1177/0956797620957998

Hoffman, Martin L. (1977). Moral internalization: Current theory and research. In Leonard Berkowitz (Ed.), *Advances in experimental social psychology* (Vol. 10). Academic Press.

Hoffmann, Carl, & Hoffmann, Arianna. (2017). The role of assessment in pilot selection. In Robert Bor, Carina Eriksen, Margaret Oakes, & Peter Scragg (Eds.), *Pilot mental health assessment and support: A practitioner's guide.* Routledge.

Hoffstein, Victor. (2005). Snoring and upper airway resistance. In Meir H. Kryger, Thomas Roth, & William C. Dement (Eds.), *Principles and practice of sleep medicine* (4th ed.). Elsevier Saunders.

Hofmann, Stefan; Curtiss, Joshua; & McNally, Richard. (2016). A complex network perspective on clinical science. *Perspectives on Psychological Science, 11*(5), 597–605. https://doi.org/10.1177/1745691616639283

Hofmann, Wilhelm; De Houwer, Jan; Perugini, Marco; Baeyens, Frank; & Crombez, Geert. (2010). Evaluative conditioning in humans: A meta-analysis. *Psychological Bulletin, 136,* 390–421.

Hofstra, Bas; Kulkarni, Vivek V.; Galvez, Sebastian M.-N.; He, Bryan; Jurafsky, Dan; & McFarland, Daniel A. (2020). The diversity–innovation paradox in science. *Proceedings of the National Academy of Sciences, 17*(117), 9284–9291. https://doi.org/10.1073/pnas.1915378117

Hogan, John D. (2003). G. Stanley Hall: Educator, organizer, and pioneer developmental psychologist. In Gregory A. Kimble & Michael Wertheimer (Eds.), *Portraits of pioneers in psychology* (Vol. 5, pp. 18–36). American Psychological Association.

Hogarth, Robin M. (2010). Intuition: A challenge for psychological research on decision making. *Psychological Inquiry, 21,* 338–353.

Hoge, Elizabeth A.; Bui, Eric; Palitz, Sophie A.; Schwarz, Noah R.; Owens, Maryann E.; Johnston, Jennifer M.; Pollack, Mark H.; & Simon, Naomi M. (2018). The effect of mindfulness meditation training on biological acute stress responses in generalized anxiety disorder. *Psychiatry Research, 262,* 328-332. https://doi.org/10.1016/j.psychres.2017.01.006

Hogg, Michael A. (2010). Influence and leadership. In Susan T. Fiske, Daniel Gilbert, & Gardner Lindzey (Eds.), *Handbook of social psychology,* Vol. 2 (pp. 1166–1207). Wiley.

Hogg, Michael A.; Adelman, Janice R.; & Blagg, Robert D. (2010). Religion in the face of uncertainty: An uncertainty-identity theory account of religiousness. *Personality and Social Psychology Review, 14*(1), 72–83. https://doi.org/10.1177/1088868309349692

Holden, Constance. (2001). Polygraph screening: Panel seeks truth in lie detector debate. *Science, 291,* 967.

Holden, Ronald R. (2008, January). Underestimating the effects of faking on the validity of self-report personality scales. *Personality and Individual Differences, 44*(1), 311–321.

Hollander, Edwin P., & Julian, James W. (1969). Contemporary trends in the analysis of the leadership process. *Psychological Bulletin, 71,* 387–397.

Hollanders, Henry. (2007). Integrative and eclectic approaches. In Windy Dryden (Ed.), *Dryden's handbook of individual therapy.* Sage.

Hollon, Steven D., & Beck, Aaron T. (2004). Behavior therapy with adults. In Michael J. Lambert (Ed.), *Bergin and Garfield's handbook of psychotherapy and behavior change* (5th ed.). Wiley.

Hollon, Steven D., & Beck, Aaron T. (2004). Behavior therapy with adults. In Michael J. Lambert (Ed.), *Bergin and Garfield's handbook of psychotherapy and behavior change* (5th ed.). Wiley.

Hollon, Steven D., & Beck, Aaron T. (2004). Behavior therapy with adults. In Michael J. Lambert (Ed.), *Bergin and Garfield's handbook of psychotherapy and behavior change* (5th ed.). Wiley.

Holman, Alison E.; Garfin, Dana; Lubens, Pauline; & Silver, Roxane C. (2020). Media exposure to collective trauma, mental health, and functioning: Does it matter what you see? *Clinical Psychological Science, 8*(1), 111–124. https://doi.org/10.1177/2167702619858300

Holmes, Thomas H., & Masuda, Minoru. (1974). Life change and illness susceptibility. In Barbara Snell Dohrenwend & Bruce P. Dohrenwend (Eds.), *Stressful life events: Their nature and effects.* Wiley.

Holmes, Thomas H., & Rahe, Richard H. (1967). The Social Readjustment Rating Scale. *Journal of Psychosomatic Research, 11,* 213–218.

Holsboer, Florian. (2009). Putative new-generation antidepressants. In Alan F. Schatzberg & Charles B. Nemeroff (Eds.), *The American Psychiatric Publishing textbook of psychopharmacology* (4th ed., pp. 503–529). American Psychiatric Publishing.

Holt-Lunstad, Julianne; Smith, Timothy; Baker, Mark; Harris, Tyler; & Stephenson, David. (2015). Loneliness and social isolation as risk factors for mortality: A meta-analytic review. *Perspectives on Psychological Science, 10,* 227–237. https://doi.org/10.1177/1745691614568352

Holt-Lunstad, Julianne; Smith, Timothy B.; & Layton, J. Bradley. (2010). Social relationships and mortality risk: A meta-analytic review. *PLOS Medicine, 7*(7), e1000316.

Holyoak, Keith J. (2005). Analogy. In Keith J. Holyoak & Robert G. Morrison (Eds.), *The Cambridge handbook of thinking and reasoning* (p. 302). Cambridge University Press.

Hölzel, Britta K.; Carmody, James; Vangel, Mark; Congleton, Christina; Yerramsetti, Sita M.; Gard, Tim; & Lazar, Sara W. (2011). Mindfulness practice leads to increases in regional brain gray matter density. *Psychiatry Research, 191,* 36–43.

Holzman, Lois. (2009). *Vygotsky at work and play.* Routledge/Taylor & Francis Group.

Homer, Bruce D.; Solomon, Todd M.; Moeller, Robert W.; Mascia, Amy; DeRaleau, Lauren; & Halkitis, Perry N. (2008). Methamphetamine abuse and impairment of social functioning: A review of the underlying neurophysiological causes and behavioral implications. *Psychological Bulletin, 134,* 301–310.

Hong, Ying-yi; Wyer, Robert S., Jr.; & Fong, Candy P. S. (2008). Chinese working in groups: Effort dispensability versus normative influence. *Asian Journal of Social Psychology, 11*(3), 187–195. https://doi.org/10.1111/j.1467-839X.2008.00257.x

Hopkins, William D., & Cantalupo, Claudio. (2005). Individual and setting differences in the hand preferences of chimpanzees (*Pan troglodytes*): A critical analysis and some alternative explanations. *Laterality, 10,* 65–80.

Hopkins, William D.; Phillips, Kimberley A.; Bania, Amanda; Calcutt, Sarah E.; Gardner, Molly; Russell, Jamie; Schaeffer, Jennifer; Lonsdorf, Elizabeth V.; Ross, Stephen R.; & Schapiro, Steven J. (2011). Hand preferences for coordinated bimanual actions in 777 Great Apes: Implications for the evolution of handedness in hominins. *Journal of Human Evolution, 60,* 605–611. https://doi.org/10.1016/j.jhevol.2010.12.008

Hordacre, Brenton; Rogasch, Nigel C.; & Goldsworthy, Mitchell R. (2016). Utility of EEG measures of brain function in patients with acute stroke. *Frontiers in Human Neuroscience, 10,*1–3. https://doi.org/10.3389/fnhum.2016.00621

Horder, Jamie; Matthews, Paul; & Waldmann, Robert. (2011). Placebo, Prozac, and PLoS: Significant lessons for psychopharmacology. *Journal of Psychopharmacology, 25*(10), 1277–1288. https://doi.org/10.1177/0269881110372544

Horner, Robert H. (2002). On the status of knowledge for using punishment: A commentary. *Journal of Applied Behavior Analysis, 35*(4), 465–467.

Horney, Karen. (1926). The flight from womanhood. In Harold Kelman (Ed.), *Feminine psychology.* Norton.

Horney, Karen. (1945). *Our inner conflicts: A constructive theory of neurosis.* Norton.

Horowitz, Alana M.; Fan, Xuelai; Bieri, Gregor; Smith, Lucas K.; Sanchez-Diaz, Cesar I.; Schroer, Adam B.; Gontier, Geraldine; Casaletto, Kaitlin B.; Kramer, Joel H.; Williams, Katherine E.; & Villeda, Saul A. (2020). Blood factors transfer beneficial effects of exercise on neurogenesis and cognition to the aged brain. *Science, 369*(6500), 167–173. https://doi.org/10.1126/science.aaw2622

Horr, Ninja; Braun, Christoph; & Volz, Kirsten G. (2014). Feeling before knowing why: The role of the orbitofrontal cortex in intuitive judgments—an MEG study. *Cognitive, Affective and Behavioral Neuroscience, 14,* 1271–1285. https://doi.org/10.3758/s13415-014-0286-7

Horvath, Jared C.; Horton, Alex J.; Lodge, Jason M.; & Hattie, John A. C. (2017). The impact of binge watching on memory and perceived comprehension. *First Monday, 22,* Issue 9. http://firstmonday.org/ojs/index.php/fm/article/view/7729/6532 https://doi.org//10.5210/fm.v22i19.7729

Hossain, Adnan. (2012). Beyond emasculation: Being Muslim and becoming hijra in South Asia. *Asian Studies Review, 36*(4), 495–513. https://doi.org/10.1080/10357823.2012.739994

Houts, Arthur C. (2002). Discovery, invention, and the expansion of the modern diagnostic and statistical manuals of mental disorders. In Larry E. Beutler & Mary L. Malik (Eds.), *Rethinking the DSM: A psychological perspective.* American Psychological Association.

Howard, Matt C. (2018, May 3). The convergent validity and nomological net of two methods to measure retroactive influences. *Psychology of Consciousness: Theory, Research, and Practice.* Advance online publication. https://doi.org/10.1037/cns0000149

Howard-Jones, Paul A. (2014). Neuroscience and education: Myths and messages. *Nature Reviews Neuroscience, 15,* 817–824. https://doi.org/10.1038/nrn3817

Howe, Mark L., & Knott, Lauren M. (2015). The fallibility of memory in judicial processes: Lessons from the past and their modern consequences. *Memory, 23,* 633–656. https://doi.org/10.1080/09658211.2015.1010709

Howland, Maryhope, & Simpson, Jeffry A. (2010). Getting in under the radar : A dyadic view of invisible support. *Psychological Science, 21,* 1827–1834. https://doi.org/10.1177/0956797610388817

Howlett, Jonathon R., & Stein, Murray B. (2016). Prevention of trauma and stressor-related disorders: A review. *Neuropsychopharmacology, 41,* 357–369. https://doi.org/10.1038/npp.2015.261.

Hoyle, Rick H., & Sherrill, Michelle R. (2006, December). Future orientation in the self-system: Possible selves, self-regulation, and behavior. *Journal of Personality, 74*(6), 1673–1696.

Hsiang, Solomon M.; Burke, Marshall; & Miguel, Edward. (2013). Quantifying the influence of climate on human conflict. *Science, 341*(6151), 1235367.

Huang, Xiao-na; Wang, Hui-shan; Zhang, Li-jin; & Liu, Xi-cheng. (2010). Co-sleeping and children's sleep in China. *Biological Rhythm Research, 41*(3), 169–181. https://doi.org/10.1080/09291011003687940.

Hubel, David H. (1995). *Eye, brain, and vision.* Scientific American Library.

Hubel, David H., & Wiesel, Torsten N. (2005). *Brain and visual perception: The story of a 25-year collaboration.* Oxford University Press.

Huber, Elizabeth; Webster, Jason M.; Brewer, Alyssa A.; MacLeod, Donald I. A.; Wandell, Brian A.; Boynton, Geoffrey M.; Wade, Alex R.; & Fine, Ione. (2015). A lack of experience-dependent plasticity after more than a decade of recovered sight. *Psychological Science, 26,* 393–401. https://doi.org/10.1177/0956797614563957

Hudson, Nathan & Fraley, Chris. (2015). Volitional personality trait change: Can people choose to change their personality traits? *Journal of Personality and Social Psychology,109,* 490–507. https://doi.org/10.1037/pspp0000021

Hudson, Nathan, & Roberts, Brent. (2014). Goals to change personality traits: Concurrent links between personality traits, daily behavior, and goals to change oneself. *Journal of Research in Personality, 53,* 68–83. https://doi.org/10.1016/j.jrp.2014.08.008

Huesmann, L. Rowell; Dubow, Eric F.; & Yang, Grace. (2013). Why it is hard to believe that media violence causes aggression. In Karen E. Dill (Ed.), *The Oxford handbook of media psychology.* Oxford University Press.

Hugdahl, Kenneth, & Westerhausen, René (Eds.). (2010). *The Two Halves of the Brain: Information Processing in the Cerebral Hemispheres.* MIT Press.

Hughes, John R. (2007). A review of sleepwalking (somnambulism): The enigma of neurophysiology and polysomnography with differential diagnosis of complex partial seizures. *Epilepsy & Behavior, 11,* 483–491.

Hulbert, Justin C.; Henson, Richard N.; & Anderson, Michael C. (2016). Inducing amnesia through systemic suppression. *Nature Communications, 7,* 11003. https://doi.org/10.1038/ncomms11003

Hum, Michelle. (2014). Paralyzed artist continues to create with help of EEG. *PSFK.* Retrieved from http://www.psfk.com/2014/09/eeg-technology-als-graffiti-writer.html

Human Rights Watch. (2020a). Central African Republic Events of 2019. https://www.hrw.org/world-report/2020/country-chapters/central-african-republic

Human Rights Watch. (2020b, May 12). COVID-19 fueling anti-Asian racism and xenophobia worldwide: National action plans needed to counter intolerance. *Human Rights Watch.* https://www.hrw.org/news/2020/05/12/covid-19-fueling-anti-asian-racism-and-xenophobia-worldwide

Human Rights Watch. (2020c). *Living in chains: Shackling of people with psychosocial disabilities worldwide.* https://www.hrw.org/report/2020/10/06/living-chains/shackling-people-psychosocial-disabilities-worldwide

Hunsley, John; Lee, Catherine M.; & Wood, James M. (2003). Controversial and questionable assessment techniques. In Scott O. Lilienfeld, Steven Jay Lynn, & Jeffrey M. Lohr (Eds.), *Science and pseudoscience in clinical psychology.* Guilford.

Hunsley, John; Lee, Catherine M.; Wood, James M.; & Taylor, Whitney. (2015). Controversial and questionable assessment technique. In Scott Lilienfeld, Steven Lynn, Jeffrey Lohr, & Carol Tarvis (Eds.), *Science and pseudoscience in clinical psychology* (2nd ed., pp. 42–82). Guilford.

Hunt, Earl. (2012). What makes nations intelligent? *Perspectives on Psychological Science, 7,* 284–306. https://doi.org/10.1177/1745691612442905

Hunt, Vivian; Layton, Dennis; & Prince, Sara. (2015). Diversity matters. *McKinsey & Company.* https://assets.mckinsey.com/~/media/857F440109AA4D13A54D9C496D86ED58.ash

Hunter, Aimee M.; Ravikumar, S.; Cook, Ian A.; & Leuchter, Andrew F. (2009). Brain functional changes during placebo lead-in and changes in specific symptoms during pharmacotherapy for major depression. *Acta Psychiatrica Scandinavica, 119*(4), 266–273.

Hurd, Yasmin L. (2020). Leading the next CBD wave—safety and efficacy. *JAMA Psychiatry.* https://doi.org/10.1001/jamapsychiatry.2019.4157

Huynh, Que-Lam; Nguyen, Angela M. D.; & Benet-Martínez, Verónica. (2011). Bicultural identity integration. In Seth J. Schwartz, Koen Luyckx, & Vivian L. Vignoles (Eds.), *Handbook of identity theory and research.* Springer.

Hyde, Janet S. (2016). Sex and cognition: Gender and cognitive functions. *Current Opinion in Neurobiology, 38,* 53–56. https://doi.org/10.1016/j.conb.2016.02.007

Hyde, Janet S.; Bigler, Rebecca S.; Joel, Daphna; Tate, Charlotte C.; & van Anders, Sari M. (2019). The future of sex and gender in psychology: Five challenges to the gender binary. *American Psychologist, 74*(2), 171–193. https://doi.org/10.1037/amp0000307

Hyde, Janet S.; Mezulis, Amy H.; & Abramson, Lyn Y. (2008). The ABCs of depression: Integrating affective, biological, and cognitive models to explain the emergence of the gender difference in depression. *Psychological Review, 115*(2), 291–313. https://doi.org/10.1037/0033-295X.115.2.291

Hyde, Janet Shibley. (2007, October). New directions in the study of gender similarities and differences. *Current Directions in Psychological Science, 16,* 259–263. https://doi.org/10.1111/j.1467-8721.2007.00516.x

Hyde, Janet Shibley. (2014). Gender similarities and differences. *Annual Review of Psychology, 65,* 373–398.

Hyman, Ira E., Jr., & Pentland, Joel. (1996). The role of mental imagery in the creation of false childhood memories. *Journal of Memory & Language, 35,* 101–117.

Hyman, Ira E., Jr.; Boss, S. Matthew; Wise, Breanne M.; McKenzie, Kira E.; & Caggiano, Jenna M. (2010). Did you see the unicycling clown? Inattentional blindness while walking and talking on a cell phone. *Applied Cognitive Psychology, 24*(5), 597–607. https://doi.org/10.1002/acp.1638

Hyman, Ray. (2010). Meta-analysis that conceals more than it reveals: Comment on Storm et al. (2010). *Psychological Bulletin, 136*(4), 486–490. https://doi.org/10.1037/a0019676

Hyman, Steven E. (2005). Neurotransmitters. *Current Biology, 15,* R154–R158. https://doi.org/10.1016/j.cub.2005.02.037

Hyman, Steven E. (2009). How adversity gets under the skin. *Nature Neuroscience 12,* 241–243.

Iacono, Diego; Markesbery, W. R.; Gross, M.; Pletnikova, Olga; Rudow, Gay; Zandi, P.; & Troncoso, Juan C. (2009). The Nun Study: Clinically silent AD, neuronal hypertrophy, and linguistic skills in early life. *Neurology, 73,* 665–673.

IJzerman, Hans, & Van Prooijen, Jan-Willem. (2008, June). Just world and the emotional defense of self. *Social Psychology, 39*(2), 117–120. https://doi.org/10.1027/1864-9335.39.2.117

Ikeda, Hiroshi. (2001). Buraku students and cultural identity: The case of a Japanese minority. In Nobuo Shimahara, Ivan Z. Holowinsky, & Saundra Tomlinson-Clarke (Eds.), *Ethnicity, race, and nationality in education: A global perspective.* Erlbaum.

Ilies, Remus; Curseu, Petru L.; Dimotakis, Nikolaos; & Spitzmuller, Matthias. (2013). Leaders' emotional expressiveness and their behavioural and relational authenticity: Effects on followers. *European Journal of Work and Organizational Psychology, 22,* 4–14. https://doi.org/10.1080/1359432X.2011.626199

Imel, Zac E.; Malterer, Melanie B.; McKay, Kevin M.; & Wampold, Bruce E. (2008). A meta-analysis of psychotherapy and medication in unipolar depression and dysthymia. *Journal of Affective Disorders, 110,* 197–206.

Inkster, Becky; Stillwell, David; Kosinski, Michal; & Jones, Peter (2016). A decade into Facebook: Where is psychiatry in the digital age? *The Lancet Psychiatry, 3,* 1087–1090. https://doi.org/10.1016/S2215-0366(16)30041-4

Innocence Project. (2015). *False confessions or admissions.* https://www.innocenceproject.org/causes/false-confessions-admissions

Insel, Thomas. (2013, April 29). Director's blog: Transforming diagnosis. *National Institutes of Mental Health.* http://www.nimh.nih.gov/about/director/2013/transforming-diagnosis.shtml

International Federation of Red Cross and Red Crescent Societies. (2020, March 23). *Remote psychological first aid during the COVID-19 outbreak.* Psychosocial Centre. https://pscentre.org/wp-content/uploads/2020/03/Remote-PFA.pdf

Ionescu, Thea. (2012). Exploring the nature of cognitive flexibility. *New Ideas in Psychology,30*(2), 190–200. https://doi.org/10.1016/j.newideapsych.2011.11.001

Irving, Julie Anne; Farb, Norman A. S.; & Segal, Zindel V. (2015). Mindfulness-based cognitive therapy for chronic depression. In Kirk Warren Brown, J. David Creswell, & Richard M. Ryan (Eds.), *Handbook of mindfulness: Theory, research, and practice.* Guilford.

Irwin, Charles E., Jr. (2005). Editorial: Pubertal timing: Is there any new news? *Journal of Adolescent Health, 37,* 343–344.

Irwin, Michael R. (2015). Why sleep is important for health: A psychoneuroimmunology perspective. *Annual Review of Psychology, 66,* 143–172. https://doi.org/10.1146/annurev-psych-010213-115205

Irwin, Michael R., & Miller, Andrew H. (2007, May). Depressive disorders and immunity: 20 years of progress and discovery. *Brain, Behavior, and Immunity, 21*(4), 374–383.

Isabella, Russell A.; Belsky, Jay; & von Eye, Alexander. (1989). Origins of infant-mother attachment: An examination of interactional synchrony during the infant's first year. *Developmental Psychology, 25,* 12–21.

Iversen, Iver H. (1992). Skinner's early research: From reflexology to operant conditioning. *American Psychologist, 47,* 1318–1328.

Ivory, James D.; Markey, Patrick M.; Elson, Malte; Colwell, John; Ferguson, Christopher J.; Griffiths, Mark D.; Savage, Joanne; & Williams, Kevin D. (2015). Manufacturing consensus in a diverse field of scholarly opinions: A comment on Bushman, Gollwitzer, and Cruz. *Psychology of Popular Media Culture, 4,* 222–229. https://doi.org/10.1037/ppm0000056

Iwamasa, Gayle Y. (1997). Asian Americans. In Steven Friedman (Ed.), *Cultural issues in the treatment of anxiety.* Guilford.

Iyadurai, Lalitha; Visser, Renée M.; Lau-Zhu, Alex; Porcheret, Kate; Horsch, Antje; Holmes, Emily A.; & James, Ella L. (2019). Intrusive memories of trauma: A target for research bridging cognitive science and its clinical application. *Clinical Psychology Review, 69,* 67–82. https://doi.org/10.1016/j.cpr.2018.08.005

Izard, Carroll E. (1990a). Facial expressions and the regulation of emotions. *Journal of Personality and Social Psychology, 58,* 487–498.

Izard, Carroll E. (1990b). The substrates and functions of emotion feelings: William James and current emotion theories. *Personality and Social Psychology Bulletin, 16,* 626–635.

Izard, Carroll E. (2007). Basic emotions, natural kinds, emotion schemas, and a new paradigm. *Perspectives on Psychological Science, 2,* 260–280.

Jack, Rachael E.; Caldara, Roberto; & Schyns, Philippe G. (2012). Internal representations reveal cultural diversity in expectations of facial expressions of emotion. *Journal of Experimental Psychology: General; 141*(1), 19–25. https://doi.org/10.1037/a0023463

Jackson, John P., Jr. (2006). Kenneth B. Clark: The complexities of activist psychology. In Donald A. Dewsbury, Ludy T. Benjamin, & Michael Wertheimer (Eds.), *Portraits of pioneers in psychology* (Vol. VI, pp. 273–286). American Psychological Association and Lawrence Erlbaum Associates.

Jackson, Lynne M. (2011). Cognitive, affective, and interactive processes of prejudice. *The psychology of prejudice: From attitudes to social action.* American Psychological Association.

Jacob, Julie A. (2016). As opioid prescribing guidelines tighten, mindfulness meditation holds promise for pain relief. *JAMA, 315,* 2385–2387. https://doi.org/10.1001/jama.2016.4875

Jacobs, Tom. (2018, March 16). Rock bands need a married square as much as they do the wild bachelor. *Pacific Standard.* https://psmag.com/economics/dont-blame-yoko

Jacobs, Tonya L.; Epel, Elissa S.; Lin, Jue; Blackburn, Elizabeth H.; Wolkowitz, Owen M.; Bridwell, David A.; Zanesco, Anthony P.; Aichele, Stephen R.; Sahdra, Baljinder K.; MacLean, Katherine A.; King, Brandon G.; Shaver, Phillip R.; Rosenberg, Erika L.; Ferrer, Emilio ; Wallace, B. Alan; & Saron, Clifford D. (2011). Intensive meditation training, immune cell telomerase activity, and psychological mediators. *Psychoneuroendocrinology, 36*(5), 664–681. https://doi.org/10.1016/j.psyneuen.2010.09.010

Jacobsen, Pamela. (2019). Mindfulness for psychosis groups; Within-session effects on stress and symptom-related distress in routine community care. *Behavioural and Cognitive Psychotherapy, 47,* 421–430. https://doi.org/10.1017/S1352465818000723

Jaffee, Sara, & Hyde, Janet Shibley. (2000). Gender differences in moral orientation: A meta-analysis. *Psychological Bulletin, 126,* 703–726.

Jagdeo, Amit; Cox, Brian J.; Stein, Murray B.; & Sareen, Jitender. (2009). Negative attitudes toward help seeking for mental illness in 2 population-based surveys from the United States and Canada. *Canadian Journal of Psychiatry/La Revue canadienne de psychiatrie, 54*(11), 757–766.

Jäkel, Sarah, & Dimou, Leda. (2017). Glial cells and their function in the adult brain: A journey through the history of their ablation. *Frontiers in Cellular Neuroscience, 11,* 1–17. https://doi.org/10.3389/fncel.2017.00024

Jakovcevski, I.; Filipovic, R.; Mo, Z.; Rakic, S.; & Zecevic, N. (2009). Oligodendrocyte development and the onset of myelination in the human fetal brain. *Frontiers in Neuroanatomy, 3,* 5. https://doi.org/10.3389/neuro.05.005.2009

James, Jenée; Ellis, Bruce J.; Schlomer, Gabriel L.; & Garber, Judy. (2012). Sex-specific pathways to early puberty, sexual debut, and sexual risk taking: Tests of an integrated evolutionary-developmental model. *Developmental Psychology, 48,* 687–702. https://doi.org/10.1037/a0026427

James, Sandy; Herman, Jody; Rankin, Susan; Keisling, Mara; Mottet, Lisa; & Anafi, Ma'ayan. (2016). *The report of the 2015 U.S. transgender survey.* National Center for Transgender Equality.

James, William. (1884). What is an emotion? *Mind, 9,* 188–205.

James, William. (1890). *Principles of psychology.* Holt.

James, William. (1892). *Psychology, briefer course.* Holt.

James, William. (1894). The physical basis of emotion. *Psychological Review, 1,* 516–529. (Reprinted in the 1994 Centennial Issue of *Psychological Review, 101,* 205–210).

James, William H. (2006). Two hypotheses on the causes of male homosexuality and paedophilia. *Journal of Biosocial Science, 38*(6), 745–761.

Jameson, Dorothea, & Hurvich, Leo M. (1989). Essay concerning color constancy. *Annual Review of Psychology, 40,* 1–22.

Jamil, Hikmet; Nassar-McMillan, Sylvia C.; & Lambert, Richard G. (2007, April). Immigration and attendant psychological sequelae: A comparison of three waves of Iraqi immigrants. *American Journal of Orthopsychiatry, 77,* 199–205.

Jansen, Petra; & Heil, Martin. (2010). Gender differences in mental rotation across adulthood. *Experimental Aging Research, 36,* 94–104. https://doi.org/10.1080/03610730903422762

Jarral, Farrah. (2020, April 29). The lockdown paradox: Why some people's anxiety is improving during the crisis. *The Guardian.* https://www.theguardian.com/commentisfree/2020/apr/29/coronavirus-lockdown-anxiety-mental-health

Jarrett, Christian. (2011). Ouch! The different ways people experience pain. *The Psychologist, 24,* 416–420.

Jarrett, Christian. (2019, May 17). Study finds microdosing psychedelics can be beneficial, but not in the way that users most expect. *Research Digest.* https://digest.bps.org.uk/2019/05/17/rare-systematic-study-of-the-effects-of-microdosing-psychedelics-finds-benefits-but-not-of-the-kind-that-users-most-expect/

Jarrett, Christian. (2020). *How lockdown may have changed your personality.* BBC. https://www.bbc.com/future/article/20200728-how-lockdown-may-have-changed-your-personality

Jason, Leonard A.; Glantsman, Olya; O'Brien, Jack; & Ramian, Kaitlyn. (2019). Introduction to the field of community psychology. Glantsman, Olya; O'Brien, Jack; & Ramian, Kaitlyn (Eds.), Introduction to Community Psychology: Becoming an agent of change. https://press.rebus.community/introductiontocommunitypsychology/chapter/intro-to-community-psychology/

Jason, Leonard A.; Pokorny, Steven B.; Adams, Monica; Topliff, Annie; Harris, Courtney; & Hunt, Yvonne. (2009). Youth tobacco access and possession policy interventions: Effects on observed and perceived tobacco use. *American Journal on Addictions, 18*(5), 367–374.

Jayasinghe, Nimali; Glosan, Cezar; Evans, Susan; Spielman, Lisa; & Difede, JoAnn. (2008, November). Anger and posttraumatic stress disorder in disaster relief workers exposed to the September 11, 2001 World Trade Center disaster: One-year follow-up study. *Journal of Nervous and Mental Disease, 196*(11), 844–846. https://doi.org/10.1097/NMD.0b013e31818b492c

Jbabdi, Saad, & Behrens, Timothy E. J. (2012). Specialization: The connections have it. *Nature Neuroscience, 15,* 171–172. https://doi.org/10.1038/nn.3031

Jean-Baptiste, Cindy Ogolla; Herring, R. Patti; Beeson, W. Lawrence; Banta, Jim E.; & Dos Santos, Hildemar. (2020a). Development of the cross-cultural stress scale. *Minerva Psichiatrica, 61*(4), 131–42. https://doi.org/10.23736/S0391-1772.20.02071-3

Jean-Baptiste, Cindy Ogolla; Herring, R. Patti; Beeson, W. Lawrence; Dos Santos, Hildemar; & Banta, Jim E. (2020b). Stressful life events and social capital during the early phase of COVID-19 in the U.S. *Social Sciences & Humanities Open, 2*(1), 100057. https://doi.org/10.1016/j.ssaho.2020.100057

Jean-Baptiste, Cindy Ogolla; Herring, R. Patti; Beeson, W. Lawrence; Banta, Jim E.; & Dos Santos, Hildemar. (2021). Assessing the validity, reliability and efficacy of the Cross-Cultural Stress Scale (CCSS) for psychosomatic studies. *Journal of Affective Disorders, 282*(1), 1110–1119. https://doi.org/10.1016/j.jad.2020.12.118

Jeckel, Cristina M. Moriguchi; Lopes, Rodrigo P.; Berleze, Maria Christina; Luz, Clarice; Feix, Leandro; Argimon, Irani I.; Stein, Lilian M.; & Bauer, Moisés E. (2010). Neuroendocrine and immunological correlates of chronic stress in 'strictly healthy' populations. *Neuroimmunomodulation, 17*(1), 9–18.

Jehn, Karen A. (Etty); & Conlon, Donald E. (2018). Are lifestyle differences beneficial? The effects of marital diversity on group outcomes. *Small Group Research 49*(4), 429–451. https://doi.org/10.1177/1046496418755920

Jensen, Mark P., & Patterson, David R. (2014). Hypnotic approaches for chronic pain management: Clinical implications of recent research findings. *American Psychologist, 69,* 167–177. https://doi.org/10.1037/a0035644

Jensen, Mark P., & Turk, Dennis C. (2014). Contributions of psychology to the understanding and treatment of people with chronic pain: Why it matters to ALL psychologists. *American Psychologist, 69,* 105–118. https://doi.org/10.1037/a0035641

Jeon, Hyeonjin; & Lee, Seung-Hwan. (2018). From neurons to social beings: Short review of the mirror neuron system research and its socio-psychological and psychiatric implications. *Clinical Psychopharmacology and Neuroscience, 16*(1), 18–31. https://doi.org/10.9758/cpn.2018.16.1.18

Jeske, Debora, & Shultz, Kenneth. (2019). Social media screening and content effects: implications for job applicant reactions. *International Journal of Manpower, 40*(1), 73–86. https://doi.org/10.1108/IJM-06-2017-0138

Jeste, Dilip V., & Lee, Ellen E. (2019) Emerging empirical science of wisdom: Definition, measurement, neurobiology, longevity, and interventions. *Harvard Review of Psychiatry, 27*(3), 127–140. https://doi.org/10.1097/HRP.0000000000000205

Jha, Amishi P.; Morrison, Alexandra B; Dainer-Best, Justin; Parker, Suzanne; Rostrup, Nina; & Stanley, Elizabeth A. (2015). Minds "at attention": Mindfulness training curbs attentional lapses in military cohorts. *PLOS ONE,10,* e0116889. https://doi.org/10.1371/journal.pone.0116889

Jha, Amishi P.; Stanley, Elizabeth A.; Kiyonaga, Anastasia; Wong, Ling; & Gelfand, Lois. (2010). Examining the protective effects of mindfulness training on working memory capacity and affective experience. *Emotion, 10,* 54–64. https://doi.org/10.1037/a0018438.

Jiang, Peihua; Josue, Jesusa; Li, Xia; Glaser, Dieter; Li, Weihua; Brand, Joseph G.; Margolskee, Robert F.; Reed, Danielle R.; & Beauchamp, Gary K. (2012). Major taste loss in carnivorous mammals. *Proceedings of the National Academy of Sciences, 109,* 4956–4961. https://doi.org/10.1073/pnas.1118360109

Joëls, Marian, & Baram, Tallie Z. (2009). The neuro-symphony of stress. *Nature Reviews Neuroscience, 10,* 459–466.

Johansen, Pål-Ørjan, & Krebs, Teri Suzanne. (2015). Psychedelics not linked to mental health problems or suicidal behavior: A population study. *Psychopharmacology, 29,* 270–279. https://doi.org/10.1177/0269881114568039

John, Oliver P. (1990). The "Big Five" factor taxonomy: Dimensions of personality in the natural language and in questionnaires. In Lawrence A. Pervin (Ed.), *Handbook of personality: Theory and research.* Guilford.

Johns, Michael; Schmader, Toni; & Martens, Andy. (2005). Knowing is half the battle: Teaching stereotype threat as a means of improving women's math performance. *Psychological Science, 16,* 175–179.

Johnson, Austin H. (2019). Rejecting, reframing, and reintroducing: trans people's strategic engagement with the medicalisation of gender dysphoria. *Sociology of Health & Illness, 41*(3), 517–532. https://doi.org/10.1111/1467-9566.12829

Johnson; Carrie. (2021, January 16). The latest on the federal investigation into the riot at the Capitol. *National Public Radio.* https://www.npr.org/2021/01/16/957593486/the-latest-on-the-federal-investigation-into-the-riot-at-the-capitol

Johnson, Kerri L.; McKay, Lawrie S.; & Pollick, Frank E. (2011). He throws like a girl (but only when he's sad): Emotion affects sex-decoding of biological motion displays. *Cognition, 119,* 265–280. https://doi.org/10.1016/ j.cognition.2011.01.016

Johnston, Lucy, & Miles, Lynden. (2007). Attributions and stereotype moderation. *New Zealand Journal of Psychology, 36*(1), 13–17.

Johnson, Marcia K.; Raye, Carol L.; Mitchell, Karen J.; & Ankudowich, Elizabeth. (2012). The cognitive neuroscience of true and false memories. In K. F. Belli (Ed.), *True and false recovered memories: Toward a reconciliation of the debate. Vol. 58: Nebraska Symposium on Motivation.* Springer.

Johnson, Paul M., & Kenny, Paul J. (2010). Dopamine D2 receptors in addiction-like reward dysfunction and compulsive eating in obese rats. *Nature Neuroscience, 13,* 635–641. https://doi.org/10.1038/nn.2519

Johnson, Sheri L.; Murray, Greg; Fredrickson, Barbara; Youngstrom, Eric A.; Hinshaw, Stephen; Bass, Julie Malbrancq; Deckersback, Thilo; Schooler, Jonathan; & Salloum, Ihsan. (2012). Creativity and bipolar disorder: Touched by fire or burning with questions? *Clinical Psychology Review, 32*(1), 1–12. https://doi.org/10.1016/j.cpr.2011.10.001

Johnson, Wendy. (2010). Understanding the genetics of intelligence: Can height help? Can corn oil? *Current Directions in Psychological Science, 19*(3), 177–182. https://doi.org/10.1177/0963721410370136

Joiner, Thomas E. (2010). *Myths about suicide.* Harvard University Press.

Joiner, Thomas E.; Brown, Jessica S.; & Wingate, LaRicka R. (2005). The psychology and neurobiology of suicidal behavior. *Annual Review of Psychology, 56,* 287–314.

Joly-Mascheroni, Ramiro M.; Senju, Atsushi; & Shepherd, Alex J. (2008). Dogs catch human yawns. *Biology Letters, 4,* 446–448.

Jones, Gary. (2003). Testing two cognitive theories of insight. *Journal of Experimental Psychology: Learning, Memory, and Cognition, 29,* 1017–1027.

Jones, Mary Cover. (1924a). The elimination of children's fears. *Journal of Experimental Psychology, 7*(5), 382–390. https://doi.org/10.1037/h0072283

Jones, Mary Cover. (1924b). A laboratory study of fear: The case of Peter. *Pedagogical Seminary and Journal of Genetic Psychology, 31*(4), 308–315. https://doi.org/10.1080/08856559.1924.9944851

Jones, Mary Cover. (1975). A 1924 pioneer looks at behavior therapy. *Journal of Behavior Therapy and Experimental Psychiatry, 6*(3), 181–187. https://doi.org/10.1016/0005-7916(75)90096-8

Jones, Steven H., & Tarrier, Nick. (2005, December). New developments in bipolar disorder. *Clinical Psychology Review, 25*(8) [Special issue: The psychology of bipolar disorder], 1003–1007.

Jones, Warren H., & Russell, Dan W. (1980). The selective processing of belief-discrepant information. *European Journal of Social Psychology, 10,* 309–312.

Jones-Eversley, Sharon D.; Rice, Johnny II; Adedoyin, Christson A.; & James-Townes, Lori. (2020). Premature deaths of young black males in the United States. *Journal of Black Studies, 51*(3), 251–272. https://doi.org/10.1177/0021934719895999

Jonides, John; Lewis, Richard L.; Nee, Derek Evan; Lustig, Cindy A.; Berman, Marc G.; & Moore, Katherine Sledge. (2008). The mind and brain of short-term memory. *Annual Review of Psychology, 59,* 193–224. https://doi.org/10.1146/annurev.psych.59.103006.093615

Jonnes, Jill. (1999). *Hep-cats, narcs, and pipe dreams: A history of America's romance with illegal drugs.* Johns Hopkins University Press.

Joseph, Stephen, & Murphy, David. (2013). Person-centered approach, positive psychology, and relational helping: Building bridges. *Journal of Humanistic Psychology, 53,* 26–51.

Josselyn, Sheena A.; Köhler, Stefan; & Frankland, Paul W. (2015). Finding the engram. *Nature Reviews Neuroscience, 16,* 521–534. https://doi.org/10.1038/nrn4000

Jost, John T. (2019). The IAT is dead, long live the IAT: Context-sensitive measures of implicit attitudes are indispensable to social and political psychology. *Current Directions in Psychological Science, 28*(1), 10–19. https://doi.org/10.1177/09637214187973

Jouriles, Ernest N.; Krauss, Alison; Vu, Nicole L.; Banyard, Victoria L.; & McDonald, Renee. (2018). Bystander programs addressing sexual violence on college campuses: A systematic review and meta-analysis of program outcomes and delivery methods. *Journal of American College Health, 66*(6), 457–466. https://doi.org/10.1080/07448481.2018.1431906

Joyce, Janine, & Herbison, G. Peter. (2015). Reiki for depression and anxiety (review). *Cochrane Database of Systematic Reviews 2015,* (4). https://doi.org/10.1002/14651858.CD006833.pub2

Jucaite, Aurelija, & Nyberg, Svante. (2012). Dopamine hypothesis of schizophrenia: A historical perspective. In Jeffrey S. Albert & Michael W. Wood (Eds.). *Targets and emerging therapies for schizophrenia.* Wiley.

Judd, Charles M., & Gawronski, Bertram. (2011). Editorial comment. *Journal of Personality and Social Psychology, 100,* 406.

Judge, Timothy; Rodell, Jessica; Klinger, Ryan; Simon, Lauren; & Crawford, Eean. (2013). Hierarchical representations of the five-factor model of personality in predicting job performance: Integrating three organizing frameworks with two theoretical perspectives. *Journal of Applied Psychology, 98,* 875–925. https://doi.org/10.1037/a0033901

Juliano, Laura M., & Griffiths, Roland R. (2004). A critical review of caffeine withdrawal: Empirical validation of symptoms and signs, incidence, severity, and associated features. *Psychopharmacology, 176,* 1–29.

Julien, Robert M. (2011). *A primer of drug action* (12th ed.). Worth.

Jun, Z.; Stephen, B.; Morag, F.; Ann Louise, K.; Carol, B.; & Jane, F. (2010). The oldest old in the last year of life: Population-based findings from Cambridge City over-75s cohort study participants aged 85 and older at death. *Journal of the American Geriatrics Society, 58*(1), 1–11.

Junco, Reynol. (2012). Too much face and not enough books: The relationship between multiple indices of Facebook use and academic performance. *Computers in Human Behavior, 28*(1), 187–198. https://doi.org/10.1016/j.chb.2011.08.026

Junco, Reynol, & Cotten, Shelia R. (2012). No A 4 U: The relationship between multitasking and academic performance. *Computers & Education, 59*(2), 505–514. https://doi.org/10.1016/j.compedu.2011.12.023

Juneau, Jen. (2021, January 27). Pete Davidson recalls the emotional moment he was diagnosed with borderline personality disorder. *People.* https://people.com/tv/pete-davidson-remembers-moment-he-was-diagnosed-with-borderline-personality-disorder

Jung, Carl G. (1931). The structure of the psyche. In Joseph Campbell (Ed.), *The portable Jung.* Penguin.

Jung, Carl G. (1936). The concept of the collective unconscious. In Joseph Campbell (Ed.), *The portable Jung.* Penguin.

Jung, Carl G. (1963). *Memories, dreams, reflections* (Richard and Clara Winston, Trans.). Random House.

Jussim, Lee; Crawford, Jarret; & Rubinstein, Rachel. (2015). Stereotype (in)accuracy in perceptions of groups and individuals. *Current Directions in Psychological Science, 24,* 490–497. https://doi.org/10.1177/0963721415605257

Kaas, Jon H.; Hui-Xin, Qi; & Stepniewska, Iwona. (2018). The evolution of parietal cortex in primates. Handbook of Clinical Neurology, 151, 31–52. https://doi.org/10.1016/B978-0-444-63622-5.00002-4

Kaas, Jon H.; O'Brien, Barbara M. J.; & Hackett, Troy A. (2013). Auditory processing in primate brains. In Randy J. Nelson, Sheri J.Y. Mizumori, & Irving B. Weiner (Eds.), *Handbook of psychology, Vol. 3: Behavioral neuroscience* (2nd ed.). Wiley.

Kabat-Zinn, Jon. (2003). Mindfulness-based interventions in context: Past, present, and future. *Clinical Psychology: Science and Practice, 10,* 144–156.

Kabat-Zinn, Jon. (2013). *Full catastrophe living: Using the wisdom of your body and mind to face stress, pain, and illness.* Random House.

Kagan, Jerome. (2004, Winter). New insights into temperament. *Cerebrum, 6,* 51–66.

Kagan, Jerome. (2010a). Emotions and temperament. In M. Bornstein (Ed.), *Handbook of cultural developmental science* (pp. 175–194). Taylor & Francis.

Kagan, Jerome. (2010b). *The temperamental thread: How genes, culture, time, and luck make us who we are.* Dana Press.

Kagan, Jerome. (2011). Three lessons learned. *Perspectives on Psychological Science 6,* 107–113. https://doi.org/10.1177/1745691611400205

Kagan, Jerome. (2016). An overly permissive extension. *Perspectives on Psychological Science, 11*(4), 442–450. https://doi.org/10.1177/1745691616635593

Kagan, Jerome, & Sinnott-Armstrong, W. (2007). Morality and its development. In Walter Sinnott-Armstrong (Ed.), *Moral psychology* (Vol. 3): *The neuroscience of morality: Emotion, brain disorders, and development* (pp. 297–312). MIT Press.

Kahn, Leah. (2019). Puberty: Onset and progression. *Pediatric Annals, 48*(4), 141–145. https://doi.org/10.3928/19382359-20190322-01

Kahneman, Daniel. (2003). A perspective on judgment and choice: Mapping bounded rationality. *American Psychologist, 58*(9), 697–720. https://doi.org/10.1037/0003-066X.58.9.697

Kahneman, Daniel, & Tversky, Amos. (1982). On the psychology of prediction. In Daniel Kahneman, Paul Slovic, & Amos Tversky (Eds.), *Judgment under uncertainty: Heuristics and biases.* Cambridge University Press.

Kalat, James W. (1985). Taste-aversion learning in ecological perspective. In Timothy D. Johnston & Alexandra T. Pietrewicz (Eds.), *Issues in the ecological study of learning.* Erlbaum.

Kaleka, Pardeep. (2013, August 4). Quoted in: Sikh temple attack victim's son and ex-skinhead form unlikely bond. http://www.cbsnews.com/news/sikh-temple-attack-victims-son-and-ex-skinhead-form-unlikely-bond/

Kaletsky, Kim. (2015, July 2). Asexual and happy. *The New York Times.* https://www.nytimes.com/2015/07/05/fashion/asexual-and-happy.html

Kalra, Gurvinder. (2012). Hijras: The unique transgender culture of India. *International Journal of Culture and Mental Health, 5,* 121–126. https://doi.org/10.1080/17542863.2011.570915

Kamin, Leon J. (1995). The pioneers of IQ testing. In Russell Jacoby & Naomi Glauberman (Eds.), *The bell curve debate: History, documents, opinions.* Times Books.

Kammeyer-Mueller, John D.; Judge, Timothy A.; & Scott, Brent A. (2009). The role of core self-evaluations in the coping process. *Journal of Applied Psychology, 94*(1), 177–195.

Kamps, Debra; Wills, Howard P.; Heitzman-Powell, Linda; Laylin, Jeff; Szoke, Carolyn; Petrillo, Tai; & Culey, Amy. (2011). Class-wide function-related intervention teams: Effects of group contingency programs in urban classrooms. *Journal of Positive Behavior Interventions, 13,* 154–167.

Kanai, Chieko; Tani, Masayuki; Hashimoto, Ryuichiro; Yamada, Takashi; Ohta, Haruhisa; & Watanabe, Hiromi. (2012). Cognitive profiles of adults with Asperger's disorder, high-functioning autism, and pervasive developmental disorder not otherwise specified based on the WAIS-III. *Research in Autism Spectrum Disorders, 6,* 58–64. https://doi.org/10.1016/j.rasd.2011.09.004

Kandel, Eric R. (2001). The molecular biology of memory storage: A dialogue between genes and synapses. *Science, 294,* 1030–1038.

Kandel, Eric R. (2006). *In search of memory: The emergence of a new science of mind.* Norton.

Kandel, Eric R. (2009). The biology of memory: A forty-year perspective. *Journal of Neuroscience, 29,* 12748–12756. https://doi.org/10.1523/jneurosci.3958-09.2009

Kandler, Christian; Zimmermann, Julia; & McAdams, Dan. (2014). Core and surface characteristics for the description and theory of personality differences and development. *European Journal of Personality,28,* 231–243. https://doi.org/10.1002/per.1952

Kane, John; Robinson, Delbert; Schooler, Nina; Mueser, Kim; Penn, David; Rosenheck, Robert; Addington, Jean; Brunette, Mary F.; Correll, Christoph U.; Estroff, Sue E.; Marcy, Patricia; Robinson, James; Meyer-Kalos, Piper S.; Gottlieb, Jennifer D.; Glynn, Shirley M.; Lynde, David W.; Pipes, Ronny; Kurian, Benji T.; Miller, Alexander L.; . . . & Heinssen, Robert. (2015). Comprehensive versus usual community care for first-episode psychosis: 2-year outcomes from the NIMH RAISE early treatment program. *American Journal of Psychiatry.* https://doi.org/10.1176/appi.ajp.2015.15050632

Kang, Sonia K., & Bodenhausen, Galen V. (2015). Multiple identities in social perception and interaction: Challenges and opportunities. *Annual Review of Psychology, 66,* 547–574. https://doi.org/10.1146/annurev-psych-010814-015025

Kann, Laura; Olsen, Emily O.; McManus, Tim; Harris, William A.; Shanklin, Shari L.; Flint, Katherine H; Queen, Barbara; Lowry, Richard; Chyen, David, Whittle, Lisa; Thornton, Jemekia; Lim, Connie; Yamakawa, Yoshimi; Brener, Nancy; & Zaza, Stephanie. (2016). Sexual identity, sex of sexual contacts, and health-related behaviors among students in grades 9–12 — United States and selected sites, 2015. *MMWR Surveillance Summaries, 65*(SS-9), 1–202. https://doi.org/10.15585/mmwr.ss6509a1

Kanner, Allen D.; Coyne, James C.; Schaefer, Catherine; & Lazarus, Richard S. (1981). Comparison of two modes of stress management: Daily hassles and uplifts versus major life events. *Journal of Behavioral Medicine, 4,* 1–39.

Kano, Fumihiro, & Hirata, Satoshi. (2015). Great apes make anticipatory looks based on long-term memory of single events. *Current Biology Report, 25,* 2513–2517.

Kanter, Jonathan W.; Williams, Monnica T.; Kuczynski, Adam M.; Manbeck, Katherine E.; Debreaux, Marlena; & Rosen, David C. (2017). A preliminary report on the relationship between microaggressions against Black people and racism among white college students. *Race and Social Problems, 9,* 291–299. https://doi.org/10.1007/s12552-017-9214-0

Kanwisher, Nancy. (2001). Faces and places: Of central (and peripheral) interest. *Nature Neuroscience, 4,* 455–456.

Kanwisher, Nancy, & Yovel, Galit. (2009) Face perception. In Gary G. Berntson & John T. Cacioppo (Eds.), *Handbook of neuroscience in the behavioral sciences.* Wiley.

Kaplan, Robert M., & Kronick, Richard G. (2006). Marital status and longevity in the United States population. *Journal of Epidemiology and Community Health, 60,* 760–765.

Kaplan, Sheila. (2019, August 30). Don't use bootleg or street vaping products, C.D.C. warns. *The New York Times.* https://www.nytimes.com/2019/08/30/health/vaping-e-cigarettes-marijuana-cdc.html?smid=nytcore-ios-share

Kaplan, Steve. (1990). Capturing your creativity. In Michael G. Walraven & Hiram E. Fitzgerald (Eds.), *Annual editions: Psychology: 1990/91.* Dushkin.

Kaptchuk, Ted J.; Friedlander, Elizabeth; Kelley, John M.; Sanchez, M. N.; Kokkotou, Efi; Singer, Joyce P.; Kowalczykowski, Magda; Miller, Franklin G.; Kirsch, Irving; Lembo, Anthony J. (2010). Placebos without deception: A randomized controlled trial in irritable bowel syndrome. *PLOS ONE, 5*(12), 1–7. https://doi.org/10.1371/journal.pone.0015591

Karau, Steven J., & Williams, Kipling D. (1993). Social loafing: A meta-analytic review and theoretical integration. *Journal of Personality and Social Psychology, 65,* 681–706.

Karera, Axelle, & Rutherford, Alexandra. (2017). Profile of Mamie Phipps Clark. In Alexandra Rutherford (Ed.), *Psychology's Feminist Voices Multimedia Internet Archive.* http://www.feministvoices.com/profiles/mamie-phipps-clark

Karlsson, Hasse. (2011). How psychotherapy changes the brain: Understanding the mechanisms. *Psychiatric Times, 28.* http://www.psychiatrictimes.com/psychotherapy/how-psychotherapy-changes-brain

Karpicke, Jeffrey D., & Roediger, Henry L. (2008). The critical importance of retrieval for learning. *Science, 319,* 966–968. https://doi.org/10.1037/a0026252

Karremans, Johan C.; Frankenhuis, Willem E.; & Arons, Sander. (2010). Blind men prefer a low waist-to-hip ratio. *Evolution and Human Behavior, 31*(3), 182–186. https://doi.org/10.1016/j.evolhumbehav.2009.10.001

Karren, Ronald J., & Zacharias, Larry. (2007, June). Integrity tests: Critical issues. *Human Resource Management Review, 17,* 221–234.

Kashdan, Todd B.; Farmer, Antonina S.; Adams, Leah M.; Ferssizidis, Patty; McKnight, Patrick E.; & Nezlek, John B. (2013). Distinguishing healthy adults from people with social anxiety disorder: Evidence for the value of experiential avoidance and positive emotions in everyday social interactions. *Journal of Abnormal Psychology, 122*(3), 645–655. https://doi.org/10.1037/a0032733

Kassin, Saul M. (2017). The killing of Kitty Genovese: What else does this case tell us? *Perspectives on Psychological Science, 12*(3), 374–381. https://doi.org/10.1177/17456916166794

Kastenbaum, Robert. (1992). *The psychology of death.* Springer-Verlag.

Kastenbaum, Robert. (2000). Death attitudes and aging in the 21st century. In Adrian Tomer (Ed.), *Death attitudes and the older adult: Theories, concepts, and applications. Series in death, dying, and bereavement.* Brunner-Routledge.

Kastenbaum, Robert. (2005). Is death better in utopia? *Illness, Crisis, & Loss, 13*(1), 31–48.

Kato, Takahiro A.; Kanba, Shigenobu; & Teo, Alan R. (2018). Hikikomori: experience in Japan and international relevance. *World Psychiatry: Official Journal of the World Psychiatric Association (WPA), 17*(1), 105–106. https://doi.org/10.1002/wps.20497

Katz, Joel, & Rosenbloom, Brittany N. (2015). The golden anniversary of Melzack and Wall's gate control theory of pain: Celebrating 50 years of pain research and management. *Pain Research & Management: The Journal of the Canadian Pain Society, 20,* 285–286.

Kaufman, Alan S. (1990). *Assessing adolescent and adult intelligence.* Allyn & Bacon.

Kaufman, Alan S. (2009). *IQ testing 101.* Springer.

Kaufman, James C.; Kaufman, Scott Barry; & Plucker, Jonathan A. (2013). Contemporary theories of intelligence. In D. Reisberg (Ed.), *The Oxford handbook of cognitive psychology* (pp. 811–822). Oxford University Press. https://doi.org/10.1093/oxfordhb/9780195376746.013.0051

Kaufman, James C., & Sternberg, Robert J. (2010). *The Cambridge handbook of creativity* Cambridge University Press.

Kaufman, Lloyd; Vassiliades, Vassias; & Noble, Richard. (2007). Perceptual distance and the moon illusion. *Spatial Vision, 20,* 155–175.

Kaufman, Scott B.; Yaden, David B.; Hyde, Elizabeth; & Tsukayama, Eli. (2019). The light vs. dark triad of personality: Contrasting two very different profiles of human nature. *Frontiers in Psychology, 10,* 1–26. https://doi.org/10.3389/fpsyg.2019.00467

Kaur, Harmeet, & Osipova, Natalia V. (2021, January 21). For flight attendants, getting people to wear masks is now one of the hardest parts of the job. *CNN Travel.* https://www.cnn.com/travel/article/flight-attendants-unruly-passengers-masks-trnd/index.html

Kaushik, Gaurav; Huber, David; Aho, Ken; Finney, Bruce; Bearden, Shawn; Zarbalis, Konstantinos; & Thomas, Michael. (2016). Maternal exposure to carbamazepine at environmental concentrations can cross intestinal and placental barriers. *Biochemical and Biophysical Research Communications, 474,* 291–295. https://doi.org/10.1016/j.bbrc.2016.04.088

Kawa, Alex B.; Allain, Florence; Robinson, Terry E.; & Samaha, Anne-Noël. (2019). The transition to cocaine addiction: The importance of pharmacokinetics for preclinical models. *Psychopharmacology, 236,* 1145–1157. https://doi.org/10.1007/s00213-019-5164-0

Kay, Aaron C.; Gaucher, Danielle; McGregor, Ian; & Nash, Kyle. (2010). Religious belief as compensatory control. *Personality and Social Psychology Review, 14*(1), 37–48.

Kaya, Aylin; Iwamoto, Derek K.; Brady, Jennifer; Clinton, Lauren; & Grivel, Margaux. (2019). The role of masculine norms and gender role conflict on prospective well-being among men. *Psychology of Men & Masculinities, 20*(1), 142–147. https://doi.org/10.1037/men0000155

Kazdin, Alan E. (2004). Cognitive-behavior modification. In Jerry M. Wiener & Mina K. Dulcan (Eds.), *The American Psychiatric Publishing textbook of child and adolescent psychiatry.* American Psychiatric Publishing.

Kazdin, Alan E. (2008). *Behavior modification in applied settings.* Waveland Press.

Kazdin, Alan E., & Blase, Stacey. (2011). Rebooting psychotherapy research and practice to reduce the burden of mental illness. *Perspectives on Psychological Science, 6*(1), 21–37. https://doi.org/10.1177/1745691610393527

Kazdin, Alan E., & Rabbitt, Sarah M. (2013). Novel models for delivering mental health services and reducing the burdens of mental illness. *Clinical Psychological Science, 1*(2), 170–191. https://doi.org/10.1177/1745691610393527

Kean, Sam. (2014, May 6). Phineas Gage, neuroscience's most famous patient. *Slate.* Retrieved from http://www.slate.com/articles/health_and_science/science/2014/05/phineas_gage_neuroscience_case_true_story_of_famous_frontal_lobe_patient.html

Kearney, Melissa, & Levine, Phillip B. (2014). Media influences on social outcomes: The impact of MTV's *16 and Pregnant* on teen childbearing (Working Paper 19795). National Bureau of Economic Research. http://www.nber.org/papers/w19795

Keel, Pamela A.; Baxter, Mark G.; & Heatherton, Todd F. (2007). A 20-year longitudinal study of body weight, dieting, and eating disorder symptoms. *Journal of Abnormal Psychology, 116,* 422–432

Keely, Matt. (2019, June 27). More people die taking selfies than by shark attacks. *Newsweek.* https://www.newsweek.com/selfies-deadlier-shark-attacks-1446363

Keltner, Dacher, & Horberg, E. J. (2015). Emotion-cognition interactions. In Mario Mikulincer, Phillip R. Shaver, Eugene Borgida, & John A. Bargh (Eds.), *APA Handbook of personality and social psychology, Volume 1: Attitudes and social cognition.* American Psychological Association. https://doi.org/10.1037/14341-020

Kemmer, Susanne. (2007, February/March). Sticking point. *Scientific American Mind,* pp. 64–69.

Kemp, Andrew H.; Krygier, Jonathan; & Harmon-Jones, Eddie. (2015). Neuroscientific perspectives of emotion. In Rafael A. Calvo, Sidney K. D'Mello, Jonathan Gratch, & Arvid Kappas (Eds.), *The Oxford handbook of affective computing.* Oxford University Press. https://doi.org/10.1093/oxfordhb/9780199942237.013.016

Kempermann, Gerd. (2012a). New neurons for "survival of the fittest." *Nature Reviews Neuroscience 13,* 727–736. https://doi.org/10.1038/nrn3319

Kempermann, Gerd. (2012b). Youth culture in the adult brain. *Science, 335,* 1175–1176. https://doi.org/10.1126/science.1219304

Kempton, Matthew J.; Salvador, Zainab; Munafò, Marcus R.; Geddes, John R.; Simmons, Andrew; Frangou, Sophia; & Williams, Steven C. R. (2011). Structural neuroimaging studies in major depressive disorder: Meta-analysis and comparison with bipolar disorder. *Archives of General Psychiatry, 68*(7), 675–690.

Kempton, Matthew J.; Stahl, Daniel; Williams, Steven C. R.; & DeLisi, Lynn E. (2010). Progressive lateral ventricular enlargement in schizophrenia: A meta-analysis of longitudinal MRI studies. *Schizophrenia Research, 120*(1–3), 54–62. https://doi.org/10.1016/j.schres.2010.03.036

Kendal, Rachel L.; Custance, Deborah M.; Kendal, Jeremy R.; Vale, Gillian; Stoinski, Tara S.; Rakotomalala, Nirina Lalaina; & Rasamimanana, Hantanirina. (2010). Evidence for social learning in wild lemurs (*Lemur catta*). *Learning & Behavior, 38*(3), 220–234. https://doi.org/10.3758/lb.38.3.220

Kendall-Tackett, K. (2010). *The psychoneuroimmunology of chronic disease: Exploring the links between inflammation, stress, and illness.* American Psychological Association.

Kendler, Kenneth S.; Gatz, Margaret; Gardner, Charles O.; & Pedersen, Nancy L. (2006). A Swedish national twin study of lifetime major depression. *American Journal of Psychiatry, 163*(1), 109–114. https://doi.org/10.1176/appi.ajp.163.1.109

Kendler, Kenneth S., & Schaffner, Kenneth F. (2011). The dopamine hypothesis of schizophrenia: An historical and philosophical analysis. *Philosophy, Psychiatry, & Psychology, 18*(1), 41–63. https://doi.org/10.1353/ppp.2011.0005

Kennedy, Carol. (2012). Frank and Lillian Gilbreth: Efficiency through studying time and motion. In *Guide to the management gurus* (5th ed.). London: Random House.

Kennedy, Lauren P. (2018, July 2). *Tiffany Haddish is positively hilarious.* WebMD. https://www.webmd.com/a-to-z-guides/features/tiffany-haddish-hilarious

Kennedy, Pagan. (2016, November 25). The thin gene. *The New York Times.* https://www.nytimes.com/2016/11/25/opinion/sunday/the-thin-gene.html

Kern, David M.; Auchincloss, Amy H.; Robinson, Lucy F.; Stehr, Mark F.; & Pham-Kanter, Genevieve. (2017). Healthy and unhealthy food prices across neighborhoods and their association with neighborhood socioeconomic status and proportion Black/Hispanic. *Journal of Urban Health, 94*(4), 494–505. https://doi.org/10.1007/s11524-017-0168-8

Kerpelman, Jennifer L., & Pittman, Joe F. (2018). Erikson and the relational context of identity: Strengthening connections with attachment theory. *Identity: An International Journal of Theory and Research, 18*(4), 306–314. https://doi.org/10.1080/15283488.2018.1523726

Kerr, David C. R.; Lopez, Nestor L.; Olson, Sheryl L.; & Sameroff, Arnold J. (2004). Parental discipline and externalizing behavior problems in early childhood: The roles of moral regulation and child gender. *Journal of Abnormal Child Psychology, 32*(4), 369–383.

Kerr, Norbert L., & Tindale, R. Scott. (2004). Group performance and decision making. *Annual Review of Psychology, 55,* 623–655. https://doi.org/10.1146/annurev.psych.55.090902.142009

Kershaw, Trina C., & Ohlsson, Stellan. (2004). Multiple causes of difficulty in insight: The case of the nine-dot problem. *Journal of Experimental Psychology: Learning, Memory, and Cognition, 30,* 3–13.

Kesebir, Selin, & Oishi, Shigehiro. (2010). A spontaneous self-reference effect in memory: Why some birthdays are harder to remember than others. *Psychological Science, 21*(10), 1525–1531.

Keshavan, M. S.; DeLisi, L. E.; & Seidman, L. J. (2011). Early and broadly defined psychosis risk mental states. *Schizophrenia Research, 126*(1–3), 1–10. https://doi.org/10.1016/j.schres.2010.10.006

Kessler, Ronald C. (2003, February). [In-cites interview with Dr. Ronald C. Kessler.] *ISI Essential Science Indicators.* Thompson Scientific. http://www.incites.com/papers/DrRonaldKessler.html

Kessler, Ronald C.; Angermeyer, Matthias; Anthony, James C.; de Graaf, Ron; Demyttenaere, Koen; Gasquet, Isabelle; de Girolamo, Giovanni; Gluzman, Semyon; Gureje, Oye; Haro, Josep Maria; Kawakami, Norito; Karam, Aimee; Levinson, Daphna; Medina Mora, Maria E.; Oakley Browne, Mark A.; Posada-Villa, José; Stein, Dan J.; Adley Tsang, Cheuk H.; Aguilar-Gaxiola, Sergio; . . . & Üstün, T. B. (2007). Lifetime prevalence and age-of-onset distributions of mental disorders in the World Health Organization's world mental health survey initiative. *World Psychiatry, 6*(3), 168–176.

Kessler, Ronald C.; Berglund, Patricia; Demler, Olga; Jin, Robert; Merikangas, Kathleen R.; & Walters, Ellen E. (2005a). Lifetime prevalence and age-of-onset distributions of DSM-IV disorders in the National Comorbidity Survey Replication. *Archives of General Psychiatry, 62*(6), 593–602. https://doi.org/10.1001/archpsyc.62.6.593

Kessler, Ronald C.; Chiu, Wai Tat; Demler, Olga; & Walters, Ellen E. (2005b). Prevalence, severity, and comorbidity of 12-month DSM-IV disorders in the National Comorbidity Survey Replication. *Archives of General Psychiatry, 62*(6), 617–627. https://doi.org/10.1001/archpsyc.62.6.617

Kessler, Ronald C.; Demler, Olga; Frank, Richard G.; Olfson, Mark; Pincus, Harold Alan; Walters, Ellen E.; Wang, Philip; Wells, Kenneth B.; & Zaslavsky, Alan M. (2005c, June 16). Prevalence and treatment of mental disorders, 1990 to 2003. *New England Journal of Medicine, 352*(24), 2515–2523. https://doi.org/10.1056/NEJMsa043266

Khan, Arif, & Brown, Walter. (2015). Antidepressants versus placebo in major depression: An overview. *World Psychiatry, 14*, 294–300. https://doi.org/10.1002/wps.20241

Khan, Sadiq. (2016, June 27). London mayor Sadiq Khan to 'Post': I have zero tolerance for anti-Semitism in my city. *Jerusalem Post.* http://www.jpost.com/Opinion/A-strict-zero-tolerance-approach-to-anti-Semitism-457805

Khan, Zafar U., & Muly, E. Chris. (2011). Molecular mechanisms of working memory. *Behavioural Brain Research.* https://doi.org/10.1016/j.bbr.2010.12.039

Khazan, Olga. (2014, July 23). When hearing voices is a good thing. *The Atlantic.* http://www.theatlantic.com/health/archive/2014/07/when-hearing-voices-is-a-good-thing/374863

Kheriaty, Aaron. (2007). The return of the unconscious. *Psychiatric Annals, 37*, 285–287.

Khoury, Bassam; Lecomte, Tania; Fortin, Guillaume; Masse, Marjolaine; Therien, Phillip; Bouchard, Vanessa; Chapleau, Marie-Andrée; Paquin, Karine; & Hofmann, Stefan G. (2013). Mindfulness-based therapy: A comprehensive meta-analysis. *Clinical Psychology Review, 33*, 763–771. https://doi.org/10.1016/j.cpr.2013.05.005

Khubchandani, Jasmine; Soni, Apurv; Fahey, Nisha; Raithatha, Nitin; Prabhakaran, Anusha; Byatt, Nancy; Moore Simas, Tiffany A.; Phatak, Ajay; Rosal, Milagros; Nimbalkar, Somashekhar; & Allison, Jeroan J. (2018). Caste matters: Perceived discrimination among women in rural India. *Archives of Women's Mental Health, 21*, 163–170. https://doi.org/10.1007/s00737-017-0790-1

Kidwell, Mallory C.; Lazarević, Ljiljana B.; Baranski, Erica; Harwicke, Tom E.; Piechowski, Sarah; Falkenberg, Lina-Sophia; Kennett, Curtis; Slowik, Agnieszka; Sonnleitner, Carina; Hess-Holden, Chelsey; Errington, Timothy M.; Fielder, Susann; & Nosek, Brian A. (2016). Badges to acknowledge open practices: A simple, low-cost, effective method for increasing transparency. *PLoS Biology, 14*(5), 1–15. https://doi.org/10.1371/journal.pbio.1002456

Kiecolt-Glaser, Janice K. (2009). Psychoneuroimmunology: Psychology's gateway to the biomedical future. *Perspectives on Psychological Science, 4*(4), 367–369. https://doi.org/10.1111/j.1745-6924.2009.01139.x

Kiecolt-Glaser, Janice K., & Glaser, Ronald. (1993). Mind and immunity. In Daniel Goleman & Joel Gurin (Eds.), *Mind/body medicine: How to use your mind for better health.* Consumer Reports Books.

Kiecolt-Glaser, Janice K., & Glaser, Ronald. (2010). Psychological stress, telomeres, and telomerase. *Brain, Behavior, and Immunology, 24*, 529–530. https://doi.org/10.1016/j.bbi.2010.02.002

Kiecolt-Glaser, Janice K; Gouin, Jean-Philippe; & Hantsoo, Liisa. (2009). Close relationships, inflammation, and health. *Neuroscience and Biobehavioral Reviews, 35*(1), 33–37.

Kiefer, Amy K., & Sekaquaptewa, Denise. (2007). Implicit stereotypes, gender identification, and math-related outcomes: A prospective study of female college students. *Psychological Science, 18*, 13–18.

Kihlstrom, John F. (2005). Dissociative disorders. *Annual Review of Clinical Psychology, 1*, 227–253. https://doi.org/10.1146/annurev.clinpsy.1.102803.143925

Kihlstrom, John F. (2007). Consciousness in hypnosis. In Philip David Zelazo, Morris Moscovitch, & Evan Thompson (Eds.), *The Cambridge handbook of consciousness.* Cambridge University Press.

Kihlstrom, John F. (2010). Social neuroscience: The footprints of Phineas Gage. *Social Cognition, 28*, 757–783.

Kihlstrom, John F.; Dorfman, Jennifer; & Park, Lillian. (2007). Implicit and explicit memory and learning. In Max Velmans & Susan Schneider (Eds.), *The Blackwell companion to consciousness.* Blackwell.

Kihlstrom, John F.; Mulvaney, Shelagh; Tobias, Betsy A.; & Tobias, Irene P. (2000). In Eric Eich, John F. Kihlstrom, Gordon H. Bower, Joseph P. Forgas, & Paula M. Niedenthal (Eds.), *Cognition and emotion.* Oxford University Press.

Kim, Bryan S. K., & Park, Yong S. (2008). East and Southeast AsianAmericans. In Garrett McAuliffe (Ed.), *Culturally alert counseling: A comprehensive introduction* (pp. 188–219). Sage.

Kim, E. Tammy. (2020, January 10). The gig economy is coming for your job. *The New York Times.* https://www.nytimes.com/2020/01/10/opinion/sunday/gig-economy-unemployment-automation.html

Kim, Jinhyun; Zhao,Ting; Petralia, Ronald S.; Yu, Yang; Peng, Hanchuan; Myers, Eugene; & Magee, Jeffrey C. (2012). mGRASP enables mapping mammalian synaptic connectivity with light microscopy. *Nature Methods, 9*, 96–102. https://doi.org/10.1038/nmeth.1784

Kim, Jinkwan.; Rapee, Roland M.; Oh, Kyung Ja; & Moon, Hye-Shin. (2008). Retrospective report of social withdrawal during adolescence and current

maladjustment in young adulthood: Cross-cultural comparisons between Australian and South Korean students. *Journal of Adolescence, 31*, 543–563. https://doi.org/10.1016/j.adolescence.2007.10.011

Kindley, Evan. (2016). *Questionnaire.* Bloomsbury Academic, An imprint of Bloomsbury Publishing.

King, Brian A.; Jones, Christopher M.; Baldwin, Grant T.; & Briss, Peter A. (2020). The EVALI and youth vaping epidemics: Implications for public health. *New England Journal of Medicine, 382*(8), 689–691. https://doi.org/10.1056/NEJMp1916171

King, Bruce M. (2013). The modern obesity epidemic, ancestral hunter-gatherers, and the sensory/reward control of food intake. *American Psychologist, 68*, 88–96.

King, David B.; DeCicco, Teresa L.; & Humphreys, Terry P. (2009). Investigating sexual dream imagery in relation to daytime sexual behaviours and fantasies among Canadian university students. *Canadian Journal of Human Sexuality, 18*, 135–146.

King, Katherine, & Ogle, Christin. (2014). Negative life events vary by neighborhood and mediate the relation between neighborhood context and psychological well-being. *PLOS ONE, 9*(4): e93539. https://doi.org/10.1371/journal.pone.0093539

King, Laura A. (2008). Personal goals and life dreams: Positive psychology and motivation in daily life. In James Y. Shah & Wendi L. Gardner (Eds.), *Handbook of motivation science.* Guilford.

Kinzler, Katherine D.; Shutts, Kristin; & Correll, Joshua. (2010). Priorities in social categories. *European Journal of Social Psychology, 40*(4), 581–592.

Kirsch, Irving. (2014a). Antidepressants and the placebo effect. *Zeitschrift für Psychologie, 222*, 128–134. https://doi.org/10.1027/2151-2604/a000176

Kirsch, Irving. (2014b). Wagstaff's definition of hypnosis. *Journal of Mind-Body Regulation, 2*, 124–125.

Kirsch, Irving, & Braffman, Wayne. (2001). Imaginative suggestibility and hypnotizability. *Current Directions in Psychological Science, 10*, 57–61.

Kirsch, Irving; Cardeña, Etzel; Derbyshire, Stuart; Dienes, Zoltan; Heap, Michael; Kallio, Sakari; Mazzoni, Giulian; Naish, Peter; Oakley, David; Potter, Catherine; Walters, Val; & Whalley, Matthew. (2011). Definitions of hypnosis and hynotizability and their relation to suggestion and suggestibility: A consensus statement. *Contemporary Hypnosis & Integrative Therapy, 28*, 107–115.

Kirsch, Irving; Deacon, Brett J.; Huedo-Medina, Tania B.; Scoboria, Alan; Moore, Thomas J.; & Johnson, Blair T. (2008). Initial severity and antidepressant benefits: A meta-analysis of data submitted to the Food and Drug Administration. *PLOS Medicine 5*(2): e45, 260–268. https://doi.org/10.1371/journal.pmed.0050045

Kirschenbaum, Howard. (2004). Carl Rogers's life and work: An assessment on the 100th anniversary of his birth. *Journal of Counseling and Development, 82*, 116–124.

Kirschenbaum, Howard, & Jourdan, April. (2005). The current status of Carl Rogers and the person-centered approach. *Psychotherapy: Theory, Research, Practice, Training, 42*(1), 37–51. https://doi.org/10.1037/0033-3204.42.1.37

Kitayama, Shinobu; Markus, Hazel Rose; & Kurokawa, Masaru. (2000). Culture, emotion, and well-being: Good feelings in Japan and the United States. *Cognition & Emotion, 14*, 93–124.

Kitayama, Shinobu, & Park, Hyekyung. (2007). Cultural shaping of self, emotion, and well-being: How does it work? *Social and Personality Psychology Compass, 1*(1), 202–222. https://doi.org/10.1111/j.1751-9004.2007.00016.x

Kitayama, Shinobu; Park, Jiyoung; Boylan, Jennifer; Miyamoto, Yuri; Levine, Cynthia; & Markus, Hazel Rose; Karasawa, Mayumi; Coe, Christopher L.; Kawakami, Norito; Love, Gayle D.; & Ryff, Carol D. (2015). Expression of anger and ill health in two cultures: An examination of inflammation and cardiovascular risk. *Psychological Science, 26*, 211–220. https://doi.org/10.1177/0956797614561268

Kitayama, Shinobu, & Uskul, Ayse K. (2011). Culture, mind, and the brain: Current evidence and future directions. *Annual Review of Psychology, 62*, 419–449. https://doi.org/10.1146/annurev-psych-120709-145357

Klasen, Fionna; Reissmann, Sina; Voss, Catharina; & Okello, James. (2015). The guiltless guilty: Trauma-related guilt and psychopathology in former Ugandan child soldiers. *Child Psychiatry & Human Development, 46*(2), 180–193. https://doi.org/10.1007/s10578-014-0470-6

Kleiman, Evan M.; Chiara, Alexandra M.; Liu, Richard T.; Jager-Hyman, Shari G.; Choi, Jimmy Y.; & Alloy, Lauren B. (2017). Optimism and well-being: A prospective multi-method and multi-dimensional examination of optimism as a resilience factor following the occurrence of stressful life events. *Cognition and Emotion, 31*, 269–283. https://doi.org/10.1080/02699931.2015.1108284

Klein, Laura C.; Bennett, Jeanette M.; Whetzel, Courtney A.; Granger, Douglas A.; & Ritter, Frank E. (2010). Caffeine and stress after salivary a-amylase activity in young men. *Human Psychopharmacology: Clinical and Experimental, 25*(5), 359–367.

Klein, Melanie. (1955). The psychoanalytic play technique. *American Journal of Orthopsychiatry, 25*(2), 223–237. https://doi.org/10.1111/j.1939-0025.1955.tb00131.x

Klein, Rachael M.; Dilchert, Stephan; Ones, Deniz S.; & Dages, Kelly D. (2015, March 30). Cognitive predictors and age-based adverse impact among business executives. *Journal of Applied Psychology, 100*, 1497–1510. https://doi.org/10.1037/a0038991

Kleinfeld, N. R. (2016, May 1). Fraying at the edges. *The New York Times.* https://www.nytimes.com/interactive/2016/05/01/nyregion/living-with-alzheimers.html

Klin, Anat, & Lemish, Dafna. (2008). Mental disorders stigma in the media: Review of studies on production, content, and influences. *Journal of Health Communication, 13*(5), 434–449. https://doi.org/10.1080/10810730802198813

Klinger, Regine; Colloca, Luana; Bingel, Ulrike; & Flor, Herta. (2014). Placebo analgesia: Clinical applications. *Pain, 155,* 1055–1058. https://doi.org/10.1016/j.pain.2013.12.007

Kluemper, Donald; Rosen, Peter; & Mossholder, Kevin. (2012). Social networking websites, personality ratings, and the organizational context: More than meets the eye? *Journal of Applied Social Psychology, 42,* 1143–1172. https://doi.org/10.1111/j.1559-1816.2011.00881.x

Knäuper, Bärbel; Roseman, Michelle; Johnson, Philip J.; & Krantz, Lillian H. (2009). Using mental imagery to enhance the effectiveness of implementation intentions. *Current Psychology, 28,* 181–186.

Knecht, S.; Dräger, B.; Deppe, M.; Bobe, L.; Lohmann, H.; Flöel, A.; Ringelstein, E.-B.; & Henningsen, H. (2000). Handedness and hemispheric language dominance in healthy humans. *Brain, 123,* 2512–2518. https://doi.org/10.1093/brain/123.12.2512

Knettel, Brandon. (2016). Exploring diverse mental illness attributions in a multinational sample: A mixed-methods survey of scholars in international psychology. *International Perspectives in Psychology: Research, Practice, Consultation, 5,* 128–140. https://doi.org/10.1037/ipp0000048

Kniffin, Kevin M.; Narayanan, Jayanth; Anseel, Frederik; Antonakis, John; Ashford, Susan P.; Bakker, Arnold B.; Bamberger, Peter; Bapuji, Hari; Bhave, Devasheesh P.; Choi, Virginia K.; Creary, Stephanie J.; Demerouti, Evangelia; Flynn, Francis J.; Gelfand, Michele J.; Greer, Lindred L.; Johns, Gary; Kesebir, Selin; Klein, Peter G.; Lee, Sun Young; . . . & van Vugt, Mark. (2021). COVID-19 and the workplace: Implications, issues, and insights for future research and action. *American Psychologist, 76*(1), 63–77. https://doi.org/10.1037/amp0000716

Knoblich, Gunther, & Öllinger, Michael. (2006, October). The Eureka moment. *Scientific American Mind, 17*(5), 38–43.

Knoll, Abby R.; Otani, Hajime; Skeel, Reid L.; & Van Horn, K. Roger. (2017). Learning style, judgements of learning, and learning of verbal and visual information. *British Journal of Psychology 108,* 544–563. https://doi.org/10.1111/bjop.12214

Knowles, Kelly A., & Olatunji, Bunmi O. (2019). Enhancing inhibitory learning: The utility of variability in exposure. *Cognitive and Behavioral Practice, 26*(1), 186–200. https://doi.org/10.1016/j.cbpra.2017.12.001

Kobylińska, Dorota, & Kusev, Petko. (2019). Flexible emotion regulation: How situational demands and individual differences influence the effectiveness of regulatory strategies. *Frontiers in Psychology, 10,* 72. https://doi.org/10.3389/fpsyg.2019.00072

Koelsch, Stefan. (2018) Investigating the neural encoding of emotion with music. *Neuron, 98*(6), 1075–1079. https://doi.org/10.1016/j.neuron.2018.04.029

Koenen, Karestan C.; Amstadter, Ananda B.; & Nugent, Nicole R. (2008). Genetic risk factors for PTSD. In Douglas L. Delahanty (Ed.), *The psychobiology of trauma and resilience across the lifespan* (pp. 23–46). Aronson.

Koenig, Anne M.; Eagly, Alice H.; Mitchell, Abigail A.; & Ristikari, Tiina. (2011). Are leader stereotypes masculine? A meta-analysis of three research paradigms. *Psychological Bulletin, 137,* 616–642. https://doi.org/10.1037/a0023557

Koester, Lynne Sanford, & Lahti-Harper, Eve. (2010). Mother-infant hearing status and intuitive parenting during the first 18 months. *American Annals of the Deaf, 155,* 5–18. https://doi.org/10.1353/aad.0.0134

Kohlberg, Lawrence. (1976). Moral stages and moralization: The cognitive developmental approach. In T. Lickona (Ed.), *Moral development and behavior: Theory, research, and social issues.* Holt, Rinehart & Winston.

Kohlberg, Lawrence. (1981). *The philosophy of moral development: Moral stages and the idea of justice: Vol. 1. Essays on moral development.* Harper & Row.

Kohlberg, Lawrence. (1984). *The psychology of moral development.* Harper & Row.

Kohlberg, Lawrence. (1988). Quoted in James W. Fowler, John Snarey, & Karen A. Denicola, *Remembrances of Lawrence Kohlberg.* Center for Research in Faith and Moral Development.

Kohls, Niko, & Benedikter, Roland. (2010). The origins of the modern concept of "neuroscience": Wilhelm Wundt between empiricism, and idealism: Implications for contemporary neuroethics. In James J. Giordano, James J. & Bert Gordijn (Eds.), *Scientific and philosophical perspectives in neuroethics* (pp. 37–65). Cambridge University Press.

Kohn, Robert. (2014). Trends, gaps, and disparities in mental health. In S. O. Okpaku (Ed.), *Essentials of global mental health* (pp. 27–38). Cambridge University Press.

Kohrt, Brandon A.; Asher, Laura; Bhardwaj, Anvita; Fazel, Mina; Jordans, Mark J. D.; Mutamba, Byamah B.; Nadkarni, Abhijit; Pedersen, Gloria A.; Singla, Daisy R.; & Patel, Vikram. (2018). The role of communities in mental health care in low- and middle-income countries: A meta-review of components and competencies. *International Journal of Environmental Research and Public Health, 15*(6), 1279. https://doi.org/10.3390/ijerph15061279

Kohrt, Brandon A.; Jordans, Mark J. D.; Tol, Wietse A.; Speckman, Rebecca A.; Maharjan, Sujen M.; Worthman, Carol M.; & Komproe, Ivan H. (2008). Comparison of mental health between former child soldiers and children never conscripted by armed groups in Nepal. *Journal of the American Medical Association, 300*(6), 691–702. https://doi.org/10.1001/jama.300.6.691

Kokaridas, Dimitrios; Maggouritsa, Georgia; Stoforos, Periklis; Patsiaouras, Asterios; Theodorakis, Yiannis; & Diggelidis, Nikolaos. (2013). The effect of a token economy system program and physical activity on improving quality of life of patients with schizophrenia. A pilot study. *American Journal of Applied Psychology, 2*(6), 80–88. https://doi.org/10.11648/j.ajap.20130206.13

Kola, Lola. (2020). Global mental health and COVID-19. *The Lancet Psychiatry, 7*(8). 655–657. https://doi.org/10.1016/S2215-0366(20)30235-2

Kolliakou, Anna; Bakolis, Ioannis; Chandran, David; Derczynski, Leon; Nomi, Werbeloff; Osborn, David P.J.; Bontcheva, Kalina; & Stewart, Robert. (2020, February 6). Mental health-related conversations on social media and crisis episodes: A time-series regression analysis. *Scientific Reports, 10,* 1342. https://doi.org/10.1038/s41598-020-57835-9

Kollndorfer, Kathrin; Kowalczyk, Knesia; Nell, Stephanie; Krajnik, Jacqueline; Mueller, Christian; & Schöpf, Veronika. (2015). The inability to self-evaluate smell performance: How the vividness of mental images outweighs awareness of olfactory performance. *Frontiers in Psychology, 6.* https://doi.org/10.3389/fpsyg.2015.00627

Kolodny, Andrew; Courtwright, David T.; Hwang, Catherine S.; Kreiner, Peter; Eadie, John L.; Clark, Thomas W., & Alexander, G. Caleb. (2015). The prescription opioid and heroin crisis: A public health approach to an epidemic of addiction. *Annual Review of Public Health, 3,* 559–574. https://doi.org/10.1146/annurev-publhealth-031914-122957

Komatsu, Hidehiko. (2006). The neural mechanisms of perceptual filling-in. *Nature Reviews Neuroscience, 7,* 220–231.

Kong, Lauren L.; Allen, John J. B.; & Glisky, Elizabeth L. (2008). Interidentity memory transfer in dissociative identity disorder. *Journal of Abnormal Psychology, 117*(3), 686–692. https://doi.org/10.1037/0021-843X.117.3.686

Konrath, Lisa; Beckius, Danièle; & Tran, Ulrich. (2016). Season of birth and population schizotypy: Results from a large sample of the adult general population. *Psychiatry Research, 242,* 245–250. https://doi.org/10.1016/j.psychres.2016.05.059

Kopp, Claire B. (2011). Development in the early years: Socialization, motor development, and consciousness. *Annual Review of Psychology. 62,* 165–87. https://doi.org/10.1146/annurev.psych.121208.131625

Koppel, Jonathan, & Berntsen, Dorthe. (2015). The peaks of life: The differential temporal locations of the reminiscence bump across disparate cueing methods. *Journal of Applied Research in Memory and Cognition, 4,* 66–80. https://doi.org/10.1016/j.jarmac.2014.11.004

Koppel, Jonathan, & Rubin, David C. (2016). Recent advances in understanding the reminiscence bump: The importance of cues in guiding recall from autobiographical memory. *Current Directions in Psychological Science, 25,* 135–140. https://doi.org/10.1177/0963721416631955

Kornell, Nate. (2008, February 1). How to study. *British Psychological Society Research Digest Blog.* https://digest.bps.org.uk/2008/02/01/how-to-study/

Kornfield, Rachel; Donohue, Julie; Berndt, Ernst R.; & Alexander, G. C. (2013). Promotion of prescription drugs to consumers and providers, 2001–2010. *PLOS ONE, 8*(3), 1–7. https://doi.org/10.1371/journal.pone.0055504

Kosslyn, Stephen M.; Ganis, Giorgio; & Thompson, William L. (2001). Neural foundations of imagery. *Nature Reviews Neuroscience, 2,* 635–642.

Kosslyn, Stephen M.; Thompson, William L.; Costantini-Ferrando, Maria F.; Alpert, Nathaniel M.; & Spiegel, David. (2000). Hypnotic visual illusion alters color processing in the brain. *American Journal of Psychiatry, 157,* 1279–1284.

Kouider, Sid; Berthet, Vincent; & Faivre, Nathan. (2011). Preference is biased by crowded facial expressions. *Psychological Science, 22,* 184–189.

Kovacs, Kristof, & Conway, Andrew R. A. (2019). What is IQ? Life beyond "general intelligence." *Current Directions in Psychological Science, 28*(2), 189–194. https://doi.org/10.1177/09637214198272

Kraemer, Helena. (2015). Research domain criteria (RDoC) and the DSM—Two methodological approaches to mental health diagnosis. *JAMA Psychiatry,72,* 1163–1164. https://doi.org/10.1001/jamapsychiatry.2015.2134

Kragel, Philip A., & LaBar, Kevin S. (2016). Decoding the nature of emotion in the brain. *Trends in Cognitive Sciences, 20*(6), 444–455. http://doi.org/10.1016/j.tics.2016.03.011

Kramer, Andrew. (2013). Russian service, and with please and thank you. *The New York Times.* http://nyti.ms/1LTqxEe

Kramer, Stephanie. (2019, December 12). U.S. has world's highest rate of children living in single-parent households. *Pew Research Center.* https://www.pewresearch.org/fact-tank/2019/12/12/u-s-children-more-likely-than-children-in-other-countries-to-live-with-just-one-parent/

Krantz, David S., & McCeney, Melissa K. (2002). Effects of psychological and social factors on organic disease: A critical assessment of research on coronary heart disease. *Annual Review of Psychology, 53,* 341–369.

Kranz, Georg; Hahn, Andreas; Kaufmann, Ulrike; Küblböck, Martin; Hummer, Allan; Ganger, Sebastian; . . . & Lanzenberger, Rupert. (2014). White matter microstructure in transsexuals and controls investigated by diffusion tensor imaging. *Journal of Neuroscience, 34,* 15466–15475. https://doi.org/10.1523%2FJNEUROSCI.2488-14.2014

Kraus, Cynthia. (2015). Classifying intersex in DSM-5: Critical reflections on gender dysphoria. *Archives of Sexual Behavior, 44*(5), 1147–1163. https://doi.org/10.1007/s10508-015-0550-0

Kraus, Michael W.; Onyeador, Ivuoma N.; Daumeyer, Natalie M.; Rucker, Julian M.; & Richeson, Jennifer A. (2019). The misperception of racial economic inequality. *Perspectives on Psychological Science, 14*(6), 899–921. https://doi.org/10.1177/174569161986304

Krebs, Dennis L., & Denton, Kathy. (2005). Toward a more pragmatic approach to morality: A critical evaluation of Kohlberg's model. *Psychological Bulletin, 112,* 629–649.

Krebs, Dennis L., & Denton, Kathy. (2006). Explanatory limitations of cognitive-developmental approaches to morality. *Psychological Bulletin, 113,* 672–675.

Kreider, Rose M. (2008, March 3). *Improvements to demographic household data in the current population survey: 2007.* U.S. Census Bureau, Housing and Household Economic Statistics Division.

Krendl, Anne C. & Pescosolido, Bernice A. (2020). Countries and cultural differences in the stigma of mental illness: The east-west divide. *Journal of Cross-Cultural Psychology, 51*(2), 149–167. https://doi.org/10.1177/0022022119901297

Krestel, Heinz; Bassetti, Claudio L.; & Walusinski, Olivier. (2018). Yawning—Its anatomy, chemistry, role, and pathological considerations. *Progress in Neurobiology, 161,* 61–78. https://doi.org/10.1016/j.pneurobio.2017.11.003

Kret, Mariska E., & de Gelder, Beatrice. (2012). A review on sex differences in processing emotional signals. *Neuropsychologia, 50,* 1211–1221. https://doi.org/10.1016/j.neuropsychologia.2011.12.022

Kring, Ann M., & Gordon, Albert H. (1998). Sex differences in emotion: Expression, experience, and physiology. *Journal of Personality and Social Psychology, 74,* 686–703.

Krippner, Stanley. (1994). Cross-cultural treatment perspectives of dissociative disorders. In Steven Jay Lynn & Judith W. Rhue (Eds.), *Dissociation: Clinical and theoretical perspectives.* Guilford.

Krishnamoorthy, Yuvaraj; Nagarajan, Ramya; Saya, Ganesh K.; & Menon, Vikas. (2020, November). Prevalence of psychological morbidities among general population, healthcare workers and COVID-19 patients amidst the COVID-19 pandemic: A systematic review and meta-analysis. *Psychiatry Research, 293,* 113382. https://doi.org/10.1016/j.psychres.2020.113382

Krohe, James. (2006). Are workplace tests worth taking? Only if you do them right—which you probably don't. *Across the Board, 43,* 16–23.

Kroll, Judith F.; Bobb, Susan C.; & Hoshino, Noriko. (2014). Two languages in mind: Bilingualism as a tool to investigate language, cognition, and the brain. *Current Directions in Psychological Science, 23,* 159–163. https://doi.org/10.1177/0963721414528511

Kross, Ethan, & Mischel Watter. (2010). From stimulus control to self-control: Toward an integrative understanding of the processes underlying willpower. In Ran R. Hassin, Kevin N. Ochsner, & Yaacov Trope (Eds.), *Self control in society, mind, and brain* (pp. 428–446). Oxford University Press.

Krueger, James M.; Frank, Marcos G.; Wisor, Jonathan P.; & Roy, Sandip. (2017). Sleep function: Toward elucidating an enigma. *Sleep Medicine Reviews, 28,* 42–50. https://doi.org/10.1016/j.smrv.2015.08.005

Kruger, Justin, & Gilovich, Thomas. (2004). Actions, intentions, and self-assessment: The road to self-enhancement is paved with good intentions. *Personality and Social Psychology Bulletin, 30*(3), 328–329.

Kruglanski, Arie W., & Kapetz, Catalina. (2010). Unpacking the self-control dilemma and its modes of resolution. In Ran R. Hassin, Kevin N. Ochsner, & Yaacov Trope (Eds.), *Self control in society, mind, and brain* (pp. 297–311). Oxford University Press.

Kryger, Meir H.; Rosenberg, Russel; & Kirsch, Douglas. (2020). *Kryger's sleep medicine review: A problem-oriented approach* (3rd ed.). Elsevier.

Krygier, Rachelle, & Faiola, Anthony. (2019, November 28). Locked up naked on a soiled mattress: Venezuela's mental health nightmare. *The Washington Post.* https://www.washingtonpost.com/world/the_americas/locked-up-naked-on-a-soiled-mattress-venezuelas-mental-health-nightmare/2019/11/27/e465f16c-0020-11ea-8341-cc3dce52e7de_story.html

Kryst, Joanna; Kawalec, Paweł; Mitoraj, Alicja M; Pilc, Andrzej; Lasoń, Władysław; & Brzostek, Tomasz. (2020). Efficacy of single and repeated administration of ketamine in unipolar and bipolar depression: A meta–analysis of randomized clinical trials. *Pharmacological Reports, 72,* 543–562. https://doi.org/10.1007/s43440-020-00097-z

Kübler-Ross, Elisabeth. (1969). *On death and dying.* Macmillan.

Kuczaj, Stan A. II. (2013). Emotions (and feelings) everywhere. In Shigeru Watanabe & Stan A. Kuczaj (Eds.), *Emotions of animals and humans: Comparative perspectives.* Springer Science + Business Media.

Kuehner, Cristine. (2017). Why is depression more common among women than among men? *The Lancet Psychiatry. 4*(2), 146-158. https://doi.org/10.1016/S2215-0366(16)30263-2

Kufahl, Peter; Li, Zhu; Risinger, Robert; Rainey, Charles; Piacentine, Linda; Wu, Gaohong; Bloom, Alan; Yang, Zheng; & Li, Shi-Jiang. (2008). Expectation modulates human brain responses to acute cocaine: A functional magnetic resonance imaging study. *Biological Psychiatry, 63,* 222–230.

Kuhl, Patricia K. (2004). Early language acquisition: Cracking the speech code. *Nature Reviews Neuroscience, 5,* 831–843.

Kuhl, Patricia K.; Williams, Karen A.; Lacerda, Francisco; Stevens, Kenneth N.; & Lindblom, Bjorn. (1992, January 31). Linguistic experience alters phonetic perception in infants by 6 months of age. *Science, 255,* 606–608.

Kuhn, Clifford C.; Nichols, Michael R.; & Belew, Barbara L. (2010). The role of humor in transforming stressful life events. In Thomas W. Miller (Ed.), *Handbook of stressful transitions across the lifespan.* Springer.

Kuhn, Deanna. (2008). Formal operations from a twenty-first century perspective. *Human Development, 51,* 48–55. https://doi.org/10.1159/000113155

Kuhn, Deanna, & Franklin, Sam. (2006). The second decade: What develops (and how)? In D. Kuhn & R. Siegler (Eds.), *Handbook of child psychology. Vol. 2: Cognition, perception, and language* (6th ed.) Wiley.

Kuikka, Jyrki T.; Tammela, Liisa; Karhunen, Leila; Rissanen, Aila; Bergström, Kim A.; Naukkarinen, Hannu; Vanninen, Esko; Karhu, Jari; Lappalainen, Raimo; Repo-Tiihonen, Eila; Tiihonen, Jari; & Uusitupa, Matti. (2001). Reduced serotonin transporter binding in binge eating women. *Psychopharmacology, 155*(3), 310–314. https://doi.org/10.1007/s002130100716

Kunz, John A., & Soltys, Florence G. (2007). *Transformational reminiscence: Life story work.* Springer.

Kuo, Ben. (2013). Collectivism and coping: Current theories, evidence, and measurements of collective coping. *International Journal of Psychology, 48,* 374–388. https://doi.org/10.1080/00207594.2011.640681

Kupferschmidt, Kai. (2014a). High hopes. *Science, 345,* 18–23.

Kurman, Jenny. (2010). Good, better, best: Between culture and self-enhancement. *Social and Personality Psychology Compass, 4*(6), 379–392.

Kurson, Robert. (2007). *Crashing through.* Random House.

Kurzban, Robert; Burton-Chellew, Maxwell N.; & West, Stuart A. (2015). The evolution of altruism in humans. *Annual Review of Psychology, 66,* 575–599. https://doi.org/10.1146/annurev-psych-010814-015355

Kuyken, Willem; Warren, Fiona C.; Taylor, Rod S.; Whalley, Ben; Crane, Catherine; Bondolfi, Guido; . . . & Dalgleish, Tim. (2016). Efficacy of mindfulness-based cognitive therapy in prevention of depressive relapse: An individual patient data meta-analysis from randomized trials. *JAMA Psychiatry, 73,* 565–574. https://doi.org/10.1001/jamapsychiatry.2016.0076

Kwan, Virginia S. Y.; Kuang, Lu Lu; & Zhao, Belinda X. (2008). In search of the optimal ego: When self-enhancement bias helps and hurts adjustment. In H. A. Wayment & J. J. Bauer (Eds.), *Transcending self-interest: Psychological explorations of the quiet ego.* American Psychological Association.

Laajaj, Rachid; Macours, Karen; Pinzon Hernandez, Daniel A.; Arias, Omar; Gosling, Samuel D.; Potter, Jeff; Rubio-Codina, Marta; & Vakis, Renos. (2019). *Science Advances, 5,* 1–13. https://doi.org/10.1126/sciadv.aaw5226

Laceulle, Odilia M.; Vollebergh, Wilma A.; & Ormel, Johan. (2015). The structure of psychopathology in adolescence: Replication of a general psychopathology factor in the TRAILS study. *Clinical Psychological Science, 3*(6), 850–860. https://doi.org/10.1177/2167702614560750

Ladabaum, Uri; Mannalithara, Ajitha; Myer, Parvathi A.; & Singh, Gurkirpal. (2014). Obesity, abdominal obesity, physical activity, and caloric intake in U.S. adults: 1988–2010. *American Journal of Medicine, 127*(8), 717–727.e12. https://doi.org/10.1016/j.amjmed.2014.02.026

Lader, Malcolm. (2008). Effectiveness of benzodiazepines: Do they work or not? *Expert Review Neurotherapy, 8,* 1189–1191. https://doi.org/10.1586/14737175.8.8.1189

Lafreniere, Denis & Mann, Norman. (2009). Anosmia: Loss of smell in the elderly. *Otolaryngologic Clinics of North America, 42*(1), 123–131.

LaFromboise, Teresa D., & Trimble, Joseph E. (1996). Obituary: Carolyn Lewis Attneave (1920-1992). *American Psychologist, 51*(5), 549. https://doi.org/10.1037/0003-066X.51.5.549

Lahey, Benjamin B. (2009). Public health significance of neuroticism. *American Psychologist, 64,* 241–256.

Laible, Deborah. (2007). Attachment with parents and peers in late adolescence: Links with emotional competence and social behavior. *Personality and Individual Differences, 43,* 1185–1197.

Laird, James D., & Lacasse, Katherine. (2014). Bodily influences on emotional feelings: Accumulating evidence and extensions of William James's theory of emotion. *Emotion Review, 6,* 27–34. https://doi.org/10.1177/1754073913494899

Lamb, Michael E.; Sternberg, Kathleen J.; & Prodromidis, Margardita. (1992). Nonmaternal care and the security of infant-mother attachment: A reanalysis of the data. *Infant Behavior and Development, 15,* 71–83.

Lamb, Michael E.; Thompson, Ross A.; Gardner, William; & Charnov, Eric L. (1985). Infant–mother attachment: The origins and developmental significance of individual differences in Strange Situation behavior. Erlbaum.

Lambert, Anthony J.; Good, Kimberly S.; & Kirk, Ian J. (2010). Testing the repression hypothesis: Effects of emotional valence on memory suppression in the think-No think task. *Consciousness and Cognition: An International Journal, 19*(1), 281–293.

Lambert, Michael J.; Garfield, Sol L.; & Bergin, Allen E. (2004). Overview, trends, and future issues. In Michael J. Lambert (Ed.), *Bergin and Garfield's handbook of psychotherapy and behavior change* (5th ed.). Wiley.

Lambert, Michael J.; Hansen, Nathan B.; & Finch, Arthur E. (2001). Patient-focused research: Using patient outcome data to enhance treatment effects. *Journal of Consulting and Clinical Psychology, 69,* 159–172.

Lambert, Michael J., & Ogles, Benjamin M. (2004). The efficacy and effectiveness of psychotherapy. In Michael J. Lambert (Ed.), *Bergin and Garfield's handbook of psychotherapy and behavior change* (5th ed.). Wiley.

Lampinen, James M.; Meier, Christopher R.; & Arnal, Jack D. (2005). Compelling untruths: Content borrowing and vivid false memories. *Journal of Experimental Psychology: Learning, Memory, and Cognition, 31,* 954–963.

The Lancet. (2015). Dementia—not all about Alzheimer's. *Lancet, 386*(10004), 1600. https://doi.org/10.1016/S0140-6736(15)00672-8

Landolt, Hans-Peter. (2008). Sleep homeostasis: A role for adenosine in humans? *Biochemical Pharmacology, 75,* 2070–2079.

Lang, Peter; Mcteague, Lisa; & Bradley, Margaret. (2016). RDoC, DSM, and the reflex physiology of fear: A biodimensional analysis of the anxiety disorders spectrum. *Psychophysiology,53,* 336–347. https://doi.org/10.1111/psyp.12462

Langan-Fox, Janice, & Grant, Sharon. (2006). The Thematic Apperception Test: Toward a Standard Measure of the Big Three Motives. *Journal of Personality Assessment, 87,* 277–291.

Lange, Carl G., & James, William. (1922). *The emotions* (I. A. Haupt, Trans.). Williams & Wilkins.

Lange, Jean, & Grossman, Sheila. (2010). Theories of aging. In Kristen L. Mauk (Ed.), *Gerontological nursing: Competencies for care* (2nd ed., pp. 50–74). Jones and Bartlett.

Lange, Tanja; Dimitrov, Stoyan; & Born, Jan. (2010). Effects of sleep and circadian rhythm on the human immune system. *Annals of the New York Academy of Sciences, 1193*(1), 48–59.

Langer, Ellen, & Rodin, Judith. (1976). The effects of choice and enhanced personal responsibility for the aged: A field experiment in an institutional setting. *Journal of Personality and Social Psychology, 34,* 191–198.

Langley, Audra K.; Cohen, Judith A.; Mannarino, Anthony P.; Jaycox, Lisa H.; Schonlau, Matthias; Scott, Molly; Walker, Douglas W.; & Gegenheimer, Kate L. (2014). Trauma exposure and mental health problems among school children 15 months post-hurricane Katrina. *Journal of Child and Adolescent Trauma, 6*(3), 143–156. https://doi.org/10.1080/19361521.2013.812171

Langlois, Judith H.; Kalakanis, Lisa; Rubenstein, Adam J.; Larson, Andrea; Hallam, Monica; & Smoot, Monica. (2000). Maxims or myths of beauty? A meta-analytic and theoretical review. *Psychological Bulletin, 126,* 390–423.

Langnickel, Robert, & Markowitsch, Hans. (2006). Repression and the unconscious. *Behavioral and Brain Sciences, 29,* 524–525. https://doi.org/10.1017/S0140525X06359110

Långström, Niklas; Rahman, Qazi; Carlström, Eva; & Lichtenstein, Paul. (2010). Genetic and environmental effects on same-sex sexual behavior: A population study of twins in Sweden. *Archives of Sexual Behavior, 39*(1), 75–80.

Lara, Antonio H.; & Wallis, Jonathan D. (2015). The role of prefrontal cortex in working memory: A mini review. *Frontiers in Systems Neuroscience, 9,* 173. https://doi.org/10.3389/fnsys.2015.00173

Larsen, Jeff T.; Norris, Catherine J.; McGraw, A. Peter; Hawkley, Louise C.; & Cacioppo, John T. (2009). The evaluative space grid: A single-item measure of positivity and negativity. *Cognition and Emotion, 23,* 453–480.

Laruelle, Marc; Kegeles, Lawrence S.; & Abi-Dargham, Anissa. (2003). Glutamate, dopamine, and schizophrenia: From pathophysiology to treatment. *Annals of the New York Academy of Sciences, 1003,* 138–158.

Lashley, Karl S. (1929). *Brain mechanisms and intelligence.* University of Chicago Press.

Lashley, Karl S. (1950). In search of the engram. *Symposia of the Society for Experimental Biology, 4,* 454–482.

Laska, Kevin M.; Gurman, Alan S.; & Wampold, Bruce E. (2014). Expanding the lens of evidence-based practice in psychotherapy: A common factors perspective. *Psychotherapy 51*(4), 467–481. https://doi.org/10.1037/a0034332

Latané, Bibb. (1981). The psychology of social impact. *American Psychologist, 36,* 343–356.

Latané, Bibb, & Darley, John M. (1968). Group inhibition of bystander intervention in emergencies. *Journal of Personality and Social Psychology, 10*(3), 215–221.

Latané, Bibb, & Darley, John M. (1970). *The unresponsive bystander: Why doesn't he help?* Appleton-Century-Crofts.

Latané, Bibb, & Nida, Steve A. (1981). Ten years of research on group size and helping. *Psychological Bulletin, 89,* 308–324.

Lau, Chi-leong; Wang, Han-Cheng; Hsu, Jung-Lung; & Liu, Mu-En. (2013). Does the dopamine hypothesis explain schizophrenia? *Reviews in the Neurosciences, 24*(4), 389–400. https://doi.org/10.1515/revneuro-2013-0011

Lau, Jennifer Y. F., & Pile, Victoria. (2015). Can cognitive bias modification of interpretations training alter mood states in children and adolescents? A reanalysis of data from six studies. *Clinical Psychological Science, 3*(1), 112–125. https://doi.org/10.1177/2167702614549596

Lavie, Nilli. (2010). Attention, distraction, and cognitive control under load. *Current Directions in Psychological Science, 19*(3), 143–148. https://doi.org/10.1177/0963721410370295

Lawler, Edward E., III. (1973). *Motivation in work organizations.* Brooks/Cole.

Lawrence, Erika; Rothman, Alexia D.; Cobb, Rebecca J.; & Bradbury, Thomas N. (2010). Marital satisfaction across the transition to parenthood: Three eras of research. In Marc S. Schulz, Marsha Kline Pruett, Patricia K. Kerig, & Ross D. Parke (Eds.), *Strengthening couple relationships for optimal child development: Lessons from research and intervention* (pp. 97–114). American Psychological Association.

Lazarus, Arnold A. (2000). Will reason prevail? From classic psychoanalysis to New Age therapy. *American Journal of Psychotherapy, 54,* 152–155.

Lazarus, Richard S. (1995). Vexing research problems inherent in cognitive-mediational theories of emotion—and some solutions. *Psychological Inquiry, 6,* 183–197.

Lazarus, Richard S. (1999). *Stress and emotion: A new synthesis.* Springer.

Lazarus, Richard S., & Folkman, Susan. (1984). *Stress, appraisal, and coping.* Springer.

Lazarus, Richard S., & Smith, Craig A. (1988). Knowledge and appraisal in the cognition-emotion relationship. *Cognition and Emotion, 2,* 281–300. https://doi.org/10.1080/02699938808412701

Le Foll, David; Rascle, Olivier; & Higgins, N. C. (2008). Attributional feedback-induced changes in functional and dysfunctional attributions, expectations of success, hopefulness, and short-term persistence in a novel sport. *Psychology of Sport and Exercise, 9,* 77–101. https://doi.org/10.1016/j.psychsport.2007.01.004

Leaper, Campbell, & Friedman, Carly Kay. (2007). The socialization of gender. In Joan E. Grusec & Paul D. Hastings (Eds.), *Handbook of socialization: Theory and research.* Guilford.

Leatherdale, Scott T. (2019). Natural experiment methodology for research: A review of how different methods can support real-world research. *International Journal of Social Research Methodology, 22*(1), 19-35, https://doi.org/10.1080/13645579.2018.1488449

Lebow, Jay L. (2008). Couple and family therapy. In Jay L. Lebow (Ed.), *Twenty-first century psychotherapies: Contemporary approaches to theory and practice* (pp. 307–346). Wiley.

Ledford, Heidi. (2014). If depression were cancer. *Nature, 515*(7526), 182–184. https://doi.org/10.1038/515182a

LeDoux, Joseph E. (1995). Emotion: Clues from the brain. *Annual Review of Psychology, 46,* 209–235.

LeDoux, Joseph E. (1996). The emotional brain: The mysterious underpinnings of emotional life. Simon & Schuster.

LeDoux, Joseph E. (2000). Emotion circuits in the brain. *Annual Review of Neuroscience, 23,* 155–184.

LeDoux, Joseph E. (2007). The amygdala. *Current Biology, 17,* R868–R874.

LeDoux, Joseph E. (2014). Coming to terms with fear. *Proceedings of the National Academy of Sciences of the United States of America, 111,* 2871–2878. https://doi.org/10.1073/pnas.1400335111

Lee, Dave. (2014). Samaritans pulls "suicide watch" Radar app. *BBC News.* http://www.bbc.com/news/technology-29962199

Lee, Evelyn, & Mock, Matthew R. (2005). Asian families: An overview. In Monica McGoldrick, Joe Giordano, & Nydia Garcia-Petro (Eds.), *Ethnicity & family therapy* (3rd ed., pp. 269–289). Guilford.

Lee, Jo Ann, & Phillips, Stephen J. (2006). Work and family: Can you have it all? *Psychologist-Manager Journal, 9*(1), 41–75.

Lee, Kibeom, & Ashton, Michael C. (2019). Not much H in the Big Five Aspect Scales: Relations between BFAS and HEXACO-PI-R scales. *Personality and Individual Differences, 144,* 164–167. https://doi.org/10.1016/j.paid.2019.03.010

Lee, Kyoung-Uk; Bahk, Won-Myong; Jon, Duk-In; Min, Kyung J.; Shin, Young C.; Woo, Young S. & Kim, Chan-Hyung. (2009). The prescription pattern and side-effect profile of bupropion. *Clinical Psychopharmacology and Neuroscience, 7*(2), 39–43.

Lee, Naomi. (2014). The Lancet Technology: November, 2014. *Lancet, 384,* 1917. https://doi.org/10.1016/s0140-6736(14)62267-4

Lee, Seung Hyun; Jin, Sang H.; & An, Jinung. (2019). The difference in cortical activation pattern for complex motor skills: A functional near-infrared spectroscopy study. *Scientific Reports, 9,* 14066. https://www.nature.com/articles/s41598-019-50644-9

Lee, Sing; Ho, Ting Pong; & Hsu, L. K. George. (1993). Fat phobic and non-fat phobic anorexia nervosa: A comparative study of 70 Chinese patients in Hong Kong. *Psychological Medicine, 23*(4), 999–1017. https://doi.org/10.1017/s0033291700026465

Lee, Sing; Ng, King Lam; Kwok, Kathleen; & Fung, Corina (2010). The changing profile of eating disorders at a tertiary psychiatric clinic in Hong Kong (1987–2007). *International Journal of Eating Disorders, 43*(4), 307–314. https://doi.org/10.1002/eat.20686

Lee, Tiane L.; Fiske, Susan T.; Glick, Peter; & Chen, Zhixia. (2010). Ambivalent sexism in close relationships: (Hostile) power and (benevolent) romance shape relationship ideals. *Sex Roles, 62,* 583–601. https://doi.org/10.1007/ s11199-010-9770-x

Lee, Yih-teen. (2010). Home versus host—identifying with either, both, or neither? The relationship between dual cultural identities and intercultural effectiveness. *International Journal of Cross Cultural Management, 10*(1), 55–76.

Legrand, Eve; Bieleke, Maik; Gollwitzer, Peter M.; & Mignon, Astrid. (2017, April 10). Nothing will stop me? Flexibly tenacious goal striving with implementation intentions. *Motivation Science, 3,* 101–118. https://doi.org/10.1037/mot0000050

Legros, Sophie, & Cislaghi, Beniamino. (2020). Mapping the social-norms literature: An overview of reviews. *Perspectives on Psychological Science, 15*(1), 62–80. https://doi.org/10.1177/17456916198664

Lehman, Barbara J.; David, Diana M.; & Gruber, Jennifer A. (2017). Rethinking the biopsychosocial model of health: Understanding health as a dynamic system. *Social and Personality Psychology Compass, 11*, 1–17. https://doi.org/10.1111/spc3.12328

Leichsenring, Falk, & Steinert, Christiane. (2017). Is cognitive behavioral therapy the gold standard for psychotherapy? The need for plurality in treatment and research. *Journal of the American Medical Association, 318*(14), 1323–1324. https://doi.org/10.1001/jama.2017.13737

Leichtman, Martin. (2004). Projective tests: The nature of the task. In Mark J. Hilsenroth & Daniel L. Segal (Eds.), *Comprehensive handbook of psychological assessment, Vol. 2: Personality assessment* (pp. 297–314). Wiley.

Leighton, Jacqueline P., & Sternberg, Robert J. (2013). Reasoning and problem solving. In Alice F. Healy, Robert W. Proctor, & Irving B. Weiner (Eds.), *Handbook of psychology, Vol. 4: Experimental psychology* (2nd ed.). Wiley.

Leighton, Jane, & Heyes, Cecilia. (2010). Hand to mouth: Automatic imitation across effector systems. *Journal of Experimental Psychology: Human Perception and Performance, 36*(5), 1174–1183.

Leising, Daniel; Scharloth, Joachim; Lohse, Oliver; & Wood, Dustin. (2014). What types of terms do people use when describing an individual's personality? *Psychological Science, 25*, 1787–1794. https://doi.org/10.1177/0956797614541285

Lemay, Edward P., Jr.; Clark, Margaret S.; & Greenberg, Aaron. (2010). What is beautiful is good because what is beautiful is desired: Physical attractiveness stereotyping as projection of interpersonal goals. *Personality and Social Psychology Bulletin, 36*(3), 339–353.

Lenert, Leslie; Muñoz, Ricardo F.; Perez, John E.; & Bansod, Aditya. (2004). Automated e-mail messaging as a tool for improving quit rates in an internet smoking cessation intervention. *Journal of the American Medical Informatics Association, 11*(4), 235–240. https://doi.org/10.1197/jamia.M1464

Lenroot, Rhoshel K., & Giedd, Jay N. (2006). Brain development in children and adolescents: Insights from anatomical magnetic resonance imaging. *Neuroscience & Biobehavioral Reviews, 30*(6), 718–729.

Lenzenweger, Mark F. (2008). Epidemiology of personality disorders. *Psychiatric Clinics of North America, 31*(3), 395–403. https://doi.org/10.1016/j.psc.2008.03.003

Leopold, David A., & Rhodes, Gillian. (2010). A comparative view of face perception. *Journal of Comparative Psychology, 124*(3), 233–251.

LePort, Aurora K. R.; Stark, Shauna M.; McGaugh, James L.; & Stark, Craig E. L. (2016). Highly superior autobiographical memory: Quality and quantity of retention over time. *Frontiers in Psychology, 6*, Article 2017. https://doi.org/10.3389/fpsyg.2015.02017

LePort, Aurora K. R.; Stark, Shauna M.; McGaugh, James L.; & Stark, Craig E. L. (2017). A cognitive assessment of highly superior autobiographical memory. *Memory, 25*, 276–288. https://doi.org/10.1080/09658211.2016.1160126

Lerman, Dorothea C., & Vorndran, Christina M. (2002). On the status of knowledge for using punishment: Implications for treating behavior disorders. *Journal of Applied Behavior Analysis, 35*, 431–464.

Lerner, Howard D. (2008). Psychodynamic perspectives. In Michael Hersen & Alan M. Gross (Eds.), *Handbook of Clinical Psychology: Vol. 1. Adults* (pp. 127–160). Wiley.

Lerner, Jennifer S.; Li, Ye; Valdesolo, Piercarlo; & Kassam, Karin S. (2015). Emotion and decision making. *Annual Review of Psychology, 66*, 799–823. https://doi.org/10.1146/annurev-psych-010213-115043

Lerner, Melvin J. (1980). *The belief in a just world: A fundamental delusion.* Plenum Press.

Leroy, Arnaud; Foucher, Jack R.; Pins, Delphine; Delmaire, Christine; Thomas, Pierre; Roser, Mathilde M.; Lefebvre, Stephanie; Amad, Ali; Fovet, Thomas; Jaafari, Nemat; & Jardri, Renaud. (2017). fMRI capture of auditory hallucinations: Validation of the two-steps method. *Human Brain Mapping, 38*(10), 4966–4979. https://doi.org/10.1002/hbm.23707

Lesonsky, Rieva. (2019, June 21). The state of freelancing in America. *Score.* https://www.score.org/resource/infographic-megaphone-main-street-gig-economy

Lester, David. (1997). *Making sense of suicide: An in-depth look at why people kill themselves.* Charles Press.

Lester, David. (2010). The final hours: A linguistic analysis of the final words of a suicide. *Psychological Reports, 106*(3), 791–797. https://doi.org/10.2466/pr0.106.3.791–797

Lester, Gregory W. (2000, November/December). Why bad beliefs don't die. *Skeptical Inquirer, 24*, 40–43.

Lester, S. Reid; Brown, Jason R.; Aycock, Jeffrey. E.; Grubbs, S. Lee; & Johnson, Roger B. (2010). Use of saliva for assessment of stress and its effect on the immune system prior to gross anatomy practical examinations. *Anatomical Sciences Education. Lester: 3*, 160–167.

Lethaby, Carol; & Harris, Patricia. (2016). Learning styles and teacher training: Are we perpetuating neuromyths? *English Language Teaching Journal, 70*, 16–27. https://doi.org/10.1093/elt/ccv051

Lett, Heather S.; Blumenthal, James A.; Babyak, Michael A.; Catellier, Diane J.; Carney, Robert M.; Berkman, Lisa F.; Burg, Matthew M.; Mitchell, Pamela; Jaffe, Allan S.; & Schneiderman, Neil. (2009). Dimensions of social support and depression in patients at increased psychosocial risk recovering from myocardial infarction. *International Journal of Behavioral Medicine, 16*(3), 248–258. https://doi.org/10.1007/s12529-009-9040-x

Leung, Paul K., & Boehnlein, James K. (2005). Vietnamese families. In Monica McGoldrick, Joseph Giordano, & Nydia Garcia-Petro (Eds.), *Ethnicity & family therapy* (3rd ed., pp. 363–373). Guilford.

Levashina, Julia; Hartwell, Christopher; Morgeson, Frederick; & Campion, Michael. (2014). The structured employment interview: Narrative and quantitative review of the research literature. *Personnel Psychology, 67*, 241–293. https://doi.org/10.1111/peps.12052

Levenson, Hanna. (2010). *Brief dynamic therapy.* American Psychological Association.

Levenson, Hanna. (2011). Time-limited dynamic psychotherapy. In Leonard M. Horowitz & Stephen Strack (Eds.), *Handbook of interpersonal psychology: Theory, research, assessment, and therapeutic interventions* (pp. 545–563). Wiley.

Levenson, Robert W. (1992). Autonomic nervous system differences among emotions. *Psychological Science, 3*, 23–27.

Levenson, Robert W. (2003). Blood, sweat, and fears: The autonomic architecture of emotion. In Paul Ekman, Joseph Campos, Richard J. Davidson, & Frans B.M. de Waal (Eds.), *Emotions inside out: 130 years after Darwin's: The expression of the emotions in man and animals.* New York University Press.

Levenson, Robert W.; Ekman, Paul; & Friesen, Wallace V. (1990). Voluntary facial action generates emotion-specific autonomic nervous system activity. *Psychophysiology, 27*, 363–384.

Levenson, Robert W.; Ekman, Paul; Heider, Karl; & Friesen, Wallace V. (1992). Emotion and autonomic nervous system activity in the Minangkabau of west Sumatra. *Journal of Personality and Social Psychology, 62*, 972–988.

Levenson, Robert W.; Lwi, Sandy J.; Brown, Casey L.; Ford, Brett Q.; Otero, Marcela C.; & Verstaen, Alice. (2017). Emotion. In John T. Cacioppo, Louis G. Tassinary, & Gary G. Berntson (Eds.), *Cambridge handbooks in psychology. Handbook of psychophysiology*, 444–464. Cambridge University Press. https://doi.org/10.1017/9781107415782.020

Levin, Ross, & Nielsen, Tore A. (2007). Disturbed dreaming, posttraumatic stress disorder, and affect distress: A review and neurocognitive model. *Psychological Bulletin, 133*, 482–528.

Levine, Robert V.; Reysen, Stephen; & Ganz, Ellen. (2008). The kindness of strangers revisited: A comparison of 24 US cities. *Social Indicators Research, 85*(3), 461–481.

Levine, Sheen; Apfelbaum, Evan; Bernard, Mark; Bartelt, Valerie; Zajac, Edward; & Stark, David. (2014). Ethnic diversity deflates price bubbles. *Proceedings of the National Academy of Sciences of the United States of America, 111*, 18524–18529. https://doi.org/10.1073/pnas.1407301111

Levinson, Douglas F. (2009). Genetics of major depression. In Ian H. Gotlib & Constance L. Hammen (Eds.), *Handbook of depression* (2nd ed., pp. 165–186). Guilford.

Lewontin, Richard. (1970, March). Race and intelligence. *Bulletin of the Atomic Scientists*, 2–8.

Liao, Jing; Head, Jenny; Kumari, Meena; Stansfeld, Stephen; Kivimaki, Mika; Singh-Manoux, Archana; & Brunner, Eric J. (2014). Negative aspects of close relationships as risk factors for cognitive aging. *American Journal of Epidemiology, 180*, 1118–1125. https://doi.org/10.1093/aje/kwu236

Libby, Lisa K.; Shaeffer, Eric M.; Eibach, Richard P.; & Slemmer, Jonathan. (2007). Picture yourself at the polls: Visual perception in mental imagery affects self-perception and behavior. *Psychological Science, 18*, 199–203.

Liberman, Zoe; Woodward, Amanda; Keysar, Boaz; & Kinzler, Katherine. (2016). Exposure to multiple languages enhances communication skills in infancy. *Development Science*, 1–11. https://doi.org/10.1111/desc.12420

Lieb, Roselind; Bronisch, Thomas; Höfler, Michael; Schreier, Andrea; & Wittchen, Hans-Ulrich. (2005). Maternal suicidality and risk of suicidality in offspring: Findings from a community study. *American Journal of Psychiatry, 162*, 1665–1671.

Lieberman, Matthew D. (2000). Intuition: A social cognitive neuroscience approach. *Psychological Bulletin, 126*, 109–137.

Lieberman, Robert Paul. (2000). The token economy. *American Journal of Psychiatry, 157*, 1398.

Liese, Bruce S.; & Monley, Corey M. (2021). Providing addiction services during a pandemic: Lessons learned from COVID-19. *Journal of Substance Abuse Treatment, 120*, 108156. https://doi.org/10.1016/j.jsat.2020.108156

Liff, Zanvel A. (1992). Psychoanalysis and dynamic techniques. In Donald K. Freedheim (Ed.), *History of psychotherapy: A century of change.* American Psychological Association.

Lilienfeld, Scott O. (2007). Psychological treatments that cause harm. *Perspectives on Psychological Science, 2*(1), 53–69. https://doi.org/10.1111/j.1745-6916.2007.00029.x

Lilienfeld, Scott O. (2011). Distinguishing scientific from pseudoscientific psychotherapies: Evaluating the role of theoretical plausibility, with a little help from Reverend Bayes. *Clinical Psychology: Science and Practice, 18*, 105–112. https://doi.org/10.1111/j.1468-2850.2011.01241.x

Lilienfeld, Scott O.; Ammirati, Rachel; & David, Michal. (2012). Distinguishing science from pseudoscience in school psychology: Science and scientific thinking as safeguards against human error. *Journal of School Psychology, 50*(1), 7–36. https://doi.org/10.1016/j.jsp.2011.09.006

Lilienfeld, Scott O., Watts, Ashley L., & Smith, Sarah F. (2015). Successful psychopathy: A scientific status report. *Current Directions in Psychological Science, 24*, 298–303. https://doi.org/10.1177/0963721415580297

Limcaoco, Gamonal R. S.; Mateos, Enrique M.; Fernández, Juan M., & Roncero, Carlos. (2020). Anxiety, worry and perceived stress in the world due to the COVID-19 pandemic, March 2020. Preliminary results. *MedRxiv*. https://doi.org/10.1101/2020.04.03.20043992

Lin, Jianfei; Jiang, Yanrui; Wang, Guanghai; Meng, Min; Zhu, Qi; Mei, Hao; Liu, Shijian; & Jiang, Fan. (2020). Associations of short sleep duration with appetite-regulating hormones and adipokines: A systematic review and meta-analysis. *Obesity Reviews, 24*(11). https://doi.org/10.1111/obr.13051

Linda, Wendy P., & McGrath, Robert E. (2017). The current status of prescribing psychologists: Practice patterns and medical professional evaluations. *Professional Psychology: Research and Practice, 48*(1), 38–45. https://doi.org/10.1037/pro0000118

Lindahl, Hans. (2019, Oct. 25). 9 young people on how they found out they were intersex. *Teen Vogue*. https://www.teenvogue.com/gallery/young-people-on-how-they-found-out-they-are-intersex

Lindau, Stacy Tessler, & Gavrilova, Natalia. (2010). Sex, health, and years of sexually active life gained due to good health: evidence from two US population based cross sectional surveys of ageing. *British Medical Journal, 340,* c810.

Linden, Michael. (2013). How to define, find and classify side effects in psychotherapy: From unwanted events to adverse treatment reactions. *Clinical Psychology and Psychotherapy, 20,* 286–296. https://doi.org/:10.1002/cpp.1765

Lindenberger, Ulman. (2014). Human cognitive aging: *Corriger la fortune? Science, 346,* 572–579.

Lindsay, D. Stephen. (2008). Source monitoring. In H. L. Roediger, III (Ed.), *Cognitive psychology of memory. Vol. 2 of Learning and memory: A comprehensive reference,* 4 Vols (pp. 325–348). Elsevier.

Lindsay, D. Stephen; Hagen, Lisa; Read, J. Don; Wade, Kimberley A.; & Garry, Maryanne. (2004a). True photographs and false memories. *Psychological Science, 15,* 149–154.

Lindsay, D. Stephen; Wade, Kimberley A.; Hunter, Michael A.; & Read, J. Don. (2004b). Adults' memories of childhood: Affect, knowing, and remembering. *Memory, 12,* 27–43.

Lindsey, Eric W. (2020). Relationship context and emotion regulation across the life span. *Emotion, 20*(1), 59–62. http://doi.org/10.1037/emo0000666

Linehan, Marsha M. (1993). *Cognitive-behavioral treatment of borderline personality disorder.* Guilford.

Linehan, Marsha M. (2009, May 2). Radical compassion: Translating Zen into psychotherapy. Presented at Meditation and Psychotherapy: Cultivating Compassion and Wisdom.

Linehan, Marsha M., & Dexter-Mazza, Elizabeth T. (2008). Dialectical behavior therapy for borderline personality disorder. In David H. Barlow (Ed.), *Clinical handbook of psychological disorders* (4th ed., pp. 365–420). Guilford.

Linnet, Jakob. (2020). The anticipatory dopamine response in addiction: A common neurobiological underpinning of gambling disorder and substance use disorder? *Progress in Neuro-Psychopharmacology and Biological Psychiatry, 98*(2), 109802. https://doi.org/10.1016/j.pnpbp.2019.109802

Lippa, Richard A. (2008). The relation between childhood gender nonconformity and adult masculinity-femininity and anxiety in heterosexual and homosexual men and women. *Sex Roles, 59*(9–10), 684–693.

Lippa, Richard A. (2010). Gender differences in personality and interests: When, where, and why? *Social and Personality Psychology Compass, 4,* 1098–1110. https://doi.org/10.1111/j.1751-9004.2010.00320.x

Lissek, Shuel; Rabin, Stephanie; Heller, Randi; Lukenbaugh, David; Geraci, Marilla; Pine, Daniel S.; & Grillon, Christian. (2010). Overgeneralization of conditioned fear as a pathogenic marker of panic disorder. *American Journal of Psychiatry, 167,* 47–55. https://doi.org/10.1176/appi.ajp.2009.09030410

Lissemore, Jennifer I.; Leyton, Marco; Gravel, Paul; Sookman, Debbie; Nordahl, Thomas E.; & Benkelfat, Chawki. (2014). OCD: Serotonergic mechanisms. In Rudi A. J. O. Dierckx, Andreas Otte, Erik F. J. de Vries, Aren van Waarde, & Johan A. den Boer (Eds.), *PET and SPECT in Psychiatry* (pp. 433–450). Springer. https://doi.org/10.1007/978-3-642-40384-2_17

Liu, Shi S.; Morris, Michael W.; Tallhelm, Thomas; & Yang, Qian. (2019). Ingroup vigilance in collectivistic cultures. *Proceedings of the National Academy of Sciences, 116*(29), 14538–14546. https://doi.org/10.1073/pnas.1817588116

Livingstone, Margaret, & Hubel, David. (1988, May 6). Segregation of form, color, movement and depth: Anatomy, physiology, and perception. *Science, 240,* 740–749.

Llenas, Bryan. (2015). Two sets of Colombian identical twins try to cope with a colossal hospital mix up. *Fox News.* http://latino.foxnews.com/latino/health/2015/08/19/two-sets-colombian-identical-twins-try-to-cope-with-colossal-hospital-mix-up/

Lobstein, Tim; Jackson-Leach, Rachel; Moodie, Marjory L.; Hall, Kevin D.; Gortmaker, Steven L.; Swinburn, Boyd A.; James, W. Philip T.; Wang, Youfa; & McPherson, Klim. (2015). Child and adolescent obesity: Part of a bigger picture. *Lancet, 385,* 2510–2520. https://doi.org/10.1016/S0140-6736(14)61746-3

LoBue, Vanessa. (2010). And along came a spider: An attentional bias for the detection of spiders in young children and adults. *Journal of Experimental Child Psychology, 107*(1), 59–66.

LoBue, Vanessa, & DeLoache, Judy S. (2008). Detecting the snake in the grass: Attention to fear-relevant stimuli by adults and young children. *Psychological Science, 19,* 284–289.

LoBue, Vanessa, & DeLoache, Judy S. (2010). Superior detection of threat-relevant stimuli in infancy. *Developmental Science, 13*(1), 22–228. https://doi.org/10.1111/j.1467-7687.2009.00872.x

Lockard, Robert B. (1971). Reflections on the fall of comparative psychology: Is there a message for us all? *American Psychologist, 26,* 168–179.

Locke, Edwin A. (1976). The nature and causes of job satisfaction. In M. D. Dunnette (Ed.), *Handbook of industrial and organizational psychology* (pp. 1297–1349). Rand McNally.

Locke, Edwin A., & Schweiger, David M. (1979). Participation in decision-making: One more look. *Research in Organizational Behavior, 1,* 265–339.

Lockhart, Robert S., & Craik, Fergus I. M. (1990). Levels of processing: A retrospective commentary on a framework for memory research. *Canadian Journal of Psychology, 44*(1), 87–112.

Locurto, Charles. (2007). Individual differences and animal personality. *Comparative Cognition & Behavior Reviews, 2,* 67–78. https://doi.org/10.3819/ccbr.2008.20004.

Lodi-Smith, Jennifer; Jackson, Joshua; Bogg, Tim; Walton, Kate; Wood, Dustin; Harms, Peter; & Roberts, Brent W. (2010). Mechanisms of health: Education and health-related behaviours partially mediate the relationship between conscientiousness and self-reported physical health. *Psychology & Health, 25*(3), 305–319.

Loeb, Tamra B.; Ebor, Megan T.; Smith, Amber M.; Chin, Dorothy; Novacek, Derek M.; Hampton-Anderson, Joya N.; Norwood-Scott, Enricka; Hamilton, Alison B.; Brown, Arleen F.; & Wyatt, Gail E. (2020). How mental health professionals can address disparities in the context of the COVID-19 pandemic. *Traumatology.* https://doi.org/10.1037/trm0000292

Loewenstein, George. (2010). Insufficient emotion: Soul-searching by a former indicter of strong emotions. *Emotion Review, 2*(3), 234–239.

Loewy, Joanne V., & Spintge, Ralph. (2011). Music soothes the savage breast. *Music and Medicine, 3,* 69–71. https://doi.org/10.1177/1943862111401626

Loftus, Elizabeth F. (1996). *Eyewitness testimony* (Rev. ed.). Harvard University Press.

Loftus, Elizabeth F. (2002). Memory faults and fixes. *Issues in Science and Technology, 18*(4), 41–50.

Loftus, Elizabeth F. (2003). Our changeable memories: Legal and practical implications. *Nature Reviews Neuroscience, 4,* 231–234.

Loftus, Elizabeth F. (2004, December 18). Dispatch from the (un)civil memory wars. *The Lancet, 364*(Suppl. 1), s20–s21.

Loftus, Elizabeth F. (2005). Planting misinformation in the human mind: A 30-year investigation of the malleability of memory. *Learning and Memory, 12,* 361–366.

Loftus, Elizabeth F. (2007). Memory distortions: Problems solved and unsolved. In Maryanne Garry & Harlene Hayne (Eds.), *Do justice and let the sky fall: Elizabeth Loftus and her contributions to science, law, and academic freedom.* Erlbaum.

Loftus, Elizabeth F. (2011). How I got started: From semantic memory to expert testimony. *Applied Cognitive Psychology, 25,* 347–348. https://doi.org/10.1002/acp.1769

Loftus, Elizabeth F. (2013). 25 years of eyewitness science……finally pays off. *Perspectives on Psychological Science, 8,* 556–557. https://doi.org/10.1177/1745691613500995

Loftus, Elizabeth F., & Cahill, Larry. (2007). Memory distortion: From misinformation to rich false memory. In James S. Nairne (Ed.), *The foundation of remembering: Essays in honor of Henry L. Roediger, III* (pp. 413-425). Psychology Press.

Loftus, Elizabeth F., & Davis, Deborah. (2006). Recovered memories. *Annual Review of Clinical Psychology, 2,* 469–498.

Loftus, Elizabeth F., & Palmer, J. C. (1974). Reconstruction of automobile destruction: An example of the interaction between language and memory. *Journal of Verbal Learning and Verbal Behavior, 13,* 585–589.

Loftus, Elizabeth F., & Pickrell, Jacqueline E. (1995). The formation of false memories. *Psychiatric Annals, 25,* 720–725.

Lohman, David F. (1998). Fluid intelligence, inductive reasoning, and working memory: Where the theory of multiple intelligences falls short. *Talent development IV: Proceedings from the 1998 Henry B. & Jocelyn Wallace National Research Symposium on talent development* (pp. 219–227). Gifted Psychology Press.

Lohr, Jeffrey M.; Hooke, Wayne; Gist, Richard; & Tolin, David F. (2003). Novel and controversial treatments for trauma-related stress disorders. In Scott O. Lilienfeld, Steven Jay Lynn, & Jeffrey M. Lohr (Eds.), *Science and pseudoscience in clinical psychology.* Guilford.

Lohse, Tina; Rohrmann, Sabine; Richard, Aline; Bop, Matthias; Faeh, David. (2017). Type A personality and mortality: Competitiveness but not speed is associated with increased risk. *Atherosclerosis, 262,* 19–24. https://doi.org/10.1016/j.atherosclerosis.2017.04.016

LoLordo, Vincent M. (2001). Learned helplessness and depression. In Marilyn E. Carroll & J. Bruce Overmier (Eds.), *Animal research and human health: Advancing human welfare through behavioral science.* American Psychological Association.

Long, Patrick, & Corfas, Gabriel. (2014). To learn is to myelinate. *Science, 346,* 298. https://doi.org/10.1126/science.1261127

Loo, Colleen. (2018). Can we confidently use ketamine as a clinical treatment for depression?. *The Lancet Psychiatry, 5*, 11–12. https://doi.org/10.1016/S2215-0366(17)30480-7

Loos, Eva; Schicktanz, Nathalie; Fastenrath, Matthias; & Coynel, David. (2020). Reducing amygdala activity and phobic fear through cognitive top-down regulation. *Journal of Cognitive Neuroscience, 32*(6), 1117–1129. https://doi.org/10.1162/jocn_a_01537

Loos, Ted. (2020, Sept. 25). A painter who puts it all on the line. *The New York Times.* https://www.nytimes.com/2020/09/25/arts/design/virginia-jaramillo-menil-houston.html?referringSource=articleShare

Lopez, Canela. (2020). Lady Gaga told Oprah she takes an antipsychotic, and without it she would 'spiral very frequently.' *Insider.* https://www.insider.com/lady-gaga-oprah-2020-tour-antipsychotic-fibromyalgia-ptsd-mental-health-2020-1

Lopez, Carla M.; Solomon, Daniel; Boulware, Susan D.; & Christison-Lagay, Emily R. (2018). Trends in the use of puberty blockers among transgender children in the United States. *Journal of Pediatric Endocrinology and Metabolism, 31*(6), 665–670. https://doi.org/10.1515/jpem-2018-0048

Lord, Charles G.; Ross, Lee; & Lepper, Mark R. (1979). Biased assimilation and attitude polarization: The effects of prior theories on subsequently considered evidence. *Journal of Personality and Social Psychology, 37*, 2098–2109.

Lorenzo, Genevieve L.; Biesanz, Jeremy C.; & Human, Lauren J. (2010). What is beautiful is good and more accurately understood: Physical attractiveness and accuracy in first impressions of personality. *Psychological Science, 21*(12), 1777–1782. https://doi.org/10.1177/0956797610388048

Louis, Winnifred R.; Esses, Victoria M.; & Lalonde, Richard N. (2013). National identification, perceived threat, and dehumanization as antecedents of negative attitudes toward immigrants in Australia and Canada: Negative attitudes toward immigrants. *Journal of Applied Social Psychology, 43*, 156–165. https://doi.org/10.1111/jasp.12044

Lowry, Brian. (October 24, 2011). Eli Roth probes evil on discovery's 'curiosity.' *Variety.* http://variety.com/2011/voices/opinion/roth-probes-nature-of-evil-on-discoverys-curiosity-1200572557

Lu, Darlene; Palmer, Julie R.; Rosenberg, Lynn; Shields, Alexandra E.; Orr, Esther H.; DeVivo, Immaculata; & Cozier, Yvette C. (2019). Perceived racism in relation to telomere length among African American women in the Black Women's Health Study. *Annals of Epidemiology, 36*, 33–39. https://doi.org/10.1016/j.annepidem.2019.06.003

Lu, Stephen M.; Hsu, David T.; Perry, Adam D.; Leipziger, Lyle S.; Kasabian, Armen K.; Bartlett, Scott P.; Thorne, Charles H.; Broer, P. Niclas; & Tanna, Neil. (2018). The public face of rhinoplasty: Impact on perceived attractiveness and personality. *Plastic and Reconstructive Surgery, 142*(4), 881–887. https://doi.org/10.1097/PRS.0000000000004731

Lubbadeh, Jens. (2005, June). Same brain for speech and sign. *Scientific American Mind, 16*(2), 86–87.

Lubinski, David; & Benbow, Camilla P. (2021). Intellectual precocity: What have we learned since Terman?. *Gifted Child Quarterly, 65*(1), 3-28. https://doi.org/10.1177/0016986220925447

Luborsky, Lester, & Barrett, Marna S. (2006). The history and empirical status of key psychoanalytic concepts. *Annual Review of Clinical Psychology, 2*, 1–19. https://doi.org/10.1146/annurev.clinpsy.2.022305.095328

Luborsky, Lester; Rosenthal, Robert; Diguer, Louis; Andrusyna, Tomasz P.; Berman, Jeffrey S.; Levitt, Jill T.; Seligman, David A.; & Krause, Elizabeth D. (2002). The dodo bird verdict is alive and well— mostly. *Clinical Psychology: Science and Practice, 9*, 2–12.

Lucas, Amelia; Repko, Melissa; Gilbert, Marc; & Berk, Christina C. (2021, January 26). Walgreens taps Starbucks operating chief Roz Brewer as its next CEO. *CNBC.* https://www.cnbc.com/2021/01/26/starbucks-coo-roz-brewer-leaving-to-become-ceo-of-publicly-traded-company.html

Lucas, Brian, & Nordgren, Loran. (2015). People underestimate the value of persistence for creative performance. *Journal of Personality and Social Psychology, 109*, 232–243. https://doi.org/10.1037/pspa0000030

Lucassen, Nicole; Tharner, Anne; van IJzendoorn, Marinus H.; Bakermans-Kranenburg, Marian J.; Volling, Brenda L.; Verhulst, Frank C.; Lambregtse-Van den Berg, Mijke P.; & Tiemeier, Henning. (2011). The association between paternal sensitivity and infant–father attachment security: A meta-analysis of three decades of research. *Journal of Family Psychology, 25*, 986–992.

Ludwig, David S., & Kabat-Zinn, Jon. (2008). Mindfulness in medicine. *Journal of the American Medical Association, 300*, 1350–1352.

Lueke, Adam, & Gibson, Bryan. (2015). Mindfulness meditation reduces implicit age and race bias: The role of reduced automaticity of responding. *Social Psychological and Personality Science, 6*, 284–291. https://doi.org/10.1177/1948550614559651

Luhrmann, Tanya Marie; Padvamati, Raman; Tharoor, Hema; & Osei, Akwasi. (2015). Differences in voice-hearing experiences of people with psychosis in the USA, India, and Ghana: Interview-based study. *British Journal of Psychiatry, 206*, 41–44. https://doi.org/10.1192/bjp.bp.113.139048

Luna, Beatriz; Paulsen, David J.; Padmanabhan, Aarthi; & Geier, Charles. (2013). The teenage brain: Cognitive control and motivation. *Current Directions in Psychological Science, 22*, 94–100. https://doi.org/10.1177/0963721413478416

Lund, Rikke; Christensen, Ulla; Nilsson, Charlotte Juul; Kriegbaum, Margit; & Rod, Naja Hulvej. (2014). Stressful social relations and mortality: A prospective cohort study. *Journal of Epidemiology and Community Health., 68*, 720–727. https://doi.org/10.1136/jech-2013-203675

Lundahl, Brad W.; Kunz, Chelsea; Brownell, Cynthia; Tollefson, Derrik; & Burke, Brian L. (2010). A meta-analysis of motivational interviewing: Twenty-five years of empirical studies. *Research on Social Work Practice, 20*(137), 137–160. https://doi.org/10.1177/1049731509347850

Lustgarten, Samuel, & Colbow, Alexander. (2017). Ethical concerns for telemental health therapy amidst governmental surveillance. *American Psychologist, 72*, 159–170. https://doi.org/10.1037/a0040321

Lutterman, Ted; Shaw, Robert; Fisher, William; & Manderscheid, Ronald. (2017, August). *Trend in psychiatric inpatient capacity, United States and each state, 1970-2014.* National Association of State Mental Health Program Directors. https://www.nasmhpd.org/sites/default/files/TACPaper.2.Psychiatric-Inpatient-Capacity_508C.pdf

Lutz, Antoine; Greischar, Lawrence L.; Rawlings, Nancy B.; Richard, Matthieu; & Davidson, Richard J. (2004, November 16). Long-term meditators self-induce high-amplitude gamma synchrony during mental practice. *Proceedings of the National Academy of Sciences, 101*, 16369–16373.

Lutz, Antoine; Slagter, Heleen A.; Rawlings, Nancy B.; Francis, Andrew D.; Greischar, Lawrence L.; & Davidson, Richard J. (2009). Mental training enhances stability of attention by reducing cortical noise. *Journal of Neuroscience, 29*, 13418–13427.

Lyn, Heidi; Greenfield, Patricia; & Savage-Rumbaugh, Sue. (2006). The development of representational play in chimpanzees and bonobos: Evolutionary implications, pretense, and the role of inter-species communication. *Cognitive Development, 21*, 199–213.

Lyn, Heidi, & Savage-Rumbaugh, Sue. (2013). The use of emotion symbols in language-using apes. In Shigeru Watanabe & Stan A. Kuczaj (Eds.), *Emotions of animals and humans: Comparative perspectives.* Springer Science + Business Media.

Lynn, Steven Jay; Fassler, Oliver; Joshua A. Knox, Joshau A.; & Lilienfeld, Scott O. (2006). Dissociation and dissociative identity disorder: Treatment guidelines and cautions. In Jane E. Fisher & William T. O'Donohue (Eds.), *Practitioner's guide to evidence-based psychotherapy.* Springer. https://doi.org/10.1007/978-0-387-28370-8_24

Lynn, Steven Jay, & Green, Joseph P. (2011). The sociocognitive and dissociation theories of hypnosis: Toward a rapprochement. *International Journal of Clinical and Experimental Hypnosis, 59*(3), 277–293.

Lynn, Steven Jay, & Kirsch, Irving. (2006). *Essentials of clinical hypnosis: An evidence-based approach.* American Psychological Association.

Lynn, Steven Jay; Kirsch, Irving; & Rhue, Judith W. (2010). An introduction to clinical hypnosis. In Steven Jay Lynn, Judith W. Rhue, & Irving Kirsch (Eds.), *Handbook of clinical hypnosis* (2nd ed., pp. 3–18). American Psychological Association.

Lynn, Steven Jay; Krackow, Elisa; Loftus, Elizabeth F.; Locke, Timothy G.; Lilienfeld, Scott O. (2015). Constructing the past: Problematic memory recovery techniques in psychotherapy. In Scott O. Lilienfeld, Steven Jay Lynn, & Jeffrey M. Lohr (Eds.), *Science and Pseudoscience in Clinical Psychology* (2nd ed.). Guilford.

Lynn, Steven Jay; Lilienfeld, Scott O.; Mercklebach, Harald; Giesbrecht, Timo; & Van Der Kloet, Dalena. (2012). Dissociation and dissociative disorders: Challenging conventional wisdom. *Current Directions in Psychological Science, 21*(1), 48–53. https://doi.org/10.1177/0963721411429457

Lynott, Dermot; Corker Katherine S.; Wortman, Jessica; Connell, Louise; Donnellan, M. Brent; Lucas, Richard E.; & O'Brien, Kerry. (2014). *Social Psychology 45*(3), 216–222. https://doi.org/10.1027/1864-9335/a000187

Ma, Ning; Dinges, David F.; Basner, Mathias; & Rao, Hengyi. (2015). How acute total sleep loss affects the attending brain: A meta-analysis of neuroimaging studies. *Sleep: Journal of Sleep and Sleep Disorders Research, 38*, 233–240.

Maccoby, Eleanor E., & Martin, John A. (1983). Socialization in the context of the family: Parent-child interaction. In Paul H. Mussen (Ed.), *Handbook of Child Psychology: Vol. 4. Socialization, personality, and social development.* Wiley.

MacCormack, Jennifer K., & Lindquist, Kristen A. (2017). Bodily contributions to emotion: Schacter's legacy for a psychological constructionist view on emotion. *Emotion Review, 9*, 36–45. https://doi.org/10.1177/1754073916639664

MacDonald, Benie, & Davey, Graham C. L. (2005). Inflated responsibility and perseverative checking: The effect of negative mood. *Journal of Abnormal Psychology, 114*, 176–182.

Macdonald, James S. P., & Lavie, Nilli. (2011). Visual perceptual load induces inattentional deafness. *Attention, Perception, & Psychophysics, 73*(6), 1780–1789. https://doi.org/10.3758/s13414-011-0144-4

Machackova, Hana. (2020). Bystander reactions to cyberbullying and cyberaggression: Individual, contextual, and social factors. *Current Opinion in Psychology, 36*, 130–134. https://doi.org/10.1016/j.copsyc.2020.06.003

Machákova, Hana; Dedkova, Lenka; Sevcikova, Anna; & Cerna, Alena. (2013). Bystanders' support of cyberbullied schoolmates. *Journal of Community and Applied Social Psychology, 23*, 25–36. https://doi.org/10.1002/casp.2135

Mack, Arien, & Rock, Irvin. (2000). *Inattentional blindness.* MIT Press.

MacKay, Donald G. (2014, May/June). The engine of memory. *Scientific American Mind, 25*, 30–38.

Macknik, Stephen L.; King, Mac; Randi, James; Robbins, Apollo; Teller; Thompson, John; & Martinez-Conde, Susana. (2008). Attention and awareness in stage magic: Turning tricks into research. *Nature Reviews Neuroscience, 9*, 871–879.

MacLean, Katherine A.; Ferrer, Emilio; Aichele, Stephen R.; Bridwell, David A.; Zanesco, Anthony P.; Jacobs, Tonya L.; King, Brandon G.; Rosenberg, Erika L.; Sahdra, Baljinder K.; Shaver, Phillip R.; Wallace, B. Alan; Mangun, George R.; & Saron, Clifford D. (2010). Intensive meditation training improves perceptual discrimination and sustained attention. *Psychological Science, 21*(6), 829–839. https://doi.org/10.1177/0956797610371339

MacLeod, Colin, & Mathews, Andrew. (2012). Cognitive bias modification approaches to anxiety. *Annual Review of Clinical Psychology, 8*, 189–217. https://doi.org/10.1146/annurev-clinpsy-032511-143052

Macmillan, Malcolm. (2000). *An odd kind of fame: Stories of Phineas Gage.* MIT Press.

Macmillan, Malcolm, & Lena, Matthew L. (2010). Rehabilitating Phineas Gage. *Neuropsychological Rehabilitation, 20*, 641–658. https://doi.org/10.1080/09602011003760527

Macpherson, Krista, & Roberts, William A. (2006). Do dogs (*Canis familiaris*) seek help in an emergency? *Journal of Comparative Psychology, 120*, 113–119. https://doi.org/10.1037/0735-7036.120.2.113

Macur, Juliet. (2020, May 1). Olympic gymnast recalls emotional abuse 'So twisted that I thought it couldn't be real.' *The New York Times.* https://www.nytimes.com/2020/05/01/sports/maggie-haney-gymnastics-abuse.html

Maddux, James E.; Volkmann, Jeffrey; & Hoyle, Rick H. (2010). Self-efficacy. In Rick H. Hoyle (Ed.), *Handbook of personality and self-regulation* (pp. 315–331). Wiley-Blackwell.

Madubata, Ijeoma, J.; Odafe, Mary O.; Talavera, David C.; Hong, Judy H.; & Walker, Rheeda L. (2018). Helplessness mediates racial discrimination and depression for African American young adults. *Journal of Black Psychology, 44*(7), 626–43. https://doi.org/10.1177/0095798418811476

Maes, Jürgen; Tarnai, Christian; & Schuster, Julia. (2012). About is and ought in research on belief in a just world: The Janus-faced just-world motivation. In E. Kals & J. Maes (Eds.), *Justice and Conflict* (pp. 93–106). Springer.

Magill, Molly; Apodaca, Timothy R.; Borsari, Brian; Gaume, Jacques; Hoadley, Ariel; Gordon, Rebecca E. F.; Tonigan, J. Scott; & Moyers, Theresa. (2018). A meta-analysis of motivational interviewing process: Technical, relational, and conditional process models of change. *Journal of Consulting and Clinical Psychology, 86*(2), 140–157. https://doi.org/10.1037/ccp0000250

Magnavita, Jeffrey J. (2008). Psychoanalytic psychotherapy. In Jay L. Lebow (Ed.), *Twenty-first century psychotherapies: Contemporary approaches to theory and practice* (pp. 206–236). Wiley.

Magruder, Kathryn M.; McLaughlin, Katie A.; & Elmore Borbon, Diane L. (2017). Trauma is a public health issue. *European Journal of Psychotraumatology, 8*(1), 1375338. https://doi.org/10.1080/20008198.2017.1375338

Maguinness, Corrina, & von Kriegstein, Katharina. (2017). Cross-modal processing of voices and faces in developmental prosopagnosia and developmental phonagnosia. *Visual Cognition, 25*, 644–657. https://doi.org/10.1080/13506285.2017.1313347

Mahon, Bradford Z., & Caramazza, Alfonso. (2011). What drives the organization of object knowledge in the brain? *Trends in Cognitive Sciences, 15*(3), 97–103.

Mahoney, Carrie E.; Cogswell, Andrew; Koralnik, Igor J.; & Scammell, Thomas E. (2019). The neurobiological basis of narcolepsy. *Nature Reviews Neuroscience, 20*(2), 83–93. https://doi.org/10.1038/s41583-018-0097-x

Mahowald, Mark W., & Schenck, Carlos H. (2005). Insights from studying human sleep disorders. *Nature, 437*, 1279–1285. https://doi.org/10.1038/nature04287

Maia, Tiago V., & Cano-Colino, Maria. (2015). The role of serotonin in orbitofrontal function and obsessive-compulsive disorder. *Clinical Psychological Science, 3*(3), 46–482. https://doi.org/10.1177/2167702614566809

Maier, Andrea; Vickers, Zata; & Inman, J. Jeffrey. (2007). Sensory-specific satiety, its crossovers, and subsequent choice of potato chip flavors. *Appetite, 49*, 419–428.

Maier, Steven F.; Seligman, Martin E.; & Solomon, Richard L. (1969). Pavlovian fear conditioning and learned helplessness: Effects of escape and avoidance behavior of (a) the CS=UCS contingency, and (b) the independence of the UCS and voluntary responding. In Byron A. Campbell & Russell M. Church (Eds.), *Punishment and aversive behavior.* Appleton-Century-Crofts.

Maier, Steven F., & Watkins, Linda R. (2000). The neurobiology of stressor controllability. In Jane E. Gillham (Ed.), *The science of optimism and hope: Research essays in honor of Martin E. P. Seligman.* Templeton Foundation Press.

Mainka, Spencer. (2019) Algorithm-based recruiting technology in the workplace, 5 *Texas A&M Journal of Property Law, 5*(3), 801–822. https://scholarship.law.tamu.edu/journal-of-property-law/vol5/iss3/8

Maj, Mario. (2012). Bereavement-related depression in the DSM-5 and ICD-11. *World Psychiatry, 11*(1), 1–2. https://doi.org/10.1016/j.wpsyc.2012.01.001

Majid, Asifa. (2014, 13 January). Quoted in Gruber, Karl, "Can you name that smell?" *Science.* http://news.sciencemag.org/brain-behavior/2014/01/can-you-name-smell

Majid, Asifa; Bowerman, Melissa; Kita, Sotaro; Haun, Daniel B. M.; & Levinson, Stephen C. (2004). Can language restructure cognition? The case for space. *Trends in Cognitive Sciences, 8*, 108–114.

Majid, Asifa, & Burenhult, Niclas. (2014). Odors are expressible in language, as long as you speak the right language. *Cognition, 130,* 266–270. https://doi.org/10.1016/j.cognition.2013.11.004

Majid, Asifa, & Kruspe, Nicole. (2018). Hunter-gatherer olfaction is special. *Current Biology, 28*, 409–413. https://doi.org/10.1016/j.cub.2017.12.014

Major, Geneviève C.; Doucet, Eric; & Trayhurn, Paul. (2007). Clinical significance of adaptive thermogenesis. *International Journal of Obesity, 31*, 204–212.

Makel, Matthew C.; Kell, Harrison J.; Lubinski, David; Putallaz, Martha; & Benbow, Camilla P. (2016). When lightning strikes twice: Profoundly gifted, profoundly accomplished. *Psychological Science.* https://doi.org/10.1177/0956797616644735

Ma-Kellams, Christine; Or, Flora; Baek, Ji; & Kawachi, Ichiro. (2016). Rethinking suicide surveillance: Google search data and self-reported suicidality differentially estimate completed suicide risk. *Clinical Psychological Science,4*(3), 480–484. https://doi.org/10.1177/2167702615593475

Makhanova, Anastasia; McNulty, James; & Maner, Jon. (2017). Relative physical position as an impression-management strategy: Sex differences in its use and implications. *Psychological Science, 28*, 1–11. https://doi.org/10.1177/0956797616688885

Makrygianni, Maria K., & Reed, Phil. (2010). A meta-analytic review of the effectiveness of behavioural early intervention programs for children with autistic spectrum disorders. *Research in Autism Spectrum Disorders, 4*(4), 577–593.

Malcolm, James P. (2008). Heterosexually married men who have sex with men: Marital separation and psychological adjustment. *Journal of Sex Research, 45*(4), 350–357.

Malhi, Gin S.; Gessler, Danielle; & Outhred, Tim. (2017). The use of lithium for the treatment of bipolar disorder: Recommendations from clinical practice guidelines. *Journal of Affective Disorders, 217*, 266–280. https://doi.org/10.1016/j.jad.2017.03.052

Malhi, Gin, & Outhred, Tim. (2016). Therapeutic mechanisms of lithium in bipolar disorder: Recent advances and current understanding. *CNS Drugs, 30*, 931–949. https://doi.org/10.1007/s40263-016-0380-1

Malinow, Roberto. (2016). Ketamine steps out of the darkness. *Nature, 533*, 477–478. https://doi.org/10.1038/nature17897

Mallett, Robyn K., & Wilson, Timothy D. (2010). Increasing positive intergroup contact. *Journal of Experimental Social Psychology, 46*(2), 382–387.

Malouff, John M.; Emmerton, Ashley J.; & Schutte, Nicola S. (2013). The risk of a halo bias as a reason to keep students anonymous during grading. *Teaching of Psychology, 40*(3), 233–237. https://doi.org/10.1177/0098628313487425

Mancini, Anthony. (2020). Heterogeneous mental health consequences of COVID-19: Costs and benefits. *Psychological Trauma: Theory, Research, Practice, and Policy, 12*(S1), S15–S16. http://dx.doi.org/10.1037/tra0000894

Mandler, George. (2013). The limit of mental structures. *Journal of General Psychology, 140*, 243–250. https://doi.org/10.1080/00221309.2013.807217

Manstead, Antony S. R., & Parkinson, Brian. (2015). Emotion theories. In Bertram Gawronski & Galen V. Bodenhausen (Eds.), *Theory and explanation in social psychology.* Guilford.

Maoz, Ifat. (2012). Contact and social change in an ongoing asymmetrical conflict: Four social-psychological models of reconciliation-aimed planned encounters between Israeli Jews and Palestinians. In John Dixon & Mark Levine (Eds.). *Beyond prejudice: Extending the social psychology of conflict, inequality and social change* (pp. 269–285). Cambridge University Press.

Maraldi, Everton O.; Costa, Adriano; Cunha, Alexandre; Flores, Douglas; Hamazaki, Edson; de Queiroz, Gregório P.; Martinez, Mateus; Siqueira, Silvana; & Reichow, Jeverson. (2021). Cultural presentations of dissociation: The case of possession trance experiences. *Journal of Trauma & Dissociation, 22*(1), 11–16. https://doi.org/10.1080/15299732.2020.1821145

Marañon, Gregorio. (1924). Contribution à l'étude de l'action émotive de l'adrenaline. *Revue Francaise d'Endocrinologie, 2*, 301–325.

Marantz, Andrew. (2013, September 16). Annals of psychology: Unreality star. *The New Yorker.* https://www.newyorker.com/magazine/2013/09/16/unreality-star

Marcus, Steven C., & Olfson, Mark. (2010). National trends in the treatment for depression from 1998 to 2007. *Archives of General Psychiatry, 67*(12), 1265–1273. https://doi.org/10.1001/archgenpsychiatry.2010.151

Marecek, Jeanne, & Gavey, Nicola. (2013). DSM-5 and beyond: A critical feminist engagement with psychodiagnosis. *Feminism & Psychology, 23*(1), 3–9. https://doi.org/10.1177/0959353512467962

Margolis, Seth, & Lyubomirsky, Sonja. (2019). Experimental manipulation of extraverted and introverted behavior and its effects on well-being. *Journal of Experimental Psychology: General, 149*(4), 719–731. https://doi.org/10.1037/xge0000668

Mari-Beffa, Paloma. (2017, May 3). Is talking to yourself a sign of mental illness? An expert delivers her verdict. *The Conversation.* https://theconversation.com/is-talking-to-yourself-a-sign-of-mental-illness-an-expert-delivers-her-verdict-77058

Marin, M; Rapisardi, Gherardo; & Tani, Franca. (2015). Two-day-old newborn infants recognize their mother by her axillary odour. *Acta Pædiatrica, 104*, 237–240. https://doi.org/10.1111/apa.12905

Marín-Burgin, Antonia; Mongiat, Lucas A.; Pardi, M. Belén; & Schinder, Alejandro F. (2012). Unique processing during a period of high excitation/inhibition: Balance in adult-born neurons. *Science 335*, 1238. https://doi.org/10.1126/science.1214956

Markman, Arthur B., & Gentner, Dedre. (2001). Thinking. *Annual Review of Psychology, 52*, 223–247.

Markowitsch, Hans J., & Staniloiu, Angelica. (2011). Memory, autonoetic consciousness, and the self. *Consciousness and Cognition: An International Journal, 20*(1), 16–39.

Markus, Hazel Rose, & Cross, Susan. (1990). The interpersonal self. In Lawrence A. Pervin (Ed.), *Handbook of personality: Theory and research.* Guilford.

Markus, Hazel Rose, & Kitayama, Shinobu. (1991). Culture and the self: Implications for cognition, emotion, and motivation. *Psychological Review, 98*, 224–253.

Markus, Hazel Rose, & Kitayama, Shinobu. (1994). The cultural construction of self and emotion: Implications for social behavior. In Shinobu Kitayama & Hazel Rose Markus (Eds.), *Emotion and culture: Empirical studies of mutual influence.* American Psychological Association.

Markus, Hazel Rose, & Kitayama, Shinobu. (1998). The cultural psychology of personality. *Journal of Cross-Cultural Psychology, 29*, 63–87.

Markus, Hazel Rose, & Kitayama, Shinobu. (2010). Culture and selves: A cycle of mutual constitution. *Perspectives on Psychological Science, 5*, 420–430. https://doi.org/10.1177/1745691610375557

Markus, Hazel Rose, & Kunda, Ziva. (1986). Stability and malleability of the self-concept. *Journal of Personality and Social Psychology, 51*, 858–866.

Markus, Hazel Rose, & Nurius, Paula. (1986). Possible selves. *American Psychologist, 41*, 954–969.

Markus, Hazel Rose, & Wurf, Elissa. (1987). The dynamic self-concept: A social psychological perspective. *Annual Review of Psychology, 38*, 299–337.

Markus, Hazel Rose; Uchida, Yukiko; Omoregie, Heather; Townsend, Sarah S. M.; & Kitayama, Shinobu. (2006). Going for the gold: Models of agency in Japanese and American contexts. *Psychological Science, 17*, 103–112.

Markwald, Rachel R.; Melanson, Edward L.; Smith, Mark R.; Higgins, Janine; Perreault, Leigh; Eckel, Robert H.; & Kenneth P. Wright, Jr. (2013). Impact of insufficient sleep on total daily energy expenditure, food intake, and weight gain. *Proceedings of the National Academy of Sciences, 110*, 5695–5700. https://doi.org/10.1073/pnas.121695111

Marmarosh, Cheri L.; Forsyth, Donelson R.; Strauss, Bernhard; & Burlingame, Gary M. (2020). The psychology of the COVID-19 pandemic: A group-level perspective. *Group Dynamics: Theory, Research, and Practice, 24*(3), 122–138. https://doi.org/10.1037/gdn0000142

Marmie, William R., & Healy, Alice F. (2004). Memory for common objects: Brief intentional study is sufficient to overcome poor recall of US coin features. *Applied Cognitive Psychology, 18*, 445–453.

Marroquín, Brett, & Nolen-Hoeksema, Susan. (2015). Emotion regulation and depressive symptoms: Close relationships as social context and influence. Journal of Personality and Social Psychology, 109, 836–855. http://doi.org/10.1037/pspi0000034

Marsh, Abigail A.; Rhoads, Shawn A.; & Ryan, Rebecca M. (2019). A multisemester classroom demonstration yields evidence in support of the facial feedback effect. *Emotion, 19*(8), 1500–1504. https://doi.org/10.1037/emo0000532

Marshall, Jamie M.; Dunstan, Debra A.; & Bartik, Warren. (2020). Treating psychological trauma in the midst of COVID-19: The role of smartphone apps. *Frontiers in Public Health, 8*, 402. https://doi.org/10.3389/fpubh.2020.00402

Martin, Annie. (2020, February 13). Jonas Brothers read 'tweet dreams' on 'Late Night Show.' *Entertainment News.* https://www.upi.com/Entertainment_News/2020/02/13/Jonas-Brothers-read-Tweet-Dreams-on-Late-Late-Show/2711581602333/

Martin, Bruce. (1998, May). Coincidences: Remarkable or random? *Skeptical Inquirer, 22*, 23–28.

Martin, Carol; Godfrey, Mary; Meekums, Bonnie; & Madill, Anna. (2011). Managing boundaries under pressure: A qualitative study of therapists' experiences of sexual attraction in therapy. *Counseling & Psychotherapy Research, 11*(4), 248–256.

Martin, Carol Lynn, & Ruble, Diane N. (2004). Children's search for gender cues: Cognitive perspectives on gender development. *Psychological Science, 13*, 67–70. https://doi.org/10.1111/j.0963-7214.2004.00276.x

Martin, Carol Lynn, & Ruble, Diane N. (2010). Patterns of gender development. *Annual Review of Psychology, 61*, 353–381.

Martin, Carol Lynn; Ruble, Diane N.; & Szkrybalo, Joel. (2004). Recognizing the centrality of gender identity and stereotype knowledge in gender development and moving toward theoretical integration: Reply to Bandura and Bussey. (2004). *Psychological Bulletin, 130*, 702–710.

Martin, Douglas; Hutchison, Jacqui; Slessor, Gillian; Urquhart, James; Cunningham, Sheila J.; & Smith, Kenny. (2014). The spontaneous formation of stereotypes via cumulative cultural evolution. *Psychological Science, 25*, 1777–1786. https://doi.org/10.1177/0956797614541129

Martin, Lisa; Neighbors, Harold; & Griffith, Derek. (2013). The experience of symptoms of depression in men vs women. *JAMA Psychiatry, 70*, 1100–1106. https://doi.org/10.1001/jamapsychiatry.2013.1985

Martinez, Isabel, & Garcia, José F. (2008). Internalization of values and self-esteem among Brazilian teenagers from authoritative, indulgent, authoritarian, and neglectful homes. *Family Therapy, 35*(1), 43–59.

Martins, Silvia S.; Sarvet, Aaron; Santaella-Tenorio, Julian; Saha, Tulshi; Grant, Bridget F.; & Hasin, Deborah S. (2017). Changes in US lifetime heroin use and heroin use disorder: Prevalence from the 2001-2002 to 2012-2013 National Epidemiologic Survey on Alcohol and Related Conditions. *JAMA Psychiatry, 74*, 445–455. https://doi.org/10.1001/jamapsychiatry.2017.0113

Marucha, Phillip T.; Kiecolt-Glaser, Janice K.; & Favagehi, Mehrdad. (1998). Mucosal wound healing is impaired by examination stress. *Psychosomatic Medicine, 60*, 362–365.

Marx, Rebecca Flynt, & Didziulis, Vytenis. (2009, February 27). A life, interrupted. *The New York Times.* http://www.nytimes.com/2009/03/01/nyregion/thecity/01miss.html

Mascaro, Jennifer S.; Rentscher, Kelly E.; Hackett, Patrick D.; Mehl, Matthias R.; & Rilling, James K. (2017). Child gender influences paternal behavior, language, and brain function. *Behavioral Neuroscience, 131*(3), 262–273. https://doi.org/10.1037/bne0000199

Mash, Clay; Novak, Elizabeth; Berthier, Neil E.; & Keen, Rachel. (2006). What do two-year-olds understand about hidden-object events? *Developmental Psychology, 42*(2), 263–271.

Maslach, Christina, & Leiter, Michael P. (2005). Stress and burnout: The critical research. In C. L. Cooper (Ed.), *Handbook of stress medicine and health* (2nd ed.). CRC Press.

Maslach, Christina, & Leiter, Michael P. (2008). Early predictors of job burnout and engagement. *Journal of Applied Psychology, 93*, 498–512.

Maslow, Abraham H. (1954). *Motivation and personality.* Harper.

Maslow, Abraham H. (1968). *Toward a psychology of being* (2nd ed.). Van Nostrand.

Maslow, Abraham H. (1970). *Motivation and personality* (2nd ed.). Harper & Row.

Masnick, Amy M., & Zimmerman, Corinne. (2009). Evaluating scientific research in the context of prior belief: Hindsight bias or confirmation bias? *Journal of Psychology of Science and Technology, 2*(1), 29–36.

Massa, Laura J., & Mayer, Richard E. (2006). Testing the ATI hypothesis: Should multimedia instruction accommodate verbalizer-visualizer cognitive style? *Learning and Individual Differences, 16*, 321–335. https://doi.org/10.1016/j.lindif.2006.10.001

Masten, Carrie L.; Telzer, Eva H.; Fuligni, Andrew J.; Lieberman, Matthew D.; & Eisenberger, Naomi I. (2012). Time spent with friends in adolescence relates to less neural sensitivity to later peer rejection. *Social Cognitive and Affective Neuroscience, 7*, 106–114. http://doi.org/10.1093/scan/nsq098

Masterpasqua, Frank. (2009). Psychology and epigenetics. *Review of General Psychology, 13*(3), 194–201.

Masters, Kevin S.; Stillman, Alexandra M.; & Spielmans, Glen I. (2007, February). Specificity of social support for back pain patients: Do patients care who provides what? *Journal of Behavioral Medicine, 30*(1), 11–20.

Mather, Mara; Cacioppo, John T.; & Kanwisher, Nancy. (2013a). Introduction to the special section: 20 Years of fMRI—What has it done for understanding cognition? *Perspectives on Psychological Science, 8*, 41–43. https://doi.org/10.1177/1745691612469036

Mather, Mara; Cacioppo, John T.; & Kanwisher, Nancy. (2013b). How fMRI can inform cognitive theories. *Perspectives on Psychological Science, 8*, 108–113. https://doi.org/10.1177/1745691612469037

Mathur, Maya B., & VanderWeele, Tyler J. (2019). Finding common ground in meta-analyses "wars" on violent video games. *Perspectives on Psychological Science, 14*(4), 705–708. https://doi.org/10.1177/1745691619850104

Matsumoto, David, & Hwang, Hyi Sung. (2011a, May). Reading facial expressions of emotion. http://www.apa.org/science/about/psa/2011/05/facial-expressions.aspx

Matsumoto, David, & Hwang, Hyi Sung. (2011b). Culture, emotion, and expression. In Kenneth Keith (Ed.), *Cross-cultural psychology: Contemporary themes and perspectives.* Wiley-Blackwell.

Matsumoto, David, & Juang, Linda. (2008). *Culture and psychology* (4th ed.). Wadsworth.

Maultsby, Katherine D., & Stutts, Lauren A. (2019). A longitudinal examination of study abroad: Student characteristics and psychological health associations. *College Student Affairs Journal, 37*(2), 183–19. https://doi.org/10.1353/csj.2019.0014

Mauriello, Marzia. (2017). What the body tells us: Transgender strategies, beauty, and self-consciousness. In: Rees E. (eds) *Talking bodies.* Palgrave Macmillan, Cham. https://doi.org/10.1007/978-3-319-63778-5_4

May, Mike. (2002, September 26). Quoted in British Broadcasting Corporation (BBC) transcript, September 26, 2002. *LiveChat: The man who learned to see.* http://www.bbc.co.uk/ouch/wyp/mikemayqa.shtml

May, Mike (2004). Quoted in Sendero Group, "Mike's journal." Retrieved from http://www.senderogroup.com/mikejournal.htm

Maybery, D. J.; Neale, Jason; Arentz, Alex; & Jones-Ellis, Jenny. (2007, June). The Negative Event Scale: Measuring frequency and intensity of adult hassles. *Anxiety, Stress & Coping, 20*(2), 163–176.

Mayer, Emeran A.; Tillisch, Kirsten; & Gupta, Arpana. (2015). Gut/brain axis and the microbiota. *The Journal of Clinical Investigation, 125*(3), 926–938. https://doi.org/10.1172/JCI76304

Mayer, John D.; Salovey, Peter; & Caruso, David R. (2004). Emotional intelligence: Theory, findings, and intelligence. *Psychological Inquiry, 15*, 197–215.

Mayer, John D.; Salovey, Peter; & Caruso, David R. (2008). Emotional intelligence: New ability or eclectic traits? *American Psychologist, 63,* 503–517.

Mayer, Richard E. (2001). *Multimedia learning.* Cambridge University Press.

Mazza, Cristina; Ricci, Eleonora; Biondi, Silvia; Colasanti, Marco; Ferracuti, Stefano; Napoli, Christian; & Roma, Paolo. (2020). A nationwide survey of psychological distress among Italian people during the COVID-19 pandemic: Immediate psychological responses and associated factors. *International Journal of Environmental Research and Public Health, 17*(9), 3165. http://doi.org/10.3390/ijerph17093165

McAdams, Dan P., & Olson, Bradley D. (2010). Personality development: Continuity and change over the life course. *Annual Review of Psychology, 61,* 517–542.

McAdams, Dan P., & Pals, Jennifer L. (2006). A new Big Five: Fundamental principles for an integrative science of personality. *American Psychologist, 61,* 204–217.

McAdams, Dan P., & Walden, Keegan. (2010). Jack Block, the Big Five, and personality from the standpoints of actor, agent, and author. *Psychological Inquiry, 21*(1), 50–56.

McAndrew, Francis T.; Akande, Adebowale; Turner, Saskia; & Sharma, Yadika. (1998). A cross-cultural ranking of stressful life events in Germany, India, South Africa, and the United States. *Journal of Cross-Cultural Psychology, 29,* 717–727.

McCabe, Marita P., & Ricciardelli, Lina A. (2004). A longitudinal study of pubertal timing and extreme body change behaviors among adolescent boys and girls. *Adolescence, 39,* 145–166.

McCall, W. Vaughn; Reboussin, David; Prudic, Joan; Haskett, Roger F.; Isenberg, Keith; Olfson, Mark; Rosenquist, Peter B.; & Sackeim, Harold A. (2013). Poor health-related quality of life prior to ECT in depressed patients normalizes with sustained remission after ECT. *Journal of Affective Disorders, 147*(1–3), 107–111. https://doi.org/10.1016/j.jad.2012.10.018

McCall, W. Vaughn; Rosenquist, Peter B.; Kimball, James; Haskett, Roger; Isenberg, Keith; Prudic, Joan; Lasater, Barbara; & Sackeim, Harold A. (2011). Health-related quality of life in a clinical trial of ECT followed by continuation pharmacotherapy: Effects immediately after ECT and at 24 weeks. *Journal of ECT, 27,* 97–102. https://doi.org/10.1097/YCT.0b013e318205c7d7

McCarley, Robert W. (2007). Neurobiology of REM and NREM sleep. *Sleep Medicine, 8,* 302–330.

McCarthy, Margaret M. (2007). GABA receptors make teens resistant to input. *Nature Neuroscience, 10,* 397–399.

McClelland, David C. (1961). *The achieving society.* Van Nostrand.

McClelland, David C. (1976). *The achieving society* (2nd ed.). Irvington.

McClelland, David C. (1985). *Human motivation.* Scott, Foresman.

McClelland, David C., & Winter, David G. (1971). *Motivating economic achievement.* Free Press.

McClintock, Martha K. (1971). Menstrual synchrony and suppression. *Nature, 229,* 244–245.

McClintock, Martha K. (1992, October). Quoted in John Easton, "Sex, rats, and videotapes: From the outside in." *University of Chicago Magazine, 85*(1), 32–36.

McClintock, Shawn M.; Trevino, Kenneth; & Husain, Mustafa M. (2009). Vagus nerve stimulation: Indications, efficacy, and methods. In Conrad M. Swartz (Ed.), *Electroconvulsive and neuromodulation therapies* (pp. 543–555). Cambridge University Press.

McCord, John-Luke; Harman, Jason L.; & Purl, Justin. (2019). Game-like personality testing: An emerging mode of personality assessment. *Personality and Individual Differences, 143,* 95–102. https://doi.org/10.1016/j.paid.2019.02.017

McCrae, Robert R., & Costa, Paul T., Jr. (1990). *Personality in adulthood.* Guilford.

McCrae, Robert R., & Costa, Paul T., Jr. (1996). Toward a new generation of personality theories: Theoretical contexts for the five-factor model. In Jerry S. Wiggins (Ed.), *The five-factor model of personality: Theoretical perspectives.* Guilford.

McCrae, Robert R., & Costa, Paul T., Jr. (2003). *Personality in adulthood: A five-factor theory perspective* (2nd ed.). Guilford.

McCrae, Robert R., & Costa, Paul T., Jr. (2006). Cross-cultural perspectives on adult personality trait development. In David K. Mroczek & Todd D. Little (Eds.), *Handbook of personality development.* Erlbaum.

McCrae, Robert R.; Scally, Matthew; Terracciano, Antonio; Abecasis, Gonçalo R.; & Costa, Paul T., Jr. (2010). An alternative to the search for single polymorphisms: Toward molecular personality scales for the five-factor model. *Journal of Personality and Social Psychology, 99*(6), 1014–1024. https://doi.org/10.1037/a0020964

McCrae, Robert R.; Terracciano, Antonio; & Members of the Personality Profiles of Cultures Project (2005). Universal features of personality traits from the observer's perspective: Data from 50 cultures. *Journal of Personality and Social Psychology, 88,* 547–561.

McDermut, Wilson, & Zimmerman, Mark. (2008). Personality disorders, personality traits, and defense mechanisms measures. In A. John Rush, Jr., Michael B. First, & Deborah Blacker (Eds.), *Handbook of psychiatric measures* (2nd ed., pp. 687–729). American Psychiatric Publishing.

McDonald, Ann. (2009). Prenatal development—The DANA Guide. *The DANA Guide to Brain Health* Retrieved from http://www.dana.org/news/brainhealth/detail.aspx?id=10050

McDonald, William M.; Meeks, Thomas W.; McCall, W. Vaughan; & Zorumski, Charles F. (2009). Electroconvulsive therapy. In Alan F. Schatzberg & Charles B. Nemeroff (Eds.), *The American Psychiatric Publishing textbook of psychopharmacology* (4th ed., pp. 861–899). American Psychiatric Publishing.

McDougall, William. (1908). *Introduction to social psychology.* Methuen.

McDuff, Daniel; Kodra, Evan; el Kaliouby, Rana; & LaFrance, Marianne. (2017) A large-scale analysis of sex differences in facial expressions. *PLoS ONE, 12*(4). https://doi.org/10.1371/journal.pone.0173942

McElhaney, Kathleen B.; Porter, Maryfrances R.; Thompson, L. Wrenn; & Allen, Joseph P. (2008). Apples and oranges: Divergent meanings of parents' and adolescents' perceptions of parental influence. *Journal of Early Adolescence, 28,* 206–229.

McGann, John P. (2017). Poor human olfaction is a 19th-century myth. *Science, 356,* 597. https://doi.org/10.1126/science.aam7263

McGaugh, James L. (2004). The amygdala modulates the consolidation of memories of emotionally arousing experiences. *Annual Review of Neuroscience, 27,* 1–28.

McGinn, Lata; Nooner, Kate; Cohen, Jonathan; & Leaberry, Kirsten. (2015). The role of early experience and cognitive vulnerability: Presenting a unified model of the etiology of panic. *Cognitive Therapy and Research, 39,* 508–519. https://doi.org/10.1007/s10608-015-9673-9

McGirr, Alexander; Berlim, M.T.; Bond, D.J.; Fleck, M.P.; Yatham, L.N.; & Lam, R.W. (2015). A systematic review and meta-analysis of randomized, double-blind, placebo-controlled trials of ketamine in the rapid treatment of major depressive episodes. *Psychological Medicine, 45,* 693–704. https://doi.org/10.1017/S0033291714001603

McGirr, Alexander; Renaud, Johanne; Seguin, Monique; Alda, Martin; Benkelfat, Chawki; Lesage, Alain; & Turecki, Gustavo. (2007). An examination of DSM-IV depressive symptoms and risk for suicide completion in major depressive disorder: A psychological autopsy study. *Journal of Affective Disorders, 97*(1–3), 203–209. https://doi.org/10.1016/j.jad.2006.06.016

McGlone, Francis, & Reilly, David. (2010). The cutaneous sensory system. *Neuroscience & Biobehavioral Reviews, 34,* 148–159.

McGoldrick, Monica; Giordano, Joseph; & Garcia-Preto, Nydia. (2005). Overview: Ethnicity and family therapy. In Monica McGoldrick, Joseph Giordano, & Nydia Garcia-Preto (Eds.), *Ethnicity & family therapy* (3rd ed., pp. 1–40). Guilford.

McGraw, A. Peter; Williams, Lawrence; & Warren, Caleb. (2013). The rise and fall of humor: Psychological distance modulates humorous responses to tragedy. *Social Psychological and Personality Science, 5,* 566–572. https://doi.org/10.1177/1948550613515006

McGregor, Douglas. (1960). *The human side of enterprise.* McGraw-Hill.

McGregor, Jacqueline C. (2009). Anxiety disorders. In Robert E. Rakel & Edward T. Bope (Eds.), *Conn's current therapy 2009* (pp. 1111–1115). Saunders Elsevier.

McGrew, Kevin S. (2009). CHC theory and the human cognitive abilities project: Standing on the shoulders of the giants of psychometric intelligence research. *Intelligence, 37,* 1–10. https://doi.org/10.1016/j.intell.2008.08.004

McGue, Matt; Bouchard, Thomas J., Jr.; Iacono, William G.; & Lykken, David T. (1993). Behavioral genetics of cognitive ability: A lifespan perspective. In Robert Plomin & Gerald E. McClearn (Eds.), *Nature, nurture, and psychology.* American Psychological Association.

McKenzie, Ian A.; Ohayon, David; Li, Huiliang; de Faria, Joana Paes; Emery, Ben; Tohyama, Koujiro; & Richardson, William D. (2014). Motor skill learning requires active central myelination. *Science, 346,* 318–322. https://doi.org/10.1126/science.1254960

McLay, Robert N.; Wood, Dennis P.; Webb-Murphy, Jennifer A.; Spira, James L.; Wiederhold, Mark D.; Pyne, Jeffrey M.; & Wiederhold, Brenda K. (2011). A randomized, controlled trial of virtual reality-graded exposure therapy for post-traumatic stress disorder in active duty service members with combat-related post-traumatic stress disorder. *Cyberpsychology, Behavior, and Social Networking, 14*(4), 223–229.

McLean, Bethany, & Elkind, Peter. (2003). *The smartest guys in the room: The amazing rise and scandalous fall of Enron.* Portfolio.

McLean, Carmen P.; Asnaani, Anu; Litz, Brett T.; & Hofmann, Stefan G. (2011). Gender differences in anxiety disorders: Prevalence, course of illness, comorbidity and burden of illness. *Journal of Psychiatric Research, 45*(8), 1027–1035. https://doi.org/10.1016/j.jpsychires.2011.03.006

McLewin, Lise A., & Muller, Robert T. (2006, September–October). Childhood trauma, imaginary companions, and the development of pathological dissociation. *Aggression and Violent Behavior, 11,* 531–545. https://doi.org/10.1016/j.avb.2006.02.001

McMurran, Mary, & Howard, Richard. (2009). Personality, personality disorder and violence: Implications for future research and practice. In Mary McMurran & Richard Howard (Eds.), *Personality, personality disorder and violence* (pp. 299–311). Wiley-Blackwell.

McNab, Fiona, & Klingberg, Torkel. (2008). Prefrontal cortex and basal ganglia access in working memory. *Nature Neuroscience, 11,* 103–107.

McNally, Richard J. (2003). Progress and controversy in the study of posttraumatic stress disorder. *Annual Review of Psychology, 54,* 229–252. https://doi.org/10.1146/annurev.psych.54.101601.145112

McNally, Richard J. (2007). Dispelling confusion about traumatic dissociative amnesia. *Mayo Clinic Proceedings, 82,* 1083–1087.

McNally, Richard J., & Geraerts, Elke. (2009). A new solution to the recovered memory debate. *Perspectives on Psychological Science, 4,* 126–134.

McNeil, Jeffrey A., & Morgan, C. A., III. (2010). Cognition and decision making in extreme environments. In Carrie H. Kennedy & Jeffrey Moore (Eds.), *Military neuropsychology.* Springer.

McNeilly, Cheryl L., & Howard, Kenneth I. (1991). The effects of psychotherapy: A reevaluation based on dosage. *Psychotherapy Research, 1,* 74–78.

McNulty, James K., & Fincham, Frank D. (2012). Beyond positive psychology: Toward a contextual view of psychological processes and wellbeing. *American Psychologist, 67,* 101–110.

McRae, Kateri, & Gross, James J. (2020). Emotion regulation. *Emotion, 20*(1), 1–9. http://doi.org/10.1037/emo0000703

McRobbie, Linda Rodriguez. (2017, February 8). Total recall: The people who never forget. *The Guardian.* https://www.theguardian.com/science/2017/feb/08/total-recall-the-people-who-never-forget

McVay, Jennifer C., & Kane, Michael J. (2010). Adrift in the stream of thought: The effects of mind wandering on executive control and working memory capacity. In A. Gruszka, G. Matthews, & B. Szymura (Eds.), *Handbook of individual differences in cognition: Attention, memory, and executive control* (pp. 321–334). Springer Science + Business Media.

Meaney, Michael J. (2001). Maternal care, gene expression, and the transmission of individual differences in stress reactivity across generations. *Annual Review of Neuroscience, 24,* 1161–1192.

Mechoulam, Raphael; Hanuš, Lumír O.; Pertwee, Roger; & Howlett, Allyn C. (2014). Early phytocannabinoid chemistry to endocannabinoids and beyond. *Nature Reviews Neuroscience, 15,* 757–764. https://doi.org/10.1038/nrn3811

Mechoulam, Raphael, & Parker, Linda A. (2013). The endocannabinoid system and the brain. *Annual Review of Psychology, 64,* 21–47. https://doi.org/10.1146/annurev-psych-113011-143739

Media for Health. (2011). Our Programs, from http://www.mediaforhealth.org/our_programs.html

Medina, Jorge H.; Bekinschtein, Pedro; Cammarota, Martin; & Izquierdo, Iván. (2008). Do memories consolidate to persist or do they persist to consolidate? *Behavioural Brain Research, 192,* 61–69.

Meduri, Mario; Bramanti, Placido; Ielitro, Giuseppe; Favaloro, Angelo; Milardi, Demetrio; Cutroneo, Giuseppina; Muscatello, Maria R. A.; Bruno, Antonio; Umberto, Micò; Pandolfo, Gianluca; La Torre, Diletta; Vaccarino, Gianluigi; & Anastasi, Giuseppe. (2010). Morphometrical and morphological analysis of lateral ventricles in schizophrenia patients versus healthy controls. *Psychiatry Research: Neuroimaging, 183*(1), 52–58. https://doi.org/10.1016/j.pscychresns.2010.01.014

Megargee, Edwin I. (2009). The California Psychological Inventory. In James N. Butcher (Ed.), *Oxford handbook of personality assessment* (pp. 323–335). Oxford University Press.

Mehall, Karissa G.; Spinrad, Tracy L.; Eisenberg, Nancy; & Gaertner, Bridget M. (2009). Examining the relations of infant temperament and couples' marital satisfaction to mother and father involvement: A longitudinal study. *Fathering, 7*(1), 2–48.

Mehler, Jacques; Bertoncini, Josiane; Barrière, M.; & Jassik-Gerschenfeld, Dora. (1978). Infant recognition of mother's voice. *Perception, 7,* 481–497. https://doi.org/10.1068/p070491

Mehrotra, Dhruv. (2020, January 28). Horror stories from inside Amazon's Mechanical Turk. *Gizmodo.* https://gizmodo.com/horror-stories-from-inside-amazons-mechanical-turk-1840878041

Meier, Jo A.; McNaughton-Cassill, Mary; & Lynch, Molly. (2006). The management of household and childcare tasks and relationship satisfaction in dual-earner families. *Marriage & Family Review, 40*(2–3), 61–88.

Meijer, Ewout H., & Verschuere, Bruno. (2010). The polygraph and the detection of deception. *Journal of Forensic Psychology Practice, 10,* 325–338. https://doi.org/10.1080/15228932.2010.481237

Meir, Irit; Sandler, Wendy; Padden, Carol; & Aronoff, Mark. (2010). Emerging sign languages. In M. Marschark & P. Spencer (Eds.) *Oxford handbook of deaf studies, language, and education* (Vol. 2). Oxford University Press.

Meissner, Karin; Bingel, Ulrike; Colloca, Luana; Wager, Tor D.; Watson, Alison; & Flaten, Magne Arve. (2011). The placebo effect: Advances from different methodological approaches. *Journal of Neuroscience, 31*(45), 16117–16124.

Melamed, David; Simpson, Brent; & Abernathy, Jered. (2020). The robustness of reciprocity: Experimental evidence that each form of reciprocity is robust to the presence of other forms of reciprocity. *Science Advances, 6*(23), 1–7. https://doi.org/10.1126/sciadv.aba0504

Meltzer, Donald. (2018). *Dream life: A re-examination of the psychoanalytic theory and technique.* The Bourne Studios (Eds.), The Harris Meltzer Trust.

Melzack, Ronald, & Wall, Patrick D. (1965). Pain mechanisms: A new theory. *Science, 150,* 971–980.

Melzack, Ronald, & Wall, Patrick D. (1996). *The challenge of pain* (2nd ed.). Penguin.

Menaker, Michael. (2003, January 10). Perspectives: Circadian photoreception. *Science, 299,* 213–214.

Menand, Louis. (2001). *The Metaphysical Club: A story of ideas in America.* Farrar, Straus & Giroux.

Mendle, Jane, & Ferrero, Joseph. (2012). Detrimental psychological outcomes associated with pubertal timing in adolescent boys. *Developmental Review, 32*(1), 49–66. https://doi.org/10.1016/j.dr.2011.11.001

Merikangas, K. R.; Akiskal, H. S.; Angst, J.; Greenberg, P. E.; Hirschfeld, R.; Petukhova, M.; & Kessler, R. C. (2007). Lifetime and 12-month prevalence of bipolar spectrum disorder in the National Comorbidity Survey replication. *Archives of General Psychiatry, 64*(5), 543–552. https://doi.org/10.1001/archpsyc.64.5.543

Merlino, Joseph P.; Jacobs, Marily S.; Kaplan, Judy Ann; & Moritz, Lynne K. (Eds.). (2008). *Freud at 150: 21st-century essays on a man of genius.* Jason Aronson.

Mervis, Carolyn B., & Rosch, Eleanor. (1981). Categorization of natural objects. *Annual Review of Psychology, 32,* 89–115.

Mesmer-Magnus, Jessica R., & Viswesvaran, Chockalingam. (2006). How family-friendly work environments affect work-family conflict: A metaanalytic examination. *Journal of Labor Research, 27,* 555–574.

Mesquita, Batja; Boiger, Michael; & De Leersnyder, Jozefien. (2016). The cultural construction of emotions. *Current Opinion in Psychology, 8,* 31–36. http://doi.org/10.1016/j.copsyc.2015.09.015

Meyer, Jerrold S. (2013). 3,4-methylenedioxymethamphetamine (MDMA): Current perspectives. *Substance Abuse and Rehabilitation, 4,* 83–99. https://doi.org/10.2147/SAR.S37258

Meyer, Julien. (2015). Whistled languages: A worldwide inquiry on human whistled speech. Springer Berlin. https://doi.org/10.1007/978-3-662-45837-2

Meyerbröker, Katharina, & Emmelkamp, Paul M. G. (2010). Virtual reality exposure therapy in anxiety disorders: A systematic review of process-and-outcome studies. *Depression and Anxiety, 27*(10), 933–944.

Meyer-Lindenberg, Andreas; Buckholtz, Joshua W.; Kolachana, Bhaskar.; Hariri, Ahmad R.; Pezawas, Lukas.; Blasi, Giuseppe; Wabnitz, Ashley; Honea, Robyn; Verchinski, Beth; Callicott, Joseph H.; Egan, Michael; Mattay, Venkata; & Weinberger, Daniel R. (2006). Neural mechanisms of genetic risk for impulsivity and violence in humans. *Proceedings of the National Academy of Sciences, 103,* 6269–6274. https://doi.org/10.1073/pnas.0511311103

Mezick, Elizabeth J.; Matthews, Karen A.; Hall, Martica; Kamarck, Thomas W.; Buysse, Daniel J.; Owens, Jane F.; & Reis, Steven. (2009). Intra-individual variability in sleep duration and fragmentation: Associations with stress. *Psychoneuroendocrinology, 34*(9), 1346–1354.

Mezulis, Amy H.; Abramson, Lyn Y.; & Hyde, Janet S. (2004, September). Is there a universal positivity bias in attributions? A meta-analytic review of individual, developmental, and cultural differences in the self-serving attributional bias. *Psychological Bulletin, 130*(5), 711–747.

Michael, Nikolaus. (2009). Hypothesized mechanisms and sites of action of electroconvulsive therapy. In Conrad M. Swartz (Ed.), *Electroconvulsive and neuromodulation therapies* (pp. 75–93). Cambridge University Press.

Michel, Christoph M., & Brunet, Denis, M. (2019). EEG source imaging: A practical review of the analysis steps. *Frontiers in Neurology, 10,* 325. https://doi.org/10.3389/fneur.2019.00325

Mikels, Joseph A.; Maglio, Sam J.; Reed, Andrew E.; & Kaplowitz, Lee J. (2011). Should I go with my gut? Investigating the benefits of emotion-focused decision making. *Emotion, 11,* 743–753.

Miklósi, Ádám, & Kubinyi, Enikö. (2016). Current trends in canine problem-solving and cognition. *Current Directions in Psychological Science, 25,* 300–306. https://doi.org/10.1177/0963721416666061

Miklowitz, David J. (2008). Bipolar disorder. In David H. Barlow (Ed.), *Clinical handbook of psychological disorders* (4th ed., pp. 421–462). Guilford.

Miklowitz, David J., & Johnson, Sheri L. (2007). Bipolar disorder. In Michel Hersen, Samuel M. Turner, & Deborah C. Beidel (Eds.), *Adult psychopathology and diagnosis* (5th ed., pp. 317–348). Wiley.

Milan, Stephanie; Snow, Stephanie; & Belay, Sophia. (2007). The context of preschool children's sleep: Racial/ethnic differences in sleep locations, routines, and concerns. *Journal of Family Psychology, 21*(1), 20–28.

Miles, Donna R., & Carey, Gregory. (1997). Genetic and environmental architecture on human aggression. *Journal of Personality and Social Psychology, 72*(1), 207.

Milgram, Stanley. (1963). Behavioral study of obedience. *Journal of Abnormal Psychology, 67,* 371–378.

Milgram, Stanley. (1965/1992). Some conditions of obedience and disobedience to authority. In John Sabini & Maury Silver (Eds.), *The individual in a social world: Essays and experiments* (2nd ed.). McGraw-Hill.

Milgram, Stanley. (1974). *Obedience to authority: An experimental view.* Harper & Row.

Miller, Christian. (2009). Social psychology, mood, and helping: Mixed results for virtue ethics. *Journal of Ethics, 13,* 145–173. https://doi.org/10.1007/s10892-009-9046-2

Miller, Cindy Faith; Trautner, Hanns Martin; & Ruble, Diane N. (2006). The role of gender stereotypes in children's preferences and behavior. In Lawrence Balter & Catherine S. Tamis-LeMonda (Eds.), *Child psychology: A handbook of contemporary issues* (2nd ed.). Psychology Press.

Miller, Claire. (2015). Can an algorithm hire better than a human? *The New York Times.* http://nyti.ms/1GIVcEl

Miller, Claude H., & Quick, Brian L. (2010). Sensation seeking and psychological reactance as health risk predictors for an emerging adult population. *Health Communication, 25*(3), 266–275.

Miller, Drew J.; Vachon, David D.; & Lynam, Donald R. (2009). Neuroticism, negative affect, and negative affect instability: Establishing convergent and discriminant validity using ecological momentary assessment. *Personality and Individual Differences, 47*(8), 873–877.

Miller, George A. (1956). The magical number seven, plus or minus two: Some limits on our capacity for processing information [Special centennial issue]. *Psychological Review, 101,* 343–352.

Miller, Greg. (2013). The promise and perils of oxytocin. *Science, 339,* 267–269. https://doi.org/10.1126/science.339.6117.267

Miller, Gregory A. (2010). Mistreating psychology in the decades of the brain. *Perspectives on Psychological Science, 5*(6), 716–743. https://doi.org/10.1177/1745691610388774

Miller, Gregory E.; Chen, Edith; & Cole, Steve W. (2009). Health psychology: Developing biologically plausible models linking the social world and physical health. *Annual Review of Psychology, 60,* 501–524.

Miller, Mark W.; Wolf, Erika J.; & Hein, Christina. (2013). Psychological effects of the marathon bombing on Boston-area veterans with posttraumatic stress disorder. *Journal of Traumatic Stress, 26*(6), 762–766. https://doi.org/10.1002/jts.21865

Miller, William R., & Rollnick, Stephen. (2012). *Motivational interviewing: Preparing people for change* (2nd ed.). Guilford.

Miller, William R., & Rose, Gary S. (2009). Toward a theory of motivational interviewing. *American Psychologist, 64,* 527–537. https://doi.org/10.1037/a0016830

Miller-Jones, Dalton. (1989). Culture and testing. *American Psychologist, 44,* 360–366.

Milner, Brenda. (1970). Memory and the medial temporal regions of the brain. In Karl H. Pribram & Donald E. Broadbent (Eds.), *Biology of memory.* Academic Press.

Milojev, Petar, & Sibley, Chris G. (2014). The stability of adult personality varies across age: Evidence from a two-year longitudinal sample of adult New Zealanders. *Journal of Research in Personality,51,* 29–37. https://doi.org/10.1016/j.jrp.2014.04.005

Minda, John Paul, & Smith, J. David. (2001). Prototypes in category learning: The effects of category size, category structure, and stimulus complexity. *Journal of Experimental Psychology: Learning, Memory, and Cognition, 27,* 775–799.

Minda, John Paul, & Smith, J. David. (2011). Prototype models of categorization: Basic formulation, predictions, and limitations. In E. M. Pothos & A. J. Wills (Eds.), *Formal approaches in categorization* (pp. 40–64). Cambridge University Press.

Mindell, Jodi A.; Sadeh, Avi; Kohyama, Jun; & How, Ti Hwei. (2010a). Parental behaviors and sleep outcomes in infants and toddlers: A cross-cultural comparison. *Sleep Medicine, 11*(4), 393–399.

Mindell, Jodi A.; Sadeh, Avi; Wiegand, Benjamin; How, Ti Hwei; & Goh, Daniel Y. T. (2010b). Cross-cultural differences in infant and toddler sleep. *Sleep Medicine, 11*(3), 274–280.

Miner, John. (2005). Chapter 13: Contingency theory of leadership. In *Organizational Behavior 1* (pp. 232–255). M.E. Sharpe.

Minihan, Elisha; Gavin, Blanaid; Kelly, Brendan D.; & McNicholas, Fiona. (2020). COVID-19, mental health and psychological first aid. *Irish Journal of Psychological Medicine, 37*(4), 259–263. https://doi.org/10.1017/ipm.2020.41

Mirandé, Alfredo. (2014). Transgender identity and acceptance in a global era: The Muxes of Juchitán. In Joseph Gelfer (Eds.), *Masculinities in a Global Era* (pp. 247–263). Springer.

Mirmiran, Majid; Maas, Yolanda G.; & Ariagno, Ronald L. (2003). Development of fetal and neonatal sleep and circadian rhythms. *Sleep Medicine Reviews, 7*(4), 321–334.

Miron, Anca M., & Branscombe, Nyla R. (2008). Social categorization, standards of justice, and collective guilt. In Arie Nadler, Thomas E. Malloy, & Jeffrey D. Fisher (Eds.), *The social psychology of intergroup reconciliation* (pp. 77–96). Oxford University Press.

Mischel, Walter. (1996). From good intentions to willpower. In Peter M. Gollwitzer & John A. Bargh (Eds.), *The psychology of action: Linking cognition and motivation to behavior.* Guilford.

Mischel, Walter; Ayduk, Ozlem; Baumeister, Roy F.; & Vohs, Kathleen D. (2004). Willpower in a cognitive-affective processing system: The dynamics of delay of gratification *Handbook of self-regulation: Research, theory, and applications* (pp. 99–129). Guilford.

Mischel, Walter, & Shoda, Yuichi. (1995). A cognitive-affective system theory of personality: Reconceptualizing situations, dispositions, dynamics, and invariance in personality structure. *Psychological Review, 102,* 246–268.

Mischel, Walter; Shoda, Yuichi; & Mendoza-Denton, Rodolfo. (2002). Situation-behavior profiles as a locus of consistency in personality. *Current Directions in Psychological Science, 11,* 50–54.

Mishel, Emma; England, Paula; Ford, Jessie; & Caudillo, Mónica L. (2018). Increases in sex with same-sex partners across U.S. cohorts born 1920–1998: A race–gender intersection. https://nyuad.nyu.edu/en/academics/divisions/social-science.html

Mistlberger, Ralph E., & Skene, Debra J. (2005). Nonphotic entrainment in humans? *Journal of Biological Rhythms, 20,* 339–352.

Mitchell, Alanah, & Zheng, Liping. (2019). Examining longhand vs. laptop debate: A replication study. *Transactions on Replication Research, 5,* 1–15. https://doi.org/10.17705/1atrr.0041

Mitchell, Colter; Hobcraft, John; McLanahan, Sara S.; Siegel, Susan Rutherford; Berg, Arthur; Brooks-Gunn, Jeanne; Garfinkel, Irwin; & Notterman, Daniel. (2014). Social disadvantage, genetic sensitivity, and children's telomere length. *Proceedings of the National Academy of Sciences, 111,* 5944–5949. https://doi.org/10.1073/pnas.1404293111

Mitchell, James E.; Roerig, James; & Steffen, Kristine. (2013). Biological therapies for eating disorders. *International Journal of Eating Disorders, 46*(5), 470–477. https://doi.org/10.1002/eat.22104

Mitchell, Jennifer M.; Bogenschutz, Michael; Lilienstein, Alia; Harrison, Charlotte; Kleiman, Sarah; Parker-Guilbert, Kelly; Ot'alora G., Marcela; Garas, Wael; Paleos, Casey; Gorman, Ingmar; Nicholas, Christopher; Mithoefer, Michael; Carlin, Shannon; Poulter, Bruce; Mithoefer, Ann; Quevedo, Sylvestre; Wells, Gregory; Klaire, Sukhpreet S.; van der Kolk, Bessel; . . . & Doblin, Rick. (2021). MDMA-assisted therapy for severe PTSD: A randomized, double-blind, placebo-controlled phase 3 study. *Nature Medicine.* https://doi.org/10.1038/s41591-021-01336-3

Mithoefer, Michael. (2016). Novel psychopharmacological therapies for psychiatric disorders: Psilocybin and MDMA. *The Lancet Psychiatry, 3,* 481–488. https://doi.org/10.1016/S2215-0366(15)00576-3

Mitka, Mike. (2009). College binge drinking still on the rise. *JAMA, 302*(8), 836–837. https://doi.org/10.1001/jama.2009.1154

Miyata, Yo. (2009). Pavlov's Nobel Prize in physiology or medicine. *Japanese Journal of Physiological Psychology and Psychophysiology, 27*(3), 225–234.

Miyatsu, Toshiya; Nguyen, Khuyen; & McDaniel, Mark A. (2018). Five popular study strategies: Their pitfalls and optimal implementations. *Perspectives on Psychological Science, 13,* 390–407. https://doi.org/10.1177/1745691617711051

Moezzi, Melody. (2015). A Persian in therapy. *The New York Times.* https://opinionator.blogs.nytimes.com/2015/03/24/a-persian-in-therapy/

Moffet, Howard H. (2008). Traditional acupuncture theories yield null outcomes: A systematic review of clinical trials. *Journal of Clinical Epidemiology, 61*(8), 741–747. https://doi.org/10.1016/S0895-4356(08)000632/j.jclinepi.2008.02.013

Moffet, Howard H. (2009). Sham acupuncture may be as efficacious as true acupuncture: A systematic review of clinical trials. *Journal of Alternative and Complementary Medicine, 15*(3), 213–216. https://doi.org/10.1089/acm.2008.0356

Mohr, Charles. (1964, March 28). Apathy is puzzle in Queens killing: Behavioral specialists hard put to explain witnesses' failure to call police. *The New York Times,* pp. 21, 40.

Moitra, Ethan; Dyck, Ingrid; Beard, Courtney; Bjornsson, Andri S.; Sibrava, Nicholas J.; Weisberg, Risa B.; & Keller, Martin B. (2011). Impact of stressful life events on the course of panic disorder in adults. *Journal of Affective Disorders.* https://doi.org/10.1016/j.jad.2011.05.029

Mojtabai, Ramin, & Olfson, Mark. (2011). Proportion of antidepressants prescribed without a psychiatric diagnosis is growing. *Health Affairs, 30,* 1434–1442. https://doi.org/10.1377/hlthaff.2010.1024

Mojtabai, R.; Olfson, M.; Sampson, N. A.; Jin, R.; Druss, B.; Wang,. P. S., & Kessler, R. C. (2011). Barriers to mental health treatment: Results from the National Comorbidity Survey Replication. *Psychological Medicine, 41*(8), 1751–1761. https://doi.org/10.1017/S0033291710002291

Molitor, Adriana, & Hsu, Hui-Chin. (2011). Child development across cultures. In Kenneth D. Keith (Ed.), *Cross-cultural psychology: Contemporary themes and perspectives.* Wiley-Blackwell.

Moore, David W. (2005, June 15). Three in four Americans believe in paranormal. Gallup News Service. http://www.gallup.com/poll/16915/Three-Four-Americans-BelieveParanormal.aspx

Moore, Jay. (2005a). Some historical and conceptual background to the development of B. F. Skinner's "radical behaviorism"—Part 1. *Journal of Mind and Behavior, 26,* 65–94.

Moore, Jay. (2005b). Some historical and conceptual background to the development of B. F. Skinner's "radical behaviorism"—Part 3. *Journal of Mind and Behavior, 26,* 137–160.

Moore, Mollie N.; Salk, Rachel H.; Van Hulle, Carol A.; Abramson, Lyn Y.; Hyde, Janet S.; Lemery-Chalfant, Kathryn.; & Goldsmith, H. Hill. (2013). Genetic and environmental influences on rumination, distraction, and depressed mood in adolescence. *Clinical Psychological Science, 1*(3), 316–322. https://doi.org/10.1177/2167702612472884

Moors, Agnes. (2009). Theories of emotion causation: A review. *Cognition & Emotion, 23,* 625–662.

Moors, Agnes; Ellsworth, Phoebe C.; Scherer, Klaus R.; & Frijda, Nico H. (2013). Appraisal theories of emotion: State of the art and future development. *Emotion Review, 5,* 119–124. https://doi.org/10.1177/1754073912468165

Moradi, Bonnie; Wiseman, Marcie C.; DeBlaere, Cirleen; Goodman, Melinda B.; Sarkees, Anthony; Brewster, Melanie E.; Huang, Yu-Ping. (2010). LGB of color and white individuals' perceptions of heterosexist stigma, internalized homophobia, and outness: Comparisons of levels and links. *Counseling Psychologist, 38,* 397–424.

Moreira, Ana L.R.; Van Meter, Anna; Genzlinger, Jacquelynne; & Youngstrom, Eric A. (2017). Review and meta-analysis of epidemiologic studies of adult bipolar disorder. *Journal of Clinical Psychiatry, 78*(9), 1259–1269. https://doi.org/10.4088/JCP.16r11165

Morelli, Gilda A.; Rogoff, Barbara; Oppenheim, David; & Goldsmith, Denise. (1992). Cultural variation in infants' sleeping arrangements: Questions of independence. *Developmental Psychology, 28,* 604–613.

Moreno, Antonio; Limousin, Fanny; Dehaene, Stanislas; & Pallier, Christophe. (2018). Brain correlates of constituent structure in sign language comprehension. *NeuroImage, 167,* 151–161. https://doi.org/10.1016/j.neuroimage.2017.11.040

Moreno, Carmen; Wykes, Til; Galderisi, Silvana; Nordentoft, Merete; Crossley, Nicolas; Jones, Nev; Cannon, Mary; Correll, Christoph U.; Byrne, Louise; Carr, Sarah; Chen, Eric Y. H.; Gorwood, Philip; Johnson, Sonia; Kärkkäinen, Hilkka; Krystal, John H.; Lee, Jimmy; Lieberman, Jeffrey; López-Jaramillo, Carlos; Männikkö, Miia; Phillips, Michael R.; . . . & Arango, Celso. (2020). How mental health care should change as a consequence of the COVID-19 pandemic. *The Lancet Psychiatry, 7*(9), 813–824. https://doi.org/10.1016/S2215-0366(20)30307-2

Moreno-Peral, Patricia; Conejo-Cerón, Sonia; Motrico, Emma; Rodríguez-Morejón, Alberto; Fernández, Anna; García-Campayo, Javier; Roca, Miquel; Serrano-Blanco, Antoni; Rubio-Valera, Maria; & Bellón, Juan. (2014). Risk factors for the onset of panic and generalised anxiety disorders in the general adult population: A systematic review of cohort studies. *Journal of Affective Disorders, 168,* 337–348. https://doi.org/10.1016/j.jad.2014.06.021

Moretti, Robert J., & Rossini, Edward D. (2004). The Thematic Apperception Test (TAT). In Mark J. Hilsenroth & Daniel L. Segal (Eds.), *Comprehensive handbook of psychological assessment, Vol. 2: Personality assessment.* Wiley.

Morgan, Christiana, & Murray, Henry A. (1935). A method of investigating fantasies: The Thematic Apperception Test. *Archives of Neurology and Psychiatry, 4,* 310–329.

Morgeson, Frederick; Campion, Michael; Dipboye, Robert; Hollenbeck, John; Murphy, Kevin; & Schmitt, Neal. (2007). Reconsidering the use of personality tests in personnel selection contexts. *Personnel Psychology, 60,* 683–729. https://doi.org/10.1111/J.1744-6570.2007.00089.X

Morin, Charles M.; Bootzin, Richard R.; Buysse, Daniel J.; Edinger, Jack D.; Espie, Colin A.; & Lichstein, Kenneth L. (2006). Psychological and behavioral treatment of insomnia: Update of the recent evidence (1998–2004). *Sleep, 29,* 1398–1414.

Morling, Beth, & Kitayama, Shinobu. (2008). Culture and motivation. In James Y. Shah & Wendi L. Gardner (Eds.), *Handbook of motivation science.* Guilford.

Morrell, Julian, & Steele, Howard. (2003). The role of attachment security, temperament, maternal perception, and care-giving behavior in persistent infant sleeping problems. *Infant Mental Health Journal, 24,* 447–468.

Morris, John S.; Scott, Sophie K.; & Dolan, Raymond J. (1999). Saying it with feeling: Neural responses to emotional vocalizations. *Neuropsychologia, 37,* 1155–1163.

Morris, Michael W., & Peng, Kaiping. (1994). Culture and cause: American and Chinese attributions for social and physical events. *Journal of Personality and Social Psychology, 67,* 949–971.

Morris, Richard G. (2013). NMDA receptors and memory encoding. *Neuropharmacology, 74,* 32–40. https://doi.org/10.1016/j.neuropharm.2013.04.014

Morrison, Anthony P.; Turkington, Douglas; Pyle, Melissa; Spencer, Helen; Brabban, Alison; Dunn, Graham; & Hutton, Paul. (2014). Cognitive therapy for people with schizophrenia spectrum disorders not taking antipsychotic drugs: A single-blind randomised controlled trial. *Lancet, 383,* 1395–1403. https://doi.org/10.1016/S0140-6736(13)62246-1

Morrison, Christopher D. (2008). Leptin resistance and the response to positive energy balance. *Physiology & Behavior, 94,* 660–663.

Morton, Katie; Beauchamp, Mark; Prothero, Anna; Joyce, Lauren; Saunders, Laura; Spencer-Bowdage, Sarah; Dancy, Bernadette; & Pedlar, Charles. (2015). The effectiveness of motivational interviewing for health behaviour change in primary care settings: A systematic review. *Health Psychology Review, 9,* 205–223. https://doi.org/10.1080/17437199.2014.882006

Moscovitch, Morris; Cabeza, Roberto; Winocur, Gordon; & Nadel, Lynn. (2016). Episodic memory and beyond: the hippocampus and neocortex in transformation. *Annual Review of Psychology, 67,* 105–134. https://doi.org/10.1146/annurev-psych-113011-143733

Moskowitz, Andrew; Schafer, Ingo; & Dorahy, Martin Justin. (2009). *Psychosis, trauma, and dissociation.* Wiley.

Moss, Jarrod; Kotovsky, Kenneth; & Cagan, Jonathan. (2011). The effect of incidental hints when problems are suspended before, during, or after an impasse. *Journal of Experimental Psychology: Learning, Memory, and Cognition, 37*(1), 140–148. https://doi.org/10.1037/a0021206

Mossbridge, Julia A., & Radin, Dean. (2018). Precognition as a form of prospection: A review of the evidence. *Psychology of Consciousness: Theory, Research, and Practice, 5,* 78–93. https://doi.org/10.1037/cns0000121

Moss-Racusin, Corinne A.; Dovidio, John F.; Brescoll, Victoria L.; Graham, Mark J.; & Handelsman, Jo. (2012). Science faculty's subtle gender biases favor male students. *Proceedings of the National Academy of Sciences, 109,* 16474–16479.

Moss-Racusin, Corinne A.; Sanzari, Christina; Caluori, Nava; & Rabasco, Helena. (2018). Gender bias produces gender gaps in STEM engagement. *Sex Roles, 79,* 651–670. https://doi.org/10.1007/s11199-018-0902-z

Motowidlo, Stephan J.; Borman, Walter C.; & Schmit, Mark J. (1997). A theory of individual differences in task and contextual performance. *Human Performance, 10,* 71–83.

Moyer, Christopher A.; Rounds, James.; & Hannum, James W. (2004). A meta-analysis of massage therapy research. *Psychological Bulletin, 130,* 3–18.

Mrazek, Michael D.; Chin, Jason M.; Schmader, Toni; Hartson, Kimberly A.; Smallwood, Jonathan; & Schooler, Jonathan W. (2011). Threatened to distraction: Mind-wandering as a consequence of stereotype threat. *Journal of Experimental Social Psychology, 47,* 1243–1248. https://doi.org/10.1016/j.jesp.2011.05.011

Mueller, Pam A., & Oppenheimer, Daniel M. (2014). The pen is mightier than the keyboard: Advantages of longhand over laptop note taking. *Psychological Science, 25,* 1159–1168. https://doi.org/10.1177/0956797614524581

Mueller, Shane T.; Seymour, Travis L.; Kieras, David E.; & Meyer, David E. (2003). Theoretical implications of articulatory duration, phonological similarity, and phonological complexity in verbal working memory. *Journal of Experimental Psychology: Learning, Memory, and Cognition, 29,* 1353–1380.

Muenchow, Susan, & Marsland, Katherine W. (2007). Beyond baby steps: Promoting the growth and development of U.S. child-care policy. In J. Lawrence Aber, Sandra J. Bishop-Josef, Stephanie M. Jones, Kathryn Taaffe McLearn, & Deborah A. Phillips (Eds.), *Child development and social policy: Knowledge for action* (pp. 97–112). American Psychological Association.

Mueser, Kim T.; Deavers, Frances; Penn, David L.; & Cassisi, Jeffrey E. (2013). Psychosocial treatments for schizophrenia. *Annual Review of Clinical Psychology, 9,* 465–497. https://doi.org/10.1146/annurev-clinpsy-050212-185620

Mulhern, Sherrill. (1991). Embodied alternative identities: Bearing witness to a world that might have been. *Psychiatric Clinics of North America, 14,* 769–786. https://doi.org/10.1016/S0193-953X(18)30300-9

Mullen, Brian; Migdal, Michael J.; & Rozell, Drew. (2003). Self-awareness, deindividuation, and social identity: Unraveling theoretical paradoxes by filling empirical lacunae. *Personality and Social Psychology Bulletin, 29,* 1071–1081. https://doi.org/10.1177/0146167203252747

Müller, Johannes, & Kretzschmar, Mirjam. (2021). Contact tracing—Old models and new challenges. *Infectious Disease Modelling, 6,* 222–231. https://doi.org/10.1016/j.idm.2020.12.005

Munakata, Yuko; Kuhn, D.; Siegler, Robert S.; Damon, William; & Lerner, Robert M. (2006). Information processing approaches to development. In William Damon & Richard M. Lerner (Eds.), *Handbook of child psychology: Vol. 2, Cognition, perception, and language* (6th ed., pp. 426–463). Wiley.

Münsterberg, Hugo. (1913). *Psychology and industrial efficiency.* Houghton Mifflin.

Murberg, Terje A., & Bru, Edvin. (2005). The role of coping styles as predictors of depressive symptoms among adolescents: A prospective study. *Scandinavian Journal of Psychology, 46*(4), 385–393.

Murdock, Logan. (2020, December 10). Kid Cudi helped a generation of kids cope with depression. I was one of them. *The Ringer.* https://www.theringer.com/2020/12/10/22166862/kid-cudi-man-on-the-moon-series-retrospective

Murnen, Sarah; Greenfield, Claire; Younger, Abigail; & Boyd, Hope. (2016). Boys act and girls appear: A content analysis of gender stereotypes associated with characters in children's popular culture. *Sex Roles, 74,* 78–91. https://doi.org/10.1007/s11199-015-0558-x

Murray, Henry A. (1938). *Explorations in personality.* Oxford University Press.

Murray, Henry A. (1943). *Thematic Apperception Test manual.* Harvard University Press.

Murray, John P. (2008). Media violence: The effects are both real and strong. *American Behavioral Scientist, 51,* 1212–1230.

Muscatell, Keely A.; Slavich, George M.; Monroe, Scott M.; & Gotlib, Ian H. (2009). Stressful life events, chronic difficulties, and the symptoms of clinical depression. *Journal of Nervous and Mental Disease, 197*(3), 154–160. https://doi.org/10.1097/NMD.0b013e318199f77b

Mustanski, Brian S.; Chivers, Meredith L.; & Bailey, J. Michael. (2002). A critical review of recent biological research on human sexual orientation. *Annual Review of Sex Research, 13,* 89–140.

Mustanski, Brian S.; Viken, Richard J.; Kaprio, Jaakko; Pulkkinen, Lea; & Rose, Richard J. (2004). Genetic and environmental influences on pubertal development: Longitudinal data from Finnish twins at ages 11 and 14. *Developmental Psychology, 40,* 1188–1198.

Musto, David F. (1991, July). Opium, cocaine and marijuana in American history. *Scientific American, 265,* 40–47.

Mutiso, V. N.; Gatonga, P.; Ndeti, D. M.; Gafna, T.; Mbwayo, A. W.; & Khasakhala, L. I. (2014). Collaboration between traditional and Western practitioners. In S. O. Okpaku (Ed.), *Essentials of global mental health* (pp. 135–143). Cambridge University Press.

Myrtek, Michael. (2007). Type A behavior and hostility as independent risk factors for coronary heart disease. In Jochen Jordan, Benjamin Bardé, & Andreas Michael Zeiher (Eds.), *Contributions toward evidence-based psychocardiology: A systematic review of the literature* (pp. 159–183). American Psychological Association.

Nader, Karim, & Wang, Szu-Han. (2006). Fading in. *Learning & Memory, 13,* 530–535.

Nadler, Joel T., & Clark, M. H. (2011). Stereotype threat: A meta-analysis comparing African Americans to Hispanic Americans. *Journal of Applied Social Psychology, 41,* 872–890.

Naeem, Farooq; Gul, Mirrat; Irfan, Muhammad; Munshi, Tariq; Asif, Aftab; Rashid, Sadaf; . . . & Ayub, Muhammad. (2015). Brief culturally adapted CBT (CaCBT) for depression: A randomized controlled trial from Pakistan. *Journal of Affective Disorders, 177,* 101–107. https://doi.org/10.1016/j.jad.2015.02.012

Nagasawa, Miho; Mitsui, Shouhei; En, Shiori; Ohtani, Nobuyo; Ohta, Mitsuaki; Sakuma, Yasuo; Onaka, Tatsushi; Mogi, Kazutaka; & Kikusui, Takefumi. (2015). Oxytocin-gaze positive loop and the coevolution of human-dog bonds. *Science, 348,* 333–336. https://doi.org/10.1126/science.1261022

Naghavi, Mohsen. (2018). Global, regional, and national burden of suicide mortality 1990 to 2016: Systematic analysis for the global burden of disease study 2016. *BMJ, 364,* l94 https://doi.org/10.1136/bmj.l94

Nai, Jared; Narayanan, Jayanth; Hernandez, Ivan; & Savani, Krishna. (2018). People in more racially diverse neighborhoods are more prosocial. *Journal of Personality and Social Psychology, 114*(4), 497–515. https://doi.org/10.1037/pspa0000103

Nairn, Ray; Coverdale, Sara; & Coverdale, John H. (2011). A framework for understanding media depictions of mental illness. *Academic Psychiatry, 35,* 202–206. https://doi.org/10.1176/appi.ap.35.3.202

Nairne, James S. (2002). Remembering over the short-term: The case against the standard model. *Annual Review of Psychology, 53,* 53–81.

Nakao, Mutsuhiro. (2010). Work-related stress and psychosomatic medicine. *BioPsychoSocial Medicine, 4,* 4.

Nancekivell, Shaylene, E.; Shah, Priti; & Gelmen, Susan A. (2020). Maybe they're born with it or maybe it's the experience: Toward a deeper understanding of the learning style myth. *Journal of Educational Psychology, 112*(2), 221–235. https://doi.org/10.1037/edu0000366

Nanda, Serena. (1999). The Hijras of India: cultural and individual dimensions of an institutionalized third gender role. *Section I: Culture, Society and Sexuality 11. Part 1: Conceptual Frameworks, 13,* 226–238.

Naselaris, Thomas; Olman, Cheryl; Stansbury, Dustin; Ugurbil, Kamil; & Gallant, Jack. (2015). A voxel-wise encoding model for early visual areas decodes mental images of remembering scenes. *NeuroImage, 105,* 215–228. https://doi.org/10.1016/j.neuroimage.2014.10.018

Nash, Michael R. (2008). Foundations of clinical hypnosis. In Michael R. Nash & Amanda J. Barnier (Eds.), *The Oxford handbook of hypnosis: Theory, research, and practice* (pp. 487–502). Oxford University Press.

Nathan, Max, & Lee, Neil. (2013). Cultural diversity, innovation, and entrepreneurship: Firm-level evidence from London. *Economic Geography, 89,* 367–394. 10.1111/ecge.12016

Nathan, Peter E., & Gorman, Jack M. (Eds.). (2007). *A guide to treatments that work* (3rd ed.). Oxford University Press.

National Academies of Science, Engineering, and Medicine. (2017). *The health effects of cannabis and cannabinoids: The current state of evidence and recommendations for research.* https://doi.org/10.17226/24625

National Academies of Sciences, Engineering, and Medicine. (2018). *Public health consequences of e-cigarettes.* https://doi.org/10.17226/24952

National Academy of Sciences, Committee on Maximizing the Potential of Women in Academic Science, Engineering (U.S.), Committee on Science, & Public Policy (U.S.). (2007). *Beyond bias and barriers: Fulfilling the potential of women in academic science and engineering.* National Academies Press.

National Association for the Education of Young Children. (2009). *Developmentally appropriate practice in early childhood programs serving children from birth through age 8.* https://www.naeyc.org/sites/default/files/globally-shared/downloads/PDFs/resources/position-statements/PSDAP.pdf

National Association of Child Care Resource & Referral Agencies. (2010). NACCRRA 2009 annual report making connections: All children, all families, all settings.

National Center for Statistics and Analysis. (2019a, April). Distracted driving in fatal crashes, 2017. (Traffic Safety Facts Research Note. Report No. DOT HS 812 700). *NHTSA.* https://www.nhtsa.gov/sites/nhtsa.dot.gov/files/documents/812_381_distracteddriving2015.pdf

National Center for Statistics and Analysis. (2019b, October). *2018 fatal motor vehicle crashes: Overview.* (Traffic Safety Facts Research Note. Report No. DOT HS 812 826). National Highway Traffic Safety Administration.

National Coalition of Anti-Violence Programs. (2017). *A crisis of hate: A a mid year report on lesbian, gay, bisexual, transgender and queer hate violence homicides.* http://avp.org/wp-content/uploads/2017/08/NCAVP-A-Crisis-of-Hate-Final.pdf

National Highway Traffic Safety Administration. (2017, March). *Asleep at the wheel: A national compendium of efforts to eliminate drowsy driving.* https://www.nhtsa.gov/sites/nhtsa.dot.gov/files/documents/12723-drowsy_driving_asleep_at_the_wheel_031917_v4b_tag.pdf

National Institute of Child Health and Human Development (NICHD). (2006). The NICHD Study of Early Child Care and Youth Development (SECCYD): Findings for children up to age 4 1/2 years (Eunice Kennedy Shriver National Institute of Child Health and Human Development, NIH publication no. 05-4318). U.S. Government Printing Office.

National Institute of Child Health and Human Development (NICHD) Early Child Care Research Network. (2003a). Does quality of child care affect child outcomes at age 4 1/2? *Developmental Psychology, 39,* 451–469.

National Institute of Child Health and Human Development (NICHD) Early Child Care Research Network. (2003b). Families matter—even for kids in child care. *Journal of Developmental & Behavioral Pediatrics, 24,* 58–62.

National Institute of Mental Health (NIMH). (n.d.). *About RDoC.* U.S. Department of Health and Human Services. https://www.nimh.nih.gov/research/research-funded-by-nimh/rdoc/about-rdoc.shtml

National Institute of Mental Health (NIMH). (2021a). *Mental Illness.* https://www.nimh.nih.gov/health/statistics/mental-illness.shtml

National Institute of Mental Health (NIMH).(2021b). *Suicide.* https://www.nimh.nih.gov/health/statistics/suicide.shtml

National Institute on Aging. (2007). U.S. Department of Health and Human Services, National Institutes of Health.

National Institute on Alcohol Abuse & Alcoholism. (2017). *Alcohol facts and statistics.* https://www.niaaa.nih.gov/alcohol-health/overview-alcohol-consumption/alcohol-facts-and-statistics

National Institute on Alcohol Abuse and Alcoholism. (2020). Alcohol facts and statistics. U.S. Department of Health and Human Services, National Institutes of Health. https://pubs.niaaa.nih.gov/publications/AlcoholFacts%26Stats/AlcoholFacts&Stats.pdf

National Institute on Drug Abuse. (2016, July). *Fake prescription drugs laced with fentanyl.* https://archives.drugabuse.gov/emerging-trends/fake-prescription-drugs-laced-fentanyl

National Institute on Drug Abuse. (2020). *Overdose death rates.* https://www.drugabuse.gov/drug-topics/trends-statistics/overdose-death-rates

National Research Council. (2003). *The polygraph and lie detection.* National Academies Press.

National Retail Federation. (2015). National retail security survey 2015 [Press release]. *NRF.* https://nrf.com/resources/retail-library/national-retail-security-survey-2015

National Survey of Student Engagement (NSSE). (2016). *Engagement insights: Survey findings on the quality of undergraduate education—Annual Results 2016.* http://nsse.indiana.edu/html/annual_results.cfm

National World War II Museum. (n.d.). *Research starters: Worldwide deaths in World War II.* https://www.nationalww2museum.org/students-teachers/student-resources/research-starters/research-starters-worldwide-deaths-world-war

Natural Standard Monographs. (2009). *Magnet therapy.* http://www.naturalstandard.com/naturalstandard/demos/patient-magnet.asp

Nature. (2017). Intelligence research should not be held back by its past [editorial]. *545*(7655), 385–386. https://doi.org/10.1038/nature.2017.22021

Nayeb, Laleh; Wallby, Thomas; Westerlund, Monica; Salameh, Eva-Kristina; & Sarkadi, Anna. (2015). Child healthcare nurses believe that bilingual children show slower language development, simplify screening procedures and delay referrals. *Acta Paediatrica, 104,* 198–205. https://doi.org/10.1111/apa.12834

Naylor, Gavin; & Bowling, Tyler. (2020). *Yearly worldwide shark attack summary.* Florida Museum. https://www.floridamuseum.ufl.edu/shark-attacks/yearly-worldwide-summary/

Neary, Martha; & Schueller, Stephen M. (2018). State of the field of mental health apps. *Cognitive and Behavioral Practice, 25*(4), 531–537. https://doi.org/10.1016/j.cbpra.2018.01.002

Neberich, Wiebke; Penke, Lars; Lehnart, Lars; & Asendorpf, Jens B. (2010). Family of origin, age at menarche, and reproductive strategies: A test of four evolutionary-developmental models. *European Journal of Developmental Psychology, 7,* 153–177.

Neel, Rebecca; Kenrick, Douglas T.; White, Andrew Edward; & Neuberg, Steven L. (2016). Individual differences in fundamental social motives. *Journal of Personality and Social Psychology, 110,* 887–907. https://doi.org/10.1037/pspp0000068

Neher, Andrew. (1991). Maslow's theory of motivation: A critique. *Journal of Humanistic Psychology, 31,* 89–112.

Neimeyer, Robert A.; Wittkowski, Joachim; & Moser, Richard P. (2004). Psychological research on death attitudes: An overview and evaluation. *Death Studies, 28*(4), 309–340.

Neisser, Ulric; Boodoo, Gwyneth; Bouchard, Thomas J., Jr.; Boykin, A. Wade; Brody, Nathan; Ceci, Stephen J.; Halpern, Diane F.; Loehlin, John C.; Perloff, Robert; Sternberg, Robert J.; & Urbina, Susana. (1996). Intelligence: Knowns and unknowns. *American Psychologist, 51,* 77–101, 298.

Nelson, Katherine, & Fivush, Robyn. (2004). The emergence of autobiographical memory: A social cultural developmental theory. *Psychological Review, 111,* 486–511. https://doi.org/10.1037/0033-295X.111.2.486

Nelson, Leif D., & Morrison, Evan L. (2005). The symptoms of resource scarcity: Judgments of food and finances influence preferences for potential partners. *Psychological Science, 16,* 167–173.

Nelson, Marcia Z. (2001). *Come and sit: A week inside meditation centers.* Skylight Paths.

Nelson, S. Katherine; Kushlev, Kostadin; & Lyubomirsky, Sonja. (2014). The pains and pleasures of parenting: When, why, and how is parenthood associated with more or less well-being? *Psychological Bulletin, 140,* 846–895. https://doi.org/10.1037/a0035444

Nelson, S. Katherine; Layous, Kristin; Cole, Steven; & Lyubomirsky, Sonja. (2016). Do unto others or treat yourself? The effects of prosocial and self-focused behavior on psychological flourishing. *Emotion, 16,* 850–861. https://doi.org/10.1037/emo0000178

Nelson-Coffey, S. Katherine. (2018). Married…with children: The science of well-being in marriage and family life. In Ed Diener, Shigehiro Oishi, & Louis Tay (Eds.), *Handbook of well-being.* DEF Publishers.

Neria, Yuval; DiGrande, Laura; & Adams, Ben G. (2011). Posttraumatic stress disorder following the September 11, 2001, terrorist attacks: A review of the literature among highly exposed populations. *American Psychologist, 66*(6), 429–446. https://doi.org /10.1037/a0024791

Nestler, Eric J., & Malenka, Robert C. (2004, March). The addicted brain. *Scientific American, 290,* 78–85.

Neumann, Craig S.; Hare, Robert D.; & Johansson, Peter T. (2013). The psychopathy checklist-revised (PCL-R), low anxiety, and fearlessness: A structural equation modeling analysis. *Personality Disorders: Theory, Research, and Treatment, 4*(2), 129–137. https://doi .org/10.1037/a0027886

Neuner, Frank; Onyut, Patience L.; Ertl, Verena; Odenwald, Michael; Schauer, Elisabeth; & Elbert, Thomas. (2008). Treatment of posttraumatic stress disorder by trained lay counselors in an African refugee settlement: A randomized controlled trial. *Journal of Consulting and Clinical Psychology, 76*(4), 686–694. https://doi.org/10.1037 /0022-006X.76.4.686

New, Joshua; Krasnow, Max M.; Truxaw, Danielle; & Gaulin, Steven J. (2007). Spatial adaptations for plant foraging: Women excel and calories count. *Proceedings of the Royal Society B: Biological Sciences, 274,* 2679–2684.

The New York Times. (2021a). *Coronavirus in the U.S.: Latest map and case count.* https://www.nytimes.com/interactive/2020/us/coronavirus-us-cases.html

The New York Times. (2021b). *Coronavirus world map: Tracking the global outbreak.* https://www.nytimes.com/interactive/2020/world/coronavirus-maps.html

Newson, Rachel S., & Kemps, Eva B. (2005). General lifestyle activities as a predictor of current cognition and cognitive change in older adults: A cross-sectional and longitudinal examination. *Journals of Gerontology, Series B: Psychological Sciences and Social Sciences, 60,* P113–P120.

Newton, Jocelyn H., & McGrew, Kevin S. (2010). Introduction to the special issue: Current research in Cattell–Horn–Carroll–based assessment. *Psychology in the Schools, 47*(7), 621–634.

Newton, Philip M. (2015). The learning styles myth is thriving in higher education. *Frontiers in Psychology, 6,* article 1908. https://doi.org/103389/fpsyg.2015.01908

Nezu, Arthur M., & Nezu, Christine M. (Eds.). (2008). *Evidence-based outcome research: A practical guide to conducting randomized controlled trials for psychosocial interventions.* Oxford University Press.

Ng, Debbie M., & Jeffery, Robert W. (2003). Relationships between perceived stress and health behaviors in a sample of working adults. *Health Psychology, 22,* 638–642.

Ng, Yu-Leung. (2016). More than social-cultural influences: A research agenda for evolutionary perspectives on prosocial media effects. *Review of General Psychology, 20,* 317–335. https://doi.org/10.1037/gpr0000084

Nguyen, Angela-MinhTu D., & Benet-Martínez, Verónica. (2013). Biculturalism and adjustment: A meta-analysis. *Journal of Cross-Cultural Psychology, 44,* 122–159. https://doi.org/10.1177/0022022111435097

Nguyen, Kim-Huong, & Gordon, Louisa. (2015). Cost-effectiveness of repetitive transcranial magnetic stimulation versus antidepressant therapy for treatment-resistant depression. *Value in Health, 18,* 597–604. https://doi.org/10.1016/j.jval.2015.04.004

Niaura, Raymond; Todaro, John F.; Stroud, Laura; Spiro, Avron; Ward, Kenneth D.; & Weiss, Scott. (2002). Hostility, the metabolic syndrome, and incident coronary heart disease. *Health Psychology, 21,* 588–593.

Niccols, Alison. (2007). Fetal alcohol syndrome and the developing socioemotional brain. *Brain and Cognition, 65,* 135–142.

Nichols, Emily S.; Wild, Conor J.; Stojanoski, Bobby; Battista, Michael E.; & Owen, Adrian M. (2020). Bilingualism affords no general cognitive advantages: A population study of executive function in 11,000 people. *Psychological Science, 31*(5), 548–567. https://doi.org/10.1177/095679762090311

Nickerson, Raymond S., & Adams, Marilyn J. (1982). Long-term memory for a common object. In Ulric Neisser (Ed.), *Memory observed: Remembering in natural contexts.* Freeman.

Nielsen, Jared A.; Zielinski, Brandon A.; Ferguson, Michael A.; Lainhart, Janet E.; & Anderson, Jeffrey S. (2013). An evaluation of the left-brain vs. right-brain hypothesis with resting state functional connectivity magnetic resonance imaging. *PLOS ONE 8,* e71275. https://doi.org/10.1371/journal.pone.0071275

Nielsen, Philip; Meyer, Urs; & Mortensen, Preben. (2016). Individual and combined effects of maternal anemia and prenatal infection on risk for schizophrenia in offspring. *Schizophrenia Research, 172,* 35–40. https://doi.org/10.1016/j.schres.2016.02.025

Nielsen, Tore A.; Stenstrom, Philippe; & Levin, Ross. (2006). Nightmare frequency as a function of age, gender, and September 11, 2001: Findings from an Internet questionnaire. *Dreaming, 16,* 145–158.

Nielsen, Tore A., & Zadra, Antonio. (2005). Nightmares and other common dream disturbances. In Meir H. Kryger, Thomas Roth, & William C. Dement (Eds.), *Principles and practice of sleep medicine* (4th ed.). Elsevier Saunders.

Nielsen, Kristy A., & Lorber, William. (2009). Enhanced post-learning memory consolidation is influenced by arousal predisposition and emotion regulation but not by stimulus valence or arousal. *Neurobiology of Learning and Memory, 92*(1), 70–79. https://doi.org/10.1016/j.nlm.2009.03.002

Niemiec, Christopher P.; Ryan, Richard M.; & Deci, Edward L. (2010). Self-determination theory and the relation of autonomy to self-regulatory processes and personality development. In Rick H. Hoyle (Ed.), *Handbook of Personality and Self-Regulation* (pp. 69–191). Wiley-Blackwell. https://doi.org/10.1002 /9781444318111

Nir, Yuval; Staba, Richard J.; Andrillon, Thomas; Vyazovskiy Vladyslav V.; Cirelli, Chiara; Fried, Ithak; Tononi, Giulio. (2011). Regional slow waves and spindles in human sleep. *Neuron, 70,* 153–169.

Nir, Yuval, & Tononi, Giulio. (2010). Dreaming and the brain: From phenomenology to neurophysiology. *Trends in Cognitive Science, 14,* 88–100. https://doi.org/10.1016/j.tics .2009.12.001

Nisbett, Richard E. (2007). Eastern and Western ways of perceiving the world. In Yuichi Shoda, Daniel Cervone, Geraldine Downey (Eds.), *Persons in context: Building a science of the individual* (pp. 62–83). Guilford.

Nisbett, Richard E.; Aronson, Joshua; Blair, Clancy; Dickens, William; Flynn, James; Halpern, Diane F.; & Turkheimer, Eric. (2012). Intelligence: New findings and theoretical developments. *American Psychologist, 67,* 130–159. https://doi.org/10.1037 /a0026699

Nisbett, Richard E., & Wilson, Timothy. D. (1977). The halo effect: Evidence for unconscious alteration of judgments. *Journal of Personality and Social Psychology, 35,* 250–256. https://doi.org/10.1037/0022-3514.35.4.250

Nivette, Amy E. (2011). Cross-national predictors of crime: A meta-analysis. *Homicide Studies, 15*(2), 103–131. https://doi.org/10.1177/1088767911406397

Nivoli, Alessandra; Murru, Andrea; Goikolea, José M.; Crespo, José M.; Montes, José M.; González-Pinto, Ana; García-Portilla, Paz; Bobes, Julio; Sáiz-Ruiz, Jerónimo; & Vieta, Eduard. (2012). New treatment guidelines for acute bipolar mania: A critical review. *Journal of Affective Disorders, 140,* 125–141. https://doi.org/10.1016/j.jad.2011.10.015

Nock, Matthew K.; Greif Green, Jennifer; Hwang, Irving; McLaughlin, Katie A.; Sampson, Nancy A.; Zaslavsky, Alan M.; & Kessler, Ronald C. (2013). Prevalence, correlates, and treatment of lifetime suicidal behavior among adolescents. *JAMA Psychiatry, 70*(3), 1–11. https://doi.org/10.1001/2013.jamapsychiatry.55

Nock, Matthew K.; Han, Georges; Millner, Alexander J.; Gutierrez, Peter M.; Joiner, Thomas E.; Hwang, Irving; King, Andrew; Naifeh, James A.; Sampson, Nancy A.; Zaslavsky, Alan M.; Stein, Murray B.; Ursano, Robert J.; & Kessler, Ronald C. (2018). Patterns and predictors of persistence of suicide ideation: Results from the Army Study to Assess Risk and Resilience in Servicemembers (army STARRS). *Journal of Abnormal Psychology, 127*(7), 650–658. https://doi.org/10.1037/abn0000379

Nofzinger, Eric A. (2006). Neuroimaging of sleep and sleep disorders. *Current Neurology and Neuroscience Reports, 6,* 149–155.

Nolan, Susan A.; & Heinzen, Thomas E. (2021). *Essentials of statistics for the behavioral sciences* (5th ed.). Worth Publishers.

Nolen-Hoeksema, Susan. (2001). Gender differences in depression. *Current Directions in Psychological Science, 10*(5), 173–176. https://doi.org/10.1111/1467-8721.00142

Nolen-Hoeksema, Susan, & Hilt, Lori M. (2009). Gender differences in depression. In Ian H. Gotlib & Constance L. Hammen (Eds.), *Handbook of depression* (2nd ed., pp. 386–404). Guilford.

Nolen-Hoeksema, Susan; Stice, Eric; & Wade, Emily. (2007, February). Reciprocal relations between rumination and bulimic, substance abuse, and depressive symptoms in female adolescents. *Journal of Abnormal Psychology, 116*(1), 198–207. https://doi.org /10.1037/0021-843X.116.1.198

Nollenberger, Natalia; Rodríguez-Planas, Núria; & Sevilla, Almudena. (2014). The math gender gap: The role of culture. *IZA Discussion Papers,* no. 8379. http://ftp.iza.org /dp8379.pdf

Noone, Peter A. (2017). The Holmes–Rahe Stress Inventory. *Occupational Medicine, 67,* 581–582. https://doi.org/10.1093/occmed/kqx099

Norasakkunkit, Vinai; Kitayama, Shinobu; & Uchida, Yukiko. (2012). Social anxiety and holistic cognition: Self-focused social anxiety in the United States and other-focused social anxiety in Japan. *Journal of Cross-Cultural Psychology, 43*(5), 742–757. https://doi.org/10.1177/0022022111405658

Nørby, Simon. (2015). Why forget? On the adaptive value of memory loss. *Perspectives on Psychological Science, 10,* 551–578. https://doi.org/10.1177/1745691615596787

Norcross, John C.; Karpiak, Christie P.; & Santoro, Shannon O. (2005). Clinical psychologists across the years: The division of clinical psychology from 1960 to 2003. *Journal of Clinical Psychology, 61,* 1467–1483.

Norcross, John C., & Lambert, Michael J. (2011). Psychotherapy relationships that work II. *Psychotherapy, 48*(1), 4–8. https://doi.org/10.1037/a0022180

Norcross, John C., & Wampold, Bruce E. (2011). Evidence-based therapy relationships: Research conclusions and clinical practices. *Psychotherapy, 48*(1), 98–102. https://doi.org/10.1037/a0022161

Nordal, Katherine C. (2010). Dr. Katherine C. Nordal on how to find a therapist. *American Psychological Association Press Releases.* http://www.apa.org/news/press /releases/2010/05/locate-a-therapist.aspx

Norouzitallab, Parisa; Baruh, Kartik; Vanrompay, Daisy; & Brossier, Peter. (2019). Can epigenetics translate environmental cues into phenotypes? *Science of the Total Environment, 647,* 1281–1293. https://doi.org/10.1016/j.scitotenv.2018.08.063

North, Adrian C., & Hargreaves, David. (2009). The power of music. *The Psychologist, 22,* 1012–1014.

Norton, Aaron, & Herek, Gregory. (2013). Heterosexuals' attitudes toward transgender people: Findings from a national probability sample of U.S. adults. *Sex Roles, 68*, 738–753. https://doi.org/10.1007/s11199-011-0110-6

Nosek, Brian A.; Greenwald, Anthony G.; & Banaji, Mahzarin R. (2007). The Implicit Association Test at age 7: A methodological and conceptual review. In J. A. Bargh (Ed.), *Automatic Processes in Social Thinking and Behavior.* Psychology Press.

Nosek, Brian A.; Smyth, Frederick L.; Sriram, N.; Lindner, Nicole M.; Devos, Thierry; Ayala, Alfonso; Bar-Anan, Yoav; Bergh, Robin; Cai, Huajian; Gonsalkorale, Karen; Kesebir, Selin; Maliszewski, Norbert; Neto, Félix; Olli, Eero; Park, Jaihyun; Schnabel, Konrad; Shiomura, Kimihiro; Tulbure, Bogdan Tudor; Wiers, Reinout W.; . . . & Greenwald, Anthony G. (2009). National differences in gender–science stereotypes predict national sex differences in science and math achievement. *Proceedings of the National Academy of Sciences, 106*, 10593–10597.

Nosofsky, Robert M.; Little, Daniel R.; Donkin, Christopher; & Fific, Mario. (2011). Short-term memory scanning viewed as exemplar-based categorization. *Psychological Review, 118*, 280–315.

Nosofsky, Robert M., & Zaki, Safa R. (2002). Exemplar and prototype models revisited: Response strategies, selective attention, and stimulus generalization. *Journal of Experimental Psychology: Learning, Memory, and Cognition, 28*, 924–940.

Notter, Michael P.; Hanke, Michael; Murray, Micah M.; & Geiser, Eveline. (2019). Encoding of auditory temporal gestalt in the human brain. *Cerebral Cortex, 29*(2), 475–484. https://doi.org/10.1093/cercor/bhx328

Novick, Laura R., & Bassok, Miriam. (2005). Problem solving. In Keith J. Holyoak & Robert G. Morrison (Eds.), *The Cambridge handbook of thinking and reasoning.* Cambridge University Press.

Novotney, Amy. (2017). A growing wave of online therapy. *Monitor on Psychology, 48*, 48–53. http://www.apamonitor-digital.org/apamonitor/201702/?pg=51&pm=2&u1=friend

Nowlan, Jamie S.; Wuthrich, Viviana M.; & Rapee, Ronald M. (2015). Positive reappraisal in older adults: A systematic literature review. *Aging & Mental Health, 19*, 475–484. https://doi.org/10.1080/13607863.2014.954528

Nowogrodzki, Anna. (2018). The world's strongest MRI machines are pushing human imaging to new limits. *Nature, 563*(7729), 24–26. https://doi.org/10.1038/d41586-018-07182-7

Nummenmaa, Lauri; Glereana, Enrico; Hari, Riitta; & Hietanend, Jari K. (2014). Bodily maps of emotions. *Proceedings of the National Academy of Sciences, 111*, 646–651. https://doi.org/10.1073/pnas.1321664111

Nurnberger, John I. (2009, June). New hope for pharmacogenetic testing. *American Journal of Psychiatry, 166*(6), 635–638.

Nutt, Roberta L. (2010). Prejudice and discrimination against women based on gender bias. In Jean L. Chin (Ed.), *The psychology of prejudice and discrimination: A revised and condensed edition* (pp. 125–137). Praeger/ABC-CLIO.

Nuzzo, Regina. (2014). Statistical errors. *Nature, 506*, 150–152.

Nyhan, Brendan, & Reifler, Jason. (2015). Does correcting myths about the flu vaccine work? An experimental evaluation of the effects of corrective information. *Vaccine, 33*, 459–464. https://doi.org/10.1016/j.vaccine.2014.11.017

Nyman, Lawrence. (2010). Documenting history: An interview with Kenneth Bancroft. *History of Psychology, 13*(1), 74–88. https://doi.org/10.1037/a0018550

O Magazine. (2005, December). Oprah talks to Jamie Foxx. *Oprah.com.* http://www.oprah.com/omagazine/Oprahs-Interview-with-Jamie-Foxx

O'Brien, Mary P.; Miklowitz, David J.; Candan, Kristin A.; Marshall, Catherine; Domingues, Isabel; Walsh, Barbara C.; Zinberg, Jamie L.; De Silva, Sandra D.; Woodberry, Kristen A.; & Cannon, Tyrone D. (2014). A randomized trial of family focused therapy with populations at clinical high risk for psychosis: Effects on interactional behavior. *Journal of Consulting and Clinical Psychology.* https://doi.org/10.1037/a0034667

O'Connor, Daryl B., & Shimizu, Mikiko. (2002). Sense of personal control, stress and coping style: A cross-cultural study. *Stress and Health, 18*, 173–183.

O'Connor, Daryl B.; Jones, Fiona; Conner, Mark; McMillan, Brian; & Ferguson, Eamonn. (2008). Effects of daily hassles and eating style on eating behavior. *Health Psychology, 27*(1), S20–S31.

O'Craven, Kathleen M., & Kanwisher, Nancy. (2000). Mental imagery of faces and places activates corresponding stimulus-specific brain regions. *Journal of Cognitive Neuroscience, 12*, 1013–1023.

O'Donnell, Sara, & Epstein, Leonard H. (2019). Smartphones are more reinforcing than food for students. *Addictive Behaviors, 90*, 124–133. https://doi.org/10.1016/j.addbeh.2018.10.018

O'Donnell, Stephanie O.; Webb, Jonathan K.; & Shine, Richard. (2010). Conditioned taste aversion enhances the survival of an endangered predator imperilled by a toxic invader. *Journal of Applied Ecology, 47*, 558–565. https://doi.org/10.1111/j.1365-2664.2010.01802.x

O'Donoghue, Gerard. (2013). Cochlear implants—Science, serendipity, and success. *New England Journal of Medicine, 369*, 1190–1193. https://doi.org/10.1056/NEJMp1310111

O'Grady, Cathleen. (2020). Famous psychologist faces posthumous reckoning. *Science, 369*(6501), 233-234. https://doi.org/10.1126/science.369.6501.233

O'Hara, Mary. (2016, December 29). Nation's first known intersex birth certificate issued in NYC. *NBC News.* http://www.nbcnews.com/feature/nbc-out/nation-s-first-known-intersex-birth-certificate-issued-nyc-n701106

O'Roark, Ann M. (2007). The best of consulting psychology 1900–2000: Insider perspectives. *Consulting Psychology Journal: Practice and Research, 59*, 189–202.

Oakley, David A., & Halligan, Peter W. (2013). Hypnotic suggestion: Opportunities for cognitive neuroscience. *Nature Reviews Neuroscience, 14*, 565–576.

Oas, Peter T. (2010). Current status on corporal punishment with children: What the literature says. *American Journal of Family Therapy, 38*(5), 413–420.

Ochsner, Kevin N.; Bunge, Silvia A.; Gross, James J.; & Gabrieli, John D. E. (2002). Rethinking feelings: An fMRI study of the cognitive regulation of emotion. *Journal of Cognitive Neuroscience, 14*(8), 1215–1229. https://doi.org/10.1162/089892902760807212

Ocklenburg, Sebastian, & Güntürkün, Onur. (2012). Hemispheric asymmetries: The comparative view. *Frontiers in Psychology, 3*, 1–9. https://doi.org/10.3389/fpsyg.2012.00005

OECD Better Life Index. (n.d.) *Work-life balance.* http://www.oecdbetterlifeindex.org/topics/work-life-balance/

Oechslin, Mathias S.; Gschwind, Markus & James, Clara E. (2018). Tracking training-related plasticity by combining fMRI and DTI: The right hemisphere ventral stream mediates musical syntax processing. *Cerebral Cortex, 28* (4), 1209–1218. https://doi.org/10.1093/cercor/bhx033

Oehen, Peter; Traber, Rafael; Widmer, Verena; & Schnyder, Ulrich. (2013). A randomized, controlled pilot study of MDMA (±3,4-Methylenedioxymethamphetamine)-assisted psychotherapy for treatment of resistant, chronic post-traumatic stress disorder (PTSD). *Journal of Psychopharmacology, 27*(1), 40–52. https://doi.org/10.1177/0269881112464827

Ogbu, John U. (1986). The consequences of the American caste system. In Ulric Neisser (Ed.), *The school achievement of minority children: New perspectives.* Erlbaum.

Ogbu, John U. (2008). *Minority status, oppositional culture, and schooling: Sociocultural, political, and historical studies in education.* Routledge.

Ogden, Cynthia L.; Carroll, Margaret D.; Fryar, Cheryl D.; & Flegal, Katherine M. (2015). *Prevalence of obesity among adults and youth: United States, 2011–2014.* NCHS Data Brief no. 219. National Center for Health Statistics.

Oh, G., & Petronis, A. (2008). Environmental studies of schizophrenia through the prism of epigenetics. *Schizophrenia Bulletin, 34*(6), 1122–1129. https://doi.org/10.1093/schbul/sbn105

Ohayon, Maurice M.; Carskadon, Mary A.; Guilleminault, Christian; & Vitiello, Michael V. (2004). Meta-analysis of quantitative sleep parameters from childhood to old age in healthy individuals: Developing normative sleep values across the human lifespan. *Sleep, 27*, 1255–1273.

Ohlsson, Stellan. (2010). *Deep learning: How the mind overrides experience.* Cambridge University Press.

Öhman, Arne. (2009). Of snakes and faces: An evolutionary perspective on the psychology of fear. *Scandinavian Journal of Psychology, 50*(6), 543–552. https://doi.org/10.1111/j.1467-9450.2009.00784.x

Öhman, Arne; Carlsson, Katrina; & Lundqvist, Daniel. (2007). On the unconscious subcortical origin of human fear. *Physiology & Behavior, 92*, 180–185.

Öhman, Arne, & Mineka, Susan. (2001). Fear, phobias, and preparedness: Toward an evolved module of fear and fear learning. *Psychological Review, 108*, 483–522.

Öhman, Arne, & Mineka, Susan. (2003). The malicious serpent: Snakes as a prototypical stimulus for an evolved module of fear. *Current Directions in Psychological Science, 12*, 5–9.

Oishi, Shigehiro; Talhelm, Thomas; & Lee, Minha. (2015). Personality and geography: Introverts prefer mountains. *Journal of Research in Personality,58*, 55–68. https://doi.org/10.1016/j.jrp.2015.07.001

Ojalehto, Bethany l., & Medin, Douglas L. (2015). Perspectives on culture and concepts. *Annual Review of Psychology, 66*, 249–275. https://doi.org/10.1146/annurev-psych-010814-015120

Okonofua, Jason A., & Eberhardt, Jennifer L. (2015). Two strikes: Race and the disciplining of young students. *Psychological Science, 26*, 617–624. https://doi.org/10.1177/0956797615570365

Olaisen, R. Henry.; Rossen, Lauren M.; Warner, Margaret; & Anderson, Robert N. (2019). *Unintentional injury death rates in rural and urban areas: United States, 1999–2017.* National Center for Health Statistics. https://www.cdc.gov/nchs/data/databriefs/db343-h.pdf

Olff, Miranda; Frijling, Jessie L.; Kubzansky, Laura D.; Bradley, Bekh; Ellenbogen, Mark A.; Cardoso, Christopher; Bartz, Jennifer A.; Yee, Jason R.; & van Zuiden, Mirjam. (2013). The role of oxytocin in social bonding, stress regulation and mental health: An update on the moderating effects of context and interindividual differences. *Psychoneuroendocrinology, 38*, 1883–94. https://doi.org/10.1016/j.psyneuen.2013.06.019

Olff, Miranda; Langeland, Willie; & Draijer, Nel. (2007, March). Gender differences in posttraumatic stress disorder. *Psychological Bulletin, 133*(2), 183–204. https://doi.org/10.1037/0033-2909.133.2.183

Olfson, Mark, & Marcus, Steven C. (2009). National patterns in antidepressant medication treatment. *Archives of General Psychiatry. 66*, 848–856. https://doi.org/10.1001/archgenpsychiatry.2009.81

Olivola, Christopher Y., & Todorov, Alexander. (2010). Fooled by first impressions? Reexamining the diagnostic value of appearance-based inferences. *Journal of Experimental Social Psychology, 46*, 315–324. https://doi.org/10.1016/j.jesp.2009.12.002

Öllinger, Michael; Jones, Gary; & Knoblich, Günther. (2008). Investigating the effect of mental set on insight problem solving. *Experimental Psychology, 55*, 269–282.

Olson-Kennedy, Johanna; Chan, Yee-Ming; Garofalo, Robert; Spack, Norman; Chen, Diane; Clark, Leslie; Ehrensaft, Diane; Hidalgo, Marco; Tishelman, Amy; & Rosenthal, Stephen. (2019). Impact of early medical treatment for transgender youth: Protocol for the longitudinal, observational trans youth care study. *JMIR Research Protocols, 8*(7), e14434. https://doi.org/10.2196/14434

Oltmanns, Thomas F., & Balsis, Steve. (2011). Personality disorders in later life: Questions about the measurement, course, and impact of disorders. *Annual Review of Clinical Psychology, 7*, 321–349. https://doi.org/10.1146/annurev-clinpsy-090310-120435

Olton, David S. (1992). Tolman's cognitive analysis: Predecessors of current approaches in psychology. *Journal of Experimental Psychology: General, 121*, 427–428.

Ong, Anthony D.; Fuller-Rowell, Thomas; & Burrow, Anthony L. (2009). Racial discrimination and the stress process. *Journal of Personality and Social Psychology, 96*, 1259–1271.

Ong, Anthony D.; Zautra, Alex J.; & Reid, M. Carrington. (2015). Chronic pain and the adaptive significance of positive emotions. *American Psychologist, 70*, 283–284. https://doi.org/10.1037/a0038816

Open Science Collaboration. (2015). Open science framework. https://osf.io/vmrgu/wiki/home/

Oppenheimer, Daniel M., & Kelso, Evan. (2015). Information processing as a paradigm for decision making. *Annual Review Psychology, 66*, 277–294. https://doi.org/10.1146/annurev-psych-010814-015148

Opris, David; Pintea, Sebastian; García-Palacios, Azucena; Botella, Cristina; Szamosközi, Stegan; & David, Daniel. (2012). Virtual reality exposure therapy in anxiety disorders: A quantitative meta-analysis. *Depression and Anxiety, 29*(2), 85–93.

Orban, Guy A. (2016). Functional definitions of parietal areas in human and non-human primates. *Proceedings of the Royal Society B, 283*. https://doi.org/10.1098/rspb.2016.0118

Oreg, Shaul, & Berson, Yair. (2018). The impact of top leader's personalities: The processes through which organizations become reflections of their leaders. *Current Directions in Psychological Science, 27*(4), 241–248. https://doi.org/10.1177/0963721417748397

Organization for Economic Cooperation and Development (OECD). (2010). *Program for International Student Assessment (PISA) 2009 results: What students know and can do: Student performance in reading, mathematics, and science* (Vol. 1). OECD. http://www.oecd.org/pisa/pisaproducts/48852548.pdf

Orne, Martin T., & Holland, Charles H. (1968). On the ecological validity of laboratory deceptions. *International Journal of Psychiatry, 6*, 282–293.

Ornell, Felipe; Schuch, Jaqueline B.; Sordi, Anne O.; & Kessler, Felix H. P. (2020). "Pandemic fear" and COVID-19: Mental health burden and strategies. *Brazilian Journal of Psychiatry, 42*(3), 232–235. https://doi.org/10.1590/1516-4446-2020-0008

Osborne, Mark. (2019, January 1). Colorado's Jared Polis, nation's 1st gay governor, signs bill banning conversion therapy for minors. *abcNEWS.* Retrieved from https://abcnews.go.com/US/colorados-jared-polis-nations-1st-gay-governor-signs/story?id=63416794

Ostrov, Jamie M., & Godleski, Stephanie A. (2010). Toward an integrated gender-linked model of aggression subtypes in early and middle childhood. *Psychological Review, 117*(1), 233–242. https://doi.org/10.1037/a0018070

Otten, Liam. (2020, Aug. 25). Obituary: Robert L. Williams II, founding director of Black Studies program, 90. *The Source.* https://source.wustl.edu/2020/08/obituary-robert-l-williams-ii-founding-director-of-black-studies-program-90/

Oud, Matthijs; Mayo-Wilson, Evan; Braidwood, Ruth; Schulte, Peter; Jones, Steven; Morriss, Richard; Kupka, Ralph; Cuijpers, Pim; & Kendall, Tim. (2016). Psychological interventions for adults with bipolar disorder: Systematic review and meta-analysis. *British Journal of Psychiatry, 208*, 213–222. https://doi.org/10.1192/bjp.bp.114.157123

Owe, Elinor; Vignoles, Vivian L.; Becker, Maja; Brown, Rupert; Smith, Peter B.; Lee, Spike W. S.; Easterbrook, Matt; Gadre, Tanuja; Zhang, Xiao; Gheorghiu, Mirona; Baguma, Peter; Tatarko, Alexander; Aldhafri, Said; Zinkeng, Martina; Schwartz, Seth J.; Des Rosiers, Sabrina E.; Villamar, Juan A.; Mekonnen, Kassahun Habtamu; Regalia, Camillo; . . . & Jalal, Baland. (2013). Contextualism as an important facet of individualism-collectivism: Personhood beliefs across 37 national groups. *Journal of Cross-Cultural Psychology, 44*(1), 24–45. https://doi.org/10.1177/0022022111430255

Owen, Adrian M.; Coleman, Martin R.; Boly, Melanie; Davis, Matthew H.; Laureys, Steven; & Pickard, John D. (2006). Detecting awareness in the vegetative state. *Science, 313*(5792), 1402. https://doi.org/10.1126/science.1130197

Owen, Jesse J., & Fincham, Frank. (2011). Young adults' emotional reactions after hooking up encounters. *Archives of Sexual Behavior, 40*, 321–330. https://doi.org/10.1007/s10508-010-9652-x

OWLLabs. (2018). *Global state of remote work.* https://www.owllabs.com/state-of-remote-work/2018

OWLLabs. (2020a). *State of remote work.* https://resources.owllabs.com/state-of-remote-work/2020

OWLLabs. (2020b). *UK state of remote work.* https://resources.owllabs.com/state-of-remote-work-uk/2020

Oyserman, Daphna, & James, Leah. (2011). Possible identities. In Seth J. Schwartz, Koen Luyckx, & Vivian L. Vignoles (Eds.), *Handbook of identity theory and research* (pp. 117–145). Springer.

Oyserman, Daphna; Bybee, Deborah; Terry, Kathy; & Hart-Johnson, Tamera. (2004). Possible selves as roadmaps. *Journal of Research in Personality, 38*, 130–149.

Oyserman, Daphna; Destin, Mesmin; & Novin, Sheida. (2015). The context-sensitive future self: Possible selves motivate in context, not otherwise. *Self and Identity, 14*, 173–188. https://doi.org/10.1080/15298868.2014.965733

Ozer, Elizabeth M., & Bandura, Albert. (1990). Mechanisms governing empowerment effects: A self-efficacy analysis. *Journal of Personality and Social Psychology, 58*, 472–486.

Ozer, Emily J.; Best, Suzanne R.; Lipsey, Tami L.; & Weiss, Daniel S. (2003). Predictors of posttraumatic stress disorder and symptoms in adults: A meta-analysis. *Psychological Bulletin, 129*, 52–73. https://doi.org/10.1037/0033-2909.129.1.52

Ozkan, Kerem, & Braunstein, Myron L. (2010). Background surface and horizon effects in the perception of relative size and distance. *Visual Cognition, 18*, 229–254.

Pace-Schott, Edward F.; Germain, Anne; & Milad, Mohammed R. (2015, April 20). Effects of sleep on memory for conditioned fear and fear extinction. *Psychological Bulletin, 141*, 835–857. https://doi.org/10.1037/bul0000014

Packer, Dominic J. (2008a). Identifying systematic disobedience in Milgram's obedience experiments: A meta-analytic review. *Perspectives on Psychological Science, 3*, 301–304.

Packer, Dominic J. (2008b). On being both with us and against us: A normative conflict model of dissent in social groups. *Personality and Social Psychology Review, 12*(1), 50–72.

Padawer, Ruth. (2016, June 28). The humiliating practice of sex-testing female athletes. *The New York Times Magazine.* https://www.nytimes.com/2016/07/03/magazine/the-humiliating-practice-of-sex-testing-female-athletes.html

Pagani, Marco; Carletto, Sara; & Ostacoli, Luca. (2019). PET and SPECT in psychiatry: The past and the future. *European Journal of Nuclear Medicine and Molecular Imaging, 46*, 1985–1987. https://link.springer.com/article/10.1007/s00259-019-04451-z

Page, Nicholas; Sivarajasingam, Vaseekaran; Matthews, Kent; Heravi, Saeed; Morgan, Peter; & Shepherd, Jonathan. (2016). Preventing violence-related injuries in England and Wales: A panel study examining the impact of on-trade and off-trade alcohol prices. *Injury Prevention, 23*, 33–39. https://doi.org/10.1136/injuryprev-2015-041884

Paivio, Allan. (1986). *Mental representations: A dual coding approach.* Oxford University Press.

Paivio, Allan. (2007). *Mind and its evolution: A dual coding theoretical approach.* Erlbaum.

Pakkenberg, Bente, & Gundersen, Hans J. G. (1997). Neocortical neuron number in humans: Effect of sex and age. *Journal of Comparative Neurology, 384*(2), 312–320. https://doi.org/10.1002/(SICI)1096-9861(19970728)384:2<312::AID-CNE10>3.0.CO;2-K

Pakkenberg, Bente; Pelvig, Dorte; Marner, Lisbeth; Bundgaard, Mads J.; Gundersen, Hans J. G.; Nyengaard, Jens R.; & Regeur, Lisbeth. (2003). Aging and the human neocortex. *Experimental Gerontology, 38*, 95–99. https://doi.org/10.1016/s0531-5565(02)00151-1

Palit, Shreela; Kerr, Kara L.; Kuhn, Bethany L.; Terry, Ellen L.; DelVentura, Jennifer L.; Bartley, Emily J.; Shadlow, Joanna O.; & Rhudy, Jamie L. (2013). Exploring pain processing differences in Native Americans. *Health Psychology, 32*, 1127–1136. https://doi.org/10.1037/a0031057

Pallavi, Krishna Priya. (2020, January 31). *Mumbai Police sets up Punishing Signal to stop unnecessary honking.* Twitter loves viral video. India Today. https://www.indiatoday.in/trending-news/story/mumbai-police-sets-up-punishing-signal-to-stop-unnecessary-honking-twitter-loves-viral-video-1642032-2020-01-31?sr=fbia

Palmer, John. (2015). Implicit anomalous cognition. In Etzel Cardeña, John Palmer, & David Marcusson-Clavertz (Eds.) *Parapsychology: A handbook for the 21st century.* McFarland.

Palmer, Stephen E. (2002). Perceptual grouping: It's later than you think. *Current Directions in Psychological Science, 11*, 101–106.

Palmiero, Massimiliano; Olivetti Belardinelli, Marta; Nardo, DAvide; Sestieri, Carlo; Di Matteo, Rosalia; D'Ausilio, Alessandro; & Romani, G. L. (2009). Mental imagery generation in different modalities activates sensory-motor areas. *Cognitive Processing, 10*, 268–271.

Palomares, Nicholas A. (2009). Women are sort of more tentative than men, aren't they? How men and women use tentative language differently, similarly, and counterstereotypically as a function of gender salience. *Communication Research, 36*(4), 538–560.

Paltrow, Gwenyth; Loehnen, Elise; Fried, Andrew; Minoprio, Shauna; & Lillegard, Dane (Executive Producers). (2020, January 24). The energy experience (Episode 5) [TV series]. The Goop Lab. Boardwalk Pictures; Netflix.

Paluck, Elizabeth Levy, & Green, Donald P. (2009). Prejudice reduction: What works? A review and assessment of research and practice. *Annual Review of Psychology, 60*, 339–367. https://doi.org/10.1146/annurev.psych.60.110707.163607

Panksepp, Jaak. (2000). The riddle of laughter: Neural and psycho-evolutionary underpinnings of joy. *Psychological Science, 9*, 183–186.

Panksepp, Jaak. (2007). Neuroevolutionary sources of laughter and social joy: Modeling primal human laughter in laboratory rats. *Behavioural Brain Research, 182,* 231–244.

Papageorgiou, Panagiotis; Deschner, James; & Papageorgiou, Spyridon. (2017). Effectiveness and adverse effects of deep brain stimulation: Umbrella review of meta-analyses. *Journal of Neurological Surgery Part A: Central European Neurosurgery, 78,* 180–190. https://doi.org/10.1055/s-0036-1592158

Parents Television Council. (2007). *Dying to entertain: Violence on primetime broadcast television 1998-2006.* Parents Television Council.

Pargament, Kenneth I., & Cummings, Jeremy. (2010). Anchored by faith: Religion as a resilience factor. In John W. Reich, Alex J. Zautra; & John Stuart Hall (Eds.), *Handbook of adult resilience.* Guilford.

Parish, Amy R., & de Waal, Frans B. M. (2000). The other "closest living relative": How bonobos (*Pan paniscus*) challenge traditional assumptions about females, dominance, intra- and intersexual interactions, and hominid evolution. *Annals of the New York Academy of Sciences, 907,* 97–13.

Park, BoKyung; & Young, Liane. (2020). An association between biased impression updating and relationship facilitation: A behavioral and fMRI investigation. *Journal of Experimental Social Psychology, 87,* 1–8. https://doi.org/10.1016/j.jesp.2019.103916

Park, Crystal L.; Armeli, Stephen; & Tennen, Howard. (2004). Appraisal-coping goodness of fit: A daily Internet study. *Personality and Social Psychology Bulletin, 30,* 558–569.

Park, Hae-Jeong, & Friston, Karl. (2013). Structural and functional brain networks: From connections to cognition. *Science, 342,* 1238411. https://doi.org/10.1126/science.1238411

Park, Samuel. (2010). The face of the Asian American male client: A clinician's assessment. In William Ming Liu, Derek Kenji Iwamoto, & Mark H. Chae (Eds.), *Culturally responsive counseling with Asian American men.* Routledge/Taylor & Francis Group.

Parker, Andrew J. (2007). Binocular depth perception and the cerebral cortex. *Nature Reviews Neuroscience, 8,* 379–391.

Parker, Elizabeth S.; Cahill, Larry; & McGaugh, James L. (2006). A case of unusual autobiographical remembering. *Neurocase, 12,* 35–49. https://doi.org/10.1080/13554790500473680

Parks-Stamm, Elizabeth J.; Gollwitzer, Peter M.; & Oettingen, Gabriele. (2007). Action control by implementation intentions: Effective cue detection and efficient response initiation. *Social Cognition, 25,* 248–266.

Parsa, Keon M.; Gao, William; Lally, Jack; Davison, Stephen P.; & Reilly, Michael J. (2019). Evaluation of personality perception in men before and after facial cosmetic surgery. *JAMA Facial Plastic Surgery, 21*(5), 369–374. https://doi.org/10.1001/jamafacial.2019.0463

Partonen, Timo, & Pandi-Perumal, S. R. (2010). *Seasonal affective disorder: Practice and research.* Oxford University Press.

Pascalis, Olivier; & Kelly, David J. (2009). The origins of face processing in humans: Phylogeny and ontogeny. *Perspectives on Psychological Science, 4*(2), 200–209.

Pascual-Leone, Alvaro; Amedi, Amir; Fregni, Felipe; & Merabet, Lotfi B. (2005). The plastic human cortex. *Annual Review of Neuroscience, 28,* 377–401.

Pashler, H.; McDaniel, M.; Rohrer, D.; & Bjork, R. (2008). Learning styles: Concepts and evidence. *Psychological Science in the Public Interest, 9,* 105–119. https://doi.org/10.1111/j.15396053.2009.01038.x

Pashler, Harold E. (1998). *The psychology of attention.* MIT Press.

Pasterski, Vickie. (2008). Disorders of sex development and atypical sex differentiation. In David L. Rowland & Luca Incrocci (Eds.), *Handbook of sexual and gender identity disorders.* Wiley.

Patihis, Lawrence. (2016). Individual differences and correlates of highly superior autobiographical memory. *Memory, 24,* 961–978. https://doi.org/10.1080/09658211.2015.1061011

Patihis, Lawrence; Ho, Lavina Y.; Tingen, Ian W.; Lilienfeld, Scott O.; & Loftus, Elizabeth F. (2014). Are the "memory wars" over? A scientist-practitioner gap in beliefs about repressed memory. *Psychological Science, 25,* 519–530.

Patrick, Christopher J. (2007). Antisocial personality disorder and psychopathy. In William T. O'Donohue, Kevin A. Fowler, & Scott O. Lilienfeld (Eds.), *Personality disorders: Toward the DSM-V* (pp. 109–166). Sage.

Patterson, Charlotte J. (2006). Children of gay and lesbian parents. *Current Directions in Psychological Science, 15,* 241–244.

Patterson, Charlotte J. (2008). Sexual orientation across the life span: Introduction to the special section. *Developmental Psychology, 44,* 1–4.

Paul, Diane B., & Blumenthal, Arthur L. (1989). On the trail of Little Albert. *The Psychological Record, 39,* 547–553.

Paulhus, Delroy L., & Williams, Kevin M. (2002). The dark triad of personality: Narcissism, Machiavellianism, and psychopathy. *Journal of Research in Personality, 36,* 556–563. https://doi.org/10.1016/S0092-6566(02)00505-6

Paunio, Tiina. (2012). Sleep modifies metabolism. *Sleep: Journal of Sleep and Sleep Disorders Research, 35,* 589–590.

Pavelko, Rachelle L., & Myrick, Jessica Gail. (2015). That's so OCD: The effects of disease trivialization via social media on user perceptions and impression formation. *Computers in Human Behavior, 49,* 251–258. https://doi.org/10.1016/j.chb.2015.02.061

Pavlov, Ivan. (1904). On conditioned reflexes. In Richard J. Herrnstein & Edwin G. Boring (Eds.), *A source book in the history of psychology.* Harvard University Press.

Pavlov, Ivan. (1927/1960). *Conditioned reflexes: An investigation of the physiological activity of the cerebral cortex* (G. V. Anrep, Trans.). Dover Books. Retrieved from http://psychclassics.yorku.ca/Pavlov/index.htm

Pavlov, Ivan. (1928). *Lectures on conditioned reflexes.* International Publishers.

Pavlova, Milena K., & Latreille, Véronique. (2018). Sleep disorders. *The American Journal of Medicine.* https://doi.org/10.1016/j.amjmed.2018.09.021

Payne, Laura A.; Ellard, Kristen K.; Farchione, T. J.; Fairholme, Christopher P.; & Barlow, David H. (2014). Emotional disorders: A unified transdiagnostic protocol. In David H. Barlow (Ed.), *Clinical handbook of psychological disorders* (5th ed.). Guilford.

Payton, Jack R. (1992, May 16). The sad legacy of Japan's outcasts. *Chicago Tribune,* Sect. 1, p. 21.

PCI Media Impact. (2018). Our programs. www.pcimedia.org/our-programs

Pedersen, Anette Fischer; Bovbjerg, Dana Howard; & Zachariae, Robert (2011). Stress and susceptibility to infectious disease. In Richard J. Contrada & Andrew Baum (Eds.), *The handbook of stress science: Biology,psychology, and health.* Springer.

Pedersen, Anette Fischer; Zachariae, Robert; & Bovbjerg, Dana Howard. (2009). Psychological stress and antibody response to influenza vaccination:A meta-analysis. *Brain, Behavior, and Immunity, 23*(4), 427–433.

Pedersen, Paul B.; Crethar, Hugh C.; & Carlson, Jon. (2008). Defining inclusive cultural empathy. In Paul B. Pedersen, Hugh C. Crethar, & Jon Carlson (Eds.), *Inclusive cultural empathy: Making relationships central in counseling and psychotherapy* (pp. 41–44). American Psychological Association.

Pedersen, Walker S.; Muftuler, L. Tugan; & Larson, Christine L. (2019). A high-resolution fMRI investigation of BNST and centromedial amygdala activity as a function of affective stimulus predictability, anticipation, and duration. *Social Cognitive and Affective Neuroscience, 14*(11), 1167–1177. https://doi.org/10.1093/scan/nsz095

Pedersen, William C.; Putcha-Bhagavatula, Anila; & Miller, Lynn C. (2010). Are men and women really that different? Examining some of Sexual Strategies Theory (SST)'s key assumptions about sex-distinct mating mechanisms. *Sex Roles,* 1–15. https://doi.org/10.1007/s11199-010-9811-5

Pedersen, William C.; Vasquez, Eduardo A.; Bartholow, Bruce D.; Grosvenor, Marianne; & Truong, Ana. (2014). Are you insulting me? Exposure to alcohol primes increases aggression following ambiguous provocation. *Personality and Social Psychology Bulletin, 40,* 1037–1049. https://doi.org/10.1177/0146167214534993

Pehrsson, Dale-Elizabeth; & Aguilera, Mary E. (2007). *Play therapy: Overview and implications for counselors* (ACAPCD-12). American Counseling Association. https://www.counseling.org/resources/library/ACA%20Digests/ACAPCD-12.pdf

Peirs, Cedric, & Seal, Rebecca P. (2016). Neural circuits for pain: Recent advances and current views. *Science, 354,* 574–584. https://doi.org/10.1126/science.aaf8933

Pennington, Charlotte R.; Litchfield, Damien; McLatchie, Neil; & Heim, Derek. (2019). Stereotype threat may not impact women's inhibitory control or mathematical performance: Providing support for the null hypothesis. *European Journal of Social Psychology, 49*(4), 717–734. https://doi.org/10.1002/ejsp.2540

Pennycook, Gordon, & Rand, David G. (2019). Lazy, not biased: Susceptibility to partisan fake news is better explained by lack of reasoning than by motivated reasoning. *Cognition, 188,* 39–50. https://doi.org/10.1016/j.cognition.2018.06.011

Pepperberg, Irene M. (2007). Grey parrots do not always "parrot": The roles of imitation and phonological awareness in the creation of new labels from existing vocalizations. *Language Sciences, 29,* 1–13. https://doi.org/10.1016/j.langsci.2005.12.002

Perdue, Bonnie M.; Snyder, Rebecca J.; Pratte, Jason; Marr, M. Jackson; & Maple, Terry L. (2009). Spatial memory recall in the giant panda (Ailuropoda melanoleuca). *Journal of Comparative Psychology, 123,* 275–279. https://doi.org/10.1037/a0016220

Perdue, Bonnie M.; Snyder, Rebecca J.; Wilson, Megan L.; & Maple, Terry L. (2013). Giant panda welfare in captivity. *Journal of Applied Animal Welfare Science, 16,* 394–395. https://doi.org/10.1080/10888705.2013.827944

Pernet, Cyril R.; McAleer, Phil; Latinus, Marianne; Gorgolewski, Krzysztof J.; Charest, Ian; Bestelmeyer, Patricia E. G.; Watson, Rebecca H.; Fleming, David; Crabbe, Frances; Valdes- Sosa, Mitchell; & Belin, Pascal. (2015). The human voice areas: Spatial organization and inter-individual variability in temporal and extra-temporal cortices. *NeuroImage, 119,* 164–174. https://doi.org/10.1016/j.neuroimage.2015.06.050

Perogamvros, Lampros; Castelnovo, Anna; Samson, David; & Dang-Vu, Thien Thanh. (2020). Failure of fear extinction in insomnia: An evolutionary perspective. *Sleep Medicine Reviews, 51.* https://doi.org/10.1016/j.smrv.2020.101277

Perret-Clermont, Anne-Nelly, & Barrelet, Jean-Marc. (2008). *Jean Piaget and Neuchatel: The learner and the scholar.* Psychology Press.

Perrotta, Valentina; Graffeo, Michele; Bonini, Nicolao; & Gottfried, Jay A. (2016). The putative chemosignal androstadienone makes women more generous. *Journal of Neuroscience, Psychology, and Economics, 9,* 89–99. https://doi.org/10.1037/npe0000055

Perry, Gina. (2013). *Behind the shock machine: The untold story of the notorious Milgram psychology experiment.* Scribe.

Perry, Gina. (2018). *The lost boys: Inside Muzafer Sherif's Robbers Cave experiment.* Scribe Publications.

Perry, Jennifer L., & Dess, Nancy K. (2012). Laboratory animal research ethics: A practical, educational approach. In Samuel J. Knapp, Michael C. Gottlieb, Mitchell M. Handelsman, Leon D. VandeCreek (Eds.), *APA handbook of ethics in psychology, Vol. 2: Practice, teaching, and research.* American Psychological Association. https://doi.org/10.1037/13272-020

Perry, Lynn K.; Smith, Linda B.; & Hockema, Stephen A. (2008). Representational momentum and children's sensori-motor representations of objects. *Developmental Science, 11*(3), F17–F23.

Pervin, Lawrence A. (1994). A critical analysis of current trait theory. *Psychological Inquiry, 5,* 103–113.

Pesant, Nicholas, & Zadra, Antonio. (2004). Working with dreams in therapy: What do we know and what should we do? *Clinical Psychology Review, 24,* 489–512.

Pescosolido, Bernice, A.; Medina, Tait R.; Martin, Jack K.; & Long, J. S. (2013). The "backbone" of stigma: Identifying the global core of public prejudice associated with mental illness. *American Journal of Public Health, 103,* 853-860. https://doi.org/10.2105/AJPH.2012.301147

Pessoa, Luiz, & Adolphs, Ralph. (2010). Emotion processing and the amygdala: From a 'low road' to 'many roads' of evaluating biological significance. *Nature Reviews Neuroscience, 11,* 773–782.

Petersen, Ronald C. (2002). *Mayo Clinic on Alzheimer's disease.* Mayo Clinic Press.

Peterson, Christopher. (2006). *A primer in positive psychology.* Oxford University Press.

Peterson, Christopher, & Park, Nansook. (2007). Explanatory style and emotion regulation. In James J. Gross (Ed.), *Handbook of emotion regulation.* Guilford.

Peterson, Christopher, & Steen, Tracy A. (2009). Optimistic explanatory style. In Shane J. Lopez & C. R. Snyder (Eds.), *Oxford handbook of positive psychology* (2nd ed.). Oxford University Press.

Peterson, Jillian K.; Skeem, Jennifer; Kennealy, Patrick; Bray, Beth; & Zvonkovic, Andrea. (2014). How often and how consistently do symptoms directly precede criminal behavior among offenders with mental illness? *Law and Human Behavior, 38,* 439–449. https://doi.org/10.1037/lhb0000075

Peterson, Lloyd R., & Peterson, Margaret J. (1959). Short-term retention of individual items. *Journal of Experimental Psychology, 58,* 193–198.

Petitto, Laura Ann; Holowka, Siobhan; Sergio, Lauren E.; Levy, Bronna; & Ostry, David J. (2004). Baby hands that move to the rhythm of language: Hearing babies acquiring sign languages babble silently on the hands. *Cognition, 93,* 43–73.

Petitto, Laura Ann; Holowka, Siobhan; Sergio, Lauren E.; & Ostry, David. (2001). Language rhythms in baby hand movements. *Nature, 413,* 35–36.

Petitto, Laura Ann, & Marentette, Paula F. (1991). Babbling in the manual mode: Evidence for the ontogeny of language. *Science, 251,* 1493–1496.

Petrovic, Predrag. (2010). Placebo analgesia and the brain. In Morten L. Kringelbach & Kent C. Berridge (Eds.), *Pleasures of the brain.* Oxford University Press.

Petrovic, Predrag; Kalso, Eija; Petersson, Karl Magnus; & Ingvar, Martin. (2002, March 1). Placebo and opioid analgesia—Imaging a shared neuronal network. *Science, 295,* 1737–1740. https://doi.org/10.1126/science.1067176

Petrow, Steven. (2016, February 8). Opening up about depression. *The New York Times.* http://nyti.ms/1UYmigk

Petty, Sara; Salame, Clara; Mennella, Julie A.; & Pepino, Marta Y. (2020). Relationship between sucrose taste detection thresholds and preferences in children, adolescents, and adults. *Nutrients, 12.* https://doi.org/10.3390/nu12071918

Peyrot des Gachons, Catherine; Beauchamp, Gary K.; Stern, Robert M.; Koch, Kenneth L.; & Breslin, Paul A. S. (2011). Bitter taste induces nausea. *Current Biology, 21*(7), R247–R248.

Phelan, Julie E., & Rudman, Laurie A. (2010). Reactions to ethnic deviance: The role of backlash in racial stereotype maintenance. *Journal of Personality and Social Psychology, 99*(2), 265–281.

Phelps, Elizabeth A. (2006). Emotion and cognition: Insights from studies of the human amygdala. *Annual Review of Psychology, 57,* 27–53.

Phelps, Elizabeth A.; O'Connor, Kevin J.; Gatenby, J. Christopher; Gore, John C.; Grillon, Christian; & Davis, Michael. (2001). Activation of the left amygdala to a cognitive representation of fear. *Nature Neuroscience, 4,* 437–441. https://doi.org/10.1038/86110

Philipps, Dave. (2015, September 19). In unit stalked by suicide, veterans try to save one another. *The New York Times.* https://www.nytimes.com/2015/09/20/us/marine-battalion-veterans-scarred-by-suicides-turn-to-one-another-for-help.html

Phillips, Deborah A., & Lowenstein, Amy E. (2011). Early care, education, and child development. *Annual Review of Psychology, 62,* 483–500.

Phillips, Michael. (1999). Problems with the polygraph. *Science, 15,* 413.

Phillips, Tommy M. (2008). Age-related differences in identity style: A cross-sectional analysis. *Current Psychology, 27*(3), 205–215.

Phillips, William L. (2011). Cross-cultural differences in visual perception of color, illusions, depth, and pictures. In K. D. Keith (Ed.), *Cross-cultural psychology: Contemporary themes and perspectives* (pp. 160–180). Wiley-Blackwell.

Philpot, Richard; Liebst, Lasse S.; Levine, Mark; Bernasco, Wim; & Lindergaard, Marie R. (2020). Would I be helped? Cross-national CCTV footage shows that intervention is the norm in public conflicts. *American Psychologist, 75*(1), 66–75. https://doi.org/10.1037/amp0000469

Piaget, Jean. (1952). *The origins of intelligence in children* (Margaret Cook, Trans.). International Universities Press.

Piaget, Jean. (1961). The genetic approach to the psychology of thought. *Journal of Educational Psychology, 52*(6), 275–281.

Piaget, Jean. (1971/1993). The epigenetic system and the development of cognitive functions. In Mark H. Johnson, Yuko Munakata, & Rick O. Gilmore (Eds.), *Brain development and cognition: A reader* (pp. 31–38). Blackwell.

Piaget, Jean. (1972). Intellectual evolution from adolescence to adulthood. *Human Development, 15,* 1–12.

Piaget, Jean. (1973). The stages of cognitive development: Interview with Richard I. Evans. In Richard I. Evans (Ed.), *Jean Piaget: The man and his ideas.* Dutton.

Piaget, Jean, & Inhelder, Bärbel. (1958). *The growth of logical thinking from childhood to adolescence: An essay on the construction of formal operational structures* (Anne Parsons & Stanley Milgram, Trans.). Basic Books.

Piaget, Jean, & Inhelder, Bärbel. (1974). *The child's construction of quantities: Conservation and atomism.* Routledge & Kegan Paul.

Pickren, Wade E., & Rutherford, Alexandra. (2010). *A history of modern psychology in context.* John Wiley.

Piernas, Carmen, & Popkin, Barry M. (2011). Increased portion sizes from energy-dense foods affect total energy intake at eating occasions in US children and adolescents: Patterns and trends by age group and sociodemographic characteristics, 1977–2006. *American Journal of Clinical Nutrition, 94,* 1324–1332.

Pietschnig, Jakob; & Voracek, Martin. (2015). One century of global IQ gains: A formal meta-analysis of the Flynn Effect. *Perspectives on Psychological Science, 10,* 282–306.

Pike, Kathleen M., & Borovoy, Amy. (2004). The rise of eating disorders in Japan: Issues of culture and limitations of the model of "Westernization." *Culture, Medicine, and Psychiatry, 28,* 493–531. https://doi.org/10.1007/s11013-004-1066-6

Pillard, Paule. (2017). WHO mental health gap action programme (mhGAP). http://www.who.int/mental_health/mhgap/en/

Pincus, David, & Sheikh, Anees A. (2009). *Imagery for pain relief: A scientifically grounded guidebook for clinicians.* Routledge/Taylor & Francis.

Pingani, Luca; Catellani, Sara; Vecchio, Valeria; Sampogna, Gaia; Ellefson, Sarah; Rigatelli, Marco; Fiorillo, Andrea; Evans-Lacko, Sara; & Corrigan, Patrick. (2016). Stigma in the context of schools: Analysis of the phenomenon of stigma in a population of university students. *BMC Psychiatry, 16,* 29. https://doi.org/10.1186/s12888-016-0734-8

Pinheiro, Andréa P.; Raney, T.J.; Thornton, Laura M.; Fichter, Manfred M.; Berrettini, Wade H.; Goldman, David; Halmi, Katherine A.; Kaplan, Allan S.; Strober, Michael; Treasure, Janet; Woodside, D. Blake; Kaye, Walter H.; & Bulik, Cynthia M. (2010). Sexual functioning in women with eating disorders. *International Journal of Eating Disorders, 43*(2), 123–129. https://doi.org/10.1002/eat.20671

Pinker, Steven. (1994). *The language instinct: How the mind creates language.* Morrow.

Pinker, Steven. (1995). Introduction: Language. In Michael S. Gazzaniga (Ed.), *The cognitive neurosciences.* MIT Press.

Pinker, Steven. (2007). *The stuff of thought: Language as a window into human nature.* Viking.

Piotrowski, Chris, & Armstrong, Terry. (2006). Current recruitment and selection practices: A national survey of Fortune 1000 firms. *North American Journal of Psychology, 8,* 489–496.

Piper, August; Lillevik, Linda; & Kritzer, Roxanne. (2008). What's wrong with believing in repression? A review for legal professionals. *Psychology, Public Policy, and Law, 14*(3), 223–242.

Pittenger, David J. (2005). Cautionary comments regarding the Myers-Briggs Type Indicator. *Consulting Psychology Journal: Practice and Research, 57,* 210–221.

Plaisier, I.; Beekman, A. T. F.; de Bruijn, J. G. M.; de Graaf, R.; ten Have, M.; Smit, J. H.; van Dyck, R.; & Penninx, B. W. J. H. (2008). The effect of social roles on mental health: A matter of quantity or quality? *Journal of Affective Disorders, 111*(2–3), 261–270.

PLAN International. (2018). The state of gender equality for U.S. adolescents. *PLAN International USA.* https://www.planusa.org/full-report-the-state-of-gender-equality-for-us-adolescents

Plant, E. Ashby, & Devine, Patricia G. (2009). The active control of prejudice: Unpacking the intentions guiding control efforts. *Journal of Personality and Social Psychology, 96*(3), 640–652. https://doi.org/10.1037/a0012960

Plassmann, Hilke; O'Doherty, John; Shiv, Baba; & Rangel, Antonio. (2008). Marketing actions can modulate neural representations of experienced pleasantness. *Proceedings of the National Academy of Sciences, 105,* 1050–1054.

Platek, Steven M.; Mohamed, Feroze B.; & Gallup, Gordon G., Jr. (2005). Contagious yawning and the brain. *Cognitive Brain Research, 23,* 448–452.

Plomin, Robert. (2003). General cognitive ability. In Robert Plomin, John C. DeFries, & Peter McGuffin (Eds.), *Behavioral genetics in the postgenomic era.* American Psychological Association.

Plomin, Robert, & Colledge, Essi. (2001). Genetics and psychology: Beyond heritability. *European Psychologist, 6,* 229–240.

Plomin, Robert; DeFries, John C.; Knopik, Valerie S.; & Neiderhiser, Jenae M. (2016). Top 10 replicated findings from behavioral genetics. *Perspectives on Psychological Science, 11*(1), 3–23. https://doi.org/10.1177/1745691615617439

Plomin, Robert; DeFries, John C.; McClearn, Gerald E.; & McGuffin, Peter. (2001). *Behavioral genetics* (4th ed.). Worth.

Plomin, Robert; Owen, Michael J.; & McGuffin, Peter. (1994). The genetic basis of complex human behaviors. *Science, 264*, 1733–1739.

Plomin, Robert, & Spinath, Frank M. (2004). Intelligence: Genetics, genes, and genomics. *Journal of Personality and Social Psychology, 86*, 112–129.

Plotnik, Joshua M.; Lair, Richard; Suphachoksahakun, Wirot; & de Waal, Frans B. M. (2011). Elephants know when they need a helping trunk in a cooperative task. *Proceedings of the National Academy of Sciences, 108*(12), 5116–5121. https://doi.org/10.1073/pnas.1101765108

Plutchik, Robert. (2001). The nature of emotions. *American Scientist, 89*(4), 344–350. https://www.jstor.org/stable/27857503

Pogue-Geile, Michael F., & Yokley, Jessica L. (2010). Current research on the genetic contributors to schizophrenia. *Current Directions in Psychological Science, 19*(4), 214–219. https://doi.org/10.1177/0963721410378490

Polderman, Tinca; Benyamin, Beben; Leeuw, Christiaan; Sullivan, Patrick; Bochoven, Arjen; Visscher, Peter; & Posthuma, Danielle. (2015). Meta-analysis of the heritability of human traits based on fifty years of twin studies. *Nature Genetics,47*, 702–709. https://doi.org/10.1038/ng.3285

Poldrack, Russell A.; Baker, Chris I.; Durnez, Joke; Gorgolewski, Krzysztof J.; Matthews, Paul M.; Munafo, Marcus R.; Nichols, Thomas E.; Poline, Jean-Baptiste; Vul, Edward; & Yarkoni, Tal. (2017). Scanning the horizon: Future challenges for neuroimaging research. *Nature Reviews Neuroscience, 18*, 115–126. https://doi.org/10.1038/nrn.2016.167

Poldrack, Russell A., & Farah, Martha J. (2015). Progress and challenges in probing the human brain. *Nature, 526*, 371–379. https://doi.org/10.1038/nature15692

Poling, Alan; Weetjens, Bart J.; Cox, Christophe; Beyene, Negussie; Bach, Håvard; & Sully, Andrew. (2010). Teaching giant African pouched rats to find landmines: Operant conditioning with real consequences. *Behavior Analysis in Practice, 3*, 19–25.

Polito, Vince, & Stevenson, Richard J. (2019). A systematic study of microdosing psychedelics. *PLOS One.* https://doi.org/10.1371/journal.pone.0211023

Poljac, Edita; Kiesel, Andrea; Koch, Iring; & Müller, Hermann. (2018). New perspectives on human multitasking. *Psychological Research, 82*, 1–3. https://doi.org/10.1007/s00426-018-0970-2

Polk, Thad A., & Newell, Allen. (1995). Deduction as verbal reasoning. *Psychological Review, 102*, 533–566.

Pompili, Maurizio; Murri, Martino B.; Patti, Sara; & Innamorati, Marco. (2016, June 3). The communication of suicidal intentions: A meta-analysis. *Psychological Medicine, 46*(11), 2239–2253. https://doi.org/10.1017/S0033291716000696

Pope, Devin; Price, Joseph; & Wolfers, Justin. (2013). Awareness reduces racial bias. *CESifo Working Paper Series No. 4675.* https://doi.org/10.3386/w19765

Pope, Kenneth S.; Butcher, James N.; & Seelen, Joyce (2006). Assessing malingering and other aspects of credibility. In Kenneth S. Pope, James N. Butcher, & Joyce Seelen (Eds.), *The MMPI, MMPI-2, & MMPI-A in court: A practical guide for expert witnesses and attorneys* (3rd. ed., pp. 129–160); American Psychological Association.

Pope, Kenneth S., & Tabachnick, Barbara G. (1993). Therapists' anger, hate, fear, and sexual feelings: National survey of therapist responses, client characteristics, critical events, formal complaints, and training. *Professional Psychology: Research and Practice, 24*, 142–152.

Population Communications International. (2004). Telling stories, saving lives. http://www.population.org/index.shtml.

Porter, Jess; Craven, Brent; Khan, Rehan M.; Chang, Shao-Ju; Kang, Irene; Judkewitz, Benjamin; Volpe, Jason; Settles, Gary; & Sobel, Noam. (2007). Mechanisms of scent-tracking in humans. *Nature Neuroscience, 10*, 27–29. https://doi.org/10.1038/nn1819

Portrat, Sophie; Barrouillet, Pierre; & Camos, Valérie. (2008). Time-related decay or interference-based forgetting in working memory? *Journal of Experimental Psychology: Learning, Memory, and Cognition, 34*, 1561–1564.

Pos, Alberta E.; Greenberg, Leslie S.; & Elliott, Robert. (2008). Experiential therapy. In Jay L. Lebow (Ed.), *Twenty-first century psychotherapies: Contemporary approaches to theory and practice* (pp. 80–122). Wiley.

Posner, Michael I., & Rothbart, Mary K. (2007). Research on attention networks as a model for the integration of psychological science. *Annual Review of Psychology, 58*, 1–23.

Poulin-Dubois, Diane, & Serbin, Lisa A. (2006). La connaissance des catégories de genre et des stéréotypes sexués chez le jeune enfant. = Infants' knowledge about gender stereotypes and categories. *Enfance, 58*(3), 283–310.

Poushter, Jacob, & Kent, Nicholas. (2020, June 25). The global divide on homosexuality persists. *Pew Research Center.* https://www.pewresearch.org/global/2020/06/25/global-divide-on-homosexuality-persists/

Powell, Lisa M.; Auld, M. Christopher; Chaloupka, Frank J.; O'Malley, Patrick M.; & Johnston, Lloyd D. (2007). Access to fast food and food prices: Relationship with fruit and vegetable consumption and overweight among adolescents. *Advances in Health Economics and Health Services Research, 17*, 23–48. https://europepmc.org/article/med/19548547

Powell, Nelson B.; Riley, Robert W.; & Guilleminault, Christian. (2005). Surgical management of sleep-disordered breathing. In Meir H. Kryger, Thomas Roth, and William C. Dement (Eds.), *Principles and practice of sleep medicine* (4th ed.). Elsevier Saunders.

Powell, Russell A.; Digdon, Nancy; Harris, Ben; & Smithson, Christopher. (2014). Correcting the record on Watson, Rayner, and Little Albert: Albert Barger as "Psychology's Lost Boy." *American Psychologist, 69*, 600–611.

Powers, Pauline M. (2009). Bulimia nervosa. In Robert E. Rakel & Edward T. Bope (Eds.), *Conn's current therapy 2009* (pp. 1115–1117). Saunders Elsevier.

Powley, Terry L. (2009). Hunger. In Gary G. Berntson, John T. Cacioppo (Eds.), *Handbook of neuroscience for the behavioral sciences* (Vol. 2, pp. 659–678). Wiley.

Pratto, Felicia, & Glasford, Demis E. (2008). Ethnocentrism and the value of a human life. *Journal of Personality and Social Psychology, 95*, 1411–1428.

Prescott, Anna T.; Sargent, James D.; & Hull, Jay G. (2017). Metaanalysis of the relationship between violent video game play and physical aggression over time. *Proceedings of the National Academy of Science, 115*(40), 9882-9888. https://doi.org/10.1073/pnas.1611617114

Pressman, Mark R. (2007). Disorders of arousal from sleep and violent behavior: The role of physical contact and proximity. *Sleep, 30*, 1039–1047.

Pressman, Sarah D., & Cohen, Sheldon. (2005). Does positive affect influence health? *Psychological Bulletin, 131*, 925–971.

Pressman, Sarah; Gallagher, Mathew; & Lopez, Shane. (2013). Is the emotion-health connection a "first-world problem"? *Psychological Science, 24*, 544–549. https://doi.org/10.1177/0956797612457382

Preston, John D.; O'Neal, John H.; & Talaga, Mary C. (2008). *Handbook of clinical psychopharmacology for therapists* (5th ed.). New Harbinger.

Preti, George; Cutler, Winnifred B.; Garcia, C. R.; Huggins, G. R.; & Lawley, H. J. (1986). Human axillary secretions influence women's menstrual cycles: The role of donor extract of females. *Hormones and Behavior, 20*, 474–482.

Price, Donald D.; Finniss, Damien G.; & Benedetti, Fabrizio. (2008). A comprehensive review of the placebo effect: Recent advances and current thought. *Annual Review of Psychology, 59*, 565–590. https://doi.org/10.1146/annurev.psych.59.113006.095941

Prieur, Jacques; Pika, Simone; Barbu, Stéphanie; & Blois-Heulin, Catherine. (2016a). A multifactorial investigation of captive chimpanzees' intraspecific gestural laterality. *Animal Behaviour, 116*, 31–43. https://doi.org/10.1016/j.anbehav.2016.03.024

Prieur, Jacques; Pika, Simone; Barbu, Stéphanie; & Blois-Heulin, Catherine. (2016b). Gorillas are right-handed for their most frequent intraspecific gestures. *Animal Behaviour, 118*, 165–170. https://doi.org/10.1016/j.anbehav.2016.06.008

Prochaska, James O., & Norcross, John C. (2014). *Systems of psychotherapy: A transtheoretical analysis* (8th ed.). Cengage Learning.

Proske, Uwe; & Gandevia, Simon. (2016). Proprioception: The sense within. *The Scientist, 30*(9), 36–42.

Pryzgoda, Jayde, & Chrisler, Joan C. (2000). Definitions of gender and sex: The subtleties of meaning. *Sex Roles, 43*, 553–569.

Przybylski, Andrew K.; Deci, Edward L.; Rigby, C. Scott; & Ryan, Richard M. (2014). Competence-impeding electronic games and players' aggressive feelings, thoughts, and behaviors. *Journal of Personality and Social Psychology, 106*, 441–457. https://doi.org/10.1037/a0034820

Psaltis, Charis; Duveen, Gerard; & Perret-Clermont, Anne-Nelly. (2009). The social and the psychological: Structure and context in intellectual development. *Human Development, 52*(5), 291–312.

Pujol, Jesus; Soriano-Mas, Carles; Gispert, Juan D.; Bossa, Matias; Reig, Santiago; Ortiz, Hector; Alonso, Pino; Cardoner, Narcís; López-Solà, Marina; Harrison, Ben J.; Deus, Joan; Menchón, José M.; Desco, Manuel; & Olmos, Salvador. (2011). Variations in the shape of frontobasal brain region in obsessive–compulsive disorder. *Human Brain Mapping, 32*(7), 1100–1108. https://doi.org/10.1002/hbm.21094

Purkey, William Watson, & Stanley, Paula Helen. (2002). The self in psychotherapy. In David J. Cain & Julius Seeman (Eds.), *Humanistic psychotherapies: Handbook of research and practice.* American Psychological Association.

Purves, Dale. (2009). Vision. In Gary G. Berntson & John T. Cacioppo (Eds.), *Handbook of neuroscience in the behavioral sciences.* Wiley.

Puterman, Eli; Lin, Jue; Blackburn, Elizabeth; O'Donovan, Aoife; Adler, Nancy; & Epel, Elissa. (2010). The power of exercise: Buffering the effect of chronic stress on telomere length. *PLOS ONE, 5*, e10837.

Puterman, Eli; Lin, Jue; Krauss, John; Blackburn, Elizabeth; & Epel, Elissa. (2015). Determinants of telomere attrition over 1 year in healthy older women: Stress and health behaviors matter. *Molecular Psychiatry,20*(4), 529–535. https://doi.org/10.1038/mp.2014.70

Pyc, Mary A., & Rawson, Katherine A. (2010, October 15). Why testing improves memory: Mediator effectiveness hypothesis. *Science, 330*, 335. https://doi.org/10.1126/science.1191465

Qin, Ping. (2011). The impact of psychiatric illness on suicide: Differences by diagnosis of disorders and by sex and age of subjects. *Journal of Psychiatric Research, 45*(11), 1445–1452. https://doi.org/10.1016/j.jpsychires.2011.06.002

Qiu, Lin; Lu, Jiahui; Yang, Shanshan; Qu, Weina; & Zhu, Tiangshao. (2015). What does your selfie say about you? *Computers in Human Behavior,52*, 443–449.

Quadflieg, Suzanne, & Penton-Voak, Ian S. (2017). The emerging science of people-watching: Forming impressions from third-party encounters. *Current Directions in Psychological Science, 26,* 383–389. https://doi.org/10.1177/0963721417694353

Quaglia, Jordan T.; Brown, Kirk Warren; Lindsay, Emily K.; Creswell, J. David; & Goodman, Robert J. (2015). From conceptualization to operationalization of mindfulness. In Kirk Warren Brown, J. David Creswell, & Richard M. Ryan (Eds.), *Handbook of mindfulness: Theory, research, and practice.* Guilford.

Queller, Sarah, & Mason, Winter. (2008). A decision bound categorization approach to the study of subtyping of atypical group members. *Social Cognition, 26*(1), 66–101.

Quenk, Naomi. L. (2009). *Essentials of Myers-Briggs type indicator assessment.* Wiley.

Quiles Marcos, Yolanda; Quiles Sebastián, María José; Pamies Aubalat, Lidia; Botella Ausina, Juan; & Treasure, Janet. (2013). Peer and family influence in eating disorders: A meta-analysis. *European Psychiatry, 28*(4), 199–206. https://doi.org/10.1016/j.eurpsy.2012.03.005

Quill, Elizabeth. (2015, May). This stroke of genius could allow you to write with your brain. *Smithsonian Magazine.* Retrieved from http://www.smithsonianmag.com/innovation/stroke-genius-could-allow-write-brain-180954961/

Quinn, Meghan E., & Joormann, Jutta. (2015). Stress-induced changes in executive control are associated with depression symptoms: Examining the role of rumination. *Clinical Psychological Science, 3*(4), 628–636. https://doi.org/10.1177/2167702614563930

Quinn, Susan. (2019). *A mind of her own: The life of Karen Horney.* Plunkett Lake Press.

Quintana, Stephen M.; & Bernal, Martha E. (1995). Ethnic minority training in counseling psychology: Comparisons with clinical psychology and proposed standards. *The Counseling Psychologist, 23*(1), 102–121. https://doi.org/10.1177/0011000095231010

Qureshi, Adil. (2020). Cultural competence in psychotherapy. In Meryam Schouler-Ocak & Marianne Kastrup (Eds.) *Intercultural psychotherapy: For immigrants, refugees, asylum seekers and ethnic minority patients* (pp. 119–130). Springer. https://doi.org/10.1007/978-3-030-24082-0_9

Rabgay, Karma; Waranuch, Neti; Chaiyakunapruk, Nathorn; Sawangjit, Ratree; Ingkaninan, Kornkanok; & Dilokthornsakul, Piyameth.(2020). The effects of cannabis, cannabinoids, and their administration routes on pain control efficacy and safety: A systematic review and network meta-analysis. *Journal of the American Pharmacists Association, 60*(1), 225–234. https://doi.org/10.1016/j.japh.2019.07.015

Rabinowitz, Amanda R.; Li, Xiaoqi; & Levin, Harvey S. (2014). Sport and nonsport etiologies of mild traumatic brain injury: Similarities and differences. *Annual Review of Psychology, 65,* 301–331. https://doi.org/10.1146/annurev-psych-010213-115103

Raboteg-Saric, Zora, & Sakic, Marija. (2014). Relations of parenting styles and friendship quality to self-esteem, life satisfaction and happiness in adolescents. *Applied Research Quality Life, 9,* 749–765. https://doi.org/10.1007/s11482-013-9268-0

Raby, Caroline R.; Alexis, Dean M.; Dickinson, Anthony; & Clayton, Nicola S. (2007). Planning for the future by western scrub-jays. *Nature, 445,* 919–921. https://doi.org/10.1038/nature05575

Rachlin, Howard. (1974). Self-control. *Behaviorism, 2,* 94–107.

Rachlin, Howard. (2000). *The science of self-control.* Harvard University Press.

Rad, Mostafa Salari; Martingano, Alison Jane; Ginges, Jeremy. (2018). Toward a psychology of *Homo sapiens*: Making psychological science more representative of the human population. *Proceedings of the National Academy of Sciences, 115*(45). 11401–11405. https://doi.org/10.1073/pnas.1721165115

Radulescu, Anca R., & Mujica-Parodi, Lilianne R. (2013). Human gender differences in the perception of conspecific alarm chemosensory cues. *PLOS ONE, 8,* e68485. https://doi.org/10.1371/journal.pone.0068485

Rafaeli, E., Cranford, J. A., Green, A. S., Shrout, P. E.; & Bolger, N. (2008). The good and bad of relationships: How social hindrance and social support affect relationship feelings in daily life. *Personality and Social Psychology Bulletin, 34,* 1703–1718.

Raghavan, Manish; Barocas, Solon; Kleinberg, Jon; & Levy, Karen. (2020). Mitigating bias in algorithmic hiring: Evaluating claims and practices. In *Proceedings of the 2020 Conference on Fairness, Accountability, and Transparency (FAT* '20),* (pp. 469–481). Association for Computing Machinery. https://doi.org/10.1145/3351095.3372828

Rahal, Danny; Huynh, Virginia; Cole, Steve; Seeman, Teresa; & Fuligni, Andrew. (2020). Subjective social status and health during high school and young adulthood. *Developmental Psychology, 56*(6), 1220–1232. https://doi.org/10.1037/dev0000919

Rahe, Richard H. (1972). Subjects' recent life changes and their nearfuture illness reports. *Annals of Clinical Research, 4,* 250–265.

Rahim-Williams, Bridgett; Riley, Joseph L. III; Williams, Ameenah K. K.; & Fillingim, Roger B. (2012). A quantitative review of ethnic group differences in experimental pain response: Do biology, psychology, and culture matter? *Pain Medicine, 13,* 522–540.

Raichle, Marcus E. (2015). The brain's default mode network. *Annual Review of Neuroscience, 38,* 433–447. https://doi.org/10.1146/annurev-neuro-071013-014030

Raj, John Dilip; Nelson, John Abraham; & Rao, K. S. P. (2006). A study on the effects of some reinforcers to improve performance of employees in a retail industry. *Behavior Modification, 30,* 848–866.

Ramachandran, Vilayanur S. (1992a, May). Blind spots. *Scientific American, 266,* 86–91.

Ramachandran, Vilayanur S. (1992b). Filling in gaps in perception: Part 1. *Current Directions in Psychological Science, 1,* 199–205.

Ramachandran, Vilayanur S.; & Hubbard, Edward M. (2001). Synaesthesia: A window into perception, thought and language. *Journal of Consciousness Studies, 8,* 3–34. http://chip.ucsd.edu/pdf/Synaesthesia%20-%20JCS.pdf

Ranehill, Eva; Dreber, Anna; Johannesson, Magnus; Leiberg, Susanne; Sul, Sunhae; & Weber, Roberto A. (2015). Assessing the robustness of power posing: No effect on hormones and risk tolerance in a large sample of men and women. *Psychological Science, 26,* 653–656. https://doi.org/10.1177/0956797614553946

Rao, Meenakshi & Gershon, Michael D. (2016). The bowel and beyond: The enteric nervous system in neurological disorders. *Nature Reviews Gastroenterology & Hepatology, 13,* 517–528. https://doi.org/10.1038/nrgastro.2016.107

Rapoport, Judith L. (1989). *The boy who couldn't stop washing: The experience and treatment of obsessive-compulsive disorder.* Dutton.

Rapoport, Roger. (2020, December 23). 'Every day is an emergency': The pandemic is worsening psychiatric bed shortages nationwide. *Stat News.* https://www.statnews.com/2020/12/23/mental-health-covid19-psychiatric-beds/

Rascoe, Rachel. (2018, September 7). How a genetic disorder drove Abby Solomon to the forefront of science and music. https://www.austinchronicle.com/music/2018-09-07/how-a-genetic-disorder-drove-abby-solomon-to-the-forefront-of-science-and-music/

Raskin, Nathaniel J., & Rogers, Carl R. (2005). Person-centered therapy. In Raymond J. Corsini & Danny Wedding (Eds.), *Current psychotherapies* (7th ed., instr. ed., pp. 130–165). Thomson Brooks/Cole.

Rasmussen, Keith G. (2009). Evidence for electroconvulsive therapy efficacy in mood disorders. In Conrad M. Swartz (Ed.), *Electroconvulsive and neuromodulation therapies* (pp. 109–123). Cambridge University Press.

Ratiu, Peter, & Talos, Ion-Florin. (2004). The tale of Phineas Gage, digitally remastered. *New England Journal of Medicine, 351,* e21. https://doi.org/10.1056/NEJMicm031024

Ravindran, Sandeep. (2016). What sensory receptors do outside of sense organs. *The Scientist,30*(9), 51–57.

Rawson, Nancy E. (2006). Olfactory loss in aging. *Science of Aging Knowledge Environment, 5,* pe6, 106.

Raymond, Jennifer. (2013). Sexist attitudes: Most of us are biased. *Nature, 495*(7439), 33–34.

Raz, Amir. (2009). Varieties of attention: A research-magician's perspective. In G. Bernston & J. Cacioppo (Eds.), *Handbook of neuroscience for the behavioural sciences* (pp. 361–369). Wiley.

Read, John; & Davies, James. (2019, January 30). The international antidepressant withdrawal crisis: Time to act. *Psychiatric Times.* https://www.psychiatrictimes.com/view/international-antidepressant-withdrawal-crisis-time-act

Reader, Simon M., & Biro, Dora. (2010). Experimental identification of social learning in wild animals. *Learning & Behavior, 38,* 265–283.

Reader, Simon M.; Kendal, Jeremy R.; & Laland, Kevin N. (2003). Social learning of foraging sites and escape routes in wild Trinidadian guppies. *Animal Behaviour, 66,* 729–739.

Recanzone, Gregg H.; & Sutter, Mitchell L. (2008). The biological basis of audition. *Annual Review of Psychology, 59,* 119–142.

Reece, Andrew G.; & Danforth, Christopher M. (2017). Instagram photos reveal predictive markers of depression. *EPJ Data Science, 6.* https://doi.org/10.1140/epjds/s13688-017-0110-z

Reece, Andrew G.; Reagan, Andrew J.; Lix, Katharina L.M.; Dodds, Peter S.; Danforth, Christopher M.; & Langer, Ellen J. (2017, October 11). Forecasting the onset and course of mental illness with Twitter data. *Scientific Reports, 7,* 13006. https://doi.org/10.1038/s41598-017-12961-9

Reece, Michael; Herbenick, Debra; Schick, Vanessa; Sanders, Stephanie A.; Dodge, Brian; & Fortenberry, J. Dennis. (2010). Sexual behaviors, relationships, and perceived health among adult men in the United States: Results from a national probability sample. *Journal of Sexual Medicine, 7,* 291–304. https://doi.org/10.1111/j.1743-6109.2010.02009.x

Rego, Simon A. (2009). Culture and anxiety disorders. In Sussie Eshun & Regan A. R. Gurung (Eds.), *Culture and mental health: Sociocultural influences, theory, and practice* (pp. 197–220). Wiley-Blackwell.

Reiber, Chris, & Garcia, Justin R. (2010). Hooking up: Gender differences, evolution, and pluralistic ignorance. *Evolutionary Psychology 8*(3), 390–404.

Reich, Stephanie M.; Black, Rebecca W.; & Foliaki, Tammie. (2018). Constructing difference: Lego® set narratives promote stereotypic gender roles and play. *Sex Roles, 79,* 285–298. https://doi.org/10.1007/s11199-017-0868-2

Reid, Pamela Trotman; Cooper, Shauna M.; & Banks, Kira Hudson. (2008). Girls to women: Developmental theory, research, and issues. In Florence L. Denmark & Michele A. Paludi (Eds.). *Psychology of women: A handbook of issues and theories* (2nd ed.). Praeger/Greenwood.

Reidy, Dennis; Berke, Danielle; Gentile, Brittany; & Zeichner, Amos. (2016). Masculine discrepancy stress, substance use, assault and injury in a survey of US men. *Injury Prevention, 22,* 370–374. https://doi.org/10.1136/injuryprev-2015-041599

Reiff, Collin M.; Richman, Elon E.; Nemeroff, Charles B.; Carpenter, Linda L.; Widge, Alik S.; Rodriguez, Carolyn I.; Kalin, Ned H.; & McDonald, William M. (2020). Psychedelics and psychedelic-assisted psychotherapy: Clinical implications. *The American Journal of Psychiatry, 177*(5), 391–410. https://doi.org/10.1176/appi.ajp.2019.19010035

Reilly, David; Neumann, David L.; & Andrews, Glenda. (2015). Sex differences in mathematics and science achievement: A meta-analysis of National Assessment of Educational Progress Assessments. *Journal of Educational Psychology, 107*(3), 645–662. https://doi.org/10.1037/edu0000012

Reilly, Michael J.; Tomsic, Jaclyn A.; Fernandez, Stephen J.; & Davison, Steven, P. (2015). Effect of facial rejuvenation surgery on perceived attractiveness, femininity, and personality. *JAMA Facial Plastic Surgery, 17*, 202–207. https://doi.org/10.1001/jamafacial.2015.0158

Reis, Elizabeth. (2004). Teaching transgender history, identity, and politics. *Radical History Review, 88*, 166–177. https://doi.org/10.1215/01636545-2004-88-166

Reis, Elizabeth. (2007). Divergence or disorder?: The politics of naming intersex. *Perspectives in Biology and Medicine, 50*(4), 535-543. https://doi.org/10.1353/pbm.2007.0054

Reis, Harry T.; Maniacci, Michael R.; Caprariello, Peter A.; Eastwick, Paul W.; & Finkel, Eli J. (2011). Familiarity does indeed promote attraction in live interaction. *Journal of Personality and Social Psychology, 101*, 557–570. https://doi.org/10.1037/a0022885

Reisenzein, Rainer. (1983). The Schachter theory of emotion: Two decades later. *Psychological Bulletin, 94*, 239–264.

Reisenzein, Rainer. (2015). A short history of psychological perspectives of emotion. In Rafael A. Calvo, Sidney K. D'Mello, Jonathan Gratch, & Arvid Kappas (Eds.), *The Oxford handbook of affective computing.* Oxford University Press. https://doi.org/10.1093/oxfordhb/9780199942237.013.014

Reisenzein, Rainer. (2017). The legacy of cognitive arousal theory. *Emotion Review, 9*, 3–6. https://doi.org/10.1177/1754073916662551

Reisenzein, Rainer, & Stephan, Achim. (2014). More on James and the physical basis of emotion. *Emotion Review, 6*, 35–46. https://doi.org/10.1177/1754073913501395

Reissig, Chad J.; Strain, Eric C.; & Griffiths, Roland R. (2009). Caffeinated energy drinks: A growing problem. *Drug and Alcohol Dependence, 99*, 1–10.

Ren, Zhiting; Shi, Liang; Wei, Dongtao; & Qiu, Jiang. (2019). Brain functional basis of subjective well-being during negative facial emotion processing task-based fMRI. *Neuroscience, 423*, 177–191. https://doi.org/10.1016/j.neuroscience.2019.10.017

Renk, Kimberly; Donnelly, Reesa; McKinney, Cliff; & Agliata, Allison Kanter. (2006). The development of gender identity: Timetables and influences. In Kam-Shing Yip (Ed.), *Psychology of gender identity: An international perspective.* Nova Science.

Renshaw, Keith D.; Steketee, Gail; Rodrigues, Camila S.; & Caska, Catherine M. (2010). Obsessive–compulsive disorder. In J. Gayle Beck (Ed.), *Interpersonal processes in the anxiety disorders: Implications for understanding psychopathology and treatment* (pp. 153–177). American Psychological Association.

Repetti, Rena; Wang, Shu-wen; & Saxbe, Darby. (2009). Bringing it all back home: How outside stressors shape families' everyday lives. *Current Directions in Psychological Science, 18*(2), 106–111.

Rescorla, Robert A. (1968). Probability of shock in the presence and absence of CS in fear conditioning. *Journal of Comparative and Physiological Psychology, 66*, 1–5.

Rescorla, Robert A. (1980). Pavlovian second-order conditioning: Studies in associative learning. Erlbaum.

Rescorla, Robert A. (1988). Pavlovian conditioning: It's not what you think it is. *American Psychologist, 43*, 151–160.

Rescorla, Robert A. (2001). Retraining of extinguished Pavlovian stimuli. *Journal of Experimental Psychology: Animal Behavior Processes, 27*, 115–124.

Rescorla, Robert A. (2003). Contemporary study of Pavlovian conditioning. *The Spanish Journal of Psychology, 6*(2), 185–195.

Rest, James R. (1983). Morality. In Paul H. Mussen, John H. Flavell, & Ellen M. Markman (Eds.), *Handbook of child psychology* (4th ed., Vol. 3). Wiley.

Rétey, Julia V.; Adam, Martin; Honegger, E. Katharina; Khatami, Ramin; Luhmann, U. F. O.; Jung, H. H.; Berger, W.; & Landolt, Hans-Peter. (2005). A functional genetic variation of adenosine deaminase affects the duration and intensity of deep sleep in humans. *Proceedings of the National Academy of Sciences, 102*, 15676–15681.

Reuters. (1982, Oct. 10). Anna Freud, psychoanalyst, dies in London at 86. *The New York Times.* https://www.nytimes.com/1982/10/10/world/anna-freud-psychoanalyst-dies-in-london-at-86.html

Revelle, William. (1995). Personality processes. *Annual Review of Psychology, 46*, 295–328, 467.

Revelle, William. (2007). Experimental approaches to the study of personality. In Richard W. Robins, R. Chris Fraley, & Robert F. Krueger (Eds.), *Handbook of research methods in personality psychology* (pp. 37–61). Guilford.

Reynolds, Megan. (2017, March 21). Police: No one reported Chicago teen's sexual assault which streamed on Facebook Live. *Jezebel.* http://jezebel.com/police-no-one-reported-chicago-teens-sexual-assault-wh-1793508939

Rhodes, Marjorie, & Chalik, Lisa. (2013). Social categories as markers of intrinsic interpersonal obligations. *Psychological Science, 24*, 999–1006. https://doi.org/10.1177/0956797612466267

Rhue, Judith W. (2010). Clinical hypnosis with children. In Steven Jay Lynn, Judith W. Rhue, & Irving Kirsch (Eds.), *Handbook of clinical hypnosis* (2nd ed.), (pp. 467–491). American Psychological Association.

Riby, Leigh Martin; Smallwood, Jonathan; & Gunn, Valerie P. (2008). Mind wandering and retrieval from episodic memory: A pilot event-related potential study. *Psychological Reports, 102*, 805–818.

Ricard, Matthieu. (2010). *Why meditate? Working with thoughts and emotions.* Hay House.

Ricard, Matthieu; Lutz, Antoine; & Davidson, Richard J. (2014, November). Mind of the meditator. *Scientific American, 311*, 38–45. https://doi.org/10.1038/scientificamerican1114-38

Riccio, David C.; Millin, Paula M.; & Gisquet-Verrier, Pascale. (2003). Retrograde amnesia: Forgetting back. *Current Directions in Psychological Science, 12*, 41–44.

Rich, Josiah D.; Green, Traci C.; & McKenzie, Michelle S. (2011). Opioids and deaths. *New England Journal of Medicine, 364*(7), 686. https://doi.org/10.1056/NEJMc1014490

Richardson, L. Song. (2015). Police racial violence: Lessons from social psychology. *Fordham Law Review, 6*, 2961–2976.

Richardson, Michelle; Abraham, Charles; & Bond, Rod. (2012). Psychological correlates of university students' academic performance: A systematic review and meta-analysis. *Psychological Bulletin, 138*, 353–387. https://doi.org/10.1037/a0026838

Richardson, Robert D. (2006). *William James: In the maelstrom of American modernism.* Houghton Mifflin.

Richarz, Allan. (2018, May 22). *The amazing psychology of Japanese train stations.* CityLab. https://www.citylab.com/transportation/2018/05/the-amazing-psychology-of-japanese-train-stations/560822/

Richtand, Neil M.; Welge, Jeffrey A.; & Logue, Aaron D. (2007, August). Dopamine and serotonin receptor binding and antipsychotic efficacy. *Neuropsychopharmacology, 32*, 1715–1726.

Riding-Malon, Ruth, & Werth, James L., Jr. (2014). Psychological practice in rural settings: At the cutting edge. *Professional Psychology: Research and Practice, 45*, 85–91. https://doi.org/10.1037/a0036172

Ridolfo, Heather; Baxter, Amy; Lucas, Jeffrey W. (2010). Social influences on paranormal belief: Popular versus scientific support. *Current Research in Social Psychology, 15*, 33–41.

Rieger, Gerulf; Chivers, Meredith L.; & Bailey, J. Michael. (2005). Sexual arousal patterns of bisexual men. *Psychological Science, 16*, 579–584.

Rieger, Gerulf; Linsenmeier, Joan A. W.; & Gygax, Lorenz. (2008, January). Sexual orientation and childhood gender nonconformity: Evidence from home videos. *Developmental Psychology, 44*(1), 46–58.

Riener, Cedar, & Willingham, Daniel. (2010, September/October). The myth of learning styles. *Change, 42*, 32–35.

Riggio, Richard E., & Reichard, Rebecca J. (2008). The emotional and social intelligences of effective leadership: An emotional and social skill approach. *Journal of Managerial Psychology, 23*, 169–185.

Riley, J. R.; Greggers, U.; Smith, A. D.; Reynolds, D. R.; & Menzel, R. (2005). The flight paths of honeybees recruited by the waggle dance. *Nature, 435*, 205–207.

Riley, Kathryn P.; Snowdon, David A.; Desrosiers, Mark F.; & Markesbery, William R. (2005). Early life linguistic ability, late life cognitive function, and neuropathology: Findings from the Nun Study. *Neurobiology of Aging, 26*, 341–317.

Ringach, Dario L. (2009). Wiring of receptive fields and functional maps in primary visual cortex. In Michael S. Gazzaniga (Ed.), *The cognitive neurosciences* (4th ed.). MIT Press.

Risen, Jane, & Gilovich, Thomas. (2007). Informal logical fallacies. In Robert J. Sternberg, Henry Roediger III, & Diane F. Halpern (Eds.), *Critical thinking in psychology.* Cambridge University Press.

Ristic, Jelena, & Enns, James T. (2015). The changing face of attentional development. *Current Directions in Psychological Science, 24*, 24–31. https://doi.org/10.1177/0963721414551165

Ritchie, Stuart J., & Tucker-Drob, Elliot M. (2018). How much does education research improve intelligence? A meta-analysis. *Psychological Science, 29*(8), 1358–1369. https://doi.org/10.1177/095679761877425

Rivara, Frederick; Adhia, Avanti; Lyons, Vivian; Massey, Anne; Mills, Brianna; Morgan, Erin; Simckes, Maayan; & Rowhani-Rahbar, Ali. (2019). The Effects of violence on health. *Health Affairs, 38*(10), 1622–1629. https://doi.org/10.1377/hlthaff.2019.00480

Rivers, Ian; Poteat, V. Paul; & Noret, Nathalie. (2008). Victimization, social support, and psychosocial functioning among children of same-sex and opposite-sex couples in the United Kingdom. *Developmental Psychology, 44*, 127–134.

Rizzolatti, Giacomo; Fadiga, Luciano; Matelli, Massimo; Bettinardi, Valentino; Paulesu, Eraldo; Perani, Daniela; & Fazio, Ferruccio. (1996). Localization of grasp representations in humans by PET: 1. Observation versus execution. *Experimental Brain Research, 111*(2), 246–252. https://doi.org/10.1007/BF00227301

Rizzolatti, Giacomo, & Sinigaglia, Corrado. (2016). The mirror mechanism: A basic principle of brain function. *Nature Reviews Neuroscience, 17*, 757–765. https://doi.org/10.1038/nrn.2016.135

Roach, Gregory D., & Sargent, Charli. (2019). Interventions to minimize jet lag after westward and eastward flight. *Frontiers in Physiology, 10.* https://doi.org/10.3389/fphys2019.00927

Roazen, Paul. (1999). *Freud: Political and social thought.* Transaction.

Roazen, Paul. (2000). *The historiography of psychoanalysis.* Transaction.

Robbins, Nicolette; Low, Kathryn; & Query, Anna. (2016). A qualitative exploration of the "coming out" process for asexual individuals. *Archives of Sexual Behavior, 45,* 751–760. https://doi.org/10.1007/s10508-015-0561-x

Roberts, Brent W.; Kuncel, Nathan R.; Shiner, Rebecca; Caspi, Avshalom; & Goldberg, Lewis R. (2007). The power of personality: The comparative validity of personality traits, socioeconomic status, and cognitive ability for predicting important life outcomes. *Perspectives on Psychological Science, 2*(4), 313–345. https://doi.org/10.1111/j.1745-6916.2007.00047.x

Roberts, Brent W.; Luo, Jing; Briley, Daniel A.; Chow, Philip I., Su, Rong; & Hill, Patrick L. (2017). A systematic review of personality trait change through intervention. *Psychological Bulletin, 143*(2), 117–141. https://doi.org/10.1037/bul0000088

Roberts, Brent W.; Walton, Kate E.; & Viechtbauer, Wolfgang. (2006). Patterns of mean-level change in personality traits across the life course: A meta-analysis of longitudinal studies. *Psychological Bulletin, 132*(1), 1–25.

Roberts, Brent W.; Wood, Dustin; & Smith, Jennifer L. (2005). Evaluating Five Factor Theory and social investment perspectives on personality trait development. *Journal of Research in Personality, 39,* 166–184. https://doi.org/10.1016/j.jrp.2004.08.002

Roberts, Gary. (2019). Fostering workplace well-being through servant leadership. In: Dhiman S. (Ed) *The Palgrave Handbook of Workplace Well-Being.* Palgrave Macmillan. https://doi.org/10.1007/978-3-030-02470-3_9-1

Roberts, P. M. (2003). Performance of Canadian adults on the Graded Naming Test. *Aphasiology, 17,* 933–946.

Roberts, Sam. (2020, September 2). Sophia Farrar dies at 92: Belied indifference to Kitty Genovese attack. *The New York Times.* https://www.nytimes.com/2020/09/02/nyregion/sophia-farrar-dead.html

Roberts, William A., & Macpherson, Krista. (2016). Of dogs and men. *Current Directions in Psychological Science, 25,* 313–321. https://doi.org/10.1177/0963721416665007

Robillard, Rebecca; Saad, Mysa; Edwards, Jodi; Solomonova, Elizaveta; Pennestri, Marie-Helen; Daros, Alexander; Veissiere, Samuel Paul Louis; Quilty, Lena; Dion, Karianne; Nixon, Ashley; Phillips, Jennifer; Bhatla, Rah; Spilg, Edward; Godbout, R.; Yazji, Bashour; Rushton, Cynda; Gifford, Wendy A.; Gautum, Mamta; Boafo, Addo; Swartz, R.; & Kendzerska, T. (2020). Social, financial and psychological stress during an emerging pandemic: Observations from a population survey in the acute phase of COVID-19. *BMJ Open, 10,* e043805. https://doi.org/10.1136/bmjopen-2020-043805

Robinson, Barbara S.; Davis, Kathleen L.; & Meara, Naomi M. (2003). Motivational attributes of occupational possible selves for low-income rural women. *Journal of Counseling Psychology, 50,* 156–164.

Robinson, David K. (2001). Reaction-time experiments in Wundt's Institute and beyond. In Robert W. Rieber & David K. Robinson (Eds.), *Wilhelm Wundt in history: The making of a scientific psychology.* Kluwer/Plenum.

Robinson, Gail. (2002). Cross-cultural perspectives on menopause. In Anne E. Hunter & Carie Forden (Ed.), *Readings in the psychology of gender: Exploring our differences and commonalities* (pp. 140–149). Allyn & Bacon.

Robinson, Jordan S., & Larson, Christine. (2010). Are traumatic events necessary to elicit symptoms of posttraumatic stress? *Psychological Trauma: Theory, Research, Practice, and Policy, 2*(2), 71–76.

Robinson, Margaret. (2019). Two-spirit identity in a time of gender fluidity. *Journal of Homosexuality,* 1–16. https://doi.org/10.1080/00918369.2019.1613853

Robles, Theodore. (2014). Marital quality and health: Implications for marriage in the 21st century. *Current Directions in Psychological Science, 23*(6), 427–432. https://doi.org/10.1177/0963721414549043

Roca, Miquel; Armengol, Silvia; Garcia-Garcia, Margarida; Rodriguez-Bayon, Antonia; Ballesta, Isabel; Serrano, Maria J.; Comas, Angels; & Gili, Margalida. (2011). Clinical differences between first and recurrent episodes in depressive patients. *Comprehensive Psychiatry, 52*(1), 26–32. https://doi.org/10.1016/j.comppsych.2010.04.011

Rock, Irvin. (1995). *Perception.* Scientific American Library.

Rodafinos, Angelo S.; Vucevic, Arso; & Sideridis, Georgios D. (2005). The effectiveness of compliance techniques: Foot in the door versus door in the face. *Journal of Social Psychology, 145*(2), 237–239.

Rodewald, Frauke; Wilhelm-Gößling, Claudia; Emrich, Hinderk M.; Reddemann, Luise; & Gast, Ursula. (2011). Axis-I comorbidity in female patients with dissociative identity disorder and dissociative identity disorder not otherwise specified. *Journal of Nervous and Mental Disease, 199*(2), 122–131. https://doi.org/10.1097/NMD.0b013e318208314e

Rodin, Judith, & Langer, Ellen. (1977). Long-term effects of a controlrelevant intervention with the institutionalized aged. *Journal of Personality and Social Psychology, 35,* 897–902.

Rodrigues, Ema; Bellinger, David; Valeri, Linda; Hasan, Muhammad; Quamruzzaman, Quazi; Golam, Mostofa; Kile, Molly L.; Christiani, David C.; Wright Robert O.; & Mazumdar, Maitreyi. (2016). Neurodevelopmental outcomes among 2- to 3-year-old children in Bangladesh with elevated blood lead and exposure to arsenic and manganese in drinking water. *Environmental Health.* https://doi.org/10.1186/s12940-016-0127-y

Rodriguez, Cameron. (2017). Personal communication.

Rodriguez-Larralde, Alvaro, & Paradisi, Irene. (2009). [Influence of genetic factors on human sexual orientation. Review]. *Investigacion Clinica, 50*(3), 377–391.

Roediger, Henry L., III. (2008). The cognitive psychology of memory: Introduction. In Henry L. Roediger (Ed.), *Cognitive psychology of memory,* Vol. 2 of *Learning and Memory: A comprehensive reference* (pp. 1–5), J. Byrne, ed. Elsevier.

Roediger, Henry L., III, & Butler, Andrew C. (2011). The critical role of retrieval practice in long-term retention. *Trends in Cognitive Science, 15*(1), 20–27. https://doi.org/10.1016/j.tics.2010.09.003

Roediger, Henry L., III; Finn, Bridgid; & Weinstein, Yana. (2012). Applications of cognitive science to education. In Sergio Della Sala & Mike Anderson (Eds.), Neuroscience in education: The good, the bad, and the ugly. Oxford University Press.

Roediger, Henry L., III, & Karpicke, Jeffrey D. (2006). Test-enhanced learning: Taking memory tests improves long-term retention. *Psychological Science, 17,* 249–255. https://doi.org/10.1111/j.1467-9280.2006.01693.x

Roediger, Henry L., III, & Karpicke, Jeffrey D. (2018). Reflections on the resurgence of interest in the testing effect. *Perspectives on Psychological Science, 13,* 236–241. https://doi.org/10.1177/1745691617718873

Roediger, Henry L., III, & Nestojko, John F. (2015). The relative benefits of studying and testing on long-term retention. In Jeroen G.W. Raaijmakers, Amy H. Criss, Robert L. Goldstone, Robert M. Nosofsky, & Mark Steyvers (Eds.), *Cognitive modeling in perception and memory: A festschrift for Richard M. Shiffrin.* Psychology Press.

Roediger, Henry L., III; Putnam, Adam L.; & Smith, Megan A. (2011). Ten benefits of testing and their applications to educational practice. In Jose P. Mestre & Brian H. Ross (Eds.), *The psychology of learning and motivation (Vol. 55): Cognition in education.* Elsevier. https://doi.org/10.1016/B978-0-12-387691-1.00001-6

Roehrs, Timothy, & Roth, Thomas. (2008). Caffeine: Sleep and daytime sleepiness. *Sleep Medicine Reviews, 12*(2), 153–162.

Roepke, Ann; Jaffee, Sara; Riffle, Olivia; McGonigal, Jane; Broome, Rose; & Maxwell, Bez. (2015). Randomized controlled trial of SuperBetter, a smartphone-based/internet-based self-help tool to reduce depressive symptoms. *Games for Health Journal, 4,* 235–246. https://doi.org/10.1089/g4h.2014.0046

Roese, Neal J., & Vohs, Kathleen D. (2012). Hindsight bias. *Perspectives on Psychological Science, 7*(5), 411–426. https://doi.org/10.1177/1745691612454303

Roetman, Philip; Tindle, Hayley; Litchfield, Carla; Chiera, Belinda; Quinton, Gillian; Kikillus, Heidy; Bruce, David; & Kays, Roland. (2017). Cat tracker South Australia: Understanding pet cats through citizen science. Discovery Circle initiative, University of South Australia, Adelaide. https://doi.org/10.4226/78/5892ce70b245a

Rogers, Carl R. (1951). *Client-centered psychotherapy.* Houghton-Mifflin.

Rogers, Carl R. (1957a). A note on "The Nature of Man." In Howard Kirschenbaum & Valerie Land Henderson (Eds.), *The Carl Rogers reader.* Houghton Mifflin.

Rogers, Carl R. (1957b). A therapist's view of the good life: The fully functioning person. In Howard Kirschenbaum & Valerie Land Henderson (Eds.), *The Carl Rogers reader.* Houghton Mifflin.

Rogers, Carl R. (1957c). The necessary and sufficient conditions of therapeutic personality change. *Journal of Consulting Psychology, 21*(2), 95–103. https://doi.org/10.1037/h0045357

Rogers, Carl R. (1959). A theory of therapy, personality, and interpersonal relationships, as developed in the client-centered framework. In S. Koch (Ed.), *Psychology: A study of a science Vol. 3. Formulations of the person and the social context.* McGraw-Hill.

Rogers, Carl R. (1961). *On becoming a person.* Houghton Mifflin.

Rogers, Carl R. (1964). Toward a modern approach to values: The valuing process in the mature person. In Howard Kirschenbaum & Valerie Land Henderson (Eds.), *The Carl Rogers reader.* Houghton Mifflin.

Rogers, Carl R. (1977). *Carl Rogers on personal power: Inner strength and its revolutionary impact.* Delacorte Press.

Rogers, Carl R. (1980). *A way of being.* Houghton Mifflin.

Rogers, Carl R., (1981/1989). Notes on Rollo May. In Howard Kirschenbaum & Valerie Land Henderson (Eds.), *Carl Rogers: Dialogues.* Houghton Mifflin.

Rogers, Carl R., & Skinner, B. F. (1956, November 30). Some issues concerning the control of human behavior: A symposium. *Science, 124,* 1057–1066.

Rogers, Katie. (2016). Instagram introduces new tools meant to curb abuse and expand privacy. *The New York Times.* http://nyti.ms/2hcGw8q

Rogers, Megan L.; Joiner, Thomas E.; & Shahar, Golan. (2020, October 31). Suicidality in chronic illness: An overview of cognitive-affective and interpersonal factors. *Journal of Clinical Psychology, 28,* 137–148. https://doi.org/10.1007/s10880-020-09749-x

Rogers, Paul; Davis, Tiffany; & Fisk, John. (2009). Paranormal belief and susceptibility to the conjunction fallacy. *Applied Cognitive Psychology, 23*(4), 524–542.

Rogowsky, Beth A.; Calhoun, Barbara M.; & Tallal, Paula. (2015). Matching learning style to instructional method: Effects on comprehension. *Journal of Educational Psychology, 107,* 64–78.https://doi.org/10.1037/a00374

Rohde, Paul; Lewinsohn, Peter M.; Klein, Daniel, N.; Seeley, John R.; & Gau, Jeff M. (2013). Key characteristics of major depressive disorder occurring in childhood, adolescence, emerging adulthood, and adulthood. *Clinical Psychological Science, 1*(1), 41–53. https://doi.org/10.1177/2167702612457599

Roisman, Glenn I.; Clausell, Eric; & Holland, Ashley. (2008, January). Adult romantic relationships as contexts of human development: A multimethod comparison of same-sex couples with opposite-sex dating, engaged, and married dyads. *Developmental Psychology, 44*(1), 91–101.

Romero, Teresa; Konno, Akitsugu; & Hasegawa, Toshikazu. (2013). Familiarity bias and physiological responses in contagious yawning by dogs support link to empathy (2013). *PLOS ONE, 8,* e71365. https://doi.org/10.1371/journal.pone.0071365

Romo, Vanessa. (2019, September 19). Teen charged in fatal stabbing of student that dozens filmed, shared on social media. *National Public Radio.* https://www.npr.org/2019/09/19/762555041/teen-charged-in-fatal-stabbing-of-student-that-dozens-filmed-shared-on-social-me

Ronen, Tammie. (1991). Intervention package for treating sleep disorders in a four-year-old girl. *Journal of Behavior Therapy and Experimental Psychiatry, 22,* 141–148.

Rook, Karen. (2015). Social networks in later life: Weighing positive and negative effects on health and well-being. *Current Directions in Psychological Science, 24*(1), 45–51. https://doi.org/10.1177/0963721414551364

Rook, Karen S.; August, Kristin J.; & Sorkin, Dara H. (2011). Social network functions and health. In Richard J. Contrada & Andrew Baum (Eds.), *The handbook of stress science: Biology, psychology, and health.* Springer.

Rosander, Michael, & Eriksson, Oskar. (2012). Conformity on the Internet—The role of task difficulty and gender differences. *Computers in Human Behavior, 28*(5), 1587–1595. https://doi.org/10.1016/j.chb.2012.03.023

Rosch, Eleanor H. (1978). Principles of categorization. In Eleanor H. Rosch & Barbara B. Lloyd (Eds.), *Cognition and categorization.* Erlbaum.

Rosch, Eleanor H. (1987). Linguistic relativity. *Et Cetera, 44,* 254–279.

Rosch, Eleanor H., & Mervis, Carolyn B. (1975). Family resemblances: Studies in the internal structure of categories. *Cognitive Psychology, 7,* 573–605.

Rose, Jed E.; Behm, Frederique M.; Westman, Eric C.; Mathew, Roy J.; London, Edythe D.; Hawk, Thomas C.; Turkington, Timothy G.; & Coleman, R. Edward. (2003). PET studies of the influences of nicotine on neural systems in cigarette smokers. *American Journal of Psychiatry, 160,* 323–333.

Rose, Steven. (2009). Should scientists study race and IQ? NO: Science and society do not benefit. *Nature, 457,* 786–788.

Rosekind, Mark. (2003, April 8). Quoted in National Sleep Foundation press release, "Sleep is important when stress and anxiety increase, says the National Sleep Foundation." Washington, DC. Retrieved from http://www.sleepfoundation.org/PressArchives/stress.cfm

Rosen, Raymond C., & Bachmann, Gloria A. (2008). Sexual well-being, happiness, and satisfaction, in women: The case for a new conceptual paradigm. *Journal of Sex & Marital Therapy, 34,* 291–297.

Rosenbaum, David A.; Carlson, Richard A.; & Gilmore, Rick O. (2001). Acquisition of intellectual and perceptual-motor skills. *Annual Review of Psychology, 52,* 453–470.

Rosenberg, Oded, & Dannon, Pinhas N. (2009). Transcranial magnetic stimulation. In Conrad M. Swartz (Ed.), *Electroconvulsive and neuromodulation therapies* (pp. 527–542). Cambridge University Press.

Rosenblat, Alex; Kneese, Tamara; & Boyd, Danah. (2014). Workplace surveillance. *Open Society Foundations' Future of Work Commissioned Research Papers 2014.* https://doi.org/10.2139/ssrn.2536605

Rosenblatt, Paul C. (2007). Culture, socialization, and loss, grief, and mourning. In Balk, David; Wogrin, Carol; Thornton, Gordon; Meagher, David (Eds.), *Handbook of thanatology: The essential body of knowledge for the study of death, dying, and bereavement.* Routledge/Taylor & Francis Group.

Rosenfield, Sarah, & Smith, Dena. (2010). Gender and mental health: Do men and women have different amounts or types of problems? In Teresa L. Scheid & Tony N. Brown (Eds.), *A handbook for the study of mental health: Social contexts, theories, and systems (2nd ed.)* Cambridge University Press.

Rosenthal, Abraham M. (1964a, May 3). Study of the sickness called apathy. *The New York Times Magazine,* Sect. VI, pp. 24, 66, 69–72.

Rosenthal, Abraham M. (1964b). *Thirty-eight witnesses.* McGraw-Hill.

Rosenwald, Michael S. (2020, December 23). 'A needle makes my blood run cold': Will the phobic get the coronavirus vaccine? *The Washington Post.* https://www.washingtonpost.com/local/needles-fear-coronavirus-vaccine/2020/12/22/1c554500-408a-11eb-8db8-395dedaaa036_story.html

Rosenzweig, Saul. (1997). Freud's only visit to America. In Wolfgang G. Bringmann, Helmut E. Lück, Rudolf Miller, & Charles E. Early (Eds.), *A pictorial history of psychology.* Quintessence.

Rosielle, Luke J., & Scaggs, W. Jeffrey. (2008). What if they knocked down the library and nobody noticed? The failure to detect large changes to familiar scenes. *Memory, 16,* 115–124.

Ross, Lee. (1977). The intuitive psychologist and his shortcomings: Distortions in the attribution process. In Leonard Berkowitz (Ed.), *Advances in experimental social psychology* (Vol. 10). Academic Press.

Ross, Lee, & Anderson, Craig A. (1982). Shortcomings in the attribution process: On the origins and maintenance of erroneous social assessments. In Daniel Kahneman, Paul Slovic, & Amos Tversky (Eds.), *Judgment under uncertainty: Heuristics and biases.* Cambridge University Press.

Ross, Michael, & Wang, Qi. (2010). Remember: Culture and autobiographical memory. *Perspectives on Psychological Science, 5*(4) 401–409. https://doi.org/10.1177/1745691610375555

Ross, Shannon E.; Niebling, Bradley C.; & Heckert, Teresa M. (1999). Sources of stress among college students. *College Student Journal, 33,* 312–317.

Ross, Stephen; Bossis, Anthony; Guss, Jeffrey; Agin-Liebes, Gabrielle; Malone, Tara; Cohen, Barry; . . . & Schmidt, Brian L. (2016). Rapid and sustained symptom reduction following psilocybin treatment for anxiety and depression in patients with life-threatening cancer: A randomized controlled trial. *Journal of Psychopharmacology, 30,* 1165–1180. https://doi.org/10.1177/0269881116675512

Rosser, Sue V. (2012). *Breaking into the lab: Engineering progress for women in science.* NYU Press.

Rossier, Jerome; Dahourou, Donatien; & McCrae, Robert R. (2005). Structural and mean level analyses of the five-factor model and locus of control: Further evidence from Africa. *Journal of Cross-Cultural Psychology, 36,* 227–246.

Roth, Thomas; Zammit, Gary; Lankford, Alan; Mayleben, David; Stern, Theresa; Pitman, Verne; Clark, David; & Werth, John L. (2010). Nonrestorative sleep as a distinct component of insomnia. *Sleep, 33,* 449–458.

Rothbart, Mary K.; Ahadi, Stephan A.; & Evans, David E. (2000). Temperament and personality: Origins and outcomes. *Journal of Personality and Social Psychology, 78*(1), 122–135. https://doi.org/10.1037/0022-3514.78.1.122

Rothbaum, Fred; Kakinuma, Miki; Nagaoka, Rika; & Azuma, Hiroshi. (2007). Attachment and AMAE: Parent-child closeness in the United States and Japan. *Journal of Cross-Cultural Psychology, 38,* 465–486.

Rothen, Nicolas; & Terhune, Devin B. (2012). Increased resting state network connectivity in synesthesia: Evidence for a neural basis of synesthetic consistency. *Journal of Neuroscience, 32,* 13641–13643. https://doi.org/10.1523/JNEUROSCI.3577-12.2012

Rotheram-Borus, Mary Jane; Swendeman, Dallas; & Chorpita, Bruce F. (2012). Disruptive innovations for designing and diffusing evidence-based interventions. *American Psychologist, 67*(6), 463–476. https://doi.org/10.1037/a0028180

Rothwell, Jonathan. (2019, December 18). Earning income on the side is a large and growing slice of American life. *The New York Times.* https://www.nytimes.com/2019/12/18/upshot/multiple-jobs-united-states.html

Rouder, Jeffrey N.; Morey, Richard D.; Cowan, Nelson; Zwilling, Christopher E.; Morey, Candice C.; & Pratte, Michael S. (2008). An assessment of fixed-capacity models of visual working memory. *Proceedings of the National Academy of Sciences, 105,* 5975–5979.

Rowe, David C. (2003). Assessing genotype-environment interactions and correlations in the postgenomic era. In Robert Plomin, John C. DeFries, Ian W. Craig, & Peter McGuffin (Eds.), *Behavioral genetics in the postgenomic era.* American Psychological Association.

Rowe, Shawn M., & Wertsch, James V. (2002). Vygotsky's model of cognitive development. In Usha Gowsami (Ed.), *Blackwell handbook of childhood cognitive development.* Blackwell.

Rowland, Christopher A. (2014). The effect of testing versus restudy on retention: A meta-analytic review of the testing effect. *Psychological Bulletin, 140,* 1432–1463. https://doi.org/10.1037/a0037559

Rowland, David L., & van Lankveld, Jacques J. D. M. (2019). Anxiety and performance in sex, sport, and stage: Identifying common ground. *Frontiers in Psychology, 10,* 1615.

Rozin, Paul. (1996). The socio-cultural context of eating and food choice. In H. L. Meiselman & H. J. H. MacFie (Eds.), *Food choice, acceptance and consumption.* Blackie Academic and Professional.

Rozin, Paul. (2007). Food and eating. In Shinobu Kitayama & Dov Cohen (Eds.), *Handbook of cultural psychology.* Guilford.

Rubin, Jennifer D.; Atwood, S.; & Olson, Kristina R. (2020). Studying gender diversity. *Trends in Cognitive Sciences, 24*(3), 163-165. https://doi.org/10.1016/j.tics.2019.12.011

Rubio-Fernández, Paula, & Glucksberg, Sam. (2012). Reasoning about other people's beliefs: Bilinguals have an advantage. *Journal of Experimental Psychology: Learning, Memory, and Cognition, 38,* 211–217. https://doi.org/10.1037/a0025162

Ruble, Diane N.; Martin, Carol Lynn; & Berenbaum, Sheri A. (2006). Gender development. In Nancy Eisenberg, William Damon, & Richard M. Lerner (Eds.), *Handbook of Child Psychology: Vol. 3, Social, emotional, and personality development* (6th ed.). Wiley.

Rudman, Laurie A., & Fairchild, Kimberly. (2004). Reactions to counter-stereotypic behavior: The role of backlash in cultural stereotype maintenance. *Journal of Personality and Social Psychology, 87*(2), 157–176.

Rudman, Laurie A., & Glick, Peter. (2012). *Social psychology of gender: How power and intimacy shape gender relations.* Guilford.

Runco, Mark A. (2007). *Creativity: Theories and themes: Research, development, and practice.* Elsevier Academic.

Ruscio, John. (1998, November/December). The perils of post-hockery. *Skeptical Inquirer, 22,* 44–48.

Russac, R. J.; Gatliff, Colleen; Reece, Mimi; & Spottswood, Diahann. (2007). Death anxiety across the adult years: An examination of age and gender effects. *Death Studies, 31*(6), 549–561.

Russell, James A. (1991). Culture and the categorization of emotions. *Psychological Bulletin, 110,* 426–450.

Russell, James A.; Bachorowski, Jo-Anne; & Fernández-Dols, José- Miguel. (2003). Facial and vocal expressions of emotions. *Annual Review of Psychology, 54,* 359–349.

Russell, Nestar John Charles. (2011). Milgram's obedience to authority experiments: Origins and early evolution. *British Journal of Social Psychology, 50,* 140–162. https://doi.org/10.1348/014466610X492205

Russon, Anne E., & Galdikas, Birute M. F. (1995). Constraints on great apes' imitation: Model and action selectivity in rehabilitant orangutan (*Pongo pygmaeus*) imitation. *Journal of Comparative Psychology, 109,* 5–17.

Rutherford, Alexandra. (2012, March). B. F. Skinner: Scientist, celebrity, social visionary. *APS Observer, 25.* http://www.psychologicalscience.org/index.php/publications/observer/2012/march-12/b-f-skinner-scientist-celebrity-social-visionary.html

Rutherford, Bret; Wall, Melanie; Glass, Andrew; & Stewart, Jonathan. (2014). The role of patient expectancy in placebo and nocebo effects in antidepressant trials. *Journal of Clinical Psychiatry, 75,* 1040–1046. https://doi.org/10.4088/JCP.13m08797

Rutledge, Thomas; Linke, Sarah E.; Olson, Marian B.; Francis, Jennifer; Johnson, B. Delia; Bittner, Vera; York, Kaki; McClure, Candace; Kelsey, Sheryl F.; Reis, Steven E.; Cornell, Carol E.; Vaccarino, Viola; Sheps, David S.; Shaw, Leslee J.; Krantz, David J.; Parashar, Susmita; & Merz, C. Noel Bairey. (2008). Social networks and incident stroke among women with suspected myocardial ischemia. *Psychosomatic Medicine, 70*(3), 282–287. https://doi.org/10.1097/PSY.0b013e3181656e09

Rutledge, Thomas; Reis, Steven E.; Olson, Marian; Owens, Jane; Kelsey, Sheryl F.; Pepine, Carl J.; Mankad, Sunil; Rogers, William J.; Merz, C. Noel Bairey; Sopko, George; Cornell, Carol E.; Sharaf, Barry; Matthews, Karen A.; & National Heart, Lung, and Blood Institute. (2004). Social networks are associated with lower mortality rates among women with suspected coronary disease: The National Heart, Lung, and Blood Institute–sponsored Women's Ischemia Syndrome Evaluation Study. *Psychosomatic Medicine, 66*(6), 882–888. https://doi.org/10.1097/01.psy.0000145819.94041.52

Rutter, Michael. (2008). Proceeding from observed correlation to causal interference: The use of natural experiments. *Perspectives on Psychological Science, 2,* 377–396.

Ruvolo, Ann Patrice, & Markus, Hazel Rose. (1992). Possible selves and performance: The power of self-relevant imagery. *Social Cognition, 10,* 95–124.

Ryan, Richard M., & Deci, Edward L. (2011). Human autonomy in cross-cultural context: Perspectives on the psychology of agency, freedom, and well-being. In Valery I. Chirkov, Richard M. Ryan, Kennon M. Sheldon (Eds.), *Cross-cultural advancements in positive psychology.* Springer.

Ryan, Richard M., & Deci, Edward L. (2012). Multiple identities within a single self: A self-determination theory perspective on internalization within contexts and cultures. In Mark R. Leary & June Price Tangney (Eds.), *Handbook of self and identity* (2nd ed., pp. 225–246). Guilford.

Ryan, Richard M., & Deci, Edward L. (2017). *Self-determination theory: Basic psychological needs in motivation, development, and wellness.* Guilford.

Ryan, Richard M., & La Guardia, Jennifer G. (2000). What is being optimized over development? A self-determination theory and basic psychological needs. In Sara Honn Qualls & Norman Abeles (Eds.), *Psychology and the aging revolution: How we adapt to longer life.* American Psychological Association.

Ryan, Shawn A., & Dunne, Robert B. (2018). Pharmacokinetic properties of intranasal and injectable formulations of naloxone for community use: a systematic review. *Pain Management, 8*(3), 231-245. https://doi.org/10.2217/pmt-2017-0060.

Rydell, Ann-Margaret; Bohlin, Gunilla; & Thorell, Lisa B. (2005). Representations of attachment to parents and shyness as predictors of children's relationships with teachers and peer competence in preschool. *Attachment & Human Development, 7,* 187–204.

Sacchi, Dario L. M.; Agnoli, Franca; & Loftus, Elizabeth F. (2007). Changing history: Doctored photographs affect memory for past public events. *Applied Cognitive Psychology, 21,* 1005–1022.

Sacks, Mike. (2016). O.C.D. in N.Y.C. *The New York Times.* http://nyti.ms/2aE5LSj

Sadler, Pamela, & Woody, Erik. (2010). Dissociation in hypnosis: Theoretical frameworks and psychotherapeutic implications. In Steven Jay Lynn, Judith W. Rhue, & Irving Kirsch (Eds.), *Handbook of clinical hypnosis* (2nd ed., pp. 151–178). American Psychological Association.

Sadoski, Mark. (2005). A dual coding view of vocabulary learning. *Reading & Writing Quarterly, 21,* 221–238.

Saeed, Sy Atezaz; Cunningham, Karlene; & Bloch, Richard M. (2019). Depression and anxiety disorders: Benefits of exercise, yoga, and meditation. *American Family Physician, 99*(10), 620–627.

Sagi, Yaniv; Tavor; Ido; Hofstetter; Shir; Tzur-Moryosef; Shimrit; Blumenfeld-Katzir; Tamar; & Assaf, Yanif. (2012). Learning in the fast lane: New insights into neuroplasticity. *Neuron, 73*(6), 1195–1203.

Saha, Sukanta; Chant, David; Welham, Joy; & McGrath, John. (2005). A systematic review of the prevalence of schizophrenia. *PLOS Medicine, 2,* 413–433. https://doi.org/10.1371/journal.pmed.0020141

Sahdra, Baljinder K.; MacLean, Katherine A.; Ferrer, Emilio; Shaver, Phillip R.; Rosenberg, Erika L.; Jacobs, Tonya L.; Zanesco, Anthony P.; King, Brandon G.;

Aichele, Stephen R.; Bridwell, David A.; Mangun, George R.; Lavy, Shiri; Wallace, B. Alan; & Saron, Clifford D. (2011). Enhanced response inhibition during intensive meditation training predicts improvements in self-reported adaptive socioemotional functioning. *Emotion, 11*(2), 299–312. https://doi.org/10.1037/a0022764

Sakheim, David K., & Devine, Susan E. (Eds.). (1992). *Out of darkness: Exploring satanism and ritual abuse.* Lexington Books.

Saks, Elyn. (2008). *The center cannot hold: My journey through madness.* Hyperion.

Saks, Elyn. (2018). *Saks Institute for Mental Health Law, Policy, and Ethics.* http://gould.usc.edu/faculty/centers/saks/

Salazar, Gloria Maria Martinez; Faintuch, Salamao; Laser, Eleanor; & Lang, Elvira. (2010). Hypnosis during invasive medical and surgical procedures. In Steven J. Lynn, Judith W. Rhue, & Irving Kirsch (Eds.), *Handbook of clinical hypnosis* (2nd ed., pp. 575–592). American Psychological Association.

Saletan, William. (2010, May 24). The ministry of truth. *Slate.* http://www.slate.com/articles/health_and_science/the_memory_doctor/2010/05/the_ministry_of_truth.html

Salloum, Alison; Garside, Laura W.; Irwin, C. Louis; Anderson, Adrian D.; & Francois, Anita H. (2009). Grief and trauma group therapy for children after Hurricane Katrina. *Social Work with Groups, 32*(1), 64–79.

Salter, Phia S.; & Adams, Glenn. (2016). On the intersectionality of cultural products: Representations of Black history as psychological affordances. *Frontiers in Psychology, 7,* 1–21. https://doi.org/10.3389/fpsyg.2016.01166

Salter, Phia S.; Adams, Glenn; & Perez, Michael J. (2018). Racism in the structure of everyday worlds: A cultural-psychological perspective. *Current Directions in Psychological Science, 27*(3), 150–155. https://doi.org/10.1177/0963721417724239

Salthouse, Timothy A. (2009). When does age-related cognitive decline begin? *Neurobiology of Aging, 30*(4), 507–514.

Sam, David L., & Berry, John W. (2010). Acculturation: When individuals and groups of different cultural backgrounds meet. *Perspectives on Psychological Science, 5*(4), 472–481. https://doi.org/10.1177/1745691610373075

Sameroff, Arnold. (2010). A unified theory of development: A dialectic integration of nature and nurture. *Child Development, 81*(1), 6–22.

Sammons, Cynthia C, & Speight, Suzette L. (2008). A qualitative investigation of changes in graduate students associated with multicultural counseling courses. *The Counseling Psychologist, 36*(6), 814–838.

Sampaio, Adriana; Soares, José M.; Coutinho, Joana; Sousa, Nuno; & Gonçalves, Óscar F. (2014). The Big Five default brain: Functional evidence. *Brain Structure Function, 219,* 1913–1922. https://doi.org/10.1007/s00429-013-0610-y

Sample, Ian. (2008, October 23). Hot drinks encourage warmer feelings. *The Guardian.* https://www.theguardian.com/science/2008/oct/24/psychology-health-food-science-colorado

Samuel, Douglas B.; Simms, Leonard J.; Clark, Lee A.; Livesley, W. John; & Widiger, Thomas A. (2010). An item response theory integration of normal and abnormal personality scales. *Personality Disorders: Theory, Research, and Treatment, 1*(1), 5–21. https://doi.org/10.1037/a0018136

Sanchez-Queija, Inmaculada; Oliva, Alfredo; Parra, Agueda. (2017). Stability, change, and determinants of self-esteem during adolescence and emerging adulthood. *Journal of Social and Personal Relationships, 34*(8), 1277–1294. https://doi.org/10.1177/0265407516674831

Sandin, Bonifacio; Sánchez-Arribas, Carmen; Chorot, Paloma; & Valiente, Rosa M. (2015). Anxiety sensitivity, catastrophic misinterpretations and panic self-efficacy in the prediction of panic disorder severity: Towards a tripartite cognitive model of panic disorder. *Behaviour Research and Therapy, 67,* 30–40. https://doi.org/10.1016/j.brat.2015.01.005

Sandler, Wendy; Meir, Irit; Padden, Carol; & Aronoff, Mark. (2005). The emergence of grammar in a new sign language. *Proceedings of the National Academy of Sciences, 102,* 2661–2665.

Sanfelippo, Augustin J. (2006). *Panic disorders: New research.* Nova Biomedical Books.

Santiago, Catherine D.; Kaltman, Stacey; & Miranda, Jeanne. (2013). Poverty and mental health: How do low-income adults and children fare in psychotherapy? *Journal of Clinical Psychology, 69*(2), 115–126. https://doi.org/10.1002/jclp.21951

Santoyo, Carlos V., & Mendoza, Brenda G. (2018). Behavioral patterns of children involved in bullying episodes. *Frontiers in Psychology, 9.* https://doi.org/10.3389/fpsyg.2018.00456

Sapolsky, Robert M. (2004). Mothering style and methylation. *Nature Neuroscience, 7,* 791–792.

Sapolsky, Robert M. (2008). Quoted in National Geographic Society. (2008). *Stress: Portrait of a killer* [Motion picture]. Randy Bean & William Free (Producers) & John Hemingway (Director).

Sar, Vedat; Koyuncu, Ahmet; Ozturk, Erdinc; Yargic, Ilhan; Kundakci, Turgut; Yazicki, Ahmet; Kuskonmaz, Ekrem; & Aksüt, Didem. (2007). Dissociative disorders in the psychiatric emergency ward. *General Hospital Psychiatry, 29*(1), 45–50. https://doi.org/10.1016/j.genhosppsych.2006.10.009

Satel, Sally, & Lilienfeld, Scott O. (2013). *Brainwashed: The seductive appeal of mindless neuroscience.* Basic Books.

Saul, Stephanie. (2007a, March 14). F.D.A. warns of odd effects of sleeping pills. http://www.nytimes.com/2007/03/14/business/15drugcnd.html

Saul, Stephanie. (2007b, March 15). F.D.A. warns of sleeping pills' strange effects. Retrieved from http://www.nytimes.com/2007/03/15/business/15drug.ready.html

Savage, Joanne, & Yancey, Christina. (2008). The effects of media violence exposure on criminal aggression: A meta-analysis. *Criminal Justice and Behavior, 35, 772–791.*

Savage-Rumbaugh, E. Sue, & Lewin, Roger. (1994, September). Ape at the brink. *Discover, 15,* 91–98.

Savi, Alexander O.; Marsman, Maarten; van der Maas, Han L. J.; & Maris, Gunter K. (2019). The wiring of intelligence. *Perspectives on Psychological Science, 14*(6), 1034-1061. https://doi.org/10.1177/1745691619866447

Savin-Williams, Ritch C. (2006). Who's gay? Does it matter? *Current Directions in Psychological Science, 15,* 40–44.

Savin-Williams, Ritch C. (2009). How many gays are there? It depends. In Debra A. Hope (Ed.), *Contemporary perspectives on lesbian, gay, and bisexual identities (pp. 5–41).* Springer.

Savin-Williams, Ritch C. (2016). Sexual orientation: Categories or continuum? Commentary on Bailey et al. (2016). *Psychological Science in the Public Interest, 17,* 37–44. https://doi.org/10.1177/1529100616637618

Saxbe, Darby E., & Repetti, Rena L. (2009). Brief report: Fathers' and mothers' marital relationship predicts daughters' pubertal development two years later. *Journal of Adolescence, 32*(2), 415–423.

Saxe, Geoffrey, & de Kirby, Kenton. (2014). Cultural context of cognitive development. *WIREs Cognitive Science, 5,* 447–461.

Saxe, Rebecca, & Powell, Lindsay J. (2006). It's the thought that counts: Specific brain regions for one component of theory of mind. *Psychological Science, 17,* 692–699.

Saxton, Tamsin K.; Lyndon, Anna; Little, Anthony C.; & Roberts, S. Craig. (2008). Evidence that androstadienone, a putative human chemosignal, modulates women's attributions of men's attractiveness. *Hormones and Behavior 54,* 597–601. https://doi.org/10.1016/j.yhbeh.2008.06.001

Scarborough, Elizabeth. (2005). Constructing a women's history of psychology. *The Feminist Psychologist, 32*(1), 6. https://www.apadivisions.org/division-35/about/heritage/women-history-psychology

Schachter, Robert. (2011). Using the group in cognitive group therapy. *Group, 35*(2), 135–149.

Schachter, Stanley, & Singer, Jerome E. (1962). Cognitive, social, and physiological determinants of emotional state. *Psychological Review, 69,* 379–399.

Schacter, Daniel L., & Loftus, Elizabeth F. (2013). Memory and law: What can cognitive neuroscience contribute? *Nature Neuroscience, 16,* 119–123.

Schaeuffele, Carmen; Schulz, Ava; Knaevelsrud, Christine; Renneberg, Babette; & Boettcher, Johanna. (2021). CBT at the crossroads: The rise of transdiagnostic treatments. *International Journal of Cognitive Therapy, 14,* 86–113. https://doi.org/10.1007/s41811-020-00095-2

Schaie, K. Warner. (1995). *Intellectual development in adulthood: The Seattle Longitudinal Study.* Cambridge University Press.

Schaie, K. Warner. (2005). *Developmental influences on adult intelligence: The Seattle Longitudinal Study.* Oxford University Press.

Schanding, G. Thomas, Jr., & Sterling-Turner, Heather E. (2010). Use of the mystery motivator for a high school class. *Journal of Applied School Psychology, 26*(1), 38–53.

Scheiber, Noam. (2016). At Trader Joe's, good cheer may hide complaints. *The New York Times.* http://nyti.ms/2ejwGjg

Schell, Jason. (2010, February 18). Design outside the box: Beyond Facebook. Presented at DICE Summit 2011. Retrieved from http://g4tv.com/videos/44277/DICE-2010-Design-Outside-the-Box-Presentation.

Schemann, Michael; Frieling, Thomas; & Enck, Paul. (2020). To learn, to remember, to forget—How smart is the gut?. *Acta Physiologica, 228*(1), e13296. https://doi.org/10.1111/apha.13296

Schenck, Carlos H. (2007). *Sleep: The mysteries, the problems, and the solutions.* Penguin.

Schenck, Carlos H.; Arnulf, Isabelle; & Mahowald, Mark W. (2007). Sleep and sex: What can go wrong? A review of the literature on sleep related disorders and abnormal sexual behaviors and experiences. *Sleep, 30,* 683–702.

Scherer, Klaus R. (2013). The nature and dynamics of relevance and valence appraisals: Theoretical advances and recent evidence. *Emotion Review, 5,* 150–162. https://doi.org/10.1177/1754073912468166

Scherer, Klaus R.; Banse, Rainer; & Wallbott, Harald G. (2001). Emotion inferences from vocal expression correlate across languages and cultures. *Journal of Cross-Cultural Psychology, 32,* 76–92.

Schiffrin, Holly H.; & Nelson, S. Katherine. (2010). Stressed and happy? Investigating the relationship between happiness and perceived stress. *Journal of Happiness Studies, 11,* 33–39. https://doi.org/10.1007/s10902-008-9104-7

Schläpfer, Thomas E., & Bewernick, Bettina H. (2009). Deep brain stimulation: Methods, indications, locations, and efficacy. In Conrad M. Swartz (Ed.), *Electroconvulsive and neuromodulation therapies* (pp. 556–572). Cambridge University Press.

Schmader, Toni. (2010). Stereotype threat deconstructed. *Current Directions in Psychological Science, 19*(1), 14–18. https://doi.org/10.1177/0963721409359292

Schmader, Toni; Forbes, Chad E.; Zhang, Shen; & Mendes, Wendy Berry. (2009). A metacognitive perspective on the cognitive deficits experienced in intellectually threatening environments. *Personality and Social Psychology Bulletin, 35*(5), 584–596. https://doi.org/10.1177/0146167208330450

Schmader, Toni; Johns, Michael; & Barquissau, Marchelle. (2004). The costs of accepting gender differences: The role of stereotype endorsement in women's experience in the math domain. *Sex Roles, 50,* 835–850.

Schmader, Toni; Johns, Michael; & Forbes, Chad. (2008). An integrated process model of stereotype threat effects on performance. *Psychological Review, 115,* 236–256.

Schmalz, Dorothy L., & Kerstetter, Deborah L. (2006). Girlie girls and manly men: Children's stigma consciousness of gender in sports and physical activities. *Journal of Leisure Research, 38,* 536–557.

Schmidt, Norman B., & Keough, Meghan E. (2010). Treatment of panic. *Annual Review of Clinical Psychology, 6,* 241–256. https://doi.org/10.1146/annurev.clinpsy.121208.131317

Schmithorst, Vincent J., & Yuan, Weihong. (2010). White matter development during adolescence as shown by diffusion MRI. *Brain and Cognition, 72*(1), 16–25.

Schmitt, David P.; Jonason, Peter K.; Byerley, Garrett J.; Flores, Sandy D.; Illbeck, Brittany E.; O'Leary, Kimberly N.; & Qudrat, Ayesha. (2012). A reexamination of sex differences in sexuality: New studies reveal old truths. *Current Directions in Psychological Science, 21*(2), 135–139.

Schmitt, David P.; Realo, Anu; Voracek, Martin; & Allik, Juri. (2008). Why can't a man be more like a woman? Sex differences in Big Five personality (traits across 55 cultures). *Journal of Personality and Social Psychology, 94,* 168–182.

Schmitt, Michael; Branscombe, Nyla; Postmes, Tom; & Garcia, Amber. (2014). The consequences of perceived discrimination for psychological well-being: A meta-analytic review. *Psychological Bulletin, 140,* 921–948. https://doi.org/10.1037/a0035754

Schnall, Simone, & Laird, James D. (2003). Keep smiling: Enduring effects of facial expressions and postures on emotional experience and memory. *Cognition & Emotion, 17,* 787–797.

Schneider, Kirk J., & Krug, Orah T. (2009). *Existential-humanistic therapy.* American Psychological Association.

Schomerus, Georg; Schwahn, Christian; Holzinger, Anita; Corrigan, Patrick. W.; Grabe, H. J.; Carta, Manolo G.; & Angermeyer, Matthais C. (2012). Evolution of public attitudes about mental illness: A systematic review and meta-analysis. *Acta Psychiatrica Scandinavica, 125,* 440–452. https://doi.org/10.1111/j.1600-0447.2012.01826.x

Schooler, Jonathan W.; Baumgart, Stephen; & Franklin, Michael. (2018). Entertaining without endorsing: The case for the scientific investigation of anomalous cognition. *Psychology of Consciousness: Theory, Research, and Practice, 5,* 63–77. https://doi.org/10.1037/cns0000151

Schueller, Stephen; & Torous, John. (2020). Scaling evidence-based treatments through digital mental health. *American Psychologist, 75*(8), 1093–1104. https://doi.org/10.1037/amp0000654

Schulenberg, J. E., & Zarrett, N. R. (2006). Mental health during emerging adulthood: Continuity and discontinuity in courses, causes, and functions. In J. J. Arnett & J. L. Tanner (Eds.), *Emerging adults in America: Coming of age in the 21st century.* American Psychological Association.

Schüll, Natasha Dow. (2012). *Addiction by design: Machine gambling in Las Vegas.* Princeton University Press.

Schupp, Harald T.; Öhman, Arne; Junghöfer, Markus; Weike, Almut I.; Stockburger, Jessica; & Hamm, Alfons O. (2004). The facilitated processing of threatening faces: An ERP analysis. *Emotion, 4,* 189–200.

Schutte, Nicola, & Malouff, John. (2014, November 13). The relationship between perceived stress and telomere length: A meta-analysis. *Stress & Health.* Advance online publication. https://doi.org/10.1002/smi.2607

Schwab, Richard J.; Kuna, Samuel T.; & Remmers, John E. (2005). Anatomy and physiology of upper airway obstruction. In Meir H. Kryger, Thomas Roth, & William C. Dement (Eds.), *Principles and practice of sleep medicine* (4th ed.). Elsevier Saunders.

Schwantes, M. (2018, April 23). Warren Buffett gave this brilliant advice to billionaires but it can instantly improve your life too. *Inc.* https://www.inc.com/marcel-schwantes/warren-buffett-gave-this-brilliant-advice-to-billionaires-but-it-can-also-improve-your-life-fast.html

Schwartz, Bennett L. (2002). *Tip-of-the-tongue states: Phenomenology, mechanism, and lexical retrieval.* Erlbaum.

Schwartz, Bennett L. (2011). The effect of being in a tip-of-the-tongue state on subsequent items. *Memory & Cognition, 39,* 245–250.

Schwartz, Earl. (2004, Summer/Fall). Why some ask why: Kohlberg and Milgram. *Judaism, 53,* 230–240.

Schwartz, Jeffrey M., & Begley, Sharon. (2002). *The mind and the brain: Neuroplasticity and the power of mental force.* Regan Books.

Schwartz, Jeffrey M.; Stoessel, Paula W.; & Phelps, Michael E. (1996). Systematic changes in cerebral glucose metabolic rate after successful behavior modification treatment of obsessive–compulsive disorder. *Archives of General Psychiatry, 53,* 109–117.

Schwartz, Seth J.; Lilienfeld, Scott O.; Meca, Alan; & Sauvigné, Katheryn C. (2016). The role of neuroscience within psychology: A call for inclusiveness over exclusiveness. *American Psychologist, 71,* 52–70. https://doi.org/10.1037/a0039678

Schwartz, Seth J.; Unger, Jennifer B.; Zamboanga, Byron L.; & Szapocznik, José. (2010). Rethinking the concept of acculturation: Implications for theory and research. *American Psychologist, 65,* 237–251.

Schwartz, Sophie. (2010). Life goes on in dreams. *Sleep, 33*(1), 15–16.

Scott, Samantha L.; Carper, Teresa Marino; Middleton, Melissa; White, Rachel; Renk, Kimberly; & Grills-Taquechel, Amie. (2010). Relationships among locus of control, coping behaviors, and levels of worry following exposure to hurricanes. *Journal of Loss and Trauma, 15*(2), 123–137.

Scoville, William Beecher, & Milner, Brenda. (1957). Loss of recent memory after bilateral hippocampal lesions. *Journal of Neurology, Neurosurgery, and Psychiatry, 20,* 11–21.

Seal, Karen H.; Bertenthal, Daniel; Maguen, Shira; Gima, Kristian; Chu, Anna; & Marmar, Charles R. (2008). Getting beyond "Don't ask, don't tell": An evaluation of U.S. Veterans Administration post-deployment mental health screening of veterans returning from Iraq and Afghanistan. *American Journal of Public Health, 98,* 714–720. https://doi.org/10.2105/AJPH.2007.115519

Seaton, Eleanor K.; Caldwell, Cleopatra H.; Sellers, Robert M.; & Jackson, James S. (2010). An intersectional approach for understanding perceived discrimination and psychological well-being among African American and Caribbean Black youth. *Developmental Psychology, 46*(5), 1372–1379. https://doi.org/10.1037/a0019869

Sebastian, Catherine; Burnett, Stephanie; & Blakemore, Sarah-Jayne. (2008). Development of the self-concept during adolescence. *Trends in Cognitive Sciences, 12*(11), 441–446.

Sedlmeier, Peter; Eberth, Juliane; Schwarz, Marcus; Zimmermann, Doreen; Haarig, Frederik; Jaeger, Sonia; & Kunze, Sonja. **(2012).** The psychological effects of meditation: A meta-analysis. *Psychological Bulletin, 138,* 1139–1171. https://doi.org/10.1037/a0028168

Seegmiller, Janelle K.; Watson, Jason M.; & Strayer, David L. (2011). Individual differences in susceptibility to inattentional blindness. *Journal of Experimental Psychology: Learning, Memory, and Cognition, 37,* 785–791. https://doi.org/10.1037/a0022474

Seelman, Kristie. (2016). Transgender adults' access to college bathrooms and housing and the relationship to suicidality. *Journal of Homosexuality, 63,* 1378–1399. https://doi.org/10.1080/00918369.2016.1157998

Seery, Mark D.; Holman, E. Alison; & Silver, Roxane Cohen. (2010). Whatever does not kill us: Cumulative lifetime adversity, vulnerability, and resilience. *Journal of Personality and Social Psychology, 99,* 1025–1041. https://doi.org/10.1037/a0021344

Seery, Mark D.; Leo, Raphael J.; Lupien, Shannon P.; Kondrak, Cheryl L.; & Almonte, Jessica L. (2013). An upside to adversity? Moderate cumulative lifetime adversity is associated with resilient responses in the face of controlled stressors. *Psychological Science, 24,* 1181–1189. https://doi.org/10.1177/0956797612469210

Segal, Nancy L. (2012). *Born together—reared apart: The landmark Minnesota Twin Study.* Harvard University Press.

Segal, Zindel V.; Bieling, Peter; Young, Trevor; MacQueen, Glenda; Cooke, Robert; Martin, Lawrence; Bloch, Richard; & Levitan, Robert D. (2010). Antidepressant monotherapy vs. sequential pharmacotherapy and mindfulness-based cognitive therapy, or placebo, for relapse prophylaxis in recurrent depression. *Archives of General Psychiatry, 67,* 1256–1264.

Segall, Marshall H. (1994). A cross-cultural research contribution to unraveling the nativist/empiricist controversy. In Walter J. Lonner & Roy Malpass (Eds.), *Psychology and culture.* Allyn & Bacon.

Segall, Marshall H.; Campbell, Donald T.; & Herskovits, Melville J. (1963). Cultural differences in the perception of geometric illusions. *Science, 193,* 769–771.

Segall, Marshall H.; Campbell, Donald T.; & Herskovits, Melville J. (1966). *The influence of culture on visual perception.* Bobbs-Merrill.

Segerdahl, Pär; Fields, William; & Savage-Rumbaugh, Sue. (2006). *Kanzi's primal language: The cultural initiation of primates into language.* Palgrave Macmillan.

Segerstrom, Suzanne C.; Castañeda, Jay O.; & Spencer, Theresa E. (2003). Optimism effects on cellular immunity: Testing the affective and persistence models. *Personality and Individual Differences, 35,* 1615–1624.

Segovia, Carolina; Hutchinson, Ian; Laing, David G.; & Jinks, Anthony L. (2002). A quantitative study of fungiform papillae and taste pore density in adults and children. *Developmental Brain Research, 138,* 135–146. https://doi.org/10.1016/s0165-3806(02)00463-7

Sela, Lee, & Sobel, Noam. (2010). Human olfaction: A constant state of change-blindness. *Experimental Brain Research, 205,* 13–29.

Seligman, Martin E. P. (1970). On the generality of the laws of learning. *Psychological Review, 77,* 406–418.

Seligman, Martin E. P. (1971). Phobias and preparedness. *Behavior Therapy, 2,* 307–320.

Seligman, Martin E. P. (1990). *Learned optimism.* Knopf.

Seligman, Martin E. P. (1992). *Helplessness: On development, depression, and death.* Freeman.

Seligman, Martin E. P., & Maier, Steven F. (1967). Failure to escape traumatic shock. *Journal of Experimental Psychology, 37B,* 1–21.

Seligman, Martin E. P.; Steen, Tracy A.; Park, Nansook; & Peterson, Christopher. (2005). Positive psychology progress: Empirical validation of interventions. *American Psychologist, 60,* 410–421. https://doi.org/10.1037/0003-066X.60.5.410

Sellbom, Martin. (2019). The MMPI-2-Restructured Form (MMPI-2-RF): Assessment of personality and psychopathology in the twenty-first century. *Annual Review of Clinical Psychology, 15,* 149–177. https://doi.org/10.1146/annurev-clinpsy-050718-095701

Sellers, Robert M.; Copeland-Linder, Nikeea; Martin, Pamela P.; & Lewis, R. L'Heureux. (2006). Racial identity matters: The relationship between racial discrimination and psychological functioning in African American adolescents. *Journal of Research on Adolescence, 16,* 187–216.

Selye, Hans. (1956). *The stress of life.* McGraw-Hill.

Selye, Hans. (1976). *The stress of life* (Rev. ed.). McGraw-Hill.

Senghas, Ann; Kita, Sotaro; & Özyürek, Asli. (2004, September 17). Children creating core properties of language: Evidence from an emerging sign language in Nicaragua. *Science, 305,* 1779–1782.

Senko, Corwin; Durik, Amanda M.; & Harackiewicz, Judith M. (2008). Historical perspectives and new directions in achievement goal theory: Understanding the effects of mastery and performance-approach. In James Y. Shah & Wendi L. Gardner (Eds.), *Handbook of motivation science.* Guilford.

Seppälä, Emma; Bradley, Christina; & Goldstein, Michael R. (2020, September 29). Research: Why breathing is so effective at reducing stress. *Harvard Business Review.* https://hbr.org/2020/09/research-why-breathing-is-so-effective-at-reducing-stress

Serchen, Josh; Doherty, Robert; Atiq, Omar; & Hilden, David. (2020) Racism and health in the United States: A policy statement from the American College of Physicians. *Annals of Internal Medicine, 173*(7), 556–557. https://doi.org/10.7326/M20-4195

Sergent, Justine; Ohta, Shinsuke; & Macdonald, Brennan. (1992). Functional neuroanatomy of face and object processing. A positron emission tomography study. *Brain. 115*(1), 15–36. https://doi.org/10.1093/brain/115.1.15

Serlin, Ilene. (2012). The history and future of humanistic psychology. *Journal of Humanistic Psychology, 51,* 428–431. https://doi.org/10.1177/0022167811412600

Serrano, Zulai. (2013, October 8). Elizabeth Smart book: Kidnapping survivor says don't ask a victim why they didn't escape sooner. http://www.hngn.com/articles/14343/20131008/elizabeth-smart-book-kidnapping-survivor-dont-ask-victim-why-didnt.htm

Seung, Sebastian. (2012). *Connectome: How the brain's wiring makes us who we are.* Houghton Mifflin.

Seurinck, Ruth; de Lange, Floris P.; Achten, Erik; & Vingerhoets, Guy. (2011). Mental rotation meets the motion after effect: The role of hV5/MT+ in visual mental imagery. *Journal of Cognitive Neuroscience, 2,* 1395–1404. https://doi.org/10.1162/jocn.2010.21525

Severus, W. Emanuel; Kleindienst, Nikolaus; Evoniuk, Gary; Bowden, Charles; Möller, Hans-Jürgen; Bohus, Martin; Fangou, Sophia; Greil, Waldemar & Calabrese, Joseph. (2009). Is the polarity of relapse/recurrence in bipolar-I disorder patients related to serum lithium levels? Results from an empirical study. *Journal of Affective Disorders, 115*(3), 466–470.

Sewart, Amy R.; & Craske, Michelle G. (2020). Inhibitory learning. In J. S. Abramowitz & S. M. Blakey (Eds.), *Clinical handbook of fear and anxiety: Maintenance processes and treatment mechanisms* (pp. 265–285). American Psychological Association. https://doi.org/10.1037/0000150-015

Shafto, Meredith A., & Tyler, Lorraine K. (2014). Language in the aging brain: The network dynamics of cognitive decline and preservation. *Science, 346,* 583–587.

Shapiro, Shauna L., & Carlson, Linda E. (2009). *The art and science of mindfulness: Integrating mindfulness into psychology and the helping professions.* American Psychological Association.

Shariatmadari, David. (2018, April 16). A real-life Lord of the Flies: The troubling legacy of the Robbers Cave experiment. *The Guardian.* https://www.theguardian.com/science/2018/apr/16/a-real-life-lord-of-the-flies-the-troubling-legacy-of-the-robbers-cave-experiment

Sharman, Stefanie J.; Garry, Maryanne; & Beuke, Carl J. (2004). Imagination or exposure causes imagination inflation. *American Journal of Psychology, 117,* 157–168.

Sharpless, Brian A. (2015a). Exploding head syndrome is common in college students. *Journal of Sleep Research, 24,* 447–449. https://doi.org/10.1111/jsr.12292

Sharpless, Brian A. (2015b, April 3). Quoted in James Hamblin, "How many beliefs are due to sleep deprivation? *The Atlantic.* http://www.theatlantic.com/health/archive/2015/04/how-many-beliefs-are-due-to-sleep-deprivation/389303

Shaw, Benjamin A.; Krause, Neal; Chatters, Linda M.; & Ingersoll-Dayton, Berit. (2004). Emotional support from parents early in life, aging, and health. *Psychology of Aging, 19,* 4–12.

Shaw, Julia, & Porter, Stephen. (2015). Constructing rich false memories of committing crime. *Psychological Science, 26,* 291–301. https://doi.org/10.1177/0956797614562862

Shedler, Jonathan. (2010). The efficacy of psychodynamic therapy. *American Psychologist, 95,* 98–109.

Shedler, Jonathan; Mayman, Martin; & Manis, Melvin. (1993). The illusion of mental health. *American Psychologist, 48,* 1117–1131.

Sheldon, B. (2011). *Cognitive-behavioural therapy: Research and practice in health and social care (2nd ed.).* Routledge.

Sheldon, Kennon M. (2008). The interface of motivation science and personology: Self-concordance, quality motivation, and multilevel personality integration. In James Y. Shah & Wendi L. Gardner (Eds.), *Handbook of motivation science.* Guilford.

Sheldon, Kennon M., & Ryan, Richard M. (2011). Positive psychology and self-determination theory: A natural interface. In Valery I. Chirkov, Richard M. Ryan, & Kennon M. Sheldon (Eds.), *Human autonomy in cross-cultural context.* Springer.

Sheldon, Kennon M.; Elliot, Andrew J.; Kim, Youngmee; & Kasser, Tim. (2001). What is satisfying about satisfying events? Testing 10 candidate psychological needs. *Journal of Personality and Social Psychology, 80,* 325–339.

Shen, Hao; Wan, Fang; & Wyer, Robert S., Jr. (2011). Cross-cultural differences in the refusal to accept a small gift: The differential influence of reciprocity norms on Asians and North Americans. *Journal of Personality and Social Psychology, 100*(2), 271–281.

Shepherd, Gordon M. (2004). Unsolved mystery: The human sense of smell: Are we better than we think? *PLOS Biology, 2,* 0572–0575.

Shepherd, Gordon M. (2006). Smell images and the flavour system in the human brain. *Nature, 444,* 316–321.

Shepherd, Jonathan. (2007). Preventing alcohol-related violence: A public health approach. *Criminal Behaviour & Mental Health, 17,* 250–264.

Sheppard, Leah D.; Goffin, Richard D.; Lewis, Rhys J.; & Olson, James. (2011). The effect of target attractiveness and rating method on the accuracy of trait ratings. *Journal of Personnel Psychology, 10*(1), 24–33.

Shergill, Sukhwinder S.; Brammer, Michael J.; Williams, Steven C. R.; Murray, Robin M.; & McGuire, Philip K. (2000). Mapping auditory hallucinations in schizophrenia using functional magnetic resonance imaging. *Archives of General Psychiatry, 57,* 1033–1038. https://doi.org/10.1001/archpsyc.57.11.1033

Sherif, Muzafer. (1956, November). Experiments in group conflict. *Scientific American, 195,* 33–47.

Sherif, Muzafer. (1966). *In common predicament: Social psychology of intergroup conflict and cooperation.* Houghton Mifflin, 502.

Sherif, Muzafer; Harvey, O. J.; White, B. Jack; Hood, William R.; & Sherif, Carolyn W. (1961). Intergroup conflict and cooperation: The Robbers Cave Experiment. University Book Exchange.

Sherman, Jeffrey W.; Stroessner, Steven J.; Conrey, Frederica R.; & Azam, Omar A. (2005). Prejudice and stereotype maintenance processes: Attention, attribution, and individuation. *Journal of Personality and Social Psychology, 89,* 607–622.

Sherwin-White, Susan. (2018). *Melanie Klein revisited: Pioneer and revolutionary in the psychoanalysis of young children.* Routledge.

Shettleworth, Sara J. (2010). *Cognition, evolution, and behavior* (2nd ed.). Oxford University Press.

Shevell, Steven K., & Kingdom, Frederick A. A. (2008). Color in complex scenes. *Annual Review of Psychology, 5,* 143–166.

Shi, Yuyan, (2017). Medical marijuana policies and hospitalizations related to marijuana and opioid pain reliever. *Drug and Alcohol Dependence, 173,* 144–150. https://doi.org/10.1016/j.drugalcdep.2017.01.006

Shiban, Youssef; Fruth, Martina; Pauli, Paul; Kinateder, Max; Reichenberger, Jonas; & Mühlberger, Andreas. (2016). Treatment effect on biases in size estimation in spider phobia. *Biological Psychology, 121,* 125–244. https://doi.org/10.1016/j.biopsycho.2016.03.005

Shidlo, Ariel, & Schroeder, Michael. (2002). Changing sexual orientation: A consumer's report. *Professional Psychology: Research and Practice, 33*(3), 249–259. Special Section: Responding to Sexual Orientation Issues. https://doi.org/10.1037/0735-7028.33.3.249

Shiffrin, Richard M., & Atkinson, Richard C. (1969). Storage and retrieval processes in long-term memory. *Psychological Review, 76,* 179–193.

Shih, Margaret J.; Pittinsky, Todd L.; & Ambady, Nalini. (1999). Stereotype susceptibility: Identity salience and shifts in quantitative performance. *Psychological Science, 10,* 80–83.

Shih, Margaret J.; Pittinsky, Todd L.; & Ho, Geoffrey C. (2012). Stereotype boost: Positive outcomes from the activation of positive stereotypes. In Michael Inzlicht & Toni Schmader (Eds.), *Stereotype threat: Theory, process, and application.* Oxford University Press.

Shih, Margaret J.; Pittinsky, Todd L.; & Trahan, Amy. (2006). Domain-specific effects of stereotypes on performance. *Self and Identity, 5,* 1–14.

Shiner, Rebecca L., & DeYoung, Colin G. (2013). The structure of temperament and personality traits: A developmental perspective. In Phillip D. Zelazo (Ed.), *The Oxford handbook of developmental psychology, Vol. 2: Self and other.* https://doi.org/10.1093/oxfordhb/9780199958474.013.0006

Shinskey, Jeanne L., & Munakata, Yuko. (2005). Familiarity breeds searching: Infants reverse their novelty preferences when reaching for hidden objects. *Psychological Science, 16,* 596–600.

Shiozawa, Pedro; Fregni, Felipe; Benseñor, Isabela M.; Lotufo1, Paulo A.; Berlim, Marcelo T.; Daskalakis, Jeff Z.; Cordeiro, Quirino; & Brunoni, André R. (2014). Transcranial direct current stimulation for major depression: An updated systematic review and meta-analysis. *International Journal of Neuropsychopharmacology, 17,* 1443–1452. https://doi.org/10.1017/S1461145714000418

Shneidman, Edwin S. (1998). *The suicidal mind.* Oxford University Press.

Shneidman, Edwin S. (2004). *Autopsy of a suicidal mind.* Oxford University Press.

Shorter, Edward. (2009). History of electroconvulsive therapy. In Conrad M. Swartz (Ed.), *Electroconvulsive and neuromodulation therapies* (pp. 167–179). Cambridge University Press.

Shrager, Yael, & Squire, Larry R. (2009). Medial temporal lobe function and human memory. In M. S. Gazzaniga, E. Bizzi, L. M. Chalupa, S. T. Grafton, T. F. Heatherton, C. Koch,... & B. A. Wandell (Eds.), *The cognitive neurosciences* (4th ed., pp. 675–690). Massachusetts Institute of Technology.

Shulman, Robert G.; & Rothman, Douglas. L. (2019). A non-cognitive behavioral model for interpreting functional neuroimaging studies. *Frontiers in Human Neuroscience, 13,* 28. https://doi.org/10.3389/fnhum.2019.00028

Shultz, Sarah; Vouloumanos, Athena; Bennett, Randi H.; & Pelphrey, Kevin. (2014). Neural specialization for speech in the first months of life. *Developmental Science, 17,* 766–774. https://doi.org/10.1016/j.neubiorev.2014.10.006

Shweder, R. A.; Much, N. C.; Mahapatra, M.; & Park, L. (1997). The "big three" of morality (autonomy, community, and divinity), and the "big three" explanations of suffering. In A. Brandt & P. Rozin (Eds.), *Morality and health.* Routledge.

Shweder, Richard A., & Haidt, Jonathan. (1993). The future of moral psychology: Truth, intuition, and the pluralist way. *Psychological Science, 4,* 360–365.

Siclari, Francesca; Baird, Benjamin; Perogamvros, Lampros; Bernardi, Giulio; LaRocque, Joshua J.; Riedner, Brady; Boly, Melanie; Postle, Bradley R.; & Tononi, Giulio. (2017, April 10). The neural correlates of dreaming. *Nature Neuroscience, 20,* 872–878. https://doi.org/10.1038/nn.4545

Siegal, Michael. (2004, September 17). Signposts to the essence of language. *Science, 305,* 1720–1721.

Siegel, Jerome M. (2005). Clues to the functions of mammalian sleep. *Nature, 437,* 1264–1271. https://doi.org/10.1038/nature04285

Siegel, Jerome M. (2009). Sleep viewed as a state of adaptive inactivity. *Nature Reviews Neuroscience 10,* 747–753. https://doi.org/10.1038/nrn2697

Siegel, Ronald D.; Gormer, Christopher K.; & Olendzki, Andrew. (2008). Mindfulness: What is it? Where does it come from? In Fabrizio Didonna (Ed.), *Clinical handbook of mindfulness.* Springer.

Siegle, Greg L.; Thompson, Wesley; Carter, Cameron S.; Steinhauer, Stuart R.; & Thase, Michael E. (2007). Increased amygdala and decreased dorsolateral prefrontal BOLD responses in unipolar depression: Related and independent features. *Biological Psychiatry, 61,* 198–209. https://doi.org/10.1016/j.biopsych.2006.05.048

Siegler, Ilene C.; Poon, Leonard W.; Madden, David J.; Dilworth- Anderson, Peggy; Schaie, K. Warner; Willis, Sherry L.; & Martin, Peter. (2009). Psychological aspects of normal aging. In Dan German Blazer and David C. Steffens (Eds.), *The American Psychiatric Publishing textbook of geriatric psychiatry* (4th ed., pp. 137–155). American Psychiatric Publishing.

Siegler, Robert S. (1992). The other Alfred Binet. *Developmental Psychology, 28,* 179–190.

Sifaki-Pistolla, Dimitra; Chatzea, Vasiliki-Eirini; Vlachaki, Sofia-Aikaterini; Melidoniotis, Evangelos; & Pistolla, Georgia. (2016). Who is going to rescue the rescuers? Post-traumatic stress disorder among rescue workers operating in Greece during the European refugee crisis. *Social Psychiatry and Psychiatric Epidemiology, 52,* 45–54. https://doi.org/10.1007/s00127-016-1302-8

Silbersweig, David A.; Stern, Emily; & Frackowaik, R. S. J. (1995, November 9). A functional neuroanatomy of hallucinations in schizophrenia. *Nature, 387,* 176–184.

Silverstein, Charles. (2009). The implications of removing homosexuality from the DSM as a mental disorder. *Archives of Sexual Behavior, 38*(2), 161–163.

Simmons, Joseph P., & Simonsohn, Uri. (2017). Power posing: P-curving the evidence. *Psychological Science, 28,* 687–693. https://doi.org/10.1177/0956797616658563

Simmons, Sarah M.; Caird, Jeff K.; Ta, Alicia; Sterzer, Franci; & Hagel, Brent E. (2020). Injury Prevention. *BMJ.* Advance online publication. https://doi.org/10.1136/injuryprev-2019-043426

Simon, Gregory; Goldberg, David P.; Von Korff, Michael; & Üstün, T. Bedirhan. (2002). Understanding cross-national differences in depression prevalence. *Psychological Medicine, 32,* 585–594. https://doi.org/10.1017/S0033291702005457

Simons, Daniel J.; Hannula, Deborah E.; Warren, David E.; & Day, Steven W. (2007). Behavioral, neuroimaging, and neuropsychological approaches to implicit perception. In Philip David Zelazo, Morris Moscovitch, & Evan Thompson (Eds.), *The Cambridge handbook of consciousness.* Cambridge University Press.

Singer, Natasha. (2018, December 31). In screening for suicide risk, Facebook takes on tricky public health role. *The New York Times.* https://www.nytimes.com/2018/12/31/technology/facebook-suicide-screening-algorithm.html

Singer, Tania; Verhaeghen, Paul; Ghisletta, Paolo; Lindenberger, Ulman; & Baltes, Paul. (2003). The fate of cognition in very old age: Six-year longitudinal findings in the Berlin Aging Study (BASE). *Psychology and Aging, 18,* 318–331.

Singh, Devendra, & Singh, Dorian. (2011). Shape and significance of feminine beauty: An evolutionary perspective. *Sex Roles, 64*(9-10), 723–731. https://doi.org/201110.1007/s11199-011-9938-z

Singh, Devendra; Dixson, Barnaby. J.; Jessop, Tim. S.; Morgan, Bethan; & Dixson, Alan F. (2010). Cross-cultural consensus for waist–hip ratio and women's attractiveness. *Evolution and Human Behavior, 31*(3), 176–181. https://doi.org/10.1016/j.evolhumbehav.2009.09.001

Singh, Maanvi. (2015, February 2). Why Cambodians never get 'depressed.' *NPR.* http://www.npr.org/blogs/goatsandsoda/2015/02/02/382905977/why-cambodians-never-get-depressed

Singh, Tushar; Arrazola, René A.; Corey, Catherine G.; Huston, Corinne G.; Neff, Linda J.; Homa, David M.; & King, Brian A. (2016). Tobacco use among middle and high school students—United States, 2011–2015. *Mortality and Morbidity Weekly Report, 65,* 361–367.

Singhal, Arvind; Cody, Michael J.; Rogers, Everett M.; & Sabido, Miguel. (Eds.). (2004). *Entertainment-education and social change: History, research, and practice.* Erlbaum.

Skeem, Jennifer; Kennealy, Patrick; Monahan, John; Peterson, Jillian; & Appelbaum, Paul. (2015). Psychosis uncommonly and inconsistently precedes violence among high-risk individuals. *Clinical Psychological Science, 4,* 40–49. https://doi.org/10.1177/2167702615575879

Skinner, B. F. (1938). *The behavior of organisms: An experimental analysis.* Appleton-Century-Crofts.

Skinner, B. F. (1948). Superstition in the pigeon. *Journal of Experimental Psychology: General, 121,* 273–274.

Skinner, B. F. (1953). *Science and human behavior.* Macmillan.

Skinner, B. F. (1956). A case history in scientific method. *American Psychologist, 11,* 221–233.

Skinner, B. F. (1961, November). Teaching machines. *Scientific American, 205,* 90–102.

Skinner, B. F. (1967). B. F. Skinner . . . an autobiography. In E. G. Boring & G. Lindzey (Eds.), *A history of psychology in autobiography* (Vol. 5). Appleton-Century-Crofts.

Skinner, B. F. (1971). *Beyond freedom and dignity.* Bantam Books.

Skinner, B. F. (1974). *About behaviorism.* Knopf.

Slagter, Heleen A.; Davidson, Richard A.; & Lutz, Antoine. (2011). Mental training as a tool in the neuroscientific study of brain and cognitive plasticity. *Frontiers in Human Neuroscience, 5,* 1–12. https://doi.org/10.3389/fnhum.2011.00017

Slobodchikoff, C. N.; Paseka, Andrea; & Verdolin, Jennifer L. (2009). Prairie dog alarm calls encode labels about predator colors. *Animal Cognition, 12,* 435–439.

Slobodskaya, Helena R., & Kozlova, Elena A. (2016). Early temperament as a predictor of later personality. *Personality and Individual Differences, 99,* 127–132. https://doi.org/10.1016/j.paid.2016.04.094

Slotnick, Scott D., & Schacter, David L. (2007). The cognitive neuroscience of memory and consciousness. In Philip David Zelazo, Morris Moscovitch, & Evan Thompson (Eds.), *The Cambridge handbook of consciousness.* Cambridge University Press.

Slutzky, Carly B., & Simpkins, Sandra D. (2009). The link between children's sport participation and self-esteem: Exploring the mediating role of sport self-concept. *Psychology of Sport and Exercise, 10*(3), 381–389.

Smalarz, Laura, & Wells, Gary L. (2015). Contamination of eyewitness self-reports and the mistaken-identification problem. *Current Directions in Psychological Science, 24,* 120–124. https://doi.org/10.1177/0963721414554394

Smallwood, Jonathan; McSpadden, Merrill; & Schooler, Jonathan W. (2007). The lights are on but no one's home: Meta-awareness and the decoupling of attention when the mind wanders. *Psychonomic Bulletin & Review, 14*(3), 527–533.

Smart, Reginald G.; Mann, Robert E.; & Stoduto, Gina. (2003). The prevalence of road rage: Estimates from Ontario. *Canadian Journal of Public Health, 94*(4), 247–250.

Smilek, Daniel; Carriere, Jonathan S. A.; & Cheyne, Allan J. (2010). Out of mind, out of sight: Eye blinking as indicator and embodiment of mind wandering. *Psychological Science, 21*(6), 786–789. https://doi.org/10.1177/0956797610368063

Smirle, Corinne. (2012). Profile of Anna Freud. In A. Rutherford (Ed.), *Psychology's Feminist Voices Multimedia Internet Archive.* https://feministvoices.com/profiles/anna-freud

Smirle, Corinne. (2013). Profile—Rosalie Rayner. *Psychology's Feminist Voices.* https://www.feministvoices.com/profiles/rosalie-rayner/

Smith, Amy M.; Floerke, Victoria A.; & Thomas, Ayanna K. (2016). Retrieval practice protects memory against acute stress. *Science, 354,* 1046–1048. https://doi.org/10.1126/science.aah5067

Smith, Brendan L. (2012, April). The case against spanking. *APA Monitor on Psychology, 43,* 60–63.

Smith, Brian; & Blumstein, Daniel. (2008). Fitness consequences of personality: A meta-analysis. *Behavioral Ecology,19,* 448–455. https://doi.org/10.1093/beheco/arm144

Smith, Craig A.; Bieke, David; & Kirby, Leslie D. (2006). Emotion-eliciting appraisals of social situations. In Joseph P. Forgas (Ed.), *Affect in social thinking and behavior.* Psychology Press.

Smith, Craig A., & Kirby, Leslie D. (2011). The role of appraisal and emotion in coping and adaptation. In Richard J. Contrada & Andrew Baum (Eds.), *The handbook of stress science: Biology, psychology, and health.* Springer.

Smith, Eliot R., & Collins, Elizabeth C. (2009). Contextualizing person perception: Distributed social cognition. *Psychological Review, 116,* 343–364.

Smith, Elke; Junger, Jessica; Derntl, Birgit; & Habel, Ute. (2015). The transsexual brain—A review of findings on the neural basis of transsexualism. *Neuroscience and Biobehavioral Reviews, 59,* 251–266. https://doi.org/10.1016/j.neubiorev.2015.09.008

Smith, J. Carson; Nielson, Kristy A.; Woodard, John L.; Seidenberg, Michael; Durgerian, Sally; Hazlett, Kathleen E.; Figueroa, Christina M.; Kandah, Cassandra C., Kay Christina D., Matthews, Monica A.; & Rao, Stephen. (2014). Physical activity reduces hippocampal atrophy in elders at genetic risk for Alzheimer's disease. *Frontiers in Aging Science, 6,* 61. https://doi.org/10.3389/fnagi.2014.00061

Smith, Jonathan A., & Rhodes, John E. (2015). Being depleted and being shaken: An interpretative phenomenological analysis of the experiential features of a first episode of depression. *Psychology and Psychotherapy: Theory, Research and Practice, 88*(2), 197–209. https://doi.org/10.1111/papt.12034

Smith, Jonathan C. (2010). *Pseudoscience and extraordinary claims: A critical thinker's toolkit.* Wiley-Blackwell.

Smith, Kristopher M., & Apicella, Coren L. (2017). Winners, losers, and posers: The effect of power poses on testosterone and risk-taking following competition. *Hormones and Behavior, 92,* 172–181. https://doi.org/10.1016/j.yhbeh.2016.11.003

Smith, Nareissa L. (2015). Built for boyhood: Proposal for reducing the amount of gender bias in the advertising of children's toys on television. *Vanderbilt Journal of Entertainment and Technology Law, 17*(4), 991–1050. https://go.gale.com/ps/anonymous?id=GALE%7CA432894720&sid=googleScholar&v=2.1&it=r&linkaccess=abs&issn=1942678X&p=AONE&sw=w

Smith, Peter B. (2010). Cross-cultural psychology: Some accomplishments and challenges. *Psychological Studies, 55*(2), 89–95.

Smith, Timothy B.; Domenech Rodríguez, Melanie; & Bernal, Guillermo. (2011). Culture. *Journal of Clinical Psychology: In Session, 67,* 166–175. https://doi.org/0.1002/jclp.20757

Smith, Timothy B.; McCullough, Michael E.; & Poll, Justin. (2005). Religiousness and depression: Evidence for a main effect and the moderating influence of stressful life events. *Psychological Bulletin, 129,* 614–636.

Smith, Tovia. (2019, Jan. 17). Backlash erupts after Gillette launches a new #MeToo-inspired ad campaign. *NPR.* https://www.npr.org/2019/01/17/685976624/backlash-erupts-after-gillette-launches-a-new-metoo-inspired-ad-campaign

Smith, Travis; Panfil, Kelsey; Bailey, Carrie; & Kirkpatrick, Kimberly. (2019). Cognitive and behavioral training interventions to promote self-control. *Journal of Experimental Psychology: Animal Learning and Cognition, 45*(3), 259–279. https://doi.org/10.1037/xan0000208

Smolen, Paul; Zhang, Yili; & Byrne, John H. (2016). The right time to learn: Mechanisms and optimization of spaced learning. *Nature Neuroscience Reviews, 17,* 77–88. https://doi.org/10.1038/nrn.2015.18

Smoller, Jordan W., & Finn, Christopher T. (2003). Family, twin, and adoption studies of bipolar disorder. *American Journal of Medical Genetics, Part C, Seminars in Medical Genetics, 123C*(1), 48–58. https://doi.org/10.1002/ajmg.c.20013

Sneddon, Ian; McKeown, Gary; McRorie, Margaret; Vukicevic, Tijana. (2011). Cross-cultural patterns in dynamic ratings of positive and negative natural emotional behaviour. *PLOS ONE, 6*(2): e14679. https://doi.org/10.1371/journal.pone.0014679

Sneed, Joel R.; Whitbourne, Susan Krauss; Schwartz, Seth J.; & Huang, Shi. (2012). The relationship between identity, intimacy, and midlife well-being: Findings from the Rochester Adult Longitudinal Study. *Psychology and Aging, 27,* 318–323. https://doi.org/10.1037/a0026378

Snitz, Beth E.; O'Meara, Ellen S.; Carlson, Michelle C.; Arnold, Alice M.; Ives, Diane G.; Rapp, Stephen R.; Saxton, Judith; Lopez, Oscar L.; Dunn, Leslie O.; Sink, Kaycee M.; & DeKosky, Steven T. (2009). Ginkgo biloba for preventing cognitive decline in older adults: A randomized trial. *JAMA: Journal of the American Medical Association, 302*(24), 2663–2670.

Snowdon, David A. (2002). *Aging with grace: What the nun study teaches us about leading longer, healthier, and more meaningful lives.* Bantam.

Snowdon, David A. (2003). Healthy aging and dementia: Findings from the Nun Study. *Annals of Internal Medicine, 139,* 450–454.

Snyder, Charles R.; Lopez, Shane J.; & (Teramoto) Pedrotti, Jennifer T. (2011). *Positive psychology: The scientific and practical explorations of human strengths.* Sage.

Snyder, Douglas K., & Balderrama-Durbin, Christina. (2012). Integrative approaches to couple therapy: Implications for clinical practice and research. *Behavior Therapy 43,* 13–24. https://doi.org/10.1016/j.beth.2011.03.004

Snyder, Hannah R.; Kaiser, Roselinde H.; Warren, Stacie L.; & Heller, Wendy. (2014). Obsessive-compulsive disorder is associated with broad impairments in executive function: A meta-analysis. *Clinical Psychological Science, 3*(2), 301–330. https://doi.org/10.1177/2167702614534210

Snyder, Rebecca J.; Perdue, Bonnie M.; Zhang, Zhihe; Maple, Terry L.; & Charlton, Benjamin D. (2016). Giant panda maternal care: A test of the experience constraint hypothesis. *Scientific Reports, 6.* https://doi.org/10.1038/srep27509

Society for Human Resource Management (SHRM). (2016). Screening and evaluating candidates. *SHRM.* https://www.shrm.org/resourcesandtools/tools-and-samples/toolkits/pages/screeningandevaluatingcandidates.aspx

Society for Human Resource Management (SHRM). (2017, April 24). *2017 employee job satisfaction and engagement: The doors of opportunity are open.* https://www.shrm.org/hr-today/trends-and-forecasting/research-and-surveys/pages/2017-job-satisfaction-and-engagement-doors-of-opportunity-are-open.aspx

Soderstrom, Nicholas C., & Bjork, Robert A. (2015). Learning versus performance: An integrative review. *Perspectives on Psychological Science, 10,* 176–199. https://doi.org/10.1177/1745691615569000

Soderstrom, Nicholas C.; Kerr, Tyson K.; & Bjork, Robert A. (2016). The critical importance of retrieval—and spacing—for learning. *Psychological Science, 27,* 223–230. https://doi.org/10.1177/0956797615617778

Sohn, Michael, & Bosinski, Hartmut A. G. (2007). Continuing medical education: Gender identity disorders: diagnostic and surgical aspects (CME). *Journal of Sexual Medicine.* 4, 1193–1208.

Sokol, Robert J., Jr.; Delaney-Black, Virginia; & Nordstrom, Beth. (2003). Fetal alcohol spectrum disorder. *Journal of the American Medical Association, 290,* 2996–2999. https://doi.org/10.1001/jama.290.22.2996

Solomon, David A.; Leon, Andrew C.; Coryell, William H.; Endicott, Jean; Li, Chunshan; Fiedorowics, Jess G.; Boyken, Lara; & Keller, Martin B. (2010). Longitudinal course of bipolar I disorder. *Archives of General Psychiatry, 67,* 339–347. https://doi.org/10.1001/archgenpsychiatry.2010.15

Solomon, Linda Zener; Solomon, Henry; & Stone, Ronald. (1978). Helping as a function of number of bystanders and ambiguity of emergency. *Personality and Social Psychology Bulletin, 4,* 318–321.

Solomon, Paul R.; Adams, Felicity; Silver, Amanda; Zimmer, Jill; & De-Veaux, Richard. (2002). Ginkgo for memory enhancement: A randomized controlled trial. *Journal of the American Medical Association, 288,* 835–840.

Solomon, Samuel G., & Lennie, Peter (2007). The machinery of colour vision. *Nature Reviews Neuroscience, 8*(4), 276–286.

Somerville, Leah H. (2013). The teenage brain: Sensitivity to social evaluation. *Current Directions in Psychological Science, 22,* 121–127. https://doi.org/10.1177/0963721413476512

Song, Alex; Severini, Thomas; & Allada, Ravi. (2017). How jet lag impairs Major League Baseball performance. *Proceedings of the National Academy of Sciences, 114,* 1407–1412. https://doi.org/10.1073/pnas.1608847114

Sørensen, Holger; Nielsen, Philip; Pedersen, Carsten; Benros, Michael; Nordentoft, Merete; & Mortensen, Preben. (2014). Population impact of familial and environmental risk factors for schizophrenia: A nationwide study. *Schizophrenia Research, 153,* 214–219. https://doi.org/10.1016/j.schres.2014.01.008

Sorenson, Karen. (2011). *Textbook opportunity.* http://karensearchformeaning.blogspot.com/2011/09/textbook-opportunity.html

Sorkhabi, Nadia. (2010). Sources of parent-adolescent conflict: Content and form of parenting. *Social Behavior & Personality: An International Journal, 38*(6), 761–782.

Soto, Christopher. (2014). Is happiness good for your personality? Concurrent and prospective relations of the Big Five with subjective well-being. *Journal of Personality,83,* 45-55. https://doi.org/10.1111/jopy.12081

Soto, Christopher J., & John, Oliver P. (2014). Traits in transition: The structure of parent-reported personality traits from early childhood to early adulthood. *Journal of Personality, 82*(3), 182–199. https://doi.org/10.1111/jopy.12044

Soto, Christopher, & Tackett, Jennifer. (2015). Personality traits in childhood and adolescence: Structure, development, and outcomes. *Current Directions in Psychological Science,24,* 358–362. https://doi.org/10.1177/0963721415589345

Soussignan, Robert. (2004). Regulatory function of facial actions in emotion processes. In Serge P. Shohov (Ed.), *Advances in Psychology Research, 31,* 173–198. Nova Science.

Southward, Matthew W.; & Cheavens, Jennifer S. (2018). Identifying core deficits in a dimensional model of borderline personality disorder features: A network analysis. *Clinical Psychological Science, 6*(5), 685–703. https://doi.org/10.1177/2167702618769560

Sowislo, Julia F.; Gonet-Wirz, Franca; Borgwardt, Stefan; Lang, Undine E., & Huber, Christian G. (2017, April 3). Perceived dangerousness as related to psychiatric symptoms and psychiatric service use- A vignette based representative population survey. *Scientific Reports, 7,* 45716. https://doi.org/10.1038/srep45716

Spalding, Kirsty L; Bergmann, Olaf; Alkass, Kanar; Bernard, Samuel; Salehpour, Mehran; Huttner, Hagen B.; . . . & Frisén, Jonas. (2013). Dynamics of hippocampal neurogenesis in adult humans. *Cell, 153,* 1219–1227.

Spanos, Nicholas P. (1991). A sociocognitive approach to hypnosis. In Steven Jay Lynn & Judith W. Rhue (Eds.), *Theories of hypnosis: Current models and perspectives.* Guilford.

Spanos, Nicholas P. (1994). Multiple identity enactments and multiple personality disorder: A sociocognitive perspective. *Psychological Bulletin, 116,* 143–165.

Spanos, Nicholas P.; Barber, T. X.; & Lang, Gerald (2005). Cognition and self-control: Cognitive control of painful sensory input. *Integrative Physiological & Behavioral Science, 40,* 119–128.

Spearman, Charles E. (1904). "General intelligence" objectively determined and measured. *American Journal of Psychology, 15,* 201–293.

Specht, Jule; Egloff, Boris; & Schmukle, Stefan. (2012). Examining mechanisms of personality maturation: The impact of life satisfaction on the development of the Big Five personality traits. *Social Psychological and Personality Science,4,* 181–189. https://doi.org/10.1177550612448197

Spencer, Natasha A.; McClintock, Martha K.; Sellergren, Sarah A.; Bullivant, Susan; Jacob, Suma; & Mennella, Julie A. (2004). Social chemosignals from breast-feeding women increase sexual motivation. *Hormones and Behavior, 46,* 362–370.

Sperry, Roger W. (1982). Some effects of disconnecting the cerebral hemispheres. *Science, 217,* 1223–1226.

Spezzaferri, Rosa; Modica, Maddalena; Racca, Vittorio; Ripamonti, Vittorino; Tavanelli, Monica; Brambilla, Gabriella; & Ferratini, Maurizio. (2009). Psychological disorders after coronary artery by-pass surgery: A one-year prospective study. *Monaldi Archives for Chest Disease, 72*(4), 200–205.

Spiers, Mary V.; Sakamoto, Maiko; Elliott, Richard J.; & Baumann, Steve. (2008). Sex differences in spatial object-location memory in a virtual grocery store *CyberPsychology & Behavior, 11,* 471–473.

Spies, Robert A.; Carlson, Janet F.; & Geisinger, Kurt F. (2010). *The mental measurements yearbook* (18th ed.), Buros Institute of Mental\Measurements/University of Nebraska Press.

Spocchia, Gino. (2021, January 17). Capitol rioters taking selfies leave digital trail of 140,000 images under FBI investigation. *Independent.* https://www.independent.co.uk/news/world/americas/us-election-2020/capitol-riot-fbi-images-video-arrested-b1788593.html

Spottiswoode, Claire; Begg, Keith; & Begg, Colleen. (2016). Reciprocal signaling in honeyguide-human mutualism. *Science, 353,* 387–389. https://doi.org/10.1126/science.aaf4885

Spradlin, Joseph E. (2002). Punishment: A primary process. *Journal of Applied Behavior Analysis, 35,* 475–477.

Sprecher, Susan, & Felmlee, Diane. (2008). Insider perspectives on attraction. In S. Sprecher, A. Wenzel & J. Harvey (Eds.), *Handbook of relationship initiation.* Psychology Press.

Squire, Larry R., & Dede, Adams J. O. (2015). Conscious and unconscious memory systems. *Cold Spring Harbor Perspectives in Biology, 7,* a021667. https://doi.org/10.1101/cshperspect.a021667

Sritharan, Rajees, & Gawronski, Bertram. (2010). Changing implicit and explicit prejudice: Insights from the associative-propositional evaluation model. *Social Psychology, 41*(3), 113–123. https://doi.org/10.1027/1864-9335/a000017

Sroufe, L. Alan. (2002). From infant autonomy to promotion of adolescent autonomy: Prospective, longitudinal data on the role of parents in development. In John G. Borkowski & Sharon Landesman Ramey (Eds.), *Parenting and the child's world: Influences on academic, intellectual, and social-emotional development.* Erlbaum.

Staats, Sara; Cosmar, David; & Kaffenberger, Joshua. (2007). Sources of happiness and stress for college students: A replication and comparison over 20 years. *Psychological Reports, 10,* 685–696.

Stacho, Martin; Herold, Christina; Rook, Noemi; Wagner, Hermann; Axer, Markus; Amunts, Katrin; & Güntürkün, Onur. (2020). A cortex-like canonical circuit in the avian forebrain. *Science, 369*(6511), 1585. https://doi.org/10.1126/science.abc5534

Stack, Dale M.; Serbin, Lisa A.; Enns, Leah N.; Ruttle, Paula L.; & Barrieau, Lindsey. (2010). Parental effects on children's emotional development over time and across generations. *Infants & Young Children, 23*(1), 52–69. https://doi.org/10.1097/IYC.1090b1013e3181c97606

Stahl, Stephen M. (2009). *Stahl's illustrated antipsychotics.* Cambridge University Press.

Stamkou, Eftychia; van Kleef, Gerben A.; Homan, Astrid C.; Gelfand, Michele J.; van de Vijver Fons J. R.; van Egmond, Marike C.; Boer, Diana; Phiri, Natasha; Ayub Nailah; Kinias, Zoe; Cantarero, Katarzyna; Treister, Dorit E.; Figueiredo, Ana; Hashimoto, Hirofumi; Hoffman, Eva B.; Lima, Renata P.; & Lee, I-Ching. (2019). Cultural collectivism and tightness moderate responses to norm violators: Effects on power perception, moral emotions, and leader support. *Personality and Social Psychology Bulletin, 45*(6), 947–964. https://doi.org/10.1177/0146167218802

Stancey, Helen, & Turner, Mark. (2010). Close women, distant men: Line bisection reveals sex-dimorphic patterns of visuomotor performance in near and far space. *British Journal of Psychology, 101,* 293–309.

Stanley, Damian A.; Sokol-Hessner, Peter; Banaji, Mahzarin R.; & Phelps, Elizabeth A. (2011). Implicit race attitudes predict trustworthiness judgments and economic trust decisions. *Proceedings of the National Academy of Sciences, 108,* 7710–7715. https://doi.org/10.1073/pnas.1014345108

Stark, Craig E. L.; Okado, Yoko; Loftus, Elizabeth F. (2010). Imaging the reconstruction of true and false memories using sensory reactivation and the misinformation paradigms. *Learning & Memory, 17,* 485–488. https://doi.org/10.1101/lm.1845710

Staub, Ervin. (1996). Cultural-societal roots of violence: The examples of genocidal violence and of contemporary youth violence in the United States. *American Psychologist, 51,* 117–132.

Stavrinos, Despina; Pope, Caitlin N.; Shen, Jiabin; & Schwebel, David C. (2018). Distracted walking, bicycling, and driving: Systematic review and meta-analysis of mobile technology and youth crash risk. *Child Development, 89*(1), 118–128. https://doi.org/10.1111/cdev.12827

Stavropoulos, Vasileios; Anderson, Emma Ela; Beard, Charlotte; Latifi, Mohammed Qasim; Kuss, Daria; & Griffiths, Mark. (2019). A preliminary cross-cultural study of Hikikomori and Internet Gaming Disorder: The moderating effects of game-playing time and living with parents. *Addictive Behaviors Reports, 9,* 100137. https://doi.org/10.1016/j.abrep.2018.10.001

Steblay, Nancy Mehrkens. (1987). Helping behavior in urban and rural environments: A meta-analysis. *Psychological Bulletin, 102,* 346–356.

Steel, Piers. (2007). The nature of procrastination: A meta-analytic and theoretical review of quintessential self-regulatory failure. *Psychological Bulletin, 133,* 65–94.

Steele, Claude M. (1997). A threat in the air: How stereotypes shape intellectual identity and performance. *American Psychologist, 52,* 613–629.

Steele, Jennifer R.; Reisz, Leah.; Williams, Amanda.; & Kawakami, Kerry. (2007). Women in mathematics: Examining the hidden barriers that gender stereotypes can impose. In Ronald J. Burke & Mary C. Mattis (Eds.), *Women and minorities in science, technology, engineering and mathematics: Upping the numbers*. Elgar.

Steg, Linda, & de Groot, Judith. (2010). Explaining prosocial intentions: Testing causal relationships in the norm activation model. *British Journal of Social Psychology, 49*(4), 725–743.

Steinberg, Laurence. (1990). Autonomy, conflict, and harmony in the family relationship. In S. Shirley Feldman & Glen R. Elliott (Eds.), *At the threshold: The developing adolescent*. Harvard University Press.

Steinberg, Laurence. (2001). We know some things: Parent–adolescent relationships in retrospect and prospect. *Journal of Research on Adolescence, 11*, 1–19.

Steinberg, Laurence. (2010). A dual systems model of adolescent risk-taking. *Developmental Psychobiology, 52*(3), 216–224. https://doi.org/10.1002/dev.20445

Stellar, Jennifer; John-Henderson, Neha; Anderson, Craig; Gordon, Amie; McNeil, Galen; & Keltner, Dacher. (2015). Positive affect and markers of inflammation: Discrete positive emotions predict lower levels of inflammatory cytokines. *Emotion, 15*(2), 129–133. https://doi.org/10.1037/emo0000033

Stellman, Jeanne Mager; Smith, Rebecca P.; Katz, Craig L.; Sharma, Vansh; Charney, Dennis S.; Herbert, Robin; Moline, Jacqueline; Luft, Benjamin J.; Markowitz, Steven; Udasin, Iris; Harrison, Denise; Baron, Sherry; Landrigan, Philip J.; Levin, Stephen M.; & Southwick, Steven. (2008). Enduring mental health morbidity and social function impairment in World Trade Center rescue, recovery, and cleanup workers: The psychological dimension of an environmental health disaster. *Environmental Health Perspectives, 116*(9), 1248–1253. https://doi.org/10.1289/ehp.11164

Stephane, Massoud; Hagen, Matthew C.; Lee, Joel T.; Uecker, Jonathan; Pardo, Patricia J.; Kuskowski, Michael A.; & Pardo, José V. (2006). About the mechanisms of auditory verbal hallucinations: A positron emission tomographic study. *Journal of Psychiatry & Neuroscience, 31*(6), 396–405.

Stephens, Benjamin R., & Banks, Martin S. (1987). Contrast discrimination in human infants. *Journal of Experimental Psychology: Human Perception and Performance, 13*, 558–565.

Steptoe, Andrew; Dockray, Samantha; & Wardle, Jane. (2009). Positive affect and psychobiological processes relevant to health. *Journal of Personality, 77*(6), 1747–1776.

Steptoe, Andrew; Shankar, Aparna; Demakakos, Panayotes; & Wardle, Jane. (2013). Social isolation, loneliness, and all-cause mortality in older men and women. *Proceedings of the National Academy of Sciences, 110*, 5797–5801. https://doi.org/10.1073/pnas.1219686110

Stern, Kathleen, & McClintock, Martha K. (1998, March 12). Regulation of ovulation by human hormones. *Nature, 392*, 177.

Stern, Peter. (2001). Sweet dreams are made of this. *Science, 294*, 1047.

Stern, Robert. (2016, March 31). Quoted in: Maese, Rick. Repeated hits to the head more significant than concussions, new study suggests. *Washington Post*. Retrieved from https://www.washingtonpost.com/sports/redskins/repeated-hits-to-head-more-significant-than-concussions-new-study-suggests/2016/03/31/58dd9c6c-f750-11e5-9804-537defcc3cf6_story.html?noredirect=on&utm_term=.addae46bf50c

Sternberg, Robert J. (1986). *Intelligence applied: Understanding and increasing your intellectual skills*. Harcourt Brace Jovanovich.

Sternberg, Robert J. (1988). A three-facet model of creativity. In Robert J. Sternberg (Ed.), *The nature of creativity*. Cambridge University Press.

Sternberg, Robert J. (1990). *Metaphors of mind: Conceptions of the nature of intelligence*. Cambridge University Press.

Sternberg, Robert J. (1995). For whom the bell curve tolls: A review of the bell curve. *Psychological Science, 6*, 257–261.

Sternberg, Robert J. (1997). The concept of intelligence and its role in lifelong learning and success. *American Psychologist, 52*, 1030–1037.

Sternberg, Robert J. (2012a). Intelligence. *Dialogues of Clinical Neuroscience, 14*(1), 19–27. https://doi.org/10.31887/DCNS.2012.14.1/rsternberg

Sternberg, Robert J. (2012b). Intelligence in its cultural context. In Michele J. Gelfand, Chi-yue Ciu, & Ying-yi Hong (Eds.), *Advances in culture and psychology* (Vol. 2). Oxford University Press.

Sternberg, Robert J. (2012c). The triarchic theory of successful intelligence. In Dawn P. Flanagan & Patti L. Harrison (Eds.) *Contemporary intellectual assessment: Theories, tests, and issues* (3rd ed.). Guilford.

Sternberg, Robert J. (2014). Teaching about the nature of intelligence. *Intelligence, 42*, 176–179. https://doi.org/10.1016/j.intell.2013.08.010

Stevenson, Harold W.; Lee, Shin-Ying; & Stigler, James W. (1986). Mathematics achievements of Chinese, Japanese, and American children. *Science, 236*, 693–698.

Stevner, A. B. A.; Vidaurre, D.; Cabral, J.; Rapuano, K.; Nielsen, S. F. V.; Tagliazucchi, E.; Laufs, H.; Vuust, P.; Deco, G.; Woolrich, M. W.; Van Someren, E.; & Kringelbach, M. L. (2019). Discovery of key whole-brain transitions and dynamics during human wakefulness and non-REM sleep. *Nature Communications, 10*. https://doi.org/10.1038/s41467-019-08934-3

Stewart, V. Mary. (1973). Tests of the "carpentered world" hypothesis by race and environment. *International Journal of Psychology, 8*, 12–34.

Sticca, Fabio, & Perren, Sonja. (2012). Is cyberbullying worse than traditional bullying? Examining the differential roles of medium, publicity, and anonymity for the perceived severity of bullying. *Journal of Youth and Adolescence, 42*, 739–750. https://doi.org/10.1007/s10964-012-9867-3

Stice, Eric, & Yokum, Sonja. (2016). Neural vulnerability factors that increase risk for future weight gain. *Psychological Bulletin, 142*(5), 447–471. https://doi.org/10.1037/bul0000044

Stickgold, Robert, & Walker, Matthew P. (2013). Sleep-dependent memory triage: Evolving generalization through selective processing. *Nature Neuroscience, 16*, 139–145.

Stinson, Danu A.; Cameron, Jessica J.; Wood, Joanne V.; Gaucher, Danielle; & Holmes, J. G. (2009). Deconstructing the "reign of error": Interpersonal warmth explains the self-fulfilling prophecy of anticipated acceptance. *Personality and Social Psychology Bulletin, 35*, 1165–1178.

Stockdale, Laura A., & Coyne, Sarah M. (2020). Bored and online: Reasons for using social media, problematic social networking site use, and behavioral outcomes across the transition from adolescence to emerging adulthood. *Journal of Adolescence, 79*, 173–183. https://doi.org/10.1016/j.adolescence.2020.01.010

Stogdill, Ralph M. (1948). Personal factors associated with leadership: A survey of the literature. *Journal of Psychology, 25*, 35–71.

Stompe, Thomas; Karakula, Hanna; Rudaleviciene, Palmira; Okribelashvili, Nino; Chaudhry, Haroon R.; Idemudia, E. E., & Gscheider, S. (2006). The pathoplastic effect of culture on psychotic symptoms in schizophrenia. *World Cultural Psychiatry Research Review, 1*(3/4),157–163.

Storm, Benjamin C., & Angello, Genna. (2010). Overcoming fixation: Creative problem solving and retrieval-induced forgetting. *Psychological Science, 21*(9), 1263–1265. https://doi.org/10.1177/0956797610379864

Stoughton, William; Thompson, Lori; & Meade, Adam. (2015). Examining applicant reactions to the use of social networking websites in pre-employment screening. *Journal of Business Psychology, 30*, 73–88. https://doi.org/10.1007/s10869-013-9333-6

Støving, René Klinkby; Andries, Alin; Brixen, Kim; Bilenberg, Niels; & Hørder, Kirsten. (2011). Gender differences in outcome of eating disorders: A retrospective cohort study. *Psychiatry Research, 186*(2–3), 362–366. https://doi.org/10.1016/j.psychres.2010.08.005

Strandwitz, Philip. (2018). Neurotransmitter modulation by the gut microbiota. *Brain Research, 1693*(Pt B), 128–133. https://doi.org/10.1016/j.brainres.2018.03.015

Strange, Deryn; Garry, Maryanne; Bernstein, Daniel M.; & Lindsay, D. Stephen. (2011). Photographs cause false memories for the news. *Acta Psychologica, 136*(1), 90–94.

Straube, Thomas; Glauer, Madlen; Dilger, Stefan; Mentzel, Hans-Joachim; & Miltner, Wolfgang H. R. (2006). Effects of cognitive-behavioral therapy on brain activation in specific phobia. *NeuroImage, 29*, 125–135. https://doi.org/10.1016/j.neuroimage.2005.07.007

Strauss, Clara; Cavanagh, Kate; Oliver, Annie; & Pettman, Danelle. (2014). Mindfulness-based interventions for people diagnosed with a current episode of an anxiety or depressive disorder: A meta-analysis of randomised controlled trials. *PLOS ONE, 9*(4), 1–13. https://doi.org/10.1371/journal.pone.0096110

Strayer, David L.; Cooper, Joel M.; Turrill, Jonna; Coleman, James; Medeiros-Ward, Nate; & Biondi, Francesco. (2013). *Measuring cognitive distraction in the automobile*. AAA Foundation for Traffic Safety.

Strayer, David L.; Drews, Frank A.; & Crouch, Dennis J. (2006). A comparison of the cell phone driver and the drunk driver. *Human Factors: The Journal of the Human Factors and Ergonomics Society, 48*, 381–391.

Streitfeld, David. (2015). Data-crunching is coming to help your boss manage your time. *The New York Times*. http://nyti.ms/1DXbXOg

Strickland, Bonnie R. (1995). Research on sexual orientation and human development: A commentary. *Developmental Psychology, 31*, 137–140.

Strickland, Brent, & Keil, Frank. (2011). Event completion: Event based inferences distort memory in a matter of seconds. *Cognition, 121*, 409–415. https://doi.org/10.1016/j.cognition.2011.04.007

Strimbu, Clark E.; Prasad, Sonal; Hakizimana, Pierre; & Fridberger, Anders. (2019). Control of hearing sensitivity by tectorial membrane calcium. *Proceedings of the National Academy of Sciences of the United States of America, 12*, 5756–764. https://doi.org/10.1073/pnas.1805223116

Stuart, Gwynedd. (2013, October 19). Show us your . . . sleeping mats for the homeless. *Chicago Reader*. https://www.chicagoreader.com/chicago/new-life-old-bags-ruth-werstler-homeless-recycle/Content?oid=11261669

Stults-Kolehmainen, Matthew, & Sinha, Rajita. (2014). The effects of stress on physical activity and exercise. *Sports Medicine,44*(1), 81–121. https://doi.org/10.1007/s40279-013-0090-5

Stump, Scott. (2020, January 24). Taylor Swift opens up about eating disorder: Photos of myself were a 'trigger'. *Today*. https://www.today.com/popculture/taylor-swift-opens-about-struggling-eating-disorder-t172463

Suarez-Morales, Lourdes; Dillon, Frank R.; & Szapocznik, Jose. (2007). Validation of the Acculturative Stress Inventory for Children. *Cultural Diversity and Ethnic Minority Psychology, 13*, 216–224.

Substance Abuse and Mental Health Services Administration (SAMHSA). (2019). *Key substance use and mental health indicators in the United States: Results from the 2018 national survey on drug use and health.* (HHS Publication No. PEP19-5068, NSDUH Series H-54). U.S. Department of Health and Human Services, Center for Behavioral Health Statistics and Quality. https://www.samhsa.gov/data/

Substance Abuse and Mental Health Services Administration (SAMHSA). (2020). *Key substance use and mental health indicators in the United States: Results from the 2019 national survey on drug use and health.* U.S. Department of Health and Human Services. https://www.samhsa.gov/data/sites/default/files/reports/rpt29393/2019NSDUHFFRPDFWHTML/2019NSDUHFFR090120.htm

Sudak, Donna M. (2011). *Combining CBT and medication: An evidence-based approach.* Wiley.

Sue, David, & Sue, Diane M. (2008). *Foundations of counseling and psychotherapy: Evidence-based practices for a diverse society.* Wiley.

Sue, Derald Wing. (2010). *Microaggressions in everyday life: Race, gender, and sexual orientation.* Wiley.

Sue, Derald Wing. (2017). Microaggressions and "evidence": Empirical and experiential reality? *Perspectives on Psychological Science, 12,* 170–172. https://doi.org/10.1177/1745691616664437

Sue, Derald Wing; Capodilupo, Christina M.; & Holder, Aisha M. B. (2008). Racial microaggressions in the life experience of black Americans. *Professional Psychology: Research and Practice, 39,* 329–336. https://doi.org/10.1037/0735-7028.39.3.329

Sue, Derald Wing, & Sue, David. (2008). *Counseling the culturally diverse: Theory and practice* (5th ed.). Wiley.

Sue, Derald Wing, & Sue, David. (2008). *Counseling the culturally diverse: Theory and practice* (5th ed.). Wiley.

Sue, Stanley. (1999). Science, ethnicity, and bias: Where have we gone wrong? *American Psychologist, 54*(12), 1070–1077.

Sue, Stanley. (2009). Ethnic minority psychology: Struggles and triumphs. *Cultural Diversity and Ethnic Minority Psychology, 15*(4), 409–415. https://doi.org/10.1037/a0017559

Sullivan, John. (2013). How Google is using people analytics to completely reinvent HR. *Talent Management and HR.* https://www.eremedia.com/tlnt/how-google-is-using-people-analytics-to-completely-reinvent-hr/

Sullivan, John Jeremiah. (2014, September 17). Donald Antrim and the art of anxiety. *The New York Times Magazine.* http://www.nytimes.com/2014/09/21/magazine/donald-antrim-and-the-art-of-anxiety.html

Sullivan, Patrick F.; Daly, Mark J.; & O'Donovan, Michael. (2012). Genetic architectures of psychiatric disorders: The emerging picture and its implications. *Nature Reviews, 13,* 537–551. https://doi.org/10.1038/nrg3240

Suls, Jerry, & Bunde, James. (2005). Anger, anxiety, and depression as risk factors for cardiovascular disease: The problems and implications of overlapping affective dispositions. *Psychological Bulletin, 131,* 260–300.

Sumter, Sindy R.; Bokhorst, Caroline L.; Steinberg, Laurence; & Westenberg, P. Michael. (2009). The developmental pattern of resistance to peer influence in adolescence: Will the teenager ever be able to resist? *Journal of Adolescence, 32*(4), 1009–1021.

Sun, Shumei S.; Schubert, Christine M.; Chumlea, William Cameron; Roche, Alex F.; Kulin, Howard E.; Lee, Peter A.; Himes, John H.; & Ryan, Alan S. (2002). National estimates of the timing of sexual maturation and racial differences among US children. *Pediatrics, 110*(5), 911–919. https://doi.org/10.1542/peds.110.5.911

Supèr, Hans, & Romeo, August. (2011). Rebound spiking as a neural mechanism for surface filling-in. *Journal of Cognitive Neuroscience, 23*(2), 491–501.

Swami, Viren; Frederick, David A.; Aavik, Toivo; Alcalay, Lidia; Allik, Jüri; Anderson, Donna; Andrianto, Sonny; Arora, Arvind; Brännström, Åke; Cunningham, John; Danel, Dariusz; Doroszewicz, Krystyna; Forbes, Gordon B.; Furnham, Adrian; Greven, Corina U.; Halberstadt, Jamin; Hao, Shuang; Haubner, Tanja; Sup, Choon; . . . & Zivcic-Becirevic, Ivanka. (2010). The attractive female body weight and female body dissatisfaction in 26 countries across 10 world regions: Results of the international body project I. *Personality and Social Psychology Bulletin, 36*(3), 309–325. https://doi.org/10.1177/0146167209359702

Swami, Viren, & Tovée, Martin J. (2006). Does hunger influence judgments of female physical attractiveness? *British Journal of Psychology, 97*(3), 353–363. https://doi.org/10.1348/000712605X80713

Swan, Daniel C., & Big Bow, Harding. (1995, Fall). Symbols of faith and belief—Art of the Native American Church. *Gilcrease Journal, 3,* 22–43.

Swanson, Sonja A.; Crow, Scott J.; Le Grange, Daniel; Swendsen, Joel; & Merikangas, Kathleen R. (2011). Prevalence and correlates of eating disorders in adolescents. *Archives of General Psychiatry, 68*(7), 714–723. https://doi.org/10.1001/archgenpsychiatry.2011.22

Swartz, Conrad M. (2009). Preface. In Conrad M. Swartz (Ed.), *Electroconvulsive and neuromodulation therapies* (pp. xvii–xxx). Cambridge University Press.

Sweeney, Gladys M. (2007). Why childhood attachment matters: Implications for personal happiness, families, and public policy. In A. Scott Loveless & Thomas B. Holman (Eds.), *The Family in the New Millennium: World Voices Supporting the "Natural" Clan:, Vol. 1: The place of family in human society* (pp. 332–346). Praeger/Greenwood.

Szyf, Moshe. (2013). How do environments talk to genes? *Nature Neuroscience, 16,* 2–4. https://doi.org/10.1038/nn.3286

Szyf, Moshe, & Bick, Johanna. (2013). DNA methylation: A mechanism for embedding early life experiences in the genome. *Child Development, 84,* 49–57.

Taber, Keith S. (2020). Mediated learning leading development—The social development theory of Lev Vygotsky. In Ben Akpan, & Teresa J. Kennedy (Eds.), *Science education in theory and practice.* Springer Texts in Education. https://doi.org/10.1007/978-3-030-43620-9_19

Tabuchi, Hiroko. (2015, October 27). Sweeping away gender-specific toys and labels. *The New York Times.* https://www.nytimes.com/2015/10/28/business/sweeping-away-gender-specific-toys-and-labels.html

Tackett, Jennifer; Slobodskaya, Helena; Mar, Raymond; Deal, James; Halverson, Charles; Baker, Spencer; Pavlopoulos, Vassilis; & Besevegis, Elias. (2012). The hierarchical structure of childhood personality in five countries: Continuity from early childhood to early adolescence. *Journal of Personality, 80,* 847–879. https://doi.org/10.1111/j.1467-6494.2011.00748.

Taheri, Shahrad; Lin, Ling; Austin, Diane; Young, Terry; & Mignot, Emmanuel. (2004, December). Short sleep duration is associated with reduced leptin, elevated ghrelin, and increased body mass index. *PLOS Medicine, 1*(3), e62, 001–008. http://www.plosmedicine.org/article/nfo%3Adoi%2F10.1371%2Fjournal.pmed.0010062

Tähkämö, Leena; Partonen, Timo; & Pesonen, Anu-Katriina. (2019). Systematic review of light exposure impact on human circadian rhythm. *Chronobiology International, 36,* 151–170. https://doi.org/10.1080/07420528.2018.1527773

Tait, Raymond C., & Chibnall, John T. (2014). Racial/ethnic disparities in the assessment and treatment of pain: Psychosocial perspectives. *American Psychologist, 69*(2), 131–141. https://doi.org/10.1037/a0035204

Taitz, Jennifer. (2020, May 20). How to reduce your risk of PTSD in a post-COVID-19 world. *The New York Times.* https://nyti.ms/3cPihuh

Takenaga, Lara. (2018). Our obituaries editor on coverage of former Mormon leader Thomas Monson. *The New York Times.* https://www.nytimes.com/2018/01/08/reader-center/thomas-monson-obituary.html

Takeuchi, Tomoka; Fukuda, Kazuhiko; Sasaki, Yuka; Inugami, Maki; & Murphy, Timothy I. (2002). Factors related to the occurrence of isolated sleep paralysis elicited during a multi-phasic sleep-wake schedule. *Sleep, 25,* 89–96.

Talarico, Jennifer M., & Rubin, David C. (2003). Confidence, not consistency, characterizes flashbulb memories. *Psychological Science, 14,* 455–461.

Talarico, Jennifer M., & Rubin, David C. (2007). Flashbulb memories are special after all; in phenomenology, not accuracy. *Applied Cognitive Psychology, 21,* 557–578.

Talhelm, T.; Zhang, X.; Oishi, S.; Shimin, C.; Duan, D.; Lan, X.; & Kitayama, S. (2014). Large-scale psychological differences within China explained by rice versus wheat agriculture. *Science, 344,* 603–608. https://doi.org/10.1126/science.1246850

Tambini, Arielle; Rimmele, Ulrike; Phelps, Elizabeth A.; & Davachi, Lila. (2017). Emotional brain states carry over and enhance future memory formation. *Nature Neuroscience, 20,* 271–278. https://doi.org/10.1038/nn.4468

Tanford, Sarah, & Penrod, Steven. (1984). Social influence model: A formal integration of research on majority and minority influence processes. *Psychological Bulletin, 95,* 189–225.

Tang, Yi-Yuan; Hölzel, Britta K.; & Posner, Michael I. (2015). The neuroscience of mindfulness meditation. *Nature Reviews Neuroscience, 16,* 213–225. https://doi.org/10.1038/nrn3916

Tang, Yi-Yuan, & Posner, Michael I. (2015). Mindfulness in the context of the attention system. In Kirk Warren Brown, J. David Creswell, & Richard M. Ryan (Eds.), *Handbook of mindfulness: Theory, research, and practice.* Guilford.

Tani, Franca; Ponti, Lucia; & Smorti, Martina. (2014). Shyness and psychological adjustment during adolescence: The moderating role of parenting style. *The Open Psychology Journal, 7.* https://doi.org/10.2174/1874350101407010033

Tanielian, Terri. (2008). Invisible wounds of war: Recommendations for addressing psychological and cognitive injuries. Testimony presented before the House Committee on Veterans' Affairs on June 11, 2008.

Tasca, Giorgio A.; Foot, Meredith; Leite, Catherine; Maxwell, Hilary; Balfour, Louise; & Bissada, Hany. (2011). Interpersonal processes in psychodynamic-interpersonal and cognitive behavioral group therapy: A systematic case study of two groups. *Psychotherapy, 48*(3), 260–273.

Tatlow, Didi (2016). On social media in China, size 0 doesn't make the cut. *The New York Times.* http://nyti.ms/1R85aly

Tavris, Carol. (2014, October). Teaching contentious classics. *Association for Psychological Science: Observer.* https://www.psychologicalscience.org/observer/teaching-contentious-classics#.WNvjfaIpB8I

Taylor, Christa L. (2017, September 21). Creativity and mood disorder: A systematic review and meta-analysis. *Perspectives on Psychological Science, 12*(6), 1040–1076. https://doi.org/10.1177/1745691617699653

Taylor, Kate. (2013). Sex on campus: She can play that game, too. *The New York Times.* Retrieved from http://www.nytimes.com/2013/07/14/fashion/sex-on-campus-she-can-play-that-game-too.html

Taylor, Marjorie; Sachet, Alison B.; Maring, Bayta L.; & Mannering, Anne M. (2013). The assessment of elaborated role-play in young children: Invisible friends, personified objects, and pretend identities. *Social Development, 22,* 75–93. https://doi.org/10.1111/sode.12011

Taylor, Marjorie; Shawber, A. B.; Mannering, A. M.; Markman, K. D.; Klein, W. M. P.; & Suhr, J. A. (2009). Children's imaginary companions: What is it like to have an invisible friend? *Handbook of imagination and mental simulation* (pp. 211–224). Psychology Press.

Taylor, Shelley E. (2006). Tend and befriend: Biobehavioral bases of affiliation under stress. *Current Directions in Psychological Science, 15*(6), 273–277. https://doi.org/10.1111/j.1467-8721.2006.00451.x

Taylor, Shelley E. (2012). Tend and befriend theory. In Paul A. M. Van Lange; Arie W. Kruglanski; & E. Tory Higgins (Eds.). *Handbook of Theories of Social Psychology* (Vol. 1). Sage. https://doi.org/10.4135/9781446249215.n3

Taylor, Shelley E., & Master, Sarah L. (2011). Social responses to stress: The tend-and-befriend model. In Richard J. Contrada & Andrew Baum (Eds.), *The handbook of stress science: Biology, psychology, and health.* Springer.

Taylor, W. S., & Martin, M. F. (1944). Multiple personality. *Journal of Abnormal and Social Psychology, 39*(3), 281–300. https://doi.org/10.1037/h0063634

Teachman, Bethany A. (2014). No appointment necessary: Treating mental illness outside the therapist's office. *Perspectives on Psychological Science, 9*(1), 85–87. https://doi.org/10.1177/1745691613512659

Telle, Nils-Torge; Senior, Carl; & Butler, Michael. (2011). Trait emotional intelligence facilitates responses to a social gambling task. *Personality and Individual Differences, 50*(4), 523–526. https://doi.org/10.1016/j.paid.2010.11.010

Tennant, Ruth; Hiller, Louise; Fishwick, Ruth; Platt, Stephen; Joseph, Stephen; Weich, Scott; Parkinson, Jane; & Stewart-Brown, Sarah. (2007). The Warwick Edinburgh mental wellbeing scale (WEMWBS): development and UK validation. *Health and Quality of Life Outcomes, 5*(63).

Teo, Alan R. (2010). A new form of social withdrawal in Japan: A review of hikikomori. *International Journal of Social Psychiatry, 56,* 178–185. https://doi.org/10.1177/0020764008100629

Teo, Alan R., & Gaw, Albert C. (2010). Hikikomori, a Japanese culturebound syndrome of social withdrawal? A proposal for DSM-5. *Journal of Nervous and Mental Disease, 198,* 444–449. https://doi.org/10.1097/NMD.0b013e3181e086b1

Terman, Lewis M. (1916). *Measurement of intelligence.* Houghton Mifflin.

Terman, Lewis M. (1926). *Genetic studies of genius* (2nd ed., Vol. I). Stanford University Press.

Terman, Lewis M., & Oden, Melita H. (1947). *Genetic Studies of Genius: Vol. IV. The gifted child grows up: Twenty-five years' follow-up of a superior group.* Stanford University Press.

Terman, Lewis M., & Oden, Melita H. (1959). *Genetic studies of genius: Vol. V. The gifted at mid-life: Thirty-five years' follow-up of the superior child.* Stanford University Press.

Terrell, Josh; Kofink, Andrew; Middleton, Justin; Rainear, Clarissa; Murphy-Hill, Emerson; Parnin, Chris; & Stallings, Jon. (2017). Gender differences and bias in open source: Pull request acceptance of women versus men. *PeerJ Computer Science, 3,* e111. https://doi.org/10.7717/peerj-cs.111

Terry, Don. (2013, Fall). The Sikh and the skinhead. *Tolerance,* issue 45. https://www.tolerance.org/magazine/number-45-fall-2013/the-sikh-and-the-skinhead

Teyber, Edward. (2009). *Interpersonal process in therapy: An integrative model* (6th ed.). Thomson Brooks/Cole.

Teymoori, Ali, & Shahrazad, Wan. (2012). Relationship between mother, father, and peer attachment and empathy with moral authority. *Ethics & Behavior, 22,* 16–29. https://doi.org/10.1080/10508422.2012.638820

Thase, Michael E., & Denko, Timothey. (2008). Pharmacotherapy of mood disorders. *Annual Review of Clinical Psychology, 4,* 53–91.

Thase, Michael E.; Larsen, Klaus G.; & Kennedy, Sidney H. (2011). Assessing the "true" effect of active antidepressant therapy *v.* placebo in major depressive disorder: Use of a mixture model. *British Journal of Psychiatry, 199,* 501–507. https://doi.org/10.1192/bjp.bp.111.093336

Thayer, Amanda, & Lynn, Steven Jay. (2006). Guided imagery and recovered memory therapy: Considerations and cautions. *Journal of Forensic Psychology Practice, 6,* 63–73.

Thibaut, Florence, & van Wijngaarden-Cremers, Patricia J. M. (2020, December 8). Women's mental health in the time of COVID-19 pandemic. *Frontiers in Global Women's Health, 1,* 588372. https://doi.org/10.3389/fgwh.2020.588372

Thøgersen-Ntoumani, Cecilie; Loughren, Elizabeth; Kinnafick, Florence-Emilie; Taylor, Ian; Duda, Joan; & Fox, Ken. (2015). Changes in work affect in response to lunchtime walking in previously physically inactive employees: A randomized trial. *Scandinavian Journal of Medicine and Science in Sports.* https://doi.org/10.1111/sms.12398

Thomas, Alexander, & Chess, Stella. (1977). *Temperament and development.* Brunner/Mazel.

Thomas, Alexander, & Chess, Stella. (1986). The New York Longitudinal Study: From infancy to early adult life. In Robert Plomin & Judith Dunn (Eds.), *The study of temperament: Changes, continuities, and challenges.* Erlbaum.

Thomas, Alexander; Chess, Stella; & Korn, Sam J. (1982). The reality of difficult temperament. *Merrill-Palmer Quarterly, 28*(1), 1–20. https://www.jstor.org/stable/23086280

Thomas, Ayanna K.; Bulevich, John B.; & Loftus, Elizabeth F. (2003). Exploring the role of repetition and sensory elaboration in the imagination inflation effect. *Memory & Cognition, 31,* 630–640.

Thompson, Clara. (1950). Some effects of the derogatory attitude toward female sexuality. In Jean Baker Miller (Ed.), *Psychoanalysis and women.* Penguin Books.

Thompson, Henry L. (2010). *The stress effect: Why smart leaders make dumb decisions—and what to do about it.* Jossey-Bass.

Thompson, J. Kevin; Roehrig, Megan; & Kinder, Bill N. (2007). Eating disorders. In Michel Hersen, Samuel M. Turner, & Deborah C. Beidel (Eds.), *Adult psychopathology and diagnosis* (5th ed., pp. 571–600). Wiley.

Thompson, Paul M.; Hayashi, Kiralee M.; de Zubicaray, Greig; Janke, Andrew L.; Rose, Stephen E.; Semple, James; . . . & Toga, Arthur W. (2003). Dynamics of gray matter loss in Alzheimer's disease. *Journal of Neuroscience, 23*(3), 994–1005. https://doi.org/10.1523/JNEUROSCI.23-03-00994.2003

Thompson, Renee J.; Mata, Jutta; Jaeggi, Susanne M.; Buschkuehl, Martin; Jonides, John; & Gotlib, Ian H. (2010). Maladaptive coping, adaptive coping, and depressive symptoms: Variations across age and depressive state. *Behaviour Research and Therapy, 48,* 459–466.

Thompson, Richard F. (1994). Behaviorism and neuroscience. *Psychological Review, 101,* 259–265.

Thompson, Richard F. (2005). In search of memory traces. *Annual Review of Psychology, 56,* 1–23.

Thompson, Robin; Emmorey, Karen; & Gollan, Tamar H. (2005). "Tip of the fingers" experiences by deaf signers. *Psychological Science, 16,* 856–860.

Thompson, Suzanne C. (2009). The role of personal control in adaptive functioning. In Shane J. Lopez & C. R. Snyder (Eds.). *Oxford handbook of positive psychology* (2nd ed.). Oxford University Press.

Thompson, Vetta L. Sanders; Bazile, Anita; & Akbar, Maysa. (2004). African Americans' perceptions of psychotherapy and psychotherapists. *Professional Psychology: Research and Practice, 35,* 19–26.

Thompson-Cannino, Jennifer; Cotton, Ronald; & Torneo, Erin. (2009). *Picking cotton: Our memoir of injustice and redemption.* St. Martin's Press.

Thorndike, Edward L. (1898). Animal intelligence: An experimental study of the associative processes in animals. *Psychological Review Monograph Supplement, 2*(Serial No. 8).

Thorndike, Edward L., & Barnhart, Clarence L. (1997). *Thorndike Barnhart junior dictionary.* Pearson Scott Foresman.

Thorndike, Robert L. (1991). Edward L. Thorndike: A professional and personal appreciation. In Gregory A. Kimble, Michael Wertheimer, & Charlotte L. White (Eds.), *Portraits of pioneers in psychology.* American Psychological Association.

Thorne, Barrie. (1993). *Gender play: Girls and boys in school.* Rutgers University Press.

Thornton, Bill, & Tizard, Hayley J. (2010). 'Not in my back yard': Evidence for arousal moderating vested interest and oppositional behavior to proposed change. *Social Psychology, 41*(4), 255–262.

Thorpy, Michael J. (2012). Classification of sleep disorders. *Neurotherapeutics, 9,* 687–701. https://doi.org/10.1007/s13311-012-0145-6

Thorpy, Michael J., & Plazzi, Giuseppe. (2010). *The parasomnias and other sleep-related movement disorders.* Cambridge University Press.

Thunberg, Monika, & Dimberg, Ulf. (2000). Gender differences in facial reactions to fear-relevant stimuli. *Journal of Nonverbal Behavior, 24,* 45–51.

Tiegs, Tom J.; Perrin, Paul B.; & Kaly, Perry W. (2007). My place or yours? An inductive approach to sexuality and gender role conformity. *Sex Roles, 56,* 449–456. https://doi.org/10.1007/s11199-007-9185-5

Tienari, Pekka, & Wahlberg, Karl-Erik. (2008). Family environment and psychosis. In Craig Morgan, Kwame McKenzie, & Paul Fearon (Eds.), *Society and Psychosis.* Cambridge University Press.

Tienari, Pekka; Sorri, Anneli; Lahti, Ilpo; Naarala, Mikko; Wahlberg, Karl-Erik; Moring, Juha; Pohjola, Jukka; & Wynne, Lyman C. (1987). Genetic and psychosocial factors in schizophrenia: The Finnish Adoptive Family Study. *Schizophrenia Bulletin, 13,* 477–484. https://doi.org/10.1093/schbul/13.3.477

Tienari, Pekka; Wahlberg, Karl-Erik; & Wynne, Lyman C. (2006, Winter). Finnish adoption study of schizophrenia: Implications for family interventions. *Families, Systems, & Health, 24*(4), 442–451.

Tienari, Pekka; Wynne, Lyman C.; Moring, Juha; Lahti, Ilpo; Naarala, Mikko; Sorri, Anneli; Wahlberg, Karl-Erik; Saarento, Outi; Seitamaa, Markku; Kaleva, Merja; & Läsky, Kristian. (1994). The Finnish Adoptive Family Study of Schizophrenia: Implications for family research. *British Journal of Psychiatry, 164*(Suppl.), 20–26. https://doi.org/10.1192/S0007125000292696

Tims, Maria; Bakker, Arnold B.; & Derks, Daantje. (2013). The impact of job crafting on job demands, job resources, and well-being. *Journal of Occupational Health Psychology, 18,* 230–240. https://doi.org/10.1037/a0032141

Tinwala, Yasmin. (2021, January 13). What is Elizabeth Smart's net worth? Rape and abduction survivor fought all odds to sell out books and help others. *Meaww.* https://meaww.com/what-is-elizabeth-smart-net-worth-abducted-brian-david-mitchell-masked-dancer-moth

Tipu, Fatima. (2015, February 22). OCD is not a quirk. *The Atlantic.* http://www.theatlantic.com/health/archive/2015/02/ocd-is-a-disorder-not-a-quirk/385562

Titchener, Edward B. (1896/2009). An outline of psychology. In Barbara Gentile & Benjamin O. Miller (Eds.), *Foundations of psychological thought. A history of psychology* (pp. 219–236). Sage.

TMZ. (2016). Ronda Rousey: I'm not ashamed of suicidal thoughts . . . I can help people. *TMZ Sports.* http://www.tmz.com/2016/02/23/ronda-rousey-im-not-ashamed-of-suicidal-thoughts-i-can-help-people/

Tobler, Irene. (2005). Phylogeny of sleep regulation. In Meir H. Kryger, Thomas Roth, & William C. Dement (Eds.), *Principles and practice of sleep medicine* (4th ed.). Elsevier Saunders.

Todd, Brenda K.; Fischer, Rico A.; Di Costa, Steven; Roestorf, Amanda; Harbour, Kate; Hardiman, Paul; & Barry, John A. (2017). Sex differences in children's toy preferences: A systematic review, meta-regression, and meta-analysis. *Infant Child Development, 27,* e2064. https://doi.org/10.1002/icd.2064

Todd, Michael. (2004). Daily processes in stress and smoking: Effects of negative events, nicotine dependence, and gender. *Psychology of Addictive Behaviors, 18,* 31–39.

Todes, Daniel P. (2014). *Ivan Pavlov: A Russian life in science.* Oxford University Press.

Todorov, Alexander; Olivola, Christopher Y.; Dotsch, Ron; & Mende-Siedlecki, Peter. (2015). Social attributions from faces: Determinants, consequences, accuracy, and functional significance. *Annual Review of Psychology, 66,* 519–545. https://doi.org/10.1146/annurev-psych-113011-143831

Toga, Arthur W., & Thompson, Paul M. (2003). Mapping brain asymmetry. *Nature Reviews Neuroscience, 4,* 37–48.

Toga, Arthur W.; Thompson, Paul M.; & Sowell, Elizabeth R. (2006). Mapping brain maturation. *Trends Neuroscience, 29*(3), 148–159. https://doi.org/10.1016/j.tins.2006.01.007

Tolman, Edward C. (1932). *Purposive behavior in animals and men.* Appleton-Century-Crofts.

Tolman, Edward C. (1948). Cognitive maps in rats and men. *Psychological Review, 55,* 189–208.

Tolman, Edward C., & Honzik, Charles H. (1930a). "Insight" in rats. *Publications in Psychology, 4,* 215–232.

Tolman, Edward C., & Honzik, Charles H. (1930b). Introduction and removal of reward, and maze performance in rats. University of California, Berkeley, *Publications in Psychology, 4,* 257–275.

Tolman, Edward C.; Ritchie, B. F.; & Kalish, D. (1946). Studies in spatial learning. I. Orientation and the short-cut. *Journal of Experimental Psychology: General, 121,* 429–434.

Tooby, John, & Cosmides, Leda. (2000). Evolutionary psychology and the emotions. In Michael Lewis & Jeanette M. Haviland-Jones (Eds.), *Handbook of emotions* (2nd ed.). Guilford.

Tooby, John, & Cosmides, Leda. (2008). The evolutionary psychology of the emotions and their relationship to internal regulatory variables. In Michael Lewis, Jeannette M. Haviland-Jones, & Lisa Feldman Barrett (Eds.), *Handbook of emotions* (3rd ed., pp. 114–137). Guilford.

Torales, Julio; Ríos-González, Carlos; Barrios, Ivan; & O'Higgins, Marcelo. (2020, October 26). Self-perceived stress during the quarantine of COVID-19 pandemic in Paraguay: An exploratory survey. *Frontiers in Psychiatry, 11,* 558691. https://doi.org/10.3389/fpsyt.2020.558691

Torges, Cynthia M.; Stewart, A.J.; & Duncan, L.E. (2009). Appreciating life's complexities: Assessing narrative ego integrity in late midlife. *Journal of Research in Personality, 43*(1), 66–74.

Torges, Cynthia M.; Stewart, Abigail J.; & Nolen-Hoeksema, Susan. (2008). Regret resolution, aging, and adapting to loss. *Psychology and Aging, 23,* 169–180.

Torpey, Elka, & Hogan, Andrew. (2016). Working in a gig economy. *Career Outlook.* https://www.bls.gov/careeroutlook/2016/article/what-is-the-gig-economy.htm

Torrey, E. Fuller; Rawlings, Robert R.; Ennis, Jacqueline M.; Merrill, Deborah Dickerson; & Flores, Donn S. (1996) Birth seasonality in bipolar disorder, schizophrenia, schizoaffective disorder and stillbirths. *Schizophrenia Research, 21,* 141–149. https://doi.org/10.1016/0920-9964(96)00022-9

Touré. (2011, April 28). Adele opens up about her inspirations, looks and stage fright. *Rolling Stone.* http://www.rollingstone.com/music/news/adele-opens-up-about-her-inspirations-looks-and-stage-fright-20120210

Tovée, Martin J.; Swami, Viren; Furnham, Adrian; & Mangalparsad, Roshila. (2006). Changing perceptions of attractiveness as observers are exposed to a different culture. *Evolution and Human Behavior, 27*(6), 443–456.

Traffanstedt, Megan; Mehta, Sheila; & LoBello, Steven. (2016). Major depression with seasonal variation: Is it a valid construct? *Clinical Psychological Science, 4*(5), 825–834. https://doi.org/10.1177/2167702615615867

Training Magazine. (2019). 2019 training industry report. https://trainingmag.com/sites/default/files/2019_industry_report.pdf

Trajanovic, Nikola N., & Shapiro, Colin M. (2010). Sexsomnias. In Michael J. Thorpy & Giuseppe Plazzi (Eds.), *The parasomnias and other sleep-related movement disorders.* Cambridge University Press.

Tran, Anh N.; Ornelas, India J.; Kim, Mimi; Perez, Georgin; Green, Melissa; Lyn, Michelle J.; & Corbie-Smith, Giselle. (2014). Results from a pilot promotora program to reduce depression and stress among immigrant Latinas. *Health Promotion Practice, 15*(3), 365–372.

Travaro, Susan F., & Travers, Joseph B. (2009). Chemical senses. In G. G. Berntson & J. T. Cacioppo (Eds.), *Handbook of neuroscience for the behavioral sciences* (Vol. 1, pp. 267–305). Wiley.

Travis, L. E. (1925). The effect of a small audience upon eye-hand coordination. *Journal of Abnormal and Social Psychology, 20,* 142–146. https://doi.org/10.1037/h0071311

Travis, Michelle A. (2021). A post-pandemic antidiscrimination approach to workplace flexibility. *Washington University Journal of Law & Policy, 64,* 1–43.

Treisman, Michel, & Lages, Martin. (2013). On the nature of sensory memory. In Charles Chubb, Barbara A. Dosher, Zhong-Lin Lu, & Richard M. Shiffrin (Eds.), *Human information processing: Vision, memory, and attention. Decade of behavior.* American Psychological Association.

Tremblay, Pascale, & Dick, Anthony Steven. (2016). Broca and Wernicke are dead, or moving past the classic model of language neurobiology. *Brain and Language, 162,* 60–71. https://doi.org/10.1016/j.bandl.2016.08.004

Triandis, Harry C. (1994). *Culture and social behavior.* McGraw-Hill.

Triandis, Harry C. (2005). Issues in individualism and collectivism. In Richard M. Sorrentino, Dov Cohen, James M. Olson, & Mark P. Zanna (Eds.), *Cultural and social behavior: The Ontario Symposium* (Vol. 10). Erlbaum.

Truitt, Brian. (June 3, 2019). 'Toy Story 4' exclusive: Check out the four comedy legends joining Woody, Buzz and the gang." USA Today. https://www.usatoday.com/story/life/movies/2019/06/03/toy-story-4-exclusive-look-whos-joining-woodys-gang/1299634001/

Trull, Timothy J., & Widiger, Thomas A. (2008). Geology 102: More thoughts on a shift to a dimensional model of personality disorders. *Social and Personality Psychology Compass, 2,* 949–967. https://doi.org/10.1111/j.1751-9004.2007.00074.x

Tsang, Laura Lo Wa; Harvey, Carol D. H.; Duncan, Karen A.; & Sommer, Reena. (2003). The effects of children, dual earner status, sex role traditionalism, and marital structure on marital happiness over time. *Journal of Family and Economic Issues, 24,* 5–26.

Tsao, Doris. (2006). A dedicated system for processing faces. *Science, 314,* 72–73.

Tsao, Doris; Freiwald, Winrich A.; Tootell, Roger B. H.; & Livingstone, Margaret S. (2006). A cortical region consisting entirely of face-selective cells. *Science, 311,* 670–674.

Tsvetkova, Milena, & Macy, Michael W. (2014). The social contagion of generosity. *PLOS ONE, 9*(2), 1–9. https://doi.org/10.1371/journal.pone.0087275

Tucker, Jeritt R.; Hammer, Joseph H.; Vogel, David L.; Bitman, Rachel L.; Wade, Nathaniel G.; & Maier, Emily J. (2013). Disentangling self-stigma: Are mental illness and help-seeking self-stigmas different? *Journal of Counseling Psychology, 60*(4), 1–12. https://doi.org/10.1037/a0033555

Tucker, William H. (2009). *The Cattell controversy: Race, science, and ideology.* University of Illinois Press.

Tucker-Drob, Elliot M.; & Bates, Timothy C. (2016). Large cross-national differences in gene x socioeconomic status interaction on intelligence. *Psychological Science 27*(2), 138–149. https://doi.org/10.1177/0956797615612727

Tufekci, Z. (2015). Algorithmic harms beyond Facebook and Google: Emergent challenges of computational agency. *Journal on Telecommunications & High Technology Law, 13,* 203–218.

Tulving, Endel. (1983). *Elements of episodic memory.* Clarendon Press/Oxford University Press.

Tulving, Endel. (1985). How many memory systems are there? *American Psychologist, 40,* 385–398.

Tulving, Endel. (2002). Episodic memory: From mind to brain. *Annual Review of Psychology, 53,* 1–25.

Tulving, Endel. (2007). Are there 256 different kinds of memory? In James S. Nairne (Ed.), *The foundations of remembering: Essays in honor of Henry L. Roediger, III.* Psychology Press.

Tulving, Endel, & Szpunar, Karl K. (2009). Episodic memory. *Scholarpedia, 4,* 3332. https://doi.org/10.4249/scholarpedia.3332

Turati, Chiara. (2004). Why faces are not special to newborns: An alternative account of the face preference. *Current Directions in Psychological Science, 13,* 5–8.

Turban, Jack. (2017, April 8). Hannah is a girl. Doctors finally treat her like one. *The New York Times.* https://www.nytimes.com/2017/04/08/opinion/sunday/hannah-is-a-girl-doctors-finally-treat-her-like-one.html?mwrsm=Email&_r=1

Turiel, Elliot. (2010). The relevance of moral epistemology and psychology for neuroscience. In P. D. Zelazo, M. Chandler, & E. Crone (Eds.), *Developmental social cognitive neuroscience* (pp. 313–331). Psychology Press.

Turk, Dennis C., & Winter, Frits. (2006). *The pain survival guide: How to reclaim your life.* American Psychological Association.

Turk, Victoria. (2019, May 14). Inside the first placebo-controlled studies testing if microdosing LSD actually works. *Wired.* https://www.wired.co.uk/article/microdosing-lsd-psilocybin-placebo-trials

Turk-Browne, & Nicholas B. (2013). Functional interactions as big data in the brain. *Science, 342,* 580–584.

Turner, C. H. (1914). An experimental study of the auditory powers of the giant silkworm moths (Saturniidæ). *The Biological Bulletin, 27*(6), 325–332. https://doi.org/10.2307/1535919

Turner, Erlanger A.; Chandler, Megan; & Heffer, Robert W. (2009). The influence of parenting styles, achievement motivation, and self-efficacy on academic performance in college students. *Journal of College Student Development,50*(3), 337–346.

Turner, John C. (2010). The analysis of social influence. In T. Postmes & N. R. Branscombe (Eds.), *Rediscovering social identity*. Psychology Press.

Turner, Monique Mitchell; Tamborini, Ron; Limon, M. Sean; & Zuckerman-Hyman, Cynthia. (2007, September). The moderators and mediators of door-in-the-face requests: Is it a negotiation or a helping experience? *Communication Monographs, 74*(3), 333–356.

Tversky, Amos, & Kahneman, Daniel. (1982). Judgment under uncertainty: Heuristics and biases. In Daniel Kahneman, Paul Slovic, & Amos Tversky (Eds.), *Judgment under uncertainty: Heuristics and biases*. Cambridge University Press.

Tversky, Amos. (1972). Elimination by aspects: A theory of choice. *Psychological Review, 80*, 281–299.

Twenge, Jean M., & Campbell, Keith W. (2019). Media use is linked to lower psychological well-being: Evidence from three datasets. *Psychiatric Quarterly*, 311–331. https://doi.org/10.1007/s11126-019-09630-7

Twenge, Jean M.; Hisler, Garrett C.; & Krizan, Zlatan. (2019). Associations between screen time and sleep duration are primarily driven by portable electronic devices: Evidence from a population-based study of U.S. children ages 0–17. *Sleep Medicine, 56*, 211–218. https://doi.org/10.1016/j.sleep.2018.11.009

Twenge, Jean; Sherman, Ryne; & Wells, Brooke. (2015). Changes in American adults' sexual behavior and attitudes, 1972-2012. *Archives of Sexual Behavior, 44*, 2273–2285. https://doi.org/10.1007/s10508-015-0540-2

Tyas, Suzanne L.; Salazar, Juan Carlos; Snowdon, David A.; Desrosiers, Mark F.; Riley, Kathryn P.; Mendiondo, Marta S.; & Kryscio, Richard J. (2007a). Transitions to mild cognitive impairments, dementia, and death: Findings from the nun study. *American Journal of Epidemiology, 165*(11), 1231–1238. https://doi.org/10.1093/aje/kwm085

Tyas, Suzanne L.; Snowdon, David A.; Desrosiers, Mark F.; Riley, Kathryn P.; & Markesbery, William R. (2007b). Healthy ageing in the Nun Study: Definition and neuropathologic correlates. *Age and Ageing, 36*(6), 650–655. https://doi.org/10.1093/ageing/afm120

Tyler, Kathryn. (2020, November 30). Measuring employee engagement during a crisis. *HR Magazine, Winter 2020*. https://www.shrm.org/hr-today/news/hr-magazine/winter2020/pages/measuring-employee-engagement-during-covid-19.aspx

Uchida-Ota, Mariko; Arimitsu, Takeshi; Tsuzuki, Daisuke; Dan, Ippeita; Ikeda, Kazushige; Takahashi, Takao; & Minagawa, Yasuyo. (2019). Maternal speech shapes the cerebral frontotemporal network in neonates: A hemodynamic functional connectivity study. *Developmental Cognitive Neuroscience, 39*. https://doi.org/10.1016/j.dcn.2019.100701

Uchino, Bert N. (2009). Understanding the links between social support and physical health: A life-span perspective with emphasis on the separability of perceived and received support. *Perspectives on Psychological Science, 4*(3), 236–255. https://doi.org/10.1111/j.1745-6924.2009.01122.x

Uchino, Bert N., & Birmingham, Wendy. (2011). Stress and support processes. In Richard J. Contrada & Andrew Baum (Eds.), *The handbook of stress science: Biology, psychology, and health.* Springer.

Uchino, Bert N.; Carlisle, McKenzie; Birmingham, Wendy; & Vaughn, Allison A. (2010). Social support and the reactivity hypothesis: Conceptual issues in examining the efficacy of received support during acute psychological stress. *Biological Psychology, 86*(2), 137–142. https://doi.org/10.1016/j.biopsycho.2010.04.003

Uji, Masayo; Sakamoto, Ayuko; Adachi, Keiichiro; & Kitamura, Toshinori. (2014). The impact of authoritative, authoritarian, and permissive parenting styles on children's later mental health in Japan: Focusing on parent and child gender. *Journal of Child and Family Studies, 23*, 293–302. https://doi.org/10.1007/s10826-013-9740-3

Uleman, James S.; Saribay, S. Adil; & Gonzalez, Celia M. (2008). Spontaneous inferences, implicit impressions, and implicit theories. *Annual Review of Psychology, 59*, 329–360.

Umberson, Debra; Williams, Kristi; Powers, Daniel A.; Chen, Meichu D.; & Campbell, Anna M. (2005). As good as it gets? A life course perspective on marital quality. *Social Forces, 84*, 493–511. https://doi.org/10.1353/sof.2005.0131

Umland, Elena M. (2008). Treatment strategies for reducing the burden of menopause-associated vasomotor symptoms. *Journal of Managed Care Pharmacy, 14*(3 Suppl), 14–19.

Unemori, Patrick; Omoregie, Heather; & Markus, Hazel Rose. (2004, October–December). Self-portraits: Possible selves in European-American, Chilean, Japanese and Japanese-American cultural contexts. *Self and Identity, 3*(4), 321–328.

UNHCR country operations profile—Central African Republic. (2015). *United Nations High Commissioner for Refugees.* http://www.unhcr.org/pages/49e45c156.html

UNICEF. (2014). *Hidden in plain sight: A statistical analysis of violence against children.* UNICEF. https://www.unicef.org/publications/index_74865.html

U.S. Census Bureau. (2008a). 2007 American Community Survey 1-year estimates: Marital status. http://factfinder.census.gov

U.S. Census Bureau. (2008b). 2007 American Community Survey 1-year estimates: Ranking table R1205: Median age at first marriage for women. http://factfinder.census.gov

U.S. Census Bureau. (2008c). 2007 American Community Survey 1-year estimates: Table S1501: Educational attainment. –http://factfinder.census.gov, 395.

U.S. Census Bureau. (2016). *Annual Social and Economic Supplement (ASEC) of the Current Population Survey (CPS), 1947 to 2016.* https://www.census.gov/programs-surveys/saipe/guidance/model-input-data/cpsasec.html

U.S. Department of Labor (DOL). (2017). *Opening doors to all candidates: Tips to ensuring access for applicants with disabilities.* https://www.dol.gov/odep/pubs/fact/opening.htm

U.S. Equal Employment Opportunity Commission (EEOC). (2017). *Best practices for employers and human resources/EEO professionals.* https://www.eeoc.gov/eeoc/initiatives/e-race/bestpractices-employers.cfm

Ur, Blase; Leon, Pedro Giovanni; Cranor, Lorrrie Faith; Shay, R., & Wang, Yang. (2012, July). Smart, useful, scary, creepy: Perceptions of online behavioral advertising. In *Proceedings of the Eighth Symposium on Usable Privacy and Security* (p. 4). ACM.

Ursano, Robert J., & Shaw, Jon A. (2007). Children of war and opportunities for peace. *Journal of the American Medical Association, 298*(5), 567–568. https://doi.org/10.1001/jama.298.5.567

Usher, Kim; Bhullar, Navjot; & Jackson, Debra. (2020). Life in the pandemic: Social isolation and mental health. *Journal of Clinical Nursing, 29*(15-16), 2756–2757. https://doi.org/10.1111/jocn.15290

Uskul, Ayse K., & Kitayama, Shinobu. (2011). Culture, mind, and the brain: Current evidence and future. *Annual Review of Psychology, 62*, 419–449.

Vale, José Sousa. (2019). Cannabis use in medical oncology: A brief review. *Revista Portuguesa Farmacoterapia, 11*, 95–102. https://doi.org/10.25756/rpf.v11i2-3.218

van Bokhoven, Irene.; van Goozen, Stephanie H. M.; van Engeland, Herman.; Schaal, Benoist.; Arseneault, Louise.; Séguin, Jean R.; Assaad, Jean-Marc; Nagin, Daniel S.; Vitaro, Frank; & Tremblay, Richard E. (2006). Salivary testosterone and aggression, delinquency, and social dominance in a population-based longitudinal study of adolescent males. *Hormones and Behavior, 50*(1), 118–125. https://doi.org/10.1016/j.yhbeh.2006.02.002

Van Cauter, Eve; Spiegel, Karine; Tasalim Esra; & Leproult, Rachel. (2008). Metabolic consequences of sleep and sleep loss. *Sleep Medicine, 9*, S23–S28.

Van Dam, Nicholas T.; van Vugt, Marieke K.; Vago, David R.; Schmalzl, Laura; Saron, Clifford D.; Olendzki, Andrew; Meissner, Ted; Lazar, Sara W.; Gorchov, Jolie; Fox, Kieran C. R.; Field, Brent A.; Britton, Willoughby B.; Brefczynski-Lewis, Julie A.; & Meyer, David E. (2018a). Reiterated concerns and further challenges for mindfulness and meditation research: A reply to Davidson and Dahl. *Perspectives on Psychological Science, 13*(1), 66–69. https://doi.org/10.1177/1745691617727529

Van Dam, Nicholas T.; van Vugt, Marieke K.; Vago, David R.; Schmalzl, Laura; Saron, Clifford D.; Olendzki, Andrew; Meissner, Ted; Lazar, Sara W.; Kerr, Catherine E.; Gorchov, Jolie; Fox, Kieran C. R.; Field, Brent A.; Britton, Willoughby B.; Brefczynski-Lewis, Julie A.; & Meyer, David E. (2018b). Mind the hype: A critical evaluation and prescriptive agenda for research on mindfulness and meditation. *Perspectives on Psychological Science, 13*(1), 36–61. https://doi.org/10.1177/1745691617709589

van de Waal, Erica; Borgeaud, Christèle; & Whiten, Andrew. (2013). Potent social learning and conformity shape a wild primate's foraging decisions. *Science, 340*, 483–485. https://doi.org/10.1126/science.1232769

Van Der Heide, Brandon; D'Angelo, Jonathan D.; & Schumaker, Erin M. (2012). The effects of verbal versus photographic self-presentation on impression formation in Facebook. *Journal of Communication, 62*(1), 98–116. https://doi.org/10.1111/j.1460-2466.2011.01617.x

van der Maas, Han L. J.; Kan, Kees-Jan; Marsman, Maarten; & Stevenson, Claire E. (2017). Network models for cognitive development and intelligence. *Journal of Intelligence, 5*, 16. https://doi.org/10.3390/jintelligence5020016

van der Vaart, Elske; Verbrugge, Rineke; & Hemelrijk, Charlotte K. (2011). Corvid caching: Insights from a cognitive model. *Journal of Experimental Psychology: Animal Behavior Processes, 37*(3), 330–340. https://doi.org/10.1037/a0022988

van der Zwaaga, Wietske; Schäferb, Andreas; Marquesa, José P.; Turner, Robert & Trampel, Robert. (2016). Recent applications of UHF-MRI in the study of human brain function and structure: A review. *NMR in Biomedicine, 29*, 1274–1288. https://onlinelibrary.wiley.com/journal/10991492

van Diermen, Linda; van den Ameele, Seline; Kamperman, Astrid M.; Sabbe, Bernard C.G.; Vermeulen, Tom; Schrijvers, Didier; & Birkenhäger, Tom K. (2018) Prediction of electroconvulsive therapy response and remission in major depression: Meta-analysis. *The British Journal of Psychiatry, 212*(2), 71–80. https://doi.org/10.1192/bjp.2017.28

Van Dyke, James Urban, & Grace, Michael S. (2010). The role of thermal contrast in infrared-based defensive targeting by the copperhead, Agkistrodon contortrix. *Animal Behaviour, 79*, 993–999.

Van Essen, David C., & Glasser, Matthew F. (2016). The Human Connectome Project: Progress and prospects. *Cerebrum: The Dana Forum on Brain Science* (Vol. 2016). Retrieved from http://www.dana.org/Cerebrum/2016/The_Human_Connectome_Project_Progress_and_Prospects/

van Geert, Paul. (1998). A dynamic systems model of basic developmental mechanisms: Piaget, Vygotsky, and beyond. *Psychological Review, 105*, 634–677.

van Heck, Guus L., & den Oudsten, Brenda L. (2008). Emotional intelligence: Relationships to stress, health, and well-being. In Ad Vingerhoets, Ivan Nyklicek, & Johan Denollet (Eds.), *Emotion regulation: Conceptual and clinical issues.* Springer Science + Business Media.

Van Horn, John Darrell; Irimia, Andrei; Torgerson, Carinna M.; Chambers, Micah C.; Kikinis, Ron; & Toga, Arthur W. (2012). Mapping connectivity damage in the case of Phineas Gage. *PLOS ONE, 7*(5): e37454. https://doi.org/10.1371/journal.pone.0037454

Van Iddekinge, Chad; Roth, Philip; Raymark, Patrick; & Odle-Dusseau, Heather. (2012). The criterion-related validity of integrity tests: An updated meta-analysis. *Journal of Applied Psychology, 97,* 499--530. https://doi.org/10.1037/a0021196

van IJzendoorn, Marinus H., & Sagi-Schwartz, Abraham. (2008). Cross-cultural patterns of attachment: Universal and contextual dimensions. In J. Cassidy & P. R. Shaver (Eds.), *Handbook of attachment: Theory, research, and clinical applications* (2nd ed., pp. 880–905). Guilford.

Van Lange, Paul; Rinderu, Maria; & Bushman, Brad. (2016). Aggression and violence around the world: A model of climate, aggression, and self-control in humans (CLASH). *Behavioral and Brain Sciences, 23,* 1–63. https://doi.org/10.1017/S0140525X16000406

van Osch, Yvette.; Breugelmans, Seger M.; Zeelenberg, Marcel.; & Boluk, Pinar. (2013). A different kind of honor culture: Family honor and aggression in Turks. *Group Processes & Intergroup Relations, 16*(3), 334–344. https://doi.org/10.1177/1368430212467475

van Vugt, Marieke K. (2015). Cognitive benefits of mindfulness. In Kirk Warren Brown, J. David Creswell, & Richard M. Ryan (Eds.), *Handbook of mindfulness: Theory, research, and practice.* Guilford.

van Zalk, Nejra; van Zalk, Maarten H. W.; & Kerr, Margaret. (2011). Socialization of social anxiety in adolescent crowds. *Journal of Abnormal Child Psychology, 39,* 1239-1249. https://doi.org/10.1007/s10802-011-9533-3

Vandell, Deborah L.; Belsky, Jay; Burchinal, Margaret; Steinberg, Laurence; & Vandergrift, Nathan. (2010). Do effects of early child care extend to age 15 years? Results from the NICHD study of early child care and youth development. *Child Development, 81*(3), 737–756. https://doi.org/10.1111/j.1467-8624.2010.01431.x

Vandello, Joseph A., & Cohen, Dov. (2003). Male honor and female fidelity: Implicit cultural scripts that perpetuate domestic violence. *Journal of Personality and Social Psychology, 84*(5), 997–1010. https://doi.org/10.1037/0022-3514.84.5.997

Vandello, Joseph A., & Cohen, Dov. (2004). When believing is seeing: Sustaining norms of violence in cultures of honor. In Mark Schaller & Christian S. Crandall (Eds.), *The psychological foundations of culture* (pp. 281–304). Erlbaum.

Vandello, Joseph A.; Cohen, Dov.; & Ransom, Sean. (2008). U.S. Southern and Northern differences in perceptions of norms about aggression: Mechanisms for the perpetuation of a culture of honor. *Journal of Cross-Cultural Psychology, 39*(2), 162–177. https://doi.org/10.1177/0022022107313862

Vander Ven, Thomas, & Beck, Jeffrey. (2009). Getting drunk and hooking up: An exploratory study of the relationship between alcohol intoxication and casual coupling in a university sample. *Sociological Spectrum, 29*(5), 626–648.

Vandervoort, Debra J. (2006). Hostility and health: Mediating Effects of belief systems and coping styles. *Current Psychology, 25*(1), 50–66.

Varela, R. Enrique; Sanchez-Sosa, Juan Jose; Biggs, Bridget K.; & Luis, Timothy M. (2009). Parenting strategies and socio-cultural influences in childhood anxiety: Mexican, Latin American descent, and European American families. *Journal of Anxiety Disorders, 23,* 609–616. https://doi.org/10.1016/j.janxdis.2009.01.012

Vargas, Ivan; Nguyen, Anna M.; Muench, Alexandria; Bastien, Célyne H.; Ellis, Jason G.; & Perlis, Michael L. (2020). Acute and chronic insomnia: What has time and/or hyperarousal got to do with it? *Brain Sciences, 10.* https://doi.org/10.3390/brainsci10020071

Varnum, Michael E. W.; Grossmann, Igor; Kitayama, Shinobu; & Nisbett, Richard E. (2010). The origin of cultural differences in cognition: The social orientation hypothesis. *Current Directions in Psychological Science, 19,* 9–13.

Varshney, Mohit; Mahapatra, Ananya; Krishnan, Vijay; Gupta, Rishab; & Deb, Koushik S. (2016). Violence and mental illness: What is the true story? *Journal of Epidemiology and Community Health, 70*(3), 223–225. https://doi.org/10.1136/jech-2015-205546

Vasquez, Kris. (2009). Learning styles as self-fulfilling prophecies. In Regan A. R. Gurung, & Loreto R. Prieto (Eds.), *Getting culture: Incorporating diversity across the curriculum.* Stylus.

Vasquez, Melba J. T. (2010). *Biography of Martha Bernal.* Society for the Psychology of Women. https://www.apadivisions.org/division-35/about/heritage/martha-bernal-biography

Vasquez, Melba J. T.; & Lope, Steve. (2002). Martha E. Bernal (1931-2001). *American Psychologist, 57*(5), 362–363. https://doi.org/10.1037//0003-066X.57.5.362

Vaughn, Brian E.; Coppola, Gabrielle; & Verissimo, Manuela. (2007). The quality of maternal secure-base scripts predicts children's secure-base behavior in three sociocultural groups. *International Journal of Behavioral Development, 31,* 65–76.

Vaughn, Kelli. (2010). Profile of Christine Ladd-Franklin. In Alexandra Rutherford (Ed.), *Psychology's Feminist Voices Multimedia Internet Archive.* http://www.feministvoices.com/profiles/christine-ladd-franklin/

Vazire, Simine. (2018). Implications of the credibility revolution for productivity, creativity, and progress. *Perspectives on Psychological Science, 13*(4), 411–417. https://doi.org/10.1177/1745691617751884

Vedantam, Shankar (Host); Boyle, Tara (Producer); & Klahr, Renee (Producer). (2017, February 14). *Hidden brain* [Audio podcast]. http://www.npr.org/2017/02/14/514578429/hookup-culture-the-unspoken-rules-of-sex-on-college-campuses

Vedel, Anna; Thomsen, Dorthe; & Larsen, Lars. (2015). Personality, academic majors and performance: Revealing complex patterns. *Personality and Individual Differences,85,* 69–76. https://doi.org/10.1016/j.paid.2015.04.030

Verdine, Brian; Golinkoff, Roberta; Hirsh-Pasek, Kathy; & Newcombe, Nora. (2017). Spatial skills, their development, and their links to mathematics. *Monographs of the Society for Research in Child Development, 82,* 7–30. https://doi.org/10.1111/mono.12280

Verheijden, Simon, & Boeckxstaens, Guy E. (2018). Neuroimmune interaction and the regulation of intestinal immune homeostasis. *American Journal of Physiology—Gastrointestinal and Liver Physiology, 314,* G75–G80. https://doi.org/10.1152/ajpgi.00425.2016

Vermetten, Eric, & Yehuda, Rachel. (2020). MDMA-assisted psychotherapy for post-traumatic stress disorder: A promising novel approach to treatment. *Neuropsychopharmacology, 45,* 217–239. https://doi.org/10.1038/s41386-019-0482-9

Vespa, Jonathan; Lewis, Jamie M.; & Kreider, Rose M. (2013). *America's families and living arrangements: 2012, current population reports, P20–570.* U.S. Census Bureau.

Viana, Ricardo B.; & de Lira, Claudio A. B. (2020). Exergames as coping strategies for anxiety disorders during the COVID-19 quarantine period. *Games for Health Journal, 9*(3), 147–149. https://doi.org/10.1089/g4h.2020.0060

Vickers, Andrew J.; Cronin, Angel M.; Maschino, Alexandra C.; Lewith, George; MacPherson, Hugh; Foster, Nadine E.; Sherman, Karen J.; Witt, Claudia M.; & Linde, Klaus; for the Accupuncture Trailists' Collaboration. (2012). Acupuncture for chronic pain: Individual patient data meta-analysis. *Archives of Internal Medicine, 172*(19), 1444–1453. https://doi.org/10.1001/archinternmed.2012.3654

Vigil, Jacob M. (2009). A socio-relational framework of sex differences in the expression of emotion. *Behavioral and Brain Sciences, 32*(5), 375–390.

Visser, Beth A.; Ashton, Michael C.; & Vernon, Philip A. (2006). Beyond *g*: Putting multiple intelligences theory to the test. *Intelligence, 34*(5), 487-502. https://doi.org/10.1016/j.intell.2006.02.004

Vita, Antonio; De Peri, Luca; Deste, Giacomo; & Sacchetti, Emilio. (2012). Progressive loss of cortical gray matter in schizophrenia: A meta-analysis and meta-regression of longitudinal MRI studies. *Translational Psychiatry, 2*(11), e190. https://doi.org/10.1038/tp.2012.116

Vogt, PJ; & Goldman, Alex. (2016a, March 9). Milk Wanted [Audio podcast]. Gimlet. https://gimletmedia.com/shows/reply-all/v4he9w

Vogt, PJ; & Goldman, Alex. (2016b, December 22). Past, Present, Future 2 [Audio podcast]. Gimlet. https://gimletmedia.com/shows/reply-all/6nh3jk

Volkow, Nora; Benveniste, Helene; McLellan, A. Thomas. (2018). Use and misuse of opioids in chronic pain. *Annual Review of Medicine, 69,* 451–465. https://doi.org/10.1146/annurev-med-011817-044739

Volkow, Nora D.; Chang, Linda; Wang, Gene-Jack; Fowler, Joanna S.; Ding, Yu-Sin; Sedler, Mark; Logan, Jean; Franceschi, Dinko; Gatley, John; Hitzemann, Robert; Gifford, Andrew; Wong, Christopher; & Pappas, Naomi. (2001). Low level of brain dopamine D2 receptors in methamphetamine abusers: Association with metabolism in the orbitofrontal cortex. *American Journal of Psychiatry, 158,* 2015–2021.

Volkow, Nora D.; Fowler, Joanna S.; Wang, Gene-Jack; Swanson, James M.; & Telang, Frank. (2007). Dopamine in drug abuse and addiction: Results of imaging studies and treatment implications. *Archives of Neurology, 64,* 1575–1579.

Volkow, Nora D.; Frieden, Thomas R.; Hyde, Pamela S.; & Cha, Stephen S. (2014). Medication-assisted therapies: Tackling the opioid-overdose epidemic. *New England Journal of Medicine, 370,* 2063–2066. https://doi.org/10.1056/NEJMp1402780

Volkow, Nora D.; Hampson, Aidan J.; & Baler, Ruben D. (2017). Don't worry, be happy: Endocannabinoids and cannabis at the intersection of stress and reward. Annual Review of Pharmacology and Toxicology, 57, 285–308. https://doi.org/10.1146/annurev-pharmtox-010716-104615

Volkow, Nora D.; Koob, George F.; & McLellan, A. Thomas. (2016). Neurobiologic advances from the brain disease model of addiction. *New England Journal of Medicine, 374,* 363–371. https://doi.org/10.1056/NEJMra1511480

Volkow, Nora D., & McLellan, A. Thomas. (2011). Curtailing diversion and abuse of opioid analgesics without jeopardizing pain treatment. *JAMA, 305*(13), 1346–1347. https://doi.org/10.1001/jama.2011.369

Volkow, Nora D.; McLellan, A. Thomas; Cotto, Jessica H.; Karithanom, Meena; & Weiss, Susan R. B. (2011a). Characteristics of opioid prescriptions in 2009. *JAMA, 305* (13), 1299–1301. https://doi.org/10.1001/jama.2011.401

Volkow, Nora D.; Wang, Gene-Jack; Fowler, Joanna S.; Tomasi, Dardo; and Telang, Frank. (2011b). Addiction: Beyond dopamine reward circuitry. *Proceedings of the National Academy of Sciences.* https://doi.org/10.1073/pnas.1010654108

Volkow, Nora D.; Wang, Gene-Jack; Telang, Frank; Fowler, Joanna S.; Logan, Jean; Childress, Anna-Rose; Jayne, Millard; Ma, Yeming; & Wong, Christopher. (2006). Cocaine cues and dopamine in dorsal striatum: Mechanism of craving in cocaine addiction. *Journal of Neuroscience, 26,* 6583–6588.

Volkow, Nora D., & Wise, Roy A. (2005). How can drug addiction help us understand obesity? *Nature Neuroscience, 8,* 555–560.

von Bartheld, Christopher S.; Bahney, Jami; & Herculano-Houzel, Suzana. (2016). The search for true numbers of neurons and glial cells in the human brain: A review of 150 years of cell counting. *The Journal of Comparative Neurology, 524*(18), 3865–3895. https://doi.org/10.1002/cne.24040

von Hippel, W., & Trivers, R. (2011). The evolution and psychology of self-deception. *Behavioral and Brain Sciences, 34*(01), 1–16. https://doi.org/10.1017/S0140525X10001354

Voorspoels, Wouter; Storms, Gert; & Vanpaemel, Wolf (2011). Representation at different levels in a conceptual hierarchy. *Acta Psychologica, 138,* 11–18. https://doi.org/10.1016/j.actpsy.2011.04.007

Voorspoels, Wouter; Vanpaemel, Wolf; & Storms, Gert. (2008). Exemplars and prototypes in natural language concepts: A typicality-based evaluation. *Psychonomic Bulletin & Review, 15,* 630–637.

Vosahlikova, Miroslava; & Svoboda, Petr. (2016). Lithium—therapeutic tool endowed with multiple beneficiary effects caused by multiple mechanisms. *Acta Neurobiologiae Experimentalis, 76*(1), 1–19. https://doi.org/10.21307/ane-2017-001

Voss, Michelle W.; Prakash, Ruchika S.; Erickson, Kirk I.; Basak, Chandramallika; Chaddock, Laura; Kim, Jennifer S.; Alves, Heloisa; Heo, Susie; Szabo, Amanda N.; White, Siobhan M.; Wójcicki, Thomas R.; Mailey, Emily L.; Gothe, Neha; Olson, Erin A; McAuley, Edward; & Kramer, Arthur F. (2010). Plasticity of brain networks in a randomized intervention trial of exercise training in older adults. *Frontiers in Aging Neuroscience, 2,* 32. https://doi.org/10.3389/fnagi.2010.00032

Voyer, Daniel; Postma, Albert; Brake, Brandy; & Imperato-McGinley, Julianne. (2007). Gender differences in object location memory: A metaanalysis. *Psychonomic Bulletin & Review, 14,* 23–38.

Vrangalova, Zhana, & Savin-Williams, Ritch C. (2012). Mostly heterosexual and mostly gay/lesbian: Evidence for new sexual orientation identities. *Archives of Sexual Behavior, 41*(1), 85–101.

Vriends, Noortje; Michael, Tanja; Schindler, Bettina; & Margraf, Jurgen. (2012). Associative learning in flying phobia. *Journal of Behavior Therapy and Experimental Psychiatry, 43,* 838–843. https://doi.org/10.1016/j.jbtep.2011.11.003

Vrij, Aldert. (2015). Deception detection. In Brian L. Cutler & Patricia A. Zapf (Eds.), *APA handbook of forensic psychology, Vol. 2: Criminal investigation, adjudication, and sentencing outcomes.* American Psychological Association. https://doi.org/10.1037/14462-008

Vrij, Aldert; Ennis, Edel; Farman, Sarah; & Mann, Samantha. (2010). People's perceptions of their truthful and deceptive interactions in daily life. *Open Access Journal of Forensic Psychology, 2,* 6–42.

Vrshek-Schallhorn, Suzanne; Mineka, Susan; Zinbarg, Richard E.; Craske, Michelle G.; Griffith, James W.; Sutton, Jonathan; Redei, Eva E.; Wolitzky-Taylor, Kate; Hammen, Constance; & Adam, Emma K. (2013). Refining the candidate environment: Interpersonal stress, the serotonin transporter polymorphism, and gene-environment interactions in major depression. *Clinical Psychologial Science, 2*(3), 235–248. https://doi.org/10.1177/2167702613499329

Vrugt, Anneke, & Vet, Carolijn. (2009). Effects of a smile on mood and helping behavior. *Social Behavior and Personality, 37*(9), 1251–1258.

Vuletich, Heidi A.; & Payne, B. Keith. (2019). Stability and change in implicit bias. *Psychological Science, 30*(6), 854–862. https://doi.org/10.1177/09567976198442

Vyazovskiy, Vladyslav V.; Olcese, Umberto; Hanlon, Erin C.; Nir, Yuval; Cirelli, Chiara; & Tononi, Giulio. (2011). Local sleep in awake rats. *Nature, 472,* 443–447. https://doi.org/10.1038/nature10009

Vygotsky, Lev S. (1978). Mind in society: The development of higher psychological processes. Harvard University Press.

Vygotsky, Lev S. (1987). *Thinking and speech* (Norris Minick, Trans.). Plenum Press.

Vytal, Katherine., & Hamann, Stephan. (2010). Neuroimaging support for discrete neural correlates of basic emotions: A voxel-based meta-analysis. *Journal of Cognitive Neuroscience, 22,* 2864–2885. https://doi.org/10.1162/jocn.2009.21366

Wachtel, Paul L.; Siegel, Judith P.; & Baer, Judith C. (2020). The scope of psychotherapy integration: Introduction to a special issue. *Clinical Social Work Journal, 48,* 231–235. https://doi.org/10.1007/s10615-020-00771-y

Wacker, Daniel; Wang, Shen; McCorvy, John D.; Betz, Robin M.; Venkatakrishnan, A. J.; Levit, Anat; . . . & Roth, Bryan L. (2017). Crystal structure of an LSD-bound human serotonin receptor. *Cell, 168,* 377–389.e12. https://doi.org/10.1016/j.cell.2016.12.033

Wade, Lisa. (2017, February 10). Sociology and the New Culture of Hooking Up on College Campuses. *Pacific Standard.* Retrieved from https://psmag.com/sociology-and-the-new-culture-of-hooking-up-on-college-campuses-e8c3cd5a7309#.pos20vyuj

Wagenmakers, Eric-Jan; Dutilh, Gilles; & Sarafoglou, Alexandra. (2018). The creativity-verification cycle in psychological science: New methods to combat old idols. *Perspectives on Psychological Science, 13*(4), 418–427. https://doi.org/10.1177/1745691618771357

Wager, Tor D., & Atlas, Lauren Y. (2015). The neuroscience of placebo effects: Connecting context, learning, and health. *Nature Neuroscience, 16,* 403–418. https://doi.org/10.1038/nrn3976

Wagner, Christopher C., & Ingersoll, Karen S. (2012). *Motivational interviewing in groups.* http://books.google.com/books?id=WIfzs84A5rcC&printsec=frontcover&dq=motivational+interviewing+in+groups&hl=en&sa=X&ei=4mthU9KmMqWysASJl4CoBw&ved=0CD8Q6AEwAA#v=onepage&q=motivational%20interviewing%20in%20groups&f=false

Wagner, Dana E.; Harrison, Patrick R.; & Mallett, Robyn K. (2011). Understanding the intergroup forecasting error. In L. R. Tropp & R. K. Mallett (Eds.), *Moving beyond prejudice reduction: Pathways to positive intergroup relations.* American Psychological Association.

Wagner, Jenny; Orth, Ulrich; Bleidorn, Wiebke; Hopwood, Christopher J.; & Kandler, Christian. (2020). Toward an integrative model of sources of personality stability and change. *Current Directions in Psychological Science,* 1–7. https://doi.org/10.1177/09637214209247

Wagstaff, Graham F. (2014). On the centrality of the concept of an altered state to definitions of hypnosis. *Journal of Mind-Body Regulation, 2,* 90–108.

Wahba, Mahmoud A., & Bridwell, Lawrence G. (1976). Maslow reconsidered: A review of research on the need hierarchy theory. *Organizational Behavior and Human Decision Processes, 15,* 212–240.

Wahl, Otto F. (2012). Stigma as a barrier to recovery from mental illness. *Trends in Cognitive Science, 16*(1), 9–10.

Wahlheim, Christopher, & DeSoto, Andrew. (2016). Study preferences for exemplar variability in self-regulated category learning. *Memory,* 231–243. https://doi.org/10.1080/09658211.2016.1152378

Wai, Jonathan; Lubinski, David; Benbow, Camilla P.; & Steiger, James H. (2010). Accomplishment in science, technology, engineering, and mathematics (STEM) and its relation to STEM educational dose: A 25-year longitudinal study. *Journal of Educational Psychology, 102*(4), 860–871. https://doi.org/10.1037/a0019454

Wainright, Jenniger L.; & Patterson, Charlotte J. (2008). Peer relations among adolescents with female same-sex parents. *Developmental Psychology, 44*(1), 117. https://doi.org/10.1037/0012-1649.44.1.117

Wakabayashi, Daisuke. (2019, May 28). Google's shadow work force: Temps who outnumber full-time employees. *The New York Times.* https://www.nytimes.com/2019/05/28/technology/google-temp-workers.html

Wakefield, Jerome C. (2013a). DSM-5: An overview of changes and controversies. *Clinical Social Work Journal, 41,* 139–154. https://doi.org/10.1007/s10615-013-0445-2

Walker, Matthew. (2011, March 22). Quoted in Yasmin Anwar, "Pulling an all-nighter can bring on euphoria and risky behavior." Retrieved from http://newscenter.berkeley.edu/2011/03/22/pulling-an-all-nighter

Walker, Matthew. (2017). *Why we sleep: Unlocking the power of sleep and dreams.* Scribner.

Walker, Matthew P. (2010). Sleep, memory and emotion. *Progress in Brain Research, 185,* 49–68.

Walker, Matthew P., & Robertson, Edwin M. (2016). Memory processing: Ripples in the resting brain. *Current Biology, 26,* R239–R240. https://doi.org/10.1016/j.cub.2016.02.028

Walker, W. Richard; Skowronski, John J.; & Thomson, Charles P. (2003). Life is pleasant—And memory helps to keep it that way! *Review of General Psychology, 7,* 203–210. https://doi.org/10.1037/1089-2680.7.2.203

Walk-Morris, Tatiana. (2016, November 29). Can mental health apps bring therapy to a wider population? *Pacific Standard.* https://psmag.com/news/can-mental-health-apps-bring-therapy-to-a-wider-population

Wallace, B. Alan. (2009). *Mind in the balance: Meditation in science, Buddhism, and Christianity.* Columbia University.

Walle, Eric A.; Reschke, Peter J.; Shannon, Roisin M.; & Main, Alexandra. (2020). The effect of emotional communication on infants' distinct prosocial behaviors. *Social Development, 29,* 1092–1114. https://doi.org/10.1111/sode.12449

Waller, Bridget M.; Cray, James J., Jr.; & Burrows, Anne M. (2008). Selection for universal facial emotion *Emotion, 8,* 435–439.

Walton, Alexander, & Toth, Amy. (2016). Variation in individual worker honey bee behavior shows hallmarks of personality. *Behavioral Ecology and Sociobiology, 70,* 999–1010. https://doi.org/10.1007/s00265-016-2084-4

Wammes, Jeffrey D.; Meade Melissa E.; & Fernandes, Myra A. (2016). The drawing effect: Evidence for reliable and robust memory benefits in free recall. *Quarterly Journal of Experimental Psychology, 69,* 1752–1776. https://doi.org/10.1080/17470218.2015.1094494

Wammes, Jeffrey D.; Ralph, Brandon C. W.; Mills, Caitlin; Bosch, Nigel; Duncan, Tracy L.; & Smilek, Daniel. (2019). Disengagement during lectures: Media multitasking and mind wandering in university classrooms. *Computers & Education, 132,* 76–89. https://doi.org/10.1016/j.compedu.2018.12.007

Wampold, Bruce E. (2015). How important are the common factors in psychotherapy? An update. *World Psychiatry, 14*(3), 270–277. https://doi.org/10.1002/wps.20238

Wamsley, Eric; Perry, Karen; Djonlagic, Ina; Reaven, Laura; & Stickgold, Robert. (2010). Cognitive replay of visuomotor learning at sleep onset: Temporal dynamics and relationship to task performance. *Sleep, 33,* 59–68.

Wanek, James E.; Sackett, Paul R.; & Ones, Deniz S. (2003). Towards an understanding of integrity test similarities and differences: An item-level analysis of seven tests. *Personnel Psychology, 56,* 873–894.

Wang, Gene-Jack; Volkow, Nora D.; Logan, Jean; Pappas, Naomi R.; Wong, Christopher T.; Zhu, W.; Netusil, Noelwah; & Fowler, Joanna S. (2001). Brain dopamine and obesity. *Lancet, 357,* 354–357.

Wang, Gene-Jack; Volkow, Nora D.; Thanos, Panayotis K.; & Fowler, Joanna S. (2004). Similarity between obesity and drug addiction as assessed by neurofunctional imaging: A concept review. *Journal of Addictive Diseases, 23,* 39–53.

Wang, Kevin H.; Penmatsa, Aravind; & Gouaux, Eric (2015). Neurotransmitter and psychostimulant recognition by the dopamine transporter. *Nature, 521,* 322–327. https://doi.org/10.1038/nature14431

Wang, Lin; & Ngai, Steven S.-y. (2020). The effects of anonymity, invisibility, asynchrony, and moral disengagement on cyberbullying perpetration among school-aged children in China. *Children and Youth Services Review, 119,* 1–9. https://doi.org/10.1016/j.childyouth.2020.105613

Wang, Philip S.; Aguilar-Gaxiola, Sergio; Alonso, Jordi; Lee, Sing; Schoenbaum, Michael; Üstün, T. Bedirhan; Kessler, Roland C.; Bruffaerts, Ronny; Borges, Guilherme; de Girolamo, Giovanni; Gureje, Oye; Haro, Josep Maria; Kostyuchenko, Stanislav; Masféty, Viviane Kovess; Levinson, Daphna; Matschinger, Herbert; Mneimneh, Zeina; Ormel, Browne; Mark Oakley Johan; . . . & Tsang, Adley. (2011). Assessing mental disorders and service use across countries: The WHO world mental health survey initiative. In Darrel A. Regier, William E. Narrow, Emily A. Kuhl, & David J. Kupfer (Eds.). *The conceptual evolution of DSM-5* (pp. 231–266). American Psychiatric Publishing.

Wang, Qi. (2001). Culture effects on adults' earliest childhood recollection and self-description: Implications for the relation between memory and the self. *Journal of Personality and Social Psychology, 81,* 220–223.

Wang, Qi. (2006). Earliest recollections of self and others in European American and Taiwanese young adults. *Psychological Science, 17,* 708–714.

Wang, Qi. (2013). *The autobiographical self in time and culture.* Oxford University Press. https://doi.org/10.1093/acprof:oso/9780199737833.001.0001

Wang, Qi. (2014). The cultured self and remembering. In Patricia J. Bauer & Robyn Fivush (Eds.), *The Wiley handbook on the development of children's memory* (pp. 605–25). Wiley-Blackwell.

Wang, Qiang; Bowling, Nathan A.; & Eschleman, Kevin J. (2010). A meta-analytic examination of work and general locus of control. *Journal of Applied Psychology, 95*(4), 761–768.

Wang, Yingxu, & Chiew, Vincent. (2010). On the cognitive process of human problem solving. *Cognitive Systems Research, 11,* 81–92. https://doi.org/10.1016/j.cogsys.2008.08.003

Wardenaar, Klaas J.; & Jonge, Peter de. (2017, February 22). The cross-national epidemiology of specific phobia in the world mental health surveys. *Psychological Medicine, 47*(10), 1744–1760. https://doi.org/10.1017/S0033291717000174

Warner, Leah R., & Shields, Stephanie A. (2007). The perception of crying in women and men: Angry tears, sad tears, and the "right way" to cry. In Ursula Hess & Pierre Philippot (Eds.), *Group Dynamics and Emotional Expression.* Cambridge University Press.

Wasserman, Edward A., & Zentall, Thomas R. (2006). *Comparative cognition: Experimental explorations of animal intelligence.* Oxford University Press.

Wasserman, John D. (2019). Deconstructing CHC. *Applied Measurement in Education, 32*(3), 249–268. https://doi.org/10.1080/08957347.2019.1619563

Wassing, Rick; Benjamins, Jeroen S.; Dekker, Kim; Moens, Sarah; Spiegelhalder, Kai; Feige, Bernd; . . . & Walker, Matthew P. (2016). Slow dissolving of emotional distress contributes to hyperarousal. *Proceedings of the National Academy of Sciences, 113,* 2538–2543. https://doi.org/10.1073/pnas.1522520113

Waterman, Alan S. (2013). The humanistic psychology–positive psychology divide: Contrasts in philosophical foundations. *American Psychologist, 68*(3), 124–133. https://doi.org/10.1037/a0032168

Watson, Jeanne C.; Goldman, Rhonda N.; & Greenberg, Leslie S. (2011). Humanistic and experiential theories of psychotherapy. In John C. Norcross, Gary R. VandenBos, & Donald K. Freedheim (Eds.), *History of psychotherapy: Continuity and change* (2nd ed., pp. 141–172). American Psychological Association.

Watson, John B. (1913). Psychology as the behaviorist views it. *Psychological Review, 20,* 158–177.

Watson, John B. (1916). The place of the conditioned-reflex in psychology. *Psychological Review, 23,* 89–116.

Watson, John B. (1919). A schematic outline of the emotions. *Psychological Review, 26,* 165–196.

Watson, John B. (1924/1970). *Behaviorism.* Norton.

Watson, John B. (1930). *Behaviorism* (Rev. ed.). University of Chicago Press.

Watson, John B., & Rayner, Rosalie. (1920). Conditioned emotional reactions. *Journal of Experimental Psychology, 3,* 1–14. (Reprinted March 2000: *American Psychologist, 55*(3), 313–317)

Watson, Nathaniel F.; Harden, Kathryn P.; Buchwald, Dedra; Vitiello, Michael V.; Pack, Allan I.; Weigle, David S.; & Goldberg, Jack. (2012). Sleep duration and body mass index in twins: A gene–environment interaction. *Sleep, 35*(5), 597–603. https://doi.org/10.5665/sleep.1810

Watters, Ethan. (2010). *Crazy like us: The globalization of the American psyche.* Free Press.

Watts, Geoff. (2012). Critics attack DSM-5 for overmedicalising normal human behaviour. *BMJ, 344,* e1020. https://doi.org/10.1136/bmj.e1020

Watts, Jonathan. (2002). Public health experts concerned about "hikikomori." *Lancet, 359*(9312), 1131. https://doi.org/10.1016/s0140-6736(02)08186-2

Watts, Richard E. (2012). On the origin of the striving for superiority and of social interest. In Jon Carlson & Michael P. Maniacci (Eds.), *Alfred Adler revisited.* Routledge /Taylor & Francis Group.

Weaver, Terri E., & George, Charles F. P. (2005). Cognition and performance in patients with obstructive sleep apnea. In Meir H. Kryger, Thomas Roth, & William C. Dement (Eds.), *Principles and practice of sleep medicine* (4th ed.). Elsevier Saunders.

Webb, Thomas L., & Sheeran, Paschal. (2007). How do implementation intentions promote goal attainment? A test of component processes. *Journal of Experimental Social Psychology, 43,* 295–302. https://doi.org/10.1016/j.jesp.2006.02.001

Wechsler, David. (1944). *The measurement of adult intelligence* (3rd ed.). Williams & Wilkins.

Wechsler, David. (1977). *Manual for the Wechsler Intelligence Scale for Children* (Rev.). Psychological Corporation.

Wechsler, Henry, & Nelson, Toben F. (2008). What we have learned from the Harvard School of Public Health College Alcohol Study: Focusing attention on college student alcohol consumption and the environmental conditions that promote it. *Journal of Studies on Alcohol and Drugs, 69*(4), 481–490.

Weems, Carl, & Silverman, Wendy. (2008). Anxiety disorders. In Theodore P. Beauchaine & Stephen P. Hinshaw (Eds.), *Child and adolescent psychopathology* (pp. 447–476). Wiley.

Weil, Rimona S., & Rees, Geraint. (2010). A new taxonomy for perceptual filling-in. *Brain Research Reviews.* https://doi.org/10.1016/j.brainresrev.2010.10.004

Weinberger, Daniel R. (1995, June). Quoted in Joel L. Swerdlow, "Quiet miracles of the brain." *National Geographic, 187,* 2–41.

Weiner, Irving B., & Meyer, Gregory J. (2009). Personality assessment with the Rorschach Inkblot Method. In James N. Butcher (Ed.), *Oxford handbook of personality assessment.* Oxford University Press.

Weinstein, N.; Brown, K. W.; & Ryan, R. M. (2009). A multi-method examination of the effects of mindfulness on stress attribution, coping, and emotional well-being. *Journal of Research in Personality, 43,* 374–385. https://doi.org/10.1016/j.jrp.2008.12.008

Weintraub, Michael I.; Wolfe, Gil I.; Barohn, Richard A.; Cole, Steven P.; Parry, Gareth J.; Hayat, Ghazala; Cohen, Jeffrey A.; Page, Jeffrey C.; Bromberg, Mark B.; Schwartz, Sherwyn L.; & the Magnetic Research Group. (2003). Static magnetic field therapy for symptomatic diabetic neuropathy: A randomized, double-blind, placebo-controlled trial. *Archives of Physical Medicine and Rehabilitation, 84*(5), 736–746. https://doi.org/10.1016/s0003-9993(03)00106-0

Weisberg, Robert W. (1988). Problem solving and creativity. In Robert J. Sternberg (Ed.), *The nature of creativity.* Cambridge University Press.

Weisberg, Robert W. (1993). *Creativity: Beyond the myth of genius.* Freeman.

Weisberg, Robert W. (2015). Toward an integrated theory of insight in problem solving. *Thinking & Reasoning, 21*(1), 5–39. https://doi.org/10.1080/13546783.2014.886625

Weisgram, Erica. (2016). The cognitive construction of gender stereotypes: Evidence for the dual pathways model of gender differentiation. *Sex Roles, 75,* 301–313. https://doi.org/10.1007/s11199-016-0624-z

Weisman, Jaclyn S.; & Rodebaugh, Thomas L. (2018). Exposure therapy augmentation: A review and extension of techniques informed by an inhibitory learning approach. *Clinical Psychology Review, 59,* 41–51. https://doi.org/10.1016/j.cpr.2017.10.010

Weiss, Alexander; Bates, Timothy C.; & Luciano, Michelle. (2008). Happiness is a personal(ity) thing: The genetics of personality and well-being in a representative sample. *Psychological Science, 19*(3), 205–210.

Weiss, Lawrence G. (2010). Considerations on the Flynn effect. *Journal of Psychoeducational Assessment, 28*(5), 482.

Weiss, Peter H.; Shah, N. Jon; Toni, Ivan; Zilles, Karl; & Fink, Gereon R. (2001). Associating colours with people: A case of chromatic-lexical synaesthesia. *Cortex, 37,* 750–753. https://doi.org/10.1016/S0010-9452(08)70631-2

Weiss, Tzipi, & Berger, Roni. (2010). Posttraumatic growth around the globe: Research findings and practice implications. In Tzipi Weiss & Roni Berger (Eds.), *Posttraumatic growth and culturally competent practice: Lessons learned from around the globe.* Wiley.

Weissman, Judith; Russell, David; Jay, Melanie; Beasley, Jeannette; Malaspina, Dolores; & Pegus, Cheryl. (2017). Disparities in health care utilization and functional limitations among adults with serious psychological distress, 2006-2014. *Psychiatric Services, 68,* 653–659. https://doi.org/10.1176/appi.ps.201600260

Weisz, John R., & Kazdin, Alan E. (2010). *Evidence-based psychotherapies for children and adolescents.* Guilford.

Wells, Gordon. (2009). The social context of language and literacy development. In O. A. Barbarin & B. H. Wasik, *Handbook of early child development and early education: Research to practice* (pp. 271–302). Guilford.

Wenger, Elisabeth; Brozzoli, Claudio; Lindenberger, Ulman; & Lövdén, Martin. (2017). Expansion and renormalization of human brain structure during skill acquisition. *Trends in Cognitive Sciences, 21*(12), 930–939. https://doi.org/10.1016/j.tics.2017.09.008

Werker, Janet, & Desjardins, Renee. (1995). Listening to speech in the 1st year of life: Experiential influences on phoneme production. *Current Directions in Psychological Science, 4,* 76–81.

Werkhoven, Peter, & van Erp, Jan. (2013). Multimodal perception and simulation. In Charles Chubb, Barbara A. Dosher, Zhong-Lin Lu, & Richard M. Shiffrin (Eds.), *Human information processing: Vision, memory, and attention. Decade of behavior.* American Psychological Association.

Werner, John S.; Pinna, Baingio; & Spillman, Lothar. (2007, March). Illusory color and the brain. *Scientific American, 296,* pp. 90–95.

Werner-Seidler, Aliza; Afzali, Mohammad H.; Chapman, Cath; Sunderland, Matthew; & Slade, Tim. (2017). The relationship between social support networks and depression in the 2007 National Survey of Mental Health and Well-being. *Social psychiatry and psychiatric epidemiology, 52*(12), 1463-1473. https://doi.org/10.1007/s00127-017-1440-7

Wertheimer, Max. (1923). Laws of organization in perceptual forms. In Barbara F. Gentile & Benjamin O. Miller (Eds.), *Foundations of psychological thought: A history of psychology* (pp. 427–440). Sage.

Wertsch, James V. (2008). From social interaction to higher psychological processes: A clarification and application of Vygotsky's theory. *Human Development, 51*(1), 66–79.

West, John D., & Bubenzer, Donald L. (2012). A basic difference between individual psychology and psychoanalysis. In Jon Carlson & Michael P. Maniacci (Eds.), *Alfred Adler revisited.* Routledge/Taylor & Francis Group.

Westen, Drew. (1998). The scientific legacy of Sigmund Freud: Toward a psychodynamically informed psychological science. *Psychological Bulletin, 124,* 333–371.

Westen, Drew. (1990). Psychoanalytic approaches to personality. In Lawrence A. Pervin (Ed.), *Handbook of personality: Theory and research.* Guilford Press.

Wethington, Elaine. (2000). Expecting stress: Americans and the "midlife crisis." *Motivation and Emotion, 24,* 85–103.

What We Know. (2018). What does the scholarly research say about the effect of gender transition on transgender wellbeing? Cornell University. https://whatweknow.inequality.cornell.edu/topics/lgbt-equality/what-does-the-scholarly-research-say-about-the-well-being-of-transgender-people/

Wheeler, Mark E.; Petersen, Steven E.; & Buckner, Randy L. (2000). Memory's echo: Vivid remembering reactivates sensory-specific cortex. *Proceedings of the National Academy of Sciences, 97,* 11125–11129.

Whisman, Mark A.; Uebelacker, Lisa A.; & Settles, Tatiana D. (2010). Marital distress and the metabolic syndrome: Linking social functioning with physical health. *Journal of Family Psychology, 24*(3), 367–370.

White, C. Michael. (2019). A review of human studies assessing cannabidiol's (CBD) therapeutic actions and potential. *The Journal of Clinical Pharmacology, 59*(7), 923–934. https://doi.org/10.1002/jcph.1387

White, Carmela A.; Uttl, Bob; & Holder, Mark D. (2019). Meta-analyses of positive psychology interventions: The effects are much smaller than previously reported. *PLoS ONE.* https://doi.org/10.1371/journal.pone.0216588

White, Elizabeth M.; Wetle, Terrie Fox; Reddy, Ann; & Baier, Rosa R. (2021). Front-line nursing home staff experiences during the COVID-19 pandemic. *Journal of the American Medical Directors Association, 22*(1), 199–203. https://doi.org/10.1016/j.jamda.2020.11.022

Whitehead, Jocelyne C., & Armony, Jorge L. (2018). Singing in the brain: Neural representation of music and voice as revealed by fMRI. *Human Brain Mapping, 39*(12), 4913–4924. https://doi.org/10.1002/hbm.24333

Whitman, M. R.; Tarescavage, Anthony M.; Glassmire, David M.; Burchett, Danielle; & Sellbom, Martin. (2019). Examination of differential validity of MMPI-2-RF scores by gender and ethnicity in predicting future suicidal and violent behaviors in a forensic sample. *2019 Faculty Bibliography,*10. https://collected.jcu.edu/fac_bib_2019/10

WHO World Mental Health Survey Consortium. (2004, June 2). Prevalence, severity, and unmet need for treatment of mental disorders in the World Health Organization mental health surveys. *Journal of the American Medical Association, 291*(21), 2581–2590. https://doi.org/10.1001/jama.291.21.2581

Whorf, Benjamin L. (1956). Science and linguistics. In J. B. Carroll (Ed.), *Language, thought, and reality: Selected papers of Benjamin Lee Whorf.* MIT Press.

Wicherts, Jelte M.; Dolan, Conor V.; Hessen, David J.; Oosterveld, Paul; Van Baal, G. Caroline M.; Boomsma, Dorret I.; & Span, Mark M. (2004). Are intelligence tests measurement invariant over time? Investigating the nature of the Flynn effect. *Intelligence, 32*(5), 509-537. https://doi.org/10.1016/j.intell.2004.07.002

Wickens, Christine M.; Mann, Robert E.; & Wiesenthal, David L. (2013). Addressing driver aggression: Contributions from psychological science. *Current Directions in Psychological Science, 22*(5), 386–391. https://doi.org/10.1177/0963721413486986

Wiech, Katja. (2016). Deconstructing the sensation of pain: The influence of cognitive processes on pain perception. *Science, 354,* 584–587. https://doi.org/10.1126/science.aaf8934

Wiederhold, Brenda K. (2020). Connecting through technology during the coronavirus disease 2019 pandemic: Avoiding "Zoom fatigue." *Cyberpsychology, Behavior, and Social Networking, 23*(7), 437–438. https://doi.org/10.1089/cyber.2020.29188.bkw

Wieland, Sandra. (2011). Dissociation in children and adolescents: What it is, how it presents, and how we can understand it. In Sandra Wieland (Ed.), *Dissociation in traumatized children and adolescents: Theory and clinical interventions* (pp. 1–27). Routledge/Taylor & Francis Group.

Wilcoxon, Hardy C.; Dragoin, William B.; & Kral, Paul A. (1971). Illness-induced aversions in rat and quail: Relative salience of visual and gustatory cues. *Science, 171,* 826–828.

Wilde, Douglass J. (2011). *Jung's personality theory quantified.* Springer-Verlag.

Wilker, Sarah, & Kolassa, Iris-Tatjana. (2013). The formation of a neural fear network in posttraumatic stress disorder: Insights from molecular genetics. *Clinical Psychological Science, 1*(4), 452–469. https://doi.org/10.1177/2167702613479583

Wilkinson, Richard G., & Pickett, Kate E. (2009). Income inequality and social dysfunction. *Annual Review of Sociology, 35,* 493–511.

Williams, Janice E. (2010). Anger/hostility and cardiovascular disease. In Michael Potegal, Gerhard Stemmler, & Charles Spielberger (Eds.), *International handbook of anger: Constituent and concomitant biological, psychological, and social processes.* Springer.

Williams, John E.; Satterwhite, Robert C.; & Best, Deborah L. (1999). Pancultural gender stereotypes revisited: The five factor model. *Sex Roles, 40,* 513–525.

Williams, Kipling D. (2007). Ostracism. *Annual Review of Psychology, 58,* 425–452. https://doi.org/10.1146/annurev.psych.58.110405.085641

Williams, Kipling D. (2009). Ostracism: A temporal need-threat model. In Zanna, Marc P. (Ed.) *Advances in experimental social psychology* (Vol. 41). Elsevier Academic Press. https://doi.org/10.1016/S0065-2601(08)00406-1

Williams, Lawrence E.; & Bargh, John A. (2008). Experiencing physical warmth promotes interpersonal warmth. *Science, 322*(5901), 606–607. https://doi.org/10.1126/science.1162548

Williams, Mark; Teasdale, John; Segal, Zindel; & Kabat-Zinn, Jon. (2007). *The mindful way through depression: Freeing yourself from chronic unhappiness.*Guilford.

Williams, Monnica T. (2020a). Microaggressions: Clarification, evidence, and impact. *Perspectives on Psychological Science, 15*(1), 3–26. https://doi.org/10.1177/1745691619827417

Williams, Monnica T. (2020b). Psychology cannot afford to ignore many harms caused by microaggressions. *Perspectives on Psychological Science, 15*(1), 38–43. https://doi.org/10.1177/1745691619898933

Williams, Nigel M.; O'Donovan, Michael C.; & Owen, Michael J. (2005). Is the dysbindin (*DTNBP1*) a susceptibility gene for schizophrenia? *Schizophrenia Bulletin, 31,* 800–805. https://doi.org/10.1093/schbul/sbi061

Williams, Robert L. (1972). *The BITCH-100: A culture-specific test* [Paper presentation]. American Psychological Association Annual Convention.

Willingham, Daniel T.; Hughes, Elizabeth M; & Dobolyi, David G. (2015). The scientific status of learning style theories. *Teaching of Psychology, 42,* 266–271. https://doi.org/10.1177/0098628315589505

Willis, Janine, & Todorov, Alexander. (2006). First impressions: Making up your mind after a 100-ms exposure to a face. *Psychological Science, 17,* 592–598. https://doi.org/10.1111/j.1467-9280.2006.01750.x

Wills, Frank. (2009). *Beck's cognitive therapy: Distinctive features.* Routledge.

Wilson, Clare. (2020). Alternative health show *The Goop Lab* on Netflix demonstrates just how easy it is to fall for bad science, says Clare Wilson. *New Scientist, 245*(3266).

Wilson, Megan L.; Snyder, Rebecca J.; Zhang, Zhi H.; Lan, Luo; Li, C. L.; & Maple, Terry L. (2009). Effects of partner on play fighting behavior in giant panda cubs. Play & culture studies. In Cindy Dell Clark (Ed.), *Transactions at play: Play and culture studies.* University Press of America.

Wilson, Nana; Kariisa, Mbabazi; Seth, Puja; Smith, Herschel IV; & Davis, Nicole L. (2020). Drug and opioid-involved overdose deaths–United States, 2017–2018. *Morbidity and Mortality Weekly Report, 69,* 290–297. https://dx.doi.org/10.15585/mmwr.mm6911a4

Winerman, Lea. (2005, October). The mind's mirror. *Monitor on Psychology, 36*(9), 8. https://www.apa.org/monitor/oct05/mirror

Winkielman, Piotr; Niedenthal, Paula; Wielgosz, Joseph; Eelen, Jiska; & Kavanagh, Liam C. (2015). Embodiment of cognition and emotion. In Mario Mikulincer, Phillip R. Shaver, Eugene Borgida, & John A. Bargh (Eds.), *APA handbook of personality and social psychology, Vol. 1: Attitudes and social cognition.* American Psychological Association. https://doi.org/10.1037/14341-004

Winkleman, Natalia. (2019, June 4). Sarah Silverman considers the link between comedy and mental health in 'It's Not That Funny' trailer. *Slate.* https://slate.com/culture/2019/06/sarah-silverman-mental-health-comedy-its-not-that-funny-trailer.html

Winkler, Connie. (2006, September). Job tryouts go virtual: Online job simulations provide sophisticated candidate assessments. *HR Magazine, 51*(9), 131–134.

Winkler, Nina; Ruf-Leuschner, Martina; Ertl, Verena; Pfeiffer, Anett; Schalinski, Inga; Ovuga, Emilio; Neuner, Frank; & Elbert, Thomas. (2015). From war to classroom: PTSD and depression in formerly abducted youth in Uganda. *Frontiers in Psychiatry, 6*, 1–10. https://doi.org/10.3389/fpsyt.2015.00002

Wintermark, Max; Sanelli, Pina C.; Anzai, Yoshimi; Tsiouris, A. John; & Whitlow, Christopher T. (2015). Imaging evidence and recommendations for traumatic brain injury: Conventional neuroimaging techniques. *Journal of the American College of Radiology, 12*(2), 1–14. https://doi.org/10.1016/j.jacr.2014.10.014

Wise, Deborah, & Rosqvist, Johan. (2006). Explanatory style and wellbeing. In Jay C. Thomas, Daniel L. Segal, & Michel Hersen (Eds.), *Comprehensive Handbook of personality and psychopathology. Vol. 1: Personality and everyday functioning* (pp. 285–305). Wiley.

Wisenberg Brin, Dinah. (2019). Employers embrace artificial intelligence for HR. *SHRM.* https://www.shrm.org/resourcesandtools/hr-topics/global-hr/pages/employers-embrace-artificial-intelligence-for-hr.aspx

Wittenberg, Alex. (2020, August 17). To get people to wear masks, try comparing them to seatbelts and helmets. *Bloomberg CityLab.* https://www.bloomberg.com/news/articles/2020-08-17/what-works-to-persuade-people-to-wear-masks

Wixted, John T. (2004). The psychology and neuroscience of forgetting. *Annual Review of Psychology, 55*, 235–269.

Wnuk, Ewelina, & Majid, Asifa. (2014). Revisiting the limits of language: The odor lexicon of Maniq. *Cognition, 131*, 125–138.

Woerle, Sandra; Roeber, Jim; & Landen, Michael G. (2007). Prevalence of alcohol dependence among excessive drinkers in New Mexico. *Alcoholism: Clinical and Experimental Research, 31*, 293–298.

Wohlschläger, Andreas, & Wohlschläger, Astrid. (1998). Mental and manual rotation. *Journal of Experimental Psychology: Human Perception and Performance, 24*, 397–412.

Wolf, Erika J., & Mori, DeAnna L. (2009). Avoidant coping as a predictor of mortality in veterans with end-stage renal disease. *Health Psychology, 28*(3), 330–337.

Wolf, Oliver T. (2017, April). Stress and memory retrieval: Mechanisms and consequences. *Current Opinion in Behavioral Sciences, 14*, 40–46. https://doi.org/10.1016/j.cobeha.2016.12.001

Wolf, Oliver T., & Kluge, Annette (2017). Commentary: Retrieval practice protects memory against acute stress. *Frontiers in Behavioral Neuroscience, 11*, article 48. https://doi.org/10.3389/fnbeh.2017.00048

Wolff, Andre; Vanduynhoven, Eric; van Kleef, Maarten; Huygen, Frank; Pope, Jason E.; & Mekhail, Nagy. (2011). Phantom pain. *Pain Practice, 11*(4), 403–413. https://doi.org/10.1111/j.1533-2500.2011.00454.x

Wolman, David. (2005, November 5). The secrets of human handedness. *New Scientist, 2524*, 36.

Wolpe, Joseph. (1958). *Psychotherapy by reciprocal inhibition.* Stanford University Press.

Wolpe, Joseph. (1982). *The practice of behavior therapy.* Pergamon Press.

Women's Sports Foundation. (2007). Title IX myths and facts. http://www.womenssportsfoundation.org/home/advocate/title-ix-and-issues/what-is-title-ix/title-ix-myths-and-facts

Wonderlic, Charles. (2005). Pre-employment testing and employee selection. furninfo.com

Wonderlic, E. F. (1998). *Wonderlic personnel test manual.* Wonderlic.

Wong, Paul T. P., & Wong, Lilian C. J. (Eds.). (2006). *Handbook of multicultural perspectives on stress and coping.* Springer.

Wong, V., & Ying, Winnie. (2006). Social withdrawal of young people in Hong Kong: A social exclusion perspective. *Hong Kong Journal of Social Work, 40* (1/2), 61–92. https://doi.org/10.1142/S0219246206000064

Wong, Wan-chi. (2009). Retracing the footsteps of Wilhelm Wundt: Explorations in the disciplinary frontiers of psychology and in Völkerpsychologie. *History of Psychology, 12*(4), 229–265.

Woo, Stephanie M., & Keatinge, Carolyn (2008). *Diagnosis and treatment of mental disorders across the lifespan.* Wiley.

Woo, Tsung-Ung W.; Canuso, Carla M.; Wojcik, Joanne D.; Brunette, Mary F.; & Green, Alan I. (2009). Treatment of schizophrenia. In Alan F. Schatzberg & Charles B. Nemeroff (Eds.), *The American Psychiatric Publishing textbook of psychopharmacology* (4th ed., pp. 1135–1169). American Psychiatric Publishing.

Wood, David; Crapnell, Tara; Lau, Lynette; Bennett, Ashley; Lotstein, Debra; Ferris, Maria; & Kuo, Alice (2018). Emerging adulthood as a critical stage in the life course. In Neal Halfon, Christopher B. Forrest, Richard M. Lerner, & Elaine M. Faustman (Eds.), *Handbook of life course health development* (pp.123–143). https://doi.org/10.1007/978-3-319-47143-3_7

Wood, Robert, & Bandura, Albert. (1991). Social cognitive theory of organizational management. In Richard M. Steers & Lyman W. Porter (Eds.), *Motivation and work behavior.* McGraw-Hill.

Wood, Wendy, & Eagly, Alice H. (2009). Gender identity. In Mark R. Leary & Rick H. Hoyle (Eds.), *Handbook of individual differences in social behavior* (pp. 109–125). Guilford.

Wood, Wendy, & Eagly, Alice H. (2010). Gender. In Susan T. Fiske, Daniel T. Gilbert, & Gardner Lindzey (Eds.), *Handbook of social psychology, 1.* Wiley

Wood Sherif, Carolyn. (1982). Needed concepts in the study of gender identity. *Psychology of Women Quarterly, 6*, 375–395.

Wood Sherif, Carolyn. (1983). Carolyn Wood Sherif. In O'Connell, A. N. & Russo, N. F. (Eds.), Models of achievement: Reflections of eminent women in psychology. (pp. 279–293). Columbia University Press.

Woodhead, Erin; Cronkite, Ruth; Moos, Rudolf H., & Timko, Christine. (2013). Coping strategies predictive of adverse outcomes among community adults. *Journal of Clinical Psychology, 70*, 1183–1195. https://doi.org/10.1002/jclp.21924

Woodhead, Erin; Northrop, Lynn; & Edelstein, Barry. (2014, August 6). Stress, social support, and burnout among long-term care nursing staff. *Journal of Applied Gerontology.* Advance online publication. https://doi.org/10.1177/0733464814542465

Woolley, Anita; Aggarwal, Ishani; & Malone, Thomas. (2015). Collective intelligence and group performance. *Current Directions in Psychological Science, 24*, 420–424. https://doi.org/10.1177/0963721415599543

Workman, Lance, & Reader, Will. (2008). *Evolutionary psychology: An introduction.* Cambridge University Press.

World Health Organization (WHO). (1998). Schizophrenia and public health. www.who.int/mental_health/media/en/55.pdf

World Heath Organization (WHO). (2017). *Depression and other common mental disorders: global health estimates.* License: CC BY-NC-SA 3.0 IGO. https://www.who.int/mental_health/management/depression/prevalence_global_health_estimates/en/

World Health Organization (WHO). (2018). *Global status report on alcohol and health 2018.* https://www.who.int/substance_abuse/publications/global_alcohol_report/en/

World Health Organization (WHO). (2019, September 9). *Suicide in the world: global health estimates.* https://www.who.int/publications/i/item/suicide-in-the-world

World Health Organization (WHO). (2020a, October 3). *COVID-19 disrupting mental health services in most countries, WHO survey.* World Health Organization News. https://www.who.int/news/item/05-10-2020-covid-19-disrupting-mental-health-services-in-most-countries-who-survey

World Health Organization (WHO). (2020b). Road traffic injuries. https://www.who.int/news-room/fact-sheets/detail/road-traffic-injuries

Wright, Brittany, & Loving, Timothy. (2011). Health implications of conflict in close relationships. *Social and Personality Psychology Compass, 5*, 552–562. https://doi.org/10.1111/j.1751-9004.2011.00371.x

Wright, Jesse H.; Thase, Michael E.; & Beck, Aaron T. (2011). Cognitive therapy. In Robert E. Hales, Stuart C. Yudofsky, & Glen O. Gabbard (Eds.), *Essentials of psychiatry.* American Psychiatric Publishing.

Wright, Jesse H.; Turkington, Douglas; Kingdon, David G.; & Basco, Monica Ramirez. (2009). *Cognitive-behavior therapy for severe mental illness: An illustrated guide.* American Psychiatric Publishing.

Wu, Ming-Shun; Chen, Kee-Hsin; Chen, I-Fan; Huang, Shihping Kevin; Tzeng Pei-Chan; Yeh, Mei-Ling; Lee, Fei-Peng; Lin, Jaung-Geng; & Chen, Chiehfeng. (2016). The efficacy of acupuncture in post-operative pain management: A systematic review and meta-analysis. *PLOS ONE, 11*(3), e0150367. https://doi.org/10.1371/journal.pone.0150367

Wu, Pei-zhe; O'Malley, Jennifer T.; de Gruttola, Victor; & Liberman, M. Charles. (2020). Age-related hearing loss is dominated by damage to inner ear sensory cells, not the cellular battery that powers them. *The Journal of Neuroscience, 40*(3), 6357–6366. https://doi.org/10.1523/JNEUROSCI.0937-20.2020

Wu, Tianchen; Jia, Xiaoqian; Shi, Huifeng; Jieqiong, Niu; Xiaohan, Yin; Xie, Jialei; & Wang, Xiaoli. (2021, February 15). Prevalence of mental health problems during the COVID-19 pandemic: A systematic review and meta-analysis. *Journal of Affective Disorders, 281*(15) 91–98. https://doi.org/10.1016/j.jad.2020.11.117

Wurtele, Sandy K. (2009). "Activities of older adults" survey: Tapping into student views of the elderly. *Educational Gerontology, 35*, 1026–1031. https://doi.org/10.1080/03601270902973557

Wyatt, Tristram D. (2009). Fifty years of pheromones. *Nature, 457*, 262–263.

Wyatt, Tristram D. (2015). The search for human pheromones: The lost decades and the necessity of returning to first principles. *Proceedings of the Royal Society B, 282*, 20142994. https://doi.org/10.1098/rspb.2014.2994

Wyer, Natalie A. (2010). You never get a second chance to make a first (implicit) impression: The role of elaboration in the formation and revision of implicit impressions. *Social Cognition, 28*(1), 1–19.

Wynn, Karen; Bloom, Paul; Jordan, Ashely; Marshall, Julia; & Sheskin, Mark. (2018). Not noble savages after all: Limits to early altruism. *Current Directions in Psychological Science, 27*, 3–8. https://doi.org/10.1177/0963721417734875

Wynne, Clive. (2016). What is special about dog cognition? *Current Directions in Psychological Science, 25*, 345–350. https://doi.org/10.1177/0963721416657540

Wynne, Lyman C.; Tienari, Pekka; & Nieminen, P. (2006, December). Genotype-environment interaction in the schizophrenia spectrum: Genetic liability and global family ratings in the Finnish adoption study. *Family Process, 45*(4), 419–434. https://doi.org/10.1111/j.1545-5300.2006.00180.x

Xie, Lulu; Kang, Hongyi; Xu, Qiwu; Chen, Michael J.; Liao, Yonghong; Thiyaga-rajan, Meenakshisundaram; O'Donnell, John; Christensen, Daniel J.; Nicholson, Charles; Iliff, Jeffrey J.; Takano, Takahiro; Deane, Rashid; & Nedergaard, Maiken. (2013). Sleep drives metabolite clearance from the adult brain. *Science, 342,* 373–377. https://doi.org/10.1126/science.124122

Xu, Fujie; Sternberg, Maya R.; & Markowitz, Lauri E. (2010a). Men who have sex with men in the United States: Demographic and behavioral characteristics and prevalence of HIV and HSV-2 infection: Results from national health and nutrition examination survey 2001–2006. *Sexually Transmitted Diseases, 37*(6), 399–405. https://doi.org/10.1097/OLQ.0b013e3181ce122b

Xu, Fujie; Sternberg, Maya R.; & Markowitz, Lauri E. (2010b). Women who have sex with women in the United States: Prevalence, sexual behavior and prevalence of herpes simplex virus type 2 infection-results from national health and nutrition examination survey 2001–2006. *Sexually Transmitted Diseases, 37*(7), 407–413. https://doi.org/10.1097/OLQ.0b013e3181db2e18

Yablonsky, Linda. (2013). Zwelethu Mthethwa's "Brave Ones." *The New York Times.* http://tmagazine.blogs.nytimes.com/2013/01/31/zwelethu-mthethwas-brave-ones/?ref=t-magazine

Yalom, Irvin D. (2005). *The theory and practice of group psychotherapy* (5th ed.). Basic Books.

Yamaguchi, Susumu, & Ariizumi, Yukari. (2006). Close interpersonal relationships among Japanese: Amae as distinguished from attachment and dependence. In Uichol Kim, Kuo-Shu Yang, & Kwang-Kuo Hwang (Eds.), *Indigenous and cultural psychology: Understanding people in context.* Springer Science + Business Media.

Yancy, George. (2011). The scholar who coined the term Ebonics: A conversation with Dr. Robert L. Williams. *Journal of Language, Identity, and Education, 10,* 41–51. https://doi.org/10.1080/15348458.2011.539967

Yang, Chunliang; Potts, Rosalind; & Shanks, David R. (2018). Enhancing learning and retrieval of new information: A review of the forward testing effect. *Science of Learning, 3.* https://doi.org/10.1038/s41539-018-0024-y

Yang, Guang; Lai, Cora Sau Wan; Cichon, Joseph; Ma, Lei; Li, Wei; & Gan, Wen-Biao. (2014). Sleep promotes branch-specific formation of dendritic spines after learning. *Science, 344,* 1173-1178.

Yarnell, Phillip R., & Lynch, Steve. (1970, April 25). Retrograde memory immediately after concussion. *Lancet, 1,* 863–865.

Ybarra, Oscar. (2002). Naive causal understanding of valenced behaviors and its implications for social information processing. *Psychological Bulletin, 128,* 421–441.

Yeh, Christine J.; Inman, Arpana C.; Kim, Angela B.; & Okubo, Yuki. (2006). Asian American families' collectivistic coping strategies in response to 9/11. *Cultural Diversity and Ethnic Minority Psychology, 12,* 134–148. https://doi:org/10.1037/1099-9809.12.1.134

Yerkes, Robert M., & Dodson, John D. (1908). The relation of strength of stimulus to rapidity of habit-formation. *Journal of Comparative Neurological Psychology, 18,* 459–482. https://doi.org/10.1002/cne.920180503

Yeung, Nelson; Lau, Joseph; Yu, Nancy; Zhang, Jianping; Xu, Zhening; Choi, Kai; Zhang, Qi; Mak, Winnie; & Lui, Wacy. (2016). Media exposure related to the 2008 Sichuan earthquake predicted probable PTSD among Chinese adolescents in Kunming, China: A longitudinal study. *Psychological Trauma: Theory, Research, Practice, and Policy, 10*(2), 253–262. https://doi.org/10.1037/tra0000121

Yiend, Jenny; Parnes, Charlotte; Shepherd, Kirsty; Roche, Mary-Kate; & Cooper, Myra J. (2014). Negative self-beliefs in eating disorders: A cognitive-bias-modification study. *Clinical Psychological Science, 2*(6), 756–766. https://doi.org/10.1177/2167702614528163

Yildirim, Baris O., & Derksen, Jan J. (2012). A review on the relationship between testosterone and life-course persistent antisocial behavior. *Psychiatry Research, 200*(2–3), 984–1010. https://doi.org/10.1016/j.psychres.2012.07.044

Yokum, Sonja, & Stice, Eric. (2019). Weight gain is associated with changes in neural response to palatable food tastes varying in sugar and fat and palatable food images: A repeated-measures fMRI study. *American Journal Clinical Nutrition, 110,* 1275–1286. https://doi.org/10.1093/ajcn/nqz204

Yong, Roseline; & Nomura, Kyoko. (2019, April 16). Hikomori is most associated with interpersonal relationships, followed by suicide risks: A secondary analysis of a national cross-sectional study. *Frontiers in Psychiatry, 10,* 247. https://doi.org/10.3389/fpsyt.2019.00247

Yonkers, Kimberly A., & Clarke, Diana E. (2011). Gender and gender-related issues in DSM-5. In Darrel A. Regier, William E. Narrow, Emily A. Kuhl, & David J. Kupfer (Eds.), *The conceptual evolution of DSM-5* (pp. 287–301). American Psychiatric Publishing.

Yoo, Seung-Schik; Gujar, Ninad; Hu, Peter; Jolesz, Ferenc A.; & Walker, Matthew P. (2007). The human emotional brain without sleep: A prefrontal-amygdala disconnect. *Current Biology, 17,* 877–878.

Yoshida, Katherine A.; Pons, Ferran; Maye, Jessica; & Werker, Janet F. (2010). Distributional phonetic learning at 10 months of age. *Infancy, 15*(4), 420–433.

Young, Antonia. (2000). *Women who become men: Albanian sworn virgins.* Berg.

Young, Liane; Cushman, Fiery; Hauser, Marc; & Saxe, Rebecca. (2007). The neural basis of the interaction between theory of mind and moral judgment. *Proceedings of the National Academy of Sciences, 104*(20), 8235–8240. https://doi.org/10.1073pnas.0701408104

Youngmisuk, Ohm. (2020, August 26). Clippers' Paul George says he dealt with anxiety, depression inside NBA bubble. *ESPN.* https://www.espn.com/nba/story/_/id/29743235/clippers-paul-george-says-dealt-anxiety-depression-bubble

Youyou, Wu; Kosinski, Michal; & Stillwell, David. (2015). Computer-based personality judgments are more accurate than those made by humans. *Proceedings of the National Academy of Sciences of the United States of America, 112,* 1036–1040. https://doi.org/10.1073/pnas.1418680112

Yudofsky, Stuart C. (2009). Contracting schizophrenia: Lessons from the influenza epidemic of 1918–1919. *Journal of the American Medical Association, 301*(3), 324–326. https://doi.org/10.1001/jama.2008.980

Yule, Morag; Brotto, Lori; & Gorzalka, Boris. (2017). Sexual fantasy and masturbation among asexual individuals: An in-depth exploration. *Archives of Sexual Behavior, 46,* 311–328. https://doi.org/10.1007/s10508-016-0870-8

Yuval, Kim; Zvielli, Ariel; & Bernstein, Amit. (2016). Attentional bias dynamics and posttraumatic stress in survivors of violent conflict and atrocities: New directions in clinical psychological science of refugee mental health. *Clinical Psychological Science, 5*(1), 64–73. https://doi.org/10.1177/2167702616649349

Zaboski, Brian A.; Kranzler, John H.; & Gage, Nicholas A. (2018). Meta-analysis of the relationship between academic achievement and broad abilities of the Cattell-Horn-Carroll theory. *Journal of School Psychology, 71,* 42–56. https://doi.org/10.1016/j.jsp.2018.10.001

Zachar, Peter; First, Michael B.; & Kendler, Kenneth S. (2017). The bereavement exclusion debate in the DSM-5: A history. *Clinical Psychological Science, 5*(5), 890–906. https://doi.org/10.1177/2167702617711284

Zachariae, Robert. (2009). Psychoneuroimmunology: A bio-psycho-social approach to health and disease. *Scandinavian Journal of Psychology, 50*(6), 645–651.

Zajonc, Robert B. (1998). Emotions. In Daniel T. Gilbert, Susan T. Fiske, & Gardner Lindzey (Eds.), *Handbook of social psychology* (4th ed.). McGraw-Hill.

Zajonc, Robert B. (2000). Feeling and thinking: Closing the debate over the independence of affect. In Joseph F. Forgas (Ed.), *Feeling and thinking: The role of affect in social cognition.* Cambridge University Press.

Zaki, Jamil, & Mitchell, Jason P. (2013). Intuitive prosociality. *Current Directions in Psychological Science, 22,* 466–470. https://doi.org/10.1177/0963721413492764

Zalsman, Gil; Stanley, Barbara; Szanto, Katalin; Clarke, Diana E.; Carli, Vladimir; & Mehlum, Lars. (2020, November 20). Suicide in the time of COVID-29: Review and recommendations. *Archives of Suicide Research, 24*(4), 477–482. https://doi.org/10.1080/13811118.2020.1830242

Zandy, Amy. (2007, July/August). If you want to lead, learn to serve. *Debt Cubed.* http://www.debt3online.com/?page=article&article_id=189

Zanos, Panos; Moaddel, Ruin; Morris, Patrick; Georgiou, Polymnia; Fischell, Jonathan; Elmer, Greg; Alkondon, Manickavasagom; Yuan, Peixiong; Pribut, Heather J.; Singh, Nagendra S.; Dossou, Katina S. S.; Fang, Yuhong; Huang, Xi-Ping; Mayo, Cheryl L.; Wainer, Irving W.; Albuquerque, Edson X.; Thompson, Scott M.; Thomas, Craig J.; Zarate, Carlos A.; & Gould, Todd. (2016). NMDAR inhibition-independent antidepressant actions of ketamine antibodies. *Nature, 533,* 481–486. https://doi.org/10.1038/nature17998

Zarate, Carlos A.; Singh, Jaskaran B.; Carlson, Paul J.; Brutsche, Nancy E.; Ameli, Rezvan; Luckenbaugh, David A.; Charney, Dennis S. & Manji, Husseini K. (2006). A randomized trial of an N-methyl-D-aspartate antagonist in treatment-resistant major depression. *Archives of General Psychiatry, 63*(8), 856–864. https://doi.org/10.1001/archpsyc.63.8.856

Zeidan, Fadel, & Vago, David R. (2016). Mindfulness meditation–based pain relief: a mechanistic account. *Annals of the New York Academy of Sciences, 1373,* 114–127. https://doi.org/10.1111/nyas.13153

Zeidan, Fadel. (2015). The neurobiology of mindfulness meditation. In Kirk Warren Brown, J. David Creswell, & Richard M. Ryan (Eds.), *Handbook of mindfulness: Theory, research, and practice.* Guilford.

Zeidan, Fadel; Johnson, Susan K.; Diamond, Bruce J.; David, Zhanna; & Goolkasian, Paula. (2010). Mindfulness meditation improves cognition: Evidence of brief mental training. *Consciousness and Cognition, 19*(2), 597–605. https://doi.org/10.1016/j.jconcog.2010.03.014

Zeidan, Fadel; Martucci, Katherine T.; Kraft, Robert A.; Gordon, Nakia S.; McHaffie, John G.; & Coghill, Robert C. (2011). Brain mechanisms supporting the modulation of pain by mindfulness meditation. *Journal of Neuroscience, 31,* 5540–5548.

Zelinski, Elizabeth M., & Kennison, Robert F. (2007). Not your parents' test scores: Cohort reduces psychometric aging effects. *Psychology and Aging, 22*(3), 546–557.

Zell, Ethan; Krizan, Zlatan; & Teeter, Sabrina. (2015). Evaluating gender similarities and differences using metasynthesis. *American Psychologist, 70,* 10–20. https://doi.org/10.1037/a0038208

Zentall, Thomas R., & Wasserman, Edward A. (Eds.). (2012). *The Oxford handbook of comparative cognition.* Oxford University Press.

Zentner, Marcel, & Shiner, Rebecca L. (2012). *Handbook of temperament.* Guilford.

Zettler, Ingo; Thielmann, Isabel; Hilbig, Benjamin E.; & Moshagen, Morten. (2020). The nomological net of the HEXACO model of personality: A large-scale meta-analytic investigation. *Perspectives on Psychological Science,* 1–38. https://doi.org/10.1177/1745691619895503

Zhang, Hualong; Zhang, Cunbao; Chen, Feng; Wei, YuanYuan. (2019). Effects of mobile phone use on pedestrian crossing behavior and safety at unsignalized intersections. *Canadian Journal of Civil Engineering,* 49(5), 381–388. https://doi.org/10.1139/cjce-2017-0649

Zhang, Tie-Yuan, & Meaney, Michael J. (2010). Epigenetics and the environmental regulation of the genome and its function. *Annual Review of Psychology, 61,* 1–28. https://doi.org/10.1146/annurev.psych.60.110707.163625

Zhao, Mengtian; Rosoff, Healther; & John, Richard S. (2019). Media disaster reporting effects on public risk perception and response to escalating tornado warnings: a natural experiment. *Risk Analysis, 39*(3). https://doi.org/10.1111/risa.13205

Zhao, Zhi-Qi. (2008). Neural mechanism underlying acupuncture analgesia. *Progress in Neurobiology, 85,* 355–375.

Zhou, Xiaoyun; Snoswell, Centaine L.; Harding, Louise E.; Bambling, Matthew; Edirippulige, Sisira; Bai, Xuejun; & Smith, Anthony C. (2020). The role of telehealth in reducing the mental health burden from COVID-19. *Telemedicine and e-Health, 26*(4), 377–379. https://doi.org/10.1089/tmj.2020.0068

Zhou, Xinyue; He, Lingnan; Yang, Qing; Lao, Junpeng; & Baumeister, Roy F. (2012). Control deprivation and styles of thinking. *Journal of Personality and Social Psychology, 102,* 460–478. https://doi.org/10.1037/a0026316

Zhou, Zi; Wang, Ping; & Fang, Ya. (2018). Social engagement and its change are associated with dementia risk among chinese older adults: A longitudinal study. *Scientific Reports, 8*(1), 1551. https://doi.org/10.1038/s41598-017-17879-w

Zhu, Bingqian; Shi, Changgui; Park, Chang G.; Zhao, Xiangxiang; & Reutrakul, Sirimon. (2019). Effects of sleep restriction on metabolism-related parameters in healthy adults: A comprehensive review and meta-analysis of randomized controlled trials. *Sleep Medicine Reviews, 45,* 18–30. https://doi.org/10.1016/j.smrv.2019.02.002

Zhu, Haiya; Huberman, Bernardo; & Luon, Yarun. (2012). To switch or not to switch: Understanding social influence in online choices. In *Proceedings of the SIGCHI Conference on Human Factors in Computing Systems,* 2257–2266.

Zhu, Jia; Kusa, Temitope; & Chan, Yee-Ming. (2018). Genetics of pubertal timing. *Current Opinion in Pediatrics, 30*(4), 532–540. https://doi.org/10.1097/MOP.0000000000000642

Zimbardo, Philip G. (2000). Prologue: Reflections on the Stanford Prison Experiment: Genesis, transformations, consequences. In Thomas Blass (Ed.), *Obedience to authority: Current perspectives on the Milgram paradigm.* Erlbaum.

Zimbardo, Philip G. (2004). A situationist perspective on the psychology of evil: Understanding how good people are transformed into perpetrators. In Arthur G. Miller (Ed.), The social psychology of good and evil. Guilford.

Zimbardo, Philip G. (2007). *The Lucifer effect: Understanding how good people turn evil.* Random House.

Zimbardo, Philip G.; Weisenberg, Matisyohu; Firestone, Ira; & Levy, Burton. (1965). Communicator effectiveness in producing public conformity and private attitude change. *Journal of Personality, 33,* 233–256.

Zimmer, Anna; Youngblood, Alix; Adnane, Adam; Miller, Brian J.; & Goldsmith, David. R. (2020). Prenatal exposure to viral infection and neuropsychiatric disorders in offspring: a review of the literature and recommendations for the COVID-19 pandemic. *Brain, Behavior, and Immunity, 19,* 756–770. https://doi.org/10.1016/j.bbi.2020.10.024

Zingrone, Nancy L.; Alvarado, Carlos S.; & Hövelmann, Gerd H. (2015). An overview of modern developments in parapsychology. In Etzel Cardeña, John Palmer, & David Marcusson-Clavertz (Eds). *Parapsychology: A handbook for the 21st century.* McFarland.

Ziomkiewicz, Anna. (2006). Menstrual synchrony: Fact or artifact? *Human Nature, 17,* 419–432.

Zitzmann, Michael. (2020). Testosterone, mood, behaviour and quality of life. *Andrology, 8*(6), 1598–1605. https://doi.org/10.1111/andr.12867

Zosuls, Kristina M.; Ruble, Diane N.; Tamis-LeMonda, Catherine S.; Bornstein, Marc H.; Greulich, Faith K.; & Shrout, Patrick E. (2009). The acquisition of gender labels in infancy: Implications for gender-typed play. *Developmental Psychology, 45,* 688–701.

Zubieta, Jon-Kar; Bueller, Joshua A.; Jackson, Lisa R.; Scott, David J.; Xu, Yanjun; Koeppe, Robert A.; Nichols, Thomas E.; & Stohler, Christian S. (2005). Placebo effects mediated by endogenous opioid activity on opioid receptors. *Journal of Neuroscience, 25,* 7754–7762.

Zucker, Kenneth J., & Cohen-Kettenis, Peggy T. (2008). Gender identity disorder in children and adolescents. In David L. Rowland & Luca Incrocci (Eds.), *Handbook of sexual and gender identity disorders.* Wiley.

Zuckerman, Marvin. (1979). *Sensation seeking: Beyond the optimal level of arousal.* Erlbaum.

Zuckerman, Marvin. (2007). *Sensation seeking and risky behavior.* American Psychological Association.

Zuckerman, Marvin. (2009). Sensation seeking. In Mark R. Leary & Rick H. Hoyle (Eds.), *Handbook of individual differences in social behavior* (pp. 455–465). Guilford.

Zulfic, Zlatan; Liu, Dennis; Lloyd, Cynthia; Rowan, Jacqueline; & Schubert, Klaus O. (2020). Is telepsychiatry care a realistic option for community mental health services during the COVID-19 pandemic? *Australian & New Zealand Journal of Psychiatry, 54*(12), 1228. https://doi.org/10.1177/0004867420937788

Zusne, Leonard, & Jones, Warren H. (1989). *Anomalistic psychology: A study of magical thinking* (2nd ed.). Erlbaum.

Zwicker, Amy, & DeLongis, Anita. (2010). Gender, stress, and coping. In J. C. Chrisler & D. R. McCreary (Eds.), *Handbook of gender research in psychology* (pp. 495–512). Springer.

NAME INDEX

SUBJECT INDEX

cued recall, 200
culture
  acculturative stress and, 445
  achievement motivation and, 272
  aggression and, 428
  of animals, 179
  attributional biases and, 405
  baby sleeping location and, 307
  beauty and, 407
  chronic negative emotions and, 453
  cognitive development and, 315
  conformity and, 416–417
  coping strategies and, 462
  culture-specific disorders and, 492–493
  dating behavior and, 320
  definition of, 14
  depressive disorders and, 486
  eating and, 272, 273
  eating disorders and, 491
  effects of on early memories, 196
  emotional expression and, 280–282
  emotion experience and, 278–279
  gender role flexibility and, 352–353
  gender-role stereotypes and, 341
  hookup, 326
  infant temperament and, 308
  intelligence tests and, 256–259
  language development and, 242–243
  meditation and, 129
  moral reasoning and, 323–324
  the Müller-Lyer illusion and, 104
  obsessive–compulsive disorder and, 483
  outward display of gender and, 352–353
  pain tolerance and, 95
  panic disorders and, 478–479
  personality traits and, 382
  peyote use and, 139
  psychotherapy and, 537, 538
  schizophrenia and, 500–501
  social loafing/social striving and, 429
  spanking and, 165–166
  stereotype threat and, 258
  therapeutic sensitivity to, 536
  top-down perception and, 99
  workforce diversity and, B-10, B-12
culture-bound syndromes, 492–493
cultures of honor, 428
cutting, 495
cyclothymic disorder, 487, 489
Cyrus, Miley, 487

D

daily hassles, 441–443
Dani languages, 242
dark triad, 383
Darley, John, 423
Darwin, Charles, 6, 13, 278, 279–280

data
  analysis of, 18–19
  big and small, B-12
  collection of in scientific method, 17–18
  interpreting, A-1–A-2
dating, 320, 326
Davidson, Pete, 495
Dávila, Armand, 479–480
day care, 309, 328
deafness, 87, 89
  babbling in babies and, 243
  facial expressions and, 280
  sign language and, 199, 239
  sign language development and, 240
  sleep-signing and, 118
  tip-of-the-fingers experience and, 199
death and dying, 331–332
  major depressive disorder and, 485
debriefing, 32
decay, of memory, 191
decay theory, 205
deception, in research, 31–32
decibel levels, 87, 89
decision making, 236–238
  in adolescence, 318
declarative memory, 196–197
deep brain stimulation (DBS), 545
defense mechanisms, 366–367
deferred imitation, 311
deindividuation, 430
delayed reinforcement, 182–183
delirium tremens, 135
delta brain waves, 117
delusions, 487, 499–500
  of being controlled, 500
  of grandeur, 500
  of persecution, 500
  of reference, 500
demand characteristics, 28
dementia, 220–222
Demerol, 135
dendrites, 41–42
denial, 332, 368, 461
deoxyribonucleic acid (DNA), 299–300, 448–449
Depakote, 542
dependent personality disorder, 494
dependent variables, 25
depolarization, 44, 45
depressants, 133–135
  alcohol, 133–135
  barbiturates and tranquilizers, 135
depression
  dying and, 332
  the gut–brain connection in, 43
  ketamine for, 141
  negative cognitive bias and, 526–527
depressive disorders, 484–489
  major depressive disorder, 485–486
  social media in diagnosis of, 472
depth perception, 100–109
Descartes, René, 5
Descent of Man, The (Darwin), 278

descriptive research, 17–18, 21–25
  case studies in, 22
  correlational studies in, 23–25
  definition of, 21
  naturalistic observation in, 21–22
  surveys, 22–23
descriptive statistics, A-2–A-10
  correlation, A-8–A-10
  definition of, A-2
  frequency distribution, A-2–A-3
  measures of central tendency, A-4–A-5
  measures of variability, A-5–A-7
  normal curve, A-7
  z-scores, A-7
designer drugs, 140–141
despair, 331
development. See lifespan development
developmental psychology, 15, 298–299
  definition of, 298
deviation, A-5–A-7
  z-scores and the normal curve, A-7
devil's advocate, 433
Diagnostic and Statistical Manual of Mental Disorders, Fifth Edition, 471–473, 475
difference thresholds, 77, A-13
difficult babies, 306–307
diffusion MRI (dMRI), 56
diffusion of responsibility, 425–426
discipline, 334
discrepancy hypothesis, B-8
discrimination, 412
  gender-based, 340
  IQ differences and, 256–259
  microaggressions, 412, 444
  against people who are transgender and intersex, 353–354
  prejudice and, 409–415
  of stimulus, 152
discriminative stimulus, 161–162
displacement, 191–192, 240, 368
display rules, 282, 343
disruptive, impulse-control, and conduct disorders, 475
dissociation, 128
dissociative amnesia, 497
dissociative anesthetic drugs, 140–141
dissociative disorders, 496–499
  definition of, 496
  dissociative amnesia and fugue, 497
  dissociative identity disorder, 497–499
dissociative experiences, 496
dissociative fugue, 497
dissociative identity disorder (DID), 497–499
distancing, 461
distorted thinking, 527
distraction, pain management and, 106
distributed practice, 34
divergence of sex development, 350–351
divergent thinking, 260

diversity, 412
  in leadership, B-9
  workplace, hiring for, B-10, B-12
division of labor, 349–350
divorce, 327
DNA, 448–449
Doctors Without Borders, 378
dogs
  classical conditioning of, 151–152
  cognitive skills of, 245–246
  learned helplessness in, 173–174
  operant conditioning of, 168
dolphins, 281
domestic and partner violence, 133
door-in-the-face technique, 432
dopamine, 48
  addiction and, 132
  amphetamines, cocaine, and, 138
  antipsychotics and, 539–541
  obesity and, 276
  schizophrenia and, 504
dorsolateral prefrontal cortex, 287
Dotson, Alison, 483
double-blind technique, 28
dreaded possible selves, 393–394
dreams and dreaming, 117, 122–124
  activation–synthesis model of, 123, 124
  definition of, 122
  Freud on, 365
  neurocognitive model of, 124
  significance of, 123–124
  sleep deprivation and, 121
  themes and imagery in, 122–123
drives, 267
drive theories of motivation, 267
driving
  cell phone use and inattention during, 114–115
  intoxicated, 133
  sleep-driving, 126
  while drowsy, 120
drug abuse, 132–133
  definition of, 132
drugs
  antianxiety, 541
  antipsychotics, 539–541
  depressants, 133–135
  for depressive and bipolar disorders, 488
  designer "club," 140–141
  effect of on neurotransmitters, 49
  fetal development and, 303
  lithium, 488, 542
  mixing, 131, 135–136
  opioids, 135–136
  for pain control, 106
  psychedelic, 139–140
  psychoactive, consciousness and, 131–141
  psychotropic, 514
  puberty blockers, 352
  sleeping pills, 124, 126
  stimulants, 136–138
  tolerance to, 131
drumming therapy, 537
DSM-5, 471–473, 475
DTs (delirium tremens), 135